Les Routiers
BRITAIN
AND IRELAND 1995

food and accommodation
RECOMMENDED
for Quality and Value

Copyright © Text and *Les Routiers* map information: Routiers Ltd. 1995
Copyright © Maps: Map Marketing Ltd. / European Map Graphics Ltd. 1995

First published in the United Kingdom in 1995
Routiers Ltd.
25 Vanston Place
London SW6 1AZ

ISBN 1-85733-141-9

All rights reserved. No part of this publication may be reproduced, stored in a retrieval system, or transmitted, in any form, or by any means, electronic, mechanical, photocopying, recording, or otherwise, without prior permission of the publishers and copyright holders.

Whilst every care has been taken to ensure that all details given in this book are correct, the publishers cannot accept any responsibility for inaccuracies or their consequences. All matters relating to the content of the book should be directed to Routiers Ltd. at the address below.

Les Routiers inspectors visit each establishment anonymously and settle their bill before revealing their identity. Complimentary meals and/or accommodation are not accepted.

Les Routiers, 25 Vanston Place, London SW6 1AZ

For reservations and further information, phone *Les Routiers Booking and Information Line* (Monday–Friday 9am–5pm): 0171 610 1856
Club Bon Viveur: 0171 610 1857
Partnership Protection Insurance: 0171 610 3266

Editor: Malcolm Morris
Assistant Editor: Stephanie Willbond

Design, Typesetting & Map Editing:	Castle House Press, Llantrisant Mid Glamorgan, Wales, UK
Digital Cartography:	European Map Graphics Ltd. Finchampstead, Berkshire, UK
Cover Design:	William Stone & Associates, London, UK
Production, Marketing & Distribution:	Kuperard (London) Ltd. No. 9 Hampstead West, 224 Iverson Road West Hampstead, London NW6 2HL, UK Tel: 0171 372 4722 / Fax: 0171 372 4599
Printed in Great Britain by:	The Bath Press, Bath, Avon, UK

CONTENTS

Les Routiers welcomes you!   Overleaf

Key to map pages
Full-colour regional maps (1–19)

A guide for all seasons   1
How to use this guide   2
Reading an entry   3
How we choose suitable establishments   4
Symbols used in this guide   6
Quality and value for money   7

Les Routiers Awards 1995   8

- The 1995 *Casserole Awards*   16
- *Les Routiers Cheeseboard Awards* 1995   21
- *Les Routiers Corps d'Elite (Wine Awards)* 1995   24

Official UK Tourist Boards   28

Les Routiers Establishments Listed by Region

- Greater London   30
- South-East England & East Anglia   54
- South-West England   98
- The Channel Islands   173
- Central England   178
- Northern England & The Isle of Man   224
- Wales   280
- Scotland   305
- Ireland   353

Les Routiers Grand Prize Draw   364
Les Routiers establishments offering Special Welcome Discounts   367
Club Bon Viveur – the Ultimate Dining Scheme!   374
Your recommendations   381

Index of *Les Routiers* establishments   383
Index of town names   394

LES ROUTIERS WELCOMES YOU!

A personal introduction from Duncan Bradbury, Managing Director of *Les Routiers*

Welcome to the *Les Routiers* guide, which lists an unrivalled choice of around 1,600 carefully selected hotels, restaurants, guest houses and inns throughout Britain and Ireland, where you can dine and stay in comfort.

We are extremely proud of our efforts to cater for a wide range of tastes and requirements. *Les Routiers* establishments range from quiet, country house hotels nestling in some of the most unspoilt corners of the British Isles to historic coaching inns in bustling spa towns, from fashionable town and city restaurants to elegant Georgian mansions in leafy suburbs. Big, small, isolated or terraced, thatched or modern, overlooking the sea or deep in the countryside, there is literally something for everyone.

You can also rediscover traditional values, such as quality food and drink in relaxed surroundings, homely accommodation and the warmest hospitality you'll find anywhere – all at excellent value. For this reason alone, we will continue to preserve these traditional values, which have earned *Les Routiers* such a proud and enviable reputation.

I hope you enjoy this guide.

Duncan Bradbury

BRITAIN AND IRELAND

KEY TO MAP PAGES

KEY TO MAP SYMBOLS

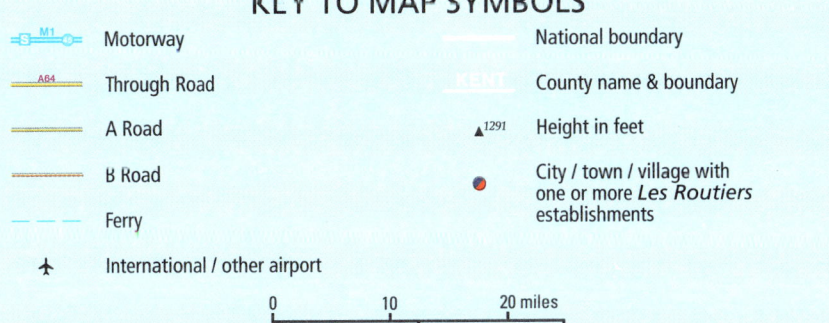

M1	Motorway
A64	Through Road
	A Road
	B Road
- - -	Ferry
✈	International / other airport
	National boundary
KENT	County name & boundary
▲1291	Height in feet
●	City / town / village with one or more *Les Routiers* establishments

Scale applies to maps 3–16 only
For maps 1–2, 17–18 and 19, see separate scale bars

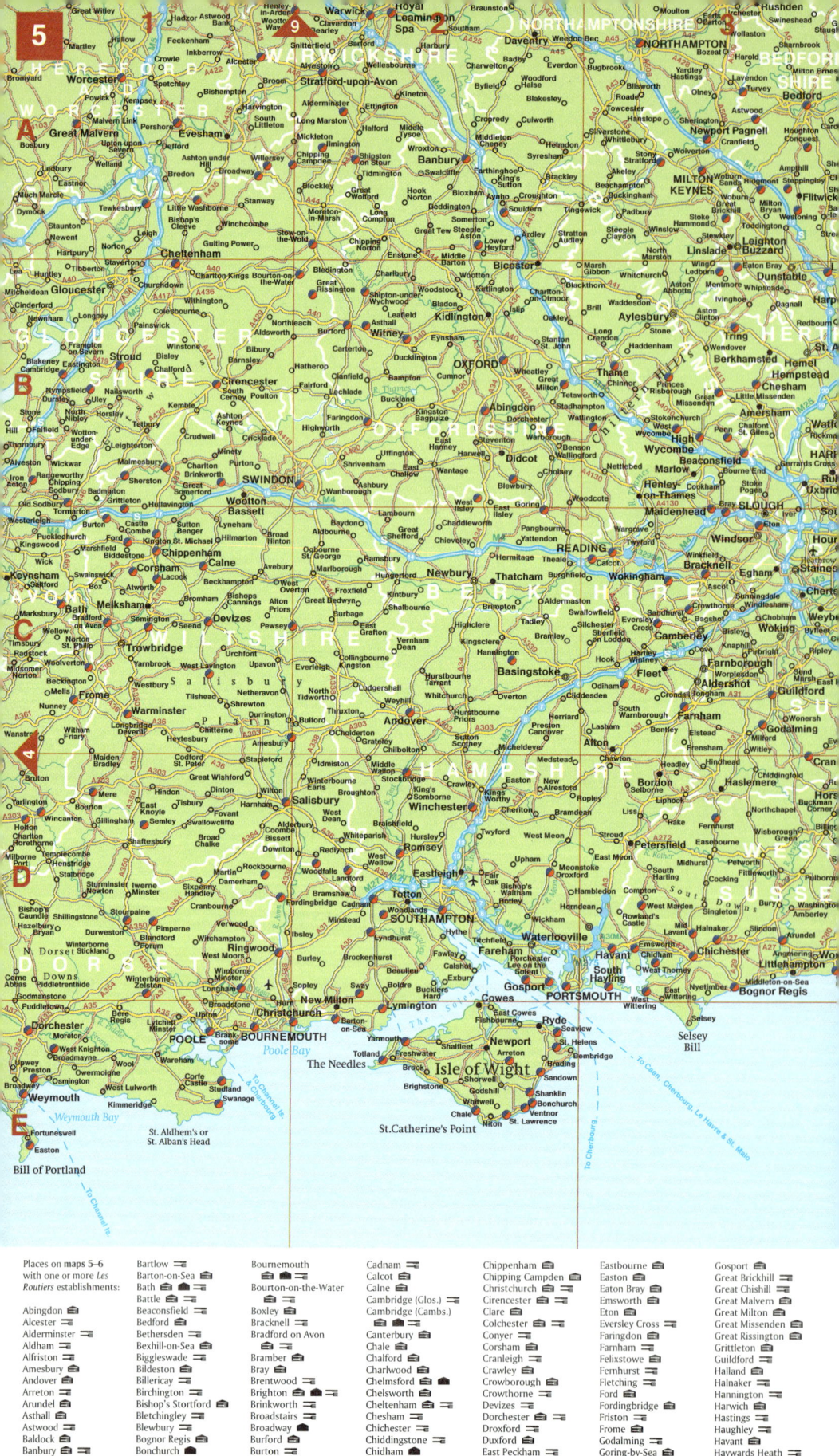

Les Routiers establishments within the M25 are located on maps 1-2

Henley-in-Arden	Lee on the Solent	Milton Keynes	Portsmouth	Rye	Shottisham	Stratford-upon-Avon
Hertford	Lenham	Minster	Preston	Saffron Walden	Sittingbourne	Stroud
High Wycombe	Lewes	Newington	Princes R'borough	Salisbury	Souldern	Studland
Hitchin	Lindfield	Newport Pagnell	Rangeworthy	Sandown	South Hayling	Swanage
Holton	Linton	Northampton	Reading	Seaford	Southampton	Sway
Horseheath	Little Washbourne	Nympsfield	Reigate	Seaview	Southend-on-Sea	Swindon
Houghton Conquest	Long Melford	Odiham	Ridgmont	Semington		Tewkesbury
Hove	Longham	Old Sodbury	Ringwood	Semley	St Helen's	Thame
Ickham	Luton	Orford	Risby	Sevenoaks	St Lawrence	Thurston
Ilmington	Lymington	Oxford	Rockbourne	Shanklin	Staple	Tonbridge
Kersey	Lyndhurst	Penn	Romsey	Sherston	Steeple Aston	Totland
Kington St Michael	Maidenhead	Penshurst	Royal Leamington	Shipbourne	Steeple Morden	Tring
Lacock	Malmesbury	Pershore	Spa	Shipley	Steppingley	Turvey
Landford	Margate	Pewsey	Royal Tunbridge Wells	Shipston on Stour	Steyning	Ventnor
Langham	Medway Services	Pimperne	Royston	Shipton-under-	Stockbridge	
Leatherhead	Mere	Pluckley		Wychwood	Stourpaine	
Ledburn	Mid Lavant	Poole		Shoeburyness	Stow-on-the-Wold	*Continued on map 8* :

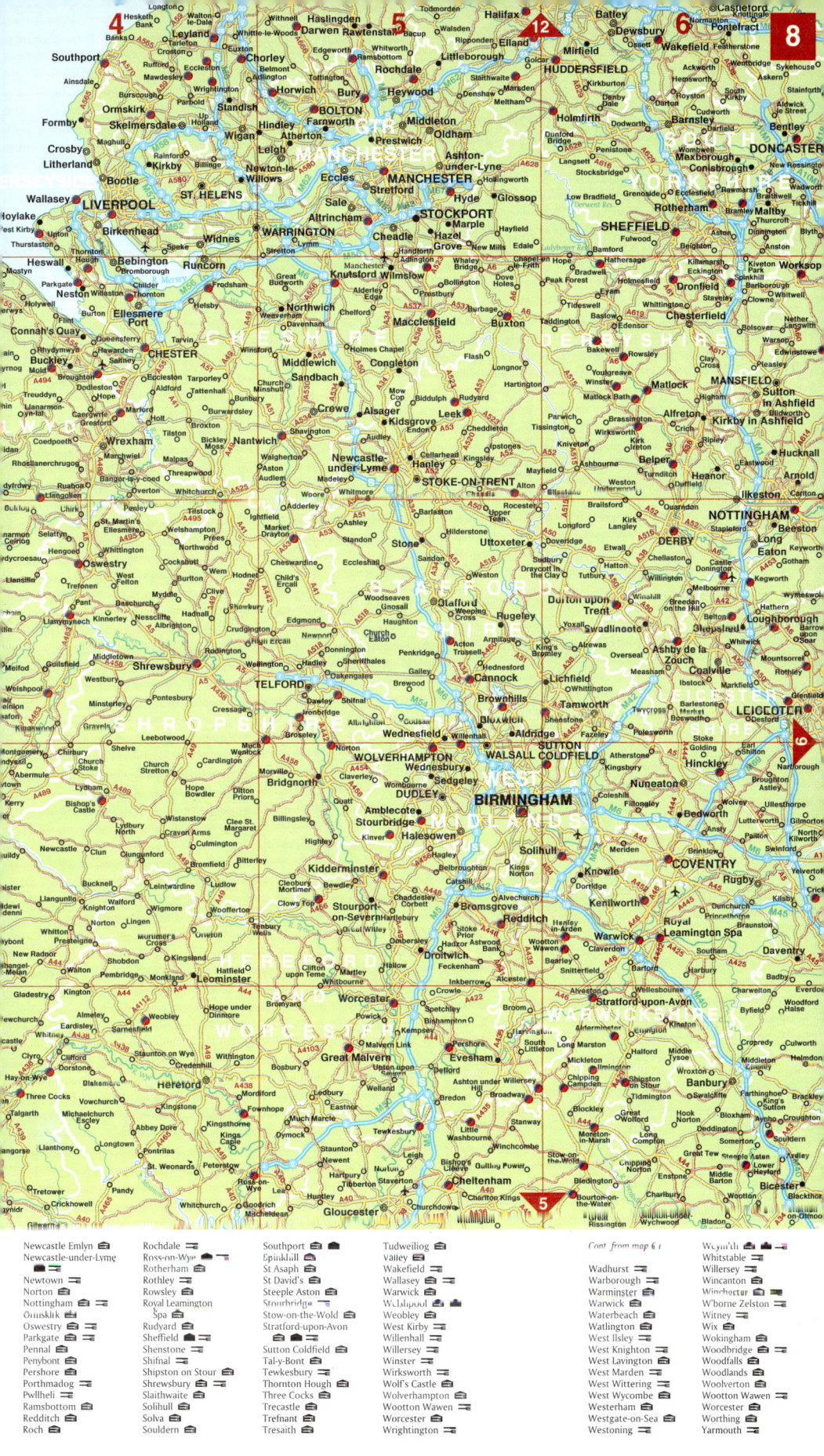

A GUIDE FOR ALL SEASONS

When planning this guide, we asked ourselves, 'Why should anyone spend good money on a guidebook they can only use once or twice a year?' Well, this is where the *Les Routiers* guide is so different from many others. Our guide is designed for use all year round, not just as an annual holiday planner.

DISCOVER EXCELLENT CUISINE
This guide enables you to choose from hundreds of specially selected places, where menus have been carefully chosen to balance colour, taste and texture in a mouthwatering combination of dishes.

In kitchens everywhere, talented chefs are being more adventurous than ever before, by cleverly combining unusual new foods and vegetables from all corners of the globe with their own inventive creations. Not only can you sample some of the best British cuisine, but many outstanding examples of Greek, Indian, Chinese, Italian, even Mongolian, as well as deliciously flavoured regional dishes, prepared from traditional revived recipes, accompanied by fine wines and real ales.

Nature's all-year-round harvest allows many exciting seasonal specialities to be enjoyed from January to December. Ward off the cold in winter with rich, full-flavoured, warming soups and dark, steaming puddings spiced with nutmeg and ginger. The arrival of spring breathes new life into the kitchen, bringing with it an abundance of crisp, tender vegetables and fresh herbs. In high summer, the tangled hedgerows provide nuts and soft, ripe, melting fruits for jams, trifles, sorbets and as a refreshing accompaniment to long, cool drinks. From the seashore comes fresh fish and seafood. And as the autumn tints change from gold to purple and game comes into season, there will be traditional favourites such as wood pigeon, hare and partridge served with delicious home-made pickles, chutney and tipsy sauces.

The 'icing on the cake', as the saying goes (excuse our pun), is improved menus offering constantly changing selections of more appetizing, interesting and unusual dishes to suit all tastes and ages.

RELAX IN COMFORTABLE ACCOMMODATION
No two *Les Routiers* establishments are alike, and in this guide you will find a superb range of comfortable accommodation to suit any occasion. Some are basic, some luxurious, but whether you favour a grand 4-poster in an isolated hunting lodge in the Scottish Isles or a contemporary suite in a London town house, all are clean and homely.

After all, if we could only offer you one style of accommodation, this would be a rather tedious guide, don't you agree? Unlike many convenience hotels, each and every *Les Routiers* establishment offers the same traditional values: a warm and friendly welcome, good food and drink, and quality and value for money.

A WARM WELCOME AWAITS
However impressive an establishment may appear, unless the host can offer guests a spontaneous greeting, the staff is polite and friendly, the service is efficient and the atmosphere warm and inviting – we simply wouldn't want to know . . . would you?

HOW TO USE THIS GUIDE

To ensure this guide is reader-friendly, we have kept everything as simple as possible to help you locate the perfect *Les Routiers* of your choice, quickly and easily.

- **REGIONAL SECTIONS**
  For your convenience, we have divided the guide into nine regional sections:

  London
  South-East England and East Anglia
  South-West England
  The Channel Islands
  Central England
  Northern England and the Isle of Man
  Wales
  Scotland
  Ireland

- **ENTRIES LISTED BY COUNTY**
  Within each regional section, individual establishments are grouped in **county order** and listed alphabetically by **town name**. Each detailed entry gives a clear, concise description of the establishment, its cuisine, accommodation, facilities, prices for food and/or accommodation, opening hours, directions and lots more, including a map reference.

- **COLOUR MAPS**
  Near the front of the book are 19 detailed full-colour regional maps of Great Britain and Ireland. As well as providing a useful touring guide, the maps show the location of all towns and villages where there is a *Les Routiers* establishment. An alphabetical list below each map tells you where you can find *Les Routiers*-recommended food, accommodation or both.

- **INDEX**
  At the back of this guide there is an A–Z index of towns and villages in which there are *Les Routiers* establishments. A second index lists establishments by name.

☎ What could be simpler? But should you have any difficulty locating a particular *Les Routiers*, please don't hesitate to call our **Information & Bookings Line** on 0171 610 1856.

READING AN ENTRY

PRICE GUIDE
Full details of food and accommodation prices are given on page 7.

MAP REFERENCE
Each entry has its own map reference number, keyed to the full-colour regional maps near the front of the book.

AYR • map 14B5

FOUTERS BISTRO
2A Academy Street, KA7 1HS
Authentic cellar restaurant serving interesting French and British dishes using the best of local produce. Fouters Bistro is renowned for the high quality of its cuisine, steak and seafood specialities. Personally run by the proprietors. On-street parking opposite Town Hall.
FOOD: from £15 to £20
Hours: lunch 12noon–2pm, dinner 6.30pm–10.30pm, Sunday 7pm–10pm, closed 4 days over Christmas and 4 days over New Year.
Cuisine: SCOTTISH / FRENCH – fine Scottish produce cooked in the French style. Vegetarians welcomed and special diets catered for.
Cards: Visa, Access, Diners, AmEx.
Other points: children welcome.
Directions: opposite Town Hall, in a cobbled stone lane.
FRAN & LAURIE BLACK ☎ (01292) 261391.

SYMBOLS
Some of these symbols represent 'special achievement' by the establishment. Refer to page 6 for details of all the symbols.

HOW WE CHOOSE SUITABLE ESTABLISHMENTS

As well as receiving personal recommendations from readers of this guide, many establishments eager to receive the *Les Routiers* recommendation approach us directly, and we have a nationwide team who visit each establishment anonymously, before sending us a detailed and comprehensive report which determines whether or not they meet our exacting standards.

One simple but successful formula we use to recognize a potential *Les Routiers* is to put ourselves in your shoes . . . if it's good enough for you – then it's good enough for us!

WHO DON'T WE INCLUDE?
There are, of course, many establishments that do not meet our required standards, by being either uncongenial or inferior in appearance, and others where the choice of cuisine is poorly presented and greatly overpriced. These we can certainly do without.

WHAT STANDARDS DO WE SET?
Good food and accommodation, value for money and a warm and friendly welcome towards guests have always been the criteria for selecting suitable establishments for the *Les Routiers* guide, and we are delighted to say that these basic but well-tested standards have met with constant customer approval for over 25 years.

MAINTAINING STANDARDS
All the establishments we have recommended in this guide are regularly re-inspected to ensure that the correct standards are being maintained. Only when we are completely satisfied do we permit an establishment to display the coveted red and blue *Les Routiers* sign.

THE *LES ROUTIERS* SIGN
The *Les Routiers* sign is a recognized and reliable standard of achievement in all types of cuisine and comfortable accommodation at hotels, restaurants, guest houses and inns throughout Britain and Ireland. It is displayed by all members demonstrating their commitment to providing quality and value for their customers. However, an establishment can only claim to be a current member if it has a current certificate with the correct proprietor's or manager's name.

Every year, there are establishments which close down or change ownership, or occasionally places which allow their standards to fall and have to be withdrawn. Unfortunately, despite our efforts, there are establishments which continue to display the sign when they are no longer members. If you know of a *Les Routiers* establishment which you do not consider worthy of bearing the sign, or which is displaying a sign without a current certificate, please let us know.

HELPING US TO HELP YOU!

☐ Every year more and more people are discovering the pleasures of dining or staying at *Les Routiers*-recommended establishments. We know this from all the many complimentary letters and comments we receive from users of our guide, and also from their recommendations to include new establishments that we didn't previously know about.

☐ This feedback is invaluable and helps us to maintain the high standards of which we are justifiably proud. At the back of this guide we have included some space for you to record your own comments, and to propose any establishments that you feel are worthy of the *Les Routiers* 'recommendation' and possible inclusion in next year's guide.

SYMBOLS USED IN THIS GUIDE

As you browse through this guide you will see that some of the entries have the following symbols. **Look out for them!**

These symbols are for 'special achievement' by an establishment, signifying that it has received one or more of our prestigious annual awards for outstanding and consistent presentation of food, wine or cheeseboards.

Casserole Award
The *Les Routiers Casserole* is awarded to any establishment that has consistently offered outstanding service and an impressive ability to present above-average cuisine to its customers. Refer to pages 16–20 for a complete list of *Casserole Award* holders.

Cheeseboard
This symbol indicates a *Les Routiers* establishment where you have the opportunity to sample a superb selection of well-chosen and prepared cheeses, including regional and less common varieties. Refer to pages 21–22 for a complete list of *Cheeseboard Award* holders.

Wine – Les Routiers 'Corps D'Elite'
Awarded to *Les Routiers* establishments that offer interesting, carefully selected wines, with a list which can be easily read and understood. Refer to pages 25–26 for a complete list of *Wine Award* holders.

There are also two other symbols you will see against certain entries. These inform you that the establishment is offering YOU one of two very special schemes:

Club Bon Viveur – The Ultimate Dining Scheme
Entries showing this sign offer – on less busy nights of the week – exceptional discounts to *Club Bon Viveur* members. To find out how you can join, refer to pages 374–375.

☆ Special Welcome Discounts
All entries showing this sign offer a 'Special Welcome' by way of an introductory discount on food or accommodation charges or, in some cases, a free bottle of house wine. Turn to pages 364–372 to see which establishments are offering a Special Welcome, and for full details of our Grand Prize Draw.

OTHER SYMBOLS
- ☎ **Telephone**
- Fax **Fax facilities available**
- **Establishment with accommodation**
- **Restaurant**
- **Establishment with accommodation and dining facilities**

QUALITY AND VALUE FOR MONEY

If you still can't believe that *Les Routiers* establishments really do offer quality and value for money, we can tell you that all their prices and services form the basis of accurate and ongoing market research undertaken by us to bring you, the customer, precisely that. There are also many places that exceed our expectations by consistently offering outstanding quality of service and above-average cuisine. These are rewarded with a *Les Routiers Casserole Award* (see page 16).

Every establishment listed in this guide includes a carefully researched estimate of cost, so that all customers know what to expect.

FOOD
☐ Prices given are based on a 3-course evening meal taken from the table d'hôte menu, excluding wine and service.

- up to £15 per person
- from £15 to £20 per person
- from £20 to £25 per person
- from £25 to £30 per person

ACCOMMODATION
☐ Prices given for **double accommodation** are per person, assuming two people sharing a double room. (Prices given *in italics* within brackets are for **single accommodation**).

- up to £20 *(£25)* per person
- from £20 to £30 *(£25 to £35)* per person
- from £30 to £40 *(£35 to £45)* per person
- from £40 to £50 *(£45 to £55)* per person
- over £50 *(£55)* per person

Please note: These price bands indicate the range of meals and accommodation available and reflect regional price variations. However, an establishment may have accommodation available at a higher or lower rate according to season and availability.

☐ **Single accommodation:** Guests staying at an establishment whose accommodation rating is 'from £25 to £35 per person' can in most instances expect to pay up to, but not more than, £35 per room.

☐ **Double accommodation:** Guests staying at an establishment whose accommodation rating is 'from £30 to £40 per person' can in most instances expect to pay up to, but not more than, £40 per person per room.

All prices are based on information supplied to us by the establishment, and although the prices quoted are correct at the time of going to press, they cannot be guaranteed.

LES ROUTIERS AWARDS 1995

All establishments listed in this guide have attained the prestigious Les Routiers recommendation only by meeting our exacting standards, providing **quality**, **value for money** and a **warm welcome**. There are some, however, whose efforts have far exceeded these standards, and our expectations, by making a concerted effort towards achieving **total customer satisfaction**, offering that something extra. In recognition of their achievements, each year we present a number of awards.

- **Restaurant of the Year**
  A restaurant or bistro that offers a full and varied menu with imaginative, mouthwatering dishes served by knowledgeable, efficient, friendly staff.

- **Hotel of the Year**
  A hotel where you start to relax the minute you arrive. Rooms should be inviting, clean and comfortable, with special touches like fresh flower arrangements, visitor information and, for the ladies, the humble hair dryer – a welcome addition, especially if they have forgotten to pack their own. Little extras such as these clearly demonstrate further consideration towards the guest. Exceptional food and welcoming hospitality are two other important ingredients of an award-winning hotel.

- **Guest House of the Year**
  A BRAND-NEW AWARD THIS YEAR! Guest houses may not offer the same comprehensive facilities as hotels and restaurants, but they certainly provide comfortable accommodation, quality and value, and the warmest welcome you'll find anywhere. For this reason alone, we have created a brand-new award this year to recognize those that offer all these qualities (and more!), leaving guests with lasting memories of a thoroughly enjoyable stay.

- **Inn of the Year**
  An establishment that echoes the true traditions of the English inn. Essential factors are a cheerful, friendly greeting, relaxed informality, a welcome for families, and the promise of traditional, wholesome food and carefully selected ales.

- **Newcomer of the Year**
  Any hotel, guest house, restaurant or inn that is being featured in the Les Routiers guide for the very first time, and is clearly already offering an outstanding level of service. Nominations for this award are usually instantly recognizable from the glowing report which follows their inspection. This year, for the first time, there is a separate Newcomer of the Year: Ireland award.

LES ROUTIERS AWARDS 1995

- **Cheeseboard of the Year**
  Awarded for the most exceptional cheeseboard at a *Les Routiers* establishment. Cheese is a serious business at this establishment, and the proprietor and staff will be able to provide customers with expert knowledge of the varieties of cheeses which they are offering.

- **Prix D'Elite (Wine of the Year)**
  The award for the most exceptional wine at a *Les Routiers* establishment. Like the *Cheeseboard* winner, wine plays a very important role in the daily programme. Although the establishment may specialize in certain varieties and vintages, the customer will find the wine list informative and easy to read and will be able to receive sound advice on the perfect selection.

- **Symbol of Excellence**
  Not an annual award, but given to an establishment that has been recommended by *Les Routiers* for at least a decade. Over this time it will have consistently provided its customers with outstanding service.

As well as having their normal full entries in the main regional listings, this year's award-winners are also specially featured in the following pages.

Restaurant of the Year

THORNTON HALL
Wirral, Merseyside

Resplendent, majestic, and sumptuous are just three words that could be used to accurately describe this year's winner of our *Restaurant of the Year Award*.

Originally the home of a major shipping family, Thornton Hall and Conference Centre is set in seven acres of gardens and has an enviable reputation for its outstanding cuisine. With an award-winning chef recognized as the best in the north-west, the restaurant is open to both guests and non-residents. Thornton Hall's table offers an excellent choice of set and à la carte menus, based on fresh local produce and creative cooking using herbs from their own gardens, all complemented by an extensive wine list.

What finer place to enjoy a delicious meal than the Oak Room, with its highly decorative copper frieze and mouldings set amongst hand-carved oak panelling, which makes this room unique yet very cosy and an ideal choice for small dinner parties or conferences? Similar to the Oak Room but larger, the Italian Room boasts magnificent oak-carved wall panels and a ceiling of hand-tooled leather with mother-of-pearl insets, providing a perfect setting for the main hotel restaurant.

Start your meal by choosing one of many inviting appetizers, such as smoked Tobermory salmon and trout with herbed cream cheese roulade and sweet pommery mustard sauce, or smoked muscovy duck breast in a pine nut vinaigrette. Mouthwatering main course dishes may include beef tenderloin medallions in a morel mushroom sauce, fresh Irish sea salmon with lime, tomato pickle and coriander butter, or possibly a seafood medley served under a pastry dome in tarragon cream.

The desserts are equally as good, and include summer pudding of wild berries on crème de menthe sauce, a large brandy snap basket filled with Bailey's ice cream on a trio of sauces, or layers of dark, white and bitter Swiss chocolate truffle torte accompanied by fresh vanilla sauce. The hotel offers a daily lunchtime smorgasbord, and traditional Sunday lunch is also served.

Hotel of the Year

RANGEWORTHY COURT
Rangeworthy, Avon

'A fine old country manor house that actually enjoys people,' they say of Rangeworthy Court, who are our undisputed winners of this award for 1995. So many customers remark on the friendly and welcoming atmosphere of the place and how they 'feel at home' that it has to be true.

Rangeworthy Court is set in its own grounds beside the church, amidst the rich farmlands and gently rolling countryside just south of the 'Edge' of the Cotswolds, offering some spectacular views across the Severn Estuary.

The hotel has an established tradition of high standards of hospitality and cleanliness, and guests can expect to be cosseted by the staff, many of whom have served loyally for a good number of years. The proprietors, Mervyn and Lucia Gillett, are always delighted to meet new customers or to renew acquaintances with old friends, and are continually developing the hotel and its services for their pleasure.

Inside, the lounges have log fires and candles in winter and fresh flowers all year round. The antique furniture, mullioned windows, sloping fireplaces, low doorways, studded oak doors and beams all contribute to the hotel's relaxing atmosphere. There are 16 comfortably furnished bedrooms, comprising five singles, nine double rooms and two triple rooms, all equipped with a range of modern facilities for maximum comfort.

Food is considered an important feature of the hotel, and the restaurant has a strong local following who come to enjoy the excellent cuisine, cooked mostly to traditional British recipes. Vegetarian and vegan dishes are also offered.

This is an establishment which thrives on company, where all guests can be sure of a warm welcome and every effort is made to ensure an enjoyable stay.

Guest House of the Year

MAES-Y-GWERNEN
Abercraf, Swansea Valley, West Glamorgan

Visitors to Abercraf in the upper Swansea Valley will most certainly find a 'welcome in the hillside' after the Maes-y-Gwernen guest house was declared the winner of our newly-created award, the *Les Routiers Guest House of the Year*.

Run by the Moore family, the Maes-y-Gwernen, a newcomer to the *Les Routiers* guide, is a well-appointed licensed guest house offering good English and French food and extremely comfortable, well-equipped accommodation to tourists and business people at rates which represent excellent value.

There are en-suite rooms, as well as rooms with separate bath and toilet facilities. All are well furnished and carry a Welsh Tourist Board 3-Crown Rating. A cosy bar, TV lounge, conservatory lounge and outside patio area are for the exclusive use of guests and their friends.

Meal times can be arranged to suit guests' requirements, and everything is home-cooked on the premises, with a special vegetarian menu available if required. A good selection of draught beers, bottled drinks, liqueurs and spirits is always available, as well as an excellent choice of fine wines at sensible prices to complement any meal. Bed and breakfast, evening meal if required, plus full bar service exclusively for guests is offered throughout the year.

The Abercraf area offers many attractions, being on the southern boundary of the Brecon Beacons National Park, and within easy reach of the Gower coastline and its excellent beaches.

✴ **NEW AWARD!** ✴

Inn of the Year

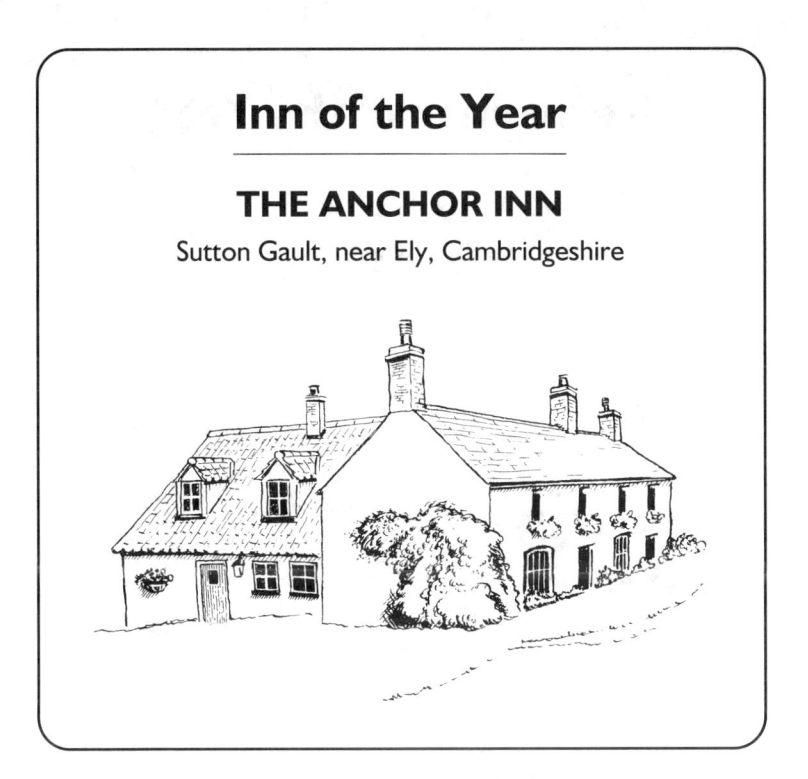

THE ANCHOR INN
Sutton Gault, near Ely, Cambridgeshire

If any establishment epitomizes this award, it is The Anchor Inn, which nestles by the river in the heart of the Cambridgeshire fens.

Approximately 350 years old, it is lit by gas lamps, with old beams, scrubbed wooden tables and chairs, all features which give this inn such tremendous character and warmth. It is popular all year round with locals and tourists alike, who come to appreciate its homely, welcoming atmosphere and excellent hearty fare, courtesy of Heather and Robin Moore.

There is an à la carte menu which changes daily, offering an extensive range of imaginative cuisine, such as fresh barracuda fillet baked with Cajun spices, Barnsley lamb chop with redcurrant-and-port sauce, and Indonesian beef with home-made spicy banana-and-date chutney. The variety of puddings and cheeses is equally impressive, and meals can be complemented with traditional ales and fine wines. Open on bank holidays, it is also a popular place for families, who come for Sunday lunch and to dine alfresco in fine weather.

The Anchor Inn is recognized in all the major guidebooks, and provides an ideal base for visiting Ely Cathedral, the Ouse Washes, Welney Wildfowl Reserve, and for those who come to discover real Fen Country.

Newcomer of the Year

TAYCHREGGAN

Kilchrenan, By Taynuilt, Strathclyde

A beautiful setting and landscape, stunning wildlife, varied country pursuits, well-prepared and presented local foods, superb wines, comfortable surroundings, and a warm welcome – these are the trademarks of the Taychreggan hotel, and the reason why they were chosen as our *Newcomer of the Year* from the hundreds of new entries in the guide this year.

Situated right on the shores of Loch Awe, Taychreggan is run by Euan and Annie Paul and a small dedicated team who enjoy living and working in this beautiful corner of Argyll, and who take pride and pleasure in making sure that house guests are comfortable and happy, enjoying the best cuisine of the Scottish Highlands and first-class wines.

Most of Taychreggan's bedrooms – including the wonderful 4-poster suite – overlook the beautiful loch, and all have private facilities. Guests can also relax in the main residents' lounge, or there is a comfortable TV lounge if preferred.

At the end of the day, a varied menu of freshly prepared and well-presented cuisine awaits in the warm, welcoming restaurant. Taychreggan's chef, Hugh Cocker, offers only the finest food available, much of which is produced or caught locally. Even the cheeseboard has a definite Scottish theme to it. Meals are complemented by a comprehensive wine list, including some half bottles, and there is an extensive range of malts.

Taychreggan is perfectly situated for guests to make the most of a variety of activities. Walkers, ramblers and wildlife enthusiasts can enjoy the numerous forest trails, whilst the fisherman is spoilt for choice. Horse-riding, golf and rough-shooting can also be arranged.

Newcomer of the Year: Ireland

THE PLOUGH INN
Hillsborough, County Down

After producing annually some outtanding places at which to eat and stay ever since *Les Routiers* expanded here, Ireland has been given its own *Newcomer of the Year* award, which for 1995 goes to the Plough Inn at Hillsborough.

Over a century old, The Plough has tremendous character and charm which attracts a mixed clientele. Its tastefully furnished interior is full of nooks and recesses which add to its calm, relaxed atmosphere. Rustic home-cooking is offered, as well as a business lunch wine bar, vegetarian dishes and an extensive global à la carte menu listing an imaginative and mouthwatering range of dishes using only the freshest of local produce.

A unique feature, the individually styled menus, provides plenty to choose from. Each offers a vast range of carefully selected and prepared delicacies. Main-course dishes include Swiss-style veal and wild mushrooms, and Caribbean-style breast of chicken. Another menu, *Marinade Parade*, lists Tuscany char-grilled chicken, venison burger, and caramelized chili and garlic fondue. On the *Harbour's Harvest* menu you will find such treats as Scottish poached salmon and chive sabayon, sautéed monkfish, and Dingle Bay shark steak with garlic prawns.

Eating at The Plough Inn is indeed a wonderful gastronomic experience, and if what you have read here has whetted your appetite then there are still further menus to select from: *From the Griddle*, *Something Different*, *Clouseau's Favourites*, *A Hint of Summer*, *Fruits of the Sea*, and others. An *After Dinner* cheese and sweet menu is also available.

Smartly-dressed uniformed staff and unobtrusive background music add the finishing touches to what is a truly remarkable establishment and a worthy winner of this award.

✳ **NEW AWARD!** ✳

THE 1995 CASSEROLE AWARDS

The *Casserole*, the *Les Routiers* mark of excellence, represents the finest culinary traditions. It is awarded annually to our members who offer that little something extra.

Whatever dish you order, it will have that extra-thoughtful finishing touch, allowing you to experience an exciting new world of wonderful sensations through the clever use of herbs and aromatic spices, combinations of carefully matched colours and varying textures, all immaculately prepared and professionally presented.

To qualify for the *Casserole Award*, an establishment must demonstrate that they have maintained the required standards for a minimum period of one year. Each year a select handful of new establishments join our list of past winners, who are allowed to display a prestigious certificate and receive a *Casserole Award* symbol against their full entry in this guide.

Look for the 🥘 symbol throughout the main regional section for full entries on the establishments listed below and overleaf.

CASSEROLE AWARDS

ENGLAND

- **Avon**
  BATH
  - The Old Malt House Hotel
  RANGEWORTHY
  - Rangeworthy Court Hotel
  WESTON-SUPER-MARE
  - The Commodore Hotel

- **Bedfordshire**
  BEDFORD
  - The Knife & Cleaver
  - Three Cranes
  BIGGLESWADE
  - La Cachette

- **Buckinghamshire**
  BEACONSFIELD
  - The Royal Standard of England
  PRINCES RISBOROUGH
  - King William IV Freehouse & Restaurant

- **Cambridgeshire**
  DUXFORD
  - Duxford Lodge Hotel
  SUTTON GAULT
  - The Anchor Inn

- **Cheshire**
  CHESTER
  - Francs Restaurant
  - Redland Hotel

PARKGATE
  - The Boathouse

- **Cornwall**
  LOOE
  - Allhays Country House
  MEVAGISSEY
  - Sharksfin Hotel & Restaurant
  PADSTOW
  - The Old Mill Country House
  PHILLEIGH
  - Smugglers Cottage Of Tolverne
  PILLATON
  - The Weary Friar Inn
  POLPERRO
  - The Kitchen
  - Penryn House Hotel
  PORT ISAAC
  - Old School Hotel
  ST IVES
  - Pedn-Olva Hotel & Restaurant
  TREGONY
  - Kea House Restaurant
  TRURO
  - Alverton Manor

- **Cumbria**
  AMBLESIDE
  - The Riverside Hotel
  BASSENTHWAITE LAKE
  - The Pheasant Inn
  BOWNESS-ON-WINDERMERE
  - Blenheim Lodge

16

GRANGE-OVER-SANDS
   Netherwood Hotel
HAWKSHEAD
   Grizedale Lodge Hotel & Restaurant
LONGTOWN
   The Sportsman's Restaurant & March Bank Hotel
MELMERBY
   Shepherds Inn
WITHERSLACK
   The Old Vicarage Country House Hotel

- **Derbyshire**
WIRKSWORTH
   Le Bistro

- **Devon**
BAMPTON
   The Swan Hotel
BOVEY TRACEY
   The Edgemoor Hotel
EXETER
   The Old Thatch Inn
LIFTON
   Lifton Hall Country House Hotel
LYNMOUTH
   Rising Sun Hotel
LYNTON
   Millslade Country House Hotel
PLYMOUTH
   Trattoria Pescatore
SOUTH MOLTON
   Stumbles Hotel & Restaurant
TORQUAY
   Jingle's Restaurant

- **Dorset**
CHRISTCHURCH
   The Fisherman's Haunt Hotel
LYME REGIS
   Bensons Restaurant
POOLE
   Allans Seafood Restaurant
TRENT
   The Rose & Crown
WEYMOUTH
   Sea Cow Restaurant

- **Co. Durham**
DURHAM
   Hallgarth Manor Hotel

- **East Sussex**
BATTLE
   Powdermills Hotel
WADHURST
   The Old Vine

- **Gloucestershire**
BOURTON ON THE WATER
   The Old Manse Hotel
CIRENCESTER
   Wild Duck Inn

CLEARWELL
   Wyndham Arms
STOW-ON-THE-WOLD
   Grapevine Hotel

- **Greater London**
HARROW
   Cumberland Hotel
   Fiddler's Restaurant
PINNER
   La Giralda
TEDDINGTON
   The Italian Place Brasserie

- **Greater Manchester**
BURY
   Rosco's Eating House

- **Guernsey**
VAZON BAY
   La Grande Mare

- **Hampshire**
GOSPORT
   Alverbank House Hotel
ODIHAM
   La Foret

- **Hereford & Worcester**
HAY-ON-WYE
   The Old Black Lion

- **Humberside**
HULL
   Kingstown Hotel

- **Isle of Man**
RAMSEY
   Harbour Bistro

- **Isle of Wight**
SEAVIEW
   Seaview Hotel & Restaurant

- **Jersey**
ST OUEN'S BAY
   The Lobster Pot Hotel & Restaurant

- **Kent**
BIRCHINGTON
   Smugglers Restaurant
EDENBRIDGE
   Castle Inn
RAMSGATE
   Morton's Fork
WESTERHAM
   The Kings Arms Hotel
WHITSTABLE
   Giovanni's Restaurant

- **Lancashire**
LANCASTER
   Springfield House Hotel & Restaurant

- **Lancashire (cont.)**
  LEYLAND
  - Runshaw College School of Catering
  LONGRIDGE
  - Corporation Arms
  PRESTON
  - The Bushells Arms
  - Ferraris Restaurant

- **Leicestershire**
  CASTLE DONINGTON
  - Le Chevalier
  OLD DALBY
  - The Crown Inn

- **Lincolnshire**
  GRANTHAM
  - The Royal Oak
  STAMFORD
  - Candlesticks Hotel & Restaurant

- **London**
  BATTERSEA
  - Buchan's
  - Jack's Place
  BLOOMSBURY
  - Academy Hotel
  CHELSEA
  - Glaisters Garden Bistro
  CLAPHAM
  - Windmill On The Common
  PUTNEY
  - Gavin's Restaurant
  WEST END
  - Don Pepe Restaurant

- **Merseyside**
  THORNTON HOUGH
  - Thornton Hall Hotel

- **Norfolk**
  SNETTISHAM
  - The Rose & Crown Freehouse

- **North Yorkshire**
  APPLETON-LE-MOORS
  - Appleton Hall Country House Hotel
  ASKRIGG
  - King's Arms Hotel & Restaurant
  HARROGATE
  - Grundy's Restaurant
  HELMSLEY
  - The Feversham Arms Hotel
  LEEMING BAR
  - Motel Leeming
  MALTON
  - Cornucopia
  NORTHALLERTON
  - Duke Of Wellington Inn
  RICHMOND
  - Peat Gate Head
  RIPON
  - Staveley Arms (Spit Roast)
  ROSEDALE ABBEY
  - The Milburn Arms Hotel
  STOKESLEY
  - Millers Restaurant
  - The Wainstones Hotel
  THIRSK
  - Nags Head Hotel & Restaurant
  - Sheppard's Hotel, Restaurant & Bistro
  WHITBY
  - The Magpie Café
  WIGGLESWORTH
  - The Plough Inn
  YORK
  - Mount Royale
  - Red Lion Motel & Country Inn

- **Northamptonshire**
  OUNDLE
  - Fitzgeralds Restaurant

- **Northumberland**
  BELLINGHAM
  - Riverdale Hall Hotel

- **Oxfordshire**
  OXFORD
  - Belfry Hotel
  SOULDERN
  - Fox Inn
  WATLINGTON
  - The Well House Restaurant & Hotel

- **Shropshire**
  LLANYMYNECH
  - Bradford Arms & Restaurant
  NORTON
  - Hundred House Hotel, Restaurant & Inn
  OSWESTRY
  - Restaurant Sebastian
  TELFORD
  - Raphaels Restaurant

- **Somerset**
  EXEBRIDGE
  - Anchor Inn Hotel
  WINCANTON
  - Holbrook House Hotel

- **South Yorkshire**
  ROTHERHAM
  - The Elton Hotel
  SHEFFIELD
  - The Old Sidings

- **Staffordshire**
  STAFFORD
  - The Moat House Restaurant

- **Suffolk**
  BILDESTON
  - The Crown Hotel
  BURY ST EDMUNDS
  - The Grange Hotel

HAUGHLEY
- The Old Counting House Restaurant

WOODBRIDGE
- Captain's Table

WRENTHAM
- Quiggins Restaurant

- **West Sussex**

CHICHESTER
- Platters Restaurant

- **West Yorkshire**

ELLAND
- Berties Bistro

HALIFAX
- Collyers Hotel
- Imperial Crown Hotel
- Rock Inn Hotel & Churchill's Restaurant

HUDDERSFIELD
- The White House

LEEDS
- Olive Tree Greek Restaurant

- **Wiltshire**

BRADFORD ON AVON
- Widbrook Grange

CHIPPENHAM
- The Three Crowns

CORSHAM
- The Rudloe Park Hotel & Restaurant

SALISBURY
- Antrobus Arms Hotel

SHERSTON
- Rattlebone Inn

WARMINSTER
- Old Bell Hotel

SCOTLAND

- **Borders**

PEEBLES
- Cringletie House Hotel
- Peebles Hotel Hydro

SELKIRK
- Philipburn House Hotel & Restaurant

- **Dumfries & Galloway**

KIRKCUDBRIGHT
- Selkirk Arms Hotel

- **Fife**

BURNTISLAND
- Kingswood Hotel

- **Grampian**

BALLATER
- Alexandra Hotel
- Auld Kirk Hotel

BANCHORY
- Banchory Lodge Hotel

BRAEMAR
- Callater Lodge Hotel

CULLEN
- Bayview Hotel

- **Highlands**

CROMARTY
- Royal Hotel

GLENFINNAN
- The Princes House

GLENMORISTON
- Cluanie Inn

ISLE OF SKYE
- Flodigarry Country House Hotel
- Kinloch Lodge
- Skeabost House Hotel

NAIRN
- Ramleh Hotel & Fingal's Restaurant

TONGUE
- Ben Loyal Hotel

- **Lothian**

EDINBURGH
- Lancers Brasserie
- The Tattler
- Verandah Tandoori Restaurant

LEADBURN
- The Leadburn Inn

- **Strathclyde**

AYR
- Fouters Bistro

GLASGOW
- Ewington Hotel
- La Fiorentina

ISLE OF MULL
- The Western Isles Hotel

KILWINNING
- Montgreenan Mansion House Hotel

STRACHUR
- The Creggans Inn

- **Tayside**

PITLOCHRY
- Green Park Hotel

- **Western Isles**

ISLE OF BENBECULA
- Dark Island Hotel

WALES

- **Clwyd**

COLWYN BAY
- Café Niçoise
- Edelweiss Hotel

- **Dyfed**

CARDIGAN
- Skippers

FISHGUARD
- Gelli Fawr Country House

LITTLE HAVEN
- The Nest Bistro

- **Dyfed (cont.)**
ST DAVID'S
- Harbour House Hotel & Restaurant

- **Gwent**
CWMBRAN
- Parkway Hotel & Conference Centre

MONMOUTH
- The Crown At Whitebrook

- **Gwynedd**
ABERSOCH
- The White House Hotel

BETWS Y COED
- Royal Oak Hotel
- Ty Gwyn Hotel

CAERNARFON
- Seiont Manor Hotel

CRICCIETH
- Bron Eifion Country House Hotel
- The Moelwyn Restaurant With Rooms

DOLGELLAU
- Clifton House Hotel

LLANBEDR
- Llew Glas

LLANBERIS
- Lake View Hotel

LLANDUDNO
- Dunoon Hotel
- Sandringham Hotel

PORTHMADOG
- Blossoms Restaurant

PWLLHELI
- Twnti Seafood Restaurant

- **Mid Glamorgan**
BRIDGEND
- Ashoka Tandoori

- **Powys**
BRECON
- Peterstone Court

LLANWDDYN
- Lake Vyrnwy Hotel

IRELAND

- **Co. Antrim**
BUSHMILLS
- Hillcrest Country House & Restaurant

LES ROUTIERS
CHEESEBOARD AWARDS 1995

'I applaud Les Routiers' *initiatives to encourage its members to provide more imaginative cheese selections. Several cheeseboard prizes are awarded each year guaranteeing that wherever you may travel in Britain and Ireland, a delicious meal with a fine cheeseboard is not far away.'*

Jenny Muir, Editor, **Good Cheese**

The variety of cheeses now generally available in the UK is wider and more unusual than ever before.

However, it is not just the selection or variety that makes a good cheeseboard. There are many important factors. We put ourselves in the customer's shoes and looked for *taste* through expert selection. We looked for *variety*, with an imaginative choice of traditional, new and local cheeses. *Presentation* requires not only good use of colour, texture and shape to create a tempting display, but careful handling and storage to bring out the best in the cheese. And finally, we looked for *knowledge* of the cheeses offered.

We hope you will discover that cheese is fun, and that in this guide there is a vast range of establishments offering an infinite and delicious choice of cheeses, from English, Scottish and Welsh cheeses to European varieties and many interesting regional specialities, complemented by well-matched vintage wines.

After careful consideration, the establishments listed below and overleaf have all been judged worthy of inclusion in the *Les Routiers* Cheeseboard Honours List. From this list, one establishment has been selected as the overall winner and receives the prestigious *Les Routiers Cheeseboard of the Year Award* 1995.

Look for the ⊕ symbol throughout the main regional section for full entries on the establishments listed below and overleaf.

CHEESEBOARD

ENGLAND

- **Bedfordshire**
BEDFORD
 ⊕ The Knife & Cleaver

- **Berkshire**
MAIDENHEAD
 ⊕ Chauntry House Hotel
WEST ILSLEY
 ⊕ The Harrow

- **Buckinghamshire**
PRINCES RISBOROUGH
 ⊕ King William IV Freehouse
   & Restaurant

- **Cambridgeshire**
BARTLOW
 ⊕ The Three Hills
SUTTON GAULT
 ⊕ The Anchor Inn

- **Cheshire**
CHESTER
 ⊕ The Blue Bell Restaurant
 ⊕ Francs Restaurant

- **Cornwall**
FALMOUTH
 ⊕ Green Lawns Hotel
LOOE
 ⊕ Allhays Country House

21

- **Cumbria**
  BROUGHTON-IN-FURNESS
  - Beswicks Restaurant
  MELMERBY
  - Shepherds Inn

- **Devon**
  LIFTON
  - Lifton Hall Country House Hotel
  TORQUAY
  - Livermead Cliff Hotel

- **Dorset**
  TRENT
  - The Rose & Crown

- **Guernsey**
  VAZON BAY
  - La Grande Mare

- **Humberside**
  HULL
  - Pearson Park Hotel

- **Lancashire**
  BOLTON-LE-SANDS
  - Deerstalker Restaurant
  CLITHEROE
  - The Inn At Whitewell
  ORMSKIRK
  - Beaufort Hotel

- **Lincolnshire**
  LEADENHAM
  - George Hotel

- **London**
  COVENT GARDEN
  - Le Café Des Amis Du Vin

- **Northumberland**
  ALNWICK
  - The Cottage Inn Hotel

- **North Yorkshire**
  HELMSLEY
  - The Feversham Arms Hotel
  LEEMING BAR
  - Motel Leeming

- **Nottinghamshire**
  NEWARK
  - New Ferry Restaurant

- **Shropshire**
  LLANYMYNECH
  - Bradford Arms & Restaurant

SHREWSBURY
- Sydney House Hotel

- **Somerset**
  WELLS
  - Fountain Inn & Boxers Restaurant

- **Suffolk**
  HAUGHLEY
  - The Old Counting House Restaurant

- **Tyne & Wear**
  GATESHEAD
  - Beamish Park Hotel

- **West Yorkshire**
  HUDDERSFIELD
  - The Lodge Hotel
  LEEDS
  - Pinewood Private Hotel

SCOTLAND

- **Grampian**
  BALLATER
  - Alexandra Hotel

- **Highlands**
  NAIRN
  - Ramleh Hotel & Fingal's Restaurant

- **Strathclyde**
  AYR
  - Fouters Bistro

- **Tayside**
  GLENSHEE
  - The Blackwater Inn

- **Western Isles**
  NORTH UIST
  - Lochmaddy Hotel

IRELAND

- **Co. Antrim**
  PORTRUSH
  - Causeway Coast Hotel & Conference Centre

- **Co. Down**
  HILLSBOROUGH
  - The Plough Inn

Cheeseboard of the Year

ALLHAYS COUNTRY HOUSE
Looe, Cornwall

'Those restaurateurs who take up the challenge to offer an interesting cheeseboard are rewarded not only with loyal customers who look forward to tasting a little bit of this, a little piece of that, and just a smidgeon of that funny-looking one over there, but also provide a valuable service to both tourists and the cheese trade. Trying local specialities is just one of the great pleasures of travelling, and the memories of good flavour stay with you long after you have eaten. From the winner of the Les Routiers Cheeseboard of the Year, you are particularly sure of a superb offering.'

Jenny Muir, Editor, **Good Cheese**

Receiving awards for their cheeseboard is certainly nothing new to the Allhays Country House. Our *Cheeseboard of the Year* winners in 1992 and holders of a *Les Routiers* cheeseboard award for five years in succession, this year they have done it again – the Allhays Country House has been declared the *Les Routiers Cheeseboard of the Year* for 1995.

A period country house standing in an English country garden with spectacular views over to Talland Bay, Allhays has an enviable reputation for its food – but the daily changing cheeseboard is quite spectacular.

British and West Country cheeses are a speciality, and the extensive list includes many less common varieties to encourage experimentation by customers. A few of them are: Charnwood, Cotswold, Huntsman, Nutcracker, Nutwood, Rutland, Red and White Stilton with ginger, mushroom and citrus, Cornish Pepper, Cornish Herb, Vulscombe Herb/Garlic Goats' Stilton, Shropshire Blue, Beenleigh Blue, Rustic, Belvoir Blue, Admirals, Applewood, and 5 Counties.

All cheeses are attractively displayed and individually presented with an imaginative, mouthwatering range of accompaniments, including fudges, Dorset cheddar wafers made with dairy cream, Miller's Damsel wheat wafers with celery seeds, and home-made biscuits.

Allhays take great pride in ensuring that all cheeses they serve are in peak condition and, in their own words, 'beautifully presented without dreadful, bland, tasteless cream crackers'. In addition to an excellent cheeseboard, visitors can also enjoy modern English cuisine based on the finest local and home-grown produce, freshly prepared and cooked in the Aga.

LES ROUTIERS CORPS D'ELITE (WINE AWARDS) 1995

Although the emphasis and care taken by both chef and proprietor over food purchase, preparation and presentation may seem ponderously slow and pedantic to the casual diner, it generally takes only one small taste of a good wine to justify the attention to detail.

Choosing a bottle of wine is a matter of personal taste, the food it is to be served with and the amount you want to spend. However, finding out about wines from different countries will make that selection so much easier. As the consumption of wine in the UK continues to enjoy tremendous growth, so too does the demand for more adventurous selections.

A well-balanced wine list should offer an interesting selection of different wines with varying tastes to suit all palates and at good value for money. Equally important is an easy-to-read wine list which is free of jargon, the provision of half-bottles throughout the range, and the enthusiasm displayed by the proprietor in giving advice on selection.

When visiting *Les Routiers* establishments you will be able to choose from an extensive range of imaginative wines from the UK and Europe, as well as from many other countries around the globe. From Australia, full-flavoured Cabernet Sauvignons have long been popular for their powerful blackcurrany taste, whilst New Zealand produces a good range of full-flavoured wines, some of which have a slightly perfumed aroma. Other countries where the wine industry has been greatly modernized in the past decade, which are currently producing some remarkable-tasting wines, include Chile, Japan, California, South Africa, China, Albania and even Romania. Be adventurous in your selections and you will not be disappointed.

The judges found all the essential qualities of a good wine list at the establishments listed opposite. From this shortlist, one establishment has been selected for the most outstanding wine list of all, and receives the coveted *Les Routiers Prix D'Elite Award* for 1995 (see page 27).

Look for the symbol throughout the main regional section for full entries on the establishments listed opposite.

CORPS D'ELITE

ENGLAND

- **Avon**
  FRESHFORD
  - Inn At Freshford

- **Bedfordshire**
  BEDFORD
  - The Knife & Cleaver
  BIGGLESWADE
  - La Cachette

- **Buckinghamshire**
  PRINCES RISBOROUGH
  - King William IV Freehouse & Restaurant

- **Cambridgeshire**
  CAMBRIDGE
  - Ancient Shepherds
  DUXFORD
  - Duxford Lodge Hotel
  SUTTON GAULT
  - The Anchor Inn

- **Cornwall**
  FALMOUTH
  - Green Lawns Hotel
  NEWQUAY
  - The Headland Hotel
  PORT ISAAC
  - The Cornish Arms

- **Cumbria**
  BOWNESS-ON-WINDERMERE
  - Blenheim Lodge
  BROUGH SOWERBY
  - The Black Bull Inn
  BROUGHTON-IN-FURNESS
  - Beswicks Restaurant
  BUTTERMERE
  - Bridge Hotel

- **Devon**
  CLAWTON
  - Court Barn Country House Hotel

- **Dorset**
  DORCHESTER
  - The Manor Hotel

- **East Sussex**
  CROWBOROUGH
  - Winston Manor Hotel

- **Essex**
  BILLERICAY
  - Duke Of York

- **Hereford & Worcester**
  WEOBLEY
  - Ye Olde Salutation Inn

- **Isle Of Wight**
  CHALE
  - Clarendon Hotel And Wight Mouse Inn

- **Jersey**
  ST HELIER
  - Millbrook House

- **Kent**
  EDENBRIDGE
  - Castle Inn
  TEYNHAM
  - The Ship Inn & Smugglers Restaurant

- **Lancashire**
  PRESTON
  - The Bushell's Arms

- **London**
  HOLBORN
  - Bleeding Heart Wine Bar
  21 LOCATIONS
  - Café Rouge

- **Merseyside**
  THORNTON HOUGH
  - Thornton Hall Hotel

- **Norfolk**
  BRANCASTER STAITHE
  - The Jolly Sailors
  GREAT YARMOUTH
  - Imperial Hotel

- **North Yorkshire**
  HELMSLEY
  - The Feversham Arms Hotel
  LEEMING BAR
  - Motel Leeming
  SETTLE
  - New Inn Hotel

- **Northumberland**
  BELLINGHAM
  - Riverdale Hall Hotel

- **Nottinghamshire**
  NEWARK
  - New Ferry Restaurant

- **Oxfordshire**
  BANBURY
  - The White Horse Inn
  SHIPTON-UNDER-WYCHWOOD
  - The Shaven Crown Hotel

25

- **Oxfordshire (cont.)**
  WATLINGTON
  - The Well House Hotel & Restaurant

- **Shropshire**
  LLANYMYNECH
  - Bradford Arms & Restaurant
  SHREWSBURY
  - Sydney House Hotel

- **South Yorkshire**
  ROTHERHAM
  - The Elton Hotel

- **Suffolk**
  HAUGHLEY
  - The Old Counting House Restaurant
  WRENTHAM
  - Quiggins Restaurant

- **West Sussex**
  CHICHESTER
  - Platters Restaurant
  WEST WITTERING
  - The Lamb Inn West Wittering

- **Wiltshire**
  PEWSEY
  - Woodbridge Inn
  SHERSTON
  - Rattlebone Inn

SCOTLAND

- **Grampian**
  BANCHORY
  - Banchory Lodge Hotel

- **Highlands**
  NAIRN
  - Ramleh Hotel & Fingal's Restaurant

ISLE OF SKYE
- Hotel Eilean Iarmain

- **Strathclyde**
  AYR
  - Fouters Bistro
  GLASGOW
  - Ewington Hotel
  STRACHUR
  - The Creggans Inn

WALES

- **Clwyd**
  COLWYN BAY
  - Café Niçoise
  LLANGOLLEN
  - Gales

- **Dyfed**
  ST DAVID'S
  - Ramsey House
  LITTLE HAVEN
  - The Nest Bistro

- **Gwent**
  MONMOUTH
  - The Crown At Whitebrook

- **Gwynedd**
  HARLECH
  - Castle Cottage Hotel & Restaurant

- **Powys**
  BRECON
  - Peterstone Court

IRELAND

- **Co. Antrim**
  BUSHMILLS
  - Hillcrest Country House & Restaurant

- **Co. Tyrone**
  OMAGH
  - The Mellon Country Inn

Prix D'Elite: Wine of the Year

THE BUSHELL'S ARMS
Goosnargh, Preston, Lancashire

Another newcomer to the Les Routiers guide they may be, but The Bushell's Arms has been chosen from almost 400 others as the overall winner of this award for what is truly an outstanding wine list.

Wine is definitely a serious business at this friendly village hostelry, and the first-class wine list has everything one would expect. Most important, though, each wine listed is accompanied by a generous, easy-to-read description to help diners make the perfect choice to balance the wide variety of international cuisine offered on the menu.

Individual wines have been selected from all round the globe, reflecting the multiplicity of flavours, textures and styles available. Although prices may vary, all have one thing in common – they are all of high quality and were selected after many visits to the cellars of the producers in the Loire, Champagne, Chablis, Cahors, Rioja, Navarra and Málaga, to name just a few. The fine selection includes varieties from France, Germany, Spain, Italy, Australia, Bulgaria, New Zealand and South Africa.

Crisply dry and fragrant whites include a 1992 Mâcon-Solutré, Domaine Paul Broyer, a really good example of a Mâcon wine. Harmans Mill White, a rich, dry white from the family-owned Willespie Vineyards in the Margaret River region of Western Australia, is a ripe and flavoursome white wine, full of tropical fruits. Rich, smooth and fruity reds include a 1982 Castillo de Ayud Reserva, Do Calatayud, aged in 500-litre oak *cubas* to produce a ripe fruit flavour with mellow overtones of soft oak. There are also full and complex reds with raspberry and woody aromas, and a 1987 Pinotage, Nobilo, full of fragrant berry-fruit aromas, which, as the list states, is an ideal accompaniment for pork, lamb, veal and ham dishes.

Rounding off the comprehensive list is a fine selection of dessert wines available in half-bottles, and several sparkling wines loaded with ripe fruit flavours – and even wines on draught.

Well-chosen, sensibly priced, there is literally something to suit every palate and pocket.

OFFICIAL UK TOURIST BOARDS

- **ENGLISH TOURIST BOARD**
  Thames Tower, Black's Road,
  Hammersmith, London W6 9EL
  ☎ 0181 846 9000

- **CUMBRIA TOURIST BOARD**
  Ashleigh, Holly Road,
  Windermere LA23 2AQ
  ☎ 015394 44444

- **EAST ANGLIA TOURIST BOARD**
  Toppesfield Hall, Hadleigh,
  Suffolk IP7 7DN ☎ 01473 822922

- **EAST MIDLANDS TOURIST BOARD**
  Exchequergate, Lincoln LN2 1PZ
  ☎ 01522 531521

- **HEART OF ENGLAND TOURIST BOARD**
  Larkhill Road, Worcester WR5 2EF
  ☎ 01905 763436

- **LONDON TOURIST BOARD**
  26 Grosvenor Gardens, London
  SW1W ODU ☎ 0171 730 3488

- **NORTHUMBRIA TOURIST BOARD**
  Aykley Heads, Durham DH1 5UX
  ☎ 0191 384 6905

- **SOUTHERN TOURIST BOARD**
  40 Chamberlayne Road,
  Eastleigh, Hants SO5 5JH
  ☎ 01703 620006

- **SOUTH EAST ENGLAND TOURIST BOARD**
  The Old Brew House, Warwick
  Park, Tunbridge Wells, Kent TN2
  5TU ☎ 01892 540766

- **WEST COUNTRY TOURIST BOARD**
  60 St. David's Hill, Exeter EX4 4SY
  ☎ 01392 211171

- **YORKSHIRE & HUMBERSIDE TOURIST BOARD**
  312 Tadcaster Road, York
  YO2 2HF ☎ 01904 707961

- **NORTHERN IRELAND TOURIST BOARD**
  St. Anne's Court, 59 North Street,
  Belfast BT1 1NB ☎ 01232 231221/246609

- **NORTHERN IRELAND TOURIST BOARD (LONDON)**
  11 Berkeley Street, London
  W1X 5AD ☎ 0171 493 0601

- **SCOTTISH TOURIST BOARD**
  23 Ravelston Terrace, Edinburgh
  EH4 3EU ☎ 0131 332 2433

- **SCOTTISH TOURIST BOARD (LONDON)**
  19 Cockspur Street, London
  SW1Y 5BL ☎ 0171 930 8661

- **WALES TOURIST BOARD**
  Brunel House, 2 Fitzalan Road,
  Cardiff CF2 1UY ☎ 01222 499909

- **WALES TOURIST BOARD (LONDON)**
  12 Lower Regent Street,
  London SW1A 4PQ ☎ 0171 409 0969

- **JERSEY TOURISM**
  Liberation Square, St. Helier,
  Jersey JE1 1BB, Channel Islands
  ☎ 01534 878000

- **STATE OF GUERNSEY TOURIST BOARD**
  PO Box 23, White Rock, St. Peter
  Port, Guernsey, Channel Islands
  ☎ 01481 723552

- **ISLE OF MAN DEPARTMENT OF TOURISM, LEISURE & TRANSPORT**
  C Terminal Building, Douglas,
  Isle of Man ☎ 01624 686801

- **NORTHERN IRELAND TOURIST BOARD**
  ☎ 01232 246609

- **DUBLIN TOURISM**
  ☎ 01 2844768

ESTABLISHMENTS LISTED BY REGION

GREATER LONDON

As one of the most exciting and vibrant cities in the world, London offers the traveller, the tourist and the casual visitor a world of adventure in places to see, places to eat and places to stay.

Scattered amongst its historical landmarks, world-famous department stores, colourful Cockney markets and quiet leafy lanes is the most extensive and diverse selection of *Les Routiers* establishments you will find anywhere. Here you can eat and drink your way around the world in a week, savouring fine food and wine of the highest quality that would cost a fortune in many other restaurants. Any absence of regional dishes is made up for by good, hearty English cooking using only the best and freshest ingredients, hand-picked from the daily markets.

After a busy day touring the capital, there is simply no better way to relax than with a drink in one of *Les Routiers'* Olde Worlde inns. There is also a superb choice of wine bars and bistros serving a wide range of delicious gastronomic snacks, prepared by first-class chefs who are not egocentrically out to dazzle customers and tickle their fancies.

The following areas are included in this chapter:

LONDON
GREATER LONDON

*L*ONDON

ALDGATE • map 2C4

THE GREAT EASTERN HOTEL
Liverpool Street, EC2M 7QN
Set in the famous Square Mile, amongst the country's leading banks and insurance companies, The Great Eastern has 163 rooms equipped with the most modern facilities. A hair-and-beauty salon is open Monday to Friday, and there are two excellent restaurants to choose from. There are 12 rooms available for hire to suit interviews, or conferences catering for 100. Close to the Barbican Arts Centre.
DOUBLE ROOM: from £40 to £50
FOOD: from £20 to £25
Hours: breakfast 7am–10am, lunch 12noon–3pm, bar snacks 11am–10.30pm, dinner 6.30pm–10pm.
Cuisine: ENGLISH – traditional carvery.
Cards: Visa, Access, Diners, AmEx.
Other points: open bank holidays, no-smoking area, afternoon teas, disabled access, residents' lounge, vegetarian meals, children welcome, residents' bar.

Rooms: 21 single rooms, 21 double rooms, 159 twin rooms, 4 quad rooms, 7 family rooms.
Directions: Liverpool Street, right by Liverpool Street station.
☎ (0171) 283 4363 Fax (0171) 283 4897.

BATTERSEA • map ID3

BUCHAN'S
62–4 Battersea Bridge Road,
SW11 3AU
An attractive shop-fronted restaurant/wine-bar which serves outstanding French cuisine in a bustling, friendly atmosphere. The service is welcoming and efficient. Although the cuisine is French, Buchan's also offers Scottish specialities such as Arbroath smokie mousse, Scotch fillet steak flambéed in whisky, and a Scottish-based cheeseboard.
FOOD: up to £15   CLUB
Hours: lunch 12noon–2.45pm, dinner 6pm–10.45pm, closed bank holidays.

Cuisine: FRENCH – specialities include some Scottish dishes. Menu changes weekly. Master chef: Alain Jeannon.
Cards: Visa, Access, Diners, AmEx.
Other points: licensed, Sunday lunch, children welcome, pets allowed.
Directions: 200 yards from Battersea bridge, on the south side of River Thames.
JEREMY & DENISE BOLAM ☎ (0171) 228 0888
[Fax] (0171) 924 1718.

JACK'S PLACE
12 York Road, SW11 3QA
This restaurant has a friendly, relaxed and informal atmosphere. The walls are covered in memorabilia, which keeps the customers interested between courses. With excellent food and substantial portions, Jack's Place is very highly recommended.
FOOD: from £15 to £20
Hours: lunch 12noon–3pm, dinner 6.30pm–11pm, closed Monday.
Cuisine: ENGLISH – steaks and fresh fish are specialities. Sunday lunch is available from September until Easter.
Cards: Visa, Access.
Other points: Sunday lunch, children welcome.
Directions: close to Clapham Junction station.
MR JACK KING ☎ (0171) 228 8519/228 1442.

BAYSWATER • map IC3

CAFE ROUGE
Whiteley's Centre, W2
Situated on the upper level at Whiteley's shopping centre, this is a café/restaurant with a genuine French feel and character, serving excellent traditional bistro food. Cappuccino and light meals are served all day, and the restaurant offers full à la carte. The atmosphere is cosmopolitan and the staff are very friendly yet professional.
FOOD: from £15 to £20
Hours: meals all day 10am–10.30pm (last orders).
Cuisine: FRENCH – with a slight British accent. Regularly changing menus. Light snacks and full à la carte.
Cards: Visa, Access, AmEx, Switch.
Other points: open-air dining, licensed, children welcome, open bank holidays.
Directions: on the second floor of Whiteley's. Nearest tubes Bayswater and Queensway.
MICHAEL CALLIA ☎ (0171) 221 1509.

GARDEN COURT HOTEL
30–31 Kensington Garden Square, W2 4BG
Situated in a calm, leafy Victorian garden square in central London, the Garden Court, built in 1870, is a family-run hotel within walking distance of many of the city's finest tourist attractions, including Kensington Palace and Portobello antique market. Its location allows easy access to buses and the tube.
DOUBLE ROOM: from £20 to £30
SINGLE ROOM: from £25 to £35
Hours: breakfast 7.30am–9.30am, open all year.

Cuisine: BREAKFAST – full English breakfast, a selection of fruits and yoghurts.
Cards: Visa, Mastercard.
Other points: children welcome, open bank holidays.
Rooms: 13 single rooms, 7 double rooms, 8 twin rooms, 1 triple room, 1 family room. All with TV, radio, tea/coffee-making facilities, hair dryer, cots.
Directions: 4-minute walk from Bayswater tube, 6 minutes from Queensway tube.
MR E. CONNOLLY ☎ (0171) 229 2553
[Fax] (0171) 727 2749.

BELGRAVIA • map IC3

NAG'S HEAD
53 Kinnerton Street, SW1X 8ED
Built in 1780, this has been called the smallest pub in London and is thought to be a former gaol. In 1921 it was sold for £11 7s 6d – almost the price of a couple of rounds of drinks today. The Nag's Head, the village pub in Belgravia, is now a free house in the real sense. Since December 1992 the pub has become an independent, one of the very few in the heart of London.
FOOD: up to £15
Hours: meals all day 12noon–10pm.
Cuisine: ENGLISH – traditional home-cooked pub food with daily specials and daily roasts: Irish stew, various curries, chilli con carne, home-made pies.
Other points: licensed, open-air dining, Sunday lunch, no-smoking area, children welcome.
Directions: near to Hyde Park Corner tube, Kinnerton Street is off Wilton Road.
KEVIN MORAN ☎ (0171) 235 1135.

TOPHAMS EBURY COURT
24–32 Ebury Court, SW1W 0LV
The hotel evokes the charm of an English Country House and yet is situated in the heart of Belgravia, one of the most exclusive residential areas in London. Owned and run by three generations of the same family, Tophams Ebury Court has a worldwide reputation for caring for their guests, who return year after year. An intimate, friendly atmosphere greets you instantly upon entering the hotel.
DOUBLE ROOM: from £50
SINGLE ROOM: over £55
FOOD: from £15 to £20
Hours: breakfast 7.30am–9.30am, lunch 12noon–2.30pm, dinner 6pm–9.30pm.
Cuisine: BRITISH – a constantly changing traditional à la carte menu.
Cards: Visa, Access, Diners, AmEx.
Other points: children welcome, pets allowed by prior arrangement, conference facilities, residents' lounge, vegetarian meals, afternoon teas.
Rooms: 16 single rooms, 15 double rooms, 10 twin rooms, 1 triple room. All with TV, telephone, hair dryer.
Directions: close to Victoria train, tube and bus stations.
NICHOLAS & MARIANNE KINGSFORD
☎ (0171) 730 8147 [Fax] (0171) 823 5966.

BISHOPSGATE • map 2C4

🍽 CITY LIMITS RESTAURANT & WINE BAR
16–18 Brushfield Street, E1 6AN
A buzzing, ground-floor wine bar with restaurant downstairs, which doubles as an evening private function room. Situated between the market and offices, with good car-parking facilities very close by.
FOOD: from £15 to £20
Hours: bar meals 11.30am–2.30pm, lunch 12noon–3pm, bar meals 5pm–8pm, closed Saturday and Sunday.
Cuisine: INTERNATIONAL – varied international foods; speciality starters, fresh fish, excellent gateaux. Imaginative wine list, international and unusual beers (non-draught).
Cards: Visa, Access, AmEx.
Other points: children welcome, parking.
Directions: situated in Spitalfields, near the Bishopsgate Institution.
DAVID HUGHES ☎ (0171) 377 9877.

BLOOMSBURY • map 1C3

🏨 ACADEMY HOTEL
17–21 Gower Street, WC1E 6HG
The Academy Hotel is a beautifully appointed hotel set in a listed building, providing comfort and personal service for tourists and business travellers. Ideally situated for theatreland and many historical places of interest, including the British Museum, Jewish Museum and Covent Garden. Conference facilities are available for 6 to 40 people.
DOUBLE ROOM: from £40 to £50
FOOD: up to £15
Hours: breakfast 7am–10.30am, lunch 12noon–2.30pm, dinner 6.30pm–12midnight.
Cuisine: ENGLISH – own club/restaurant, GHQ, with *Les Routiers Golden Casserole* award-winning cuisine, predominantly European/English dishes. Good, reasonably priced wine list.
Cards: Visa, Access, Diners, AmEx.
Other points: licensed, Sunday lunch, children welcome, afternoon tea, garden, conferences, library.
Directions: Nearest tube: Goodge Street, Tottenham Court Road or Russell Square.
METTE DOESSING ☎ (0171) 631 4115
Fax (0171) 636 3442.

🏨 THE BONNINGTON IN BLOOMSBURY
Southampton Row, WC1B 4BH
Owned and run by the Frame family since its construction in 1911, the Bonnington, with its Edwardian facade, offers up-to-the-minute standards of comfort at value-for-money prices. With 200 comfortable bedrooms, imposing lounges and a splendid dining room, an 80-year tradition of friendly service and hospitality awaits. The hotel offers eight flexibly designed function rooms and provides the ideal venue for anything from a small committee meeting to a major conference or luncheon. Its central location makes it ideal for visitors to London.
DOUBLE ROOM: from £40 to £50
SINGLE ROOM: from £55
FOOD: from £15 to £20 CLUB
Hours: breakfast 7am–10am, lunch 12noon–2pm, bar snacks 12noon–2.30pm, dinner 5.30pm–10.30pm, bar snacks 5pm–9.30pm, restaurant closed Saturday and Sunday lunch.
Cuisine: INTERNATIONAL – à la carte and table d'hôte menus.
Cards: Visa, Access, Diners, AmEx.
Other points: children welcome, open bank holidays, no-smoking rooms, afternoon tea, disabled access, pets allowed, residents' lounge, vegetarian meals, conferences, functions, foreign exchange, 24hr reception, residents' bar, baby-listening device, baby-sitting, cots.
Rooms: 108 single rooms, 43 double rooms, 44 twin rooms, 20 family rooms. All with TV, radio, telephone, tea/coffee-making facilities, hair dryer, trouser-press.
Directions: in the heart of London, just minutes from Holborn tube station.
BONNINGTON HOTELS LTD ☎ (0171) 242 2828 Fax (0171) 831 9170.

🏨 EURO AND GEORGE HOTELS
51–53 Cartwright Gardens, WC1H 9EL
The Euro and George Hotels are situated in a quiet crescent of historically-listed buildings. Both provide a high standard of service and comfort at good-value prices. Their central position offers easy access to the West End and local attractions such as the British Museum.
DOUBLE ROOM: from £40 to £50
Hours: breakfast 7.30am–9am.
Cuisine: BREAKFAST.
Cards: Visa, Access, AmEx.
Other points: children welcome, residents' lounge, garden, in-house films, tennis, garden, cots.
Rooms: 23 single rooms, 10 double rooms, 10 twin rooms, 16 triple rooms, 16 quad rooms. All with TV, radio, alarm, telephone, tea/coffee-making facilities.
Directions: close to King's Cross, Euston and Russell Square tube stations.
MR A. MESROPIANS ☎ (0171) 387 8777/387 6789 Fax (0171) 383 5044.

CHELSEA • map 1D3

🍽 CAFE ROUGE
390 King's Road, SW3 5UZ
Cheerful French café with lively and vibrant atmosphere. Varied clientele attests to Café Rouge's continuing popularity. Cappuccino and à la carte food available all day. Warm and courteous staff make you welcome.
FOOD: up to £15
Hours: meals all day 10am–11pm, Sunday 10am–10.30pm.
Cuisine: FRENCH – traditional French food. Full à la carte. Light meals available. Good wine list. Regional specialities.
Cards: Visa, Access, AmEx.
Other points: open bank holidays, children welcome, licensed.
Directions: nearest tube is Sloane Square.
☎ (0171) 352 2226 Fax (0171) 352 8006.

GLAISTER'S GARDEN BISTRO
4 Hollywood Road, SW10 9HW

One of the many inviting features at Glaister's is the beautiful garlanded garden where one can dine alfresco enjoying excellent home-cooked cosmopolitan dishes prepared with great care at very reasonable prices. And if it rains, there's an automatic roof which rolls back to keep you dry! High chairs and children's portions are a feature of bustling Sunday lunches. The garden is also an ideal location for cocktail parties, wedding receptions and birthday parties for up to 40 guests. Balloons or flowers can be supplied, and every effort is taken to ensure your party is a success.
FOOD: up to £15
Hours: lunch 12noon–3pm, Sunday 12noon–4pm, dinner 7.30pm–11.30pm.
Cuisine: ENGLISH / COSMOPOLITAN – delicious daily specials.
Cards: Visa, Access, Diners, AmEx.
Other points: Sunday lunch, vegetarian meals, open air dining, licensed.
Directions: off Fulham Road, opposite the new Chelsea and Westminster Hospital.
STEPHEN GLAISTER & JAMES WRAITH
☎ (0171) 352 0352.

CHISWICK • map 1C2

CAFE ROUGE
227–229 Chiswick High Road, W4

A lively, Parisian-style café with genuine French feel and character, serving excellent traditional bistro food. Light meals and cappuccino served all day. Full à la carte. Continental atmosphere conducive to lingering. Prominently located in the heart of Chiswick shopping area.
FOOD: from £15 to £20
Hours: meals all day 10am–11pm (last orders), Sunday 10am–10.30pm.
Cuisine: FRENCH – with a slight British accent. Regularly changing menus. Light snacks and full à la carte.
Cards: Visa, Access, AmEx, Switch.
Other points: open-air dining, licensed, children welcome, open bank holidays.
Directions: halfway between Turnham Green and Chiswick Park.
GIAMPIEROT MARTIGNONI ☎ (0181) 742 7447.

CHISWICK HOTEL
73 Chiswick High Road, W4 2LS

A well-appointed, luxuriously furnished Victorian hotel offering an ideal base for families visiting London. Under the same ownership for 19 years, it has a warm and welcoming atmosphere and has been steadily improved to an extremely high standard with many modern facilities. Special weekend rates are available on request.
DOUBLE ROOM: from £30 to £40
SINGLE ROOM: over £50
FOOD: up to £15
Cuisine: ENGLISH.
Cards: Visa, Access, Diners, AmEx, Switch.
Other points: parking, children welcome, open bank holidays, pets allowed, residents' lounge, vegetarian meals, garden.
Rooms: 16 single rooms, 3 double rooms, 14 twin rooms.
Directions: turn north on Chiswick Lane from A4, between M4 and Hammersmith at Hogarth roundabout. The hotel is at the junction with Chiswick High Road. Nearest tube Turnham Green (District Line). 30 minutes to Heathrow Airport.
BRYN DREW ☎ (0181) 994 1712 Fax (0181) 742 2585.

LES ROUTIERS
Information & Bookings Line
☎ 0171 610 1856

CLAPHAM • map 1D3

WINDMILL ON THE COMMON
Southside, Clapham Common, SW4 9DE

First mentioned in local records in 1729, the Windmill retains much of its Victorian character and charm. Prize-winning traditional beers are complemented by modern hotel accommodation offering peace and tranquility. An ideal venue for meetings, luncheons, wedding receptions and cocktail parties. Clapham Common is nearby.
DOUBLE ROOM: from £30 to £40
FOOD: up to £15 ☆
Hours: breakfast 7am–10am, bar snacks 12noon–2.30pm, dinner 7pm–10pm, bar snacks 7pm 10pm.
Cuisine: BRITISH.
Cards: Visa, Access, Diners, AmEx.
Other points: parking, children welcome, no-smoking area, disabled access, pets, garden, vegetarian meals, open-air dining.
Rooms: 30 twin rooms.
Directions: follow South Circular to where it crosses A24, turn towards central London on A24; quarter of a mile along on Common side.
MR R. & MRS H. WILLIAMSON ☎ (0181) 673 4578 Fax (0181) 675 1486.

CLERKENWELL • map 2C4

THE HELLENIK RESTAURANT
86 St John Street, EC1M 4EH

A family-run, fully licensed Greek/Cypriot restaurant where good food at reasonable prices matters. Situated near Smithfield and the Barbican, it is ideal for business and pre- or post-theatre meals.
FOOD: up to £15
Hours: lunch 11.45am–3pm, dinner 6pm–11pm, closed in August for three weeks, closed Sunday and bank holidays.
Cuisine: GREEK / CYPRIOT – kleftico, moussaka, meze, souvlaki. Special lunch menu: 11 dips and dishes for £8.50 per person.
Cards: Visa, Access, AmEx.
Other points: children welcome, street parking.
Directions: 500 yards from Smithfield market. Farringdon and Barbican tube stations.
MR P. & MRS A. KRASE ☎ (0171) 253 0754.

COVENT GARDEN • map 1C3

⇛ FOOD FOR THOUGHT
31 Neal Street, WC2 9PA
Ideal for the hungry traveller, this lively vegetarian restaurant provides a warm welcome and quick, friendly service. Menu changed twice a day. Take-away meals and snacks also available.
FOOD: up to £15
Hours: meals all day 9.30am–8pm, Sunday 10.30am–4.30pm, closed Christmas and New Year.
Cuisine: VEGETARIAN – wide range of imaginative vegetarian dishes, all prepared on premises from fresh produce; daily specials.
Other points: no-smoking area, children welcome, parking.
Directions: close to Covent Garden tube. NCP car park in St Martin's Lane.
JERZY PAJDAK & VANESSA GARRETT ☎ (0171) 836 9072 [Fax] (0171) 379 1249.

⇛ FUNG-SHING
15 Lisle Street, WC2 7BE
Fung-Shing is situated in a converted Victorian warehouse. Customers can enjoy a wide variety of competently served Cantonese dishes.
FOOD: up to £15
Hours: meals all day 12noon–11.30pm.
Cuisine: CANTONESE – crispy duck, sizzling prawns.
Cards: Visa, Access, Diners, AmEx.
Other points: licensed, Sunday lunch, private dining.
Directions: in Chinatown.
JIMMY CHIM ☎ (0171) 437 1539.

⇛ HENRY'S CAFE BAR (COVENT GARDEN)
27–29 Endell Street, WC2 7PQ
Set amongst a terrace of small shops, Henry's is modelled on an American-style café-bar. It has a quiet, relaxing atmosphere, dark wooden furniture, Art Deco lamps and a magnificent stained-glass ceiling. Diners can choose from an extensive range of international fast-food, complemented by some interesting wines. Royal Opera House, Covent Garden market, Transport Museum and many more attractions nearby.
FOOD: up to £15
Cuisine: INTERNATIONAL.
Cards: Visa, Access, AmEx.
Other points: children welcome, no-smoking area, afternoon teas, disabled access, vegetarian meals, fully air-conditioned.
Directions: nearest tube is Covent Garden.
MISS V. CUMMINS ☎ (0171) 379 8500.

⇛ LE CAFE DES AMIS DU VIN
12 Hanover Place (off Long Acre), WC2E 9JP
This restaurant offers good value for money in that the food is well prepared, cooked and served, the service is friendly and you can enjoy your meal amidst pleasant surroundings. Popular basement wine bar for theatre-goers. Adjacent to the Royal Opera House. Les Routiers Cheeseboard Award 1991, 1992, 1993, 1994 and 1995.
FOOD: from £15 to £20 🍷 [CLUB]

Hours: meals all day 11.30am–11.30pm.
Cuisine: FRENCH – charcuterie, plats du jour. French cheese and wines.
Cards: Visa, Access, Diners, AmEx.
Other points: open-air dining, children welcome.
Directions: nearest tube Covent Garden, on the Piccadilly Line.
MR P. NOTTAGE/CAFE DES AMIS LIMITED ☎ (0171) 379 3444 [Fax] (0171) 379 9124.

CRYSTAL PALACE • map 2D4

⇛ JOANNA'S
56 Westow Hill, SE19 1RX
Situated in the heart of Crystal Palace, this popular bistro is convenient for Dulwich Picture Gallery, Horniman Museum and the National Sports Centre. There is a distinct North American influence, with wall-mounted pictures, posters and celebrity photographs throughout. The atmosphere is lively and is reminiscent of a true North American restaurant.
FOOD: up to £15
Hours: lunch 12noon–2.30pm, dinner 6pm–11.30pm, meals all day Saturday and Sunday 12noon–11.30pm.
Cuisine: AMERICAN – freshly prepared North American and Asian dishes. Features special low-cost menus as well as a good à la carte menu.
Cards: Visa, Access, Diners, AmEx, Switch.
Other points: parking, children welcome, no-smoking area, open-air dining, vegetarian meals.
Directions: 1 mile south of Dulwich village on the A214. Close to Crystal Palace Sports Centre.
JOHN & CHRIS ELLNER ☎ (0181) 670 4052 [Fax] (0181) 670 8306.

EALING • map 1C2

⇛ ANNE-MARIE AT THE 'TASTE OF THE TAJ'
4 Norbreck Parade, NW10 7HR
The warmth and efficiency of the staff here make this a pleasant and enjoyable place to spend an evening, sampling cuisine of a high quality. The proprietor, Anne-Marie, is pleased to guide you through the many different dishes, which are offered at varying levels of hotness. The service is friendly and efficient and the atmosphere calm and welcoming.
FOOD: up to £15
Hours: lunch 12noon–2.30pm, dinner, 6pm–11.30pm, closed for lunch Saturday and Sunday, closed Christmas.
Cuisine: INDIAN – comprehensive choice of fine Indian-style cuisine.
Cards: Visa, Access, Diners, AmEx.
Other points: licensed, children welcome, disabled access, vegetarian meals, open bank holidays, street parking.
Directions: on Hanger Lane gyratory system – telephone for directions, which are essential . . . .
ANNE-MARIE DUBREIL ☎ (0181) 991 5366/ 991 5209.

LONDON

CAFE ROUGE
17 The Green, W5
A delightful French bistro, cheerfully decorated in traditional café style. Friendly staff contribute to the warm, continental atmosphere. Popular with all ages.
FOOD: from £15 to £20
Hours: meals all day 10am–11pm (last orders), Sunday 10am–10.30pm.
Cuisine: FRENCH – with a slight British accent. Regularly changing menus. Light snacks and full à la carte.
Cards: Visa, Access, AmEx, Switch.
Other points: open-air dining, licensed, children welcome, open bank holidays.
Directions: close to Ealing Broadway and almost opposite Ealing Studios.
PATRICK LECUYER ☎ (0181) 579 2788.

LONDON HOME TO HOME
19 Mount Park Crescent, W5 2RN
A booking agency specializing in high-quality bed-and-breakfast accommodation in private homes in Ealing and other parts of West London (Hammersmith, Chiswick, Kensington and Parsons Green). Homes offer guest rooms for 1 to 4 people, including family rooms, many with private or en suite bathrooms, with full cooked breakfasts. Rates range from £19 to £40. Brochure and listings upon application.
Hours: office is open Monday to Friday 9.30am–5pm.
Cards: Visa, Eurocard, MasterCard.
Other points: children welcome, pets not allowed, parking.
ANITA HARRISON & ROSEMARY RICHARDSON ☎ (0181) 566 7976. Fax (0181) 655 7976.

EALING COMMON • map 1C2

CARNARVON HOTEL
Ealing Common, W5 3HN
A modern, well-appointed hotel overlooking Ealing Common, offering both the business visitor and tourist a convenient and comfortable base just 15 minutes from central London. Spacious and comfortable lounges with a well-stocked residents' bar. The Gunnersby Suite is ideal for meetings and training seminars. Ideally located for quick and easy access to motorways, airport and tube stations.
DOUBLE ROOM: from £50
SINGLE ROOM: over £50
FOOD: from £15 to £20 ★
Hours: breakfast 7am–9.30am, lunch 12.30am–2.30pm, bar snacks 12noon–2.30pm, dinner 6.30pm–9.30pm.
Cuisine: ENGLISH – à la carte and snack menus available.
Other points: licensed.
Rooms: 145 bedrooms.
Directions: located at the junction of the A406 North Circular and Uxbridge Road A4020, overlooking Ealing Common.
CARNARVON HOTELS LTD ☎ (0181) 992 5399 Fax (0181) 992 7082.

CHARLOTTE'S PLACE
16 St Matthews Road, Ealing Common, W5 3JT
A small, cosy restaurant providing imaginative French/English cuisine. Candlelit tables, nostalgic music and friendly staff add to the overall ambience.
FOOD: from £15 to £20 CLUB
Hours: lunch 12.30am–2pm, dinner 7.30pm–10pm, closed Saturday lunch and Sunday.
Cuisine: FRENCH / ENGLISH – complemented by a comprehensive wine list. Fixed-price lunch menu.
Cards: Visa, Access, Diners, AmEx.
Other points: licensed, children welcome, vegetarian meals.
Directions: just off Uxbridge Road, overlooking Ealing Common.
JOHN & CHARLOTTE KEARNS ☎ (0181) 567 7541.

EARLS COURT • map 1C3

KENSINGTON COURT HOTEL
33 Nevern Place, SW5 9NP
Built in the 1970s, this hotel has undergone recent refurbishment. Catering for businessmen and tourists, it is an ideal location for short-stay guests. Nearby for South Kensington museums.
DOUBLE ROOM: from £20 to £30
FOOD: up to £15
Hours: breakfast 7am–9.30am.
Cuisine: BREAKFAST.
Cards: Visa, Access, Diners, AmEx.
Other points: parking, children welcome.
Rooms: 10 twin rooms. All with TV, radio, alarm, tea/coffee-making facilities.
Directions: off Earls Court Road, just a few minutes' walk from Earls Court tube.
MR S. KADIR ☎ (0171) 370 5151 Fax (0171) 370 3499.

KENSINGTON INTERNATIONAL HOTEL
4 Templeton Place, SW5 9LZ
A delightful Victorian hotel, recently renovated to a high standard. An inventive decorating scheme means every floor follows a different theme; Art Deco, Chinese, Tudor. Imaginative lunch and dinner scheme involving local restaurants. Extremely friendly, helpful staff. Altogether outstanding value for money.
DOUBLE ROOM: from £30 to £40
SINGLE ROOM: from £55
FOOD: up to £15
Hours: bar meals 6pm–11pm, breakfast 8am–10am.
Cuisine: ENGLISH / CONTINENTAL – substantial continental or English breakfast. Lunch and dinner provided by local Chinese, Italian or Indian restaurants using hotel voucher.
Cards: Visa, Access, Diners, AmEx.
Other points: room service, conservatory, residents' bar, children welcome, residents' lounge, garden, cots, 24hr reception, left luggage, vegetarian meals.
Rooms: 15 single rooms, 15 double rooms, 24 twin rooms, 2 triple rooms. All with TV, telephone, tea/coffee-making facilities.
Directions: close to Earl's Court tube, between

Warwick Road and Earls Court Road.
DENZIL RATNAM ☎ (0171) 370 4333
[Fax] (0171) 244 7873.

FINCHLEY • map 1B3

🍽 **RANI VEGETARIAN RESTAURANT**
7 Long Lane, Finchley Central, N3 2PR
A high-class and well-known speciality restaurant, offering an extensive choice of Indian vegetarian dishes. All produce is freshly prepared by family chefs. Bright and welcoming, with a warm and friendly atmosphere.
FOOD: up to £15 [CLUB] ☆
Hours: lunch 12.15am–4pm, dinner 6pm–12midnight, closed lunchtime Monday, Saturday and Christmas day.
Cuisine: INDIAN VEGETARIAN.
Cards: Visa, Access, AmEx.
Other points: children welcome, Sunday lunch, open bank holidays, no-smoking area, disabled access.
Directions: 5-minute walk from Finchley Central tube.
JYOTINDRA PATTNI ☎ (0181) 349 4386
[Fax] (0181) 349 4386.

FOREST HILL • map 2D4

🍽 **BABUR BRASSERIE**
119 Brockley Rise, SE23 1JP
A stylish, upmarket restaurant providing comfortable dining in smart surroundings. The Moghul-style menu spoils you for choice, ranging from the tasty appetizers through the Tandoori selection, to fish, prawn and vegetable dishes. Babur specialities: Shugati Masala (chicken in spices and a masala sauce enriched with coconut and poppy seeds) and Babur-e-Bhojan (a selection of Murgh Tikka, Boti Kebab, Sali Jardaloo and Makhani, with nan and basmati rice). Although not listed separately, the chef will prepare any traditional dishes, such as Rogan Josh, Dupeaza or Dhansak at your request.
FOOD: up to £15
Hours: lunch 12noon–2.30pm, dinner 6pm–11.30pm, closed Christmas day and Boxing day.
Cuisine: MOGHUL.
Cards: Visa, Access, Diners, AmEx.
Other points: licensed, Sunday buffet lunch, children welcome.
Directions: Brockley Rise is off the South Circular–Stansted Road.
BABUR LTD ☎ (0181) 291 2400/291 4881.

FULHAM • map 1D3

🍽 **CAFE ROUGE**
855 Fulham Road, SW6 5HJ
A café/restaurant with a genuine French feel and character, serving excellent traditional bistro food. Cappuccino and light meals are served all day, and the restaurant offers full à la carte. The atmosphere is cosmopolitan and the French staff are very friendly yet professional. Popular with all ages.
FOOD: up to £15
Hours: meals all day 10am–11pm, Sunday 10am–10.30pm.
Cuisine: FRENCH – traditional French cuisine. Menu changes every 3 months, but generally includes marmite dieppoise, entrecôte béarnaise. Lighter meals also served.
Cards: Visa, Access, AmEx.
Other points: licensed, Sunday lunch, children welcome, open bank holidays, afternoon tea.
Directions: on corner of Munster Road.
CAFE ROUGE LTD ☎ (0171) 371 7600.

🍽 **LA TERRAZA**
53 Fulham Broadway, SW6 1AE
A light, bright and airy Spanish restaurant, decorated with plants and paintings to create comfortable, authentic surroundings. All dishes from the large, varied menu are fresh and the servings are plentiful. The newly opened La Terraza is a welcome addition for local residents and business people. It is also popular with visitors to the Fulham area.
FOOD: up to £15
Hours: lunch 12noon–3pm, dinner 6pm–10.30pm.
Cuisine: SPANISH – typical Spanish dishes, with both à la carte and Tapas menus available.
Cards: Visa, Access.
Other points: children welcome, no-smoking area, vegetarian meals.
Directions: situated 100 yards from Fulham Broadway tube station.
ARTHUR & TONY ROSA ☎ (0171) 385 9272.

GREENWICH • map 2C4

🍽 **SPREAD EAGLE RESTAURANT**
1&2 Stockwell Street, SE10 9JN
A tavern since before the 1650s and later a thriving coaching inn and hostelry. Strong 19th century music hall connections. The Spread Eagle is a truly fascinating place steeped in history, much of it still visible. Provides business lunches, bar snacks and pre-theatre suppers. Three dining areas. Private party facilities. A visit is highly recommended.
FOOD: from £15 to £20
Hours: lunch 12noon–3pm, dinner 6.30pm–10.30pm (last orders).
Cuisine: FRENCH – a constantly changing menu. Lunch menu available from £8.
Other points: children welcome, disabled access, vegetarian meals.
Directions: situated just off the A2 and A206, opposite the Greenwich Theatre.
MR R. MOY ☎ (0181) 853 2333 [Fax] (0181) 305 1666.

HAMMERSMITH • map 1C3

🏠 **DALMACIA HOUSE**
71 Shepherd's Bush Road, W6 7LS
This recently refurbished Victorian terraced house offers comfortable accommodation and value for

money. The family who run the hotel speak French and Serbo-Croat. Situated midway between central London and Heathrow. Olympia and Kensington nearby.
DOUBLE ROOM: up to £20
Hours: breakfast 7am–9.30am, dinner 6pm–8.30pm.
Cuisine: BREAKFAST.
Cards: Visa, Access, Diners, AmEx.
Other points: children welcome, cots, left luggage.
Rooms: 3 single rooms, 3 doubles, 6 twins, 4 triples. All with TV, telephone.
Directions: on A219, north of Hammersmith tube. Identified in 'Airbus' leaflet.
GEORGE KRIVOSIC ☎ (0171) 603 2887
[Fax] (0171) 602 9226.

ST PETERS HOTEL
407–411 Goldhawk Road, W6 0SA
A small, personally-run hotel offering clean and comfortable accommodation to suit both business and tourist clientele. On the bus route for Kew Gardens, the River Thames and the West End.
DOUBLE ROOM: from £20 to £30
SINGLE ROOM: from £25 to £35
Hours: breakfast 7am–9.30am.
Cuisine: ENGLISH.
Cards: Visa, Access, AmEx.
Other points: children welcome, open bank holidays, afternoon tea, residents' lounge, residents' bar.
Rooms: 4 single rooms, 4 double rooms, 10 twin rooms.
Directions: opposite Stamford Brook tube station. Close to M4. Junction: Goldhawk Road and Chiswick High Road.
MR M. COSIC ☎ (0181) 741 4239 [Fax] (0181) 748 3845.

HAMPSTEAD • map 2C3

CAFE ROUGE
19 High Street, NW3 1PX
A French café/restaurant, serving traditional bistro food in an informal but professional atmosphere. Serves cappuccino and light meals all day in the café area, and the restaurant offers full à la carte.
FOOD: up to £15
Hours: meals all day 10am–11pm, Sunday 10am–10.30pm.
Cuisine: FRENCH – traditional French cuisine. Menu changes every three months, but generally offers marmite dieppoise, cochonaille and plats du jour.
Cards: Visa, Access, AmEx.
Other points: licensed, Sunday lunch, no-smoking area, children welcome, open bank holidays.
Directions: nearest tube is Hampstead.
CAFE ROUGE LTD ☎ (0171) 433 3404.

HARROW • map 1B2

THE HARROW HOTEL
Roxborough Bridge, 12–22 Pinner Road, HA1 4HZ
Situated within easy travelling distance of Wembley Stadium and Conference Centre and the heart of London, The Harrow Hotel is popular with business people and tourists alike. Warm and courteous service is displayed at all times, whether relaxing in the luxurious lounge and bar or dining in the superb restaurant. A pleasant stay is assured.
DOUBLE ROOM: from £30 to £40
SINGLE ROOM: from £55
FOOD: from £15 to £20 ☆
Hours: breakfast 7am–9.30am, lunch 12noon–2pm, dinner 6.45pm–9.45pm.
Cuisine: ENGLISH.
Cards: Visa, Access, Diners, AmEx.
Other points: parking, children welcome, no-smoking area, disabled access, garden, vegetarian meals.
Rooms: 58 bedrooms. All with en suite, TV, radio, telephone, tea/coffee-making facilities, hair dryer.
Directions: at the junction of the A404 and A312 at the Harrow Town end of Pinner Road.
MR I.F. HARTOG ☎ (0181) 427 3435
[Fax] (0181) 861 1370.

HIGHGATE • map 1B3

CAFE ROUGE
6–7 South Grove, N6 6BS
Cavern-type French café with lively decor. Frothy cappuccino complements the vibrant continental atmosphere. Cheerful service and good food.
FOOD: up to £15
Hours: meals all day 10am–11pm, Sunday 10am–10.30pm.
Cuisine: FRENCH – traditional French cuisine including marmite dieppoise, saucisses fumées and sandwiches. Good wine list.
Cards: Visa, Access, AmEx.
Other points: open bank holidays, licensed.
Directions: near Highgate tube.
☎ (0181) 342 9797 [Fax] (0181) 342 9503.

HOLBORN • map 1C3

BLEEDING HEART WINE BAR
Bleeding Heart Yard, Greville Street, EC1N 8SJ
The Bleeding Heart is well-hidden beneath historic Bleeding Heart Yard off Greville Street, near Farringdon tube. Not only does the Yard feature in Dickens' novel Little Dorrit – hence the Dickensian atmosphere and first editions - but it is said to be haunted by the ghost of Lady Hatton. Terrace for outdoor eating in summer.
FOOD: from £15 to £20
Hours: lunch 12noon–3pm, dinner 5.30pm–10.30pm, closed Saturday and Sunday.
Cuisine: FRENCH charcoal-grilled meats, French regional dishes (especially Provençal). Over 200 wines, many by the glass.
Cards: Visa, Access, Diners, AmEx.
Other points: licensed, open-air dining, coaches by prior arrangement.
Directions: nearest tube Farringdon.
MR R. WILSON ☎ (0171) 242 8238/242 2056.

HODGSON'S
115 Chancery Lane, WC2A 1PP

This attractive restaurant, once the legal book depository for Sotheby's, serves beautifully presented food in generous portions. The à la carte menu is changed every 6 weeks, and there is a daily table d'hôte lunch menu offering a choice of three starters, main courses and desserts, representing excellent value for money.
FOOD: from £15 to £20
Hours: lunch 12noon–2.30pm, bar meals 11am–11pm, dinner 5pm–11pm, closed Saturday and Sunday.
Cuisine: CONTINENTAL – nouvelle cuisine-style à la carte and table d'hôte menus. Includes roast monkfish teriyaki, magret of duck, roast rack of lamb.
Cards: Visa, Access, Diners, AmEx.
Other points: children welcome.
Directions: off Fleet Street.
☎ (0171) 242 2836.

HOLLAND PARK • map IC3

HOLLAND PARK HOTEL
6 Ladbroke Terrace, W11 3PG

Situated in a quiet tree-lined area close to Kensington Palace, this Victorian town house has been extensively renovated and restored to provide fine accommodation in relaxed and comfortable surroundings. There is an elegant sitting room and a beautiful garden. Close to shops and restaurants, with major train, bus and tube services just minutes away.
DOUBLE ROOM: from £20 to £25
Cuisine: BREAKFAST – continental breakfast.
Cards: Visa, Access, Diners, AmEx.
Other points: licensed, children welcome, residents' lounge, garden, cots, 24hr reception.
Rooms: 11 single rooms, 7 double rooms, 5 twin rooms, 2 triple rooms.
Directions: situated north of Holland Park Road, near Holland Park tube station.
MR BELLHOUSE ☎ (0171) 792 0216
[Fax] (0171) 727 8166.

KENSINGTON • map IC3

ABCONE HOTEL
10 Ashburn Gardens, SW7 4DG

Located in a quiet street in the heart of Kensington, the Abcone is ideal for business or pleasure. All rooms are equipped with many modern facilities, including in-house video and satellite movies. Full secretarial services are available to all business clients. Just a short walk away from Hyde Park, the Natural History and Victoria & Albert Museums, and the world-famous Harrods.
DOUBLE ROOM: from £30 to £40
SINGLE ROOM: from £35 to £45
Hours: breakfast 7.30am–9.30am.
Cards: Visa, Access, Diners, AmEx.
Other points: residents' lounge, children welcome.
Rooms: 17 single rooms, 14 double rooms, 4 twin rooms.
Directions: off Cromwell Road, turn on to Ashburn Gardens.
MR A.A. SADDUDDIN ☎ (0171) 370 3383
[Fax] (0171) 373 3082.

ATLAS HOTEL
24–30 Lexham Gardens, W8 5JE

This well-maintained Victorian terraced hotel is situated in a desirable part of Kensington, close to Earls Court and Olympia exhibition centres, Natural History Museum, Victoria & Albert Museum, Science Museum, Kensington Gardens and Hyde Park. Recently refurbished to provide tasteful and comfortable accommodation, the Atlas Hotel is an ideal place to stay when visiting London on business or pleasure.
DOUBLE ROOM: from £20 to £30
SINGLE ROOM: from £45 to £55
Hours: breakfast 7.30am–9.30am.
Cuisine:.
Cards: Visa, Access, Diners, AmEx.
Other points: children welcome, residents' lounge, residents' bar.
Rooms: 19 single rooms, 5 double rooms, 20 twin rooms, 6 triple rooms. All with TV, telephone, radio. Most rooms are en suite.
Directions: off Cromwell Road (A4), first turn on left after Cromwell Hospital. Within easy walking distance of High Street Kensington, Gloucester Road and Earls Court tube stations.
KEITH FENTON ☎ (0171) 835 1155
[Fax] (0171) 370 4853.

BEAVER HOTEL
57–59 Philbeach Gardens, SW5 9ED

Situated in a quiet, tree-lined crescent of late Victorian houses, Beaver Hotel is ideally placed for Earls Court, Olympia and central London. Car park for hotel guests. Rooms with en suite facilities also have TV, hairdryer and telephone. Basic rooms have telephone and radio.
DOUBLE ROOM: from £20 to £30
SINGLE ROOM: from £35 to £45
Hours: breakfast 7.30am–9.30am.
Cuisine: BREAKFAST.
Cards: Visa, Access, AmEx.
Other points: children welcome, pets allowed, baby-sitting, cots, left luggage, residents' lounge, residents' bar.
Rooms: 18 single rooms, 6 double rooms, 10 twin rooms, 4 triple rooms. Many rooms are en suite.
Directions: off Warwick Road, between Earls Court Exhibition Centre and A4 Cromwell Road.
JAN LIS ☎ (0171) 373 4553 [Fax] (0171) 373 4555.

CAFE ROUGE
2 Lancer Square (off Kensington Church Street), W8 5EB

A delightful French bistro, cheerfully decorated in traditional café style. Friendly staff contribute to the warm, continental atmosphere. Good location, with easy access to shops.
FOOD: up to £15

LONDON

Hours: meals all day 10am–11pm, Sunday 10am–10.30pm.
Cuisine: FRENCH – traditional French food. Full à la carte with a good wine list. Light meals available all day.
Cards: Visa, Access, AmEx.
Other points: children welcome, open bank holidays, licensed.
Directions: a few minutes' walk from High Street Kensington tube.
☎ (0171) 938 4200.

IL PORTICO
277 Kensington High Street, W8 6SA
A popular high street restaurant, offering a good selection of Italian-style cuisine. The atmosphere is warm and friendly, attracting a regular, mostly local clientele. Ideally situated for visiting the famous Albert Hall, Hyde Park and many other London tourist attractions.
FOOD: from £20 to £25
Hours: lunch 12noon–3pm, dinner 6pm–11.30pm.
Cuisine: ITALIAN – à la carte menu, offering a wide range of Italian-style cuisine. Vegetarian dishes available.
Cards: Visa, Access, AmEx.
Other points: no-smoking area, children welcome, vegetarian meals.
Directions: easy to locate – situated almost opposite the Commonwealth Institute.
ANNA & PINO CHIAVARINI ☎ (0171) 602 6262.

LA SALA ROMANA
1st Floor, 117 Gloucester Road, SW7 4ST
Newly decorated, La Sala Romana offers diners a cosy, relaxed atmosphere in which to enjoy the freshly prepared Italian dishes. Close to the museums and the many hotels in the area, the restaurant is not only frequented by locals but also by tourists of all nationalities.
FOOD: from £20 to £25 [CLUB]
Hours: lunch 12noon–2.30pm, dinner 6.30pm–9.30pm, closed Christmas eve, Christmas day and Boxing day.
Cuisine: ITALIAN – freshly prepared Italian dishes from an extensive à la carte menu.
Cards: Visa, Access, Diners, AmEx.
Other points: children welcome, vegetarian meals.
Directions: located near Gloucester Road tube station.
MATTHEW NELSON ☎ (0171) 373 3678
[Fax] (0171) 370 1316.

SCOFFS EATING HOUSE
267 Kensington High Street, W8 6NA
The decor of this popular 'eating house' is reminiscent of North Italian restaurants, with brick floors, white plaster walls and wooden beams. The food is made from fresh produce, and the good-sized portions are served by pleasant, efficient staff.
FOOD: up to £15
Hours: meals all day 10am–12midnight.
Cuisine: ITALIAN.
Cards: Visa, Access, Diners, AmEx.
Other points: children welcome.

Directions: next to the Odeon Cinema in Kensington High Street.
MR L. SBUTTONI AND MS P. MANCINI
☎ (0171) 602 6777.

KEW • map 1D2

CAFE ROUGE
Firth Street, TW9 3IU
A lively, Parisian-style café with genuine French feel and character, serving excellent traditional bistro food. Light meals and cappuccino served all day. An ideal place to rest after a walk in Kew Gardens.
FOOD: from £15 to £20
Hours: meals all day 10am–11pm (last orders), Sunday 10am–10.30pm.
Cuisine: FRENCH – with a slight British accent. Regularly changing menus. Light snacks and full à la carte.
Cards: Visa, Access, AmEx.
Other points: open-air dining, licensed, children welcome, open bank holidays.
Directions: close to Kew Gardens and the tube station.
CATHY SUE HOPE ☎ (0181) 332 2882.

KING'S CROSS • map 1C3

THE GREAT NORTHERN HOTEL
Pancras Road, N1 9AN
Opened in 1854, The Great Northern Hotel is situated between King's Cross and St Pancras main line stations. The atmosphere is of a warm and friendly modern establishment. Squires Carving Restaurant is an ideal venue for lunch and dinner, before retiring to the Potters Bar. The hotel also has a choice of 13 meeting rooms, and private catering arrangements with seating for up to 100.
DOUBLE ROOM: from £40 to £50
FOOD: from £15 to £20 [CLUB]
Hours: breakfast 7am–10am, Sunday 8am–10.30am, lunch 12noon–3pm, weekends 12noon–2pm, dinner 5.30pm–10pm, weekends 5.30pm–9pm, closed Christmas eve until Boxing day.
Cuisine: ENGLISH.
Cards: Visa, Access, Diners, AmEx.
Other points: parking, children welcome, afternoon teas, vegetarian meals, residents' lounge, residents' bar.
Rooms: 13 single rooms, 60 double rooms, 16 family rooms. All with TV, telephone, tea/coffee-making facilities.
Directions: access from Pancras Road.
☎ (0171) 837 5454 [Fax] (0171) 278 5270.

KNIGHTSBRIDGE • map 1C3

CAFE ROUGE
27–31 Basil Street, SW3
A French café/restaurant, serving traditional bistro food in an informal but professional atmosphere. Serves cappuccino and light meals all day as well as a full à la carte menu. Perfect for relaxing after a shopping expedition at Harrods.
FOOD: from £15 to £20

Hours: meals all day 10am–11pm (last orders), Sunday 10am–10.30pm.
Cuisine: FRENCH – with a slight British accent. Regularly changing menus. Light snacks and full à la carte.
Cards: Visa, Access, AmEx, Switch.
Other points: open-air dining, licensed, children welcome, open bank holidays.
Directions: opposite the rear entrance to Harrods.
IAN WILD ☎ (0171) 584 2345.

LEADENHALL • map 2C4

BEAUCHAMPS RESTAURANT
25 Leadenhall Market, EC3V 1LR
A turn-of-the-century city restaurant, tastefully furnished in dark wood and brass, situated within the confines of Leadenhall Market. A range of quality fish speciality dishes are available. The restaurant is unique in London by owning its own fishmonger, 'Ashdown,' with live holding-tanks for shellfish. Attractions nearby include Lloyds, Stock Exchange and Bank of England. Evening parties welcome by appointment.
FOOD: from £20 to £25 [CLUB]
Hours: morning coffee 9.30am–11.30am, meals all day 11.30am–3.30pm, closed bank holidays.
Cuisine: SEAFOOD – excellent selection of fish speciality dishes, including lobster with ginger and spring onion, halibut steak with thyme, parsley and cream. Often two or three daily specials.
Cards: Visa, Access, Diners, AmEx.
Other points: licensed, children welcome, vegetarian meals, hard to park.
Directions: take either the Bank or Monument tube. Just off Leadenhall Street.
JOHN BEAUCHAMP BLACKETT ☎ (0171) 621 1331 [Fax] (0171) 626 5889.

LONDON BRIDGE • map 2C4

CAFE ROUGE
Hays Galleria, Tooley Street, SE1 2HD
Lively French café with warm, vibrant decor. Continental atmosphere conducive to lingering after a meal. Friendly, efficient service and frothy cappuccino. Pétanque pitch outside all summer.
FOOD: up to £15
Hours: meals all day - weekdays 10am–10pm, weekends 10am–6pm.
Cuisine: FRENCH – lively French cuisine. Light meals available. French pizzeria open at lunch time.
Cards: Visa, Access, Diners, AmEx.
Other points: open bank holidays, children welcome.
Directions: a few minutes' walk from London Bridge tube station.
☎ (0171) 378 0097 [Fax] (0171) 378 6317.

MAIDA VALE • map 1C3

CAFE ROUGE
30 Clifton Road, W9
A delightful French bistro, cheerfully decorated in traditional café style. Friendly staff contribute to the warm, continental atmosphere. Conveniently located for exploring Little Venice.
FOOD: from £15 to £20
Hours: meals all day 10am–11pm (last orders), Sunday 10am–10.30pm.
Cuisine: FRENCH – with a slight British accent. Regularly changing menus. Light snacks; full à la carte.
Cards: Visa, Access, AmEx, Switch.
Other points: open-air dining, licensed, children welcome, open bank holidays.
Directions: Clifton Road is just off Edgware Road. Nearest tube Warwick Avenue.
GILLES GAUBERT ☎ (0171) 286 2266.

MAYFAIR • map 1C3

DINO'S (MAYFAIR)
33 North Audley Street, W1Y 1WG
Forming part of an attractive Edwardian terrace, Dino's is divided into three sections and decorated accordingly: coffee bar, trattoria and restaurant. It offers a typical Italian menu and the atmosphere is lively, with an upmarket clientele.
FOOD: up to £15 [CLUB]
Hours: meals all day 8am–11.30pm.
Cuisine: ITALIAN.
Cards: Visa, Access, Diners, AmEx.
Other points: children welcome, afternoon teas, disabled access, vegetarian meals.
Directions: situated just off Oxford Street, close to Selfridges and minutes from the tube.
☎ (0171) 629 7070 [Fax] (0171) 370 1316.

NOTTING HILL • map 1C3

192 RESTAURANT
192 Kensington Park Road, W11 2ES
This appealing modern restaurant and wine bar, with pavement tables where you can enjoy dining alfresco in the summer months, is light and airy, with a modern feel to it. This is reflected in the good-sized portions, attractively presented by the courteous, friendly staff. Very popular with local residents, business people and visitors.
FOOD: from £15 to £20
Hours: lunch (Mon-Fri) 12.30am–3pm, Sunday 1pm–3.30pm, dinner (Mon-Fri) 7pm–11.30pm, Sunday 7pm–11pm.
Cuisine: BRITISH – freshly made modern British dishes from the à la carte and table d'hôte menus.
Cards: Visa, Access, Diners, AmEx.
Other points: vegetarian meals, traditional Sunday lunch.
Directions: 5 minutes' walk from Notting Hill Gate tube station.
ANTHONY MACKINTOSH ☎ (0171) 229 0482.

CAFE ROUGE
31 Kensington Park Road, W11 2EU
A traditional French bistro/bar open for meals and snacks throughout the day. Whether you dine à la carte or choose a lighter snack, all dishes are very well cooked, using fresh ingredients. A welcoming and relaxed atmosphere prevails, and the professional but young and friendly staff will go out of their way to ensure that you enjoy your visit.
FOOD: up to £15

Hours: meals all day 10am–11pm, closed August bank holiday, closed Christmas day.
Cuisine: FRENCH – traditional French cuisine such as marmite dieppoise, entrecôte béarnaise and plats du jour. Also French snacks and sandwiches.
Cards: Visa, Access, AmEx.
Other points: licensed, Sunday lunch, children welcome, functions.
Directions: close to Portobello market.
CAFE ROUGE LTD ☎ (0171) 221 4449
[Fax] (0171) 738 5301.

OVAL • map 1D3

THE OLD CALCUTTA
64A Brixton Road, SW9 6BP
This highly acclaimed and popular restaurant is lavishly decorated in a pleasant colour scheme, with fine Indian art displayed on the walls and plenty of plants to decorate the room. The menu is extensive, and although many of the dishes listed are not instantly recognizable, the helpful staff will advise you on selection. The Old Calcutta is situated close to the Oval Cricket Ground, Imperial War Museum, Old Vic Theatre and only a short cab-ride away from the Houses of Parliament.
FOOD: up to £15 [CLUB] ☆
Hours: lunch 12noon–2.30pm, dinner 6pm–12midnight, closed Christmas day.
Cuisine: INDIAN – Tandoori and curries made daily from the freshest produce available.
Cards: Visa, Access, Diners, AmEx.

Other points: children welcome, parking, vegetarian meals, no-smoking area.
Directions: a short walk from Oval tube station.
MR ABDUL MAZID ☎ (0171) 582 1415.

PADDINGTON • map 1C3

ASHLEY HOTEL
15 Norfolk Square, W2 1RU
The Ashley Hotel is flanked by its sister hotels, the Tregaron and the Oasis; all three adjoin one another and are interconnected. Very centrally situated in a pretty garden square, a few minutes' bus ride from Oxford Street and close to Paddington station. The Norfolk gardens were redesigned in 1990 to re-create the Victorian era. A lovely and quiet place to sit and take your ease.
DOUBLE ROOM: from £20 to £30
SINGLE ROOM: from £25 to £35
Hours: breakfast 7.30am–9am, closed Christmas.
Cuisine: BREAKFAST full English breakfast.
Cards: Visa, Access.
Other points: central heating, children welcome, no evening meal, residents' lounge, left luggage.
Rooms: 12 single rooms, 14 double rooms, 14 twin rooms, 1 triple room, 5 family rooms. All with IV, radio, tea/coffee-making facilities. Many rooms are en suite.
Directions: situated between Praed Street and Sussex Gardens. 3 minutes from Paddington station.
MR W.J. & MR D.E. GEORGE ☎ (0171) 723 3375 [Fax] (0171) 723 0173.

Ashley Hotel

LONDON

A charming and pretty Garden Square, where you can relax quietly by the lawns and flowers, with London's traffic just a distant hum. It's so peaceful here, it's hard to believe that you're in the centre of London, and just 10 minutes away from Piccadilly Circus.

And the Hotel? Well, we're just across the road from the Gardens, a quiet 52-room Hotel, owned by the same Welsh family for over 25 years. The bedrooms are very attractive, most have private showers and toilets, all have colour T.V's and tea-making facilities, and the full English breakfasts are really excellent. The prices are good too, for this is centre-of-town accommodation that won't burn a hole in your pocket.

Most of our guests are return visits, and it's easy to see why.

We are... **ASHLEY HOTEL**
15 NORFOLK SQUARE
HYDE PARK, LONDON W2 1RU
(Tel: 071-723-3375) (Fax: 071-723-0173)

LONDON

◆ MITRE HOUSE HOTEL
178–184 Sussex Gardens, W2 1TU

The Mitre House Hotel has been run by the same family for over 30 years, and this is reflected in its comfortable atmosphere and ambience. Ideally located on the north side of Hyde Park. Central London is easily accessible, and should you require a hired car or a sightseeing tour, the helpful staff will be happy to assist.
DOUBLE ROOM: from £30 to £40
SINGLE ROOM: from £45 to £55
Hours: breakfast 7.30am–9am.
Cards: Visa, Access, Diners, AmEx.
Other points: children welcome.
Rooms: 6 single rooms, 27 double rooms, 27 twin rooms, 7 family rooms, 3 junior suites. All with TV, radio, telephone. Suites also have trouser-press, fridge, Jacuzzi bath.
Directions: south of Paddington tube, parallel to Praed Street.
ANDREW & MICHAEL CHRIS ☎ (0171) 723 8040 [Fax] (0171) 402 0990.

PICCADILLY • map 1C3

≡€ HENRY'S CAFE BAR (PICCADILLY)
80 Piccadilly, W1V 9HF

An attractive café-bar with Art Deco interior, serving an extensive range of international fast-food dishes, speciality cocktails and American beers. Very popular with businessmen and tourists and busy at lunchtimes. Near to many major tourist attractions, including Buckingham Palace and the Royal Academy.
FOOD: up to £15
Hours: meals all day 8am–11pm.
Cuisine: INTERNATIONAL.
Cards: Visa, Access, AmEx.
Other points: children welcome, open bank holidays, afternoon teas, no-smoking area, disabled access, vegetarian meals.
MR M. GLANCY ☎ (0171) 491 2544.

PUTNEY • map 1D3

≡€ CAFE ROUGE
200–204 Putney Bridge Road, SW15 2NA

A French café/restaurant, serving traditional bistro food in an informal but professional atmosphere. Cappuccino and light meals are served all day in the café area, and the restaurant offers full à la carte (à la carte menu also available in the café area). Attractively decorated in reds and dark wood, the atmosphere is busy yet relaxing. Popular with all ages.
FOOD: up to £15
Hours: meals all day 10am–11pm, closed Christmas day.
Cuisine: FRENCH – French dishes such as Normandy fish stew, entrecôte béarnaise. Snacks include baguette du Café Rouge (hot steak sandwich), croque-monsieur.
Cards: Visa, Access, AmEx.
Other points: licensed, open-air dining, Sunday lunch, children welcome, street parking.

Directions: left off Putney High Street at the Cannon Cinema. Very close to Putney Bridge.
☎ (0181) 788 4257 [Fax] (0181) 785 9608.

≡€ GAVIN'S RESTAURANT
5 Lacy Road, SW15 1NH

This lively Putney restaurant has an interesting menu with imaginative brasserie-style dishes and an excellent choice of fresh pasta with a wide selection of sauces, all complemented by a well-selected wine list. It has a great atmosphere and a well-established local reputation.
FOOD: up to £15
Hours: lunch 12noon–3.30pm, dinner 6pm–11pm.
Cuisine: ECLECTIC CONTINENTAL – à la carte menu specializing in brasserie and fresh pasta dishes.
Cards: Visa.
Other points: Sunday lunch, children welcome.
Directions: Lacy Road runs off Putney High Street, opposite Marks & Spencer.
MARK MILTON & GAVIN BARLOW ☎ (0181) 785 9151 [Fax] (0181) 788 1703.

≡€ MYRA RESTAURANT
240 Upper Richmond Road, SW15 6TG

This cosy, Victorian-fronted restaurant is situated close to the junction with Putney High Street and welcomes family groups to complement its strong local patronage. Theme nights are a popular 'speciality', so book ahead to avoid disappointment! Traditional English fayre, all home-cooked by Myra, and a warm welcome guarantee satisfaction.
FOOD: from £15 to £20 [CLUB]
Hours: lunch 12noon–2.30pm, Sunday 12.30am–4pm, dinner 6.30pm–11pm.
Cuisine: ENGLISH – à la carte, fixed price three-course menu.
Cards: Visa, Access, Diners, AmEx.
Other points: licensed, open-air dining, Sunday lunch, children welcome, garden.
Directions: on South Circular, near Putney Bridge.
MISS MOLONY ☎ (0181) 788 9450.

≡€ SAMRATT INDIAN CUISINE
18–20 Lacy Road, SW15 1NL

This spacious and airy restaurant is pleasantly decorated, and although it is a popular restaurant, it is also peaceful and relaxing. The extensive menu offers an impressive selection of meat, chicken, seafood and vegetable dishes, complemented by a well-stocked bar and wine cellar.
FOOD: from £15 to £20
Hours: lunch 12noon–3pm, dinner 6pm–11.30pm.
Cuisine: INDIAN – the house speciality is Kurchi-style dishes.
Cards: Visa, Access, AmEx.
Other points: parking, children welcome, no-smoking area, vegetarian meals.
Directions: Lacy Road is situated opposite Marks and Spencer, Putney High Street.
SATYENDRANATH DATTA ☎ (0181) 788 9110/ 785 4487.

TRAPPERS
148 Upper Richmond Road, SW15 2SW
Decorated in the style of a Canadian log cabin close to Putney High Street. Very popular with all ages with its interesting selection of dishes, cocktail list and special children's menu.
FOOD: up to £15
Hours: dinner – weekdays 6pm–11.30pm, weekends 12noon–11pm, closed Easter Sunday and Christmas day.
Cuisine: INTERNATIONAL – dishes include char-grilled steaks, burgers and chicken. Pasta, pizza, curry and vegetarian dishes. Plus a selection of daily specials.
Cards: Visa, Access, Diners, AmEx.
Other points: open-air dining, Sunday lunch, children welcome.
Directions: on the South Circular road, 3 minutes' walk from East Putney tube.
MR J. CORY ☎ (0181) 788 6324 Fax (0181) 780 1728.

LES ROUTIERS
Your assurance of Quality and Value

SHEEN • map 1D2

CAFE ROUGE
248 Upper Richmond Road, SW14 8AG
French café and brasserie restaurant offering an extensive range of imaginative French dishes and fine wines. The atmosphere is relaxing and the staff are very friendly yet professional.
FOOD: from £15 to £20
Hours: meals all day 10am–11pm (last orders), Sunday 10am–10.30pm.
Cuisine: FRENCH – with a slight British accent. Regularly changing menus. Light snacks and full à la carte.
Cards: Visa, Access, AmEx, Switch.
Other points: licensed, children welcome, open bank holidays.
Directions: on the South Circular in the centre of Sheen.
ODILE GUITARDE ☎ (0181) 878 8897.

SHEPHERD'S BUSH • map 1C3

BALZAC BISTRO
4 Wood Lane, W12 7DT
A typical bistro-style restaurant offering regional French cuisine of a high quality. A pleasant, warm and friendly atmosphere abounds. Metered parking during the day.
FOOD: from £15 to £20 ★
Hours: lunch, 12noon–2.30pm, dinner 7pm–11pm, closed Saturday lunchtime and Sunday, closed bank holidays.
Cuisine: FRENCH.
Cards: Visa, Access, Diners, AmEx.
Other points: children welcome, vegetarian meals.
Directions: corner of Shepherd's Bush Green and Wood Lane.
MR P. TARELLI ☎ (0181) 743 6787.

SOHO • map 1C3

CAFE ROUGE
15 Frith Street, W1V 5TS
Cheerful French café with a vibrant, Bohemian atmosphere. Varied clientele attests to Café Rouge's continuing popularity. Cappuccino and à la carte food available all day. Warm and courteous staff make you welcome.
FOOD: from £15 to £20
Hours: meals all day 10am–11pm (last orders), Sunday 10am–10.30pm.
Cuisine: FRENCH – with a slight British accent. Regularly changing menus. Light snacks and full à la carte.
Cards: Visa, Access, AmEx.
Other points: open-air dining, licensed, children welcome, open bank holidays.
Directions: nearest tube Leicester Square. Close to Prince Edward Theatre.
LEONID RODZMAND ☎ (0171) 437 4307.

MING
35 Greek Street, W1V 5LN
Ming offers an extensive à la carte menu of traditional and imaginative Chinese dishes and an additional four set menus. The food is beautifully cooked and the large choice ensures plenty of scope for exploration of new dishes for even the most regular customers. The simple decor is in keeping with the calm, relaxed atmosphere of the restaurant.
FOOD: up to £15 CLUB
Hours: closed Sunday except Chinese New Year, closed Christmas and Boxing days, meals all day 12noon–11.45pm.
Cuisine: CHINESE – Northern Chinese. Special menu with more unusual, innovative dishes. Ming bowl menu featuring one-dish meal, and pre-theatre menu.
Cards: Visa, Access, Diners, AmEx.
Other points: licensed, no-smoking area, children welcome, private dining.
Directions: corner of Greek Street and Romilly Street. Nearest tube: Leicester Square.
CHRISTINE YAU ☎ (0171) 734 2721 Fax (0171) 435 0812.

STOKE NEWINGTON • map 2B4

THE FOX REFORMED
176 Stoke Newington Church Street, N16 0JL
Formerly a restaurant, The Fox Reformed is now a popular wine bar and brasserie, offering a good selection from the well-stocked bar, tasty meals amd courteous, friendly service. In the warmer months, the patio to the rear of the restaurant allows for pleasant outdoor dining.
FOOD: from £15 to £20
Hours: lunch 12noon–2.30pm, dinner 6.30pm–10.30pm.
Cuisine: FRENCH / INTERNATIONAL – delicious home-made dishes. The ice cream is a must!
Cards: Visa, Access, Switch.
Other points: children welcome, garden, open-air dining, vegetarian meals.

Directions: just off A10, at junction with Stoke Newington High Street.
ROBBIE & CAROL RICHARDS ☎ (0171) 254 5975.

SYDENHAM • map 2D4

■ BE MY GUEST
79 Venner Road, SE26 5HU

This spacious and luxurious Victorian home offers guests comfortable accommodation in elegant surroundings and a warm and friendly atmosphere. Off-street parking is available, and with two British Rail stations within 6 minutes' walk, it is ideal for visitors to London.
DOUBLE ROOM: from £20 to £30
Hours: breakfast 7.30am–9am, dinner 7pm–8pm.
Cuisine: ENGLISH – breakfast and evening meals, vegetarian meals by prior arrangement.
Cards: Visa, Access, AmEx.
Other points: parking, children welcome, residents' lounge, vegetarian meals.
Rooms: 3 bedrooms. All with TV, tea/coffee-making facilities, telephone, radio, hair dryer, trouser-press. All rooms have twin-linked beds and can be reserved as single, twin or double accommodation. Extra beds can be provided for family rooms.
Directions: take the A212 to Sydenham, then A213 into Newlands Park. Venner Road is the third on the right.
KATHY THOMPSON ☎ (0181) 659 5413
Fax (0181) 776 8151.

THE CITY • map 2C4

≒ CAFE ROUGE
Limburner Lane, EC4M 7HY

A city bistro/bar open for meals and snacks throughout the day. All dishes are cooked to order using fresh ingredients. A welcoming and relaxed atmosphere prevails, and the friendly, professional staff will go out of their way to ensure that you enjoy your visit.
FOOD: from £15 to £20
Hours: meals all day 10am–10.30pm (last orders), closed Saturday and Sunday.
Cuisine: FRENCH – with a slight British accent. Regularly changing menus. Light snacks and full à la carte.
Cards: Visa, Access, AmEx, Switch.
Other points: licensed, children welcome, open bank holidays.
Directions: first street on left of Ludgate Hill going towards St Paul's Cathedral.
PETER MYERS ☎ (0171) 329 1234.

≒ CAFE ROUGE
140 Fetter Lane, EC4

Warm and friendly French café with lively decor and atmosphere. Good location in London's hectic business centre. Here you can take refuge from the busy world outside and let the efficient, friendly staff make you feel welcome.
FOOD: from £15 to £20
Hours: meals served all day Monday to Friday 10am–10pm (last orders).
Cuisine: FRENCH – with a slight British accent. Regulary changing menus. Light snacks and full à la carte.
Cards: Visa, Access, AmEx, Switch.
Other points: licensed, children welcome, open bank holidays.
Directions: just off Fleet Street. Nearest tubes Chancery Lane and Blackfriars.
☎ (0171) 242 3469.

TWICKENHAM • map 1D2

≒ CAFE DE BONHEUR
55 Church Street, TW1 3NR

A French-style bistro/brasserie situated in an historical and picturesque part of Twickenham, close to the River Thames. There are two seating areas: the light and airy ground-floor level and a more intimate dining area upstairs.
FOOD: up to £15 CLUB
Hours: meals all day 9.45am–11pm.
Cuisine: FRENCH.
Cards: Visa, Access.
Other points: parking adjacent, children welcome, no-smoking area, disabled access, vegetarian meals, open-air dining.
Directions: off the junction of King Street and York Street in Twickenham.
IAN STANTON ☎ (0181) 891 6338.

WANDSWORTH • map 1D3

≒ CALICO CAFE BAR RESTAURANT
573 Garratt Lane, Earlsfield, SW18

A local neighbourhood bar and restaurant with a bustling yet relaxed atmosphere, with a large patio for alfresco dining in summer and an open fire for cosy winter visits. Traditional Sunday lunch is very popular with families – children are genuinely welcome. Calico offer excellent-value two- and three-course menus as well as imaginative brasserie cooking, with an extensive, reasonably priced wine list.
FOOD: up to £15
Hours: open for lunch and dinner 7 days, open all day Saturday and Sunday.
Cuisine: CONTINENTAL.
Cards: Visa, Access, Diners, AmEx.
Other points: children welcome, open-air dining, vegetarian meals, traditional Sunday lunch.
Directions: 300 yards from Earlsfield station.
☎ (0181) 947 9616.

WAPPING • map 2C4

≒ HENRY'S CAFE BAR (WAPPING)
Tobacco Dock, E1 9SG

A glass-fronted, wooden-beamed building, which was opened as part of the Tobacco Dock development project. Serving an extensive range of international fast-food, it has a robust atmosphere with warm, courteous waitress service. The Tower of London and St Katherine's Dock are within easy reach.

FOOD: up to £15
Hours: meals all day 11am–11pm.
Cuisine: INTERNATIONAL.
Cards: Visa, Access.
Other points: parking, children welcome, open bank holidays, no-smoking area, afternoon teas, disabled access, vegetarian meals.
MR P. MOULLET ☎ (0171) 481 0004.

WEST END • map IC3

ARRAN HOUSE HOTEL (ARRAN HOUSE)
77–79 Gower Street, WC1 6HJ
A small English family-run hotel offering warmth and hospitality, which has brought back the same dedicated clientele for many years. A 200-year-old Georgian building in the centre of 'Literary Bloomsbury', it offers guests a wide range of modern facilities to ensure a comfortable stay. Within walking distance of the British Museum, Piccadilly Circus, Oxford Street and London's theatreland.
DOUBLE ROOM: from £20 to £30
Hours: breakfast 7.30am–9am, Sunday 8am–9.30am.
Cuisine: ENGLISH.
Other points: licensed.
Directions: situated in Gower Street, between Chenies Street and Torrington Place.
MR J. RICHARDS ☎ (0171) 637 1140/636 2186 Fax (0171) 436 5328.

BICKENHALL HOTEL
119 Gloucester Place, W1H 3PJ
This spacious and elegant hotel in the heart of London provides guests with comfortable, well-appointed accommodation of a very good standard. Popular with business people and holiday-makers, the hotel has an atmosphere similar to that of a small country house hotel. It is conveniently located for Madame Tussaud's, the Planetarium and the Wallace Collection.
DOUBLE ROOM: from £30 to £40
SINGLE ROOM: from £35 to £45
Hours: breakfast 7.30am–10am.
Cards: Visa, Access, Diners, AmEx.
Other points: children welcome, pets allowed, residents' lounge.
Rooms: 5 single rooms, 3 double rooms, 2 twin rooms, 8 triple rooms, 2 family rooms. All with TV, telephone, radio, alarm, hair dryer, tea/coffee-making facilities.
Directions: at top end of Gloucester Place, close to Marylebone Road. Nearest tube Baker Street.
IRENE AGHABEGIAN ☎ (0171) 935 3401 Fax (0171) 224 0614.

CAFE IN THE CRYPT
St Martin-In-The-Fields, WC2N 4JS
A unique café, situated immediately underneath the famous church of St Martin-In-The-Fields, Trafalgar Square. Generous portions of wholesome food are offered at outstanding value for money. Meals can be enjoyed beneath the vaulted ceilings in what must be one of the most unusual eating places in London. Centrally situated and very close to the National Gallery.
FOOD: up to £15
Hours: meals all day 10am–9pm, Sunday 12noon–6pm.
Cuisine: ENGLISH – English home-cooking. Self-service. Menu changes daily.
Cards: Visa, Access.
Other points: licensed, Sunday lunch, children welcome, afternoon tea.
Directions: nearest tubes Leicester Square and Charing Cross. Entrance: Duncannon Street.
ALYSON HARGREAVES ☎ (0171) 839 4342.

CAFE ROUGE
46–48 James Street, W1M 5HS
Warm and friendly French café with lively decor and atmosphere. Good location in London's busy West End, with good access to shops, cinemas and theatres. Efficient, friendly staff make you feel welcome. Continental ambience will make you want to linger.
FOOD: up to £15
Hours: meals all day 10am–11pm, Sunday 9am–4pm.
Cuisine: FRENCH – traditional French cuisine. Full à la carte. Light meals available. Good selection of wines.
Cards: Visa, Access, AmEx.
Other points: children welcome, open bank holidays.
Directions: closest tube station is Bond Street.
☎ (0171) 487 4847 Fax (0171) 935 2631.

DON PEPE RESTAURANT
99 Frampton Street, NW8 8NA
Founded by the present owner 20 years ago, this was one of London's first Tapas bars. Today it is undoubtedly one of the capital's premier Spanish restaurants, offering a wide range of excellent Spanish cuisine. This popular restaurant offers live music and alfresco dining in summertime. Ideal for Lord's cricket ground and Little Venice canal.
FOOD: up to £15
Hours: lunch 12noon–3pm, dinner 7pm–1am, closed Sunday evenings and Christmas day.
Cuisine: SPANISH.
Other points: children welcome, vegetarian meals, open bank holidays.
Directions: just off Edgware Road, between Lisson Grove and Edgware Road itself.
☎ (0171) 262 3834/723 9749 Fax (0171) 724 8305.

EDWARD LEAR HOTEL
28–30 Seymour Street, W1H 5WD
Formerly the home of the famous Victorian painter and poet Edward Lear. The hotel offers cheerful rooms with all the usual facilities and is in the perfect location, just minutes away from Hyde Park, Speakers' Corner and Oxford Street.
DOUBLE ROOM: from £20 to £30
SINGLE ROOM: from £25 to £35
Hours: breakfast 7.30am–9.15am.
Cuisine: BREAKFAST.
Cards: Visa, Access.
Other points: children welcome, in-house films,

baby-listening device, cots, residents' lounge.
Rooms: 1 single room, 1 double room, 29 twin rooms. All with TV, radio, telephone, tea/coffee-making facilities.
Directions: close to Marble Arch tube and a minute's walk from Oxford Street.
PETER EVANS ☎ (0171) 402 5401 [Fax] (0171) 706 3766.

● GARTH HOTEL
69 Gower Street, WC1E 6HJ
A privately-owned Georgian terrace hotel in the heart of London, offering guests a friendly, peaceful atmosphere with clean and comfortable rooms. The Garth is centrally located and very reasonably priced for central London.
DOUBLE ROOM: up to £20
SINGLE ROOM: from £25 to £35
Hours: breakfast 7.30am–8.45am.
Cards: Visa, Access.
Other points: children welcome.
Rooms: 3 single rooms, 4 double rooms, 5 twin rooms, 3 triple rooms, 2 family rooms. All with TV.
Directions: situated in Gower Street, between Oxford Street and Euston Road, opposite London University.
SIMON HOARE ☎ (0171) 636 5761 [Fax] (0171) 637 4854.

⊨ LA MADELEINE
5 Vigo Street, W1X 1AH
For a great selection of French meals or snacks, superbly cooked and attractively presented, look no further than La Madeleine. Situated in the heart of the West End, it is conveniently accessible from theatreland and all the West End attractions. The delectable pastries are a must!
FOOD: up to £15
Hours: Sundays, all day 8am–7pm, closed Sundays, party room available every evening and Sunday for private functions.
Cuisine: FRENCH – a delicious and varied à la carte menu. The pastries are marvellous and the fish soup is highly recommended.
Cards: Visa, Access, Switch.
Other points: children welcome, no-smoking area, vegetarian meals, afternoon teas.
Directions: located off Regent Street between Piccadilly and Oxford Street.
JOEL CARRERAS & CORINNE VANDERHAEGEN ☎ (0171) 734 8353 [Fax] (0171) 287 9554.

● LONDON CONTINENTAL HOTEL
88 Gloucester Place, Baker Street, W1H 3HN
This centrally located hotel offers guests comfortable accommodation in newly decorated and furnished surroundings. The bedrooms are coordinated in soothing pastel tones to a very high standard. With a cheery and bright atmosphere, this is a highly recommended hotel, suitable for business people and holidaymakers alike.
DOUBLE ROOM: from £20 to £30
Other points: children welcome, residents' lounge, no-smoking area.
Rooms: 8 single rooms, 8 double rooms, 6 twin rooms, 3 triple rooms. All with satellite TV, telephone, radio, alarm, hair dryer, tea/coffee-making facilities. Most rooms are en suite.
Directions: 5 minutes from Baker Street tube station.
AZHAR AHMED KHAN ☎ (0171) 486 8670 [Fax] (0171) 486 8671.

⊨ MARCHE RESTAURANT – THE SWISS CENTRE
1 Swiss Court, WIV 1FJ
Continental café meets outdoor market. Choose the ingredients for your meal from diverse stations, then watch it being cooked before your eyes. An unusual set-up, but the cheerful, café-type decor and helpful service make for an interesting, enjoyable meal.
FOOD: up to £15 [CLUB]
Hours: breakfast 7am–11am, meals all day 11am–12midnight, closed Christmas day.
Cuisine: SWISS / GERMAN – Swiss with Germanic influence. Fresh ingredients, varied menu at reasonable prices.
Cards: Visa, Access, Diners, AmEx.
Other points: licensed, Sunday lunch, no-smoking area, children welcome, open bank holidays.
Directions: closest tube stations Piccadilly Circus and Leicester Square.
☎ (0171) 494 0498 [Fax] (0171) 494 0502.

● PARKWOOD HOTEL
4 Stanhope Place, W2 2HB
An attractive town house situated in a quiet, residential street, but just a short walk away from Oxford Street, Marble Arch and Hyde Park. The Parkwood is under excellent management, offering spotlessly clean and airy bedrooms serviced by friendly and efficient staff.
DOUBLE ROOM: from £20 to £30
SINGLE ROOM: from £45 to £55
Hours: breakfast 7.30am–9.15am.
Cuisine: BREAKFAST.
Cards: Visa, Access.
Other points: children welcome, in-house films, left luggage, baby-listening device, cots, left luggage, hairdryers, satellite TV.
Rooms: 5 single rooms, 2 double rooms, 7 twin rooms, 4 family rooms. All with TV, radio, alarm, telephone, tea/coffee-making facilities.
Directions: a minute's walk from Marble Arch tube station.
PETER EVANS ☎ (0171) 402 2241 [Fax] (0171) 402 1574.

⊨ PICCADILLY RESTAURANT
31 Great Windmill Street, W1V 7PG
Centrally situated in the heart of theatreland and on the fringes of Soho. The restaurant is on two levels, and both have a cosy, informal atmosphere. Excellent for eating either before or after the theatre.
FOOD: from £15 to £20
Hours: lunch 12noon–2.30pm, dinner 5.30pm–11.15pm, closed Sunday and bank holidays.
Cuisine: ITALIAN – Italian cuisine.
Cards: Visa, Access, AmEx.

Other points: children welcome, guide dogs.
Directions: nearest tube Piccadilly Circus.
CLAUDIO MUSSI ☎ (0171) 734 4956.

ST GILES HOTEL
Bedford Avenue, WC1B 3AS

A modern international 3-star hotel of 600 bedrooms, located at the eastern end of Oxford Street. Just 50 yards from Tottenham Court Road tube station, it is within easy walking distance of all the West End shops and theatres. All the bedrooms have been recently refurbished, and guests have free access to the pool and leisure facilities situated in the same building. Café Bagatelle, the hotel's street café on Tottenham Court Road, features English and Continental cuisine at reasonable prices. The Clock Bar offers a large selection of drinks and pub food throughout the day.
DOUBLE ROOM: over £50
SINGLE ROOM: over £55
FOOD: from £15 to £20
Hours: breakfast 7am–10.30am, meals or snacks all day.
Cuisine: ENGLISH / INTERNATIONAL.
Cards: Visa, Access, Diners, AmEx.
Other points: open bank holidays, residents' lounge, vegetarian meals.
Rooms: 600 bedrooms.
Directions: situated on the corner of Tottenham Court Road and Bedford Avenue.
MR D. TAYLOR ☎ (0171) 636 8616
Fax (0171) 631 1031.

WEST HAMPSTEAD • map 1C3

CHARLOTTE RESTAURANT & GUEST HOUSE
221 West End Land, NW6 1UX

An old-established restaurant and guest house, 2 minutes from West Hampstead tube (Jubilee Line) and direct British Rail link to Gatwick and Luton Airports. A free London Travel Card is issued to guests staying one week or more. The restaurant is tastefully decorated and the ample portions are served by cheerful staff. The accommodation is unbeatable value and comfortable.
DOUBLE ROOM: up to £20
FOOD: up to £15
Hours: breakfast 7.30am–11.30am, lunch 12noon–4pm, dinner 6pm–11pm, closed Sunday.
Cuisine: ENGLISH / CONTINENTAL – from liver Bavaria and deubreziner sausages to stir-fried vegetables with rice and prawn, and poussin à la diable.
Other points: children welcome.
Rooms: 12 single rooms, 24 double rooms. All with TV.
Directions: 2 minutes from West Hampstead tube (Jubilee Line).
MR L KOCH ☎ (0171) 794 6476 Fax (0171) 431 3584.

No. 77 WINE BAR
77 Mill Lane, NW6 1NB

A popular wine bar decorated in pine with old film bills on the walls. International theme evenings such as Burns Night, July 4th, Greek Evening. The in-house club sails and plays cricket, rugby and golf tournaments.
FOOD: from £15 to £20
Hours: lunch 12noon–3pm, dinner 6pm–11pm, closed bank holidays, Good Friday and Christmas.
Cuisine: ENGLISH – home-made soups, lamb Shrewsbury.
Cards: Visa, Access.
Other points: children welcome, street parking.
Directions: Mill Lane is off the Edgware Road between Kilburn and Cricklewood.
DAVID BLAKEMORE ☎ (0171) 435 7787.

WESTMINSTER • map 1C3

BUMBLES RESTAURANT
16 Buckingham Palace Road, SW1W 0QP

Friendly English restaurant with cartoons and old prints lining the walls, padded bench-style seating set in alcoves, and a spacious basement which is also air-conditioned. Private room available for functions. Places of interest nearby include Buckingham Palace, Westminster Abbey and local theatres.
FOOD: from £15 to £20 CLUB
Hours: lunch 12noon–2.15pm, dinner 6pm–10.45pm, closed Saturday lunch and Sunday, closed bank holidays.
Cuisine: ENGLISH / INTERNATIONAL – fresh fish, lamb, duck, game in season, home-made pies. Super puddings. Extensive wine list.
Cards: Visa, Access, Diners, AmEx.
Other points: children welcome, functions.
Directions: 200 yards from Victoria station going towards Buckingham Palace.
PHILIP BARNETT ☎ (0171) 828 2903.

HANOVER SQUARE WINE BAR & GRILL
25 Hanover Square, W1

Don Hewitson's spacious and stylish addition to the Mayfair eating-and-drinking scene. Award-winning wine bar food where the 'South of France meets California', plus an ever-changing selection of charcoal grills. A full-service restaurant, 'Don's Room', at lunch. The wine list features the '200 Wines From All Around The World' made famous at the Cork and Bottle – many, including champagne, available by the glass. An excellent central London venue for evening events (private room for parties up to 60). The entire place is available at weekends (parties up to 150).
FOOD: from £15 to £20
Hours: lunch 12noon–4pm, dinner 6pm–10.30pm, bar meals 12noon–11pm.
Cuisine: CALIFORNIAN / SOUTHERN FRENCH.
Cards: Visa, Access, AmEx.
Other points: vegetarian meals.
Directions: nearest tubes Oxford Circus, Bond Street.
DON & NOELENE HEWITSON ☎ (0171) 408 0935 Fax (0171) 783 2230.

WIMBLEDON • map 1D3

CAFE ROUGE
26 High Street, SW19 5BY

A lively, Parisian-style café with genuine French feel and character, serving excellent traditional

47

bistro food. Light meals and cappuccino served all day. Full à la carte. Continental atmosphere conducive to lingering.
FOOD: up to £15
Hours: meals all day 10am–11pm, Sunday 10am–10.30pm.
Cuisine: FRENCH – traditional French cuisine. House speciality marmite dieppoise. Good selection of wines. Light meals available.
Cards: Visa, Access, AmEx.
Other points: open bank holidays, children welcome.
Directions: nearest tube is Wimbledon.
☎ (0181) 944 5131 Fax (0181) 947 6610.

GOURMET RESTAURANT
2a King's Road, SW19 8QN
A modern-style restaurant situated just off Wimbledon Broadway and close to the theatre, offering an excellent mix of French cuisine with continental influence. The spacious and comfortable interior is attractively decorated around a large central chimney feature, amidst subtle lighting and gentle background music, providing a perfect setting for diners. The staff are friendly and efficient, and in summer alfresco dining on pavement tables is an additional attraction.
FOOD: up to £15 CLUB
Hours: lunch 10am–3pm, dinner 5.30pm–11.30pm.
Cuisine: FRENCH.
Cards: Visa, Access, Diners, AmEx.
Other points: children welcome, Sunday lunch, open bank holidays, vegetarian meals.
Directions: just off Wimbledon Broadway.
ABDDOLLAH SHIRAZI ☎ (0181) 540 5710/ 543 6416.

GREATER LONDON

CROYDON • map 1E3

BRIARLEY HOTEL
8 Outram Road, CR0 6XE
A Victorian exterior, but inside, everything you expect from a hotel in the 1990s, including colour TV, tea facilities and direct-dial telephone. Quietly situated but excellent for public transport. Private car park. Launderette.
DOUBLE ROOM: from £40 to £50
FOOD: up to £15
Hours: Sunday lunch 12noon–1.30pm, dinner (except Sunday) 6.30pm–10pm.
Cuisine: ENGLISH – traditional home-made food with soups, steaks, Briarley burger and fresh vegetables, and all the usual favourites associated with the à la carte menu.
Cards: Visa, Access, Diners, AmEx.
Other points: licensed, Sunday lunch, children welcome, baby-listening device, cots, bar, lounge, central heating.
Rooms: 18 single rooms, 7 double rooms, 8 twin rooms, 5 family rooms. All with TV, radio, telephone, tea/coffee-making facilities, alarm.
Directions: Outram Road runs between the A232 and A222, near East Croydon station.
MRS S.P. MILLS ☎ (0181) 654 1000
Fax (0181) 656 6084.

MARKINGTON HOTEL
9 Haling Park Road, CR2 6NG
This comfortable, friendly hotel is situated in a quiet area, yet is very close to the commercial centre of Croydon. After a day's shopping in the covered shopping centre, you can relax in the bar lounge.
DOUBLE ROOM: from £20 to £30
SINGLE ROOM: from £25 to £35
FOOD: up to £15
Hours: breakfast 7am–9am, dinner 6.30pm–8.30pm.
Cuisine: ENGLISH.
Cards: Visa, Access, AmEx.
Other points: children welcome, garden, vegetarian meals, parking, residents' lounge, bar.
Rooms: 9 single rooms, 10 double rooms, 3 twin rooms, 1 family room. All with TV, radio, telephone, tea/coffee-making facilities, hair dryer, video, trouser-press.
Directions: just off A235 to Brighton, opposite Croydon bus garage.
MR & MRS MICKELBURGH ☎ (0181) 681 6494 Fax (0181) 688 6530.

ENFIELD • map 2A4

OAK LODGE HOTEL
80 Village Road, Bush Hill Park, EN1 2EU
An exclusive country-style hotel set in secluded gardens, offering a personal atmosphere and service. English Tourist Board 3-Crown 'Highly Commended', it has a reputation as the 'Director's Choice'. Favoured at weekends by visiting family wedding guests or newlyweds who are attracted by the romantic atmosphere. Luxurious and well-appointed with a unique personal charm.
DOUBLE ROOM: from £30 to £40
SINGLE ROOM: from £55
FOOD: from £15 to £20 CLUB ☆
Hours: breakfast 7am–10am, dinner 7pm–10pm.
Cuisine: ENGLISH / CONTINENTAL – connoisseur à la carte and table d'hôte menus available. A la carte menu also available for celebratory dinner parties, for up to 14 persons.
Cards: Visa, Access, Diners, AmEx.
Other points: licensed, Sunday lunch, children welcome, pets by prior arrangement, parking, residents' lounge, garden, honeymoon suite, functions.
Rooms: 5 bedrooms.
Directions: 1 mile from A10. Turn right at seventh set of lights from exit 25 of M25.
JOHN BROWN ☎ (0181) 360 7082.

GREATER LONDON

GREENFORD • map IC2

🛏 THE BRIDGE HOTEL
Western Avenue, UB6 8ST
A tasteful combination of the 'old' and the 'new', The Bridge Hotel has always enjoyed an excellent reputation for its quality beers and delightful atmosphere. Ideally situated on the A40, it is easily accessible from all routes. The private bedrooms have every modern facility, including satellite TV, and the lounge and saloon bars proudly boast their beautiful, original wood panelling. The new, superbly appointed restaurant offers a wide range of appetizing alternatives to the most discerning of palates.
DOUBLE ROOM: from £40 to £50
SINGLE ROOM: from £55
FOOD: from £15 to £20
Cuisine: ENGLISH.
Other points: parking, disabled facilities, residents' lounge, vegetarian meals.
Rooms: 68 bedrooms.
Directions: on A4127, off the A40. Greenford tube (Central Line) is a few minutes' walk from the hotel.
☎ (0181) 566 6246 Fax (0181) 566 6140.

HAMPTON COURT • map ID2

🛏 MITRE HOTEL
Hampton Court Road, KT8 9BN
Rich with its own history, the Mitre was built in 1665 on the orders of Charles II to accommodate an overflow of guests at nearby Hampton Court Palace. While retaining the original charm, the hotel now offers modern facilities in comfortable and elegant surroundings with wonderful views over the palace, the Thames and the courtyard. The Mitre has always been famed for its excellent food and wines: what better place to appreciate the chef's skills than in the magnificent Mitre Restaurant, with its superb view over the Thames? Highly recommended.
DOUBLE ROOM: over £50
FOOD: from £15 to £20
Hours: breakfast 7am–9.30am, lunch 12noon–2pm, dinner 7pm–10pm.
Cuisine: INTERNATIONAL – only fresh ingredients used; the chef is keen to provide well balanced menus and healthy options.
Cards: Visa, Access, Diners, AmEx.
Other points: parking, children catered for (please check for age limits), conference facilities, vegetarian meals.
Rooms: 14 double rooms, 21 twin rooms, 1 suite. All with en suite, TV, telephone, radio, hair dryer, trouser-press, room service, tea/coffee-making facilities.
Directions: situated adjacent to Hampton Court Bridge on the Thames.
☎ (0181) 979 9988 Fax (0181) 979 9777.

HARROW • map IB2

🛏 CRESCENT LODGE HOTEL
58–62 Welldon Crescent, HA1 1QR
This is a family-owned and run hotel situated in Harrow, providing guests with personal service and a comfortable, carefree stay. Happy to cater for conferences. A genuinely warm welcome is extended to all visitors, and the accommodation is of a very high standard.
DOUBLE ROOM: from £30 to £40
FOOD: up to £15
Hours: breakfast 7.30am–9am.
Cuisine: ENGLISH – varied menu, including vegetarian. Dishes may include venison in red wine, nut Wellington provençal, chicken satay with noodles, steaks.
Cards: Visa, Access, AmEx.
Other points: children welcome, open bank holidays, conferences, secretary available, children welcome, baby-listening device, cots, 24hr reception, foreign exchange, left luggage, vegetarian meals, residents' bar, residents' lounge.
Rooms: 9 single rooms, 3 double rooms, 7 twin rooms, 1 triple room, 1 quad room. All with satellite TV, radio, telephone, tea/coffee-making facilities, refrigerator.
Directions: off Headstone Road, onto Hindes Road, then Welldon Crescent.
ZENNIE & SHIRAZ JIVRAJ ☎ (0181) 863 5491
Fax (0181) 427 5965.

🛏 CUMBERLAND HOTEL
St John's Road, HA1 2EF
Relax in the unrushed, peaceful atmosphere of this long-established hotel. The restaurant offers generous portions of freshly prepared food to suit all tastes. Every care is taken by the attentive staff to make all visitors feel relaxed and welcome. Highly recommended. When booking, please quote 'Les Routiers'.
DOUBLE ROOM: from £20 to £30
SINGLE ROOM: from £25 to £35
FOOD: from £15 to £20
Hours: breakfast 7am–9am, lunch 12noon–2pm, dinner 7pm–9pm.
Cuisine: FRENCH / CONTINENTAL – dishes are mainly French on the à la carte menu, with vegetarian and healthy option meals available. Also a speciality children's menu. Les Routiers Casserole Award winner.
Cards: Visa, Access, Diners, AmEx.
Other points: Sunday lunch, no-smoking area, conferences, gym facilities, sauna, children welcome, baby-listening device, cots, 24hr reception, parking, disabled access.
Rooms: 31 single rooms, 28 double rooms, 16 twin rooms, 5 family rooms. All with satellite TV, radio, telephone, tea/coffee-making facilities, trouser-press.
Directions: leave M4 at exit 3. Follow the A312 to Harrow.
MR M.A.K. SMITH ☎ (0181) 863 4111.

🍴 FIDDLER'S RESTAURANT
221–225 High Road, Harrow Weald, HA3 5EE
Part of a 1930s row of shops, Fiddler's has a black and white mock-Tudor frontage. Inside, Tudor decor, bric-a-brac and mirrors create warm, attractive surroundings in which to enjoy the excellent food. All dishes are well cooked and well

49

GREATER LONDON

presented. Everything is done to ensure that customers enjoy their meal, and the service and atmosphere is warm and welcoming.
FOOD: up to £15 🍽 CLUB ☆
Hours: lunch 12noon–2.30pm, dinner 7pm–1am (7pm–2am Fri, Sat).
Cuisine: ITALIAN / FRENCH – wide selection of Italian and French cuisine such as duck with orange sauce; beef al pepe (with a crushed pepper, brandy and cream sauce); calamari fritti.
Cards: Visa, Access, Diners, AmEx, MasterCard.
Other points: licensed, Sunday lunch, no-smoking area, children welcome, entertainment, conferences, functions, air-conditioned.
Directions: on A409, between Harrow Wealdstone station and Uxbridge Road roundabout.
ANTONIO BRANCA ☎ (0181) 863 6066/ 427 1931 Fax (0181) 861 2807.

🍽 OLD ETONIAN RESTAURANT
38 High Street, Harrow on the Hill, HA1 3LL
An 18th century French bistro-style restaurant, situated in the town centre near the famous Harrow Public School, combining the qualities of excellent food and service with comfortable and relaxed surroundings.
FOOD: up to £15
Hours: lunch 12noon–2.30pm, dinner 7pm–11pm, closed Saturday lunch, Sunday and bank holidays.
Cuisine: FRENCH – featuring seafood pancake, steak dijon, roast duck in orange sauce with guava, chocolate mousse, creme brulée.
Cards: Visa, Access, Diners, AmEx.
Other points: licensed, children welcome, parking.
Directions: off Uxbridge road, in the town centre, near the school.
MR PELAEZ ☎ (0181) 422 8482.

KEW • map 1D2

🍽 JASPER'S BUN IN THE OVEN
11 Kew Green, TW9 3AA
French/international cuisine is served in this charming Georgian house overlooking Kew Green. Jasper's offers winter dining in front of log fires and summer dining in the courtyard. Great-value set-price menu, extensive à la carte menu and special Sunday menu. Open for lunch and dinner except Sunday evening. Extensive wine list. Private room available for business lunches/dinners. Parties and weddings catered for.
FOOD: from £15 to £20
Hours: lunch 12.30am–3pm, dinner 7pm–11pm, closed Sunday evening, Good Friday, Christmas eve, Christmas day and Boxing day.
Cuisine: FRENCH – complemented by an extensive wine list.
Cards: Visa, Access, Diners, AmEx.
Other points: licensed, garden, children welcome, vegetarian meals, private rooms available.
Directions: situated on Kew Green.

MR CARVOSSO ☎ (0181) 940 3987 Fax (0181) 940 6387.

🍽 PISSARRO'S WINE BAR
1 Kew Green, Richmond, TW9 3AA
A roaring open fire, oak beams, a host of antique curios, some 50 wines and a delicious selection of home-made foods are all there to welcome and tempt you. Pissarro once painted the buildings where this enchanting wine bar now stands.
FOOD: up to £15
Hours: bar 11.30am–11pm, Sunday 12noon–3pm, 7pm–10.30pm, closed Easter Sunday and Christmas.
Cuisine: ENGLISH – home-made country pies, delicious soups, fresh vegetables, a hearty selection of cheeses, plus a daily cold buffet with special slimmers' salads, mouthwatering desserts and a traditional Sunday lunch.
Cards: Visa, Access.
Other points: licensed, open-air dining, Sunday lunch, disabled access, no children.
Directions: on the A205 (South Circular), south of Kew Bridge, just off Kew Green.
PAUL & PENNY CARVOSSO ☎ (0181) 940 3987.

KINGSTON-UPON-THAMES
map 1D2

🏨 CHASE LODGE HOTEL
10 Park Road, Hampton Wick, KT1 4AS
Set on a quiet residential street in Hampton Wick, this tranquil hotel is a real gem. Tastefully furnished with a conservatory and a well-tended garden, it strives to provide personal service and attention to detail, and offers a welcome retreat in a busy world.
DOUBLE ROOM: from £20 to £30
SINGLE ROOM: from £25 to £35
FOOD: up to £15
Hours: breakfast 7am–9am, dinner 7pm–9.30pm.
Cuisine: ENGLISH – traditional English cuisine with imaginative sauces. Prepared to a high standard. Good selection of wines.
Cards: Visa, Access, AmEx.
Other points: no-smoking area, parking, residents' lounge, garden, vegetarian meals, Sunday dinner.
Rooms: 1 single room, 5 double rooms, 3 twin rooms.
Directions: Kingston-upon-Thames, near Hampton Court.
MR & MRS STAFFORD HAWORTH ☎ (0181) 943 1862 Fax (0181) 943 9363.

PINNER • map 1B2

🍽 FRIENDS RESTAURANT
11 High Street, HA5 5PJ
Situated in the heart of picturesque Pinner High street, Friends Restaurant is a charming 400-year-old building with oak beams, open fireplaces and lots of character. The weekly changing set menu and the seasonally changing à

la carte menu offer superb meals made from fresh local produce.
FOOD: from £15 to £20
Hours: lunch 12noon–2.30pm, dinner 6.30pm–10pm, closed Sunday evening, Christmas day and Boxing day.
Cuisine: MODERN ENGLISH / FRENCH – innovative dishes professionally presented.
Cards: Visa, Access, Diners, AmEx.
Other points: children welcome, conference facilities, no-smoking area, vegetarian meals, traditional Sunday lunch.
Directions: follow A404 from Harrow; in the centre of Pinner.
TERRY FARR ☎ (0181) 866 0286.

LA GIRALDA
66 Pinner Green, HA5 2AB
Situated just north of Pinner village amongst a parade of shops, this tastefully furnished restaurant has 4 rooms of different Spanish styles and serves authentic Spanish cuisine. Fixed-price menu using finest fresh produce. Believed to own one of the finest lists of Spanish wine in Britain.
FOOD: up to £15
Hours: lunch 12noon–2.30pm, dinner 6.30pm–10.30pm, closed Sunday evening and Monday.
Cuisine: SPANISH – paella, fish. Fixed-price menus.
Cards: Visa, Access, AmEx.
Other points: licensed, children welcome, street parking.
Directions: situated north of Pinner village on A404.
MR D. BROWN ☎ (0181) 868 3429/868 3193
Fax (0181) 868 1218.

RAINHAM • map 2C5

PORKY'S
Unit 1, Manor Way Business Centre, Fairview Industrial Estate, RM13 8UG
Quite unlike any other eating establishment in the UK, Porky's may be described as having a hint of original Les Routiers French truck-stop café whilst serving exceptional traditional British food. Situated on a large, modern industrial estate, it is extremely popular with intercontinental truckers, and even operates a timed phone-in delivery service to businesses on the estate. The attractive decor compromises dark timber furniture, circular tables, saloon-style chairs, a full bar and seating for 80 people.
FOOD: up to £15
Hours: meals all day 7am–11pm, Saturday 7am–12noon, closed Sunday.
Cuisine: ENGLISH.
Other points: parking, children welcome, no-smoking area, afternoon tea, disabled access, vegetarian meals.
Directions: Manor Way, off A13, alongside Rainham Steel.
☎ (01708) 630552/630553.

GREATER LONDON

RICHMOND • map 1D2

CAFE ROUGE
7a Petersham Road, TW10 6UH
A lively bar and restaurant, with rear conservatory, polished wood floors, chandeliers, oil paintings and posters. The food is fresh, of excellent quality and served in ample portions. River Thames, Kew Gardens, Richmond Park and Hampton Court nearby.
FOOD: up to £15
Hours: meals all day 10am–11pm, Sunday 10am–10.30pm.
Cuisine: FRENCH – traditional French cuisine. Menu changes every three months, but generally offers Toulouse sausages, marmite dieppoise and plats du jour.
Cards: Visa, Access, AmEx.
Other points: Sunday lunch, no-smoking area, children welcome, afternoon tea, open bank holidays.
Directions: through Richmond from A3, follow one-way to Petersham, past Odeon Cinema.
CAFE ROUGE LTD ☎ (0181) 332 2423
Fax (0181) 332 2534.

CAFFE MAMMA
24 Hill Street, TW9 1TN
Decorated in the style of a Neapolitan café with typical Italian ambience. Situated in the main shopping area of Richmond, not far from the river. Caffe Mamma enjoys a good reputation in the area and is popular with all ages.
FOOD: up to £15
Hours: meals all day 12noon–12midnight, closed Christmas day and New Year's day.
Cuisine: ITALIAN – Italian, specializing in pasta dishes.
Cards: Visa, Access, AmEx, Switch.
Other points: Sunday lunch, children welcome.
Directions: in the centre of Richmond, near Odeon Cinema.
TIM DIXON-NUTTALL ☎ (0181) 940 1625
Fax (0181) 948 7330.

HENRY'S CAFE BAR (RICHMOND)
Riverside Development, Riverside, TW9 1TJ
A popular split-level café/bar serving an extensive range of international fast-food, American and non-alcoholic beers and speciality cocktails. Comfortable, friendly interior; live music at weekends. Ideal location for those wanting to take a riverboat excursion along the Thames.
FOOD: up to £15
Hours: meals all day 11am–10pm.
Cuisine: INTERNATIONAL.
Cards: Visa, Access.
Other points: children welcome, open bank holidays, no-smoking area, afternoon teas, disabled access, vegetarian meals.
Directions: situated behind the town hall.
MR R. McKAY ☎ (0181) 332 2494.

THE RIVER TERRACE
The Tower, Bridge Street, TW9 1TQ
A Regency-style building, recently renovated, with a balcony which overlooks the River Thames. The

chef prides himself on his imaginative dishes, one of which is a scooped-out pineapple filled with seafood, herbs and spices, vegetables and rice in a coconut sauce, served with a tropical salad. Service is very efficient, and staff are pleased to offer advice on various dishes.
FOOD: up to £15
Hours: meals all day 11am–11pm.
Cuisine: INTERNATIONAL – breast of duckling with blueberries, char-grilled swordfish steak with yoghurt and coriander, fillet of beef with oyster sauce and noodles.
Cards: Visa, Access, Diners, AmEx.
Other points: licensed, open-air dining, Sunday lunch, children welcome.
Directions: situated on the Richmond side of Richmond Bridge, overlooking river.
RIVER TERRACE LTD ☎ (0181) 332 2524
Fax (0181) 332 6136.

RUISLIP • map 1B1

RUISLIP TANDOORI
115 High Street, HA4 8JW
A 60-seater Tandoori restaurant serving Nepalese cuisine. The atmosphere is set by subdued lighting and soft background music. Well patronized by the locals. Established since 1980.
FOOD: up to £15
Hours: lunch 12noon–2.30pm, dinner 6pm–11.30pm, closed Christmas day.
Cuisine: NEPALESE – chicken zhal frazi, chicken gurkhali, butter chicken, chicken Nepal, chicken chili massala. Karai dishes and Kathmandu dishes. Set Nepalese Thali and set dinner. Special Sunday lunch buffet: 12 dishes to choose from at £6.95 for adults and £3.50 for children.
Cards: Visa, Access, Diners, AmEx.
Other points: Sunday lunch, children catered for (please check for age limit), no service charge.
Directions: situated centrally on Ruislip High Street.
K.B. RAICHHETRI ☎ (01895) 632859/674890.

STAINES • map 1D1

THE ANGEL INN
24 High Street, TW18 4EE
The coaching inn was originally built in 1685. It was carefully rebuilt at the turn of the century and has recently been refurbished and redecorated to a very good standard. All the bedrooms are comfortable and well furnished. The brasserie-style restaurant offers freshly prepared food and caters for all tastes.
DOUBLE ROOM: from £30 to £40
FOOD: up to £15
Hours: breakfast 7am–9am, lunch 12noon–2.30pm, dinner 5.30pm–9.45pm, bar meals 11am–10pm.
Cuisine: INTERNATIONAL – a brasserie-style menu with a good selection of English, French and Eastern dishes.

Cards: Visa, Access, AmEx.
Other points: parking, children welcome, pets allowed by arrangement, no-smoking area, garden, open-air dining, vegetarian meals, afternoon teas, traditional Sunday lunch.
Rooms: 3 single rooms, 3 double rooms, 6 twin rooms. All with TV, tea/coffee-making facilities.
Directions: on the main High Street, opposite Debenhams.
GALLEON TAVERNS LTD ☎ (01784) 452509
Fax (01784) 458336.

SUTTON • map 1E3

ASHLING TARA HOTEL
44–50 Rosehill, SM1 3EU
A family-run hotel with a friendly and welcoming atmosphere, situated within easy walking distance of Sutton town centre and directly opposite the Rose Hill tennis centre and sports complex. With the comfort of her guests in mind, Mrs Harold has succeeded in offering a combination of tasty home-cooked meals to complement comfortable, attractive accommodation. A pleasure to visit.
DOUBLE ROOM: from £20 to £30
FOOD: up to £15
Hours: breakfast 7.30am–8.45am, dinner 7pm–9pm.
Cuisine: ENGLISH.
Cards: Visa, Access, Diners, AmEx.
Other points: children welcome, open bank holidays, residents' lounge, garden, launderette, fax.
Rooms: 4 single rooms, 5 double rooms, 5 twin rooms, 2 family rooms. All with TV, radio, bar, telephone, tea/coffee-making facilities.
Directions: near Angel Hill.
CATHERINE HAROLD ☎ (0181) 641 6142
Fax (0181) 644 7872.

THATCHED HOUSE HOTEL
135 Cheam Road, SM1 2BN
Situated a short walk from Sutton centre and Cheam village, this lovely thatched cottage has been completely modernized and offers good food, comfortable accommodation and a friendly welcome. Close proximity to Epsom Downs, Wimbledon Tennis, Hampton Court, Windsor Castle and RHS Gardens at Wisley. Golf can be arranged at Banstead Downs only a mile from the hotel.
DOUBLE ROOM: from £20 to £30
FOOD: up to £15
Hours: breakfast 7.30am–9am, dinner 7pm–9pm.
Cuisine: ENGLISH – chef's specials daily.
Cards: Visa, Access, MasterCard.
Other points: licensed, children welcome, afternoon tea, functions, conferences, garden.
Rooms: 5 single rooms, 11 double rooms, 10 twin rooms, 2 four-poster rooms. All with TV, telephone, tea/coffee-making facilities.
Directions: on the A232, opposite Sutton cricket and squash club.
MR & MRS P. SELLS ☎ (0181) 642 3131
Fax (0181) 770 0684.

TEDDINGTON • map ID2

🏨 THE CLARENCE HOTEL
Park Road, TW11 0AB
The hotel is conveniently situated just 5 miles from Heathrow Airport and very close to Hampton Court, Bushey Park and the River Thames. Within its attractive listed Victorian exterior are 20 recently refurbished en suite bedrooms, a Victorian-style bar and Parisian-style restaurant, all offering good value for money.
DOUBLE ROOM: from £40 to £50
FOOD: up to £15
Hours: breakfast 7am–9am, lunch 12noon–3pm, dinner 6pm–9.45pm.
Cuisine: ENGLISH – home-cooking from daily changing menu.
Cards: Visa, Access, Diners, AmEx.
Other points: parking, children welcome, pets allowed by arrangement, open-air dining, vegetarian meals, afternoon teas, traditional Sunday lunch.
Rooms: 7 single rooms, 7 double rooms, 3 twin rooms. All with en suite, TV, telephone, radio, alarm, hair dryer, trouser-press, tea/coffee-making facilities.
Directions: over Kingston Bridge and follow A310 past Bushey Park. The hotel is opposite the police station.
GALLEON TAVERNS LTD ☎ (0181) 977 8025
[Fax] (0181) 977 8698.

🍴 THE ITALIAN PLACE BRASSERIE
38 High Street, TW11 8EW
An excellent Italian restaurant in the centre of Teddington. The menu offers an extensive choice of authentic and creative Italian dishes at very reasonable prices, with all meals freshly cooked and well presented. Highly recommended for the excellent food and welcoming service in a lively yet relaxed atmosphere.
FOOD: from £15 to £20
Hours: lunch 12noon–2.30pm, Sunday 12noon–3pm, dinner 6.30pm–11pm, Sunday 7pm–10.30pm, open bank holidays.
Cuisine: ITALIAN – dishes may include polenta con funghi, fettuccine Federico, manzo alla mostarda, insalata marinara. Specials change daily.
Cards: Visa, Access, Diners, AmEx, Switch, Delta.
Other points: licensed, Sunday lunch, no-smoking area.
Directions: on Teddington High Street.
FEDERICO SECOLA ☎ (0181) 943 2433.

WOODFORD GREEN • map 2B4

🏨 PACKFORD'S HOTEL
16 Snakes Lane, IG8 0BS
A turn-of-the-century house where the proprietors have imaginatively retained the original Victorian features while at the same time incorporating discreet innovations. The hotel provides a well-organized banqueting and conference service; weddings and private parties are a speciality. Situated within easy reach of the unspoilt Epping Forest, Packford's Hotel is just a 30-minute trip from the heart of London.
DOUBLE ROOM: from £40 to £50
SINGLE ROOM: from £45 to £55
FOOD: from £15 to £20
Hours: breakfast 7.30am–8.30am, dinner 6.30pm–8pm.
Cuisine: ENGLISH.
Cards: Visa, Access, AmEx, Switch, Delta.
Other points: parking, children welcome, pets allowed, conference facilities, banqueting, residents' lounge, garden, vegetarian meals.
Rooms: 11 bedrooms. All with en suite, TV, telephone, iron, baby-listening device, tea/coffee-making facilities.
Directions: exit junction 26 on M25, follow signs to Woodford.
SIMON & DEBRA PACKFORD ☎ (0181) 504 2642 [Fax] (0181) 505 5778.

SOUTH-EAST ENGLAND & EAST ANGLIA

However long your stay, you will not exhaust the pleasures and hearty welcome offered by these beautiful regions, from the wide-open skies of East Anglia to the rolling North and South Downs, from the charming chocolate-box villages of the Thames and Chilterns to the famous South-East holiday coastline.

This is an area where the opportunities to sample really fine food have increased immensely over the past few years. It is rich in quality restaurants run by a new generation of chefs who have successfully created a new Anglo-French cuisine with a greener, leaner image.

There are endless comfortable inns in which to spend a relaxing evening enjoying good home-cooked treats and the very best of ethnic cuisine, with a first-class choice for vegetarians. The Essex coastline, in particular, is world-famous for its fresh fish and seafood, notably Colchester oysters, which have been farmed here since Roman times. Look out also for Staithe mussels, Aylesbury duckling and Norfolk crab, country pies, toasted savouries, traditional roasts and succulent steaks, all complemented by a mouth-watering selection of market-fresh vegetables.

The following counties are included in this chapter:

BEDFORDSHIRE
BUCKINGHAMSHIRE
CAMBRIDGESHIRE
EAST SUSSEX
ESSEX
(other Essex entries appear in the preceding chapter)

HERTFORDSHIRE
KENT
NORFOLK
SUFFOLK
SURREY
(other Surrey entries appear in the preceding chapter)
WEST SUSSEX

BEDFORDSHIRE

BEDFORD • map 9E3

EDWARDIAN HOUSE HOTEL
Shakespeare Road, MK40 2DZ

On a beautiful tree-lined road in the poets area of Bedford, just a few minutes from the town centre, this charming, family-run hotel offers modern facilities, excellent service and a friendly atmosphere. The hotel is very tastefully decorated and the accommodation is of a high standard. Enjoy good, freshly prepared food in the restaurant and relax in the hotel's bar and lounge.
DOUBLE ROOM: from £20 to £30
SINGLE ROOM: from £25 to £35
FOOD: up to £15
Hours: breakfast 7.30am–9am, bar meals 6.30pm–8.45pm.
Cuisine: ENGLISH.

BEDFORDSHIRE • SE ENGLAND & EAST ANGLIA

Cards: Visa, Access, AmEx.
Other points: children welcome, conferences, vegetarian meals.
Rooms: 11 single rooms, 5 double rooms, 2 twin rooms, 1 family room. All with TV, telephone, tea/coffee-making facilities, alarm, heating.
Directions: centrally located in Bedford, a few minutes from railway station.
JOHN & ROSSLYN ALLAN ☎ (01234) 11156.

THE KNIFE & CLEAVER
The Grove, Houghton Conquest, MK45 3LA
In a prominent position opposite the medieval church in Houghton Conquest. The restaurant is an airy Victorian-style conservatory, and the innovative menu, which changes monthly, incorporates seasonal specialities made from the finest fresh produce. Fresh shellfish, lobster and vegetarian dishes. List of 100 well-chosen wines, many by the glass. Flowery terrace and other open-air dining areas. Within easy reach of Woburn Abbey and Luton Airport.
DOUBLE ROOM: from £20 to £30
SINGLE ROOM: from £35 to £45
FOOD: from £15 to £20
Hours: breakfast 7.30am, weekends 8.30am, lunch 12noon–2.30pm, bar meals 12noon–2.30pm, dinner 7pm–9.30pm, bar meals 7pm–9.30pm; both hotel and restaurant are closed on Sunday evening, but arrangements can be made in advance for accommodation.
Cuisine: MODERN ENGLISH / FRENCH – a speciality is the 'Knife & Cleaver Hors d'Oeuvre', almost a meal in itself.
Cards: Visa, Access, Diners, AmEx.
Other points: licensed, Sunday lunch, children welcome, pets allowed, open bank holidays, functions.
Rooms: 4 double rooms, 5 twin rooms. All with en suite, TV, radio, tea/coffee-making facilities, alarm, refrigerators.
Directions: between A6 and B530, 5 miles south of Bedford and 2 miles north of Ampthill.
DAVID & PAULINE LOOM ☎ (01234) 740387 [Fax] (01234) 740900.

THE LAWS HOTEL
High Street, Turvey, MK43 8DB
Situated in the pleasant village of Turvey, northwest of Bedford, this hotel offers attractive and comfortable accommodation. The restaurant serves well-presented meals and provides excellent service in a light and relaxed atmosphere. Close to Woburn Abbey and Whipsnade Park Zoo.
DOUBLE ROOM: from £20 to £30
FOOD: from £15 to £20
Hours: breakfast 7am–8.30am, lunch 12noon–2pm, dinner 7pm–9.45pm.
Cuisine: ENGLISH / SEAFOOD – a wide selection of dishes on the à la carte menu, plus a table d'hôte menu featuring specials: fillet steak and lobster tail, queen scallops, Dover sole.
Cards: Visa, Access, AmEx.
Other points: licensed, open-air dining, Sunday lunch, children welcome, afternoon tea, pets allowed, residents' lounge, residents' bar.

Rooms: 2 single rooms, 17 double rooms. All with TV, radio, alarm, telephone, tea/coffee-making facilities, hair dryer, trouser-press.
Directions: follow A6, take exit for A428 to Bedford. Continue to Turvey.
JEROME & FRANCESCA MACK ☎ (01234) 881213 [Fax] (01234) 888864.

THREE CRANES
High Street, Turvey, MK43 8EP
Set in the centre of the attractive village of Turvey, next to the ancient Turvey church, the Three Cranes offers very good food, a welcoming atmosphere and excellent service. All meals are well-cooked and presented, served by friendly and efficient staff. The Three Cranes is a very popular pub and well worth a visit.
DOUBLE ROOM: up to £20
SINGLE ROOM: from £25 to £35
FOOD: up to £15
Hours: breakfast 7.30am–9.30am; bar meals lunchtime 12noon–2pm, Sunday to Wednesday 6.30pm–9.30pm, Thursday to Saturday 6.30pm–10pm.
Cuisine: ENGLISH – wide choice of dishes such as Crane's mixed grill, salads, steaks. Blackboard specials including fresh fish dishes, especially at the weekend.
Cards: Visa, Access.
Other points: licensed, open-air dining, Sunday lunch, beer garden.
Rooms: 2 single rooms, 1 double room, 2 twin rooms.
Directions: on A428, midway between Bedford and Northampton.
DAVID & SANDRA ALEXANDER ☎ (01234) 881305.

BIGGLESWADE • map 10E4

LA CACHETTE
61 Hitchin Street, SG18 8BE
A welcoming restaurant offering an imaginative menu and excellently cooked, fresh food. A separate menu caters for vegetarian guests and provides an equally good choice and high standard of cuisine. With a warm atmosphere and excellent service, La Cachette is definitely worth a visit.
FOOD: from £15 to £20
Hours: dinner 7pm–10pm, closed Sunday and Monday.
Cuisine: FRENCH / CONTINENTAL – imaginative cuisine which also features speciality dishes from around the world. Dishes may include wild sea trout stuffed with prawns and mushrooms, loin of lamb with orange and redcurrant sauce, shank of pork.
Cards: Visa, Access, AmEx.
Other points: licensed, children welcome, street parking.
Directions: From the A1M, follow signs to the town centre. Two minutes' walk from market square.
RICHARD & MARGARET POOL ☎ (01767) 313508.

55

SE ENGLAND & EAST ANGLIA • BEDFORDSHIRE

DUNSTABLE • map 9E3

🏨 BELLOWS MILL
Bellows Mill, Eaton Bray, LU6 1QZ
For a truly memorable break, this delightful mill, set in its own grounds and dating back to the Domesday Book, is idyllic. The accent is on highly personal attention to your needs, and facilities include an all-weather tennis court, pool table, and even fishing by arrangement. Bellows Mill is also ideal for private receptions and small conferences (marquee for larger functions). Children and pets are welcome by prior arrangement.
DOUBLE ROOM: from £20 to £30
SINGLE ROOM: from £35 to £45
FOOD: up to £15
Hours: breakfast 7am–10.30am, dinner 7pm–9pm, open all year.
Cuisine: HOME COOKING – fixed-price menu. Dishes may include pheasant normande, chicken in lemon and coriander (Indian-style), and lamb noisettes. Vegetarian dishes by arrangement.
Cards: Visa, Access.
Other points: licensed, open-air dining, residents' lounge, garden, disabled access, parking, children welcome, pets by prior arrangement, open bank holidays.
Rooms: 5 double rooms, 1 family room. All with TV, telephone, tea/coffee-making facilities.
Directions: follow signs for zoo, and at Plough Pub take road to Eaton Bray off B489; easy access to M1.
RACHAEL HODGE ☎ (01525) 220548/220536.

LES ROUTIERS
Your assurance of Quality and Value

LUTON • map 9E3

🏨 LEASIDE HOTEL
72 New Bedford Road, LU3 1BT
A Victorian hotel, set in its own well-tended gardens with large patio. Pleasantly decorated with comfortable furnishings and serving well-cooked food, attractively presented from a comprehensive menu. The light, pleasant atmosphere attracts tourists and business persons alike.
DOUBLE ROOM: from £20 to £30
SINGLE ROOM: from £35 to £45
FOOD: from £15 to £20
Hours: breakfast 7am–9am, lunch 12noon–2pm, dinner 7pm–9.30pm, closed Christmas day and Boxing day.
Cuisine: ENGLISH – à la carte menu, fixed-price three-course menu, bar meals/snacks and vegetarian meals available.
Cards: Visa, Access, Diners, AmEx.
Other points: licensed, Sunday lunch, children welcome, garden.
Rooms: 11 single rooms, 2 double rooms, 1 twin room, 1 family room.
Directions: on A6 near Moor Park.
MRS C.A. GILLIES ☎ (01582) 417643
[Fax] (01582) 34961.

RIDGMONT • map 5A3

🍽 THE ROSE & CROWN
89 High Street, MK43 0TY
A 300-year-old country pub with a prize-winning large garden. Patio for barbecues. Games room, conference and private party facilities. Recommended for its traditional ales; also offers an extensive wine list. 20 years in the Good Beer Guide. The pub has recently bought its own camping and caravanning site.
FOOD: up to £15
Hours: dinner 6.30pm–10pm, lunch 12noon–2pm.
Cuisine: ENGLISH – bar: a comprehensive menu including specials of the day, e.g., tarragon lamb, lemon chicken, beef olives, etc.
Cards: Visa, Access, Diners, AmEx.
Other points: open-air dining, Sunday lunch.
Directions: on the main street in Ridgmont (A507), 2 miles from junction 13 of M1.
NEIL & ELIZABETH McGREGOR ☎ (01525) 280245.

STEPPINGLEY • map 5A3

🍽 THE FRENCH HORN
Rectory Road, MK45 5AU
This beautiful old-world inn, restored to its original character, has gained a proud reputation in and around the picturesque village of Steppingley, near Woburn Abbey, for its imaginative, freshly prepared menus and friendly hospitality. The intimate, candlelit restaurant and timber-beamed bars with roaring fires are warm and inviting. A range of real ales and fine wines available.
FOOD: from £15 to £20
Hours: lunch 12noon–3.30pm, bar meals 12noon–3.30pm, dinner 7pm–10.30pm, bar meals 6pm–10pm.
Cuisine: ENGLISH – traditional fare with a flair for fresh fish and game.
Cards: Visa, Access.
Other points: parking, children welcome, pets allowed, no-smoking area, open-air dining, vegetarian meals, traditional Sunday lunch.
Directions: Take junction 12 off M1 through Toddington and Flitwick. Restaurant is on left opposite Bury Lawn School.
DEAN SINGER ☎ (01525) 712051.

WESTONING • map 5A3

🍽 THE CHEQUERS
Park Road, MK45 5LA
A 17th century thatched inn, retaining all of its original character. The stables have been tastefully redecorated to form an outstanding restaurant offering good value for money. Very highly recommended.
FOOD: up to £15
Hours: Monday to Saturday 11am–11pm, Sunday 12noon–3pm and 7pm–10.30pm, meals all day.
Cuisine: ENGLISH / INTERNATIONAL – fixed-price menu. English cuisine. Dishes include char-grilled

BUCKINGHAMSHIRE

steaks, lamb steaks, Cajun chicken. Extensive bar food menu. Daily specials on blackboards.
Cards: Visa, Access, Diners, AmEx, Switch.
Other points: children welcome, courtyard, Sunday lunch.
Directions: on A5120, in centre of village.
PAUL WALLMAN ☎ (01494) 713125
Fax (01525) 716702.

BEACONSFIELD • map 5B3

THE ROYAL STANDARD OF ENGLAND
Forty Green, HP9 1XT

Famous old English pub boasting a beautiful country atmosphere, in character with its surroundings. Reputed to be one of the oldest public houses in England. English and continental draught beers.
FOOD: up to £15
Hours: lunch 11am–3pm, dinner 5.30pm–11pm.
Other points: licensed, open-air dining, Sunday lunch, children welcome, pets allowed.
Directions: between Beaconsfield and Forty Green.
MR P.W. ELDRIDGE ☎ (01494) 673382.

CHESHAM • map 5B3

THE OLD ROSE & CROWN
The Vale, Hanridge Common, near Cholesbury, HP5 2UQ

Situated in the Vale of Chesham, this 17th century inn is full of character, with open log fires and a raised candlelit restaurant area offering excellent home-cooked meals, using only the finest fresh produce. It has a fine selection of real ales. A beautiful garden with views across the valley.
FOOD: from £15 to £20
Hours: lunch 12.30am–2.30pm, bar meals 12noon–2.30pm, dinner 7pm–10pm, bar meals 6pm–10pm.
Cuisine: FRENCH / SWISS / ENGLISH.
Cards: Visa, Access, Switch.
Other points: parking, children welcome, pets allowed, open-air dining, vegetarian meals, traditional Sunday lunch.
Directions: The Vale, between Chesham and Cholesbury.
FRASER & LINDA CARRUTH ☎ (01494) 758386.

GREAT MISSENDEN • map 5B3

THE GEORGE
94 High Street, HP16 0BG

Many levelled, old beamed and tastefully furnished pub, which offers excellent food, competent service and a pleasant atmosphere at very good value.
DOUBLE ROOM: from £20 to £30
FOOD: up to £15 CLUB ☆
Hours: lunch 12noon–2pm, dinner 7pm–11.30pm, last orders 9.45pm, bar snacks all day.

Cuisine: ENGLISH / CONTINENTAL – steaks, pasta and vegetarian selections.
Cards: Visa.
Other points: licensed, open-air dining, Sunday lunch, children welcome.
Rooms: 4 double rooms, 6 twin rooms, 2 family rooms.
Directions: quarter of a mile from A413, between Amersham and Wendover. In town's main street.
GUY & SALLY SMITH ☎ (01494) 862084
Fax (01494) 865622.

HIGH WYCOMBE • map 5B3

DRAKE COURT HOTEL
141 London Road, HP11 1BT

A small, friendly hotel situated close to the centre of historic High Wycombe. The staff are welcoming and efficient. Convenient for the M40 London–Oxford motorway and for touring the Thames Valley, Oxford and the Cotswolds.
DOUBLE ROOM: up to £20
SINGLE ROOM: up to £25
FOOD: up to £15
Hours: breakfast 7.30am–8.30am, dinner 7pm–9.30pm.
Cuisine: ENGLISH / CONTINENTAL – traditional English and continental cuisine.
Cards: Visa, Access, Diners, AmEx.
Other points: licensed, children welcome, open bank holidays, residents' lounge, swimming pool.
Directions: On A40 London Road, close to High Wycombe. Approximately 1 mile from M40 motorway.
☎ (01494) 523639 Fax (01494) 472696.

LEDBURN • map 5B3

HARE & HOUNDS
Near Leighton Buzzard, LU7 0QB

A large country inn steeped with unique character, situated in open countryside. It caters for the discerning diner, with freshly prepared home-cooked meals, and the real-ale enthusiast. The delightful restaurant and bar are enhanced by an impressive open fire.
FOOD: up to £15
Hours: lunch 12noon–3pm, dinner 6.30pm–10pm.
Cuisine: ENGLISH.
Cards: Visa, Access.
Other points: parking, children welcome, garden, open-air dining, vegetarian meals, traditional Sunday lunch.

Directions: out of Leighton Buzzard on the A418, turn left onto B4032, then left to Ledburn.
MARK FICKEN & ANGELA DURRANT
☎ (01525) 373484.

MILTON KEYNES • map 5A3

🍴 MOGHUL PALACE
7a St Paul's Court, High Street, Stony Stratford, MK11 1LT
A fully-licensed restaurant serving an extensive choice of traditional Indian cuisine, with a good range of chef's specialities and set menus. Other dishes include Balti, seafood, lamb, poultry and Tandoori specialities.
FOOD: up to £15
Hours: lunch 12noon–2.30pm, dinner 6pm–11pm.
Cuisine: INDIAN.
Cards: Visa, Access, Diners, AmEx, Switch.
Other points: parking, children welcome, vegetarian meals.
ALI ANFOR ☎ (01908) 566577.

🍴 THE NAVIGATION INN
Thrupp Road, Castlethorpe Road, MK19 7BE
Situated on the banks of the Grand Union Canal with ample moorings and overlooking the south Northamptonshire countryside, The Navigation Inn is a must when travelling through the area. The best of English cuisine is on offer from the table d'hôte, bar snacks and daily changing blackboard menu. There are two pianos in the aptly named Piano Bar, offering both impromptu and arranged musical happenings, particularly at weekends.
FOOD: up to £15
Hours: lunch 12noon–2.30pm, Sunday 12noon–2pm, dinner 7pm–9.30pm.
Cuisine: ENGLISH – a wide range of excellent dishes to please everybody; the Sunday lunches are highly recommended.
Cards: Visa, Access.
Other points: parking, children welcome, open-air dining, vegetarian meals, traditional Sunday lunch.
Directions: 6 miles from M1 junction 15, off A508 towards Stony Stratford. From Stony Stratford, take second turn on right, marked Cosgrove, then first left after approximately 200 yards. The inn is visible on the left.
GORDON BRADSHAW ☎ (01908) 543156.

🍴 OLD GREEN MAN
Watling Street, Little Brickhill, MK17 9LU
This elegant country inn has become a major feature of the village, with its tasteful exterior and outstanding floral displays, and the old-world ambience of the restaurant with its beamed bars and inglenook fireplace. Good home-cooked locally-produced fare is always available. The range of real ales, fine wines and friendly hospitality is second to none.
FOOD: up to £15
Hours: lunch 12noon–2.30pm, dinner 6.30pm–11pm.
Cuisine: ENGLISH.

Cards: Visa, Access.
Other points: parking, children welcome, vegetarian meals, traditional Sunday lunch.
Directions: off A5 to Little Brickhill, turn right at roundabout, 500 yards on the right.
PETER & PAM MORRIS ☎ (01525) 261253.

NEWPORT PAGNELL • map 5A3

🍴 MYSORE INDIAN CUISINE
97–101 High Street, MK16 8EN
The Mysore restaurant offers a wide range of high-quality traditional Indian and Persian cuisine, with take-away menu also available. For special occasions a Mysore table of Murgh Masala or Kurzi Lamb can be ordered for four or more people at 48 hours' notice. On Sundays a special hot buffet lunch is available for a very reasonable set price. Best in Britain Award Top 30 1994 by Real Curry Restaurant guide, Patak's Restaurant of the Year 1993/1994, second in Curry Club 1994.
FOOD: up to £15
Hours: lunch 12noon–2.30pm, dinner 6pm–11.30pm, closed Christmas, bank holidays.
Cuisine: INDIAN – Tandoori specialities.
Cards: Visa, Access, AmEx.
Other points: licensed, Sunday lunch, no-smoking area, children welcome.
Directions: Take M1 junction 14. Situated in centre of Newport Pagnell.
MR ODUD ☎ (01908) 216426 Fax (01908) 216726.

🍴 THE OLD SWAN
Main Road, Astwood, MK16 9JS
Visit this 14th century thatched inn, situated in the heart of the pretty village of Astwood, and step back in time. It boasts an open fire, low timbered beams, flagstone floors and that old-world ambience. Sample home-cooked local produce in the intimate, candlelit restaurant, or relax with one of their real ales by a roaring fire.
FOOD: up to £15
Hours: lunch 12noon–2.30pm, dinner 6pm–9.30pm.
Cuisine: ENGLISH.
Cards: Visa, Access.
Other points: parking, children welcome, open-air dining, vegetarian meals, traditional Sunday lunch.
Directions: just off A422 Newport Pagnell road.
PHIL & KAREN STRINGER ☎ (01234) 391351.

PENN • map 5B3

🍴 THE OLD QUEENS HEAD
Hammersley Lane, Tylers Green, HP10 8EV
This impressive, heavily beamed country inn is situated at Penn in the heart of the beautiful Buckinghamshire countryside. It boasts excellent food, an old English cheese counter, real ales and fine wines, with an old-charm ambience of its own. The warm, candlelit bars and restaurant make this the perfect venue for any occasion.
FOOD: up to £15

Hours: bar meals 12noon–2.30pm, dinner 7pm–9.30pm, bar meals 6pm–9.30pm, bar 11am–11pm.
Cuisine: ENGLISH – bar: traditional and creative bar snacks. Restaurant: full à la carte and daily specials board.
Cards: Visa, Access, Switch.
Other points: parking, children welcome, garden, open-air dining, vegetarian meals, traditional Sunday lunch.
Directions: junction 3 off M40, head for High Wycombe on A40, turn right into Hammersley Lane. At the top of the road on the right.
MARK ROBERTS & LOUISE PRATAP
☎ (01494) 813371.

PRINCES RISBOROUGH • map 5B3

KING WILLIAM IV FREEHOUSE & RESTAURANT
Hampden Road, Speen, HP27 ORU
A Grade II listed building, originally an old farmhouse dating from 1668, offering a combination of good food and unobtrusive expert service. The fresh flowers on every table are an additional bonus. Ideally situated for visiting Hughenden Manor and the Home of Rest for Horses
FOOD: from £15 to £20
Hours: lunch 12noon–3pm, dinner 7pm–11pm, last orders 9.30pm, closed Sunday evening.
Cuisine: ENGLISH – a two- or three-course set menu is available. For lighter dining a two-course supper menu at £9.95 per person is displayed on a chalkboard and changes daily alongside other freshly prepared specials. Some examples are fresh salmon and dill fishcakes with a spicy tomato and herb sauce, and braised sirloin of beef in port wine gravy with shallots. Single-course light lunches are always available.
Cards: Visa, Access, Switch.
Other points: licensed, open-air dining, Sunday lunch, no-smoking area, children welcome, parking, open bank holidays.
Directions: from High Wycombe, take Hughenden Valley road (A4128).
GEOFFREY & SANDRA CARTER ☎ (01494) 488329 [Fax] (01494) 488301.

TRING • map 5B3

THE WHITE LION
Startops End, Marsworth, HP12 4LJ
This 15th century inn is idyllically situated on the Grand Union Canal at Marsworth Lock, an ideal stop for longboats, walkers and fishermen. Its unique character, with open fires, low beams, real ales and home-cooked food using only fresh local produce, makes this inn well worth a visit.
FOOD: from £15 to £20
Hours: meals all day 12noon–11pm.
Cuisine: ENGLISH – bar meals and à la carte restaurant menu.
Cards: Visa, Access.
Other points: parking, children welcome, pets allowed, vegetarian meals, traditional Sunday lunch.
Directions: 1 mile out of Tring on Grand Union Canal, B489.
GLEN & WENDY SMITH ☎ (01442) 822325.

WEST WYCOMBE • map 5B3

GEORGE & DRAGON
High Street, HP14 3AB
This charming country inn is situated in a National Trust village, with several tourist attractions within walking distance. Renowned for traditional English home-cooking, the George & Dragon offers superior accommodation for that special stay. Private room available for functions.
DOUBLE ROOM: from £20 to £30
FOOD: up to £15
Hours: lunch 12noon–2pm, dinner 6pm–9.30pm.
Cuisine: ENGLISH – home-cooking, local game in season.
Cards: Visa, Access, Diners, AmEx.
Other points: licensed, open-air dining, Sunday lunch.
Directions: on the A40 in West Wycombe village, 3 miles west of High Wycombe.
PHILIP TODD ☎ (01494) 464414 [Fax] (01494) 462432.

CAMBRIDGESHIRE

BARTLOW • map 10E4

THE THREE HILLS
Near Cambridge, CB1 6AW
A 16th century village inn set in glorious countryside off the beaten track, but well worth checking out. The bar and restaurant boasts a wealth of old beams, with an inglenook fire in winter. For the summer, there is a walled garden and covered patio. A popular pub with a growing reputation.
FOOD: up to £15
Hours: lunch 12noon–1.45pm, dinner 7pm–9.30pm.
Cuisine: ENGLISH – home-made specials every day plus fine steaks, grills and fresh fish. Only fresh local produce used when possible. The Three Hills is noted for its selection of vegetarian meals.
Cards: Visa, Access, MasterCard.
Other points: licensed, open-air dining, vegetarian meals, parking.

Directions: one mile off the A604 Cambridge to Haverhill road (Linton by-pass).
SUE & STEVE DIXON ☎ (01223) 891259.

CAMBRIDGE • map 10D4

ANCIENT SHEPHERDS
High Street, Fen Ditton, CB5 8ST
A very friendly country inn, c.1540, serving well-cooked and presented food. Very pleasant atmosphere, with a good cross-section of business people, students and locals.
FOOD: from £15 to £20
Hours: lunch 12noon–2pm; bar meals 12noon–2.15pm, 6.30pm–9.30pm; dinner Monday to Thursday 6.30pm–9.30pm, Friday and Saturday 6.30pm–10pm; closed Sunday night and for one week at Christmas.
Cuisine: ENGLISH / CONTINENTAL – varied à la carte menu, including moules marinière and fresh fish. Bar meals include chicken ancient shepherds (chicken with apricots, brandy and cream).
Cards: Visa, Access.
Other points: children catered for (please check for age limits), pets allowed, garden, open bank holidays.
Directions: 2 miles from the centre of Cambridge, off Newmarket Road.
HILTON ROSE ☎ (01223) 293280.

LES ROUTIERS ACCOMMODATION DIRECTORY

This handy directory is ideal for those looking for somewhere to stay at great value.
It lists a huge choice of Les Routiers-recommended places throughout the British Isles offering comfortable accommodation, good food and a warm welcome amid relaxed surroundings.

Available from selected
Les Routiers establishments
or direct from the publishers.

Price £2

ARUNDEL HOUSE HOTEL
53 Chesterton Road, CB4 3AN
Overlooking the River Cam and Jesus Green, the Arundel House Hotel is one of the few privately-owned hotels in Cambridge. Within easy walking distance of the city centre and university colleges. An elegant conversion of fine Victorian terraced houses, with a reputation for some of the best food in the area.
DOUBLE ROOM: from £30 to £40
SINGLE ROOM: from £45 to £55
FOOD: up to £15
Hours: lunch 12.15am–1.45pm, dinner 6.30pm–9.30pm.
Cuisine: FRENCH / ENGLISH – children's, vegetarian and extensive range of bar meals also available.
Cards: Visa, Access, Diners, AmEx.
Other points: licensed, Sunday lunch, children welcome, limited disabled access.

Rooms: 5 single rooms, 33 double rooms, 24 twin rooms, 6 family rooms. All with TV, radio, telephone, tea/coffee-making facilities, hair dryer. Most rooms are en suite.
Directions: on the A1303. Exit junction 13 on M11.
☎ (01223) 67701 Fax (01223) 67721.

BRIDGE HOTEL
Clayhithe, near Waterbeach, CB5 9NZ
The historic Bridge Hotel is not only one of the most popular luncheon and dinner rendezvous in the area, but is internationally famous as a riverside hotel. The riverside restaurant offers you excellent service and personal attention, and a delicious full à la carte menu is always available. Sited beside the River Cam, with a lawn sweeping down to the water's edge. Residents have fishing rights on the river from the garden.
DOUBLE ROOM: from £20 to £30
FOOD: up to £15
Hours: breakfast 7.30am–9am, bar meals 12noon–2pm, dinner 7pm–9pm, bar meals 6.30pm–9.30pm.
Cuisine: ENGLISH.
Cards: Visa, Access, AmEx.
Other points: parking, children welcome, pets allowed, no-smoking area, vegetarian meals, open-air dining, traditional Sunday lunch.
Rooms: 6 single rooms, 10 double rooms, 10 twin rooms, 2 family rooms. All with en suite, TV, telephone, tea/coffee-making facilities.
Directions: 4 miles north of Cambridge off A10, pass through Waterbeach. The hotel is on the left.
MARGARET MANSON ☎ (01223) 860252 Fax (01223) 440448.

HENRY'S CAFE BAR (CAMBRIDGE)
Quayside, CB5 8AB
A popular café-bar in the centre of this beautiful university town, close to Magdalen College. Serving an extensive range of international food, it is extremely popular with businessmen, students and tourists.
FOOD: up to £15
Hours: meals all day 11am–11pm.
Cuisine: INTERNATIONAL.
Cards: Visa, Access.
Other points: children welcome, open bank holidays, no-smoking area, afternoon teas, disabled access, vegetarian meals.
JON SHAW ☎ (01223) 324649.

REGENT HOTEL
The Regent Hotel is a fine listed building, situated in the heart of Cambridge. The location offers easy access to various business amenities and cultural attractions, and provides superb views over the famous Parker's Piece. Recently refurbished, the hotel maintains the tradition of friendly service, sumptuous meals in an elegant and luxurious environment, and reasonably priced, quality accommodation.
DOUBLE ROOM: from £30 to £40
SINGLE ROOM: from £45 to £55
FOOD: up to £15
Hours: breakfast 7.30am–9.30am, lunch 12noon–

2pm, dinner 7pm–10pm, closed 24th December until 2nd January.
Cuisine: CONTINENTAL – with a menu to suit all tastes, the hotel has an excellent reputation for superb cuisine.
Cards: Visa, Access, Diners, AmEx, Switch.
Other points: children welcome, conference facilities, residents' lounge, no-smoking area, vegetarian meals, afternoon teas.
Rooms: 6 single rooms, 17 double/twin rooms, 2 family rooms. All with en suite, TV, telephone, radio, alarm, hair dryer, trouser-press, room service, baby-listening device, tea/coffee-making facilities.
Directions: situated in the centre of Cambridge.
PAOLO PASCHALIS ☎ (01223) 351470
Fax (01223) 566562.

THE SUFFOLK HOUSE
69 Milton Road, CB4 1XA
A spacious 1930s gable-fronted detached house, set in a large secluded garden. A high standard of comfort and cleanliness is maintained by Mary and Michael Cuthbert, who extend a warm welcome to their guests. Less than 20 minutes' walk from the city centre.
DOUBLE ROOM: from £20 to £30
SINGLE ROOM: from £35 to £45
Hours: breakfast weekdays 8am–8.45am, weekends 8.30am–9.15am.
Cuisine: BREAKFAST.
Cards: Visa, Access.
Other points: central heating, children welcome, residents' lounge, garden.
Rooms: 4 double rooms, 4 twin rooms, 2 family rooms. All with TV.
Directions: situated on the A1309 – leave the A45 at A10 Ely and A1309 junction.
MR & MRS CUTHBERT ☎ (01223) 352016.

TATTIES
26–28 Regent Street, CB2 1DB
Tatties has been completely refurbished and enlarged, whilst still retaining its original character. Decorated with a wealth of traditional metal advertising signs (1890–1930), antique cooking utensils, garden tools, market barrows and other interesting items of a bygone era. The restaurant also has a large roof garden, overlooking the grounds of Downing College. It is conveniently located in the centre of the city and is a popular venue for undergraduates and tourists.
FOOD: up to £15
Hours: breakfast 8.30am–10.30am, meals all day 10.30am–10.50pm, open 7 days.
Cuisine: ENGLISH – specializing in baked potatoes: here the jacket spud is plucked from its humble roots and transformed into a mouth-watering meal in its own right! Charcoal-grilled chicken, fish and steaks, salads and pasta dishes also available.
Other points: licensed, children welcome, disabled facilities, guide dogs welcome, open-air dining, vegetarian meals.
Directions: located in the centre of Cambridge next to Downing College.
BARRY PAIN & MIKE LAMBOURN-BROWN
☎ (01223) 358478 Fax (01228) 359703.

CHITTERING • map 10D4

TRAVELLERS REST
Ely Road, CB5 9PH
A 300-year-old beamed public house with its own restaurant, decorated throughout with a cottage theme, providing a perfect atmosphere for families and caravanners. Carvery offering 3-course meals. Ideal location for visiting Anglesey Abbey and Wicken Fen, or for touring Cambridge, Bury St Edmunds and Newmarket.
FOOD: up to £15
Hours: lunch 12noon–2.30pm, dinner Monday to Saturday 6pm–9.30pm, Sunday 7pm–9pm.
Cuisine: ENGLISH / CONTINENTAL – quality à la carte.
Cards: Visa, Access, AmEx.
Other points: parking, children welcome, no-smoking area, disabled access, vegetarian meals, open-air dining.
Directions: on A10, exactly halfway between Ely and Cambridge (8 miles each way).
KEITH & ALEXANDRA RICHARDSON
☎ (01223) 860751.

DUXFORD • map 10E4

DUXFORD LODGE HOTEL
Ickleton Road, CB2 4RU
Duxford Lodge has been carefully converted and refurbished to form a luxurious country house hotel. The accommodation is outstanding, with all bedrooms individual in design. The restaurant serves a high standard of traditional cuisine, cooked by the proprietor, at excellent value for money and within attractive, elegant surroundings. Duxford Lodge is an ideal choice for a meal or overnight stay.
DOUBLE ROOM: from £30 to £40
SINGLE ROOM: from £55
FOOD: from £15 to £20
Hours: breakfast 7.15am–9.30am, lunch 12noon–2pm, dinner 7pm–9.30pm.
Cuisine: ENGLISH – table d'hôte and à la carte menus. Dishes may include Dover sole, chicken Duxford, rack of lamb, steak au poivre.
Cards: Visa, Access, Diners, AmEx.
Other points: licensed, Sunday lunch, conferences, functions.
Rooms: 15 bedrooms.
Directions: the first or second right turn after exiting from the M11 onto the A505 eastbound will bring you directly to the hotel.
RONALD & SUZANNE CRADDOCK ☎ (01223) 836444 Fax (01223) 832271.

ELY • map 10D4

CHEZ TON TON
The Basement, 60 Market Street, CB7 4LS
An excellent restaurant offering the highest standards of French cuisine, with a strong emphasis on individual customer attention. The attractive walled garden is a very popular venue for dining alfresco in the summer, but for the

cooler months or for those who would rather dine indoors, the temperature-controlled restaurant provides tastefully decorated, comfortable surroundings in which to enjoy a superb meal. Disabled access to the garden only.
FOOD: up to £15
Hours: lunch 12noon–3pm, dinner from 6.30pm, closed Sunday and Monday.
Cuisine: FRENCH – classical French cuisine with a modern approach.
Cards: Visa, Access.
Other points: children welcome, vegetarian meals, garden dining, limited disabled access.
Directions: located in the centre of Ely, 2 minutes from the cathedral.
NIGEL SMITH ☎ (01353) 669668.

LES ROUTIERS AWARDS 1995
Our award-winners are featured on pages 10–15, 23 and 27.

GREAT CHISHILL • map 10E4

THE PHEASANT
24 Heydon Road, near Royston, SG8 8JH
This charming country inn, situated in the beautiful village of Great Chishill, has been tastefully refurbished with character and features an impressive inglenook fireplace, flagstone floors and candlelit restaurant, giving a warm and cosy atmosphere with excellent home-cooked food and real ales. It has a large raised garden with panoramic views across the countryside.
FOOD: up to £15
Hours: lunch 12noon–2.30pm, dinner 7pm–10pm.
Cuisine: ENGLISH – from simple bar food to haute cuisine.
Cards: Visa, Access, Switch.
Other points: parking, children welcome, open-air dining, vegetarian meals, traditional Sunday lunch.
Directions: Barley/Barkway turning off A505, heading east out of Royston; after about 2 to 3 miles, turn right into village.
JOHN & LIZ MANN ☎ (01763) 838535.

HORSEHEATH • map 10E4

THE OLD RED LION
Linton Road, CB1 6QF
This beautiful 17th century country inn is situated on the A604 close to Cambridge, offering good food, real ales and fine wines. Totally refurbished with flagstone floors, open fire and timber beams and a wealth of character. It boasts elegantly furnished en suite letting rooms. Close by is Chilford Hall Vineyard and Linton Zoo.
DOUBLE ROOM: from £30 to £40
FOOD: up to £15
Hours: breakfast 7.30am–9.30am, meals all day 11am–10.30pm.
Cuisine: ENGLISH – traditional cuisine with European and Asian influences.
Cards: Visa, Access.

Other points: parking, children welcome, pets allowed, conference facilities, garden, open-air dining, vegetarian meals, traditional Sunday lunch.
Rooms: 14 bedrooms. All with TV, telephone, radio, alarm, hair dryer, trouser-press, tea/coffee-making facilities.
Directions: on the main A604 between Linton and Haverhill, 14 miles outside Cambridge.
JOHN & ANGELA ERA ☎ (01223) 892909
Fax (01223) 894217.

HUNTINGDON • map 10D4

THE OLD FERRY BOAT INN
Holywell, St Ives, PE17 3TG
This charming thatched riverside inn claims to be the oldest in England, with the spirit of over a thousand years of good hospitality. Judging by the number of visitors, this reputation is still upheld. One sad spirit still exists: the ghost of young Juliette, whose gravestone forms part of the ancient floor in the bar.
DOUBLE ROOM: from £20 to £30
SINGLE ROOM: from £35 to £45
FOOD: up to £15
Hours: breakfast 7.30am–10am, lunch 12noon–2pm, dinner 6.30pm–10pm, Sunday 7pm–9.30pm.
Cuisine: INTERNATIONAL – including traditional English. Daily specials, extensive choice of bar meals and weekend specials. Real ales available.
Cards: Visa, Access, Switch.
Other points: children welcome, parking, disabled access, vegetarian meals.
Rooms: 7 bedrooms. All ensuite.
Directions: from the A604, take the B1040 towards St Ives, followed by the A1123. At Needingworth, take the road on the right to Holywell.
MISS PADDOCK ☎ (01480) 463227.

LINTON • map 10E4

THE CROWN INN
High Street, CB1 6HS
A lime-washed Georgian pub, situated in the centre of the pleasant village of Linton, offering a choice of tasty bar meals or an interesting à la carte menu in their restaurant. Excellent service, and a very warm welcome typical of a charming village pub, make a visit here well worthwhile.
DOUBLE ROOM: up to £20
FOOD: up to £15
Hours: lunch 12noon–2pm, dinner 6.30pm–9.30pm, bar 12noon–3pm and 5.30pm–11pm, no food Sunday evenings.
Cuisine: INTERNATIONAL – home-cooked food using fresh ingredients.
Cards: Visa, Access.
Other points: licensed, open-air dining, Sunday lunch, no-smoking area, children welcome, garden.
Rooms: 1 double room, 3 twin rooms. All with en suite, TV, tea-making facilities.
Directions: off A604, near the water tower.
JOEL PALMER ☎ (01223) 891759.

CAMBRIDGESHIRE • SE ENGLAND & EAST ANGLIA

PETERBOROUGH • map 10D4

BELL INN HOTEL
Great North Road, PE7 3RA
This hotel has been built around the courtyard of an ancient inn. It offers old-world charm, relaxing comfort and modern facilities. The inn dates from 1500 and is a dream for history lovers.
DOUBLE ROOM: from £20 to £30
FOOD: from £15 to £20
Hours: breakfast 7am–9am, lunch 12noon–2pm, dinner 7pm–9.30pm.
Cuisine: ENGLISH – à la carte. Dishes include Byron fillet of beef, wild salmon dumpling, vegetable filo parcels.
Cards: Visa, Access, AmEx, Switch.
Other points: open-air dining, Sunday lunch, no-smoking area, garden, conferences.
Rooms: 2 single rooms, 13 double rooms, 3 twin rooms, 1 family room.
Directions: half a mile off A1 northbound; 5 miles south of Peterborough.
MR & MRS McGIVERN ☎ (01733) 241066.

ST IVES • map 10D4

THE DOLPHIN HOTEL
Bridge Foot, London Road, PE17 4EP
The Dolphin is a family-owned hotel on the banks of the Great Ouse in the old market town of St Ives. Guests enjoy good food, friendly but efficient service and panoramic views of the river and surrounding meadows. The large riverside terrace is the perfect setting for a refreshing drink or a light meal served in a relaxed atmosphere. For the convenience of the guests, there is a large car park and mooring for 20 boats.
DOUBLE ROOM: from £30 to £40
SINGLE ROOM: over £55
FOOD: up to £15
Hours: breakfast 7.30am–9.30am, lunch 12noon–2pm, dinner 7pm–9.30pm.
Cuisine: ENGLISH / CONTINENTAL – with a good selection of wines from an extensive list. Special carvery Sunday lunch.
Cards: Visa, Access, Diners, AmEx.
Other points: fully licensed.
Rooms: 2 single rooms, 13 double rooms (2 have been adapted for disabled persons), 31 twin rooms, 2 family rooms. All with TV, radio, telephone, tea/coffee-making facilities, hair dryer.
Directions: from A14 take B1040 towards St Ives, left at first roundabout, then immediately right; the Dolphin is about 800 yards, by the old river bridge.
H.R. WADSWORTH ☎ (01480) 466966
[Fax] (01480) 495597.

OLIVER'S LODGE HOTEL & RESTAURANT
Needingworth Road, near Cambridge, PE18 4JP
Originally a Victorian building, it was sympathetically extended in 1990/91 and now has 16 first-class rooms, a brand-new restaurant, real-ale bar and several function rooms, together with an attractive garden and patio areas. Situated in a residential area in the historic riverside market town of St Ives, just 3 minutes' walk from the town centre and close to the river (special rates for use of the hotel's own boat). The hotel is 20 minutes from Cambridge and makes an ideal touring centre for Cambridge and the surrounding area.
DOUBLE ROOM: from £30 to £40
SINGLE ROOM: from £45 to £55
FOOD: from £15 to £20
Hours: breakfast 7.30am–9.30am, lunch 12noon–2pm, dinner 7pm–9.30pm.
Cuisine: ENGLISH / CONTINENTAL – fish and game specialities when in season.
Cards: Visa, Access, AmEx, MasterCard.
Other points: parking, children welcome, pets allowed, conference facilities, functions, residents' lounge, garden, open-air dining, vegetarian meals, traditional Sunday lunch, afternoon teas.
Rooms: 1 single room, 6 double rooms, 6 twin rooms, 3 family rooms. All with en suite, satellite TV, telephone, radio, alarm, hair dryer, trouser-press, iron, baby-listening device, tea/coffee-making facilities.
Directions: from M11, A45 or A1, take A14 towards St Ives; leave A14 where signposted to St Ives (A1096). Straight across first roundabout, left at next roundabout and turn first right into Needingworth Road. The hotel is 200 yards along on the right.
CHRIS & LIZ LANGLEY ☎ (01480) 463252
[Fax] (01480) 461150.

SUTTON GAULT • map 10D4

THE ANCHOR INN
Sutton, near Ely, CB6 2BD
A traditional Fen riverside pub, approximately 350 years old, lit by gas lamps and with old beams, scrubbed wooden tables and chairs. Frequented by locals and tourists alike, the atmosphere is homely and welcoming, and the service is efficient. Recognized in all the guides. Ideal base for visiting Ely Cathedral, the Ouse Washes, Welney Wildfowl Reserve and for exploring the real Fen country. Cambridge and Newmarket within easy reach. Five en suite rooms are planned for spring 1995. (See special feature on page 13.)

LES ROUTIERS
INN of the Year 1995

FOOD: from £15 to £20
Hours: lunch, 12noon–2.30pm, dinner 6.30pm–11pm, last orders 9.30pm, closed Sunday evening October until Easter.
Cuisine: ENGLISH – à la carte menu, offering an extensive range of imaginative dishes, changes daily.
Cards: Visa, Access, AmEx.
Other points: licensed, open-air dining, Sunday lunch, no-smoking area, children catered for (please check for age limits), open bank holidays.
Directions: signposted to Sutton Gault, just south of Sutton Village (B1301). 7 miles west of Ely.
HEATHER & ROBIN MOORE ☎ (01353) 778537 [Fax] (01353) 776180.

63

EAST SUSSEX

ALFRISTON • map 6D4

DRUSILLAS PARK
Alfriston, BN26 5QS
The attractive Toucans thatched restaurant forms part of a leisure park that includes a zoo, known as the best small zoo in the south. Set in large well-kept grounds, it was established in 1924 and is still a family-run business. Toucans was Egon Ronay's Family Restaurant of the Year 1991. Toy boxes and Sunday lunchtime entertainment.
FOOD: up to £15
Hours: lunch 12noon–6pm, closed evenings.
Cuisine: INTERNATIONAL – family menu in Toucans Restaurant. Pub food in Inn at the Zoo.
Cards: Visa, Access.
Other points: licensed, Sunday lunch, children welcome, zoo, playland.
Directions: off the A27 between Lewes and Polegate.
MR M. ANN ☎ (01323) 870656 Fax (01323) 870846.

BATTLE • map 6D5

BURNT WOOD HOUSE HOTEL
Powdermill Lane, TN33 0SU
An Edwardian country house set in 18 acres of lawns, gardens and woodland. Ideal location for exploring this historic area. Excellent French and English cuisine, with a good selection of wines. Warm and relaxing atmosphere, in the heart of the tranquil Sussex countryside.
DOUBLE ROOM: from £30 to £40
FOOD: from £15 to £20
Hours: breakfast 7.30am–9.30am, lunch 12noon–2pm, dinner 7pm–9.30pm (last orders), restaurant closed Sunday evening.
Cuisine: ENGLISH / FRENCH – à la carte, table d'hôte and bar meals.
Cards: Visa, Access, Diners, AmEx.
Other points: parking, children welcome, swimming pool, tennis, croquet, pets, residents' lounge, vegetarian meals, garden dining.
Rooms: 2 single rooms, 7 double rooms, 1 twin room.
Directions: turn right onto B2095 Catsfield Road, 1½ miles on left, between Battle and Catsfield.
MR M. HOGGARTH ☎ (01424) 775151.

POWDERMILLS HOTEL
Powdermill Lane, TN33 0SP
Set in 150 acres of park-like grounds and with fishing lakes and woodlands, this Georgian country house hotel is ideal for those wanting to return to nature. The Orangery Restaurant serves imaginative and exciting meals, and the hotel offers accommodation of a very high standard. Highly recommended.
DOUBLE ROOM: from £30 to £40
SINGLE ROOM: from £45 to £55
FOOD: from £20 to £25

Hours: breakfast 7.30am–9.30am, lunch 12noon–2pm, dinner 7pm–9pm.
Cuisine: ENGLISH – full à la carte menu, table d'hôte and bar snacks. Vegetarian menu.
Cards: Visa, Access, AmEx.
Other points: licensed, open-air dining, Sunday lunch, children welcome, morning tea, afternoon tea, swimming pool, golf nearby, riding, dogs allowed, disabled access, vegetarian meals, residents' lounge, residents' bar.
Rooms: 11 double rooms, 12 twin rooms. All with TV, telephone.
Directions: through Battle towards Hastings, first right turn into Powdermill Lane.
D. & J. COWPLAND ☎ (01424) 775511 Fax (01424) 774540.

THE SQUIRREL INN
North Trade Road, TN33 9LJ
A free-house with its own restaurant serving traditional fare, including bar snacks. Close to Battle Abbey, Bodiam Castle, Drusillas Zoo and many other attractions.
FOOD: up to £15
Hours: lunch 12noon–2.30pm, dinner (Mon-Sat) 6pm–9.30pm, Sunday 7pm–9.30pm, closed Sunday night in winter.
Cuisine: ENGLISH.
Cards: Visa, Access, AmEx.
Other points: parking, children welcome, Sunday lunch, open bank holidays, no-smoking area, disabled access, pets allowed, vegetarian meals, open-air dining, licensed.
Directions: located on A271, just before approaching A2100 and Battle.
BOB & KATH BRITT ☎ (01424) 772717.

BEXHILL-ON-SEA • map 6D5

THE NORTHERN HOTEL
72–78 Sea Road, TN40 1JN
Adjacent to the seafront, the hotel is just one minute's walk from the sea. Comfortable accommodation, decorated and furnished to a high standard. The Georgian-style restaurant serves well-prepared, well-presented food at very good value for money. Quiet and relaxing atmosphere, as is the tradition of a family-run hotel.
DOUBLE ROOM: from £30 to £40
SINGLE ROOM: from £35 to £45
FOOD: up to £15
Hours: breakfast 8am–9.30am, lunch 12noon–2pm, dinner 6pm–8pm.
Cuisine: ENGLISH – varied high-quality selection on table d'hôte, à la carte and bar snack menu. Vegetarians catered for.
Cards: Visa, Access, AmEx.
Other points: licensed, children welcome, afternoon tea, pets allowed, disabled access.
Rooms: 6 single rooms, 7 double rooms, 21 twin rooms, 1 family room.

ESTABLISHED 1934

LES ROUTIERS

WHETHER YOU ARE A REGULAR VISITOR TO FRANCE or planning a first visit, Les Routiers France 1995 is the perfect travelling companion and will help you to discover the rich variety of scenery, gastronomy and relaxed, convivial lifestyle of this alluring country.

It is your key to over 1,600 Relais Routiers offering some of the finest food and wine in the world, simply furnished but comfortable accommodation and a warm Gallic welcome.

Choose from friendly, family-run country hotels, lively brasseries, simple roadside cafés and local bars. Every establishment featured has been awarded the distinctive red and blue Les Routiers symbol – the true sign of quality and value in France today.

Whatever your itinerary, Les Routiers France deserves a place in any travel bag!

Les Routiers
have been inspecting and recommending the finest places to eat and stay in France for 60 years

Look for the red and blue symbol on your travels!

Les Routiers
FRANCE
1995

- Over 1,600 entries listed by region
- Details of opening times, facilities and prices
- New regional, full-colour maps
- Hints on eating out
- Useful expressions

288 pages | UK £ 9.99
| USA $17.95

Available from your bookseller or direct from the publishers

Les Routiers

25 VANSTON PLACE LONDON SW6 1AZ TEL: 0171-385 6644 FAX: 0171-385 7136

HARROW HOTEL

12-22 Pinner Road, Harrow, Middlesex HA1 4HZ

English Cuisine

Luxurious Lounge & Bar

Superb Restaurant

TEL: 0181-427 3435   ◊   FAX: 0181-861 1370

For full details see London, Harrow

WHITE HOUSE HOTEL

S·U·P·E·R·B   I·N·T·E·R·N·A·T·I·O·N·A·L   C·U·I·S·I·N·E

TEL
01923
237316

FAX
01923
233109

UPTON ROAD, WATFORD, HERTS, WD1 2EL

For full details see Hertfordshire, Watford

Directions: off the A259.
THE SIMS FAMILY ☎ (01424) 212836
[Fax] (01424) 213036.

BRIGHTON & HOVE • map 6E5

■ BRIGHTON MARINA HOUSE HOTEL
8 Charlotte Street, off Marine Parade, BN2 1AG
A cosy, well-maintained, well-run hotel, comfortably furnished and centrally located. The staff at the hotel will endeavour to make your stay truly memorable by the quality of their service and attention. The hotel lies in the heart of Kemp Town, the Regency side of Brighton, in a quiet street leading to the beach, with the seafront a minute's walk away.
DOUBLE ROOM: from £20 to £30
SINGLE ROOM: up to £25
FOOD: up to £15
Hours: breakfast 7.30am–10am.
Cards: Visa, Access, Diners, AmEx.
Other points: children welcome, residents' lounge.
Rooms: 10 double rooms, 3 twin rooms, 1 triple room, 6 family rooms. All with TV, telephone, radio, alarm, hair dryer, tea/coffee-making facilities.
Directions: just off Marine Parade, fourth street on left from roundabout facing Palace Pier.
S. JUNG ☎ (01273) 605349/679484
[Fax] (01273) 605349.

■ COSMOPOLITAN HOTEL
31 New Steine, Marine Parade, BN2 1PD
Overlooking the beach and Palace Pier, the Cosmopolitan Hotel is a friendly, comfortable place to stay and popular with holiday-makers and business visitors alike. There is a cosy residential licensed bar, and the hotel is very central for shopping, entertainments and conference centres.
DOUBLE ROOM: from £20 to £30
SINGLE ROOM: from £25 to £35
Hours: breakfast 8am–9am.
Cuisine: BREAKFAST.
Cards: Visa, Access, Diners, AmEx.
Other points: children welcome, TV lounge, residents' bar.
Rooms: 10 single rooms, 1 double room, 4 twin rooms, 9 family rooms. All with TV, radio, telephone, tea/coffee-making facilities, alarm, heating. Many rooms are en suite.
Directions: A23 to Brighton seafront, turn left onto A259 Marine Parade – ¼ mile.
C. PAPANICHOLA ☎ (01273) 682461
[Fax] (01273) 622311.

≡ DONATELLO RESTAURANT
3 Brighton Place, The Lanes, BN1 1HJ
A popular and well-run Italian restaurant specializing in pasta dishes, pizzas and Italian ice cream. The menu offers an extensive choice of dishes at good value for money. A lively restaurant with friendly service and a warm, relaxed atmosphere.
FOOD: up to £15 [CLUB]
Hours: meals all day 11.30am–11.30pm.

Cuisine: ITALIAN – extensive menu of Italian dishes including pasta, pizzas, fish and meat dishes. Italian ice cream.
Cards: Visa, Access, Diners, AmEx, Switch.
Other points: licensed, Sunday lunch, children welcome.
Directions: in centre of Brighton's Lanes.
MR PIETRO ADDIS ☎ (01273) 775477
[Fax] (01273) 677659.

≡ ENGLISH'S OYSTER BAR & SEAFOOD RESTAURANT
29–31 East Street, BN1 1HL
The restaurant is housed in three fishermen's cottages on the edge of Brighton's historic Lanes. For more than 200 years, English's Oyster Bar has been a family business, selling oysters and fish without a break in tradition. Enjoy the pleasures of dining alfresco on the outside terrace, where a full menu and barbeque are served.
FOOD: up to £15
Hours: meals all day 12noon–10.15pm, Sunday 12.30am–9.30pm, closed Christmas eve, Christmas day, Boxing day and New Year's day.
Cuisine: SEAFOOD – seafood, including oysters, Dover sole, plaice, monkfish, mussels, fresh crab and lobsters. Special two-course menu for £5.95. Daily specialities.
Cards: Visa, Access, Diners, AmEx, Switch.
Other points: Sunday lunch, no-smoking area, children welcome, open bank holidays.
Directions: in the heart of Brighton's Lanes, 2 minutes' walk from the Royal Pavilion.
MRS P.M. LEIGH JONES ☎ (01273) 327980/ 325661.

■ KEMPTON HOUSE HOTEL
33–34 Marine Parade, BN2 1TR
A friendly, family-run hotel situated opposite the beach and the famous Palace Pier and within minutes of all amenities. Mr and Mrs Swaine assure a warm welcome and real 'home from home' atmosphere. With a high standard of accommodation, a patio overlooking the seafront, residential bar and comfortable surroundings, an enjoyable stay is guaranteed.
DOUBLE ROOM: from £20 to £30
SINGLE ROOM: from £35 to £45
Hours: breakfast 8.30am–9am, dinner 6pm.
Cuisine: ENGLISH.
Cards: Visa, Access, Diners, AmEx.
Other points: children welcome, pets allowed, residents' lounge, garden, vegetarian meals, street parking, residents' bar.
Rooms: 7 double rooms, 2 twin rooms, 3 family rooms. All with en suite, satellite TV, radio, alarm, telephone, trouser-press, tea/coffee-making facilities.
Directions: A23 London Road until Palace Pier roundabout. Left onto A259. 200 yards on left.
PHILIP & VALERIE SWAINE ☎ (01273) 570248
[Fax] (01273) 570248.

■ KIMBERLEY HOTEL
17 Atlingworth Street, BN2 1PL
A friendly, family hotel with clean, comfortable rooms, a residents' lounge and bar facilities. Centrally situated, being only two minutes from

the seafront, with the Royal Pavilion, Palace Pier and marina nearby.
DOUBLE ROOM: up to £20
SINGLE ROOM: up to £25
Hours: breakfast – weekdays 8am–9am, weekends 8.30am–9.30am.
Cuisine: BREAKFAST.
Cards: Visa, Access, Diners, AmEx.
Other points: children catered for (please check for age limits), open bank holidays, residents' lounge.
Rooms: 3 single rooms, 2 double rooms, 7 twin rooms, 3 family rooms. All with TV, tea/coffee-making facilities.
Directions: situated between Brighton Marina and Palace Pier off the A259.
MRS R. LISS & MRS M. ROLAND ☎ (01273) 603504 [Fax] (01273) 603504.

▲ MELFORD HALL HOTEL
41 Marine Parade, BN2 1PE

A seafront hotel on a corner position of a garden square and close to all main amenities. Melford Hall also overlooks the beach. The accommodation is en suite, and ground-floor rooms and four-poster bedrooms are available. Under the personal supervision of the resident proprietors.
DOUBLE ROOM: from £20 to £30
SINGLE ROOM: from £25 to £35
Hours: breakfast 8am–9am.
Cuisine: BREAKFAST.
Cards: Visa, Access, Diners, AmEx.
Other points: children catered for (please check for age limits), residents' lounge.
Rooms: 2 single rooms, 11 double rooms, 11 twin rooms, 1 quad room. All with TV, radio, alarm, tea/coffee-making facilities.
Directions: A259 Newhaven to Brighton road, on Marine Parade, close to Palace Pier.
IAN DIXON ☎ (01273) 681435 [Fax] (01273) 624186.

▲ NEW STEINE HOTEL
12A New Steine, BN2 1PB

A Grade II listed building in a Regency square, within easy walking distance of the town centre, conference centre and the famous Royal Pavilion. Pleasantly decorated and comfortably furnished. An enjoyable stay is assured.
DOUBLE ROOM: up to £20
Hours: breakfast 8am–9am.
Cuisine: BREAKFAST.
Other points: children catered for (please check for age limits), pets allowed, central heating, residents' lounge, street parking.
Rooms: 3 single rooms, 6 double rooms, 2 twin rooms. All with TV, tea/coffee-making facilities.
Directions: in a Regency square just off the main promenade.
MR SHAW & MR MILLS ☎ (01273) 681546.

≈ PINOCCHIO
22 New Road, BN1 1UF

A traditional Italian meal at a reasonable price in pleasant, unpretentious and relaxed surroundings. This is a very popular restaurant with travellers and locals alike. It is also a regular haunt for theatre-goers and actors – you will often spot a famous face.
FOOD: up to £15 [CLUB]
Hours: dinner weekdays 5pm–11.30pm, lunch weekdays 12noon–2.30pm, meals all day, weekends 12noon–11.30pm.
Cuisine: ITALIAN / CONTINENTAL – pizza and pasta. Selection of chicken, veal and fish dishes.
Cards: Visa, Access, Diners, AmEx, Switch.
Other points: Sunday lunch, children welcome.
Directions: easily located opposite the Pavilion Theatre.
MR PIETRO ADDIS ☎ (01273) 677676 [Fax] (01273) 677659.

≈ REGENCY RESTAURANT
131 King's Road, BN1 2HH

A friendly, relaxed restaurant with welcoming staff where good food can be enjoyed throughout the day. The restaurant specializes in locally caught fresh fish, with a wide choice of other dishes, including roasts, grills and steaks. All food is well cooked and offers good value for money. In fine weather, tables are available outside on the seafront.
FOOD: up to £15 [CLUB]
Hours: meals all day 10am–11pm, closed Christmas 23rd December until 10th January.
Cuisine: SEAFOOD / ENGLISH – a wide range of meals, with locally caught fresh fish a speciality.
Cards: Visa, Access, Diners.
Other points: licensed, Sunday lunch, children welcome, morning tea, afternoon tea, parking.
Directions: On A259, opposite West Pier on Brighton seafront.
ROVERTOS & EMILIO SAVVIDES ☎ (01273) 325014.

▲ ST CATHERINE'S LODGE HOTEL
Seafront, Kingsway, BN3 2RZ

A 150-year-old Victorian gabled hotel, centrally situated on the seafront, with full accommodation facilities. Good food at value-for-money prices is served by well-trained attentive staff in attractive surroundings. Located nearby is the King Alfred Leisure Centre with swimming pools, waterslides and ten-pin bowling.
DOUBLE ROOM: from £30 to £40
SINGLE ROOM: from £45 to £55
FOOD: up to £15 [CLUB]
Hours: breakfast 7.45am–9.30am, lunch 12.30am–2pm, dinner 7pm–9pm.
Cuisine: ENGLISH – extensive à la carte. Dishes include roast carved at the table.
Cards: Visa, Access, Diners, AmEx.
Other points: Sunday lunch, children welcome, garden, games room, residents' lounge, afternoon tea, conferences, functions, residents' bar, vegetarian meals, parking, foreign exchange.
Rooms: 10 single rooms, 22 double rooms, 12 twin rooms, 4 family rooms, 2 suites. All with TV, telephone.
Directions: hotel is on A259 coast road, on the seafront in the centre of Hove. Near King Alfred Leisure Centre.
JOHN HOULTON ☎ (01273) 778181 [Fax] (01273) 774949.

TROUVILLE HOTEL
11 New Steine, BN2 1PB

A Regency Grade II listed town-house tastefully restored and furnished, enhanced with window boxes, conveniently situated in a seafront square. The town centre, marina, Pavilion, Lanes and conference centre are all within easy walking distance.
DOUBLE ROOM: up to £20
SINGLE ROOM: up to £25
Hours: breakfast weekdays 8.15am–9am, weekends 8.45am–9.15am.
Cuisine: BREAKFAST.
Cards: Visa, Access, AmEx.
Other points: central heating, children welcome, residents' lounge.
Rooms: 2 single rooms, 4 double rooms, 2 twin rooms. All with TV, tea/coffee-making facilities.
Directions: just off the seafront, 300 yards east of Palace Pier, off A259.
MR & MRS J.P. HANSELL ☎ (01273) 697384.

CROWBOROUGH • map 6D4

WINSTON MANOR HOTEL
Beacon Road, near Tunbridge Wells, TN6 1AD

This large, late-Victorian hotel is set in the heart of the Ashdown Forest within easy reach of Gatwick Airport and the South Coast, offering excellent facilities including a leisure club. The atmosphere is quiet and relaxed and the food and service outstanding.
DOUBLE ROOM: from £30 to £40
SINGLE ROOM: fro £35 to £45
FOOD: from £15 to £20
Hours: breakfast 7.30am–9.30am, dinner 7.30pm–9.30pm, meals all day 7.30am–10pm.
Cuisine: FRENCH / ENGLISH – à la carte, table d'hôte and coffee shop menus. Children's menu available. Imaginative dishes for vegetarians.
Cards: Visa, Diners, AmEx, Switch.
Other points: licensed, Sunday lunch, no-smoking area, children welcome, garden, pets allowed, afternoon tea, conferences, functions, baby-listening device, baby-sitting, cots, 24hr reception, residents' lounge, residents' bar, swimming pool, vegetarian meals, parking.
Rooms: 54 bedrooms. All with TV, telephone, tea/coffee-making facilities.
Directions: the hotel is on the A26 between Tunbridge Wells and Uckfield.
MRS MORGAN ☎ (01892) 652772
Fax (01892) 665537.

EASTBOURNE • map 6D4

THE CHATSWORTH HOTEL
Grand Parade, BN21 3YR

The Chatsworth Hotel is a traditional English hotel in an elegant Edwardian building. It is ideally situated on the Grand Parade only a minute away from the beach and promenade. With the staff always ready to help in any way, the Chatsworth is a very comfortable three-star hotel.
DOUBLE ROOM: from £30 to £40
SINGLE ROOM: from £35 to £45
FOOD: from £15 to £20
Hours: breakfast 8am–9.45am, lunch 12noon–2.05pm, Sunday lunch 12.30am–2pm, dinner 7pm–8.30pm.
Cuisine: ENGLISH – a wide range of food including dishes such as avocado and prawns, soup, rosette of lamb, escalope of turkey, strawberry gateaux and crepes normand.
Cards: Visa, Access, AmEx.
Other points: licensed, Sunday lunch, children welcome, pets allowed, conferences, cots.
Rooms: 12 single rooms, 8 double rooms, 27 twin rooms, 2 family rooms. All with TV, radio, telephone.
Directions: on corner of the Grand Parade and Hartington Place, very near the bandstand.
PETER HAWLEY ☎ (01323) 411016
Fax (01323) 643270.

WEST ROCKS HOTEL
Grand Parade, BN21 4DL

A friendly, family-owned/managed hotel, occupying one of Eastbourne's finest seafront locations. Three elegant and spacious lounges afford magnificent views over the parades and the Channel. The 54 comfortable bedrooms – the majority with sea views – have many modern facilities, and there is also a passenger lift. As one of the sunniest resorts in Great Britain, Eastbourne is the ideal place for your summer holiday.
DOUBLE ROOM: from £20 to £30
SINGLE ROOM: from £25 to £35
FOOD: up to £15
Hours: breakfast 8am–9.30am, bar snacks 12noon–2pm, dinner 6.45pm–8pm, closed mid-November until mid-March.
Cuisine: ENGLISH / CONTINENTAL.
Cards: Visa, Access, Diners, AmEx.
Other points: children catered for (please check for age limits), no-smoking area, residents' lounge, vegetarian meals, residents' bar, wheelchair ramp.
Rooms: 6 single rooms, 17 double rooms, 28 twin rooms, 3 family rooms. All with TV, telephone, tea/coffee-making facilities.
Directions: at western end past the bandstand.
MR K.B. SAYERS ☎ (01323) 725217
Fax (01323) 720421.

WISH TOWER HOTEL
King Edward's Parade, BN21 4EB

Ideally situated on the seafront, the Wish Tower Hotel provides splendid views across to the Esplanade and beach beyond. There is a friendly, relaxing atmosphere in which to enjoy the well-cooked food, with locally caught fish and seafood always available. With efficient, courteous service and comfortable furnishings, the Wish Tower is a popular rendezvous.
DOUBLE ROOM: from £30 to £40
SINGLE ROOM: from £35 to £45
FOOD: up to £15
Hours: breakfast 7am–9.30am, lunch 12noon–2pm, Sunday 12.30am–2pm, dinner 7pm–8.45pm.
Cuisine: ENGLISH – table d'hôte menu. Fish is the speciality, but dishes include roast sirloin of

Scotch beef with burgundy wine sauce.
Lunchtime hot and cold buffet.
Cards: Visa, Access, Diners, AmEx.
Other points: licensed, Sunday lunch, no-smoking area, children catered for (please check for age limits), afternoon tea, pets allowed, conferences.
Rooms: 25 single rooms, 11 double rooms, 29 twin rooms.
Directions: on the promenade overlooking The Wish Tower, museum and sea.
☎ (01323) 722676 Fax (01323) 721474.

FLETCHING • map 6D4

THE ROSE & CROWN
High Street, near Uckfield, TN22 3ST
This 16th century country inn, with a charm all of its own, offers diners a good choice of delicious meals from the à la carte, table d'hôte and bar menus. With a good selection of wines and ales and courteous service, The Rose & Crown is popular with locals and with visitors to the many nearby tourist attractions.
FOOD: up to £15
Hours: lunch 12noon–2pm, dinner 7pm–9.30pm.
Cuisine: ENGLISH – fresh, home-made dishes. Children's menu available.
Cards: Visa, Access, AmEx.
Other points: parking, children welcome, no-smoking area, open-air dining, vegetarian meals, traditional Sunday lunch.
Directions: Fletching is situated off A272, between Uckfield and Haywards Heath.
ROGER & SHEILA HAYWOOD ☎ (01825) 722039.

HASTINGS • map 6D5

RESTAURANT TWENTY SEVEN
27 George Street, Hastings Old Town, TN34 3EA
Attractive French restaurant set in the old part of town near the seafront. All food is freshly prepared for each customer and, with its Impressionist paintings and soft Gallic-style music, the atmosphere is both intimate and relaxing.
FOOD: from £15 to £20
Hours: dinner 7pm–10.30pm, closed Monday.
Cuisine: FRENCH – French dishes including salad maconnaise, seafood croustade, filet de porc dijonaise, magret de canard, steak au poivre. Traditional Sunday lunch.
Cards: Visa, Access, AmEx.
Other points: licensed, Sunday lunch.
Directions: east end of the seafront, in pedestrianized area of the old town.
P. ATTRILL & E. GIBBS ☎ (01424) 420060.

LEWES • map 6D4

LA CUCINA RESTAURANT
13 Station Street, BN7 2DA
Outstanding food and excellent service can be found at this Italian restaurant in the centre of Lewes. The menu offers an extensive choice of authentic Italian dishes, superbly cooked and served in generous portions. Highly recommended for the high standard of cuisine and service within an atmosphere of peace and calm.
FOOD: up to £15
Hours: closed Sunday/bank holidays, dinner Monday to Saturday 6.30pm–10.30pm, lunch Thursday to Saturday 12noon–2pm.
Cuisine: ITALIAN – seasonal specialities may include fresh mussels marinara, pesce misto marinara, pollo alla cacciatora, Sussex lamb, strawberries and cream or maraschino, fagiano, brill, venison.
Cards: Visa, Access, AmEx.
Other points: licensed, children welcome, parking.
Directions: 200 metres from station towards the high street.
JOSE VILAS MAYO ☎ (01273) 476707.

WHITE HART HOTEL
High Street, BN7 1XE
A historic 16th century coaching house with a modern extension, tastefully blended to the original architecture. Well placed for exploring the Sussex coast, the hotel offers comfort, good food and warm hospitality.
DOUBLE ROOM: from £30 to £40
SINGLE ROOM: from £45 to £55
FOOD: up to £15
Hours: breakfast 8am–9.30am, lunch 12.30am–2pm, dinner 7pm–10.15pm.
Cuisine: ENGLISH / FRENCH – à la carte, English and French. Carvery (set price), with fish or vegetarian option.
Cards: Visa, Access, Diners, AmEx.
Other points: licensed, Sunday lunch, children welcome, pets allowed, conferences, afternoon tea.
Rooms: 50 bedrooms.
Directions: 7 miles from Brighton on A27.
MR AYRIS ☎ (01273) 476694.

RYE • map 6D5

LANDGATE BISTRO
5–6 Landgate, TN34 7LH
This Grade II listed building in the historic town of Rye offers unpretentious yet comfortable surroundings in which to enjoy a fine meal from the good selection available. The comprehensive wine list and the relaxed, informal atmosphere ensure an enjoyable meal out.
FOOD: from £15 to £20
Hours: dinner 7pm–9.30pm, closed Sunday and Monday.
Cuisine: BRITISH – modern cuisine made with the freshest produce.
Cards: Visa, Access, Diners, AmEx.
Other points: children welcome, licensed.
Directions: situated 50 yards below Landgate Arch.
NICK PARKIN & TONI FERGUSON-LEES
☎ (01797) 222829.

THE OLD FORGE RESTAURANT
24 Wish Street, TB8 17DA
Originally a forge, the building was bought and converted by the present owner. Highly recommended for its good food within a reasonable price limit, friendly service and informal atmosphere. A large open fire adds to the character and atmosphere of the restaurant during winter.
FOOD: up to £15
Hours: lunch 12.30am–2pm, dinner 6.30pm–10pm, closed Sunday, Monday, Tuesday lunch and Wednesday lunch.
Cuisine: ENGLISH – specialities include fresh local fish, shellfish and char-grilled steaks.
Cards: Visa, Access.
Other points: licensed, children welcome, street parking.
Directions: on western side of Rye, where Wish Street joins the main A259.
DEREK BAYNTUN ☎ (01797) 223227.

THE SHIP INN
Strand Quay, TN31 7AY
An attractive 16th century inn, set amongst the historic Strand Quay warehouses, where confiscated contraband was once stored by revenue men, as records show. All bedrooms are equipped with modern facilities for maximum comfort, and the inn provides guests with details of where to visit and what to see in the area. Special breaks are available throughout the year.
DOUBLE ROOM: from £20 to £30
SINGLE ROOM: from £35 to £45
FOOD: up to £15
Hours: breakfast 8am–9.45am, lunch 12.30am–2.30pm, dinner 7.30pm–9.15pm, bar snacks 12noon–3pm, 7pm–9.30pm.
Cuisine: ENGLISH.
Cards: Visa, Access.
Other points: parking, children welcome, residents' lounge, vegetarian meals.
Rooms: 1 single room, 6 double rooms, 4 twin rooms, 1 triple room.
Directions: among 18th century warehouses on Strand Quay, at foot of Mermaid Street.
MR M. GREGORY ☎ (01797) 222233
[Fax] (01797) 223892.

SEAFORD • map 6D4

THE OLD PLOUGH
20 Church Street, BN25 1HG
A delightful 17th century coaching inn situated in the town, which is set in the beautiful East Sussex Downs, bordering Newhaven. The inn is extremely popular with tourists who are attracted to the area, which is steeped in history as a result of the Norman Conquests. The nearby Heritage Centre is well worth a visit.
FOOD: up to £15 [CLUB]
Hours: lunch 12noon–2.30pm, dinner 7pm–10pm, open all year.
Cuisine: ENGLISH – traditional home-style cooking, offering an extensive selection of dishes, including speciality home-made pies and steamed puddings. Cut-to-order steaks, fresh fish, luxury desserts.

Cards: Visa, Access, Diners, Switch.
Other points: licensed, Sunday lunch, no-smoking area, children catered for (please check for age limits), parking, garden terrace.
Directions: situated off A259 in Seaford, adjoining the parish church.
JOHN BOOTS ☎ (01323) 892379.

UCKFIELD • map 6D4

HALLAND FORGE HOTEL & RESTAURANT
Halland, near Lewes, BN8 6PW
All dishes are cooked to order for the restaurant, whereas the coffee shop is self-service. A family-run hotel in its own grounds, which include lawns, flower beds and woodlands. Its location is ideal for the South Downs, Ashdown Forest and the coast at Eastbourne and Brighton.
DOUBLE ROOM: from £20 to £30
SINGLE ROOM: from £45 to £55
FOOD: up to £15 ☆
Hours: breakfast 8am–12noon, lunch 12noon–2pm, dinner 7pm–9.30pm.
Cuisine: ENGLISH / FRENCH / ITALIAN – only fresh ingredients. Both à la carte and table d'hôte menus in the restaurant and carvery.
Cards: Visa, Access, Diners, AmEx.
Other points: Sunday lunch, children catered for (please check for age limits), residents' lounge, residents' bar.
Rooms: 11 double rooms, 9 twin rooms. All with TV, radio, telephone, tea/coffee-making facilities, heating.
Directions: at the junction of the A22 and B2192, 4 miles south of Uckfield.
MR & MRS J.M. HOWELL ☎ (01825) 840456
[Fax] (01825) 840773.

WADHURST • map 6D5

THE GREYHOUND
St James Square, TN5 6NP
An historic coaching inn with heavily beamed and half-panelled bar, inglenook fireplace and photographs of past eras. Variety of draught lagers and real ales, plus a fine selection of wines.
FOOD: up to £15
Hours: lunch 12noon–2pm, dinner 7pm–9.30pm.
Cuisine: ENGLISH – house menu contains a large range of fish, poultry, veal and beef dishes, all of very high standard. Separate Sunday roast luncheon menu.
Cards: Visa, Access.
Other points: Sunday lunch, children welcome.
Directions: situated in the centre of Wadhurst.
ROBIN & TANNIA HEALE ☎ (01892) 783224/784090.

THE OLD VINE
Cousley Wood, TN5 6ER
The Old Vine provides an extensive choice of excellently cooked food in the bar and restaurant. All meals are freshly prepared and attractively presented while offering excellent value for money. The service is friendly and efficient, in keeping with

the busy, convivial atmosphere. Very highly recommended by the Les Routiers inspector.
FOOD: from £15 to £20
Hours: Sunday lunch 12noon–2pm, bar meals 12noon–2pm, 6pm–9.30pm, dinner 7pm–11.30pm, last orders 9.30pm.
Cuisine: CONTINENTAL – modern European cuisine with a good vegetarian selection. Dishes may include peppered sirloin, chicken caprice.
Cards: Visa, Access, Diners.
Other points: licensed, Sunday lunch, children welcome, pets allowed, reservations, entertainment.
Directions: off the A21 at Lamberhurst onto B2100, direction Wadhurst.
ANTHONY PEEL ☎ (01892) 782271.

ESSEX

Towns in Essex that are actually part of Greater London can be found in *Greater London*, pages 30–53.

BILLERICAY • map 6B5

DUKE OF YORK
Southend Road, South Green, CM11 2PR
A pub and restaurant offering good-value meals and efficient, friendly service. The Duke of York was a beer house in 1868, and the restaurant has since been sympathetically added to complement the original building. Customers will find a warm, cosy atmosphere in which to enjoy their meal.
FOOD: from £20 to £25
Hours: lunch and bar snacks 12noon–2pm, dinner and bar snacks 7pm–10pm, no food Sunday evenings.
Cuisine: FRENCH / ENGLISH – choice of menus. Large choice of bar snacks. Hot and cold bar snacks Sunday lunchtime as well as a traditional Sunday roast (£4.25).
Cards: Visa, Access, Diners, AmEx.
Other points: licensed, children welcome.
Directions: On A129 Billericay to Wickford road, 1 mile from Billericay High Street.
MRS EDNA WHITE ☎ (01277) 651403.

BRENTWOOD • map 6B4

THE BLACK HORSE
Ongar Road, Pilgrims Hatch, CM15 9JN
Dating back to the 14th century, this delightful converted farmhouse retains its rustic charm and atmosphere. Warm and friendly staff make guests welcome. Substantial, well-prepared meals are complemented by a good range of beers.
FOOD: up to £15
Hours: meals all day from 11am to 11pm. Last orders 10pm.
Cuisine: ENGLISH – traditional English steak-and-kidney pie, mixed grills, fresh fish, steaks.
Cards: Visa, Access.
Other points: licensed, children catered for (please check for age limits), garden, parking, disabled access.
Directions: in the village of Pilgrim's Hatch on A128, 4 miles from Brentwood.
DAVID AND JAYNE TAYLOR ☎ (01277) 372337.

CHELMSFORD • map 6B5

MIAMI HOTEL
Princes Road, CM2 9AJ
The Miami Hotel has been a family-run business for the past 30 years, with three generations working in the hotel. 55 bedrooms, all twin/double size, but let as single if required. All rooms have colour television, Sky TV, trouser-press and tea-making facilities. Easy access from all main routes, M25, A12 and A1016. Close to all major airports for the international traveller. The Miami Hotel offers value, comfort and hospitality.
DOUBLE ROOM: from £20 to £30
Hours: breakfast 7.30am–9am, dinner 6.30pm–9.30pm, lunch 12noon–2.30pm.
Cuisine: CONTINENTAL – filet mignon, steak au poivre, beef stroganoff.
Cards: Visa.
Other points: Sunday lunch, children welcome.
Rooms: 16 double rooms, 39 twin rooms. All with TV, tea/coffee-making facilities.
Directions: by the A1016 Billericay roundabout.
MR C. NEWCOMBE ☎ (01245) 269603/ 264848 Fax (01245) 259860.

SOUTH LODGE HOTEL
196 New London Road, CM2 0AR
A busy commercial hotel close to the town centre and County Cricket Ground. South Lodge is a converted Victorian residence standing in its own mature gardens. Full conference, function and leisure facilities available.
DOUBLE ROOM: from £20 to £30
SINGLE ROOM: from £45 to £55
FOOD: up to £15
Hours: breakfast 7.30am–9.30am, lunch 12.30am–2.30pm, dinner 7pm–10pm.
Cuisine: ENGLISH / INTERNATIONAL – international and new English cuisine.
Cards: Visa, Access, Diners, AmEx.
Other points: licensed, Sunday lunch, no-smoking area, children welcome, cots.
Rooms: 20 single rooms, 11 double rooms, 10 twin rooms. All with TV, telephone, tea/coffee-making facilities.
Directions: off the A12, close to the town centre.
MR A.A. SOLDANI ☎ (01245) 264564 Fax (01245) 492827.

CLACTON-ON-SEA • map 6B6

THE ROBIN HOOD
221 London Road, CO15 4ED
Originally a farmhouse, this delightful pub has retained its rustic charm. Hot, home-style meals at affordable prices and friendly staff will make you feel at home. There is a family atmosphere, as children are particularly welcome.
FOOD: up to £15
Hours: meals all day from 11am to 11pm.
Cuisine: ENGLISH – good selection of pub-style food. Blackboard specials daily. Children's menu. Enormous portions at extremely reasonable prices.
Cards: Visa, Access.
Other points: licensed, children catered for (please check for age limits), open bank holidays.
Directions: on A133, follow signs to Clacton centre. The Robin Hood is on the right.
JOHN AND BARBARA TAYLOR ☎ (01255) 421519.

COLCHESTER • map 6A5

JACKLINS RESTAURANT
147 High Street, CO1 1PG
A first-floor restaurant, situated in the town centre on the site of the pottery shops of Roman Colchester. Delightful oak-panelled rooms, where breakfasts, lunches and afternoon teas are served. Also specialist shop downstairs for tobacco products, teas and confectionery.
FOOD: up to £15 [CLUB]
Hours: meals all day 9.15am–5pm, closed Sunday and bank holidays.
Cuisine: ENGLISH – breakfasts, lunches, light meals and afternoon teas.
Cards: Visa, Access, AmEx.
Other points: children welcome, parking.
Directions: 100 yards west of the town hall in the high street.
MR S.H. JACKLIN ☎ (01206) 572157.

THE OLD QUEEN'S HEAD
Ford Street, Aldham, CO6 3PH
Following a major refurbishment, this traditional 17th century inn now boasts an abundance of charm and character with open fires, timber beams and flagstone floors, specializing in good food, real ales and fine wines in warm and friendly surroundings. A main feature of this pub is a beautiful 150 seater canopied patio.
FOOD: up to £15
Hours: lunch 12noon–2pm, dinner 6pm–10pm.
Cuisine: ENGLISH – traditional home-cooked fare.
Cards: Visa, Access.
Other points: parking, children welcome, open air dining, vegetarian meals, traditional Sunday lunch.
Directions: on A604, off A12.
RICHARD & PATRICIA BROWN ☎ (01206) 241584.

ROSE & CROWN HOTEL
East Street, CO1 2TZ
The original style of this Tudor building has been carefully retained, while extensively refurbished inside, and is the oldest inn in Britain's oldest recorded town. The restaurant has a cosy cocktail bar and offers fresh home-made food every day of the year. A delightful place for lovers of history. Easy access to all town amenities.
DOUBLE ROOM: from £50
SINGLE ROOM: from £55
FOOD: up to £15
Hours: breakfast 7am–9.30am, lunch 12noon–2pm, dinner 7pm–10pm.
Cuisine: FRENCH / ENGLISH – à la carte, fixed-price menu.
Cards: Visa, Access, Diners, AmEx.
Other points: licensed, children welcome, conferences, residents' lounge, residents' bar, off-street parking.
Rooms: 13 single rooms, 11 double rooms, 2 twin rooms, 4 family rooms. All with TV, telephone, tea/coffee-making facilities.
Directions: in town centre off A12. Follow signs for university/Rollerworld.
MR BAGHERZADEH ☎ (01206) 866677 [Fax] (01206) 866616.

THE SHEPHERD & DOG
Moor Road, Langham, CO4 5NR
Set in a small village near Colchester, this pub offers tasty meals presented with care. As this is a free-house, there is a good selection of beers. Booking recommended, as restaurant can be busy.
FOOD: up to £15 [CLUB]
Hours: lunch 11am–3pm, dinner 6pm–12midnight, last orders 10pm, bar meals 11am–2.30pm, bar meals 6pm–11pm.
Cuisine: ENGLISH / CONTINENTAL – bar and restaurant meals. Predominantly English and continental cuisine.
Cards: Visa, Access, Diners, AmEx.
Other points: licensed, open-air dining, Sunday lunch, children welcome, open bank holidays, pets allowed.
Directions: first exit off A12 north of Colchester (sign-posted to Langham).
MR PAUL BARNES & MISS JANE GRAHAM ☎ (01206) 272711.

THE WAREHOUSE BRASSERIE
12 Chapel Street North, CO2 7AT
A converted chapel with a unique layout, the Brasserie is an enticingly different restaurant to any other in the area. The menu combines the best of traditional English, provincial French and Mediterranean dishes, presented simply but attractively. This is a very well-known and popular restaurant.
FOOD: from £15 to £20
Hours: lunch 12noon–2pm, dinner 7pm–10pm, closed Sunday evening.
Cuisine: ENGLISH / FRENCH – 2-course lunch £7.95.
Cards: Visa, Access, Switch.
Other points: children welcome, no-smoking area, disabled access, vegetarian meals, air-conditioned, no music.
Directions: Located off St John's Street, which can be found at the junctions of Butt Road and Head Street in Colchester town centre.
MR M. BURLEY & MR M. BROOKS ☎ (01206) 765656.

HARWICH • map 6A6

CLIFF HOTEL
Marine Parade, Dovercourt, CO12 3RE
Overlooking the seafront, this large Victorian hotel is decorated and furnished in keeping with the character of the building. Attractively presented meals are served by friendly, competent staff, and the accommodation is very comfortable. Ideally located on the seafront for holiday-makers.
DOUBLE ROOM: from £20 to £30
SINGLE ROOM: from £45 to £55
FOOD: up to £15
Hours: breakfast 7.30am–9.30am, lunch 12.30am–2pm, dinner 6.30pm–9pm, bar meals 12noon–2pm, 6pm–9pm.
Cuisine: ENGLISH – wide choice of dishes including fresh fish.
Cards: Visa, Access, Diners, AmEx.
Other points: licensed, Sunday lunch, children welcome, open bank holidays, afternoon tea.
Rooms: 1 single room, 11 double rooms, 10 twin rooms, 5 family rooms.
Directions: on seafront at Dovercourt.
A. BALAAM & D. LOFTS ☎ (01255) 503345
[Fax] (01255) 240358.

NEW FARM HOUSE
Spinnel's Lane, Wix, CO11 2UJ
A large modern farmhouse, set in its own well-tended gardens situated on the outskirts of the quiet village of Wix. Comfortable, clean bedrooms complemented by a relaxing and friendly atmosphere.
DOUBLE ROOM: from £20 to £30
SINGLE ROOM: up to £25
FOOD: up to £15
Hours: breakfast 8am–10am, dinner 6.30pm–7pm.
Cuisine: ENGLISH.
Cards: Visa, Access.
Other points: children welcome, playland, pets allowed, vegetarian meals.
Rooms: 1 single room, 1 double room, 3 twin rooms, 5 family rooms. All with TV, tea/coffee-making facilities.
Directions: follow A120 from Colchester to Harwich. Turn into Wix village.
THE MITCHELL FAMILY ☎ (01255) 870365
[Fax] (01255) 870837.

TOWER HOTEL
Main Road, Dovercourt, CO12 3PJ
Built in 1885, the main feature of the building is a tower in the north-east corner. Inside, it retains many original architectural features with friezes, cornices and architraves. The Pattrick Suite is a magnificent function room, which is available for private hire.
DOUBLE ROOM: from £20 to £30
FOOD: up to £15
Hours: breakfast 8am–9.30am, lunch 12noon–2pm, dinner 6.30pm–9.30pm.
Cuisine: ENGLISH / SEAFOOD – fresh local lobster and Dover sole.
Cards: Visa, Access, Diners, AmEx.
Other points: licensed, Sunday lunch, children welcome.

Rooms: 3 single rooms, 8 double rooms, 15 twin rooms, 2 family rooms.
Directions: on the left side of A136 (Harwich bound) near Dovercourt station.
DOUGLAS HUTCHINS ☎ (01255) 504952.

SAFFRON WALDEN • map 6A4

SAFFRON HOTEL
10–18 High Street, CB10 1AY
This listed building with 16th century origins, in "Lovejoy country", has recently been refurbished. The award-winning restaurant enjoys an excellent reputation for a high standard of imaginatively prepared cuisine. You can enjoy table d'hôte and à la carte meals in the elegant conservatory restaurant, or bar meals in the popular bar, with real ales. The accommodation is comfortable and well-equipped and includes three rooms with four-poster beds.
DOUBLE ROOM: from £30 to £40
SINGLE ROOM: from £45 to £55
FOOD: from £15 to £20
Hours: breakfast 7.30am, lunch 12noon–2.15pm, dinner 6.45pm–9.30pm.
Cuisine: ENGLISH – steak-and-kidney pie, bread-and-butter pudding.
Cards: Visa, Access, Diners, AmEx.
Other points: Sunday lunch, children welcome, residents' lounge, functions, garden.
Rooms: 20 bedrooms, 17 en suite.
Directions: take M11 junction 9. The hotel is on the High Street in the centre of Saffron Walden.
DAVID BALL ☎ (01799) 522676 [Fax] (01799) 513979.

SHOEBURYNESS • map 6B5

THE POLASH RESTAURANT
84–86 West Road, SS3 9DS
Authentic Bangladeshi and Indian music unobtrusively relaxes diners and gives an aura of tranquility. One of the top 30 out of 10,500 Indian restaurants in the United Kingdom, nominated by Pataks for food, quality and service.
FOOD: up to £15 [CLUB]
Hours: lunch 12noon–3pm, dinner 6pm–12midnight.
Cuisine: BANGLADESHI – Bangladeshi food: Kim's dish, Kipling's favourites, Passage to India, Sunset in Ganges. Authentic Tandoori and Bhoona dishes.
Cards: Visa, Access, Diners, AmEx.
Other points: Sunday lunch, children welcome, air-conditioned.
Directions: On A127/A13 Southend-on-Sea road.
MR A. KHALIQUE ☎ (01702) 293989/294721.

SOUTHEND-ON-SEA • map 6B5

LA POUBELLE
50A Hamlet Court Road, Westcliff, SS0 7LX
A small, friendly, family-run restaurant with an emphasis on good, honest, fresh food in

comfortable surroundings. An informal atmosphere provides the ideal ambience for pleasant dining. Very popular locally, so booking is advised.
FOOD: up to £15
Hours: Sunday lunch 12.30am–2.15pm, dinner 7pm (last orders 10.30pm), closed Sunday evening and Monday.
Cuisine: INTERNATIONAL – paella, chicken breast in Stilton sauce, local fish, home-smoked produce. A varied and interesting menu: all dishes home-prepared and cooked. Set-price menus.
Cards: Visa, Access.
Other points: licensed, Sunday lunch in winter, children welcome.
Directions: on shopping street near Westcliff railway station, 5 minutes from seafront and Cliffs Pavilion.
MR & MRS R.C. BERNER ☎ (01702) 351894.

THE MAYFLOWER HOTEL
6 Royal Terrace, SS1 1DY
Built in 1792, this Grade II listed house still retains many original Georgian features. A mass of flowers in hanging baskets are draped over the balcony and on the terrace. The hotel overlooks the Thames estuary and the pier.
DOUBLE ROOM: up to £20
Hours: breakfast 6.45am–9am, closed Christmas.
Cuisine: BREAKFAST.
Other points: central heating, no evening meal, children welcome, residents' lounge.
Rooms: 7 single rooms, 9 double rooms, 5 twin rooms, 3 family rooms. All with TV.
Directions: On A127 to Southend-on-Sea; hotel overlooks the Thames estuary.
CHRISTOPHER POWELL ☎ (01702) 340489.

ROSLIN HOTEL
Thorpe Esplanade, Thorpe Bay, SS1 3BG
Situated on the seafront, the Roslin Hotel boasts one of the finest views of the Thames estuary in residential Thorpe Bay. Facilities for golfing, sailing, tennis, bowling, horse-riding, ten-pin bowling. Weekend bargain breaks. Temporary membership of local leisure centre for residents.
DOUBLE ROOM: from £30 to £40

SINGLE ROOM: from £35 to £45
FOOD: up to £15
Hours: lunch 12.30am–2pm, dinner 6.30pm–9.30pm.
Cuisine: ENGLISH – noisette of lamb gascoigne, veal milanese, local trout with chestnut and cucumber. Sunday lunches. Vegetarian menu. A la carte and table d'hôte menus.
Cards: Visa, Access, Diners, AmEx.
Other points: Sunday lunch, children welcome, residents' lounge, residents' bar, disabled access.
Rooms: 18 single rooms, 20 double/twin rooms. All with satellite TV, radio, alarm, telephone, tea/coffee-making facilities, hair dryer.
Directions: close to the seafront.
MR K.G. OLIVER ☎ (01702) 586375.

TOWER HOTEL AND RESTAURANT
146 Alexandra Road, SS1 1HE
Built in 1901 as a unique gentleman's residence, Taranaki, it first became a hotel in 1923. Fully renovated and restored in the elegant ambience of the era, it combines every modern convenience and luxury. The 'tower' rooms afford views of the Thames estuary and the Kentish coastline. To complement a comfortable stay in luxurious accomodation, a superb English breakfast is served daily. Just a few minutes' walk from the town's finest amenities.
DOUBLE ROOM: from £20 to £30
SINGLE ROOM: from £35 to £45
FOOD: up to £15
Hours: breakfast weekdays 7am–9am, weekends 8am–10am; dinner 6.30pm–9.30pm, bar snacks 6.30pm–11pm; closed Sunday evening.
Cuisine: ENGLISH.
Cards: Visa, Access, Diners, AmEx.
Other points: children welcome, Sunday lunch, disabled access, pets allowed, residents' lounge, vegetarian meals.
Rooms: 13 single rooms, 10 double rooms, 6 twin rooms, 3 family rooms.
Directions: phone hotel for verbal or faxed directions.
MR M. TAYLOR ☎ (01702) 348635
Fax (01702) 433044.

HERTFORDSHIRE

BALDOCK • map 6A4

THE JESTER HOTEL
116 Station Road, Odsey, SG7 5RS
Set in pleasant gardens, The Jester Hotel offers comfortable accommodation and well-presented meals at value-for-money prices. Popular with locals, the hotel enjoys a relaxed atmosphere.
DOUBLE ROOM: from £20 to £30
SINGLE ROOM: from £35 to £45
FOOD: up to £15
Hours: breakfast 7am–10am, lunch 12noon–3pm, dinner 7pm–10pm, bar meals 11.30am–2.30pm, 6.30pm–10pm.

Cuisine: ENGLISH – serving bar snacks, table d'hôte and full à la carte menu. Dishes may include hot avocado and crabmeat, Dover sole, flambés, choice of sweets.
Cards: Visa, Access, Diners, AmEx, Switch.
Other points: licensed, open-air dining, Sunday lunch, no smoking area, children welcome, garden
Rooms: 3 single rooms, 8 double rooms, 3 twin rooms.
Directions: between Royston and Baldock. Turn off Steeple Morden, opposite Ashwell and Morden station.
MR MILDENHALL-CLARKE ☎ (01462) 742011
Fax (01462) 742011.

BISHOP'S STORTFORD • map 6B4

PEARSE HOUSE
Parsonage Lane, CM23 5BQ
Pearse House is an established management training and conference centre, offering residential conference facilities of the highest standard. It is easily accessible by road, rail and air and just one hour from London. All rooms are equipped with the most modern business facilities. The attractive modern bedrooms offer comfortable accommodation, and leisure facilities are also available on site and close by.
DOUBLE ROOM: from £20 to £30
SINGLE ROOM: from £35 to £45
FOOD: from £15 to £20
Hours: breakfast 7.30am–9am, lunch 12noon–2pm, dinner 6.30pm–9pm, bar snacks 7pm–10.30pm.
Cuisine: BRITISH – there is a good selection of fine wines to accompany your meal.
Cards: Visa, Access, AmEx.
Other points: parking, children welcome, limited disabled access, residents' lounge, vegetarian meals, conferences.
Rooms: 23 single rooms, 9 double rooms.
Directions: situated in Parsonage Lane off Dunmow Road (B1250), which leads from town centre to M11. From motorway (M11), 2 minutes' drive following signs to Bishop's Stortford; or follow signs from Stansted Road (B1184). Ten minutes from Stansted Airport.
VALERIE McGREGOR ☎ (01279) 757400
[Fax] (01279) 506591.

HERTFORD • map 6B4

SALISBURY ARMS HOTEL
Fore Street, SG14 1BZ
Hertford's oldest hostelry, offering guests the opportunity to enjoy excellent food, traditional ales and a warm welcome in surroundings that retain all the character and charm of a bygone age. The oak-beamed and wood-panelled restaurant offers exceptional cuisine, and the well-appointed bedrooms are furnished in a blend of subtle pastel shades, complementing the cottage atmosphere.
DOUBLE ROOM: from £30 to £40
SINGLE ROOM: from £45 to £55
FOOD: from £15 to £20
Hours: breakfast 7am–9am, lunch 12noon–2pm, dinner 7pm–10pm.
Cuisine: INTERNATIONAL.
Cards: Visa, Access, Diners, AmEx.
Other points: licensed.
Rooms: 29 bedrooms.
Directions: A414 to Hertford from A10.
MR JOEY O'REGAN ☎ (01992) 583091
[Fax] (01992) 552510.

HITCHIN • map 6A4

REDCOATS FARMHOUSE HOTEL
Redcoats Green, SG4 7JR
A 15th century farmhouse set in beautiful grounds amid the rolling Hertfordshire countryside near Little Wymondley village, yet only minutes from the A1. Full of English charm, with its beamed and comfortable interior, bar and lounge, the intimate quiet of the dining rooms and individual character of the bedrooms, Redcoats exudes an air of peace and tranquility. Excellent food and efficient service. Ideally situated for visiting Knebworth and Woburn parks. Bargain-break weekends available.
DOUBLE ROOM: from £30 to £40
SINGLE ROOM: from £35 to £45
FOOD: from £20 to £25 ☆
Hours: breakfast 7am–9am, club lunch 12noon–2pm, club supper from 7pm, dinner, 7pm–9.30pm, lunch 12noon–1.30pm.
Cuisine: ENGLISH / FRENCH.
Cards: Visa, Access, Diners, AmEx.
Other points: parking, children welcome, no-smoking area, residents' lounge, vegetarian meals, open-air dining.
Rooms: 1 single room, 10 double rooms, 3 twin rooms.
Directions: junction 8 on A1M. South of Little Wymondley. Follow signs for Todds Green, then Redcoats Green.
PETER BUTTERFIELD & JACKIE GAINSFORD
☎ (01438) 729500 [Fax] (01438) 723322.

ROYSTON • map 6A4

See also GREAT CHISHILL (Cambridgeshire), page 62.

BRITISH RAJ BANGLADESHI RESTAURANT
55 High Street, SG8 9AW
Reputed to be one of East Anglia's best Indian restaurants and one of the top 100 curry houses. In a varied menu, dishes may include such specialities as shooting bird bhuna, fixed bayonet poussin and crab rezalla. Silver Award winner in Best Menu category, Top 30 in Best Britain category, listed in Pataks Real Curry Restaurant guide and Good Curry guide amongst others. Highly recommended.
FOOD: up to £15 [CLUB] ☆
Hours: lunch 12noon–3pm, dinner 6pm–12midnight.
Cuisine: BANGLADESHI-INDIAN – lamb masala: a whole leg of lamb cooked for four. Tandoori, royal, karai dishes. English menu also available. Thalia dishes including wedding feast. Weekday business lunch and Saturday/Sunday buffet lunch.
Cards: Visa, Access, Diners, AmEx.
Other points: children welcome.
Directions: situated in Royston, on the A10.
NAZIR UDDIN CHOUDHURY ☎ (01763) 241471.

WATFORD • map 5B3

UPTON LODGE
Upton Road, WD1 2EL
Upton Lodge is owned by the same family-run company that operates The White House Hotel, situated directly across the road. This cosy lodge is well designed and appointed to a high level of

comfort. Although the reception is at The White House Hotel, guests receive their own key to the front door of the Lodge and are most welcome to use the facilities of the main hotel.
DOUBLE ROOM: from £20 to £30
SINGLE ROOM: from £25 to £35
Hours: breakfast 6.45am–9.30am.
Other points: parking, children welcome, pets allowed, no-smoking areas, garden.
Rooms: 22 bedrooms. All with TV, telephone, tea/coffee-making facilities, hair dryer. No-smoking rooms available.
Directions: just off the ring road at the junction with Cassio Road, near Watford town centre.
MR I.F. HARTOG ☎ (01923) 237316
Fax (01923) 233109.

THE WHITE HOUSE HOTEL
Upton Road, WD1 2EL
Privately-owned and run by a professional, caring staff,

The White House is popular with both discerning business executives and well-travelled tourists. A high standard prevails throughout this well-appointed hotel, which offers luxury three-star accommodation and superb international cuisine. (See also UPTON LODGE, page 74.)
DOUBLE ROOM: from £30 to £40
SINGLE ROOM: from £55
FOOD: from £15 to £20
Hours: breakfast.
Cuisine: BRITISH / INTERNATIONAL.
Cards: Visa, Access, Diners, AmEx.
Other points: children welcome, parking.
Rooms: 58 bedrooms. All with TV, telephone, radio, hair dryer, trouser-press, tea/coffee-making facilities. No-smoking rooms available.
Directions: Just off the ring road at the junction of Cassio Road, near the town centre.
MR I.F. HARTOG ☎ (01923) 237316
Fax (01923) 233109.

KENT

ASHFORD • map 6C5

THE ROYAL STANDARD
Ashford Road, Bethersden, TN26 3LF
A popular free-house with a warm and friendly atmosphere, offering a very good selection of meals at reasonable prices. Dine in the restaurant or the bar, beside the warmth of log fires in winter or in the large garden during summer. A visit at any time of the year is memorable.
FOOD: up to £15
Hours: lunch 12noon–2pm, dinner 7pm–9.30pm, open every day including bank holidays.
Cuisine: ENGLISH – traditional, featuring home-made dishes including a vegetarian selection. Large no-smoking area in the restaurant.
Cards: Visa, Eurocard, MasterCard.
Other points: parking, garden, patio, play area, no-smoking area.
Directions: On A28, 1 mile west of Bethersden.
ROGER HAMBERG ☎ (01233) 820280.

BIRCHINGTON • map 6C6

SMUGGLERS RESTAURANT
212 Canterbury Road, CT7 9AB
A comfortable, welcoming restaurant, which offers a very extensive choice of well-cooked food. The cuisine is predominantly French, with dishes ranging from salmon with a prawn-and-dill sauce to fillet steak cooked in brandy and French mustard. All dishes are made from fresh ingredients and attractively presented. The quality of the food is complemented by excellent service.
FOOD: from £15 to £20
Hours: lunch 12noon–2pm, dinner 7pm–10pm, closed Monday lunch.
Cuisine: FRENCH / ENGLISH – table d'hôte menus and extensive à la carte menu. Duckling

aux cerises, châteaubriand, fish dishes.
Cards: Visa, Access, Diners, AmEx.
Other points: licensed, open-air dining, Sunday lunch, children welcome, functions.
Directions: on road to Margate from Thanet Way, just past Birchington roundabout.
BOB & SUE SHERMAN ☎ (01843) 841185.

DISCOVER FRANCE FOR ONLY £9.99!

The *Les Routiers Guide to France* is the only official fully translated guide to the French *Routiers*, listing over 1,600 recommended restaurants, cafés and hotels throughout this alluring country.

Available from all good bookshops, or direct from the publishers, price £9.99.

BROADSTAIRS • map 6C6

THE TARTAR FRIGATE
Harbour Street, CT10 1EU
An attractive 17th century flint pub with superb views over Broadstairs harbour. The first-floor seafood restaurant is beautifully appointed, and the menu is a culinary delight, with many unique dishes. With the restaurant being so close to the harbour, you may feel inclined to walk a delicious meal off along the seafront.
FOOD: from £15 to £20
Hours: lunch 12noon–2.30pm, dinner 6.30pm–10pm.
Cuisine: SEAFOOD – à la carte and table d'hôte menu, freshly cooked dishes in generous portions.
Cards: Visa, Access, Diners, AmEx.
Other points: parking, children welcome, vegetarian meals, traditional Sunday lunch.
Directions: opposite picturesque Broadstairs harbour.
THORLEY TAVERNS ☎ (01843) 862013
Fax (01843) 230231.

BROMLEY • map 6C4

🍽 HENRY'S CAFE BAR (BROMLEY)
2–4 Ringers Road
Situated just off Bromley High Street, this popular café-bar serves an extensive range of international fast-food, American, continental and non-alcoholic beers and speciality cocktails. Busy at lunchtimes.
FOOD: up to £15
Hours: meals all day 10am–6pm, closed Sunday.
Cuisine: INTERNATIONAL.
Cards: Visa, Access, AmEx.
Other points: children welcome, open bank holidays, afternoon teas, disabled access, vegetarian meals.
Directions: off High Street, Bromley South.
MR G. COLLINS ☎ (0181) 313 0980.

CANTERBURY • map 6C5

🏠 THE GREEN MAN
Shatterling, near Wingham, CT3 1JR
Old English country inn with garden, set in an area known for its hop-growing and vine culture. Two 'bat & trap pitches'. Easy access to Dover and Ramsgate ports.
DOUBLE ROOM: up to £20
FOOD: up to £15
Hours: breakfast 7.45am–9am, lunch 12noon–2pm, dinner 7pm–8.45pm, closed Sunday evening to non-residents.
Cuisine: ENGLISH – genuine English home-cooking.
Cards: Visa, Access.
Other points: open-air dining, Sunday lunch, children welcome, coaches by prior arrangement.
Rooms: 4 twin rooms, 1 family room. All with TV, tea/coffee-making facilities.
Directions: on the A257 between Wingham and Ash.
MR FERNE & MR GREENWOOD ☎ (01304) 812525.

🏠 MILLER'S ARMS
2 Mill Lane, CT1 2AW
The Miller's Arms stands beside the River Stour, the meandering chief waterway of East Kent. The inn has recently undergone a careful programme of modernization, aimed at preserving the features of the original building, and now offers guests a maximum level of comfort and modern convenience. The bars downstairs, part of the Miller's Arms free house, are homely and friendly, capturing the very essence of an English country pub.
DOUBLE ROOM: from £20 to £30
SINGLE ROOM: from £25 to £35
FOOD: up to £15
Hours: breakfast 7.30am–9.30am, lunch 12noon–2.30pm, bar meals 12noon–2.30pm, 6pm–7pm, dinner 6pm–9pm.
Cuisine: ENGLISH – appealingly presented, freshly prepared traditional fare.
Cards: Visa, Access, Diners, AmEx.
Other points: children welcome, pets allowed, garden, vegetarian meals, traditional Sunday lunch.

Rooms: 4 single rooms, 6 double rooms, 3 twin rooms, 1 family room. All with TV, telephone, tea/coffee-making facilities.
Directions: though only 2 minutes' walk from the heart of Canterbury, the inn is tucked away in a quiet location: follow signs to Marlowe Theatre car park.
MR P. STOCKDALE ☎ (01227) 456057.

🏠 THE THREE TUNS INN
Staple, CT3 1LN
A family-run free-house situated 9 miles from Canturbury and 5 miles from the historic town of Sandwich. Here you can enjoy good home-cooked meals in a friendly atmosphere or stay in the new, tastefully furnished chalet accommodation, whilst visiting this beautiful part of England.
DOUBLE ROOM: from £20 to £30
SINGLE ROOM: from £25 to £35
FOOD: up to £15 ⭐
Hours: breakfast, lunch and dinner served daily.
Cuisine: BRITISH – steaks, fresh fish, vegetable dishes: good, wholesome traditional meals.
Cards: Visa, Access, AmEx.
Other points: parking, children welcome, conference facilities, residents' lounge, garden, open-air dining, vegetarian meals, traditional Sunday lunch, payphone available.
Rooms: 8 bedrooms. All with en suite, TV, radio, alarm, tea/coffee-making facilities.
Directions: take the A2 to Barham, followed by the B2046 to Wingham. The Three Tuns Inn may be found by following signs towards Staple.
RICHARD GUNNER ☎ (01304) 812317
Fax (01304) 812317.

EDENBRIDGE • map 6C4

🍽 CASTLE INN
Chiddingstone, TN8 7AH
The Castle Inn is a delightful oak-beamed pub in the centre of one of Kent's most unspoilt villages. Enjoy traditional English bar food from the comfort of the Saloon Bar or in the pretty cottage garden during summertime. There is a separate restaurant with formal waiter service and an ever-changing menu. Extensive list of over 150 wines and three hand-pumped draught beers.
FOOD: from £15 to £20 🍴
Hours: lunch 12noon–2pm, dinner 7.30pm–9.30pm.
Cuisine: ENGLISH / CONTINENTAL – mainly British with European overtones. Roast rib beef, roast rack of lamb, local game, fresh fish, fresh vegetables.
Cards: Visa, Access, Diners, AmEx.
Other points: licensed, Sunday lunch, children welcome.
Directions: 1½ miles south of the B2027 Edenbridge to Tonbridge road.
NIGEL D. LUCAS ☎ (01892) 870247.

🍽 THE VILLAGE TEA SHOP
3 The Village, Chiddingstone, TN8 7AH
The Village Tea Shop in the Old Coach House helps to set the scene in the picturesque historic

village of Chiddingstone. Inside this lovely restaurant, the aroma of freshly-made coffee and home-baked scones will entice you to relax over morning coffee, afternoon tea or enjoy a tasty lunch, before continuing on your expedition around this beautiful village.
FOOD: up to £15
Hours: lunch 11am–3pm, afternoon tea until 5.30pm.
Cuisine: ENGLISH – hearty traditional meals with a vegetarian selection. Lunch menu from £2.95.
Other points: children welcome, no-smoking area, disabled access.
Directions: off B2027 between Tonbridge and Edenbridge, within the National Trust village of Chiddingstone.
MR D. AITCHISON ☎ (01892) 870326
Fax (01892) 870326.

GILLINGHAM • map 6C5

MEDWAY PAVILION LODGE AT MEDWAY PAVILION SERVICE AREA
Between junctions 4 and 5, M2 Motorway, ME8 8PQ

The Lodge provides excellent accommodation at a competitive price and offers the facilities to make travelling a pleasure. Convenient for London, Dover, the Channel Ferries and Tunnel – the gateway to Europe.
DOUBLE ROOM: from £20 to £30
FOOD: up to £15
Hours: open 24 hours.
Cuisine: BRITISH / INTERNATIONAL – offered within the service building.
Cards: Visa, Access, Diners, AmEx.
Other points: parking, children welcome, disabled access, no-smoking area, forecourt shop, Burger King.
Rooms: 58 bedrooms. All with en suite, satellite TV, radio, alarm, hair dryer, trouser-press, tea/coffee-making facilities.
Directions: M2, between junctions 4 and 5.
DAVID VERNAZZA ☎ (01634) 377337
Fax (01634) 263187.

ICKHAM • map 6C5

THE DUKE WILLIAM
The Street, CT3 1QP

A 16th century free house in a picturesque village surrounded by farmlands. There is a lovely garden to the rear, with ponds, a fountain and flowers, as well as swings for the children. Situated only ten minutes from Canterbury, Ickham is central for Kent's many tourist attractions.
FOOD: from £20 to £25
Hours: open every day 11am–2.30pm and 6pm–10.30pm – food available during these hours in both bar and restaurant.
Cuisine: ENGLISH / INTERNATIONAL – extensive seafood menu, beef, lamb, poultry, veal. In the bar: omelettes, fish, home-made soup, chilli, home-baked bread. Exciting bar meals.
Cards: Visa, Access, Diners, AmEx.

Other points: licensed, open-air dining, Sunday lunch, children welcome, pets allowed, conservatory, garden.
Directions: in the centre of Ickham, which is signposted from the A257.
MR A. ROBIN & MRS C.A. McNEILL ☎ (01227) 721308.

MAIDSTONE • map 6C5

BOXLEY HOUSE HOTEL
Boxley Village, ME14 3DZ

This lovely 17th century house, set in 20 acres of parkland, has been carefully modernized to include all aspects of comfort, while retaining the full character of a period home. Fully licensed and centrally heated throughout, the hotel is an ideal setting for both business and pleasure. The restaurant, with its unique Minstrels gallery and dance floor, caters for every taste, from a superb intimate dinner to a wedding reception for up to 120 guests.
DOUBLE ROOM: from £20 to £30
SINGLE ROOM: from £35 to £45
FOOD: from £15 to £20 CLUB ★
Hours: breakfast 7am–9.15am, lunch 12noon–2pm, dinner 7pm–9.15pm, bar snacks available.
Cuisine: COSMOPOLITAN.
Cards: Visa, Access, Diners, AmEx.
Other points: parking, children welcome, disabled access, residents lounge, garden, open-air dining, vegetarian meals, afternoon teas.
Rooms: 5 single rooms, 7 double rooms, 4 twin rooms, 2 family rooms. All with TV, tea/coffee-making facilities, telephone, radio.
Directions: located in Boxley Village, reached via junction 6 of the M20, or exit 3 of the M2.
MALCOM FOX ☎ (01622) 692269
Fax (01622) 683536.

THE LIMETREE RESTAURANT AND HOTEL
The Limes, The Square, ME17 2PQ

Situated in the picturesque old Kentish village of Lenham, this family-run establishment is steeped in history, boasting timber frames dating back to the 14th century. Sympathetically renovated and refurbished, the hotel still retains many traditional features of a 600-year-old building. The seven en suite bedrooms are all comfortably furnished, and the restaurant specializes in classic French and continental cuisine. The atmosphere is relaxed and informal. Small weddings and parties can be catered for. Ideally located for motorway and channel ports, with the beautiful Leeds Castle just five miles away.
DOUBLE ROOM: from £20 to £30
FOOD: from £30
Hours: breakfast 7am–9am, lunch 12noon–2.30pm, bar snacks 12noon–2.30pm, dinner 7pm–10.30pm, bar snacks 7pm–10.30pm.
Cuisine: ENGLISH / FRENCH – an extensive à la carte menu and set menu Monday to Sunday.
Other points: parking, children welcome, Sunday lunch, open bank holidays, no-smoking area, afternoon tea, vegetarian meals, open-air dining, garden, licensed.

Rooms: 2 double rooms, 3 twin rooms, 1 family rooms, 1 four-poster room. All with TV, telephone, tea/coffee-making facilities.
Directions: situated in the square just off the A20.
MUSA KIVRAK ☎ (01622) 859509 [Fax] (01622) 850096.

MARGATE • map 6C6

🏨 IVYSIDE HOTEL
25 Sea Road, Westgate-on-Sea, CT8 8SB
The Ivyside overlooks the sea, standing in its own grounds. Tourists, conference delegates and families blend well to make an excellent atmosphere. Good value, open 24 hours, with super sports complex and pools.
DOUBLE ROOM: from £30 to £40
SINGLE ROOM: from £25 to £35
FOOD: up to £15
Hours: breakfast 7am–10am, lunch 12.30am–2.30pm, bar meals 12noon–2pm & 6pm–10pm, dinner 6.30pm–9pm.
Cuisine: TRADITIONAL ENGLISH – à la carte and vegetarian, junior menu.
Cards: Visa, Access, AmEx.
Other points: indoor swimming pool, spa pool, paddling pool, steam room, sauna, massage, squash, children welcome, family suites, baby-listening device, baby-sitting, outdoor pool, entertainment.
Rooms: 75 bedrooms. All en suite.
Directions: A28 from Canterbury or A299 from M2. Close to Canterbury and Ramsgate.
MICHAEL WISEMAN ☎ (01843) 831082
[Fax] (01843) 831082.

🏨 KINGSDOWN HOTEL
59–61 Harold Road, Cliftonville, CT9 2HS
A Victorian hotel, situated near the main shopping area and seafront, offering pleasantly decorated and spotlessly clean accommodation. The warm and courteous service and welcoming atmosphere attracts business people and tourists alike.
DOUBLE ROOM: up to £20
SINGLE ROOM: up to £25
FOOD: up to £15 ☆
Hours: breakfast 9am–9.30am, bar snacks 12.30am–2pm, dinner 6pm.
Cuisine: ENGLISH – winner of Thanet Clean Food Award and Kent Heart Beat Award.
Cards: Visa, Access, AmEx.
Other points: children welcome, afternoon tea, parking.
Rooms: 4 single rooms, 5 double room, 10 twin rooms.
Directions: follow A28 to Margate or follow the Isle of Thanet signs.
MR JAMES WILLIAMS ☎ (01843) 221672.

PENSHURST • map 6C4

🍴 THE SPOTTED DOG
Smarts Hill, TN11 8EE
Originally established in 1520, having started life as a row of cottages. The pub sign was intended to represent the coat of arms of the Sydney family who resided at Penshurst Place. A short-sighted painter mistook the leopard on the family crest for a spotted hunting dog, since when the pub has been known as The Spotted Dog. A typical Kentish pub with good food and a warm, hearty welcome. A large garden and terraced area complements the warm atmosphere inside.
FOOD: up to £15
Hours: bar meals 12noon–2.15pm, bar meals 7pm–9.45pm, dinner 7.15pm–10pm.
Cuisine: ENGLISH / FRENCH – traditional English and French, complemented by a fine wine list. Dishes may include roast half-rack of lamb and monkfish, king prawn and scallop ragout.
Cards: Visa, Access, Diners, Switch.
Other points: licensed, open-air dining, Sunday lunch, children welcome, parking, vegetarian meals.
Directions: B2176 and B2110. Through Penshurst village, third turning on the right.
ANDY & NIKKI TUCKER ☎ (01892) 870253.

PLUCKLEY • map 6C5

🍴 THE DERING ARMS
Station Road, near Ashford, TN27 0RR
Originally built as a hunting lodge for the Dering family, the inn has some unusual features such as the curved Dutch gables and the windows. Visitors to The Dering Arms are assured of a varied choice of real ales and fine wines. Good home-made food is served seven days a week, and comfortable accommodation is available throughout the year. Friendly and welcoming.
DOUBLE ROOM: up to £20
SINGLE ROOM: from £25 to £35
FOOD: up to £15
Hours: dinner 6.30pm–11pm, last orders 2pm and 10pm, lunch (Monday–Saturday) 12noon–3pm, Sundays 12noon–2pm.
Cuisine: ENGLISH – continually changing menu: seafood specials and daily specials. Restaurant and bar menus.
Cards: Visa, Access, AmEx.
Other points: licensed, Sunday lunch, garden.
Rooms: 2 double rooms, 1 twin room.
Directions: on Bethersden Road, 100 yards from Pluckley railway station.
MR JAMES BUSS ☎ (01233) 840371
[Fax] (01233) 840498.

RAMSGATE • map 6C6

🏨 MORTON'S FORK
42 Station Road, Minster, CT12 4BZ
A charming 17th century restaurant and wine bar, situated in a quiet, historical village, only 5 miles from Ramsgate. Charming ambience with a menu that offers good regional and imaginative dishes. The guest rooms have been attractively refurbished, retaining character yet providing modern conveniences.
DOUBLE ROOM: from £20 to £30
SINGLE ROOM: from £35 to £45

FOOD: from £15 to £20 🍳 [CLUB]
Hours: lunch 11.30am–2pm, dinner 6.30pm–10pm.
Cuisine: BRITISH / CONTINENTAL – including salmon parcel and chicken stuffed with crab. Good vegetarian dishes available.
Cards: Visa, Access, Diners, AmEx.
Other points: Sunday lunch, children welcome, parking, vegetarian meals, residents' bar, disabled access.
Rooms: 3 double rooms. All with TV, telephone, tea/coffee-making facilities.
Directions: follow the A28, exit onto A253. Turn left for Minster village.
MR DAVID J. SWORDER ☎ (01843) 823000.

ROYAL TUNBRIDGE WELLS
map 6D4

🍴 PORTOVINO'S RESTAURANT
Church Road, TN4 0XY

An attractive Edwardian-style house, with a delightfully furnished green and white interior and fresh flowers. Comfortable, clean and very efficiently run, offering fine food and wine in a restful and pleasing atmosphere.
FOOD: from £15 to £20 [CLUB]
Hours: lunch 12noon–2.30pm, dinner 7pm–10pm; closed Sunday evening, Monday, 1st January until 7th January.
Cuisine: ENGLISH / CONTINENTAL – à la carte and table d'hôte menus, offering an extensive selection of dishes, complemented by a fine wine list. Vegetarian meals also available.
Cards: Visa, Access, AmEx.
Other points: licensed, Sunday lunch, children welcome, parking.
Directions: off Southborough Common on A26 between Tunbridge and Tunbridge Wells.
ANDREW BOND ☎ (01892) 513161
[Fax] (01892) 513161.

🏨 RUSSELL HOTEL
80 London Road, TN1 1DZ

The Russell Hotel is a large Victorian house furnished to a high standard. It is situated facing the common and is only a few minutes' walk from the town centre. This hotel offers generous portions of appetizing meals, cooked from local fresh produce. The staff are welcoming and helpful, making a stay here very comfortable. Residents' lounge in annexe.
DOUBLE ROOM: from £40 to £50
FOOD: up to £15
Hours: breakfast 7am–9.30am, Sunday 8am–10am, dinner 7pm–9.30pm, Sunday 7pm–9pm.
Cuisine: MODERN ENGLISH – à la carte menu, fixed three-course menu, bar snacks. Dishes include stuffed mushrooms, veal cooked in marsala and cream, and grilled steak in mustard sauce.
Cards: Visa, Access, Diners, AmEx.
Other points: children welcome, foreign exchange, residents' lounge, residents' bar, vegetarian meals, parking.

Rooms: 2 single rooms, 11 double rooms, 13 twin rooms. All with TV, telephone, tea/coffee-making facilities.
Directions: take M25 exit 5. Follow A21 south and join A26. On A26 near A264 junction.
MR & MRS K.A. WILKINSON ☎ (01892) 544833 [Fax] (01892) 515846.

SEVENOAKS • map 6C4

🏨 MOORINGS HOTEL
97 Hitchen Hatch Lane, TN13 3BE

A small, friendly family hotel offering a high standard of accommodation for tourists and business travellers. One especially pleasant feature is the range of garden patio bedrooms, which are arranged like a small motel around a secluded lawn. Sevenoaks is a pleasant Kentish market town within easy reach of many places of historical interest. The newly refurbished restaurant opened January 1994.
DOUBLE ROOM: from £20 to £30
SINGLE ROOM: from £25 to £35
FOOD: up to £15 [CLUB] ☆
Hours: breakfast weekdays 7.30am–9am, weekends 8am–9am, dinner 7pm–9pm.
Cuisine: INTERNATIONAL.
Cards: Visa, Access, AmEx.
Other points: children welcome, no-smoking area, vegetarian meals, garden, residents' bar, residents' lounge, parking.
Rooms: 24 bedrooms.
Directions: situated on the A224, two minutes from the M25. 200 yards from Sevenoaks BR station.
FIONA & TIM RYAN ☎ (01732) 452589 [Fax] (01732) 456462.

🏨 SEVENOAKS PARK HOTEL
Seal Hollow Road, TN13 3SH

The Sevenoaks Park Hotel is a charming building standing in 3 acres of Elizabethan gardens overlooking superb views of Knole Park. Offering well-cooked and presented cuisine and attractive comfortable accommodation, the hotel provides guests with a pleasant and welcoming atmosphere. An ideal base for touring areas of interest such as Royal Tunbridge Wells and Leeds Castle.
DOUBLE ROOM: up to £20
FOOD: up to £15
Hours: breakfast 7am–9.30am, dinner 7pm–9.30pm.
Cuisine: MODERN ENGLISH – à la carte, table d'hôte: dishes include poached salmon served in lemon and mustard sauce, breast of duck fried and served with strawberry and blackcurrant.
Cards: Visa, Access, Diners, AmEx.
Other points: licensed, open-air dining, Sunday lunch, children welcome, afternoon tea, swimming pool.
Rooms: 2 single rooms, 10 double rooms, 20 twin rooms, 1 family room. All with TV, radio, telephone.
Directions: off A225.
MR NOBLE & MR HUNTLEY ☎ (01732) 454245 [Fax] (01732) 457468.

SITTINGBOURNE • map 6C5

🏨 CONISTON HOTEL
70 London Road, ME10 1NT
The hotel is very well placed for visiting Kent's many sights and attractions. The ballroom can seat 160 people and is available for private hire.
DOUBLE ROOM: from £20 to £30
FOOD: up to £15
Hours: breakfast 7.30am–9.30am, lunch 12noon–2.30pm, dinner 7pm–10pm, open 7 days.
Cuisine: ENGLISH / SEAFOOD – speciality: Dover sole.
Cards: Visa, Access, Diners, AmEx.
Other points: traditional Sunday lunch, children welcome, coaches by prior arrangement, charge for pets.
Rooms: 16 single rooms, 14 double rooms, 16 twin rooms, 5 family rooms. All with TV, telephone, tea/coffee-making facilities.
Directions: on the A2, half a mile from the town centre.
MR S. KLECKOWSKI ☎ (01795) 472131/ 427907 [Fax] (01795) 428056.

LES ROUTIERS
Information & Bookings Line
☎ 0171 610 1856

🏨 NEWINGTON MANOR HOTEL & RESTAURANT
Callaways Lane, Newington, ME9 7LU
This fine example of a 14th century hall house is a splendid Tudor building, combining a wealth of oak beams, mullioned windows, massive chimneys and inglenooks with such present-day luxuries as four-poster beds and real log fires. Set in its own beautiful gardens, the hotel offers two beautifully appointed dining rooms plus a small conference or private functions room. There is an extensive cellar of carefully chosen wines and a fully stocked bar for residents and diners. The outstanding beauty and character of Newington Manor lends itself perfectly for any special occasion.
DOUBLE ROOM: from £30 to £40
SINGLE ROOM: from £45 to £55
FOOD: from £15 to £20
Hours: breakfast 7.30am–9.30am, lunch 12noon–2pm, dinner 7pm–10pm, restaurant closed bank holidays, hotel closed 27th December until 30th December.
Cuisine: EUROPEAN – an exceptionally high standard of cuisine, served in delightful surroundings with excellent service.
Cards: Visa, Access, Diners, AmEx.
Other points: parking, conference facilities, garden, vegetarian meals, traditional Sunday lunch, afternoon teas.
Rooms: 11 double rooms, 1 twin room. All with en suite, TV, telephone, hair dryer, tea/coffee-making facilities.
Directions: off Bull Lane, south from A2 in Newington village.
CHRISTOPHER & ANGELIKA EATON
☎ (01795) 842053 [Fax] (01795) 844273.

TEYNHAM • map 6C5

🍽 THE SHIP INN & SMUGGLERS RESTAURANT
Conyer Quay, near Sittingbourne, ME9 9HR
Hidden away in the picturesque village of Conyer, which nestles amongst the orchards and hopfields of the marsh farms, but well worth searching for. An attractive pub and restaurant offering good food and a warm and friendly atmosphere. The interior is full of character. Les Routiers Corps d'Elite 1991, 1992, 1993 and 1994 for their excellent wine list; over 60 bottled beers and 250 different whiskies.
FOOD: from £20 to £25 🍽
Hours: lunch 12noon–2.30pm, dinner 7pm–10.30pm.
Cuisine: ENGLISH / CONTINENTAL – moules marinière, King Neptune's banquet, steak au poivre. Huge choice of whiskies, rums, brandies, liqueurs, wine, real ales, draught and bottled beers.
Cards: Visa, Access, AmEx.
Other points: licensed, open-air dining, Sunday lunch, children welcome, pets allowed.
Directions: 2 miles off the A2 in village of Conyer. On water's edge.
ALEC HEARD ☎ (01795) 521404.

TONBRIDGE • map 6C4

🏨 THE CHASER INN
Stumble Hill, Shipbourne, TN11 9PE
Built in the 1880s, The Chaser Inn is an attractive colonial-style building. An extensive and imaginative range of food is offered in the bars and a creative set menu can be enjoyed in the restaurant, which features a beamed vaulted ceiling and panelled walls. Only minutes from the M25, M20 and M26 motorway networks, The Chaser Inn is well placed to greet travellers.
DOUBLE ROOM: from £20 to £30
SINGLE ROOM: from £45 to £55
FOOD: from £20 to £25
Hours: breakfast 7.30am–9.30am, lunch 12.30am–2pm, dinner 7.30pm–9.30pm, bar meals 12noon–2pm, 7pm–9.30pm.
Cuisine: ENGLISH / FRENCH – table d'hôte menu in restaurant. Dishes may include lamb fillet on a raspberry and mint sauce, lemon sole. Also bar snacks.
Cards: Visa, Access, AmEx.
Other points: licensed, open-air dining, Sunday lunch, children welcome, functions, baby-listening device, cots, 24hr reception, residents' bar, vegetarian meals, parking, residents' lounge, disabled access.
Rooms: 5 single rooms, 6 double rooms, 4 twin rooms. All with TV, telephone, tea/coffee-making facilities.
Directions: On A227, north of Tonbridge. Next to Shipbourne church and opposite green.
MICHAEL AND VIVIEN NIX ☎ (01732) 810360 [Fax] (01732) 810941.

THE HARP
Hale Street, East Peckham, TN12 5JB
An enticing country inn adorned with flower baskets, which is popular with locals and an ideal stopping place for travellers. There is an extensive menu, and all dishes are freshly prepared and cooked on the premise: no frozen microwave meals here! Conveniently located for the Whitbread Hop Farm and Brookside Garden Centre.
FOOD: up to £15
Hours: meals all day 12noon–9.30pm.
Cuisine: ENGLISH – traditional meals with weekly specials.
Other points: parking, children welcome, open-air dining, vegetarian meals, traditional Sunday lunch.
Directions: on A228 at junction of Severn Mile Lane.
PATRICIA ROBINSON ☎ (01622) 872334
Fax (01622) 873404.

THE OFFICE WINE BAR
163 High Street, TN9 1TX
A 16th century half-brick timbered building in Tonbridge High Street, offering a very warm and friendly bistro-style atmosphere. The menu and wine list are extensive, the service polite and efficient. An ideal stop-off for tourists who wish to visit Tonbridge Castle, Penshurst Place, Tunbridge Wells, and the beautiful Kent countryside.
FOOD: up to £15
Hours: lunch 12noon–2pm, dinner 7pm–9.30pm, bar 10.30am–2.30pm, bar 6pm–11pm, closed Sunday and bank holidays.
Cuisine: ENGLISH – bistro-style menu, with an added touch of French. Wide choice of dishes, nicely presented. Vegetarian dishes also available.
Cards: Visa, Access, Diners, AmEx.
Other points: licensed, children welcome.
Directions: situated at north end of the High Street, near Tonbridge School.
JERRY HALFHIDE ☎ (01732) 353660.

WESTERHAM • map 6C4

THE KINGS ARMS HOTEL
Market Square, TN16 1AN
A privately-owned, elegant Georgian coaching inn offering a relaxed, peaceful atmosphere, comfortable accommodation and professional, welcoming staff. The restaurant provides traditional but imaginative dishes, freshly prepared and cooked to order. The good food is complemented by a comprehensive wine list. Ideal location for business and pleasure
DOUBLE ROOM: from £50
SINGLE ROOM: from £55
FOOD: from £15 to £20 [CLUB]
Hours: bar meals 12noon–2pm, bar meals 7pm–10pm, breakfast weekdays 7.30am–9.30am, weekends 8am–10am, lunch 12noon–2pm, dinner 7pm–10pm.
Cuisine: ENGLISH – table d'hôte and à la carte menus using fresh ingredients. Dishes may include pot-roasted guinea fowl, supreme of chicken, rosettes of lamb.
Cards: Visa, Access, Diners, AmEx.
Other points: licensed, open-air dining, Sunday lunch, children welcome, residents' lounge, garden, conferences, terrace bar.
Rooms: 1 single room, 9 double rooms, 16 twin rooms, 1 family room.
Directions: M25 junction 6, then follow A25 into Westerham.
KEN EATON ☎ (01959) 562990 Fax (01959) 564240.

WHITSTABLE • map 6C5

GIOVANNI'S RESTAURANT
49-55 Canterbury Road, CT5 4HH
This fully air-conditioned cocktail bar and restaurant is very popular and booking is recommended. Established in 1968, Giovanni's is owner-managed, with an enthusiastic continental staff.
FOOD: from £15 to £20
Hours: lunch 12noon–2.30pm, dinner 6pm–10.30pm, closed Sunday evening and all day Monday.
Cuisine: ITALIAN / FRENCH.
Cards: Visa, Access, Diners, AmEx.
Other points: licensed, Sunday lunch, children welcome.
Directions: on the A290 near the railway bridge.
GIOVANNI FERRARI ☎ (01227) 273034.

NORFOLK

ACLE • map 10C6

MANNINGS HOTEL & RESTAURANT
South Walsham Road, NR13 3ES
A small family-run hotel, set in peaceful landscaped gardens. All rooms are elegantly furnished and comfortable. The licensed restaurant is open to non-residents, offering cuisine which is believed to be the best in the area. Centrally situated for touring the Norfolk Broads and for exploring the beautiful Norfolk countryside.
DOUBLE ROOM: from £20 to £30
FOOD: up to £15
Hours: breakfast 7.30am–9am, lunch 12noon–2pm, bar meals 12noon–2pm, dinner 7pm–9.30pm.
Cuisine: ENGLISH – full à la carte and table d'hôte menus offering a very high standard of catering, using only the freshest of produce.
Cards: Visa, Access, AmEx.
Other points: licensed, open-air dining, Sunday lunch, children welcome, pets allowed, parking,

garden, vegetarian meals.
Rooms: 3 single rooms, 4 double rooms, 3 twin rooms. All with TV, radio, telephone, tea/coffee-making facilities.
Directions: midway between Great Yarmouth (9 miles) and Norwich (11 miles).
ROBERT MANNING ☎ (01493) 750377
[Fax] (01493) 751220.

BRANCASTER STAITHE • map 10C5

THE JOLLY SAILORS
Brancaster Staithe, PE13 8BJ
Records of The Jolly Sailors date back to 1789 – a popular haunt with locals, where beer is still drawn by hand pumps. It is ideally situated for good beaches, sailing, bird reserves and many places of interest, including Sandringham House and Holkham Hall. Award-winning wine list.
FOOD: up to £15 [CLUB]
Hours: lunch 12noon–2pm, dinner 7pm–9pm, meals all day July and August, closed Christmas.
Cuisine: ENGLISH – Staithe mussels, lasagne, game casserole. All food prepared and cooked on the premises. Bar food and restaurant meals available.
Cards: Visa, Access.
Other points: licensed, open-air dining, Sunday lunch, pets allowed, children welcome, log fire, no music, playland, tennis court.
Directions: on A149 coast road, halfway between Hunstanton and Wells-Next-The-Sea.
ALISTER BORTHWICK ☎ (01485) 210314
[Fax] (01485) 210158.

BRESSINGHAM • map 10D5

THE OLD GARDEN HOUSE
Thetford Road, IP22 2AG
This charming, heavily-beamed, thatched inn has a cosy, warm ambience of its own. The imaginative home-cooked food, selection of real ales and excellent wines, coupled with roaring fires and flagstone floors, make this the ideal setting for any occasion. It is situated opposite the Bressingham Steam Railway Museum and Blooms Garden Centre.
FOOD: from £15 to £20
Hours: lunch 12noon–2.30pm, dinner 7pm–9pm.
Cuisine: ENGLISH / CONTINENTAL.
Cards: Visa.
Other points: parking, children welcome, no-smoking area, open-air dining, vegetarian meals, traditional Sunday lunch.
Directions: on the main Thetford–Diss road, opposite Bressingham Church.
ANDY & LINDA MOORE ☎ (01379) 88405.

BRISTON • map 10C5

THE JOHN H. STRACEY
West End, near Melton Constable, NR24 2JA
Professional and friendly staff take special care to make guests feel at home. Mr Fox is at present offering Bargain Breaks. With the good food and relaxing surroundings, this promises to be a popular bargain indeed.
DOUBLE ROOM: up to £20
FOOD: up to £15 [CLUB]
Hours: lunch 12noon–2.15pm, bar meals 12noon–2.15pm, dinner 7pm–9.30pm, bar meals 7pm–10pm.
Cuisine: INTERNATIONAL – comprehensive menu including salmon à la Stracey (fresh salmon steaks, poached in white wine, with prawns and parsley).
Cards: Visa.
Other points: licensed, Sunday lunch, children welcome, vegetarian meals, afternoon tea.
Rooms: 2 double rooms, 1 twin room. All with TV.
Directions: on B1354 close to Melton Constable and en route to Aylsham and Fakenham.
MR & MRS R.E. FOX ☎ (01263) 860891.

CASTLE ACRE • map 10C5

THE OSTRICH INN
Stocks Green, near King's Lynn, PE32 2AE
Large 16th century coaching inn with two big open fires in the lounge bar. On the A1065 in a typical, small Norfolk village which has the Peddars Way running through it. Many National Trust attractions nearby.
DOUBLE ROOM: up to £20
FOOD: up to £15
Hours: bar meals 12noon–2pm, bar meals 7.30pm–10.30pm, closed Christmas.
Cuisine: INTERNATIONAL – bar meals ranging from sausages to caviar, cockles to T-bone steaks. Daily specials from all over the world, cooked by the chef/proprietor.
Other points: licensed, Sunday lunch, children welcome, children welcome, coaches by prior arrangement.
Rooms: 2 twin rooms.
Directions: on the A1065 between Swaffham and Fakenham, on the village green.
RAYMOND H. WAKELEN ☎ (01760) 755398.

DOWNHAM MARKET • map 10C4

THE CROWN HOTEL
Bridge Street, PE38 9DH
This impressive old coaching inn, dating back to the 13th century, is situated in the centre of Downham Market. It has recently been restored to its former glory, with log fires and flagstone floors, boasting ten letting rooms, restaurant, stables bar, locals bar and function room. The hotel has all the facilities, together with its warm and friendly atmosphere, to offer something for everyone.
DOUBLE ROOM: from £30 to £40
FOOD: from £15 to £20
Hours: breakfast 7.30am–10am, lunch 12noon–2.30pm, dinner 7pm–10pm.
Cuisine: ENGLISH.
Cards: Visa, Access.
Other points: parking, children welcome, pets allowed, conference facilities, residents' lounge,

vegetarian meals, traditional Sunday lunch.
Rooms: 10 bedrooms. All with TV, telephone, tea/coffee-making facilities.
Directions: 1 mile off A10 London to King's Lynn road, 9 miles from King's Lynn.
TIM & KATH SMITH ☎ (01366) 382322.

GREAT YARMOUTH • map 10C6

THE CLIFF HOTEL
Cliff Hill, Gorleston-on-Sea, NR31 6DH

A welcoming business and holiday hotel overlooking the harbour on the quieter side of Great Yarmouth. The chefs and their staff provide a large selection of English dishes, offering the opportunity to sample the best from the produce of Norfolk farms and market gardens.
DOUBLE ROOM: from £20 to £30
FOOD: from £15 to £20
Hours: breakfast 7.30am–9.45am, lunch 12.30am–2pm, dinner 7pm–9.30pm, open all year.
Cuisine: ENGLISH – traditional roasts.
Cards: Visa, Access, Diners, AmEx.
Other points: Sunday lunch, children welcome.
Directions: overlooking the harbour at Great Yarmouth, on A47
MR R.W. SCOTT ☎ (01493) 662179.

THE GALLON POT
Market Place, NR30 1NB

A traditional town-centre public house, which has built up a fine reputation for good-quality bar food at very reasonable prices. Popular with locals of all ages, the pub also appeals to seasonal holiday-makers. A relaxed and comfortable atmosphere.
FOOD: up to £15
Hours: bar 10am–11pm, lunch 11.30am–2.30pm, Sunday lunch 12noon–2.30pm, dinner 7pm–10pm, Sunday dinner 7pm–9.30pm, snacks served throughout afternoon Monday to Saturday.
Cuisine: ENGLISH – traditional pub food. Special weekend and lunchtime menus.
Other points: licensed, open-air dining, children welcome, parking.
Directions: in town centre, in open market square. Next to large public car park.
MICHAEL & MARIA SPALDING ☎ (01493) 842230.

IMPERIAL HOTEL
North Drive, NR30 1EQ

For many years the Imperial has enjoyed an outstanding reputation for its quality of food and wine. The Rambouillet, with its quiet intimacy, offers a wide range of dishes to appeal to both the gourmet and traditional diner. The excellently appointed rooms are equipped with all modern facilities, and many have glorious sea views. A perfect base for touring East Anglia.
DOUBLE ROOM: from £30 to £40
FOOD: from £15 to £20
Hours: breakfast 7.30am–9.30am, lunch 12.30am–2.30pm, dinner 7pm–10pm, open all year.
Cuisine: ENGLISH / FRENCH – regional English and French cuisine of the highest quality, complemented by a superb wine list. Special

gastronomic weekends are held each year.
Cards: Visa, Access, Diners, AmEx.
Other points: licensed, Sunday lunch, children welcome, afternoon tea, residents' lounge, pets allowed, conferences.
Rooms: 4 single rooms, 23 double rooms, 12 twin rooms. All with satellite TV, radio, telephone, tea/coffee-making facilities, hair dryer, trouser-press.
Directions: on seafront, opposite the Waterways.
ROGER MOBBS ☎ (01493) 851113
[Fax] (01493) 852229.

REGENCY HOTEL
5 North Drive, NR30 1ED

A modern seaside hotel offering comfortable accommodation in a good seafront location. Guests can choose from table d'hôte or à la carte menus at dinner, and there is a good choice at breakfast. The Regency Hotel is popular with holiday-makers and business people alike.
DOUBLE ROOM: from £20 to £30
SINGLE ROOM: from £25 to £35
FOOD: up to £15
Hours: breakfast 8am–9.30am, dinner 6pm–8.30pm.
Cuisine: ENGLISH.
Cards: Visa, Access, Diners, AmEx, Switch.
Other points: licensed.
Rooms: 3 single rooms, 9 double rooms, 1 family room. All en suite.
Directions: on the seafront in Great Yarmouth.
J. BARNETT ☎ (01493) 843759.

HUNSTANTON • map 10C4

CALEY HALL MOTEL & RESTAURANT
Old Hunstanton, PE36 6HH

The resident proprietors of Caley Hall have skillfully converted the outbuildings of their 17th century manor house to provide a comfortable bar and restaurant facilities. Chalets have been sympathetically added and are closely in keeping with the overall architectural style. The restaurant serves a wide range of good food, which is well presented and offers good value for money.
DOUBLE ROOM: from £20 to £30
SINGLE ROOM: from £25 to £35
FOOD: up to £15
Hours: breakfast 8am–9.30am, lunch 12noon–2pm, dinner 7pm–9pm.
Cuisine: FRENCH / BRITISH – table d'hôte and à la carte menus. Specializing in steaks and fish. Children's portions available.
Cards: Visa, Access.
Other points: licensed, Sunday lunch, children welcome, pets allowed, residents' lounge.
Rooms: 1 single room, 12 double rooms, 12 twin rooms. All rooms are en suite. Most rooms are on the ground floor, providing easy access for wheelchairs.
Directions: On A149, just off the coast road between Brancaster and Hunstanton.
CLIVE KING ☎ (01485) 533486 [Fax] (01485) 533348.

GATE LODGE GUEST HOUSE
2 Westgate, PE36 5AL

Gate Lodge is a family-run guest house offering comfortable accommodation and meals of a high standard. The beach, leisure complex, shopping centre and bus station are all within easy reach. Gate Lodge provides an ideal base for touring the unspoilt north Norfolk Heritage coast and countryside. Sandringham is within easy reach. Bird-watching, windsurfing, bowling, tennis and croquet.
DOUBLE ROOM: up to £20
SINGLE ROOM: up to £25
FOOD: up to £15
Hours: breakfast 8.45am, dinner 6.45pm, closed December.
Cuisine: ENGLISH – menus are chosen daily, prepared with fresh seasonal produce to a very high standard.
Other points: security parking, pets allowed, residents' lounge, vegetarian meals, special diets, disabled access, children catered for (please check for age limits).
Rooms: 3 double rooms, 3 twin rooms. All with en suite, TV, tea/coffee-making facilities, heating.
Directions: A149 from King's Lynn. Left at Hunstanton roundabout. Down hill and turn right.
GUY & ROISIN WELLARD ☎ (01485) 533549.

NORTHGATE HOUSE
46 Northgate, PE36 6DR

Northgate House is a family-run guest house with comfortable, spacious accommodation, close to Hunstanton's Blue Flag beach, shops and theatre. Nearby are bird reserves, golf courses, several stately homes, Peddars Way and the Norfolk coast path.
DOUBLE ROOM: up to £20
SINGLE ROOM: up to £25
FOOD: up to £15
Hours: breakfast 8.30am–9am, dinner 6.30pm.
Cuisine: BREAKFAST.
Other points: central heating, vegetarian meals, children welcome, residents' lounge.
Rooms: 2 single rooms, 3 double rooms, 1 twin room. All with TV, tea/coffee-making facilities.
Directions: off the A149, turn right into Austin Street, which leads to Northgate.
MR & MRS M.R. SNARE ☎ (01485) 533269.

KING'S LYNN • map 10C4

GUANOCK HOTEL
Southgates, PE30 5JG

Close to the historic Southgates and adjacent to Jubilee Gardens. Just a few minutes from the town centre in a pleasant area of town.
DOUBLE ROOM: up to £20
SINGLE ROOM: up to £25
FOOD: up to £15
Hours: breakfast 7am–8.30am, dinner 6pm–7pm.
Cuisine: BREAKFAST – full English, or your choice from a large selection.
Cards: Visa, Access, AmEx.
Other points: central heating, children welcome, residents' lounge, roof patio garden, pool room.
Rooms: 5 single rooms, 4 double rooms, 3 twin rooms, 5 family rooms. All with TV, radio, tea/coffee-making facilities, iron, hair dryer.
Directions: on the London road, enter King's Lynn via Southgates.
TERRY PARCHMENT ☎ (01553) 772959
Fax (01553) 772959.

NORWICH • map 10C6

GRANGE HOTEL
230 Thorpe Road, NR1 1TJ

Formerly an old manor house and now tastefully restored, the Grange Hotel provides comfortable accommodation to the casual visitor and businessman alike. The comfortable bar is an ideal spot in which to spend a relaxing evening or enjoy a pre-dinner drink. Sauna and solarium. Available for special and private function hire. Ideal for touring Norfolk.
DOUBLE ROOM: from £30 to £40
FOOD: from £15 to £20 ☆
Hours: breakfast 7.30am–9am, dinner 6.30pm–9.30pm, closed Christmas until New Year.
Cuisine: ENGLISH – à la carte and table d'hôte. Dishes may include roast Aylesbury duckling, lamb cutlets Marchale, supreme of chicken, darne of salmon rouge. Vegetarian.
Cards: Visa, Access, Diners, AmEx.
Other points: licensed, no-smoking area, children welcome, parking, residents' lounge, disabled access, children welcome, cots, functions, vegetarian meals, residents' bar.
Rooms: 16 single rooms, 12 double rooms, 6 twin rooms, 1 quad room. All with TV, telephone, tea/coffee-making facilities, alarm.
Directions: 1 mile from Norwich station, travelling towards Great Yarmouth.
ROBERT HARGREAVES ☎ (01603) 34734
Fax (01603) 34734.

REEDHAM • map 10C6

REEDHAM FERRY & INN
Near Norwich, NR13 3HH

Situated on the River Yare, adjacent to the ferry crossing, this popular old inn provides a pleasant stop for locals and tourists alike. Well-presented, well-served, good-value meals and welcoming family atmosphere. Riverside tables and chairs with garden. Adjoining the Inn is the Reedham Ferry Camping & Caravan Park, four acres of landscaped grounds and modern facilities next to the river Yare.
FOOD: up to £15
Hours: lunch 12noon–2.15pm, dinner 7pm–10pm.
Cuisine: ENGLISH – a changing seasonal menu using only fresh produce, with prime meat from local butchers and hand-picked fish from Lowestoft Market. Chef's own daily specials, vegetarian and diet-conscious dishes. A selection of salads, fresh filled rolls and sandwiches.
Cards: Visa, Access.
Other points: open-air dining, Sunday lunch, children welcome, pets allowed.

SUFFOLK • SE ENGLAND & EAST ANGLIA

Directions: just off the B1140 in Reedham on the north side of the ferry.
MR D.N. ARCHER ☎ (01493) 700429.

SNETTISHAM • map 10C5

THE ROSE & CROWN FREEHOUSE
Old Church Road, PE32 2HN
Situated just off the A149, this 14th century pub offers good food, real ales and a friendly, welcoming atmosphere. A large collection of old farming implements is on display. Children have their own menu and a large, separate room, personally supervised by the proprietor.
DOUBLE ROOM: up to £20
SINGLE ROOM: up to £25
FOOD: up to £15
Hours: dinner 6.30pm–10.30pm, lunch 12noon–2pm.
Cuisine: ENGLISH – rare roast beef, quality steaks, good selection of vegetarian dishes, dish of the day: good home-cooking.
Cards: Visa, Access.
Other points: open-air dining, Sunday lunch, children welcome, coaches by prior arrangement, garden.
Rooms: 1 double room, 2 twin rooms.
Directions: from King's Lynn, take A149 north for 10 miles; follow signs for Snettisham.
MARGARET GODDARD ☎ (01485) 541382.

STALHAM • map 10C6

SUTTON STAITHE HOTEL
Sutton Staithe, Sutton, NR12 9QS
Situated by the waterside at the head of Sutton Broad, the inn is popular with boat people. The food is plentiful, well-cooked and well-presented.
DOUBLE ROOM: from £30 to £40
FOOD: up to £15
Hours: lunch 12noon–2pm, dinner 7pm–9.30pm.
Cuisine: ENGLISH / SEAFOOD – local game and fish in season.
Cards: Visa, Access, Diners, AmEx.
Other points: licensed, open-air dining, Sunday lunch, children welcome, fishing.
Directions: just off the A149 Yarmouth to North Walsham road.
M.K. & D.P. TAYLOR ☎ (01692) 580244.

WELLS-NEXT-THE-SEA • map 10B4

CROWN HOTEL & RESTAURANT
The Buttlands, NR23 1EX
The hotel is ideally situated for visiting historic churches, priories and stately homes, including Holkham Hall and Sandringham. Both table d'hôte and à la carte menus are available in the restaurant.
DOUBLE ROOM: from £30 to £40
FOOD: up to £15
Hours: lunch 12noon–2pm, dinner 7pm–9.30pm.
Cuisine: ENGLISH / FRENCH – sea and shellfish, steak-and-kidney pie, home-made soups, pâté and French specialities. Local produce used where possible.
Cards: Visa, Access, Diners, AmEx.
Other points: licensed, Sunday lunch, children welcome.
Rooms: 1 single room, 5 double rooms, 5 twin rooms, 1 family room.
Directions: The Buttlands is a tree-lined square in the centre of town.
MR & MRS W. FOYERS ☎ (01328) 710209.

SUFFOLK

BILDESTON • map 10E5

THE CROWN HOTEL
104 High Street, IP7 7EB
A 15th century coaching inn in the heart of the Suffolk countryside. Along with excellent food and accommodation, The Crown Hotel offers guests the chance to spot one of its several ghosts!
DOUBLE ROOM: from £20 to £30
FOOD: up to £15
Hours: breakfast 7.30am–10am, lunch 12noon–2pm, Sunday 12.30am–2.30pm, dinner 7pm 9.30pm.
Cuisine: ENGLISH – traditional English. Victorian diable mixed meats in a spicy sauce is a speciality.
Cards: Visa, Access.
Other points: licensed, open-air dining, Sunday lunch, children welcome, garden, afternoon tea, residents' bar, baby-listening device, baby-sitting
Rooms: 1 single room, 8 double rooms, 5 twin rooms, 1 triple room. All with TV.
Directions: in the village on the B1115.

MR HENDERSON ☎ (01449) 740510
Fax (01449) 740224.

BURY ST EDMUNDS • map 10D5

THE GRANGE HOTEL
Thurston, IP31 3PQ
Attractive mock-Tudor country house hotel set in its own beautiful grounds. It has a resident chef/proprietor, Gordon Wagstaff, who, together with his wife Wanda, has run the hotel for 20 years. Together with their staff they create a welcoming and relaxed atmosphere. The Grange is just four miles from the historic market town of Bury St Edmunds, home to the beautiful National Trust-owned theatre. It is well placed for the picturesque city of Cambridge, and the Newmarket racecourse is close by.
DOUBLE ROOM: from £20 to £30
FOOD: from £15 to £20
Hours: breakfast 7am–9.30am, lunch 12noon–

2.30pm, bar meals 12noon–2.30pm, dinner 7pm–10pm, bar meals 7pm–10pm.
Cuisine: ENGLISH / FRENCH – wherever possible local produce is used, to ensure that meat, fish and vegetables are all fresh and of a high standard.
Cards: Visa, Access.
Other points: licensed, traditional Sunday lunch, children welcome, pets allowed, open bank holidays, bargain breaks.
Rooms: 8 double rooms, 4 twin rooms, 2 family rooms. All with TV, telephone, hair dryer, tea/coffee-making facilities.
Directions: A14 (was A45) to Bury St Edmunds, exit at Bury Central and follow A143 to Great Barton and Thurston.
MR & MRS E.G. WAGSTAFF ☎ (01359) 231260
[Fax] (01359) 231260.

THE WHITE HORSE
Old Newmarket Road, Risby, IP28 6NJ
A 17th century inn offering accommodation, good home-cooked food and real ales in a very romantic atmosphere with a candlelit dining room, open fire and soft background music. The inn is well worth a visit.
DOUBLE ROOM: from £20 to £30
FOOD: up to £15
Hours: lunch 12noon–2pm, dinner 7pm–10.30pm.
Cuisine: ENGLISH.
Cards: Visa, Access.
Other points: parking, children welcome, pets allowed, open-air dining, vegetarian meals, traditional Sunday lunch.
Rooms: 2 bedrooms. Both with TV, tea/coffee-making facilities.
Directions: Risby turn-off on A14, 10 miles east of Newmarket.
DAVID MEARS & GEORGINA SMITH
☎ (01284) 810686.

CHELSWORTH • map 10E5

THE PEACOCK INN
The Street, IP7 7HV
A genuine 14th century oak-timbered inn with inglenook fireplaces and unique character. It is a prominent feature of the picturesque village of Chelsworth, opposite the River Brett. The Peacock prides itself on imaginative home-cooked meals with a selection of real ales and fine wines, coupled with quaint letting rooms. The village inn is the ideal traveller's rest.
DOUBLE ROOM: from £20 to £30
FOOD: up to £15
Hours: breakfast 9am–10am, lunch 12noon–2pm, dinner 7pm–9.30pm.
Cuisine: ENGLISH / MEDITERRANEAN.
Cards: Visa, Access.
Other points: children welcome, pets allowed, open-air dining, traditional Sunday lunch.
Rooms: 4 bedrooms. All with TV, tea/coffee-making facilities.
Directions: on the A1115 between Stowmarket and Lavenham.
NIGEL & CAROL RAMSBOTTOM ☎ (01449) 740758.

CLARE • map 10E5

THE CLARE HOTEL
Nethergate Street, CO10 8NP
Recently renovated 17th century inn, in a picturesque market town, close to the market place, park and castle ruins. Large bar and restaurant, decorated with antiques, serving excellent cuisine accompanied by a superb wine list. Beautiful landscaped garden with garden restaurant for summer evenings.
DOUBLE ROOM: from £20 to £30
FOOD: up to £15
Cuisine: ENGLISH / FRENCH – café/restaurant-style.
Cards: Visa, Access, AmEx.
Other points: licensed, Sunday lunch, children welcome, pets allowed.
Rooms: 1 single room, 2 double rooms, 5 twin rooms.
Directions: easy to locate in the town centre.
MR & MRS ROSS ☎ (01787) 277449
[Fax] (01787) 278270.

FELIXSTOWE • map 6A6

MARLBOROUGH HOTEL
Sea Front, IP11 8BJ
An Edwardian building facing the sea, offering panoramic views from many of the rooms. The staff are very friendly and promote a high standard of service, all the rooms being very clean and the food well-cooked and prepared. Conveniently situated, close to Felixstowe leisure centre and the Spa Pavilion.
DOUBLE ROOM: from £20 to £30
FOOD: up to £15 ★
Hours: breakfast 7pm–9.30pm; lunch 12noon–2.30pm; bar meals 12noon–2.30pm; dinner Friday to Saturday 7pm–9.45pm, Monday to Thursday 6.30pm–9pm, Sunday 6.30pm–8.45pm; bar meals Monday to Saturday 6.30pm–9.30pm, Sunday 7pm–9pm.
Cuisine: ENGLISH / FRENCH – traditional cuisine, including carvery. Good wine list.
Cards: Visa, Access, AmEx.
Other points: licensed, Sunday lunch, no-smoking area, children welcome, pets allowed, afternoon tea, open bank holidays, baby-listening device, cots, foreign exchange.
Rooms: 5 single rooms, 20 double rooms, 22 twin rooms. All with TV, telephone, tea/coffee-making facilities.
Directions: second turn off roundabout at end of A45, to port. At port, take first turning. Proceed over traffic lights, taking first left. Hotel is 250 yards on the left.
MICHAEL HOLLMAN ☎ (01394) 285621.

THE WAVERLEY HOTEL
Wolsey Gardens, IP11 7DF
The Waverley is a beautiful, recently refurbished Victorian-style hotel standing high on the cliff, offering spectacular views of the sea and promenade. Wolsey's Restaurant provides an excellent à la carte menu as well as specially

priced, changing daily menus. There is always a selection of fresh fish and seafood, game, poultry and meat dishes available. Lighter meals available in Gladstones Bar and Brasserie, where a selection of real ales is always available.
DOUBLE ROOM: from £20 to £30
SINGLE ROOM: from £45 to £55
FOOD: up to £15
Hours: lunch 12noon–2pm, dinner 7pm–9.30pm.
Cuisine: ENGLISH / CONTINENTAL – varied à la carte menu in the restaurant. Bar meals include steaks, fresh fish, chilli, lasagne, salads and home-made pies, with daily changing specials.
Cards: Visa, Access, Diners, AmEx.
Other points: Sunday lunch, children welcome, weekend breaks, Christmas packages, functions.
Rooms: 4 single rooms, 9 double rooms, 6 twin rooms, 1 family room. All with en suite, satellite TV, telephone, tea/coffee-making facilities, radio, hair dryer, trouser-press. Most rooms have sea views; some have lovely balconies.
Directions: above Under Cliff Road, one minute from main high street.
MR KEVIN AVERY ☎ (01394) 282811
Fax (01394) 670185.

FRAMLINGHAM • map 10D6

THE OLD MILL HOUSE
Saxtead Green, IP13 9QE
This delightful pub has been beautifully restored with open fires, flagstone floors and timber beams. It offers an excellent menu, a special lunchtime buffet, coupled with a range of fine cask ales. Families welcome. The garden has a large fishpond and is situated on the village green, opposite the famous windmill. A must for connoisseurs of good food, ales and wines.
FOOD: from £15 to £20
Hours: lunch 12noon–2pm, dinner 7pm–9pm.
Cuisine: ENGLISH / CONTINENTAL.
Cards: Visa, Access, MasterCard.
Other points: parking, children welcome, no-smoking area, open-air dining, vegetarian meals, traditional Sunday lunch.
Directions: situated on the village green at Saxtead Green, on B1119.
NICK BARLOW & RUTH SHEPHERD
☎ (01728) 685064.

HAUGHLEY • map 10D5

THE OLD COUNTING HOUSE RESTAURANT
Near Stowmarket, IP14 3NR
Typical Suffolk timber-framed house dating back to the 1500s when it was a bank. Now you may dine at tables set with damask linen, fine glassware and classic cutlery.
FOOD: from £15 to £20
Hours: lunch (Monday to Friday) 12noon–2pm, dinner (Monday to Saturday) 7.15pm–9.30pm, closed Sunday.
Cuisine: ENGLISH / FRENCH – lunch: two- or three-course table d'hôte plus à la carte. Dinner:

four-course table d'hôte, six choices for each course, changed every three weeks. Also bistro menu available for lunch and dinner.
Cards: Visa, Access, Diners, AmEx.
Other points: licensed, children welcome.
Directions: 3 miles west of Stowmarket, 1½ miles along A14. At Haughley centre.
MR & MRS P. WOODS ☎ (01449) 673617.

KERSEY • map 10E5

THE BELL INN
The Street, near Ipswich, IP7 6DY
Built in 1320, this timber-framed inn is situated in one of the prettiest villages in Suffolk. The beautiful inn with its restaurant and two bars offers a friendly, informal atmosphere in delightful surroundings. It is the perfect venue for a romantic dinner for two, private parties or a relaxing evening, sampling the excellent selection of real ales and fine wines.
FOOD: from £15 to £20
Hours: lunch 12noon–2.30pm, dinner 7pm–9.30pm.
Cuisine: ENGLISH / CONTINENTAL – creative cuisine.
Cards: Visa, Access.
Other points: parking, children welcome, pets allowed, no-smoking area, open-air dining, vegetarian meals, traditional Sunday lunch.
Directions: north of A1071 (Hadleigh to Lavenham).
JIMMY & ORLA CULLEN ☎ (01473) 823229.

LONG MELFORD • map 10E5

THE COCK & BELL INN
Hall Street, CO10 9JR
This beautiful Grade II listed coaching inn is situated in the centre of Long Melford, well-known for its antiques. It offers a wealth of English charm with a quiet, intimate restaurant, ideal for families, and with letting rooms, making this the perfect destination for tourists.
DOUBLE ROOM: up to £20
FOOD: from £15 to £20
Hours: breakfast 8.30am–10am, lunch 11.30am–3pm, dinner 6pm–10pm.
Cuisine: ENGLISH.
Cards: Visa, Access.
Other points: parking, children welcome, pets allowed, no-smoking area, conference facilities, vegetarian meals, traditional Sunday lunch.
Rooms: 2 bedrooms. Both with tea/coffee-making facilities.
Directions: from Sudbury, follow signs off Bury Road, on A134.
MARK BELLERBY & KAREN BROWN ☎ (01787) 379807 Fax (01787) 379807.

CROWN INN HOTEL
Hall Street, CO10 9JL
This historic family-run inn, originally built in 1610, still retains many of its interesting architectural features. The warm and friendly hospitality of the

inn prevails throughout, whether relaxing in the comfortable bar or enjoying a home-cooked meal in the intimate restaurant. The lovely Suffolk countryside provides many enjoyable walks and popular attractions nearby.
DOUBLE ROOM: from £20 to £30
FOOD: up to £15 [CLUB]
Hours: breakfast 8am–9.30am, lunch 12noon–2pm, bar snacks 12noon–2pm, dinner 7pm–9pm, bar snacks 7pm–9pm.
Cuisine: ENGLISH.
Cards: Visa, Access.
Other points: parking, children welcome, no-smoking area, residents' lounge, garden, open-air dining, vegetarian meals, traditional Sunday lunch.
Rooms: 11 bedrooms. All with TV, tea/coffee-making facilities.
Directions: located in the centre of Long Melford.
MR & MRS QUINCEY ☎ (01787) 377666 [Fax] (01787) 311325.

LOWESTOFT • map 10D6

WHERRY HOTEL
Bridge Road, Oulton Broad, NR32 3LN
Easy access and a first-class setting allow guests from far and near to relax in the hotel or take in the sights along the delightful inland waterways, renowned as the famous Norfolk Broads. The Wherry Hotel has been completely refurbished and offers a variety of amenities for the guests' requirements and comfort. Large conference facilities, catering for up to 140, are available for functions and conferences.
DOUBLE ROOM: from £30 to £40
SINGLE ROOM: from £45 to £55
FOOD: from £15 to £20
Hours: breakfast 7.30am–9am, lunch 12noon–2pm, bar meals 12noon–2pm, dinner 7pm–10pm, bar meals 7pm–9pm.
Cards: Visa, Access, Diners, AmEx, Switch.
Other points: children welcome, parking, vegetarian meals, pets.
Rooms: 32 twin rooms.
Directions: On A117. From London, A12 towards Lowestoft, follow signs to Oulton Broad.
MR A. LOCK ☎ (01502) 573521 [Fax] (01502) 501350.

MILDENHALL • map 10D5

THE SMOKE HOUSE
Beck Row, IP28 8DH
Tony and Inez Warin extend a warm welcome to this atmospheric 16th century establishment, set in the heart of the East Anglian countryside. It has an established reputation for its friendly staff and caring attitude, good food and accommodation. Ideal for the country lover and sportsman, offering fishing, shooting, riding, and horse-racing at nearby Newmarket. Ten golf courses nearby.
DOUBLE ROOM: from £40 to £50
SINGLE ROOM: from £55
FOOD: from £15 to £20 [CLUB]

Hours: breakfast 7am–9.30am, lunch 12noon–2pm, dinner 5pm–10pm, bar meals 11am–2.30pm, bar meals 5pm–11pm, open all year.
Cuisine: ENGLISH – à la carte and table d'hôte, offering a wide range of traditional English dishes.
Cards: Visa, Access, Diners, AmEx, Switch.
Other points: licensed, Sunday lunch, no-smoking area, children welcome, afternoon tea, residents' lounge, garden, parking, baby-listening device, 24hr reception, foreign exchange.
Rooms: 18 double rooms, 83 twin rooms. All with TV, radio, alarm, telephone, tea/coffee-making facilities.
Directions: 4 miles from A11 Barton Mills roundabout on A1101, near Mildenhall.
TONY & INEZ WARIN ☎ (01638) 713223 [Fax] (01638) 712202.

ORFORD • map 10E6

CROWN & CASTLE HOTEL
Near Woodbridge, IP12 2LJ
Set in the market square next to Orford Castle, on the beautiful Suffolk coast, the Crown & Castle is tastefully and comfortably furnished and provides good, traditional fare. Popular with all ages, the hotel enjoys a pleasant, relaxed atmosphere. Ten en suite rooms have private access to a garden overlooking the castle.
DOUBLE ROOM: from £20 to £30
FOOD: up to £15
Hours: breakfast 8am–9.30am, lunch 12noon–2pm, dinner 7pm–9pm.
Cuisine: ENGLISH – predominantly English cuisine.
Cards: Visa, Access, Diners, AmEx.
Other points: licensed, open-air dining, Sunday lunch, children welcome, open bank holidays, afternoon tea, pets allowed.
Rooms: 2 single rooms, 6 double rooms, 12 twin rooms. All with TV, telephone, tea/coffee-making facilities.
Directions: turn off the A12 at Woodbridge.
SARAH MANN ☎ (01394) 450205 [Fax] (01394) 450176.

SAXMUNDHAM • map 10D6

THE OLD CHEQUERS
Aldeburgh Road, Friston, IP17 1NP
This ever-popular, attractive country inn has established an excellent reputation for its fine cuisine, specializing in local fresh fish and game. The delightful decor of the restaurant and bar have been tastefully refurbished to create a warm and friendly atmosphere. Situated just a few miles from Aldeburgh on the Suffolk coast, it is well worth a visit.
FOOD: from £15 to £20
Hours: lunch 12noon–2pm, dinner from 7pm.
Cuisine: ENGLISH / EUROPEAN.
Cards: Visa, Access.
Other points: parking, children welcome, open-air dining, vegetarian meals, traditional Sunday lunch.

SUFFOLK • SE ENGLAND & EAST ANGLIA

Directions: 3 miles off A12 on the way to Aldeburgh.
DAVID & SALLY GRIMWOOD ☎ (01728) 688270.

SOUTHWOLD • map 10D6

SUTHERLAND HOUSE RESTAURANT
56 High Street, IP18 6DN
Built in the 16th century, Sutherland House was once the headquarters of an admiral who became King of England, James II. Today it carefully preserves its historic past and specializes in good food and refreshment of high quality. You can be assured of welcoming service, well-presented, fresh home-cooked food, and good value-for-money prices.
DOUBLE ROOM: from £20 to £30
FOOD: up to £15
Hours: breakfast 9am–10am, Sunday lunch 12noon–2pm, dinner 7pm–9pm, open for dinner 7 days in summer.
Cuisine: ENGLISH – a daily menu featuring all fresh, home-cooked local produce. Fresh, local fish dishes are a speciality. Informal brasserie-style cuisine.
Cards: Visa, Access.
Other points: licensed, Sunday lunch, no smoking in bedrooms.
Rooms: 3 double rooms. All with TV, tea/coffee-making facilities.
Directions: 4 miles from A12, on High Street in the centre of Southwold.
PAUL & MARGARET SAMAIN ☎ (01502) 722260.

WOODBRIDGE • map 10E6

BULL HOTEL
Market Hill, IP12 4LR
A 16th century coaching inn on the A12 in the centre of town. Facilities for conferences, private hire and receptions.
DOUBLE ROOM: from £20 to £30
FOOD: up to £15
Hours: breakfast 7.30am–9.30am, lunch 12noon–2pm, dinner 7pm–10pm.
Cuisine: ENGLISH – home-made soup, steaks, bar snacks.
Cards: Visa, Access, Diners, AmEx.
Other points: Sunday lunch, no-smoking area, children welcome, residents' lounge, residents' bar.
Rooms: 4 single rooms, 10 double rooms, 7 twin rooms, 2 triple rooms, 1 family room. All with TV, telephone, tea/coffee-making facilities.
Directions: on A12 in town centre.
NEVILLE & ANNE ALLEN ☎ (01394) 382089
Fax (01394) 384902.

CAPTAIN'S TABLE
3 Quay Street, IR12 1BX
This fish and seafood restaurant has a timbered interior with a distinct nautical flavour to the decor. Very close to the river and the town centre.
FOOD: from £15 to £20

Hours: lunch 12noon–2pm, dinner 6.30pm–9.30pm, closed Monday.
Cuisine: SEAFOOD – local seafood.
Cards: Visa, Access, Diners, AmEx.
Other points: open-air dining, no-smoking area, children welcome.
Directions: close to the quayside and town centre.
MR A.J. PRENTICE ☎ (01394) 383145.

WOOD HALL HOTEL & COUNTRY CLUB
Shottisham, IP12 3EG
Set in ten acres of magnificent grounds, this imposing Elizabethan manor house has been completely refurbished to a luxurious standard. The hotel offers individually decorated, luxury bedrooms, three intimate candlelit restaurants, an elegant lounge with a real log fire, a superb banqueting suite, its own exclusive leisure club and 'Woodies' unique night-club.
DOUBLE ROOM: from £30 to £40
SINGLE ROOM: from £45 to £55
FOOD: up to £15 CLUB
Hours: breakfast 7.30am–9.30am, lunch 12noon–3pm, dinner 7pm–10pm, bar snacks 12noon–3pm, bar snacks 6pm–9pm.
Cuisine: MODERN ENGLISH / FRENCH – all dishes are carefully prepared with special attention to detail.
Cards: Visa, Access, Diners, AmEx.
Other points: parking, children welcome, no-smoking area, disabled access, vegetarian meals.
Rooms: 15 bedrooms. All en suite.
Directions: take the A12 north through Woodbridge to the A1152 junction. Turn right towards Melton and after two miles take the B1083 south to Shottisham.
HARVEY AND CAROLE STORCH ☎ (01394) 411283 Fax (01394) 410007.

WRENTHAM • map 10D6

QUIGGINS RESTAURANT
2 High Street, near Beccles, NR34 7HB
An elegant yet comfortable and relaxing, beamed restaurant, decorated with plants, family pictures and knick-knacks to create a homely atmosphere. The food is well-cooked and presented. A choice of main course may include filet au fromage, Brigit's plum duck and prawn creole, among others. Warm and courteous service. Wide range of wines with emphasis on New World varieties. Quiggins adhere to the BTA's 'Restaurant Customers Charter'.
FOOD: from £15 to £20 CLUB
Hours: lunch 11.30am–2pm, dinner 7pm–10pm, closed Sunday evening and Monday.
Cuisine: ENGLISH / INTERNATIONAL – all made from fresh ingredients, including English puddings. Established reputation for quality seafood.
Cards: Visa, Access, Switch, Delta.
Other points: licensed, open-air dining, Sunday lunch, no-smoking area, children welcome, close to beach.
Directions: situated on crossroads in centre of Wrentham. On the A12.
DUDLEY & JILL McNALLY ☎ (01502) 675397.

SURREY

Towns in Surrey that are actually part of Greater London can be found in *Greater London*, pages 30–53.

BLETCHINGLEY • map 6C4

WILLIAM IV
Little Common Lane, RH1 4QG

A traditional, unspoilt British village pub with compact bars and an old English garden. The pub offers an extensive à la carte and bar-meals menu, with dishes ranging from salmon en croute to home-made steak-and-kidney pie. Friendly, efficient service complements the warm, bustling atmosphere of the pub. Ideally situated for walks over the North Downs and Tillgates Gardens.
FOOD: up to £15
Hours: lunch 12noon–2pm, dinner 7pm–9.15pm.
Cuisine: ENGLISH / INTERNATIONAL – extensive menu including grills, home-made pies, curries, pizzas, fish dishes. Daily specials and bar meals. Dining room.
Cards: Visa, Access.
Other points: licensed, open-air dining, children welcome, beer garden, pets allowed (under control).
Directions: Little Common Lane is located at top of Bletchingley High Street (A25). Signposted to Merstham.
BRIAN & SANDRA STRANGE ☎ (01883) 743278.

CHARLWOOD • map 6C4

RUSS HILL HOTEL
Russ Hill, near Gatwick, RH6 0EL

Built in the late 1800s as a fine country manor house, this hotel is rich in Victorian charm and elegance, enjoying panoramic views of Surrey's hills. All 150 air-conditioned bedrooms feature the most modern facilities, with furnishings of the highest standard. Superb health and leisure centre, conference and banqueting facilities are also available. Ideal for Gatwick Airport and many nearby places of interest. A courtesy coach to Gatwick Airport is available to guests.
DOUBLE ROOM: from £20 to £30
FOOD: up to £15
Hours: bar snacks 12noon–12midnight, breakfast 6.30am–10am, dinner 7pm–10pm.
Cuisine: INTERNATIONAL.
Other points: parking, children catered for (please check for age limits), open bank holidays, Sunday dinner, disabled access, pets allowed, residents' lounge, vegetarian meals, conferences, garden, leisure club.
Rooms: 19 single rooms, 96 double rooms, 25 twin rooms, 12 family rooms.
Directions: from A23 follow signs to Charlwood. At the end of the village turn left into Rectory Lane: the hotel is at the top of the hill. Close to Gatwick Zoo.
MR H.E. SKALNIK ☎ (01293) 862171
Fax (01293) 862390.

CHERTSEY • map 5C3

THE CROWN HOTEL
7 London Street, KT16 8AP

This comfortable hotel is popular with tourists and locals alike, whether relaxing in the bar or soaking up the atmosphere and sampling the fine food in the restaurant. The private bedrooms have every possible modern facility to make you feel at home. The special conference suite, accommodating up to 100 people, can also be used for private celebrations and dinner dances. Ideally located for London, Heathrow and Gatwick and also the tourist areas of Hampton Court, Windsor and Windsor Great Park.
DOUBLE ROOM: from £30 to £40
SINGLE ROOM: over £55
FOOD: up to £15
Hours: breakfast 7am–10am, lunch 12noon–2pm, bar snacks 12noon–2.30pm, dinner 7pm–10pm, closed Saturday lunch.
Cuisine: ENGLISH.
Other points: parking, children welcome, no-smoking area, disabled access, pets allowed, residents' lounge, garden, vegetarian meals, open-air dining.
Rooms: 30 bedrooms. All with TV, telephone, tea/coffee-making facilities.
Directions: off M25, junction 11, follow signs for Chertsey town centre. Situated behind Sainsbury Centre.
MR W. PETTERS ☎ (01932) 564657
Fax (01932) 570839.

COBHAM • map 5C3

WOODLANDS PARK HOTEL
Woodlands Lane, Stoke D'Abernon, KT11 3QB

The Woodlands Park Hotel is a magnificent Victorian mansion, pleasantly set in its own landscaped grounds. At the turn of the century, the then Prince of Wales and the famous actress Lillie Langtry were frequent visitors. Today the hotel is ideally located for touring the picturesque Surrey and Berkshire countryside, the great gardens and stately homes.
DOUBLE ROOM: from £50
SINGLE ROOM: over £55
FOOD: from £15 to £20
Hours: breakfast 7am–9.30am, lunch 12.30am–2.30pm, dinner 7pm–9.30pm, brasserie 11am–11pm, closed 24th December until 31st December.
Cuisine: ENGLISH / FRENCH.
Cards: Visa, Access, Diners, AmEx.
Other points: parking, children welcome, open-air dining, conference facilities, vegetarian meals.
Rooms: 5 single rooms, 35 double rooms,

13 twin rooms, 5 suites. All with tea-making facilities, TV, telephone, radio, hair dryer, trouser-press, room service.
Directions: on A245, junction 10 off M25, or Cobham off A3.
MR M. DICKSON ☎ (01372) 843933 Fax (01372) 842704.

CRANLEIGH • map 5D3

BRICKS RESTAURANT
Smithbrook Kilns, GU5 8PT
Situated in a multi-workshop craft centre in an old brickworks. Self-service from kitchen counter with table service for drinks, desserts and coffee. Waitress service in evenings.
FOOD: up to £15
Hours: lunch 12noon–2pm, dinner 7.30pm–9.45pm, closed bank holidays, 25th December until 27th December and New Year's day.
Cuisine: INTERNATIONAL – menus change daily, offering a selection of casseroles with hot potatoes, salads, French bread and butter. All desserts are made on the premises.
Cards: Visa, Access.
Other points: open-air dining, Sunday lunch, children welcome, coaches by prior arrangement
Directions: on A281, just north of crossroads with B2127.
MRS H. RUSSELL-DAVIS ☎ (01483) 276780.

LA SCALA RESTAURANT
High Street, GU6 8RF
A well-established and popular restaurant under the current ownership for over 20 years. Situated on the first floor above a jeweller's shop on the high street. The menu offers an interesting selection of Italian favourites and regional cuisine.
FOOD: up to £15 CLUB
Hours: lunch 12noon–2pm, dinner 6.30pm, closed Sunday and Monday.
Cuisine: ITALIAN – veal escalopa a la crema, sole Isoladoro, fettucini crema, mussels.
Cards: Visa, Access.
Other points: open-air dining, children welcome.
Directions: on A281 Guildford to Horsham road.
ROSARIO MAZZOTTA ☎ (01483) 274900.

EPSOM • map 1E2

EPSOM DOWNS HOTEL
9 Longdown Road, KT17 3PT
A friendly hotel with a cosy, inviting atmosphere and excellent, individual service. Comfortably furnished and attractively decorated, the hotel offers well-appointed accommodation and very good food. All dishes are tasty and served in generous portions. You are guaranteed the warmest of welcomes by the manager, Jenny Clark, and her staff.
DOUBLE ROOM: from £30 to £40
FOOD: from £15 to £20
Hours: breakfast weekdays 7.30am–9.30am, weekends 8.30am–10.30am, lunch 12.30am–2pm, dinner 7.30pm–9.30pm, closed for one week over Christmas.
Cuisine: ENGLISH / CONTINENTAL – traditional English and continental cuisine such as lemon sole, rack of lamb roasted with honey and served with a herb and garlic sauce.
Cards: Visa, Access, Diners, AmEx.
Other points: licensed, children welcome, residents' lounge, garden, children welcome, cots, 24hr reception.
Rooms: 9 single rooms, 3 double rooms, 2 twin rooms. All with TV, telephone, tea/coffee-making facilities.
Directions: quiet, residential area on the eastern (Banstead) side of Epsom.
JENNY CLARK (manager) ☎ (01372) 740643 Fax (01372) 723259.

ESHER • map 1E2

ALBERT ARMS
82 High Street, KT10 9QS
Situated close to Hampton Court and to Sandown Park and Kempton race courses, The Albert Arms is a traditional pub with a restaurant extension.
FOOD: up to £15
Hours: breakfast 10.30am–12noon, lunch 12noon–3pm, dinner 7.30pm–10pm, bar meals 11am–3pm, 7.30pm–10pm.
Cuisine: ENGLISH / ITALIAN – wide range of dishes including grills, salads, steaks, pies, casseroles and Italian specialities.
Cards: Visa, Access, Diners, AmEx.
Other points: licensed, Sunday lunch, children welcome.
Directions: off the A3 London–Guildford road, on the A304 in Esher.
JEAN & BRUCE MONTGOMERY ☎ (01372) 465290 Fax (01372) 469217.

FARNHAM • map 5C3

SEVENS WINE BAR & BISTRO
7 The Borough, GU9 7NA
An 18th century beamed black-and-white restaurant situated in the centre of Farnham, serving tasty, well-prepared food. In summer you can dine in the garden, but whatever the month and setting the food is always good and the service excellent. The friendly, welcoming staff and relaxing, informal atmosphere makes this bistro a pleasure to visit. Fully air-conditioned.
FOOD: up to £15
Hours: morning coffee 9.30am–12noon, lunch 12noon–2.30pm, afternoon tea 2.30pm–6.30pm, dinner 6.30pm–11pm, closed Sunday.
Cuisine: FRENCH – French-style bistro, including home-made dishes, home-made sweets. Menus change monthly and blackboard specials daily.
Cards: Visa, Access.
Other points: licensed, children welcome, garden, afternoon tea, barbecues.
Directions: in the centre of Farnham, very close to Castle Street and market.
MR A.C. GREEN ☎ (01252) 715345.

SE ENGLAND & EAST ANGLIA • SURREY

GODALMING • map 5C3

THE MONGOLIAN
10–14 Wolf Street, GU7 1NQ
Discover the unique style of eating which exemplifies an age-old tradition from the homelands of Mongolia. Fill your bowl with a selection of meat or fish, then your choice of vegetables and noodles. Add to this a mixture of delicious marinades and sauces, aromatic herbs and spices and watch your meal being barbecued on the large, curved hotplate in the centre of the restaurant. Fun, friendly and enthusiastic crowd. There is a baby changing-room with full changing facilities, bottle-warmers, etc., and special offers throughout the year for children.
FOOD: up to £15 ☆
Hours: dinner from 6pm, Saturday from 4.30pm, open all day Sunday from 12.30am, closed Christmas day and New Year's day.
Cuisine: MONGOLIAN – barbecue-style cuisine, enhanced with aromatic spices and seasonings.
Cards: Visa, Access, AmEx.
Other points: licensed, Sunday lunch, children welcome.
Directions: on junction of B3001 and B2130, opposite the police station.
GLENN & CLARE WATERFALL ☎ (01483) 414155.

GUILDFORD • map 5C3

KINGS SHADE COFFEE HOUSE
20 Tunsgate, GU1 3QS
Well situated between the famous Guildhall clock and the superb Castle gardens. Kings Shade Coffee House is open all day and is a very popular venue in which to enjoy a meal or snack. The menu is extensive, the atmosphere bustling and the service friendly and efficient. The home-made sweets are particularly recommended.
FOOD: up to £15 CLUB
Hours: meals all day 8.30am–6pm, closed Sunday.
Cuisine: ENGLISH – house specialities include steak-and-kidney pie, chicken and spinach gratin, lasagne. Salads, toasted savouries, stuffed baked potatoes, sandwiches. Morning coffee, lunch, light meals and afternoon tea are also available.
Other points: licensed, afternoon tea, air-conditioned.
Directions: off the high street, opposite the Guildhall.
DAVID GOLDSBY ☎ (01483) 576718.

LEATHERHEAD • map 6C4

THE STAR
Kingston Road, KT22 0DP
In a convenient position close to Chessington World of Adventures and the M25, The Star serves good-quality bar meals. A very popular, busy pub.
FOOD: up to £15
Hours: lunch 12noon–2pm, dinner 5.30pm–10pm.
Cuisine: ENGLISH – house speciality: fresh Scottish beef steaks cooked over charcoal.

Cards: Visa, Access, Diners, AmEx.
Other points: licensed, open-air dining, Sunday lunch, coaches by prior arrangement
Directions: on the A243 one mile from Leatherhead. Close to Chessington and M25.
COLIN & IRENE SUCKLING ☎ (0137284) 2416.

REIGATE • map 6C4

CRANLEIGH HOTEL
41 West Street, RH2 9BL
The Cranleigh Hotel is set in one of the last unspoilt towns fringing the magnificent forested North Downs, famous for its pilgrims, Romans and spring-waters. Owned and managed by the Bussandri family for over 20 years, who have in this time achieved an unsurpassable reputation for friendliness, care and quality hospitality. The house has been carefully restored to include luxurious bedrooms, fine public rooms and a grand conservatory, leading on to their pride: a garden and orchard, overlooking a swimming pool and tennis courts.
DOUBLE ROOM: from £20 to £30
SINGLE ROOM: from £35 to £45
FOOD: up to £15 ☆
Hours: breakfast 7.30am–9.30am, dinner 7pm–9pm, closed 24th December until 26th December (inclusive).
Cuisine: INTERNATIONAL.
Other points: parking, children welcome, residents' lounge, garden, vegetarian meals, open-air dining.
Rooms: 9 bedrooms.
Directions: on A25, at end of Reigate High Street going west.
MR G. BUSSANDRI ☎ (01737) 223417
Fax (01737) 223734.

THE MARKET HOTEL
High Street, RH2 9AY
Situated in the centre of Reigate, this lively pub does much to justify its continuing popularity. A good selection of real ales, bottled and continental lagers make the perfect complement to well-cooked food, all at reasonable prices.
FOOD: up to £15
Hours: meals all day 12noon–9.30pm, open all year including bank holidays.
Cuisine: ENGLISH – traditional English pub food, prepared to a high standard. Generous portions complemented by a fine selection of wines, ales and lagers.
Cards: Visa, Access.
Other points: licensed, open-air dining, Sunday lunch, no-smoking area, children welcome, morning tea, afternoon tea, garden.
Directions: at centre of town, by clocktower.
MARKET TAVERNS LIMITED ☎ (01737) 240492 Fax (01737) 226221.

WALTON-ON-THAMES • map 1E1

SIXTIES WINE BAR
New Zealand Avenue, KT12 1QB
The small bar area of the 36-seater wine bar leaves plenty of room for the restaurant. The cosy

92

atmosphere, varied wine list and good food make this a popular spot with the locals.
FOOD: from £15 to £20
Hours: lunch 12noon–2.15pm, dinner 6pm–10.15pm, closed Sunday and Monday evening.
Cuisine: ENGLISH – fresh, local produce. Each dish cooked to order. No frozen foods.
Cards: Visa, Access, Diners, AmEx.
Other points: LICENSED.
Directions: Walton-on-Thames is situated one mile from the A3.
MR & MRS NEIL BARKBY ☎ (01932) 221685.

WEST SUSSEX

ARUNDEL • map 5D3

SWAN HOTEL
27–29 High Street, BN18 9AG
Situated in the heart of historic Arundel, the Swan Hotel has been been lovingly restored to its former Victorian splendour. Many of the hotel's original features, including English oak flooring and wall panelling, are still very much in evidence, creating a wonderful ambience in the hotel's bar and lounge areas. The Grade II listed building offers luxurious accommodation, combining traditional comforts with modern facilities. The hotel is close to Arundel's 12th century castle, the River Arun, cathedral and parks.
DOUBLE ROOM: from £20 to £30
SINGLE ROOM: from £45 to £55
FOOD: from £15 to £20
Hours: breakfast 6.30am–10.30am, lunch 12noon–2.30pm, dinner 6.30pm–9.30pm.
Cuisine: ENGLISH – locally acclaimed chef Michael Collis has created a range of succulent dishes to suit all tastes, with seasonal and local produce used extensively throughout the à la carte menu. Wines can be selected from the original 200-year-old cellar, which stocks a wide choice of quality wines from around the world. Local traditional ales.
Cards: Visa, Access, Diners, AmEx.
Other points: vegetarian meals, afternoon teas, traditional Sunday lunch.
Rooms: 15 bedrooms. All with en suite, TV, telephone, hair dryer, tea/coffee-making facilities, room service.
Directions: Arundel is just off the A27, midway between Chichester and Worthing. The hotel is located on the High Street.
ARUNDEL BREWERY ☎ (01903) 882314 [Fax] (01903) 733381.

BOGNOR REGIS • map 5D3

THE ROYAL HOTEL
The Esplanade, PU21 I52
A Victorian hotel situated only yards from the sea, with unimpeded views from the restaurant, bars and coffee shop.
DOUBLE ROOM: from £20 to £30
FOOD: from £15 to £20 [CLUB]
Hours: breakfast 7.30am–9.30am, lunch 12noon–2.30pm, bar meals 11.30am–10.30pm, dinner 6pm–10.30pm.
Cuisine: ENGLISH / CONTINENTAL – prawns, pasta, lobster.
Cards: Visa, Access, Diners, AmEx.
Other points: licensed, Sunday lunch, children welcome, coaches by prior arrangement
Directions: on Bognor Regis seafront, 50 yards west of the pier.
DAVID M. COOMBS ☎ (01243) 864665/864666.

CHICHESTER • map 5D3

ANGLESEY ARMS
Halnaker, PO18 0NQ
A small, friendly, traditional pub serving real ales. The single bar and attractive garden are both very popular. Only two miles from Goodwood Racecourse and four miles from Chichester harbour. There is a separate restaurant area.
FOOD: up to £15
Hours: lunch 12noon–2pm, dinner 7.30pm–12midnight, last orders 10pm, closed Christmas day and New Year's day.
Cuisine: ENGLISH – peppered fillet steak, fresh Selsey lobster and crab, locally smoked salmon and ham, traditional roast Sunday lunch.
Cards: Visa, Access, Diners, AmEx.
Other points: licensed, children welcome.
Directions: close to the A27. Take the A285 to Halnaker. The pub is one mile up on the right, just after Halnaker cross-roads.
CHRISTOPHER & TESSA HOUSEMAN
☎ (01243) 773474 [Fax] (01243) 530034.

BULL'S HEAD AND SUSSEX BARN
Main Road, Fishbourne, PO19 3JP
This 17th century pub, in the small village of Fishbourne on the outskirts of Chichester, offers a very attractive bar and good home-cooked food. A wide selection of first-class pub food is available daily for lunch and dinner, served by the friendly, efficient staff, under the supervision of Roger Jackson. Close to the coast, the pub is within easy travelling distance of Portsmouth and Hayling Island.
FOOD: up to £15
Hours: lunch 12noon–3pm, dinner 7pm–10.30pm, bar snacks also available.
Cuisine: ENGLISH – fresh food is used in preparing all meals.
Cards: Visa, Access, AmEx.
Other points: children welcome, parking, vegetarian meals.
Directions: located on the A259, off the A27 Chichester to Portsmouth Road.
ROGER JACKSON ☎ (01243) 785707.

EARL OF MARCH
Mid Lavant, PO18 0BQ
Excellent service by well-trained staff will make this a good stop for those travelling in the area. Comfortable surroundings and good food can be found here.
FOOD: up to £15
Hours: lunch 12.30am–2pm, dinner 6pm–11pm, last orders 10pm, Sunday 7pm–9.30pm.
Cuisine: ENGLISH – varied selection of traditional cuisine. Special vegetarian dishes. Bar food.
Cards: Visa, Access.
Other points: licensed, open-air dining, Sunday lunch, children welcome, pets allowed.
Directions: 2 miles from Chichester on the A286.
MR A.L. LAURIN ☎ (01243) 774751.

EASTON HOUSE
Chidham Lane, Chidham, PO18 8TF
A former 16th century farmhouse situated on the Chidham peninsula. Within easy reach of Goodwood, Chichester, Portsmouth and the New Forest. Uncrowded and peaceful waterside walks within 5 minutes of the house. The bedrooms overlook either farmland, the harbour or the garden.
DOUBLE ROOM: from £20 to £30
Hours: breakfast 8am–9am.
Cuisine: BREAKFAST.
Other points: central heating, no evening meal, children welcome, residents' lounge, garden.
Directions: 1 mile south of the A259.
MRS C.M. HARTLEY ☎ (01243) 572514.

MICAWBER'S RESTAURANT
13 South Street, PO19 1EH
Situated just south of the Cross, this popular restaurant has a provincial French character. The fruits de mer are cooked by the chef directly after he gets them from the local fishermen.
FOOD: up to £15 CLUB
Hours: closed Sunday, dinner 6pm–10.30pm, lunch 11.30am–2.30pm.
Cuisine: FRENCH / ENGLISH – wide selection of fish dishes and shellfish, fresh meat and vegetables, all from local markets.
Cards: Visa, Access, Diners, AmEx.
Other points: children welcome, French spoken.
Directions: situated just south of the Cross at Chichester.
PHILIP COTTERILL & THIERRY BOISHU
☎ (01243) 786989.

PLATTERS RESTAURANT
15 Southgate, PO19 1ES
A sumptuous meal in this Mediterranean-style restaurant is assured, with very personal attention from the friendly staff. House specialities change from day to day, and you may even be treated to an explanation of the more interesting ingredients, such as local wild mushrooms. Chefs enjoying a break from their own restaurants are known to dine here – high praise indeed.
FOOD: from £15 to £20 CLUB
Hours: lunch 12noon–2pm, dinner 7pm, closed Sunday and Tuesday.
Cuisine: MEDITERRANEAN – à la carte and table d'hôte offering a range of imaginative dishes with daily changes. Vegetarian dishes always available.
Cards: Visa, Access.
Other points: licensed, open-air dining, children welcome, street parking.
Directions: 100 yards north of railway and bus station, opposite magistrates' court.
NIK WESTACOTT ☎ (01243) 530430.

CRAWLEY • map 6D4

GOFFS PARK HOTEL
Goffs Park Road, near Gatwick, RH11 8AX
Goffs Park Hotel is a modern country house situated in a peaceful residential area, close to Crawley town centre and within easy reach of the M23 and Gatwick airport. The newly refurbished restaurant offers imaginative table d'hôte and à la carte menus, complemented by an interesting wine list. All rooms are furnished to a very high standard, with many modern facilities.
DOUBLE ROOM: from £30 to £40
SINGLE ROOM: from £55
FOOD: up to £15
Hours: breakfast 7am–9.30am, Sunday 8am–10am, lunch 12.30am–2pm, closed Saturday lunch, dinner 7pm–9.30pm.
Cuisine: ENGLISH / ITALIAN.
Cards: Visa, Access, Diners, AmEx.
Other points: licensed.
Rooms: 13 single rooms, 21 double rooms, 25 twin rooms, 2 family rooms. All rooms are en suite.
Directions: M23, junction 11, fourth exit off the roundabout (A23 Crawley). Follow dual carriageway, go over first roundabout, turn right at second roundabout. Goffs Park Road is second turning on right. Hotel is on the left.
STEVE DUNFORD ☎ (01293) 535447
Fax (01293) 542050.

FERNHURST • map 5D3

THE RED LION
The Green, GU27 3HY
One of the oldest buildings in the village, The Red Lion is an attractive stone-built inn overlooking the village green. With exposed beams and open log fires to add to the cosy atmosphere, you will find the good food and Mrs Heath's hospitality hard to pass by. This free-house also offers real ales and an extensive wine list.
FOOD: up to £15
Hours: lunch 12noon–2.30pm, dinner 7pm–10.30pm.
Cuisine: ENGLISH / CONTINENTAL – including breast of pigeon in a blackberry sauce, peppered chicken in a cream and Dijon sauce.
Cards: Visa, Access.
Other points: licensed, Sunday lunch, no-smoking area, children welcome, garden.
Directions: off the A286, situated in Fernhurst, 3 miles from Haslemere, Surrey.
MRS BRENDA HEATH ☎ (01428) 643112/653304.

HAYWARDS HEATH • map 6D4

INN THE PRIORY
Syresham Gardens, RH16 3LB
A lovely restaurant set in the surroundings of a Victorian priory chapel, with stained-glass windows, ornate wood carvings and a turret clock. Offers a freshly prepared carvery menu of high quality and good value. Conference facilities available. National Trust gardens and Bluebell steam railway located nearby.
FOOD: from £15 to £20 [CLUB] ☆
Hours: lunch 12noon–3pm, Sunday 11.45am–4pm, dinner 7pm–11.30pm.
Cuisine: ENGLISH – traditional English carvery. Fish and vegetarian menus available.
Cards: Visa, Access, Diners, AmEx.
Other points: licensed, Sunday lunch, children welcome.
Directions: take Caxton Way off Sussex Square roundabout on South Road.
DAVID & MARTINA WHITE ☎ (01444) 459533
[Fax] (01444) 459340.

THE SLOOP INN
Freshfield Lock, RH17 7NP
This attractive public house offers good-quality bar meals in comfortable surroundings. The service is warm and courteous and the pub enjoys a friendly, welcoming atmosphere.
FOOD: up to £15
Hours: lunch 12noon–2pm, dinner 7pm–9.30pm (Sunday to Thursday), 7pm–10pm (Friday and Saturday).
Cuisine: ENGLISH – extensive menu displayed on blackboards: changes daily.
Cards: Visa, Access, Diners, AmEx, Switch.
Other points: licensed, open-air dining, children welcome, pets allowed, beer garden, games room.
Directions: Off the A272 at Scaynes Hill near Haywards Heath. Approximately 1½ miles down Church Lane.
MR & MRS MILLS ☎ (01444) 831219.

HORSHAM • map 5D3

COUNTRYMAN INN
Shipley, RH13 8PL
A traditional old country pub with a very friendly atmosphere, set in 3,000 acres of Sussex farmland. Customers can enjoy delicious home-cooked meals, especially the deep-dish pies, which are made with fresh meat from the local farm. A very popular pub with the local community and country walkers. Places of interest nearby include Knepp Castle and Shipley Mill.
FOOD: up to £15 ☆
Hours: lunch 12noon–2pm, bar meals 12noon–2pm, dinner 7pm–9.30pm, bar meals 7pm–9pm.
Cuisine: ENGLISH – rural English cuisine, including speciality deep-dish pies and fresh fish. Good wine list.
Cards: Visa, Access.
Other points: open-air dining, Sunday lunch, children welcome, open bank holidays, functions.
Directions: follow A24 to Worthing, then A272

signs to Billingshurst. Second turn left, then 1 mile to bottom of lane.
ALAN VAUGHAN ☎ (01403) 741383.

LINDFIELD • map 6D4

BENT ARMS
98 High Street, RH16 2HP
The Bent Arms is part of a 16th century coaching inn, which sits in a typical English village with half-timbered houses, a lake and swans. It is popular with locals and has a friendly and relaxed atmosphere.
DOUBLE ROOM: from £20 to £30
SINGLE ROOM: from £25 to £35
FOOD: up to £15 [CLUB]
Hours: breakfast 7.30am, lunch 12noon–2.15pm, dinner 6.15pm–10.15pm.
Cuisine: ENGLISH – à la carte, bar meals/snacks. The speciality is spit-roast beef in the bar – sliced to order, hot.
Cards: Visa, Access, Diners, AmEx.
Other points: licensed, open-air dining, Sunday lunch, children welcome, garden, pets allowed.
Rooms: 9 bedrooms. All with en suite, TV, tea/coffee-making facilities.
Directions: 2 miles outside Haywards Heath station.
MR HOYLE ☎ (01444) 483146.

STEYNING • map 5D3

OLD TOLLGATE RESTAURANT & HOTEL
The Street, Bramber, BN44 3WE
Travellers passing through Bramber were, at one time, obliged to interrupt their journey to pay a few pence at a tollgate for the right to continue on their way. Today many still stop there, but only to enjoy the good food and hospitality offered by this establishment, which stands on the original site. Ideal for touring, or for visiting the ruins of nearby Bramber Castle.
DOUBLE ROOM: from £30 to £40
SINGLE ROOM: from £55
FOOD: from £15 to £20
Hours: breakfast 7.30am–9.30am, lunch 12noon–2pm, bar meals 12noon–2pm, dinner 7pm–9.30pm, open all year.
Cuisine: ENGLISH – traditional old-English cuisine, including shellfish, meats and salads, roasts, casseroles, poultry and savoury pies. Special Christmas menu.
Cards: Visa, Access, Diners, AmEx.
Other points: licensed, Sunday lunch, children welcome, residents' lounge, garden, parking, functions, conferences, residents' bar, disabled access, vegetarian meals.
Rooms: 31 bedrooms. All with satellite TV, telephone, tea/coffee-making facilities, hair dryer, trouser-press.
Directions: on A283; situated in Bramber village, 4 miles from Shoreham–by–Sea.
PETER SARGENT ☎ (01903) 879494
[Fax] (01903) 813399.

SE ENGLAND & EAST ANGLIA • WEST SUSSEX

● SPRINGWELLS HOTEL
9 High Street, BN4 3GG
A delightful 17th century Georgian hotel, with ivy wall-covering and large Georgian windows, situated on the High Street of the charming, unspoilt town of Steyning. Under the personal supervision of the owners, this hotel has been arranged and fitted to ensure maximum comfort for guests by providing attractive bedrooms and a large, sunny dining room for a hearty English breakfast.
DOUBLE ROOM: from £20 to £30
Hours: breakfast 7.15am–10am.
Cuisine: BREAKFAST.
Cards: Visa, Access, Diners, AmEx.
Other points: children welcome, swimming pool, residents' lounge, garden, vegetarian meals.
Directions: off A283.
MRS J. HESELGRAVE ☎ (01903) 812446/ 812043.

WEST MARDEN • map 5D3

≔ VICTORIA INN
Near Chichester, PO18 9EN
A deservedly popular pub in the heart of the Sussex countryside. The inn is family-run and enjoys a friendly atmosphere. Well-cooked and presented meals are served in the bar and in the small restaurant, and the emphasis is on home-cooked dishes. Vegetarian dishes on request. The inn has a well-appointed garden and terrace. Draught beers, including Gibbs Mews, Bishops Tipple and Bass.
FOOD: up to £15
Hours: lunch 12noon–2pm, dinner 7pm–9.30pm, Sunday 7pm–9pm.
Cuisine: ENGLISH – all dishes home-cooked. Daily blackboard menu served in both bar and restaurant.
Cards: Visa, Access, AmEx.
Other points: licensed, Sunday lunch, beer garden, open bank holidays.
Directions: on the B2146 road between the coast and Petersfield, situated nine miles west of Chichester.
JAMES NEVILLE ☎ (01705) 631330
Fax (01705) 631722.

WEST WITTERING • map 5D3

≔ THE LAMB INN
WEST WITTERING
Chichester Road, PO20 8QA
This traditional Sussex country freehouse specializes in real ales and home-cooking; the pies and toasted sandwiches are particularly recommended. The evening menu also features a range of local fresh fish, and during summer months (weather permitting) food is available in the pretty pub garden. With its good value and warm welcome, The Lamb Inn is popular with locals, visiting sailors and windsurfers.
FOOD: up to £15 ≔

Hours: lunch 12noon–2pm, dinner 7pm–9pm, bar 11am–2.30pm and 6pm–11pm, Sunday 12noon–3pm and 7pm–10.30pm.
Cuisine: ENGLISH – home-made food including pies and fresh fish (evenings).
Cards: Visa, Access.
Other points: licensed, open-air dining, limited Sunday lunch menu, no-smoking area, open bank holidays, dogs allowed (on lead), barbecues, parking, vegetarian meals.
Directions: on B2179, 500 yards beyond Itchenor turn. Sign opposite pub.
MR NIGEL CARTER ☎ (01243) 511105.

WORTHING • map 5D3

● THE COURT HOUSE
Sea Lane, Goring-by-Sea, BN12 4NY
Goring is just west of Worthing town. The Court House is an historic listed building within walking distance of the sea. There are train and bus services to the town centre, Sussex and London. Local attractions include yachting and windsurfing, the National Bowls Centre and other sports facilities.
DOUBLE ROOM: up to £20
SINGLE ROOM: up to £25
Hours: breakfast 8.15am–9am.
Cuisine: BREAKFAST.
Cards: Visa, Access, Eurocard, MasterCard.
Other points: children welcome, pets allowed, residents' lounge, garden, German spoken, French spoken, Dutch spoken.
Rooms: 1 single room, 4 twin rooms, 2 family rooms.
Directions: A259 from Worthing, 2 miles.
MRS I. GOMME ☎ (01903) 248473.

● KINGSWAY HOTEL
Marine Parade, BN11 3QQ
This four-storey hotel, ideally situated for the promenade, town centre shopping and entertainments, has been under the personal supervision of the Howlett family for over 20 years. Offering good cuisine, with a choice of à la carte, carvery or bar meals, the Kingsway Hotel has very comfortable accommodation, complemented by friendly and attentive service.
DOUBLE ROOM: from £30 to £40
SINGLE ROOM: from £45 to £55
FOOD: up to £15 ☆
Hours: breakfast 7.30am–9.30am, lunch 12noon–2pm, dinner 6.30pm–9pm, Sunday 6.30pm–8.30pm.
Cards: Visa, Access, Diners, AmEx, Switch.
Other points: fully licensed, traditional Sunday lunch, children welcome, afternoon tea, pets allowed, lift, residents' lounge, patio, functions, bar, parking.
Rooms: 14 single rooms, 7 double rooms, 8 twin rooms. All with satellite TV, radio, bar, telephone, tea/coffee-making facilities, hair dryer.
Directions: on Marine Parade, near the pier, to the west.
BRIAN & ANN HOWLETT ☎ (01903) 237542/ 237543 Fax (01903) 204173.

For full details see Essex, Southend-on-Sea

For full details see Hampshire, Lyndhurst

MILLBROOK HOUSE

Rue De Trachy, St Helier, Jersey, C. I. Tel. (0534) 33036

For full details see Channel Islands, Jersey

LES ROUTIERS

For further information on

Les Routiers

or to book your accommodation...

telephone **(0171) 610 1856**

(Mondays to Fridays 9am-5pm)

(0171) 385 7136 *facsimile*

LES ROUTIERS   25 VANSTON PLACE   LONDON SW6 1AZ

WINDSOR HOUSE HOTEL
14-20 Windsor Road, BN11 2LX

This family-owned and run hotel is situated close to the sea and a short walk from the town centre. Well maintained and attractively decorated, it offers a friendly atmosphere and good service to both business people and holiday-makers. The hotel enjoys an attractive bar and gardens and three comfortable lounges. It also has a private car park.

DOUBLE ROOM: from £30 to £40
SINGLE ROOM: from £35 to £45
FOOD: up to £15

Hours: breakfast 7.30am–9.15am, lunch 12.30am–2.30pm, dinner 6pm–9.30pm.

Cuisine: ENGLISH – à la carte menu, fixed-price three-course menu, bar meals/snacks and vegetarian meals.
Cards: Visa, Access, AmEx, Eurocard.
Other points: licensed, Sunday lunch, garden, afternoon tea, children catered for (please check for age limits), baby-listening device, cots.
Rooms: 1 single room, 14 double rooms, 12 twin rooms, 3 quad rooms. All with TV, radio, alarm, telephone, tea/coffee-making facilities, hair dryer, trouser-press.
Directions: take A24 to A259.
MR & MRS ARMSTRONG ☎ (01903) 239655
Fax (01903) 210763.

SOUTH-WEST ENGLAND

The counties of the South-West that make up England's most popular holiday areas offer the traveller or tourist a constantly changing choice of magnificent scenery, as well as first-class food complemented by fine wines and traditional cask ales.

The undulating coastline, with its secret coves and windswept, grassy cliffs, firm, sandy beaches and picturesque fishing villages, yields an abundance of locally-caught fish and seafood specialities.

Travel further inland through picture-book villages with cottage gardens full of old-fashioned sweet-scented flowers to discover hearty, home-made cooking, prepared from old recipes passed down from generation to generation and served in bounteous proportions to satisfy the most insatiable of appetites. Round it all off perhaps with a Devonshire cream tea or a medley of the region's excellent farmhouse cheeses.

Whether you opt for a traditional steak-and-kidney pudding or dine continental, it will be a gourmet experience you'll never forget. And if your stay is for a day or longer, you'll find it hard to ignore the warm, friendly hospitality of your hosts in the true *Les Routiers* spirit.

The following counties are included in this chapter:

AVON	HAMPSHIRE
BERKSHIRE	ISLE OF
CORNWALL	WIGHT
DEVON	SOMERSET
DORSET	WILTSHIRE

AVON

BATH • map 4B5

APSLEY HOUSE HOTEL
141 Newbridge Hill, BA1 3PP
Built in 1830, reputedly for the Duke of Wellington, the family-run Apsley House Hotel rates among Britain's finest small hotels. The interior is tastefully decorated with antiques and oil paintings, providing an atmosphere more like a country home than a hotel.
DOUBLE ROOM: from £30 to £40
SINGLE ROOM: from £35 to £45
Hours: breakfast 8am–9am, light snacks available on request, open all year.
Cards: Visa, Access, MasterCard.
Other points: parking, children welcome, no-smoking area, residents' lounge, garden.
Rooms: 5 double rooms, 2 twin rooms. All with en suite, TV, telephone, alarm, hair dryer, trouser-press.
Directions: 1 mile from Bath city centre on A4 to Bristol, proceed along Upper Bristol Road to second set of traffic lights, turn right into Newbridge Hill.
MR AND MRS C. AND A. BAKER ☎ (01225) 336966 [Fax] (01225) 425462.

BATH TASBURGH HOTEL
Warminster Road, BA2 6SH
Built in 1890, this charming Victorian house, with panoramic views over the lovely Avon Valley, is set in two acres of beautifully tended gardens and five acres of sweeping pasture with canal frontage. Located near the city centre, the guest house has been extensively refurbished and offers 13 bedrooms combining Victorian elegance and

charming decor with all the modern comforts of a good hotel. Service is paramount, and the efficient staff will tend to your requirements in a warm and friendly manner.
DOUBLE ROOM: from £30 to £40
SINGLE ROOM: from £35 to £45
Hours: breakfast 8am–9.30am, open all year round.
Cards: Visa, Access, Diners, AmEx.
Other points: children welcome, parking, residents' lounge, conservatory, garden, no-smoking area, vegetarian meals, licensed, croquet lawn.
Rooms: 6 double rooms, 2 family rooms, 2 four-poster rooms. All with tea/coffee-making facilities, TV, telephone, radio, hair dryer, trouser-press, baby-listening device.
Directions: leave M4 at exit 18, take A46, then A36. From the city centre, take A36, travel approximately 1 mile east.
BRIAN & AUDREY ARCHER ☎ (01225) 425096
[Fax] (01225) 463842.

BROMPTON HOUSE
St Johns Road, BA2 6PT
A former Georgian rectory of 1777, now converted and extended, it is set amidst a prize-winning garden. All rooms have been tastefully furnished to an extremely high standard with guests' comfort in mind, and although remodernized, the building still retains the Georgian era, with oil paintings, furniture and fittings of the period. A very friendly and courteous welcome is assured from both the management and helpful staff in the relaxing, informal atmosphere.
DOUBLE ROOM: from £30 to £40
SINGLE ROOM: from £25 to £35
Hours: breakfast 8.15am–9.30am, closed 23rd December until 2nd January.
Cuisine: BREAKFAST.
Cards: Visa, Access, AmEx, Eurocard, MasterCard.
Other points: parking, children welcome, open bank holidays, no-smoking area, residents' lounge, vegetarian meals, garden.
Rooms: 2 single rooms, 11 double rooms, 4 twin rooms, 1 family room. All with TV, radio, telephone, tea/coffee-making facilities.
Directions: exit 17 or 18 off M4 to A4, Bath Road. At traffic lights take A35, Warminster Road, crossing Cleveland bridge first right. Brompton House is on left next to church.
DAVID & SUSAN SELBY ☎ (01225) 420972
[Fax] (01225) 420505.

CANARY CAFE
3 Queen Street, BA1 1HE
The Canary Café has become one of Bath's most popular and well-established restaurants. The chefs produce an array of international dishes to suit all tastes and times of the day. Tea time is a speciality, and the Canary was winner of the Tea Council's Top Tea Place Award of the Year in 1989. Over 40 different types of tea are served, with an impressive selection of patisserie.
FOOD: up to £15
Hours: meals all day from 9am to 8pm (Sundays 11am to 6pm), closed Christmas day, Boxing day, New Year's day.
Cuisine: INTERNATIONAL – varied and interesting range of international cuisine, with award-winning speciality teas.
Cards: Visa, Access.
Other points: children catered for (please check for age limits), parking.
Directions: on A4, 9 miles off M4 on A46.
MR DAVIES ☎ (01225) 424846.

THE COMPASS ABBEY HOTEL
North Parade, BA1 1LG
Originally built as a wealthy merchant's house in the 1740s, The Compass Abbey Hotel reopened in May 1990 after a complete refurbishment. Just a minute's walk from the abbey, Roman baths and Pump Room, it offers comfortable accommodation with many luxuries, including Sky TV. Wedgwood's restaurant, coffee house and bar make ideal meeting places while you are exploring the European Heritage City of Bath. The Fernley and Orchard rooms are available for meetings and for conference hire.
DOUBLE ROOM: from £30 to £40
FOOD: from £15 to £20
Hours: breakfast 7.15am–9.30am, bar snacks 10am–6pm, lunch 12noon–2pm, dinner 7.15pm–9.15pm.
Cuisine: ENGLISH.
Cards: Visa.
Other points: children welcome, no-smoking area, afternoon teas, disabled access, pets, residents' lounge, vegetarian.
Rooms: 12 single rooms, 26 double rooms, 54 twin rooms.
Directions: right in the city centre.
DAVID PRIOR ☎ (01225) 461603 [Fax] (01225) 447758.

COURT HOTEL
Emborough, Chilcompton, BA3 4SA
An attractive Victorian stone manor house, this recently refurbished hotel is set in the beautiful countryside of Avon. Tastefully decorated, the rooms are light and airy with good views. Superb food is served in the tranquil dining room. Conference facilities.
DOUBLE ROOM: from £30 to £40
FOOD: up to £15
Hours: breakfast 6.45am–9.30am, lunch 12.15am–2.15pm, dinner 7.30pm–9.30pm.
Cuisine: ENGLISH – mainly traditional English and French cuisine. Imaginative cooking. Good selection of wines.
Cards: Visa, Access, AmEx.
Other points: licensed, open-air dining, Sunday lunch, children welcome, open bank holidays, afternoon tea, residents' lounge, garden.
Rooms: 3 single rooms, 5 double rooms, 3 twin rooms, 1 family room. All with TV, tea/coffee-making facilities.
Directions: take A367 from Bath to Radstock, then Wells Road.
MISS COLLINS ☎ (01761) 232237
[Fax] (01761) 233730.

CROSS KEYS INN
Midford Road, Combe Down, BA2 5RZ

An attractive olde-worlde pub with a friendly, welcoming atmosphere. The food is well cooked and offers variety and good value for money. The B3110 is a scenic alternative to the main A36 and is worth taking even if only to visit the Cross Keys for its good food, warm welcome and friendly service. In the garden there is an interesting, well-stocked aviary.
FOOD: up to £15
Hours: lunch 12noon–1.50pm, dinner 7pm–9.50pm (for last orders).
Cuisine: ENGLISH – bar meals including a large selection of home-made foods.
Other points: licensed, Sunday lunch, children welcome, garden, pets allowed.
Directions: on B3110 overlooking Bath. Near St Martin's Hospital.
MARK & CAROLINE PALMER ☎ (01225) 832002.

DORIAN HOUSE
1 Upper Oldfield Park, BA2 3JX

A gracious Victorian home with free parking. Situated on the southern slopes overlooking Bath, yet only ten minutes' stroll to the city centre. There are eight charming bedrooms, all en suite. The lounge and small licensed bar provide a pleasant atmosphere for friends to meet. There is a full English breakfast menu and a warm welcome for all guests.
DOUBLE ROOM: from £30 to £40
SINGLE ROOM: from £35 to £45
Hours: breakfast 8am–9am.
Cuisine: BREAKFAST.
Cards: Visa, Access, Diners, AmEx.
Other points: children welcome, residents' lounge, garden, vegetarian meals.
Rooms: 1 single room, 3 double rooms, 2 four-poster rooms, 2 family rooms. All with TV, radio, alarm, telephone, tea/coffee-making facilities.
Directions: up A367 Wells Road for 250 metres to left-hand bend. First right, then third house on left.
IAN & DOREEN BENNETTS ☎ (01225) 426336 Fax (01225) 444699.

GEORGES HOTEL
2–3 South Parade, BA2 4AA

Situated in the very heart of historic Bath, the hotel is part of an elegant terrace built in the 1740s. Guests can enjoy well-appointed accommodation and a well-stocked Georgian bar. For a touch of Greece, the Acropolis Restaurant below the hotel offers a wide range of traditional Greek and English dishes. Private parties and weddings are a speciality.
DOUBLE ROOM: from £20 to £30
FOOD: up to £15
Hours: breakfast 7.30am–9.30am, restaurant 11am–11pm.
Cuisine: GREEK / ENGLISH.
Cards: Visa.
Other points: children welcome, open Sunday lunch, open bank holidays, no-smoking area, afternoon tea, open Sunday dinner, residents' lounge, disabled access, pets allowed, weddings, vegetarian meals, conferences.
Rooms: 7 double rooms, 8 twin rooms, 4 family rooms. All with TV, telephone.
Directions: junction 18 off M4, signed towards Bath. Located on North Parade Bridge in centre of Bath.
MR G.M. PAPANICOLAOU ☎ (01225) 464923 Fax (01225) 425471.

LEIGHTON HOUSE
139 Wells Road, BA2 3AL

A well-appointed Victorian residence that has been tastefully furnished by Kathy and Dave Slape, who have successfully created a warm and friendly haven for their guests. With the emphasis on comfort, warm hospitality and attention to detail, guests can be assured of an enjoyable stay. Situated just 10 minutes from the city centre, Leighton House comes highly recommended.
DOUBLE ROOM: from £20 to £30
SINGLE ROOM: from £35 to £45
Hours: breakfast 8am–9am.
Cards: Visa, Access.
Other points: children welcome, residents' lounge, garden, special breaks, baby-listening device, cots.
Rooms: 3 double rooms, 3 twin rooms, 1 triple room, 1 quad room. All with en suite, TV, radio, telephone, tea/coffee-making facilities.
Directions: situated on the southern side of Bath on the A367 Exeter road.
DAVE & KATHY SLAPE ☎ (01225) 314769 Fax (01225) 314769.

THE OLD MALT HOUSE HOTEL
Radford, Timsbury, BA3 1QF

Only 6 miles from Bath, the hotel is an excellent base to explore the West Country, and guests are welcome at the farm run by the same family, with its famous Shire horses. The comfortable, relaxed restaurant is renowned for its excellent English food. Full English breakfast is included in all B&B rates.
DOUBLE ROOM: from £30 to £40
SINGLE ROOM: from £35 to £45
FOOD: from £15 to £20
Hours: breakfast 7.45am–9am, lunch 12noon–2pm, dinner 7pm–8.30pm, closed 25th December to 1st January.
Cuisine: ENGLISH – traditional English, including pheasant, duck, venison, steak, rabbit and vegetarian dishes.
Cards: Visa, Access, Diners, AmEx.
Other points: licensed, open-air dining, parking, children by arrangement, afternoon tea, residents' lounge, garden, disabled access, vegetarian meals, residents' bar.
Rooms: 1 single room, 4 double rooms, 3 twin rooms, 2 triple rooms. All with en suite, TV, telephone, tea/coffee-making facilities.
Directions: off A367, take B3115. Follow the 'Radford Farm' signs.
MICHAEL & MARGUERITE HORLER ☎ (01761) 470106 Fax (01761) 470106.

AVON • SW ENGLAND

🏨 PRIORY HOTEL
Weston Road, BA1 2XT

This 19th century Gothic-style listed building is part of a row of elegant residences on the west side of Bath. Set in two acres of award-winning gardens, the Priory is individually furnished with choice antique furniture, plush rugs and objets d'art. The atmosphere is peaceful and comfortable and the helpful staff are courteous and efficient, making you immediately at ease.
DOUBLE ROOM: from £50
SINGLE ROOM: over £55
FOOD: from £20 to £25
Hours: breakfast 7.30am–9.30am, lunch 12noon–2.30pm, dinner 7pm–9.30pm.
Cuisine: FRENCH.
Cards: Visa, Access, Diners, AmEx.
Other points: children welcome, parking, conference facilities, residents' lounge, residents' garden, swimming pool, Sunday lunch, no-smoking area, vegetarian meals.
Rooms: 3 single rooms, 8 double rooms, 9 twin rooms, 1 four-poster room. All with TV, telephone, radio, hair dryer, trouser-press, fresh fruit and flowers.
Directions: Located one mile west of Bath city centre.
MR T. CONBOY ☎ (01225) 331922
Fax (01225) 448276.

🍴 RASCALS BISTRO
8 Pierrepont Place, BA1 1JX

Rascals is situated in a listed building in converted cellars and is entered via a main staircase. Its original stone walls give it a warm, intimate atmosphere, where you can sample imaginative international cuisine and an excellent wine list. The friendly staff and the emphasis on value for money make for a relaxed and informal ambience. Definitely not to be missed!
(See advertisement below.)
FOOD: up to £15 [CLUB]
Hours: bar snacks 11.30am–2.30pm, lunch 11.30am–2.30pm, dinner weekdays 6pm–10.30pm, weekends 5.30pm–11pm, closed Sunday lunch.
Cuisine: INTERNATIONAL – all meals are prepared on the premises and all ingredients are bought fresh each day.
Cards: Visa, MasterCard, Switch.
Other points: children welcome, open bank holidays, no-smoking area, pets allowed, vegetarian meals, open-air dining.
Directions: near Pulteney Bridge off Pierrepont Street, through stone pillars behind Compass Hotel.
NICK ANDERSON & NIGEL MANNING-MORTON ☎ (01225) 330201.

Rascals Bistro

8 Pierrepoint Place, Bath, Avon BA1 1JX
Telephone: Bath (0225) 330201

A warm welcome and value for money is guaranteed at Rascals!

3 course lunches from £5.25 inc.
3 course dinner from £9.25 inc.

Try Us
– You Won't Be Disappointed!

101

THE ROOKERY
Wells Road, Radstock, BA3 3RS
Set amidst a pleasant garden with flowers and shrubs, this 200-year-old country house is now a homely guest house offering every comfort, good food, personal attention, a happy and friendly atmosphere and olde-worlde charm. Separate guest lounge is available for small conferences. Ideal location for touring the West Country.
DOUBLE ROOM: from £20 to £30
SINGLE ROOM: from £25 to £35
FOOD: up to £15 [CLUB]
Hours: breakfast 7.30am–9.30am, lunch 12noon–2pm, dinner 7pm–9.30pm, bar snacks 12noon–2pm, bar snacks 7pm–9.30pm, closed Christmas day (to non-residents).
Cuisine: ENGLISH.
Cards: Visa, Access, Diners.
Other points: parking, children welcome, open bank holidays, no-smoking area, afternoon tea, disabled access, pets allowed, residents' lounge, vegetarian meals, garden, licensed.
Rooms: 4 double rooms, 3 twin rooms, 3 family rooms. All with TV, telephone, tea/coffee-making facilities, iron.
Directions: take A367 from Bath to Radstock, approximately 8 miles to The Rookery.
ANN & ROGER SIMS ☎ (01761) 432626.

THE WIFE OF BATH RESTAURANT
12 Pierrepont Street, BA1 1LA
This well-established bistro-style restaurant is close to Bath Abbey and the famous Pump Rooms. A series of Georgian cellars of great character open onto a walled garden. The atmosphere is informal and staff are welcoming and friendly. The good food is complemented by an interesting wine list. Attractive decor, with quarry-tiled floors, stone walls and Provençal printed fabrics.
FOOD: up to £15
Hours: lunch 12noon–2.15pm, dinner 5.30pm–11pm, closed Sunday lunch.
Cuisine: ENGLISH – casseroles, stuffed peppers, steaks, fresh fish, daily specials, toasted sandwiches at lunchtime.
Cards: Visa, Access, AmEx.
Other points: licensed, open-air dining, children welcome, vegetarian meals, garden.
Directions: situated close to Bath Abbey.
DICK & AINSLIE ENSOM ☎ (01225) 461745.

BRISTOL • map 4B5

51 PARK STREET
51 Park Street, BS1 5NT
Prominently positioned in Bristol's shopping area, 51 Park Street is well-decorated and offers a wide variety of dishes at value-for-money prices. Frequented by holiday-makers and locals alike, and of appeal to all age groups.
FOOD: from £15 to £20 [CLUB]
Hours: closed Monday, Christmas day and New Year's day, meals all day 12noon–11pm, Sunday 12noon–10pm.
Cuisine: INTERNATIONAL – mainly English with French and Asiatic influences. Specialities include modern American dishes and European brasserie food.
Cards: Visa, Access, Diners, AmEx.
Other points: licensed, open-air dining, Sunday lunch, no-smoking area, children welcome, afternoon tea.
Directions: from city centre follow route to Bristol University.
MRS H.L. TIMMONS ☎ (0117) 926 8016.

ARCHES HOTEL
132 Cotham Brow, BS6 6AE
This early-Victorian house hotel offers comfortable accommodation and a warm welcome to Les Routiers visitors. Situated just off the A38, it is convenient for the central stations, theatres, waterfront, exhibition and shopping centres, and is located in an area renowned for its diverse restaurants.
DOUBLE ROOM: from £20 to £30
SINGLE ROOM: up to £25
Hours: breakfast weekdays 7.15am–8.30am, Saturday 8am–9am, Sunday 8.30am–9.30am, closed Christmas and New Year.
Cuisine: BREAKFAST – choice of continental or 6 cooked breakfasts, with traditional, vegetarian and vegan tastes catered for.
Cards: Visa, AmEx, MasterCard.
Other points: no-smoking areas, children welcome, pets allowed, open bank holidays.
Rooms: 3 single rooms, 4 double rooms, 1 twin room, 2 family rooms. All with TV, tea/coffee-making facilities.
Directions: half a mile from bus station, north on A38, turn left at first mini-roundabout, 100 yards on the left.
MR & MRS D. LAMBERT ☎ (0117) 924 7398.

THE GANGES
368 Gloucester Road, Horfield, BS7 8TP
A friendly restaurant, tastefully decorated in Indian style, with intimate alcoves for romantic dining. The service is courteous and efficient, and the menu includes some lesser-known Indian dishes.
FOOD: from £15 to £20
Hours: lunch 12noon–2.30pm, dinner 6pm–11.30pm, closed Christmas day.
Cuisine: INDIAN – north Indian.
Cards: Visa, Access, Diners, AmEx.
Other points: licensed, Sunday lunch, children welcome.
Directions: on the A38 Gloucester road.
MR CHOWDHURY ☎ (0117) 942 8505/ 924 5234.

GLASS BOAT
Welsh Back, near Bristol Bridge, BS1 4SB
The Glass Boat is – as the name would have you believe – a boat, anchored on the riverside in the centre of Bristol. The quiet aspect overlooking the harbour with the swans swimming by is very

relaxing and adds to the wonderful atmosphere. You can choose from the à la carte or table d'hôte menus and be assured of refreshing excellence.
FOOD: from £15 to £20
Hours: breakfast 7.30am–10.30am, lunch 12noon–2.30pm, dinner 6pm until late, closed Christmas day, Boxing day and on New Year's day.
Cuisine: ENGLISH / FRENCH – the restaurant has an excellent reputation for freshly prepared food at reasonable prices.
Cards: Visa, Access, AmEx.
Other points: children welcome, no-smoking area, vegetarian meals.
Directions: situated by Bristol Bridge in the centre of Bristol.
ARNE RINGNER ☎ (0117) 929 0704.

GRASMERE COURT HOTEL
22–24 Bath Road, Keynsham, BS15 1SN

Situated approximately halfway between Bath and Bristol city centre, this hotel has recently been renovated and modernized to provide a compact 'country-style' hotel with a friendly atmosphere. The hotel offers a haven of peace in which to relax in comfort after a strenuous day exploring the nearby Mendip Hills, shopping or sightseeing.
DOUBLE ROOM: from £20 to £30
SINGLE ROOM: from £35 to £45
FOOD: up to £15
Hours: breakfast 7.30am–9.30am, dinner 6pm–7.30pm, bar snacks 12noon–2pm, 6pm–9.30pm.
Cuisine: ENGLISH / COSMOPOLITAN – attractively presented, home-style meals.
Cards: Visa, Access, AmEx.
Other points: parking, children welcome, open bank holidays, no-smoking rooms, afternoon tea, residents' lounge, vegetarian meals, garden.
Rooms: 1 single room, 12 double rooms, 3 twin rooms.
Directions: on main road between Bristol and Bath.
JOHN BARRINGTON LLEWELLIN & M. LLEWELLIN ☎ (0117) 986 2662 Fax (0117) 986 2762.

HENRY AFRICA'S HOTHOUSE
65 Whiteladies Road, Clifton, B28 2LY

This lively restaurant with its extensive cocktail list, busy happy hour and Cajun and Tex-Mex specialities is extremely popular, whether for snacks and drinks at the bar, or for a full meal in the attractive upstairs restaurant.
FOOD: from £15 to £20
Hours: meals served all day 12noon–11pm; Sunday breakfast 10am–1pm, meals served all day 1pm–10.30pm.
Cuisine: CAJUN / TEX-MEX – grills, barbecue, Cajun and Tex-Mex specialities. Magnificent selection of cocktails, wines and beers, including a choice of non-alcoholic drinks.
Cards: Visa, Access, AmEx.
Other points: licensed, Sunday lunch, no-smoking area, children welcome, afternoon tea, open bank holidays.

Directions: just north of the BBC on Whiteladies Road, Clifton, Bristol.
CRAIG COLLINS ☎ (0117) 923 8300
Fax (0117) 946 7893.

JUBILEE INN
Flax Bourton, BS19 3QX

An olde-worlde stone-built inn, covered by creepers and hanging baskets. Fresh produce is used to provide well-cooked meals, and all dishes offer good value for money. Traditional English dishes are cooked with an imaginative touch. For warmer days there is an attractive garden for customers' use.
DOUBLE ROOM: from £20 to £30
SINGLE ROOM: from £25 to £35
FOOD: up to £15
Hours: breakfast 8.15am–9.15am, lunch 12noon–2pm, dinner 7.30pm–10pm.
Cuisine: ENGLISH – traditional English home-made dishes. Specialities include the special seafood pie (fresh salmon, white fish and prawns, topped with potato).
Other points: licensed, Sunday lunch, garden, pets allowed.
Rooms: 3 bedrooms.
Directions: between Bristol and Weston-Super-Mare.
BRIAN HAYDOCK ☎ (01275) 462741.

LINDEN HOTEL
51–59 High Street, Kingswood, BS15 4AD

A deceptively large hotel offering first-class accommodation, excellent food and luxurious reception rooms, the Linden Hotel is conveniently situated close to Bristol. The helpful and courteous staff are always on hand to ensure that all guests requirements are provided for.
DOUBLE ROOM: from £20 to £30
FOOD: up to £15
Hours: breakfast 7am–9.30am, lunch 12noon–2pm, dinner 6.30pm–9pm.
Cuisine: ENGLISH.
Cards: Visa, Access, Diners, AmEx.
Other points: parking, children welcome, pets allowed, no-smoking area, disabled access, vegetarian meals, residents' lounge.
Rooms: 5 single rooms, 10 double rooms, 10 twin rooms, 3 triple rooms, 3 family rooms.
Directions: 4 miles east of Bristol city centre on the north side of the A420 Bristol–Chippenham road.
R.A. FAY ☎ (0117) 967 4331 Fax (0117) 961 5871.

NATRAJ TANDOORI (NEPALESE & INDIAN CUISINE)
185 Gloucester Road, Bishopston, BS7 8BG

Natraj offers an excellent mix of traditional Tandoori with more unusual Nepalese dishes. Try momocha (spiced minced lamb in pastry served with Nepalese pickle) as one of the many Nepalese specialities on offer, or one of the set menus. Friendly, helpful staff will help you choose from

the extensive menu. Generous helpings of food in comfortable, Oriental surroundings.
FOOD: up to £15
Hours: lunch (Fri-Sat 12noon–2pm), dinner (Monday–Thursday) 6pm–12midnight, Friday and Saturday 6pm–12.30am, Sunday 6pm–12midnight.
Cuisine: NEPALESE / INDIAN – specialities of the house include gurkha chick, momocha, murgi mussalam, thuckpa. Continental dishes and à la carte or special buffet.
Cards: Visa, Access, Diners, AmEx.
Other points: licensed, no-smoking area, children welcome, functions.
Directions: A38, north of city centre. Opposite Bristol North swimming baths.
MR D. KARKI ☎ (0117) 924 8145.

LES ROUTIERS AWARDS 1995
Our award-winners are featured on pages 10–15, 23 and 27.

RAINBOW CAFE
9–10 Waterloo Street, Clifton, BS8 4BT
The combination of home-made meat and vegetarian dishes on offer has made this small restaurant very popular. Quality second-hand books on sale and monthly exhibitions of work by local artists.
FOOD: up to £15
Hours: snacks 10am–5.30pm, lunch 12noon–2.30pm, closed Sunday, bank holidays and Christmas until New Year.
Cuisine: ENGLISH / VEGETARIAN – fish and meat dishes. The lunch menu varies daily and all food is fresh each day.
Other points: licensed, no-smoking area, children welcome.
Directions: from Bristol city centre, follow Clifton signs. Off Princess Street.
ALISON MOORE & TIM ANSELL ☎ (0117) 973 8937.

SEVERN VIEW PAVILION LODGE AT SEVERN VIEW SERVICE AREA
Junction 21, M4 Motorway, BS2 3BH
The Lodge provides excellent accommodation at a competitive price and offers the facilities to make travelling a pleasure. Located close to the Severn Bridge with views over the river. Convenient for Bristol, Bath and Cheddar Gorge.
DOUBLE ROOM: from £20 to £30
FOOD: up to £15
Hours: open 24 hours.
Cuisine: BRITISH / INTERNATIONAL.
Cards: Visa, Access, Diners, AmEx.
Other points: parking, children welcome, no-smoking area, disabled access, forecourt shop, Pizzaland.
Rooms: 51 bedrooms. All with en suite, satellite TV, telephone, radio, alarm, hair dryer, trouser-press, baby-listening device, tea/coffee-making facilities.
Directions: situated off M4 at junction 21.
TOM CASSIDY ☎ (01454) 633313 Fax (01454) 632482.

CLEVEDON • map 4B5

CASA TOMAS RISTORANTE
Millcross, Southern Way, BS21 5HX
For a true taste of Italy, one need go no further than this lively restaurant in the heart of Clevedon. Warm, friendly service and a vibrant atmosphere complement the first-class Italian food.
FOOD: from £15 to £20
Hours: dinner 7.30pm–10.30pm, closed Sunday.
Cuisine: ITALIAN – distinctive Italian cuisine, with vegetarian meals also provided.
Cards: Visa, Access.
Other points: children welcome.
Directions: half a mile off junction 20 of M5.
TOMAS MEDINA ☎ (01275) 343578.

FRESHFORD • map 4B5

INN AT FRESHFORD
Freshford Village, BA3 6EG
Updated yet retaining all its original charm, this fine example of an old coaching inn is decorated throughout in an olde-worlde style, providing an enchanting atmosphere in which to enjoy a fine meal. Stephen Turner and his helpful staff have worked hard to achieve the enviable reputation they now hold for superb food and an award-winning wine list.
FOOD: up to £15
Hours: lunch 12noon–2pm, Sunday 12noon–2.15pm, dinner 6pm–10pm, Sunday 7pm–9.30pm.
Cuisine: ENGLISH / FRENCH – a blackboard menu and an extensive à la carte selection, both at reasonable prices.
Cards: Visa, Access.
Other points: parking, children welcome, no-smoking area, garden, open-air dining, vegetarian meals, traditional Sunday lunch.
Directions: off A36, 5 miles south of Bath between Limpley Stoke and Bradford on Avon.
STEPHEN TURNER ☎ (01225) 722250.

OLD SODBURY • map 4A5

SODBURY HOUSE HOTEL
Badminton Road, BS17 6LU
Set in large, attractive grounds with ample off-road parking, this former 1830s farmhouse has been tastefully converted into a hotel retaining the character but providing the facilities that today's guest expects. All 13 rooms are en suite and have direct-dial telephone, colour TV, hair dryer, trouser-press and welcome tray. Most rooms have mini-bars. A self-contained conference facility is situated in the Coach House. The hotel caters for small weddings and private dinner parties. Bed & Breakfast is provided at an all-inclusive rate. Ideally situated for visiting Bath, Bristol and the Cotswolds. An ideal stopover en route to the West Country, Wales and Ireland.
DOUBLE ROOM: from £30 to £40
SINGLE ROOM: from £35 to £45
Hours: breakfast weekdays 7.30am–8.30am,

AVON • SW ENGLAND

weekends and bank holidays 8.30am–9.30am, closed 24th December until 4th January.
Cuisine: BREAKFAST – supper menu is available Monday to Wednesday.
Cards: Visa, Access, AmEx, MasterCard, Switch.
Other points: parking, children welcome, open bank holidays, afternoon tea, pets by prior arrangement, vegetarian meals, garden, open-air dining, residents' lounge.
Rooms: 6 single rooms, 2 double rooms, 2 twin rooms, 3 family rooms. All with TV, bar, telephone, tea/coffee-making facilities.
Directions: from M4 junction 18, take A46 for 3 miles, left at traffic lights on A432. 12 miles from junction 14 on M5.
DAVID & MARGARET WARREN ☎ (01454) 312847 [Fax] (01454) 273105.

RANGEWORTHY • map 4A5

RANGEWORTHY COURT HOTEL
Church Lane, Wotton Road, BS17 5ND

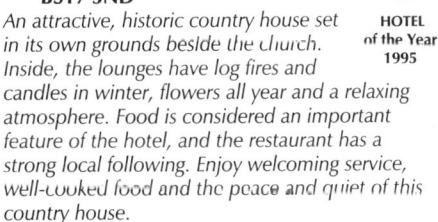

LES ROUTIERS

An attractive, historic country house set in its own grounds beside the church. Inside, the lounges have log fires and candles in winter, flowers all year and a relaxing atmosphere. Food is considered an important feature of the hotel, and the restaurant has a strong local following. Enjoy welcoming service, well-cooked food and the peace and quiet of this country house.
(See special feature on page 11.)

HOTEL of the Year 1995

DOUBLE ROOM: from £30 to £40
SINGLE ROOM: from £45 to £55
FOOD: from £15 to £20 ☕ [CLUB] ☆
Hours: breakfast 7.15am–9.30am, lunch 12noon–2pm, dinner 7pm–9pm.
Cuisine: ENGLISH – dishes may include devilled crab, lamb steak in Madeira and rosemary sauce, fresh salmon, turbot. Vegetarian and vegan dishes.
Cards: Visa, Access, Diners, AmEx.
Other points: licensed, Sunday lunch, garden, pets allowed, functions, conferences, children welcome, baby-listening device, cots, residents' bar, residents' lounge, vegetarian meals, parking, swimming pool.
Rooms: 5 single rooms, 9 double rooms, 2 triple rooms. All with TV, radio, telephone, tea/coffee-making facilities.
Directions: from Bristol, M32 exit 1, then B4058 to Rangeworthy.
MERVYN & LUCIA GILLETT ☎ (01454) 228347 [Fax] (01454) 228945.

WESTON-SUPER-MARE • map 1D5

CARRINGTON HOTEL
28 Knightstone Road, BS23 2AN

A Victorian terraced house overlooking the beach and the pier, with a patio to the front laid with tables and umbrellas for alfresco dining in summer. Situated near to the Winter Gardens, and with all the facilities of a British seaside town on the doorstep.
DOUBLE ROOM: from £20 to £30
FOOD: up to £15
Hours: breakfast 8.30am–9.30am, lunch 11.30am–3pm, dinner 6pm–9.30pm, bar meals 11am–9.30pm.
Cuisine: ENGLISH – in the restaurant, steaks, grills, salads, omelettes, fish. In the bar, home-made steak-and-kidney pie, cottage pie, home-made sweets.
Cards: Access.
Other points: licensed, open-air dining, Sunday lunch, no-smoking area, children welcome.
Directions: on the seafront between the Grand Pier and Marine Lake.
MR & MRS ARNAOUTI ☎ (01934) 626621.

THE COMMODORE HOTEL
Beach Road, Sand Bay, BS22 9UZ

On the seafront at Sand Bay, with extensive views across the Bristol Channel and the local countryside. Good access to West Country attractions and several National Trust walks. Golfing discounts and riding can be arranged.
DOUBLE ROOM: from £30 to £40
SINGLE ROOM: from £45 to £55
FOOD: up to £15 ☕
Hours: breakfast weekdays 7.30am–9.30am, weekends 8am–10am, lunch 12noon–2pm, dinner 6.30pm–9.30pm.
Cuisine: MODERN ENGLISH – lounge buffet-carvery and à la carte restaurant with international and modern English cuisine.
Cards: Visa, Access, Diners, AmEx.
Other points: licensed, Sunday lunch, disabled access, children welcome, functions, conferences.
Rooms: 18 bedrooms.
Directions: overlooking beach in Sand Bay, 1½ miles north of Weston on Toll Road.
JOHN STOAKES ☎ (01934) 415778 [Fax] (01934) 636483.

PEARL DE MARE CHINESE CUISINE
15–18 Alexandra Parade, BS23 1QT

An opportunity to sample excellent cuisine in delightful surroundings. The restaurant is tastefully furnished and comfortable, with pleasant, restful background music. Service is highly efficient and courteous. Executive business lunches available. Situated within easy reach of many major tourist attractions, from the seafront to the beautiful surrounding countryside.
FOOD: up to £15 [CLUB]
Hours: lunch 12noon–2pm, dinner 6pm–11.30pm, closed Sunday lunch.
Cuisine: CHINESE – Cantonese and Peking cuisine of an extremely high standard and beautifully presented. Fixed-price executive lunches available.
Cards: Visa, Access, Diners, AmEx.
Other points: licensed, children welcome, disabled access, vegetarian meals, street parking.
Directions: situated in the town centre, opposite the Odeon cinemas.
MR CHIM ('JIM') ☎ (01934) 621307/626104.

105

BERKSHIRE

BRACKNELL • map 5C3

🍴 OSCARS
South Hill Park Arts Centre, RG12 4PA
Situated in a large, elegant mansion now used as an arts centre. The food is excellently prepared: an ideal accompaniment to an evening at the theatre or cinema on the same site.
FOOD: from £15 to £20
Hours: bar meals 12noon–2pm, 6.15pm–7.30pm, dinner 6.30pm–9.30pm, closed Sunday, Monday and Christmas day.
Cuisine: INTERNATIONAL – ethnic, vegetarian, seafood, steaks, game and special supper parties and wines. All main dishes freshly cooked to order.
Cards: Visa.
Other points: licensed, children welcome, coaches by prior arrangement, disabled access, parking.
Directions: from the A3095 or the A322 follow signs to South Hill Park.
MARK BRIDGES ☎ (01344) 59031 Fax (01344) 411427.

MAIDENHEAD • map 5C3

🍴 ANTONIA'S BAR BISTRO
11 Bridge Street, SL6 8LR
Originally an old pub and now tastefully redecorated in bistro style, offering a cosy, warm welcome in pleasant surroundings. The River Thames and Boulters Lock are just two of the many nearby points of interest to visit and explore.
FOOD: from £15 to £20
Hours: lunch 12noon–2.30pm, dinner 7pm–10.30pm, closed Monday.
Cuisine: CONTINENTAL – freshly prepared food cooked to order. Tapas. Classic pasta dishes. French, Spanish and Italian cuisine.
Cards: Visa, Access.
Other points: licensed, open-air dining, no-smoking area, open bank holidays, parking.
Directions: situated off the A4.
ANTONIA TARTAGLIONE ☎ (01628) 23670.

🏨 CHAUNTRY HOUSE HOTEL
Bray-on-Thames, SL6 2AB
An outstanding 18th century country-house hotel situated in a delightful village close to Windsor and Heathrow Airport. No visitor can fail to be impressed by the friendly and relaxed atmosphere in this intimate restaurant.
DOUBLE ROOM: from £40 to £50
SINGLE ROOM: from £55
FOOD: from £15 to £20 ⓖ
Hours: breakfast 7.30am–9.30am, lunch 12noon–2pm, dinner 7.30pm–9.30pm.
Cuisine: ENGLISH – imaginative English cuisine. Menu changes seasonally.
Cards: Visa, Access, Diners, AmEx.
Other points: licensed, open-air dining, conferences, functions.

Rooms: 2 single rooms, 9 double rooms, 5 twin rooms. All with en suite, satellite TV, telephone, radio, alarm, tea/coffee-making facilities, baby-listening device.
Directions: M4 junction 8 or 9, A308 to Windsor, B3028 to Bray. Last building on right.
RAY HAND ☎ (01628) 73991 Fax (01628) 773089.

🏨 THAMES RIVIERA HOTEL
Bridge Road, SL6 8DW
Edwardian in origin, the Thames Riviera Hotel is situated at one of the most picturesque points on the River Thames. There are 53 luxurious en suite bedrooms situated in two buildings, most of the rooms having river views. There is a superb ground floor opening onto a riverside terrace, comprising a piano bar, à la carte restaurant and separate coffee shop, collectively known as 'Jerome's'. Sample the riverside hospitality.
DOUBLE ROOM: over £50
SINGLE ROOM: from £55
FOOD: from £20 to £25
Hours: breakfast 6.30am–8.30am, lunch 12noon–2pm, dinner 7pm–10pm, bar meals 12noon–5pm, closed 26th December until 30th December.
Cuisine: ENGLISH / FRENCH – all meals are freshly prepared from quality produce. Plus a more casual coffee shop, open 9am–5pm for snacks etc.
Cards: Visa, Access, Diners, AmEx, Switch.
Other points: parking, children welcome, conference facilities, garden, open-air dining, vegetarian meals, traditional Sunday lunch, afternoon teas.
Rooms: 53 bedrooms. All with satellite TV, telephone, alarm, hair dryer, trouser-press, tea/coffee-making facilities.
Directions: situated on the bank of the Thames on A4, off junction 7 of M4.
GALLEON TAVERNS LTD ☎ (01628) 74057 Fax (01628) 776586.

READING • map 5C3

🏨 CALCOT HOTEL
98–100 Bath Road, Calcot, RG3 5QN
The recently extended and refurbished Calcot Hotel offers 78 well-appointed bedrooms, informal lively restaurants, traditional bars, well-equipped conference rooms and popular banqueting facilities. In addition to being an ideal venue for the business traveller, the Calcot's location brings many popular sights and attractions within easy reach.
DOUBLE ROOM: from £30 to £40
SINGLE ROOM: from £35 to £45
FOOD: up to £15
Hours: breakfast 7am–9am, lunch 12.15am–2pm, dinner 7pm–10pm.
Cuisine: ENGLISH – a range of modern and imaginative dishes freshly prepared. A traditional

carvery roast is available on Sunday.
Cards: Visa, Access, Diners, AmEx, Switch.
Other points: parking, children welcome, no-smoking area, disabled access, residents' lounge, vegetarian meals, open-air dining, garden.
Rooms: 78 bedrooms.
Directions: situated on the A4 Bath road, 4 miles east of Reading.
JOHN CALCOT ☎ (01734) 416423
[Fax] (01734) 451223.

HONG HONG RESTAURANT
14 West Street, RG1 1TT
A friendly, traditional Chinese restaurant serving an interesting selection of regional Chinese specialities, wines and liqueurs.
FOOD: from £15 to £20
Hours: meals all day (Monday–Thursday) 12noon–11.30pm, Friday 12noon–12midnight, Saturday 12noon–12midnight, Sunday 1pm–11.30pm.
Cuisine: CANTONESE / PEKINESE – Peking, Cantonese and Szechuan food: crispy aromatic duck, Peking-style imperial hors d'ouvres, Cantonese-style spicy Szechuan prawn.
Cards: Visa, Access, Diners, AmEx.
Other points: licensed, Sunday lunch, children welcome, functions.
Directions: in the town centre opposite the Co-op, next to Prontaprint.
NGHU CHAN & GENEVIEVE ONG ☎ (01734) 585372/507472.

WEST ILSLEY • map 5B2

THE HARROW
West Ilsley, RG16 0AR
A village pub standing on the edge of the cricket green opposite the duck pond. The village is situated on the edge of the Berkshire Downs. Beer garden and children's play area. The interior structure has been refurbished, giving increased space. Visitors enjoy a high standard of home-cooking using fresh ingredients, with the emphasis on traditional British dishes.
FOOD: up to £15
Hours: lunch 12noon–2.15pm, dinner 6pm–9.15pm.
Cuisine: ENGLISH – rabbit pie with lemon, herbs and bacon. Traditional English puddings. English farmhouse cheese.
Cards: Visa, Access.
Other points: open-air dining, Sunday lunch, children welcome, coaches by prior arrangement.
Directions: one mile off the A34 – follow the signs to West Ilsley.
MRS HEATHER HUMPHREYS ☎ (01635) 281260.

WINDSOR • map 5C3

CHRISTOPHER HOTEL
110 High Street, Eton, SL4 6AN
A former coaching inn situated in Eton High Street, close to the famous school and within walking distance of Windsor Castle. The restaurant serves

BERKSHIRE • SW ENGLAND

an excellent selection of home-cooked meals.
DOUBLE ROOM: from £50
SINGLE ROOM: from £55
FOOD: from £15 to £20
Hours: breakfast 7.30am–9.30am, lunch 12noon–2.30pm, dinner weekends 7pm–10pm, weekdays 6.30pm–9.30pm.
Cuisine: ENGLISH / FRENCH – traditional cuisine.
Cards: Visa, Access, Diners, AmEx.
Other points: open-air dining, children welcome, pets allowed, baby-listening device, cots, left luggage.
Rooms: 8 single rooms, 17 double rooms, 5 twin rooms, 3 triples, 3 family rooms. All with TV, telephone, tea/coffee-making facilities.
Directions: 2 miles off M4. 10 miles from M25/Heathrow Airport.
MRS MARTIN ☎ (01753) 852359/857091.

WOKINGHAM • map 5C3

CANTLEY HOUSE HOTEL / MARYLINE'S BRASSERIE
Milton Road, RG11 5QG
A converted Victorian country house set in pleasant parklands with easy access to the M4. The Penguin & Vulture Pub and Maryline's Brasserie are situated in a converted 17th century barn in a secluded courtyard. A charming, character restaurant with old oak beams and sunken lounge around a warming log fire.
DOUBLE ROOM: from £30 to £40
SINGLE ROOM: from £55
FOOD: from £15 to £20
Hours: breakfast 7.30am–10am, lunch 12noon–2pm.
Cuisine: MODERN ENGLISH – fine modern English cuisine.
Cards: Visa, Access, Diners, AmEx.
Other points: Sunday lunch, pets allowed, children welcome.
Rooms: 15 single rooms, 12 double rooms, 2 twin rooms.
Directions: from M4 junction 10, follow signs to Wokingham. Off A321 towards Henley.
MR MAURICE MONK ☎ (01734) 789912
[Fax] (01734) 774294.

EDWARD COURT HOTEL
Wellington Road, RG11 2AN
Situated in the heart of Berkshire and easily accessible by rail and road, this hotel provides comfortable accommodation and well-cooked, well-presented meals. Local produce is used wherever possible.
DOUBLE ROOM: from £30 to £40
FOOD: up to £15
Hours: breakfast 7.30am–9am, lunch 12noon–2pm, dinner 7.30pm–9.30pm, closed Christmas 24th December until 2nd January.
Cuisine: FRENCH – dishes may include smoked mackerel salad with grated apple and horseradish sauce, sauté of veal strips in creamy sauce with apple.
Cards: Visa, Access, Diners, AmEx.
Other points: licensed, conferences, functions.

Rooms: 8 single rooms, 17 double rooms.
Directions: leave M4 junction 10, onto A329M. Follow signs for Wokingham, 100 yards from BR station.
JUDITH SIMPSON ☎ (01734) 775886
Fax (01734) 772018.

THE HANSOM CABIN
Lower Wokingham Road, Crowthorne, RG11 3NG
The Hansom Cabin is an attractive cabin-like restaurant surrounded by roses. Inside, you will find pine panelling and pictorial reference to hansom cabs. Fresh ingredients are used imaginatively to produce well-cooked meals, simply and thoughtfully presented. Good, welcoming service and a happy and relaxed atmosphere prevails.
FOOD: up to £15
Hours: lunch 12noon–2pm, dinner 7pm–12.30am, Sunday 7pm–9.30pm, last orders 9.30pm, closed Saturday lunch and Sunday lunch.
Cuisine: ENGLISH – starters range from sliced smoked trout, fresh soup or prawns. House specialities are duck or salmon en croute. Desserts includes home-made ice creams.
Cards: Visa, Access.
Other points: licensed.
Directions: alongside A321.
MR JOHN HANSOM ☎ (01344) 772450.

CORNWALL

BODMIN • map 3D2

ASTERISK RESTAURANT WITH ROOMS
A30 Mount Pleasant, Roche, PL26 8LH
Situated west of Bodmin, this is an ideal spot from which to visit Land's End and many other fascinating places of interest. Offering good home-cooking, dishes may include fillet in stout, beef fillet, duck chartreuse and pork fillet Oriental. Tasty desserts.
DOUBLE ROOM: up to £20
FOOD: up to £15
Hours: breakfast as required, dinner 7pm–10pm.
Cuisine: ENGLISH.
Cards: Visa, Access, AmEx.
Other points: parking, children welcome, open bank holidays, Sunday dinner, pets allowed, residents' lounge, vegetarian meals, garden.
Directions: on A30 two miles due west of Bodmin roundabout.
MR F. ZOLA ☎ (01726) 890863.

BUDE • map 3C2

COOMBE BARTON INN
Crackington Haven, EX23 0JG
Recently refurbished, the inn is charmingly decorated throughout. The warm and friendly service complements the high standard of food and accommodation on offer. A wide variety of freshly prepared and cooked meals is served every lunchtime and evening in the public bar or the bar/restaurant.
DOUBLE ROOM: up to £20
SINGLE ROOM: up to £25
FOOD: up to £15
Hours: breakfast 8.45am–9.30am, bar snacks 11am–3pm, dinner 6pm–10pm, bar snacks 6pm–10pm.
Cuisine: ENGLISH – large and comprehensive menu, with fresh fish being the speciality.
Cards: Visa, Access, Diners.
Other points: parking, children welcome, no-smoking area, pets allowed, residents' lounge, vegetarian meals, open-air dining.
Rooms: 1 single room, 6 double rooms.
Directions: turn off the A39 at Wainhouse Corner towards Crackington Haven.
JOHN COOPER ☎ (01840) 230345
Fax (01840) 230788.

THE FALCON HOTEL
Breakwater Road, EX23 8SD
Character hotel in unique position overlooking the historic Bude Canal and yet only a short stroll from the sandy beaches and shops. Renowned for the quality of the food, whether for the high-class menu in the Candlelit Restaurant, or from the extensive bar snack menu in the Coachmans Bar.
DOUBLE ROOM: from £30 to £40
SINGLE ROOM: from £25 to £35
FOOD: from £15 to £20
Hours: breakfast 8am–9.30am, lunch 12noon–2pm, dinner 7pm–9pm, closed Christmas day.
Cuisine: ENGLISH / FRENCH / INTERNATIONAL – à la carte and table d'hôte menus of an English and French style are served in the restaurant. An international menu of great variety is available in the bar.
Cards: Visa, Access, Diners, AmEx.
Other points: licensed, children welcome, pets allowed, garden, car park.
Rooms: 4 single rooms, 12 double rooms, 4 twin rooms. All with TV, tea/coffee-making facilities.
Directions: on western side of Bude, easily seen from the main road.
TIM & DOROTHY BROWNING ☎ (01288) 352005 Fax (01288) 356359.

MAER LODGE HOTEL
Crooklets Beach, EX23 8NG
Maer Lodge Hotel serves excellent and extremely varied home-cooked food. The quality of the ingredients and the care in preparation and presentation are paramount. A friendly, family hotel with first-class personal service.
DOUBLE ROOM: from £20 to £30
SINGLE ROOM: from £25 to £35

CORNWALL • SW ENGLAND

FOOD: up to £15 CLUB ☆
Hours: breakfast 8.30am–9.15am, lunch 12.30am–1.30pm, dinner 7pm–7.45pm.
Cuisine: ENGLISH / CONTINENTAL.
Cards: Visa, Access, Diners, AmEx.
Other points: pets allowed, children welcome, baby-listening device, baby-sitting, cots, 18hr reception, foreign exchange, left luggage, residents' lounge, residents' bar.
Rooms: 4 single rooms, 7 double rooms, 4 twin rooms, 4 family rooms. All with TV, radio, alarm, telephone, tea/coffee-making facilities.
Directions: overlooking golf course and close to the beach.
MR & MRS STANLEY ☎ (01288) 353306
Fax (01288) 353306.

🏨 MORNISH HOTEL
20 Summerleaze Crescent, EX23 8HL
The Mornish Hotel offers magnificent views from a prime location in Bude overlooking the beach. Centrally situated, with shops, golf course and beach nearby.
DOUBLE ROOM: up to £20
SINGLE ROOM: up to £25
FOOD: up to £15
Hours: breakfast 8.30am–9am, dinner 6.30pm–7pm to be ordered by 5.30pm, closed November to February.
Cuisine: ENGLISH – B&B includes a full English breakfast. Dinner: home-cooking to a very high standard (£8.50 for five courses – if you can manage them!).
Cards: Visa, Access, Diners, AmEx.
Other points: central heating, children welcome, residents' lounge, vegetarian meals.
Rooms: 5 double rooms, 2 twin rooms, 3 family rooms. All with en suite, TV, tea/coffee-making facilities.
Directions: from town centre, turn left at post office corner, towards sea.
JOHN & JULIA HILDER ☎ (01288) 352972.

CARLYON BAY • map 3E2

🏨 PORTH AVALLEN HOTEL
Sea Road, PL25 3SG
Situated in several acres of gardens with panoramic views over Carlyon Bay and its rugged coastline, this well-appointed hotel offers perfect peace and quiet. The oak-panelled residents' lounge opens onto the terrace, and is a cosy retreat during the winter months. The 40-seater restaurant maintains a very high standard, as does the accommodation. Ideal base for touring.
DOUBLE ROOM: from £40 to £50
SINGLE ROOM: from £45 to £55
FOOD: from £15 to £20
Hours: breakfast 7.30am–9.30am, lunch 12noon–2pm, dinner 7pm–9pm, closed Christmas day until 2nd January.
Cuisine: BRITISH – with a touch of French. Dishes may include: magret of duck, roast rack of lamb, Scottish fillet steak and Dover sole. Vegetarian dishes.
Cards: Visa, Access, AmEx, Switch.

Other points: licensed, Sunday lunch, children welcome, afternoon tea, residents' lounge, garden, parking, functions, conferences.
Rooms: 3 single room, 10 double rooms, 6 twin rooms, 5 family rooms. All with TV, radio, tea/coffee-making facilities, hair dryer, trouser-press.
Directions: from Plymouth, take A390 – 45 minutes. On outskirts of St Austell.
N. & M. PERRETT & G. & K. SIM ☎ (01726) 812802/812183 Fax (01726) 817097.

COVERACK • map 3E2

🏨 THE BAY HOTEL
Near Helston, TR12 6TF
Set in the unspoilt Cornish countryside of the beautiful Lizard peninsular, providing the perfect location for that away-from-it-all feeling. Furnished to an extremely high standard, most rooms have wonderful sea views. Cornish proprietors Lorraine and David Goldsworthy have succeeded in providing a comfortable and friendly atmosphere.
DOUBLE ROOM: from £20 to £30
FOOD: up to £15
Hours: breakfast 8.30am–9.30am, bar snacks 12noon–2pm, dinner 6.30pm–8.30pm, closed November until February, open Christmas and New Year.
Cuisine: ENGLISH – all meals are cooked to order with fresh local produce.
Cards: Visa, Access.
Other points: parking, Sunday lunch, open bank holidays, disabled access, pets allowed, residents' lounge, vegetarian meals, garden, licensed, central heating.
Rooms: 1 single room, 10 double rooms, 3 twin rooms. All with TV, tea/coffee-making facilities.
Directions: from Helston take B3292 to St Keverne; Coverack is signed.
LORRAINE & DAVID GOLDSWORTHY
☎ (01326) 280464.

FALMOUTH • map 3E2

🏨 GREEN LAWNS HOTEL
Western Terrace, TR11 4QJ
An elegant château-style hotel situated midway between town and beaches. Renowned à la carte restaurant and full banqueting/conference facilities available. The hotel's 'Garras Leisure Complex' consists of indoor heated swimming pool, Jacuzzi, sauna, solarium and gymnasium. Honeymoon and Executives suites available.
DOUBLE ROOM: from £30 to £40
SINGLE ROOM: from £35 to £45
FOOD: from £15 to £20
Hours: breakfast 7am–9.30am, lunch 12noon–2pm, dinner 6.45pm–10pm.
Cuisine: MODERN ENGLISH – fresh local seafood and speciality steaks.
Cards: Visa, Access, Diners, AmEx.
Other points: licensed, Sunday lunch, children welcome, coaches by prior arrangement, honeymoon suite, children welcome, baby-listening device, baby-sitting, cots, 24hr reception.

109

Rooms: 6 single rooms, 11 double rooms, 23 twin rooms. All with TV, radio, alarm, telephone, tea/coffee-making facilities.
Directions: on the main road into Falmouth heading towards the main beaches.
☎ (01326) 312734 Fax (01326) 211427.

THE GROVE HOTEL
Grove Place, TR11 4AU

Overlooking the harbour, close to shops, quays, railway station and ideally situated for exploring the Cornish coastline, the Grove Hotel was established in 1946. Although the building itself has been changed, you will still find the same relaxed and friendly atmosphere under the second generation of the Corks.
DOUBLE ROOM: from £20 to £30
SINGLE ROOM: from £25 to £35
FOOD: up to £15 CLUB ☆
Hours: breakfast 8am–9am, dinner 7pm–9pm.
Cuisine: ENGLISH / INTERNATIONAL – vegetarian meals.
Cards: Visa, Access, Diners, AmEx.
Other points: central heating, children welcome, residents' lounge, street parking.
Rooms: 2 single rooms, 5 double rooms, 4 twin rooms, 4 family rooms. All with en suite, TV, tea/coffee-making facilities.
Directions: off the A39. Take harbour road to Grove Place near the dinghy hard.
PETER & JANET CORK ☎ (01326) 319577
Fax (01326) 319577.

GYLLYNGVASE HOUSE HOTEL
Gyllyngvase Road, TR11 4DJ

Personally supervised by the owners, this is a small hotel which extends the warmest of welcomes to all its guests. The fine cuisine includes seafood specialities, and even special diets and picnic lunches can be arranged. There is an attractive lounge bar and garden terrace, and comfortably furnished rooms in colour co-ordinated schemes. Gyllyngvase is Falmouth's main beach, a wide sweep of golden sands, making it an ideal location for a family holiday.
DOUBLE ROOM: from £20 to £30
FOOD: up to £15
Hours: breakfast 8.30am–9am, dinner 6.30pm–7pm, closed mid-December until mid-January.
Cuisine: ENGLISH.
Other points: children welcome, no-smoking area, vegetarian meals, afternoon teas, pets, residents' lounge, garden, parking.
Rooms: 3 single rooms, 7 double rooms, 3 twin rooms, 2 family rooms.
Directions: from Truro take A3078 to traffic lights, go straight on to Melville Road. Hotel on right.
MR C. LE MAITRE ☎ (01326) 312956.

FOWEY • map 3E2

STANTON'S RESTAURANT
11 The Esplanade, PL23 1HY

Family-owned and run restaurant with superb views over moorings on the River Fowey estuary and harbour. The emphasis is on quality, freshness and real home-cooking. Established and renowned since 1980, Stanton's is 35 yards along the Esplanade on the left-hand side (almost invisible until you reach it).
FOOD: from £15 to £20
Hours: dinner 7pm–10.30pm (reservations appreciated), closed Monday.
Cuisine: COSMOPOLITAN – local seafood and fish, char-grilled steaks. Vegetarian and vegan meals are always available. Meals may be taken on the balcony – weather permitting.
Cards: Visa, Access, Diners, AmEx.
Other points: children welcome, no dogs.
Directions: descend hill into Fowey. Turn right into The Esplanade. 35 yards on left.
PETER & ANN WILKES ☎ (01726) 832631
Fax (01726) 832631.

GRAMPOUND • map 3E2

EASTERN PROMISE CHINESE RESTAURANT
1 Moorview, TR2 4RT

Attractive and roomy, beautifully decorated with matching furnishings, flowers on the tables, and comfortable chairs. Excellent cuisine, efficient and personal service, and a quiet, friendly atmosphere all adds to the overall ambience of this professional restaurant.
FOOD: from £15 to £20
Hours: closed Wednesday.
Cuisine: CHINESE – à la carte and table d'hôte menus, offering dishes of the highest quality of China's most famous regional cuisine, such as Cantonese, Peking and Szechuan, complemented by an extensive wine list. Vegetarian meals available.
Cards: Visa, Access, Diners, AmEx.
Other points: licensed, children catered for (please check for age limits), vegetarian meals, parking, open bank holidays.
Directions: between Truro and St Austell.
PHILIP & LISA TSE ☎ (01726) 883033.

HELSTON • map 3E1

NANPLOUGH FARM
Cury, White Cross, TR12 7BQ

Nanplough Farm is a Victorian farmhouse situated in the small, attractive village of Cury. It has been completely modernized and luxuriously furnished throughout. The house itself sits in 26 acres of its own grounds with lovely views all round. The gardens are lovely and are there for all to share.
DOUBLE ROOM: from £20 to £30
SINGLE ROOM: from £25 to £35
FOOD: up to £15
Hours: breakfast 8.30am–9.15am, dinner 6pm.
Cuisine: ENGLISH – traditional home-cooked meals using predominantly home-grown produce.
Cards: Visa, Access.
Other points: parking, children welcome, vegetarian meals, residents' lounge, garden,

heated swimming pool, games room, play area, barbecue area.
Rooms: 2 double rooms, 1 twin room. All with en suite, satellite TV, hair dryer, tea/coffee-making facilities.
Directions: leave Helston on Lizard Road, through R.N.A.S. and follow signs to Cury.
LAWRENCE JOHN MAKIN ☎ (01326) 241088.

LAND'S END • map 3E1

OLD SUCCESS INN HOTEL
Sennen Cove, TR19 7DG
With excellent views of the coast and sea, this spacious 17th century inn is the perfect place to relax. In the restaurant you can expect the presentation of the food and the food itself to be first-class. The comfortable bedrooms, including two bridal suites, are all of a very high standard, and the service throughout is warm and friendly, but, most importantly, it is genuine.
DOUBLE ROOM: from £30 to £40
SINGLE ROOM: up to £25
FOOD: up to £15
Hours: breakfast 8.30am–9.30am, lunch 12noon–2.30pm, dinner 7pm–9.30pm.
Cuisine: ENGLISH – house specialities are seafood and carvery.
Cards: Visa, Access, Eurocard, MasterCard.
Other points: children welcome, parking, residents' lounge, vegetarian meals, no-smoking area.
Rooms: 1 single room, 8 double rooms, 2 twin rooms, 1 family room.
Directions: A30 towards Land's End, turn right at Sennen Cove sign.
BRIAN WARREN (PROPRIETOR), GEOFFREY WELLS (MANAGER) ☎ (01736) 871232
Fax (01736) 871457.

LIZARD • map 3E1

THE CAERTHILLIAN
Helston, TR12 7NQ
A Victorian building in the centre of the village, retaining much of its character with some of the original furnishings and fireplaces, yet recently refurbished to provide modern standards of comfort. Set in the beautiful surroundings of the Lizard Peninsula. Restaurant serves a selection of sensibly priced home-cooked food, offering quality and real value.
DOUBLE ROOM: up to £20
FOOD: up to £15 CLUB
Hours: breakfast 8.30am–9.30am, lunch 12noon–2pm, dinner 6pm–9pm, restaurant closed Sunday evening, Monday and Tuesday (winter only).
Cuisine: INTERNATIONAL – international cuisine, with Italian bias. Dishes may include guinea fowl and mushrooms in red wine, grilled whole lemon sole, home-made pasta dishes.
Cards: Visa, Access, AmEx.
Other points: licensed, Sunday lunch, children welcome, pets by prior arrangement, parking, vegetarian meals.
Rooms: 2 double rooms, 1 twin room, 1 family room. All with TV, radio, tea/coffee-making facilities, alarm.
Directions: in Lizard village, opposite the post office.
JACK & PENNY GAYTON ☎ (01326) 290019.

LOOE • map 3D2

ALLHAYS COUNTRY HOUSE
Talland Bay, PL13 2JB
Allhays is a period country house standing in 'an English country garden' with spectacular views over to Talland Bay. A Victorian-style conservatory extends the dining room into the garden for dining alfresco whatever the weather. Allhays has an enviable reputation for its food, and most particularly for its impressive and daily-changing cheeseboard. (See special feature on pages 21–23.)

LES ROUTIERS
CHEESE-BOARD of the Year 1995

DOUBLE ROOM: from £30 to £40
FOOD: up to £15
Hours: breakfast 8.30am–9am, dinner 7pm.
Cuisine: MODERN ENGLISH – new English cuisine using the finest local and home-grown produce, freshly prepared and cooked in the Aga by chef/patronne Lynda Spring. British cheeses.
Cards: Visa, Access, Diners, AmEx.
Other points: pets allowed, children welcome, vegetarian meals, parking, residents' bar, residents' lounge, disabled access.
Rooms: 4 double rooms, 3 twin rooms. All with TV, radio, telephone, tea/coffee-making facilities, alarm, hair dryer.
Directions: turn left 2½ miles from Looe on A387. Follow hotel signposts.
BRIAN & LYNDA SPRING ☎ (01503) 72434
Fax (01503) 72929.

COOMBE FARM
Widegates, PL13 1QN
A lovely country house surrounded by lawns, meadows, woods and streams with superb views to the sea. Log fires. Delicious home-cooking. Candlelit dining. Licensed. All bedrooms are en suite and have colour TV, radio, tea- and coffee-making facilities and direct-dial telephone. In the grounds are many animals and flowers, a swimming pool (heated in summer), croquet lawn and a stone barn for snooker and table tennis. Nearby are golf, fishing, tennis, horse-riding and glorious walks and beaches. The perfect centre for visiting all parts of Cornwall and Devon.
DOUBLE ROOM: from £20 to £30
SINGLE ROOM: up to £25
FOOD: up to £15
Hours: breakfast 8.30am–9am, dinner 7pm–7.30pm, closed November until February.
Cuisine: ENGLISH – traditional home-cooking.
Other points: central heating, children welcome, residents' lounge, garden, swimming pool.
Rooms: 3 double rooms, 3 twin rooms, 3 family rooms. All with en suite, TV, hair dryer, radio, telephone, tea/coffee-making facilities.
Directions: Just south of Widegates on the B3253, between Looe and Hessenford.
ALEXANDER & SALLY LOW ☎ (01503) 240223.

PELYNT DAGGER RESTAURANT
14 Barton Meadow, Pelynt by Looe, PL13 2LW

A warm welcome awaits you at this popular family-run restaurant, serving quality meals prepared from local produce at value-for-money prices. Comfortable lounge area to sit and make your choice from the comprehensive menu, in a relaxing and friendly atmosphere.
FOOD: up to £15 CLUB ☆
Hours: dinner 6pm–11.30pm, last orders 8.45pm, closed October until Easter.
Cuisine: ENGLISH / CONTINENTAL – local beef, steak Portuguese, award-winning duckling, roast Sunday lunch.
Cards: Visa, Access, AmEx, Eurocard, MasterCard.
Other points: licensed, open-air dining, Sunday lunch, children welcome, parking, no-smoking area.
Directions: 4 miles from Looe on B3359 in Pelynt village.
JOHN & JOAN BLAKE ☎ (01503) 220386.

PUNCHBOWL INN
Lanreath, near Looe, PL13 2NX

This oak-beamed inn is over 400 years old and has served as the court house, a coaching inn and smugglers' distribution house in its time! It now offers visitors a chance to enjoy traditional hospitality within its historic walls.
DOUBLE ROOM: from £20 to £30
FOOD: up to £15 CLUB
Hours: breakfast 8.30am–9.30am, lunch 12noon–2pm, dinner 7pm–9pm.
Cuisine: ENGLISH – table d'hôte and à la carte. Traditional English, seasonal fish menu and ice cream specialities. Bar snack menu.
Cards: Visa, Access.
Other points: licensed, Sunday lunch, no-smoking area, children welcome, pets allowed, beer garden, vegetarian meals, residents' bar, residents' lounge, parking.
Rooms: 14 twin rooms. All with TV, tea/coffee-making facilities.
Directions: off the B3359 in the centre of Lanreath village.
HARVEY & SYLVIA FRITH ☎ (01503) 220218.

LOSTWITHIEL • map 3D2

TREWITHEN RESTAURANT
3 Fore Street, PL2 0AD

A personally-run restaurant with a cottage atmosphere, where all the food is home-cooked. The cuisine reflects the proprietors' international background and offers both à la carte and blackboard menus. Situated next door to the Duchy Palace, with Restormel Castle, Lanhydroch House and Bodmin all close by.
FOOD: from £20 to £25
Hours: dinner 7pm–9.30pm (last orders), closed Sunday and Monday.
Cuisine: INTERNATIONAL – including summer seafood, lobster and winter game.
Cards: Visa, Access, Diners.
Other points: children welcome, no pets,

disabled access, vegetarian meals.
Directions: A390, halfway between Liskeard and St Austell, 5 miles south of Bodmin.
B.F. & L.J. ROLLS ☎ (01208) 872373.

MEVAGISSEY • map 3E2

HARBOUR LIGHTS
Polkirt Hill, near St Austell, PL26 6UR

A family-run fully licensed freehouse with letting accommodation in one of the finest locations in Cornwall. Situated on the cliff top with panoramic views over Mevagissey and St Austell Bay from all public rooms and most of the bedrooms. Comfort and atmosphere are guaranteed.
DOUBLE ROOM: from £20 to £30
SINGLE ROOM: up to £25
FOOD: up to £15
Hours: breakfast 8.30am–9am, lunch 12noon–2pm, dinner 6.30pm–9pm.
Cuisine: ENGLISH – extensive bar menu served in public bar or dining room, where smoking is not permitted.
Cards: Visa, Access, Eurocard.
Other points: licensed, Sunday lunch, children catered for (please check for age limits), parking, no dogs.
Rooms: 7 bedrooms. All with TV, telephone, tea/coffee-making facilities. Most en suite.
Directions: B3273 to Mevagissey from A390. Follow Gorren Haven signpost.
MR & MRS SHENTON & MR & MRS QUINN ☎ (01726) 843249.

MR BISTRO
East Quay, PL26 6QH

This restaurant is situated facing the harbour in a town with a long-established fishing history. The menu, needless to say, specializes in fish dishes. The 'Dish of the Day' depends on the fishermen's catch of the day!
FOOD: from £15 to £20
Hours: lunch 12noon–2pm, dinner 7pm–10pm, closed November until January.
Cuisine: ENGLISH / SEAFOOD – fresh fish and shellfish, sweet trolley.
Cards: Visa, Access, Diners, AmEx.
Other points: Sunday lunch, children welcome.
Directions: on the harbour front.
CHRIS & ROMER ROBINS ☎ (01726) 842432.

SHARKSFIN HOTEL & RESTAURANT
The Quay, PL26 6QU

The Sharksfin Hotel and Restaurant occupies a commanding position on the quay, overlooking this quaint and busy fishing harbour. The bar and restaurant provide a warm welcome with a high standard of decor and friendly service. Most of the 11 well-equipped bedrooms have views of the harbour and sea. The location makes the hotel an ideal place from which to tour Cornwall and the many nearby places of interest. For golfers, no Cornish course is more than one hour away and play-as-you-please golf can be arranged to suit all individual requirements.

DOUBLE ROOM: from £20 to £30
FOOD: from £15 to £20
Hours: breakfast from 8am, lunch 12noon–2.30pm, dinner 7pm–9.30pm, closed January and February.
Cuisine: ENGLISH / FRENCH – the French head chef offers the best of French and English cuisine using fresh local fish, shellfish and West Country produce. Full à la carte, three-course and five-course gourmet menus.
Cards: Visa, Access, Diners, AmEx.
Other points: children welcome, afternoon teas, vegetarian meals, residents' lounge.
Rooms: 2 single rooms, 8 double rooms, 1 family room. All with TV, radio, bar, telephone, tea/coffee-making facilities.
Directions: Sharksfin Hotel is an old historic building situated right on the quay in the picturesque fishing village of Mevagissey, accessed by the B3273.
J. & A. GOODHEW ☎ (01726) 843241
Fax (01726) 842552.

MYLOR BRIDGE • map 3E2

THE PANDORA INN
Restronguet Creek, near Falmouth, TR11 5ST
A beautiful 13th century thatched inn reputedly owned by Captain Edwards of Bounty mutiny fame. Flagstone floors, low, beamed ceilings and gleaming brasswork complete the picturebook setting. Come by car or by boat (yachts may be moored on the 140ft pontoon at the front) and enjoy the famous, fine cuisine.
FOOD: up to £15 ☆
Hours: bar meals 12noon–2.15pm, dinner 7pm–12midnight, last orders 10pm, bar meals 6.30pm–10pm.
Cuisine: ENGLISH – local fresh fish and fresh produce. Cornish specialities. Afternoon teas.
Cards: Visa, Access.
Other points: licensed, open-air dining, Sunday lunch, disabled access, pets allowed, afternoon tea, vegetarian meals.
Directions: from A39 in Falmouth take Mylor turn, then downhill to Pandora.
MR & MRS R. HOUGH ☎ (01326) 372678.

NEWQUAY • map 3D2

CORISANDE MANOR HOTEL
Riverside Avenue, Pentire, TR7 1PL
Built in 1900 of Austrian design, standing in three acres of grounds with private foreshore. The Painters have owned and run the hotel since 1968 and they offer many facilities, such as rowing boats, a putting green, croquet and giant outdoor chess. Advance booking is strongly recommended.
DOUBLE ROOM: from £20 to £30
SINGLE ROOM: up to £25
FOOD: up to £15
Hours: breakfast 8.30am–9.30am, bar meals 12.30am–1.30pm, dinner 7pm–7.30pm, closed 15th October until 6th May.

Cuisine: ENGLISH.
Cards: Visa, Access.
Other points: central heating, children catered for (please check for age limits), residents' lounge, garden.
Rooms: 5 single rooms, 8 double rooms, 3 twin rooms, 3 triple rooms. All with TV, radio, tea/coffee-making facilities. Most rooms are en suite.
Directions: located off the B3282 on the Gannel estuary.
DAVID PAINTER ☎ (01637) 872042.

THE GREAT WESTERN HOTEL
Cliff Road, TR7 2PT
An imposing cream building perched on the cliff above Great Western Beach, offering magnificent seaviews. The hotel comprises a lawned garden, indoor swimming pool and Jacuzzi, and serves traditional English food with warm hospitality.
DOUBLE ROOM: from £20 to £30
SINGLE ROOM: from £25 to £35
FOOD: up to £15 CLUB
Hours: breakfast 8am–9.30am, lunch 12noon–2pm, bar meals 12noon–2pm, dinner 7pm–8.45pm, bar meals 6pm–9.30pm.
Cuisine: ENGLISH – home-made dishes.
Cards: Visa, Access, Diners, AmEx.
Other points: licensed, Sunday lunch, coaches by prior arrangement, children welcome, baby-listening device, cots, foreign exchange, residents' lounge, residents' bar, swimming pool.
Rooms: 12 single rooms, 21 double rooms, 18 twin rooms, 18 triple rooms, 3 quad rooms. All with TV, radio, alarm, telephone, tea/coffee-making facilities.
Directions: on the cliff road near the railway station.
MR D. FITTER ☎ (01637) 872010 Fax (01637) 874435.

THE HEADLAND HOTEL
Fistrol Bay, TR7 1EW
The 'Great British Holiday' revisited at one of the UK's most outstanding locations: 10 acres of private headland with the sea on three sides. Enjoy old-fashioned service provided by friendly staff, good Cornish food and excellent-value wines.
DOUBLE ROOM: from £30 to £40
SINGLE ROOM: from £35 to £45
FOOD: from £15 to £20
Hours: lunch 12.30am–2pm, dinner 7.30pm–9pm, closed mid-November until mid-March, open New Year and February half term.
Cuisine: ENGLISH – including local crab and lobster. Table d'hôte and à la carte. Snacks, home-made cakes and scones served in coffee shop.
Cards: Visa, Access, Diners, AmEx.
Other points: children welcome, pets allowed, residents' lounge, residents' bar, garden, swimming pool, tennis, billiards, putting green, licensed, afternoon tea.
Rooms: 100 bedrooms. All with en suite, TV, telephone and tea/coffee-making facilities. Most with superb sea views.
Directions: follow directions to Fistral Beach.
MR & MRS ARMSTRONG ☎ (01637) 872211.

🛏 TREGURRIAN HOTEL
Watergate Bay, TR8 4AB
A modern hotel overlooking the surf beach of Watergate Bay. Offering comfortable accommodation, there are excellent facilities for family holidays, with heated swimming pool, games room, laundry room, etc. A wide range of bar meals are available. Only 100 yards from the beach, it is suitable for all ages and offers excellent surfing conditions. Central location for all of Cornwall.
DOUBLE ROOM: from £20 to £30
SINGLE ROOM: up to £25
FOOD: up to £15
Hours: breakfast 8.30am–9.15am, lunch 12.30am–1.30pm, dinner 6.45pm–7.30pm.
Cuisine: ENGLISH.
Cards: Visa, Access.
Other points: children welcome, garden, afternoon tea, pets allowed.
Rooms: 4 single rooms, 11 double rooms, 5 twin rooms, 7 family rooms.
Directions: 3 miles from Newquay, on the B3276.
MR & MRS MOLLOY ☎ (01637) 860280.

🛏 TYGWYN
107 Pentire Avenue, TR7 1PF
A luxury split-level chalet bungalow set high on the cliff top overlooking the beach, with sea views from every room. On the food side, the emphasis is on fresh produce with a choice of menu. The Tygwyn may be small, but the welcome is warm and served with true Cornish hospitality. Tygwyn offers its guests the convenience of on-site parking.
DOUBLE ROOM: up to £20
FOOD: up to £15
Hours: breakfast 8.30am–9am, dinner 6pm–8pm, closed November until February.
Cuisine: ENGLISH – special diets and vegetarians also catered for.
Other points: central heating, children catered for (please check for age limits), residents' lounge, garden, sun patio.
Rooms: 1 single room, 3 double rooms, 1 twin room, 1 family room. All with TV, tea/coffee-making facilities. Most en suite.
Directions: from the centre of Newquay, take the road to Pentire headland.
MEL, CLIVE & MARK GRIFFIN ☎ (01637) 874480.

🛏 WATERGATE BAY HOTEL
Watergate Bay, near Newquay, TR8 4AA
Set in countryside-by-the-sea, this family-owned and run hotel has grounds that include a sandy beach and the famous coastal path. Watergate is a magical place away from the bustle of the town, with a wonderful range of indoor/outdoor leisure facilities, good food and friendly service in a happy, relaxed atmosphere.
DOUBLE ROOM: from £20 to £30
SINGLE ROOM: from £25 to £35
FOOD: up to £15
Hours: breakfast 8.30am–9.45am, lunch 12.30am–1.45pm, bar meals 10.30am–6pm, dinner 7pm–8.30pm, closed mid-November until March.

Cuisine: ENGLISH – a good selection of traditional and modern English cuisine with vegetarian and continental dishes.
Cards: Visa, Access.
Other points: children welcome, traditional Sunday lunch, surfing, heated indoor swimming pool, heated outdoor swimming pool, sports hall, badminton, squash, tennis, skittles, snooker, sauna, solarium, spa bath, live music, dancing, entertainment, pets allowed, parking, special golf rates.
Rooms: 8 single rooms, 20 double rooms, 4 twin rooms, 7 triple rooms, 18 family rooms/family suites. All with en suite, TV, telephone, radio, baby-listening device, tea/coffee-making facilities.
Directions: from A30 after Bodmin, follow A3059 to airport, then B3276 to Watergate Bay.
JOHN & MARY ASHWORTH ☎ (01637) 860543 [Fax] (01637) 860333.

🛏 WHIPSIDERRY HOTEL
Trevelgue Road, Porth, TR7 3LY
The Whipsiderry commands a superb position overlooking Porth beach and bay, with breathtaking views of both sea and country. Whether exploring the rugged Cornish coastland or venturing inland, the hotel provides a friendly retreat. On fine summer evenings enjoy a barbecue on the terrace, and at night, watch the badgers feed and play only a few feet away.
DOUBLE ROOM: from £20 to £30
FOOD: up to £15
Hours: breakfast 8.30am–9am, lunch 12noon–2pm, dinner 6.30pm–8pm, closed November until March, open Christmas.
Cuisine: ENGLISH – varied table d'hôte menu changes daily.
Other points: licensed, open-air dining, Sunday lunch, central heating, children welcome, pets allowed, swimming pool, sauna, billiards, launderette.
Rooms: 14 double rooms, 3 twin rooms, 4 family rooms, 2 suites. All with TV, radio, tea/coffee-making facilities, baby-listening device.
Directions: Trevelgue Road leads off Watergate Road (the seafront).
RICHARD & ANN DRACKFORD ☎ (01637) 874777.

🛏 WHITE LODGE HOTEL
Mawgan Porth, TR8 4BN
Family-owned and run, the hotel is beautifully situated in an elevated position, just 100 yards from the golden sands of Mawgan Porth. Excellent views of the sea and cliffs from the dining room, bar and most of the bedrooms. Comments from recent visitors highly praise the White Lodge and commend the comfortable accommodation, good food and welcoming, friendly service.
DOUBLE ROOM: from £20 to £30
SINGLE ROOM: up to £25
FOOD: up to £15
Hours: breakfast 8am–9am, bar snacks 12noon–2pm, dinner 6pm–7.30pm, closed November until February.
Cuisine: ENGLISH.
Cards: Visa, Access, AmEx.

Other points: children welcome, afternoon tea, pets allowed, residents' lounge, picnic lunches, vegetarian meals, games room, garden.
Rooms: 1 single room, 4 double rooms, 7 twin rooms, 6 family rooms. All with TV, tea/coffee-making facilities, heating, baby-listening device.
Directions: B3276 coast road between Newquay and Padstow. 5 miles from Newquay.
JOHN & DIANE PARRY ☎ (01637) 860512.

PADSTOW • map 3D2

THE OLD MILL COUNTRY HOUSE
Little Petherick, PL27 7QT

This 16th century converted corn mill complete with water wheel is situated in the pretty village of Little Petherick and is a Grade II listed building set within its own gardens next to a stream that dawdles into the Carmel estuary. It retains much of its original character and charm whilst providing guests with modern amenities amidst a welcoming and friendly atmosphere. A unique feature of The Old Mill is the kitchen, which is available for residents' inspection of the cuisine, of which the proprietors Michael and Pat Walker are justly proud.
DOUBLE ROOM: from £20 to £30
FOOD: up to £15
Hours: breakfast 8.45am–9.15am, dinner 7pm, closed November until February.
Cuisine: TRADITIONAL – freshly prepared and traditionally cooked.
Other points: parking, no-smoking area, residents' lounge, garden, vegetarian meals, residents' bar.
Rooms: 4 double rooms, 2 twin rooms. All with tea/coffee-making facilities.
Directions: A39, then A389.
MICHAEL & PAT WALKER ☎ (01841) 540388.

PENZANCE • map 3E1

CARNSON HOUSE HOTEL
East Terrace, TR18 2TD

This small, comfortable, private hotel enjoys one of Penzance's most central positions. Close to harbour and beaches, it is an ideal base for touring the Land's End peninsula with its dramatic scenery of coves and cliffs. Tourist information and excursion booking service available. French and German spoken.
DOUBLE ROOM: up to £20
SINGLE ROOM: up to £25
Hours: breakfast 8am–8.30am, dinner 6.15pm – orders to be made by 4pm.
Cuisine: ENGLISH.
Cards: Visa, Access, Diners, AmEx.
Other points: central heating, residents' lounge, garden.
Rooms: 3 single rooms, 3 double rooms, 2 twin rooms. All with TV, tea/coffee-making facilities. Some en suite.
Directions: on the right side of main road entering Penzance from the A30 east.
RICHARD & TRISHA HILDER ☎ (01736) 65589.

LYNWOOD GUEST HOUSE
41 Morrab Road, TR18 4EX

A comfortable, well-appointed family guest house built in Victorian times. Situated between the promenade and the town centre, Lynwood is convenient for all amenities and close to the sub-tropical gardens. An ideal base for visiting Land's End and the Lizard peninsula, St Michael's Mount and the Isles of Scilly.
DOUBLE ROOM: up to £20
Hours: breakfast 8am–8.45am.
Cuisine: BREAKFAST.
Cards: Visa, Access, Diners, AmEx.
Other points: central heating, children welcome, no evening meal, residents' lounge.
Rooms: 1 single room, 1 double room, 2 twin rooms, 3 family rooms. All with TV, radio, alarm, tea/coffee-making facilities.
Directions: Morrab Road is a turning off the seafront.
MRS JOAN WOOD ☎ (01736) 65871.

UNION HOTEL
Chapel Street, TR18 4AL

Steeped in history, the hotel dates back to the 17th century. It was here that news of Nelson's victory and death at the Battle of Trafalgar was first announced. Today, well-cooked and presented meals are served in a cosy atmosphere, and the accommodation is comfortable. Log fires in winter add to the warm welcome extended to all guests.
DOUBLE ROOM: from £30 to £40
FOOD: up to £15
Hours: breakfast 8am–9.30am, bar meals 12noon–2pm, dinner 6pm–9.30pm, bar meals 6pm–9pm.
Cuisine: ENGLISH – full à la carte menu, table d'hôte and bar snacks.
Cards: Visa, Access, Diners, AmEx.
Other points: licensed, Sunday lunch, children welcome.
Directions: take the A30 or A394 to Penzance. Follow town centre one-way system.
☎ (01736) 62319.

PERRANPORTH • map 3D1

BEACH DUNES HOTEL
Ramoth Way, Reen Sands, TR6 0BY

Roomy, comfortably furnished hotel, with colour-coordinated decor and pleasant, cheerful atmosphere. The hotel is situated in the sand dunes above the beach, and adjoins the golf course.
DOUBLE ROOM: from £20 to £30
FOOD: up to £15
Hours: breakfast 8.15am–9.30am, bar meals 12noon–2pm, dinner 6pm–11pm, closed November and December.
Cuisine: ENGLISH – traditional English home-cooked food. Fixed menu which changes daily.
Cards: Visa, Access, AmEx.
Other points: no-smoking area, children welcome, afternoon tea, parking, residents' lounge, garden, indoor swimming pool, squash.
Rooms: 4 double rooms, 2 twin rooms, 2 quad rooms. All with TV, radio, telephone, tea/coffee-making facilities.

Directions: B3285. Situated along a private road, 400 metres from main road.
KEITH WOOLDRIDGE ☎ (01872) 572263
Fax (01872) 573824.

🍴 THE GALLEON RESTAURANT
St Pirrans Road, TR6 0BJ
Excellent service in spacious surroundings makes this a highly popular restaurant with business people, locals and tourists alike. Although there are many delious alternatives all prepared from the freshest produce available, locally caught seafood is a prevailing feature of The Galleon.
FOOD: up to £15
Hours: lunch 12noon–2pm, dinner 6.30pm–9.30pm.
Cuisine: ENGLISH – fresh fish and steaks are the specialities from the good selection of home-cooked meals.
Cards: Visa, Access, Diners, Eurocard, Switch.
Directions: located in Perranporth High Street.
MR & MRS T. & V. SUTTON ☎ (01872) 572066.

PHILLEIGH • map 3E2

🍴 SMUGGLERS COTTAGE OF TOLVERNE
Near Truro, TR2 5NG
This 500-year-old thatched cottage has been run by the Newman family for over 60 years. It is situated on the banks of the River Fal, near the King Harry car ferry on the Roseland Peninsula, with own landing stage and moorings. Smugglers Cottage offers a selection of over 70 different malt whiskies.
FOOD: from £15 to £20 🍲
Hours: morning coffee 10.30am, lunch 12noon–2pm, cream teas 3pm–5.30pm, dinner 7.30pm–9pm.
Cuisine: ENGLISH – daily changing menu of home-cooked dishes using fresh local produce, particularly fish and seafood. Daily buffet.
Cards: Visa, Access.
Other points: open-air dining, children catered for (please check for age limits).
Directions: near King Harry car ferry on Roseland peninsula.
ELIZABETH & PETER NEWMAN ☎ (01872) 580309 Fax (01872) 580216.

PILLATON • map 3D3

🏠 THE WEARY FRIAR INN
Near Saltash, PL12 6QS
A famous old 12th century inn situated next to the church of St Odolphus, where you will find true character and atmosphere. Today The Weary Friar welcomes you to imaginative food of a high standard, superb surroundings and comfortable accommodation. Highly recommended for its high-quality food and the excellent combination of modern comforts with 12th century character.
DOUBLE ROOM: from £20 to £30
SINGLE ROOM: from £25 to £35
FOOD: up to £15 🍲

Hours: breakfast 8am–9am, lunch 12noon–2pm, dinner 7pm–9.30pm.
Cuisine: MODERN ENGLISH – dishes may include fillets of sole champagne, honey roast saddle of lamb, smokey carpetbag steak (with oysters), vegetable and nut salousie.
Cards: Visa, Access.
Other points: licensed, open-air dining, Sunday lunch, children welcome, afternoon tea, residents' lounge.
Directions: between Saltash and Callington, two miles west of A388. Near St Mellion.
SUE & ROGER SHARMAN ☎ (01579) 50238.

POLPERRO • map 3E2

🍴 THE KITCHEN
The Coombes, PL13 2RQ
A small, informal, licensed restaurant specializing in high-quality dishes prepared by the owners, who have a well-deserved reputation for imaginative food.
FOOD: from £15 to £20 🍲 CLUB
Hours: closed Sunday–Thursday from November until March, dinner 7pm–9.30pm.
Cuisine: MODERN ENGLISH – fish, lobster, crab, duck, steak, lamb and vegetarian menu.
Cards: Visa, Access.
Other points: parking, disabled access.
Directions: on the walk down to the harbour.
IAN & VANESSA BATESON ☎ (01503) 72780.

🍴 NELSON'S RESTAURANT
Big Green, PL13 2QT
A large, olde-worlde restaurant with a distinct nautical flavour, reflecting the proprietor's long connection with the sea. The table d'hôte menu changes with the availability of fresh produce. An intimate restaurant with a friendly atmosphere.
FOOD: up to £15 ★
Hours: lunch 11.45am–2pm, dinner 7pm–10pm, closed Saturday lunch and Monday, closed mid-January until mid-February.
Cuisine: ENGLISH / FRENCH / SEAFOOD – fresh seafood, roasts, grills, game.
Cards: Visa, Access, Diners, AmEx.
Other points: licensed, Sunday lunch, children welcome, pets by prior arrangement.
Directions: on the Saxon bridge in Polperro.
PETER NELSON ☎ (01503) 72366.

🏠 PENRYN HOUSE HOTEL
The Coombes, PL13 2RG
Located on the main village road in a tranquil setting, the hotel offers imaginative food using mostly local fresh produce. Enjoy extra-individual attention and quality of service, whilst relaxing in the comfortable surroundings. An exciting range of 'special interest holidays' are also offered, including Watercolour Painting Weekends, Walking Weekends and Murder Mysteries.
DOUBLE ROOM: from £20 to £30
FOOD: from £15 to £20 🍲 CLUB
Hours: breakfast 9am–9.30am, dinner 7pm–9.30pm, open all year.
Cuisine: ENGLISH / CONTINENTAL – a varied

selection of vegetarian dishes are also available.
Cards: Visa, Access, Diners.
Other points: licensed, open-air dining, no-smoking area, children welcome, pets allowed, parking, residents' lounge, afternoon tea, open bank holidays.
Directions: A387 to Polperro from A38.
MS C. KAY ☎ (01503) 72157 [Fax] (01503) 73055.

PORT ISAAC • map 3D2

BAY HOTEL & RESTAURANT
1 The Terrace, PL29 3SG
Small, friendly, family-run hotel at the top of this Cornish fishing village, with views out to sea and cliffs. Ideal for a quiet holiday. 3- and 4-night mini-breaks available out of main season.
DOUBLE ROOM: up to £20
FOOD: up to £15
Hours: breakfast 8.30am–9.30am, dinner 7pm–8pm, bar snacks 11am–10pm, closed November until Easter.
Cuisine: ENGLISH / CONTINENTAL – fresh local crab and seafood, including lobster, home-baked pies and pastries. Vegetarians catered for.
Other points: licensed, Sunday lunch, children welcome.
Rooms: 2 single rooms, 3 double rooms, 1 twin room, 2 family rooms. All with tea/coffee-making facilities.
Directions: on the B3267 at the top of the cliff, opposite main public car park.
JIM & MARY ANDREWS ☎ (01208) 880380.

THE CORNISH ARMS
Pendoggett, PL30 3HH
This typical Cornish 16th century coaching inn, located in the heart of the small village of Pendoggett, is indeed charming. The excellent cuisine is served in a relaxed and friendly atmosphere, and the choice of fresh seafood, from the local fishing villages, makes it well worth a visit!
DOUBLE ROOM: from £30 to £40
SINGLE ROOM: from £35 to £45
FOOD: up to £15 [CLUB]
Hours: breakfast 8.30am–9.30am, lunch 12.30am–2pm, dinner 7.15pm–12midnight, last orders 9.30pm.
Cuisine: ENGLISH / SEAFOOD – à la carte and bar menu. Fresh local lobster, crab, lemon sole and fillet steak filled with sautéed mushrooms and smoked oysters, specialities.
Cards: Visa, Access, Diners, AmEx, Switch.
Other points: licensed, open-air dining, Sunday lunch, no-smoking area, pets allowed, children welcome, disabled access, residents' lounge, residents' bar, vegetarian meals.
Rooms: 3 double rooms, 4 twin rooms. All with TV, telephone, tea/coffee-making facilities.
Directions: off A30, follow A395 until A39 T-junction. Left, then first right onto B3314.
JOHN ROBINSON & MERVYN GILMOUR
☎ (01208) 880263 [Fax] (01208) 880335.

OLD SCHOOL HOTEL
Fore Street, PL29 3RB
The Old School dates from 1875 and stands sentinel on the cliff top overlooking the harbour and out to sea. The accommodation is excellent, tastefully furnished to provide a high standard of comfort yet retaining the original character of the building. The restaurant specializes in local fish and seafood. Deep-sea fishing, riding, golf and sailing are all available nearby.
DOUBLE ROOM: from £20 to £30
FOOD: up to £15
Hours: breakfast 8am–11am, lunch 11am–3pm, bar snacks 11am–9.30pm, dinner 7pm–9.30pm, open all year.
Cuisine: SEAFOOD – restaurant specializes in fish and seafood dishes such as whole grilled lemon sole, lobster Thermidor, mariner's fish pie. Bar meals.
Cards: Visa, Access.
Other points: licensed, open-air dining, Sunday lunch, children welcome, afternoon tea, residents' lounge, pets allowed, garden, barbecues, medieval banquets.
Rooms: 6 double rooms, 1 twin room, 3 family rooms, 3 suites. All with TV.
Directions: 9 miles north of Wadebridge on B3314 until left turn on B3267.
MICHAEL WARNER ☎ (01208) 880721.

ROCK • map 3D2

ROSKARNON HOUSE HOTEL
Rock, near Wadebridge, PL27 6LD
By the golden sands of Rock and the open sea of the Camel estuary, the Roskarnon House Hotel is an ideal place in which to enjoy the delights of a holiday in Cornwall. This small, unpretentious hotel offers all the essentials and amenities to make your stay a happy one. Simple, home-cooked food.
DOUBLE ROOM: from £20 to £30
SINGLE ROOM: up to £25
FOOD: up to £15
Hours: breakfast 8.30am–9.30am, dinner 7pm–8pm, lunch 12noon–1.30pm.
Cuisine: ENGLISH – dishes include vegetarian lasagne, roast chicken and poached salmon with butter sauce.
Cards: AmEx.
Other points: children welcome, garden, afternoon tea.
Rooms: 12 bedrooms. Most rooms are en suite.
Directions: overlooking Camel estuary. Off A39 and B3314.
IAN VEALL ☎ (01208) 862329.

ST AGNES • map 3E1

PENKERRIS
Penwinnick Road, TL5 OPA
Enchanting Edwardian residence with garden and large lawn in an unspoilt Cornish village. Dramatic cliff walks, beaches, swimming and surfing all nearby. Superb home-cooking: traditional roasts,

home-made fruit tarts with local fresh produce. Touches of the exotic with excellent curries, pastas and vegetable dishes.
DOUBLE ROOM: up to £20
FOOD: up to £15
Hours: breakfast 8.30am, dinner 6.30pm.
Cuisine: ENGLISH / INTERNATIONAL.
Cards: Visa, Access.
Other points: central heating, children welcome, residents' lounge, garden, piano, log fire, video.
Directions: take B3277 off A30 at Chiverton roundabout. 3 miles into village.
DOROTHY GILL-CAREY ☎ (01872) 552262.

ST IVES • map 3E1

BOSKERRIS HOTEL
Carbis Bay, TR26 2RU
A family-run hotel, set in private gardens with a heated swimming pool, noted for its fine wines and good food. Overlooks Carbis Bay, with magnificent views across to St Ives harbour on one side and Godrevy Head on the other.
DOUBLE ROOM: from £20 to £30
FOOD: up to £15
Hours: breakfast 8.30am–9.30am, bar meals 12.30am–1.30pm, dinner 7pm–8.30pm.
Cuisine: ENGLISH.
Cards: Visa, Access, Diners.
Other points: children welcome, pets allowed, afternoon tea, open bank holidays, special breaks.
Directions: along A30 to St Ives. Third turning on right as you enter Carbis Bay.
MR & MRS MONK ☎ (01736) 795295
Fax (01736) 798632.

CHY-AN-DOUR HOTEL
Trelyon Avenue, TR26 2AD
This 19th century former sea captain's home has been extended to form a most attractive hotel with superb panoramic views over St Ives Bay and harbour. All bedrooms are en suite, most with breathtaking views.
DOUBLE ROOM: from £20 to £30
FOOD: from £15 to £20
Hours: breakfast 8.30am–9.30am, bar meals 12noon–2pm, dinner 7pm–8pm.
Cuisine: ENGLISH – six-course table d'hôte dinner menu. Main-course dishes include a choice of meat, fish, salad and vegetarian.
Cards: Visa, Access.
Other points: licensed, no-smoking area, children welcome, residents' lounge, garden, residents' bar, baby-listening device, baby-sitting, cots.
Rooms: 10 double rooms, 10 twin rooms, 3 family rooms. All with TV, radio, telephone, tea/coffee-making facilities.
Directions: A3074, on main road into St Ives.
DAVID & RENEE WATSON ☎ (01736) 796436
Fax (01736) 795772.

CHY-AN-GWEDHEN
St Ives Road, Carbis Bay, TR26 3JW
This delightful, welcoming guest house, a haven for non-smokers, is exceptionally decorated throughout and offers splendid views of St Ives Bay. The superb bedrooms are outstanding in design and offer many facilities for that comfortable home-away-from-home feeling. Located in St Ives, adjacent to the coastal footpath, it is ideal for visiting St Ives' Tate Gallery or Land's End, or relaxing on one of the magnificent beaches nearby, or just walking the wonderful coastline. Watersports, golf, riding close by.
DOUBLE ROOM: up to £20
SINGLE ROOM: up to £25
Hours: breakfast 7am–9am, closed Christmas and New Year.
Cuisine: ENGLISH – breakfast only. Excellent selection of traditional and vegetarian breakfasts. Locally oak-smoked fish.
Cards: Visa, Access, AmEx, Eurocard, MasterCard.
Other points: parking, central heating, no-smoking area, patio, garden, sun loungers, telephone available.
Rooms: 3 double rooms, 2 twin rooms. All with en suite, TV, hair dryer, tea/coffee-making facilities, clock/radio/alarm.
Directions: from A30 take A3074, the main road into St Ives. The guest house is on the right, 500 yards from Cornish Arms Inn.
LESLIE & MARY HART ☎ (01736) 798684.

THE COUNTRYMAN AT TRINK
Old Coach Road, TR26 3JQ
This attractive hotel, sympathetically restored to retain many of its 17th century features, is set in two acres of landscaped gardens with a trout stream, pond and paddock. Each of the spacious, newly refurbished bedrooms enjoys views of either the gardens or the countryside. Whether indulging in a freshly cooked meal in the candlelit restaurant or relaxing in the cosy 17th century lounge, you will be ensured a pleasant stay.
DOUBLE ROOM: from £20 to £30
SINGLE ROOM: from £25 to £35
FOOD: up to £15
Hours: breakfast 8am–9am, dinner 7pm–9pm.
Cuisine: ENGLISH – specialities include local fish, steaks, chicken, duck.
Cards: Visa, Access, Diners, AmEx.
Other points: parking, children catered for (please check for age limits), no-smoking area, vegetarian meals, garden, residents' lounge.
Rooms: 8 double rooms. All with TV, tea/coffee-making facilities, hair dryer.
Directions: situated on the B3311 to St Ives.
KATHY & HOWARD MASSEY ☎ (01736) 797571.

HUNTERS RESTAURANT
St Andrew's Street, TR26 1AH
A delightful 18th century terraced building houses this popular, tastefully decorated restaurant. The menu is varied and all meals are professionally served by the excellent staff.
FOOD: up to £15
Hours: breakfast weekends only 7.30am–9.30am, dinner 6.30pm–10.30pm.
Cuisine: ENGLISH / CONTINENTAL – traditional and continental cuisine specializing in local seafood and some game.
Cards: Visa, Access, Diners, AmEx.

CORNWALL • SW ENGLAND

Other points: vegetarian meals, children welcome.
Directions: Follow A30, then A3074, turn right at the parish church.
JONATHAN GIBBARD ☎ (01736) 793955.

🏨 PEDN-OLVA HOTEL & RESTAURANT
Porthminster Beach, TR26 2EA
'Pedn-Olva' means 'look-out on the headland', and this hotel, built with its series of towers, is situated on a rocky promontory overlooking the ancient town, the harbour and bay. Beautifully presented and served, the quality of food and wine offered here only just surpasses the restaurant's seascape view. Attractive balcony bedrooms provide guests with a relaxing holiday setting.
DOUBLE ROOM: from £40 to £50
FOOD: from £15 to £20
Hours: breakfast 8am–9.15am, lunch 12noon–2pm, dinner 6.30pm–9.30pm.
Cuisine: ENGLISH – wide selection of table d'hote or à la carte menu, using fresh quality produce, including seafood specialities.
Cards: Visa, Access.
Other points: licensed, Sunday lunch, children welcome, afternoon tea, swimming pool, residents' lounge, pets allowed.
Directions: on A3074 – the hotel overlooks the town, harbour and bay.
KENNETH GEORGE EVANS ☎ (01736) 796222.

🏨 SKIDDEN HOUSE HOTEL & RESTAURANT
Skidden Hill, TR26 2DU
Welcoming and comfortable, the Skidden House Hotel is set in the centre of St Ives and dates back through almost 500 years of history. Today, under the ownership of Michael and Dennis, the hotel enjoys a fine reputation for its cuisine and comfortable accommodation. With a peaceful, olde-world atmosphere, it is an ideal place to relax and enjoy the delights of Cornwall.
DOUBLE ROOM: from £30 to £40
SINGLE ROOM: from £35 to £45
FOOD: from £15 to £20 CLUB
Hours: breakfast 8.30am–9.30am, lunch 12noon–1.30pm, dinner 7pm–8.30pm.
Cuisine: ENGLISH – à la carte and table d'hôte menus. Dishes may include wild salmon poached in wine with king scallops and served in scallop and cream sauce, or tornedos rossini.
Cards: Visa, Access, Diners, AmEx.
Other points: licensed, no-smoking area, children welcome, afternoon tea, pets allowed, vegetarian meals, residents' bar, residents' lounge.
Rooms: 7 double/twin rooms. All with TV, telephone, tea/coffee-making facilities.
Directions: take A30, then A3074 to St Ives. Turn right after bus/train station.
MR HOOK & MR STOAKES ☎ (01736) 796899
Fax (01736) 798619.

🏨 THE ST UNY HOTEL
Carbis Bay, TR26 2NQ
Superb position overlooking the bay, with excellent views from most rooms. Originally a private mansion, now a thoroughly refurbished hotel with an atmosphere of calm and relaxation. Standing in two acres of sheltered gardens with semi-tropical trees and shrubs.
DOUBLE ROOM: from £30 to £40
SINGLE ROOM: from £25 to £35
FOOD: from £15 to £20
Hours: breakfast 8.45am–9.30am, bar snacks 12noon–2pm, dinner 7pm–8pm.
Cuisine: ENGLISH.
Cards: Visa, Access.
Other points: Sunday lunch, children welcome, parking, afternoon tea.
Rooms: 30 bedrooms.
Directions: from A30 take the A3074; the hotel is close to Carbis Bay station.
T. & B.C. CARROLL ☎ (01736) 795011.

ST JUST • map 3E1

🏨 BOSCEAN COUNTRY HOTEL
Bosweddon Road, TR19 7QP
This peaceful Edwardian hotel is an ideal place to 'get away from it all'. Surrounded by fields and moorlands, the stately building overlooks the sea and, with its spacious oak-panelled interior, is a delightful holiday spot. Friendly staff and loyal clientele give it a welcoming atmosphere.
DOUBLE ROOM: up to £20
FOOD: up to £15
Hours: breakfast 8.30am–9.15am, dinner 7pm.
Cuisine: ENGLISH – traditional home-cooked English cuisine. Fresh produce. Fixed daily menu with ample choice of appetizers and sweets.
Cards: Visa.
Other points: children welcome, pets allowed by prior arrangement, garden, parking.
Rooms: 4 double rooms, 4 twin rooms, 4 family rooms. All with tea/coffee-making facilities.
Directions: A3071 to St Just Square. Turn left by Barclays Bank into Boswedden Road.
ROY & JOYCE LEE ☎ (01736) 788748.

🏨 WELLINGTON HOTEL
Market Square, TR19 7HD
In the centre of St Just, the Wellington Hotel is well located to explore Cornwall. Extensively modernized in recent years, this comfortable, family-run hotel is noted for its excellent food. All room bookings include a full English breakfast, and a menu with daily specials is available for non-residents at lunch and dinner times. Ideal centre for walking, climbing, water sports and relaxing holidays, golf and beaches.
DOUBLE ROOM: up to £20
SINGLE ROOM: from £25 to £35
FOOD: up to £15
Hours: breakfast 8am–8.30am, lunch 12noon–2pm, dinner 6pm–8.30pm, open all year.
Cuisine: ENGLISH – cuisine for all the family, pub-style, including traditional Sunday lunch and children's menu. Vegetarians also catered for. Fresh local fish and crab, steaks, etc.
Cards: Visa, Access.
Other points: licensed, open-air dining, Sunday lunch, children welcome, open bank holidays, pets allowed.
Rooms: 13 twin rooms. All with TV, telephone.

Directions: take A3071 from Penzance to St Just (6 miles).
RODERICK & JENNIFER GRAY ☎ (01736) 787319/787906.

ST MAWES • map 3E2

🛏 PENDOWER BEACH HOUSE HOTEL
Gerrans Bay, Ruan High Lanes, Portscatho, TR2 5LW

The hotel occupies a prime position on the beautiful Roseland Peninsula. It boasts extensive grounds where peacocks and ducks roam freely. The choice of cuisine is excellent, specializing in local fresh fish served in a relaxing atmosphere.
DOUBLE ROOM: from £50
FOOD: from £15 to £20
Hours: breakfast 8.45am–9.15am, lunch 12noon–2pm, dinner 7.30pm–9pm.
Cuisine: ENGLISH – à la carte, fixed five-course menu or light lunches available.
Cards: Visa, Access.
Other points: licensed, open-air dining, no-smoking area, children welcome, afternoon tea, garden, pets allowed.
Rooms: 7 double rooms, 4 twin rooms, 1 family room.
Directions: A3078, turning 6 miles north of St Mawes. End of lane to 'Pink Hotel', on the beach.
PETER & CAROL BEETHAM ☎ (01872) 501241.

🛏 HOUSEL BAY HOTEL
Housel Bay, TR12 7PG

An elegant Victorian hotel in a spectacular clifftop position, with a secluded sandy cove and extensive grounds. Offers well-equipped, comfortable rooms and value-for-money food. Kynance Cove, the Lizard and Goonhilly Downsall nearby.
DOUBLE ROOM: from £20 to £30
SINGLE ROOM: from £25 to £35
FOOD: from £15 to £20
Hours: breakfast 8.30am–10am, bar meals 12noon–1.45pm, dinner 7.30pm–9.30pm, bar meals 7.30pm–8.45pm, closed 1st January–31st January.
Cuisine: ENGLISH – traditional English cuisine, including fresh fish and seafood.
Cards: Visa, Access, AmEx.
Other points: Sunday lunch, no-smoking area, children welcome, pets allowed, afternoon tea, open bank holidays, disabled access, residents' lounge, residents' bar.
Rooms: 4 single rooms, 11 double rooms, 8 twin rooms. All with TV, radio, alarm, telephone, tea/coffee-making facilities.
Directions: at The Lizard town signpost, take the left fork, following hotel signs.
FREDA & DEREK OSWALD ☎ (01326) 290417
[Fax] (01326) 290359.

TINTAGEL • map 3D2

🍴 THE PORT WILLIAM
Trebarwith Strand, PL34 0HB

Beautifully situated on top of the cliffs at Trebarwith, overlooking the bay, this cheerful 19th century pub provides good food and a vibrant atmosphere in which to enjoy it. An excellent selection of home-cooked food and seafood at reasonable prices. Live music in the evenings.
FOOD: up to £15
Hours: lunch 12noon–2.30pm, dinner 6pm–9.30pm, closed Christmas day.
Cuisine: ENGLISH – à la carte menu offering traditional home-style cooking. Speciality dishes include shellfish and seafood, with daily changing blackboard specials.
Cards: Visa, Access.
Other points: licensed, open-air dining, Sunday lunch, children welcome, pets allowed, parking, afternoon tea, open bank holidays, disabled access.
Directions: follow the B3263, off the Tintagel/Camelford road (3 miles).
PETER HALE ☎ (01840) 770230.

TREGONY • map 3E2

🍴 KEA HOUSE RESTAURANT
69 Fore Street, TR2 5RW

A two-storey stone building facing the main street, tastefully decorated with a warm, welcoming atmosphere. Excellent cuisine with seafood and fish specialities (in season), and special selection of malt whiskies.
FOOD: from £15 to £20
Hours: lunch summer 10.30am–4.30pm, dinner 7pm, closed Sunday, closed 1st November until 30th November.
Cuisine: ENGLISH – chicken with fresh herbs and spices fried in filo pastry served in plum sauce; also fish and cheeseboard.
Cards: Visa, Access, AmEx.
Other points: licensed, disabled access.
Directions: on the B3287, west of Truro.
MR & MRS A. NIXON ☎ (01872) 530642.

TRURO • map 3E2

🛏 ALVERTON MANOR
Tregolls Road, TR1 1XQ

Situated in the heart of Truro, this building was in the Tweedy family for over 150 years. The interior is tastefully decorated and furnished to a high standard. In a pleasant atmosphere and delightful, elegant surroundings, you can enjoy 'superbly cooked and presented' meals. Highly recommended.
DOUBLE ROOM: from £40 to £50
FOOD: from £15 to £20
Hours: breakfast 7.30am–9.45am, lunch 12noon–1.45pm, dinner 7pm–9pm.
Cuisine: MODERN ENGLISH – dishes may include pepper mousse with salad, baked loin of pork with an apple-and-plum tartlet, fresh peaches in champagne.
Cards: Visa, Access, Diners, AmEx.
Other points: licensed, open-air dining, Sunday lunch, no-smoking area, children welcome, open bank holidays, afternoon tea, pets allowed.
Rooms: 34 bedrooms.

DEVON • SW ENGLAND

Directions: on A390 approach road to Truro from St Austell.
MS MICHELLE MARKS ☎ (01872) 76633
[Fax] (01872) 222989.

THE GANGES RESTAURANT
St Clement Street, TR1 1EQ
The Ganges is close to the city centre, with a large car park opposite. The restaurant is beautifully set out and decorated in traditional Indian style. Seating for 78 persons in comfort and calm atmosphere. Discreet lighting adds to the delicate aroma of Indian spices and sauces. A most pleasant and relaxing restaurant, with happy and attentive staff. Prices are very reasonable and meals can be taken in an unhurried and peaceful ambience.
FOOD: up to £15
Hours: lunch 12noon–2.15pm, dinner 6pm–11.15pm, Friday and Saturday 11.45pm.
Cuisine: INDIAN – fresh ingredients used, all meals prepared daily and cooked to order.
Cards: Visa, Access, AmEx.
Other points: children welcome, no-smoking area, vegetarian meals.
Directions: off A39, close to Truro police station.
BAHAR UDDINE ☎ (01872) 42535.

MARCORRIE
20 Falmouth Road, TR1 2HX
A Victorian family-run hotel in a conservation area, 5 minutes' walk from the city centre and cathedral. Centrally situated for touring Cornwall and for visiting the nearby country houses, gardens and coast.
DOUBLE ROOM: from £20 to £30
SINGLE ROOM: up to £25
FOOD: up to £15
Hours: breakfast 7.30am–8.45am, dinner from 7pm.
Cuisine: ENGLISH – home-cooking.
Cards: Visa, Access, Diners, AmEx.
Other points: parking, chidren welcome, conference facilities, pets allowed, residents' lounge, no-smoking area, garden, swimming pool.
Rooms: 2 single rooms, 3 double rooms, 4 twin rooms, 1 triple room, 2 family rooms.
Directions: located on Falmouth Road, about 500 yards south of Truro city centre.
MRS P. TRESEDER ☎ (01872) 77374
[Fax] (01872) 44461.

THE WITHIES
Penmount Farm, Newquay Road,
An interesting old farmhouse which has been upgraded to a fine restaurant, offering fine traditional cuisine using fresh garden produce. A friendly old-world atmosphere prevails. Morning coffee and tea are served, and customers can purchase willow baskets, herbs, preserves and dried flowers.
FOOD: up to £15
Hours: lunch 10.30am–5pm, dinner 7pm–11pm, closed Monday and Saturday from October until June.
Other points: parking, children welcome, Sunday lunch, no-smoking area, disabled access, vegetarian meals, open-air dining.
Directions: 2 miles from Truro on A3076.
MR C.J. ELLIS ☎ (01872) 70007.

WADEBRIDGE • map 3D2

THE MOLESWORTH ARMS HOTEL
Molesworth Street, PL27 7DP
True Cornish hospitality can be found at this 16th century coaching inn. The traditional furnishings and old, beamed ceilings retain the character and olde-worlde elegance of the inn while providing comfortable surroundings in which to enjoy the best in fresh local produce and the friendly, caring atmosphere.
DOUBLE ROOM: from £20 to £30
FOOD: up to £15
Hours: breakfast 8am–10am, bar meals 12noon 2.30pm, dinner 7pm–9.30pm, bar meals 6.30pm–9.30pm.
Cuisine: ENGLISH – traditional English cuisine using local produce. Cornish produce includes local shell fish, salmon and speciality steaks.
Cards: Visa, Access, AmEx.
Other points: licensed, open-air dining, Sunday lunch, children welcome, afternoon tea, pets allowed, residents' lounge, conferences.
Rooms: 2 single rooms, 5 twin rooms, 2 family rooms. All with TV, tea/coffee-making facilities.
Directions: A30 to Bodmin, A389 to Wadebridge. Left over bridge. Parking at rear.
NIGEL CASSIDY ☎ (01208) 812055
[Fax] (01208) 814254.

DEVON

AXMINSTER • map 1C4

THE NEW COMMERCIAL INN
Trinity Square, EX13 5AN
This restaurant is found in a natural stone Victorian building in the centre of Axminster and offers excellent service and menu variety, including a special children's menu. The value for money is outstanding.
FOOD: up to £15 ☆
Hours: breakfast 7.30am–12noon, lunch 12noon– 2pm, afternoon tea 2pm–5.30pm, dinner 6pm–10.30pm.
Cuisine: ENGLISH / INTERNATIONAL – hot meals served all day from 7.30am. Children's menu. Dishes include trout, burgers, cod, plaice, steak, gammon and vegetarian options.
Cards: Visa, Access, Diners, AmEx.
Other points: licensed, children welcome, afternoon tea, street parking, bread shop.
Directions: In the main square in Axminster.
THE WALDEN FAMILY ☎ (01297) 33225.

SW ENGLAND • DEVON

AXMOUTH • map 4D4

THE SHIP INN
Near Seaton, EX12 4AF
A small, popular pub on the road from Seaton serving an extensive range of lunchtime and evening meals in both bars and the garden. Real ales.
FOOD: up to £15 ☆
Hours: lunch 12noon–2pm, dinner 7.30pm–9pm.
Cuisine: ENGLISH – deep sea surprise, baked plaice with seafood stuffing, accent on local game and seafood in season. Home-grown fruit, vegetables and herbs.
Other points: children welcome, garden, games room.
Directions: 1 mile south of the A3052 Lyme Regis–Exeter road towards Seaton.
MR & MRS C. CHAPMAN ☎ (01297) 21838.

BAMPTON • map 4C4

THE SWAN HOTEL
Station Road, EX16 9NG
A 15th century building which retains its old charm and character. Originally, The Swan housed the stone masons who built the nearby church. Close to Exmoor, Bickley Mill and Wimbleball Lake.
DOUBLE ROOM: from £20 to £30
FOOD: up to £15
Hours: breakfast 8am–9.30am, lunch 12noon–2pm, bar meals 12noon–2pm, dinner 7pm–10pm, bar meals 6pm–10pm.
Cuisine: ENGLISH – home-style traditional cooking, using fresh produce such as local trout and fresh vegetables.
Cards: Visa, Access, Diners.
Other points: licensed, Sunday lunch, open bank holidays, children welcome, pets allowed, afternoon tea.
Directions: on main Barnstable–Taunton road on B3227. Close to public car park.
BRIAN & PAM DUNESBY ☎ (01398) 331257.

BEER • map 4D4

GARLANDS
Stovar Long Lane, EX12 3EA
An Edwardian character house set in an acre of ground on the main coast road between Seaton and Beer. There are superb views from the house both of the sea and the Devon countryside; the beach is within easy walking distance. Fishing trips can be arranged – and your catch cooked for supper.
DOUBLE ROOM: up to £20
SINGLE ROOM: up to £25
FOOD: up to £15
Hours: breakfast 8.30am–9.30am, dinner 6.30pm–9.30pm, to be ordered by 12noon.
Cards: Visa, Access.
Other points: central heating, children welcome, residents' lounge.
Rooms: 1 single room, 2 double rooms, 1 twin room, 3 family rooms. All with en suite, TV, tea/coffee-making facilities.
Directions: turn south off A3052 at Hangmans Stone onto B3174. The hotel is signposted.
ANN & NIGEL HARDING ☎ (01297) 20958.

BICKINGTON • map 3C3

THE DARTMOOR HALFWAY
Near Newton Abbot, TQ12 6JW
A charming pub, aptly named, half-way between Ashburton and Newton Abbot. The Dartmoor Halfway offers first-class food and service.
FOOD: up to £15
Hours: full restaurant menu, specialities and bar meals 11am–10.30pm, closed Christmas day.
Cuisine: ENGLISH – home-cooking.
Cards: Visa, Access, Diners, AmEx.
Other points: licensed, Sunday lunch, children welcome, caravan facilities.
Directions: on the A383, half-way between Ashburton and Newton Abbot.
MR B.R. & MRS M.D. HUGGINS ☎ (01626) 821270.

BIDEFORD • map 3C3

DURRANT HOUSE HOTEL
Heywood Road, Northam, EX39 3QB
This outstandingly impressive hotel has been completely modernized to provide guests with superb facilities and comfortable, quality accommodation. The sumptuously furnished restaurant and bar provide perfect surroundings in which to relax after a day spent enjoying the many local activities that can be arranged by the helpful, enthusiastic staff, or for the less energetic who may have spent the day lounging by the swimming pool.
DOUBLE ROOM: from £30 to £40
SINGLE ROOM: from £55
FOOD: up to £15
Hours: breakfast 7.30am–9.30am, lunch 12noon–2pm, dinner 7.30pm–9.30pm.
Cuisine: ENGLISH / FRENCH – an excellent choice of first-class dishes.
Cards: Visa, Access, Diners, AmEx.
Other points: parking, children welcome, pets allowed, no-smoking area, conference facilities, function suite, gym facilities, sauna, solarium, swimming pool, residents' lounge, garden, vegetarian meals, traditional Sunday lunch, afternoon teas.
Rooms: 20 double rooms, 95 twin rooms, 2 suites. All with en suite, TV, telephone, radio, alarm, hair dryer, tea/coffee-making facilities.
Directions: exit 27 from M5, A361 to Barnstaple, A39 to Bideford. Cross Torridge Bridge and continue onto the roundabout. Take third exit towards Westward Ho. Entrance via Durrant Lane.
VINCENT & MARIA BORG ☎ (01237) 472361 Fax (01237) 421709.

RIVERSFORD HOTEL
Limers Lane, EX39 2RG
A country house hotel in 3 acres of gardens, affording magnificent views of the River Torridge. Ideal touring centre for beaches and countryside or for discovering the hidden charms of Devon and Exmoor.

122

DOUBLE ROOM: from £30 to £40
FOOD: up to £15 [CLUB] ☆
Hours: open all year.
Cuisine: ENGLISH – home-made country fare, home-made sweets, Devonshire cream teas and interesting wines. Traditional Sunday lunch. Extensive snack meals.
Cards: Visa, Access, Diners, AmEx.
Other points: licensed, open-air dining, Sunday lunch, children welcome.
Directions: Limers Lane is on the right, 1 mile north of Bideford on the A386.
MAURICE & MERRILYN JARRAD ☎ (01237) 474239/470381 [Fax] (01237) 421661.

BOVEY TRACEY • map 4D4

THE EDGEMOOR HOTEL
Lowerdown Cross, Haytor Road, TQ13 9LE
A 19th century country house, surrounded by extensive well-tended lawns and gardens, lovingly decorated and comfortably furnished in keeping with the era. Offering good-quality food, excellently cooked and presented, complemented by a distinguished wine list and attentive, well-trained staff. A delightful establishment, not to be missed. Highly recommended.
DOUBLE ROOM: from £40 to £50
SINGLE ROOM: from £35 to £45
FOOD: from £15 to £20
Hours: breakfast 8am–9.30am, lunch 12noon–2pm, dinner 7.30pm–9pm.
Cuisine: FRENCH / ENGLISH – dishes include curried cream prawns in a filo pastry croustade, roast duck glazed with orange and Cointreau, roast sirloin of beef with red wine and mushrooms.
Cards: Visa, Access, Diners, AmEx.
Other points: licensed, Sunday lunch, children welcome, garden, afternoon tea, pets allowed.
Rooms: 3 single rooms, 6 double rooms, 12 twin rooms, 1 family room.
Directions: 7 minutes from A38, 1 mile from Bovey Tracey.
ROD & PATRICIA DAY ☎ (01626) 832466 [Fax] (01626) 834760.

BRAUNTON • map 3C3

PRESTON HOUSE HOTEL
Saunton, EX33 1LG
A grand Victorian country house overlooking the 10-mile sweep of Barnstaple's sandy bay. Built in 1895, the stained-glass windows, moulded ceilings, period furnishings, paintings and ornaments all re-create the glory of the period. Golf, riding, fishing and water sports are all available nearby, and the hotel has its own heated outdoor swimming pool.
DOUBLE ROOM: from £30 to £40
SINGLE ROOM: from £25 to £35
FOOD: up to £15 ☆
Hours: breakfast 8.30am–9.30am, lunch 12noon–2pm, dinner 7pm–8.30pm.
Cuisine: ENGLISH – table d'hôte menu changes daily. All dishes prepared and cooked on the premises.

Cards: Visa, Access.
Other points: licensed, Sunday lunch, solarium, sauna, spa bath, residents' lounge, garden, conservatory, residents' bar, swimming pool.
Rooms: 2 single rooms, 5 double rooms, 7 twin rooms. All with TV, radio, alarm, telephone, tea/coffee-making facilities.
Directions: take the A361 to Braunton. Follow signposts to Saunton.
ANN COOK ☎ (01271) 890472 [Fax] (01271) 890555.

BRIXHAM • map 4D4

THE QUAYSIDE HOTEL
41 King Street, TQ5 9TJ
This friendly and welcoming hotel, which over many years has been built up from six quayside cottages, has everything that would be expected of a hotel of this repute. The excellent restaurant offers both English and French cuisine. There is a choice of two bars: the residents' bar for a cosy drink, or the more vibrant Ernie Lister bar, where you can enjoy your favourite tipple and chat or listen to the tales of the local seafarers. With spectacular views and a wealth of history, The Quayside Hotel comes highly recommended.
DOUBLE ROOM: from £20 to £30
SINGLE ROOM: from £45 to £55
FOOD: from £15 to £20
Hours: breakfast 8am–9.30am, bar meals 12noon–2pm, dinner 7pm–9.15pm, dinner 7pm–9.30pm.
Cuisine: FRENCH / ENGLISH – a variety of local produce, not least the famous fresh Brixham fish, straight from the decks of local fishing boats, along with fine wines to complement your meal.
Cards: Visa, Access, Diners, AmEx, Switch.
Other points: parking, children welcome, pets allowed, no-smoking area, residents' lounge, vegetarian meals.
Rooms: 30 bedrooms. All with en suite, TV, telephone, radio, alarm, baby-listening device, tea/coffee-making facilities.
Directions: take A3022 to Brixham; follow signs to harbour.
JEAN-MARIE LAUZIER ☎ (01803) 855751 [Fax] (01803) 882733.

RADDICOMBE LODGE
120 Kingswear Road, TQ5 0EX
The latticed windows and pitched ceilings give this country house a cottage atmosphere. Most rooms have a fine sea or country view. A good base for touring the Devon coast and Dartmoor.
DOUBLE ROOM: up to £20
SINGLE ROOM: up to £25
Hours: breakfast 8am–9am.
Cuisine: BREAKFAST.
Cards: Visa, Access, Diners.
Other points: central heating, children welcome, residents' lounge, garden, vegetarian meals.
Rooms: 3 double rooms, 2 twin rooms, 2 family rooms. All with TV, tea/coffee-making facilities.
Directions: on the B3205 between Brixham and Dartmouth.
MR & MRS GLASS ☎ (01803) 882125.

CHAGFORD • map 3D3

🏨 THE THREE CROWNS HOTEL
Dartmoor, TQ13 5AJ
Situated in the pretty village of Chagford, within the Dartmoor National Park, this 13th century inn retains an olde-worlde charm with its open fires and four-poster beds.
DOUBLE ROOM: from £20 to £30
SINGLE ROOM: from £25 to £35
FOOD: from £15 to £20
Hours: breakfast 8.30am–9.30am, lunch 12noon–2pm, dinner 7pm–9.30pm.
Cuisine: ENGLISH – bar menu, e.g., home-made steak-and-kidney pie, ploughman's, seafood; special vegetarian meals and table d'hôte menus.
Cards: Visa, Access, AmEx.
Other points: Sunday lunch, children welcome.
Rooms: 18 bedrooms.
Directions: 3 miles off A382 (B3206). Situated within the village.
MR & MRS J. GILES ☎ (01647) 433444
[Fax] (01647) 433117.

CLAWTON • map 3C3

🏨 COURT BARN COUNTRY HOUSE HOTEL
Near Holsworthy, EX22 6PS
A country house of great character and charm, with antiques, pictures and flowers throughout, Court Barn is the perfect touring hotel for Dartmoor, Bodmin and Exmoor. Les Routiers/Mercier Wine List of the Year 1989, Corps d'Elite 1990, 1991, 1992, 1993 and 1994. Tea Council 'Best Teas in Britain' 1987 and 1989. National Awards for cuisine. Devon's 'Hotel of Distinction'.
DOUBLE ROOM: from £30 to £40
SINGLE ROOM: from £25 to £35
FOOD: from £15 to £20 [CLUB]
Hours: morning coffee 10am–12noon, lunch 12noon–2pm, afternoon tea 3pm–5pm, dinner 7.30pm–9pm, closed 1st January until 7th January.
Cuisine: ENGLISH / FRENCH – Cordon Bleu cuisine. Five-course candlelit dinners. Fresh local produce. Vegetarian dishes. Menu changes daily. Award-winning cream teas and restaurant awards.
Cards: Visa, Access, Diners, AmEx.
Other points: licensed, traditional Sunday lunch, children welcome, pets allowed, garden, tennis, croquet, residents' lounge, library, residents' bar.
Rooms: 1 single room, 4 double rooms, 3 twin rooms. All with TV, telephone, tea/coffee-making facilities.
Directions: 3 miles south of Holsworthy, off A388. Next to 12th century church.
ROBERT & SUSAN WOOD ☎ (01409) 271209
[Fax] (01409) 271309.

COCKWOOD • map 4D4

🍴 THE ANCHOR INN
Near Starcross, EX6 8RA
The Anchor Inn, an attractive 16th century inn, is refreshingly different in many ways. Although there is a wide range of meat, fish and vegetarian dishes available, the speciality is undoubtedly the mussel selection. The 'Moules Menu' consists of 30 variations of sauces and serving styles to accompany the ever-popular mussel. The ambience is warm and welcoming and the service is friendly but professional.
FOOD: up to £15
Hours: lunch 12noon–2.30pm, dinner 6.30-10pm.
Cuisine: ENGLISH / SEAFOOD – all meals are made from only the freshest produce available, but the speciality is mussels.
Cards: Visa, Access, Switch, Delta.
Other points: parking, children welcome, vegetarian meals, no-smoking area.
Directions: take the A38, A380, B3381, A379 and follow signs to Cockwood.
MR TERRENCE W. MORGAN ☎ (01626) 890203.

COMBE MARTIN • map 3B3

🏨 RONE HOUSE HOTEL
King Street, EX34 OAD
A small, privately-run hotel where the emphasis is on comfort, relaxation and superb food and service. Nearby are fine, sandy beaches, Exmoor, beautiful hills and valleys such as Valley of the Rocks, Watersmeet and Doone, and the famous Dartington Glass Factory.
DOUBLE ROOM: up to £20
SINGLE ROOM: up to £25
FOOD: from £15 to £20 [CLUB]
Hours: breakfast 8.30am–9.15am, lunch 12.30am–2pm, dinner 6.30pm–9pm.
Cuisine: MODERN ENGLISH.
Cards: Visa, Access.
Other points: garden, children welcome, special breaks, pets allowed, swimming pool.
Rooms: 10 bedrooms.
Directions: junction 27 on M5. Then follow A369 link road to the sign for Combe Martin.
GRAHAM & ELSPETH COTTAGE ☎ (01271) 883428.

🏨 SANDY COVE HOTEL
Berrynarbor, EX31 4Q7
The hotel stands in 20 acres of gardens featuring woods, cliffs and coves. Other facilities include indoor swimming pool, sauna and whirlpool.
DOUBLE ROOM: from £30 to £40
FOOD: up to £15
Hours: breakfast 8.30am–9.30am, bar 11am–11pm, lunch 12.30am–2.30pm, afternoon tea 3pm–5pm, dinner 7pm–9.30pm.
Cuisine: INTERNATIONAL – fondue, kebabs, five variations of lobster. Large à la carte menu.
Other points: licensed, Sunday lunch, children welcome, coaches by prior arrangement, vegetarian meals, disabled access, swimming pool, residents' bar.
Rooms: 2 single rooms, 15 double rooms, 5 twin rooms, 11 family rooms. All with TV, telephone, tea/coffee-making facilities.
Directions: on the A399 (coast road), 1 mile from Combe Martin.
MRS DARLINGTON ☎ (01271) 882243/882888
[Fax] (01271) 883830.

CULLOMPTON • map 4C4

MANOR HOUSE HOTEL
Fore Street, EX15 1JL
Built in 1603, the Manor House has a particularly elegant timbered facade and has been carefully restored to its former glory. The Manor boasts a delightfully intimate restaurant where you can expect a top-class meal, a splendid character bar and, most importantly, excellent, well-appointed accommodation.
DOUBLE ROOM: from £20 to £30
FOOD: up to £15
Hours: breakfast 7.15am–9am, lunch 12.15am–1.45pm, dinner 7pm–9pm.
Cuisine: ENGLISH / FRENCH – a very wide choice of dishes, freshly prepared, to suit all tastes.
Cards: Visa, Access.
Other points: parking, children welcome, pets allowed, conference facilities, residents' lounge, vegetarian meals, traditional Sunday lunch.
Rooms: 1 single room, 4 double rooms, 3 twin rooms, 1 family room, 1 four-poster room. All with en suite, TV, telephone, radio, alarm, hair dryer, trouser-press, tea/coffee-making facilities.
Directions: junction 28 off M5; turn to Cullompton and continue to T-junction; turn left and hotel is 400 yards on the right.
MALCOLM POWELL ☎ (01884) 32281
Fax (01884) 38344.

DARTMOUTH • map 4E4

ROYAL CASTLE HOTEL
The Quay, TQ6 9PS
Standing on the quayside of the River Dart, this hotel was a coaching inn and has a fascinating history. The ceiling of the bar is reputed to have been constructed with timber from the wreckage of the Armada. The hotel's elegant atmosphere is reflected in the traditional English cooking and service.
DOUBLE ROOM: from £30 to £40
SINGLE ROOM: from £35 to £45
FOOD: up to £15
Hours: breakfast 8am–9.30am, bar meals 12noon–9.45pm, lunch 12.30am–2.15pm, dinner 7pm–9.45pm.
Cuisine: ENGLISH – seafood, traditional roasts.
Cards: Visa, Access.
Other points: Sunday lunch, children welcome, afternoon tea, pets allowed, weekend breaks, Jacuzzi, parking.
Rooms: 21 double rooms, 4 twin rooms. All with satellite TV, radio, telephone, tea/coffee-making facilities, heating. Some four-poster rooms with Jacuzzi bath.
Directions: from A38 take A384 to Totnes, A381 to Halwell, then B3207.
MR NIGEL WAY ☎ (01803) 833033
Fax (01803) 835445.

SLOPING DECK RESTAURANT
The Butterwalk, TP6 9PZ
The Sloping Deck consists of a bakery on the ground floor and a restaurant on the first floor, both offering quality food at very good value.
Situated in one of Dartmouth's most famous historic buildings.
FOOD: up to £15
Hours: meals all day 9am–5.30pm.
Cuisine: ENGLISH – home-cooking, including fresh fish and steak-and-kidney pie.
Cards: Visa, Access.
Other points: licensed, Sunday lunch, no-smoking area, children welcome, pets allowed, afternoon tea.
Directions: a historic building at centre of town, in The Butterwalk.
MR & MRS BARNES ☎ (01803) 832758.

STOKE LODGE HOTEL
Stoke Fleming, TQ6 0RA
Situated on the scenic coastal road between historic Dartmouth and Kingsbridge, this charming hotel is very popular locally and offers first-class service and comfort with fresh local food, 3 acres of grounds with large gardens, and every facility for a truly relaxing holiday.
DOUBLE ROOM: from £30 to £40
FOOD: from £15 to £20
Cuisine: ENGLISH / FRENCH – a large variety of English and French cuisine using only the best local fresh ingredients, e.g., poached salmon with hollandaise sauce.
Cards: Visa, Access.
Other points: licensed, outdoor swimming pool, indoor swimming pool, Jacuzzi, tennis, sauna, fishing, river trips, bird-watching, garden, pets allowed, children welcome, baby-listening device, baby-sitting, cots.
Rooms: 3 single rooms, 9 double rooms, 8 twin rooms, 4 triple rooms, 3 suites. All with en suite, TV, radio, alarm, telephone, tea/coffee-making facilities.
Directions: on A379, 2 miles south of Dartmouth.
STEVEN MAYER ☎ (01803) 770523
Fax (01803) 770851.

DAWLISH • map 4D4

LANGSTONE CLIFF HOTEL
Mount Pleasant Road, Dawlish Warren, EX7 0NA
Set in 19 acres of wooded grounds and only 500 yards from the beach, this hotel offers the warmest of welcomes and the best in friendly service, with special consideration for families and children. Superbly decorated, the hotel provides a high standard of food and accommodation, and there is a host of activities for all ages to enjoy. Set in an area of outstanding beauty.
DOUBLE ROOM: from £30 to £40
FOOD: up to £15
Hours: breakfast 7.30am–10am, lunch 12.30am–2pm, dinner 7pm–9pm.
Cuisine: ENGLISH – traditional English cuisine. Table d'hôte dinner menu and carvery. Coffee shop offering light refreshments.
Cards: Visa, Access, Diners, AmEx.
Other points: licensed, Sunday lunch, children welcome, games room, tennis, swimming pool, dinner dances, conferences, children welcome,

baby-listening device, baby-sitting, cots, 24hr reception, residents' lounge, residents' bar.
Rooms: 6 single rooms, 21 double rooms, 25 triple rooms, 16 quad rooms. All with TV, radio, telephone, tea/coffee-making facilities, alarm.
Directions: 1 mile off the A379; 1 mile north of Dawlish.
GEOFFREY ROGERS ☎ (01626) 865155 [Fax] (01626) 867166.

EXETER • map 4D4

🍴 THE ANGLER'S REST
Fingle Bridge, Drewsteignton, EX6 6PW
A family-run restaurant and lounge bar with riverside terraces. Adjoining Fingle Bridge on the banks of the River Teign deep in Fingle Gorge, The Angler's Rest provides a starting point for miles of walks, fishing and birdwatching.
FOOD: up to £15
Hours: lunch summer 11am–5.30pm, winter 11am–2.30pm; dinner summer 7pm–9pm, winter (Saturday only) 7pm–9pm.
Cuisine: ENGLISH / INTERNATIONAL – steak-and-kidney pie, Devon steaks, salmon, trout. Bar meals. Devonshire cream teas. Vegetarian dishes. Home-made speciality curries and pasta dishes.
Cards: Visa, Access.
Other points: open-air dining, Sunday lunch, children catered for (please check for age limits), functions.
Directions: next to Fingle Bridge in Drewsteignton.
THE PRICE FAMILY ☎ (01647) 281287.

🍴 COWICK BARTON INN
Cowick Lane, St Thomas, EX2 9JG
A medieval country inn and restaurant within the city of Exeter, where you will discover some of the charm and tranquility which only a much loved ancient building can radiate. Unlatch the four-foot-wide door and prepare to be impressed by the amazing interior! But it is not only the superb surroundings you will be impressed by: dining and wining at the Cowick Barton is an extremely pleasant experience, and the Uphills are proud of the reputation they have achieved, with the help of their head chef David Williams, for the high standard of their cuisine.
FOOD: up to £15
Hours: lunch 12noon–2pm, bar meals 12noon–2pm, dinner 7.30pm–10pm, bar meals 7pm–9.30pm.
Cuisine: ENGLISH – delicious country fare.
Cards: Visa, Access, AmEx.
Other points: parking, children welcome, no-smoking area, conference facilities, open-air dining, vegetarian meals, traditional Sunday lunch.
Directions: take Exeter junction off A30, turn left at first traffic lights into Cowick Lane, follow signs to Exwick, 500 yards on right.
PETER UPHILL ☎ (01392) 70411 [Fax] (01392) 211736.

🍴 LAMB'S
Under the Iron Bridge, 15 Lower North Street, EX4 3ET
A Grade II listed building approximately 200 years old, providing modern English food in a delightful, friendly setting. The restaurant has a courtyard at the rear alongside the original Roman city wall. Ideal location for exploring Exeter and for visiting Devon's many attractions.
FOOD: from £15 to £20 [CLUB]
Hours: lunch (Tuesday–Friday) 12noon–2.30pm, dinner (Tuesday–Saturday) 6pm–12midnight.
Cuisine: ENGLISH.
Cards: Visa, Access, MasterCard, Switch, Delta.
Other points: vegetarian meals.
Directions: 100 yards from Harlequin car park, under the Iron Bridge.
IAN & ALISON ALDRIDGE ☎ (01392) 54269 [Fax] (01392) 431145.

🛏 THE OLD THATCH INN
Cheriton Bishop, EX6 6HG
Traditional 16th century thatched free house, originally built as a coaching house. Just 10 miles from Exeter and inside the eastern border of Dartmoor National Park. Les Routiers of the Year 1985.
DOUBLE ROOM: from £20 to £30
SINGLE ROOM: from £25 to £35
FOOD: up to £15 🍴
Hours: lunch 12noon–2.15pm, dinner 6.30pm–9.30pm, Sunday 7pm–9pm.
Cuisine: ENGLISH – home-made food using traditional recipes. Dishes may include steak-and-kidney pudding, Thatch mixed grill, baked stuffed aubergine, fish rolls with sesame sauce.
Cards: Visa, Access, Eurocard.
Other points: licensed, traditional Sunday lunch, children catered for (please check for age limits).
Rooms: 3 double rooms. All with TV, radio, alarm, tea/coffee-making facilities.
Directions: from the A30, 10 miles west of Exeter, take Cheriton Bishop road.
BRIAN & HAZEL BRYON-EDMOND ☎ (01647) 24204.

● PARK VIEW HOTEL
8 Howell Road, EX4 4LG
A popular hotel in the centre of Exeter, which offers comfortable accommodation and excellent full breakfasts. Attractively decorated, Park View Hotel provides a comfortable, welcoming base from which to visit Exeter, whether on business or for pleasure. Very close to the university and station.
DOUBLE ROOM: up to £20
SINGLE ROOM: up to £25
Hours: breakfast 7.30am–9am, breakfast Sunday 8.30am–9.30am, closed Christmas day.
Cuisine: BREAKFAST.
Cards: Visa, Access.
Other points: children welcome, residents' lounge.
Rooms: 4 single rooms, 9 double/twin rooms, 2 family rooms. All with TV, telephone, tea/coffee-making facilities, heating. Some rooms are en suite.

DEVON • SW ENGLAND

Directions: from M5 (junction 30), first roundabout fourth exit, second roundabout second exit (signposted B3183 city centre), straight on for 3 miles until the Clock Tower roundabout, third exit (Elm Grove Road), at end of road turn left into Howell Road, Park View Hotel is 100 metres on the right.
MR & MRS BATHO ☎ (01392) 71772.

🏨 WHITE HART HOTEL
66 South Street, EX1 1EE
This appealing 600-year-old coaching inn has an attractive listed exterior, large courtyard, wine patio and garden, and ancient protected doorways. The interior of the hotel is extremely old and beautifully kept, the original fireplace still stands, and many artefacts, dating back centuries, adorn the public areas. The accommodation is of an excellent standard, as is the fine food available in the comfortable restaurant.
DOUBLE ROOM: from £30 to £40
FOOD: up to £15
Hours: breakfast 7.30am–9.30am, lunch 12noon–2pm, dinner 7pm–10pm.
Cuisine: ENGLISH – traditional fare.
Cards: Visa, Access, Diners, AmEx, Switch.
Other points: parking, children welcome, conference facilities, residents' lounge, open-air dining, vegetarian meals, traditional Sunday lunch.
Rooms: 18 single rooms, 40 double rooms. All with en suite, TV, radio, alarm, trouser-press.
Directions: the White Hart Hotel may be found in Exeter city centre, just within the city walls.
GRAHAM STONE ☎ (01392) 79897
[Fax] (01392) 79897.

EXMOUTH • map 4D4

🏨 BALCOMBE HOUSE HOTEL
Stevenstone Road, EX8 2EP
This is an oasis of peace and tranquility with over half an acre of pretty gardens. Just a short distance away from the seafront, with 2 miles of golden sands and a wealth of leisure activities. The town centre and River Exe nature reserve are both close at hand. Very comfortably furnished to a high standard, with a warm and homely atmosphere. The hotel has a well-stocked bar in a sunny lounge overlooking the garden, and a second no-smoking lounge. The extended hours of service allow guests to dine early or late, choosing from the many varied dishes on offer. The hotel is affiliated to the nearby Cranford Sports Club, where guests can enjoy the facilities free of charge all year round. The hotel offers a special Christmas programme.
DOUBLE ROOM: from £20 to £30
FOOD: up to £15
Hours: breakfast 8am–9.30am, lunch 12noon–1pm, dinner 6.30pm–9pm, open all year.
Cuisine: ENGLISH.
Cards: Visa, Diners, AmEx, MasterCard.
Other points: parking, no-smoking area, afternoon teas, disabled access, residents' lounge, garden, vegetarian meals, functions, sports facilities, children catered for (please check for age limits).

Rooms: 2 single rooms, 4 double rooms, 4 twin rooms, 2 family rooms. All with en suite, TV, radio, alarm, tea/coffee-making facilities, hair dryer.
Directions: follow road to Sandy Bay, bear right at Littleham Cross, third turn on left.
MR O. SMALDON ☎ (01395) 266349.

HONITON • map 4C4

🍽 THE FLINTLOCK INN
**Marsh, near Honiton,
EX14 9AJ**
A charming inn offering value-for-money food, good service and standards. All set in a rural traditional theme. The menus are created to use fresh products whenever possible and are largely home-made.
FOOD: from £15 to £20
Hours: lunch (bar) 12noon–2pm, dinner 7pm–9.45pm, closed Christmas day evening and Boxing day.
Cuisine: ENGLISH / EUROPEAN – wide choice of dishes catering for all tastes. The à la carte menu changes periodically. The good-sized portions are always attractively presented. Coeliac and vegetarian meals available.
Cards: Visa, Access, Switch.
Other points: parking, no-smoking area, vegetarian meals, traditional Sunday lunch.
Directions: situated off the A303 between Honiton and Ilminster.
JOHN & MAGGIE WARDELL ☎ (01460) 234403.

🏨 THE HEATHFIELD
Walnut Road, EX14 8UG
This 16th century traditional thatched Devon longhouse was once a farmhouse. Retaining many of its original features, it is now a busy free house and restaurant, with accommodation. The restaurant offers an excellent à la carte menu, and a large selection of wines, real ales and spirits is available from the bar. The luxurious bedrooms have all been furnished to a five-star standard.
DOUBLE ROOM: from £20 to £30
SINGLE ROOM: from £25 to £35
FOOD: up to £15
Hours: breakfast 8am–9am, bar meals 12noon–2pm, dinner 7pm–10pm (Friday and Saturday), bar meals 7pm–10pm, kitchen closed Sunday evening.
Cuisine: ENGLISH / VEGETARIAN.
Cards: Visa, Access, AmEx.
Other points: parking, vegetarian meals, conference facilities, residents' garden, open-air dining.
Rooms: 2 double rooms, 3 twin rooms. All with tea/coffee-making facilities, TV, telephone, radio, trouser-press.
Directions: from the A30 London–Exeter Road, take the A375 towards Sidmouth. The Heathfield is well signposted from the mini-roundabout after the railway bridge.
ANDREW FORD ☎ (01404) 45321
[Fax] (01404) 45321.

ILFRACOMBE • map 3B3

DEDES HOTEL AND WHEEL INN, PUB AND RESTAURANT
1–3 The Promenade, EX34 9BD
Situated on the Victorian promenade overlooking the sea, incorporating the wheel room. A delightful character restaurant and bar featuring exposed stonework, beams and old coaching wheels.
DOUBLE ROOM: up to £20
FOOD: up to £15
Hours: breakfast 8am–10am, lunch 12noon–2pm, dinner 6pm–10pm.
Cuisine: MODERN ENGLISH – quality steaks and fresh, local seafood in season, including fresh lobster.
Cards: Visa, Access, Diners, AmEx.
Other points: Sunday lunch, disabled access, children welcome, cots.
Rooms: 5 single rooms, 3 double rooms, 3 twin rooms, 4 triple rooms, 2 quad rooms. All with TV, tea/coffee-making facilities.
Directions: A361 to Ilfracombe, situated on the promenade.
MR & MRS C.I. CAWTHORNE ☎ (01721) 862545.

EPCHRIS HOTEL
Torrs Park, EX34 8AZ
A small, friendly family hotel, offering good accommodation and delicious home-cooked meals. All the bedrooms are large and airy, and there is an outdoor swimming pool and two acres of gardens. Conveniently located for Exmoor and the wonders of the Devon coast, and within walking distance of Ilfracombe's attractions.
DOUBLE ROOM: up to £20
SINGLE ROOM: up to £25
FOOD: up to £15
Hours: breakfast 9am, dinner 6.30pm, closed January.
Cuisine: ENGLISH – home-cooking.
Cards: Visa, Access, Eurocard.
Other points: licensed, parking, children welcome, no-smoking area, swimming pool, garden, residents' lounge, bar, vegetarian meals.
Rooms: 1 single room, 8 family rooms. All rooms have TV, tea/coffee-making facilities. Most rooms are en suite.
Directions: from Barnstaple take A361 to Ilfracombe town centre, turn left at signs for seafront, turn left again. Torrs Park is ahead and the hotel is on the left.
ANN BARLEYCORN ☎ (01271) 862751.

HEADLANDS HOTEL
7 Capstone Crescent, EX34 9BT
A 100-year-old terraced hotel set in its own cliff garden in a popular holiday resort. Offering good wholesome food, nothing is too much trouble for the proprietors, whose aim is to please. Older, retired clientele. Near to harbour.
DOUBLE ROOM: up to £20
SINGLE ROOM: up to £25
FOOD: up to £15 ☆
Hours: breakfast 8.30am, dinner 6.15pm.
Other points: licensed, children catered for (please check for age limits).
Rooms: 19 bedrooms.
Directions: in the harbour area, near Britannia public hotel.
MR & MRS ANGOLD ☎ (01271) 862887.

THE ILFRACOMBE CARLTON
Runnacleave Road, EX34 8AR
Situated in a central location adjacent to the beach, this hotel offers fresh, well-cooked food in pleasant surroundings. The accommodation is comfortable and the service friendly and attentive. Ilfracombe offers its visitors a choice of recreational and sporting activities, a spectacular coastline and secluded bays.
DOUBLE ROOM: from £20 to £30
SINGLE ROOM: from £25 to £35
FOOD: up to £15 ☆
Hours: breakfast 8.30am–9.30am, lunch 12noon–2pm, dinner 7pm–8.30pm.
Cuisine: ENGLISH – traditional English food.
Cards: Visa, Access, Diners, AmEx.
Other points: Sunday lunch, children welcome, afternoon tea, baby-listening device, cots, 24hr reception, residents' lounge, residents' bar.
Rooms: 8 single rooms, 15 double rooms, 24 twin rooms, 1 family room. All with TV, radio, alarm, telephone, tea/coffee-making facilities.
Directions: off the A361, close to the seafront.
DAWN MARSHALL ☎ (01271) 862446
Fax (01271) 865379.

ST BRANNOCKS HOUSE HOTEL
St Brannocks Road, EX34 8EQ
A detached Victorian hotel set in its own grounds and close to the beautiful Bicclescombe Park, Cairn Nature Reserve, town centre and seafront. The cosy, well-stocked bar is an ideal place to relax and socialize, and the dining room offers generous portions of good home-cooked food and a selection of table wines. An ideal place for a perfect family holiday, special break or business trip.
DOUBLE ROOM: up to £20
SINGLE ROOM: up to £25
FOOD: up to £15
Hours: breakfast 8.30am–9am, dinner 6.30pm.
Cuisine: ENGLISH.
Cards: Visa, Access, AmEx.
Other points: children welcome, pets welcome, residents' lounge, garden, parking, special diets catered for.
Rooms: 16 bedrooms. All with TV, radio, tea/coffee-making facilities. Many rooms are en suite.
Directions: approach from Barnstaple on A361. Hotel is on left side heading into town.
MRS B. CLARKE ☎ (01271) 863873.

TORRS HOTEL
Torrs Park, EX34 8AY
This hotel is in a commanding position at the end of the Torrs Walk, which follows the cliff along the coast. The hotel has lovely views of the surrounding countryside.
DOUBLE ROOM: from £20 to £30
FOOD: up to £15

Hours: breakfast 8.30am–9.30am, dinner 6.30pm–7.30pm, closed November until February.
Cuisine: ENGLISH – roasts, grills, home-cooked dishes.
Cards: Visa, Access, Diners, AmEx.
Other points: licensed, open-air dining, Sunday lunch, special diets, children welcome.
Directions: off the A399 or A361 at the end of the Torrs Walk.
MR R.I. COOK ☎ (01271) 862334.

TRAFALGAR HOTEL
Larkstone Terrace, Hillsborough Road, EX34 9NU

A Victorian hotel, retaining many of its original features and furnished to a high standard. Offering excellent sea and woodland views from comfortable rooms, a pleasant, relaxing stay is assured.
DOUBLE ROOM: from £20 to £30
SINGLE ROOM: from £25 to £35
FOOD: up to £15 [CLUB]
Hours: breakfast 8.30am–9.30am, bar snacks 12noon–2pm, dinner 6.30pm–8pm, bar snacks 6pm–9pm.
Cuisine: ENGLISH.
Cards: Visa, Access, Diners, AmEx.
Other points: parking, children welcome, afternoon teas, residents' lounge, vegetarian meals.
Rooms: 4 single rooms, 10 double rooms, 11 twin rooms.
Directions: continuation of High Street from A361 direction.
TONY & JUNE WHITE ☎ (01271) 862145/863745.

UPSTAIRS RESTAURANT
Mullacott Cross, EX34 8AY

High above Ilfracombe with unrestricted views to Lundy Island, the Welsh coast and Exmoor.
FOOD: up to £15
Hours: dinner 6pm–10pm, closed October until Easter.
Cuisine: MODERN ENGLISH – carvery with best-quality steaks. Children's menu.
Cards: Visa, Access, Diners, AmEx.
Other points: open-air dining, Sunday lunch, children welcome.
Directions: found on the A361 Mullacott roundabout.
MRS C.J. NAPPER ☎ (01271) 863780/865500.

IVYBRIDGE • map 3D3

IMPERIAL INN
28 Western Road, PL21 9AR

A charming olde-worlde village pub adorned with window boxes, with a large, welcoming open fire and a warm welcome to match. There is a large beer garden and a separate children's play area with playground equipment.
FOOD: up to £15
Hours: lunch 12noon–2pm, dinner 6pm–10pm.
Cuisine: MODERN ENGLISH – many daily specials, from home-cooked meals to hot beef curry, with a variety of local fresh fish including

fresh Avon mussels in wine and cream sauce, and from sautéed lamb's kidneys to chicken marengo – and much more.
Other points: open-air dining, Sunday lunch, children welcome, coaches by prior arrangement.
Directions: follow the A38 from Plymouth (7 miles).
PHILIP GRIMES ☎ (01752) 892269.

KINGSBRIDGE • map 3E3

THE ASHBURTON ARMS
West Charleton, TQ7 2AH

A very friendly pub, serving excellent home-made food at good value for money. The steaks are particularly good, served on hot stones so they continue to cook at the table, and there is a good wine list. The pub is set on a main tourist route, in an area of outstanding natural beauty. Well worth visiting.
DOUBLE ROOM: up to £20
SINGLE ROOM: up to £25
FOOD: up to £15
Hours: lunch 12noon–1.45pm, dinner 7pm–9pm.
Cuisine: ENGLISH – dishes include speciality 'steak on the rocks', served on hot stones. Vegetarian dish of the day. Desserts such as pavlova and treacle tart. All home-made. Fresh fish always on the menu. No-smoking area in the restaurant.
Cards: Visa, Access.
Other points: Sunday lunch, no-smoking area, children catered for (please check for age limits).
Rooms: 2 single rooms, 2 double rooms. All with TV, radio, tea/coffee-making facilities, alarm.
Directions: on A379, 1½ miles east of Kingsbridge on Tor crossroads.
BRIAN & ELIZABETH SAUNDERS ☎ (01548) 531242.

WHITE HOUSE HOTEL
Chillington, TQ7 2JX

The White House Hotel is a lovely Georgian house set in an acre of lawned and terraced gardens and is just two miles from the coast. It offers excellent food and friendly service in peaceful and relaxed surroundings.
DOUBLE ROOM: from £30 to £40
SINGLE ROOM: from £35 to £45
FOOD: up to £15
Hours: breakfast 8.30am–9.30am, dinner 7pm–8.05pm.
Cuisine: ENGLISH – All dishes are home-made, with constant change of fixed menu, e.g., roast rack of lamb, fresh lemon sole. The wine list is interesting and most reasonably priced.
Cards: Visa, Access.
Other points: licensed, children welcome, pets by prior arrangement, residents' lounge.
Rooms: 7 bedrooms. All with TV, tea/coffee-making facilities, telephone.
Directions: on A379 between Kingsbridge and Dartmouth.
MICHAEL ROBERTS & DAVID ALFORD
☎ (01548) 580580 [Fax] (01548) 581124.

LYDFORD • map 3D3

THE CASTLE INN HOTEL
Near Okehampton, EX20 4BH
A delightful 16th century free house, overlooked by Lydford Castle, and set in one of the loveliest parts of Devon. Featured in the film The Hound of the Baskervilles, The Castle Inn is a traditional West Country inn, offering good food, fine ales, comfortable accommodation and a very warm welcome. Nearby visitor attractions include Lydford Gorge and the beautiful wild moors.
DOUBLE ROOM: from £20 to £30
FOOD: up to £15
Hours: breakfast 8am–9am, dinner 7pm–9.30pm, bar meals 12noon–2.30pm, bar meals 6.30pm–9.30pm.
Cuisine: ENGLISH – à la carte and table d'hôte menus, using freshly cooked food and local produce. Dishes may include guinea fowl, whiskied steak, and salmon cutlets.
Cards: Visa, Access, Diners, AmEx.
Other points: licensed, open-air dining, Sunday lunch, no-smoking area, children welcome, pets allowed, parking, garden, disabled access, residents' lounge, vegetarian meals, cots, 24hr reception, left luggage.
Rooms: 2 double rooms, 6 twin rooms. All with TV, radio, tea/coffee-making facilities.
Directions: take the Lydford turning off A386 between Okehampton and Tavistock.
CLIVE & MO WALKER ☎ (0182282) 242
Fax (01822882) 454.

LYNMOUTH • map 3B3

THE BATH HOTEL
Lynmouth Street, EX35 6EL
Centrally located by picturesque Lynmouth harbour, the hotel has a relaxed, friendly atmosphere in an ideal position for exploring Exmoor and many local attractions. The sun lounge, serving traditional afternoon teas, is open to non-residents. Two bars serve bar lunches, and in the restaurant a set 5-course dinner menu is available, offering excellent value and a wide choice of different dishes.
DOUBLE ROOM: from £30 to £40
SINGLE ROOM: from £25 to £35
FOOD: up to £15
Hours: breakfast 8.30am–9.30am, lunch 12.30am–2pm, bar meals 12noon–2.15pm, dinner 7pm–8.30pm, closed November until mid-March.
Cuisine: ENGLISH – bar snacks, lunches, teas and set dinner menu featuring specials and a vegetarian dish. A speciality is wild Lyn salmon, caught in their own trap. Lynmouth lobster dishes.
Cards: Visa, Access, Diners, AmEx.
Other points: licensed, Sunday lunch, no-smoking area, children welcome, afternoon tea, pets allowed, parking.
Rooms: 1 single room, 11 double rooms, 8 twin rooms, 4 family rooms. All with en suite, tea/coffee-making facilities, TV, telephone, baby-listening device, radio/alarm.

Directions: situated on the A39 at Lynmouth.
MRS DALGARNO ☎ (01598) 752238.

CORNER HOUSE
Riverside Road, EX35 6EH
A pleasant and comfortable establishment with a large restaurant, spacious, airy rooms and a garden with attractive shrubs and flowers, overlooking the rivers and Lyn Valley. Ideal for visiting Exmoor, the Valley of Rocks and Watersmeet. Outside paved area for alfresco dining at umbrella tables.
DOUBLE ROOM: from £20 to £30
SINGLE ROOM: from £25 to £35
FOOD: up to £15
Hours: breakfast 8.30am–11am, bar snacks 11.30am–5pm, dinner 6pm until late, last orders 9pm, closed November until February.
Cuisine: ENGLISH – cream teas available during the afternoon.
Cards: Visa, Access, Switch.
Other points: residents' parking, children catered for (please check for age limits), Sunday lunch, open bank holidays, afternoon tea, vegetarian meals, open-air dining, licensed.
Rooms: 3 double rooms. All with en suite, TV, tea/coffee-making facilities, views.
Directions: follow A39; on entry into Lynmouth you will see the black and white umbrellas along the river.
ROBERT & PENELOPE WHITWELL ☎ (01598) 53300.

RISING SUN HOTEL
Harbourside, EX35 6EQ
A lovely 14th century thatched smugglers' inn overlooking a small picturesque harbour and Lynmouth Bay. The hotel offers free salmon-fishing for residents. The buildings were once smugglers' cottages, with a wealth of intriguing staircases and narrow passages.
DOUBLE ROOM: from £30 to £40
SINGLE ROOM: from £35 to £45
FOOD: from £20 to £25
Hours: breakfast 8.30am–9.30am, lunch 12.30am–2pm, dinner 7pm–9pm, open all year.
Cuisine: ENGLISH – seafood, game in season.
Cards: Visa, Access, AmEx.
Other points: licensed, open-air dining, Sunday lunch, coaches by prior arrangement, baby-listening device, cots, residents' bar, residents' lounge, vegetarian meals, parking, children catered for (please check for age limits).
Rooms: 1 single room, 11 double rooms, 3 twin rooms, 1 suite. All with TV, radio, alarm, telephone, tea/coffee-making facilities.
Directions: exit 23 on the M5, then A39 to Lynmouth. Opposite sea harbour.
MR F. ST H. JEUNE ☎ (01598) 53223
Fax (01598) 53480.

ROCK HOUSE HOTEL
The Waterfront, EX35 6EN
Perched on the water's edge overlooking Lynmouth's picturesque harbour, the Rock House Hotel has a backdrop of wooded trees. Tastefully decorated, the rooms are spacious and airy. Serving quality food at good-value prices, the hotel

is very popular with locals and holiday-makers alike, with its cheerful atmosphere.
DOUBLE ROOM: from £20 to £30
FOOD: up to £15
Hours: breakfast 8.45am–9.45am, lunch 12noon–2pm, dinner 7pm–9pm.
Cuisine: INTERNATIONAL – large and varied menu. Dishes include crab soup, escargots bourguignonne, guinea fowl, Hawaiian duck, peppered steak, steak Exmoor and a variety of sweets.
Cards: Visa, Access, Diners, AmEx.
Other points: licensed, open-air dining, Sunday lunch, garden, afternoon tea, pets by prior arrangement, picnic lunches.
Rooms: 6 bedrooms.
Directions: A39 to Lynton, then follow the short road down to Lynmouth.
MRS N. WESTON ☎ (01598) 53508.

SHELLEYS COTTAGE HOTEL
Watersmeet Road, EX35 6EP
A quiet, peaceful hotel and restaurant set in its own shrub gardens in a beautiful Devon village. The proprietors personally supervise the day to day running of the hotel, ensuring that every guest's need is catered for. Ideal base from which to explore the Valley of Rocks, Glen Lyn gorge and the Devon countryside.
DOUBLE ROOM: up to £20
FOOD: up to £15
Hours: breakfast 8.30am–9.30am, lunch 12noon–2.30pm, dinner 7pm–9pm, closed December until January except New Year.
Cards: Visa, Access, AmEx.
Other points: children welcome, no-smoking area, pets allowed, residents' lounge, vegetarian meals, garden.
Rooms: 10 twin rooms. All with TV, radio, tea/coffee-making facilities.
Directions: A39, end of Watersmeet Road, bottom of Lynmouth Hill.
MRS & MR PRIDEAUX ☎ (01598) 53219.

LYNTON • map 3B3

THE EXMOOR SANDPIPER INN
Countisbury, EX31 4Q7
A long, white 13th century building of considerable charm and character at the top of Countisbury hill, with stunning views over Exmoor. The area is distinctly rural, with sheep roaming the grounds, but the food and accommodation are sophisticated yet homely. An excellent base for walkers.
DOUBLE ROOM: from £30 to £40
SINGLE ROOM: from £45 to £55
FOOD: from £15 to £20 [CLUB]
Hours: breakfast 8.30am–9.30am, lunch 12noon–2.30pm, dinner 7pm–10pm, bar 11am–11pm.
Cuisine: ENGLISH – large selection of table d'hôte evening meals, including garlic prawns, local venison in red wine, steaks, lobster, cold seafood platter, home-made soups.
Other points: licensed, open-air dining, Sunday lunch, children welcome, pets by prior arrangement,

parking, residents' lounge, residents' bar.
Rooms: 12 double rooms, 2 twin rooms, 2 family rooms. All with TV, radio, tea/coffee-making facilities.
Directions: on the A39 at the top of Countisbury hill, outside Lynton.
PERSONALLY RUN HOTELS LTD ☎ (015987) 263 [Fax] (015987) 358.

MILLSLADE COUNTRY HOUSE HOTEL
Brendon, EX35 6PS
An 18th century country house set in 9 acres of grounds in a quiet spot on the edge of Brendon village, surrounded by the forest and River Lynn. The hotel has fishing rights (salmon and trout) for their guests to enjoy, and there are plenty of local attractions, including Doone Valley, Barnstaple and Minehead.
DOUBLE ROOM: from £30 to £40
FOOD: from £15 to £20 🍽 [CLUB]
Hours: breakfast 8.30am–9.30am, dinner 7pm–9.30pm, lunch 12noon–2.30pm.
Cards: Visa.
Other points: licensed, Sunday lunch, children welcome, pets allowed, afternoon tea, open bank holidays, residents' lounge, garden.
Directions: two miles from Lynton, just off the A39.
E.M. FREWER ☎ (015987) 322.

ROCKVALE HOTEL
Lee Road, EX35 6HW
The hotel stands in its own grounds in a delightfully sunny and quiet, yet central, position and enjoys extensive views over Lynton village and the surrounding hills to Exmoor and Countisbury. Judith and David offer their guests comfortable accommodation, an excellent range of freshly cooked meals, and extremely friendly hospitality in a pleasant atmosphere.
DOUBLE ROOM: from £20 to £30
SINGLE ROOM: up to £25
FOOD: up to £15
Hours: closed November until February.
Cuisine: ENGLISH – traditional up-market home-cooking.
Cards: Visa, Access.
Other points: parking, children catered for (please check for age limits), no-smoking area, residents' lounge, vegetarian meals.
Rooms: 1 single room, 5 double rooms, 1 triple room, 1 family room. All with en suite, TV, telephone, radio, alarm, tea/coffee-making facilities.
Directions: on a private road left of the Town Hall in the centre of Lynton.
JUDITH & DAVID WOODLAND ☎ (01598) 52279/53343.

MORTEHOE • map 3B3

LUNDY HOUSE HOTEL
Chapel Hill, Woolacombe, EX34 7DZ
Spectacularly situated on the cliff-side opposite a secluded beach, with magnificent sea views over Morte Bay to Lundy Island. Terraced gardens, comfortable licensed lounge bar, separate colour

TV, video and satellite TV lounges. Traditional 'home from home' cooking. Vegetarian and special diets catered for.
DOUBLE ROOM: up to £20
SINGLE ROOM: up to £25
FOOD: up to £15
Hours: breakfast 8.30am–9.30am, dinner 7.30pm, closed November until January.
Cuisine: ENGLISH.
Other points: pets allowed, special breaks.
Rooms: 9 bedrooms.
Directions: situated between Woolacombe and Mortehoe off the A361 on the B3343.
ROGER & DENA SELLS ☎ (01271) 870372.

PAIGNTON • map 4D4

THE INN ON THE GREEN
Seafront, TQ4 6BG

A holiday complex set in 2 acres right on the seafront, yet within a 2-minute walk from shops, theatre and other attractions. The menu is very extensive, offering a wide range of dishes, well-cooked and presented, and the apartments are very comfortable. An ideal place for family holidays, as children are well catered for, with sandpits, a Wendy House and their own discos.
DOUBLE ROOM: up to £20
FOOD: up to £15 [CLUB]
Hours: lunch 12noon–3pm, dinner 6.30pm–12midnight, Sunday 7pm–10.30pm.
Cuisine: INTERNATIONAL – very extensive menu, including traditional English, Indian and Italian dishes. Children's own menu. Desserts include olde-English puddings.
Other points: Sunday lunch, children welcome, pets allowed, garden, playland, swimming pool, launderette, games room.
Directions: end of M5 to Torbay. Directly on seafront opposite the pier.
BRIAN SHONE ☎ (01803) 557841
[Fax] (01803) 550344.

REDCLIFFE HOTEL
Marine Drive, TQ3 2NL

Situated in one of Britain's most popular seaside resorts. This is an ideal location from which to visit Paignton Zoo and explore the Devon countryside.
DOUBLE ROOM: from £40 to £50
SINGLE ROOM: from £35 to £45
FOOD: up to £15
Hours: breakfast 8am–9.30am, bar snacks 12noon–2pm, Sunday lunch 12.45am–2pm, dinner 7pm–8.30pm.
Cuisine: ENGLISH/FRENCH.
Cards: Visa, Access.
Other points: parking, children welcome, afternoon teas, residents' lounge, vegetarian meals, garden, leisure centre, indoor pool.
Rooms: 12 single rooms, 23 double rooms, 23 twin rooms.
Directions: take the A385 or A380 and head for Paignton seafront. The hotel is at the Torquay end of Paignton Green.
MR S. TWIGGER ☎ (01803) 526397
[Fax] (01803) 528030.

ROSSLYN HOTEL
16 Colin Road, TQ3 2NR

This comfortably furnished, privately-owned hotel is situated just off the seafront and is convenient for visiting Torquay and Brixham. The hotel offers many homely attributes, which serve to enhance the general feeling of welcome.
DOUBLE ROOM: up to £20
SINGLE ROOM: up to £25
FOOD: up to £15 ☆
Hours: breakfast 8.30am–9am, dinner 6pm–7pm, bar snacks all day.
Cuisine: ENGLISH – table d'hôte menu.
Other points: parking, children welcome, no-smoking area, residents' lounge, vegetarian meals.
Rooms: 1 single room, 5 double rooms, 1 twin room, 3 family rooms.
Directions: just off the seafront.
VALERIE ADAMS ☎ (01803) 525578.

SOUTH SANDS HOTEL
12 Alta Vista Road, TQ4 6BZ

South Sands Hotel, situated close to Goodrington Sands, enjoys outstanding views of the bay. Under the personal supervision of the proprietors, visitors are assured of a warm welcome, comfortable, well-equipped bedrooms and superb, freshly prepared food. Very good value for money. Ideally located for the beach, town centre and water adventure park. Free car park.
DOUBLE ROOM: from £20 to £30
SINGLE ROOM: up to £25
FOOD: up to £15
Hours: breakfast 8am–9am, dinner 6pm–7pm.
Cuisine: ENGLISH / CONTINENTAL.
Cards: Visa, MasterCard.
Other points: children welcome, vegetarian meals, afternoon tea, pets allowed, garden, residents' lounge, children welcome, baby-listening device, baby-sitting, cots, left luggage.
Rooms: 2 single rooms, 3 double rooms, 6 twin rooms, 8 family rooms. All with TV, radio, alarm, tea/coffee-making facilities.
Directions: keep Paignton harbour on left, go over top of hill. First hotel on right.
TONY & CECILE CAHILL ☎ (01803) 557231/529947 [Fax] (01803) 551871.

PLYMOUTH • map 3D3

BOUGIE FRENCH BRASSERIE
Nykredit House, Princess Street, PL1 2EX

Strategically located in the heart of businessland and within one minute's walk from the prestigious Theatre Royal is this Plymouth landmark restaurant. A modern brasserie with innovative French-style cooking served in a relaxed atmosphere. This charming, stylish restaurant is a real find for the 'gastronauts'. The cassoulet de Toulouse cooked by Martial, from Paris, is the favourite with regulars. An excellent wine list complements the excellent food.
FOOD: from £15 to £20
Hours: lunch 12noon–3pm, dinner 6pm–12midnight, closed Saturday lunch and all day Sunday, closed Christmas day and New Year's day.

Cuisine: FRENCH – with an emphasis on seafood. Plat du jour served 12noon–2.30pm and 6pm–7.30pm at £9.50 for one course or £12.50 for two courses. Full à la carte is always available.
Cards: Visa, Access, MasterCard.
Other points: children welcome, no-smoking area, vegetarian meals.
Directions: in city centre, behind Theatre Royal.
EDMOND RENE DAVARI ☎ (01752) 221177
[Fax] (01752) 221177.

CRANBOURNE HOTEL
282 Citadel Road, The Hoe, PL1 2PZ
A clean, family-run town-house hotel close to the city centre with all its attractions. Cranbourne Hotel is a convenient two-minute walk from the ferry port and has its own hairdressing salon.
DOUBLE ROOM: up to £20
Hours: breakfast 7am–9am.
Cuisine: BREAKFAST.
Cards: Visa, Access, AmEx.
Other points: children welcome, pets allowed, parking.
Rooms: 2 single rooms, 2 double rooms, 7 twin rooms, 3 family rooms. All with TV, tea/coffee-making facilities, alarm, video.
Directions: close to city centre, 200 yards from Hoe promenade.
PETER & VALERIE WILLIAMS ☎ (01752) 661400 [Fax] (01752) 263858.

SMEATONS TOWER HOTEL
40–44 Grand Parade, The Hoe, PL1 3DJ
A small, friendly, family-run hotel situated close to the seafront and 12–15 minutes' walk from the city centre. A popular holiday and commercial hotel.
DOUBLE ROOM: up to £20
FOOD: up to £15
Hours: breakfast 7am–9am, lunch 12noon–2pm, bar meals 12noon–3pm, dinner 6pm–8.30pm, bar meals 6pm–11pm.
Cuisine: ENGLISH / CONTINENTAL – table d'hôte and full à la carte menus.
Cards: Visa, Access.
Other points: licensed, Sunday lunch, no smoking area, children welcome, afternoon tea.
Rooms: 10 double rooms, 4 twin rooms, 4 family rooms. All with TV, telephone, tea/coffee-making facilities.
Directions: adjacent to Plymouth Hoe.
BRIAN & MAY MASON ☎ (01752) 221007
[Fax] (01752) 221664.

THE SPORTSMAN'S INN
Exeter Road, Ivybridge, PL21 0BQ
This attractive, long, old coaching inn has recently been refurbished throughout to very attractive standards. With an extensive selection of well-cooked dishes, complemented by a wide range of wines, the inn has justifiably proved to be very popular with locals and travellers alike.
DOUBLE ROOM: from £20 to £30
SINGLE ROOM: from £25 to £35
FOOD: up to £15
Hours: breakfast 7.30am–9am, meals all day 11.30am–9.30pm, open every day.
Cuisine: ENGLISH – wide choice of traditional dishes.

Cards: Visa, Access, AmEx, Eurocard, MasterCard, Switch, Delta.
Other points: parking, children welcome, pets allowed, no-smoking area, vegetarian meals, traditional Sunday lunch.
Rooms: 2 single rooms, 7 double rooms, 1 twin room, 1 family room. All with satellite TV, telephone, radio, alarm, hair dryer, tea/coffee-making facilities. Doubles can be used as singles.
Directions: just off the A38 Plymouth–Exeter road.
MS DONNA O. HIBBERT ☎ (01752) 892280
[Fax] (01752) 690714.

TRATTORIA PESCATORE
36 Admiralty Street, Stonehouse, PL1 3RU
A small Italian restaurant situated in an old Victorian building. Hand-painted murals on the walls add to the truly Italian atmosphere of the restaurant. All food is freshly cooked to order, and seafood is the house speciality. Delicious food and friendly, efficient service. Highly recommended.
FOOD: from £15 to £20
Hours: lunch 12noon–2pm, dinner 7pm–11pm, closed Saturday lunch, Sunday and bank holidays.
Cuisine: ITALIAN – the traditional Italian cuisine selection includes giant prawns tossed in garlic butter, and special vegetarian pastas. Also, chef's specials available from the blackboard.
Cards: Visa, Access.
Other points: licensed, open-air dining, children welcome.
Directions: approximately 1 mile from city centre, near Plymouth to Roscoff ferry port.
GIAN PIERO CALIGARI & RITA ATKINSON
☎ (01752) 600201.

SHALDON • map 4D4

THE NESS HOUSE HOTEL
Marine Parade, near Teignmouth, TQ14 0HP
Formerly a private country house, the hotel sits in beautiful gardens and enjoys wonderful views of the coast and the Teign Estuary. A friendly hotel serving good food.
DOUBLE ROOM: from £30 to £40
SINGLE ROOM: from £35 to £45
FOOD: from £15 to £20 [CLUB]
Hours: breakfast 8am–10am, lunch 12noon–2pm, dinner 7pm–10pm, bar meals 12noon–2pm, bar meals 6.30pm–10pm.
Cuisine: FRENCH – a large choice of traditional French dishes. Coquilles Saint-Jacques au saffran, mignon de veau aux fraises.
Cards: Visa, Access, AmEx.
Other points: licensed, open-air dining, Sunday lunch, children welcome, afternoon tea, garden, residents' bar, residents' lounge.
Rooms: 10 double rooms, 2 family rooms. All with telephone, tea/coffee-making facilities, heating, satellite TV. The rooms are of varying standards and prices; all can be used as singles when required.
Directions: on A379 (Teignmouth–Torquay road) in Shaldon, set in parkland.
PETER REYNOLDS ☎ (01626) 873480
[Fax] (01626) 873486.

SIDFORD • map 4D4

THE BLUE BALL INN
Near Sidmouth, EX10 9QL
Dating back to 1385, The Blue Ball Inn is thatched and made of cob and flint. Fresh flowers add to the tasteful decor of the building, and outside customers can enjoy barbecues in the garden during summer. Run by the same family since 1912, the pub provides well-cooked food in a busy but relaxed atmosphere. Excellent, friendly service.
DOUBLE ROOM: from £20 to £30
FOOD: up to £15
Hours: breakfast 8.30am–10am, lunch 10.30am–2pm, dinner 6.30pm–10pm.
Cuisine: ENGLISH – home-made specialities include steak-and-kidney pie, chicken mornay, chilli con carne, and local fish.
Cards: Visa, Access.
Other points: licensed, open-air dining, Sunday lunch, children welcome, garden, barbecues, pets allowed, functions.
Rooms: 3 twin rooms.
Directions: on the A3052, located just outside Sidmouth.
MR ROGER NEWTON ☎ (01395) 514062.

SIDMOUTH • map 4D4

FORTFIELD HOTEL
Station Road, EX10 8NU
Privately-owned country house-style hotel, stunning sea views, lovely grounds with putting green and private parking. Indoor heated pool, sauna, solarium and beauty treatments. All rooms en suite, passenger lift, superb traditional English cuisine, old-fashioned quality service assured. Open all year.
DOUBLE ROOM: from £20 to £30
SINGLE ROOM: up to £25
FOOD: up to £15
Hours: breakfast 8am–9.30am, lunch 12noon–2pm, dinner 6.30pm–8pm.
Cuisine: ENGLISH – prawn and apple cocktail, deep-fried mushroom rossini, pork fillet cider and apple sauce, escalope of veal Italian, traditional steak-and-kidney pudding.
Cards: Visa, Access, Diners, AmEx, Switch.
Other points: licensed, open-air dining, Sunday lunch, no-smoking area, children welcome, beauty therapy, gym facilities, afternoon tea, pets allowed.
Rooms: 6 single rooms, 11 double rooms, 33 twin rooms, 5 family rooms. All with TV, radio, telephone, tea/coffee-making facilities.
Directions: from Exeter take A3052. Turn right at Bowd Inn. Hotel on right just before seafront.
ANDREW TORJUSSEN ☎ (01395) 512403
Fax (01395) 512403.

KINGSWOOD HOTEL
Esplanade, EX10 8AX
An excellent family-run establishment on the seafront with an award-winning and colourful, terraced garden. Fully modernized, the interior is spacious, and many of the rooms look out over the Devon coast. Personally supervised by the proprietors, the food and service are excellent. The Kingswood is now licensed, with a good selection of reasonably priced wines
DOUBLE ROOM: from £20 to £30
FOOD: up to £15
Hours: breakfast 8.15am–9.15am, lunch 12.30am–12.45am, dinner 6.45pm–7.30pm.
Cuisine: ENGLISH.
Other points: central heating, children welcome, pets allowed, residents' lounge, baby-listening device, picnic lunches.
Rooms: 8 single rooms, 6 double rooms, 7 twin rooms, 5 family rooms. All with TV, telephone, tea/coffee-making facilities.
Directions: on the seafront.
JOY, COLIN, MARK & JOANNA SEWARD
☎ (01395) 516367/513185 Fax (01395) 513185.

SOUTH MOLTON • map 3C3

STUMBLES HOTEL & RESTAURANT
131–134 East Street, EX36 3BU
Stumbles is situated on the edge of Exmoor in a bustling market town, with many fine antique shops and historic buildings. The attractive and spacious 30-seater restaurant, with its secluded tables and soft lighting, offers fresh food daily. Stumbles have their own hotel offering very comfortable accommodation, all en suite. The bar and courtyard are open for morning coffees and lunches, with barbecues in summmer.
DOUBLE ROOM: from £20 to £30
FOOD: up to £15
Hours: breakfast 8am–9am, lunch 12.30am–2pm, dinner 7pm–9.30pm, restaurant closed Sunday.
Cuisine: ENGLISH/FRENCH – fresh produce used for the daily changing menu.
Cards: Visa, Access.
Other points: parking, children welcome, no-smoking area, disabled access, pets, residents' lounge, garden, vegetarian meals, open-air dining.
Rooms: 3 single rooms, 5 double rooms, 3 twin rooms. All with TV, telephone, tea/coffee-making facilities, hair dryer.
Directions: in town centre, just off the square.
MR & MRS M. POTTER ☎ (01769) 574145
Fax (01769) 572558.

TAVISTOCK • map 3D3

THE OLD PLOUGH INN
Bere Ferrers, near Yelverton, PL20 7JL
A 16th century inn, situated beside the River Tavy in the scenic village of Bere Ferrers, in an unspoilt area of outstanding beauty. A wide range of home-made food and ales is offered in the bar, restaurant or beer garden. Open log fires in winter.
FOOD: up to £15
Hours: lunch 12noon–3pm, dinner 7.30pm–10.30pm, closed Christmas evening only.
Cuisine: ENGLISH – menus change daily, including, when available, fresh fish and 'Maggies Monster' home-made pies. Locally grown vegetables. All dishes home-made.
Cards: Visa, Access, AmEx.

Other points: licensed, open-air dining, Sunday lunch.
Directions: from Plymouth, take A386, following signs for Bere Alston and Bere Ferrers.
ADRIAN & MARGARET HOOPER ☎ (01822) 840358.

TEIGNMOUTH • map 4D4

RATHLIN HOUSE HOTEL
Upper Hermosa Road, TQ14 9JW
A beautiful Victorian villa, built in 1892, standing in its own enclosed gardens with a large terrace. Located in a quiet residential area, this is a small private hotel with the atmosphere of a large family home. The hotel is ten minutes' walk from the town centre, the harbour and the seafront.
DOUBLE ROOM: up to £20
SINGLE ROOM: up to £25
FOOD: up to £15
Hours: breakfast 8.15am–9am, dinner 6.30pm, closed November until March.
Cuisine: ENGLISH – traditional dishes; gluten-free diets and vegetarians catered for.
Other points: parking, children welcome, residents, lounge, garden, vegetarian meals.
Rooms: 2 double rooms, 1 twin room, 4 family rooms. All with en suite, TV, tea/coffee-making facilities.
Directions: M5, A38, A380, B3192; continue down the hill in Teignmouth, then turn right into Yannom Drive.
TERENCE FALLON ☎ (01626) 774473.

THROWLEIGH • map 3D3

WELL FARM
Near Okehampton, EX20 2JQ
Relax in beautiful and peaceful surroundings at Well Farm, a Grade II listed medieval Dartmoor longhouse. It is a working family-run dairy and outdoor pig farm, with peacocks, ornamental pheasants and free-range poultry. Fresh produce is served in a relaxed, family atmosphere.
DOUBLE ROOM: up to £20
SINGLE ROOM: up to £25
FOOD: up to £15
Hours: breakfast 9am, dinner 8pm–9pm, closed Christmas.
Cuisine: ENGLISH.
Other points: children welcome, residents' lounge, vegetarian meals, working farm.
Rooms: 1 twin room, 2 family rooms. All with en suite, tea/coffee-making facilities, heating.
Directions: 1½ miles from the A30 in the Dartmoor National Park.
MRS SHEELAGH KNOX ☎ (01647) 231394.

TIVERTON • map 4C4

BICKLEIGH COTTAGE COUNTRY HOTEL
Bickleigh Bridge, EX16 8RJ
Situated on the bank of the River Exe near Bickleigh Bridge, a landmark famous for its scenic beauty, Bickleigh Cottage Country Hotel – built circa 1640 – has been privately owned by the Cochrane family since 1933. This partly thatched cottage still retains its low-beamed ceilings and genuine old fireplaces, while providing comfortable, beautifully decorated bedrooms and excellent fresh cuisine in a wonderful, homely atmosphere.
DOUBLE ROOM: from £20 to £30
SINGLE ROOM: from £25 to £35
FOOD: up to £15
Hours: breakfast 8.30am–9.15am, dinner 7pm, closed November until March.
Cuisine: ENGLISH – the daily-chosen menus are announced at breakfast.
Cards: Visa, Access.
Other points: parking, no-smoking area, residents' lounge, garden.
Rooms: 2 single rooms, 4 double rooms, 3 twin rooms. All with en suite, tea/coffee-making facilities.
Directions: 4 miles south of Tiverton, 10 miles north of Exeter on the A396.
STUART & PAULINE COCHRANE ☎ (01884) 855230.

BRIDGE GUEST HOUSE
23 Angel Hill, EX16 6PE
Situated on the main road bridge over the River Exe in the centre of the town, all rooms overlooking the river. There is a pleasant riverside tea garden. Fishing rights.
DOUBLE ROOM: up to £20
FOOD: from £15 to £20
Hours: breakfast 7.30am–9am, dinner 6.30pm–7.30pm, open all year.
Cuisine: ENGLISH.
Other points: central heating, children welcome, residents' lounge, bar.
Rooms: 1 single room, 2 double rooms, 5 twin rooms, 2 family rooms. All with TV, tea/coffee-making facilities.
Directions: off M5 at junction 27, link road to town centre, beside River Exe.
BOB & SUE COXALL ☎ (01884) 252804.

THE HARTNOLL COUNTRY HOUSE HOTEL
Bolham Road, Bolham, EX16 7RA
This lovely Georgian hotel has a cosy and intimate atmosphere, which is very welcome after an active day prowling through the surrounding Devon countryside. A mill-stream runs through the hotel grounds, giving you a delightful feeling of 'getting away from it all'. Friendly and courteous staff help make your stay memorable.
DOUBLE ROOM: from £20 to £30
SINGLE ROOM: from £35 to £45
FOOD: from £15 to £20
Hours: breakfast 7.30am–10am, dinner 7pm–9pm, lunch 12noon–2pm.
Cuisine: ENGLISH / FRENCH – mixture of traditional English and French cuisine. Regular à la carte.
Cards: Visa, Access.
Other points: licensed, open-air dining, Sunday lunch, children welcome, pets allowed, open

bank holidays, residents' lounge, residents' bar, vegetarian meals, parking, disabled access.
Directions: after junction 27 on the M5, take the first roundabout (6 miles). The A396 is the third exit right.
SALLY PRICE AND MAGDI SOLIMAN
☎ (01884) 252777.

THE MERRIEMEADE HOTEL
1 Lower Town, Sampford Peverell, EX16 7BJ

Formerly a Georgian-style gentleman's residence, The Merriemeade Hotel overlooks the Blackdown Hills. This hotel caters for all ages, with a children's play area in the rear garden. Its food is both varied and excellently cooked. The rooms are also of high standard. Great value for money.
DOUBLE ROOM: from £20 to £30
SINGLE ROOM: from £25 to £35
FOOD: up to £15
Hours: breakfast 7.30am–9am, lunch 11.30am–2pm, Sunday 12noon–2.30pm, dinner 6.45pm–9pm, Sunday 7pm–9.30pm.
Cuisine: ENGLISH / FRENCH – à la carte menu, bar meals and snacks.
Cards: Visa, Access, AmEx.
Other points: licensed, open-air dining, Sunday lunch, children welcome, pets by arrangement.
Rooms: 1 single room, 1 double room, 1 twin room, 2 family rooms.
Directions: 1 mile from junction 27 of the M5 and North Devon link road. On A373.
MR L.J. AFFLECK & MR P.J.P. COURT
☎ (01884) 820270 Fax (01884) 821614.

TORQUAY • map 4D4

THE DEVONSHIRE HOTEL
Parkhill Road, TQ1 2DY

A large, luxurious and quiet 100-year-old hotel where guests are warmly welcomed with porter service. Distinctive features are the original doors and high, corniced ceilings, leading to the beautiful dining rooms and bar lounges, which have been decorated in restful colours. Convenient for theatre visits and boat excursions.
DOUBLE ROOM: from £30 to £40
FOOD: up to £15
Hours: bar snacks 12noon–2.30pm, dinner 7pm–8.45pm, bar snacks 6.30pm–8.45pm.
Cuisine: ENGLISH – traditional cuisine and grill options.
Cards: Visa, Access, Diners.
Other points: parking, children welcome, open bank holidays, afternoon teas, disabled access, pets allowed, residents' lounge, vegetarian meals, garden, residents' bar, swimming pool.
Rooms: 8 single rooms, 14 double rooms, 40 twin rooms, 9 family rooms. All with TV, telephone, tea/coffee-making facilities.
Directions: at the harbour clock, turn right along the harbour side and proceed up the hill towards Meadfoot Beach. The hotel is at the crest of the hill.
THE DEVONSHIRE HOTEL (TORQUAY) LTD
☎ (01803) 291123 Fax (01803) 291710.

INGOLDSBY HOTEL
Chelston Road, TQ2 6PT

A truly delightful hotel where you can relax in the attractive garden or take a short stroll to the seafront or into Cockington village. The spacious dining room overlooks the garden, and there are comfortable bedrooms and a quiet television room. An ideal base for a family hotel or seasonal break.
DOUBLE ROOM: up to £20
Hours: breakfast 8.45am–9.30am, bar snacks all day, dinner 6pm–7pm.
Cuisine: ENGLISH.
Cards: Visa, Access.
Other points: parking, children welcome, open bank holidays, disabled access, residents' lounge, vegetarian meals, garden.
Directions: from seafront, turn right by Grand Hotel, first left, then right at crossroads.
MR R. WELLS ☎ (01803) 607497.

JINGLE'S RESTAURANT
34 Torwood Street, TQ1 1EB

An American-themed restaurant offering a good variety of very well-cooked dishes to suit all tastes. The choice includes char-grilled steaks, hamburgers and vegetarian meals. House specialities are Mexican dishes such as sizzling fajita, a traditional Mexican style of cooking. The good food is complemented by generous portions and welcoming service. International beers.
FOOD: up to £15
Hours: lunch summer only 12noon–3pm, closed Sunday lunch, dinner 6pm–11pm.
Cuisine: AMERICAN / MEXICAN – wide choice of dishes including char-grilled steaks, Cajun dishes, Mexican dishes, vegetarian meals, hamburgers and deep-pan pizzas.
Cards: Visa, Access, AmEx.
Other points: licensed, children welcome, parking nearby.
Directions: 100 yards from clock tower on harbourside.
JOHN & PAT GOLDER ☎ (01803) 293340.

LANSDOWNE HOTEL
Babbacombe Road, TQ1 1PW

A relaxed but lively south-facing holiday hotel, spacious and comfortable, with a sun-trap patio, swimming pool, and full central heating for those cooler evenings. Nightly entertainment is provided, with cabaret, live music and a family disco in the spacious ballroom, with special entertainment for children. Good traditional cuisine with a wide choice of drinks and cocktails. Many nearby attractions.
DOUBLE ROOM: from £20 to £30
FOOD: up to £15
Hours: breakfast 8.30am–10am, lunch 12noon–1.30pm, dinner 7pm–8.30pm.
Cuisine: ENGLISH.
Cards: Visa, Access.
Other points: parking, children welcome, no-smoking area, pets, residents' lounge, vegetarian meals, garden.
Directions: to Torquay Harbour, turn left at clock tower. The hotel is ¼ mile on the left.
MR & MRS RIDLER ☎ (01803) 299599.

DORSET • SW ENGLAND

LIVERMEAD CLIFF HOTEL
Sea Front, TQ2 6RQ
A comfortable family hotel situated on the seafront at the water's edge, yet only a few minutes' level walk from the centre of town and the English Riviera Centre. The hotel is tastefully decorated and offers a high standard of comfort, which is complemented by the friendly and efficient service. All meals are cooked on the premises using fresh ingredients.
DOUBLE ROOM: from £30 to £40
SINGLE ROOM: from £25 to £35
FOOD: from £15 to £20
Hours: lunch 1pm–2pm, bar meals 12noon–2pm, 6.30pm–8.30pm, dinner 7pm–8.30pm, open all year.
Cuisine: ENGLISH / CONTINENTAL – locally caught fish, Devon meats and poultry.
Cards: Visa, Access, Diners, AmEx.
Other points: licensed, Sunday lunch, children welcome, afternoon tea, swimming pool, solarium, garden, conferences, baby-listening device, cots, baby-sitting, vegetarian meals, parking, residents' bar, residents' lounge, disabled access.
Rooms: 64 bedrooms. All with TV, radio, alarm, telephone, tea/coffee-making facilities.
Directions: from M5, exit onto A380 to Torquay, right at seafront, 600 yards.
MR JOHN PERRY ☎ (01803) 299666
Fax (01803) 294496.

TOTNES • map 4D4

OLD CHURCH HOUSE INN
Torbryan, Ipplepen, TQ12 5UR
Many kings of England have wined and dined at this inn, which is steeped in history. Recognized as one of the most haunted inns in the West Country, it offers comfortable accommodation in individually heated rooms and good traditional English cuisine. The Locals Bar is well known for the quality of its beer and wide range of spirits and liqueurs. Filmed for numerous television and radio programmes.
DOUBLE ROOM: from £20 to £30
FOOD: up to £15
Hours: breakfast 8.30am–10am, lunch 12noon–3pm, dinner 7pm–10.30pm, open all year.
Cuisine: ENGLISH.
Cards: Visa, Access.
Other points: licensed.
Directions: turn off the A381 Newton Abbot to Totnes road towards Ipplepen. Go through the village to Orley Common, and then follow signs to the inn.
MR E.G. PIMM ☎ (01803) 812372.

WOOLACOMBE • map 3B3

BAYCLIFFE HOTEL
Chapel Hill, Mortehoe, EX34 7AZ
Small, family-run hotel offering good service, comfortable rooms and superb views of the bay. Beaches are just a few minutes away, and places of interest include an 11th century church. Also, being adjacent to National Trust land, walkers will find this an ideal spot.
DOUBLE ROOM: from £20 to £30
FOOD: up to £15
Hours: breakfast 9am–10am, dinner 7pm–8pm.
Cuisine: ENGLISH.
Cards: Visa, Access.
Other points: licensed.
Directions: B3343 to Mortehoe village.
MR & MRS McFARLANE ☎ (01271) 870393.

DORSET

BLANDFORD FORUM • map 4C6

ANVIL HOTEL AND RESTAURANT
Salisbury Road, Pimperne, DT11 8UQ
Situated in the pretty Dorset village of Pimperne, this beautifully maintained 16th century thatched hotel, just two minutes from Blandford, is steeped in history. The well-appointed restaurant, with log fire and beams, offers a mouthwatering menu with delicious desserts, prepared by a Savoy-trained chef and personally supervised by Carolann Palmer. Very comprehensive tasty bar meals are served in the Forge Bar. Ideally situated for touring Dorset and the surrounding counties of Wiltshire, Hampshire, Somerset and Devon. Enquire about clay pigeon tuition.
DOUBLE ROOM: from £30 to £40
SINGLE ROOM: from £35 to £45
FOOD: from £15 to £20
Hours: breakfast 7.30am–9.30am, lunch 12noon–2pm, bar snacks 12noon–2.30pm, dinner 7pm–9.45pm, bar snacks 7pm–10pm.
Cuisine: ENGLISH / CONTINENTAL – varied menu, freshly prepared. Bar snacks also available.
Cards: Visa, Access, Diners, AmEx.
Other points: parking, children welcome, open bank holidays, disabled access, pets allowed, vegetarian meals, garden, entertainment, residents' bar, cots.
Rooms: 1 single room, 5 double rooms, 2 twin rooms, 1 family room. All with TV, telephone, tea/coffee-making facilities.
Directions: 2 miles out of Blandford on A354 road to Salisbury.
CAROLANN PALMER ☎ (01258) 453431/ 480182.

BOURNEMOUTH • map 4D6

BAY VIEW COURT HOTEL
35 East Overcliff Drive, East Cliff, BH1 3AH
A 64-bedroom hotel, completely refurbished recently, situated in its own delightful garden with

137

breathtaking views across the bay. This hotel offers the highest standards for business customers, conference delegates and holiday-makers, all of whom can enjoy the indoor pool, snooker room, games room and bars. The hotel is family-run, and a warm welcome with excellent food and service are guaranteed.
DOUBLE ROOM: from £30 to £40
SINGLE ROOM: from £35 to £45
FOOD: from £15 to £20 [CLUB]
Hours: breakfast 8am–9.30am, dinner 6.30pm–8.30pm, bar snacks 12noon–2pm, 6.30pm–8.30pm.
Cuisine: ENGLISH / CONTINENTAL – very high quality. Vegetarian meals available on request.
Other points: parking, children welcome, Sunday lunch, open bank holidays, no-smoking area, vegetarian meals, functions, indoor swimming pool.
Rooms: 9 single rooms, 28 double rooms, 16 twin rooms, 11 family rooms.
Directions: from A338 Bournemouth ring road (Wessex Way) take A35 turning at St Pauls roundabout near Central Station to Christchurch Road. Turn left to Manor Road and continue to East Overcliff Drive, overlooking the sea.
MR L. COX ☎ (01202) 294449 [Fax] (01202) 292883.

■ BRAMCOTE HALL HOTEL
1 Glen Road, Boscombe, BH5 1HR
The house was built in 1894 for Lady Jane Shelley, daughter-in-law of the famous poet, and became a hotel in 1926. Great improvements have since been made, but many delightful aspects have remained unchanged. Children are particularly well catered for, with games provided and a special children's menu. The hotel is very close to Boscombe Pier and beach.
DOUBLE ROOM: up to £20
SINGLE ROOM: up to £25
FOOD: up to £15
Hours: breakfast 8.30am–9am, dinner 6pm–7pm, refreshments served to order throughout the day.
Cuisine: ENGLISH – all meals are freshly cooked to order; even the bread is baked on the premises.
Cards: Visa, Access, Diners, AmEx.
Other points: parking, children welcome, pets allowed, vegetarian meals.
Rooms: 3 single rooms, 4 double rooms, 1 twin room, 4 triple rooms, 2 family rooms. All with TV, radio, tea/coffee-making facilities.
Directions: from Boscombe shopping area, take road signposted Boscombe Pier and Percy Road; the hotel is the first in Glen Road.
JILL & ALLAN DALE ☎ (01202) 395555.

■ BURLEY COURT HOTEL
Bath Road, BH1 2NP
A well-known hotel, in the same family for over 40 years, where the continuing aims are good-quality food, courteous service and a high standard of cleanliness. The hotel is large enough to offer every luxury, yet not too large to be personally supervised throughout. A friendly, comfortable hotel. Children are most welcome, and

accommodation is free when sharing with two adults. There is a beach hut on the main promenade for guests' use.
DOUBLE ROOM: from £30 to £40
FOOD: up to £15
Hours: breakfast 8am–9.30am, bar meals 12noon–2.30pm, dinner 6.30pm–8.30pm.
Cuisine: ENGLISH – traditional English dishes. Snack lunches available in lounge bar or by the pool. Vegetarian meals by arrangement.
Cards: Visa, Access.
Other points: licensed, open-air dining, Sunday lunch, children welcome, afternoon tea, pets allowed, residents' lounge, lift, games room, swimming pool, solarium.
Rooms: 5 single rooms, 11 double rooms, 11 twin rooms, 9 family rooms.
Directions: East Cliff, near Bournemouth railway station.
MASLYN & JAN HASKER ☎ (01202) 552824 [Fax] (01202) 298514.

■ CHINE HOTEL
25 Boscombe Spa Road, BH5 1AX
Constructed during 1874 on Sir Henry Drummond-Wolff's estate, the Chine overlooks Poole Bay and the beautifully landscaped Boscombe Chine Gardens. Excellent service and old-world charm combine to create a warm, friendly atmosphere. The Bay Restaurant enjoys sea views and offers a high standard of freshly prepared meals for guests and non-residents.
DOUBLE ROOM: from £40 to £50
Hours: breakfast 8am–9.30am, lunch 12.30am–2pm, dinner 7pm–8.30pm.
Cuisine: ENGLISH – dishes include fillet steak topped with mushroom and stilton, paupiette of plaice with asparagus. Lunchtime cold buffet and carvery.
Cards: Visa, Access, Diners, AmEx.
Other points: licensed, Sunday lunch, children welcome, garden, afternoon tea.
Rooms: 9 single rooms, 30 double rooms, 39 twin rooms, 19 family rooms.
Directions: M3, M27 to A31 and Wessex Way, Bournemouth ring road, turn at St Paul's roundabout to Christchurch Road and Boscombe Spa Road. Hotel overlooks the sea and Poole Bay to the south.
MR J.G.J. BUTTERWORTH ☎ (01202) 396234.

■ CHINEHURST HOTEL
Studland Road, Alum Chine, BH4 8SA
A family-run hotel overlooking the beautiful Alum Chine. Tastefully decorated throughout, this is a medium-sized establishment with all the facilities of a large hotel. Close to the sea and shops on the West Cliff. Entertainment weekly. Separate special Italian restaurant: 'Mr Macaws'.
DOUBLE ROOM: from £20 to £30
FOOD: up to £15
Hours: breakfast 7.30am–9.30am, lunch 12noon–2.30pm, bar meals 12noon–1.45pm, dinner 6.30pm–10.30pm.
Cuisine: ENGLISH – wide selection table d'hôte menu changes daily: roasts, sole in white wine,

DORSET • SW ENGLAND

steaks. A la carte menu also available.
Cards: Visa, Access, Diners, AmEx.
Other points: licensed, Sunday lunch, no-smoking area, children welcome, pets by prior arrangement, afternoon tea, garden, barbecues, residents' lounge, residents' bar.
Rooms: 2 single rooms, 15 double rooms, 6 twin rooms, 6 family rooms. All with TV, radio, telephone, tea/coffee-making facilities, heating, baby-listening device, hair dryer.
Directions: west of the pier overlooking Alum Chine, close to the seafront.
MR C.K. GRIFFIN ☎ (01202) 764583
[Fax] (01202) 765854.

THE CLIFFESIDE HOTEL
East Overcliff Drive,
BH1 3AQ

The Cliffeside Hotel, overlooking the sea, is suitable for all ages. Well-cooked food and friendly, efficient service are complemented by the comfortable furnishings throughout. In an excellent position, close to shops, theatres, the BIC, and with plenty of activities: golf, wind-surfing, tennis and pony-trekking to name a few. Complimentary membership to Queensbury Leisure Club.
DOUBLE ROOM: from £30 to £40
SINGLE ROOM: from £35 to £45
FOOD: from £15 to £20
Hours: breakfast 8am–9.30am, lunch 12.45am–2pm, Sunday lunch 12.30am–2pm, dinner 6.45pm–8.30pm.
Cuisine: ENGLISH – dishes include grilled lamb cutlet garni and grilled whole dover sole maître d'hôtel. Cold buffet.
Cards: Visa, Access, Diners, AmEx, Switch.
Other points: licensed, parking, vegetarian meals, Sunday lunch, no-smoking area, children welcome, pets by prior arrangement, afternoon tea, swimming pool, games room, conferences.
Rooms: 61 bedrooms.
Directions: from M3, M27 to A31 and A338 Wessex Way, Bournemouth Ring Road to East Overcliff Drive.
COLIN YOUNG ☎ (01202) 555724.

CORIANDER RESTAURANT
14 Richmond Hill, BH2 6ES

A long-established town-centre restaurant catering for many tastes, including vegetarian. Open all day, so travellers and visitors are able to obtain almost anything, from a light snack and Mexican beer to full three-course meal.
FOOD: up to £15
Hours: open all day, Monday–Saturday 12noon–10.30pm, Sunday 6pm–10.30pm.
Cuisine: MEXICAN / INTERNATIONAL – wide selection of authentic Mexican dishes, plus 'Gringo' steaks, chicken and fish. Special vegetarian dishes. Daily blackboard specials. Home-made sweets.
Cards: Visa, Access, Switch, Delta.
Other points: children welcome (children's menu up to age 12), no-smoking area, coaches by prior arrangement
Directions: in the heart of Bournemouth.
CHRISTINE MILLS ☎ (01202) 552202.

CUMBERLAND HOTEL
East Overcliff Drive, BH1 3AF

A purpose-built hotel providing luxurious accommodation and facilities. Situated on the famous East Cliff, there are superb sea views, from the Purbeck Hills to the Isle of Wight. The elegant oak-panelled restaurant offers a varied menu, carefully selected wine list and efficient, courteous service. A family-run hotel which provides excellent standards. Guests have use of the nearby Queensbury Leisure Club.
DOUBLE ROOM: from £30 to £40
SINGLE ROOM: from £35 to £45
FOOD: from £15 to £20
Hours: breakfast 8am–9.30am, lunch 12.30am–1.45pm, bar meals 12.30am–2pm, dinner 7pm–8.30pm, bar meals 7pm–8.30pm.
Cuisine: MODERN ENGLISH – four-course table d'hôte menu. Dishes may include poached fillet of sole, medallions of pork tenderloin with a Calvados cream sauce. Bar snacks.
Cards: Visa, Access, AmEx.
Other points: licensed, Sunday lunch, no-smoking area, children welcome, residents' lounge, swimming pool, garden, conferences, parking, vegetarian meals, disabled access, residents' bar.
Rooms: 12 single rooms, 32 double rooms, 44 twin rooms, 8 triple rooms, 4 quad rooms. All with TV, radio, alarm, telephone, tea/coffee-making facilities.
Directions: M3, then M27, follow Wessex Way to East Cliff.
ARTHUR YOUNG HOTELS LTD ☎ (01202) 290722 [Fax] (01202) 311394

DEAN PARK HOTEL
41 Wimborne Road, BH2 6NB

A privately-owned hotel situated close to the town centre, Dean Park Cricket Ground, West Hants Tennis Club, Meyrick Golf Club and Bournemouth Conference Centre. The atmosphere is relaxed and friendly, the food is well prepared and the comfortable accommodation is of a very good standard.
DOUBLE ROOM: from £20 to £30
FOOD: up to £15
Hours: breakfast 8am–10am, dinner 7pm–9.30pm.
Cuisine: ENGLISH – à la carte and table d'hôte menus.
Cards: Visa, Access, AmEx.
Other points: parking, children welcome, conference facilities, pets allowed, residents' lounge, games room, residents' bar, central heating.
Rooms: 6 single rooms, 12 twin rooms. All with TV, radio, telephone, tea-making facilities.
Directions: from Wessex Way (Bournemouth by-pass, A338), turn off at Richmond roundabout and follow Wimborne Road, A337, to next island. The hotel is on the right.
LEONARD WALLEN ☎ (01202) 552941
[Fax] (01202) 556400.

DURLSTON COURT HOTEL
47 Gervis Road, East Cliff, BH1 3DD

Situated on Bournemouth's East Cliff in a quiet tree-lined road close to the cliff top, town centre and pavilion. Here, you can enjoy excellent food in comfortable surroundings, from a sandwich to a

139

candlelit dinner. The hotel is equipped with sauna, solarium, Jacuzzi and mini-gymnasium. There are several bars to choose from offering a wide range of drinks.
DOUBLE ROOM: from £20 to £30
FOOD: up to £15
Hours: breakfast 8am, bar snacks 12.30am–1.45pm, dinner 7pm–7.30pm.
Cuisine: ENGLISH / CONTINENTAL – fresh produce used where possible.
Cards: Visa, Access, Diners, AmEx.
Other points: parking, children welcome, no-smoking area, disabled access, pets allowed, residents' lounge, vegetarian meals, garden.
Rooms: 60 twin rooms. All with TV, radio, telephone, tea/coffee-making facilities.
Directions: approximately half a mile from Bournemouth travel interchange.
MS Z. INVERNE ☎ (01202) 291488
[Fax] (01202) 290335.

EMBASSY HOTEL
Meyrick Road, East Cliff, BH1 3DW
Set in a prime position on Bournemouth's beautiful East Cliff, close to the sea and within walking distance of the town-centre shops, the Embassy offers high standards, comfortable accommodation and a friendly atmosphere. It is set in attractive gardens with its own large heated swimming pool, presenting an ideal location for holiday or business visitors.
DOUBLE ROOM: from £20 to £30
SINGLE ROOM: from £25 to £35
FOOD: from £15 to £20
Hours: breakfast 8am–9am, bar snacks 11.30am–2pm, dinner 6.30pm–8.30pm.
Cuisine: ENGLISH / FRENCH.
Other points: parking, children welcome, open bank holidays, afternoon tea, pets allowed, residents' lounge, vegetarian meals.
Rooms: 8 single rooms, 22 double rooms, 32 twin rooms, 12 family rooms.
Directions: leave A338 to East Cliff and head for Lansdowne roundabout. Meyrick Road can be found second left off roundabout.
ANTHONY EDEN ☎ (01202) 290751
[Fax] (01202) 557459.

GRANGE HOTEL
Southbourne Overcliffe Drive, Southbourne, BH6 3NL
Situated in a premier position by the sea overlooking beautiful Bournemouth Bay, with scenic views from the Isle of Wight in the east to the Isle of Purbeck in the west. Offering quality accommodation and service, many rooms have balconies with excellent sea views. A passenger lift (wheelchair-friendly) serves all floors. The sun terrace and barbecue area are open during the summer season.
DOUBLE ROOM: from £30 to £40
SINGLE ROOM: from £25 to £35
FOOD: up to £15 [CLUB]
Hours: breakfast 8am–9.30am, Sunday lunch 12noon–2.30pm, dinner 6.30pm–8.30pm, bar snacks 6pm–11pm.
Cuisine: ENGLISH / CONTINENTAL.
Cards: Visa, Eurocard, MasterCard, Switch.

Other points: children welcome, parking, no-smoking area, afternoon teas, disabled access, pets, residents' lounge, vegetarian meals.
Rooms: 6 single rooms, 16 double rooms, 6 twin rooms, 3 family rooms.
Directions: on seafront between Christchurch and Boscombe (Fisherman's Walk).
GORDON & KAY BLAKEY ☎ (01202) 433093/433094 [Fax] (01202) 424228.

HOTEL MON BIJOU
47 Manor Road, East Cliff, BH1 3EU
Formerly a Victorian coach house, the building, set in a lovely tree-lined avenue, has been skillfully converted to provide a luxurious and elegantly furnished small private hotel. Poole Harbour and sandbanks are a short distance to the west, with ferries to Swanage and Studland Bay. The historic towns of Wimborne Minster and Ringwood (for the New Forest) are within easy reach, and Christchurch Priory is just a few minutes' drive away. Also ideal for Beaulieu Motor Museum, Compton Acres, Bournemouth beach and shopping centre.
DOUBLE ROOM: from £20 to £30
SINGLE ROOM: from £35 to £35
FOOD: up to £15 [CLUB] ☆
Hours: breakfast 8am–9am, lunch 12.30am–2pm, dinner 6.30pm–7.30pm, à la carte dinner 7.30pm–9pm.
Cuisine: ENGLISH – classic dishes.
Cards: Visa, Access, Diners, AmEx.
Other points: parking, children welcome, afternoon teas, disabled access, pets allowed, residents' lounge, vegetarian meals, open-air dining, garden.
Rooms: 7 bedrooms.
Directions: from Bournemouth town centre, take the town bypass along Wessex Way on the A338. The hotel is on Manor Road, adjacent to Eastcliff.
SYLVIA & VIC SHEARS ☎ (01202) 551389.

MAE-MAR HOTEL
91–93 Westhill Road, West Cliff, BH2 5PQ
An attractive hotel situated in the heart of the Westcliff area. Within walking distance of both beach and town, the Mae-Mar provides a friendly family retreat at the end of the day.
DOUBLE ROOM: up to £20
Hours: breakfast 8am–9.15am, dinner 6pm–6.30pm, last orders 4.30pm, open all year.
Cuisine: BREAKFAST.
Cards: Visa, Access.
Other points: central heating, children welcome, pets by prior arrangement, residents' lounge, lift.
Rooms: 9 single rooms, 12 double rooms, 1 twin room, 6 family rooms. All with TV, tea/coffee-making facilities, video.
Directions: A31 to Bournemouth; situated in Westcliff area.
MRS JANET CLEAVER ☎ (01202) 553167
[Fax] (01202) 311919.

OAK HALL HOTEL
9 Wilfred Road, Boscombe Manor, BH5 1ND
A comfortable, family-run hotel with a homely atmosphere, which has been thoroughly refurbished and modernized while retaining many

DORSET • SW ENGLAND

of its old-world features. Resident proprietors Margaret and Joe McDonnell and their staff extend a warm, hearty welcome to all. Oak Hall is adjacent to Shelley Park with its bowls and tennis courts and is just a short walk away from the seafront.
DOUBLE ROOM: from £20 to £30
FOOD: up to £15
Hours: breakfast 9am–10am, dinner 6pm–7pm, closed New Year.
Cuisine: ENGLISH.
Cards: Visa, Access, AmEx.
Other points: parking, children welcome, pets, residents' lounge, vegetarian meals, garden.
Rooms: 2 single rooms, 5 double rooms, 13 twin rooms, 6 family rooms.
Directions: A35 Christchurch road into Bournemouth or Bournemouth ring road (Wessex Way); observe signpost for Boscombe and Boscombe Pier.
J. & M. McDONNELL ☎ (01202) 395062.

THE QUEEN'S HOTEL
Meyrick Road, East Cliff, BH1 3DL
A comfortable family-run hotel, which caters for every taste, offering full à la carte, table d'hôte and bar menus. Situated on the East Cliff, a minute's walk from the town centre and a host of local amenities. Other attractions like Lulworth Cove and Brownsea Island are also within easy reach. New leisure club, including indoor pool, sauna, Jacuzzi and steam room.
DOUBLE ROOM: from £30 to £40
SINGLE ROOM: from £35 to £45
FOOD: from £15 to £20
Hours: breakfast 7.30am–9.45am, lunch 12.45am–1.45pm, dinner 7pm–9pm, bar meals 12noon–3pm, 6pm–10pm.
Cuisine: ENGLISH / FRENCH.
Cards: Visa, Access.
Other points: licensed, Sunday lunch, children welcome, pets allowed, open bank holidays, conferences.
Rooms: 14 single rooms, 36 double rooms, 42 twin rooms, 12 family rooms, 6 suites. All with TV, radio, telephone, tea/coffee-making facilities, hair dryer.
Directions: A338 Wessex Way into Bournemouth, then follow signs to East Cliff.
DAVID BURR ☎ (01202) 554415 Fax (01202) 294810.

TROUVILLE HOTEL
Priory Road, West Cliff, BH2 5DH
Centrally situated within walking distance of all the main amenities in Bournemouth, the Trouville provides high standards of food and accommodation. The restaurant overlooks the town and offers first-class table d'hôte cuisine, excellently presented and served in pleasant and relaxed surroundings. The leisure facilities include a sauna, gymnasium, spa pool, indoor swimming pool and solarium.
DOUBLE ROOM: from £20 to £30
SINGLE ROOM: from £35 to £45
FOOD: from £15 to £20
Hours: breakfast 7.30am–9.30am, lunch

12.15am–1.45pm, dinner 7pm–8.30pm.
Cuisine: ENGLISH – dishes may include cubes of salmon, monkfish and scampi in tarragon cream and a flaky pastry case, braised Scotch steak, roast loin of pork.
Cards: Visa, Access, AmEx.
Other points: licensed, Sunday lunch, no-smoking area, children welcome, afternoon tea, residents' lounge, pets allowed, leisure centre, conferences, 24hr reception, baby-listening device, baby-sitting, cots, residents' bar.
Rooms: 11 single rooms, 21 double rooms, 24 twin rooms, 24 family rooms. All with TV, telephone, tea/coffee-making facilities, hair dryer.
Directions: adjacent to Bournemouth International Centre. Very central.
DAVID ARTHUR YOUNG ☎ (01202) 552262 Fax (01202) 293324.

BRIDPORT • map 4D5

BURTON CLIFF HOTEL
Cliff Road, Burton Bradstock, DT6 4RB
The hotel, standing on the cliffs overlooking Lyme Bay, is surrounded by Heritage Coast countryside. Well-furnished, spacious bedrooms enjoy wonderful views. Steps lead to the beach. Ground-floor rooms have access for wheelchair users. The restaurant offers delicious à la carte, table d'hôte, vegetarian and bar menus. Golf course 1½ miles. Photography and walking are special interests of the owners. Darkroom facilities are available.
DOUBLE ROOM: from £20 to £30
SINGLE ROOM: from £25 to £35
FOOD: up to £15
Hours: breakfast 8.30am–9.15am, lunch 12noon–2pm, dinner 7pm–8.30pm, bar meals 7pm–10pm, closed December until February.
Cuisine: ENGLISH – only fresh produce used in preparation of all meals.
Cards: Visa, Access.
Other points: parking, children welcome, fully licensed lounge bar, vegetarian meals.
Rooms: 4 single rooms, 6 double rooms, 8 twin rooms.
Directions: from A35 Bridport take B3157 to Burton Bradstock.
DAVID & JUNE BARNIKEL ☎ (01308) 897205 Fax (01308) 898111.

THE GEORGE INN
Chideock, DT6 6JD
A 16th century thatched inn offering an extensive menu with daily extras and prices to suit all pockets. Restaurant, beer garden, family room with pool, darts and skittles. A true local welcome is assured in this very popular Dorset pub. Reservations are advisable.
FOOD: up to £15
Hours: lunch 12noon–2pm, dinner 6.45pm–9.30pm, open all year.
Cuisine: ENGLISH – specialities: omelettes with various fillings, steaks including massive mixed grill, salads, fish, gammon. Daily specials, e.g., venison, lamb, trout. Popular 'sizzler' meals. Heartbeat Award.

141

Other points: licensed, open-air dining, Sunday lunch, children welcome.
Directions: on the A35, 2 miles west of Bridport in the east of Chideock.
MIKE & MARILYN TUCK ☎ (01297) 89419.

HADDON HOUSE HOTEL
West Bay, DT6 4EL
Regency-style 3-star country house hotel with a reputation for fine cuisine. Situated approximately 300 yards from the picturesque harbour and coast of West Bay, overlooking Dorset's beautiful countryside. Amenities available to visitors include deep-sea fishing, riding, tennis and 18-hole golf course opposite hotel. Ideally situated for touring Dorset, Devon and Somerset.
DOUBLE ROOM: from £20 to £30
FOOD: up to £15
Hours: breakfast 7.45am–9.15am, lunch 12noon–1.30pm, dinner 7pm–9pm.
Cuisine: ENGLISH – fresh local fish, grills, own-lable wines.
Cards: Visa, Access, Diners, AmEx.
Other points: Sunday lunch, children welcome, coaches by prior arrangement, residents' bar.
Rooms: 2 single rooms, 6 double rooms, 3 twin rooms, 2 family rooms. All with TV, radio, alarm, telephone, tea/coffee-making facilities, heating, hair dryer, trouser-press.
Directions: half a mile south of main A35 at Bridport. Follow signs to West Bay.
MR & MRS P.W. LOUD ☎ (01308) 423626/425323 Fax (01308) 423748.

CHARMOUTH • map 4D5

HENSLEIGH HOTEL
Lower Sea Lane, DT6 6LW
A comfortable, well-equipped, family-run hotel in a quiet position. A friendly, homely atmosphere is complemented by good home-cooking using local produce. The rolling hills of Dorset and stunning cliff walks are on the doorstep.
DOUBLE ROOM: from £20 to £30
SINGLE ROOM: up to £25
FOOD: up to £15 ☆
Hours: breakfast 8am–9am, lunch 12noon–2pm, dinner 6.30pm–7.45pm, closed November until February.
Cuisine: ENGLISH.
Other points: central heating, children welcome, pets allowed, residents' lounge, garden.
Rooms: 2 single rooms, 3 double rooms, 4 twin rooms, 2 family rooms. All with en suite, TV, tea/coffee-making facilities.
Directions: midway between the village and beach, off the A35.
MALCOLM & MARY MacNAIR ☎ (01297) 560830.

NEWLANDS HOUSE
Stonebarrow Lane, DT6 6RA
A former 16th century farmhouse, family-run and situated in approximately 2 acres of garden and old orchard at the foot of Stonebarrow Hill, which is part of the National Trust Golden Cap Estate. Newlands House makes an ideal centre for walking and touring and is just minutes away from the famous fossil cliffs and beaches of Lyme Bay. Six miles east of Axminster. No smoking except in the bar lounge. Ample off-road parking for cars.
DOUBLE ROOM: from £20 to £30
SINGLE ROOM: up to £25
FOOD: up to £15
Hours: breakfast 8.30am–9.15am, dinner 7pm–7.30pm, open March to October.
Cuisine: ENGLISH / CONTINENTAL – home-produced dishes.
Other points: licensed, no-smoking areas, children catered for (please check for age limits), pets by prior arrangement, residents' lounge, garden.
Rooms: 3 single rooms, 4 double rooms, 3 twin rooms, 2 family rooms. All with TV, tea/coffee-making facilities.
Directions: via A35, 7 miles west of Bridport at foot of Stonebarrow Lane.
ANNE & VERNON VEAR ☎ (01297) 560212.

CHRISTCHURCH • map 4D6

THE COPPER SKILLET
17 Church Street, BH23 1BW
A licensed steak house and family restaurant situated in the old part of Christchurch, close to the town quay, priory and castle ruins.
FOOD: up to £15 CLUB
Hours: meals all day 9am–9pm, closed Christmas day.
Cuisine: ENGLISH – steaks and grills, weekly fresh fish and vegetarian specialities.
Cards: Visa, Access.
Other points: Sunday lunch, children welcome, coaches by prior arrangement
Directions: off main A35 into Christchurch High Street; take Church Street towards priory.
MICHAEL DEVALL ☎ (01202) 485485
Fax (01202) 475866.

THE FISHERMAN'S HAUNT HOTEL
Salisbury Road, Winkton, BH23 7AS
Superior 2-star/4-crowns country house hotel on the banks of the River Avon. The restaurant overlooks the river, and there is an attractive beer garden with children's play area. Situated on the edge of the New Forest. A freehouse serving real ales.
DOUBLE ROOM: from £30 to £40
SINGLE ROOM: from £35 to £45
FOOD: from £15 to £20
Hours: breakfast 7.30am–9.30am, Sunday 8am–9.30am; lunch 12noon–2pm; dinner 7pm–10pm; bar 10am–2.30pm, 6pm–11pm, Sunday 12noon–3pm, 7pm–10.30pm; closed Christmas day.
Cuisine: ENGLISH – fresh Christchurch salmon, Avon trout, steak-and-kidney pie.
Cards: Visa, Access, Diners, AmEx.
Other points: licensed, open-air dining, Sunday lunch, children welcome.
Rooms: 20 bedrooms.
Directions: on the B3347 between Christchurch and Ringwood.
MR J. BOCHAN ☎ (01202) 477283.

DORSET • SW ENGLAND

LE PETIT ST TROPEZ
3 Bridge Street, BH23 1DY
The ambience, cuisine and service at Le Petit St Tropez combine to make dining here a special experience. This genuine French family-run restaurant has a choice of fixed-price or à la carte menu, including their own seasonal specialities.
FOOD: up to £15
Hours: lunch 12noon, dinner 7pm.
Cuisine: FRENCH – traditional French from Provence. Seasonal specialities.
Cards: Visa, Access.
Other points: open-air dining, children welcome, open bank holidays, functions.
Directions: between the two bridges, 100 metres from the civic offices.
MARCEL & DEBORAH DUVAL ☎ (01202) 482522 [Fax] (01202) 470048.

DORCHESTER • map 4D5

THE ACORN INN HOTEL
28 Fore Street, Evershot, DT2 0JW
Dating from the 16th century, The Acorn Inn Hotel nestles in an unspoilt and peaceful village, set in the heart of Thomas Hardy's Dorset. A warm welcome awaits you from the resident owners and their friendly staff in this totally refurbished establishment. An imaginative à la carte menu is available, from plain and simple cooking to the diverse, using local produce when in season.
DOUBLE ROOM: from £30 to £40
FOOD: up to £15
Hours: breakfast 8am–9.30am, lunch 12noon–2pm, dinner 6.30pm–9.45pm, open all year.
Cuisine: ENGLISH – dishes may include game bordeaux, pork Wellington, and duck with orange and Grand Marnier. Speciality main course changes daily. Excellent wine selection.
Cards: Visa, Access.
Other points: licensed, open-air dining, traditional Sunday lunch, no-smoking area, children welcome, residents' lounge, garden, pets allowed.
Directions: off A37 towards Evershot, in main street before church.
DENISE MORLEY ☎ (01935) 83228.

JUDGE JEFFREYS RESTAURANT
6 High West Street, DT1 1UJ
In 1685 the notorious Judge Jeffreys lodged at this famous Dorchester House during the time of 'The Bloody Assize'. Today the original beamed building houses a restaurant, which provides very good food and polite, friendly service. Highly recommended for its warm welcome, good food and value-for-money prices.
FOOD: up to £15
Hours: morning coffee 9.30am–12noon, lunch 12noon–2.30pm, afternoon tea 2.30pm–5pm, dinner 7pm–9.30pm.
Cuisine: ENGLISH – wide range of lunchtime specials, which change daily. Evening à la carte menu. Morning coffee and afternoon teas.
Cards: Visa, Access.
Other points: licensed, no-smoking area, children welcome, pets allowed, afternoon tea.

Directions: in centre of town on main road. Public car parks nearby.
IAN & PAT McLELLAN ☎ (01305) 264369.

THE MANOR HOTEL
Beach Road, West Bexington, DT2 9DF
17th century manor house 500 yards from Chesil Beach. Panoramic views from most bedrooms of unspoilt Dorset coastline. Three real ales served in character cellar bar. Log fires. Private dining room for up to 40. Facilities for conferences, buffets, receptions.
DOUBLE ROOM: from £30 to £40
SINGLE ROOM: from £35 to £45
FOOD: from £15 to £20 ☆
Hours: breakfast 8.30am–9.30am, lunch 12noon–2pm, dinner 7pm–10pm.
Cuisine: ENGLISH / SEAFOOD – local seafood and imaginative dishes.
Cards: Visa, Access, Diners, AmEx.
Other points: licensed, Sunday lunch, children welcome, parking.
Rooms: 1 single room, 9 double rooms, 3 twin rooms. All with TV, radio, telephone, tea/coffee-making facilities.
Directions: on the B3157 Bridport to Weymouth coast road.
RICHARD & JAYNE A. CHILDS ☎ (01308) 897616 [Fax] (01308) 897035.

NEW INN
West Knighton, DT2 8PE
Attractive old pub with hanging baskets and jasmine creeper. Cheerful, relaxed atmosphere. Efficient service provided by friendly staff.
FOOD: up to £15 [CLUB]
Hours: lunch 12noon–2pm, dinner 7pm–9pm, open all year.
Cuisine: ENGLISH – well-cooked traditional pub food. Wide selection. Sunday lunches and sizzling dishes a speciality. Extensive specials board. Vegetarian menu.
Cards: Visa, Access.
Other points: licensed, open-air dining, Sunday lunch, children welcome, pets allowed.
Directions: situated off the A352 Wareham road at West Knighton.
ROGER & JULIA GILBEY ☎ (01305) 852349.

WESSEX ROYALE HOTEL
32 High Street, DT1 1UP
Dating back to the 1600s, the hotel was originally built as a town house for the Earl of Ilchester. The hotel has been substantially refurbished to provide a friendly, relaxing atmosphere. The generously proportioned rooms have feature fireplaces. Bedrooms are attractively furnished with many modern facilities, and the restaurant offers a high standard of continental and English cuisine. A conservatory is available for banquets and weddings for up to 100 people. Ideal location for the leisure traveller exploring Dorset.
DOUBLE ROOM: from £20 to £30
SINGLE ROOM: up to £25
FOOD: up to £15
Hours: breakfast 7.30am–10am, dinner 6pm–10.30pm.

143

SW ENGLAND • DORSET

Cuisine: ENGLISH / CONTINENTAL.
Cards: Visa, Access, Diners, AmEx, MasterCard, Switch, Delta.
Other points: children welcome, no-smoking area, residents' lounge, garden, pets, vegetarian meals, open bank holidays.
Rooms: 2 single rooms, 16 double rooms, 5 twin rooms.
Directions: on main road in centre of Dorchester.
MR M. BOWLEY ☎ (01305) 262660
[Fax] (01305) 251941.

LONGHAM • map 4C6

ANGEL INN
Near Wimborne, BH22 9AD
Situated on the busy A438 road from Ferndown to Poole or Wimborne Minster. The menu is varied and quite extensive, with the emphasis on fresh, well-cooked, generous portions of food. The inn offers a large beer garden at the rear, a children's play area with an additional area for children to eat, and plenty of car parking where you are welcome to park your car while enjoying one of the many interesting walks nearby.
FOOD: up to £15
Hours: lunch 12noon–2pm, dinner 6pm–9.30pm.
Cuisine: ENGLISH – Dorset pâté, steak-and-kidney pie, steaks, daily specials.
Cards: Visa, Access.
Other points: Sunday lunch, children welcome, garden, playland.
Directions: on the A348 road from Ferndown to Poole, or approach from the A31 Southampton to Poole road.
MR B. SIMS ☎ (01202) 873778.

LULWORTH COVE • map 4D6

MILL HOUSE HOTEL & BISHOP'S COTTAGE
West Lulworth, Wareham, BH20 5RQ
At one time the Bishop of Salisbury's home, the house stands in its own grounds on the edge of the Cove and is sheltered by Bindon Hill. The grounds have direct access to coastal heritage cliffs and the Cove.
DOUBLE ROOM: from £20 to £30
FOOD: up to £15
Hours: bar meals 12noon–2.30pm, bar meals 6pm–10pm, breakfast 8am–9.30am, dinner, 6pm–10pm, lunch 12noon–2.30pm, open all year.
Cuisine: SEAFOOD – seafood, local fish, vegetarian dishes.
Cards: Visa, Access.
Other points: licensed, Sunday lunch, children welcome, swimming pool, pets allowed.
Rooms: 3 single rooms, 21 double rooms, 2 family rooms. All with TV, radio, telephone, tea/coffee-making facilities, baby-listening device.
Directions: overlooking Lulworth Cove.
MRS ELIZABETH RUDD ☎ (0192941) 261/404.

LYME REGIS • map 4D5

BELL CLIFF RESTAURANT
5–6 Broad Street, DT 3QD
A small, homely restaurant, slightly Dickensian in appearance, with excellent service, quality and ambience. The building dates from the 16th century and was used in the film The French Lieutenant's Woman as the 'Old Fossil Depot'. Well placed in the centre of town and popular with both locals and holidaymakers.
FOOD: up to £15 [CLUB]
Hours: meals all day: summer 8.30am–6pm, winter 9am–5pm.
Cuisine: ENGLISH – home-cooking: specialities include home-made sweets and cakes.
Other points: licensed, Sunday lunch, children welcome, disabled access, pets allowed, afternoon tea, parking.
Directions: off A35 on A3052 or A3070. At sea end of main thoroughfare (A3052).
RICHARD & AUDREY EVANS ☎ (01297) 442459.

BENSONS RESTAURANT
65 Broad Street, DT7 3QF
A small, elegantly furnished restaurant offering outstanding food at reasonable prices. The à la carte menu provides a good choice of imaginative, excellently cooked and presented dishes. Welcoming and efficient service and a good wine list complement the quality of the food. A menu priced under £10 for two courses is available from Monday to Thursday.
FOOD: up to £15
Hours: dinner 7pm–9.30pm (or later for bookings), closed Sunday and also Monday from mid-October until Easter.
Cuisine: FRENCH – predominantly French-style cuisine. House specialities include Benson's mushrooms, deep-fried camembert, garlic prawns, tournedos Oporto, sole dieppoise, Dorset pork, salmon tarragon, spicy chicken, treacle-and-walnut tart, profiteroles.
Cards: Visa, Access, Diners, AmEx.
Other points: licensed, children welcome, booking advisable.
Directions: at bottom of hill on main street, next to car park, opposite sea.
BOB, IRENE & JENNY BENSON ☎ (01297) 442049.

KERSBROOK HOTEL & RESTAURANT
Pound Road, DT7 3HX
A thatched 18th century listed house, set in its own gardens overlooking Lyme Bay. Carefully modernized to retain the original character of the building and to offer a high level of comfort and convenience. The food is of a good standard, and the restaurant boasts an extensive wine list for every occasion.
DOUBLE ROOM: from £30 to £40
FOOD: from £15 to £20 [CLUB] ☆
Hours: breakfast 8.30am–9.30am, lunch 12.15am–2.15pm, dinner 7.30pm–9pm.
Cuisine: ENGLISH / CONTINENTAL – full à la carte menu and table d'hôte.

Cards: Visa, Access, Diners, AmEx.
Other points: licensed, residents' lounge, garden.
Rooms: 10 bedrooms.
Directions: from main Lyme Regis–Exeter road, turn right opposite main car park.
ERIC HALL STEPHENSON ☎ (01297) 442596.

ROYAL LION HOTEL
Broad Street, DT7 3QF
A 17th century coaching inn in the centre of this attractive little town, equipped with a large games room with snooker and table tennis. Apart from being the home town of many writers, artists and artisans, Lyme Regis is famous as the location of United Artists' The French Lieutenant's Woman.
FOOD: up to £15
Hours: breakfast 8.30am–9.30am, lunch 12noon–2pm, dinner 6.30pm–9.30pm.
Cuisine: ENGLISH – fresh sirloin steak.
Cards: Visa, Access, Diners, AmEx.
Other points: Sunday lunch, children welcome, coaches by prior arrangement, leisure centre, swimming pool.
Directions: in the centre of Lyme Regis.
MR & MRS B.A. SIENESI ☎ (012974) 445622/ 442014.

POOLE • map 4D6

ALLANS SEAFOOD RESTAURANT
8 Bournemouth Road, BH14 OES
A small seafood restaurant offering extremely fresh, perfectly prepared seafood of all types. The exterior is unpretentious and the interior has the feel of a French rural restaurant, in keeping with the very helpful, friendly service. Considering the high cost of seafood, this restaurant offers excellent value for money. Highly recommended.
FOOD: from £15 to £20
Hours: lunch 12noon–2pm, dinner 6.30pm till late.
Cuisine: SEAFOOD – fresh local fish, fresh lobster and crab, all year. Alternative dishes include steaks, veal, duck and chicken. Special lunch menu.
Cards: Visa, Access.
Other points: licensed, street parking.
Directions: main Bournemouth–Poole road (A35).
A.D. TOMLINSON ☎ (01202) 741489.

CORKERS CAFE BAR & RESTAURANT
1 High Street, The Quay, BH15 1AB
Adjacent to and overlooking Poole harbour and quay, the ground floor is a café-bar, the first floor a licensed restaurant and the second floor bed & breakfast accommodation.
DOUBLE ROOM: up to £20
FOOD: from £15 to £20
Hours: lunch 12noon–2pm, dinner 7pm–11pm, café-bar 10am–12midnight, café-bar Sunday 10am–10.30pm.
Cuisine: ENGLISH / SEAFOOD – seafood a speciality.
Cards: Visa, Access, Diners, AmEx.
Other points: disabled access, children welcome.
Rooms: 1 double room, 4 twin rooms.
Directions: adjacent to quayside, with good

views of the waterfront and sea-going vessels.
NICHOLAS CONSTANDINOS ☎ (01202) 681393.

HAVEN HOTEL
Banks Road, Sandbanks, BH13 7QL
An attractive building standing on the seafront, with magnificent views across to the Purbeck Hills and Poole Harbour. Like its sister hotels, the Sandbanks and Chine, an informal atmosphere reigns despite its size and sophistication. The Haven Hotel has a purpose-built sports and leisure centre, and a newly-built business centre complex.
DOUBLE ROOM: from £50
SINGLE ROOM: from £55
FOOD: from £15 to £20
Hours: breakfast 8am–10am, lunch 12.30am–2.30pm, dinner 7pm–9.30pm.
Cuisine: ENGLISH / INTERNATIONAL – traditional and international cuisine. 'La Roche', the hotel's gourmet restaurant, is open 6 days a week.
Cards: Visa, Access, Diners, AmEx.
Other points: licensed, Sunday lunch, vegetarian meals, residents' lounge, residents' bar, leisure club.
Rooms: 18 single rooms, 39 double rooms, 32 twin rooms, 3 quad rooms, 2 family rooms. All with TV, telephone, tea/coffee-making facilities.
Directions: from Bournemouth and Poole, follow Sandbanks signs. The hotel is adjacent to the ferry in the Sandbanks area of Poole.
BROWNSEA HAVEN PROPERTIES ☎ (01202) 707333 [Fax] (01202) 708796.

SANDBANKS HOTEL
15 Banks Road, Sandbanks, BH13 7QL
Sandbanks occupies a superb position right on the beach, with lovely views of the sea and Poole harbour. The beach has the coveted EU Blue Flag Award for clean beaches. A large, fully-equipped hotel with the atmosphere and charm of a smaller establishment.
DOUBLE ROOM: from £40 to £50
SINGLE ROOM: from £35 to £45
FOOD: from £15 to £20
Hours: breakfast 8am–9.45am, lunch 12.30am–2pm, dinner 7pm–9pm.
Cuisine: ENGLISH – table d'hôte menu changes daily: steaks, game, fish dishes. A la carte restaurant also available.
Cards: Visa, Access, Diners, AmEx.
Other points: licensed, Sunday lunch, children welcome, garden.
Rooms: 105 bedrooms.
Directions: from Bournemouth, follow signs to Sandbanks ferry. On the seafront.
SANDBANKS HOTEL LIMITED ☎ (01202) 707377 [Fax] (01202) 708885.

PORTLAND • map 4D5

ALESSANDRIA HOTEL AND ITALIAN RESTAURANT
71 Wakeham, Easton, DT5 1HW
An excellent family-run hotel and Italian restaurant, ideally situated to explore Portland's historic interests, yet close to the beach and

SW ENGLAND • DORSET

shopping centre of Weymouth and the beautiful Dorset coast. Accommodation is of a very high standard, and the à la carte menu offers a wide range of traditional Italian, English and French dishes.
DOUBLE ROOM: from £20 to £30
SINGLE ROOM: from £25 to £35
FOOD: from £15 to £20
Hours: breakfast 7.30am–9.30am, dinner 7pm–9pm.
Cuisine: CONTINENTAL / ENGLISH – all fresh produce, cooked to order by Giovanni, chef and proprietor for 30 years, with 5-star experience. Most salads and vegetables from their own garden.
Cards: Visa, Access, Diners, AmEx.
Other points: parking, children welcome, open bank holidays, disabled access, residents' lounge, vegetarian meals, residents' bar.
Rooms: 4 single rooms, 7 double rooms, 3 twin rooms, 3 family rooms. All with TV, tea/coffee-making facilities.
Directions: from Weymouth, take the A354 main road for Portland.
GIOVANNI BISOGNO ☎ (01305) 822270/ 820108.

SHAFTESBURY • map 4C6

THE BENETT ARMS
Semley, SP7 9AS
Built in the 17th century, The Benett Arms overlooks the village green. A choice of freshly cooked, interesting meals and knowledgeable advice on wine make this traditional pub extremely popular with both locals and many foreign travellers. In summer, you can enjoy a barbecue on the common itself. Special events such as steam rallies, jazz bands, etc. are sometimes organized.
DOUBLE ROOM: from £20 to £30
SINGLE ROOM: from £25 to £35
FOOD: from £15 to £20 [CLUB] ☆
Hours: breakfast 8.30am–9.30am, lunch 12noon–2pm, dinner 7pm–10pm.
Cuisine: ENGLISH / CONTINENTAL – dishes in the restaurant may include steaks, chicken trois frères, traditional bar meals in the bar.
Cards: Visa, Access, Diners, AmEx.
Other points: licensed, Sunday lunch, children welcome, garden, pets allowed, vegetarian meals, parking, residents' bar, disabled access, residents' lounge.
Rooms: 5 twin rooms. All with TV, telephone, tea/coffee-making facilities.
Directions: 2 miles off the A350, north of Shaftesbury. Turn right to Semley (1 mile).
J.C.M. DUTHIE ☎ (01747) 830221
[Fax] (01747) 830152.

STOURPAINE • map 4C6

THE WHITE HORSE
Shaston Road, DT11 8TA
Situated in a very attractive Dorset village on a main route to Shaftesbury, The White Horse is well known and respected for well-prepared, fresh country food. The menu is varied and is complemented by a good wine list. A warm welcome awaits everyone calling at this public house for a full meal, a snack or just a drink.
FOOD: up to £15
Hours: lunch 12noon–2pm, dinner 7pm–10pm.
Cuisine: ENGLISH – all dishes on the varied menu are prepared to a very high standard.
Other points: children welcome, pets allowed, no-smoking area, garden, open-air dining, vegetarian meals, traditional Sunday lunch.
Directions: located on the A350 between Blandford Forum and Shaftesbury.
JOHN & MARILYN HURLOW ☎ (01258) 453535.

STUDLAND • map 4D6

THE MANOR HOUSE
Beach Road, Studland Bay, BH19 3AU
An 18th century Gothic manor in 16 acres of secluded, mature grounds with two tennis courts, overlooking the sea and 3 miles of sandy beach. The house has been in the Rose family since 1950 and has been fully modernized whilst retaining the original features and character. Wonderful coastal walks.
DOUBLE ROOM: from £30 to £40
SINGLE ROOM: from £35 to £45
FOOD: from £15 to £20 [CLUB]
Hours: breakfast 8.30am–9.30am, lunch 12noon–2pm, dinner 7pm–8.30pm, closed 18th December until 28th December.
Cuisine: ENGLISH – local venison, duckling and fresh local seafood. There is a large terrace outside where bar meals may be served – weather permitting.
Cards: Visa, Access.
Other points: open-air dining, Sunday lunch, children catered for (please check for age limits), golf nearby, tennis, residents' lounge, residents' bar.
Rooms: 6 double rooms, 6 twin rooms, 2 triple rooms, 6 quad rooms. All with TV, radio, telephone, tea/coffee-making facilities.
Directions: 3 miles from Swanage, 3 miles from Sandbanks ferry.
MR RICHARD ROSE ☎ (01929) 450288.

SWANAGE • map 4D6

HAVENHURST HOTEL
Cranborne Road, BH19 1EA
A comfortable hotel standing in its own grounds, just a short stroll from the shops, the safe, sandy beach and all other amenities. With good home-cooked food, a comfortable lounge bar and a spacious colour TV lounge, Havenhurst also offers a high standard of accommodation. The proprietors extend a warm and friendly welcome to all guests.
DOUBLE ROOM: from £20 to £30
SINGLE ROOM: from £25 to £35
FOOD: up to £15
Hours: breakfast 8.30am–9.15am, bar meals 12noon–2pm, dinner 7pm.
Cuisine: ENGLISH.
Other points: children welcome, garden,

afternoon tea, TV lounge, hair dryers.
Rooms: 3 single rooms, 8 double rooms, 4 twin rooms, 2 family rooms. All with tea/coffee-making facilities.
Directions: close to the beach, off Rempstone Road.
MRS CHERRETT & MRS ROBSON ☎ (01929) 424224.

MOWLEM RESTAURANT
Shore Road, BH19 1DD
Situated on the beach road, with views over the beach and bay. Very popular with families, as it has a special children's menu, and everyone can enjoy watching their meals being prepared in front of them.
FOOD: from £15 to £20
Hours: lunch 12noon–2pm, dinner 7pm–10pm, closed Christmas day.
Cuisine: ENGLISH – seafood, steaks, salads, children's menu.
Cards: Visa, Access.
Other points: Sunday lunch, children welcome, coaches by prior arrangement
Directions: on the beach road.
MICHAEL POLLARD ☎ (01929) 422496.

TRENT • map 4C5

THE ROSE & CROWN
Near Sherborne, DT9 4SL
A 16th century part-thatched freehouse, which could have been plucked from a picture postcard. There are three open fires and stone floors – a traditional atmosphere in which to sample fine ales and cider and tasty home-cooked food, without the intrusion of juke-boxes or fruit machines. Won national awards for cuisine in 1989 and 1990. Children are especially welcome here – there is a children's room where food is available and a playground at the rear of the premises.
FOOD: up to £15
Hours: lunch 12noon–2pm, bar meals 12noon–1.45pm, dinner 7pm–11pm, bar meals 7pm–9.30pm, closed Christmas day.
Cuisine: INTERNATIONAL – fish and game, using local ingredients. The menu changes weekly. Specialities: Cajun and Creole cuisine from Louisiana.
Cards: Visa, Access, AmEx.
Other points: licensed, open-air dining, Sunday lunch, children welcome, children's room, play area, pets allowed, no-smoking area.
Directions: A30 between Sherborne and Yeovil, take Trent turn, approximately 1–2 miles
MR C.F. MARION-CRAWFORD ☎ (01935) 850776.

WEST LULWORTH • map 4D6

THE CASTLE INN
Main Street, BH20 5RN
A charming thatched building dating back to the 1600s and close to the famous Lulworth Cove. The large garden is very popular – barbecues are held in summer.
DOUBLE ROOM: from £20 to £30
FOOD: up to £15
Hours: breakfast 7am–9.30am, lunch 12noon–2.30pm, dinner 7.30pm–11pm, bar meals 11am–2.30pm, 7pm–11pm.
Cuisine: ENGLISH – home-made raised pies, fillet Stilton, spicy lamb, pork in whisky.
Cards: Visa, Access, Diners, AmEx.
Other points: licensed, open-air dining, Sunday lunch, children welcome, coaches by prior arrangement.
Rooms: 2 single rooms, 8 double rooms, 15 twin rooms, 1 family room.
Directions: on the B3070 road from Wareham, in the centre of West Lulworth.
GRAHAM & PATRICIA HALLIDAY ☎ (0192941) 311.

WEYMOUTH • map 4D5

BEECHCROFT HOTEL
128–9 The Esplanade, DT4 7EU
The Beechcroft Hotel is situated in a prime seafront position, only 5 minutes' level walk to the city centre and the stations.
DOUBLE ROOM: up to £20
FOOD: up to £15
Hours: breakfast 8.30am–9am, dinner 6pm, last orders 4.30pm, closed October until March.
Cuisine: ENGLISH.
Cards: Visa, Access.
Other points: children welcome, pets by prior arrangement, residents' lounge.
Rooms: 8 single rooms, 6 double, 4 twin rooms, 12 family rooms. All with TV.
Directions: A354 or A353 to Weymouth; the hotel is on The Esplanade between the pier bandstand and jubilee clock.
MR THOMPSON, MR CLAYDEN & MR EVANS-JONES ☎ (01305) 786608.

THE CHATSWORTH
14 The Esplanade, DT4 8EB
An attractive Georgian building with excellent views over Weymouth Bay, the sands to the front, and the picturesque harbour to the rear. The Chatsworth offers a friendly and comfortable base for short breaks and family holidays. All the amenities of an English seaside town are nearby, and it is an ideal centre from which to tour Hardy's Dorset.
DOUBLE ROOM: from £20
SINGLE ROOM: up to £25
Hours: breakfast 8am–9am, dinner 6pm–7pm, closed Christmas.
Cuisine: ENGLISH.
Cards: Visa, Access, AmEx.
Other points: central heating, children welcome, pets allowed, residents' lounge, garden.
Rooms: 9 bedrooms.
Directions: situated on The Esplanade, opposite Alexandra Gardens.
MR S. ROBERTS ☎ (01305) 785012
Fax (01305) 766342.

SW ENGLAND • DORSET

🛏 MOONFLEET MANOR
Moonfleet, DT3 4ED
A complete resort hotel set in 5 acres of countryside by the sea. Many sports facilities including indoor pool, gymnasium, 4-rink indoor bowls hall, 9-pin automatic skittles, 2 tennis courts, 1 squash court, 2 snooker tables, children's indoor and outdoor play areas.
DOUBLE ROOM: from £30 to £40
SINGLE ROOM: from £25 to £35
FOOD: up to £15
Hours: bar snacks 12noon–2pm, dinner 7pm–9pm.
Cuisine: ENGLISH – Trenchards: carvery, buffet, Sunday roasts, table d'hôte.
Cards: Visa, Access, Diners, AmEx.
Other points: licensed, Sunday lunch, no-smoking area, children welcome, vegetarian meals, parking, residents' bar, residents' lounge, disabled access.
Rooms: 38 bedrooms.
Directions: take the B3157 to Weymouth, turn towards sea at Chickerell.
JAN HEMINGWAY ☎ (01305) 786948.

🛏 THE PEBBLES GUEST HOUSE
18 Kirtleton Avenue, DT4 7PT
Situated in a quiet and peaceful residential area of Weymouth, with the beach and town shopping centre just minutes away. A warm and courteous welcome is assured, and the accommodation, like the traditional English cooking, is of a high standard. An ideal base for guests wishing to explore beautiful Dorset.
DOUBLE ROOM: up to £20
SINGLE ROOM: up to £25
FOOD: up to £15 ☆
Hours: breakfast 8am–9am, dinner 5.30pm–6.30pm.
Cuisine: ENGLISH.
Other points: children catered for (please check for age limits), no-smoking area, residents' lounge, vegetarian meals, garden, parking.
Rooms: 2 single rooms, 3 double rooms, 3 family rooms.
Directions: A354 Dorchester to Weymouth road; just before entering the centre of Weymouth, turn into Carlton Road North. Kirtleton Avenue is first on left. Hotel is on the left.
SHEILA & BARRY SINGLE ☎ (01305) 784331.

🍴 SEA COW RESTAURANT
7 Custom House Quay, DT4 8BE
With a prominent quayside position, this restaurant specializes in fresh fish and also offers a wide variety of meat, poultry and game. Very popular with visitors to this picturesque town.
FOOD: from £15 to £20 🍲
Hours: lunch 12noon–2pm, dinner 7pm–10.15pm, fully licensed bar serving light meals and continental dishes during lunch and early evening.
Cuisine: ENGLISH – fresh mussels and scallops in season, fresh local lobster, skate, lemon sole. Game in season, Dorset blue steak. Chocolate mousse.
Cards: Visa, Access, Eurocard, MasterCard.
Other points: Sunday lunch, children welcome,

street parking, vegetarian meals, function facilities.
Directions: on the quayside.
MR & MRS T.M. WOOLCOCK ☎ (01305) 783524.

🍴 THE SHIP INN RESTAURANT
Custom House Quay, DT4 8BE
Overlooking the harbour, this traditional quayside pub has an upstairs restaurant offering food at excellent value for money. There is also a full range of children's facilities and a wide range of home-cooked bar snacks.
FOOD: up to £15
Hours: lunch 10.30am–2.30pm, Sunday 12noon–2.30pm, dinner 7pm–10.30pm.
Cuisine: ENGLISH / SEAFOOD – fresh local seafood.
Cards: Visa, Access, Diners.
Other points: Sunday lunch, children welcome.
Directions: on the quayside.
R. BALL ☎ (01305) 773879 Fax (01305) 761206.

🛏 SOU'WEST LODGE HOTEL
Rodwell Road, DT4 8QT
An extremely pleasant, well-kept hotel with first-class furnishings throughout. A warm, friendly atmosphere has been created by Michael and June Moxham, who will endeavour to make your stay enjoyable. There is a cosy, intimate bar to relax in at the end of the day.
DOUBLE ROOM: from £20 to £30
SINGLE ROOM: up to £25
FOOD: up to £15
Hours: breakfast 7.30am–8.30am, dinner 6pm, last orders 3pm, closed Christmas.
Cuisine: ENGLISH.
Other points: children welcome, pets allowed, residents' lounge, patio.
Rooms: 5 double rooms, 1 twin room, 2 family rooms. All with en suite, TV, tea/coffee-making facilities.
Directions: situated off harbour road to Portland, over Boot Hill.
MICHAEL & JUNE MOXHAM ☎ (01305) 783749.

🛏 SUNNINGDALE HOTEL
Preston Road, Preston, DT3 6QD
Set in 1½ acres of grounds, with all bedrooms enjoying fine views over the gardens or fields. Only 600 yards from the sea, yet the heated outdoor swimming pool is always popular, especially with small children.
DOUBLE ROOM: up to £20
FOOD: up to £15
Hours: breakfast 8.15am–9.15am, dinner 6.15pm–7.15pm, closed mid-October until March.
Cuisine: ENGLISH.
Cards: Visa, Access, Diners.
Other points: children welcome, residents' lounge, garden, swimming pool, putting green, games room, pets allowed.
Rooms: 1 single room, 8 double rooms, 6 twin rooms, 1 family room. All with radio, tea/coffee-making facilities.

HAMPSHIRE • SW ENGLAND

Directions: off the A353, through Preston village towards the sea.
MR & MRS TONY FLUX ☎ (01305) 832179.

WINTERBORNE ZELSTON • map 4C6

THE BOTANY BAY INNE
Winterborne Zelston, DT11 9ET
A friendly country pub with a delightful restaurant offering a wide variety of home-cooked fresh food, served in immaculate and comfortable surroundings. Ideal as a refreshment stop for lunch or excellent bar snacks while visiting some of the places of interest within the idyllic countryside. A relaxing and sophisticated atmosphere.
FOOD: up to £15
Hours: lunch 11am–2.30pm, dinner 6pm–10pm, closed Christmas day.
Cuisine: ENGLISH / CONTINENTAL.
Cards: Visa, Access, Diners.
Other points: children welcome, parking, vegetarian meals, pets, open-air dining.
Directions: A31, between Wimborne and Dorchester.
CHRIS & BEVERLEY MASSEY ☎ (01929) 459227.

HAMPSHIRE

ANDOVER • map 5C2

WHITE HART
Bridge Street, SP10 1BH
Centrally located in the town centre, this delightful family-run hotel dates back to the 15th century. It is comfortably furnished and decorated, with a spacious bar and reception area. The hotel offers the finest quality cuisine and well-furnished, homely bedrooms. Well located for journeys throughout Hampshire, including Stonehenge, Salisbury and Winchester.
DOUBLE ROOM: from £30 to £40
SINGLE ROOM: from £55
FOOD: up to £15
Hours: breakfast 7am–9am, lunch 12.30am–2.30pm, dinner 6.30pm–9pm.
Cuisine: ENGLISH / CONTINENTAL.
Cards: Visa, Access, Diners, AmEx.
Other points: parking, children welcome, pets allowed, conference facilities, vegetarian meals, traditional Sunday lunch, afternoon teas.
Rooms: 2 single rooms, 12 double rooms, 6 twin rooms. All with en suite, telephone, radio, hair dryer, trouser-press, tea/coffee-making facilities.
Directions: M3 junction 8 onto A303, second exit onto A3057. Follow signs for town centre: Bridge Street runs along the bottom of High Street.
SIMON HUGHES ☎ (01264) 352266
Fax (01264) 323767.

BARTON-ON-SEA • map 5E2

HOTEL GAINSBOROUGH
39 Marine Drive East, BH25 7QX
A small family-run hotel in a good location facing the sea, close to the New Forest, Lymington, the Isle of Wight and Christchurch Priory. The five en suite bedrooms provide a comfortable night's rest, while the residents' dining room offers good-quality English fare of a very high standard.
DOUBLE ROOM: from £20 to £30
SINGLE ROOM: up to £25
FOOD: from £15 to £20
Hours: breakfast 8am–9am, dinner 6.30pm–7pm.
Cuisine: ENGLISH – good-quality English fare.
Other points: parking, pets allowed, residents' lounge, licensed.
Rooms: 1 single room, 3 double rooms, 1 twin room.
Directions: take the A337 Lymington to Christchurch Road. At New Milton, follow the signposts to Barton-on-Sea.
JILL RENNIE ☎ (01425) 610541.

BROCKENHURST • map 5D2

THE WATERSPLASH HOTEL
The Rise, SO42 7ZP
A family-run Victorian country house hotel set in 2 acres of secluded gardens. The hotel is noted for good food, friendly service and comfortable accommodation. The menu offers imaginative, well-cooked food. Situated in the centre of the New Forest.
DOUBLE ROOM: from £40 to £50
FOOD: from £15 to £20 CLUB
Hours: bar meals 12noon–2pm, lunch 1pm–2pm, dinner 7.30pm–8.30pm.
Cuisine: ENGLISH – specialities include pot roast haunch of New Forest venison.
Cards: Visa, Access.
Other points: licensed, open-air dining, Sunday lunch, no-smoking area, children welcome, garden, pets allowed, afternoon tea.
Directions: off A337 south of Lyndhurst. Turning to The Rise opposite Shell garage.
ROBIN & JUDY FOSTER ☎ (01590) 22344.

CADNAM • map 5D2

THE WHITE HART
Old Romsey Road, SO40
A superb family-run pub/restaurant, extensively refurbished recently to a very high standard, yet retaining a warm and welcoming atmosphere. The bar and restaurant are spacious, and there is a delightful garden to the rear to be enjoyed in the warmer months. All food is freshly prepared daily by family members, and a varied menu is provided for both lunch and dinner.
FOOD: up to £15
Hours: lunch 11am–2pm, Sunday 12noon–2pm,

149

dinner 6pm–9.30pm, Sunday 7pm–9pm.
Cuisine: ENGLISH – a varied menu with a wide choice to suit all tastes, all freshly prepared.
Cards: Visa, Access, AmEx.
Other points: parking, children welcome, pets allowed, no-smoking area, garden, vegetarian meals, traditional Sunday lunch.
Directions: from exit 1 of M27 take Lyndhurst sign to Cadnam roundabout; turn left to A31 and The White Hart is immediately on the left.
SUE & NICK EMBERLEY ☎ (01703) 812277
[Fax] (01703) 814632.

DROXFORD • map 5D2

HURDLES PUB AND RESTAURANT
Station Road, SO3 1QU

The Hurdles is a warm and cosy pub/restaurant, superbly run by the proprietors, Pam and Paul Mulle. Open fires in winter, red velvet-style benches, a long bar with open-plan restaurant and a wide variety of delicious meals all help to maintain its popularity. A warm welcome awaits all. Well worth a visit.
FOOD: up to £15
Hours: lunch 12noon–2pm, dinner 7pm–10pm.
Cuisine: ENGLISH – a varied menu using fresh produce.
Other points: parking, vegetarian meals.
Directions: from A32 Alton to Fareham road, take B2150 just north of Droxford. Positioned on the right immediately after old railway bridge.
PAUL & PAM MULLE ☎ (01489) 877451.

DISCOVER FRANCE FOR ONLY £9.99!

The *Les Routiers Guide to France* is the only official fully translated guide to the French *Routiers*, listing over 1,600 recommended restaurants, cafés and hotels throughout this alluring country.

Available from all good bookshops, or direct from the publishers, price £9.99.

EMSWORTH • map 5D3

JINGLES
77 Horndean Road, PO10 7PU

A homely Victorian building flanked by open countryside. All bedrooms are individually decorated and provide comfortable accommodation. Under the personal supervision of Kit and Angela Chapman. The atmosphere and service are welcoming and friendly. Weekend rates available.
DOUBLE ROOM: from £20 to £30
FOOD: up to £15
Hours: breakfast 7.15am–9am, dinner 7pm–9pm, lunch Sunday 12noon–2pm.
Cuisine: ENGLISH / INTERNATIONAL.
Cards: Visa, Access.
Other points: children welcome, central heating, residents' lounge, pets allowed, garden, swimming pool, afternoon tea, vegetarian meals, disabled access, parking, residents' bar.
Rooms: 4 single rooms, 5 double rooms, 2 twin rooms, 1 family room. All with TV, tea/coffee-making facilities.
Directions: follow the A259 to Emsworth. Proceed north from village onto B2148.
KIT & ANGELA CHAPMAN ☎ (01243) 373755.

EVERSLEY CROSS • map 5C3

LE TOAD AND STUMPS BISTRO
The Green, near Wokingham, RG27 0NS

A popular bar/bistro offering fine English and continental cuisine. Attractively furnished throughout, it has a distinct cosmopolitan atmosphere. A live guitarist often plays in the bistro.
FOOD: up to £15
Hours: lunch 12noon–2.30pm, bar snacks 12noon–10pm, dinner 7pm–10.30pm.
Cuisine: ENGLISH / CONTINENTAL.
Other points: parking, children welcome, disabled access, vegetarian meals, open-air dining.
Directions: leave the M3 at junction 4 and travel through Blackwater and Yateley. The establishment is situated on the B3272 at Eversley Cross, just before Eversley.
MR T. PAINE ☎ (01734) 731126 [Fax] (01734) 731126.

FORDINGBRIDGE • map 5D1

LIONS COURT RESTAURANT & HOTEL
29–31 High Street, SP6 1AS

Set on the edge of the New Forest with all its amenities and rural pursuits. The delightful sleepy town of Fordingbridge is ideally centered for the cathedral city of Salisbury, Bournemouth, Stonehenge and many places of interest. The Lions Court is a charming 17th century family hotel with six en suite bedrooms and one 4-poster. The à la carte restaurant has a reputation for excellent cuisine in a relaxed, intimate atmosphere. A classic English setting with gardens extending to the River Avon. Fishing, golf, horse-riding available locally.
DOUBLE ROOM: from £20 to £30
SINGLE ROOM: from £35 to £45
FOOD: from £15 to £20
Hours: breakfast 7.30am–9.30am, lunch 12noon–2.30pm, dinner 6.30pm–9.30pm.
Cuisine: ENGLISH / CONTINENTAL – a varied menu favouring fresh local produce. Specialities include salad of smoked venison, grilled calf's liver with a bacon and mushroom concasse flavoured with basil. Unusual fish and many vegetarian dishes. Reservations are advised. Chef: Danny Wilson.
Cards: Visa, Access, Diners, AmEx.
Other points: parking, children welcome, pets allowed, vegetarian meals, traditional Sunday lunch.
Rooms: 2 single rooms, 3 double rooms, 1 twin room. All with en suite, TV, tea/coffee-making facilities.
Directions: half-way between Salisbury and Ringwood on the A338.
MICHAEL & JENNY EASTICK ☎ (01425) 652006 [Fax] (01425) 657946.

HAMPSHIRE • SW ENGLAND

GOSPORT • map 5D2

ALVERBANK HOUSE HOTEL
Stokesbay Road, Alverstoke, PO12 2QT
Victorian country house comfortably furnished and decorated with excellent views of the bay. Popular with both holiday-makers and locals, this establishment enjoys a lively atmosphere. Offering generous portions of good food, first-class service, and accommodation of a high quality.
DOUBLE ROOM: from £20 to £30
FOOD: up to £15
Hours: breakfast 7am–9am, lunch 12noon–2.30pm, bar meals 12noon–2.30pm, dinner 7pm–9.30pm, bar meals 7pm–9.30pm.
Cuisine: BRITISH / INTERNATIONAL – à la carte and fixed-price menus, using local fresh produce where possible.
Cards: Visa, Access, Diners, AmEx.
Other points: fully licensed, open-air dining, Sunday lunch, children welcome, afternoon tea, parking, vegetarian meals, disabled access.
Rooms: 1 single room, 5 double rooms, 2 twin rooms. All with TV, telephone, tea/coffee-making facilities.
Directions: exit M27 to Fareham, follow A32 for 3 miles, signposted Stokes Bay.
MR PATRICK DOYLE ☎ (01705) 510005
[Fax] (01705) 520864.

BELLE VUE HOTEL
39 Marine Parade East, Lee on the Solent, PO13 9BW
Situated on the seafront, overlooking the Solent, this modern yet traditional hotel offers comfortable accommodation for a wide range of visitors. The food in the restaurant can be enjoyed in relaxed surroundings.
DOUBLE ROOM: from £30 to £40
SINGLE ROOM: from £45 to £55
FOOD: up to £15
Hours: breakfast 7.15am–9.15am, lunch 12noon–2pm, bar meals 12noon–2pm, dinner 7pm–9.45pm, open bank holidays.
Cuisine: ENGLISH – menu includes a good selection of fish, meat, grills and vegetarian dishes and may feature potted prawns and avocado fans. Grilled whole lemon sole, rack of English lamb set in a delicious sauce.
Cards: Visa, Access, AmEx, Switch.
Other points: licensed, open-air dining, Sunday lunch, no-smoking area, children welcome, patio, entertainment.
Rooms: 4 single rooms, 19 double rooms, 27 twin rooms.
Directions: M27 junction 8 or 11 to Fareham; to Lee on the Solent takes approximately 8 minutes.
MR T. BELLASIS ☎ (01705) 550258
[Fax] (01705) 552624.

HAVANT • map 5D3

OLD MILL GUEST HOUSE
Mill Lane, Old Bedhampton, PO9 3JH
This is an outstanding family-run Georgian guest house of immense charm and interest, with a lake and large grounds housing wild life, fish and water fowl. A place for complete relaxation and with most comfortable, spacious accommodation. John Keats rested here while finishing his poem Eve of St Agnes.
DOUBLE ROOM: up to £20
SINGLE ROOM: up to £25
FOOD: up to £15
Hours: breakfast 7am–9am, evening snacks available on request.
Cuisine: BREAKFAST – English breakfast, cooked to order. Picnic snacks can be prepared if requested.
Other points: children welcome, residents' lounge, garden, swimming pool.
Rooms: 1 twin room, 4 family rooms.
Directions: From A3(M) take the A27 and follow signs for Havant and Bedhampton.
MR & MRS D. & J. KELLY ☎ (01705) 454948
[Fax] (01705) 499677.

HAYLING ISLAND • map 5D3

NEWTOWN HOUSE HOTEL
Manor Road, West Town, PO11 0QR
An 18th century converted farmhouse set in its own large gardens, Newtown House Hotel provides a cosy bar and lounge, an à la carte restaurant, comfortable accommodation and an indoor leisure complex. Well suited to families, this hotel is an ideal place to stay throughout the year, due to its location near the sea and the indoor leisure complex.
DOUBLE ROOM: from £20 to £30
SINGLE ROOM: from £45 to £55
FOOD: from £15 to £20
Cuisine: FRENCH / ENGLISH – predominantly French cuisine. Specialities include filet de boeuf Diane, tournedos Rossini, rack of lamb roasted with honey and garlic. Bar meals available.
Cards: Visa, Access, Diners, AmEx.
Other points: licensed, Sunday lunch, pets allowed, garden, afternoon tea, leisure centre, swimming pool, Jacuzzi, gym facilities, steam room, sauna, tennis, children welcome, baby-listening device, cots.
Rooms: 7 single rooms, 13 double rooms, 4 twin rooms, 2 family rooms. All with TV, radio, alarm, telephone, tea/coffee-making facilities.
Directions: take the A3023 into South Hayling. Close to shops and shore.
N & M PROPERTIES ☎ (01705) 466131
[Fax] (01705) 461366.

KINGSCLERE • map 5C2

THE VINE INN
Hannington, RG26 5TY
An exceptional country inn in a prime location off the A339 in this charming village. The Vine incorporates a large freehouse pub, new 42-seater conservatory, and an à la carte restaurant offering varied menus seven days a week. The Matthews have gained a considerable reputation locally for their food.

151

FOOD: up to £15
Hours: lunch 12noon–2pm, dinner 6.30pm–9.30pm.
Cuisine: ENGLISH – famous pies, reputable steaks, choice of vegetarian meals in bar and conservatory, and a seasonally changing à la carte menu.
Cards: Visa, Access, Diners, AmEx.
Other points: open-air dining, children welcome.
Directions: off the A339 Newbury–Basingstoke road.
MR & MRS MATTHEWS ☎ (01635) 298525.

LYMINGTON • map 5E2

🍴 PEELERS BISTRO
Gosport Street, SO41 9BE

Built in 1700 as a police station, Peelers no longer dishes out law and order but rather serves a wide range of delicious food, with a well-deserved reputation for its fish. This is an extremely popular restaurant, especially in the evenings. It is situated close to the Isle of Wight ferry, in a mainly cobbled road. It was acclaimed as 'Restaurant of the Year' in 1992 by Where to eat in Hants/Wilts.
DOUBLE ROOM: up to £20
SINGLE ROOM: up to £25
FOOD: from £15 to £20
Hours: breakfast 8.30am–9am, lunch 12noon–1.45pm, dinner 7pm–10.15pm (July–September 6.30pm–10.30pm).
Cuisine: MODERN ENGLISH – fresh fish and pasta.
Cards: Visa, Access, Diners, AmEx.
Other points: licensed, open-air dining, Sunday lunch, children welcome.
Rooms: 2 double/twin rooms. All with TV.
Directions: at bottom of Lymington High Street, turn left into Gosport Street, Peelers is 100 yards along on the left-hand side.
MR & MRS W.J. SMITH ☎ (01590) 676165.

🏨 THE WHITE ROSE HOTEL
Village Centre, Sway, SO41 6BA

A family-run hotel of immense charm, offering accommodation and food of the finest quality. The hotel is situated in the New Forest village of Sway, close to the coast and with many places of interest to visit nearby. Southampton and Bournemouth are within easy travelling distance, as are such wonderful New Forest locations as Beaulieu, Brockenhurst, Lyndhurst and Lymington. Standing in 5 acres of gardens with a swimming pool, the hotel is an ideal spot to stay when visiting or touring Hampshire.
DOUBLE ROOM: from £30 to £40
FOOD: up to £15
Hours: breakfast 8am–9.30am, lunch 12noon–2pm, dinner 7pm–9pm, bar snacks available.
Cuisine: ENGLISH / CONTINENTAL – a varied menu of home-made meals.
Cards: Visa, Access, AmEx.
Other points: parking, children welcome, pets allowed, no-smoking area, residents' lounge, garden, swimming pool, open-air dining, vegetarian meals, traditional Sunday lunch.
Rooms: 7 double rooms, 3 twin rooms, 2 family rooms. All with TV, telephone, radio, tea/coffee-making facilities. Most rooms are en suite.
Directions: from junction 1 (M27), follow A337 to Lyndhurst and Brokenhurst and turn right onto B3055 to Sway (centre of village).
PAUL & ANNE WINCHCOMBE ☎ (01590) 682754.

LYNDHURST • map 5D2

🏨 BUSKETTS LAWN HOTEL
174 Woodlands Road, Woodlands, SO40 7GL

A superb family-run country hotel offering a sheltered, quiet and peaceful location with a warm and comfortable atmosphere, where you can enjoy the modern amenities of a hotel retaining the charm and elegance of yesteryear. The resident proprietors take a personal interest in the comfort of all guests and have established a reputation for high standards of excellence, service and cuisine.
DOUBLE ROOM: from £30 to £40
FOOD: from £15 to £20
Hours: breakfast (weekdays) 7.30am–9.15am, lunch 12noon–2pm, dinner 7pm–8.30pm.
Cuisine: ENGLISH / CONTINENTAL – an excellent table is offered, with fine, homely cuisine served by cheerful and helpful staff.
Cards: Visa, Access, Diners, AmEx.
Other points: parking, children welcome, pets allowed, residents' lounge, heated swimming pool, golf, croquet lawn, garden, open-air dining, vegetarian meals.
Rooms: 4 single rooms, 6 double rooms, 3 twin rooms, 1 family room. All with en suite, TV, telephone, radio, alarm, hair dryer, trouser-press, tea/coffee-making facilities.
Directions: A35 road from Southampton and Bournemouth. At the village of Ashurst take turning for Woodlands Road.
MR & MRS HAYES ☎ (01703) 292272 Fax (01703) 292272.

🏨 ORMONDE HOUSE
Southampton Road, SO43 7BT

A superb family-run guest house situated in the attractive village of Lyndhurst, with many places of interest nearby. The accommodation is first-class, with some views of the New Forest. All meals are prepared under the strict supervision of the proprietor. An ideal place to stay within the county of Hampshire, with Dorset and Wiltshire within easy travelling distance.
DOUBLE ROOM: from £20 to £30
SINGLE ROOM: from £25 to £35
FOOD: up to £15
Hours: breakfast 8am–9.30am, dinner 6.30pm–7.30pm.
Cuisine: ENGLISH.
Cards: Visa, Access, AmEx.
Other points: parking, children welcome, pets allowed, no-smoking area, vegetarian meals.
Rooms: 1 single room, 12 double rooms, 1 family room. All with TV, telephone, radio, tea/coffee-making facilities.
Directions: A35 from Southampton to Bournemouth; Ormonde House is on the right just before entering Lyndhurst.
PAUL AMES ☎ (01703) 282806 Fax (01703) 283775.

HAMPSHIRE • SW ENGLAND

THE PENNY FARTHING HOTEL
Village Centre, SO43 7AA

This attractive family-run guest house, situated 150 yards from the centre of the village, provides comfortable en suite rooms with remote colour TV and tea/coffee facilities. Lyndhurst is the New Forest capital and offers the main visitor centre and museum, as well as a charming selection of shops, inns and restaurants. The hotel also provides a comfortable bar with satellite TV for guests and a large car park to the rear.
DOUBLE ROOM: from £20 to £30
SINGLE ROOM: from £25 to £35
FOOD: up to £15
Hours: breakfast 8am–9.30am, closed Christmas day and Boxing day.
Cuisine: ENGLISH – although only breakfast was available at the time of going to press, further selections are planned: please check with the hotel for details of additional meals.
Cards: Visa, Access.
Other points: parking, children welcome, pets allowed, no-smoking areas, residents' lounge.
Rooms: 1 single room, 7 double rooms, 2 twin rooms. All with TV, tea/coffee-making facilities.
Directions: from M27, take the A337 Romsey Road. The Penny Farthing can be found just before entering Lyndhurst.
JANE & MIKE ☎ (01703) 284422 Fax (01703) 284488.

ODIHAM • map 5C3

LA FORET
High Street, RG25 1LB

This intimate French restaurant, situated on the main street of the delightful country town of Odiham, provides excellently cooked French cuisine in attractive, comfortable surroundings. Using an imaginative menu which has obviously been devised by a creative and caring chef, you will find that excellent service and candlelit surroundings complement your gastronomic delights.
FOOD: from £20 to £25
Hours: lunch 12.30am–2pm, dinner 7pm–9.45pm.
Cuisine: FRENCH – classic French cuisine, including extensive selection of fish specialities.
Cards: Visa, Access, Diners, AmEx.
Other points: licensed, Sunday lunch, children welcome.
Directions: on the main street in Odiham.
MR & MRS HOULKER ☎ (01256) 702697.

PORTSMOUTH • map 5D2

BEAUFORT HOTEL
71 Festing Road, Southsea, PO4 0NQ

The Beaufort Hotel has achieved an outstanding reputation for comfort and excellence. You can relax in the warm and friendly atmosphere, where the emphasis is on service and quality, confident that your stay will be an enjoyable and memorable one. The hotel is situated in a beautiful part of Southsea, overlooking the canoe lake and the colourful rose garden, with the seafront and promenade just a short stroll away.
DOUBLE ROOM: from £30 to £40
FOOD: up to £15
Other points: licensed.
Directions: Festing Road is a quiet road 250 yards from the seafront.
PENNY & TONY FREEMANTLE ☎ (01705) 823707 Fax (01705) 870270.

SEAFARER STEAK HOUSE & FISH RESTAURANT
177–185 Elm Grove, Southsea, PO5 1LU

A steak-house-style restaurant, situated 5 minutes by car from the continental ferry port near the central shopping centre, offering good grills, interesting fish dishes and a daily market-produce board. Friendly and efficient service and a welcoming pre dinner bar.
FOOD: up to £15 CLUB
Hours: Monday to Friday 7pm–10pm, Saturday 6pm–11pm, closed Sunday.
Cuisine: ENGLISH – English, with strong European influence, using fresh daily market produce.
Cards: Visa, Access.
Other points: children welcome.
Directions: M275 to Portsmouth; first exit at roundabout, over 3 roundabouts, restaurant on right.
TIM HUNT ☎ (01705) 827188.

UPLAND PARK HOTEL
Garrison Hill, Droxford, SO3 1QL

Set in the heart of the beautiful Meon Valley, this superb hotel and excellent restaurant is a gem of a place to stay in, offering guests a welcoming atmosphere in which to enjoy the quality accommodation, spacious dining room, and cosy bar with homely log fire in winter. For summer visitors there is a large pool, and space to relax or explore the lovely surrounding countryside.
DOUBLE ROOM: from £30 to £40
SINGLE ROOM: from £25 to £35
FOOD: up to £15
Hours: breakfast 7am–10am, lunch 12noon–2.30pm, dinner 7pm–10pm, bar meals all day.
Cuisine: ENGLISH / CONTINENTAL – a varied menu including a good selection of fresh fish dishes.
Cards: Visa, Access, Diners, AmEx.
Other points: parking, pets allowed, conference facilities, no-smoking area, swimming pool, garden, open-air dining, vegetarian meals, afternoon teas, traditional Sunday lunch.
Rooms: 3 single rooms, 9 double rooms, 3 twin rooms, 2 family rooms. All with en suite, TV, telephone, trouser-press, tea/coffee-making facilities.
Directions: situated on the A32 Alton to Fareham road at Droxford, south of Alton.
BRIAN LAY ☎ (01489) 878507 Fax (01489) 877853.

UPLANDS
34 Granada Road, Southsea,
PO4 0RH

Two minutes from seafront, ten minutes from continental car ferries. Reduced rates for children sharing parents' room. Special rates for OAPs in September. Stay seven nights – pay for six nights! Or 20% discount for two persons sharing (two nights minimum).
DOUBLE ROOM: up to £20
Hours: breakfast 6am–9am, dinner 6pm.
Cuisine: BREAKFAST.
Cards: Visa, Access.
Other points: children welcome, TV lounge, satellite TV.
Rooms: 2 single rooms, 2 double rooms, 11 twin rooms, 3 family rooms.
Directions: off M27 to Portsea, follow the Southsea sign to South Parade pier.
MRS H. ZANELLOTTI ☎ (01705) 821508
Fax (01705) 870126.

RINGWOOD • map 5D1

THE OLD COTTAGE RESTAURANT
14 West Street, BH14 1DZ

A unique and beautiful 14th century thatched restaurant, reported to be the oldest building in the area. Retaining many historical features, it offers excellent English and continental cuisine in an atmosphere of olde-worlde charm. The proprietors personally supervise the day to day running of this extremely popular restaurant in a beautiful part of England.
FOOD: from £15 to £20
Hours: lunch 12noon–2.30pm, dinner 7pm–10.30pm, closed Boxing day.
Cuisine: ENGLISH / CONTINENTAL.
Cards: Visa, Access, AmEx.
Other points: parking, children welcome, Sunday lunch, open bank holidays, no-smoking area, disabled access, vegetarian meals, open-air dining.
Directions: A31 across New Forest towards Bournemouth, turn off at A31 Ringwood roundabout and proceed to the High Street. West Street is a continuation of High Street.
TRICIA & PAUL HARPER ☎ (01425) 474283.

ROCKBOURNE • map 5D1

ROSE & THISTLE
Rockbourne, near Fordingbridge,
SP6 3NL

A beautiful 16th century thatched roof inn, situated in a picture-postcard village in the New Forest. A popular haunt of tourists and walkers who are drawn by the warm, homely atmosphere and the olde-worlde interior, which offers log fires, oak beams and low ceilings. Fine-quality, imaginative fresh food, with excellent wines and real ales available daily.
FOOD: up to £15 CLUB
Hours: lunch 12noon–2.30pm, dinner 7pm–10pm, open all year.
Cuisine: BRITISH – fresh fish and shellfish available daily, including lobster Thermidor and a huge Dover sole. Also traditional Scottish grouse, pheasant and beef.
Cards: Visa, Access, Switch.
Other points: licensed, open-air dining, Sunday lunch, children welcome, afternoon tea, disabled access, pets allowed.
Directions: from Fordingbridge A3078, look for Sandleheath sign for the Roman Villa.
TIM NORFOLK ☎ (017253) 236.

ROMSEY • map 5D2

COBWEB TEA ROOMS
49 The Hundred, SO51 8GE

Situated in the town centre of Romsey, this friendly tea room has a restful atmosphere with a soft green colour scheme inside and an attractive tea garden. Broadlands and Romsey Abbey are nearby places of interest to visit.
FOOD: up to £15
Hours: morning coffee 10am–12noon, lunch 12noon–2pm, afternoon tea 2pm–5.30pm, closed Sunday and Monday, open bank holidays.
Cuisine: ENGLISH – home-made cakes and sweets. Toasted sandwiches. Light lunches.
Other points: open-air dining, children welcome, limited disabled access, no-smoking area.
Directions: in the main street in Romsey on the A27, 100 yards from Broadlands estate.
MISS ANGELA WEBLEY ☎ (01794) 516434.

SOUTH GARDEN CANTONESE & PEKINESE CUISINE
9 Bell Street, SO5 8GY

An elegant restaurant in the centre of Romsey, offering excellent food in comfortable surroundings. All dishes are cooked from fresh ingredients and beautifully presented. Cantonese cuisine is based on freshness and stir-fry cooking, while Pekinese cuisine is more spicy and aromatic. The wine list includes Chinese wines. Excellent, welcoming service.
FOOD: up to £15 ☆
Hours: lunch (Thursday–Sunday) 12.15am–2.15pm, dinner 6pm–11.30pm.
Cuisine: CANTONESE / PEKINESE – including sizzling dishes and a wide choice of seafood dishes. Extensive menu. Set dinners and English dishes also available.
Cards: Visa, Access, AmEx.
Other points: licensed, Sunday lunch, no-smoking area, children welcome, parking.
Directions: in centre of Romsey, approximately 200 yards from Romsey Abbey. Behind town hall.
JASON MAN ☎ (01794) 514428.

SOUTHAMPTON • map 5D2

AVENUE HOTEL
Lodge Road, SO2 0QR

Privately owned, the Avenue Hotel is situated in a tree-lined avenue. A friendly welcome awaits you at this modern, comfortably furnished hotel. The restaurant offers fine food and wine served in a

convivial ambience, so providing an excellent venue to entertain and in which to be entertained. Conveniently located, with direct access from motorways to the city centre.
DOUBLE ROOM: from £20 to £30
FOOD: up to £15
Hours: breakfast 7am–9.30am, lunch 12noon–2.30pm, Sunday 12noon–3pm, dinner 6.30pm–10pm, Sunday 6.30pm–9.30pm.
Cuisine: ENGLISH – à la carte and table d'hôte menus. All dishes are home-made.
Cards: Visa, Access, AmEx.
Other points: licensed, Sunday lunch, no-smoking area, children welcome, afternoon tea, pets allowed, conferences, functions.
Directions: off the A33.
A. WYLIE ☎ (01703) 229023.

LA MARGHERITA RESTAURANT
6 Commercial Road, SO1 0GE
A busy, friendly bistro-type restaurant near the Mayflower Theatre. Popular with theatre goers and TV stars. Repartee and good humour flow as fast as the Italian red wine.
FOOD: up to £15 [CLUB]
Hours: dinner 6.30pm–11.30pm, lunch 12noon–2.30pm, open bank holidays.
Cuisine: CONTINENTAL – langostinos, steak Diane, freshly-made pizzas and home-made lasagne. Desserts include creme caramel.
Cards: Visa, Access, Diners, AmEx.
Other points: disabled access, children welcome.
Directions: from main BR station, turn right at traffic lights into Commercial Road.
FRANCESCO FANTINI ☎ (01703) 333390.

LANGLEY'S BISTRO
10–11 Bedford Place, SO1 2DB
Situated in a busy area, this is a popular city-centre bistro offering fine English and continental dishes to a sophisticated business clientele. Spacious, with an attractive bar and furnishings, and a comfortable atmosphere prevails.
FOOD: up to £15
Hours: lunch 12noon–2pm, dinner 6.30pm–10.30pm.
Cuisine: ENGLISH / CONTINENTAL.
Cards: Visa.
Other points: children welcome, open bank holidays, disabled access, vegetarian meals.
Directions: via Winchester, from M3 motorway take A33 to Southampton.
MR TUCKER ☎ (01703) 224551.

STOCKBRIDGE • map 5D2

THE GAME LARDER RESTAURANT
New Street, SO20 6HG
Situated close to the city of Winchester, Romsey, Andover and Salisbury, this beautiful 18th century converted malthouse has a wealth of oak beams, an enormous open log fire, and a minstrel's gallery which overlooks the main restaurant. There is on offer a wide and interesting menu, complemented by a wine list of 72 bins. This is the ideal setting for a romantic dinner for two, a family party or a quiet business meal, and is perfect also for wedding receptions. A very warm welcome awaits you from Terry and Kerry Jayne and their friendly, efficient staff.
FOOD: from £20 to £25 [CLUB]
Hours: lunch 12noon–2pm, dinner 7pm–10pm, closed Sunday dinner and Monday.
Cuisine: ENGLISH – good à la carte menu with dishes made from fresh local produce. Game in season.
Cards: Visa, Access, Diners, AmEx.
Other points: parking, children welcome, vegetarian meals, traditional Sunday lunch.
Directions: on the A30, 7 miles south of Andover. The Game Larder can be found just off the High Street in Stockbridge.
TERRY & KERRY JAYNE ☎ (01264) 810414.

THE GREYHOUND HOTEL
High Street, SO20 6EY
This small hotel situated in a delightful, small Hampshire town has log fires and oak beams, and the restaurant offers a wide selection of seafood dishes, including lobster, crepe fruits de mer and smoked trout. The hotel has its own stretch of the famous River Test (day tickets available). Golf day fees can also be arranged, along with clay pigeon shooting.
DOUBLE ROOM: from £30 to £40
FOOD: up to £15
Hours: breakfast 7.30am–9.30am, lunch 12noon–2pm, dinner 6pm–9.30pm.
Cuisine: ENGLISH / SEAFOOD – à la carte including a range of seafood, crepes, and ploughman's.
Cards: Visa, Access, AmEx.
Other points: licensed, open-air dining, Sunday lunch, children welcome, afternoon tea, garden, pets allowed.
Directions: Stockbridge is located at the intersection of the A30 and A3057.
MR GUMBRELL ☎ (01264) 810833.

WINCHESTER • map 5D2

THE ABBEY BAR & COURTYARD CAFE
The Guildhall, The Broadway, SO22 6EN
Situated within the delightful Victorian building of Winchester Guildhall, this is an ideal place to stop, meet and visit. Winchester Guildhall is a perfect venue for banqueting, promotions and conferences. Good food is provided in comfortable, friendly surroundings.
FOOD: up to £15 [CLUB]
Hours: morning coffee 10am–12noon, lunch 12noon–2pm, open bank holidays.
Cuisine: ENGLISH – serving morning coffee, bar meals, salad bar and carvery. Afternoon tea in the Café.
Other points: Sunday lunch, no-smoking area, parking nearby.
Directions: approximately 75 yards from King Alfred statue in city centre and 200 yards from Winchester Cathedral.
MRS SHIRLEY MORRISSEY ☎ (01962) 848368 [Fax] (0196) 878458.

SW ENGLAND • HAMPSHIRE

CATHEDRAL VIEW GUEST HOUSE
9A Magdalen Hill, SO23 8HJ

Cathedral View is a small guest house of a very high standard. A good-quality, home-cooked breakfast can be enjoyed in the residents' dining room, and the tastefully decorated bedrooms ensure a comfortable night's rest. The guest house is well sited for the City of Winchester, Salisbury, Stonehenge, New Forest and many other places of interest.
DOUBLE ROOM: up to £20
FOOD: up to £15
Hours: breakfast 7.45am–8.45am.
Cuisine: ENGLISH – a good-quality breakfast can be enjoyed in the residents' dining room.
Other points: parking, children welcome, garden.
Rooms: 3 double rooms, 1 twin room, 1 family room.
Directions: on entering Winchester from the east along the B3404, the guest house is situated on the right-hand side, just before entering the city centre.
MR & MRS CRONAN ☎ (01962) 863802.

LES ROUTIERS ACCOMMODATION DIRECTORY

This handy directory is ideal for those looking for somewhere to stay at great value.
It lists a huge choice of *Les Routiers*-recommended places throughout the British Isles offering comfortable accommodation, good food and a warm welcome amid relaxed surroundings.

Available from selected
Les Routiers establishments
or direct from the publishers.

Price £2

HARESTOCK LODGE HOTEL & RESTAURANT
Harestock Road, SO22 6NX

The hotel is situated on the edge of historic Winchester, once the capital of England. Built in 1885, it is owned by the Bishop family. There is a large, secluded garden and rooms furnished in country house style. Facilities include an open-air swimming pool and indoor spa pool. The superb restaurant offers fine food from the à la carte and table d'hôte menus. Everything is here for a relaxing stay.
DOUBLE ROOM: from £30 to £40
FOOD: up to £15
Hours: breakfast 7.30am–9am, dinner 6.30pm–10pm, lunch 12noon–2.30pm.
Cuisine: ENGLISH.
Cards: Visa, Access, AmEx.
Other points: parking, children welcome, afternoon teas, disabled access, pets, residents' lounge, garden, vegetarian meals, open-air dining.
Directions: 1 mile north of Winchester, on dual-carriageway A34.
PETER & NICK BISHOP ☎ (01962) 881870
Fax (01962) 880038.

THE ROYAL HOTEL
St Peter Street, SO23 8BS

Formally a bishop's residence, The Royal Hotel was built in the 16th century and has been a hotel for about 150 years. The restaurant offers well-cooked, imaginative dishes using predominantly fresh local produce. The hotel is furnished and decorated to a very high standard, providing attractive surroundings and comfortable accommodation. Two minutes from main shopping street.
DOUBLE ROOM: from £30 to £40
FOOD: from £15 to £20
Hours: breakfast weekdays 7am–9.30am, weekends 8am–10am, bar meals 12noon–2.30pm, dinner Sunday 7pm–9.30pm.
Cuisine: MODERN ENGLISH – à la carte and table d'hôte menus. Dishes may include baked local pink trout, navarin of spring lamb, medallions of beef cooked in a green peppercorn sauce.
Cards: Visa, Access, Diners, AmEx.
Other points: licensed, open-air dining, Sunday lunch, afternoon tea, residents' lounge, special breaks, children welcome, residents' bar, vegetarian meals, parking, disabled access.
Rooms: 75 bedrooms. All en suite.
Directions: from the M3, take exit 9. Follow the one-way system to St George's Street, then turn right.
TONY & PAMELA SMITH ☎ (01962) 840840
Fax (01962) 841582.

WOODFALLS • map 5D2

THE WOODFALLS INN
The Ridge, SO5 2LN

Located in the village of Woodfalls, nestling on the north edge of the New Forest, Woodfalls has provided hospitality to travellers seeking rest and refreshment since 1870. On arrival, guests will find that the hospitality and welcome remain as warm as ever. A well-stocked bar includes a fine choice of properly stored cask-conditioned ales. Ideal for touring the New Forest.
DOUBLE ROOM: from £20 to £30
SINGLE ROOM: from £25 to £35
FOOD: up to £15 CLUB ☆
Hours: breakfast 7.30am–11.45am, lunch 12noon–3pm, bar meals 11.30am–3pm, dinner 6.30pm–9.30pm, bar meals 6.30pm–10pm.
Cuisine: ENGLISH – traditional and wholesome English cooking. Frequently changing menus to suit every palate, using a wide variety of fresh, locally grown produce.
Cards: Visa, Access.
Other points: licensed, open-air dining, Sunday lunch, no-smoking area, children welcome, pets allowed, afternoon tea, parking, residents' lounge, residents' bar, disabled access, vegetarian meals.
Rooms: 4 double rooms, 6 twin rooms, 2 suites.
Directions: exit from M27 at junction 1. Take the B3078 to Telegraph Corner, then the B3080 to Woodfalls.
MR M. ELVIS ☎ (01725) 513222 Fax (01725) 513220.

ISLE OF WIGHT

CHALE • map 5E2

CLARENDON HOTEL AND WIGHT MOUSE INN
St Catherine's Down, PO38 2HA
A charming 17th century inn overlooking Chale Bay in the south of the island, a few minutes from Blackgang Chine. The hotel enjoys a fine reputation for good food, wine, comfort and hospitality. With over 365 whiskies, 6 real ales and open fires, a warm, friendly atmosphere is assured! Children are most welcome.
DOUBLE ROOM: from £20 to £30
SINGLE ROOM: from £25 to £35
FOOD: up to £15 CLUB
Hours: open all day (Monday–Saturday) 11am until late, Sunday 12noon–3pm and 7pm–10.30pm, open all year round.
Cuisine: INTERNATIONAL – Wight Mouse Inn: island steaks, local fish, crab, home-made pizzas, curries, lasagne, chilli, daily specials etc., all home-made. Clarendon Hotel: fresh vegetables, fresh local fish, meat and vegetarian menu.
Cards: Visa, Access, MasterCard.
Other points: open-air dining, Sunday lunch, entertainment, children welcome, baby-listening device, cots, vegetarian meals, parking, residents' bar, residents' lounge.
Rooms: 3 double rooms, 5 quad rooms, 2 suites. All with TV, radio, alarm, hair dryer, baby-listening device, tea/coffee-making facilities.
Directions: on B3399, 50 yards from the Military Road, B3055, in Chale.
JOHN & JEAN BRADSHAW ☎ (01983) 730431
Fax (01983) 730431.

NEWPORT • map 5E2

THE BARN BISTRO
Arreton, near Newport, PO30 3AA
For a good country bistro-style meal and a great atmosphere in appealing country surroundings, look no further than The Barn Bistro and pub. This attractive old farm building is located in the centre of a popular craft centre. Here you can enjoy home-cooked meals made from fresh local produce at excellent value-for-money prices. Live jazz-style music at weekends.
FOOD: up to £15
Hours: lunch 12noon–2.30pm, dinner 7pm–10.30pm, bar is open all day.
Cuisine: FRENCH / ENGLISH – speciality sauces. Fresh local duck, chicken and fish.
Cards: Visa, Access.
Other points: parking, children welcome, no-smoking area, open-air dining, traditional Sunday lunch, afternoon teas.
Directions: on A3056 Sandown to Newport road, at Arreton country craft village.
JENNIFER HOWARD ☎ (01983) 825950
Fax (01983) 528004.

SANDOWN • map 5E2

CULVER LODGE HOTEL
17 Albert Road, PO36 8AW
A family-run hotel with glass frontage, which looks out on shrubs and flower beds. Just a few minutes from beaches and entertainment for all ages, summer theatre and shops.
DOUBLE ROOM: up to £20
SINGLE ROOM: up to £25
FOOD: up to £15
Hours: breakfast 8.30am–9am, lunch 12noon–2pm, dinner 6pm–7pm.
Cuisine: MODERN ENGLISH – table d'hôte menu.
Cards: Visa, Access, Diners, AmEx.
Other points: licensed, special diets, children welcome, cots, residents' lounge, residents' bar.
Rooms: 3 single rooms, 9 double rooms, 7 twin rooms, 1 triple room, 1 family room. All with TV, radio, tea/coffee-making facilities.
Directions: Albert Road runs off the main shopping street, parallel to the high street, half a mile to the train station.
MRS LE LIEVRE ☎ (01983) 403819.

THE OAKLANDS HOTEL
Yarbridge, PO36 0AB
A friendly, family-run licensed hotel at the foot of the Brading Downs, offering cheerful, efficient service. Local activities include fishing, swimming, golf and sailing. Ideal for walking holidays. The pool is heated to at least 82 degrees Fahrenheit from June to September.
DOUBLE ROOM: from £30 to £40
Hours: breakfast 8.30am–9am, dinner (low season) 6.30pm–7pm, bar meals (high season) 9pm–10.30pm.
Cuisine: ENGLISH.
Cards: Visa, Access.
Other points: children welcome, garden, pets allowed, swimming pool, floodlit boules, aerospa, vegetarian meals.
Directions: on Ryde–Sandown road, 1 mile from Sandown in direction of Brading.
JOAN RAWLINGS & FAMILY ☎ (01983) 406197.

SEAVIEW • map 5E2

SEAVIEW HOTEL & RESTAURANT
High Street, PO34 5EX
This Victorian hotel is situated in the heart of the pretty sailing village of Seaview. It is possible to while away many hours looking at the unique collection of prints of old ships and liners that once passed the hotel. Frequented by local characters and the visiting yachtsmen. Les Routiers Restaurant of the Year 1989.
DOUBLE ROOM: from £30 to £40
FOOD: from £15 to £20

Hours: breakfast 7am–9.30am, lunch 12noon–2pm, dinner 7.30pm–9.45pm.
Cuisine: BRITISH – local produce, seafood and game, home-grown vegetables and herbs, island asparagus, garlic, lobster and wine.
Cards: Visa, Access, Diners, AmEx.
Other points: open-air dining, traditional Sunday lunch, children welcome, residents' lounges, no-smoking area, residents' bar, vegetarian meals, parking.
Rooms: 4 double rooms, 10 twin rooms, 2 suites. All with en suite, TV, telephone, room service. Some with sea view.
Directions: take B3330 to Seaview. At Nettlestone Green turn left into village. Continue down to sea: hotel on left.
MR & MRS NICHOLAS HAYWARD ☎ (01983) 612711 Fax (01983) 613729.

SHANKLIN • map 5E2

BRAEMAR HOTEL
1 Grange Road, PO37 6NN
The Braemar is tucked away in Shanklin's old village. Probably the island's most attractive corner, it is ideally placed for the beach, chine, shops and countryside. All bedrooms are tastefully decorated, providing a cosy, relaxing retreat. A large sunbathing balcony is available to all guests, and at mealtimes, individual tables with waitress service make dining here a real pleasure. Entertainment is provided in the comfortable surroundings of the Olde Worlde Thatched bar, which also has its own dance floor. A happy, friendly atmosphere prevails.
DOUBLE ROOM: up to £20
FOOD: up to £15
Hours: breakfast 8.45am, dinner 6pm.
Cuisine: ENGLISH – with a touch of continental style.
Cards: Visa, Access, AmEx.
Other points: parking, children welcome, no-smoking area, pets, vegetarian meals.
Directions: Grange Road is directly off Shanklin High Street.
MRS P. WILSON ☎ (01983) 863172.

BURLINGTON HOTEL
6 Chine Avenue, PO37 6AG
An attractive stone building, constructed in the reign of Queen Victoria as a gentleman's residence. Standing in its own grounds overlooking the sea, it is a comfortable family hotel for those seeking the customary seaside holiday. Traditional home-cooking, with a pleasant lounge bar and residents' lounge with sea views.
DOUBLE ROOM: from £20 to £30
Other points: parking, children welcome, residents' lounge, vegetarian meals, garden, residents' bar, cots.
Rooms: 3 single rooms, 4 double rooms, 1 twin room, 5 family rooms. All with TV, tea/coffee-making facilities.
Directions: follow the B3328 to Chine Avenue, then turn right.
MR J.W. ELLYATT ☎ (01983) 862090.

THE HAMBLEDON HOTEL
11 Queens Road, PO37 6AW
A detached family-run hotel surrounded by well-kept gardens. Tastefully decorated in a traditional style to a high standard, the accommodation is very comfortable. This is an ideal place to stay if you have young children, as there are special provisions for very young children, including baby-sitting: Mrs Birch is a trained nursery nurse.
DOUBLE ROOM: up to £20
SINGLE ROOM: up to £25
Hours: breakfast 8.30am–9am, dinner 6.30pm.
Cuisine: BREAKFAST.
Cards: Visa, Access.
Other points: children welcome, garden, nursery, special diets.
Rooms: 1 single room, 6 double rooms, 1 twin room, 3 family rooms. All with TV, radio, telephone, hair dryer.
Directions: from Fishbourne ferry, take A3055 to Shanklin. Near Cliff Top lift.
NORMAN & BERYL BIRCH ☎ (01983) 862403.

QUEENSMEAD HOTEL
Queen's Road, PO37 6AN
Positioned close to the famous Keats' Green area of Shanklin, just minutes from the sea, town and old village. An elegant Victorian villa with modern additions, the hotel has a large, heated outdoor swimming pool and a sheltered rose arbour in the garden. The dining room is also open to non-residents, space permitting. Guaranteed personal all-day service.
DOUBLE ROOM: from £30 to £40
SINGLE ROOM: from £25 to £35
FOOD: up to £15
Hours: breakfast 8.30am–9am, lunch 12noon–2.30pm, dinner 6.30pm, closed December until end of February, open Christmas.
Cuisine: ENGLISH.
Cards: Visa, Access.
Other points: children catered for (please check for age limits), vegetarian meals, garden, residents' lounge.
Rooms: 2 single rooms, 12 double rooms, 10 twin rooms, 6 family rooms. All with TV, tea/coffee-making facilities.
Directions: opposite the church of St Saviour (very tall spire) on the cliff.
KEN & JEAN CHAPMAN ☎ (01983) 862342.

WEST COOMBE HOTEL
West Hill Road, PO37 6PT
Situated in a delightful secluded garden at the end of a tree-lined drive on the edge of Shanklin's old village. The tranquility of the gardens is reflected by the mood and decor of the hotel, making for a quiet, relaxing stay. With a cosy bar and restaurant opening out onto the sun terrace, dining is a double pleasure. West Coombe has an enviable reputation for a quality menu, with service to match.
DOUBLE ROOM: up to £20
FOOD: up to £15
Hours: breakfast 8.30am–9am, dinner 6.15pm–7pm, closed November until February.
Cuisine: ENGLISH / CONTINENTAL.

Cards: Visa, Access, AmEx.
Other points: parking, no-smoking area, residents' lounge, bar lounge, vegetarian meals, garden.
Rooms: 4 single rooms, 5 double rooms, 6 twin rooms, 3 family rooms. All with en suite, TV, tea/coffee-making facilities.
Directions: turn off Victoria Avenue at the sign for the cricket club.
MRS B. STARKEY ☎ (01983) 866323.

ST HELEN'S • map 5E2

ST HELEN'S RESTAURANT
Lower Green Road, PO33 1TS

This cosy English restaurant, which has a big log fire in winter, has a cheerful, relaxed atmosphere and overlooks the largest green in England. The home-cooking is excellent value and tastes delicious!
FOOD: from £15 to £20 CLUB ★
Hours: lunch 12noon–2pm, dinner 6.30pm–0.30am, last orders 10pm, closed Monday.
Cuisine: ENGLISH – à la carte menu, fixed three-course menu. Mainly traditional English with vegetarian choice.
Cards: Visa, Access.
Other points: licensed, Sunday lunch, children welcome.
Directions: B3330 to St Helen's, right onto Lower Green.
FRANK & ROSEMARY BALDRY ☎ (01983) 872303.

TOTLAND BAY • map 5E2

SENTRY MEAD HOTEL
Madeira Road, PO39 0BJ

An imposing Victorian country house on the west-coast headland, within two minutes' walk from the beach, providing good-quality, comfortable accommodation in attractive, pleasant surroundings. You can be assured of a warm welcome from resident proprietors Mike and Julie Hodgson. This makes an ideal base for countryside and coastal walking. Freephone 0500 131277 for reservations.
DOUBLE ROOM: from £20 to £30
FOOD: up to £15
Hours: breakfast 8.30am–9.15am, lunch 12noon–2pm, dinner 7pm–8pm.
Cuisine: ENGLISH – fixed-price menu. Imaginative home-style cooking. Dishes may include turkey breast in a cream and brandy sauce, lemon sole and lamb Maroc.
Cards: Visa, Access, AmEx.
Other points: children welcome, garden, pets allowed.
Rooms: 2 single rooms, 5 double rooms, 3 twin rooms, 3 triple rooms, 1 family room. All with TV, radio, tea/coffee-making facilities.
Directions: situated on the headland, opposite Turf Walk.
MIKE & JULIE HODGSON ☎ (01983) 753212.

VENTNOR • map 5E2

MADEIRA HALL
Trinity Road, Bonchurch, PO38 1NS

This beautiful, well-appointed, Grade II listed mansion house, set in its own secluded grounds, offers outstanding accommodation. This haven for non-smokers is classically decorated throughout. All guests are assured a warm welcome and a wonderful and memorable stay.
DOUBLE ROOM: from £20 to £30
SINGLE ROOM: from £25 to £35
Hours: breakfast 8.30am–9.30am.
Cards: Visa, Access.
Other points: parking, residents' lounge, garden.
Rooms: 3 four-poster rooms. All with en suite, TV, telephone, radio, alarm, trouser-press, iron, tea/coffee-making facilities.
Directions: A3055 Shanklin to Ventnor road; turn left at parish church.
PETER & CINDY WITHERIDGE ☎ (01983) 852624 [Fax] (01983) 854906.

OLD PARK HOTEL
St Lawrence, PO38 1XS

Games room, under-fives supper between 4.30pm and 5.30pm, sauna, solarium, swimming pool, and no danger from traffic – all this plus comfortable accommodation, good food and a friendly atmosphere, adds up to a fantastic family holiday. Mr Thornton has created a fun safe-haven for children, while providing all the qualities of a good hotel.
DOUBLE ROOM: from £20 to £30
FOOD: up to £15
Hours: breakfast 8.30am–9.30am, bar meals 12noon–2pm, dinner 7.30pm–8.30pm.
Cuisine: ENGLISH – extensive fixed-price five-course menu (pies, pasties – traditional English).
Cards: Visa, Access.
Other points: licensed, children welcome, garden, afternoon tea, pets allowed, sauna, solarium, swimming pool, special breaks, residents' lounge, residents' bar, foreign exchange.
Rooms: 1 single room, 6 double rooms, 4 twin rooms, 3 family rooms, 20 suites. All with TV, tea/coffee-making facilities.
Directions: A3055 to St Lawrence.
MR R.W. THORNTON ☎ (01983) 852583 [Fax] (01983) 854920.

ST MAUR HOTEL
Castle Road, PO38 1LG

St Maur is beautifully situated on a level with the town, only minutes from Ventnor beach and Steephill cove. All bedrooms have views over the hotel gardens, and some have sea views.
DOUBLE ROOM: up to £20
SINGLE ROOM: up to £25
FOOD: up to £15
Hours: breakfast 8.30am–9am, dinner 6.30pm–7pm, closed December until February.
Cuisine: ENGLISH.
Cards: Visa, Access, Diners, AmEx.
Other points: children catered for (please check for age limits).
Directions: west of Ventnor, St Maur is 100 yards

SW ENGLAND • SOMERSET

up Castle Road at end of Park Avenue (A3055).
D.J. GROOCOCK ☎ (01983) 852570
Fax (01983) 852306.

YARMOUTH • map 5E2

GARRICK'S AT MAYNARD'S
High Street, PO41 0PL

This stylish restaurant and bistro, specializing in local seafood dishes and French cuisine, is situated in the centre of Yarmouth High Street. Owned and operated by a well-known resident of the island, the character of the restaurant is popular with locals and tourists alike. Ideally located for the ferry terminal, Yarmouth Castle and harbour.
FOOD: up to £15
Hours: meals all day 10am–3pm, dinner 6.30pm–10pm.
Cuisine: ENGLISH / CONTINENTAL – seafood.
Cards: Visa, Access, AmEx, Switch.
Other points: children welcome, no-smoking area, vegetarian meals, traditional Sunday lunch.
Directions: situated towards the centre of Yarmouth High Street, a short walk from the ferry terminal.
MARTIN & CAROLYNE SMITH ☎ (01983) 760014.

SOMERSET

BRENT KNOLL • map 4B4

BATTLEBOROUGH GRANGE COUNTRY HOTEL
Bristol Road, TA9 4HJ

This hotel and restaurant nestles in its own grounds at the foot of the historic Iron Age fort known as Brent Knoll. Both the restaurant and bar offer imaginative, well-presented home-made food. The proprietors and their staff ensure that each guest enjoys their visit.
DOUBLE ROOM: from £20 to £30
FOOD: from £15 to £20
Hours: breakfast 7.30am–9.30am, lunch 12noon–2pm, bar meals 12noon–2pm, dinner 7pm–9pm.
Cuisine: MODERN ENGLISH – Peking prawns, scampi Pernod, Grange fillet steak.
Cards: Visa, Access, Diners, AmEx.
Other points: licensed, open-air dining, Sunday lunch, afternoon tea.
Directions: 1 mile from M5 junction 22, on A38.
TONY & CAROL WILKINS ☎ (01278) 760208.

BRIDGWATER • map 4C4

WALNUT TREE INN
North Petherton, TA6 6QA

Set in the heart of Somerset, this fully modernized 18th century coaching inn makes an ideal touring centre for many attractions. Two popular restaurants, friendly bar, spacious decorated luxury bedrooms, including a four-poster and suites. Quietly located, the Walnut Tree offers everything for a touring holiday base or restful short break. Ample parking.
DOUBLE ROOM: from £20 to £30
SINGLE ROOM: from £25 to £35
FOOD: up to £15
Hours: lunch 12noon–2pm, dinner 7pm–10pm.
Cuisine: ENGLISH – local produce, fresh meat, duck, local dishes.
Cards: Visa, Access, Diners, AmEx.
Other points: Sunday lunch, children welcome, baby-listening device, baby-sitting, cots, disabled access, 24hr reception, foreign exchange, residents' bar, residents' lounge, central heating, vegetarian meals, parking.
Rooms: 2 single rooms, 20 double rooms, 6 twin rooms. All with TV, radio, alarm, telephone, tea/coffee-making facilities.
Directions: exit 24 of M5 to Taunton (¼ mile). Follow signs to North Petherton. On A38.
RICHARD & HILARY GOULDEN ☎ (01278) 662255 Fax (01278) 663946.

CREWKERNE • map 4C5

THE GEORGE HOTEL & RESTAURANT
Market Square, near Yeovil, TA18 7LP

An interesting building with a fascinating history dating back to the 17th century. With an excellent function room, restaurant and accommodation of the highest standard, it provides an ideal base for touring the counties of Somerset, Dorset and the Devon coastline. Also a good area for walking, cycling, golf, horse-riding, etc.
DOUBLE ROOM: from £20 to £30
SINGLE ROOM: from £25 to £35
FOOD: up to £15
Hours: breakfast 7.30am–9.30am, lunch 12noon–2pm, dinner 6.30pm–9.30pm.
Cuisine: ENGLISH / CONTINENTAL.
Cards: Visa, Access, Diners, AmEx.
Other points: children welcome, Sunday lunch, residents' lounge, vegetarian meals.
Rooms: 3 single rooms, 4 double rooms, 5 twin rooms, 1 suite. All with TV, tea/coffee-making facilities. Bridal suite with Jacuzzi.
Directions: half-way between Yeovil and Chard.
FRANK & LINA JOYCE ☎ (01460) 73650 Fax (01460) 72974.

THE MANOR ARMS
North Perrott, TA18 7SG

The Manor Arms is a 16th century Grade II listed building, which has been lovingly restored and refurbished. It is full of olde-worlde charm and character, with its exposed stone, inglenook fireplace and original oak beams. The restaurant and bar menu offer only home-made dishes, and

160

comfortable accommodation is available in the adjacent Olde Coach House, which has also been carefully restored.
DOUBLE ROOM: from £20 to £30
SINGLE ROOM: from £25 to £35
FOOD: up to £15
Hours: breakfast 7.30am–9am, lunch 12noon–1.45pm, dinner 7pm–9pm.
Cuisine: ENGLISH / FRENCH – à la carte and bar menus available.
Cards: Visa, Access.
Other points: parking, children welcome, no-smoking area, conference facilities, garden, open-air dining, vegetarian meals, traditional Sunday lunch.
Rooms: 3 double rooms, 2 twin rooms. All with TV, tea/coffee-making facilities.
Directions: from A30 take A3066, signposted for Bridport. North Perrott is 1½ miles along this road.
REX & JANE GILMORE ☎ (01460) 72901.

DULVERTON • map 4C4

THE LION HOTEL
Bank Square, BS23 1LN
Set in the heart of the Exmoor National Park, the Lion is an ideal base for exploring this beautiful, unspoilt corner of England. It offers a warm welcome, comfortable accommodation and good food at excellent value for money. The wide range of holiday breaks cater for every interest, including those who fancy a trip in a hot air balloon.
DOUBLE ROOM: from £20 to £30
FOOD: from £15 to £20
Hours: breakfast 8.30am–9.30am, lunch 12noon–2pm, dinner 6.30pm–9pm, Sunday 7pm–9pm.
Cuisine: ENGLISH – fresh Exmoor produce including salmon, trout, game birds and venison, traditionally cooked and available in the restaurants and bars.
Cards: Visa, Access.
Other points: Sunday lunch, children welcome, pets allowed (charge), special breaks, shooting, hunting, fishing.
Rooms: 4 single rooms, 4 double rooms, 4 twin rooms, 1 family room. All with TV, telephone, tea/coffee-making facilities.
Directions: junction 27 off M5. Then off A396, between Liverton and Minehead.
DUNCAN & JACKIE MACKINNON (MANAGERS) ☎ (01398) 23444.

DUNSTER • map 4B4

THE TEA SHOPPE
3 High Street, TA24 6SF
15th century tea rooms in lovely medieval village close to National Trust castle. Norman and Pam can boast 32 years' experience and specialize in home-cooking. A well-presented tea room offering all sorts of unusual teas, jams, coffees, etc.
FOOD: up to £15
Cuisine: ENGLISH – home-made soups and traditional recipes. Delicious puddings and home-made cakes.

Cards: Visa, Access.
Other points: licensed, traditional Sunday lunch, no-smoking area, children welcome, pets allowed.
Directions: situated in the town's main road at the end nearest the castle.
NORMAN & PAM GOLDSACK ☎ (01643) 821304.

EXEBRIDGE • map 4C4

ANCHOR INN HOTEL
Near Dulverton, TA22 9AZ
A 300-year-old residential inn on the banks of the River Exe, with fishing from the hotel grounds. Standing in an acre of grounds, the Anchor Inn provides a high standard of comfort and tranquility. The restaurant is set in a converted stable block overlooking the lawned garden and river. Excellent à la carte menu includes trout from the River Exe. Ideal base for exploring Exmoor.
DOUBLE ROOM: from £30 to £40
FOOD: from £15 to £20
Hours: breakfast 8.30am–9.30am, lunch 12noon–2pm, dinner 7pm–9pm, open all year.
Cuisine: MODERN ENGLISH – good home-cooking with local produce used where possible; the chef bakes his own bread and makes home-made desserts.
Cards: Visa, Access.
Other points: open-air dining, beer garden, reservations, children welcome, playland.
Rooms: 3 double rooms, 6 twin rooms.
Directions: on the B3222, just off the A396, north-east of Bampton.
JOHN & JUDY PHRIPP ☎ (01398) 323433.

EXFORD • map 4B4

THE EXMOOR WHITE HORSE INN
Near Minehead, EX31 4QT
Your dream of an olde-worlde inn with log fires comes true before your eyes, standing on the green by the side of a trickling stream in one of Exmoor's most beautiful villages. Horses all around, the blacksmith busy over the road, and rolling moors await you at the edge of the village.
DOUBLE ROOM: from £40 to £50
SINGLE ROOM: from £45 to £55
FOOD: up to £15
Hours: breakfast 8.30am–9.30am, lunch 12noon–2.30pm, dinner 7pm–9.30pm.
Cuisine: ENGLISH – steaks, seafood, venison and extensive bar snacks.
Other points: licensed, Sunday lunch, children welcome, garden, vegetarian meals, residents' lounge, residents' bar, parking, disabled access.
Rooms: 12 double rooms, 3 twin rooms, 3 family rooms. All with TV, radio, tea/coffee-making facilities, heating.
Directions: from Taunton take the A358, then the B224 to Exford.
MRS D DARLINGTON ☎ (0164383) 229.

EXMOOR • map 4C4

🍴 THE REST & BE THANKFUL INN
Wheddon Cross, TA24 7DR

Blazing log fires and a warm, courteous welcome await you at this charming, olde-style inn with a patio and views over the moors. Good food in a friendly atmosphere and comfortable accommodation ensure a restful stay and an entirely enjoyable visit. Children are especially welcome, with the Buttery Bar dedicated to parents with children and a games room with skittles and videos.
DOUBLE ROOM: from £20 to £30
SINGLE ROOM: up to £25
FOOD: up to £15
Hours: breakfast 8am–9.30am, lunch 12noon–2pm, dinner 7pm–10pm.
Cuisine: ENGLISH – traditional English bar meals. Full menu with recommended house specials.
Cards: Visa, Access, AmEx.
Other points: licensed, open-air dining, Sunday lunch, no-smoking area, children catered for (please check for age limits), residents' lounge, open bank holidays.
Directions: 9 miles south of Minehead on A396 to Tiverton.
MR M. WEAVER ☎ (01643) 841222.

🍴 THE ROYAL OAK INN
Withypool, TA24 7QP

Set in the beautiful village of Withypool in the middle of Exmoor, this is an ideal base from which to ride, hunt, shoot, fish or simply take a leisurely walk. All bedrooms are individually furnished, with their own character, and the two bars with their beamed ceilings are everything you would expect of an old country inn. R.D. Blackmore stayed here while writing his famous novel Lorna Doone.
DOUBLE ROOM: from £30 to £40
SINGLE ROOM: from £35 to £45
FOOD: from £15 to £20 ✩
Hours: breakfast 8.30am–9.30am, bar snacks 12noon–2pm, 6.30pm–9.30pm, dinner 7pm–9pm.
Cuisine: ENGLISH / CONTINENTAL.
Cards: Visa, Access, Diners, AmEx.
Other points: parking, children catered for (please check for age limits), pets allowed, residents' lounge, vegetarian meals, open-air dining.
Rooms: 7 double rooms, 1 twin room.
Directions: leave the M5 at Tiverton and take the A361. Turn left for North Molton and Withypool. The establishment is in the centre of Withypool.
MR M. BRADLEY ☎ (0164383) 506/507
Fax (0164383) 659.

EXMOOR NATIONAL PARK

🍴 THE ROYAL OAK INN
Winsford, TA24 7JE

Nestling in the picturesque village of Winsford on the edge of the Exmoor National Park, the inn dates from the 12th century. Its charming thatched roof, open fireplaces and oak beams have been subtly combined with many modern facilities to ensure guests' comfort. The restaurant prides itself on its freshly cooked cuisine, and the lounges are furnished to a high standard of elegance, as are the bedrooms, which maintain cosiness and charm. This is a superb location for exploring Exmoor and its ancient history. A winner of many outstanding awards, including Les Routiers Accommodation of the Year 1994.
DOUBLE ROOM: from £40 to £50
SINGLE ROOM: from £45 to £55
FOOD: from £15 to £20 ✩
Hours: bar 11.30am–2.30pm & 6pm–11pm, open all year.
Cuisine: ENGLISH.
Other points: parking, children welcome, open bank holidays, afternoon teas, pets, residents' lounge, garden dining, vegetarian meals.
Rooms: 1 single room, 10 double rooms, 2 twin rooms, 1 family room, 1 suite.
Directions: M5 south, turn off at junction 27 onto A396 north.
CHARLES STEVEN ☎ (0164385) 455
Fax (0164385) 388.

FROME • map 4B5

🍴 THE GEORGE HOTEL
Market Place, BA11 1AF

An old coaching inn, now completely modernized but retaining its original character. There is a choice of bars and a dining room where you can enjoy good food at very reasonable prices. The menu changes frequently to use the best of seasonal produce. The bedrooms are comfortable and attractively furnished with local wooden furniture. A cheerful, friendly hotel.
DOUBLE ROOM: from £30 to £40
FOOD: up to £15 CLUB
Hours: breakfast 7.30am–9.30am, lunch 12noon–2pm, bar meals 12noon–2pm, dinner 7pm–9.30pm, bar meals 6.30pm–9.30pm, closed January until February (inclusive) and weekdays in November and December.
Cuisine: ENGLISH – home-made soups and traditional recipes, à la carte, table d'hôte and bar menus. English cuisine, with char-grills a speciality.
Cards: Visa, Access, Diners, AmEx.
Other points: licensed, Sunday lunch, children welcome, afternoon tea, residents' lounge, pets allowed, disabled access, residents' bar, vegetarian meals, parking.
Directions: from the A36/361 west from Bath, travel to Frome. In town centre.
MR N.J. BICKHAM ☎ (01373) 462584.

GLASTONBURY • map 4B5

🍴 THE LION AT PENNARD
Glastonbury Road, West Pennard, BA6 8NH

Built around 1678, the Red Lion has been sympathetically restored to retain the original flagstone floors, log fires and beam and stone interior. The atmosphere is relaxed and friendly, enhanced by welcoming staff, and provides an

SOMERSET • SW ENGLAND

ideal setting in which to enjoy the excellent food. All dishes are individually prepared, beautifully presented and in generous portions.
DOUBLE ROOM: from £30 to £40
FOOD: up to £15 ☆
Hours: breakfast 8am–9.30am, lunch 12noon–2.30pm, dinner 7pm–9pm.
Cuisine: ENGLISH / CONTINENTAL – restaurant menu and bar snacks. Dishes may include breast of duck with cherry sauce, veal Portuguese. All dishes individually prepared.
Cards: Visa, Access, AmEx.
Other points: licensed, Sunday lunch, children welcome.
Directions: A361 between Shepton Mallet and Glastonbury in West Pennard.
BOB BUSKIN, LORRAINE JESSEMEY & PARTNERS ☎ (01458) 832941.

HOLTON • map 4C5

THE OLD INN
Near Wincanton, BA9 8AR

The Old Inn is a 350-year-old coaching inn with a small, intimate restaurant. The bar has an original flagstone floor and inglenook fireplace. The inn is situated half-way between London and the West Country.
FOOD: up to £15
Hours: lunch 12noon–2pm, dinner 7pm–12midnight, last orders 10pm; bar Saturday 11.30am 11pm, Sunday 12noon–3pm, 7pm–10.30pm, weekdays 11.30am–3pm.
Cuisine: ENGLISH – à la carte menu, extensive wine list. Four-course Sunday lunch if booked by previous Saturday. Wide range of bar meals, from sandwiches to steaks.
Cards: Visa, Access.
Other points: licensed, open-air dining, Sunday lunch, beer garden, pets allowed, coaches by prior arrangement
Directions: just off A303 in centre of Holton, one mile from Wincanton.
MARTIN & LINDA LUPTON ☎ (01963) 32002.

MINEHEAD • map 4B4

BEACONWOOD HOTEL
Church Road, North Hill, TA24 5SB

A 16-bedroom Edwardian country house hotel, which stands in over two acres of terraced gardens, with panoramic views over Exmoor and the sea. A warm welcome awaits you, and the quiet, friendly atmosphere guarantees a peaceful and relaxing stay. There is a bar decorated like an old country inn, a spacious dining room serving good food, and the accommodation is of a very high standard.
DOUBLE ROOM: from £20 to £30
Hours: breakfast 8.30am–9.15am, lunch 12noon–1pm, dinner 6.30pm–8pm.
Cuisine: ENGLISH.
Cards: Visa, Access.

Other points: children welcome, garden, pets allowed, special breaks, tennis, swimming pool.
Rooms: 1 single room, 6 double rooms, 7 twin rooms, 2 family rooms. All with TV, radio, telephone, tea/coffee-making facilities, alarm, baby-listening device.
Directions: close to St Michaels Church, off St Michaels Road.
MR T. ROBERTS ☎ (01643) 702032.

MONTACUTE • map 4C5

KINGS ARMS INN

A 16th century inn constructed of local stone and set in one of Somerset's most picturesque villages. It provides an ideal touring base for those wishing to explore the West Country, offering a relaxing stay in comfortable, attractively furnished accommodation. The elegant Abbey Room restaurant has a wide selection of classical and unusual dishes, complemented by a good wine list.
DOUBLE ROOM: from £30 to £40
FOOD: from £15 to £20
Hours: breakfast 8am–9am, lunch 12noon–2pm, bar snacks 12noon–2pm, dinner 7.30pm–9pm, bar snacks 7pm 9pm, closed Christmas day and Boxing day.
Cuisine: ENGLISH / CONTINENTAL.
Cards: Visa, Access, Diners, AmEx.
Other points: traditional Sunday lunch, parking, children welcome, no-smoking area, disabled access, afternoon teas, vegetarian meals, open-air dining, residents' lounge, garden.
Rooms: 8 double rooms, 11 twin rooms.
Directions: on A3088, 3 miles west of Yeovil, just off main A303.
MICHAEL & VICKI HARRISON ☎ (01935) 822513 Fax (01935) 826549.

PANBOROUGH • map 4B5

THE PANBOROUGH INN
Near Wells, BA5 1PN

A late-17th century inn situated in the hamlet of Panborough, and offering a quiet, relaxing atmosphere. The well-maintained frontage with hanging baskets and manicured gardens are a joy in summer. Good, traditional food in delightful surroundings!
FOOD: up to £15
Hours: dinner 6.30pm–10pm, lunch 11.30am–2.30pm, open all year.
Cuisine: ENGLISH – à la carte and table d'hôte menus offering a wide range of traditional-style dishes. Good choice of steaks. Vegetarian dishes also available.
Cards: Visa, Access.
Other points: licensed, open-air dining, Sunday lunch, children welcome, pets allowed, open bank holidays, disabled access.
Directions: situated on the B3139 Burnham-on-Sea/Wedmore/Wells road.
JOHN HALLIWELL & KENNETH HARGREAVES ☎ (01934) 712554.

RODE • map 4B5

⚞ THE BELL INN
13 Frome Road, BA3 6PW

Having undergone thorough modernization, the inn still retains the olde-worlde charm of yesteryear. The cuisine is traditional English and international, but the fish specialities come highly recommended. The superb wine list offers 28 wines from around the world to complement any dish selected. After a sumptuous meal you can relax in the comfortable lounge or bar over a post-dinner drink and take in the warm, friendly atmosphere.
FOOD: from £15 to £20
Hours: lunch 12noon–2.30pm, dinner 6pm–10pm, open all year.
Cuisine: INTERNATIONAL – an excellent reputation for speciality fish cuisine, and lobster when available.
Cards: Visa, Access, MasterCard, Switch.
Other points: parking, children welcome, garden, open-air dining, tradtional Sunday lunch, vegetarian meals.
Directions: follow A361 Trowbridge to Frome road for approximately 5 miles. The restaurant is on the right when entering Rode.
MIKE & LEZA PRICE ☎ (01373) 830356.

TAUNTON • map 4C4

⚞ THE CAREW ARMS
Crowcombe, TA4 4AD

Nestling in the Somerset countryside yet conveniently situated for access to the South-West, the Carew Arms is the ideal place to stay when exploring the West Country.
DOUBLE ROOM: up to £20
FOOD: up to £15
Hours: breakfast 8am–9am, dinner 8pm–9pm.
Cuisine: ENGLISH.
Cards: Visa, Access.
Other points: children welcome.
Rooms: 4 double rooms, 4 twin rooms.
Directions: off A358 Taunton to Minehead road. Situated 10 miles from Taunton, 4 miles from Williton.
MRS C. BREMNER ☎ (019848) 631.

⚞ THE CORNER HOUSE
Park Street, TA1 4QD

A Victorian hotel of character, situated close to the centre of Taunton. Lunch and dinner is served in the Parkfield Restaurant, offering food and wine of fine quality, and the staff are efficient and friendly. Close to Exmoor, Dartmoor, the Quantocks, and Yeovilton Air Museum.
DOUBLE ROOM: from £20 to £30
SINGLE ROOM: from £45 to £55
FOOD: up to £15
Hours: breakfast 7am–9.30am, lunch 12noon–1.30pm, dinner 7pm–9pm.
Cuisine: ENGLISH / FRENCH – including trout served with almonds and Chateaubriand. Good wine list.

Cards: Visa, Access.
Other points: licensed, no-smoking area, children welcome, open bank holidays, vegetarian meals, parking, residents' lounge, residents' bar, disabled access.
Rooms: 6 single rooms, 20 double/twin rooms, 4 family rooms. All with en suite, TV, radio, telephone, tea/coffee-making facilities, alarm.
Directions: A38, on south side of Taunton town centre.
MR R. IRISH ☎ (01823) 284683.

WATCHET • map 4B4

⚞ WEST SOMERSET HOTEL
Swain Street, TA23 0AB

A 2-crown town pub situated in the ancient port of Watchet. The hotel can arrange sea, freshwater fishing, clay pigeon shooting, golf and horse-riding. For fossil hunters, the local cliffs are of interest. Also an ideal base for cycling and walking holidays in Somerset and Devon.
DOUBLE ROOM: up to £20
FOOD: up to £15
Hours: breakfast 8.30am–10am, lunch 12noon–2pm, dinner 7pm–10pm.
Cuisine: ENGLISH – imaginative cuisine using local produce plus standard back-up menu and daily specials. Wine list includes interesting and excellent locally produced wines.
Cards: Visa, Access.
Other points: open-air dining, Sunday lunch, children welcome, pets allowed.
Directions: on the A358 in Watchet.
MR & MRS CLIFFORD & VICTORIA BARBER ☎ (01984) 34434.

WELLS • map 4B5

⚞ THE BULL TERRIER
Croscombe, BA5 3QJ

An old stone-built country pub with stone flagged floors, open inglenook fireplace and an attractive garden. With a reputation for good food and value for money, The Bull Terrier has an atmosphere which is warm and inviting to locals and holiday-makers alike.
DOUBLE ROOM: from £20 to £30
FOOD: up to £15
Hours: breakfast 8.15am–9am, lunch 12noon–2pm, Sunday 12noon–1.45pm, dinner 7pm–9.30pm, Sunday 7pm–9pm, closed all day Monday, 1st October until 31st March.
Cuisine: ENGLISH / CONTINENTAL – dishes include tuna and egg mayonnaise, scampi, turkey cordon bleu, spiced Brazil nut roast, hot butterscotch and walnut fudge cake.
Cards: Visa, Access.
Other points: licensed, Sunday lunch, garden, children welcome, real ales.
Rooms: 1 single room, 1 double room, 3 twin rooms.
Directions: on A371, in the village of Croscombe, east of Wells.
MR & MRS LEA ☎ (01749) 343658.

CROSSWAYS INN
North Wootton, BA4 4AG
Located in the heart of the country, off the A361 and midway between Wells, Glastonbury and Shepton Mallet. Overlooking the historic Valley of Avon and Glastonbury Tor. Advance booking recommended.
DOUBLE ROOM: up to £20
FOOD: from £15 to £20
Hours: lunch 12noon–2.30pm, dinner 7pm–10pm.
Cuisine: ENGLISH – full à la carte menu plus daily specials in the buffet bar, hot and cold bar meals.
Cards: Visa, Access.
Other points: Sunday lunch, children welcome, coaches by prior arrangement
Directions: on the A361 midway between Wells, Glastonbury and Shepton Mallet.
JOHN KIRKHAM ☎ (01749) 890237/890476.

FOUNTAIN INN & BOXERS RESTAURANT
1 St Thomas Street, BA5 2UU
Georgian-style building, 50 yards from Wells Cathedral, enjoying a local reputation for fine food using the freshest ingredients. Good selection of Spanish wines. Restaurant decorated with pine, local prints and Laura Ashley fabrics.
FOOD: up to £15
Hours: lunch 11.30am–2pm, dinner 6pm–10pm, closed Christmas day.
Cuisine: MODERN ENGLISH – local produce mainly used; lamb with redcurrant and rosemary sauce. Fresh fish daily. Interesting selection of West Country cheeses.
Cards: Visa, Access, AmEx.
Other points: licensed, Sunday lunch, children welcome, real ales.
Directions: in the centre of town behind the cathedral.
ADRIAN LAWRENCE ☎ (01749) 672317.

WINCANTON • map 4C5

HOLBROOK HOUSE HOTEL
Holbrook, BA9 8BS
A genuine country house hotel, set in 15 acres of its own grounds in unspoilt countryside. Behind the walled garden and dovecote lie the squash and tennis courts. The old orchard provides a delightful setting for the outdoor heated pool. A splendid wine list complements the interesting variety of well-cooked food. A lovely hotel that provides visitors with a relaxing and pleasant atmosphere.
DOUBLE ROOM: from £30 to £40
SINGLE ROOM: from £35 to £45
FOOD: up to £15
Hours: breakfast 8.15am–9.15am, lunch 1pm–2pm, dinner 7.30pm–8.30pm.
Cuisine: ENGLISH – à la carte, table d'hôte, using freshest ingredients available. Dining room open to non-residents for lunch only.
Cards: Visa, Access, Diners, AmEx.
Other points: licensed, traditional Sunday lunch, pets allowed, tennis, squash, swimming pool, games room, golf, riding, fishing, croquet, residents' lounge, children welcome, baby-listening device, cots, residents' bar.
Rooms: 7 single rooms, 4 double rooms, 5 twin rooms, 2 triple rooms, 2 quad rooms. All with radio, alarm, telephone, tea/coffee-making facilities, heating, baby-listening device, cots.
Directions: 1½ miles outside Wincanton off A303, on the A371 towards Castle Cary and Shepton Mallet.
MR & MRS G.E. TAYLOR ☎ (01963) 32377.

WOOLVERTON • map 4B5

WOOLVERTON HOUSE HOTEL
Near Bath, BA3 6QS
Woolverton House was built in the early 19th century as a rectory, and has been sympathetically converted to a splendid hotel. Set in its own 2½-acre grounds with scenic views, it offers all the facilities you would expect from an elegant country house. Surrounded by beautiful countryside, this is an ideal location for a leisurely break.
DOUBLE ROOM: from £20 to £30
SINGLE ROOM: from £35 to £45
FOOD: from £15 to £20
Hours: breakfast 7.30am–9am, lunch 12noon–2pm, dinner 7pm–9pm, closed 24th December until 3rd January.
Cuisine: ENGLISH.
Cards: Visa, Access, Diners, AmEx.
Other points: parking, children welcome, open bank holidays, no-smoking area, disabled access, pets allowed, residents' lounge, vegetarian meals, open-air dining, residents' garden.
Rooms: 3 single rooms, 13 double rooms.
Directions: 9 miles south of Bath on A36.
GEORGE & VERA WILKES ☎ (01373) 830415
Fax (01373) 830415.

WILTSHIRE

BRADFORD ON AVON • map 5G1

GONGOOZLER RESTAURANT
Bradford on Avon Marina, Trowbridge Road, BA15 1UD
This fully licensed restaurant is situated on the water's edge of Bradford's very own marina. The entire frontage presents a panoramic view of the water and the multi-coloured long-boats bobbing up and down in their berths. The beautiful wood panelling, beams and natural stone blend together in total harmony, creating an air of complete relaxation. A comprehensive wine list complements the good menu, offering great value for money in a spectacular location.
FOOD: up to £15

Hours: lunch 12noon–2.30pm, dinner 7pm–10pm.
Cuisine: ENGLISH – a good selection from a varied à la carte menu.
Cards: Visa, Access, Diners, AmEx.
Other points: parking, children welcome, vegetarian meals, no-smoking area, traditional Sunday lunch.
Directions: take the A363 from Trowbridge to Bradford on Avon. The Gongoozler can be found in Widbrook on the right-hand side, 200 yards from the bottom of the hill.
M. & D.J. GRIGGS ☎ (01225) 862004
Fax (01225) 862004.

RIVERSIDE INN HOTEL & RESTAURANT
49 St Margaret's Street, BA15 1BE
Overlooking the Avon River, this charming 17th century inn has a long tradition of hospitality and good service. Well located to serve as a base from which to explore the many nearby attractions, the Riverside offers comfortable accommodation and excellent home-cooking. Their succulent steak-and-kidney pies are renowned.
DOUBLE ROOM: up to £20
SINGLE ROOM: up to £25
FOOD: up to £15 ☆
Hours: bar meals 12noon–2.30pm, 6pm–10pm, breakfast 7.30am–9am, dinner 6pm–10pm.
Cuisine: ENGLISH – traditional home-made English cuisine. A la carte or table d'hôte menus available. Bar meals also available.
Cards: Visa, MasterCard, Switch.
Other points: open-air dining, Sunday lunch, children welcome, open bank holidays.
Rooms: 4 double rooms, 6 twin rooms, 2 family rooms.
Directions: into town centre and over bridge, first right turn.
NOAH STEFANICKI ☎ (01225) 863526
Fax (01225) 868082.

THE SWAN HOTEL
1 Church Street, BA15 1LN
A delightful, privately-owned hotel and restaurant, situated in the centre of historic Bradford on Avon, 8 miles from the Georgian city of Bath. The atmosphere is warm, friendly and relaxing. The bar has an excellent selection of well-kept real ales, wines and spirits, and the Moonrakers restaurant is widely known for superb food at sensible prices. The Coach House Room is available for weddings, functions and conferences, offering facilities for over 100 people.
DOUBLE ROOM: from £20 to £30
SINGLE ROOM: from £35 to £40
FOOD: from £15 to £20
Hours: breakfast 7.30am–9.30am, weekends 8am–9.30am, lunch 12noon–3pm, last orders 2pm, dinner 7pm–10.30pm, last orders 9pm.
Cuisine: ENGLISH / INTERNATIONAL – a varied menu offering an excellent choice.
Cards: Visa, Access, AmEx, Switch.
Other points: parking, children welcome, pets by arrangement, conference facilities, residents' lounge, open-air dining, vegetarian meals, traditional Sunday lunch.
Rooms: 2 single rooms, 6 double rooms, 2 twin rooms, 1 family room, 1 four-poster room. All with TV, telephone, radio, alarm, tea/coffee-making facilities.
Directions: situated in the centre of Bradford on Avon, next to the Avon Bridge. 8 miles from Bath.
JOHN & ANNE AMBLER ☎ (01225) 868686
Fax (01225) 868681.

WIDBROOK GRANGE
Trowbridge Road, BA15 1UH
An impressive building set in 11 acres, expertly converted to provide luxurious accommodation while retaining the atmosphere of a traditional English farmhouse. Inside, the decor and furnishings are elegant and provide the best in comfort. Widbrook Grange enjoys a welcoming, gracious atmosphere and is highly recommended as a delightful place to stay or as an elegant conference venue.
DOUBLE ROOM: from £30 to £40
SINGLE ROOM: from £35 to £45
FOOD: from £15 to £20
Hours: breakfast 7.30am–9.45am, dinner 6.30pm–8pm.
Cuisine: INTERNATIONAL – an evening meal is available Monday to Thursday. Fresh, local produce is used in preparing the daily changing menu. Orders for dinner are requested by 6pm.
Cards: Visa, Access, Diners, AmEx.
Other points: children welcome, residents' lounge, garden, conferences, indoor swimming pool.
Rooms: 1 single room, 10 double rooms, 8 twin rooms, 1 family room. All with TV, telephone, tea/coffee-making facilities.
Directions: 1 mile from town centre, 200 meters past canal towards Trowbridge.
JOHN & PAULINE PRICE ☎ (01225) 864750/ 863173 Fax (01225) 862890.

CALNE • map 5C1

LANSDOWNE STRAND HOTEL
The Strand, SN11 0JR
Situated in the picturesque market town of Calne on the edge of the Marlborough Downs, this original 16th century coaching inn with its courtyard and medieval brewhouse is of particular historic interest. Today, after thoughtful refurbishment, it offers many modern amenities, with well-appointed bedrooms, three friendly bars and an excellent restaurant serving imaginative fare. The area is steeped in history, and this is an ideal touring base.
DOUBLE ROOM: from £20 to £30
FOOD: up to £15 CLUB
Hours: breakfast 7am–9.30am, lunch 12noon–2.30pm, dinner 7pm–9.30pm.
Cuisine: ENGLISH.
Cards: Visa, Access, Diners, AmEx.
Other points: bar, children welcome, parking, disabled access, pets allowed, vegetarian meals.
Rooms: 22 twin rooms. All with TV, radio, alarm, telephone, tea/coffee-making facilities.
Directions: right in the centre of Calne.
MR TILSDEN ☎ (01249) 812488 Fax (01249) 815323.

CHIPPENHAM • map 5C1

THE CROWN INN
Giddeahall, Bristol Road, SN14 7ER

Formerly four cottages and a farm building with a small pub at the front, dating back to the 15th century. The interior has maintained its original style and has open log fires and beams, with brasses and farming implements. Offering farmhouse cooking and dishes from the Far East, it is very popular with locals and tourists alike.
DOUBLE ROOM: up to £20
SINGLE ROOM: up to £25
FOOD: up to £15
Hours: breakfast 7am–9.30am, lunch 12noon–2.30pm, bar snacks 12noon–2.30pm, dinner 7pm–9.30pm, bar snacks 7pm–9.30pm.
Cuisine: ENGLISH.
Cards: Visa, Access, AmEx.
Other points: parking, children welcome, no-smoking area, residents' lounge, vegetarian meals, outdoor dining.
Rooms: 1 single room, 1 double room, 1 family room.
Directions: from Chippenham proceed along the A420 for approximately 3 miles. The pub is situated on the left before the ford.
MRS I. OLDLAND & JULIE McCUTCHEON
☎ (01249) 782229.

THE JOLLY HUNTSMAN
Kington St Michael, SN14 6JB

Originally a village brewery and tap room, this 17th century Grade II listed building is now the highly popular Jolly Huntsman. With a very good reputation, the restaurant provides a good selection of traditional English country cuisine, cooked to the highest standards and presented by the friendly, helpful staff. The oak-panelled Colonial Room is the perfect place to relax over a quiet drink. A wide range of beverages is on offer, featuring up to seven real ales at any one time.
DOUBLE ROOM: up to £20
FOOD: up to £15
Hours: breakfast as required, lunch 12noon–2.30pm, dinner 6.30pm–10pm, open all year.
Cuisine: ENGLISH / INTERNATIONAL – 4 seasonal menus, and blackboard menu constantly updated.
Cards: Visa, Access.
Other points: children welcome, parking, pets allowed, residents' lounge, conference facilities, garden, open-air dining, vegetarian meals, traditional Sunday lunch.
Rooms: 1 double room, 1 family room, 1 four-poster room. All with TV, tea/coffee-making facilities, radio, hair dryer, trouser-press.
Directions: from M4, junction 17 toward Chippenham, turn right at first set of traffic lights on dual carriageway, then proceed for half a mile.
MICHAEL LAWRENCE ☎ (01249) 750305
[Fax] (01249) 758846.

NEELD ARMS INN
The Street, Grittleton, SN14 6AP

This charming 17th century Cotswold-stone country inn offers comfortable accommodation and delicious home-cooked food in the unspoiled village of Grittleton. There are four bed & breakfast rooms, three twin bedrooms and one family room. All rooms are en suite (bath or shower), with colour TV, tea/coffee-making facilities and a radio/alarm. The rooms are comfortable and cosy, in keeping with the rest of the 17th century inn. Each room is individually decorated, and no rooms are the same. A fine range of wines, spirits and traditional ales is available in the bar, which you can enjoy in front of open log fires.
DOUBLE ROOM: up to £20
SINGLE ROOM: from £25 to £35
FOOD: up to £15
Hours: breakfast 7am–9am, lunch 12noon–2pm, dinner Tuesday–Thursday 7pm–9pm, dinner Friday–Sunday 7pm–9.30pm.
Cuisine: ENGLISH – traditional home-cooked meals. Gluten-free food.
Other points: parking, vegetarian meals, children welcome, conference facilities, pets allowed, open-air dining, central heating.
Rooms: 3 twin rooms, 1 family room. All en suite.
Directions: 3½ miles from junction 17 on the M4, 2 miles from Castle Combe, Bath 14 miles, Badminton 3 miles.
NEILL & ELIZABETH SAINT ☎ (01249) 782470.

THE OLD HOUSE AT HOME
Burton, SN14 7LT

Originally a 17th century coaching inn built in soft Cotswold stone, with oak beams and leaded windows throughout. Offering good home-cooked English and continental cuisine, for which it has a renowned reputation, this is a truly up-market public house with a loyal clientele.
FOOD: up to £15 [CLUB]
Hours: lunch 12noon–2pm, dinner 7pm–8pm, Sunday dinner 7pm–9.30pm, closed Christmas day, Boxing day and Tuesday lunch.
Cuisine: ENGLISH / CONTINENTAL – good choice of meals cooked fresh daily; vegetarian options are available.
Cards: Visa, Access.
Other points: parking, open bank holidays, no-smoking area, disabled access, vegetarian meals, garden, open-air dining.
Directions: off A46 from Bath; or from Bristol, take M4 junction 18 to Acton Turville. Situated on the B4039.
DAVE & SALLY WARBURTON ☎ (01454) 218227.

THE THREE CROWNS
Brinkworth, SN15 5AF

A stone-built 18th century pub situated on the village green. There is an extensive menu with an emphasis on fresh produce. All dishes are cooked to order and served with a minimum of six fresh vegetables. The Three Crowns is justifiably proud of its award-winning cuisine. Good service and a relaxed, friendly atmosphere will add to the enjoyment of your meal.
FOOD: up to £15
Hours: lunch 12noon–2pm, dinner 6pm–

SW ENGLAND • WILTSHIRE

9.30pm, Sunday 7pm–9.30pm.
Cuisine: ENGLISH – blackboard menu changes daily according to the availability of fresh produce, e.g., locally smoked chicken, rack of lamb, steaks, fresh fish.
Cards: Visa, Access, AmEx, Switch.
Other points: licensed, Sunday lunch, children welcome, garden, pets allowed (in bar only).
Directions: on the B4042, next to the village church in Brinkworth.
MR A. WINDLE ☎ (01666) 510366.

CORSHAM • map 5C1

THE RUDLOE PARK HOTEL & RESTAURANT
Leafy Lane, SN13 0PA
A peaceful 19th century country house hotel set in 4 acres of beautiful gardens with extensive views to and beyond the Georgian city of Bath. The restaurant has received many awards for their wine and cheeseboard. Les Routiers Cheeseboard of the Year 1993, and Casserole Award holder.
DOUBLE ROOM: from £30 to £40
FOOD: from £15 to £20
Hours: breakfast 7.30am–9.30am, lunch 12noon–2pm, dinner 7pm–10pm.
Cuisine: ENGLISH – large fixed-price menus with freshly cooked food. Vegetarian and dietary meals available. Lounge food. Extensive selection of excellent cheeses and wines.
Cards: Visa, Access, Diners, AmEx.
Other points: licensed, Sunday lunch, no-smoking area, children welcome, pets allowed.
Rooms: 8 double rooms, 3 twin rooms. All with TV, radio, telephone, tea/coffee-making facilities. Twin rooms are furnished so they can be used as family rooms. All rooms can be let as singles.
Directions: on the A4 between Bath and Chippenham, at the top of Box Hill.
IAN & MARION OVEREND ☎ (01225) 810555
Fax (01225) 811412.

DEVIZES • map 5C1

THE BEAR HOTEL
Market Place, 1HS SN10
A 16th century coaching inn where you will find friendly, helpful service and many historic associations. Within easy reach of Bath, Swindon, Salisbury and a host of stately homes and gardens. Weekend breaks.
DOUBLE ROOM: from £30 to £40
FOOD: from £15 to £20
Hours: lunch 12noon–2pm, dinner 7pm–9.30pm.
Cuisine: ENGLISH – Devizes pie, roast joints carved at your table daily, charcoal grills in the Lawrence room.
Cards: Visa, Access, AmEx.
Other points: open-air dining, Sunday lunch, children welcome.
Directions: 15 miles off M4, A350 to Melksham, then A365 to Devizes.
MR W.K. DICKENSON ☎ (01380) 722444
Fax (01380) 2450.

THE WHEATSHEAF INN
High Street, West Lavington, SN10 4HQ
This family-owned 16th century coaching inn at the gate to the west of England offers guests comfortable accommodation, a full à la carte restaurant, classic English pub bars with real ales, and a suite designed for conferences and functions. To add to the pleasure of your stay, the inn is tastefully decorated throughout, and the helpful staff will always offer a warm and friendly welcome.
DOUBLE ROOM: from £20 to £30
SINGLE ROOM: from £25 to £35
FOOD: up to £15
Hours: breakfast 7.30am–9.30am, lunch 12noon–3pm, dinner 6.30pm–10.30pm.
Cuisine: ENGLISH / INTERNATIONAL – fresh fish and home-made pasta dishes are the house speciality.
Cards: Visa, Access, MasterCard, Switch.
Other points: parking, pets by arrangement, no-smoking area, residents' lounge, conference facilities, vegetarian meals, traditional Sunday lunch.
Rooms: 2 single rooms, 5 double rooms, 1 twin room, 1 family room. All with TV, radio, alarm, tea/coffee-making facilities. Most rooms are en suite.
Directions: on A360, 5 miles south of Devizes on the Salisbury Road, in the village of West Lavington.
MAUREEN DOWNS & ANDREA SLEEMAN
☎ (01380) 813392 Fax (01380) 818038.

FORD • map 5C1

WHITE HART HOTEL
Near Chippenham, SN14 8RP
Reputedly built in 1533 and listed as being of architectural and historical interest, this attractive West Country inn was featured in the film Dr Doolittle. In spring and summer, the terrace overlooking the Bybrook River is an ideal spot to eat, drink and contemplate the abundance of nature. The interior is pleasantly decorated, and there is a wealth of oak beams. The atmosphere lends itself well to the olde-worlde image, and the inn has a proud reputation for good food and ale at value-for-money prices.
DOUBLE ROOM: from £20 to £30
SINGLE ROOM: from £35 to £45
FOOD: up to £15
Hours: breakfast 7.15am–9.30am, lunch 12noon–2pm, dinner 7pm–9.30pm, open all year.
Cuisine: ENGLISH / FRENCH.
Cards: Visa, Access, Diners, AmEx.
Other points: licensed.
Rooms: 10 double rooms, 1 twin room.
Directions: situated on the A420, exit junction 17 or 18 from Chippenham.
MR & MRS PHILLIPS ☎ (01249) 782213
Fax (01249) 783075.

LACOCK • map 5C1

CARPENTER'S ARMS
22 Church Street, SN15 2LB
Originally a 16th century coaching house named the White Hart, the Carpenter's Arms is now a free

WILTSHIRE • SW ENGLAND

house and serves many fine real ales. The restaurant offers superb home-made meals, and the bedrooms have been decorated in the style of the 18th century. Situated in the centre of Lacock village. There are many tourist attractions within easy travelling distance.
DOUBLE ROOM: up to £20
SINGLE ROOM: from £25 to £35
FOOD: from £15 to £20
Hours: breakfast 8.30am, lunch 12noon–2pm, dinner 6pm–10pm, bar snacks available throughout the day, closed Christmas day.
Cuisine: ENGLISH – traditional home-cooking.
Cards: Visa, Access, Diners, AmEx.
Other points: parking, children welcome, no-smoking area, disabled access, residents' lounge, vegetarian meals.
Rooms: 3 double rooms.
Directions: take A350 from Chippenham towards Melksham. Turn left opposite the Garden Centre and follow signs to Lacock. The Carpenter's Arms can be found by taking the first left after the bridge in the village.
MR F. GALLEY ☎ (01249) 730203.

MALMESBURY • map 5B1

THE SMOKING DOG
62 High Street, SN16 9AT
A Grade II listed building with polished wooden floors, oak beam ceilings, Cotswold stone walls and a large open log fire, this most attractive pub has farmhouse appeal. Boasting a good reputation for quality and service in a friendly atmosphere, The Smoking Dog offers a tasty selection of meals accompanied by a good wine list.
DOUBLE ROOM: up to £20
SINGLE ROOM: from £25 to £35
FOOD: up to £15
Hours: breakfast 8.30am–9.30am, lunch 12noon–2pm, dinner 7pm–9.30pm.
Cuisine: ENGLISH / CONTINENTAL.
Cards: Visa, Access, AmEx.
Other points: children welcome, pets allowed, garden, vegetarian meals, open-air dining.
Rooms: 2 double rooms.
Directions: located at the lower end of the High Street, Malmesbury.
DAVID & SUSAN ROBSON ☎ (01666) 825823 [Fax] (01666) 825944.

MERE • map 5D1

THE BUTT OF SHERRY
Castle Street, BA12 6JE
A 17th century pub with atmospheric low ceilings and uneven floors, offering a fine selection of traditional home-made cuisine. Popular with locals and tourists alike. The staff are friendly and efficient, while the proprietor speaks fluent French and is popular with holiday-makers from France. An ideal stop-off point for touring the Wiltshire countryside.
FOOD: up to £15
Hours: lunch 12noon–2.30pm, dinner 6.30pm–9.30pm, open all year.
Cuisine: ENGLISH – superb home-cooking.
Cards: Visa, Access.
Other points: licensed, open-air dining, Sunday lunch, children welcome, pets allowed, parking, disabled access, playland.
Directions: on the B3092, situated just off A303 on the edge of the village.
PAULINE BASHFORD ☎ (01747) 860352.

THE TALBOT HOTEL
The Square, BA12 6DR
The Talbot Hotel dates from 1580 and is situated in the centre of the delightful Wiltshire country town of Mere, facing the square and the clock tower. Although the hotel has been modernized, it still retains the original features throughout. The stylish restaurant and bar have earned a fine reputation for providing good food at reasonable prices.
DOUBLE ROOM: from £20 to £30
SINGLE ROOM: from £25 to £35
FOOD: up to £15
Hours: breakfast 7.30am–9.30am, Sunday 8am–10am, lunch 12noon–2.30pm, dinner 6.30pm–9.30pm.
Cuisine: ENGLISH / INTERNATIONAL – traditional English, continental and Eastern cuisine cooked to a high standard.
Cards: Visa, Access, AmEx, MasterCard.
Other points: parking, children welcome, pets by prior arrangement, no-smoking area, conference facilities, residents' lounge, garden, open-air dining, vegetarian meals, traditional Sunday lunch.
Rooms: 1 single room, 2 double rooms, 1 twin room, 3 family rooms. All with TV, radio, alarm, tea/coffee-making facilities. Most rooms are en suite.
Directions: situated in the centre of the village, opposite the clock tower on B3095.
PETER & HELEN AYLETT ☎ (01747) 860427.

PEWSEY • map 5C2

WOODBRIDGE INN
North Newnton, SN9 6JZ
This popular 17th century country riverside inn, located in the tranquil Vale of Pewsey, is unique in offering the best of both worlds. The inn is busy and lively with a friendly atmosphere, yet not rowdy. The award-winning food and drink are imaginatively different and excellent. The rooms are comfortable and well-appointed, and you can really relax. Yet if you want to see the sights, you can make this location your ideal base: Stonehenge 15 minutes, Bath 55 minutes, Avebury 10 minutes, Marlborough 10 minutes, Salisbury 25 minutes, the South Coast 1 hour.
DOUBLE ROOM: up to £20
SINGLE ROOM: from £25 to £35
FOOD: up to £15 [CLUB] ☆
Hours: meals all day 11am–11pm, Sunday lunch 12noon–3pm, Sunday dinner 7pm–10.30pm.
Cuisine: INTERNATIONAL – a wide range of international dishes featuring Cajun, Indonesian, classical French and English, and Mexican

169

specialities such as sizzling fajita, vegetable chimichanga, chicken burrito. Traditional Sunday roasts. Reservations essential to avoid disappointment.
Cards: Visa, Access, Diners, AmEx, Switch.
Other points: licensed, open-air dining, Sunday lunch, children welcome, beer garden, pétanque pistes, caravan/camping facilities, conferences, cots, trout fishing.
Rooms: 2 double room, 1 twin room. All with TV, radio, telephone, tea/coffee-making facilities.
Directions: 3 miles south of Pewsey on the A345, on the roundabout.
MR T. VERTESSY ☎ (01980) 630266
[Fax] (01980) 630266.

ROWDE • map 4B6

THE GEORGE AND DRAGON
High Street, SN10 2PN
This olde-worlde 17th century village inn has a well-deserved reputation for quality and value for money. Owner Tim Withers prepares the delicious meals, specializing in fresh fish dishes, cooked to order and served in the same informal atmosphere whether in the restaurant, bar or garden.
FOOD: from £15 to £20
Hours: lunch 12noon–2pm, dinner 7pm–10pm, no meals Sunday and Monday, closed Christmas day, Boxing day and New Year's day.
Cuisine: INTERNATIONAL – fresh fish and other fresh food cooked to order.
Cards: Visa, Access, Switch.
Other points: parking, garden, open-air dining.
Directions: on A342 Chippenham–Devizes road, 1 mile from Devizes.
TIM & HELEN WITHERS ☎ (01380) 723053.

SALISBURY • map 5D1

ANTROBUS ARMS HOTEL
15 Church Street, Amesbury, SP4 7EY
Situated on a quiet thoroughfare, the Antrobus Arms Hotel is a traditional hotel offering a warm welcome, good food in both the bar and the renowned Fountain Restaurant, and comfortable accommodation with large public rooms and open fires in winter. There is a large Victorian walled garden with a three-tier fountain in the centre. There is excellent fishing nearby on the River Avon. Also golf and tennis. Stonehenge is only 2 miles from the hotel, and the cathedral city of Salisbury is 6 miles.
DOUBLE ROOM: from £20 to £30
SINGLE ROOM: from £25 to £35
FOOD: up to £15
Hours: breakfast 7.30am–9.30am, lunch 12noon–2.30pm, bar meals 12noon–2.30pm, 7pm–9.30pm, dinner 7pm–9.30pm.
Cuisine: ENGLISH – serving bar snacks, full à la carte menu and table d'hôte. Vegetarian meals available. Fresh produce and home-grown vegetables.
Cards: Visa, Access, Diners, AmEx, MasterCard.
Other points: licensed, open-air dining, Sunday lunch, children welcome, afternoon tea, pets allowed.
Rooms: 7 single rooms, 6 double rooms, 6 twin rooms, 1 family room. Includes four-poster Garden Room.
Directions: 6 miles north of Salisbury A345, half a mile off the A303, 11 miles west of Andover.
JOHN HALLIDAY ☎ (01980) 623163
[Fax] (01980) 622112.

FINDERS KEEPERS
Southampton Road, Landford, SP5 2ED
This cottage-style building is surrounded by well-kept grounds, which are lit up at night. It is decorated in a light, attractive colour scheme and comfortably furnished. Serving well-presented and cooked meals, the atmosphere is relaxed and is complemented by the soft tones of music in the background. Excellent value.
FOOD: up to £15 [CLUB] ☆
Hours: lunch 10.30am–5.30pm, dinner (Tuesday–Saturday) 6.30pm–9.30pm.
Cuisine: ENGLISH – a wide variety of traditional fare and local dishes, with the emphasis on fresh produce and all home-made sweets.
Cards: Visa, Access, AmEx.
Other points: licensed, Sunday lunch, children welcome, garden, afternoon tea.
Directions: on A36, on the left travelling west from Southampton.
KIM & SUZANNE SPROAT ☎ (01794) 390331.

GEORGE & DRAGON
85 Castle Street, SP1 3SP
A small family pub dating back to the early 16th century, within 5 minutes' walk of the city centre. Real ales, keg bitters, bottled beers and an extensive wine list are offered to complement the variety of meals available. Enjoy the riverside garden – or barbecue your own meal in summer.
FOOD: up to £15 [CLUB]
Hours: lunch 12noon–2.30pm, dinner 6pm–9pm, closed Christmas day.
Cuisine: ENGLISH – grills, roasts, salads and daily specials. All meals prepared with fresh vegetables and produce wherever possible.
Cards: Visa, Access, Diners, AmEx.
Other points: open-air dining, Sunday lunch, pets allowed, barbecues.
Directions: by the river in Salisbury.
JOHN & WENDY WADDINGTON ☎ (01722) 333942.

THE KINGS ARMS HOTEL
7A–11 St John's Street, SP1 2SB
Standing in the heart of Salisbury and surrounded by picturebook English countryside, this hotel is full of lovely old oak beams, slanting staircases and sloping floors. Evenings can be spent dining by candlelight in the informal atmosphere of the restaurant. The Snug Bar offers real timeless character, while the bedrooms are individually decorated to a very high standard. Stonehenge and Salisbury Cathedral are nearby.
DOUBLE ROOM: from £30 to £40
FOOD: up to £15

Hours: breakfast 7.30am–9am, lunch 12noon–2.30pm, bar snacks 11.30am–3pm, dinner 6pm–10pm, bar snacks 6pm–10pm.
Cuisine: ENGLISH / CONTINENTAL.
Cards: Visa, Access, Diners, AmEx.
Other points: parking, children welcome, Sunday lunch, no-smoking area, pets, residents' lounge, vegetarian meals.
Rooms: 1 single room, 3 double rooms, 15 twin rooms, 1 family room.
Directions: opposite St Anne Gate to the cathedral, in St John's Street.
MR & MRS R. STOKES ☎ (01722) 327629
Fax (01722) 414246.

PEMBROKE ARMS HOTEL
Minster Street, SP2 0BH
A Georgian-style hotel and restaurant, set in an attractive garden complete with a small stream. The accommodation is outstanding, and the restaurant offers very good food at reasonable prices. With welcoming service and a friendly atmosphere, the Pembroke Arms is well worth a visit.
DOUBLE ROOM: from £30 to £40
FOOD: up to £15
Hours: breakfast 7am–9.30am, lunch 12noon–2pm.
Cuisine: CONTINENTAL – dishes may include beef Wellington, duck à l'orange, scampi provençale, mushroom stroganoff.
Cards: Visa, Access, Diners, AmEx.
Other points: licensed, open-air dining, Sunday lunch, afternoon tea, residents' lounge, garden, 24hr reception, children welcome, baby-listening device, cots, vegetarian meals, residents' bar, disabled access.
Rooms: 1 single room, 5 double rooms, 2 twin rooms. All with TV, radio, alarm, telephone, tea/coffee-making facilities.
Directions: A36, opposite Wilton House stately home. Approximately 2 miles from the city centre.
MR R. TAYLOR ☎ (01722) 743328
Fax (01722) 744886.

SHERSTON • map 5B1

RATTLEBONE INN
Church Street, SN16 0LR
An old Cotswold pub in the time-honoured setting opposite the church. The lounge bar is full of nooks and crannies, while the roof of the dining room is festooned with tankards, water jugs and bottles. The Games Bar walls are covered with boozy cartoons, and the attractive walled garden has a boules pitch.
FOOD: up to £15
Hours: lunch 12noon–2pm, dinner 7pm–9.45pm.
Cuisine: ENGLISH – a wide range of meat, fish and vegetarian dishes, together with constantly changing blackboard specials, with fresh vegetables.
Cards: Visa.
Other points: licensed, Sunday lunch, children welcome, disabled access.
Directions: situated 5 miles from Malmesbury on the B4040 heading towards Bristol.
MR & MRS D. AND I. REES ☎ (01666) 840871
Fax by prior arrangement.

SWINDON • map 5B2

BLUNSDON HOUSE HOTEL
Blunsdon, SN2 3AD
In private grounds, with a 15-mile view to the Cotswolds, this hotel caters for every type of traveller. Family-owned and managed, with a pleasing, friendly, relaxed atmosphere.
DOUBLE ROOM: from £40 to £50
SINGLE ROOM: over £55
FOOD: up to £15
Hours: breakfast 7am–9.30am, lunch 12noon–2.15pm, dinner 7pm–10pm, open 24 hours.
Cuisine: ENGLISH – ranges from excellent bar snacks in Carrie's, via a fixed-price menu in the Carvery, to top-class modern-English-style à la carte in the elegant Ridge restaurant.
Cards: Visa, Access, Diners, AmEx, MasterCard.
Other points: leisure facilities include indoor pool, spa, saunas, steam rooms, sunbeds, beauty therapy, squash, tennis, and an immaculate 9-hole par 3 golf course, making Blunsdon very popular with families.
Rooms: 88 bedrooms. All with en suite, satellite TV, radio, telephone, tea/coffee-making facilities. Family rooms, four-poster rooms and suites available.
Directions: located at Blunsdon, 7 miles along the A419 dual carriageway north from junction 15 of the M4. If southbound on the A419, turn left into Broad Blunsdon at the top of Blunsdon Hill.
MR J. CLIFFORD ☎ (01793) 721701
Fax (01793) 721056.

TROWBRIDGE • map 5C1

EDWARD'S DINING ROOM AT HIGHFIELD HOUSE
High Street, Semington, BA14 6JN
This attractive Grade II listed 18th century Georgian farmhouse has been tastefully converted, while maintaining the style of the Georgian era. The restaurant successfully blends old-fashioned hospitality with the very best of modern English cuisine. Conveniently situated for Bath, Bradford on Avon, Devizes and Warminster, it is ideally suited for business entertaining, informal dining, special parties and overnight accommodation.
DOUBLE ROOM: up to £20
SINGLE ROOM: up to £25
FOOD: from £15 to £20
Hours: breakfast 7am–9.30am, lunch 12noon–2pm, dinner 7pm–9.30pm, Sunday evening and Monday open by booking only.
Cuisine: MODERN ENGLISH – the emphasis is on good food that is well presented and offers great value for money.
Cards: Visa, Access, AmEx.
Other points: parking, children welcome, residents' lounge, vegetarian meals, open-air dining.

Rooms: 2 double rooms.
Directions: situated on the A350 Chippenham to Westbury road, on the High Street in Semington.
EDWARD STREET ☎ (01380) 870554.

WARMINSTER • map 5C1

THE FARMERS HOTEL
1 Silver Street, BA12 8PS
Centrally located in the town centre, this family-run hotel, whose buildings date back to the 17th century, is comfortably furnished and decorated. The hotel offers good-quality food and accommodation in pleasant surroundings. Ideal for exploring West Country attractions, including Longleat and Stonehenge.
DOUBLE ROOM: from £20 to £30
FOOD: up to £15
Hours: breakfast 7am–9.30am, lunch 12noon–2pm, dinner 6.15pm–12midnight, last orders 10.45am.
Cuisine: ENGLISH / CONTINENTAL – English, French and Italian cooking, extensive à la carte and set menus and bar meals. Dishes include fettucine alla carbonara, veal marsala and steak-and-kidney pie.
Cards: Visa, Access, Diners, AmEx.
Other points: disabled access, children welcome, functions, coaches, parking, vegetarian meals.

Directions: situated on the A36.
MR G. BRANDANI ☎ (01985) 213815/212068.

OLD BELL HOTEL
42 Market Place, BA12 9AN
Part of the Old Bell dates from 1483, and much of the character and old-English charm has been retained while adding modern comforts. Enjoy the high standard of English cuisine in the candlelit restaurant, or good bistro and bar meals. On warm days relax in the attractive courtyard, or by the open log fires in winter. Luxury accommodation and excellent, welcoming service.
DOUBLE ROOM: from £20 to £30
FOOD: up to £15 CLUB
Hours: breakfast 7.30am–9.30am, lunch 12noon–2.30pm, bar meals 12noon–2.30pm, dinner 7pm–10.30pm, bar meals 7pm–9pm, closed Christmas eve until Boxing day inclusive.
Cuisine: ENGLISH / INTERNATIONAL – à la carte and bistro menus and bar meals. Mexican, Italian and American.
Cards: Visa, Access, AmEx.
Other points: licensed, Sunday lunch, children welcome, pets allowed, residents' lounge, functions, residents' bar.
Rooms: 3 single rooms, 11 double rooms, 4 twin rooms, 2 family rooms. All with TV, telephone, tea/coffee-making facilities.
Directions: in the centre of Warminster.
MERVYN PARRISH ☎ (01985) 216611
Fax (01985) 217111.

THE CHANNEL ISLANDS

For those seeking real solitude, the Channel Islands of Jersey, Guernsey, Alderney and Sark are the perfect location for a relaxing holiday or weekend break.

Guernsey may be very different from Jersey, but it still has an unmistakeably French atmosphere complemented by excellent cuisine ranging from classical dishes to shellfish and seafood specialities, from the highest standard of international dishes to daily changing selections of traditional English pub food. Vegetarian, vegan and other special diets are all adequately catered for.

For the ultimate peace, tiny Sark – known as the 'Gem of the Channel Islands' is unspoiled by aircraft or cars. The traditional and leisurely way to travel the island is by horse-drawn carriage, although bicycles may be hired for exploring the many superb cliff walks.

The range of accommodation is good, too: country manors set in rambling grounds, quaint farmhouses with cobbled courtyards, harbour-side inns, and modern hotels with every convenience. The Channel Islands has it all!

The following islands are included in this chapter:

ALDERNEY   ISLAND OF SARK
GUERNSEY   JERSEY

THE ISLANDS

ALDERNEY • map 4D5

INCHALLA HOTEL
St Anne's
A modern hotel with first-class facilities, including sauna, Jacuzzi and solarium. A pleasant and relaxing atmosphere in a hotel situated in lovely grounds overlooking the sea.
DOUBLE ROOM: from £20 to £30
SINGLE ROOM: single
FOOD: up to £15 [CLUB]
Hours: breakfast 8.30am–9.30am, Sunday lunch 1pm–2pm, dinner 7pm–8.30pm.
Cuisine: ENGLISH / FRENCH.
Cards: Visa, Access, AmEx.
Other points: central heating, children welcome, residents' lounge, garden.
Rooms: 4 double rooms, 4 twin rooms, 2 family rooms. All with satellite TV, radio, bar, telephone, tea/coffee-making facilities, heating.
Directions: at the edge of St Anne's overlooking the sea.
MRS VALERIE WILLS ☎ (01481) 823220.

ROSE & CROWN
Le Huret, St Anne's
Constructed of Alderney granite around 1770, this hotel is situated in one of the most attractive yet peaceful parts of St Anne's. It offers a friendly, homely atmosphere and is tastefully furnished to a very high standard, with added comfort. Picnic lunches are available to those who wish to spend the day walking, exploring or relaxing on the beach. Attractive garden.
DOUBLE ROOM: from £20 to £30
SINGLE ROOM: from £25 to £35
FOOD: up to £15
Hours: breakfast 9am–9.30am, bar meals 12noon–2pm, 6.30pm–9pm.
Cuisine: ENGLISH / INTERNATIONAL – traditional English pub cuisine, and a wide choice of international specialities. Daily blackboard specials. Vegetarians catered for.
Cards: Visa, Access, AmEx, MasterCard.
Other points: licensed, open-air dining, picnic lunches, children welcome.
Rooms: 6 bedrooms.

Directions: situated in the centre of St Anne's in a quiet area.
BASIL BLUMBERG ☎ (01481) 823414
Fax (01481) 823615.

GUERNSEY • map 4E5

🛏 IMPERIAL HOTEL, BARS & RESTAURANT
Pleinmont, Torteval, GY8 0PS

The Imperial has proved a popular rendezvous with tourists and locals alike for over 100 years, with its unequalled views of the west coast and safe, sandy beaches. The cuisine too is excellent, with seafood specialities and shellfish fresh from the bay. The main restaurant offers superb cuisine for that special candlelit dinner with fine wines and friendly service. In the bars, meals are served all year round; in the summer you can enjoy your lunch or supper in the garden or on the terrace.
DOUBLE ROOM: from £20 to £30
SINGLE ROOM: up to £25
FOOD: up to £15
Hours: breakfast 8.15am–9.15am, lunch 12noon–1.30pm, dinner 6.30pm–9pm, bar meals 12noon–2pm, bar meals 7pm–9pm, closed (hotel only) November until March.
Cuisine: FRENCH – traditional French haute cuisine with seafood specialities. A la carte, table d'hôte and bar menus.
Cards: Visa, Access.
Other points: licensed, Sunday lunch, children welcome, disabled access.
Rooms: 1 single room, 9 double rooms, 4 twin rooms, 3 family rooms. All with TV, telephone, tea/coffee-making facilities.
Directions: at south-western tip of the island, overlooking Rocquaine Bay.
PATRICK & DIANA LINDLEY ☎ (01481) 64044
Fax (01481) 66139.

🛏 LA GRANDE MARE
Castel, Vazon Bay, GY5 7LL

La Grande Mare, situated in its own grounds of over 100 acres, enjoys delightful views. Friendly, caring and efficient service complements the high-quality food on offer at this hotel, golf and country club. The restaurant specializes in seafood, shellfish and top-class à la carte cuisine, and an extensive wine list. Casserole Award winner 1990, 1991, 1992 and 1993; also Corps D'Elite.
DOUBLE ROOM: from £50
FOOD: from £20 to £25
Hours: lunch 12noon–2pm, dinner 7pm–9.45pm.
Cuisine: CONTINENTAL – fresh seafood, shellfish, flambé and the modern interpretation of classical dishes using the best of home-grown and local produce. Extensive wine list. *Restaurant of the Year* 1992.
Cards: Visa, Access, Diners, AmEx.
Other points: licensed, Sunday lunch, no-smoking area, children welcome, swimming pool, spa bath, golf, fishing.
Directions: fronts directly onto Vazon Bay. Only 15 minutes from St Peter Port and 10 minutes from the airport.

MR P.M. VERMEULEN ☎ (01481) 56576
Fax (01481) 56532.

🍴 LE NAUTIQUE RESTAURANT
Quay Steps, St Peter Port

Black oak beams and whitewashed walls adorned with various fishing items all add up to create a nautical ambience. Meals of the highest quality are served by friendly, efficient staff. Frequented by business people and locals alike, Le Nautique has its fair share of regulars: a tribute to the consistently good food and service. Established for 33 years, 18 of them under Mr Graziani.
FOOD: from £20 to £25
Hours: lunch 12noon, dinner 7pm, closed Sunday, closed 26th December until 10th January, open bank holidays.
Cuisine: SEAFOOD – fish dishes a speciality. Dishes may include huitres de sur epinars au currie, turbot grillé au poche – sauce hollandaise.
Cards: Visa, Access, Diners, AmEx.
Other points: private dining.
Directions: town centre; on seafront overlooking St Peter Port yacht marina.
CARLO GRAZIANI ☎ (01481) 721714.

🛏 MARINE HOTEL
Well Road, St Peter Port, GY1 1WS

A comfortable town hotel enjoying a delightful view of the harbour and islands. Guests can relax on the attractive sun patio overlooking the sea. There are many good restaurants offering reasonably priced meals within walking distance of the hotel, and the picturesque shopping centre is close by.
DOUBLE ROOM: up to £20
SINGLE ROOM: up to £25
Hours: breakfast 8am–8.45am.
Cuisine: BREAKFAST – packed lunches also, if ordered the day before.
Cards: Visa, Eurocard, MasterCard.
Other points: children welcome, vegetarian meals, picnic lunches, lounge.
Rooms: 1 single room, 4 double rooms, 3 twin rooms, 3 family rooms. All with TV, tea/coffee-making facilities, heating.
Directions: 30 yards from seafront and new marina. Off Glategny Esplanade.
MR & MRS CLEGG ☎ (01481) 724978.

ISLAND OF SARK • map 4E5

🛏 DIXCART HOTEL
Sark

Sark, an ancient, feudal and magical isle, is traffic-free and virtually untouched by the 20th century. Dixcart Hotel has played an important part in Sark's history, and today's visitors will discover the same beauty, flora and fauna enjoyed by Victor Hugo and others. Dixcart occupies the original 16th century feudal farm longhouse of La Jaspellerie Tenement and still controls its own extensive acreage of medieval hand-terraced gardens, fields, cliff paths and the densely wooded valley of Dixcart. The family-owned and managed hotel is open all year and offers its guests the very

JERSEY • CHANNEL ISLANDS

best facilities, service and relaxed atmosphere. You will never want to leave!
DOUBLE ROOM: from £30 to £40
SINGLE ROOM: from £25 to £35
FOOD: up to £15
Hours: breakfast 8.30am–10am, lunch 12noon–2pm, dinner 7pm–9pm.
Cuisine: LOCAL – Channel Island cuisine, especially fish and crustaceans.
Cards: Visa, Access, Diners, AmEx.
Other points: children welcome, dogs allowed, garden, bay, residents' lounges, conference facilities, open-air dining, vegetarian meals, afternoon teas, Sunday lunch.
Rooms: 3 single rooms, 7 double/twin rooms, 5 family rooms. All with en suite, tea/coffee-making facilities.
Directions: sited at the head of Dixcart Valley on the southern coast of the island.
☎ (01481) 832015   Fax (01481) 832164.

JERSEY • map 4E5

ANNE PORT BAY HOTEL
St Martin, Anne Port, JE3 6DT

Situated in the picturesque and unspoilt bay of Anne Port, this small country inn, taking 26 guests, is owned and run by a Jersey family. Over several years, they have built a fine reputation for excellent food and a high level of personal service and comfort. The beach is quiet, sandy and safe for bathing. There are many exciting places of interest to visit nearby.
DOUBLE ROOM: from £20 to £30
FOOD: up to £15
Hours: breakfast 8.30am–9.15am, bar meals 12noon–1.45pm, dinner 6.30pm–7.15pm, closed November until March.
Cuisine: ENGLISH – à la carte and table d'hôte menus, offering home-style cuisine. Vegetarians catered for.
Cards: Visa, Access.
Other points: licensed, children welcome, parking, residents' lounge, baby-listening device, cots, left luggage.
Rooms: 2 single rooms, 8 double rooms, 4 twin rooms. All with TV, radio, tea/coffee-making facilities.
Directions: first bay north of Gorey on east of Jersey.
MRS RUTH CAVEY ☎ (01534) 852058
Fax (01534) 857887.

BELLE PLAGE HOTEL
Green Island, St Clement, JE2 6SD

A small family-run hotel where personal attention is paid to guests by a friendly management and staff. A genuine seaside location. Cosy bar and lounge available for guests to relax in at the end of the day. Varied menus and a selected wine list are available in the restaurant.
DOUBLE ROOM: from £20 to £30
Hours: breakfast 8.30am–9.30am, dinner 7pm–8pm, closed October until March.
Cuisine: ENGLISH.
Cards: Visa, Access, AmEx.

Other points: children welcome, vegetarian meals, swimming pool.
Rooms: 20 bedrooms.
Directions: seaside location at St Clement.
F.B. HOUSE & W.B. YATES ☎ (01534) 853750
Fax (01534) 853894.

THE BERKSHIRE HOTEL & LILLIE LANGTRY BAR
La Motte Street, St Helier, JE2 4SY

Situated in the business district and near the yacht harbour, the main shopping precinct, park and leisure complex, this is an ideal base for touring St Helier. Offers good meals with an emphasis on fresh seafood, and comfortable accommodation. Frequented by mixed ages, the hotel enjoys a convivial atmosphere.
DOUBLE ROOM: from £20 to £30
SINGLE ROOM: from £25 to £35
FOOD: up to £15   CLUB
Hours: lunch 12noon–3pm, dinner 7pm–10pm, restaurant closed on Sundays.
Cuisine: CONTINENTAL – predominantly continental cuisine such as moules Lillie Langtry, fruits de mer, chicken camembert, lobster, daily specials.
Cards: Visa, Access, Diners, AmEx.
Other points: licensed, open-air dining.
Rooms: 8 single rooms, 24 double rooms, 24 twin rooms, 8 family rooms. All with TV, radio, tea/coffee-making facilities.
Directions: at top of main shopping precinct.
MICHAEL BARNES ☎ (01534) 23241
Fax (01534) 32986.

BRYN-Y-MOR
**Route de la Haule, Beaumont,
St Aubin's Bay, JE3 8BA**

A large Georgian house, set in well-tended gardens, with a magnificent view of the beautiful bay of St Aubin's. Friendly, attentive service combines with comfortable surroundings and a fine location. Its situation, just 200 yards from 3 miles of golden beach, makes the Bryn-y-Mor a must for all visitors, be it on business or leisure. Open throughout the year.
DOUBLE ROOM: from £20 to £30
SINGLE ROOM: from £25 to £35
FOOD: up to £15
Hours: breakfast 8.30am–9.30am, dinner 6.30pm–7.30pm.
Cuisine: ENGLISH / CONTINENTAL.
Cards: Visa, Access, Diners, AmEx.
Other points: children welcome, TV lounge, picnic lunches, pets allowed.
Rooms: 14 bedrooms.
Directions: on the A1, situated on the main south coast road.
MISS M.F. TEMPLETON ☎ (01534) 20295
Fax (01534) 24262.

COTE DU NORD HOTEL
Côte Du Nord, Trinity, JE3 5BN

Standing in its own grounds on the north-east coast, the Côte Du Nord has a spectacular view of the sea and surrounding country, and is within walking distance of the harbour and village of

175

Rozel. The restaurant is known locally for the high standard of cuisine and service it offers.
DOUBLE ROOM: from £20 to £30
FOOD: from £15 to £20
Hours: breakfast 8am–9.30am, lunch 12noon–2pm, dinner 7pm–10pm, closed Christmas.
Cuisine: BRITISH / FRENCH – à la carte, table d'hôte and bar menus. French cuisine: seafood a speciality.
Cards: Visa, Access, Diners, AmEx.
Other points: licensed, open-air dining, Sunday lunch, children welcome, afternoon tea.
Rooms: 2 single rooms, 4 double rooms, 2 twin rooms, 2 family rooms. All with TV, radio, tea/coffee-making facilities.
Directions: off the C93, on left towards Rozel.
MR HODSON ☎ (01534) 861171/861122
Fax (01534) 865119.

GLENTHORNE HOTEL
Elizabeth Place, St Helier, JE2 3PN
A welcoming hotel situated close to the town and beach. The Glenthorne is family-run and offers a friendly, homely atmosphere, good home-cooking and good value for money. The proprietors are always at hand to assist guests and to ensure that your stay in Jersey is enjoyable.
DOUBLE ROOM: from £20 to £30
SINGLE ROOM: up To £25
FOOD: up to £15
Hours: breakfast 8.30am–9am, dinner 6.30pm–7pm, bar 5.45pm–1am.
Cuisine: ENGLISH.
Cards: Visa, Access, Diners, AmEx, Eurocard, Switch.
Other points: children catered for (please check for age limits), pets allowed, afternoon tea, residents' lounge, garden, picnic lunches, safe facilities.
Rooms: 2 single rooms, 9 double rooms, 4 twin rooms, 3 family rooms. All with TV, radio, alarm, telephone, tea/coffee-making facilities.
Directions: 5 minutes' walk to St Helier and beach.
MR & MRS WAYNE & ANN RHODES
☎ (01534) 22817 Fax (01534) 58002.

GREENWOOD LODGE
Roseville Street, St Helier, JE2 4PL
Situated in a quieter part of St Helier, this family-run hotel is decorated to a high standard. The accommodation is bright and airy and more than comfortable. The quality food is prepared under the personal supervision of the proprietors. Staff are helpful and friendly, adding to the hotel's popularity with holiday-makers.
DOUBLE ROOM: up to £20
SINGLE ROOM: up to £25
FOOD: up to £15
Hours: breakfast 8.30am–9.30am, dinner 6.30pm–7.30pm, closed mid-November until end February.
Cuisine: ENGLISH – a good selection of traditional English cuisine, specializing in seafood.
Cards: Visa, AmEx, MasterCard, Switch.
Other points: children catered for (please check for age limits), pets allowed, vegetarian meals,

residents' lounge, open bank holidays, parking.
Rooms: 2 single rooms, 15 double rooms, 12 twin rooms, 4 family rooms. All with en suite, TV, radio, alarm, telephone, baby-listening device, tea/coffee-making facilities.
Directions: from Weighbridge, go through the tunnel and take second right. The lodge is the first building on the left.
HOWARD & SUE SNOW ☎ (01534) 67073
Fax (01534) 67876.

THE LOBSTER POT HOTEL & RESTAURANT
L'Etacq, St Ouen's Bay, JE3 2FB
A 17th century French-style granite farmhouse enjoying sweeping panoramic views of the Atlantic ocean. The restaurant is internationally famous for its cuisine and offers a mouthwatering selection of seafood. The seafaring name of the restaurant is reflected in the decor, and the walls are festooned with lobster pots. Excellent food in a friendly and comfortable atmosphere.
DOUBLE ROOM: from £30 to £40
FOOD: up to £15
Hours: breakfast 8am–9.15am, lunch 12.30am–2.15pm, bar meals 10.30am–6pm, dinner 7.30pm–12.30am, last orders 10.15pm.
Cuisine: SEAFOOD / INTERNATIONAL – lobster, shellfish, fish, steak and veal dishes.
Cards: Visa, Access, Diners, AmEx.
Other points: licensed, open-air dining, Sunday lunch, children welcome, afternoon tea.
Rooms: 9 double rooms, 3 twin rooms, 1 family room. All with satellite TV, telephone, tea/coffee-making facilities.
Directions: set on the seafront at St Ouen's Bay.
GERALD HOWE ☎ (01534) 482888
Fax (01534) 481574.

MILLBROOK HOUSE
Rue de Trachy, St Helier, JE2 3JN
This elegant Georgian residence has been sympathetically modernized and extended to create a hotel of outstanding character. The 10 acres of gardens and park and the stupendous views overlooking St Aubin's Bay give an immediate sense of ease, tranquillity, peace and quiet. Millbrook House is an ideal setting for an away-from-it-all restful holiday. Comprehensive menu, extensive wine list and comfortable accommodation.
DOUBLE ROOM: from £20 to £30
SINGLE ROOM: from £25 to £35
FOOD: up to £15
Hours: breakfast 7.30am–9.30am, dinner 6.30pm–8.30pm.
Cuisine: ENGLISH.
Cards: AmEx.
Other points: children catered for (please check for age limits), lift, special diets, vegetarian meals.
Rooms: 3 single rooms, 10 double rooms, 9 twin rooms, 2 family rooms. All with en suite, TV, telephone, tea/coffee-making facilities.
Directions: off the A1, 1½ miles west of St Helier.
MR G. PIROUET – G.T.P. (JERSEY) LTD
☎ (01534) 33036 Fax (01534) 24317.

MONT MILLAIS HOTEL
Mont Millais, St Helier, JE2 4RA

Set in own attractive terraced gardens, only 5 minutes away from town centre. Decorated in light shades of welcoming colours and offering accommodation of a high standard. The restaurant enjoys a friendly atmosphere in which you can indulge in a really good meal, made even more enjoyable by the excellent service. Highly recommended.
DOUBLE ROOM: from £20 to £30
FOOD: up to £15
Hours: breakfast 8.15am–9.30am, bar meals 12noon–2pm, dinner 7pm–9pm, closed January until April.
Cuisine: ENGLISH / CONTINENTAL – home-made soups and sweets. Fresh local fish.
Cards: Visa, Access.
Other points: licensed, Sunday lunch, children welcome, afternoon tea, coaches by prior arrangement, dry cleaning, picnic lunches.
Directions: from Howard Davis Park, approximately 400 metres towards Five Oaks.
COLIN KIRKHAM ☎ (01534) 30281
Fax (01534) 66849.

THE STAR & TIPSY TOAD BREWERY
St Peter's village, St Peter

Originally a small Victorian pub and now recently refurbished and extended, this is the first pub in Jersey to house its own brewery. Very popular with locals and families alike, and customers can view the brewery by prior arrangement. Nearby tourist attractions include a German underground hospital, a car museum and an excellent beach for surfing.
FOOD: up to £15
Hours: lunch 12noon–2.15pm, dinner 6pm–8.15pm.
Cuisine: ENGLISH – extensive menu offering steak, prawn, chicken, fish, salad and pork dishes. Children's menu. Chef's specials. Vegetarian dishes available. Good wine list.
Other points: licensed, open-air dining, children welcome, pets allowed, parking, garden, patio, disabled access, playland.
Directions: on the A12 in St Peter's village, near airport.
STEVE & SARAH SKINNER ☎ (01534) 485556
Fax (01534) 485559.

WATERS EDGE HOTEL
Les Charrières du Bouley, Bouley Bay, JE3 5AF

Set in its own terraced gardens in a commanding position of outstanding natural beauty. Panoramic windows in nearly all public areas take advantage of the vista afforded by Bouley Bay, the boats and the coast of France. There is outdoor dining in the beautiful terraced gardens, and a swimming pool, heated from April to October.
DOUBLE ROOM: from £40 to £50
SINGLE ROOM: from £45 to £55
FOOD: from £20 to £25
Hours: breakfast 8am–9.30am, lunch 12.30am–1.45pm, dinner 7pm–9.45pm, bar snacks 12noon–1.45pm.
Cuisine: FRENCH – à la carte and table d'hôte lunch and dinner menus. Wide choice of dishes and local fresh fish specialities. The hotel offers an extensive wine list and a selection of banqueting menus for up to 140 people.
Cards: Visa, Access, Diners, AmEx.
Other points: children welcome, pets allowed, afternoon tea, residents' lounge, garden, parking, licensed.
Rooms: 7 single rooms, 18 double rooms, 19 twin rooms, 3 family rooms, 3 deluxe suites. All with TV, radio, phone, tea/coffee-making facilities, hair dryer.
Directions: take the A8/B31 from St Helier; 300 metres from Trinity Church, turn left.
MR B. OLIVER ☎ (01534) 862777 Fax (01534) 863645.

CENTRAL ENGLAND

No other part of England offers greater variety of countryside, town or village than can be found in the 'Heart of England' – and the food is no exception either!

There are hundreds of places offering an unrivalled choice of excellent cuisine and the heartiest of welcomes. Choose from a superb combination of dishes with an emphasis on fresh produce: Shropshire chicken, Cotswold trout, beef Wellington, smoked quail, rabbit pie, Bakewell pudding, Ashbourne gingerbread, black pudding or pork pies from Melton Mowbray, followed by a tempting home-made dessert.

For those who prefer to eat informally, there is a superb selection of character inns displaying the warmth and comfort of a traditional pub combined with really excellent food for around a pound or two, such as hot pie lunches, filling salads and tangy ploughman's. And if you are 'guest-housing', start your day with a fine British breakfast – still an important part of our culinary heritage.

No visitor to this lovely part of England will have trouble in finding good cooking and a range of comfortable accommodation, with the accent on quality and service.

The following counties are included in this chapter:

CHESHIRE	NORTHAMPTONSHIRE
DERBYSHIRE	NOTTINGHAMSHIRE
GLOUCESTERSHIRE	OXFORDSHIRE
HEREFORD & WORCESTER	SHROPSHIRE
	STAFFORDSHIRE
LEICESTERSHIRE	WARWICKSHIRE
LINCOLNSHIRE	WEST MIDLANDS

*C*HESHIRE

ADLINGTON • map 8B5

LIBERTY CITY
London Road, SK10 4DU
The restaurant has an excellent reputation for all things American. There is an extensive bar (and cocktail bar open Friday and Saturday evenings) where you can enjoy a pre- or post-dinner cocktail or liqueur from the wide selection. Although this is a busy restaurant, the service is always warm and courteous and a fun-filled atmosphere prevails. There is children's entertainment every Sunday from noon until 3pm, and party nights with DJ or live band every Friday.

FOOD: up to £15 ★
Hours: meals all day 12noon–11pm, Sunday 12noon–10pm, closed Christmas day and Boxing day.
Cuisine: AMERICAN – food of the Americas, including burgers, steaks, ribs, Tex-Mex and chicken.
Cards: Visa, Access, AmEx, Switch.
Other points: parking, children welcome, no-smoking area, vegetarian meals, disabled toilet.
Directions: located between Poynton and Macclesfield on the A523.
LAWRENCE & DIANE WILLIAMS ☎ (01625) 829681. Fax (01625) 829681.

BROUGHTON • map 8B4

🍴 THE SPINNING WHEEL TAVERN
The Old Warren, near Chester, CH4 0EG
Old roadside pub, attractively furnished and decorated with copper antiques and brass horse artifacts. Freshly prepared traditional meals are served in a convivial, welcoming atmosphere. Friendly staff and efficient service make the meal complete. Good value for money.
FOOD: up to £15
Hours: lunch 11.30am–2.30pm, dinner 6pm–10.30pm.
Cuisine: ENGLISH / INTERNATIONAL – specialities may include 'sole spinning wheel' (with white wine, mushrooms, prawns and cream), tournedos Rossini. Blackboard specials change daily.
Cards: Visa, Access, Diners, AmEx.
Other points: licensed, Sunday lunch, children welcome, open bank holidays, functions.
Directions: on old main road from Broughton to Buckley, 6 miles from Chester.
MIKE & MAGGIE VERNON ☎ (01244) 531068/ 533637.

CHESTER • map 8B4

🍴 THE BLUE BELL RESTAURANT
65 Northgate Street, CH1 2HQ
The Blue Bell is Chester's oldest surviving domestic structure and the city's only example of a medieval inn. Dating back to the 15th century, the Blue Bell has been beautifully restored as a restaurant and displays a wealth of antique furniture, and a resident ghost. Serving fine English food combining tradition with imagination and noted for its extensive wine list, the Blue Bell offers discreet and efficient service and is the perfect venue for a relaxing lunch or evening meal. Excellent value for money!
FOOD: up to £15 🍷
Hours: lunch 12noon–2.30pm, dinner 7pm–10pm.
Cuisine: ENGLISH / FRENCH.
Cards: Visa, Access, Switch.
Other points: licensed, Sunday lunch and evening meals, no-smoking area, children welcome, garden.
Directions: 9 miles south of M53 and M56 intersection.
MRS GLENYS EVANS ☎ (01244) 317758.

🏨 CHEYNEY LODGE HOTEL
77–79 Cheyney Road, CH1 4BS
Half a mile from the city's Roman Wall, Cheyney Lodge was originally three houses. Recently completely refurbished, the hotel is now attractively decorated and provides good quality accommodation, a cosy bar, small dining room and separate lounge. A small, well-furnished hotel with a welcoming atmosphere and tasty, home-cooked meals, offering good value for money.
DOUBLE ROOM: up to £20
SINGLE ROOM: up to £25
FOOD: up to £15

Hours: breakfast 8am–9am, lunch 12noon–2pm, dinner 6.30pm–8pm.
Cuisine: ENGLISH.
Cards: Visa, Access.
Other points: children welcome, residents' lounge, ETB – 3 crowns.
Rooms: 5 double rooms, 2 twin rooms, 1 family room. All with TV, radio, tea/coffee-making facilities.
Directions: from the city centre, take A540 to Hoylake; left into Cheyney Road.
KEVIN DIXON ☎ (01244) 381925.

🍴 FRANCS RESTAURANT
14 Cuppin Street, CH1 2BD
A 17th century oak-beamed building within the city walls serving top-quality, exclusively French cuisine. Wide choice of dishes, whether you are looking for 'un petit morceau' or a whole feast. The wine list has been produced to complement their menus, and there is a wide range of French aperitifs and liqueurs. A friendly, relaxing and informal atmosphere.
FOOD: up to £15 🍷 🍷
Hours: à la carte menu 11am–11pm, plats du jour 11am–6pm.
Cuisine: FRENCH – provincial French cuisine. House specialities include traditional French savoury crepes, boudins and vegetarian dishes.
Cards: Visa, Access, AmEx.
Other points: licensed, children welcome, parking, air-conditioned.
Directions: off Grosvenor Road, near main North Wales roundabout and police station.
D. JOHNSTON-CREE ☎ (01244) 317952
[Fax] (01244) 342767.

🍴 MAMMA MIA
St Werburgh Street, CH1 2DY
A friendly Italian pizzeria with a lively atmosphere. Diners can watch chefs preparing and cooking pizzas in the traditional way in the open-plan kitchen. Popular with locals and tourists alike.
FOOD: up to £15
Hours: lunch 12noon–2.30pm, dinner 6pm–11pm, Sunday 6pm–8pm, closed Sunday lunch.
Cuisine: ITALIAN – authentic Italian dishes: pizzas, pasta, calamari, sirloin.
Cards: Visa, Access, Diners, AmEx.
Other points: licensed, children welcome.
Directions: next to the cathedral.
GIUSEPPE & ANNA LABELLA ☎ (01244) 314663.

🏨 REDLAND HOTEL
64 Hough Green, CH3 8JY
An exquisite hotel with a unique Victorian ambience re-created with genuine antiques, tasteful period furnishings and original wood panelling. Each of the rooms has been individually decorated. It has all the facilities of a large hotel but with great character, charm and friendliness. The Redland turns a night away from home into a special experience.
DOUBLE ROOM: from £30 to £40
FOOD: from £25 to £30 🍷
Hours: breakfast 7.30am–9.30am.

CENTRAL ENGLAND • CHESHIRE

Cuisine: BREAKFAST.
Other points: children welcome, pets by prior arrangement, residents' lounge, honeymoon suite, garden.
Directions: on the A5104, 1 mile from the city centre.
MRS THERESA WHITE ☎ (01244) 671024.

ROWTON HALL HOTEL
Rowton Lane, Whitchurch Road, CH3 6AD
A Georgian manor house converted to a hotel in 1955, 3 miles from Chester city. Set in 8 acres of gardens, the hall stands on Rowton Moor, site of one of the major battles in the English Civil War. The health and leisure club, Hamiltons, provides excellent facilities.
DOUBLE ROOM: from £40 to £50
FOOD: from £15 to £20
Hours: lunch 12noon–2pm, dinner 7pm–9.30pm.
Cuisine: FRENCH / ENGLISH – game (in season), local salmon and trout.
Cards: Visa, Access, Diners, AmEx.
Other points: licensed, Sunday lunch, children welcome, leisure centre.
Directions: just off the A41 Chester to Whitchurch road. Take junction 13 from M53.
S.D. BEGBIE ☎ (01244) 335262.

ELLESMERE PORT • map 8B4

BROOK MEADOW HOTEL
Heath Lane, Childer Thornton, L66 7NS
This mock-Tudor country mansion in a green belt area overlooks the hotel's 3½ acres of grounds on one side and market gardens on the other. An air of contentment pervades throughout the tastefully decorated, peaceful hotel and restaurant. The general atmosphere and the service are relaxed, informal and very friendly.
DOUBLE ROOM: from £20 to £30
FOOD: up to £15
Hours: breakfast 7.30am–9.30am, lunch 12noon–2pm, dinner 7pm–7.30pm, closed Christmas day and Boxing day.
Cuisine: CONTINENTAL – à la carte and table d'hôte menus available, also regularly changing specials.
Other points: children welcome, parking, no-smoking area, conference facilities, garden, open-air dining, vegetarian meals, afternoon teas, Sunday lunch.
Rooms: 4 bedrooms. All with TV, tea/coffee-making facilities, radio.
Directions: exit M53 at junction 5 and take A41 to A550. Brook Meadow Hotel is located on Heath Lane in Childer Thornton.
WENDY JONES ☎ (0151) 339 9350.

FRODSHAM • map 8B4

OLD HALL HOTEL
Main Street, WA6 7AB
This 15th century house has been beautifully renovated and modernized and is set among other old buildings in the centre of Frodsham. The restaurant serves an imaginative variety of dishes, all of which are beautifully presented and served by friendly, attentive staff.
DOUBLE ROOM: from £40 to £50
FOOD: from £15 to £20
Hours: breakfast 6am–10am, lunch 12noon–2pm, dinner 7pm–10pm.
Cuisine: ENGLISH – à la carte menu. Dishes include sea bass champagne, roast duckling cerises.
Cards: Visa, Access, Diners, AmEx.
Other points: licensed, open-air dining, Sunday lunch, children welcome, garden, afternoon tea, pets allowed, parking, residents' lounge, residents' bar.
Rooms: 23 twin rooms. All with TV, telephone, tea/coffee-making facilities.
Directions: M5, junction 12.
MR & MRS WINDFIELD ☎ (01928) 732052.

KNUTSFORD • map 8B5

KNUTSFORD PAVILION SERVICE AREA
Between junctions 18 and 19, M6 Motorway, WA16 0TL
When travelling along the M6 by day or by night, you can rely on the Knutsford Pavilion Services to offer a welcoming place to break your journey. Whether you require a light snack, a complete wholesome meal or simply to stock up on light refreshments, all your needs will be catered for.
FOOD: up to £15
Hours: open 24 hours.
Cuisine: BRITISH – international specialities also available.
Cards: Visa, Access, Diners, AmEx.
Other points: parking, children welcome, disabled access, vegetarian meals, forecourt shop, Burger King.
Directions: off the M6, between junctions 18 and 19.
MR S. PITHERS ☎ (01565) 634167
[Fax] (01565) 634742.

LONGVIEW HOTEL & RESTAURANT
Manchester Road, WA16 0L6
A period hotel, recently refurbished to enhance its Victorian splendour. With many antiques, this hotel offers a relaxed and comfortable atmosphere, from its open log fires to the quality of its award-winning restaurant and welcome. Just minutes away from M6 junction 19. Set overlooking the common in this attractive Cheshire market town.
DOUBLE ROOM: from £30 to £40
SINGLE ROOM: from £35 to £45
FOOD: from £15 to £20
Cuisine: BRITISH / CONTINENTAL – an ever-changing menu, which draws on the best of continental foods as well as the rich heritage of British cooking.
Cards: Visa, Access, Diners, AmEx.
Other points: children welcome, pets allowed, open bank holidays.
Rooms: 5 single rooms, 11 double room, 7 twin rooms. All with TV, radio, telephone, tea/coffee-making facilities, baby-listening device.

CHESHIRE • CENTRAL ENGLAND

Directions: junction 19 off M6, follow A556 towards Chester. Left at lights, left at roundabout.
PAULINE & STEPHEN WEST ☎ (01565) 632119 [Fax] (01565) 652402.

MACCLESFIELD • map 8B5

SUTTON HALL
Bullocks Lane, Sutton, SK11 0HE
Once the baronial residence of the Sutton family and more recently a convent, Sutton Hall has been sympathetically restored to create a unique 'inn' of distinction, affording the weary traveller superb food, good ales and truly sumptuous accommodation. The fully licensed lounge bar, open to non-residents, boasts a wealth of 16th century oak beams and three open log fires.
DOUBLE ROOM: from £40 to £50
SINGLE ROOM: over £55
FOOD: from £15 to £20
Hours: breakfast 7.30am–10am, lunch 12noon–2.30pm, dinner 7pm–10pm, open all year.
Cuisine: INTERNATIONAL – international cuisine: a changing range of fresh seasonal dishes traditionally prepared from the finest fresh ingredients. Fine ales and wines.
Cards: Visa, Access.
Other points: licensed, open-air dining, Sunday lunch, garden, pets allowed.
Rooms: 10 double/twin rooms. All with TV, telephone, tea/coffee-making facilities, trouser-press.
Directions: south of Macclesfield via A523, left at Byrons Lane, right at Bullocks Lane.
ROBERT BRADSHAW ☎ (01260) 253211 [Fax] (01260) 252538.

NANTWICH • map 8B5

THE MALBANK HOTEL
14 Beam Street, CW5 5LL
Situated close to the heart of Nantwich, this comfortable, well-equipped, family-run hotel is an ideal base for business or pleasure. The Malbank's attractively furnished restaurant has a good reputation for its attentive service, fine food and pleasant ambience. The recently refurbished bars create the atmosphere of a good English pub – an ideal place to meet friends and enjoy fine beers and a wide range of wines and spirits.
DOUBLE ROOM: from £20 to £30
FOOD: up to £15
Hours: breakfast 7am–10am, food served all day 11am–10pm.
Cuisine: ENGLISH – fresh home-made English meals are available in both the restaurant and the bar.
Cards: Visa, Access, Diners, AmEx.
Other points: children welcome, no-smoking area, afternoon teas, Sunday lunch, vegetarian meals.
Rooms: 11 bedrooms. All with en suite, TV, telephone, tea/coffee-making facilities.
Directions: located in Nantwich town centre.
CHRISTOPHER EVANS ☎ (01270) 626011.

ROOKERY HALL HOTEL
Worleston, CW5 6DQ
Rookery Hall is poised on a hill near the historic town of Nantwich. Built in or around 1815 by a wealthy English landowner, the house is set in 200 acres of gardens and pastures fringing the banks of the River Weaver, which ensures complete tranquility and the atmosphere of bygone ages. A visit is highly recommended.
DOUBLE ROOM: from £50
SINGLE ROOM: over £55
FOOD: from £25 to £30 [CLUB]
Hours: breakfast 7am–9.30am, lunch 12noon–2pm, dinner 7pm–10pm.
Cuisine: MODERN EUROPEAN.
Cards: Visa, Access, Diners, AmEx, Switch.
Other points: children welcome, parking, pets by prior arrangement, conference facilities, residents' lounge, residents' garden, no-smoking area, Sunday lunch, vegetarian meals.
Rooms: 45 bedrooms. All with TV, telephone, tea/coffee-making facilities, hair dryer, trouser-press.
Directions: from the North, junction 18 off M6, follow A54, A530 and A51, then B5074; Rookery Hall is one mile up the road towards Worleston. From the south, junction 16 off M6, then A5000, A51, B5074.
MR P. PARKER ☎ (01270) 610016 [Fax] (01270) 626017.

PARKGATE • map 8A4

THE BOATHOUSE
1 The Parade, L64 6RN
This is an establishment that certainly has a history. First recorded on this site was The Beer House in 1664. Today, The Boathouse has been recently refurbished and pleasantly decorated. Good portions of value-for-money meals are served in a quiet and friendly atmosphere.
FOOD: up to £15 [CLUB]
Hours: lunch 12noon–2pm, dinner 6.30pm–9.30pm, bar meals 12.30am–2.30pm, open bank holidays.
Cuisine: WELSH – classical home-cooking, which has won many awards. Dishes may include Welsh trimmed lamb with elderberry sauce, saddle of hare or barbary duck.
Cards: Visa, Access, AmEx, Switch.
Other points: licensed, open-air dining, Sunday lunch, children welcome.
Directions: 4 miles off M56; off A540.
MR JOHN CLARKE ☎ (0151) 336 4187 [Fax] (0151) 353 0230.

PARKGATE HOTEL
Boathouse Lane, L64 6RD
This Victorian country-style manor is warm and cosy, not only in its decor but also its ambience. The hotel is decorated to a high standard throughout, with constant attention paid to the appearance and facilities offered. The silver service restaurant is reputed for the excellent quality and value of the meals, made from fresh local produce.
DOUBLE ROOM: from £30 to £40
SINGLE ROOM: from £45 to £55

181

FOOD: from £15 to £20
Hours: breakfast 7am–10am, lunch 12noon–2.20pm, bar meals 12noon–7.30pm, dinner 7pm–10.30pm.
Cuisine: ENGLISH / CONTINENTAL – quality meals at value-for-money prices.
Cards: Visa, Access, AmEx.
Other points: parking, children welcome, pets allowed, conference facilities, residents' lounge, garden, no-smoking area, vegetarian meals, afternoon teas, traditional Sunday lunch.
Rooms: 1 single room, 10 double rooms, 12 twin rooms, 3 family rooms. All with en suite, satellite TV, telephone, radio, alarm, hair dryer, trouser-press, tea/coffee-making facilities.
Directions: the hotel is on B5135 off the A540, a few minutes off M53; 10 miles from Chester on the banks of the River Dee.
JOHN & JACQUELINE CAMPBELL ☎ (0151) 336 5001 Fax (0151) 336 8504.

DERBYSHIRE

ASHBOURNE • map 9B2

THE BENTLEY BROOK INN
Fenny Bentley, DE6 1LF
This traditional timbered inn, set in 2 acres of well-tended gardens, provides wonderfully cooked food using only the freshest produce – no frozen food here! With a daily changing menu, you will find their tasty main dishes with crispy fresh vegetables and home-made sweets a delight, especially when teamed with their comprehensive list of wines. Good accommodation and welcome.
DOUBLE ROOM: from £20 to £30
SINGLE ROOM: up to £25
FOOD: up to £15 CLUB
Hours: breakfast 7am–10am, meals all day 11am–9.30pm.
Cuisine: ENGLISH – dishes include savoury Derbyshire oatcake, prime steaks, selection of home-made sweets.
Cards: Visa, Access, Diners, AmEx.
Other points: licensed, Sunday lunch, children welcome, garden, pets allowed.
Rooms: 1 single room, 8 double rooms, 1 self-catering cottage. All with TV, radio, telephone, tea/coffee-making facilities.
Directions: on intersection of the A515 to Buxton and the B5056 to Bakewell.
MR & MRS ALLINGHAM ☎ (01335) 350278 Fax (01335) 350422.

STANSHOPE HALL
Stanshope, DE6 2AD
A 17th century country house with beautiful south-facing views, standing on the brow of a hill above Dovedale in the Peak National Park. The rooms are large and comfortable, featuring unusual decorations such as hand-painted walls. Atmosphere of a country house and family home, combined with the standards and features of a hotel. Ideal for walkers. 30 minutes to Alton Towers.
DOUBLE ROOM: from £20 to £30
FOOD: from £15 to £20
Hours: breakfast 8.30am–9.30am.dinner 7.30pm.
Cuisine: ENGLISH – 3-course dinner. Home-cooking and vegetables from the garden. Home-made chocolates served with the coffee. Vegetarians welcome. Light snacks available.
Other points: licensed, children welcome, pets allowed, garden, residents' lounge, payphone.
Rooms: 2 double rooms, 1 twin room. All with en suite, TV, tea/coffee-making facilities.
Directions: off A515 Ashbourne to Buxton road, in the hamlet of Stanshope.
NAOMI CHAMBERS & NICK LOURIE
☎ (01335) 310278 Fax (01335) 310470.

BAKEWELL • map 9B2

ASHFORD HOTEL & RESTAURANT
Church Street, Ashford-in-the-Water, DE4 1QB
An 18th century Grade II listed building with traditional oak beams and open fires. A family-run hotel with a warm welcome and personal service. Good food is beautifully presented in the restaurant, and a wide range of bar meals is also available. Behind the hotel and extending down to the River Wye is a large beer garden, a perfect place to enjoy a snack in summer.
DOUBLE ROOM: from £30 to £40
FOOD: up to £15
Hours: breakfast 8am–9.30am, bar meals 12noon–2pm, Sunday lunch 12noon–2pm, dinner 7pm–9.30pm.
Cuisine: FRENCH – specializing in fish dishes including salmon, Dover sole and trout. À la carte and table d'hôte menus.
Cards: Visa, Access.
Other points: licensed, open-air dining, Sunday lunch, children welcome, beer garden, afternoon tea, pets allowed, residents' lounge.
Rooms: 1 single room, 3 double rooms, 2 four-poster rooms, 7 twin rooms.
Directions: 2½ miles outside Bakewell, off the A6 towards Buxton.
JOHN & SUE DAWSON ☎ (01629) 812725.

BELPER • map 9B2

DANNAH FARM COUNTRY GUEST HOUSE
Bowmans Lane, Shottle, DE56 2DR
Dannah is a beautiful 18th century Georgian farmhouse, with its own tranquil atmosphere and character. The house has been lovingly restored and is renowned for providing its guests with the

very best in friendly, personal service. Enjoy a relaxing meal, imaginatively cooked and beautifully served in the unique licensed restaurant. Winner of the 1992 National Award for Farmhouse Cooking and of the ADAS/Sunday Telegraph award for excellence and innovation, Dannah has rapidly gained a reputation for good food and wine served in relaxed surroundings.
DOUBLE ROOM: from £20 to £30
SINGLE ROOM: from £35 to £45
FOOD: from £15 to £20
Hours: breakfast 7.30am–9.30am, dinner 6.45pm–7.45pm, closed Christmas day and Boxing day.
Cuisine: ENGLISH – imaginative menu, changed daily.
Cards: Visa, Access, Eurocard, MasterCard.
Other points: parking, children welcome, conference facilities, residents' lounge, no-smoking area, garden, vegetarian meals.
Rooms: 1 single room, 5 double rooms, 1 triple room, 1 family room. All with en suite, TV, radio, alarm, hair dryer, baby-listening device, tea/coffee-making facilities.
Directions: from Derby, take A6 Matlock road. At Duffield, turn left onto B5023 towards Wirksworth. Turn right at traffic lights onto A517 towards Belper, then take first turn left to Shottle. Bowmans Lane is 100 yards past the crossroads.
MR & MRS JOAN & MARTIN SLACK ☎ (01773) 550273/273630 [Fax] (01773) 550590.

BUXTON • map 9B1

THE HAY-WAY
35 High Street, SK17 6HA
At first glance this is an appealing restaurant with an attractive water garden right inside. Upon closer inspection, it is cosy and relaxing, offering a warm atmosphere, friendly service and, most importantly, delicious meals and good wines. Conveniently situated for Buxton Baths and Spa, Bakewell, Chatsworth and the Derby Dales.
FOOD: from £15 to £20
Hours: lunch 12noon–3pm, cream teas (summer only) 3pm–5pm, dinner 7pm–11pm, closed Sunday evening and all day Monday except bank holidays.
Cuisine: ENGLISH / FRENCH – a good selection of freshly cooked meals.
Cards: Visa, Access, AmEx.
Other points: children welcome, no-smoking area, vegetarian meals, traditional Sunday lunch, afternoon teas.
Directions: A515 from Ashbourne.
HAYDEN & KATHRYN TAYLOR ☎ (01298) 78388.

OLD HALL HOTEL
The Square, SK17 6BB
This historic hotel dating back to the 16th century has entertained thousands of visitors including Mary Queen of Scots. Overlooking the Pavilion Gardens and Opera House, it is an ideal base for those wishing to visit the theatre. Good food and comfortable accommodation.

DOUBLE ROOM: from £30 to £40
FOOD: up to £15
Hours: breakfast 7.30am–9.30am, lunch 12noon–2.30pm, bar meals 6pm–11pm, dinner 6pm–11pm.
Cuisine: ENGLISH – serving bar snacks, full à la carte menu and table d'hôte.
Cards: Visa.
Other points: licensed, open-air dining, Sunday lunch, children welcome, afternoon tea, functions, conferences, foreign exchange, residents' lounge, residents' bar.
Rooms: 38 twin rooms. All with TV, telephone, tea/coffee-making facilities.
Directions: centre of Buxton, past The Crescent.
GEORGE & LOUISE POTTER ☎ (01298) 22841 [Fax] (01298) 72437.

DERBY • map 9C2

HOTEL RISTORANTE LA GONDOLA
220 Osmaston Road, DE3 8JX
The Hotel Ristorante La Gondola is situated 5 minutes from Derby city centre, 15 minutes from the scenic Peak District. The hotel is elegantly decorated and very comfortable. Meals are cooked from fresh produce and served in generous portions, which are enjoyed by locals and holiday-makers alike. Staff are friendly and pleasant, adding to the relaxed atmosphere of the hotel.
DOUBLE ROOM: over £50
SINGLE ROOM: from £45 to £55
FOOD: from £15 to £20
Hours: breakfast 7am–9am, lunch 12.15am–2pm, dinner 7pm–10pm.
Cuisine: ENGLISH / CONTINENTAL – traditional English and continental cuisine. Dishes include pork cutlet pizzaiola, rainbow trout, roast duckling.
Cards: Visa, Access, Diners, AmEx.
Other points: licensed, children welcome, afternoon tea, conferences, baby-listening device, cots, 24hr reception, residents' lounge, residents' bar, parking, vegetarian meals, disabled access.
Rooms: 11 double rooms, 2 twin rooms, 7 triple rooms, 1 family room. All with TV, radio, alarm, bar, telephone, tea/coffee-making facilities.
Directions: the hotel is located off the A514 dual carriageway into Derby.
MR R. GIOVANNELLI ☎ (01332) 332895 [Fax] (01332) 384512.

HATHERSAGE • map 8B6

LONGLAND'S EATING HOUSE
Main Road, S30 1BB
Large country-style café/restaurant with exposed beams and wood floor, offering well-presented, generous portions of good food at excellent value for money. Situated in the main street of an attractive Peak District village.
FOOD: up to £15
Hours: breakfast weekends 9am–11.30am, meals all day 11.30am–5pm, dinner 6.45pm–9.30pm, closed evenings except Saturday.
Cuisine: INTERNATIONAL – the menu is

CENTRAL ENGLAND • DERBYSHIRE

half-vegetarian: vegetable and nut risotto, spicy chick peas. Old English beef in ale, steak teriyaki.
Cards: Visa, Access.
Other points: children welcome, afternoon tea, pets allowed.
Directions: off the A625, situated on the main road in Hathersage.
MR P.J.N. LONGLAND ☎ (01433) 651978.

THE PLOUGH INN
Leadmill Bridge, S31 1BA

A 17th century building on the banks of the River Derwent in the midst of the Peak District. The cosy atmosphere, log fires and excellent restaurant ensure its popularity with tourists and visitors to the National Parks area.
DOUBLE ROOM: from £20 to £30
FOOD: from £15 to £20
Hours: breakfast 8am–9.15am, lunch 11.30am–2.30pm, dinner 6.30pm–9.30pm.
Cuisine: ENGLISH – traditional home-cooking.
Cards: Visa, Access, Switch.
Other points: children welcome, traditional Sunday lunch, vegetarian meals, no pets allowed, parking.
Rooms: 3 bedrooms.
Directions: situated 1 mile from centre of Hathersage village.
MR R. EMERY ☎ (01433) 650319 Fax (01433) 650180.

KEGWORTH • map 9C2

KEGWORTH HOTEL
Packington Hill, DE74 2DF

The Kegworth Hotel is situated on the A6 in a quiet village setting, ideally positioned near Loughborough, Nottingham, Derby and Leicester and conveniently located for Alton Towers, Nottingham Castle, Mount St Bernard's Abbey and American Adventure. A warm welcome awaits you at this well-appointed, confortable hotel, and the helpful staff are always willing to assist you, whether your stay is for a weekend break, a holiday or a business conference.
DOUBLE ROOM: from £20 to £30
SINGLE ROOM: from £35 to £45
FOOD: up to £15 ☆
Hours: breakfast 7am–9.30am, lunch 12.30am–2pm, dinner 7pm–9.30pm, bar snacks available all day.
Cuisine: ENGLISH / INTERNATIONAL.
Cards: Visa, Access, AmEx.
Other points: parking, children welcome, disabled access, pets allowed, residents' lounge, vegetarian meals, traditional Sunday lunch, open-air dining, conference facilities, swimming pool, Jacuzzi, solarium, gym, sauna, squash, function suite.
Rooms: 6 single rooms, 33 double rooms, 13 twin rooms. All with en suite, TV, telephone, radio, alarm, hair dryer, tea/coffee-making facilities.
Directions: situated on the A6, just south of junction 24 (M1).
JOHN MARSHALL ☎ (01509) 672427
Fax (01509) 674664.

MATLOCK • map 9B2

BOWLING GREEN INN
East Bank, Winster, DE4 2ES

Situated in a popular and picturesque Derbyshire village, the Bowling Green Inn is thought to be of 15th century origin, with a characteristic fireplace. Along with the resident ghost, Dave and Marilyn Bentley extend a warm and friendly welcome to all. The inn is centrally located when touring nearby attractions, such as Chatsworth House, Haddon Hall, Tissington and Dove Dale.
FOOD: up to £15
Hours: lunch (weekends only) 12noon–2pm, meals from 6pm, Sunday from 7pm, bar open all day Saturday.
Cuisine: ENGLISH – good selection with fresh daily specials, including vegetarian speciality dishes. Traditional Sunday roast of beef, lamb or pork. Good selection of home-made sweets.
Cards: Visa, Access.
Other points: open-air dining, Sunday lunch, children welcome, disabled access, parking, open bank holidays, vegetarian meals, garden.
Directions: from Matlock, take A6 north for 1½ miles. Turn left onto B5057 for 2½ miles.
DAVID & MARILYN BENTLEY ☎ (01629) 650219.

THE ELIZABETHAN RESTAURANT
4 Crown Square, DE4 3AT

This attractive restaurant is located right in the centre of the picturesque town of Matlock on the A6. It offers a warm, friendly welcome and excellent food in idyllic surroundings.
FOOD: up to £15
Hours: morning coffee 10am–12noon, lunch 12noon–3pm, afternoon tea 3pm–5pm, dinner 7.30pm–10pm, open every day.
Cuisine: ENGLISH / CONTINENTAL – steak-and-kidney pie, savoury filled pancakes. Home-made continental dishes. Roasts daily.
Cards: Visa, Access.
Other points: Sunday lunch, children welcome, coaches by prior arrangement
Directions: on the A6 in the centre of town.
MR G.E. FAULKNER ☎ (01629) 583533.

THE JARVIS PEACOCK HOTEL
Rowsley, DE4 2EB

This imposing 17th century country house is beautifully decorated throughout and adorned with antiques of interest. Here you can enjoy traditional English food in the Garden Restaurant, a relaxing drink in the Peacock Bar and charming bedrooms to unwind in. The hotel is the perfect setting for weddings, conferences and that much-needed break away.
DOUBLE ROOM: from £40 to £50
SINGLE ROOM: from £55
FOOD: from £20 to £25
Hours: breakfast 7.30am–9.30am, lunch 12.30am–2pm, dinner 7pm–9pm.
Cuisine: ENGLISH – traditional cuisine of a very high standard.
Cards: Visa, Access, Diners, AmEx, Switch.
Other points: parking, children welcome, pets

allowed, conference facilities, vegetarian meals, traditional Sunday lunch, afternoon teas.
Rooms: 14 bedrooms. All with en suite, TV, telephone, radio, alarm, hair dryer, trouser-press, room service, tea/coffee-making facilities.
Directions: off A6, midway between Matlock and Bakewell in the centre of Rowsley.
PAT A. GILLSON ☎ (01629) 733518
Fax (01629) 732671.

SUNNYBANK GUEST HOUSE
37 Clifton Road, Matlock Bath, DE4 3PW
This attractive Victorian house offers guests comfortable accommodation, wonderful home-cooked meals and friendly service in a homely atmosphere. This is an ideal base to discover the many attractions nearby. Local activities include walking, climbing, fishing, sailing, canoeing, caving, horse-riding – the list just goes on and on! Well worth a visit.
DOUBLE ROOM: from £20 to £30
SINGLE ROOM: up to £25
FOOD: up to £15
Hours: breakfast 8.30am (or earlier by arrangement), dinner 7pm (residents only), closed 24th December until 27th December.
Cuisine: ENGLISH.
Cards: Visa, Access.
Other points: children catered for (please check for age limits), no-smoking area, residents' lounge, garden, vegetarian meals.
Rooms: 1 single room, 2 double rooms, 2 twin rooms. All with tea/coffee-making facilities. Some rooms have TV.
Directions: from Matlock, travel south along A6 towards Derby. At southern end of Matlock Bath, just before the New Bath Hotel, turn right into Clifton Road: 250 yards on left.
PETER & DAPHNE WEST ☎ (01629) 584621.

LES ROUTIERS
Your assurance of Quality and Value

THE TAVERN AT TANSLEY
Nottingham Road, Tansley, DE4 5FR
Situated in the midst of the delightful village of Tansley, this 18th century inn offers guests excellent service, whether enjoying a traditional bar meal in the charming lounge bar or a sumptuous meal in the restaurant. The Tavern At Tansley is an ideal place to use as a base for exploring the Peak District.
DOUBLE ROOM: from £20 to £30
FOOD: from £15 to £20
Hours: breakfast 7.30am–9.30am, lunch 12noon–2.30pm, dinner 6.30pm–9.15pm.
Cuisine: ENGLISH – varied menu including vegetarian.
Cards: Visa, Access.
Other points: parking, children welcome, vegetarian meals, traditional Sunday lunch.

Rooms: 2 double rooms, 1 twin room. All with TV, tea/coffee-making facilities.
Directions: located on the A615 between Matlock and Alfreton.
ERIC & INGEBORG TRAVIS ☎ (01629) 57735.

SPINKHILL • map 8B6

PARK HALL HOTEL
Near Sheffield, S31 9YD
This magnificent 16th century manor house, set in beautiful gardens, has recently had extensive restoration work and careful modernization carried out in order to preserve the most interesting features but provide guests with modern, luxurious accommodation. Occasions of all kinds are catered for, from an intimate dinner for two to conferences, wedding receptions and business lunches. A highly rated hotel.
DOUBLE ROOM: from £30 to £40
SINGLE ROOM: from £55
FOOD: from £20 to £25
Hours: breakfast 7.30am–9.30am, Sunday luncheon 12.30am–2pm, bar meals 12.30am–2pm, dinner 7.30pm–9.45pm, open all year.
Cuisine: MODERN ENGLISH – an extensive menu based on fresh local produce.
Cards: Visa, Access, Diners, AmEx.
Other points: parking, children catered for (please check for age limits), no-smoking area, garden, conference facilities, vegetarian meals, traditional Sunday lunch.
Rooms: 5 double rooms, 3 twin rooms. All with en suite, TV, telephone, radio, alarm, trouser press, tea/coffee-making facilities.
Directions: take M1 to junction 30, follow A616 to Blacksmiths Arms, turn right to Spinkhill, follow road to village and turn right at the crossroads to hotel. Four minutes from M1.
MRS JAN CLARK ☎ (01246) 434897
Fax (01246) 436282.

WIRKSWORTH • map 9B2

LE BISTRO
13 St John Street, DE4 4DR
Built in 1760, this is a candlelit cellar restaurant approached by a spiral staircase from the reception bar. Situated in the centre of this quaint market town, the freshly prepared, rural French-style cuisine is very popular. The friendly, efficent service complements a wonderful meal. International evenings monthly. Highly recommended.
FOOD: from £15 to £20
Hours: dinner 6.30pm–9.30pm, closed Sunday.
Cuisine: FRENCH – sauce dishes, such as half Norfolk duckling in Grand Marnier and fresh orange sauce, steaks, seafood and an extensive vegetarian menu. Game in season.
Cards: Visa, Access, Diners, AmEx.
Other points: licensed, parking.
Directions: in the centre of Wirksworth, opposite Lloyds Bank.
MARK FOX ☎ (01629) 823344.

GLOUCESTERSHIRE

BOURTON-ON-THE-WATER
map 4A6

BO-PEEP TEA ROOMS
Riverside, GL54 2DP

'Olde worlde' riverside tea rooms and licensed restaurant. The spacious interior has fitted carpets, panelling and exposed Cotswold stone walls. A homely, comfortable atmosphere prevails and the service is efficient and welcoming. All dishes are freshly cooked, well-served and presented. The menu offers a good choice including vegetarian dishes. A beautiful setting. Chosen by the Tea Council as one of the top ten places in Britain for 1992, 1993 and 1994.
FOOD: up to £15
Hours: summer 10am–8pm, winter (closed some weekdays) 10am–5.30pm.
Cuisine: ENGLISH – home-made. Large Cornish clotted-cream teas.
Cards: Visa, Access, Diners, AmEx.
Other points: licensed, Sunday lunch, no-smoking area, children welcome, afternoon tea, pets allowed, open bank holidays.
Directions: off A429 Fosse Way. Opposite side of river to village green.
JUDY & BOB HISCOKE ☎ (01451) 822005.

THE OLD MANSE HOTEL
Victoria Street, GL54 2BX

Built in 1748 as the home of the Reverend Benjamin Beddome, the village's Baptist pastor, this traditional Grade II listed Cotswold stone building stands on the south bank of the River Windrush, which flows leisurely by. A spacious 60-seater restaurant, elegantly decorated and furnished, offers excellent cuisine, using fresh local produce wherever possible, complemented by an extensive wine list. Special dishes can be prepared on request. Places of interest within the village include Birdland, perfumery, motor museum, model village and model railway exhibition.
DOUBLE ROOM: from £20 to £30
SINGLE ROOM: from £35 to £45
FOOD: from £15 to £20
Hours: breakfast 8am–9am, Sunday 8.30am–9.30am, Sunday lunch 12noon–2.30pm, bar meals 11.30am–2.30pm, Sunday 11am–2.30pm, dinner and bar meals 6pm–9pm, Sunday 7pm–9pm, bar 11am–11pm, Sunday 11am–3pm, 7pm–10.30pm.
Cuisine: ENGLISH / FRENCH.
Cards: Visa, Access, Diners, AmEx.
Other points: children welcome, parking, disabled access, pets, residents' lounge, garden, vegetarian meals, open-air dining.
Rooms: 12 bedrooms. All with TV, telephone, tea/coffee-making facilities.
Directions: Bourton-on-the-Water is off the A429 (Fosse Way) running between Stow-on-the-Wold and Cirencester. The hotel is located in the conservation area in the centre of the village.

stands on the river bank, overlooking the village green and the high street.
OSWALD & AUDREY DOCKERY ☎ (01451) 820082 Fax (01451) 810381.

OLD NEW INN
GL54 2AS

A traditional country inn built in 1709, situated in the heart of the Cotswolds on the banks of the River Windrush and set in attractive gardens. Antique furnishings, warming log fires and traditional home-cooking set the atmosphere. Run by the Morris family for over 60 years.
DOUBLE ROOM: from £30 to £40
SINGLE ROOM: from £25 to £35
FOOD: up to £15
Hours: breakfast 8.15am–9.15am, lunch 12.30pm–1.30pm, dinner 7.30pm–8.30pm, closed Christmas day.
Cuisine: ENGLISH – traditional home-cooking.
Cards: Visa, Access.
Other points: open-air dining, Sunday lunch, children welcome, pets allowed.
Rooms: 1 single room, 7 double rooms, 4 twin rooms. All with TV, tea/coffee-making facilities.
Directions: off the A429. Turn off Fosse Way down to the high street.
PETER MORRIS ☎ (01451) 820467 Fax (01451) 810236.

CAMBRIDGE • map 4A5

THE GEORGE INN
Bristol Road, CB2 4AG

Nestling on the banks of the River Cam, The George Inn is the ideal stepping stone to many of Gloucestershire's premier tourist attractions. The oak-beamed dining areas have a unique style, with tables made from original Singer sewing-machine treadles. Meals also available in the garden or on the patio.
FOOD: up to £15 CLUB
Hours: lunch 12noon–2pm, dinner 7pm–11pm, last orders 10pm.
Cuisine: ENGLISH / INTERNATIONAL – from traditional Gloucestershire fare to international cuisine.
Cards: Visa, Access, Diners, AmEx.
Other points: licensed, open-air dining, Sunday lunch, children welcome, garden, coaches by prior arrangement
Directions: on the A38, 3 miles south of junction 13, M5.
ALISTAIR & JANE DEAS ☎ (01453) 890270.

CHELTENHAM • map 4A6

BELOW STAIRS RESTAURANT
103 Promenade, GL50 1NW

Situated in the town centre, with front entrance from the Promenade and rear access with evening

GLOUCESTERSHIRE • CENTRAL ENGLAND

and weekend parking in Montpellier Street. Cooking is personally supervised by the chef/proprietor.
FOOD: up to £15 [CLUB] ☆
Hours: lunch 12noon, dinner 6pm, closed Sunday, closed bank holidays.
Cuisine: ENGLISH / SEAFOOD – fresh seafood is a speciality. Traditional cooking and fresh vegetables. Vegetarian and vegan dishes are available.
Cards: Visa, Access, Diners, AmEx.
Other points: open-air dining, no-smoking area, children welcome.
Directions: in the town centre.
MR J.B. LINTON ☎ (01242) 234599.

COTSWOLD GRANGE HOTEL
Pittville Circus Road, GL52 2QH
Built as the fine country house of a London solicitor, this attractive, mellow, Cotswold-stone building is set in a tree-lined avenue in a pleasant location close to the centre of Cheltenham. The hotel is a friendly, family-run establishment and offers quality food and accommodation at excellent prices.
DOUBLE ROOM: from £20 to £30
SINGLE ROOM: from £35 to £45
FOOD: up to £15
Hours: breakfast 7.15am–9am, lunch 12noon–2pm, dinner 6pm–7.30pm, restaurant closed after breakfast on Sundays, hotel closed Christmas to New Year.
Cuisine: ENGLISH.
Cards: Visa, Access, Diners, AmEx.
Other points: licensed, no-smoking area, children welcome, connecting rooms, pets welcome, baby-sitting, baby-listening device, cots, residents' lounge, residents' bar, parking.
Rooms: 9 single rooms, 9 double rooms, 5 twin rooms, 2 family rooms. All with en suite, TV, radio, telephone, tea/coffee-making facilities, alarm, hair dryer.
Directions: at roundabout on Prestbury road, take right for Pittville Circus.
MR PAUL WEAVER ☎ (01242) 515119 [Fax] (01242) 241537.

THE RETREAT
10–11 Suffolk Parade, GL50 2AB
Lively, friendly bar with fresh food cooked daily on the premises. Its central location and distinctive atmosphere makes The Retreat a popular rendezvous.
FOOD: up to £15
Hours: lunch 12noon–2.15pm, closed Sunday.
Cuisine: INTERNATIONAL – prepared in their own kitchen using fresh produce. Wide range of cold meats, salads and fish from servery. Home-made puddings, cheesecakes, tarts. Extensive hot menu with a wide range of vegetarian food.
Cards: Visa, Access, Diners, AmEx.
Other points: open-air dining, children welcome.
Directions: in the centre of Cheltenham's antique area of town.
MIKE DEY ☎ (01242) 235436.

CHIPPING CAMPDEN • map 8E6

NOEL ARMS HOTEL
High Street, GL55 6AT
This 14th century hotel has been welcoming travellers for more than six centuries. Although the faces have changed, the welcome is still the epitome of traditional hospitality. A freshly prepared meal from the extensive menu may be enjoyed in the delightful and impressive oak-panelled restaurant; or if you simply wish to relax over a quiet drink, the cosy lounge bar with its oak beams and open fire offers a congenial atmosphere.
DOUBLE ROOM: from £30 to £40
SINGLE ROOM: from £55
FOOD: from £15 to £20
Hours: breakfast 7.30am–9.30am, lunch Monday to Saturday on request, bar meals 12noon–2pm, dinner 7pm–9.30pm.
Cuisine: MODERN ENGLISH.
Cards: Visa, Access, Diners, AmEx, Switch.
Other points: parking, children welcome, pets allowed, conference facilities, residents' lounge, traditional Sunday lunch, vegetarian meals.
Rooms: 11 double rooms, 13 twin rooms, 2 four-poster rooms. All with TV, telephone, radio, alarm, tea/coffee-making facilities.
Directions: located in the centre of Chipping Campden, near the Old Market Hall.
NEIL JOHN ☎ (01386) 840317 [Fax] (01386) 841136.

CIRENCESTER • map 4A6

THE CROWN OF CRUCIS HOTEL & RESTAURANT
Ampney Crucis, GL7 5RS
A well-patronized, pleasant hotel and restaurant with good home-cooking. On fine days the tables beside the stream are very popular with families. Facilities for private parties of up to 100 people.
DOUBLE ROOM: from £20 to £30
SINGLE ROOM: from £25 to £35
FOOD: up to £15
Hours: dinner 7pm–10pm, lunch 12noon–2.30pm, open all year.
Cuisine: ENGLISH – daily specials, home-made desserts, traditional English cooking including award-winning steak-and-kidney pies.
Cards: Visa, Access, Diners, AmEx.
Other points: licensed, open-air dining, Sunday lunch, parking, garden, children welcome, baby-listening device, baby-sitting, cots, left luggage.
Rooms: 8 double rooms, 17 twin rooms. All with TV, radio, telephone, tea/coffee-making facilities.
Directions: on the A417 between Cirencester and Fairford.
MR R.K. MILLS ☎ (01285) 851806 [Fax] (01285) 851735.

THE HARE & HOUNDS
Foss Cross, near Chedworth, GL54 4NW
Located in open countryside, the pub dates back to the 17th century, with many original features. They now offer a separate function area. All food is

187

CENTRAL ENGLAND • GLOUCESTERSHIRE

home-made. Registered caravan site for up to 5 vehicles adjacent.
FOOD: up to £15
Hours: bar weekdays 11am–3pm, 6pm–11pm, weekends 12noon–3pm, 7pm–10.30pm, bar meals from 7pm, closed Christmas day.
Cuisine: ENGLISH – steak-and-kidney with dumplings cooked in ale, grills and a selection of various home-made dishes, including vegetarian.
Cards: Visa, Access, Diners, AmEx.
Other points: licensed, open-air dining, Sunday lunch, children welcome, coaches by prior arrangement, functions.
Directions: half-way between Cirencester and Northleach on A429.
THE TURNER FAMILY ☎ (01285) 720288.

HARRY HARE'S RESTAURANT & BRASSERIE
3 Gosditch Street, GL7 2AG
The wide-ranging menu at this restaurant and brasserie caters for all tastes, from those wanting an à la carte lunch or dinner to those seeking a traditional breakfast or just coffee and a cake. The menu changes monthly and includes steaks, pasta, salads, and sautéed king prawns in garlic butter on a julienne of vegetables. All are very fresh, as local suppliers deliver twice daily.
FOOD: up to £15
Hours: meals all day 11am–11pm, open for lunch Christmas day.
Cuisine: ENGLISH / CONTINENTAL – very varied brasserie-style food including breakfast, brunch and tea.
Cards: Visa, Access, AmEx.
Other points: licensed, open-air dining, Sunday lunch, children welcome, open bank holidays, afternoon tea.
Directions: just off West Market Place, 200 yards from parish church.
MARK R. STEPHENS ☎ (01285) 652375
Fax (01285) 641691.

KINGS HEAD HOTEL
Market Place, GL7 2MR
Retaining its old-world charm, this delightful hotel has an inn-keeping tradition that dates back 300 years. Paintings, panelling and high ceilings add atmosphere, while the accommodation has been furnished with attention to comfort
DOUBLE ROOM: from £30 to £40
FOOD: up to £15
Hours: breakfast 7.30am–9.15am, Sunday and bank holidays 8.30am–10am, lunch 12.15am–2pm, dinner 7pm–9pm, closed 27th December until 30th December.
Cuisine: ENGLISH – appetizing traditional English fare; creative omelettes a house speciality.
Cards: Visa, Access, Diners, AmEx.
Other points: licensed, Sunday lunch, children welcome, pets allowed, residents' lounge, open bank holidays, children welcome, baby-listening device, cots, residents' bar.
Rooms: 15 single rooms, 20 double rooms, 26 twin rooms, 5 family rooms. All with TV, radio, telephone, tea/coffee-making facilities.

Directions: situated in the town centre opposite prominent church tower.
MR & MRS BANNERMAN ☎ (01285) 653322
Fax (01285) 655103.

THE VILLAGE PUB
Barnsley, GL7 3EF
A traditional Cotswold-stone country pub in the centre of Barnsley village. The food is well cooked and presented and served in generous portions. The country-style accommodation boasts low beams, welcoming service and a friendly atmosphere.
DOUBLE ROOM: from £20 to £30
SINGLE ROOM: from £25 to £35
FOOD: up to £15 CLUB
Hours: breakfast 7.30am–9am, lunch 12noon–2pm, dinner 7pm–9.30pm, closed Christmas day.
Cuisine: ENGLISH – bar meals and à la carte menu. Dishes include local Bibury trout, deep-fried halibut, gammon steak, bean and vegetable casserole.
Cards: Visa, Access, AmEx.
Other points: licensed, Sunday lunch, children welcome, garden, pets allowed, afternoon tea.
Rooms: 4 double rooms, 1 twin room.
Directions: on B4425 in the centre of Barnsley.
MRS S. WARDROP ☎ (01285) 740421.

WILD DUCK INN
Drakes Island, Ewen, GL7 6BY
The Wild Duck Inn is a unique 15th century inn set in its own grounds, with a delightful garden for dining alfresco and open fires in the winter. You will find very good food, piping hot and in plentiful portions, complemented by a wide selection of traditional ales and wines.
DOUBLE ROOM: from £30 to £40
FOOD: up to £15 ☆
Hours: breakfast 8am–10am, lunch 12noon–2pm, dinner 7pm–10pm.
Cuisine: FRENCH / CONTINENTAL – French and bistro-style. Extensive choice.
Cards: Visa, Access, AmEx.
Other points: licensed, Sunday lunch, children welcome, garden, afternoon tea, pets allowed.
Directions: off the A419.
MR & MRS MUSSELL ☎ (01285) 770310
Fax (01285) 770310.

CLEARWELL • map 4A5

TUDOR FARMHOUSE HOTEL
Near Coleford, GL16 8JS
Delightful 13th century stone farmhouse in a peaceful village setting. The hotel features an abundance of oak beams, original wall-panelling and a 15th century spiral staircase. Ideal for the Forest of Dean and Wye Valley.
DOUBLE ROOM: from £20 to £30
FOOD: up to £15
Hours: breakfast 7.30am–9.30am, dinner 7.30pm–9pm.
Cuisine: ENGLISH / INTERNATIONAL – à la carte and table d'hôte, with menu changes daily. Dishes may include Cajun whitefish, roast rack of lamb, guinea fowl. Vegetarian dishes.

GLOUCESTERSHIRE • CENTRAL ENGLAND

Cards: Visa, Access, AmEx.
Other points: licensed, open-air dining, children welcome, pets allowed, disabled access, 24hr reception, residents' bar, residents' lounge, cots, baby-listening device.
Rooms: 6 double rooms, 3 family rooms. All with TV, telephone, tea/coffee-making facilities, alarm.
Directions: Clearwell is north of the A48 and east of A466.
DEBORAH & RICHARD FLETCHER ☎ (01594) 833046 [Fax] (01594) 837093.

WYNDHAM ARMS
Near Coleford, GL16 8JT
Situated within easy reach of Chepstow and Lydney, yet peaceful and secluded, off the main route. The Wyndham Arms has beautifully decorated rooms and offers food of excellent quality. It deservedly won the Les Routiers Accommodation of the Year Award *in 1990*.
DOUBLE ROOM: from £20 to £30
SINGLE ROOM: from £35 to £45
FOOD: up to £15
Hours: lunch 12noon–2pm, dinner 7pm–9.30pm.
Cuisine: ENGLISH – fresh food using home-grown fruit and vegetables in season. Fresh Wye and Severn salmon. Home-made puddings.
Cards: Visa, Access, Diners, AmEx.
Other points: licensed, Sunday lunch, children welcome, pets allowed, 24hr reception, patio, bar meals daily.
Rooms: 2 single rooms, 6 double rooms, 9 twin rooms. All with en suite, TV, radio, telephone, tea/coffee-making facilities, alarm, hair dryer, trouser-press, baby-listening device, cots available.
Directions: in the centre of Clearwell village, 2 miles from Coleford.
MR J. STANFORD ☎ (01594) 833666
[Fax] (01594) 836450.

COLEFORD • map 4A5

OREPOOL INN & MOTEL
St Briavels Road, Sling, near Coleford, GL16 8LH
Charming motel and inn dating from the mid-17th century. Friendly staff ensure a warm welcome. Busy family atmosphere. Conference facilities. Coach parties welcome by prior appointment. C.L. site (five caravans at any one time).
DOUBLE ROOM: up to £20
FOOD: up to £15
Hours: bar snacks 11am–10.30pm, breakfast 7am–9.30am.
Cuisine: ENGLISH – substantial English or continental breakfast. Extensive bar menu and specials board, which changes on a daily basis.
Cards: Visa, Access, AmEx.
Other points: licensed, open-air dining, Sunday lunch, afternoon tea, children welcome, disabled access.
Rooms: 2 single rooms, 4 double rooms, 2 twin rooms, 2 family rooms. All with TV, telephone, tea/coffee-making facilities.
Directions: take B4228 Coleford–Chepstow road.
JIM & JOAN WILSON ☎ (01594) 833277.

GREAT RISSINGTON • map 5B2

THE LAMB INN
GL54 2LP
Situated in the heart of the Cotswolds, Great Rissington is popular with tourists. Locally there is the Cotswold Wildlife Park and, slightly further afield, Oxford and Stratford-upon-Avon. Here, at The Lamb Inn, you will find warm hospitality, fine ales and wines, excellent food and comfortable accommodation in rooms with chintz and antique furniture.
DOUBLE ROOM: from £20 to £30
SINGLE ROOM: from £35 to £45
FOOD: up to £15
Hours: breakfast 8.30am–9am, dinner weekdays 7pm–9pm, dinner weekends 7pm–9pm, lunch 12noon–1.45pm.
Cuisine: ENGLISH – steaks, Cotswold trout, pâtés, soups, casseroles.
Cards: Visa, Access.
Other points: children welcome.
Rooms: 10 double rooms, 3 suites.
Directions: A40 from Oxford to Cheltenham; turn right to the Barringtons and Rissingtons.
MR & MRS CLEVERLY ☎ (01451) 820388
[Fax] (01451) 820724.

LITTLE WASHBOURNE • map 5A1

THE HOBNAILS INN
Near Tewkesbury, GL20 8NQ
Dating back to 1474, the inn has been run by the same family since 1743. A delightful location in a valley sweeping down to the River Severn at the foot of the Cotswolds.
FOOD: from £15 to £20
Hours: bar meals 12noon–2pm, dinner Friday 7pm–9.30pm, Saturday 7pm–9.30pm, bar meals 7pm–10pm, closed Christmas day.
Cuisine: ENGLISH – hobnails baps: soft round rolls with 52 different fillings, from sausage to steak and mushrooms. Home-made gateaux and flans.
Cards: Visa, Access.
Other points: open-air dining, Sunday lunch, children welcome, pets allowed.
Directions: situated on the B4077 Tewkesbury to Stow road.
MR & MRS S. FARBROTHER ☎ (01242) 620237.

MORETON-IN-MARSH • map 8E6

THE MARSHMALLOW
High Street, GL56 0AT
This Grade II listed, ivy-clad licensed restaurant offers outstanding, olde-worlde surroundings in which to relax, contemplate life and enjoy a sumptuous meal or light snack. The extensive menu is an indication of Valerie's dedication to providing her valued guests with the very best cuisine and service. Well worth a visit.
FOOD: up to £15
Hours: meals all day 10am–9.30pm, menu changes at 6pm.

189

Cuisine: ENGLISH / CONTINENTAL – good menu, well-presented dishes using fresh local produce. Candlelit suppers amongst a profusion of hanging baskets.
Cards: Visa, Access.
Other points: children welcome, no-smoking area, open-air dining, vegetarian meals, afternoon teas, traditional Sunday lunch.
Directions: northern end of the High Street.
VALERIE WEST ☎ (01608) 651536.

NYMPSFIELD • map 5B1

ROSE & CROWN INN
Stonehouse, GL10 3TU

A 300-year-old coaching inn in an extremely quiet Cotswold village. Close to the Cotswold Way and Nympsfield Gliding Club. A friendly, local inn which is an ideal base for touring, and within easy access of the M4 and M5.
DOUBLE ROOM: from £20 to £30
SINGLE ROOM: from £25 to £35
FOOD: up to £15
Hours: breakfast 8am–9am, lunch 12noon–2pm, bar meals 6.30pm–9.30pm.
Cuisine: ENGLISH / INTERNATIONAL – good bar food with sandwiches, salads, steaks, fish meals, spicy dishes. Packed lunch available. Choice of over 55 main meals.
Cards: Visa, Access, AmEx.
Other points: licensed, Sunday lunch, children welcome, coaches by prior arrangement
Rooms: 4 family rooms. All rooms can be let as twins.
Directions: off the B4066 Dursley to Stroud road. Situated in village centre.
BOB & LINDA WOODMAN & NEIL SMITH
☎ (01453) 860240. Fax (01453) 860240.

PARKEND • map 4A5

PARKEND HOUSE HOTEL
Near Lydney, GL15 4HL

A small country house hotel set in three acres of parkland. Over 200 years old, the house has been tastefully converted to retain its country house atmosphere. The restaurant offers a varied menu of well-cooked dishes at good value for money, served in pleasing surroundings. A welcoming hotel where guests can relax within the peaceful surroundings of the Royal Forest of Dean.
DOUBLE ROOM: from £20 to £30
SINGLE ROOM: from £25 to £35
FOOD: up to £15
Hours: bar meals 12noon–2pm, breakfast 8.30am–9.30am, dinner 7pm–8pm.
Cuisine: ENGLISH / CONTINENTAL – table d'hôte menu with a of choice of English and continental dishes.
Cards: Visa, Access.
Other points: licensed, children welcome, afternoon tea, pets allowed, residents' lounge, garden, croquet.
Rooms: 5 double rooms, 3 twin rooms. All with TV.

Directions: A48 Chepstow–Gloucester road to Lydney. In Lydney take B4234 to Parkend.
MRS ROBERTA POOLE ☎ (01594) 563666.

ROYAL FOREST OF DEAN
map 4A5

LAMBSQUAY HOUSE HOTEL
Near Coleford, GL16 8QB

An elegant Georgian country house, full of charm and character, dating back to the 17th century, situated in a pleasant area high up in the Forest of Dean. This friendly, family-run hotel has nine individually decorated comfortable bedrooms and a fine restaurant offering a blend of English and continental food. All meals are prepared using fresh produce, from the hotel garden whenever possible. A warm welcome awaits you, and you will be assured of the best attention throughout your stay.
DOUBLE ROOM: from £20 to £30
SINGLE ROOM: up to £25
FOOD: up to £15
Hours: breakfast weekdays 7am–9am, weekends and bank holidays 7.30am–9.30am, dinner 7pm–9pm.
Cuisine: ENGLISH – traditional home-cooked dishes.
Cards: Visa, Access.
Other points: parking, children welcome, pets by arrangement, conference facilities, residents' lounge, garden, vegetarian meals.
Rooms: 2 single rooms, 4 double rooms, 2 twin rooms, 1 family room. All with TV, telephone, tea/coffee-making facilities.
Directions: 1½ miles south of Coleford on B4228 Coleford to Chepstow road.
MIKE & LESLEY HARDY ☎ (01594) 833127
Fax (01594) 833127.

STOW-ON-THE-WOLD • map 8E6

GRAPEVINE HOTEL
Sheep Street, GL54 1AU

Award-winning 17th century hotel in antiques centre. Romantic conservatory restaurant with beautiful furnishings, crowned by magnificent historic vine. Caring staff. Rosette for fine cuisine. Hotel of the Year 1991. Bargain breaks from £47 per person, dinner, bed and breakfast.
DOUBLE ROOM: from £50
SINGLE ROOM: from £55
FOOD: from £15 to £20 🍴 CLUB ☆
Hours: breakfast 8.30am–9.45am, bar meals 12noon–2pm, dinner 7pm–9.30pm, bar meals 7pm–9.30pm, closed 24th December until 11th January.
Cuisine: FRENCH / ENGLISH – bar: delicious selection of unusual dishes. Restaurant: English and French haute cuisine. Changing menu with fresh ingredients. Typically local and national traditional dishes.
Cards: Visa, Access, Diners, AmEx.
Other points: licensed, open-air dining, Sunday lunch, children welcome, afternoon tea, garden, baby-listening device, cots, left luggage, tennis.

GLOUCESTERSHIRE • CENTRAL ENGLAND

Rooms: 1 single room, 9 double rooms, 11 twin room, 2 quad rooms. All with ensuite, TV, alarm, radio, telephone, tea/coffee-making facilities. There are deluxe garden rooms with trouser press and mini-bar available.
Directions: from A429, take A436 towards Chipping Norton; 150 yards on right.
MRS SANDRA ELLIOTT ☎ (01451) 830344
[Fax] (01451) 832278.

THE OLD STOCKS HOTEL
The Square, GL54 1AF
A 17th century Grade II listed hotel, one of the original buildings in the square, and facing the quiet village green on which the original penal stocks still stand. Refurbished to combine modern comforts with original charm and character. Friendly and caring staff make this an ideal base for exploring the beautiful Cotswolds.
DOUBLE ROOM: from £30 to £40
SINGLE ROOM: from £35 to £45
FOOD: from £15 to £20
Hours: breakfast 8.15am–9.15am, lunch 12noon–2pm, dinner 7pm–9pm.
Cuisine: ENGLISH / VEGETARIAN – extensive table d'hôte and very popular special-value menu, specializing in traditional home-cooked dishes and also catering for the vegetarian.
Cards: Visa, Access, MasterCard.
Other points: licensed, Sunday lunch, pets allowed, children welcome, garden, patio, disabled access.
Rooms: 1 single room, 14 double rooms, 2 twin rooms, 1 family room. All with TV, tea/coffee-making facilities.
Directions: take A429 to Stow-on-the-Wold. Hotel in town centre next to the green.
ALAN ROSE ☎ (01451) 830666.

THE WHITE HART HOTEL
Market Square, GL54 1AF
A 17th century coaching inn, which still retains much of its old character and ambience. It provides an ideal base for touring the Cotswolds, and the food and service are of a high standard.
DOUBLE ROOM: up to £20
SINGLE ROOM: up to £25
FOOD: up to £15
Hours: breakfast 8.15am–9.15am, lunch 11.45am–2.15pm, dinner 6pm–10pm, Sunday 7pm–9pm.
Cuisine: ENGLISH – home-made traditional pies, local grilled trout.
Cards: Visa, Access, Diners, AmEx.
Other points: Sunday lunch, children welcome.
Rooms: 4 double rooms, 4 family room. All with TV, tea/coffee-making facilities.
Directions: off A429. Turn off at town centre sign; on left side of main square.
COLIN & ALISON HEWETT & CLARE PEASTON
☎ (01451) 830674 [Fax] (01451) 830090.

STROUD • map 4A6

BELL HOTEL & RESTAURANT
Wallbridge, GL5 3JA
Situated in the town centre of Stroud, this delightful Victorian hotel has 12 newly refurbished bedrooms, a fine restaurant, wine bar and beer garden. The service is welcoming and the general ambience is jovial.
DOUBLE ROOM: up to £20
SINGLE ROOM: from £25 to £35
FOOD: up to £15
Hours: breakfast 7.30am–9am, lunch 12noon–2pm, dinner 7pm–9.30pm.
Cuisine: ENGLISH / CONTINENTAL – all meals freshly cooked to order and great value for money.
Cards: Visa, Access.
Other points: parking, children welcome, pets allowed, no-smoking area, garden, open-air dining, Sunday lunch, vegetarian meals.
Rooms: 1 single room, 7 double rooms (2 with whirlpool bath), 3 twin rooms, 1 four-poster room.
Directions: follow directions to Stroud. The Bell Hotel & Restaurant is near to the town centre.
MICHAEL & CHRISTINE WILLIAMS ☎ (01453) 763556.

LONDON HOTEL
30–31 London Road, GL5 2AJ
A very friendly, welcoming hotel situated in the small industrial town of Stroud, where five valleys meet in the beautiful Cotswolds. The food in the candlelit restaurant is of excellent quality, and the accommodation is very comfortable. Places of interest nearby include Gatcombe Park, Gloucester Cathedral and Slimbridge Wild Fowl Trust.
DOUBLE ROOM: from £20 to £30
FOOD: up to £15
Hours: breakfast 7.30am–9.30am, lunch 12noon–2pm, dinner 7pm–9.30pm.
Cuisine: CONTINENTAL – dishes including sirloin steak Francaise, Hawaiian duck and Romany chicken. À la carte, table d'hôte and bar meals. Good wine list.
Cards: Visa, Access, Diners, AmEx.
Other points: licensed, no-smoking area, children welcome, open bank holidays, residents' lounge, afternoon tea, children welcome, baby-listening device, cots.
Rooms: 4 single rooms, 5 double rooms, 3 twin rooms. All with TV, radio, alarm, telephone, tea/coffee-making facilities.
Directions: from Stroud town centre, take A419 towards Cirencester.
MR & MRS PORTAL ☎ (01453) 759992
[Fax] (01453) 753363.

THE RAGGED COT INN
Hyde, Chalford, GL16 8PE
Located in a supremely ideal position, deep in the heart of the Cotswolds and surrounded by a wealth of picturesque villages, this inn is personally supervised by the owners. The cosy, intimate restaurant offers imaginative award-winning food, and all bedrooms are equipped with the most modern facilities to provide a comfortable, relaxing stay. The bar is warm and friendly, with lots of character and open log fires. Ideal base for visiting the many important equestrian events which are held annually in this area.
DOUBLE ROOM: from £20 to £30
FOOD: up to £15 [CLUB]
Hours: breakfast 8am–9.30am, lunch 12noon–

2.30pm, dinner 7pm–9.30pm, closed Christmas day.
Cuisine: ENGLISH.
Cards: Visa, Access, AmEx.
Other points: children welcome, disabled access, vegetarian meals, open-air dining, garden, no-smoking area, parking.
Rooms: 10 twin rooms.
Directions: junction 15 off M4, A419 to Cirencester or junction 13 off M5 to Stroud. Follow signs to Hyde out of Chalford and turn left at junction.
MARGARET ANN & MICHAEL CASE ☎ (01453) 884643/731333 Fax (01453) 731166.

TEWKESBURY • map 8E5

GUPSHILL MANOR
Gloucester Road, GL20 5SY
This is a timbered 15th century manor house and the site of the 1491 Battle of Tewkesbury. Margaret of Anjou is rumoured to have watched the battle from the precarious safety of one of the bedrooms. The battles are over now, and Gupshill has been tastefully restored, offering a peaceful setting to enjoy good food.
FOOD: from £15 to £20
Hours: bar meals 12noon–2.15pm, dinner 7pm–9.30pm, bar meals 7pm–9.30pm.
Cuisine: ENGLISH – all home-cooked. Menu in carvery changes daily.
Cards: Visa, Access, Diners, AmEx.
Other points: licensed, open-air dining, Sunday lunch, children welcome.
Directions: situated on the A38 on the edge of Tewkesbury, only about five minutes from the M5.
MARK & KAY RATCLIFFE ☎ (01684) 292278.

HEREFORD & WORCESTER

BROADWAY • map 8E5

BELL INN
Main Street, Willersey, WR12 7PJ
A large public house built in traditional Cotswold stone, the Bell Inn serves excellent food within comfortable, relaxed surroundings. The food is made from fresh local produce and is superbly cooked and presented. Highly recommended for its welcoming service and excellent food at very good value for money.
FOOD: up to £15
Hours: lunch 12noon–2pm, dinner 6pm–9.30pm, Sunday 7pm–9pm.
Cuisine: ENGLISH – daily changing menu. Dishes may include lemon sole, salmon en croute, traditional game pie, steak au poivre, as well as a standard menu.
Cards: Visa, Access, AmEx.
Other points: licensed, open-air dining, Sunday lunch, children welcome, beer garden.
Directions: B4632 Broadway (1½ miles) to Stratford-upon-Avon. By the duck pond.
WILLIAM MOORE ☎ (01386) 858405.

LEASOW HOUSE
Laverton Meadows, WR12 7NA
A most appealing Cotswold stone farmhouse with superb gardens, this has a very high standard. Beautifully decorated throughout, it offers guests accommodation of the highest quality with a warm and welcoming ambience. Impressed and satisfied guests keep returning again and again, and this is surely a high recommendation.
DOUBLE ROOM: from £20 to £30
Hours: breakfast 7am–9am.
Cards: Visa, Access, AmEx.
Other points: parking, children welcome, pets allowed, disabled access, no-smoking area, residents' lounge, garden, vegetarian meals.
Rooms: 7 bedrooms. All with en suite, TV, telephone, radio, alarm, tea/coffee-making facilities. There is one room for disabled guests.
Directions: from Broadway take B4632 to Cheltenham, and turn right at sign for Wormington and Dumbleton. First house on the right.
BARBARA MEEKINGS ☎ (01386) 584526 Fax (01386) 584596.

FOWNHOPE • map 8E4

THE GREEN MAN INN
HR1 4PE
A 15th century country inn set in the heart of the beautiful Wye Valley, popular for businessmen, families, wedding parties or small functions. Ideal centre for fishing, with some of England's best salmon reaches nearby.
DOUBLE ROOM: from £20 to £30
FOOD: up to £15
Hours: breakfast 8.15am–9am, lunch 12noon–2pm, bar meals 12noon–2pm, dinner 7pm–9pm, bar meals 6pm–10pm.
Cuisine: ENGLISH – à la carte and bar food menus. Dishes include beef, mushroom and ale pie.
Cards: Visa, Access, AmEx.
Other points: open-air dining, Sunday lunch, children welcome.
Rooms: 13 double rooms, 20 twin rooms.
Directions: on B4224, midway between Ross-on-Wye and Hereford.
ARTHUR & MARGARET WILLIAMS ☎ (01432) 860243 Fax (01432) 860207.

GREAT MALVERN • map 8E5

MOUNT PLEASANT HOTEL
Belle Vue Terrace, WR14 4PZ
An attractive early Georgian building and orangery set in 1.5 acres of mature terraced gardens with

HEREFORD & WORCESTER • CENTRAL ENGLAND

lovely views across the town. Close to the theatre and shops yet only seconds from the Malvern Hills rising behind the hotel. An informal hotel with all the facilities of a larger establishment.
DOUBLE ROOM: from £30 to £40
FOOD: up to £15 ☆
Hours: breakfast 7.45am–9.30am, lunch 12noon–2pm, bar meals 12noon–2pm, dinner 7pm–9.30pm, bar meals 7pm–9pm, coffee shop 10am–6pm, closed Christmas day.
Cuisine: INTERNATIONAL – in the restaurant: salmon in plum sauce, paella, gazpacho, guacamole, turkey guajalote and vegetarian menu. Excellent home-cooked bar meals, and table d'hôte menu.
Cards: Visa, Access, Diners, AmEx.
Other points: licensed, Sunday lunch, children welcome, conferences, functions, cots, left luggage, vegetarian meals, lounge bar, residents' lounge.
Rooms: 2 single rooms, 6 double rooms, 6 twin rooms. All with TV, radio, telephone, tea/coffee-making facilities, alarm.
Directions: take M5 exit 7, follow A449 to Malvern. Near Priory church in town centre.
SOL & GEOFF PAYNE ☎ (01684) 561837
Fax (01684) 569968.

HAY-ON-WYE • map 8E4

THE OLD BLACK LION
Lion Street, HR3 5AD
Oliver Cromwell is reputed to have stayed at the Old Black Lion while the Roundheads besieged Hay Castle, which was a Loyalist stronghold. Whether you be Loyalist or Roundhead, this old coaching inn extends a warm welcome to all who visit today by serving delicious country cooking. Hay is the world centre for secondhand books, with over 2 million books in 27 bookshops.
DOUBLE ROOM: from £20 to £30
SINGLE ROOM: up to £25
FOOD: from £15 to £20
Hours: breakfast 8.30am–9.15am, lunch 12noon–2.30pm, dinner 7pm–9pm.
Cuisine: INTERNATIONAL – home country cooking with international flair, house specials being steaks, seafood, game and vegetarian. 44 wines from around the world and a choice of 6 malt whiskies.
Cards: Visa, Access, AmEx.
Other points: licensed, Sunday lunch, children welcome, pets allowed, fishing.
Rooms: 1 single room, 4 double rooms, 4 twin rooms, 1 family room. All with TV, radio, telephone, tea/coffee-making facilities.
Directions: 50 yards off the B4352 Hereford to Hay road.
JOHN & JOAN COLLINS ☎ (01497) 820841.

SIDNEY HOUSE
40 Worcester Road, WR14 4AA
An attractive, white Georgian listed building standing in an elevated position in Great Malvern, with stunning views over the Severn Valley, towards the Vale of Evesham and the Cotswolds. The town centre, Winter Gardens, Malvern Festival Theatre, Priory Park and the hills are only a few minutes' walk away.
DOUBLE ROOM: from £20 to £30
SINGLE ROOM: up to £25
FOOD: from £15 to £20
Hours: breakfast 8am–9am, dinner 7pm by arrangement.
Cuisine: BREAKFAST.
Cards: Visa, Access, AmEx.
Other points: central heating, children welcome, pets by prior arrangement, residents' lounge.
Rooms: 1 single room, 4 double rooms, 2 twin rooms, 1 family room. All with TV, hair dryer, radio, alarm, tea/coffee-making facilities.
Directions: on the A449, 150 yards on right from junction with Church Street.
TOM J.S. & MARGARET E. HAGGETT
☎ (01684) 574994.

KIDDERMINSTER • map 8D5

THE COLLIERS ARMS
Clows Top, DY14 9HA
This two-storey rendered country pub is set in its own gardens with delightful pergola and surrounded by pleasant, open countryside. It provides excellent service and value for money. Daily chef's specials.
FOOD: up to £15
Hours: lunch 12noon–2pm, dinner 7pm–10pm, closed Sunday evening - winter.
Cuisine: ENGLISH.
Cards: Visa, Access.
Other points: licensed, Sunday lunch, children welcome, garden, pets allowed.
Directions: A456 at Clows Top. Highest point locally.
THE SANKEY FAMILY ☎ (01299) 832242.

LES ROUTIERS
Information & Bookings Line
☎ 0171 610 1856

STONE MANOR HOTEL
Stone, DY10 4PJ
Located in a rural setting of 25 acres, this is the perfect setting for a most attractive country house hotel. The peace and tranquillity of the surroundings truly sets off the sumptuous interior of this superb hotel. A warm welcome and courteous service make any stay a memorable one.
DOUBLE ROOM: from £20 to £30
FOOD: from £15 to £20
Cuisine: FRENCH / ENGLISH – seasonal dishes. Only fresh produce used.
Cards: Visa, Access, Diners, AmEx.
Other points: children welcome, parking, room service.
Rooms: 52 bedrooms. All with TV, telephone.
Directions: on the junctions of the A450 and A448, approximately 2 miles west of Kidderminster.
CALCOT HOTELS LTD ☎ (01562) 777555
Fax (01562) 777834.

PERSHORE • map 8E5

🛏 CHEQUERS INN
Chequers Lane, Fladbury, WR10 2PZ
Situated at the end of a quiet lane in Fladbury, this old English village inn, parts of which date from the 14th century, offers exceptional accommodation and is renowned for its hospitality and excellent food. Warm and comfortable, there is a traditional country lounge bar with magnificent open fire, cosy restaurant and endless beams. Ideal location for both tourists and business people.
DOUBLE ROOM: from £20 to £30
FOOD: up to £15 [CLUB] ☆
Hours: breakfast 7.15am–9.30am, lunch 12noon–2pm, bar snacks 12noon–2pm, dinner 7.30pm–10pm, bar snacks 6pm–10pm.
Cuisine: ENGLISH.
Cards: Visa, Access.
Other points: parking, children welcome, Sunday lunch, open bank holidays, vegetarian meals, garden.
Rooms: 4 double rooms, 8 twin rooms.
Directions: between Evesham and Pershore. Off A44 or off B4084.
MR A. & MRS D. CORFIELD ☎ (01386) 860276 [Fax] (01386) 860527.

REDDITCH • map 8D5

🛏 HOTEL MONTVILLE & GRANNY'S RESTAURANT
101 Mount Pleasant, Southcrest, B76 4JE
A fine 16-bedroomed hotel, offering exceptional quality. The latest addition is Granny's Restaurant, where the majority of guests dine, which is also popular with the locals. The residents' lounge is comfortably furnished and has a writing desk. The hotel can arrange for guests to play squash, snooker, golf and use the gymnasium.
DOUBLE ROOM: from £30 to £40
SINGLE ROOM: from £25 to £35
FOOD: up to £15
Hours: breakfast 7.30am–9.30am, lunch 12noon–2pm, dinner 6.30pm–9.30pm.
Cuisine: ENGLISH – English home-cooking, using freshly cooked vegetables and salads, with traditional home-made puddings. Vegetarians are also well catered for.
Cards: Visa, Access, Diners, AmEx.
Other points: Sunday lunch, no-smoking area, children welcome, pets allowed, residents' lounge, parking.
Rooms: 16 bedrooms.
Directions: Redditch ring road. Left for Southcrest, turn right into Tunnel Drive.
MARY WARNER ☎ (01527) 544411.

ROSS-ON-WYE • map 8E4

🛏 ARCHES HOTEL
Walford Road, HR9 5PT
A small, family-run hotel set in half an acre of lawned gardens only 10 minutes' walk from the town centre. Easy access to many places of interest in the beautiful Wye valley. All bedrooms are decorated and furnished to a high standard and overlook the gardens. Renowned for good food and a warm and friendly atmosphere with personal service.
DOUBLE ROOM: up to £20
Hours: breakfast 8am, dinner 7pm, closed Christmas.
Cuisine: ENGLISH – dinner is available on request. An excellent and varied menu offers home-cooked dishes using local home-grown produce whenever possible.
Other points: central heating, children welcome, residents' lounge, garden, pets by prior arrangement.
Rooms: 1 single room, 4 double rooms, 2 twin rooms, 1 family rooms. All with TV, tea/coffee-making facilities.
Directions: A40, then onto B4234.
JEAN JONES ☎ (01989) 563348.

🍴 LOUGHPOOL INN
Sellack, HR9 6LX
A 16th century pub with oak beams, a large open fireplace and original flagstone flooring. Outside, the inn is set in a large garden, facing a pool surrounded by willows. On the main Hoarwithy road – a popular tourist route.
FOOD: up to £15
Hours: lunch 12noon–2.30pm, dinner 7pm–9.30pm, open all year.
Cuisine: ENGLISH / INTERNATIONAL.
Cards: Visa, Access.
Other points: open-air dining, Sunday lunch, garden.
Directions: turn off the A49, to the Sellack to Hoarwithy road. The Loughpool Inn is midway between Hoarwithy and Ross.
PHILIP & JANET MORAN ☎ (01989) 730236.

🛏 THE OLD COURT HOTEL & RESTAURANT
Symonds Yat West, HR9 6DA
This old 16th century manor house is situated in a most beautiful part of the Wye Valley. The carefully selected menus in the Tudor restaurant offer a wide variety of dishes, and the charming Cotswold bar serves a wide choice of hot and cold bar food and a comprehensive selection of ales, lagers and wines. Excellent accommodation and service.
DOUBLE ROOM: from £20 to £30
SINGLE ROOM: from £35 to £45
FOOD: from £15 to £20
Hours: bar meals 12noon–2pm, bar meals 6pm–10pm, dinner 7pm–9.30pm.
Cuisine: ENGLISH – fixed three-course menu and bar menu.
Cards: Visa, Access, Diners, AmEx.
Other points: licensed, open-air dining, Sunday lunch, no-smoking area, children welcome, afternoon tea, pets allowed, swimming pool, conservatory.
Rooms: 17 double rooms, 3 twin rooms.
Directions: within the Wye valley on A40, 6 miles from end of M50.
JOHN & ELIZABETH SLADE ☎ (01600) 890367.

WEOBLEY • map 8E4

🍴 YE OLDE SALUTATION INN
Market Pitch, HR4 8SJ
Dating back over 500 years, this former Ale & Cider house offers a traditional setting and friendly atmosphere in which to spend a pleasant lunchtime or evening out. A main feature of the comfortable lounge is a large inglenook fireplace, leading into the 40-seater Oak Room Restaurant. The local area offers many activities, including fishing, horse-riding, hiking and golf.
DOUBLE ROOM: from £20 to £30
SINGLE ROOM: from £25 to £35
FOOD: from £15 to £20 🍴
Hours: breakfast 9am–9.30am (enquire for early breakfast), lunch 12noon–2pm, dinner 7pm–9pm.
Cuisine: ENGLISH – traditional English fare of excellent quality, using fresh local produce. All dishes are cooked to order. Vegetarian dishes also available.
Cards: Visa, Access, Diners, AmEx.
Other points: licensed, open-air dining, Sunday lunch, no-smoking area, pets allowed, lounge, bar, baby-listening device.
Rooms: 3 double rooms, 1 twin room. All with TV, radio, tea/coffee-making facilities, alarm.
Directions: situated 8 miles from Leominster on the A4112 Brecon road.
CHRISTOPHER ANTHONY ☎ (01544) 318443
[Fax] (01544) 318216.

WORCESTER • map 8E5

🏨 LENCHFORD HOTEL
Shrawley, WR6 6TB
Stephen and Karen Horn offer you a warm welcome and personal attention in the relaxed atmosphere of this splendid late Georgian house, which still retains many of its original features. Log fires in winter and riverside lawns in summer. The large restaurant offers superb views across the River Severn, which flows gently by. A 100-seater banqueting suite is available for hire.
DOUBLE ROOM: from £20 to £30
SINGLE ROOM: from £25 to £35
FOOD: from £15 to £20 [CLUB]
Hours: breakfast 7.30am–9am, bar meals 12noon–2pm, dinner 7pm–9.30pm, closed Christmas 24th December until 30th December.
Cuisine: ENGLISH / CONTINENTAL – extensive à la carte lunch and dinner menus Monday–Saturday. Carvery Sunday lunchtimes. Bar meals available.
Cards: Visa, Access, Diners, AmEx.
Other points: licensed, open-air dining, Sunday lunch, children welcome, parking, residents' lounge, garden, vegetarian meals, cots, residents' bar.
Rooms: 1 single room, 7 double rooms, 8 twin rooms. All with TV, radio, alarm, telephone, tea/coffee-making facilities.
Directions: on the A443–B1496, 6 miles north of Worcester. 7 miles from M5 junctions 5 and 6.
STEPHEN & KAREN HORN ☎ (01905) 620229.

LEICESTERSHIRE

ASHBY DE LA ZOUCH • map 9C2

🍴 LA ZOUCH RESTAURANT
2 Kilwardby Street, LE6 5FQ
A renovated Georgian building, tastefully decorated and furnished and with a walled garden, cottage-style with pebble water feature. There is a small intimate bar with a larger lounge bar upstairs, and private functions and dinner parties can be arranged. The restaurant offers a large selection of English and continental dishes.
FOOD: from £15 to £20 [CLUB]
Hours: lunch 12noon–2pm, dinner 7pm–10pm, closed Sunday evening, Monday, and from 1st to 15th January and 1st to 14th July.
Cuisine: ENGLISH / CONTINENTAL – grilled salmon and cucumber sauce, rump steak and mustard sauce. Home-made sweets. Speciality; Colston Bassett Stilton.
Cards: Visa, Access, Diners, AmEx.
Other points: licensed, open-air dining, Sunday lunch, children welcome, parking, vegetarian meals.
Directions: at the crossroads of the A50 and B5006 in town centre.
GEOFFREY & LYNNE UTTING ☎ (01530) 412536.

🍴 THE MEWS WINE BAR & RESTAURANT
8 Mill Lane, LE6 5HP
Situated in a pedestrian mews in this historic market town, this popular Queen Anne listed building in a conservation area has a reputation for excellent home-cooked food in its Garden Room restaurant. Under same ownership for 12 years.
FOOD: up to £15
Hours: lunch 12noon–2.30pm, dinner 6pm–10.30pm, closed Sunday and Monday.
Cuisine: ENGLISH – traditional cooking with a different menu using only fresh supplies.
Cards: Visa, Access, AmEx.
Other points: no-smoking area, children welcome.
Directions: 30 yards from the junction of the A50/A453.
IAN G. BRIDGE ☎ (01530) 416683
[Fax] (01530) 415111.

BOTTESFORD • map 9C3

🍴 THE RUTLAND ARMS
2 High Street, NG13 0AA
Built in the early 1900s, this listed building is home to a popular bar and restaurant. The local patrons have opted to congregate here because of its lively

atmosphere, good selection available from the well-stocked bar, and the tasty home-cooked meals on offer. Being in such a prominent position, The Rutland Arms is also a highly popular stop for travellers, being only 3 miles from Belvoir Castle.
FOOD: from £15 to £20
Hours: lunch 12noon–2pm, dinner 7pm–9.30pm.
Cuisine: ENGLISH – an excellent choice: grills, full à la carte menu, chef's daily specials, freshly baked pizzas to eat in or take away.
Cards: Visa, Access, Switch.
Other points: parking, children welcome, no-smoking area, vegetarian meals, traditional Sunday lunch, disabled facilities.
Directions: main road location off A52 Grantham to Nottingham road.
ANN KATRINA ASHLEY ☎ (01949) 843031
Fax (01949) 843031.

BURTON ON THE WOLDS
map 9C2

GREYHOUND INN
25 Melton Road, LE12 5AG
A traditional coaching inn renovated in 1991. All the food is home-cooked and supported by a comprehensive wine list. British Institute of Innkeeping (East Midlands Section) 'Pub of the Year' 1988 and 1989. Greenhalls Catering 'Pub of the Year' 1993.
FOOD: up to £15 CLUB
Hours: lunch 12noon–2pm, dinner 7pm–10pm.
Cuisine: ENGLISH – home-cooked specials. 'Big Steak Night' every Thursday.
Cards: Visa.
Other points: open-air dining, Sunday lunch, children welcome, coaches by prior arrangement
Directions: B676 Loughborough to Melton Mowbray road.
PHILIP & ANN ASHLEY ☎ (01509) 880860
Fax (01509) 881709.

CASTLE DONINGTON • map 9C2

DONINGTON MANOR HOTEL
High Street, DE74 2PP
An 18th century Regency coaching inn, refurbished in period style. Donington Manor provides the epitome of traditional British hospitality.
DOUBLE ROOM: from £30 to £40
SINGLE ROOM: from £45 to £55
FOOD: from £15 to £20
Hours: last orders 9.30pm, closed 27th December until 30th December.
Cuisine: ANGLO-FRENCH – Melton fillet, fresh duckling, game dishes and fresh fish in season.
Cards: Visa, Access, Diners, AmEx.
Other points: Sunday lunch, conference facilities.
Rooms: 14 single rooms, 14 double rooms, 8 twin rooms, 1 family suite.
Directions: off M1 at junction 24, 2 miles along A6 to Derby, turn left at B6540.
MR N. GRIST ☎ (01332) 810253.

LE CHEVALIER
2 Borough Street, DE7 2LA
A small, intimate, personally run restaurant with a well-established reputation for its good food and friendly atmosphere. It now has a number of lovely rooms around the rear courtyard and makes an ideal base for exploring the surrounding area, with Donington Park Racetrack, Nottingham, Derby and Alton Towers nearby.
DOUBLE ROOM: from £20 to £30
FOOD: up to £15   CLUB
Hours: breakfast 7.30am–8.30am, lunch 12noon–2pm, dinner 6.30pm–11pm.
Cuisine: FRENCH / CONTINENTAL – specialities including boudin à l'Anglaise and filet de boeuf Chevalier.
Cards: Visa, Access, Diners, AmEx.
Other points: licensed, children welcome, open bank holidays, garden.
Rooms: 2 double rooms, 1 twin room, 1 family room. All with TV, radio, alarm, telephone, tea/coffee-making facilities.
Directions: just off B6540 (junction 24 of M1). On main street of Castle Donington.
MR JAD OTAKI & LYNN OTAKI ☎ (01332) 812106/812005.

HINCKLEY • map 9D2

WOODSIDE FARM GUEST HOUSE
Ashby Road, Stapleton, LE9 8JE
A working farm in a rural and tranquil setting, where Julia Furniss and her husband provide a warm welcome for all guests. Comfortable lounge and dining room with traditional farmhouse furniture. Ideally situated for visiting nearby Bosworth Battle Centre, Kirkby Mallory Race Track and Twycross Zoo.
DOUBLE ROOM: from £20 to £30
SINGLE ROOM: from £25 to £35
FOOD: from £15 to £20
Hours: breakfast 7am–9am, dinner 6.30pm–9.30pm, open all year.
Cuisine: ENGLISH – good homely cooking using the freshest of local produce, cooked and served by the owners.
Cards: Visa, Access, AmEx, Switch.
Other points: licensed, open-air dining, Sunday lunch, vegetarian meals, residents' lounge, garden, parking, children welcome, cots.
Rooms: 4 single rooms, 3 double rooms, 2 twin rooms, 1 triple room. All with TV, radio, tea/coffee-making facilities.
Directions: 3 miles north of Hinckley on left-hand side, past Woodlands Nursery.
JULIA FURNISS ☎ (01455) 291929
Fax (01455) 291929.

LEICESTER • map 9C2

THE JOHNSCLIFFE HOTEL & RESTAURANT
73 Main Street, LE6 0AF
The Johnscliffe provides a varied and exciting menu served by friendly and efficient staff. Set in its own

wooded grounds, this elegant building has sunlit rooms and a quiet, relaxing atmosphere. Places to visit include Bradgate park (the home of Lady Jane Grey) and Castle Donington race track.
DOUBLE ROOM: from £30 to £40
FOOD: from £15 to £20
Hours: lunch 12noon–2pm, dinner 7pm–9.30pm.
Cuisine: ENGLISH / CONTINENTAL – crab, chicken, pheasant, fish and steak in interesting sauces.
Cards: Visa, Access, AmEx.
Other points: licensed, Sunday lunch, children welcome, pets allowed.
Rooms: 2 single rooms, 12 double rooms, 1 twin room, 1 family room.
Directions: 5 minutes from junction 22 off the M1.
MR & MRS DEVONPORT ☎ (01530) 242228.

OLD TUDOR RECTORY
Main Street, Glenfield, LE3 8DG
A Tudor hotel with Jacobean and Queen Anne additions, set in its own acre of well-tended gardens, offering attractive and comfortable accommodation. The tasteful, well-selected interior adds to the friendly relaxed atmosphere and outstanding hospitality of Mrs Weston.
DOUBLE ROOM: from £20 to £30
FOOD: up to £15
Hours: breakfast 7.30am–9am, bank holidays 8.30am–9.45am, dinner 7pm–9.30pm.
Cuisine: ENGLISH / CONTINENTAL.
Cards: Visa, Access, Diners, AmEx.
Other points: children welcome, garden, pets allowed, beauty therapy, gym facilities, disabled access, parking, vegetarian meals, residents' lounge, residents' bar.
Rooms: 3 single rooms, 8 double rooms, 3 twin rooms, 2 family rooms. All with TV, telephone, tea/coffee-making facilities.
Directions: leave M1 at exit 22. Take the A50 to Leicester. Opposite Forge Berni Inn.
MR I. PHILLIPS ☎ (0116) 2320220 Fax (0116) 2876002.

LOUGHBOROUGH • map 9C2

COSSINGTON MILL
Cossington, LE7 4UZ
This Grade II listed building standing on the banks of the canal is a popular restaurant and bar. The reputation it has earned is justified by the excellent cuisine, prepared and cooked by the chef who takes pride in all details of his creations. There is an ambience of friendliness and discretion in the excellently furnished medieval restaurant.
FOOD: up to £15
Hours: lunch 12noon–2.30pm, bar meals 12noon–2.30pm, dinner 6.30pm–10.30pm, bar meals 6.30pm–1am, closed Monday.
Cuisine: ENGLISH / FRENCH – a good selection of dishes complemented by a fine wine list.
Cards: Visa, Access, Diners, AmEx.
Other points: parking, children welcome, no-smoking area, garden, open-air dining, vegetarian meals, traditional Sunday lunch.

Directions: located on the B5328, from A6 or A46.
ROBERT & JAN KING ☎ (01509) 812205 Fax (01509) 812205.

THE EAST MIDLANDS HOTEL
Nottingham Road, LE11 1ET
In the reception foyer at the heart of the hotel you will be lulled by the sound of gently cascading waterfalls, the strains of a soft melody playing in the background, and the sight of trellising foliage creeping from the lantern-light glass roof two storeys above. The well-appointed bedrooms are tastefully decorated, and the intimate coves of the candlelit Victorian Restaurant will ensure a pleasant dining experience or stay.
DOUBLE ROOM: from £20 to £30
SINGLE ROOM: from £45 to £55
FOOD: from £15 to £20
Hours: breakfast 7am–10am, lunch 12noon–2pm, bar meals 11am–3pm, dinner 7pm–10pm, bar meals 6pm–11pm.
Cuisine: ENGLISH – delicious cuisine complemented by good wine list in an atmosphere of olde-worlde charm.
Cards: Visa, Access, Diners, AmEx, Switch.
Other points: parking, children welcome, pets allowed, swimming pool, sauna, gym facilities, conference facilities, function suite, residents' lounge, no-smoking area, vegetarian meals, traditional Sunday lunch.
Rooms: 18 double rooms, 31 twin room, 4 executive suites. All with en suite, satellite TV, telephone, radio, alarm, hair dryer, trouser-press, tea/coffee-making facilities.
Directions: junction 24 off M1, A6 to Loughborough, follow signs for Belton Road Industrial Estate (left at traffic lights). Close to Loughborough railway station.
ROBERT STEWART ☎ (01509) 233056 Fax (01509) 268665.

THE GEORGE HOTEL
17 Market Place, Belton, LE12 9UH
This old coaching inn dating back to 1753 is set in the rural village of Belton near the church. It offers a warm welcome and good wholesome food to travellers and locals alike. Near Castle Donnington race track and East Midlands Airport.
DOUBLE ROOM: from £20 to £30
SINGLE ROOM: from £25 to £35
FOOD: from £20 to £25
Hours: breakfast 7.30am–9.30am, lunch 12noon–2.30pm, dinner 7pm–10.30pm, bar meals 12noon–2.30pm, 7pm–10.30pm.
Cuisine: ENGLISH – home-made bar meals and very good à la carte menu available.
Cards: Visa, Access, Diners, AmEx.
Other points: licensed, Sunday lunch, vegetarian meals, children welcome, pets allowed, afternoon tea, disabled access, parking.
Rooms: 1 single room, 9 double rooms, 11 twin room, 2 family rooms.
Directions: 5 minutes from M1, junction 23 or 24, via A42.
MR HOUSTON ☎ (01530) 222426 Fax (01530) 222426.

CENTRAL ENGLAND • LEICESTERSHIRE

THE PACKE ARMS
Rempstone Arms, Hoton, LE12 5SJ
This pub has undergone a £500,000 refurbishment. There are facilities for all the family, with a beer garden, play area, barbecue and pétanque available. Private parties and receptions catered for.
FOOD: up to £15
Hours: lunch 12noon–2pm, Sunday 12noon–2.30pm, dinner (Friday–Saturday) 6pm–10pm, dinner (Monday–Thursday) 6.30pm–9pm, (Sunday) 7pm–9pm.
Cuisine: Extensive menu plus specials of the day. Most dishes are home-made. Vegetarian dishes always available.
Cards: Visa, Access, AmEx.
Other points: open-air dining, Sunday lunch, children welcome, playland, coaches by prior arrangement, beer garden.
Directions: on A60 Loughborough to Nottingham road.
PETER & SANDRA NEWMAN ☎ (01509) 880662.

LYDDINGTON • map 9D3

OLD WHITE HART COUNTRY INN & RESTAURANT
51 Main Street, LE15 9LS
Situated in an unspoilt village, this stone building with its walled garden is opposite the village green. Decorated to a high standard, it is furnished with good, solid yet comfortable furniture. In the restaurant you can enjoy quality food, appealingly presented and served in generous portions. The staff are skilled and helpful while the atmosphere is friendly and relaxed. Pétanque (French boules), for 60 persons on site, can be played by all ages. Private parties welcomed (French food and boules).
FOOD: up to £15
Hours: lunch 12noon–2pm, dinner 6.30pm–10am.
Cuisine: ENGLISH – full restaurant and bar menus: most popular dishes are mushrooms Lyddington, chicken in filo pastry with asparagus sauce, and Sussex pond pudding.
Cards: Visa, Access.
Other points: licensed, Sunday lunch, garden, pets allowed.
Directions: 1 mile south of Uppingham, follow 'Bede House' signs.
DIANE & BARRY BRIGHT ☎ (01572) 821703 [Fax] (01572) 821965.

MELTON MOWBRAY • map 9C3

SYSONBY KNOLL HOTEL & RESTAURANT
Asfordby Road, LE13 0HP
A family-run hotel, set in 2 acres of grounds with river frontage, the Sysonby Knoll has beautifully decorated rooms with quality furnishings. The restaurant offers an imaginative menu, which, our inspector comments, 'gives excellent value for money'.
DOUBLE ROOM: from £20 to £30
SINGLE ROOM: from £35 to £45
FOOD: up to £15
Hours: breakfast 7.30am–9.30am, lunch 12noon–2pm, dinner 7pm–9pm.
Cuisine: ENGLISH – extensive à la carte menu, which includes a vegetarian selection.
Cards: Visa, Access, Diners, AmEx.
Other points: Sunday lunch, pets allowed, garden, children welcome, cots, vegetarian meals, parking, residents' lounge, residents' bar, disabled access.
Rooms: 6 single rooms, 10 double rooms, 6 twin rooms, 2 triple rooms. All with TV, radio, alarm, telephone, tea/coffee-making facilities.
Directions: take A606/607 to Melton Mowbray. Follow A6006; half a mile from town centre.
STELLA BOOTH ☎ (01664) 63563.

OLD DALBY • map 9C3

THE CROWN INN
Debdale Hill, near Melton Mowbray, LE14 3LF
Tucked away in a corner of the village and approached through the large car park, the Crown Inn offers the facilities of a croquet lawn, large garden and a pétanque pitch. The beer is drawn straight from the wood, and the bar menu is interesting and extensive. Games room, snug and tap room with some no-smoking areas. Routiers Pub of the Year 1991.
FOOD: from £15 to £20
Hours: lunch 12noon–2pm, dinner 6pm–9.30pm.
Cuisine: MODERN ENGLISH – fresh, seasonal dishes.
Other points: licensed, open-air dining, Sunday lunch, children welcome.
Directions: off the A46 and the A606 in Old Dalby.
LYNNE BRYAN & SALVATORE INGUANTA ☎ (01664) 823134.

ROTHLEY • map 9C2

THE RED LION INN
933 Loughborough Road, LE7 7NJ
A coaching inn, trading since about 1725. Bar platters and snacks are served every day. Extensive table d'hôte.
FOOD: up to £15
Hours: lunch 12noon–2pm, dinner 7pm–10pm, bar meals 12noon–2pm, 6pm–10pm, restaurant closed Saturday lunch and Sunday dinner, open all year.
Cuisine: MODERN ENGLISH – regional French and English dishes complemented by an extensive wine list. Traditional Sunday lunch. Extensive bar snacks. Vegetarian menu. Summer barbecue.
Cards: Visa, Access, Diners, AmEx, Switch.
Other points: licensed, Sunday lunch, children welcome, playland, disabled access.
Directions: between Leicester and Loughborough at Rothley crossroads. B5328 and Loughborough road.
MRS IRENE DIMBLEBEE & MISS JENNIFER TEBBOTT ☎ (01116) 2302488.

LINCOLNSHIRE • CENTRAL ENGLAND

UPPINGHAM • map 9C3

FALCON HOTEL
High Street East, LE15 9PY
This renowned coaching inn of great charm and character, in the former county of Rutland, offers warmth and comfort in a convivial atmosphere, where you will be welcomed by the efficient and friendly staff. The hotel has long served as a popular meeting place on Uppingham's market square, with its traditional architecture and Dickensian-style shop fronts, which reflect a timeless quality. Situated a short distance from the A1 and M1 motorways, there are many nearby attractions, including Rutland Water, which is famous for its water sports and fishing, Burghley House and Rockingham Castle.
DOUBLE ROOM: from £20 to £30
FOOD: up to £15
Hours: breakfast 7.30am–9.30am, weekends 8am–10am, lunch 12noon–2pm, dinner 7pm–9.30pm.
Cuisine: ENGLISH / INTERNATIONAL.
Cards: Visa, Access, Diners, AmEx.
Other points: licensed, parking, children welcome, Sunday lunch, open bank holidays, afternoon tea, disabled access, pets allowed, residents' lounge, vegetarian meals, open-air dining.
Rooms: 5 single rooms, 12 double rooms, 6 twin rooms, 2 suites. All with TV, telephone, tea/coffee-making facilities.
Directions: near to Corby/Kettering on A6003 to Oakham.
RICHARD & JOANNE BATTERSBY ☎ (01572) 823535 [Fax] (01572) 821620.

WYMONDHAM • map 9C3

HUNTERS ARMS HOTEL
Edmondthorpe Road, Wymondham, LE14 2AD
Old stone-built country house offering beautifully cooked cuisine in the restaurant and a good snack to the traveller passing through. The hotel has a large garden at the rear, real ales, and warm and friendly service.
DOUBLE ROOM: up to £20
FOOD: up to £15
Hours: bar meals 12noon–2pm, dinner 7pm–9.30pm, bar meals 7pm–9.30pm, closed Monday.
Cuisine: ENGLISH – medallion of fillet steak flamed with brandy, mushroom and cream. Specials of the day, e.g., lambs liver Provençale, fillet of lemon sole, prawn and cream sauce, beef Wellington, bouillabaisse.
Cards: Visa, Access, Diners, AmEx.
Other points: licensed, Sunday lunch, vegetarian meals, pets allowed, children welcome.
Rooms: 2 twin rooms.
Directions: from the A607 onto the B676, past Wymondham.
MR & MRS M. MASCARO ☎ (01572) 787633.

LINCOLNSHIRE

GEDNEY DYKE • map 10C4

THE CHEQUERS
Near Spalding, PE12 0AJ
This is a small, homely country freehouse with restaurant. A new conservatory dining room has been added, which overlooks the garden and is non-smoking. The bar has low ceilings with exposed beams and has been attractively furnished. Good food and a friendly, welcoming atmosphere have made this restaurant and freehouse deservedly popular.
FOOD: up to £15
Hours: lunch 12noon–1.45pm, dinner 7pm–9.30pm, dinner (Monday–Wednesday) 7pm–9pm, no meals Christmas day and Boxing day, no meals Sunday evenings November to March.
Cuisine: ENGLISH – cooked on the premises, with local fresh fish and vegetables, and light meals in the bar. Full à la carte menu in the comfortably furnished restaurant.
Cards: Visa, Access, Diners, AmEx.
Other points: licensed, open-air dining, Sunday lunch, children welcome, garden.
Directions: take B1359 north of the A17 and turn left at the post office.
JUDITH & ROB MARSHALL ☎ (01406) 362666.

GRANTHAM • map 9C3

THE ROYAL OAK
Swayfield, near Grantham, NG33 4LL
This traditional stone-built country inn has been excellently maintained and is set amidst the attractive Lincolnshire countryside. Offering well-cooked and presented food, with 'special dishes' each day, served by helpful and friendly staff. Outside dining in well-tended beer garden during the summer months. Listed in the Good Beer Guide.
DOUBLE ROOM: up to £20
SINGLE ROOM: from £25 to £35
FOOD: up to £15
Hours: lunch 11am–2.30pm, Sunday 12noon–3pm, dinner 6pm–10.30pm, Sunday 7pm–10.30pm.
Cuisine: ENGLISH – à la carte with special Sunday lunch menu and special Sunday supper menu. Monday to Friday lunch, three-course table d'hôte and à la carte.
Cards: Visa, Access, AmEx.
Other points: licensed, Sunday lunch, children welcome, garden, pets allowed.
Rooms: 2 double rooms, 2 twin rooms, 1 family room. All en suite.
Directions: A1 south from Grantham. Left at

CENTRAL ENGLAND • LINCOLNSHIRE

Colsterworth roundabout. 2 miles, follow signs for Swayfield.
DAVID COOKE ☎ (01476) 550247.

LEADENHAM • map 9B3

GEORGE HOTEL
High Street, LN5 0PN
A family-run old coaching inn on the A17. The George is renowned for its well-stocked bar – a whisky-drinkers' delight, with over 500 varieties of whisky and drinks from around the world.
DOUBLE ROOM: up to £20
FOOD: up to £15
Hours: lunch 10.30am–2.30pm, dinner 6pm–11pm, last orders 10pm.
Cuisine: ENGLISH – steaks, Lincolnshire duckling à l'orange, Georgian trout.
Cards: Visa, Access, Diners, AmEx.
Other points: open-air dining, Sunday lunch, children welcome.
Rooms: 2 single rooms, 2 double rooms, 3 twin rooms. All with TV, tea/coffee-making facilities.
Directions: at the junction of the A17 and the A607, 8 miles from the A1.
MR G.M. WILLGOOSE ☎ (01400) 72251.

LINCOLN • map 9B3

HILLCREST HOTEL
15 Lindum Terrace, LN2 5RT
A former Victorian rectory situated in a quiet avenue, yet only 5 minutes' walk to the cathedral, museums and shops. The Hillcrest offers a chance to relax and enjoy a drink or meal in the wonderful conservatory, with views over the garden and parkland. Non-smoking restaurant and some non-smoking bedrooms.
DOUBLE ROOM: from £20 to £30
SINGLE ROOM: from £35 to £45
FOOD: up to £15 ☆
Hours: breakfast 7.15am–9am, lunch 12noon–2pm, dinner 7pm–8.45pm, bar meals (except Sunday) 7.30pm–9.30pm.
Cuisine: MODERN ENGLISH – dishes may include lamb noisettes, gammon in peaches and honey, steaks, vegetarian dishes, pork with honey and apple.
Cards: Visa, Access, AmEx, Switch.
Other points: licensed, no-smoking area, children welcome, pets allowed, afternoon tea, baby-listening device, cots, left luggage, vegetarian meals, parking, residents' bar, residents' lounge.
Rooms: 6 single rooms, 5 double rooms, 4 twin rooms, 2 family rooms. All with TV, radio, alarm, telephone, tea/coffee-making facilities.
Directions: off the A115 Wragby road, close to the cathedral.
JENNIFER BENNETT ☎ (01522) 510182
Fax (01522) 510182.

KINGS HEAD
31 High Street, Navenby, LN5 0EE
Situated in the attractive village of Navenby, this is a friendly and welcoming inn, frequented by the locals. Proprietors Cliff and Beryl Freeman both wait and serve at the bar to ensure personal service at all times. The ancient Viking Way passes nearby.
DOUBLE ROOM: up to £20
FOOD: up to £15 CLUB
Hours: lunchtime 11am–2.30pm, evening 5pm–11pm, Saturday 11am–11pm.
Cuisine: ENGLISH / CONTINENTAL – cooked to a high standard. Constantly changing menu.
Cards: Visa, Access.
Other points: parking, children welcome, open bank holidays, no-smoking area, disabled access, vegetarian meals, open-air dining.
Rooms: 2 double rooms, 2 twin rooms.
Directions: on the A607 between Lincoln and Grantham.
CLIFF & BERYL FREEMAN ☎ (01522) 810367.

PORTLAND HOTEL
49–55 Portland Street, LN5 7JZ
Situated 5 minutes from the city centre and close to the railway and coach stations, this guest house is ideally situated for the passing traveller or for visitors to the city. The reception is friendly and cheerful.
DOUBLE ROOM: up to £20
Hours: breakfast 7.30am–9am, open all year.
Cuisine: BREAKFAST.
Cards: Visa.
Other points: central heating, no evening meal, children welcome, residents' lounge, games room, garden.
Rooms: 7 single rooms, 3 double rooms, 3 twin rooms, 1 family room. All with TV.
Directions: off high street, opposite Ritz Theatre.
DAVID HALLGATH ☎ (01522) 521098.

WASHINGBOROUGH HALL COUNTRY HOUSE HOTEL
Church Hill, Washingborough, LN4 1BE
Set in 3 acres of lawns and woodland, on the edge of Washingborough village. The bar serves real ales, and the Wedgwood dining room serves an interesting and comprehensive menu as well as an excellent wine list. Outdoor heated swimming pool.
DOUBLE ROOM: from £30 to £40
SINGLE ROOM: from £45 to £55
FOOD: up to £15 ☆
Hours: breakfast 7.30am–9am, dinner 7pm–9pm.
Cuisine: ENGLISH – traditional cuisine.
Cards: Visa, Access, Diners, AmEx.
Other points: licensed, Sunday lunch, no-smoking area, children welcome, pets allowed, afternoon tea, heated swimming pool, residents' lounge, residents' bar, vegetarian meals, parking.
Rooms: 6 double rooms, 6 twin rooms.
Directions: from Lincoln town centre, take B1190 for Bardney. Turn right after 2 miles.
MARY & BRIAN SHILLAKER ☎ (01522) 790340
Fax (01522) 792936.

LOUTH • map 10A4

BRACKENBOROUGH ARMS HOTEL
Cordeaux Corner, LN11 0SZ
Set in the heart of the Lincolnshire Wolds, the hotel is situated in pleasant surroundings noted for

its natural beauty and within easy reach of all major routes. The bedrooms feature the best in home comforts, with many modern facilities. A beautifully furnished lounge boasts traditional low beams and log fire, and there is a superb dining room offering the finest in fresh cuisine. Nearby are the coastal towns of Mabelthorpe and Skegness, Market Rasen racecourse and Cadwell park, with historical Lincoln just an hour away.
DOUBLE ROOM: from £20 to £30
SINGLE ROOM: from £45 to £55
FOOD: from £15 to £20
Hours: breakfast 7am–10.30am, lunch 12noon–3pm, bar snacks 12noon–3pm, dinner 7pm–11pm, bar snacks 6.30pm–11pm, closed Christmas day and Boxing day.
Cuisine: ENGLISH.
Cards: Visa, Access, Diners, AmEx.
Other points: children welcome, open-air dining, vegetarian meals, garden, parking, disabled access.
Rooms: 18 bedrooms.
Directions: A16 Louth to Grimsby, 1 mile outside Louth.
J., D. & A. LIDGARD ☎ (01507) 609169
Fax (01507) 609413.

MR CHIPS FISH RESTAURANT
17–21 Aswell Street, LN11 9BA
A bright and roomy restaurant, which provides excellent value in both quantity and quality. Seating for 300. Self-service.
FOOD: up to £15
Hours: all day 9am–11pm, closed Sunday, closed Christmas, Boxing day and New Year's day, open bank holidays.
Cuisine: ENGLISH – fresh North Sea haddock, cod, plaice, scampi with chips and mushy peas. Lincolnshire sausages, Norfolk chicken, vegetarian meals. Selection of sweets.
Other points: licensed, no-smoking area, children catered for (please check for age limits), parking, air-conditioned, coaches by prior arrangement, baby changing room, disabled access and toilet.
Directions: from Market Place, turn into Queen Street, then first right into Aswell Street.
THE HAGAN FAMILY ☎ (01507) 603756
Fax (01507) 601255.

SKEGNESS • map 10B4

THE CRAWFORD HOTEL
104 South Parade, PE25 3HR
A very attractive, well-organized hotel, offering a high standard of service, with comfortable rooms and good food. Mr and Mrs Willis ensure their guests have every satisfaction: a full English breakfast is provided, but vegetarian, continental and any other dietary requirement is catered for on request.
DOUBLE ROOM: from £20 to £30
FOOD: up to £15
Hours: breakfast 8.30am–9.15am, lunch 12.30am–1.30pm, dinner 6pm.
Cuisine: BREAKFAST.
Cards: Visa, Access.
Other points: children welcome, afternoon tea, residents' lounge, swimming pool, sauna, solarium.
Rooms: 3 single rooms, 9 double rooms, 8 family rooms. All with TV, radio, alarm, tea/coffee-making facilities.
Directions: A52. Clock tower: right end of parade.
MR & MRS WILLIS ☎ (01754) 764215.

CROWN HOTEL
Drummond Road, PE25 3AB
Completely refurbished, the Crown Hotel provides first-class service with an ambience of quiet unobtrusiveness and efficiency in full traditional English style. Enjoy a swim in the hotel pool or a game of golf on one of the many nearby well-known professional courses. Ideally situated for touring the area's many attractions, such as the famous Gibraltar Point nature reserve.
DOUBLE ROOM: from £30 to £40
SINGLE ROOM: from £45 to £55
FOOD: up to £15
Hours: breakfast 7.30am–10am, lunch 12noon–2pm, bar meals 12noon–2pm, dinner 7pm–9.30pm.
Cuisine: ENGLISH – à la carte and table d'hôte menus. Dishes may include pork escalope with cider cream and apples, poached salmon steak. Vegetarian and children's dishes.
Cards: Visa, Access, Diners, AmEx.
Other points: licensed, Sunday lunch, parking, children welcome, residents' lounge, garden, functions, conferences.
Rooms: 1 single room, 4 double rooms, 13 twin rooms, 7 family rooms, 1 suite. All with TV, telephone, tea/coffee-making facilities.
Directions: A52 to Skegness. Lumley Road. Take last turning right before seafront.
PETER McGONAGLE ☎ (01754) 610760
Fax (01754) 610847.

STRAND RESTAURANT
The Savoy Hotel, 12 North Parade, PE25 2UB
The Strand Restaurant at The Savoy Hotel is a friendly, family-run business offering a very high standard of cuisine and service provided by warm and courteous staff. An excellent wine list complements the splendid dishes available from the table d'hôte and à la carte menus.
DOUBLE ROOM: from £20 to £30
FOOD: up to £15
Hours: breakfast 8am–9.30am, lunch 12noon–2pm, dinner 6pm–9.30pm.
Cuisine: ENGLISH – well-presented home-cooking with fresh local produce.
Cards: Visa, Access, Diners.
Other points: parking, children welcome, vegetarian meals, no-smoking area.
Directions: Situated on the Skegness seafront, close to the pier.
MR & MRS R. UNDERWOOD ☎ (01754) 763371.

SLEAFORD • map 9B3

MILLERS WINE BAR
Mill Court, Carre Street, NG4 7TR
A delightful 150-year-old red-brick barn set in the market town of Sleaford, it has been carefully renovated to provide a wine bar of character, with

CENTRAL ENGLAND • LINCOLNSHIRE

large oak beams and attractive patterned furnishings. Set in a secluded situation, it offers garden dining during the summer months and is extremely popular with people of all ages. Good location for visiting the RAF Museum at Cranwell and Heckington Mill.
FOOD: up to £15 [CLUB]
Hours: lunch 12noon–2pm, dinner 7pm–12midnight, bookings only on Sunday, closed Christmas day.
Cuisine: ENGLISH – healthy, wholesome and delicious.
Cards: Visa, AmEx, MasterCard, Switch, Delta.
Other points: parking, children welcome, open bank holidays, disabled access, pets allowed, vegetarian meals, open-air dining.
Directions: A153 to Skegness into centre of Sleaford, turn right opposite church and right into the carpark.
ROWENA MARY DROWLEY ☎ (01529) 413383.

SPALDING • map 10C4

THE RED LION HOTEL
Market Place, PE11 1SU

Sympathetically refurbished 18th century town centre hotel offering en suite accommodation, real ales, real food, a warm welcome and value for money. Local facilities include beautiful gardens and nurseries, fishing, clay pigeon shooting and golf.
DOUBLE ROOM: from £20 to £30
SINGLE ROOM: from £35 to £45
FOOD: up to £15 [CLUB] ☆
Hours: breakfast 7.30am–9.30am, lunch 12noon–2pm, dinner 7pm–9.30pm.
Cuisine: ENGLISH / CONTINENTAL.
Cards: Visa, Access, Diners, AmEx, Switch.
Other points: Sunday lunch, children welcome, disabled access.
Rooms: 1 single room, 7 double rooms, 7 twin rooms. All with TV, telephone, tea/coffee-making facilities.
Directions: centre of Spalding.
MRS J.M. & MR N.J. WILKINS ☎ (01775) 722869.

SPILSBY • map 10B4

RED LION INN / LE BARON RESTAURANT
Raithby-by-Spilsby, PE23 4DS

A pleasant Tudor-style country pub (a listed building), attractively furnished with brick-tiled floor, original beams and comfortable seating. The atmosphere is warm and friendly, as locals and tourists mix together to enjoy good food. Nearby places of interest include Wesley Chapel, Old Bolingbroke Castle and the famous Lincolnshire Wolds.
DOUBLE ROOM: up to £20
SINGLE ROOM: up to £25
FOOD: up to £15
Hours: breakfast 7.30am–10am, lunch by arrangement 12noon–2.30pm, dinner 7.15pm–10.30pm, bar meals every evening 7.15pm–10.30pm, bar meals weekends and bank holidays 12noon–3pm.
Cuisine: ENGLISH / FRENCH – with fish and game speciality dishes. Vegetarian meals available.
Cards: Visa, Access, AmEx.
Other points: licensed, open-air dining, Sunday lunch, pets allowed, disabled access, residents' lounge, parking, open bank holidays.
Rooms: 2 double rooms, 2 twin rooms.
Directions: Lincoln road out of Spilsby; turn right after Hundleby for Raithby.
ROGER & MAGGIE SMITH ☎ (01790) 753727.

STAMFORD • map 9C3

CANDLESTICKS HOTEL & RESTAURANT
1 Church Street, PE9 2JU

Occupying the corner unit of a stone Victorian building, this hotel has been established for over 18 years. During that time the restaurant has gained a fine reputation for the very high standard of food and for good-value prices. After an enjoyable meal, it is worth taking a walk around the historic stone-built town of Stamford. Highly recommended.
DOUBLE ROOM: from £20 to £30
FOOD: up to £15 🍲
Hours: continental breakfast taken in bedroom, lunch 12noon–2pm, dinner 7pm–9.30pm, Sunday 7pm–8.45pm, closed all day Monday and Tuesday morning.
Cuisine: FRENCH / CONTINENTAL – specialities include Portuguese dishes. Menu changes monthly.
Cards: Visa, Access.
Other points: licensed, Sunday lunch, children welcome, no-smoking area, parking, vegetarian meals.
Rooms: 2 single rooms, 3 double rooms, 3 twin rooms. All with en suite, satellite TV, telephone, tea/coffee-making facilities, fridge.
Directions: opposite St Martins church.
MANUEL PINTO ☎ (01780) 64033
[Fax] (01780) 56071.

WOODHALL SPA • map 10B4

EAGLE LODGE HOTEL
The Broadway, LN10 6ST

Purpose-built as an hotel in 1891, the Eagle Lodge reigned supreme when Woodhall Spa was as well known to high society in London as it now is to the golfing fraternity of the world. As one of the foremost hotels in Lincolnshire, the Eagle offers superb accommodation, a titillating choice of dishes in the Garden Restaurant, lovely garden views to enjoy while taking morning or afternoon tea in the Rose Lounge, and a great atmosphere in the well-stocked Regency Bar.
DOUBLE ROOM: from £20 to £30
FOOD: up to £15
Hours: breakfast 7.30am–9am, lunch 12noon–2pm, dinner 7pm–9.30pm.
Cuisine: ENGLISH – daily changing à la carte menu, including local game.

NORTHAMPTONSHIRE • CENTRAL ENGLAND

Cards: Visa, Access, Diners, AmEx, Switch.
Other points: parking, children welcome, pets allowed, conference facilities, residents' lounge, garden, open-air dining, vegetarian meals, traditional Sunday lunch, afternoon teas.
Rooms: 23 bedrooms. All with en suite, TV, telephone, radio, alarm, room service, tea/coffee-making facilities.
Directions: 45 minutes to A1, 30 miles from East Coast.
MICHAEL ARAM ☎ (01526) 353231
[Fax] (01526) 352797.

NORTHAMPTONSHIRE

CRICK • map 9D2

EDWARDS OF CRICK
The Wharf, NN6 7XT
Situated on the canal side, an ideal location for those seeking the more leisurely pace of life. Enjoy a romantic candlelit dinner in the spacious upstairs restaurant, or a pot of fresh-ground coffee in the informal ground-floor coffee house. While waiting for your meal, you can play bagatelle or solitaire, read the magazines, feed the ducks, or simply watch the boats go by.
FOOD: from £15 to £20
Hours: meals all day 10.30am, closed Sunday evening and Monday.
Cuisine: ENGLISH – à la carte menu, offering an interesting selection of freshly home-made dishes, in both restaurant and coffee house. Coffee house menu from £1.50.
Cards: Visa, Access, Diners, AmEx.
Other points: licensed, open air dining, Sunday lunch, children welcome, afternoon tea, disabled access, vegetarian meals, parking.
Directions: situated at the eastern end of Crick, off the A428. Near junction 18 of M1.
RICHARD COLEMAN ☎ (01788) 822517.

KETTERING • map 9D3

THE STAR INN
2 Bridge Street, Geddington, NN14 1AD
Peter and Ann welcome you to The Star Inn, where you will enjoy traditional ales, a good selection of fine wines and home-cooked food. Located in the attractive village of Geddington, this lovely 300-year-old public house and restaurant offers superb surroundings in which to enjoy the friendly atmosphere, whether relaxing over a drink or sampling the delicious cuisine. Log fires in winter.
FOOD: from £15 to £20
Hours: lunch weekdays 12noon–2pm, weekends 12noon–3pm, dinner 7pm–10pm, Sunday 7pm–9.30pm.
Cuisine: ENGLISH – a high standard of freshly prepared meals. Afternoon teas in summer.
Cards: Visa, Access, Diners.
Other points: parking, children welcome, no-smoking area, conference facilities, vegetarian meals, traditional Sunday lunch, afternoon teas.
Directions: mid-way between Kettering and Corby on the A43, only minutes from the M1–A1 link (A14).
ANN CAREY & PETER SMART ☎ (01536) 742386 [Fax] (01536) 742386.

NORTHAMPTON • map 9D3

COACH HOUSE HOTEL
8–10 East Park Parade, Kettering Road, NN1 4LA
Popular among business people, this charming Victorian hotel offers comfortable accommodation, good food and friendly service at reasonable prices. Close to the centre of town.
DOUBLE ROOM: from £20 to £30
FOOD: up to £15 [CLUB]
Hours: breakfast 7.30am–10am, dinner 7pm–9.30pm.
Cuisine: ENGLISH – traditional English cooking. Generous portions at reasonable prices. Real ales.
Cards: Visa, Access, Diners, AmEx.
Other points: licensed, children welcome, afternoon tea, pets allowed, residents' lounge, residents' bar, vegetarian meals, parking, satellite TV.
Directions: half a mile from town centre on A43 Northampton to Kettering road.
MRS LONG ☎ (01604) 250981.

RED LION HOTEL
Main Street, East Haddon, NN6 8BU
Its welcoming old-world atmosphere, comfortable decor and good food has given this establishment a well-deserved reputation as the ideal location for a peaceful weekend break. It is within easy reach of Althorp House, Guilsbrough Wild Life Park and facilities for golf, trout fishing, sailing and horse riding.
DOUBLE ROOM: up to £20
FOOD: from £15 to £20 [CLUB]
Hours: breakfast 7.30am–9.30am, lunch 12.30am–2pm, dinner 7pm–9.30pm, open all year.
Cuisine: ENGLISH – traditional English cooking with some more adventurous menu items. Examples of what you may find on the menu include fresh crab claws, rabbit and hare pie, supreme of chicken Roquefort.
Cards: Visa, Access, Diners, AmEx.
Other points: licensed, open-air dining, Sunday lunch, children welcome, residents' lounge, garden.
Rooms: 1 single room, 2 double rooms, 2 twin rooms. All with tea/coffee-making facilities.
Directions: off A428 between Northampton and Rugby, 7 miles from Junction 18 (M1).
IAN KENNEDY ☎ (01604) 770223 [Fax] (01604) 645866.

CENTRAL ENGLAND • NOTTINGHAMSHIRE

OUNDLE • map 9D3

FITZGERALDS RESTAURANT
26 West Street, PE8 4EF

A 17th century Grade II listed building in the heart of Oundle, which has been converted to a 32-seat restaurant with walled courtyard. All dishes are home-made using fresh, seasonal produce. The Routiers inspector was impressed by the very well-cooked food and welcoming service. Exposed oak beams and solid pine furniture add to the cosy, homely atmosphere. Good value.
FOOD: up to £15
Hours: morning coffee 10.30am–12noon, dinner 7pm–10pm, closed Sunday.
Cuisine: ENGLISH / FRENCH – an English country bistro offering regional French cuisine and traditional English fare.
Cards: Visa, Access.
Other points: licensed, open-air dining, children welcome, patio.
Directions: A605. 300 metres beyond Oundle War Memorial, towards Corby.
NIALL FITZGERALD ☎ (01832) 273242.

THE MILL AT OUNDLE
Barnwell Road

A friendly pub/restaurant, set in an 11th century restored watermill, offering a choice of eating and drinking venues on the banks of the River Nene. The mill race can be seen from the bars, and it is situated close to Barnwell Country Park and Oundle Marina.
FOOD: up to £15 CLUB
Hours: lunch 12noon–3pm, dinner 7pm–11pm.

Cuisine: ENGLISH – Granary restaurant serving English fare, and La Trattoria serving continental dishes with pizzas, steaks, fajitas, kebabs and seafood.
Cards: Visa, Access, AmEx.
Other points: open-air dining, Sunday lunch, no-smoking area, children welcome, open bank holidays.
Directions: off A605 to Oundle. Signs to Barnwell Country Park.
MR & MRS N. & L. TULLEY ☎ (01832) 272621
Fax (01832) 272166.

WELFORD • map 9D2

THE SHOULDER OF MUTTON INN
12 High Street, NN6 7HT

Charming 17th century low-beamed village inn on the A50. There is a large beer garden, and the play area will keep the liveliest children amused! Good home-cooked food served with a ready smile.
FOOD: up to £15
Hours: lunch 12noon–2pm. dinner 7pm–9.30pm.
Cuisine: INTERNATIONAL – varied menu to suit all tastes, in addition to daily home-made specials, i.e., Indian curries, beef stroganoff and chicken dishes.
Cards: Visa, Access, AmEx.
Other points: licensed, open-air dining, Sunday lunch, children welcome, free house.
Directions: on the A50, midway between Leicester and Northampton. Near junction 1 of A14 (A1–M1 link).
ARTHUR & JUDY CORLETT ☎ (01858) 575375.

NOTTINGHAMSHIRE

COLSTON BASSETT • map 9C3

THE MARTINS ARMS INN
School Lane, NG12 3FD

Housed in an attractive period building, The Martins Arms offers excellent food and and a warm welcome. Only fresh produce is used, and the menu offers a good choice of very well-cooked and presented dishes. During summer, drinks and meals can be enjoyed in the garden. The establishment is under the same ownership as The Crown Inn, Old Dalby, the winner of the Les Routiers Pub of the Year Award 1991.
FOOD: from £15 to £20
Hours: lunch 12noon–2pm, dinner 6pm–9.30pm.
Cuisine: ENGLISH / CONTINENTAL – dishes may include roast rack of English lamb served with a fresh tarragon and cream sauce, freshly-made tagliatelle with spicy chicken pieces.
Other points: licensed, open-air dining, Sunday lunch, beer garden.
Directions: A46 Bingham roundabout, left on A52, 1 mile, first right for Langar and Colston Bassett.
LYNNE BRYAN & SALVATORE INGUANTA
☎ (01949) 81361.

GUNTHORPE • map 9B3

THE TOLL HOUSE RESTAURANT
Riverside, NG14 7FB

First-class service is upheld in this small, friendly restaurant. The building itself used to be the toll house to the first Gunthorpe bridge built in 1875.
FOOD: from £15 to £20
Hours: dinner 7pm–10pm, closed Sunday evenings.
Cuisine: ENGLISH / FRENCH – moules marinière, salmon and smoked salmon mousse, fish, meat and fresh pasta dishes, with a selection of desserts and cheeses.
Cards: Visa, Access.
Other points: licensed, Sunday lunch, no-smoking area, Sunday lunch.
Directions: from Nottingham, turn left immediately before Gunthorpe bridge.
MR CLIVE HARRIS ☎ (0115) 9663409.

MANSFIELD • map 9B2

MAID MARIAN RESTAURANT
8 Church Street, Edwinstowe, NG21 9QA

Legend has it that Maid Marian and Robin Hood

204

NOTTINGHAMSHIRE • CENTRAL ENGLAND

were married in the church opposite this restaurant. Still celebrating the occasion, the à la carte menu offers dishes such as Will Scarlett's Feast and Robin's Reward.
FOOD: up to £15
Hours: meals all day 9am–10pm.
Cuisine: ENGLISH – extensive grill, snack, table d'hôte and à la carte menus. Excellent choice and good value for money.
Cards: Visa, Access, Diners, AmEx.
Other points: Sunday lunch, children welcome, coaches by prior arrangement
Directions: situated on the B6034 in the heart of Sherwood forest.
MR & MRS C.A. BENNETT ☎ (01623) 822266.

NEWARK-ON-TRENT • map 9B3

THE GRANGE HOTEL
73 London Road, NG24 1RZ
Set in a quiet residential park of Newark, The Grange Hotel is an attractive gabled town house, providing guests with modern, comfortable accommodation and excellent friendly service. The restaurant offers an à la carte menu, a table d'hôte menu and a vegetarian menu. Candlelight and soft music give the perfect setting for an enjoyable meal.
DOUBLE ROOM: from £30 to £40
FOOD: up to £15
Hours: breakfast 7.15am–8.45am, lunch by arrangement, dinner 7pm–9pm.
Cuisine: ENGLISH.
Cards: Visa, Access, Diners, AmEx, Switch, Delta.
Other points: parking, children welcome, conference facilities, residents' lounge, no-smoking area, vegetarian meals.
Rooms: 2 single rooms, 5 double rooms, 5 twin rooms, 1 triple room, 1 family room, 1 four-poster room. All with en suite, TV, telephone, radio, alarm, hair dryer, trouser-press, tea/coffee-making facilities.
Directions: south approach from A1.
CLIFF & CHRISTINE EDMONDSON ☎ (01636) 703399 [Fax] (01636) 702328.

THE GRIFFINS HEAD
Grantham Road, Whatton, NG13 9EA
Comfort, quality and value are the main concerns at this popular pub and restaurant, offering good, home-cooked meals and friendly, efficient service. Conveniently situated for Belvoir Castle and Newark market place.
FOOD: up to £15
Hours: lunch 12noon–2pm, dinner 6.30pm–10pm.
Cuisine: ENGLISH – traditional, fresh food.
Cards: Visa, Access, Diners, AmEx.
Other points: parking, children welcome, garden, vegetarian meals, traditional Sunday lunch.
Directions: A52 side of main Nottingham to Grantham road.
JAMES RENWICK ☎ (01949) 50214.

NEW FERRY RESTAURANT
Riverside, Farndon, NG24 3SX
Standing attractively by the River Trent, the New Ferry Restaurant serves generous portions of well-cooked food in a relaxed and friendly atmosphere. The menus offer a wide choice of dishes, and the specialities change three times a week to make use of the best in fresh produce. The high standard of the food is complemented by a good, varied wine list. 1994 Corps d'elite.
FOOD: up to £15 [CLUB]
Hours: lunch 12noon–2pm, dinner 7pm–10pm, open bank holidays, closed Monday.
Cuisine: MEDITERRANEAN – Mediterranean-influenced cuisine. Dishes may include fresh salmon with a fennel and cream sauce, or rack of lamb with a redcurrant and port sauce. Fresh lobster, shellfish, etc. always available.
Cards: Visa, Access, Diners, AmEx.
Other points: licensed, open-air dining, Sunday lunch, children welcome.
Directions: off A46, Nottingham to Newark road. 5 minutes from Newark. Next to River Trent.
JOSE & PAM GOMES ☎ (01636) 76578.

THE WILLOW TREE INN
Front Street, Barnby-in-the-Willows, NG24 2SA
This delightful 17th century inn was a former stop for drivers on the heavy horse route from Newark to the coast. Retaining its welcoming aspect and atmosphere, this heavily beamed, typical country inn is nestled in the conservation village of Barnby-in-the-Willows and makes a charming resting place for anyone who appreciates good food and good beer. Horse-riding and livery can be arranged locally.
DOUBLE ROOM: up to £20
SINGLE ROOM: up to £25
FOOD: up to £15 [CLUB]
Hours: breakfast 7.45am–9am, lunch 12noon–2pm, dinner 7pm–12midnight, last orders 10.30pm, bar meals 7pm–10.30pm, closed Christmas day.
Cuisine: ENGLISH – traditional English cuisine with regular daily specials. Menu features traditional main courses such as rabbit pie, game pie. Good desserts.
Cards: Visa, Access, AmEx, MasterCard.
Other points: licensed, Sunday lunch, children welcome, cots, parking, vegetarian meals, no dogs.
Rooms: 1 single room, 2 double rooms, 2 family rooms. All with TV, clock/radio, tea/coffee-making facilities.
Directions: near Newark golf course. Turn off A17 (signposted Barnby).
DONALD & MARY-ANNE GRANT ☎ (01636) 626613 [Fax] (01636) 626613.

NOTTINGHAM • map 9C2

BELL INN
Old Market Square, NG1 6HL
A 15th century traditional inn, situated in the historic heart of Nottingham, offering well-presented, appetizing English fare complemented by warm and courteous service. Owned and operated by the same family for over 95 years, the Bell Inn, with its original oak beams and ancient flagstones, makes a pleasant lunchtime stop for

205

locals and tourists alike.
FOOD: up to £15 [CLUB]
Hours: lunch 11.30am–2.15pm, closed evenings, restaurant closed Sunday.
Cuisine: ENGLISH – good English fare at reasonable prices.
Cards: Visa, Access, Diners, AmEx.
Other points: children welcome, pets allowed, street parking.
Directions: situated in Old Market Square in the centre of Nottingham.
DAVID R. JACKSON ☎ (0115) 9475241
[Fax] (0115) 9475502.

THE HAVEN
Grantham Road, Whatton, NG13 9EU
The Haven is a pleasant, homely hotel, situated in 5 acres of grassland in the beautiful Vale of Belvoir. Offers food of fine quality, in generous proportions, at very good value for money.
DOUBLE ROOM: from £20 to £30
SINGLE ROOM: from £25 to £35
FOOD: up to £15
Hours: breakfast 7am–9.30am, lunch 12noon–2pm, dinner 6pm–10pm.
Cuisine: ENGLISH.
Cards: Visa, Access, AmEx.
Other points: licensed, open-air dining, Sunday lunch, no-smoking area, children catered for (please check for age limits), pets allowed, open bank holidays, afternoon tea.
Rooms: 33 bedrooms.
Directions: between Nottingham and Grantham. Corner of A52 and road to Belvoir Castle.
LESLIE & BETTY HYDES ☎ (01949) 50800.

JALLANS
9 Byard Lane, NG1 2GJ
A Victorian flagged-floor building situated up a small alley in the heart of the city of Nottingham, providing an ideal meeting place for lunch amid a friendly and lively atmosphere. The decor is bright and welcoming, with dried flower arrangements, patterned table cloths and wooden chairs, and the food is well presented, with good use of garnishes. Ideal location for visitors to the city, with Tales of Robin Hood, the Theatre Royal, concert hall and shops all within walking distance.
FOOD: up to £15 [CLUB]
Hours: meals all day 11am–7pm, closed Christmas day and New Year's day.
Cuisine: INTERNATIONAL.
Cards: Visa, Access, Diners, AmEx.
Other points: children welcome, open bank holidays, afternoon tea, disabled access, vegetarian meals, licensed.
Directions: situated in the city centre, off Bridlesmith Gate, opposite Paul Smith.
MR ROMER, MR VIGGERS, MR BRADFIELD
☎ (0115) 9506684.

THE OLD SHIP
Main Street, Lowdham, NG14 7BE
This 18th century converted cottage with a nautical theme offers visitors a welcoming atmosphere in which to enjoy a traditional, freshly cooked meal or simply relax with friends over a drink from the well-stocked bar. The Old Ship is popular with locals and travellers of all ages.
FOOD: up to £15
Hours: lunch 12noon–2pm, dinner 6.30pm–10pm.
Cuisine: ENGLISH – traditional dishes and chef's daily specials.
Cards: Visa, Access.
Other points: parking, children welcome, garden, vegetarian meals, traditional Sunday lunch.
Directions: centre of Lowdham village.
JAMES RENWICK ☎ (0115) 9663049.

THE TOWN HOUSE
8–10 Low Pavement, NG1 7DL
The Town House restaurant and coffee house are two Grade II listed buildings in Victorian Gothic and Edwardian style, set in a pedestrianized area in the heart of the city of Nottingham. Popular with the local business community, it has an informal atmosphere where you can enjoy good food in generous portions. Upstairs is a new self-service restaurant offering a wide range of food, including various vegetarian meals and cakes. Ideal for shopping or for visiting Nottingham Castle.
FOOD: up to £15
Hours: meals all day Monday, Tuesday, Friday and Saturday 8.30am–6pm, Wednesday and Thursday 8.30am–9pm, closed Sunday.
Cuisine: MODERN BRITISH.
Cards: Visa.
Other points: children welcome, vegetarian meals, no-smoking area, open-air dining, baby-listening device, changing room.
Directions: situated in the heart of the city.
CHRIS & LINDSAY DEERING ☎ (0115) 9470074.

WALTON'S HOTEL
North Lodge, The Park, NG7 1AG
Originally the hunting lodge to the Castle Deer Park, Walton's Hotel is a Regency house furnished with antiques and offering food and accommodation of a very high standard. The atmosphere is pleasant and welcoming, and guests can relax and enjoy the good food and wine in the comfort of the elegant dining room. Within walking distance of the city centre, theatres and castle.
DOUBLE ROOM: from £40 to £50
SINGLE ROOM: over £50
FOOD: up to £15 [CLUB]
Hours: breakfast 7.30am–10am, dinner 7.30pm–9.30pm, lunch 12.30am–2pm.
Cuisine: FRENCH – dishes include scallops in ginger sauce, chicken in hazelnut sauce and a large selection of steaks, but fish is their speciality.
Cards: Visa, Access, AmEx.
Other points: licensed, open-air dining, Sunday lunch, children welcome, garden, afternoon tea, pets allowed, residents' lounge.
Rooms: 4 single rooms, 14 double rooms, 3 twin rooms, 1 family room.
Directions: A6200. From A52 follow city centre signs. 200 yards from police station.
G.L. FLANDERS & T.W.K. WALTON ☎ (0115) 9475215 [Fax] (0115) 9475053.

THURGARTON • map 9B3

THE RED LION
Southwell Road, NG14 7GP
An attractive 16th century olde-worlde inn, the tasteful decor in keeping with the period and style of the inn throughout. The food is reputable, the well-stocked bar will quench any thirst, and the service and atmosphere are both very warm and friendly.
FOOD: up to £15
Hours: lunch 12noon–2pm, dinner 7pm–10pm.
Cuisine: ENGLISH – traditional à la carte menu; also daily chef's choice.
Cards: Visa, Access, Diners, AmEx, Switch, Delta.
Other points: parking, children welcome, garden, open-air dining, vegetarian meals, traditional Sunday lunch.
Directions: on the main Nottingham to Southwell road.
JAMES RENWICK ☎ (01636) 830351.

WORKSOP • map 9B2

LION HOTEL
112 Bridge Street, S80 1HT
A 16th century coaching inn, the Lion Hotel is situated in the centre of Worksop, offering a warm welcome and comfortable accommodation. The restaurant provides well-cooked and presented meals with a good choice of traditional and more imaginative dishes. Bar meals are served in the popular, lively bar adjoining the restaurant. It is close to Sherwood Forest, Clumber Park and Creswell Crags.
DOUBLE ROOM: from £20 to £30
SINGLE ROOM: from £45 to £55
FOOD: from £20 to £25 ★
Hours: breakfast 7am–9.30am, lunch 12noon–2pm, bar meals 11.30am–2.30pm, dinner 7pm–9.45pm, bar meals 7pm–9.30pm.
Cuisine: ENGLISH / CONTINENTAL – carte de jour and table d'hôte menus featuring traditional English and more imaginative dishes. Good vegetarian menu available. Traditional Sunday lunch.
Cards: Visa, Access, AmEx.
Other points: licensed, Sunday lunch, children welcome, pets allowed, residents' lounge, gym facilities, sauna, solarium, functions.
Rooms: 32 bedrooms.
Directions: Market Square, turn right at Eyres furniture store, then sharp right.
COOPLANDS (DONCASTER) LTD ☎ (01909) 477925 [Fax] (01909) 479038.

OXFORDSHIRE

ABINGDON • map 5B2

THE DOG HOUSE HOTEL
Frilford Heath, OX13 6QJ
The Dog House is set in the idyllic countryside of the Vale of the White Horse and is the ideal place to spend a couple of days to get away from it all. There are beautiful panoramic views of the Downs in the distance at all times of the year and always plenty to do in the surrounding area. Each of the comfortable en suite bedrooms is attractively furnished to make your stay as relaxing as possible.
DOUBLE ROOM: from £30 to £40
SINGLE ROOM: from £35 to £45
FOOD: up to £15
Hours: breakfast weekdays 7.30am–9am, weekends 9am–10am, lunch 12noon–2.30pm, dinner 7pm–10pm, Sunday 7pm–9pm.
Cuisine: ENGLISH – an excellent range of meals, always with an emphasis on quality and variety.
Cards: Visa, Access, Diners, AmEx.
Other points: parking, children welcome, pets allowed, conference facilities, residents' lounge, garden, vegetarian meals, traditional Sunday lunch.
Rooms: 19 bedrooms. All with TV, telephone, radio, alarm, hair dryer, tea/coffee making facilities.
Directions: off A34 at Abingdon South junction, onto A415 to Masham, first right, then approximately 3 miles.
TIM ALLEN ☎ (01865) 390830 [Fax] (01865) 390860.

ASTHALL • map 5B2

THE MAYTIME INN
Near Burford, OX8 4HW
Situated in a tiny hamlet, 2½ miles from Burford, The Maytime Inn has retained much of its centuries-old Cotswold charm. In addition to a spacious bar, there is a dining room seating 80 where one can wine and dine in style and comfort.
DOUBLE ROOM: from £20 to £30
FOOD: up to £15 [CLUB]
Hours: breakfast 8am–11am, lunch 11am–2.30pm, dinner 7pm–10pm, open bank holidays.
Cuisine: ENGLISH / INTERNATIONAL – daily specials, e.g., steak-and-kidney pie, fish pie, medallions of fillet steak Chinese-style, fresh local salmon.
Cards: Visa, Access, AmEx.
Other points: licensed, open-air dining, Sunday lunch, children welcome.
Rooms: 2 double rooms, 6 twin rooms.
Directions: down a narrow country lane from the A40 between Witney and Burford.
T.M. & M. MORGAN ☎ (0199382) 2068.

LES ROUTIERS
Information & Bookings Line
☎ 0171 610 1856

CENTRAL ENGLAND • OXFORDSHIRE

BANBURY • map 5A2

🏠 EASINGTON HOUSE & FARMHOUSE RESTAURANT
50 Oxford Road, OX16 9AN
Malcolm and Gwynneth Hearne ensure that all guests are greeted with warmth and guenuine courtesy at this delightful 400-year-old country house hotel. Style and elegance are evident in every room, whether you are relaxing in the intimate lounge, sampling cuisine of a very high standard in the Farmhouse Restaurant or preparing for a restful night in one of the tastefully decorated bedrooms.
DOUBLE ROOM: from £30 to £40
SINGLE ROOM: from £45 to £55
FOOD: up to £15
Hours: breakfast 7.30am–9am, dinner 7pm–9.30pm.
Cuisine: ENGLISH / CONTINENTAL – fresh local produce used.
Cards: Visa, Access, Diners, AmEx.
Other points: parking, pets allowed, conference facilities, residents' lounge, garden, open-air dining, vegetarian meals.
Rooms: 12 bedrooms. All with TV, telephone, tea/coffee-making facilities.
Directions: 300 yards south of Banbury Cross on B4100.
MALCOLM & GWYNNETH HEARNE
☎ (01295) 270181 Fax (01295) 269527.

🏠 THE MOON & SIXPENCE
Hanwell, OX17 1HW
Snuggling in the old Anglo-Saxon village of Hanwell, deep in the Oxfordshire countryside, the Moon & Sixpence offers luxurious accommodation. The attractive split-level restaurant seats up to 100 in comfort, who all come to enjoy the excellent freshly prepared cuisine and fine wines. The Oak Room is available for private hire, as are many other rooms: details on request. Large car park for guests.
DOUBLE ROOM: from £20 to £30
FOOD: from £20 to £25 ★
Hours: lunch 12noon–2pm (last orders), dinner 7pm–10pm, closed part of August.
Cuisine: INTERNATIONAL – finest Scottish beef dishes. Poached Scotch salmon and grilled Dover sole feature among the fresh fish selection. Involtini della mamma!
Cards: Visa, Access.
Other points: licensed, patio, children welcome, residents' lounge, parking, disabled access.
Rooms: 2 double rooms, 1 twin room. Let as a suite for 1–6 guests.
Directions: close to junction 11 of M40 between A423 and B4100, north from Banbury.
LEONARDO & GILLIAN DE FELICE ☎ (01295) 730544 Fax (01295) 730147.

🍴 RED LION INN
High Street, Bloxham, OX15 4LX
With its good range of first-rate home-cooked bar meals and CAMRA commendation for their excellent selection of beers, there is no cause to doubt the inn's popularity. Paul and Carol provide warm and friendly hospitality and even offer a free mini-bus service (for four or more diners) within a 10-mile radius, so you can relax and enjoy yourself without worrying about the ever-present drink/driving problem.
FOOD: up to £15
Hours: lunch 12noon–2pm, dinner 7pm–10pm.
Cuisine: ENGLISH – a wide range of grills, home-cooked fare and bar meals.
Cards: Visa, Access, AmEx.
Other points: parking, children welcome, pets allowed, garden, open-air dining, vegetarian meals, traditional Sunday lunch.
Directions: on Main Road, centre of Bloxham Road from Banbury to Chipping Norton.
PAUL COOPER ☎ (01295) 720352
Fax (01295) 720007.

🏠 ROEBUCK INN
Drayton, OX15 6EN
The 16th century stone-built village pub offers excellent-value bar meals and a good à la carte menu with fish, steak and vegetarian specialities, served in a friendly atmosphere.
DOUBLE ROOM: up to £20
FOOD: up to £15
Hours: breakfast 8am–9am, lunch 11.30am–2pm, dinner 7pm–9.30pm.
Cuisine: ENGLISH – à la carte.
Cards: Visa, Access.
Other points: licensed, Sunday lunch, children welcome.
Rooms: 1 double room, 1 twin room.
Directions: A422, just outside Banbury.
MICHAEL & LIZ BROWN ☎ (01295) 730542.

🏠 THE WHITE HORSE INN
Duns Tew, OX6 4JS
A Grade I listed 17th century inn, constructed of Cotswold stone. The interior is heavily beamed and the walls adorned with saddlery and horse-brasses, which add to the quaintness. As the only pub in the village, it is a firm favourite with locals who visit regularly. Nearby places of interest are Blenheim Palace, Oxford (15 miles) and Stratford (18 miles). The hotel now has its own 18-hole golf course, par 72, 6,100 yards.
DOUBLE ROOM: from £20 to £30
FOOD: up to £15
Hours: breakfast 8.30am–9.30am, lunch 12.30am–2pm, dinner 7.30pm–9.30pm.
Cuisine: ENGLISH – à la carte and table d'hôte menus offering traditional English fare.
Cards: Visa, Access.
Other points: licensed, open-air dining, Sunday lunch, children welcome, residents' lounge, parking, disabled access, vegetarian meals, air-conditioned.
Rooms: 6 double rooms, 7 twin rooms. All with TV, tea/coffee-making facilities.
Directions: five miles from junction 10 on M40. Two miles south of Deddington.
E. SINCLAIR ☎ (01869) 40272 Fax (01869) 47732.

BURFORD • map 5B2

🏠 COTSWOLD GATEWAY
Cheltenham Road Roundabout, OX18 4HX
Situated in the enchanting town of Burford with its

1,000 inhabitants, the Cotswold Gateway has for more than 200 years provided a welcome stopover for travellers. Today, guests can expect personal and caring attention in a friendly and intimate atmosphere from the highly trained staff. Burford, set on the valley side of the River Windrush and surrounded by old hay meadows and cornfields, has changed little since the early 17th century and is also an important centre for reputable antique dealers.
DOUBLE ROOM: from £30 to £40
FOOD: from £15 to £20
Hours: breakfast 7.30am–9.30am, lunch 12noon–2pm, bar snacks 12noon–2pm, dinner 7pm–9.30pm, bar snacks 7pm–9.30pm.
Cuisine: MODERN ENGLISH – great attention paid to quality and presentation.
Cards: Visa, Access, Diners, AmEx.
Other points: parking, children welcome, Sunday lunch, open bank holidays, afternoon tea, disabled access, pets allowed, residents' lounge, vegetarian meals, licensed.
Rooms: 1 single room, 9 double rooms, 16 twin rooms, 4 family rooms.
Directions: on the A40 main road, right by the roundabout at the top of Burford Hill.
RAY & JOYCE FORD ☎ (01993) 822695
[Fax] (01993) 823600.

DIDCOT • map 5B2

THE RED LION
Nottingham Fee, Blewbury, OX11 9PQ
A very old, traditional country pub, tucked away in the pretty village of Blewbury. The interior has an olde-worlde appearance and an informal, relaxed atmosphere in which to enjoy the good bar meals.
FOOD: up to £15
Hours: lunch 12noon–2pm, dinner 6pm–9.30pm, Sunday evening 7pm–7.30pm.
Cuisine: ENGLISH – bar meals including daily specials, especially fresh fish.
Cards: Visa, Access, Diners, AmEx.
Other points: licensed, Sunday lunch, children welcome, garden, disabled access.
Directions: off the A417.
ROGER SMITH ☎ (01235) 850403.

FARINGDON • map 5B2

THE CROWN HOTEL
Market Square, SN7 7HU
An outstanding hotel by all accounts, The Crown Hotel offers splendid accommodation, excellent cuisine and superb hospitality to all who dine or stay there. The building surrounds a charming, historic cobbled courtyard where you can sit out and enjoy a meal or snack during the summer months; in the winter you can eat by a log fire in the cosy, panelled Crown Bar. The hotel has a restaurant, a ballroom and conference facilities. Highly recommended.
DOUBLE ROOM: from £20 to £30
SINGLE ROOM: from £35 to £45
FOOD: up to £15

OXFORDSHIRE • CENTRAL ENGLAND

Hours: breakfast 7am–9am, Sunday lunch 12.30am–2.30pm, bar meals 11.30am–2.30pm, dinner 7.30pm–9pm, bar meals 6pm–10.30pm, closed Christmas day and Boxing day.
Cuisine: ENGLISH – à la carte restaurant menu and bar meals.
Cards: Visa, Access.
Other points: parking, children welcome, pets allowed, conference facilities, wedding receptions, garden, open-air dining, vegetarian meals, afternoon teas, traditional Sunday lunch.
Rooms: 3 single rooms, 7 double rooms, 1 twin room. All with TV, telephone, television, tea/coffee-making facilities, room service, baby-listening device.
Directions: take Faringdon town centre turn from A420 or A417.
ANDREW & BECKY BRYSON ☎ (01367) 242744 [Fax] (01367) 240058.

GORING • map 5C2

THE MILLER OF MANSFIELD HOTEL
High Street, RG8 9AW
A beautiful 18th century building decorated in line with the period and with many antiques. The hotel is situated close to the river in the village centre. The Goring Gap is an area of outstanding natural beauty. 9 miles from Reading, 15 miles from Oxford, and with easy access from the M4. Special weekend rates, except bank holidays.
DOUBLE ROOM: from £20 to £30
SINGLE ROOM: from £25 to £35
FOOD: up to £15
Hours: breakfast 7.30am–9am, lunch 12noon–2pm, dinner 7pm–10pm.
Cuisine: ENGLISH – varied à la carte menu including grills, plus extensive bar food menus.
Cards: Visa, Access.
Other points: licensed, children welcome, parking, vegetarian meals.
Rooms: 10 bedrooms. All with TV, radio, tea/coffee-making facilities. 5 rooms are en suite.
Directions: from A329, take the B4009 at Streatley, cross river, 200 yards on left.
MARTIN WILLIAMSON ☎ (01491) 872829 [Fax] (01491) 874200.

OXFORD • map 5B2

BELFRY HOTEL
Brimpton Grange, Milton Common, OX9 2TN
Set in the Oxfordshire countryside approximately 10 minutes from Oxford. Decorated and furnished to a high standard and enjoying a friendly atmosphere. Good food and comfortable accommodation. Highly recommended.
DOUBLE ROOM: from £40 to £50
SINGLE ROOM: over £55
FOOD: from £20 to £25
Hours: breakfast weekdays 7.30am–9.30am, weekends 8.30am–9.30am, lunch 12.30am–2pm, bar meals 12.30am–2pm, dinner 7.30pm–9.30pm, closed 24th December until 31st December.

209

Cuisine: ENGLISH – serving bar snacks, full à la carte menu and table d'hôte.
Cards: Visa, Access, Diners, AmEx.
Other points: licensed, Sunday lunch, children welcome, leisure centre, conferences, baby-sitting, cots, 24hr reception.
Rooms: 11 single rooms, 36 double rooms, 30 twin rooms. All with TV, radio, phone, tea/coffee-making facilities.
Directions: situated on the A40 between junctions 7 and 8 of the M40.
MR BARBER ☎ (01844) 279381 Fax (01844) 279624.

HOPCROFTS HOLT HOTEL
Steeple Aston, OX5 3QQ

A large 15th century coaching inn, which has been extensively refurbished to offer well-appointed bedrooms, good food and a relaxed informal atmosphere. Situated very close to the delightful village of Steeple Aston, the hotel is an ideal base for touring North Oxfordshire and the Northern Cotswolds.
DOUBLE ROOM: from £20 to £30
FOOD: from £15 to £20 CLUB
Hours: breakfast 7.30am–9.30am, lunch 12noon–2pm, dinner 7pm–9.45pm, Sunday 7pm–8.30pm.
Cuisine: MODERN ENGLISH – escalope of salmon and crunchy vegetables with lemon butter, fillet beef with a celery and Stilton jus, poached supreme of chicken and fresh salad.
Cards: Visa, Access, Diners, AmEx.
Other points: licensed, Sunday lunch, children welcome, garden, afternoon tea, pets allowed, parking, vegetarian meals, residents' lounge, residents' bar, disabled access.
Directions: midway between Oxford and Banbury on A4260.
☎ (01869) 40259 Fax (01869) 40865.

PICKWICKS
17 London Road, Headington, OX3 7SP

A comfortable, quiet and efficiently managed hotel with first-class decor and facilities. Large, clean, well-appointed dining room and a comfortable residents' lounge. A welcoming and helpful attitude will be found here.
DOUBLE ROOM: from £20 to £30
SINGLE ROOM: from £25 to £35
FOOD: up to £15
Hours: breakfast 7am–8.30am, Sunday 8am–9am.
Cuisine: BREAKFAST.
Cards: Visa, Access, Diners, AmEx, MasterCard.
Other points: children welcome, garden.
Rooms: 15 bedrooms.
Directions: quarter of a mile from Oxford centre on London Road (A420).
G.J. & P. MORRIS ☎ (01865) 750487/69413 Fax (01865) 742208.

THE WHITE HOUSE HOTEL
315 Iffley Road, OX4 4AG

Situated conveniently for access in and out of Oxford, this town house hotel offers their guests a warm and friendly atmosphere in a good location. The hotel has been well decorated with comfort in mind, for that relaxed home-away-from-home feeling.
DOUBLE ROOM: from £20 to £30
FOOD: up to £15
Hours: breakfast 7am–9.20am, dinner 6pm–7.30pm.
Cuisine: ENGLISH.
Cards: Visa, Access.
Other points: children welcome, parking, no-smoking area, pets allowed, residents' lounge, garden.
Rooms: 3 double rooms, 2 twin rooms, 1 family room. All with TV, tea/coffee-making facilities.
Directions: approaching Oxford on the A40, take the city centre route along London Road. At the roundabout junction of the A40/A4158, head south along Iffley Road. The White House can be found approximately 1¼ miles down, on the left.
DIANE & DENIS DUVNJAK ☎ (01865) 244524 Fax (01865) 244524.

SHIPTON-UNDER-WYCHWOOD
map 5B2

THE SHAVEN CROWN HOTEL
Chipping Norton, OX7 6BA

Built c.1380 as a hospice to Bruern Abbey, The Shaven Crown is now one of the ten oldest inns in England. An attractive building of honey-coloured stone around a medieval courtyard with a fountain, in the heart of the Cotswolds. In fine weather, dine alfresco in the courtyard.
DOUBLE ROOM: from £30 to £40
FOOD: up to £15
Hours: breakfast 8.30am–9.30am, bar meals 12noon–2pm, dinner 7.30pm–9.30pm, Sundays 7.30pm–9pm, bar meals 7pm–9.30pm.
Cuisine: ENGLISH – an excellent selection of à la carte and bar meal dishes.
Cards: Visa, Access.
Other points: licensed, open-air dining, Sunday lunch, children welcome, afternoon tea.
Rooms: 9 bedrooms.
Directions: 4 miles north of Burford on the A361, opposite the church and green.
TREVOR & MARY BROOKES ☎ (01993) 830330.

SOULDERN • map 5A2

FOX INN
Fox Lane, OX6 9JW

A traditional 19th century stone-built inn, situated 7 miles north of Bicester off the B4100 in a beautiful Cotswold stone village. Ideal for Oxford, Stratford, the Cotswolds, Warwick and Silverstone motor racing circuit.
DOUBLE ROOM: up to £20
FOOD: from £15 to £20
Hours: breakfast 8am–9.30am, lunch 12noon–2pm, bar meals 12noon–2pm, dinner 7pm–12midnight, last orders 9.30pm, bar meals 7pm–9.30pm, no food Sunday evening.
Cuisine: EUROPEAN – roast Sunday lunch, table d'hôte and à la carte menu, daily specials in both bar and restaurant.
Cards: Visa, Access, AmEx.

OXFORDSHIRE • CENTRAL ENGLAND

Other points: open-air dining, Sunday lunch, children welcome, fishing nearby, golf nearby.
Rooms: 3 double rooms, 1 twin room. All with TV, tea/coffee-making facilities.
Directions: follow Souldern signs off the B4100; situated on left in village, 200 yards past pond. 3 miles from junction 10 of M40.
IAN MACKAY ☎ (01869) 345284 [Fax] (01869) 40074.

THAME • map 5B3

ABINGDON ARMS
21 Cornmarket, OX9 2BL
A large Victorian public house, which adequately caters for families and tourists to the area. There is a large beer garden with children's climbing frame, swing and sandpit. Barbecues are frequently held in the garden or barn, which is available for private hire, and live bands and discos can be provided. Jazz bands play in the barn on a regular basis.
DOUBLE ROOM: up to £20
SINGLE ROOM: from £25 to £35
FOOD: up to £15
Hours: breakfast 8am–10.30am, lunch 12noon–2.30pm, dinner 6pm–9pm.
Cuisine: ENGLISH / CONTINENTAL.
Cards: Visa, Access.
Other points: children welcome, parking, disabled access, vegetarian meals, open-air dining.
Rooms: 5 twin rooms.
Directions: enter Thame from Oxford direction, in main high street at first zebra crossing and lights: on the right.
WAYNE BONNER ☎ (01844) 260116 [Fax] (01844) 260338.

DISCOVER FRANCE FOR ONLY £9.99!

The *Les Routiers Guide to France* is the only official fully translated guide to the French *Routiers*, listing over 1,600 recommended restaurants, cafés and hotels throughout this alluring country.

Available from all good bookshops, or direct from the publishers, price £9.99.

WARBOROUGH • map 5B2

THE SIX BELLS
The Green South, OX10 7DN
A delightful 15th century thatched inn housing its own restaurant, offering outstanding British cuisine with nouvelle cuisine influences. It has undergone considerable refurbishment to provide a comfortable atmosphere with attractive furnishings. The River Thames, Dorchester Abbey, Henley on Thames and the city of Oxford are within easy reach.
FOOD: up to £15 ☆

Hours: bar snacks 12noon–2.30pm, dinner 7pm–10pm.
Cuisine: BRITISH.
Cards: Visa, Access.
Other points: parking, Sunday lunch, open bank holidays, no-smoking areas, disabled access, vegetarian meals, open-air dining.
Directions: A329, 2 miles from Wallingford off Henley to Oxford road.
MR C. DAVEY ☎ (0186732) 8265 [Fax] (0186732) 8556.

WATLINGTON • map 5B3

THE WELL HOUSE RESTAURANT & HOTEL
34–40 High Street, OX9 5PY
An elegant 15th century house in a small picturesque town at the foot of the Chilterns, some 40 miles from London and 30 minutes from Heathrow Airport. The Well House restaurant comprises an attractive cocktail bar and dining room with inglenook fireplace. Close to National Trust woodlands.
DOUBLE ROOM: from £20 to £30
FOOD: from £15 to £20 🍷 🍴 [CLUB]
Hours: lunch 12noon–2pm, dinner 7.30pm–9.30pm.
Cuisine: ENGLISH / INTERNATIONAL – seasonal specials, e.g., boned quail with hazelnut stuffing, salmon en croute with ginger and herb sauce. Chocolate velvet cake and creme brulée.
Cards: Visa, Access, Diners, AmEx.
Other points: Sunday lunch, children welcome.
Rooms: 1 single room, 5 double rooms, 4 twin rooms. All with TV, telephone.
Directions: on the main street in Watlington, 2 miles from M40 at junction 6.
ALAN & PAT CRAWFORD ☎ (01491) 613333 [Fax] (01491) 612025.

WITNEY • map 5B2

THE COUNTRY PIE
63 Corn Street, OX8 7DQ
A 16th century building of Cotswold stone, a short walk from Buttercross. Recent extensive modernization has not detracted from the old-world charm. Here, good food is served in congenial surroundings with an air of calm efficiency.
FOOD: from £15 to £20
Hours: lunch 12noon–2pm (Tuesday–Sunday), dinner 7pm–9.45pm (Tuesday–Sunday), closed Sunday evening and all day Monday.
Cuisine: ENGLISH / CONTINENTAL – traditional English and continental cuisine. Table d'hôte and à la carte menus available.
Cards: Visa, Access, Diners, AmEx.
Other points: licensed, open-air dining, Sunday lunch, coaches by prior arrangement, children welcome, street parking.
Directions: from the A40, follow signs to town centre.
JANET & ALAN DIXEY ☎ (01993) 703590.

SHROPSHIRE

BISHOPS CASTLE • map 8D4

THE BOARS HEAD
Church Street, SY9 5AE
A 16th century inn and restaurant in a historic Shropshire market town. The inn has a comfortable dining area with an extensive menu ranging from bar snacks to full à la carte meals. The stable block behind The Boars Head has been converted to provide four comfortable bedrooms. All food is well cooked and provides good value for money. A relaxed, friendly atmosphere prevails.
DOUBLE ROOM: from £20 to £30
SINGLE ROOM: from £25 to £35
FOOD: up to £15 CLUB ☆
Hours: breakfast 8am–9am, bar meals 12noon–2pm, dinner 7pm–9.30pm, bar meals 7pm–10pm.
Cuisine: ENGLISH – bar snacks and à la carte meals. Predominantly English cuisine.
Cards: Visa, Access.
Other points: licensed, children welcome, pets allowed, cots, parking.
Rooms: 1 double room, 2 twin rooms, 1 family room. All with TV, telephone, tea/coffee-making facilities, alarm.
Directions: from A488, follow signs to livestock market and continue to car park before crossroads.
GRANT PERRY ☎ (01588) 638521.

LLANYMYNECH • map 8C4

BRADFORD ARMS & RESTAURANT
Near Oswestry, SY22 6EJ
Old coaching inn on A483, which was 'Victorianized' in 1902. Comfortably and traditionally furnished with soft lighting, Victorian marble fireplace and mahogany bar. Sheltered patio area to the side. Large car park to the rear and on-road parking.
FOOD: up to £15
Cuisine: MODERN ENGLISH – bar (all home-made): soups, bread, filled brioches, mushrooms in port, hot baked avocado and prawns, devilled crab, steak kebabs, salmon and mushroom au gratin. Restaurant: loin of lamb in garlic sauce, vegetarian dishes. Always fresh vegetables and home-made desserts. Large selection of farmhouse cheeses.
Other points: licensed, open-air dining, children welcome.
Directions: off the A483, situated on the main road in Llanymynech.
ANNE & MICHAEL MURPHY ☎ (01691) 830582.

MARKET DRAYTON • map 8C5

BOWMANS
High Street, TF9 1PG
Built in 1774 as an old coaching inn, this is now Ellesmere's premier hotel, having undergone extensive refurbishment and modernization. There are tastefully furnished rooms for overnight stays and a lovely function suite for weddings and parties. Located in the town centre, it offers a wide variety of good food and drink in hospitable surroundings.
FOOD: up to £15
Hours: meals all day 9am–1am.
Cuisine: BRITISH.
Cards: Visa, Access, Diners.
Other points: children welcome, vegetarian meals, garden, disabled access, parking.
Directions: on the town square, opposite The Corset Arms Hotel.
MR PAUL ALCOCK ☎ (01630) 658728.

THE WHITE LION
Knighton, TF9 4HJ
Jayne and John offer a menu of an exceptional standard using only fresh ingredients, with all dishes entirely home-made. Aside from the superb meal you will undoubtedly enjoy, take note of the excellent service and the relaxed atmosphere that prevails. The wooden floors and furniture of The Famous Bar provide a haven for those seeking to escape the tide of modernism which has engulfed so many pubs and inns.
FOOD: up to £15
Hours: lunch 12noon–2.30pm, dinner 7pm–9.30pm.
Cuisine: FRENCH / BRITISH – a French-based menu, with the best of British cuisine also.
Cards: Visa, Access, AmEx, MasterCard.
Other points: parking, children welcome, vegetarian meals, traditional Sunday lunch.
Directions: on B5026 (B5145) at south end of village. Turn off A51 at Pipegate and continue for 1 mile.
JAYNE GREEN & JOHN BIRCH ☎ (01630) 647300.

MUCH WENLOCK • map 8C5

THE WENLOCK EDGE INN
Hilltop, Wenlock Edge, TF13 6DJ
Stone-built in the 17th century, this traditional country inn is family-run and provides a delightful rural retreat. The inn is comfortable and the home-cooking is of a high standard. Welcoming service and a relaxed atmosphere ensure an enjoyable meal or stay. Highly recommended.
DOUBLE ROOM: from £20 to £30
FOOD: up to £15
Hours: breakfast 8.30am–9.30am, lunch 12noon–2pm, dinner 7pm–9pm.
Cuisine: ENGLISH – traditional English cuisine. Pies and puddings are house specialities.
Cards: Visa, Access.
Other points: Sunday lunch, no-smoking area, children welcome, open bank holidays, pets allowed.

Rooms: 4 twin rooms.
Directions: from Much Wenlock take B4371. Approximately 4 miles along on left side.
THE WARING FAMILY ☎ (0174636) 403.

NORTON • map 8D5

HUNDRED HOUSE HOTEL, RESTAURANT & INN
Bridgnorth Road, near Telford, TF11 9EE
An award-winning, family-run, country inn with character, charm and a warm atmosphere. It has patchwork-themed bedrooms with antique furnishings and all facilities, and offers superb European and English food. Only 45 minutes from Birmingham International Airport, Conference and Exhibition Centres and an ideal location to explore Ironbridge Gorge museums and the Severn Valley.
DOUBLE ROOM: from £30 to £40
SINGLE ROOM: over £55
FOOD: from £20 to £25
Hours: breakfast 7.30am–9.30am, lunch 11.30am–2.30pm, dinner 6pm–10pm.
Cuisine: ENGLISH / CONTINENTAL – varied menu, which changes frequently: local game, char-grilled meats, traditional roasts, home-made steak-and-kidney pies, lasagne and bruschetta.
Cards: Visa, Access, AmEx.
Other points: licensed, open-air dining, Sunday lunch, children welcome, garden.
Rooms: 10 bedrooms.
Directions: situated on the A442 Bridgnorth–Telford road, in Norton village.
HENRY, SYLVIA & DAVID PHILLIPS ☎ (01952) 730353 [Fax] (01952) 730355.

OSWESTRY • map 8C4

RESTAURANT SEBASTIAN
45 Willow Street, SY11 1AQ
Pleasantly decorated with oak beams and panelling, Restaurant Sebastian enjoys a relaxed atmosphere. The French provincial cuisine is of the highest standard and elegantly presented. A popular restaurant, highly recommended for its outstanding food, welcoming service and attractive surroundings.
FOOD: from £15 to £20
Hours: lunch 12noon–2pm, dinner 6.30pm–10.30pm, closed all day Sunday and Monday, closed Tuesday and Saturday lunch.
Cuisine: FRENCH – table d'hôte and à la carte menus featuring predominantly French cuisine. The restaurant also offers a three-course *Routiers* menu at £15.95 (including a half bottle of wine per person and coffee) and a Tourist menu at £15.95 (2 course menu with choices). Lunchtime consists of French-style snacks from £1.99. Both set meals are also available.
Cards: Visa, Access, AmEx.
Other points: licensed.
Directions: close to the town centre.
MICHELLE & MARK SEBASTIAN FISHER
☎ (01691) 655444 [Fax] (01691) 653452.

STARLINGS CASTLE
Bron y Garth, SY10 7NU
An 18th century sandstone farmhouse, previously a shooting lodge, surrounded by the deep foliage of rhododendrons and conifers and standing within sight of Offa's Dyke, the plain of Shropshire and the hidden valleys and mountains of Berwyn. Ideally situated within reach of many interesting activities: salmon and trout fishing, walking, horse and pony trekking, canoeing, canal cruising and golf. Chirk Castle, Erddig Hall and the medieval flower town of Shrewsbury are all just a short distance away.
DOUBLE ROOM: up to £20
FOOD: from £15 to £20 [CLUB]
Hours: breakfast 8am–9.30am, Sunday lunch 12.30am–2.30pm, dinner 7.30pm–9.30pm.
Cuisine: ECLECTIC.
Cards: Visa, Access, Diners, AmEx.
Other points: parking, children welcome, disabled access, pets, residents' lounge, vegetarian meals, garden, open-air dining.
Rooms: 2 single rooms, 4 double rooms, 8 twin rooms.
Directions: situated off B4579.
MR A. & MRS J. PITT ☎ (01691) 718464
[Fax] (01691) 718464.

SHREWSBURY • map 8C4

RENOIRS
School Chambers, School Gardens, SY1 2AL
Once the home of the headmaster of Shrewsbury school, the restaurant is situated in the school gardens, adjacent to the former Shrewsbury school where Charles Darwin was a pupil. This first-class restaurant has the ambience of a Parisian bistro – close your eyes, listen to Piaf playing softly in the background and inhale the enticing aromas, and you will imagine that you really are in Paris!
FOOD: from £15 to £20
Hours: meals all day 10am–11pm.
Cuisine: CONTINENTAL / FRENCH – an excellent selection of freshly prepared and cooked meals from the à la carte menu and daily specials listed on the blackboard.
Cards: Visa, Access, Diners, AmEx.
Other points: vegetarian meals, traditional Sunday lunch, afternoon teas.
Directions: in the main town centre, just off Castle Street.
JANET HARRIS & TOM BATES ☎ (01743) 350006.

SHELTON HALL HOTEL
Shelton, SY3 8BH
A manor house set in $3\frac{1}{2}$ acres of beautiful landscaped gardens. Extensive facilities for weddings, parties, meetings and conferences. The bedrooms are comfortably furnished with TV, radio, direct-dial telephone and tea/coffee facilities.
DOUBLE ROOM: from £30 to £40
FOOD: from £15 to £20
Hours: breakfast 7.30am–9.30am, lunch 12.30am–2pm, dinner 7.30pm–9.30pm, closed Boxing day.

CENTRAL ENGLAND • STAFFORDSHIRE

Cuisine: ENGLISH – fixed-price menus with variety of dishes, e.g., rainbow trout Cleopatra, roast duck Olde Englande, steak chasseur. Popular for Sunday lunch.
Other points: Sunday lunch, children welcome.
Rooms: 1 single room, 4 double rooms, 2 twin rooms, 2 family rooms. All with TV, radio, telephone, tea/coffee-making facilities.
Directions: 1½ miles north-west of the town on the old A5.
MR GEOFFREY LARKIN ☎ (01743) 343982
Fax (01743) 241515.

SYDNEY HOUSE HOTEL
Coton Crescent, Coton Hill, SY1 2LJ
This Edwardian Hotel is within ten minutes' walk of Shrewsbury's historical town centre. The restaurant boasts an extensive wine list and some excellent ports. You are assured of a warm welcome at the restaurant, as the owners aim to make all guests feel at home.
DOUBLE ROOM: from £20 to £30
SINGLE ROOM: from £35 to £45
FOOD: up to £15
Hours: breakfast 7.30am–9am, dinner 7.30pm–9pm, last orders 8.30pm, closed 1 week over Christmas.
Cuisine: ENGLISH – fixed-price menu.
Cards: Visa, Access, AmEx.
Other points: licensed, no-smoking restaurant, children welcome.
Rooms: 2 single rooms, 2 double rooms, 2 twin rooms, 1 family room. All with TV, radio, alarm, telephone, tea/coffee-making facilities. Many rooms are en suite.
Directions: off the A528 and B5067, just outside the town centre.
TERENCE & PAULINE HYDE ☎ (01743) 354681/130243 Fax (01743) 354681.

TELFORD • map 8C5

RAPHAELS RESTAURANT
4 Church Street, Shifnal, TF11 9AA
Highly recommended by the Routiers inspector, Raphaels Restaurant offers an imaginative menu of excellently cooked dishes to suit vegetarians and non-vegetarians alike. The quality of the food and service is outstanding. An ideal choice for excellent food in attractive and comfortable surroundings.
FOOD: from £15 to £20
Hours: Sunday lunch 12noon–2.30pm, dinner 7.30pm–12midnight, last orders 9.30pm, closed Sunday evening and Monday.
Cuisine: FRENCH / BRITISH / VEGETARIAN – French, British and vegetarian gourmet food. A la carte and table d'hôte menus. Dishes may include guinea fowl with redcurrant sauce, halibut with Chardonnay sauce, and a fine selection of gourmet vegetarian dishes.
Cards: Visa, Access.
Other points: licensed, no-smoking area, children welcome.
Directions: 2 miles from junction 4, M54. Off A464 in centre of Shifnal, on one-way street.
ROGER & MARY WILD ☎ (01952) 461136.

THE VALLEY HOTEL
Ironbridge, TF8 7DW
Originally an 18th century country house, this beautifully refurbished Georgian listed building is set in its own secluded and spacious grounds. The industrious owner, Mr Arthur Maw, conducted his tile manufacturing business in the nearby gorge, which is now the Jackfield Tile Museum. The Chez Maw Restaurant offers an extensive range of fine cuisine, and there are exceptional conference and business facilities available. All bedrooms are equipped with the most up-to-date facilities. A superb location for exploration in a stunning setting.
DOUBLE ROOM: from £30 to £40
SINGLE ROOM: from £55
FOOD: up to £15
Hours: breakfast 7.30am–9.30am, lunch 12noon–2pm, bar snacks 12noon–3pm, dinner 7pm–10pm.
Cuisine: INTERNATIONAL – innovative cooking.
Cards: Visa, Access, AmEx.
Other points: parking, children welcome, open bank holidays, disabled access, no-smoking area, afternoon teas, Sunday dinner, residents' lounge, vegetarian meals, garden, open-air dining, conferences.
Rooms: 34 bedrooms. All with TV, telephone.
Directions: M6 onto M54 to junction 6 onto A5223 to Ironbridge.
MR P. CASSON ☎ (01952) 432247
Fax (01952) 432308.

STAFFORDSHIRE

ALTON • map 8B5

WILD DUCK INN
New Road, ST10 4AF
A country house built by Earl John, the Wild Duck Inn is an elegant bar and family restaurant with comfortable and reasonably priced letting bedrooms. Set in Churnet Valley overlooking Alton Towers Leisure Park.
DOUBLE ROOM: from £20 to £30
FOOD: up to £15
Hours: breakfast 8.30am–9.30am, dinner 7pm–9pm.
Cuisine: ENGLISH – traditional pub food in the bar. English-style food and snacks in the restaurant.
Cards: Visa, Access.
Other points: licensed, children welcome, coaches by prior arrangement
Rooms: 6 twin rooms, 4 family rooms.
Directions: off the B5032. Follow directions for Alton Towers.
MR & MRS KEITH MURDOCH ☎ (01538) 702218.

STAFFORDSHIRE • CENTRAL ENGLAND

BURTON UPON TRENT
map 8C6

THE HORSESHOE INN
Main Street, DE13 9SD
This attractive country inn, dating back to 1600, stands in its own gardens with a large car park and children's play area. Its traditional cask ales and Sunday roasts are very popular.
FOOD: up to £15
Hours: lunch (Monday–Saturday) 12noon–2pm, Sunday lunch (bookings only) and bar snacks 12noon–1.30pm, dinner (Monday–Saturday) 6pm–9.30pm.
Cuisine: ENGLISH – à la carte menu. Dishes include steaks, salmon steak, duckling and chicken with stilton sauce. Bar snacks include home-made steak-and-kidney pie.
Cards: Visa, Access, MasterCard, Switch, Delta.
Other points: children welcome, coaches by appointment, parking, disabled access, vegetarian meals.
Directions: 1 mile from the A38 (Branston exit) signposted Tatenhill. Turn right at crossroads.
MR M. BOULD ☎ (01283) 564913
Fax (01283) 511314.

CANNOCK • map 8C5

SALEEM BAGH
Queens Square, WS11 1EA
A popular air-conditioned restaurant offering an extensive menu of traditional Indian cuisine with speciality dishes, all freshly prepared. A four-course businessman's lunch is also available.
FOOD: up to £15
Hours: lunch 12noon–2.30pm, dinner 5pm–11pm, closed Sunday, open Christmas day.
Cuisine: INDIAN.
Cards: Visa, Access, Diners, AmEx.
Other points: children catered for (please check for age limits), open bank holidays, no-smoking area, disabled access, vegetarian meals.
Directions: close to town centre on the ringway.
MR N. MIAH ☎ (01543) 505089.

LEEK • map 8B5

HOTEL RUDYARD
Lake Road, Rudyard, ST13 8RN
An impressive Victorian building overlooking Rudyard Lake in an attractive rural setting. The hotel enjoys a relaxed, family atmosphere, and the accommodation is of a high standard. With friendly and efficient service, well-cooked food and generous portions, the Carvery restaurant provides an enjoyable meal at excellent value for money.
DOUBLE ROOM: from £20 to £30
FOOD: up to £15
Hours: bar 11am–3pm, 6pm–11pm.
Cuisine: ENGLISH – carvery and bar meals.
Cards: Visa, Access.
Other points: licensed, open-air dining, Sunday lunch, children welcome, disabled access, residents' lounge.

Directions: 1 mile along the Leek to Macclesfield (A523) road, turn left for Rudyard.
RONALD WILLIAM & JEAN LLOYD
☎ (0153833) 208 Fax (0153833) 249.

THE THREE HORSESHOES INN & RESTAURANT
Buxton Road, Blackshaw Moor, ST13 8TW
Situated in a lovely country setting with beautiful views towards the moors and Pennines. First-class accommodation in cottage-style bedrooms. Dinner/dance at weekends.
DOUBLE ROOM: from £20 to £30
FOOD: up to £15
Hours: breakfast 7.30am–9.30am, lunch 12noon–2pm, dinner 7pm–9.30pm.
Cuisine: ENGLISH – bar carvery at lunch and evening, plus restaurant à la carte and table d'hôte menus in the evening.
Cards: Visa, Access.
Other points: Sunday lunch, children welcome, garden.
Rooms: 4 double rooms, 2 twin rooms. All with TV, radio, alarm, telephone, tea/coffee-making facilities.
Directions: located on A53 Leek to Buxton road.
WILLIAM KIRK ☎ (01538) 300296 Fax (01538) 300320.

LICHFIELD • map 8C6

THE BULLS HEAD
Birmingham Road, Shenstone, WS14 0JR
Having undergone extensive refurbishment throughout, The Bulls Head now offers a relaxed and friendly atmosphere in pleasant surroundings. It is very popular with locals and tourists alike, who come to sample the good, wholesome English cuisine. Close to the famous Belfry Golf Club.
FOOD: up to £15
Hours: meals all day 11am–10pm.
Cuisine: ENGLISH – traditional-style menu, offering mixed grill specialities and imaginative desserts. Children's menu. Daily specials. Traditional beers.
Cards: Visa, Access, MasterCard.
Other points: licensed, open-air dining, Sunday lunch, no-smoking area, children welcome, children's play area, disabled access, parking.
Directions: take A5127 off A5 or A38 to Sutton Coldfield. Half a mile on right.
WARREN ASHCROFT ☎ (01543) 480214.

NEWCASTLE-UNDER-LYME
map 8B5

BRUNSWICKS RESTAURANT
10 Brunswick Street, ST5 1HL
A Victorian-type building, brightly and tastefully decorated, only 2 minutes' walk from the town centre. This restaurant serves a range of European dishes in a bright and busy atmosphere.

FOOD: from £15 to £20
Hours: lunch Tuesday–Friday 12noon–2pm, dinner 6.30pm, closed Monday and Sunday.
Cuisine: EUROPEAN – house specialities are steaks served with a variety of sauces and evening blackboard specials, featuring many fresh fish dishes.
Cards: Visa, Access, AmEx.
Other points: licensed, children welcome.
Directions: on Brunswick Street between Fatty Arbuckle's nightclub and baths. Opposite Berkley Court.
MRS M. ARCHER ☎ (01782) 635999.

GABLES HOTEL
570–572 Etruria Road, ST5 0SU
The Gables is a fine Edwardian townhouse set in extensive gardens. Situated next to the New Victoria Theatre and ideal for visitors to Stoke-on-Trent's pottery factories (e.g., Wedgwood, Spode and Royal Doulton) and to Alton Towers.
DOUBLE ROOM: up to £20
Hours: breakfast 7.15am–8.45am, dinner 6pm–8.30pm.
Cuisine: ENGLISH.
Other points: central heating, children welcome, pets allowed, residents' lounge, garden.
Directions: on the A53 half a mile from the town centre, next to New Victoria Theatre.
☎ (01782) 619748.

STAFFORD • map 8C5

THE MOAT HOUSE RESTAURANT
Lower Penkridge Road, Acton Trussell, ST17 0RJ
A 13th century moated manor house set in six acres of landscaped grounds and overlooking the canal, yet only one mile from the M6. The delightful restaurant provides excellent food, with all dishes home-made, including the bread and petit fours. The food is of the highest quality and is beautifully served in generous portions. The Moat House is an outstanding restaurant in every respect.
FOOD: from £20 to £25
Hours: lunch 12noon–2pm, bar meals 12noon–2pm, dinner 7pm–9.30pm, closed Sunday evening.
Cuisine: ENGLISH – traditional English cuisine. A la carte menu in evenings and table d'hôte luncheon and dinner during the week. Traditional Sunday lunch.
Cards: Visa, Access, AmEx.
Other points: licensed, open-air dining, Sunday lunch, no-smoking area, children welcome, patio, disabled access, functions, conservatory.
Directions: junction 13, M6. A449 towards Stafford. First right to village. Near church.
JOHN & MARY LEWIS ☎ (01785) 712217
Fax (01785) 715364.

WARWICKSHIRE

ALCESTER • map 9D1

ROSSINI RESTAURANT
50 Birmingham Road, B49 5EP
The Rossini is a well-maintained, traditional Italian restaurant, which offers good food and wine in comfortable, friendly surroundings. The 100-year-old Victorian building is pleasantly furnished throughout, and the service is highly efficient. Nearby places of interest include Ragley Hall, Coughton Court, and Stratford-upon-Avon.
FOOD: from £15 to £20 CLUB ☆
Hours: lunch 12noon–2pm, dinner 6.30pm–10.30pm.
Cuisine: ITALIAN – à la carte and table d'hôte menus. Traditional Italian-style cuisine, including a wide choice of pasta dishes, complemented by a good wine list.
Cards: Visa, Access, Diners, AmEx.
Other points: licensed, Sunday lunch, children welcome, disabled access, parking.
Directions: situated on the main Evesham to Birmingham A435 road.
CARMINE SACCO ☎ (01789) 762764.

ALDERMINSTER • map 9E2

BELL BISTRO
CV37 8NY
Standing on the A3400, the Bell is an old coaching inn with flagstones, beams and fireplaces. All food is freshly prepared and cooked on the premises, and because of the use of fresh produce, the menu changes daily. Traditional, predominantly English cuisine is imaginatively cooked. A friendly atmosphere prevails.
FOOD: up to £15
Hours: lunch 12noon–2.30pm, dinner 7pm–11pm.
Cuisine: ENGLISH – menu written on blackboards: changes daily. Fresh fish and seafood is a speciality. Low fat and vegetarian dishes always available. All dishes are freshly prepared.
Cards: Visa, Access.
Other points: licensed, Sunday lunch, no-smoking area, children welcome, conference facilities.
Directions: on the A3400, 4 miles south of Stratford-upon-Avon.
KEITH & VANESSA BREWER ☎ (01789) 450414 Fax (01789) 450998.

WARWICKSHIRE • CENTRAL ENGLAND

HENLEY-IN-ARDEN • map 9D1

ARDEN TANDOORI RESTAURANT
137 High Street, B95 5BJ
Situated right in the centre of the historic town of Henley-in-Arden. The interior has been tastefully decorated with an air of subdued elegance. The Arden offers a warm welcome and excellent food. There is a private room available for parties.
FOOD: up to £15 [CLUB]
Hours: lunch 12noon–2.30pm, dinner 5.30pm–11.30pm.
Cuisine: INDIAN – kurzi lamb, lamb pasanda nawabi, makhon chicken and balti dishes.
Cards: Visa, Access, Diners, AmEx.
Other points: open-air dining, Sunday lunch, coaches by prior arrangement, children welcome.
Directions: on the A34 between Solihull and Stratford-upon-Avon.
NANU MIAH ☎ (01564) 792503.

ILMINGTON • map 9E2

THE HOWARD ARMS
Lower Green, CV36 4LN
This tranquil 16th century inn provides a delightful setting in which to sample some delectable English cuisine. Fresh ingredients and an imaginative, constantly changing menu can tempt even the most particular palate.
DOUBLE ROOM: from £20 to £30
FOOD: up to £15
Hours: lunch 12noon–2pm, dinner (Sunday–Thursday) 7pm–9pm.
Cuisine: ENGLISH – classic English cuisine with a regularly changing menu, served in bar, restaurant or garden.
Cards: Visa, Access, AmEx.
Other points: licensed, open-air dining, Sunday lunch, children welcome, garden.
Rooms: 1 double room, 1 twin room. Both with TV, tea/coffee-making facilities.
Directions: from Stratford-upon-Avon, a turn-off on the A3400 Shipston on Stour road: turn right, then 4 miles.
MR SMART & MR THOMPSON ☎ (01608) 682226. [Fax] (01608) 682226.

KENILWORTH • map 9D2

CLARENDON ARMS
44 Castle Hill, CV8 1NB
An olde-worlde inn in a historic, picture-postcard location opposite the entrance to Kenilworth Castle. Dine in the small, intimate bar, or in the larger dining area on the first floor – either way, the cheerful ambience and good home-cooked fare are sure to please.
FOOD: up to £15
Hours: lunch 11am–3pm, Sunday 12noon–3pm, dinner 5.30pm–11pm, Sunday 7pm–10.30pm.
Cuisine: ENGLISH / INTERNATIONAL – giant char-grilled steaks, chicken teriyaki, traditional pub meals.

Cards: Visa, Access, Diners, AmEx.
Other points: licensed, open-air dining, Sunday lunch, children welcome.
Directions: opposite the entrance to Kenilworth Castle.
PATRICK McCOSKER & MAURICE KUTNER
☎ (01926) 52017 [Fax] (01926) 50229.

ROYAL LEAMINGTON SPA
map 9D2

EATON COURT HOTEL
1–7 St Marks Road, CV32 6DL
The Eaton family are directly involved in running this comfortable hotel, located in a calm backwater close to the centre of Leamington Spa. The spacious and comfortable bedrooms are furnished to a high standard and provide a convenient base from which to explore the Warwickshire countryside. The superb cuisine uses a wide range of freshly prepared produce, and special diets can be arranged. Ideal for the business traveller, and conferences and weddings can also be catered for. Some rooms are no-smoking.
DOUBLE ROOM: from £30 to £40
FOOD: up to £15 [CLUB] ★
Hours: breakfast 7am–9.30am, lunch by arrangement, dinner 7pm–12midnight.
Cuisine: ENGLISH / FRENCH.
Cards: Visa, Access.
Other points: parking, children welcome, no-smoking area, pets, residents' lounge, garden, vegetarian meals, open-air dining.
Directions: off A452 Leamington–Warwick road on northern side of Leamington town.
VINCE & BARBARA EATON ☎ (01926) 885848
[Fax] (01926) 885848.

SHIPSTON ON STOUR
map 9E2

THE HORSESHOE INN
Church Street, CV36 4AP
This popular inn, situated in the centre of Shipston on Stour, is a favourite with travellers and locals alike. The menu is varied and the service is efficient and friendly. The bedrooms are comfortable and clean, the perfect place to rest your weary head after a day's sightseeing in nearby Stratford-upon-Avon, Warwick and Stow-on-the-Wold.
DOUBLE ROOM: up to £20
SINGLE ROOM: up to £25
FOOD: up to £15 [CLUB]
Hours: breakfast 8am–10.30am, lunch 12noon–3pm, dinner 7pm–10pm.
Cuisine: ENGLISH.
Cards: Visa, Access, Diners, AmEx.
Other points: children welcome, parking, disabled access, pets allowed, vegetarian meals, open-air dining.
Rooms: 3 twin rooms.
Directions: located in the centre of Shipston on Stour.
MRS A. WILLIAMS ☎ (01608) 661225
[Fax] (01608) 663762.

STRATFORD-UPON-AVON
map 9E2

● BROOK LODGE
192 Alcester Road, CV37 9DR
This well-appointed guest house with its tasteful decorations and furnishings provides a comfortable and enjoyable place to stay. Located within 5 minutes' walk of Anne Hathaway's cottage, Brook Lodge is in an ideal position for visiting Stratford-upon-Avon, Warwick, the Cotswolds and the many other nearby places of interest.
DOUBLE ROOM: from £20 to £30
Hours: breakfast 8.30am–9.15am, closed Christmas.
Cuisine: BREAKFAST.
Cards: Visa, Access, AmEx.
Other points: central heating, children welcome, parking, residents' lounge.
Rooms: 3 double rooms, 1 twin room, 3 family rooms. All with en suite, TV, hair dryer, clock/radio.
Directions: leave M40 from Warwick and take A46. Exit left onto A422 towards Stratford-upon-Avon.
YVONNE & ROB CHARLETT ☎ (01789) 295988.

● CRAIG CLEEVE HOUSE
67–69 Shipston Road, CV37 7LW
A licensed private hotel retaining a family atmosphere where the sole aim is to make guests feel comfortable and welcome. Good, friendly service, comfortable rooms of a high standard, and a breakfast where no one is left feeling hungry! Quality, value for money and a warm welcome are guaranteed. Only 5 minutes' walk from the town centre and within easy reach of the Cotswolds.
DOUBLE ROOM: up to £20
Hours: breakfast 7.30am–9am.
Cuisine: BREAKFAST.
Cards: Visa, Access, Diners, AmEx.
Other points: children welcome, afternoon tea, pets allowed, residents' lounge, parking, coaches by prior arrangement.
Rooms: 2 single rooms, 7 double rooms, 4 twin rooms, 2 family rooms. All with TV, tea/coffee-making facilities.
Directions: A3400 Stratford to Oxford Road. Five minutes' walk to town centre.
TERRY & MARGARITA PALMER ☎ (01789) 296573 [Fax] (01789) 299452.

● MARLOWES RESTAURANT
18 High Street, CV37 6AU
Marlowes, originally an Elizabethan town house, is now a first-class restaurant with an enviable clientele, including actors Anthony Quayle, Vanessa Redgrave, Sir John Gielgud, Sir Alec Guinness and many more. It has enjoyed a long association with the Royal Shakespeare Theatre and was once the home of Denny Gilkes, the famous opera singer and actress. Enjoy excellent cuisine, from the charcoal grill to fish, meat and poultry dishes, including vegetarian specials. The restaurant will also cook any speciality or gourmet/party meal, with prior notice.
FOOD: from £15 to £20
Hours: lunch 12noon–2.30pm, dinner 5.45pm–10.30pm.
Cuisine: ENGLISH.
Cards: Visa, Access, Diners, AmEx.
Other points: Sunday lunch, open bank holidays, vegetarian.
Directions: centre of Stratford-upon-Avon.
MR GEORGE KRUSZYNSKYI ☎ (01789) 204999 [Fax] (01789) 204171.

● MOONRAKER HOUSE
40 Alcester Road, CV37 9DB
Moonraker House comprises three attractive white houses situated in a pleasant area in the north-west of the town. Very tastefully decorated and comfortably furnished throughout, the atmosphere is friendly and relaxed. An ideal location for touring Shakespeare country, the Cotswolds and the many castles and places of interest nearby.
DOUBLE ROOM: from £20 to £30
Hours: breakfast 8am–9.30am.
Cuisine: BREAKFAST.
Cards: Visa, Access.
Other points: central heating, children welcome, pets by prior arrangement, residents' lounge, garden, patio.
Directions: on the A422 in the centre of town, close to railway station.
MR & MRS M.S. SPENCER ☎ (01789) 267115/299346 [Fax] (01789) 295504.

● THE OPPOSITION RESTAURANT
13 Sheep Street, CV37 6EF
A 500-year-old, half-timbered Grade II listed 16th century building, converted to a popular bistro with candlelit dining. Home-made Italian, American and continental dishes. Dine before or after the theatre, which is only 3 minutes away.
FOOD: up to £15
Hours: morning coffee 11am–12noon, lunch 12noon–2pm, dinner 5.30pm–11pm.
Cuisine: AMERICAN / CONTINENTAL – eclectic bistro.
Cards: Visa, Access, AmEx, MasterCard.
Other points: licensed, Sunday lunch, children welcome, garden, street parking.
Directions: 3 minutes from Royal Shakespeare Theatre.
MR NIGEL LAMBERT ☎ (01789) 269980.

● SEQUOIA HOUSE PRIVATE HOTEL
51 Shipston Road, CV37 7LN
Beautifully appointed, quietly run, private licensed hotel, superbly situated across the River Avon opposite the Royal Shakespeare Theatre. Large private car park. Delightful garden walk to the theatre, riverside gardens and town centre. Fully air-conditioned dining room and conference facility.
DOUBLE ROOM: from £20 to £30
SINGLE ROOM: from £35 to £45
Hours: breakfast 7.30am–9am.
Cuisine: BREAKFAST.
Cards: Visa, Access, Diners, AmEx.
Other points: central heating, children welcome, residents' lounge, air-conditioned, conferences, vegetarian meals.

Rooms: 24 double/twin rooms.
Directions: located on A34 approach road from the south, near Clopton bridge.
MR P.L. EVANS ☎ (01789) 268852.

🏨 SWAN HOUSE HOTEL
The Green, Wilmcote, CV37 9XJ

An attractive listed building overlooking Mary Arden's House. Swan House occupies a rural setting, yet is close enough to Birmingham to be a good centre for business conferences etc.
DOUBLE ROOM: from £20 to £30
SINGLE ROOM: from £25 to £35
FOOD: up to £15
Hours: breakfast 7.30am–9.30am, lunch 12noon–2.30pm, dinner 7.30pm–9.30pm, closed 3rd to 6th January.
Cuisine: ENGLISH – extensive range of home-made bar meals: steak-and-mushroom pie, lasagne. A la carte: duckling, salmon, peppered sirloin.
Cards: Visa, Access, AmEx.
Other points: Sunday lunch, children welcome, disabled access.
Rooms: 1 single room, 3 double room, 2 twin rooms, 1 family room. All with TV, radio, alarm, tea/coffee-making facilities.
Directions: from the A3400, 3 miles north-west of Stratford, take the Wilmcote turn-off.
DIANA SYKES ☎ (01789) 267030 [Fax] (01789) 204875.

LES ROUTIERS ACCOMMODATION DIRECTORY

This handy directory is ideal for those looking for somewhere to stay at great value.
It lists a huge choice of *Les Routiers*-recommended places throughout the British Isles offering comfortable accommodation, good food and a warm welcome amid relaxed surroundings.

Available from selected
Les Routiers establishments
or direct from the publishers.

Price £2

🍴 THE VINTNER CAFE, WINE BAR
5 Sheep Street, CV37 6ES

The Vintner's name derives from 1601 when John Smith lived at this address working as a vintner, and the Elizabethan decor reflects this association. An extensive, international wine, beer and spirits list and prompt service make this café/wine bar popular with theatre-goers and locals alike. Open for coffees to three-course meals. Family run.
FOOD: up to £15
Hours: meals all day 10.30am–11.30pm, closed Christmas day and Boxing day.
Cuisine: MODERN ENGLISH – wide selection of home-cooked soups, vegetarian dishes, steaks and salads. Superb sweets. Full menu is accompanied by many daily changing chef's specials.
Cards: Visa, Access, AmEx.

Other points: licensed, Sunday lunch, children welcome, pets by prior arrangement, coaches by prior arrangement.
Directions: off A34, first right approaching theatre, on waterside near town hall.
MR N. MILLS ☎ (01789) 297259.

WARWICK • map 9D2

🏨 TUDOR HOUSE INN
West Street, CV34 6AW

A privately-owned inn of great charm and character. Dating from 1472, it retains a wealth of timbers, many of which were used in old warships. It is also one of the few buildings to survive the great fire of Warwick in 1694. The inn offers good, plentiful food at reasonable prices in a very friendly and welcoming atmosphere, along with good-value wines.
DOUBLE ROOM: from £20 to £30
SINGLE ROOM: up to £25
FOOD: up to £15 [CLUB]
Hours: breakfast 7am–9.30am, lunch 12noon–3pm, dinner 6pm–11pm.
Cuisine: ENGLISH/INTERNATIONAL – traditional English and varied international dishes.
Cards: Visa, Access, Diners, AmEx, Switch, Delta.
Other points: licensed, open-air dining, Sunday lunch, children welcome, afternoon tea, garden, residents' bar.
Rooms: 3 single rooms, 4 double rooms, 4 twin rooms. All with TV, telephone, tea/coffee-making facilities. One double room has a four-poster bed.
Directions: on the A429, almost opposite the entrance to Warwick Castle.
MR P. McCOSKER & MR M. KUTNER
☎ (01926) 495447.

WOOTTON WAWEN • map 9D1

🍴 NAVIGATION INN
Stratford Road, B95 6BZ

A friendly, family pub, serving good-quality food in generous portions. An excellent place to take children, as it has a large garden and adventure playground and, being situated on the canal side, there are walks along the tow-path with plenty of narrow boats to look at.
FOOD: up to £15
Hours: lunch 11.30am–3pm, bar meals 11.30am–3pm, dinner 6pm–10pm, bar meals 6pm–10pm.
Cuisine: ENGLISH / INTERNATIONAL – home-made dishes, with grills, seafood casserole, lasagne and crispy chicken. Home-made sweets include apple pie and cheesecake. Sunday roast lunches.
Cards: Visa, Access, Diners, AmEx.
Other points: licensed, traditional Sunday lunch, children welcome, pets allowed, open bank holidays.
Directions: located on the main A3400 Birmingham to Stratford road, 6 miles north of Stratford.
MARK SMITH ☎ (01564) 792676 [Fax] (01564) 792228.

WEST MIDLANDS

BIRMINGHAM • map 8D5

FOUNTAIN COURT HOTEL
Fountain Court Hotel, 339–343 Hagley Road, B17 8NN
A friendly, family-run hotel located on a main road about 3 miles west from the city centre. Good location for access to M5 and the International Conference Centre. The hotel is well maintained and has recently been refurbished. Especially popular with business travellers and weekenders.
DOUBLE ROOM: from £20 to £30
SINGLE ROOM: from £35 to £45
FOOD: up to £15
Hours: breakfast 6.45am–9am, dinner 6.30pm–8.30pm.
Cuisine: ENGLISH – table d'hôte menu. Dishes may include roast duck, chilli con carne, grilled gammon. Everything is home-made.
Cards: Visa, Access, Diners, AmEx.
Other points: licensed, children welcome, garden, afternoon tea, pets allowed.
Rooms: 13 single rooms, 6 double rooms, 6 twin rooms. All with TV, telephone, tea/coffee-making facilities.
Directions: A456. Corner of Hagley Road and Fountain Road. (2 miles from junction 3, M5.)
GLADYS, STELLA & RICHARD SMITH ☎ (0121) 429 1754 [Fax] (0121) 429 1209.

HAGLEY COURT HOTEL
229 Hagley Road, Edgbaston, B16 9RP
A Georgian mansion, set back from the main road leading into the city. The International Conference Centre is only one mile from the hotel, making it an ideal place for delegates to stay. The hotel is renowned for its comfortable and homely accommodation.
DOUBLE ROOM: from £20 to £30
SINGLE ROOM: from £25 to £35
FOOD: up to £15
Hours: breakfast 7am–9am, dinner 6pm–9.30pm.
Cuisine: FRENCH / ENGLISH – à la carte, table d'hôte and bar menus. Steaks, chicken, fish.
Cards: Visa, Diners, AmEx, MasterCard, Switch.
Other points: licensed, children welcome, cots, residents' bar, residents' lounge, parking.
Rooms: 8 single rooms, 16 double rooms, 3 twin rooms. All with satellite TV, radio, alarm, cots, telephone, tea/coffee-making facilities, heating.
Directions: on A456.
CHRISTOPHER PHILIPPIDES ☎ (0121) 454 6514 [Fax] (0121) 456 2722.

HEATH LODGE HOTEL
117 Coleshill Road, Marston Green, B37 7HT
Family-run hotel, with cosy lounge and coal-effect fire, quietly situated just a short distance away from NEC and Birmingham International Airport. Courtesy car available for airport travellers, and long-term car parking.
DOUBLE ROOM: up to £20

FOOD: up to £15
Hours: dinner 6.30pm–9pm.
Cuisine: INTERNATIONAL – farmhouse grill, fillet steak, chicken kiev, salmon, halibut.
Cards: Visa, Access, Diners, AmEx.
Other points: licensed, children welcome, pets allowed, open bank holidays, residents' bar, residents' meals, vegetarian meals, parking.
Rooms: 8 single rooms, 4 double rooms, 6 twin rooms. All with TV, telephone, tea/coffee-making facilities.
Directions: hotel located 1 mile from entrance to Birmingham Airport.
SIMEON COLLINS ☎ (0121) 779 2218 [Fax] (0121) 779 5673.

HENRY'S CAFE BAR (BIRMINGHAM)
1 Victoria Square, B1 1BD
A popular café-bar situated in the city centre, close to shops and serving an extensive range of international fast-food, American beers and speciality cocktails. Lively and very popular; lunchtimes are busy.
FOOD: up to £15
Hours: meals all day 10.30am–9.30pm, closed Sunday.
Cuisine: INTERNATIONAL.
Cards: Visa, Access.
Other points: children welcome, open bank holidays, no-smoking area, afternoon teas, disabled access, vegetarian meals.
Directions: 5-minute walk from International Conference Centre.
MR D. SAMPSON ☎ (0121) 631 3827/ 631 3834.

LYNDHURST HOTEL
135 Kingsbury Road, Erdington, B24 8QT
Family-owned and run. Recently refurbished to a high standard, but maintaining a relaxed, family atmosphere. On the route of the 114 and 116 buses, which go to the city centre.
DOUBLE ROOM: from £20 to £30
FOOD: up to £15
Hours: breakfast 7.30am–8.30am, closed Christmas, dinner 6.30pm–8.30pm.
Cuisine: ENGLISH.
Cards: Visa, Access, Diners, AmEx.
Other points: central heating, children welcome, residents' lounge, garden, vegetarian meals.
Rooms: 8 single rooms, 4 twin rooms, 2 family rooms. All with TV, tea/coffee-making facilities, hair dryer.
Directions: on the A38, half mile from M6 turn-off at junction 6.
MR & MRS R. WILLIAMS ☎ (0121) 373 5695 [Fax] (0121) 373 5695.

PINOCCHIO'S RESTAURANT
Chad Square, Hawthorne Road, B15 3TQ
A traditional Italian decor sets the scene in which to enjoy quality Italian meals generously served. With its warm, friendly and relaxed atmosphere, it

is the perfect place for a quiet or romantic dinner. Fresh fish and vegetables are bought daily. Situated just minutes from the city on the Harborne/Edgbaston border, Pinocchio's is a real taste of Italy in Birmingham.
FOOD: from £20 to £25 [CLUB]
Hours: lunch 12noon–2.30pm, dinner 7pm–11pm, closed Sunday and bank holidays.
Cuisine: ITALIAN – extensive menu: dishes may include filetto farfalla, calamari alla livornese, sogliola di Dover grigliata, pollo alla Pinocchio.
Cards: Visa, Access, Diners, AmEx.
Other points: licensed, children welcome.
Directions: opposite White Swan pub, just off Harborne Road. Near Botanical Gardens.
MR SILVIO NOVELLI ☎ (0121) 454 8672.

VALENTINOS
73 High Street, Harborne, B17 9NS
A very popular restaurant situated close to the Botanical Gardens, canal, ICC and NEC. The decor sets the scene perfectly for this traditional Italian style restaurant. The staff are very efficient, giving excellent service even at the busiest times.
FOOD: from £15 to £20
Hours: lunch 12noon–2.30pm, dinner 6.30pm–11pm.
Cuisine: ITALIAN – excellent menu, attractively presented. Fresh fish is the speciality.
Cards: Visa, Access, Diners, AmEx.
Other points: parking, children welcome, no-smoking area, traditional Sunday lunch, vegetarian meals.
Directions: located on Harborne High Street, five miles west of Birmingham.
MAURIZIO & BARBARA GUGLIA ☎ (0121) 427 2560 [Fax] (0121) 427 2560.

WESTBOURNE LODGE HOTEL
27–29 Fountain Road, Edgbaston, B17 8NJ
Family-run hotel ideally situated for ICC, NEC, National Indoor Arena and Edgbaston cricket ground. Located 1½ miles from the city in a quiet suburb, 200 yards off the A456 Hagley Road. A warm welcome, good food, free parking, and all rooms en suite.
DOUBLE ROOM: from £20 to £30
FOOD: up to £15
Hours: breakfast 7am–9am, lunch 12.30am–2pm, dinner 6pm–9pm, closed Christmas.
Cuisine: ENGLISH.
Cards: Visa, Access, AmEx.
Other points: central heating, children welcome, patio, garden, residents' lounge, vegetarian meals.
Directions: off the A456, 200 yards from the corner of Hagley and Fountain Roads.
MR & MRS J.H. HANSON ☎ (0121) 429 1003 [Fax] (0121) 429 7436.

YEW TREE COTTAGE BALTI & TANDOORI RESTAURANT
43 Stoney Lane, Yardley Village, B25 8RE
Established for over 15 years, the Yew Tree Cottage is a venue of style, character and food beyond compare. A very stylish Indian restaurant, recommended by many good food guides. The genuine and authentic food served here is

prepared by chefs who have been acclaimed as experts in the culinary art. The ingredients are bought fresh daily and all meals are cooked to order. For the true taste of India, this is a must!
FOOD: up to £15
Hours: dinner 5.30pm–12midnight, closed Christmas day.
Cuisine: INDIAN – Northern Indian and Mughal Empire delicacies; unusual North Bengali cuisine.
Cards: Visa, Access, Diners, AmEx.
Other points: parking, children welcome, vegetarian meals.
Directions: near to NEC, ICC, A45 and M6. A to Z reference 5B 76.
JAMAL CHAUDHURI ☎ (0121) 784 0707/786 1814.

BROWNHILLS • map 8C5

TERRACE RESTAURANT
9 Watling Street, Newtown, WS8 6JR
A superbly appointed restaurant with all modern facilities. Set in award-winning gardens with parking facilities for over 100 cars. Disabled facilities available.
FOOD: up to £15 [CLUB]
Hours: lunch 12noon–2.30pm, dinner 7pm–10pm, closed Sunday evening.
Cuisine: ENGLISH – traditional English cuisine. Specialities include beef Wellington and fresh fish. Vegetarians also catered for. Advance booking essential on Saturdays and Sundays.
Cards: Visa, Access, Diners, AmEx, Switch.
Other points: licensed, Sunday lunch, children welcome, functions, conferences.
Directions: situated on the main A5 trunk road. 7 miles east of M6. 5 miles north-east of Walsall.
MR ADSHEAD ☎ (01543) 378291/360456.

COVENTRY • map 8D6

LADY GODIVA HOTEL
80–90 Holyhead Road, CV1 3AS
Situated on the main Coventry–Birmingham road, only 11 miles from Birmingham Airport. Good facilities for conferences and private functions of up to 300. Central for the Cotswolds and Shakespeare Country.
DOUBLE ROOM: from £30 to £40
FOOD: from £15 to £20
Hours: breakfast 7am–9.30am, lunch 12.30am–2.30pm, dinner 7.30pm–10pm.
Cuisine: MODERN ENGLISH – nouvelle cuisine, e.g., salmon with maltaise sauce, mille-feuilles of scampi tomato, garlic, herbs.
Cards: Visa, Access, Diners, AmEx.
Other points: Sunday lunch, children welcome, coaches by prior arrangement, parking, disabled access, lift.
Rooms: 60 single rooms, 9 double rooms, 105 twin rooms.
Directions: 10 minutes' walk from city centre; 9 miles from NEC.
MR GAUNT ☎ (01203) 258585 [Fax] (01203) 225547.

SOLIHULL • map 8D6

🍴 FLEMINGS HOTEL
141 Warwick Road, Olton, B92 7HW

A patron-run hotel situated only 5½ miles from the centre of Birmingham. A high standard of comfort and service are provided at reasonable prices, and the restaurant offers both à la carte and table d'hôte menus. All the homely friendliness of a small hotel.
DOUBLE ROOM: from £20 to £30
FOOD: from £15 to £20
Hours: lunch 12noon–2pm, dinner 6.30pm–9.30pm, Christmas day lunch only.
Cuisine: ENGLISH – seafood specials, steaks, beef stroganoff.
Cards: Visa, Access, Diners, AmEx.
Other points: licensed, Sunday buffet lunch, open-air dining, children welcome, pets allowed.
Rooms: 51 single rooms, 16 double rooms, 7 twin rooms, 4 family rooms. All with TV, radio, alarm, tea/coffee-making facilities, heating.
Directions: on A41, 250 yards from Olton station.
W. FLEMING ☎ (0121) 706 0371 [Fax] (0121) 706 4494.

STOURBRIDGE • map 8D5

🍴 KINFARE HOTEL & RESTAURANT
41 High Street, Kinver, DY7 6HF

Built in 1690, the Kinfare was originally the Crown public house and still retains its distinctive olde-worlde charm. Hanging flower baskets and wooden beams add to a pleasant atmosphere, where you can enjoy well-cooked food and friendly service.
DOUBLE ROOM: from £20 to £30
FOOD: up to £15 [CLUB]
Hours: breakfast 7am–9am, lunch 12noon–2.30pm, dinner 7pm–10pm, open all year, open bank holidays.
Cuisine: ENGLISH.
Cards: Visa, Access.
Other points: licensed, Sunday lunch, no-smoking area, children welcome, afternoon tea, residents' lounge, garden.
Directions: situated off the A449, 7 miles south of Wolverhampton.
MR & MRS WILLIAMS ☎ (01384) 872565
[Fax] (01384) 877724.

🍴 THE RETREAT
157 Hagley Road, Old Swinford, DY8 2JJ

A stylish and popular bar and bistro, situated in the village of Old Swinford, serving fine, quality food and drink, six days per week. The brasserie-style menu offers light snacks and full meals, served in an informal atmosphere in pleasant surroundings. Places of interest nearby include Hagley Hall, Harvington Hall and an interesting glassworks.
FOOD: up to £15
Hours: lunch 12noon–2.30pm, dinner (Thursday–Saturday) 6.30pm–11pm, dinner (Monday–Wednesday) 7pm–11pm, closed Christmas day and Boxing day.

Cuisine: ENGLISH / MEDITERRANEAN – full à la carte menu, offering a wide selection of imaginative dishes. Vegetarian meals available. Business lunches and small parties catered for.
Cards: Visa, Access, AmEx.
Other points: licensed, disabled access, vegetarian meals, open bank holidays.
Directions: 1 mile outside the town centre on the left of the A491.
PAT & PETER GULLY ☎ (01384) 396290.

SUTTON COLDFIELD
map 8D6

🍴 SUTTON COURT HOTEL
60–66 Lichfield Road, near Birmingham, B74 2NA

Privately owned and convenient for Birmingham International Airport and the NEC. Six golf courses within 15-minute drive. The restaurant enjoys a fine reputation for its international cuisine. Free car parking.
DOUBLE ROOM: from £30 to £40
SINGLE ROOM: over £55
FOOD: from £15 to £20 ☆
Hours: breakfast 7.30am–9.30am, lunch 12noon–2pm, dinner 7pm–10pm, bar meals 12noon–2pm and 7pm–10pm,.
Cuisine: FRENCH – table d'hôte and à la carte menus available, traditional French dishes, vegetarian meals available.
Cards: Visa, Access, Diners, AmEx, Switch.
Other points: children under 14 get complementary accommodation if sharing with parents (meals extra), airport nearby, baby-sitting available, cots, 24hr reception, foreign exchange.
Rooms: 64 bedrooms. All with en suite, satellite TV, telephone, trouser-press, hair dryer, tea/coffee-making facilities.
Directions: off A38 on corner of A5127 and A453.
PETER JOHN BENNETT ☎ (0121) 355 6071
[Fax] (0121) 355 0083.

WILLENHALL • map 8C5

🍴 YE OLDE TOLL HOUSE RESTAURANT
40 Walsall Street, WV13 2ER

An 18th century toll house, which has been renovated to a high standard incorporating original features such as oak beams. Table d'hôte menu includes starter, main course, cheese and biscuits, wine and liqueur coffee.
FOOD: from £15 to £20
Hours: lunch 12noon–3pm, dinner 7pm–9.30pm.
Cuisine: ENGLISH – large, varied selection of fresh fish. Fresh vegetables, home-made desserts.
Cards: Visa, Access.
Other points: children welcome.
Directions: situated on A454 in the centre of Willenhall.
MR BRIAN FRENCH ☎ (01902) 605575
[Fax] (01902) 605575.

WEST MIDLANDS • CENTRAL ENGLAND

WOLVERHAMPTON • map 8D5

HILTON PARK PAVILION LODGE AT HILTON PARK SERVICE AREA
Between junctions 10A and 11, M6 Motorway, WV11 2AT

The Lodge provides excellent accommodation at a competitive price and offers the facilities to make travelling a pleasure. Convenient for Alton Towers, Black Country Museum, NEC and ICC.
DOUBLE ROOM: from £20 to £30
FOOD: up to £15
Hours: open 24 hours.

Cuisine: BRITISH / INTERNATIONAL – offered within the service building.
Cards: Visa, Access, Diners, AmEx.
Other points: parking, children welcome, disabled access, no-smoking area, vegetarian meals, forecourt shop, Burger King.
Rooms: 64 bedrooms. All with en suite, satellite TV, telephone, radio, alarm, hair dryer, trouser-press, tea/coffee-making facilities.
Directions: on the M6 between junctions 10A and 11.
STUART RICHARDS ☎ (01922) 412237
Fax (01922) 418762.

NORTHERN ENGLAND & THE ISLE OF MAN

The north of England is a region of tremendous scenic diversity, steeped in history: from the lush, green pastures and rolling fells of Yorkshire and Humberside to the rugged wild countryside of Northumberland with its miles of unspoilt coastline, from the incomparable beauty of the Cumbrian Lakes to the open sweeping moors of Lancashire. Whether you come to climb, hill-walk, cave, sail or simply absorb the breathtaking scenery at your leisure, this region offers endless scope for visitors of all ages.

This is predominantly 'dales' country, where the local folk know the true meaning of a good wholesome feast, and how to marry local ingredients with their own native wit. There is simply no better way to round off the day than with a substantial supper at a sound hostelry. Choose from Westmoreland lamb, Coniston char plucked from the sparkling clear fern-lined waters of a babbling hill-stream that very morning, Cumberland Tattie Pot, Grizedale venison, farmhouse grills – barbecued, flamed or just cold, the choice of excellent cuisine is endless.

For those who enjoy a more vibrant atmosphere, the city centres are the places to visit. Here you will find a superb selection of café-bars and bistros serving a wide range of imaginative dishes, tasty beers and colourful speciality cocktails at great value for money.

The following counties are included in this chapter:

CLEVELAND	LANCASHIRE
COUNTY DURHAM	MERSEYSIDE
CUMBRIA	NORTH YORKSHIRE
GREATER MANCHESTER	NORTHUMBERLAND
	SOUTH YORKSHIRE
HUMBERSIDE	TYNE & WEAR
ISLE OF MAN	WEST YORKSHIRE

*C*LEVELAND

BILLINGHAM • map 12C5

BILLINGHAM ARMS HOTEL
The Causeway, TS23 2HD
A conveniently located, modern hotel, five minutes from Billingham railway station and ten miles from Teeside Airport. Berties Restaurant is renowned for its good food and friendly service. An ideal hotel for tourists and business-people alike.
DOUBLE ROOM: from £30 to £40
SINGLE ROOM: from £35 to £45
FOOD: up to £15
Hours: breakfast 7am–10am, lunch 12noon–2pm, dinner 6pm–11pm.
Cuisine: ENGLISH / CONTINENTAL – croissant filled with diced chicken and bacon in a cream cheese and mushroom sauce, strips of beef cooked at your table in a sherry and oyster sauce.
Cards: Visa, Access, Diners, AmEx.
Other points: licensed, Sunday lunch, pets

allowed, coaches by prior arrangement, children welcome, disabled access, residents' lounge, residents' bar, vegetarian meals.
Rooms: 17 single rooms, 41 double rooms, 10 twin rooms, 1 suite. All with telephone, tea/coffee-making facilities, satellite TV, trouser-press. Some doubles are available as singles when required.
Directions: from A19, in town square next to Forum sports centre and theatre.
MR SNAITH & MR HUGHES ☎ (01642) 553661/360880 [Fax] (01642) 552104.

HARTLEPOOL • map 12C5

GRAND HOTEL
Swainson Street, TS24 8AA
A Grade II listed Victorian hotel situated in the town centre. Victoria's Lounge Bar serves popular bar food Monday to Saturday lunchtime, while Piper's Restaurant provides a Carvery and à la carte menus. The food is well cooked and served in generous portions. Excellent, welcoming service adds to the relaxed, friendly atmosphere of the Grand Hotel.
DOUBLE ROOM: from £30 to £40
SINGLE ROOM: from £35 to £45
FOOD: up to £15
Hours: breakfast 7.30am–9.30am, lunch 12noon–2pm, dinner 7.30pm–10pm, Sunday 7.30pm–9pm.
Cuisine: ENGLISH / CONTINENTAL – carvery and à la carte menu. The specialities are steaks: steak Diane, surf and hoof, etc.
Cards: Visa, Access, Diners, AmEx.
Other points: licensed, Sunday lunch, children welcome, afternoon tea, pets allowed, conferences, functions, 24hr reception, foreign exchange, residents' bar, residents' lounge, baby-listening device, cots, disabled access.
Rooms: 15 single rooms, 15 double rooms, 17 twin rooms. All with TV, radio, alarm, telephone, tea/coffee-making facilities, hair dryer, trouser-press.
Directions: town centre by Civic Centre and Cenotaph.
WEST HARTLEPOOL HOTELS LTD ☎ (01429) 266345 [Fax] (01429) 265217.

KRIMO'S
8 The Front, Seaton Carew, TS25 1BS
An outstanding restaurant with Mediterranean-style decor, popular with both locals and visitors and offering a relaxed, welcoming atmosphere. The food is well-cooked, well-presented and highly recommended.
FOOD: from £15 to £20
Hours: lunch 12noon–1.30pm, dinner 7.30pm–9.30pm, closed Saturday lunch, Sunday and Monday.
Cuisine: MEDITERRANEAN – Mediterranean food: steaks, fish.
Cards: Visa, Access.
Other points: licensed, children welcome, street parking.
Directions: on seafront, off A689.
KRIMO BOUABDA ☎ (01429) 266120.

THORNABY-ON-TEES • map 12C5

GOLDEN EAGLE HOTEL
Trenchard Avenue, TS17 0DA
Set in the heart of Teeside's commercial centre, the Golden Eagle is an excellent venue for conferences, yet provides prompt and easy access to the North Yorkshire Moors National Park. The hotel is situated only a few minutes from the A19 and is close to both mainline rail and air communications. There is easy access to the A1 and M1 motorways.
DOUBLE ROOM: from £20 to £30
SINGLE ROOM: from £35 to £45
FOOD: up to £15 ★
Hours: breakfast 7am–10am, dinner 7pm–10pm, bar meals 11am–9.30pm.
Cuisine: ENGLISH.
Cards: Visa, Access, Diners, AmEx, Switch.
Other points: parking, children welcome, disabled access, pets, vegetarian meals, restaurant, bar.
Rooms: 15 single rooms, 16 double rooms, 26 twin rooms. All rooms can be double or single occupancy.
Directions: leave A19 onto A174, turn left at traffic lights and hotel is half a mile on the right.
JOHN SNAITH & EDWARD HUGHES ☎ (01642) 766511 [Fax] (01642) 750336.

COUNTY DURHAM

BISHOP AUCKLAND • map 12C4

BISHOPS BISTRO
17 Cockton Hill Road, DL14 6EN
Old converted cottages with plenty of character, situated in the main street from the town centre. Personally run by the chef/proprietor, there is a restaurant, and a separate bar area where diners may enjoy pre-dinner drinks. Efficient service and well-cooked cuisine in an informal atmosphere.
FOOD: from £15 to £20
Hours: lunch 12noon–1.30pm, dinner 7pm–9pm, last orders 9pm, closed Sunday and Monday.
Cuisine: ENGLISH / CONTINENTAL – dishes may include honey roast breast of duckling, braised guinea fowl, escalope of veal. Daily specials displayed on blackboard. Choice of vegetarian dishes.
Cards: Visa, Access, Diners, AmEx.
Other points: licensed, children welcome.
Directions: 2 minutes from the new railway station opposite the hospital.
CHARLES & KATE DAVIDSON ☎ (01388) 602462.

CONSETT • map 12B4

ROYAL DERWENT HOTEL
Hole Row, Allensford, DH8 9BB
The Royal Derwent has the ambience and style of a medieval mansion. Timber-beamed bedrooms are furnished with either queen- or king-size beds and equipped with many modern facilities. Enjoy fine cuisine in the Cutlers Restaurant, with its crackling winter log fire, or morning and afternoon teas in the lounge. This hotel is an ideal venue for visiting Hadrian's Wall, Beamish Museum, Durham Cathedral, the north Pennines and Lake District.
DOUBLE ROOM: from £20 to £30
SINGLE ROOM: from £45 to £55
FOOD: up to £15
Hours: breakfast 7am–10am, lunch 12noon–2.30pm, bar meals 12noon–2.45pm, 7pm–9.45pm, dinner 7pm–9.45pm.
Cuisine: ENGLISH.
Cards: Visa, Access, Diners, AmEx.
Other points: parking, children welcome, no-smoking area, afternoon teas, disabled access, pets, residents' lounge, vegetarian meals, residents' bar.
Rooms: 11 double rooms, 28 twin rooms. All with TV, telephone, tea/coffee-making facilities.
Directions: 1 mile north of Castleside.
MISS A. BURGESS ☎ (01207) 592000
[Fax] (01207) 502472.

DARLINGTON • map 12C4

GEORGE HOTEL
Piercebridge, DL2 3SW
This 17th century coaching inn is set on the grassy banks of the River Tees. The restaurant offers excellent value-for-money dishes, complemented by a varied selection of good wines. Comfortable accommodation and friendly, efficient service.
DOUBLE ROOM: from £20 to £30
Hours: breakfast 7.30am–11am, lunch 11.30am–3pm, dinner 6.30pm–10pm.
Cuisine: ENGLISH – à la carte menu and bar meals.
Cards: Visa, Access, Diners, AmEx.
Other points: licensed, open-air dining, Sunday lunch, children welcome, garden, afternoon tea, coaches by prior arrangement, disabled access, vegetarian meals, residents' lounge, residents' bar.
Rooms: 35 bedrooms. All en suite.
Directions: follow A1; exit to B6275 to Piercebridge. Hotel located in village.
MR & MRS WAIN ☎ (01325) 374576
[Fax] (01325) 374577.

DURHAM • map 12C4

HALLGARTH MANOR HOTEL
Pittington, DH6 1AB
Located in the small village of Pittington 3½ miles from Durham city, this hotel is brightly yet tastefully decorated. Frequented by all ages, the hotel enjoys a relaxed atmosphere. First-class food and accommodation of a high standard.
DOUBLE ROOM: from £20 to £30

SINGLE ROOM: from £45 to £55
FOOD: up to £15   [CLUB]
Hours: breakfast 7.30am–9.30am, lunch 12noon–2pm, dinner 7pm–9.15pm, bar snacks 12noon–2pm, 5.30pm–9.30pm.
Cuisine: ENGLISH – à la carte menu, table d'hôte and bar snacks.
Cards: Visa, Access, Diners, AmEx.
Other points: licensed, open-air dining, Sunday lunch, children welcome, afternoon tea, pets allowed.
Rooms: 5 single rooms, 12 double rooms, 6 twin rooms.
Directions: 3½ miles northeast of Durham city centre.
ALAN DUMIGHAM & TERENCE ROBSON
☎ (0191) 372 1188 [Fax] (0191) 372 1249.

KENSINGTON HALL HOTEL
Kensington Terrace, Willington, Crook, DL15 0PJ
A delightful old village hall, which has been tastefully converted to a hotel of a very high standard. It is widely renowned for its excellent cuisine. The Regency function suite is available for private hire. Good base for exploring Durham Cathedral and Beamish Museum.
DOUBLE ROOM: from £20 to £30
SINGLE ROOM: from £25 to £35
FOOD: up to £15 ☆
Hours: lunch 11.30am–2pm, dinner 7pm–9.30pm.
Cuisine: ENGLISH.
Cards: Visa, Access, Diners, AmEx.
Other points: licensed.
Rooms: 10 bedrooms.
Directions: on A690, 8 miles from Durham, 2 miles from Crook.
RON & JOYCE SMEATON ☎ (01388) 745071
[Fax] (01388) 745800.

NEVILLE'S CROSS HOTEL
Darlington Road, Neville's Cross, DH1 4JX
A small, family-run hotel on the outskirts of Durham, with open fires which create a warm, convivial atmosphere.
DOUBLE ROOM: up to £20
SINGLE ROOM: from £25
FOOD: up to £15
Hours: breakfast (except Sunday) 8am–9am, lunch 12noon–2pm, bar meals 12noon–2pm, dinner 7pm–9pm, bar meals 6.30pm–9.30pm.
Cuisine: ENGLISH – home-made steak-and-kidney pie, steaks grilled in red wine, veal flambé.
Cards: Visa, Access, AmEx.
Other points: Sunday lunch, children catered for (please check for age limits), pets allowed, coaches by prior arrangement.
Directions: on the crossroads of the A167 and A690.
MR & MRS J.B. HOLLAND ☎ (0191) 384 3872.

RAMSIDE HALL HOTEL
Carrville, DH6 1BN
A country-house-type hotel set in 280 acres of maturing golf course. Choice of three eating areas, and musical entertainment seven nights a week.

The Ramside Hall Hotel provides an ideal venue for conferences, functions and weddings.
DOUBLE ROOM: from £40 to £50
SINGLE ROOM: from £55
FOOD: from £15 to £20
Hours: breakfast 7.30am–10.30am, lunch 12noon–2pm, dinner 7pm–9.30pm.
Cuisine: ENGLISH – three eating areas: à la carte restaurant (fixed price), carvery, grill room.
Cards: Visa, Access, Diners, AmEx.
Other points: Sunday lunch, no-smoking area, children welcome, coaches welcome.
Rooms: 2 single rooms, 46 double rooms, 30 twin rooms, 2 suites. All with TV, radio, telephone, tea/coffee-making facilities.
Directions: on A690, just off the A1 motorway, northeast of Durham.
MR R.J. SMITH ☎ (0191) 386 5282 [Fax] (0191) 386 0399.

SEVEN STARS INN
Shincliffe Village, DH1 2NU
A 1725 coaching inn set in a charming village, in a conservation area one mile from Durham City. The atmosphere is very relaxed and friendly, the food is well-prepared and served in generous proportions, and the accommodation is very comfortable with all major facilities, plus thoughtful extra touches. Close to Durham Cathedral, castle and museums.
DOUBLE ROOM: from £20 to £30
SINGLE ROOM: from £35 to £45
FOOD: up to £15
Hours: breakfast 8am–9am, lunch 12noon–2pm, bar meals 12noon–2pm, dinner 7pm–9pm, bar meals 7pm–9.30pm.
Cuisine: ENGLISH – with traditional roasts, home-made lasagne, pies, and steaks.
Cards: Visa, Diners, AmEx.
Other points: Sunday lunch, no-smoking area, children welcome, open bank holidays, residents' lounge, Hungarian spoken.
Rooms: 1 single room, 6 double rooms, 1 twin room. All with TV, radio, alarm, telephone, tea/coffee-making facilities.
Directions: from A1 take A177 to Bowburn, then main road into Shincliffe village.
ANDREW WINTERHALTER ☎ (0191) 384 8454.

NEWTON AYCLIFFE • map 12C4

THE GRETNA HOTEL & RESTAURANT
Great North Road, DL5 7UT
Situated just a short drive away from Darlington InterCity railway, the Gretna is an ideal place to stay when touring the north-east, with its many interesting attractions. Formerly the Wedding Inn, it has recently undergone extensive refurbishment to provide a high level of comfort. A function room is available for private hire for up to 100 guests.
DOUBLE ROOM: from £20 to £30
FOOD: up to £15
Hours: breakfast 7am–9.30am, lunch 11.30am–2pm, dinner 6.30pm–10pm.
Cuisine: ENGLISH / INTERNATIONAL – home-cooked to a high standard.
Cards: Visa, Access.
Other points: parking, children welcome, Sunday lunch, open bank holidays, afternoon tea, disabled access, pets allowed, vegetarian meals, open-air dining, garden.
Rooms: 9 twin rooms. All with TV, telephone, tea/coffee-making facilities, alarm.
Directions: A167 junction of A1M, through village of Newton Aycliffe.
MR G. HAMILTON ☎ (01325) 300100 [Fax] (01325) 300949.

CUMBRIA

AMBLESIDE • map 11D2

COMPSTON HOUSE HOTEL
Compston Road, LA22 9DJ
A family-run hotel, beautifully situated opposite park and fells. Ann and Graham Smith offer excellent food and friendly service in cosy surroundings. Most rooms have views of the park, where you may play tennis, croquet and bowls, or test your skills on the putting green. Guided fell-walking, rock-climbing, pony-trekking and riding can be arranged. Excellent water-sports nearby. Guests receive free membership to an exclusive private leisure club with pool.
DOUBLE ROOM: from £20 to £30
FOOD: from £15 to £20
Hours: breakfast 8.30am–9am, dinner 7pm (to be ordered by 5pm).
Cuisine: ENGLISH.
Other points: central heating, children catered for (please check for age limits), lounge, patio, vegetarian meals, special diets, licensed, residents' bar.
Rooms: 6 double rooms, 1 twin room, 1 family room. All with TV, tea/coffee-making facilities.
Directions: leave M6 at junction 36. Follow A590/591, bypassing Kendal and Windermere and leading straight on to the centre of Ambleside village. The hotel is situated on the corner, overlooking the park.
ANN & GRAHAM SMITH ☎ (015394) 32305.

THE RIVERSIDE HOTEL
Near Rothay Bridge, Upper Loughrigg, LA22 9LJ
A small, family-run hotel in a peaceful riverside setting in a typical English country lane. The Haineys are Scots with a welcome to match in their classic hotel. Excellent food: booking highly recommended. A few minutes from the centre of Ambleside.
DOUBLE ROOM: from £30 to £40
FOOD: from £15 to £20

NORTHERN ENGLAND • CUMBRIA

Hours: breakfast 8.30am–9.30am, dinner 7pm–8pm.
Cuisine: ENGLISH – à la carte and table d'hôte menu: changes daily.
Cards: Visa, Access.
Other points: licensed.
Rooms: 8 double rooms, 2 twin rooms. All with TV, radio, alarm, telephone, tea/coffee-making facilities.
Directions: from A591 take A593 to Coniston; left over Rothay bridge, then right.
JIM & JEAN HAINEY ☎ (015394) 32395.

APPLEBY-IN-WESTMORELAND
map 11C3

NEW INN
Brampton, CA16 6JS

The New Inn is in fact a very old inn, built around 1730 and charmingly restored with hanging baskets, which enhance its appearance. Inside, low beams, open log fires and flagstone floors take you back to a bygone era. A delightful setting in the Vale of Eden, and an ideal stop for the tourist.
DOUBLE ROOM: up to £20
FOOD: up to £15 ☆
Hours: breakfast 7.30am–9.30am, lunch 12noon–2pm, dinner 7.30pm–9.30pm.
Cuisine: ENGLISH – steaks, grills, curried nut roast, pork chops in cider, Westmoreland sweetbake, chocolate fudge cake.
Other points: licensed, open-air dining, Sunday lunch, children welcome, beer garden.
Rooms: 2 double rooms, 1 twin room. All with TV, tea/coffee-making facilities.
Directions: from Appleby, follow signs to Brampton, 1½ miles away.
ROGER & ANNE CRANSWICK ☎ (017683) 51231 [Fax] (017683) 53130.

BASSENTHWAITE LAKE
map 11C2

THE PHEASANT INN
Near Cockermouth, CA13 9YE

The hotel is an excellent base from which to tour the Lake District, as well as the Roman Wall and Border country, the Eden Valley and Cumbrian coast. It has all the charm and character of a typical old inn and is well known for its excellent English cooking, service and friendliness. Les Routiers Symbol of Excellence award-winner 1993.
DOUBLE ROOM: from £40 to £50
FOOD: from £15 to £20
Hours: breakfast 8.30am–9.45am, lunch 12noon–2pm, dinner 7pm–10.30pm, closed Christmas.
Cuisine: ENGLISH – roast meats: pheasant, venison (in season), roast duckling with orange sauce, Silloth shrimps.
Cards: Visa, Access.
Other points: licensed, Sunday lunch, no-smoking area, children welcome, parking.
Rooms: 5 single rooms, 14 double rooms, 20 twin rooms.
Directions: just off the A66, 7 miles west of Keswick.

MR W.E. BARRINGTON WILSON ☎ (017687) 76234 [Fax] (017687) 76002.

BORROWDALE • map 11C2

YEW TREE COUNTRY RESTAURANT
Seatoller, CA12 5XN

Originally two cottages built in 1628, the Yew Tree today boasts a wide and varied choice on their extensive à la carte menu, and a fine reputation. Each dish is freshly prepared to order, with many recipes derived from traditional Cumbrian origins.
FOOD: from £15 to £20
Hours: lunch 12noon–2.30pm, dinner 6.30pm–9.30pm, teas available throughout the day, closed January.
Cuisine: BRITISH – the fine cuisine is authentic Cumbrian home-cooking.
Cards: Visa, Access.
Other points: children welcome, no-smoking area, open-air dining, vegetarian meals.
Directions: located at the foot of Honister, on the B5289 Borrowdale road from Keswick.
ANDREW & JAN LYSSER ☎ (017687) 77634 [Fax] (017687) 77273.

BOWNESS-ON-WINDERMERE
map 11D2

BLENHEIM LODGE
Brantfell Road, LA23 3AE

A beautiful Lakeland hotel overlooking Lake Windermere, Blenheim Lodge offers peace and quiet, yet is close to the lake and shops. Jacqueline Sanderson is an expert in traditional English cuisine, and guests' admiration for the food has resulted in the Sandersons' own award-winning cookbook. Repeat visits vouch for the warm welcome and quality that are to be found here. Winner of Les Routiers Accommodation of the Year in 1992 and Casserole Award in 1991, 1992, 1993, 1994 and 1995.
DOUBLE ROOM: from £20 to £30
SINGLE ROOM: from £25 to £35
FOOD: up to £15
Hours: breakfast 8.30am–9am, dinner 7pm.
Cuisine: ENGLISH – traditional and Victorian dishes. All home-made. Fresh home-grown produce. Extensive vegetarian fare.
Cards: Visa, Access, Diners, AmEx, MasterCard.
Other points: licensed, no-smoking area, children welcome, residents' lounge.
Rooms: 3 single rooms, 5 double rooms, 1 twin room, 1 family room.
Directions: from M6 turn left off A591 to Windermere. Opposite St Martins church.
FRANK SANDERSON ☎ (015394) 43440.

DAMSON DENE HOTEL
Crosthwaite, Lyth Valley, LA8 8JE

Lying in the heart of the Lyth Valley in the beautiful Lake District National Park, the Damson Dene is luxury throughout. Log fires in winter, patios and three acres of landscaped gardens to enjoy in summer. Both the restaurant and bar enjoy

stunning views across the fields to the fells beyond. Excellent leisure facilities including a swimming pool and squash court, and an entertainment suite with dance floor for special functions. An ideal base for touring the lakes.
DOUBLE ROOM: from £40 to £50
FOOD: from £15 to £20
Hours: breakfast 8am–9.30am, Sunday lunch 12noon–2pm, bar meals 12noon–2pm, dinner 7pm–9pm.
Cuisine: ENGLISH.
Cards: Visa, Access.
Other points: children welcome, Sunday lunch, parking, no-smoking area, afternoon teas, disabled access, residents' lounge, garden, vegetarian meals, garden dining.
Directions: exit 36 of the M6; take the A590, then the A5074.
MR PHILIP COULSON ☎ (015395) 68676
[Fax] (015395) 68227.

KNOLL HOTEL
Lake Road, LA23 2JF
A large Victorian country house set in an acre of gardens and woodland, offering superb views over Lake Windermere, yet within easy reach of the shops and the bay.
DOUBLE ROOM: from £20 to £30
SINGLE ROOM: from £25 to £35
FOOD: up to £15
Hours: breakfast 8.45am–9.15am, dinner 7pm–7.30pm.
Cuisine: ENGLISH.
Cards: Visa, Access.
Other points: children catered for (please check for age limits), garden, leisure centre.
Rooms: 4 single rooms, 5 double rooms, 1 twin room, 2 family rooms. All with TV, telephone, tea/coffee-making facilities. Most rooms are en suite.
Directions: between Windermere station and pier.
MRS BERRY ☎ (015394) 43756.

QUINN'S RESTAURANT
Royal Square, LA23 3DB
A corner-site restaurant in Royal Square, on two floors. Tastefully and simply decorated with cane furniture and pretty Lakeland pictures. A friendly atmosphere is created with unobtrusive background music in which to enjoy well-cooked and well-presented cuisine.
FOOD: up to £15
Hours: lunch 12noon–2.30pm, dinner 6pm–10pm, closed mid-January until mid-February, open all day during summer.
Cuisine: BRITISH – full à la carte and table d'hôte menus. Sunday roasts.
Cards: Visa, Access, Diners, AmEx.
Other points: licensed, children welcome.
Directions: in Royal Square in Bowness.
MR & MRS QUINN ☎ (015394) 45510

BRAMPTON • map 11B3

ABBEY BRIDGE INN
Lanercost, CA8 2HG
This inn is in a superb setting on the banks of the River Irthing amid the Borders and gently rolling fells. Proprietor Philip Sayers is an authority on 'real ale', and up to 15 real ales are offered every week. The rooms in the hotel are attractively furnished in shades of bright pastel. The excellent cuisine attracts local and foreign tourists visiting Hadrian's Wall and the many other nearby attractions.
DOUBLE ROOM: from £20 to £30
SINGLE ROOM: up to £25
FOOD: from £15 to £20
Hours: breakfast 8am–9am, lunch 12noon–2.30pm, dinner 7pm–9.30pm, closed Christmas day.
Cuisine: ENGLISH – mainly modern English, but also includes some international flavour.
Cards: Visa, Access.
Other points: parking, children welcome, no-smoking area, disabled access, pets, residents' lounge, vegetarian meals, open-air dining, garden.
Rooms: 1 single room, 4 double rooms, 2 twin rooms.
Directions: 1 mile off A69, north of Brampton.
MR P. SAYERS ☎ (016977) 2224.

BROUGH SOWERBY • map 11C3

THE BLACK BULL INN
Near Kirkby Stephen, CA17 4EG
A country inn where the staff are keen to make guests feel at home, the food is professionally prepared and the steaks are served in particularly generous portions. Situated within easy reach of the Yorkshire Dales and the Lake District National Park.
FOOD: up to £15
Hours: bar meals 11.30am–2pm, bar meals 6pm until late.
Cuisine: INTERNATIONAL – barbequed spare ribs, chicken kiev, lasagne and bar snacks.
Other points: licensed, Sunday lunch, no-smoking area, beer garden, afternoon tea, children welcome, pets allowed.
Directions: on A685 between Brough and Kirkby Stephen in the Upper Eden Valley.
MR G. DUTTON ☎ (017683) 41413.

BROUGHTON-IN-FURNESS map 11D2

BESWICKS RESTAURANT
Langholme House, The Square, LA20 6JF
A traditional Lakeland house facing the square in the village of Broughton, well-decorated and comfortably furnished. The five-course set menu offers a good choice of English/French dishes. The tranquil and unhurried atmosphere, unobtrusive classical music and excellent service ideally complement the high standard of cuisine, with all dishes freshly cooked to order.
FOOD: from £20 to £25
Hours: dinner 7.30pm–12midnight, last orders 9.30pm, generally closed Sunday until Tuesday.
Cuisine: ENGLISH / FRENCH – five-course table d'hôte menu with regular changes. Main courses

may include rack of lamb with Cumberland sauce, roast quail and poached salmon steak.
Cards: Visa, Access, Diners, AmEx, Switch, Delta.
Other points: licensed, no-smoking area, children welcome.
Directions: junction of A595 and A593, in the centre of Broughton-in-Furness.
CHRISTINE ROE ☎ (01299) 716285.

BUTTERMERE • map 11C2

BRIDGE HOTEL
CA13 9UZ
In a beautiful and unspoilt Lakeland valley with easy access to both Buttermere Lake and Crummock Water, this hotel is set in superb unrestricted walking country with wonderful mountain scenery. The home-made food is freshly prepared daily. The comfortable, inviting lounges provide an ideal place in which to relax.
DOUBLE ROOM: from £30 to £40
SINGLE ROOM: from £25 to £35
FOOD: from £15 to £20
Hours: bar meals 12noon–9.30pm, open all year.
Cuisine: ENGLISH / CUMBRIAN – traditional Cumbrian dishes and English cuisine; Cumberland hot-pot with black pudding, Cumbrian sausages.
Other points: Sunday lunch, children welcome, pets allowed, self-catering apartments available.
Rooms: 22 bedrooms.
Directions: on the B5289 Keswick to Buttermere road.
PETER McGUIRE ☎ (017687) 70252/70266
Fax (017687) 70252.

CARLISLE • map 11B2

ANGUS HOTEL & RESTAURANT
14 Scotland Road, CA3 9DG
At the Angus hotel you will find a warm welcome and an emphasis on making guests feel at home. Good home-cooked food is available from our licenced restaurant, open six evenings per week. Fresh soup and home-baked bread complement a menu which offers very good value for money. The spotlessly clean and comfortable accommodation offers tea- and coffee-making facilities, radio/alarms and colour TVs in all rooms. En suite rooms have hair dryers too! A friendly place to stay, at very reasonable prices.
DOUBLE ROOM: from £20 to £30
SINGLE ROOM: from £25 to £35
FOOD: up to £15 CLUB
Hours: breakfast 7.30am–8.45am, dinner 6.30pm–9pm, open all year.
Cuisine: BRITISH.
Cards: Visa, Access, AmEx.
Other points: children welcome, pets allowed, vegetarian meals, residents' lounge.
Rooms: 2 single rooms, 2 double rooms, 4 twin rooms, 4 family rooms.
Directions: leave M6/A74 at junction 44. Hotel at sixth set of lights, on A7.
ELAINE & GEOFF WEBSTER ☎ (01228) 23546.

GREYHOUND INN
Bothel, CA5 2HS
An attractive country inn with an excellent roadside location, offering warm and friendly hospitality in newly refurbished surroundings. The inn is very popular with locals of all ages and is a convenient place to stop off for a meal, or to stay when travelling through the Lake District.
DOUBLE ROOM: up to £20
FOOD: up to £15
Hours: breakfast 7.30am–9.30am, lunch 12noon–2pm, bar meals 6pm–9pm.
Cuisine: ENGLISH – traditional Cumberland fare.
Other points: parking, children welcome, open-air dining, vegetarian meals, traditional Sunday lunch.
Rooms: 2 double rooms.
Directions: located seven miles east of Cockermouth on A595.
GEOFF & LINDA MITCHELL ☎ (016973) 20601.

THE ROYAL OAK
Scotby, CA4 8BP
A very popular public house in the attractive North Cumbrian village of Scotby. The Royal Oak has a good reputation locally for its well-cooked bar meals. Welcoming staff and a friendly atmosphere. Only three miles from the historic city of Carlisle.
FOOD: up to £15
Hours: bar meals 12noon–2pm, dinner 6pm–8.30pm, Sunday 7pm–8.30pm.
Cuisine: ENGLISH – bar meals including goujons of plaice, farmhouse grill, Cumberland sausage, lasagne, Mediterranean bake, T-bone steak, salads and rolls.
Other points: licensed, open-air dining, Sunday lunch, children welcome, pets allowed, beer garden, open bank holidays.
Directions: 2 miles east of Carlisle on A69. Cross M6, take first right to Scotby.
☎ (01228) 513463.

CONISTON • map 11D2

CONISTON LODGE HOTEL
Sunny Brow, LA21 8HH
A family-run-hotel offering very high standards of comfort, yet retaining a homely feel with country-cottage-style furnishing. The dining room serves excellent home-made cuisine, presented with originality and flair. Comfortable accommodation with beautiful views. The warm welcome and good service is vouched for by the large number of repeat bookings every year.
DOUBLE ROOM: from £30 to £40
FOOD: from £15 to £20
Hours: breakfast 8.30am–9.30am, dinner 7pm–7.30pm, closed Christmas.
Cuisine: ENGLISH – traditional English and local dishes such as freshly caught Coniston char. Full Lakeland-style breakfast.
Cards: Visa, Access, AmEx.
Other points: licensed, no-smoking area, residents' lounge, vegetarian meals.
Rooms: 3 double rooms, 3 twin rooms. All with

TV, radio, tea/coffee-making facilities.
Directions: turn up hill at crossroads by filling station on A593.
ANTHONY & ELIZABETH ROBINSON
☎ (015394) 41201.

FAR SAWREY • map 11D2

THE SAWREY HOTEL
Near Ambleside, LA22 0LQ
This family-run country hotel provides a welcoming and friendly service and excellent home-cooking. Close to Windermere car ferry and Hawkshead; ideally situated for touring the Lake District.
DOUBLE ROOM: from £20 to £30
SINGLE ROOM: up to £25
FOOD: up to £15
Hours: lunch 11am–2.30pm, Sunday 12noon–2.30pm, dinner 7pm–8.45pm, closed mid-December until end December.
Cuisine: ENGLISH – Windermere char (in season), fresh and smoked Esthwaite trout, home-made soups and gateaux.
Other points: fully licensed, Sunday lunch, children welcome, vegetarian meals to order, special winter breaks.
Rooms: 4 single rooms, 7 double rooms, 5 twin rooms, 6 family rooms. All with TV, telephone, tea/coffee-making facilities.
Directions: on the B5285 road to Hawkshead, 1 mile from Windermere car ferry.
DAVID D. BRAYSHAW ☎ (015394) 43425.

GRANGE-OVER-SANDS map 11D2

NETHERWOOD HOTEL
Lindale Road, LA11 6ET
An imposing hotel enjoying a prime position overlooking Morecambe Bay on the fringe of the Lake District. Inside, the oak panelling and log fires provide an atmosphere of old-world luxury and comfort. In the restaurant, dishes include roast rack of venison Caroline, local venison roasted pink, served on a bed of tagliatelle with wild mushrooms, and a sauce Robert.
DOUBLE ROOM: from £40 to £50
SINGLE ROOM: from £45 to £55
FOOD: from £15 to £20
Hours: breakfast 7.30am–10am, lunch 12.30am–2pm, dinner 7pm–9.30pm, open all year.
Cuisine: MODERN ENGLISH – imaginative home-cooked dishes using local produce; breast of chicken filled with Cumberland sausagemeat, apples and cranberries, wrapped in puff pastry.
Cards: Visa, Access, Switch.
Other points: Sunday lunch, children welcome, swimming pool, spa bath, beauty salon, solarium, steam room.
Rooms: 3 single rooms, 6 double rooms, 11 twin room, 9 family rooms.
Directions: 600 yards from Grange-over-Sands railway station.
MR J.D. & MR M.P. FALLOWFIELD ☎ (015395) 32552 Fax (015395) 34121.

HAWKSHEAD • map 11D2

GRIZEDALE LODGE HOTEL & RESTAURANT
Hawkshead, LA22 0QL
Situated two miles south of Hawkshead on the Satterthwaite road in the heart of Grizedale Forest, midway between Coniston Water and Lake Windermere. The hotel is approached down a small country road and provides an elegant and relaxing retreat in a superb, peaceful setting. Les Routiers Newcomer of the Year 1986.
DOUBLE ROOM: from £30 to £40
SINGLE ROOM: from £35 to £45
FOOD: from £15 to £20
Hours: breakfast 8.30am–9.15am, lunch 12.15am–1.45pm, dinner 7pm–8pm, closed January until mid-February.
Cuisine: ENGLISH / FRENCH – Cumbrian specialities such as Derwentwater duck, Grizedale venison and Lake Esthwaite trout. Bar lunches available.
Cards: Visa, Access.
Other points: licensed, residents' lounge, residents' bar.
Rooms: 9 double rooms. All with en suite, TV, tea/coffee-making facilities, telephone. All rooms are non-smoking.
Directions: on the road to Grizedale visitor centre from Hawkshead.
JACK & MARGARET LAMB ☎ (015394) 36532 Fax (015394) 36572.

KINGS ARMS HOTEL
The Square, LA22 0NZ
Situated in the picturesque village of Hawkshead, close to Beatrix Potter's house, this 16th century pub is ideally positioned for fishing and walking. Fishing holidays arranged at no extra charge
DOUBLE ROOM: from £20 to £30
FOOD: up to £15 CLUB
Hours: lunch 12noon–2.30pm, Sunday 12noon–2.30pm, dinner 6pm–9.30pm, Sunday 7pm–9.30pm, bar open 11am–11pm, Sunday 12noon–3pm.
Cuisine: ENGLISH – home-cooking, e.g., steak-and-kidney pie, Kings Arms chicken supreme.
Cards: Visa, Access.
Other points: Sunday lunch, children welcome, pets allowed.
Rooms: 4 double rooms, 12 twin rooms, 2 family rooms.
Directions: situated within the village of Hawkshead on B5285.
MRS R. JOHNSON ☎ (015394) 36372.

KENDAL • map 11D3

FINKLES RESTAURANT
Yard 34, Finkle Street, LA9 4BW
A 300 year old building occupying one of Kendal's famous labyrinthine 'yards' behind the main street. A variety of dishes are served by friendly, efficient staff. Seating now available for up to 130 people.
FOOD: up to £15 CLUB ☆
Hours: meals all day 9.30am–9.30pm, closed Sunday.

Cuisine: CONTINENTAL – crepes, pizzas, gateaux.
Other points: pets allowed, coaches by prior arrangement, children welcome, afternoon tea.
Directions: behind the main street in Kendal.
MR & MRS STANWORTH ☎ (01539) 727325.

THE KENDAL ARMS HOTEL
72 Milnthorpe Road, PR2 2NL
A listed building, around 150 years old, serving wholesome good pub food in pleasant surroundings. It is a typical town-style pub, very popular with locals and business people working nearby. Ideal location from which to tour and explore all other Lakeland amenities.
DOUBLE ROOM: up to £20
FOOD: up to £15
Hours: breakfast 7am–9.30am, lunch 12noon–2pm, dinner 7pm–9pm.
Cuisine: ENGLISH – a mixture of classic and modern English cuisine prepared to a high standard.
Cards: Visa, Access.
Other points: garden, residents' lounge, open bank holidays, pets allowed, licensed.
Directions: M5, junction 17 onto A4018. Right at second roundabout, then right at junction.
GEORGE WARDMAN ☎ (01539) 720956
Fax (01772) 722470.

KESWICK • map 11C2

HIGHFIELD HOTEL
The Heads, CA12 5ER
Friendly, family-run hotel with superb views of Derwentwater and the mountains. The hotel is opposite the miniature golf course, on a quiet road only minutes from the lake and market square. Bread baked on the premises, and fresh produce used in all dishes.
DOUBLE ROOM: from £20 to £30
FOOD: up to £15
Hours: breakfast 8.30am–9.15am, dinner 6.30pm–7.30pm (to be ordered by 6pm), closed November until March.
Cuisine: BRITISH.
Other points: central heating, children welcome, residents' lounge, garden.
Rooms: 5 single room, 8 double rooms, 3 twin rooms, 3 family rooms. Most rooms are en suite.
Directions: A66 to Keswick, second entry to Keswick via roundabout, left at T-junction, next right signed Borrowdale, second right after petrol station.
MR & MRS R.M. JORDAN ☎ (017687) 72508.

IVY HOUSE HOTEL
Braithwaite, CA12 5SY
Once a 17th century yeoman farmer's house, this beautiful oak-beamed building is tucked away in the corner of a typical Cumbrian village. The restaurant offers an interesting and imaginative menu, and both the proprietors and staff pride themselves in offering a warm welcome and personal service.
DOUBLE ROOM: from £40 to £50

FOOD: up to £15
Hours: breakfast 8.30am–9am, dinner 7pm–7.30pm, closed January.
Cuisine: MODERN ENGLISH – chicken stuffed with mango served with a creamy saffron sauce; salmon with ginger and sultanas; haunch of venison with port wine and redcurrant sauce.
Cards: Visa, Access, Diners, AmEx.
Other points: licensed, no-smoking area, pets by prior arrangement.
Directions: north-west from Keswick on A66; Braithwaite is signposted after two miles.
NICK & WENDY SHILL ☎ (017687) 78338.

KITCHINS BISTRO & CELLAR BAR
18–20 Lake Road, CA12 5BX
This friendly, family-run bistro and cellar-bar is as equally popular with the locals as it is with travellers and tourists. The first-class cuisine is predominantly traditional English with distinct French overtones and is complemented by a superb wine list. Nearby visitor attractions include the beautiful Lake District and Keswick Motor Museum.
FOOD: up to £15 CLUB
Hours: lunch 11.30am–2pm, dinner 4pm–9.30pm, closed Christmas day.
Cuisine: ENGLISH / FRENCH.
Cards: Visa, Access.
Other points: licensed.
Directions: from Westbourne take the Avenue to Canford Cliffs village.
GEOFFREY KITCHIN ☎ (017687) 72990.

QUEENS HOTEL
Main Street, CA12 5JF
An old coaching inn, originally the posting house. The town is on the busy A66 to the north of the Lakes. The hay loft and stables have been converted to provide a cosy bar known as Ye Olde Queens Head.
DOUBLE ROOM: from £20 to £30
FOOD: up to £15
Hours: breakfast 8am–9.30am, lunch 10am–5pm, bar meals 12noon–9pm, dinner 6.30pm–9pm.
Cuisine: ENGLISH – traditional British dishes.
Cards: Visa, Access, Diners, AmEx.
Other points: licensed, Sunday lunch, children welcome, coaches by prior arrangement
Rooms: 9 single rooms, 20 double rooms, 8 family rooms.
Directions: in the market square in Keswick. Off the A66.
PETER JAMES WILLIAMS ☎ (017687) 73333
Fax (017687) 71144.

KIRKBY LONSDALE • map 11D3

THE COPPER KETTLE
3–5 Market Street, LA62 AU
A 16th century building on the main street of this busy market town. Mr Gamble is a member of the Société Gastronomique Française, evident in the excellent meals produced. Kirkby Lonsdale is a charming market town, and a good base for

touring the Lakes and the Yorkshire Dales.
DOUBLE ROOM: up to £20
SINGLE ROOM: up to £25
FOOD: up to £15
Hours: meals all day 12noon–9pm, lunch 12noon–3pm, high tea 3pm–6.30pm, dinner 6.30pm–9pm.
Cuisine: ENGLISH – roasts, steaks and dishes cooked in wine.
Cards: Visa, Access, Diners, AmEx.
Other points: licensed, Sunday lunch, children welcome.
Rooms: 4 bedrooms. All with TV, tea/coffee-making facilities.
Directions: from M6 junction 36, follow signs to Kirkby Lonsdale; Market Street is on left.
MR & MRS GAMBLE ☎ (015242) 71714.

LAKE ULLSWATER • map 11C2

WREAY FARM COUNTRY GUEST HOUSE
Lake Ullswater, Watermillock, CA11 0LT
Built in 1787, Wreay Farm has been completely modernized to provide a high standard of comfort. Situated on the brow of a hill near Bennet Head in a quiet, peaceful area, it affords spectacular views of Lake Ullswater. Offering exceptional cuisine using only the freshest of local produce, it is an ideal choice for a family hotel. A list of places to visit is provided for all guests.
DOUBLE ROOM: from £20 to £30
SINGLE ROOM: up to £25
FOOD: up to £15
Hours: breakfast 8.30am, dinner 7.30pm, closed December until January (inclusive).
Cuisine: ENGLISH.
Other points: parking, children welcome, dogs allowed, residents' lounge, vegetarian meals.
Rooms: 10 bedrooms.
Directions: come to Lake Ullswater, turn right, go up lake for two miles until you reach the Brackenrigg Hotel, turn right, go up hill and the guest house is at the top on the right.
D.H.N. WINDLE ☎ (017684) 86296.

LONGTOWN • map 11B2

THE SPORTSMAN'S RESTAURANT & MARCH BANK HOTEL
Scotsdyke, CA6 5XP
The 'Last Hotel in England' is an old country house with beautiful views over the River Esk. Personally run by the Moore family, you are assured of a warm welcome and excellent service in both the hotel and restaurant. The food is of a very high standard, yet offers excellent value for money. Highly recommended. Fishing available. A Les Routiers Casserole Award winner for four years running.
DOUBLE ROOM: from £20 to £30
SINGLE ROOM: from £25 to £35
FOOD: up to £15
Hours: breakfast 8am–9am, lunch 12noon–2pm, dinner 6pm–9pm.
Cuisine: BRITISH – specialities include locally smoked salmon, whole roast leg of lamb (for four persons at 24 hours' notice), Scotch steaks, game.
Cards: Visa, Access, AmEx.
Other points: licensed, Sunday lunch, no-smoking area, children welcome, fishing.
Rooms: 1 single room, 3 double rooms. All with TV, tea/coffee-making facilities.
Directions: 3 miles north of Longtown on the A7. 9 miles from M6, junction 44.
THE MOORE FAMILY ☎ (01228) 791325.

MELMERBY • map 11C3

SHEPHERDS INN
Near Penrith, CH10 1HF
An 18th century pub, built of traditional Cumberland stone, nestling at the foot of Hartside Pass in the northern Pennines. Serves fine traditional beers and extensive, original, home-prepared meals. Winner of the 1990 Les Routiers Cheeseboard Award for their outstanding cheese selection. Casserole Award winner 1991, 1992, 1993, 1994 and 1995. 1993 Publican Catering Pub of the Year. Holiday cottages available in village – brochure on request.
FOOD: up to £15
Hours: lunch 11am–2.30pm, Sunday 12noon–2pm, dinner 6pm–10pm, Sunday 7pm–10pm, closed Christmas day.
Cuisine: INTERNATIONAL – many home-made dishes such as spare ribs, chicken Leoni, rogan gosht. Choice of 26 different cheeses for ploughmans, and a range of exotic pickles.
Cards: Visa, Access, Diners, AmEx, Switch.
Other points: open-air dining, Sunday lunch, children welcome.
Directions: on the A686 in Melmerby.
MARTIN & CHRISTINE BAUCUTT
☎ (01768) 881217.

PENRITH • map 11C3

KNOTTS MILL COUNTRY LODGE
Watermillock, Ullswater, CA11 0JN
Originally a sawmill, Knott's Mill has recently been refurbished to provide comfortable accommodation in the beautiful Ullswater countryside. The house is set in a secluded position, and all rooms have views of the fells. Sailing boats and windsurfers may be hired in Glenridding, and a steamer trip offers a scenic trip of the lake. Many nearby picturesque valleys and villages.
DOUBLE ROOM: from £20 to £30
SINGLE ROOM: from £25 to £35
FOOD: up to £15
Hours: breakfast 8.15am–9.15am, dinner 6.30pm–8.30pm, last orders 8.30pm, open all year.
Cuisine: BRITISH – à la carte menu, offering a range of traditional home-style cuisine.
Cards: Visa, Access.
Other points: licensed, children welcome, morning tea, afternoon tea, garden, parking.

Rooms: 6 double rooms, 1 twin room, 2 family rooms. All with TV, tea/coffee-making facilities.
Directions: from junction 40 on M6, follow A66 towards Keswick, then A592 for six miles.
JANE JONES ☎ (017684) 86472 Fax (017684) 86699.

TEBAY MOUNTAIN LODGE HOTEL
Orton, CA10 3SB

Tebay Mountain Lodge is a beautiful new concept in hotel accommodation. Each studio is custom-built, offering every modern-day comfort, and enjoying magnificent views of the Cumbrian hills. Not only does it provide a stop-over for business travellers and families, but it is also an excellent base for holidaying and exploring the unspoilt valleys and historical attractions.
DOUBLE ROOM: from £30 to £40
FOOD: up to £15 ☆
Hours: breakfast 7.30am–9am, dinner 7pm–9pm, open all year.
Cuisine: ENGLISH / CONTINENTAL – à la carte menu, offering a combination of home-made English, continental and vegetarian dishes.
Cards: Visa, Access, Diners, AmEx.
Other points: licensed, no-smoking area, children catered for (please check for age limits), pets allowed, residents' lounge, parking.
Rooms: 30 bedrooms.
Directions: 1 mile north of junction 38 of M6 motorway northbound/southbound; leave at Tebay services and follow signs.
MR BULT ☎ (015396) 24351 Fax (015396) 24354.

YANWATH GATE INN
Yanwath, CA10 2LF

A lovely olde-worlde inn of 300 years, providing all patrons with a warm welcome, excellent service and a homely atmosphere – not forgetting the superb, home-cooked meals on offer. Situated in the village of Yanwath, the inn is conveniently located for visiting Penrith town, Ullswater Lake and Lowther Park.
FOOD: up to £15
Hours: lunch 12noon–2pm, dinner 6.30pm–9.30pm.
Cuisine: FRENCH / BRITISH – home-cooked meals offering excellent value for money.
Cards: Visa, Access, AmEx.
Other points: parking, children welcome, open-air dining, vegetarian meals, traditional Sunday lunch.
Directions: take the A6 from Penrith south towards Shap; turn right after Eamont Bridge.
IAN & SUE RHIND ☎ (01768) 62386.

SEDBERGH • map IID3

THE DALESMAN COUNTRY INN
Main Street, LA10 5BN

An olde-worlde stone-built country inn, renovated by local craftsmen and situated in a village 'frozen in time'. Decorated in a country style throughout, with traditional log fires, this is a popular retreat for locals and tourists alike. A nice place to 'get away from it all'. Winter breaks very popular.

DOUBLE ROOM: from £20 to £30
SINGLE ROOM: from £35 to £45
FOOD: up to £15
Hours: breakfast 8.30am–9.30am, lunch 12noon–2pm, dinner 6pm–9.30pm.
Cuisine: ENGLISH – grills and steaks, gammon, daily specials and roasts every Sunday.
Cards: Visa, Access.
Other points: licensed, Sunday lunch, children welcome, afternoon tea, vegetarian meals.
Rooms: 1 double room, 2 twin rooms, 3 family rooms. All with TV, tea/coffee-making facilities, iron, hair dryer, toiletries. One of the family rooms is a cottage with double room and single room.
Directions: first pub on left entering Sedbergh, 5 miles from junction 37 of the M6.
BARRY & IRENE GARNETT ☎ (015396) 21183.

THIRLMERE • map IIC2

STYBECK FARM
CA12 4TN

A working mixed farm with a friendly, non-smoking atmosphere. Situated at the foot of the Helvellyn range of mountains, central for touring, walking, fishing and sailing on Lake Thirlmere.
DOUBLE ROOM: up to £20
SINGLE ROOM: up to £25
Hours: breakfast 8.30am–9am, dinner 7pm, closed Christmas day.
Cuisine: BRITISH.
Other points: central heating, children welcome, residents' lounge.
Rooms: 1 single room, 1 double room, 1 twin room. All with tea/coffee-making facilities.
Directions: A591, near the junction with the B5322, 5 miles from Keswick.
JOSEPH & JEAN HODGSON ☎ (017687) 73232.

ULVERSTON • map IID2

HILL FOOT HOTEL
Pennington Lane, LA12 7ES

Within easy reach of the magnificence of the Lake District, this excellent family-run hotel is set in a charming cobbled market town and boasts meat-suppliers appointed by Her Majesty the Queen. An ideal base for a relaxing vacation. The well-equipped bedrooms and facilities and friendly service ensure your personal comfort, while the superb cuisine offers maximum satisfaction.
DOUBLE ROOM: from £20 to £30
FOOD: up to £15
Hours: breakfast 7.30am–9am, lunch 11.30am–2.30pm, dinner 6.30pm–9.30pm, open all year, open bank holidays.
Cuisine: ENGLISH – good-quality English cooking. Charcoal-grilled steaks a house speciality. Daily chef's specials.
Cards: Visa, Access, AmEx.
Other points: licensed, open-air dining, Sunday lunch, children welcome, pets allowed.
Directions: situated on the A590 past Ulverston, by a garden centre.
MARGARET NICOLSON ☎ (01229) 580300.

WINDERMERE • map 11D2

■ BECKMEAD HOUSE
5 Park Avenue, LA23 2AR
Delightful stone-built Victorian house, with a good reputation for high standards, comfort and friendliness. The breakfasts are famous. Convenient for lake, shops, restaurants and golf course.
DOUBLE ROOM: up to £20
Hours: breakfast 8.30am–9am.
Cuisine: BREAKFAST.
Other points: central heating, children welcome, residents' lounge, no evening meal, vegetarian meals.
Rooms: 1 single room, 2 double rooms, 1 twin room, 1 family room. All with TV, tea/coffee-making facilities.
Directions: M6 junction 36, westbound on A590 for three miles. A591 to Windermere.
MRS DOROTHY HEIGHTON ☎ (015394) 42757.

■ GREEN GABLES GUEST HOUSE
37 Broad Street, LA23 2AB
A small, friendly guest house with very pretty bedrooms providing clean, comfortable accommodation, close to local amenities, bus and railway station. Guests are assured of a warm welcome, for the Green Gables' motto is 'cleanliness, friendliness and a good hearty breakfast'.
DOUBLE ROOM: up to £20
SINGLE ROOM: up to £25
Hours: breakfast 8.30am, closed Christmas and New Year's day.
Cuisine: BREAKFAST.
Other points: central heating, children welcome, residents' lounge, special breaks, no evening meal.
Rooms: 2 single rooms, 3 double rooms, 2 family rooms. All with TV, hair dryer, tea/coffee-making facilities. Some rooms are en suite.
Directions: leave M6 at junction 36, A591 to Windermere.
MRS SHEILA LAWLESS ☎ (015394) 43886.

■ THE HIDEAWAY HOTEL
Phoenix Way, LA23 1DB
A delightful Victorian stone building, The Hideaway has a reputation for good food, value and service. The easy access to the Lakes, a beautifully tended garden and well-appointed rooms keep people returning
DOUBLE ROOM: from £30 to £40
SINGLE ROOM: from £25 to £35
FOOD: up to £15
Hours: breakfast 8.30am–9.30am, dinner 7.30pm–8.30pm, open February until December.
Cuisine: ENGLISH / CONTINENTAL – modern English cuisine with continental influences. Menu changes daily.
Other points: children welcome, afternoon tea, residents' lounge, garden, pets allowed.
Rooms: 2 single rooms, 5 double rooms, 5 twin rooms, 3 family rooms. All with TV, telephone, tea/coffee-making facilities.
Directions: situated on Phoenix Way off Ambleside Road (A591).
MRS GORNALL & MR SUMMERLEE ☎ (015394) 43070.

■ OLDFIELD HOUSE
Oldfield Road, LA23 2BY
Bob and Maureen Theobald welcome you to Oldfield House, which has a friendly, informal atmosphere within a traditionally-built Lakeland residence. Ideally situated close to Windermere village, yet away from the busy main road. Fully centrally heated, with a comfortable lounge and pleasant dining room. Guests are permitted to use the facilities at nearby Parklands Country Club.
DOUBLE ROOM: from £20 to £30
Hours: breakfast 8.30am–9am, open all year.
Cuisine: BREAKFAST.
Cards: Visa, Access.
Other points: children welcome, residents' lounge, parking, baby-listening device, cots.
Rooms: 1 single room, 4 double rooms, 2 twin rooms, 1 triple room. All with TV, radio, alarm, telephone, tea/coffee-making facilities.
Directions: junction 36 of M6. A591 to Windermere, through village. Off lake, turn left into Ellerthaite Road, then second right and first left into Oldfield Road.
BOB & MAUREEN THEOBALD ☎ (015394) 88445.

■ ST JOHN'S LODGE
Lake Road, LA23 2EQ
A small, private hotel centrally situated for touring the Lake District and only ten minutes' walk from the Lake Pier. Mini-breaks off-season. Facilities of local country sports club available to residents.
DOUBLE ROOM: up to £20
SINGLE ROOM: up to £25
FOOD: up to £15
Hours: breakfast 8.15am–9am, dinner 7pm (to be ordered by 6pm), closed December and January.
Cuisine: ENGLISH – all dishes made from fresh, local produce. Will cater for vegetarians.
Cards: Visa, Access.
Other points: central heating, children welcome, residents' lounge, residents' bar.
Rooms: 1 single room, 8 double rooms, 2 twin rooms, 3 family rooms. All with en suite, TV, tea/coffee making facilities.
Directions: midway between Windermere village and Bowness on the A5074.
RAY & DOREEN GREGORY ☎ (015394) 43078.

■ THORNBANK HOTEL
Thornbarrow Road, LA23 2EW
Thornbank is a family-run hotel Ideally situated in a pleasant residential area of Windermere in the beautiful Lake District, just a short distance from the lake shore. Bedrooms are fully-equipped with many modern facilities, including Sky TV, and there is a comfortable guest lounge with ample tourist information. Windermere is an excellent location for touring and exploring, with endless amenities.
DOUBLE ROOM: up to £20
SINGLE ROOM: up to £25
FOOD: up to £15 ☆
Hours: breakfast 8.45am, dinner 6.45pm.
Cuisine: ENGLISH.
Cards: Visa, Access, AmEx.
Other points: parking, children welcome, open

bank holidays, no-smoking area, residents' lounge, vegetarian meals.
Rooms: 9 bedrooms, 4 en suite, 1 deluxe four-poster. All rooms have TV, tea/coffee-making facilities.
Directions: A591, turn left at Windermere Hotel towards Bowness; ¾ mile along is Thornbarrow Road.
MR R. & MRS P. CHARNOCK ☎ (015394) 43724.

WITHERSLACK • map 11D2

🏠 THE OLD VICARAGE COUNTRY HOUSE HOTEL
Church Road, LA11 6RS
This outstanding establishment, a delightful Georgian-period country vicarage, offers all the necessary qualities for a truly memorable evening. The ambience, cuisine and service combine to make dining here a pleasure, totally in keeping with its setting in the peaceful and unspoiled countryside where it nestles under Yewbarrow Scar. Les Routiers Regional Newcomer 1991.
DOUBLE ROOM: from £50
SINGLE ROOM: from £55
FOOD: from £20 to £25
Hours: breakfast 8.30am–9.30am, dinner 7.30pm for 8pm.
Cuisine: ENGLISH – regional cooking.
Cards: Visa, Access.
Other points: licensed, afternoon tea, residents' lounge, garden, special breaks, children catered for (please check for age limits).
Rooms: 1 single room, 10 double rooms, 3 twin rooms. All with TV, radio, alarm, telephone, tea/coffee-making facilities.
Directions: off the A590 Barrow road, take right turning to village, then first left in Witherslack village after the phone box.
MR R. BURRINGTON BROWN ☎ (015395) 52381 Fax (015395) 52373.

GREATER MANCHESTER

ALTRINCHAM • map 8A5

🍴 FRANCS RESTAURANT
2 Goose Green, WA14
Francs Restaurant, overlooking Goose Green conservation area, offers first-class French cuisine in an informal and relaxed atmosphere which truly captures the essence of France. Furnished in typically French style, the service is friendly and efficient, making it a very popular choice with both tourists and local businessmen. Very highly recommended.
FOOD: up to £15 CLUB
Hours: lunch 12noon–3pm, dinner 6pm–10.30pm, dinner (Fri-sa) 6pm–11pm.
Cuisine: FRENCH.
Cards: Visa, Access, Diners, AmEx.
Other points: parking, children welcome, Sunday lunch, open bank holidays, vegetarian meals, open-air dining.
Directions: off New Stanford Road, turn left after Barclays Bank.
MR N.J. BANKS ☎ (0161) 941 3954.

🏠 WOODLAND PARK HOTEL
Wellington Road, Timperley, WA15 7RG
The Woodland Park is a delightful family-owned hotel, set in spacious grounds in a secluded residential area. Brian and his attentive, courteous staff pride themselves on personal care and attention to detail. All the bedrooms are individually designed and furnished, while the restaurant, conservatory, bar and reception have all been designed in an appealing country house style with a warm, rustic colour scheme.
DOUBLE ROOM: from £50
SINGLE ROOM: from £55
FOOD: from £15 to £20
Hours: breakfast 7am–9.30am, lunch 12noon–2pm, dinner 7pm–10pm.
Cuisine: ENGLISH – mainly traditional dishes made from fresh produce.
Cards: Visa, Access, Diners, AmEx.
Other points: parking, children welcome, vegetarian meals, no-smoking area, residents' lounge.
Rooms: 45 bedrooms. All with en suite, TV, telephone, radio, hair dryer, tea/coffee-making facilities.
Directions: M56 from Manchester Airport, exit onto A560 to Altrincham.
MR B.N. WALKER ☎ (0161) 928 8631 Fax (0161) 941 2821.

BOLTON • map 8A5

🏠 GEORGIAN HOUSE HOTEL
Manchester Road, Blackrod, BL6 5RU
This large Georgian building is decorated to a high standard and provides a very comfortable stay. Attractive meals are presented in the relaxed atmosphere of the restaurant. With its five conference suites and banqueting facilities, it is ideal for either weddings or conferences. Dinner dances on Fridays and Saturdays in the Regency Restaurant.
DOUBLE ROOM: from £30 to £40
SINGLE ROOM: from £55
FOOD: from £15 to £20
Hours: breakfast 7am–10am, bar snacks 11am–3pm, lunch 12noon–2pm, dinner 7pm–10pm.
Cuisine: ENGLISH / CONTINENTAL – dishes may include Georgian house pâté, egg and prawn Marie Rose, supreme of chicken, quenelles of seafood. Flambé specialities on the à la carte menu.
Cards: Visa, Access, Diners, AmEx, Switch.

Other points: licensed, Sunday lunch, children welcome, afternoon tea, pets allowed, leisure centre.
Rooms: 15 single rooms, 49 double rooms, 26 twin rooms, 3 family rooms, 8 suites. All with TV, radio, telephone, tea/coffee-making facilities, hair dryer, satellite TV, trouser-press.
Directions: on the A6, 1½ miles from M61 junction 6.
MRS DIANE NORBURY ☎ (01942) 814598.

🍴 RIVINGTON PAVILION SERVICE AREA
Between junctions 6 and 8, M61 Motorway, Horwich, BL6 5UZ
When travelling along the M61 by day or by night, you can rely on the Rivington Pavilion Services to offer a welcoming place to break your journey. Whether you require a light snack, a complete wholesome meal or simply to stock up on light refreshments, your needs will be catered for. The Lodge is scheduled to open May 1995.
FOOD: up to £15
Hours: open 24 hours.
Cuisine: BRITISH – varying daily specials, continental choices also available.
Cards: Visa, Access, Diners, AmEx.
Other points: parking, children welcome, disabled access, no-smoking area, vegetarian meals, forecourt shop.
Directions: off M61 between junctions 6 and 8.
NICK BROOKES ☎ (01204) 68641
[Fax] (01204) 695444.

🍴 WATERGATE TOLL
Watergate Drive, Over Hulton, BL5 1BU
This attractive converted old farmhouse is a very popular meeting point with people of all ages, whether local or just passing through. With good food, attentive service and a congenial atmosphere, this is a restaurant/bar that you will want to return to again and again.
FOOD: up to £15
Hours: meals all day (Sunday–Thursday) 11.30am–9pm, Friday 11.30am–9.30pm, Saturday 11.30am–10pm.
Cuisine: ENGLISH / INTERNATIONAL – à la carte menu, speciality menu, bar snacks and children's menu.
Cards: Visa, Access, Diners, AmEx.
Other points: parking, children welcome, vegetarian meals, traditional Sunday lunch, afternoon tea.
Directions: take exit 4 on M61, turn left and then second exit off roundabout, first exit right into Service Road.
MR CANNON ☎ (01204) 64989.

BURY • map 8A5

🏨 THE BOLHOLT
Walshaw Road, BL8 1PU
A large, extended country house set in 50 acres of parkland and lakes. The warm and courteous hospitality, open fires and elegant surroundings make this hotel a joy to visit.
DOUBLE ROOM: from £20 to £30

SINGLE ROOM: from £45 to £55
FOOD: up to £15
Hours: breakfast 7am–8.45am, lunch 12noon–2pm, dinner 7pm–9.30pm.
Cuisine: ENGLISH – à la carte. Traditional English, fillet steak Wellington.
Cards: Visa, Access, Diners, AmEx.
Other points: licensed, Sunday lunch, children welcome, garden, pets allowed.
Rooms: 10 single rooms, 28 double rooms, 9 twin rooms.
Directions: A58 from Bury towards Bolton, fork right for Tottington, fork extreme left at Dusty Miller Pub.
STEFAN SIKORSKI ☎ (0161) 763 7007
[Fax] (0161) 763 1789.

🍴 ROSCO'S EATING HOUSE
173 Radcliffe Road, BL9 9LN
Owned and run by two chefs, the atmosphere is definitely 'foody'. The unassuming frontage hides a simple and welcoming restaurant which specializes in original dishes served in a distinctive style. The charcoal grill is placed so that everyone can see their steaks cooking. Booking advisable at weekends, as Rosco's is very popular with locals and other caterers – hence the late opening.
FOOD: up to £15 👍
Hours: dinner Friday 6.30pm–4am, Saturday, 4.30pm–4am, Sunday 7.30pm–12midnight, Wednesday–Thursday 7.30pm–12midnight, closed Monday and Tuesday.
Cuisine: ENGLISH / INTERNATIONAL – from simple meals costing a few pounds to original dishes with imaginative sauces freshly made to order. Large selection of fresh vegetables.
Cards: Visa, Access.
Other points: Sunday lunch, limited disabled access, children welcome, coaches by prior arrangement
Directions: Whitfield Road from centre, right at traffic lights near Pack Horse Pub.
STUART & JACQUELINE RUSCOE ☎ (0161) 797 5404.

HYDE • map 8A5

🏨 NEEDHAMS FARM
Uplands Road, Werneth Low, Gee Cross, near Hyde, SK14 3AQ
A small working farm, dating from the 16th century, which offers very comfortable accommodation and food of an excellent standard. The inspector declared it 'a wonderful place to stay', and noted it was ideal for children, as there are many friendly animals on the farm. Perfect base for walking, riding and golf, with many local places of interest nearby. Highly recommended.
DOUBLE ROOM: up to £20
SINGLE ROOM: up to £25
FOOD: up to £15
Hours: breakfast 6.30am–11am, dinner 7pm–9.30pm.
Cuisine: ENGLISH.
Cards: Visa, Access, AmEx.
Other points: children welcome, special breaks, residents' lounge, cots.

Rooms: 1 single room, 4 double rooms, 1 triple room, 1 family room. All with TV, radio, alarm, telephone, tea/coffee-making facilities. Some rooms are en suite.
Directions: junction 15 on M66; off A560. Between Werneth Low Country Park and Etherow Valley.
MRS WALSH ☎ (0161) 368 4610 Fax (0161) 367 9106.

MANCHESTER • map 8A5

ELM GRANGE HOTEL
561 Wilmslow Road, Withington, M20 4GJ
A family-run commercial hotel situated approximately 20 minutes' drive from the city centre, exhibition centre and the airport. In a main road position with a good bus service to the main shopping area, it is easily located by following the signposts to Christie Hospital, which is opposite the hotel. Good food from an extensive menu.
DOUBLE ROOM: from £20 to £30
SINGLE ROOM: from £25 to £35
FOOD: up to £15 CLUB
Hours: breakfast 7.15am–9.45am.
Cuisine: ENGLISH.
Cards: Visa, Access, AmEx.
Other points: children welcome, central heating, residents' lounge, residents' bar.
Rooms: 32 bedrooms. All with TV, telephone, tea/coffee-making facilities, radio, alarm, iron, video, trouser-press.
Directions: from A34 at West Didsbury, take B5117 to Didsbury; hotel 1 mile on right.
GORDON W. DELF ☎ (0161) 445 3336
Fax (0161) 445 3336.

GARDENS HOTEL
55 Piccadilly, M1 2AP
Located in the heart of the city, Gardens Hotel is only minutes away from Piccadilly Station and within easy access to Manchester International Airport and the famous G-Mex centre. Overlooking the Piccadilly Gardens, it provides stylish comfort and is an ideal base for both businessmen and tourists alike. Ed's Bar is available for private functions, and there are also three conference suites accommodating up to 70 people.
DOUBLE ROOM: from £30 to £40
FOOD: from £15 to £20 CLUB
Hours: breakfast 7am–9.30am, lunch 12noon–2pm, dinner 6.30pm–10pm, bar snacks 12noon–10pm.
Cuisine: ENGLISH.
Cards: Visa, Access, Diners, AmEx.
Other points: children welcome, pets, entertainment.
Rooms: 100 bedrooms. All en suite.
Directions: on Piccadilly, in the heart of the city.
MR B. CROWLEY ☎ (0161) 236 5155
Fax (0161) 228 7287.

HENRY'S CAFE BAR (MANCHESTER)
Parsonage Gardens, M3 2LE
A lively, popular café-bar serving an extensive range of international fast-food, American and non-alcoholic beers and speciality cocktails. Very busy at lunchtimes.
FOOD: up to £15
Hours: meals all day 10.30am–11pm, closed Sunday.
Cuisine: INTERNATIONAL.
Cards: Visa, Access.
Other points: children welcome, open bank holidays, no-smoking area, afternoon teas, disabled access, vegetarian meals.
Directions: behind Kendals, off Deansgate.
☎ (0161) 832 7935.

THAT CAFE
1031–3 Stockport Road, Levenshulme, M19 2TB
Situated three miles from Manchester city centre, That Café offers a good variety of both meat and vegetarian dishes. The atmosphere and decor are unique, with open fires, bric-a-brac, and 1930s and '40s music.
FOOD: up to £15
Hours: Sunday lunch 12.30am–2.30pm, dinner 7pm–11pm, closed Sunday evenings.
Cuisine: ENGLISH / CONTINENTAL – special £12.95 table d'hôte menu, exclusive of coffee or tea, Monday, Tuesday, Wednesday and Thursday evenings. Weekly menu change. Fresh fish. Three-course Sunday lunch £10.95, main courses £5.95. A la carte menu changes monthly.
Cards: Visa.
Other points: Sunday lunch, children welcome, functions.
Directions: on the A6 between Manchester and Stockport.
JOSEPH QUINN & STEPHEN KING ☎ (0161) 432 4672.

RAMSBOTTOM • map 8A5

OLD MILL HOTEL & RESTAURANT
Springwood, BL0 9DS
Originally an old mill, this hotel has been completely refurbished, achieving an attractive yet comfortable atmosphere. With a combination of a good choice of food and wine and attentive service, both restaurants are well worth a visit.
DOUBLE ROOM: from £30 to £40
FOOD: up to £15
Hours: breakfast 7.30am–9.30am, lunch 12noon–2pm, dinner 6.30pm–10.30pm.
Cuisine: FRENCH / ITALIAN – two restaurants. French cuisine: fish, steak, shellfish, casseroles. Comprehensive wine list. Italian cuisine: pastas, pizzas.
Cards: Visa, Access, Diners, AmEx.
Other points: licensed, Sunday lunch, swimming pool, sauna, solarium, leisure centre, children welcome, residents' lounge, garden.
Rooms: 12 single rooms, 12 double rooms, 12 twin rooms. All with TV, telephone, tea/coffee-making facilities.
Directions: off junction M66 with A56, situated on A676 north of Manchester.
KAREN SACCO ☎ (0170682) 2991.

HUMBERSIDE • NORTHERN ENGLAND

ROCHDALE • map 8A5

AFTER EIGHT RESTAURANT
2 Edenfield Road, OL11 5AA
This sumptuously decorated Victorian-style restaurant offers a wide choice of superb dishes from the à la carte menu. With excellent service and a relaxing atmosphere, it is well worth a visit.
FOOD: from £15 to £20
Hours: dinner from 7pm, closed first week of May.
Cuisine: MODERN ENGLISH / CONTINENTAL – among the house specialities are the salmon and asparagus parcel, baked fillet of brill, and duck breast én croute.
Cards: Visa, Access, AmEx.
Other points: children welcome, vegetarian meals, no-smoking area, garden.
Directions: on the A680 Blackburn Road, 5 minutes from Rochdale town centre.
GEOFFREY TAYLOR ☎ (01706) 46432.

HUMBERSIDE

BEVERLEY • map 12E6

THE LAIRGATE HOTEL
Lairgate, HU17 8EP
A delightful Georgian house in the centre of this busy market town, famous for its Minster, racecourse and Saturday market. The hotel has a relaxed, happy atmosphere with friendly, conscientious staff. Live duo entertainment in the restaurant. Private car park at the rear of the hotel.
DOUBLE ROOM: up to £20
FOOD: from £15 to £20
Hours: meals all day 7.30am–9.30pm.
Cuisine: ENGLISH / CONTINENTAL – all dishes are home-made. Fisherman's pie, steak-and-kidney pie, moussaka and steaks. Flambée and fondue served in the piano bar atmosphere.
Cards: Visa, Access.
Other points: Sunday lunch, no-smoking area, children welcome, coaches by prior arrangement.
Directions: in the centre of Beverley; Lairgate runs parallel to Market Square.
PETER WALSHAW ☎ (01482) 882141/ 861901.

RUDSTONE WALK FARM
South Cave, Brough, HU15 2AH
A beautiful 400-year-old farmhouse mentioned in the Domesday Book, nestling into the foot of the Yorkshire wolds in an area steeped in history and charm. The farm offers unrivalled views across the countryside towards nearby York, Beverley and the East Riding. Luxurious, serviced, self-contained cottages in the grounds are available for hire all year round. Convenient for the M62.
DOUBLE ROOM: from £20 to £30
SINGLE ROOM: from £35 to £45
FOOD: from £15 to £20
Hours: breakfast 7am–8.30am, dinner 7pm–8.20pm.
Cuisine: ENGLISH – traditional home-cooking.
Cards: Visa, Access, Eurocard, MasterCard.
Other points: central heating, children welcome, TV lounge, garden, vegetarian meals, licensed.
Rooms: 7 double rooms, 7 twin rooms. All with TV, tea/coffee-making facilities.
Directions: situated on the B1230, off M62.
MRS PAULINE GREENWOOD ☎ (01430) 422230 Fax (01430) 424552.

BRIDLINGTON • map 12D6

SEACOURT HOTEL
76 South Marine Drive, YO15 3NS
The Seacourt Hotel stands quietly in a prime position overlooking the beautiful South Bay, with panoramic views of the old harbour, town and Flamborough Head. A refurbishment project has transformed this former large Edwardian house into a delightful small hotel of distinction. Bridlington and the surrounding area offer a virtually endless combination of attractions.
DOUBLE ROOM: from £20 to £30
FOOD: from £15 to £20
Hours: lunch 12noon–2pm, dinner 6.30pm–10pm, open all year.
Cuisine: ENGLISH – table d'hôte and à la carte menus, with fish dishes, a house speciality and fresh local market produce. Children's menu.
Cards: Visa, Access.
Other points: licensed, Sunday lunch, no-smoking area, children catered for (please check for age limits), meals all day, residents' lounge, functions.
Rooms: 3 single rooms, 3 double rooms, 5 twin rooms, 1 family room. All with telephone, tea/coffee-making facilities, heating, satellite TV.
Directions: on South Marine Drive overlooking the bay.
ANNE & GEOFFREY HOLMES ☎ (01262) 400872.

WINSTON HOUSE HOTEL
5 South Street, YO15 3BY
Situated near the seafront in Bridlington, this newly refurbished hotel offers guests excellent accommodation and a very good English restaurant with a continental theme. The daily-changing menu provides diners with a freshly prepared meal cooked to high standards.
DOUBLE ROOM: up to £20
SINGLE ROOM: up to £25
FOOD: up to £15
Hours: breakfast 8am–8.45am, dinner 5pm–5.50pm.
Cards: Visa, Access.
Other points: children welcome, residents' lounge, no-smoking area, vegetarian meals.
Rooms: 2 single rooms, 10 double rooms, 2 twin rooms, 1 family room. All with satellite TV, tea/coffee-making facilities.

239

NORTHERN ENGLAND • HUMBERSIDE

Directions: A165/A166, follow signs for South Beach; turn off seafront at lifeboat station.
DAVID & CAROL BOTHAM ☎ (01262) 670216
[Fax] (01262) 670216.

Other points: Sunday lunch, children welcome.
Directions: in the market place behind the Dolphin Hotel.
MR P. & MR K. OLIVER ☎ (01472) 692644.

BRIGG • map 9A3

🛏 ARTIES MILL
Wressle Road, Castlethorpe, DN20 9LF
This charming old windmill dates back to 1790, and the adjoining grain sheds have been converted into bars and restaurants with a pleasant and friendly atmosphere, while still retaining the fascinating mill features. Good food, comfortable accommodation and the warm friendly welcome from the proprietors combine to make this hotel 'highly recommended'.
DOUBLE ROOM: from £20 to £30
FOOD: up to £15 [CLUB]
Hours: breakfast 7am–9am, dinner 7pm–10pm, bar meals 11am–10pm.
Cuisine: ENGLISH – à la carte, table d'hôte, bar meals.
Cards: Visa, Access, Diners, AmEx.
Other points: licensed, open-air dining, Sunday lunch, children welcome, garden, functions, private dining, children welcome, cots, 24hr reception, left luggage.
Rooms: 7 double rooms, 25 twin rooms, 1 family room.
Directions: 1 mile from Brigg on the A18 and 5 miles from Scunthorpe.
IAN & DOREEN BRIGGS ☎ (01652) 652094
[Fax] (01652) 657107.

CLEETHORPES • map 10A4

🍴 AGRAH INDIAN RESTAURANT
7–9 Seaview Street, DN38 8EU
The Agrah Indian Restaurant is decorated with brightly coloured pictures illustrating a story, and with Muslim-style wall panels. A broad clientele, including many thespians from the seasonal summer shows.
FOOD: up to £15
Hours: lunch 12noon–2.30pm, dinner 6pm–12midnight.
Cuisine: INDIAN – Tandoori dishes.
Cards: Visa, Access.
Other points: licensed, open-air dining, Sunday lunch, children welcome.
Directions: Cleethorpes is four miles south of Grimsby on A46 and A16.
BASHIR MIAH ☎ (01472) 698669.

🍴 STEELS CORNER HOUSE RESTAURANT
11–13 Market Street, DN35 8LY
A popular and friendly restaurant, which continues to provide excellent value for money.
FOOD: up to £15
Hours: breakfast 9am–11am, meals all day 9am–10pm.
Cuisine: ENGLISH – fish and chips. Grills. Business lunches.
Cards: Visa, Access.

COTTINGHAM • map 12E6

🍴 MANDARIN RESTAURANT
119 Hallgate, HU16 4DA
A typically furnished Chinese-style restaurant, offering excellent cuisine in a friendly, warm atmosphere. Conveniently located. Helpful staff assist you in making a selection so that you will be sure to enjoy your meal.
FOOD: up to £15
Hours: lunch 12noon–2pm, dinner 5pm–12midnight.
Cuisine: ORIENTAL / VEGETARIAN – Peking, Cantonese and vegetarian cuisine. Coffee specialities.
Cards: Visa, Access, Diners, AmEx.
Other points: licensed, Sunday lunch, children welcome, parking.
Directions: situated in Cottingham village centre.
WAI LUN CHUNG ☎ (01482) 843475
[Fax] (01482) 875795.

ELLERKER • map 12E5

🍴 KINGSTONS BLACK HORSE INN
Church Lane, HU15 2DN
Set in the pretty little village of Ellerker, 14 miles outside Hull, the Black Horse offers excellent value for money. A combination of low-lighting and an interesting use of mirrors give a continental feel, even though the food is predominantly English. You can be sure of a warm welcome in this popular and atmospheric pub.
FOOD: up to £15
Hours: lunch 12noon–3pm, dinner 6.30pm–12midnight, last orders 10pm, closed Monday lunch and Tuesday lunch, open all year.
Cuisine: CONTINENTAL – with a variety of steaks, fish, chicken and venison on offer. Dishes include Dover sole Veronique, chicken à la Pernod, fillet steak princess.
Other points: licensed, open-air dining, Sunday lunch, children welcome.
Directions: situated 1 mile off the A63 in the village of Ellerker.
BARBARA & MICHAEL KINGSTON ☎ (01430) 423270.

HULL • map 12E6

🛏 KINGSTOWN HOTEL
Hull Road, Hedon, HU12 8DJ
A family-run luxury hotel with very high standards and a friendly, welcoming atmosphere. Good food excellently served in the restaurant and bar. Ideally situated for the continental ferry, rural Holdferness with its seaside resorts, the historic towns of Hedon and Beverley, and the important city of Hull.

240

DOUBLE ROOM: from £30 to £40
SINGLE ROOM: from £45 to £55
FOOD: from £15 to £20
Hours: breakfast 7am–9.30am, lunch 12noon–2.30pm, dinner 7pm–10pm.
Cuisine: ENGLISH – à la carte and table d'hôte menus served in the dining room and lounge bar.
Cards: Visa, Access, AmEx.
Other points: fully licensed, Sunday lunch, no-smoking area, children welcome, guide dogs, residents' lounge, conferences, baby-sitting, cots, 24hr reception, left luggage.
Rooms: 10 single rooms, 20 double rooms, 4 twin rooms. All with satellite TV, radio, telephone, tea/coffee-making facilities.
Directions: on eastern outskirts of Hull, opposite continental ferry terminal.
SALLY READ ☎ (01482) 890461 Fax (01482) 890713.

PEARSON PARK HOTEL
Pearson Park, HU5 2TQ
Delightfully situated within a public ornamental park, one mile north of the city centre. Very popular with families and businessmen. The establishment has been under the same ownership for the last 27 years. Coffee-shop service weekday lunchtimes.
DOUBLE ROOM: from £30 to £40
FOOD: up to £15
Hours: breakfast 7.30am–9.15am, dinner 6.30pm–9pm, lunch 12.30am–2pm.
Cuisine: FRENCH / ENGLISH – daily specials, fresh local produce.
Cards: Visa, Access, Diners, AmEx.
Other points: Sunday lunch, children welcome, cots, 24hr reception, parking, residents' bar, residents' lounge, disabled access.
Rooms: 9 single rooms, 16 double rooms, 6 twin rooms, 1 family room.
Directions: take A1079 Beverley Road from city centre. After Mobil garage turn left onto Pearson Avenue. This leads into the park.
MR & MRS D.A. ATKINSON ☎ (01482) 43043.

SCUNTHORPE • map 9A3

BRIGGATE LODGE INN
Ermine Street, Broughton, DN20 0NQ
An attractive hotel offering comfortable acommodation and fine cuisine using only the freshest of produce. Dishes may include mustard-glazed lamb chops, supreme of chicken fromage, and poached salmon steak with a lime sauce.
DOUBLE ROOM: from £30 to £40
SINGLE ROOM: over £55
FOOD: from £20 to £25
Hours: breakfast 7am–10am, lunch 12noon–2pm, dinner 7pm–10pm, bar snacks 11am–11pm.
Cuisine: ENGLISH / FRENCH.
Cards: Visa, Access, Diners, AmEx.
Other points: parking, children welcome, Sunday lunch, open bank holidays, no-smoking area, afternoon tea, Sunday dinner, disabled access, residents' lounge, vegetarian meals, garden.
Rooms: 50 bedrooms.
Directions: 200 meters from junction 4 on M180. A18/A15.
MR M.A. MIDDLETON ☎ (01652) 650770 Fax (01652) 650495.

ISLE OF MAN

DOUGLAS • map 14E5

INGLEWOOD HOTEL
Queens Promenade, IM2 4NF
The Inglewood is a homely, Manx family-run hotel with a fine open outlook over the sea, sky and headlands. It is reputed for providing guests with good quality accommodation and excellent food and service at very competitive rates. Situated close to all local amenities, the horse trams pass just outside the hotel as a means of convenient transport, and there are several lovely glens and walks within easy reach.
DOUBLE ROOM: up to £20
SINGLE ROOM: up to £25
FOOD: up to £15
Hours: breakfast 9am–9.30am (earlier by arrangement), 6pm–7pm (later by arrangement), snacks 5pm–10pm.
Cuisine: BRITISH – traditional Manx cuisine using fresh farm produce.
Other points: children welcome, residents' lounge, no-smoking dining room, vegetarian meals, baby-sitting.
Rooms: 3 single rooms, 2 doubles rooms, 3 twin rooms, 13 family rooms. All with TV, hair dryer, tea/coffee-making facilities.
Directions: on the seafront, midway betweeen boat arrival pier and electric tram station. Horse trams pass the hotel.
BRIAN & ANNE HEAP ☎ (01624) 674734 Fax (01624) 674734.

LA BRASSERIE
The Empress Hotel, Central Promenade, IM2 4RA
An excellent restaurant situated below the Empress Hotel, serving an extensive choice of meals throughout the day. All dishes are prepared from fresh produce, well-cooked and attractively presented in generous proportions. The high quality food is complemented by a good wine list and excellent service. Enjoy your meal in comfortable surroundings with a pleasant, relaxed atmosphere.
DOUBLE ROOM: from £30 to £40
SINGLE ROOM: over £55
FOOD: up to £15

Hours: meals all day 10am–10.45pm, children's menu available until 7.30pm, open all year.
Cuisine: INTERNATIONAL – extensive menu, featuring fresh scallops wrapped in bacon with garlic butter, kidney and guiness pie, salmon hollandaise. Complemented by a good wine list.
Cards: Visa, Access, AmEx.
Other points: children catered for (please check for age limits), open all day, no-smoking area, afternoon tea, street parking, vegetarian meals, disabled access.
Rooms: 102 bedrooms. All with en suite, TV, radio, telephone, tea/coffee-making facilities, alarm.
Directions: directly beneath the Empress Hotel, Douglas Promenade. On seafront.
MR JOHN TURNER ☎ (01624) 661155
Fax (01624) 673554.

🏨 MIDLAND HOTEL
Loch Promenade, IM1 2LY
At the Midland you can expect the personal attention of the owners, an excellent combination of good value and fine service, and comfortable accommodation. The hotel is in a perfect position, overlooking the bay and convenient for the shopping centre and the travel terminus. Visit the legendary Isle of Man and discover for yourself the many charms of this remarkable island.
DOUBLE ROOM: up to £20
SINGLE ROOM: up to £25
FOOD: up to £15
Hours: breakfast 8.30am–9.15am, dinner 5.30pm, closed October until March.
Cuisine: BRITISH – appetizing meals available to residents.
Cards: Visa, Access, Diners, AmEx.
Other points: children welcome, residents' lounge, vegetarian meals, afternoon teas.
Rooms: 17 bedrooms. All with radio, alarm, iron, baby-listening device.
Directions: from the sea terminal, the Midland is 10 minutes' walk along the seafront.
DEREK & SYLVIA AKERMAN ☎ (01642) 674990.

🏨 SEFTON HOTEL
Harris Promenade, IM1 2RM
Adjacent to the Gaiety Theatre, this hotel offers special 'Island Theatre Weekends'. Whether you wish to enjoy a play or two, or simply relax, the Sefton Hotel is ideal. Good food is served in a pleasantly relaxed atmosphere. With a health club, indoor heated swimming pool and comfortable accommodation, this is just the place to return to after discovering the island. There are two bedrooms suitable for the disabled.
DOUBLE ROOM: from £30 to £40
FOOD: up to £15
Hours: breakfast 7.30am–9.45am, lunch 12.30am–2pm, bar snacks 9.45am–11pm, dinner 7.15pm–9.30pm, open bank holidays.
Cuisine: MODERN ENGLISH – dishes may include mushroom crepes with sauce mornay, grilled salmon with cucumber sauce, Manx ice cream.
Cards: Visa.
Other points: licensed, poolside bar, no-smoking area, children welcome, afternoon tea, solarium,

gym facilities, swimming pool, beauty therapy, sauna, coffee shop, conferences, disabled access.
Rooms: 13 single rooms, 31 double rooms, 80 twin rooms, 4 family rooms.
Directions: centre of Douglas Promenade, next to the Gaiety Theatre.
CHRIS ROBERTSHAW ☎ (01624) 626011
Fax (01624) 676004.

PORT ERIN • map 14E5

🏨 THE FALCON'S NEST HOTEL
Station Road, IM9 6AF
This attractive, family-run Georgian hotel, restored to its former elegance, provides comfort and a relaxing atmosphere, with superb quality service and cuisine to suit the most discerning visitor, whether on business or on holiday. The hotel is situated in the picturesque south-west of the island, overlooking Port Erin Bay and only two minutes' walk from the sheltered sandy beach.
DOUBLE ROOM: from £20 to £30
FOOD: up to £15
Hours: breakfast 7am–9.30am, lunch 12noon–2pm, bar meals 12noon–2pm, dinner 6pm–9pm, bar meals 6pm–7.30pm.
Cuisine: CONTINENTAL.
Cards: Visa, Access, AmEx.
Other points: parking, children welcome, pets allowed, conference facilities, residents' lounge, traditional Sunday lunch.
Rooms: 50 bedrooms. All with TV, telephone, radio, alarm, hair dryer, baby-listening device, tea/coffee-making facilities.
Directions: five miles south-west of airport, in centre of Port Erin.
ROBERT POTTS ☎ (01624) 834077
Fax (01624) 835370.

RAMSEY • map 14E5

🍴 HARBOUR BISTRO
5 East Street, IM8 1DN
Comfortably furnished and enjoying a relaxed atmosphere, the Harbour Bistro offers an extensive menu with an emphasis on seafood. All dishes are well-cooked, attractively presented and served by helpful, friendly staff. Good wine list. Popular with locals and holiday-makers alike. The atmosphere is welcoming and relaxed.
FOOD: up to £15 🍷
Hours: lunch, 12noon–2pm, dinner 6.30pm–10.30pm, closed Tynwald Day, closed for 2 weeks in October.
Cuisine: CONTINENTAL – dishes may include traditional roast duck with walnut stuffing, baked chicken breast and asparagus. Seafood specialities, and fresh lobster and Dover sole when available.
Cards: Visa, Access.
Other points: licensed, Sunday lunch, children welcome, special diets, street parking.
Directions: between harbour and Parliament Street.
KEN & PATRICK DEVANEY ☎ (01624) 814182.

SULBY • map 14E5

PEPPER MILL RESTAURANT
Sulby Mill
Situated in the heart of the beautiful countryside, this former woollen mill – now extensively refurbished – offers good food and friendly service in an informal setting. Excellent wine list and well-stocked bar. Nearby visitor attractions include Sulby Claddagh and a wildlife park.
FOOD: up to £15
Hours: lunch 12noon–2.30pm, dinner 6pm–10pm, open all year.
Cuisine: BRITISH – a wide choice of dishes, including Junior Gourmet's selection. Vegetarian dishes available.
Cards: Visa, Access.
Other points: licensed, open-air dining, Sunday lunch, children welcome, parking, vegetarian meals.
Directions: turn off Snaefell mountain road at bungalow. Centre of Sulby Glen.
KARL MEIER ☎ (01624) 897436.

LANCASHIRE

BLACKBURN • map 11E3

MAY HOUSE RESTAURANT
208 Preston New Road, BB2 6PS
This delightful restaurant offers diners a superb meal in a very friendly and welcoming atmosphere. Relax over an enjoyable meal with the soft tones of selected classical, jazz and easy-listening music helping to ease away the strains and pressures of the day.
FOOD: up to £15
Hours: lunch 12noon–2pm, dinner 6pm–9.30pm (last orders).
Cuisine: MODERN ENGLISH/CONTINENTAL – à la carte menu changes monthly, table d'hôte changes weekly.
Cards: Visa, Access.
Other points: parking, children welcome, private room, no-smoking area, open-air dining, vegetarian meals.
Directions: exit M6 from junction 31 and take A677 towards Blackburn. The May House may be found half a mile past The Moat House on the left.
MARK BROADBENT ☎ (01254) 53160.

MILLSTONE HOTEL
Church Lane, Mellor, BB2 7JR
Set in a small Lancashire village, the Millstone combines the cosy atmosphere of a traditional country inn with all the conveniences of a modern hotel. Bedrooms are very well-appointed and boast fine furnishings and delightful decor. The restaurant specializes in local market produce, selected according to the season and freshly prepared for the table. Within easy reach of the remote Trough of Bowland, with Blackpool just 45 minutes away.
DOUBLE ROOM: from £40 to £50
FOOD: from £15 to £20 [CLUB]
Hours: breakfast 7am–9.30am, dinner 7pm–9.45pm, lunch 12noon–2pm.
Cuisine: ENGLISH / CONTINENTAL.
Cards: Visa.
Other points: children welcome, parking, no-smoking area, pets, residents' lounge, vegetarian meals, residents' bar, disabled access.
Rooms: 6 single rooms, 12 double rooms, 1 twin room, 1 family room. All with TV, radio, alarm, telephone, tea/coffee-making facilities.
Directions: A59/A667. 10 minutes' drive from junction 31 of M6.
☎ (01254) 813333 Fax (01254) 812628.

BLACKPOOL • map 11E2

COASTERS BAR & DINER
Ocean Boulevard, FY4 1EZ
An exciting restaurant reminicent of a 1920s casino. The atmosphere is always fun-filled, enhanced by the young and efficient staff. The menu is everything you would expect from a good Tex-Mex restaurant, featuring old favourites like burgers, southern fried chicken, barbecued ribs and a selection of fajitas.
FOOD: up to £15
Hours: open bank holidays.
Cuisine: AMERICAN / TEX-MEX – good-sized portions of favourite American-style dishes.
Cards: Visa, Access, Diners, AmEx.
Other points: parking, children welcome, no-smoking area, vegetarian meals.
Directions: located on Blackpool Promenade, close to Blackpool Pleasure Beach.
SIMON RUSSELL ☎ (01253) 401771
Fax (01253) 401098.

HILL'S TUDOR ROSE HOTEL
435-7 South Promenade, FY1 6BQ
A comfortable, medium-sized family hotel overlooking the sea and only a few minutes away from the Sandcastle. Friendly, personal service will ensure that your stay is as enjoyable as possible. The lounge bar makes a good rendezvous for a drink before dinner.
DOUBLE ROOM: from £20 to £30
Hours: breakfast 8.30am–9.30am, dinner 5.30pm.
Cuisine: ENGLISH.
Cards: Visa, Access, Diners, AmEx.
Other points: children welcome, snack lunches.
Rooms: 6 single rooms, 15 double rooms, 9 family rooms.
Directions: on the Promenade near the South Pier.
STAN HILL ☎ (01253) 342656.

NEWLYN PRIVATE HOTEL
31–33 Northumberland Avenue, North Shore, FY2 9SA

Family-run hotel noted for good food and hospitality. In quiet North Shore area, adjacent to Queens Promenade, yet close to all Blackpool's amenities. An ideal base for touring the Forest of Bowland, Lakes or Dales.
DOUBLE ROOM: up to £20
SINGLE ROOM: up to £25
FOOD: up to £15
Hours: breakfast 8.30am–9am (if required earlier, continental breakfast can be served to your room), dinner 5pm.
Cuisine: ENGLISH.
Cards: Visa, Access.
Other points: children welcome, licenced, residents' lounge.
Rooms: 3 single rooms, 7 double rooms, 3 twin rooms, 2 family rooms. En suite bedrooms with TV, tea/coffee-making facilities. Basic rooms with tea/coffee-making facilities.
Directions: off Queens Promenade.
MRS S. HARGREAVES ☎ (01253) 353230.

NEWLYN REX HOTEL
56–58 Central Drive, FY1 5QR

A resort hotel, traditionally furnished. There is a separate lounge and bar room, with two good-size dining rooms in the basement. Ideal for conference delegates, being only 100 yards from main conference halls. Bookings welcomed from illumination parties. The famous tower and town centre are close by.
DOUBLE ROOM: up to £20
FOOD: up to £15
Hours: breakfast 9am–9.30am, bar snacks 11am–4pm, dinner 5pm–5.30pm, open Christmas and New Year.
Cuisine: ENGLISH.
Cards: Visa, Access, Diners.
Other points: children welcome, afternoon tea, pets allowed, vegetarian meals, TV lounge, special breaks.
Rooms: 6 single rooms, 20 double rooms, 2 twin rooms, 6 family rooms. All with TV, telephone, tea/coffee-making facilities, heating.
Directions: situated at the far end of municipal car park, corner of Hornby Road.
TERENCE DOHERTY ☎ (01253) 25444.

SUNRAY
42 Knowle Avenue, off Queens Promenade, FY2 9TQ

A cheerful and comfortable guest house that has been family-run for the past 21 years under the capable hands of Mrs Jean Dodgson. With all your needs catered for by this friendly and welcoming establishment, you will find the Sunray an ideal place to stay while in the area. It provides the facilities you expect from a large hotel: direct-dial telephone, TV, hair dryer and more. Special rates can be arranged for pensioners.
DOUBLE ROOM: from £20 to £30
FOOD: up to £15 ☆
Hours: breakfast 8.30am–9.15am, dinner 5.30pm until after shows.

Cuisine: BREAKFAST.
Cards: Visa, Access.
Other points: children welcome, garden, pets allowed, vegetarian meals.
Rooms: 3 single rooms, 2 double rooms, 9 twin rooms, 2 family rooms.
Directions: 2 miles north of Blackpool Tower, along Promenade. Turn right at Uncle Tom's Cabin.
JEAN & JOHN DODGSON ☎ (01253) 351937.

WHITE TOWER RESTAURANT
Balmoral Road, FY4 1EZ

The White Tower Restaurant serves excellent food and wine in very pleasant, elegant surroundings. From its penthouse position, high in the exciting 'Wonderful World Building', the restaurant has splendid views overlooking the Promenade and the famous Illuminations.
FOOD: up to £15 CLUB
Hours: Sunday lunch 12noon–4pm, dinner 7pm–10.45pm, closed January.
Cuisine: CONTINENTAL – extensive à la carte menu. Dishes may include Chateaubriand, Dover sole. continental dishes. Excellent wine list.
Cards: Visa, Access, Diners, AmEx.
Other points: Sunday lunch, children welcome, guide dogs, conferences, functions.
Directions: M55. Yeadon Way, near Pleasure Beach/Sandcastle Centre.
BLACKPOOL PLEASURE BEACH LTD
☎ (01253) 346710/341036 Fax (01253) 401098.

BOLTON-LE-SANDS • map 11D3

DEERSTALKER RESTAURANT
4 Main Road, LA4 8DH

A three-storey stone-built restaurant, decorated in olde-worlde style, with many interesting pieces of railway memorabilia. The food is freshly prepared and beautifully presented, complemented by a good wine list. The service is excellent, very efficient yet warm and friendly.
FOOD: up to £15
Hours: lunch 12noon–2pm, dinner 6.30pm–9.30pm, closed Monday.
Cuisine: ENGLISH / CONTINENTAL – with dishes such as filet mignon, boeuf bourguignon, tournedos Deerstalker and sole meunière.
Cards: Visa, MasterCard.
Other points: licensed, Sunday lunch, children welcome.
Directions: exit 35 off M6, then take A6. Near garage.
MR & MRS WOODS ☎ (01524) 732841.

CHORLEY • map 8A4

SHAW HILL HOTEL, GOLF & COUNTRY CLUB
Preston Road, Whittle-le-Woods, PR6 7PP

Set in beautiful countryside midway between Chorley and Preston, Shaw Hill is a perfect venue for golf, business seminars, weddings and private functions. Vardons Restaurant is, without doubt,

one of the finest à la carte dining facilities in the north-west. The luxuriously furnished suites offer quiet and comfort, with magnificent views over the golf course and greens.
DOUBLE ROOM: from £30 to £40
FOOD: from £15 to £20
Hours: breakfast weekdays 7am–9.30am, lunch 12noon–2pm, bar meals 11am–7pm, dinner 7pm–9.45pm.
Cuisine: INTERNATIONAL – fillet with truffle, pheasant with asparagus, corn-fed supreme of chicken with scallops. Fresh fish daily.
Cards: Visa, Access, AmEx.
Other points: licensed, Sunday lunch, children welcome, pets allowed, afternoon tea, parking, residents' lounge, garden, special breaks.
Directions: junction 28 of M6, follow signs for Whittle-le-Woods. Junction of A6, one mile from junction 8.
J.S. STOKES & CO LTD ☎ (01257) 269221
Fax (01257) 261223.

CLITHEROE • map 11E3

BAYLEY ARMS
Hurst Green, near Whalley, BB7 9QB
Situated in the delightful village of Hurst Green, the Bayley Arms offers warm hospitality all year round. Comfortable chairs, gleaming brass and welcoming log fires contribute to a relaxing, unhurried atmosphere.
DOUBLE ROOM: from £20 to £30
SINGLE ROOM: from £35 to £45
FOOD: up to £15
Hours: breakfast 7.30am–10am, lunch 12noon–2pm, dinner 7pm–9.30pm.
Cuisine: ENGLISH/CONTINENTAL – imaginative chef-prepared restaurant menu and bar snacks.
Cards: Visa, AmEx, MasterCard.
Other points: licensed, Sunday lunch, open bank holidays, children welcome, cots.
Rooms: 5 double rooms (doubles can be let as singles), 1 twin room, 2 family rooms. All with TV, tea/coffee-making facilities.
Directions: in village of Hurst Green close to Stonyhurst College.
MR TAYLOR ☎ (01254) 826478 Fax (01254) 826797.

CALF'S HEAD HOTEL
Worston, BB7 1QA
Nestling in the historic village of Worston, the hotel offers a variety of dining locations, including a beautiful walled garden with stream and rustic bridge for warm summer days. In winter, roaring fires in the à la carte dining room or intimate Tudor Room and Bar Lounge area will melt away the chill. Private parties catered for.
DOUBLE ROOM: from £20 to £30
FOOD: up to £15
Hours: breakfast 7.30am–10am, lunch 12noon–2pm, dinner 7pm–9.30pm.
Cuisine: ENGLISH – full à la carte menu, bar meals, Sunday 'Hot Galfey' (12noon–6pm). Barbeques on request. All food home-made using fresh, local produce.

Cards: Visa, Access, Diners, AmEx.
Other points: open-air dining, Sunday lunch, pets allowed, children welcome, weekend breaks.
Rooms: 1 single room, 4 double rooms, 1 twin room. All with en suite, satellite TV, telephone, tea/coffee-making facilities, baby-listening device, hair dryer, video, trouser-press.
Directions: situated just off A59.
MR & MRS DAVIS ☎ (01200) 441218
Fax (01200) 441510.

THE INN AT WHITEWELL
Forest of Bowland, BB7 3AT
A lovely riverside setting with six miles of salmon, sea-trout and trout-fishing for residents. Log fires and antique furniture create a homely atmosphere. The inn has magnificent views across the trough of Bowland and provides an ideal location for exploring the surrounding countryside on foot.
DOUBLE ROOM: from £30 to £40
SINGLE ROOM: from £35 to £45
FOOD: from £15 to £20
Hours: bar open 11am–3pm and 6pm–11pm, dinner 7.30pm–9.30pm.
Cuisine: ENGLISH – home-made soups. Steak, kidney and mushroom pie. Local lamb. Home-made ice cream.
Cards: Visa, Access, Diners, AmEx.
Other points: licensed, children welcome.
Directions: follow signs to Whitewell from roundabout in Longridge centre.
RICHARD & PAM BOWMAN ☎ (01200) 448222.

SPREAD EAGLE HOTEL (SAWLEY) LTD
Sawley, BB7 4NH
Owing to its popularity, it is advisable to book for Sunday lunch, Friday and Saturday dinner. Situated on a bend of the River Ribble, with lovely views across the river to the surrounding countryside. An excellent base from which to tour the Dales and the Lake District.
DOUBLE ROOM: from £40 to £50
FOOD: from £15 to £20
Hours: lunch 12.30am–2pm, dinner 7pm–9pm, open all year.
Cuisine: ENGLISH / CONTINENTAL – à la carte menu, including beef from Aberdeen Angus stock. Regional specialities.
Cards: Visa, Access, Diners, AmEx.
Other points: licensed, Sunday lunch, children welcome.
Rooms: 2 single rooms, 3 double rooms, 5 twin rooms. All with TV, radio, telephone, tea/coffee-making facilities.
Directions: off the A59, half a mile down the road to Sawley village.
THE TRUEMAN FAMILY ☎ (01200) 441202/ 441406 Fax (01200) 441973.

DARWEN • map 11E3

WHITEHALL HOTEL & RESTAURANT
Springbank, BB3 2JU
A large country house, standing in its own tended grounds and pleasingly furnished throughout. It

offers guests a high standard of comfort, with en suite rooms, indoor heated swimming pool and a highly recommended restaurant. The hotel is conveniently located for access to Ribble Valley, the Lake District and the north-west coast.
DOUBLE ROOM: from £20 to £30
SINGLE ROOM: from £45 to £55
FOOD: up to £15 [CLUB]
Hours: breakfast 7.30am–9.30am, lunch 12noon–2pm, dinner 7pm–10pm.
Cuisine: ENGLISH.
Cards: Visa, Access, Diners, AmEx.
Other points: indoor swimming pool, sauna, solarium, snooker room.
Rooms: 15 bedrooms.
Directions: located off the A666 Bolton to Blackburn road.
MR & MRS JOSEPH & MARIE WHITEHEAD
☎ (01254) 701595 [Fax] (01254) 773426.

ECCLESTON • map 8A4

THE COURTYARD AT THE BLUE ANCHOR
Towngate, PR7 5QR

A varied menu of freshly-cooked, well-presented meals is available at this attractive Victorian pub and restaurant. You can relax in the appealing cottage-style restaurant and oak-beamed bar, and when the weather is fine you can enjoy your tasty meal alfresco on the patio or in the garden. The good food and friendly efficient service are popular with locals and travellers alike.
FOOD: up to £15
Hours: meal all day 11.30am–10pm, Sunday 12noon–10pm, open every day for food Easter until September.
Cuisine: ENGLISH / CONTINENTAL – a good selection from the à la carte and table d'hôte menus. Bar snacks available lunchtimes and evenings.
Cards: Visa, Access, Switch.
Other points: parking, children welcome, garden, open-air dining, vegetarian meals, traditional Sunday lunch, afternoon teas.
Directions: from junction 27 on M6 Motorway, take the B5250 west from Chorley. The Blue Anchor is located in Eccleston town centre.
MARY FLANAGAN & CHARLES ADAMS
☎ (01257) 451159.

THE ORIGINAL FARMERS ARMS
Towngate, PR7 5QS

A country-style pub with a warm, family atmosphere. Friendly staff combined with a wide choice of good food served in generous portions illustrate why the Farmers Arms enjoys such popularity. For those wishing to stay in the area, or for travellers on the M6, there are four comfortable bedrooms.
DOUBLE ROOM: up to £20
FOOD: up to £15
Hours: breakfast 7am–9am, meals all day 12noon–10pm, dinner 5.30pm–10pm.
Cuisine: ENGLISH / INTERNATIONAL – wide choice of dishes such as home-made steak-and-kidney pie, rack of lamb and mixed grill. Plus a vast selection of home-made specials, which are written on the blackboard.
Cards: Visa, Access.
Other points: licensed, open-air dining, Sunday lunch, children welcome, children welcome, beer garden, afternoon tea.
Rooms: 2 double rooms, 2 twin rooms. All with TV, radio, alarm, tea/coffee-making facilities.
Directions: B5250 west of M6 near Chorley. 2 miles from Charnock Richard service area on M6.
BARRY S. NEWTON ☎ (01257) 451594
[Fax] (01257) 453329.

LANCASTER • map 11E3

FORTON PAVILION LODGE AT FORTON SERVICE AREA
Between junctions 32 and 33, M6 Motorway, LA2 9DU

The Lodge provides excellent accommodation at a competitive price and offers the facilities to make travelling a pleasure. Convenient for the historic city of Lancaster, Blackpool, Morecambe, Last Drop Village and Martin Mere Bird Sanctuary.
DOUBLE ROOM: from £20 to £30
FOOD: up to £15
Hours: open 24 hours.
Cuisine: BRITISH / INTERNATIONAL – offered within the service building.
Cards: Visa, Access, Diners, AmEx.
Other points: parking, children welcome, disabled access, no-smoking area, vegetarian meals, forecourt shop, Burger King.
Rooms: 41 bedrooms. All with en suite, satellite TV, radio, alarm, hair dryer, trouser-press, tea/coffee-making facilities.
Directions: between junctions 32 and 33 at services on M6 motorway.
IAN MALLOCH ☎ (01524) 792227
[Fax] (01524) 791703.

SPRINGFIELD HOUSE HOTEL & RESTAURANT
Wheel Lane, Pilling, PR3 6HL

A Georgian country house hotel set in extensive, attractive grounds with walled gardens and pools. The two dining rooms, The Corless Room and Miss Ciceleys, are sympathetically decorated in keeping with the 1840s style of building. Very well-cooked and presented meals offering outstanding value for money are served in a relaxed atmosphere by polite, efficient staff.
DOUBLE ROOM: from £30 to £40
SINGLE ROOM: from £25 to £35
FOOD: from £15 to £20 [CLUB]
Hours: lunch 12noon–2pm, dinner 7pm–9pm.
Cuisine: INTERNATIONAL – monthly changing table d'hôte menu may include trout Dundee (in a whisky and orange sauce), duckling, steak, chicken Maryland and medallions Carribean.
Cards: Visa, Access.
Other points: licensed, Sunday lunch, children welcome, pets allowed, afternoon tea, residents' lounge, garden, functions.

Rooms: 7 bedrooms.
Directions: off A588 Blackpool to Lancaster road, to the west of Pilling village.
GORDON & ELIZABETH COOKSON
☎ (01253) 790301 Fax (01253) 790907.

LEYLAND • map 8A4

RUNSHAW COLLEGE SCHOOL OF CATERING
Langdale Road, near Preston, PR5 2DQ
The Fox Holes Restaurant is part of a tertiary college, allowing students an opportunity to practise skills in food service and kitchen work.
FOOD: up to £15
Hours: lunch 11.45am–2pm (last orders 12.45am), dinner 6.30pm–10pm (last orders 7.45pm), closed July until August, closed Saturday and Sunday.
Cuisine: ENGLISH / FRENCH / CONTINENTAL – a varied menu. Dishes include steak pie, tagliatella carbonara, champignons stroganoff, tournedos de saumon avec beurre citron.
Other points: parking, children welcome, no-smoking area, disabled access, vegetarian meals.
Directions: from M6 junction 28, follow signs for Leyland, take second road on left (Bent Lane). Follow to end, turn right and first left for Langdale Road.
MR LITTLEWOOD ☎ (01772) 642010
Fax (01772) 622295.

LONGRIDGE • map 11E3

CORPORATION ARMS
Lower Road, near Preston, PR3 2YJ
Situated in the wilds of Lancashire on the borders of the Fell Country, this pub provides a warm and friendly welcome to its customers. The food and service are excellent, making it highly recommended.
FOOD: up to £15
Hours: lunch 12.15am–2pm, dinner 7pm–9.30pm, Sunday 12noon–9.30pm, closed Christmas day.
Cuisine: ENGLISH – pan-fried chicken, beef stroganoff, home-made steak, kidney and mushroom pie, stuffed mushrooms, hot chocolate fudge cake, hot sticky toffee pudding.
Cards: Visa, Access, Diners, AmEx.
Other points: Sunday lunch and evening meals.
Directions: on the B6245 Longridge to Blackburn road, half a mile from Longridge centre.
MR A. GORNALL ☎ (01772) 782644.

LYTHAM–ST-ANNES • map 11E2

BEDFORD HOTEL
307–311 Clifton Drive South, FY8 1HN
Exclusive family-run hotel, with a reputation for comfort and cuisine. Situated 200 yards from shops, beach and swimming pool, with four golf-courses nearby. Other places of nearby interest include Blackpool, Liverpool Docks, Wigan Pier and the Lake District, which are all easily accessible, as the motorway is ten minutes away.
DOUBLE ROOM: from £30 to £40
FOOD: up to £15
Hours: breakfast 7.30am–9.30am, lunch 12noon–5pm, dinner 6.30pm–8.30pm.
Cuisine: ENGLISH / CONTINENTAL.
Cards: Visa, Access.
Other points: licensed, Sunday lunch, no-smoking area, children welcome, pets allowed, leisure centre.
Directions: off M6 to M55. Turn off at junction 4, then left, following signs.
J.P. & T. BAKER ☎ (01253) 724636
Fax (01253) 729244.

CHADWICK HOTEL & LEISURE COMPLEX
South Promenade, FY8 1NP
A modern, family-run hotel commanding lovely sea views. Spacious lounges overlook the seafront and indoor leisure pool. Other facilities include a spa bath, Turkish room, sauna, solarium, soft play adventure area and games room. The restaurant serves generous portions of very good food, and the bedrooms are comfortable and well furnished.
DOUBLE ROOM: from £20 to £30
SINGLE ROOM: from £35 to £45
FOOD: up to £15
Hours: breakfast 7.30am–10am, lunch 1pm–2pm, dinner 7pm–8.30pm, bar meals 12noon–2pm, 24hr room and lounge service, open all year.
Cuisine: ENGLISH – traditional English cooking, local seafood specialities.
Cards: Visa, Access, Diners, AmEx.
Other points: children welcome, baby-listening device, cots, 24hr reception, foreign exchange, parking, vegetarian meals, residents' lounge, residents' bar, disabled access, live entertainment.
Rooms: 72 bedrooms. All with en suite, satellite TV and movies. Some rooms have spa baths and four-poster beds.
Directions: off the M6 to M55, take junction 4. Turn left following signposts.
MR MILES CORBETT ☎ (01253) 720061
Fax (01253) 714455.

FERNLEA HOTEL & LEISURE COMPLEX
15 South Promenade, FY8 1LU
Situated on St Annes' South Promenade, the Fernlea is a large, comfortable, family-run hotel, with lots of fun things to do. They serve well-prepared, generous portions of food and the accommodation is of a high standard.
DOUBLE ROOM: from £30 to £40
SINGLE ROOM: from £25 to £35
FOOD: from £15 to £20 CLUB
Hours: breakfast 8am–9.30am, lunch 12.30am–1.30pm, dinner 7pm–8.30pm.
Cuisine: ENGLISH – fixed-price four-course menu, and bar snacks at lunchtime.
Cards: Visa, Access, Diners, AmEx.
Other points: licensed, Sunday lunch, children welcome, pets allowed, swimming pool, gym facilities, solarium, squash, aerobics, sauna.
Rooms: 19 single rooms, 15 double rooms, 30 twin rooms, 44 family rooms, 2 suites. All with TV,

NORTHERN ENGLAND • LANCASHIRE

radio, alarm, tea/coffee-making facilities.
Directions: five miles from Blackpool. Close to the pier.
TONY P. CROSTON ☎ (01253) 726726.

THE LINDUM HOTEL
63–67 South Promenade, FY8 1LZ

Open all year round, The Lindum Hotel has 80 bedrooms, all with private bath, and modern facilities. Lounge entertainment and children's parties are held regularly throughout the season. The food is all home-cooked and offers good value for money.
DOUBLE ROOM: from £20 to £30
SINGLE ROOM: from £25 to £35
FOOD: up to £15
Hours: breakfast 8.30am–9.15am, Sunday lunch 12.45am–1.45pm, bar meals 12noon–2pm, dinner 6pm–7pm.
Cuisine: ENGLISH – dishes include sardines with saffron rice, roast beef and Yorkshire pudding, poached salmon with cucumber sauce, sticky toffee pudding.
Cards: Visa, Access, AmEx.
Other points: licensed, Sunday lunch, children welcome, pets allowed, sauna, solarium, Jacuzzi, night porter.
Rooms: 78 bedrooms.
Directions: near St Annes pier, on the seafront.
LINDUM HOTEL LTD ☎ (01253) 721534.

MAWDESLEY • map 8A4

ROBIN HOOD INN
Bluestone Lane, LA40 2RG

A small family pub set in a rural area and humming with local life. Prompt friendly service and special Robin Hood dishes such as the Friar Tuck grill.
FOOD: up to £15
Hours: lunch 12noon–2pm, dinner 6.30pm–9.30pm.
Cuisine: ENGLISH – traditional, varied menu available in bar. Restaurant menu: steaks, fish, chicken.
Cards: Visa, Access.
Other points: licensed, Sunday lunch, Sunday afternoon tea, children welcome, open bank holidays.
Directions: take B5246 to Mawdesley. Through village, turn left.
DAVID CROPPER ☎ (01704) 822275.

MORECAMBE • map 11D2

CRAIGWELL HOTEL & TEDDY'S RESTAURANT
372 Marine Road East, LA4 5AH

A terraced bay-fronted property on the seafront with splendid views to the Lakeland hills. The hotel has been extensively refurnished to provide guests with a high level of comfort and convenience. Teddy's Restaurant provides well-cooked and attractively presented food, served by warm and courteous staff.
DOUBLE ROOM: up to £20
FOOD: up to £15
Hours: breakfast 8am–9.30am, Sunday lunch 12.30am–3.30pm, dinner 6pm–9.30pm.
Cuisine: ENGLISH – table d'hôte menu and à la carte menu.
Cards: Visa, Access, AmEx.
Other points: parking, vegetarian meals, licensed, children welcome, specials breaks, central heating.
Rooms: 5 single rooms, 5 double rooms, 13 twin rooms, 2 family rooms.
Directions: between the town hall and Broadway.
MR N. PETERS ☎ (01524) 410095.

ORMSKIRK • map 8A4

BEAUFORT HOTEL
High Lane, Burscough, L40 7SN

A welcoming hotel offering excellent food and comfortable accommodation. These high standards are matched by friendly and efficient service, and the prices, especially in the restaurant, are very reasonable. Close to M6 and M58, the hotel is within easy travelling distance of Liverpool and Southport.
DOUBLE ROOM: from £30 to £40
SINGLE ROOM: from £55
FOOD: from £15 to £20
Hours: breakfast 7am–9.30am, lunch 12noon–2pm, dinner 7pm–10pm.
Cuisine: ENGLISH / CONTINENTAL – French table d'hôte and à la carte menus.
Cards: Visa, Access, Diners, AmEx.
Other points: licensed, Sunday lunch, children welcome, pets allowed.
Rooms: 2 single rooms, 9 double rooms, 10 twin rooms.
Directions: 2 miles north of Ormskirk on A59, at corner of Pippin Street and High Lane.
M. SHELBOURNE ☎ (01704) 892655
Fax (01704) 895135.

PRESTON • map 11E3

THE BUSHELL'S ARMS
Church Lane, Goosnargh, PR3 2BH

LES ROUTIERS

A friendly village hostelry, which offers a superb variety of dishes. There is both a standard menu and a 'specials' board. The ever-changing but comprehensive wine list is selected to complement the style of food. All meals are home-made and the puddings are sumptuous. Visitors can enjoy all this at very reasonable prices and relax in the friendly surroundings. (See the special feature on pages 24–27.)

PRIX D'ELITE (WINE) of the Year 1995

FOOD: up to £15
Hours: lunch 12noon–2.30pm, dinner 7pm–10pm, closed occasional Mondays, closed Christmas day.
Cuisine: INTERNATIONAL – Dublin coddle, kefta tagine, jambalaya. Comprehensive choice of 'specials'. Changing wine list. Vegetarian meals.
Other points: licensed, open-air dining, Sunday lunch, no-smoking area, children welcome, beer garden.

Directions: M6 junction 32, north on A6 towards Garstang, turn right at lights.
DAVID BEST ☎ (01772) 865235.

CARAVELA RESTAURANT
Preston New Road, Freckleton, PR4 1HP

A Portuguese restaurant, attractively decorated with pinewood furniture, fishing nets and old schooner paintings to create a Portuguese feel. The à la carte menu offers a wide choice of Portuguese dishes while the table d'hôte provides a more British alternative. Excellently cooked and presented food and friendly, efficient service. Good selection of Portuguese wines.
FOOD: from £15 to £20
Hours: lunch 12noon–2pm, dinner 6.30pm–10.30pm, closed Saturday lunch and Monday.
Cuisine: PORTUGUESE – three-course weekday lunch menu, Sunday lunch menu and à la carte. Wide choice of Portuguese specialities.
Cards: Visa, Access.
Other points: licensed, Sunday lunch, vegetarian meals, children welcome.
Directions: A584 Preston to Lytham road.
A. FIGUEIRA & M. DE NOBREGA ☎ (01772) 632308.

FERRARIS RESTAURANT
West End, Great Eccleston, PR3 OYL

An excellent English and continental restaurant in the village of Great Eccleston. The interior is very Italian in style, with an accent on Ferrari cars, and provides attractive, comfortable surroundings in which to enjoy the first-class cuisine. The meals are beautifully cooked and presented, complemented by welcoming and efficient service. Excellent food and atmosphere.
FOOD: from £15 to £20
Hours: Sunday lunch 12noon–3pm, dinner 6.30pm–10.30pm.
Cuisine: ENGLISH / CONTINENTAL – table d'hôte and extensive à la carte menu.
Cards: Visa, Access, Switch.
Other points: licensed, children welcome.
Directions: from M55 at Kirkham, take A585 to Larbreck, then right on A586.
SUSAN & VIRGINIO FERRARI ☎ (01995) 670243.

YE HORN'S INN
Horns Lane, Goosnargh, PR3 2FJ

This delightful oak-beamed inn offers good, home-cooked English country fare, using local farm produce. Private parties catered for. Small private rooms available. Set in rural countryside, the inn provides an ideal base from which to visit nearby beauty spots, such as Beacon Fell, The Trough of Bowland and the Hodder Valley.
DOUBLE ROOM: from £40 to £50
FOOD: from £15 to £20
Hours: lunch 12noon–2pm, dinner 7pm–9.15pm, closed Monday lunch.
Cuisine: ENGLISH – home-cooking, e.g., roast duckling.

Cards: Visa, Access, Diners, AmEx.
Other points: Sunday lunch, no-smoking area, children welcome, disabled access, residents' bar, vegetarian meals.
Rooms: 6 twin rooms. All with TV, telephone, tea/coffee-making facilities.
Directions: M6 exit 36. Off the B5269 near Whittingham Hospital.
MRS E. WOODS ☎ (01772) 865230.

RIBCHESTER • map 11E3

MILES HOUSE RESTAURANT
Blackburn Road, Dutton, near Preston, PR3 3ZQ

A traditional Ribble Valley farmhouse is home to Miles House Restaurant, a very comfortable and relaxed place to dine, whether getting together with friends or family, or enjoying a quiet evening or lunch with that special person. The atmosphere is very warm and inviting and the staff are friendly and helpful.
FOOD: up to £15
Hours: lunch 11am–3pm, dinner from 7pm, afternoon high tea 2.30pm–5pm.
Cuisine: ENGLISH/FRENCH à la carte menu, featuring tempting dishes such as lobster Thermidor, halibut cooked in yoghurt and honey, served on a bed of tomato puree and grapefruit. Traditional farmhouse soup is also a speciality.
Cards: Visa, Access, AmEx.
Other points: children welcome, parking, no-smoking area, designated wildlife garden, open-air dining, vegetarian meals.
Directions: located half a mile south of Ribchester, close to the Ribble Bridge on the B6245.
MR & MRS RICHARD & CHRISTINE MARSHALL ☎ (01254) 878204.

WRIGHTINGTON • map 8A4

HIND'S HEAD HOTEL & RESTAURANT
Mossy Lea Road, WN6 9RN

The Hind's Head is a lovely village pub, offering locals and visitors alike a comfortable and relaxed place to enjoy a good meal and a chance to sample their wide selection of fine ales, beers, wines and spirits. It is conveniently situated for visiting Wigan Pier, Camelot Theme Park and Martin Mere Wildfowl Trust.
FOOD: up to £15
Hours: lunch 12noon–2pm, dinner 6pm–9.30pm, meals all day Sunday.
Cuisine: ENGLISH / CONTINENTAL – an innovative menu with regularly changing specials.
Cards: Visa, Access, AmEx.
Other points: parking, children welcome, no-smoking area, open-air dining, vegetarian meals, afternoon teas, Sunday lunch.
Directions: leave the M6 at junction 27. Wrightington is approximately one mile to the west.
JOAN DOBSON ☎ (01257) 421168.

MERSEYSIDE

LIVERPOOL • map 8A4

DEL SECOLO
Temple Court
The Del Secolo is the flagship of this Italian restaurant complex. With a vast and interesting menu, an extensive range of wines and excellent service, it is no wonder that this restaurant has been acclaimed for its excellent reputation. Below the comfortable and intimate Del Secolo is the Casa Italia, a bustling pizzeria. If a choice of two styles of Italian cuisine is not enough, at the back of the Casa Italia, accessed by Temple Court, is the Villa Italia, a trattoria in true Italian style.
FOOD: from £15 to £20
Hours: lunch 12noon–2.30pm, dinner 7.30pm–10.30pm.
Cuisine: ITALIAN – pizza, pasta and fish dishes are the house specialities.
Cards: Visa, Access, Diners, AmEx.
Other points: children welcome, vegetarian meals, disabled access.
Directions: in the Cavern Quarter.
CARLO CAMPOLUCCI-BORDI ☎ (0151) 236 1040 Fax (0151) 236 9985.

LA BOUFFE
48a Castle Street, L2 7LQ
Located in the basement area of a listed building, this French-style bistro offers diners a popular place to meet, good food and a great atmosphere. There is a regular live jazz band to enhance the ambience: check for details of live music.
FOOD: from £15 to £20
Hours: lunch 12noon–3pm, dinner 6.30pm–10.30pm, closed Monday evenings, Saturday lunch and all day Sunday.
Cuisine: CONTINENTAL – an ever changing menu, made with fresh produce. The selection of wines and sprits is of an excellent standard, perfectly complementing the imaginative menu and the fantastic cheeseboard.
Cards: Visa, Access, Diners, AmEx.
Other points: children welcome, vegetarian meals, afternoon teas, guide dogs allowed.
Directions: located in Liverpool City Centre.
DEBORAH HOLDEN ☎ (0151) 236 3375.

MAYFLOWER RESTAURANT
48 Duke Street, L1 5AS
A large, modern Chinese restaurant with a warm and relaxed atmosphere. The restaurant serves Pekingese, Cantonese and Schezuan dishes, including crispy fragrant duck served with pancakes. As the restaurant is open until 4am, it is ideal for anyone looking for a peaceful restaurant in which to enjoy good food, but outside the more usual opening hours.
FOOD: up to £15 CLUB
Hours: meals all day 12noon–4am.
Cuisine: PEKINGESE / CANTONESE – Peking and Cantonese cuisine, with vegetarian and seafood specialities.

Cards: Visa, Access, Diners, AmEx, Switch.
Other points: licensed, children welcome, air-conditioned, parking, disabled access.
Directions: two minutes from main shopping area, near Pier Head and Albert Dock.
MR SIM ☎ (0151) 709 6339.

SOUTHPORT • map 8A4

THE AMBASSADOR PRIVATE HOTEL
13 Bath Street, PR9 0DP
Situated in an early Victorian terrace and family-run since 1964. This small hotel offers a good standard of accommodation and is centrally situated for the main shopping areas and promenade, water sports and golf courses. The relaxed and comfortable surroundings are complemented by the friendly welcome provided by the proprietors Margaret and Harry Bennett.
DOUBLE ROOM: from £20 to £30
SINGLE ROOM: from £25 to £35
FOOD: up to £15
Hours: breakfast 7.30am–9.30am, bar snacks 12.30am–2pm, dinner 6pm–7pm, bar snacks 9pm–11pm, closed Christmas and New Year.
Cuisine: ENGLISH – predominantly English.
Cards: Visa, Access.
Other points: no-smoking area, pets allowed, residents' lounge, parking, children welcome.
Rooms: 1 single room, 2 double rooms, 2 twin rooms, 3 family rooms. All with en suite, TV, radio, tea/coffee-making facilities, hair dryer.
Directions: from Lord Street, turn at traffic lights towards promenade, then second on the right.
MARGARET & HARRY BENNETT ☎ (01704) 543998/0704 530459 Fax (01704) 536269.

THE CRIMOND HOTEL
Knowsley Road, PR9 0HN
A small, family-run hotel offering excellent facilities including indoor swimming pool, sauna and Jacuzzi. The good food, excellent service and comfortable accommodation combine to make this a pleasant and relaxing stay for tourists and businessmen alike. Conference facilities, including slide projector, TV and video.
DOUBLE ROOM: from £20 to £30
SINGLE ROOM: from £35 to £45
FOOD: up to £15 ☆
Hours: breakfast 7.30am–9.30am, lunch 12noon–2pm, dinner 7pm–9pm.
Cuisine: MODERN ENGLISH – Northern lamb chops glazed with a redcurrant sauce, Aunty Neddy's special fruit meringue nests.
Cards: Visa, Access, Diners, AmEx.
Other points: no-smoking area, garden, pets allowed, conferences, functions.
Rooms: 4 single rooms, 4 double rooms, 2 twin rooms, 2 family rooms. All with TV, radio, telephone, tea/coffee-making facilities, hair dryer, trouser-press.

Directions: situated in Southport, off Park Road West. Near municipal golf links.
PAT & GEOFF RANDLE ☎ (01704) 536456
[Fax] (01704) 548643.

■ THE GILTON HOTEL
7 Leicester Street, PR9 OER
A Victorian house with an attractive, well-kept garden, situated in the centre of Southport. Gilton Hotel is traditionally decorated to provide a comfortable place to stay for tourists and business people alike. Mrs Cunliffe extends a warm welcome to all her guests, and the hotel enjoys a friendly, homely atmosphere. Particularly attractive for golfers, with five courses nearby.
DOUBLE ROOM: to £20.00
Hours: breakfast 7.30am–9am, dinner 5.30pm–8pm, bar meals 7pm–10pm.
Cuisine: ENGLISH.
Cards: Visa, Access.
Other points: children welcome, garden, TV lounge, residents' lounge, games room, table-tennis, golf nearby, children welcome, baby-sitting, baby-listening device, cots.
Rooms: 1 single room, 5 double rooms, 7 twin rooms. All with TV, radio, alarm, tea/coffee-making facilities.
Directions: M6 exit M62. Follow till M57, exit A565. Signposted Southport.
MR & MRS CUNLIFFE ☎ (01704) 530646.

THORNTON HOUGH • map 8B4

■ THORNTON HALL HOTEL
Wirral, L63 1JF

LES ROUTIERS
RESTAURANT of the Year 1995

Formerly the home of a major shipping family, Thornton Hall is a magnificent residence set in seven acres of gardens. Splendid wood carvings and panelling adorn the main staircase and many rooms. The Italian Room provides a perfect setting for the hotel restaurant, with a ceiling of hand-tooled leather and mother of pearl. Suitably located in the lovely Wirral countryside. (See special feature on page 10.)
DOUBLE ROOM: from £30 to £40
SINGLE ROOM: from £55
FOOD: from £20 to £25
Hours: breakfast 7am–9.30am, dinner 7pm–10pm.
Cuisine: MODERN INTERNATIONAL – excellent choice of set and à la carte menus based on local produce and creative cooking. Comprehensive wine list complements their award-winning chef, recognized as one of the best in the north-west.
Cards: Visa, Access, AmEx.
Other points: licensed, open-air dining, Sunday lunch, children welcome, pets allowed, afternoon tea, parking, functions, special breaks, baby-listening device, baby-sitting cots, 24hr reception, foreign exchange, left luggage.
Rooms: 63 bedrooms. All with TV, radio, telephone, tea/coffee-making facilities.
Directions: exit junction 4 of M53 and take B5151; turn off right onto B5136.
COLIN FRASER ☎ (0151) 336 3938 [Fax] (0151) 336 7864.

WALLASEY • map 8A4

■ GROVE HOUSE HOTEL & RESTAURANT
Grove Road, Wirral, L45 3HT
A well-appointed Victorian hotel and restaurant, situated in its own attractive gardens in a quiet residential area of Wallasey. Offering fine cuisine using a comprehensive menu, including an extensive selection of vegetarian dishes. Excellent accommodation and warm, courteous service.
DOUBLE ROOM: from £30 to £40
FOOD: from £15 to £20
Hours: breakfast 7.30am–9.30am, lunch 12noon–2pm, dinner 7pm–9.30pm.
Cuisine: FRENCH / CONTINENTAL – comprehensive à la carte menu, featuring French and continental dishes.
Cards: Visa, Access.
Other points: licensed, Sunday lunch, children welcome, garden, functions, conferences.
Directions: off the A554.
MR N.J. BURN ☎ (0151) 639 3947.

■ LEASOWE CASTLE
Leasowe, Moreton, L46 3RF
This 16th century castle has been converted to accommodate an excellent restaurant with varied table d'hôte and à la carte menus. The Stables restaurant has recently opened and serves continental and English dishes in a very relaxed atmosphere. Sea views, outstanding accommodation, fine cuisine and excellent service combine to make Leasowe Castle a delightful place to visit.
DOUBLE ROOM: from £40 to £50
FOOD: up to £15 ★
Hours: breakfast 7am–10am, lunch 12noon–3pm, dinner 4.30pm–11pm, dinner 7pm–10pm.
Cuisine: ENGLISH / CONTINENTAL – à la carte and fixed three-course menu, bar meals/snacks. A second restaurant has recently opened, serving continental and English dishes.
Cards: Visa, Access, Diners, AmEx.
Other points: licensed, Sunday lunch, no-smoking area, children welcome, garden, afternoon tea, 24hr reception, foreign exchange, residents' lounge, baby-listening device, baby-sitting, cots.
Rooms: 23 double rooms, 23 twin rooms, 3 triple rooms. All with TV, radio, alarm, telephone, tea/coffee-making facilities.
Directions: Wallasey is situated at the end of the M53, 3 miles from Liverpool.
MR HARDING ☎ (0151) 606 9191.

■ MONROES
45 Wallasey Road, L45 4NN
A bistro-style restaurant with a Marilyn Monroe theme, offering tasty and well-presented food in a happy and relaxed atmosphere. Friendly, attentive service will assist you in your choice of more than 24 steak dishes, vegetarian dishes and specials. 14-page menu and children's menu.
FOOD: up to £15
Hours: dinner 6pm–10.30pm, Sunday 5.30pm–10pm.
Cuisine: ENGLISH / INTERNATIONAL – specialities

include over 24 steak dishes. Home-made profiteroles, cheesecake and apple pie, plus vegetarian menu. Siumai, Cantonese beef balls, Texas rib starters, buffalo pie, surf'n'turf chicken, pork marsala.
Cards: Visa, Access, AmEx.
Other points: children welcome.
Directions: situated in Liscard, 2km north-west of Wallasey town centre.
DAVID W. CULLEN ☎ (0151) 638 3633.

WEST KIRBY • map 8A4

SURFERS RESTAURANT
136–140 Banks Road, L48 0RF
Suited to people of all ages, this restaurant is popular with the locals and tourists. Surfers is a relaxed and informal American-style restaurant with friendly, efficient personal service and a great variety of excellent dishes, just waiting to tempt you. Children are most welcome here (3-D kids' collect-a-menu available), so look out for the special offers and make this a family event to remember.
FOOD: up to £15
Hours: meals all day, Monday–Friday 5pm–10.30pm, Saturday–Sunday 1pm–11pm.
Cuisine: CONTINENTAL / AMERICAN – à la carte menu. All dishes are made from fresh supplies delivered daily. Three-course meal for £4.95 between 5pm and 7pm.
Other points: vegetarian meals.
Directions: located 400 yards south of town centre.
GUY LAWRENSON ☎ (0151) 625 1757.

NORTH YORKSHIRE

APPLETON-LE-MOORS • map 12D5

APPLETON HALL COUNTRY HOUSE HOTEL
Appleton-le-Moors, YO6 6TF
Enjoy elegance, comfort and tranquility in this delightful country house. Set in 2½ acres of beautiful gardens and with lovely views over the Yorkshire Moors, the hotel is an ideal base for exploring the Moors and the Dales. Offering the very best of English cuisine and using local produce whenever posssible, their aim is to make your stay a memorable one.
DOUBLE ROOM: from £30 to £40
FOOD: from £15 to £20
Hours: breakfast 8.15am–9.15am, dinner 7pm–8.30pm, open all year.
Cuisine: ENGLISH.
Cards: Visa, Access, AmEx.
Other points: licensed, Sunday lunch, afternoon tea, pets allowed, children catered for (please check for age limits), lift, parking, residents' lounge, residents' bar.
Rooms: 3 single rooms, 5 double rooms, 2 twin rooms. All with TV, radio, telephone, tea/coffee-making facilities. 1 double and 1 twin with private lounge.
Directions: less than 2 miles from the A170. Follow signs for Appleton-le-Moors.
GRAHAM & NORMA DAVIES ☎ (01751) 417227/417452 [Fax] (01751) 417540.

ASKRIGG • map 11D3

KING'S ARMS HOTEL & CLUBROOM RESTAURANT
Askrigg in Wensleydale, DL8 3HQ
A Grade II listed coaching inn of atmosphere and character, which began life as the famous 18th century racing stable of John Pratt. The bars – once the tack and harness rooms – are familiar to many as the 'Drovers Arms' of Darrowby in the BBC TV series of James Herriot's All Creatures Great and Small. Famous for good food, comfort and hospitality.
DOUBLE ROOM: from £30 to £40
FOOD: from £25 to £30
Hours: breakfast 8.30am–9.30am, bar meals 12noon–2pm, dinner 7pm–9pm, bar meals 6.30pm–9pm.
Cuisine: ENGLISH / FRENCH – meat, game, fresh fish and vegetarian dishes cooked to order in restaurant, grill room and bars.
Cards: Visa, Access.
Other points: licensed, open-air dining, Sunday lunch, no-smoking area, disabled access, children welcome.
Directions: 1 mile off the A684 at Bainbridge, in the market square in Askrigg.
LIZ & RAY HOPWOOD ☎ (01969) 650258 [Fax] (01969) 650635.

BAINBRIDGE • map 11D3

RIVERDALE COUNTRY HOUSE HOTEL
Bainbridge, Leyburn, DL8 3EW
Situated in the centre of a country village in Upper Wensleydale among hills and moors, Riverdale Country House is an ideal base for touring and walking. Used in the filming of James Herriot's novels.
DOUBLE ROOM: from £20 to £30
FOOD: up to £15
Hours: breakfast 8.30am–9am, dinner 7.30pm, closed December until February.
Cuisine: ENGLISH.
Other points: central heating, children welcome, residents' lounge.
Rooms: 5 double rooms, 14 twin rooms, 2 family rooms.
Directions: follow A684 to Bainbridge; the hotel overlooks the green.
MRS A. HARRISON ☎ (01969) 50311.

NORTH YORKSHIRE • NORTHERN ENGLAND

CASTLETON • map 12C5

MOORLANDS HOTEL
55 High Street, YO21 2DB
A 100-year-old stone building with modern furnishings and walls decorated with pictures by a local artist. Good traditional cuisine and à la carte menu. Located in the heart of the North Yorkshire Moors National Park.
DOUBLE ROOM: from £20 to £30
SINGLE ROOM: from £25 to £35
FOOD: from £15 to £20
Hours: breakfast 8.30am–9.30am, dinner 7pm–10pm, bar snacks 10am–10pm.
Cuisine: ENGLISH / INTERNATIONAL.
Cards: Visa, Access, AmEx.
Other points: children catered for (please check for age limits), parking, pets, garden, vegetarian meals, open-air dining, residents' lounge, residents' bar.
Rooms: 8 bedrooms. All with TV, tea/coffee-making facilities.
Directions: 4 miles south of A171 Whitby to Middlesborough road. 15 miles west of Whitby, 40 miles north of York.
A. & A. ABRAHAMS ☎ (01287) 660206.

FAIRBURN • map 12E5

THE BAY HORSE
Silver Street, WF11 9JA
The Bay Horse is near the turn-off between Ferrybridge and Selby Fork, and is easily accessible from both carriageways of the A1.
FOOD: up to £15
Hours: lunch 12noon–2pm, dinner 7pm–10pm.
Cuisine: ENGLISH / CONTINENTAL – dishes may include pork cordon bleu, chicken angélique, sole bonne femme.
Cards: Visa, Access, Diners, Switch.
Other points: open-air dining, Sunday lunch, children welcome, functions.
Directions: on the A1 northbound at the Fairburn turn off.
J.M. & P.S. PALFREYMAN ☎ (01977) 607265
Fax (01977) 670553.

FILEY • map 12D6

SEAFIELD HOTEL
9–11 Rutland Street, YO14 9JA
A pleasant, family-run guest house, conveniently situated for the beautiful Crescent Gardens in the traditional seaside resort of Filey. Close to the railway and bus stations. Offering good food, comfortable accommodation and a friendly 'home from home' atmosphere.
DOUBLE ROOM: up to £20
SINGLE ROOM: up to £25
FOOD: up to £15 ☆
Hours: breakfast 8.45am–9am, dinner 6pm.
Cuisine: ENGLISH.
Cards: Visa, Access.
Other points: children welcome, residents' lounge, special breaks, children welcome, baby-listening device, cots, left luggage.
Rooms: 1 single room, 1 double room, 11 twin room, 1 family room. All with TV, tea/coffee-making facilities.
Directions: Rutland Street runs off The Crescent.
JILL & DON DRISCOLL ☎ (01723) 513715.

GOATHLAND • map 12D5

INN ON THE MOOR
YO22 5LZ
Rooms are comfortably furnished and service in the restaurant is friendly, yet prompt. The Inn overlooks the Yorkshire Moors, offering the ideal opportunity to explore the countryside. Places of interest in the area include the waterfalls and the Roman Road.
DOUBLE ROOM: from £20 to £30
FOOD: up to £15
Hours: breakfast 8.45am–9.30am, lunch 12noon–2pm, dinner 7pm–8.30pm.
Cuisine: ENGLISH.
Cards: Visa, Access, AmEx.
Other points: licensed, Sunday lunch, children welcome, pets allowed, parking.
Rooms: 24 twin rooms. All with TV, telephone, tea/coffee-making facilities.
Directions: 9 miles from Whitby, 14 miles from Pickering.
MALCOLM SIMPSON ☎ (01947) 896296
Fax (01947) 896484.

GRASSINGTON • map 12D4

GRASSINGTON HOUSE HOTEL
Skipton, BD23 5AQ
Built in the early 18th century and situated in the renowned cobbled square, the hotel enjoys an atmosphere of warmth and friendliness. The food is outstanding, imaginatively cooked from fresh ingredients and beautifully presented. The traditional decor of the dining room is delightful and forms an ideal setting for your meal. Well situated in the heart of the Yorkshire Dales, Grassington House was Les Routiers Newcomer of the Year in 1992.
DOUBLE ROOM: from £20 to £30
SINGLE ROOM: from £25 to £35
FOOD: from £15 to £20 CLUB
Hours: breakfast 8am–9am, bar meals 12noon–2pm and 7pm–9.30pm, dinner 7pm–9.30pm.
Cuisine: ENGLISH – monthly changing table d'hôte dinner menu; guinea fowl, venison.
Cards: Visa, Access, Eurocard.
Other points: licensed, children welcome, pets allowed, residents' lounge.
Rooms: 2 single rooms, 5 double rooms, 2 twin rooms, 1 family room. All with TV, telephone, tea/coffee-making facilities.
Directions: B6265 from Skipton or Ripon. In Grassington Square.
GORDON & LINDA ELSWORTH ☎ (01756) 752406 Fax (01756) 752135.

253

HARROGATE • map 12E4

🏨 ARDEN HOUSE HOTEL
69–71 Franklin Road, HG1 5EH

A comfortable, family-run hotel offering a warm and personal welcome. Situated within easy walking distance of the town centre, Valley Gardens and Royal Hall. It is tastefully decorated and noted for its high standards of traditional English cooking. A popular meeting place is the Victorian bar, where guests can relax.
DOUBLE ROOM: from £20 to £30
SINGLE ROOM: from £25 to £35
FOOD: up to £15
Hours: breakfast 8.45am–9am, dinner 7pm, closed Christmas day and New Year's day.
Cuisine: ENGLISH.
Cards: Visa, Access, AmEx.
Other points: parking, children welcome, no-smoking area, afternoon teas, pets, residents' lounge, vegetarian meals, garden, residents' bar, cots.
Rooms: 4 single rooms, 5 double rooms, 5 twin rooms. All with TV, radio, telephone, tea/coffee-making facilities, alarm, hair dryer and trouser-press.
Directions: A61 Harrogate, Kings Road, Strawberry Dale Avenue, then turn left to Franklin Road.
MR & MRS W.J. LYNCH ☎ (01423) 509224
Fax (01423) 561170.

🏨 BRITANNIA LODGE HOTEL
16 Swan Road, HG1 2SA

A family-run hotel in a very good position for all the attractions of Harrogate. Refurbished to a high standard, the hotel provides comfortable facilities for its guests and prides itself on personal service. Weekend/midweek breaks available at most times.
DOUBLE ROOM: from £20 to £30
FOOD: up to £15
Hours: breakfast 7.30am–9am, dinner 6.30pm–8pm.
Cuisine: ENGLISH – full English breakfast. Evening menu consists of traditional Yorkshire home-cooking.
Cards: Visa, Access, AmEx.
Other points: children welcome.
Rooms: 4 single rooms, 4 double rooms, 3 twin rooms, 1 family room. All with satellite TV, radio, telephone, tea/coffee-making facilities, alarm, video.
Directions: close to Royal Hall, Valley Gardens and exhibition complex.
P. & E.M.J. CULLING ☎ (01423) 508482
Fax (01423) 508482.

🍴 GRUNDY'S RESTAURANT
21 Cheltenham Crescent, HG1 1DH

This is an excellent restaurant serving first-class meals in comfortable surroundings. The cuisine is predominantly Modern English and all dishes are freshly cooked to order. The outstanding food is complemented by a good wine list, excellent service and a friendly, warm atmosphere. The fixed-price menu offers particularly good value for money.
FOOD: up to £15

Hours: dinner 6.30pm–10pm, closed Sunday, bank holidays, 2 weeks in July/August, 2 weeks in January.
Cuisine: MODERN ENGLISH – menu may feature baked fresh salmon with watercress cream sauce, English lamb with honey and sherry sauce. Table d'hôte and à la carte.
Cards: Visa, Access, AmEx.
Other points: licensed.
Directions: in town centre, approx 2 minutes' walk from Royal Hall/conference centre.
VAL & CHRIS GRUNDY ☎ (01423) 502610.

🏨 THE LANGHAM HOTEL
21–27 Valley Drive, HG2 0JL

Run by three members of the Ward family, this beautiful old hotel is in the heart of Harrogate, overlooking the renowned Valley Gardens. The Langham is a friendly, comfortable establishment, offering good food, with the table d'hôte menu being of particularly good value. National parks, stately homes and golf courses are nearby.
DOUBLE ROOM: from £40 to £50
SINGLE ROOM: from £35 to £45
FOOD: from £15 to £20
Hours: dinner 7.30pm–9.30pm.
Cuisine: ENGLISH / FRENCH – traditional English and French cuisine.
Cards: Visa, Access, Diners, AmEx.
Other points: licensed, Sunday lunch, children welcome, open bank holidays, vegetarian meals, residents' bar, residents' lounge.
Rooms: 50 bedrooms. All with TV, telephone, tea/coffee-making facilities.
Directions: take A1, exit onto the A59 for Harrogate. Opposite Valley Gardens.
THE WARD FAMILY ☎ (01423) 502179.

🏨 SHANNON COURT HOTEL
65 Dragon Avenue, HG1 5DS

A beautiful Victorian house with character and charm, bordering on the 'Stray' in High Harrogate. This family-run hotel offers its guests a warm and friendly atmosphere in pleasant surroundings, and your stay would be a happy one with Tricia and Mike on hand to welcome you. Within easy driving distance of the Yorkshire Dales and North Yorkshire Moors National Park.
DOUBLE ROOM: from £20 to £30
FOOD: up to £15
Hours: breakfast 8am–9am, dinner 7pm.
Cuisine: ENGLISH – traditional.
Cards: Visa, Access.
Other points: children welcome, residents' lounge, vegetarian meals, no-smoking area.
Rooms: 2 single rooms, 3 double rooms, 1 twin room, 2 family rooms. All with en suite, TV, tea/coffee-making facilities.
Directions: off the A59 Skipton road.
TRICIA & MIKE YOUNG ☎ (01423) 509858
Fax (01423) 530606.

🏨 STUDLEY HOTEL
Swan Road, HG1 2SA

Attractively situated adjacent to the beautiful Valley Gardens but within easy walking distance of Harrogate town centre, the Studley Hotel has all

amenities. All bedrooms have private facilities. Le Breton French Restaurant has a genuine charcoal grill, and in addition there is a meeting room/private party room available for up to 15 people.
DOUBLE ROOM: from £30 to £40
FOOD: up to £15
Hours: breakfast 7.30am–10am, lunch 12.30pm–2pm, dinner 7pm–10pm.
Cuisine: INTERNATIONAL – extensive à la carte menu, including charcoal-grilled steaks, fish, chicken, seafood, kebabs. Luncheon: steak-and-kidney pie. Bar snacks available.
Cards: Visa, Access, Diners, AmEx.
Other points: licensed, Sunday lunch, pets by prior arrangement, vegetarian meals, children welcome.
Rooms: 15 single rooms, 10 double rooms, 11 twin room. All with satellite TV, radio, telephone, tea/coffee-making facilities.
Directions: adjacent to Valley Gardens.
MR G.G. DILASSER ☎ (01423) 560425
[Fax] (01423) 530967.

HELMSLEY • map 12D5

THE FEVERSHAM ARMS HOTEL
1 High Street, YO6 5AG
Attractive, historic coaching inn, modernized but retaining its old charm, set in the North Yorkshire Moors National Park. There are 18 bedrooms including five 4-poster rooms, one suite and six ground-floor bedrooms. Tennis court, heated outdoor swimming pool (May–October) and gardens for guests' use. Golf and riding nearby. Les Routiers Cheeseboard of the Year 1994.
DOUBLE ROOM: from £30 to £40
SINGLE ROOM: from £55
FOOD: from £15 to £20
Hours: breakfast 7.30am–10am, lunch 12noon–3pm, last orders 1.30pm, dinner 7pm–11pm, last orders 9.30pm.
Cuisine: ENGLISH / CONTINENTAL – fresh shellfish, game (in season), Spanish paella (if booked in advance). Wide range of continental dishes complemented by an impressive Spanish and clarets wine list.
Cards: Visa, Access, Diners, AmEx.
Other points: licensed, Sunday lunch, children welcome, special breaks, parking, vegetarian meals, residents' bar, residents' lounge, disabled access.
Rooms: 4 double rooms, 8 twin rooms, 5 four-poster rooms, 1 suite. All with radio, telephone, tea/coffee-making facilities, hair dryer, satellite TV, trouser-press, safe.
Directions: at the junction of the A170 and B1257 in Helmsley.
THE FEVERSHAM ARMS HOTEL LTD
☎ (01439) 770766 [Fax] (01439) 770346.

PHEASANT HOTEL
Harome, YO6 5JE
Near the North Yorkshire Moors National Park in the charming village of Harome. The hotel was originally two blacksmiths' cottages and a shop, which have been carefully converted, with spacious rooms and much character. Many of the rooms overlook the village pond.
DOUBLE ROOM: from £30 to £40
FOOD: up to £15
Hours: breakfast 8.30am–9.30am, lunch 12noon–2pm, dinner 7.30pm–8pm, bar lunches every day, closed 1st January until 28th February.
Cuisine: ENGLISH – steak-and-kidney pie, fresh local meat, fish and poultry.
Other points: licensed, open-air dining, no-smoking area, indoor swimming pool.
Rooms: 2 single rooms, 5 double rooms, 12 twin rooms.
Directions: 3 miles from Helmsley off the A170 in the direction of Scarborough.
MR & MRS K. & MR & MRS C. BINKS
☎ (01439) 771241.

KIRKBYMOORSIDE • map 12D5

GEORGE & DRAGON
17 Market Place, YO6 6AA
Situated in the ancient cobbled market square of Kirkbymoorside, the George & Dragon has provided travellers with hospitality perfected over centuries. Full of olde-worlde charm and antiquity, this delightful hotel dating from the 13th century combines comfort, service and excellent cuisine with true Yorkshire tradition. An ideal centre for holiday and business guests.
DOUBLE ROOM: from £30 to £40
SINGLE ROOM: from £35 to £45
FOOD: up to £15 [CLUB]
Hours: breakfast 7.30am–9.30am, lunch 12noon–2pm, dinner 7pm–9.15pm, bar snacks 12noon–2pm, 6.30pm–9.30pm.
Cuisine: ENGLISH.
Cards: Visa, Access.
Other points: licensed.
Rooms: 19 bedrooms. All en suite.
Directions: situated in the town centre, just off the A170 between Thirsk and Scarborough.
MR S.G. COLLING ☎ (01751) 433334
[Fax] (01751) 433334.

LEEMING BAR • map 12D4

MOTEL LEEMING
Great North Road, Bedale, DL8 1DT
Motel Leeming has easy access to both carriageways of the A1 and is open and serving meals 24 hours a day.
DOUBLE ROOM: from £20 to £30
FOOD: up to £15
Hours: open 24 hours.
Cuisine: ENGLISH – farmhouse platter, cheese fritters, traditional Sunday lunch, fresh fish dishes. Award-winning cheeseboard. Only fresh produce from local suppliers is used.
Cards: Visa, Access, Diners, AmEx.
Other points: Sunday lunch, children welcome.
Rooms: 10 single rooms, 18 double rooms, 40 twin rooms, 4 family rooms.
Directions: take A1; exit at the A684. Bedale sits on the A1/A684 junction.
CARL LES ☎ (01677) 422122/423611
[Fax] (01677) 424507.

LONG PRESTON • map 11E3

MAYPOLE INN
Near Skipton, BD23 4PH
17th century village inn situated on the Maypole Green in the Yorkshire Dales National Park. Interesting selection of real ales in cosy bars with open fires, and a restaurant with a good local following, serving generous portions of home-cooked food. Close to Malham, the Settle/Carlisle railway and the starting point for many beautiful walks. Easy drive to the Lake District and Forest of Bowland.
DOUBLE ROOM: up to £20
SINGLE ROOM: from £25 to £35
FOOD: up to £15 ☆
Hours: lunch weekdays 12noon–2pm, dinner 6.30pm–9pm, Saturday 5.30pm–9.30pm, Sunday 5pm–9pm, closed Christmas.
Cuisine: ENGLISH – traditional home-cooking: beef in ale pie, braised shoulder of lamb, trout, Yorkshire ham and eggs, 20oz rump, vegetarian selection and daily blackboard specials.
Cards: Visa, Access, Diners, AmEx.
Other points: licensed, Sunday lunch, children welcome, coaches by prior arrangement, residents' lounge.
Rooms: 1 single room, 3 double rooms, 2 family rooms. All rooms are en suite.
Directions: on the A65 between Settle and Skipton.
ROBERT & ELSPETH PALMER ☎ (01729) 840219.

MALTON • map 12D5

CORNUCOPIA
87 Commercial Street, Norton, YO17 9HY
Set in the heart of the horse-racing capital of the North, the restaurant is appropriately adorned with horse-racing memorabilia. The menu is extensive and innovative, with a wine list to suit most palates. An award-winning pub and a finalist in the Steak-and-Kidney Pie Competition.
FOOD: up to £15
Hours: dinner 6.30pm–10pm, lunch 12noon–2pm.
Cuisine: ENGLISH – halibut, salmon and prawn mornay, boned duckling, traditional Sunday lunch. Braised beef simmered in ale and herb dumplings, pork casserole and apple fritters.
Cards: Visa, Access.
Other points: licensed, open-air dining, Sunday lunch, children welcome, beer garden.
Directions: off the A64 in the centre of Norton.
HAROLD ST QUINTON ☎ (01653) 693456.

KINGS HEAD HOTEL
5 Market Place, YO17 0LP
A delightful welcome awaits you when you visit this establishment. Serving good food at value-for-money prices, in a down to earth, homely and relaxing atmosphere.
FOOD: up to £15 CLUB ☆
Hours: lunch 12noon–2pm, bar snacks 11am–2.30pm, dinner 7pm–9.30pm, last orders 9pm, bar snacks 7pm–9.30pm.
Cuisine: BRITISH – menu features Wensleydale mushrooms, Yorkshire puddings in onion gravy, a large range of traditional home-made dishes, together with steaks and grills.
Cards: Visa, Access, Diners, AmEx.
Other points: Sunday lunch, children welcome, parking.
Directions: located at top of market place.
CHRISTOPHER BARLOW ☎ (01653) 692289.

THE MOUNT HOTEL
Yorkersgate, YO17 0AB
An attractive hotel with a fascinating interior in the form of over 700 jugs and a collection of horse-racing memorabilia, Malton being a racehorse-breeding centre. Very popular with local racing folk who gather in the old-fashioned mahogany bar to enjoy the excellent home-cooking. Ideal location for touring the North Yorkshire Moors and visiting Castle Howard and Eden Camp.
DOUBLE ROOM: from £20 to £30
FOOD: up to £15
Hours: lunch 12noon–2pm, dinner 7pm–9pm.
Cuisine: BRITISH – home-cooked country fare at value-for-money prices.
Cards: Visa, Access.
Other points: street parking, children welcome, no-smoking area, afternoon tea, open all day, disabled access, vegetarian meals, air-conditioned, residents' garden.
Rooms: 4 single rooms, 2 double rooms, 12 twin rooms, 3 family rooms.
Directions: off the A64 York to Scarborough road. First hotel on left in Malton.
MR GIBSON ☎ (01653) 692608 Fax (01653) 692608.

MIDDLETON TYAS • map 12D4

SHOULDER OF MUTTON INN
Richmond, DL11 7JH
Built 300 years ago as a farmhouse, the Shoulder of Mutton has been tastefully restored retaining all the charm and character of a bygone era. The Shoulder of Mutton makes an ideal stop-over en route to Scotland.
FOOD: from £15 to £20
Hours: lunch 12noon–2pm, bar meals 12noon–2pm, dinner 7pm–10pm, bar meals 7pm–10pm.
Cuisine: ENGLISH – steaks, fish, poultry. Menu changes weekly.
Cards: Visa, Access, AmEx.
Other points: licensed, Sunday lunch, children welcome.
Directions: half a mile from the Scotch Corner roundabout on the A1.
MR & MRS TWEEDY ☎ (01325) 377271.

NORTHALLERTON • map 12D4

DUKE OF WELLINGTON INN
Welbury, DL6 2SG
A family-run, rural village inn with a warm, welcoming atmosphere enhanced by real log fires in winter. All food is fresh, well-cooked and

attractively presented, and the service is warm and courteous. For a friendly, relaxed atmosphere, good food and service, the Duke of Wellington is well worth a visit. Adjoining the inn is a cottage available for holiday let.
FOOD: up to £15
Hours: bar meals 12noon–2pm & 7pm–10pm, closed Monday and Tuesday lunch.
Cuisine: ENGLISH – traditional home-made cuisine. Dishes may include duck à l'orange, steak Diane, steak-and-kidney pie. Vegetarian dishes.
Cards: Visa, Access.
Other points: licensed, children welcome, beer garden, playland.
Directions: between A19 and A167. 7 miles north of Northallerton, 3 miles west of A19.
MR & MRS THOMPSON ☎ (01609) 882464.

OSMOTHERLEY • map 12D5

THREE TUNS INN
South End, near Northallerton, DL6 3BN
Situated on the edge of the beautiful North Yorkshire Moors in an old village, the Three Tuns is an early 18th century inn, with a walled garden. An ideal place for a relaxing meal at good-value prices, especially after tackling one of the nearby walks: Lyke Wake, Hambleton Hobble and Cleveland Way.
DOUBLE ROOM: from £40 to £50
FOOD: up to £15
Hours: lunch 12noon–2.30pm, dinner 7pm–9.30pm.
Cuisine: ENGLISH / FRENCH – home-cooked, using fresh produce, the speciality being seafood.
Cards: Visa, Access.
Other points: licensed, Sunday lunch, children welcome, pets allowed.
Directions: from north or south, take A19, turn left at sign for Northallerton/Osmotherley.
H. & J. DYSON ☎ (01609) 883301.

REETH • map 12D4

KINGS ARMS HOTEL
High Row, near Richmond, DL11 6SY
An 18th century listed building situated in the heart of Swaledale. Original beams and open log fires add to the cosy and friendly atmosphere of this village 'local'.
DOUBLE ROOM: from £20 to £30
SINGLE ROOM: from £25 to £35
FOOD: up to £15
Hours: bar meals 12noon–2pm, bar meals 6.30pm–9pm.
Cuisine: ENGLISH.
Other points: licensed, open-air dining, children welcome, coaches by prior arrangement.
Rooms: 1 double room, 1 twin room, 2 family rooms.
Directions: leave the A6108 at Richmond and take B6270 to Reeth.
ASHLEY MARKHAM & ARTHUR COOK
☎ (01748) 884259.

RICHMOND • map 12D4

A66 MOTEL
Smallways, DL11 7QW
The A66 Motel was originally a 17th century farm. Situated close to the Dales and areas of historic interest, the motel is conveniently placed for visiting this beautiful part of England.
DOUBLE ROOM: from £20 to £30
FOOD: from £15 to £20
Hours: bar meals 12noon–2.30pm, bar meals 7pm–10.30pm, breakfast 7am–10am, lunch 12noon–2pm, dinner 7pm–10.30pm.
Cuisine: MODERN ENGLISH – fresh salmon salad, Aylesbury duckling, steaks with sauce Espagnole.
Cards: Visa, Access, Diners, AmEx.
Other points: licensed, Sunday lunch, children welcome, pets allowed, garden.
Directions: on the A66, near Scotch Corner.
SONIA HALL ☎ (01833) 27334 Fax (01833) 627334.

PEAT GATE HEAD
Low Row In Swaledale, DL11 6PP
A 300-year-old Dales house standing in two acres of grounds with magnificent and memorable views update to the Pennines and down to Richmond. An ideal stop for travellers to explore the bewitching countryside. All food is home-made and uses fresh, seasonal produce. Special diets, likes and dislikes are all catered for. A friendly, welcoming place to stay.
DOUBLE ROOM: up to £20
FOOD: from £15 to £20
Hours: breakfast 8.30am, dinner 7pm.
Cuisine: ENGLISH.
Other points: central heating, children welcome, residents' lounge, garden, vegetarian meals.
Directions: situated off B6270 on Langthwaite road.
ALAN EARL ☎ (01748) 86388.

SCOTCH CORNER PAVILION LODGE AT SCOTCH CORNER SERVICE AREA
Junction A1/A66, Scotch Corner, DL10 6PA
The Lodge provides excellent accommodation at a competitive price, with the facilities to make travelling a pleasure. Convenient for Richmond, Herriot country, Lightwater Valley and Beamish Museum.
DOUBLE ROOM: from £20 to £30
FOOD: up to £15
Hours: reception open 24 hours, meals all day 7.30am–10pm.
Cuisine: BRITISH / INTERNATIONAL – table-service restaurant in service building.
Cards: Visa, Access, Diners, AmEx.
Other points: parking, children welcome, disabled access, no-smoking area, Sunday lunch, vegetarian meals, forecourt shop.
Rooms: 50 bedrooms. All with en suite, satellite TV, telephone, radio, alarm, hair dryer, trouser-press, baby-listening device, tea/coffee-making facilities.
Directions: at junction of A1 and A66 (Scotch Corner).
HILLARY LOCKWOOD ☎ (01325) 377177
Fax (01325) 377890.

NORTHERN ENGLAND • NORTH YORKSHIRE

RIPON • map 12D4

STAVELEY ARMS (SPIT ROAST)
North Stainley, HG4 3HT
Charming country pub oozing with atmosphere. Flagged floors, log fires and candlelight. Bygone farming paintings and country tools adorn the walls. Delightful rural setting, 3 miles from Fountains Abbey, 1 mile from Lightwater Valley Theme Park, on the main A6108 road to the beautiful Yorkshire Dales.
DOUBLE ROOM: up to £20
FOOD: up to £15
Hours: lunch 12noon–2pm, dinner 7pm–9.30pm, bar meals 7pm–9.30pm.
Cuisine: ENGLISH – famous Lightwater Carvery Thursday–Sunday. Excellent bar meals every evening. Choose from the blackboard; vegetarian dishes available.
Cards: Visa, Access.
Other points: licensed, open-air dining, Sunday lunch, children welcome, parking.
Rooms: 1 single room, 2 double rooms. All with en suite, TV, tea/coffee-making facilities.
Directions: A6108 north out of Ripon, 4 miles towards North Stainley.
R.M. STAVELEY ☎ (01765) 635439
Fax (01765) 635359.

ROSEDALE ABBEY • map 12D5

BLACKSMITH'S ARMS HOTEL
Hartoft End, near Pickering, YO18 8EN
A family-run hotel at the foot of Rosedale in the North Yorkshire Moors National Park, an area renowned for its scenic beauty. The original farmhouse dates back to the 16th century and commands extensive views of the surrounding moors and dales. Ideal centre for touring and riding.
DOUBLE ROOM: from £40 to £50
SINGLE ROOM: from £45 to £55
FOOD: from £20 to £25
Hours: lunch 12noon–2pm, dinner 7pm–9pm.
Cuisine: FRENCH / ENGLISH – hot or cold meals available in bar, e.g. supreme of chicken filled with garlic butter. Table d'hôte, e.g., fresh local lobster.
Cards: Visa, Access, AmEx.
Other points: children welcome.
Rooms: 14 bedrooms.
Directions: set within the North Yorkshire Moors National Park.
ANTHONY & MARGARET FOOT ☎ (017515) 331.

THE MILBURN ARMS HOTEL
Near Pickering, YO18 8RA
Set in the heart of the North Yorkshire Moors National Park, this hotel is an ideal centre for walking and touring, as many places of scenic and historical interest are within easy reach. The atmosphere is most convivial, with low beams, log fires and real ales. Award-winning cuisine.
DOUBLE ROOM: from £30 to £40
FOOD: up to £15
Hours: breakfast 8am–9.30am, dinner 7pm–8.30pm, lunch 12noon–2pm.
Cuisine: ENGLISH – extensive range of bar food including grilled Farndale goats' cheese, Lastingham lamb hot-pot, pan-fried supreme of salmon, home-made steamed treacle and ginger pudding.
Cards: Visa, Access, Diners.
Other points: licensed, open-air dining, Sunday lunch, children welcome, parking, vegetarian meals, no dogs.
Rooms: 9 double rooms, 2 twin rooms. All with TV, telephone, tea/coffee-making facilities.
Directions: from the A170 at Wrelton, follow the sign to Rosedale Abbey.
TERRY & JOAN BENTLEY ☎ (017515) 312
Fax (017515) 312.

SCARBOROUGH • map 12D6

AMBASSADOR HOTEL
**Centre of the Esplanade,
South Cliff, YO11 2AY**
Scarborough's premier Ambassador is a gracious Victorian building commanding spectacular views of the South Bay. It is opposite the famous Italian Gardens and 150 yards from the cliff lift to the beach, spa entertainments and conference complex. Excellent five-course table d'hôte dinners and full English breakfasts are served in the Bay View Restaurant, with tasteful entertainment in the Bay View Lounge. Bar, lift, ample unrestricted free parking. This family-owned and managed hotel ensures a pleasant and relaxing break, with Yorkshire hospitality plus super value.
DOUBLE ROOM: from £20 to £30
SINGLE ROOM: from £25 to £35
FOOD: up to £15 ☆
Hours: breakfast 8am–9.30am, bar meal 12noon–1.30pm, dinner 6pm–7.45pm, closed November until February (inclusive), open New Year.
Cuisine: ENGLISH – special dietary meals available on request.
Cards: Visa, Access, AmEx.
Other points: no-smoking area, afternoon teas, morning coffee, garden, lounge bar, sun bed, special breaks.
Rooms: 12 single rooms, 12 double rooms, 11 twin room, 14 family rooms. All with en suite, telephone, satellite TV, tea/coffee-making facilities, hair dryer, radio/alarm.
Directions: on the corner of Avenue Victoria and the Esplanade, South Cliff.
RICHARD, KATHRYN & DAVID FRANK
☎ (01723) 362841 Fax (01723) 362841.

ATTENBOROUGH HOTEL
28–29 Albemarle Crescent, YO11 1XX
A welcoming hotel set in a Victorian crescent, overlooking attractive gardens. Located in the centre of town; the train and bus station are only a short distance away.
DOUBLE ROOM: up to £20
FOOD: up to £15
Hours: breakfast 8.30am–9.15am, dinner 6pm.
Cuisine: ENGLISH – traditional English cooking

with continental influence. Daily fixed menu.
Other points: central heating, children welcome, residents' lounge, garden, vegetarian meals.
Directions: A170, A171 or A165 to Scarborough. Located in centre of town.
MR & MRS J. SNOW ☎ (01723) 360857.

AVONCROFT HOTEL
Crown Terrace, YO11 2BL
A comfortable, family-run private hotel in the centre of a Georgian terrace overlooking Crown Gardens and within minutes' walk of the beach, town centre, entertainments, spa complex, road and rail terminals. There is a quiet, comfortable lounge with well-stocked bar and games room, which provide ideal meeting points. Good British tradition, comfort and hospitality.
DOUBLE ROOM: up to £20
SINGLE ROOM: up to £25
FOOD: up to £15
Hours: breakfast 8.30am–9.15am, bar meals 11am–4pm, dinner 5.30pm–6.15pm, bar meals 7pm–11pm, closed late December until early January.
Cuisine: ENGLISH – a daily changing menu, prepared with fresh ingredients.
Other points: children welcome, open bank holidays, afternoon tea, pets allowed, residents' lounge, vegetarian meals.
Rooms: 34 bedrooms.
Directions: from town centre take A165 Filey Road across Valley Bridge; at St Andrews Church turn left into Albion Road. First left into Crown Crescent, then first right into Crown Terrace.
CHRISTINE WILDE ☎ (01723) 372737.

THE BLACKSMITHS ARMS INN
High Street, Cloughton, YO13 0AE
An old country pub, with oak beams and fires, set in a village near the North Yorkshire Moors. The staff are very friendly, and the food is not only excellently cooked but also offers superb value for money. Ideal base for exploring the Moors and Whitby and for enjoying golf and pony-trekking.
DOUBLE ROOM: from £20 to £30
FOOD: up to £15
Hours: breakfast 9am–9.30am, lunch 12noon–2pm, dinner 7pm–10pm.
Cuisine: MODERN ENGLISH – house specialities include fresh poached salmon in a white wine sauce, and trout grenobloise fried with prawns, capers and lemon. Vegetarian dishes.
Cards: Visa, Access.
Other points: Sunday lunch, children welcome, pets allowed, open bank holidays.
Rooms: 6 double rooms. All with TV, tea/coffee-making facilities.
Directions: 5 miles north of Scarborough, on the A171 Whitby to Scarborough road.
JEAN ANN ARNALL ☎ (01723) 870244.

THE CENTRAL HOTEL
1–3 The Crescent, YO11 2PW
Elegant yet comfortable, this newly refurbished hotel offers the discerning holiday maker or business person a chance to relax. Situated on Scarborough's elegant Georgian Crescent overlooking the gardens, yet only a short walk from all the major attractions of the town. Ideal for exploring the nearby North Yorkshire Moors. Jazz sessions Saturday and Sunday lunchtimes.
DOUBLE ROOM: from £30 to £40
FOOD: up to £15 [CLUB]
Hours: breakfast 8am–9.30am, bar snacks 12noon–2pm, dinner 7pm–10.30pm.
Cuisine: ENGLISH.
Cards: Visa, Access, Diners.
Other points: parking, children welcome, open all year, no-smoking area, afternoon tea, disabled access, residents' lounge, vegetarian meals.
Rooms: 3 single rooms, 13 double rooms, 33 twin rooms, 6 family rooms.
Directions: A64 from York, A171 from Whitby, A165 from Bridlington. 3 minutes from the railway station.
FRANK & YVONNE MILLARD ☎ (01723) 365766 [Fax] (01723) 360448.

THE COPPER HORSE
15 Main Street, Seamer, YO12 4RF
Traditional good home-style cooking in a delightful pub atmosphere, with efficient and helpful service in comfortable surroundings. Ideally located for visiting Scarborough and touring the North Yorkshire Moors.
FOOD: up to £15 [CLUB]
Hours: lunch 12noon, dinner 6.30pm–9.30pm, open all year.
Cuisine: ENGLISH – traditionally cooked food, beautifully presented. Dishes may include crispy boned half duckling, large fillet of haddock, plus steaks, grills and fish.
Cards: Visa, Access.
Other points: licensed, Sunday lunch, no-smoking area, children welcome.
Directions: situated off the A64 in the main street of Seamer.
MR S.T. QUINTON ☎ (01723) 862029.

EAST AYTON LODGE
COUNTRY HOTEL & RESTAURANT
Moor Lane, East Ayton, YO13 9EW
An attractive country residence built in the early 19th century and skilfully converted to a small but luxurious hotel and restaurant. Situated three miles from Scarborough in a beautiful three-acre setting in the National Park, close to the River Derwent.
DOUBLE ROOM: from £20 to £30
SINGLE ROOM: from £35 to £45
FOOD: from £15 to £20 [CLUB]
Hours: lunch 12noon–2pm, dinner 6pm–9pm.
Cuisine: ENGLISH / FRENCH – home-grown produce in season. Good selection of vegetarian meals.
Cards: Visa, Access.
Other points: licensed, open-air dining, Sunday lunch, children welcome, beer garden, baby-listening device, cots, 24hr reception.
Rooms: 13 double rooms, 3 twin rooms, 1 family room. All with TV, telephone, tea/coffee making facilities. All rooms are let as singles when required.
Directions: turn left off A170 (to Scarborough) in East Ayton. Close to post office.
BRIAN GARDNER ☎ (01723) 864227 [Fax] (01723) 862680.

THE FALCON INN
Whitby Road, Cloughton, YO13 0DY

A select free-house on the edge of the North Yorkshire Moors, with open views of the sea. Good food served by friendly, attentive staff. Three-times winner of 'Scarborough in Bloom'. Log fires in winter.
DOUBLE ROOM: from £20 to £30
FOOD: up to £15
Hours: lunch 12noon–2pm, dinner 7pm–9.30pm, open all year.
Cuisine: ENGLISH – bar meals, with carvery on Saturday evenings, and Sunday lunchtimes in the restaurant.
Other points: licensed.
Rooms: 4 double rooms, 4 twin rooms. All with TV, tea/coffee-making facilities.
Directions: 9 miles from Scarborough on A171 to Whitby. Take second Ravenscar turn-off.
MR STEWART & MR ROBERTS ☎ (01723) 870717.

GOLDEN GRID FISH RESTAURANT
4 Sandside, YO11 1PE

The restaurant is bright and cheerful, with a nautical theme throughout. The seafood is brought in daily, ensuring that your selection is always fresh. This is a very busy restaurant with high standards of food preparation and presentation.
FOOD: up to £15
Hours: breakfast 10.30am, full menu to 10pm, check opening December and January.
Cuisine: ENGLISH – an extensive menu, with fish being the speciality.
Cards: Visa, Access.
Other points: children welcome, no-smoking area, disabled access, vegetarian meals.
Directions: situated on the Scarborough seafront, opposite the harbour.
JOHN SENIOR ☎ (01723) 360922.

LILMONT HOTEL
44 Castle Road, YO11 1XE

Ideally situated for both bays and town centre, this is a family hotel with all modern amenities and a reputation for their excellent table and warm Yorkshire hospitality. Nearby attractions include the harbour, castle, swimming pool, water theme park, minature railway, cricket ground, indoor bowls centre, plus Scarborough's new multi-million-pound Brunswick Pavilion shopping centre.
DOUBLE ROOM: up to £20
FOOD: up to £15
Hours: breakfast 8.30am–9.15am, dinner 6pm, bar snacks 8.30pm–11pm, closed 2 weeks in October or November.
Cuisine: ENGLISH – home-cooked meals from a daily menu. Orders taken at breakfast.
Cards: Visa, Access.
Other points: children welcome, open bank holidays, no-smoking area, residents' lounge, vegetarian meals, parking, special breaks.
Rooms: 2 single rooms, 2 double rooms, 2 twin rooms, 2 family rooms. All with TV, radio, alarm, tea/coffee-making facilities.
Directions: from A64 to town centre at railway station; turn left; at traffic lights turn right; ¼ mile on left.
SHEILA & WES SWIFT ☎ (01723) 363687.

MANOR HEATH HOTEL
67 Northstead Manor Drive, YO12 6AF

An attractive, well-appointed, detached hotel overlooking Peasholm Park and North Bay. Ideally situated close to all the attractions of this English seaside resort: the beach, swimming pools, Kinderland, miniature railway and Mr Marvel's Fun Park, as well as golf links, bowling and county cricket.
DOUBLE ROOM: up to £20
SINGLE ROOM: up to £25
FOOD: up to £15
Hours: breakfast 9am, dinner 6pm, closed Christmas day and New Year's day.
Cuisine: ENGLISH.
Other points: central heating, children welcome, TV lounge.
Rooms: 1 single room, 8 double rooms, 1 twin room, 4 family rooms. All with TV, tea/coffee-making facilities.
Directions: from Whitby, turn right just before Peasholm Park traffic lights.
MRS JANET MOORE ☎ (01723) 365720.

RED LEA HOTEL
Prince of Wales Terrace, YO11 2AJ

One of Scarborough's most popular hotels, having undergone sympathetic conversion from six elegant Victorian houses. Located on Scarborough's fashionable South Cliff, it provides an ideal base for summer holidays, weekend breaks and conferences. Guests are assured of a warm and sincere welcome. Superb heated indoor swimming pool and fitness facilities.
DOUBLE ROOM: from £30 to £40
SINGLE ROOM: from £25 to £35
FOOD: up to £15
Hours: breakfast 8.30am–9.30am, bar meals 12noon–2pm, Sunday lunch 12.30am–1.30pm, dinner 6.30pm–10pm.
Cuisine: ENGLISH.
Cards: Visa, Access.
Other points: licensed, children welcome, Sunday lunch, open bank holidays, no-smoking area, residents' lounge, vegetarian meals, 24hr reception, residents' bar, swimming pool, cots.
Rooms: 18 single rooms, 12 double rooms, 69 twin rooms, 1 family room. All with TV, radio, alarm, telephone, tea/coffee-making facilities.
Directions: Prince of Wales Terrace runs between the Esplanade and Filey Road.
BRUCE & VALERIE LEE ☎ (01723) 362431 Fax (01723) 371230.

SOUTHLANDS HOTEL
15 West Street, South Cliff, YO11 2QW

Southlands Hotel is ideally situated on Scarborough's select South Cliff, enjoying close proximity to the Italian Rose Gardens, Esplanade and South Bay. All bedrooms in this centrally heated hotel are well appointed, with many facilities. The Windsor Restaurant offers an à la carte and table d'hôte menu, and pre-luncheon

drinks can be enjoyed in the Windsor Bar. Evening dances are held throughout the season, and in-house conference facilities can cater for 20–100 delegates.
DOUBLE ROOM: from £30 to £40
SINGLE ROOM: from £35 to £45
FOOD: up to £15
Hours: breakfast 8am–9.30am, bar snacks 12noon–1.45pm, dinner 6.30pm–8.30pm.
Cuisine: ENGLISH.
Cards: Visa, Access, Diners, AmEx.
Other points: licensed.
Rooms: 58 bedrooms.
Directions: A64, turn right at Mere to Filey road, turn left and second right.
MR & MRS H. DIXON ☎ (01723) 361461
Fax (01723) 376035.

WILLOW DENE
110 Columbus Ravine, YO12 7QZ
A family-run private hotel situated in Scarborough's prime holiday area, within minutes of all the North Bay attractions and only a short walk to the town centre. The hotel has been well maintained by the resident proprietors and offers the comforts and amenities that today's holiday-maker requires.
DOUBLE ROOM: up to £20
SINGLE ROOM: up to £25
FOOD: up to £15 ☆
Hours: breakfast 9am, dinner 5.15pm.
Cuisine: ENGLISH – traditional English fare.
Other points: parking, children catered for (please check for age limits), no-smoking area, residents' lounge, vegetarian meals.
Rooms: 2 single rooms, 2 double rooms, 2 twin rooms, 3 family rooms. The family rooms may be used as double rooms.
Directions: located near Peasholm Park, north of Scarborough town centre.
ROBERT & ELIZABETH BRIGGS ☎ (01723) 365173.

SETTLE • map 11E3

NEW INN HOTEL
Clapham, LA2 8HH
The New Inn is over 200 years old and has provided a welcome stop for visitors to the Lake District, Scotland and the Yorkshire Dales since the 18th century. This coaching inn offers a relaxing and friendly atmosphere, comfortable accommodation and well-cooked food in generous portions. Under the personal supervision of the resident proprietors.
DOUBLE ROOM: from £20 to £30
FOOD: up to £15 CLUB
Hours: breakfast 8.30am–9.30am, lunch 12noon–2pm, dinner 7pm–9.30pm.
Cuisine: ENGLISH – restaurant and bar meals. Dishes include cheese and leek pie, game pie and sticky toffee pudding.
Cards: Visa, Access, AmEx.
Other points: licensed, Sunday lunch, garden, afternoon tea, pets allowed, games room, real ales, children welcome, cots, residents' bar,

residents' lounge, parking, vegetarian meals.
Rooms: 10 double rooms, 3 twin rooms. All with TV, telephone, tea/coffee-making facilities.
Directions: situated on A65 to Lake District. Clapham is 5 miles north of Settle.
KEITH & BARBARA MANNION ☎ (015242) 51203 Fax (015242) 51496.

SKIPTON • map 12E4

RANDELL'S HOTEL & LEISURE
Keighley Road, Snaygill, BD23 2TA
Randell's nestles in the Aire valley, next to the historic Leeds and Liverpool canal, with foothills to the Dales as a backdrop. Whether on business or pleasure, your every need is catered for. A health and beauty suite offers a tremendous range of treatments, while the ozone-purified swimming pool ensures total relaxation. Extensive conference and banqueting facilities for up to 350 people.
DOUBLE ROOM: from £40 to £50
SINGLE ROOM: over £55
FOOD: from £15 to £20
Hours: breakfast 7am–10am, bar meals 11am–7pm, dinner 7pm–10pm, open all year.
Cuisine: ENGLISH – fixed-price menu, offering fine dining in attractive and comfortable setting. Vegetarians catered for.
Cards: Visa.
Other points: licensed, Sunday lunch, children welcome, state-registered children's nursery, pets allowed, afternoon tea, leisure centre, squash, gym facilities, parking, indoor pool.
Rooms: 27 double rooms, 29 twin rooms, 20 family rooms. All with satellite TV, radio, alarm, telephone, tea/coffee-making facilities, hair dryer.
Directions: 1 mile from the centre of Skipton, on the main A629 Keighley road.
CHRISTOPHER HULL ☎ (01756) 700100
Fax (01756) 700107.

STOKESLEY • map 12C5

MILLERS RESTAURANT
9 Bridge Road, TS9 5AA
An attractive, family-run restaurant with an excellent reputation locally. Bookings are required for dinner. The lunchtime menu offers simpler meals at a very reasonable price. Lunch or dinner, all meals are well cooked and excellently served.
FOOD: up to £15 ☆
Hours: lunch 12noon–2pm, dinner 7.30pm–9.30pm, last orders 9pm, closed Sunday and Monday.
Cuisine: FRENCH / ENGLISH – evening à la carte menu including breast of barbarie duck aux cerises. Lighter meals served on the lunchtime menu.
Cards: Visa, Access, Diners, AmEx.
Other points: licensed, reservations, street parking.
Directions: off Stokesley High Street (A172), by River Leven.
KATHRYN ABBOTT ☎ (01642) 710880.

NORTHERN ENGLAND • NORTH YORKSHIRE

THE WAINSTONES HOTEL
31 High Street, Great Broughton, TS9 7EW

A most attractive village hotel with a real 'local' bar. The restaurant has a homely atmosphere and serves both à la carte and table d'hôte meals within its bright and airy setting. Great care and consideration is shown to all guests, and the accommodation is of a high standard.
DOUBLE ROOM: from £20 to £30
FOOD: up to £15
Hours: breakfast 7am–9.30am, lunch 12noon–2pm, bar meals 12noon–2pm, dinner 7pm–10pm, bar meals 5pm–10pm.
Cuisine: MODERN ENGLISH – savoury cheese fritters, medallions of pork fillet, home-made beef burgers.
Cards: Visa, Access, AmEx.
Other points: open-air dining, Sunday lunch, children welcome, conferences, guide dogs.
Rooms: 4 single rooms, 8 double rooms, 11 twin room. All with satellite TV, radio, telephone, tea/coffee-making facilities, heating, hair dryer.
Directions: situated 2 miles southeast of Stokesley on the B1257 Helmsley road.
JAMES KEITH PIGG ☎ (01642) 712268
Fax (01642) 711560.

LES ROUTIERS
Your assurance of Quality and Value

THIRSK • map 12D4

ANGEL INN
Long Street, Topcliffe, YO3 3RW

Dating back to the 17th century, the Angel Inn is steeped in history, being one of the main stopping points between the north and south in the days of stage coach travel. In recent years it has been tastefully extended into a charming country inn and is renowned for its warm, friendly atmosphere, excellent food and traditional Yorkshire ales. A choice of suites provide the perfect setting for private functions and conferences. Car and coach park for 150 vehicles.
DOUBLE ROOM: from £20 to £30
SINGLE ROOM: from £25 to £35
FOOD: up to £15 CLUB ★
Hours: breakfast 7am–9.15am, lunch 12noon 2.30pm, dinner 6.30pm–9.30pm.
Cuisine: ENGLISH / INTERNATIONAL – a wide choice including home-made steak-and-kidney pie, chicken Switzerland, leek and Gruyère Pithivier.
Cards: Visa, Access, Switch, Delta.
Other points: parking, children welcome, open bank holidays, afternoon tea, residents' lounge, vegetarian meals, garden, open-air dining, fishing, conferences, functions.
Rooms: 2 single rooms, 8 double rooms, 4 twin rooms, 1 family room. All with TV, bar, telephone, tea/coffee-making facilities.
Directions: on A167, just off A168. 3 miles from the A1 and A19.
TONY & TRISH ARDRON ☎ (01845) 577237
Fax (01845) 578000.

NAG'S HEAD HOTEL & RESTAURANT
Pickhill, YO7 4JG

There has been an inn on this site for over 200 years, providing food and rest for travellers and horses using the A1, which was then the only road connecting London and Edinburgh. Today, the Nag's Head has been upgraded to an excellent standard, with comfortable rooms, superb cuisine and a wide selection of real ales and wines. Highly recommended.
DOUBLE ROOM: from £20 to £30
FOOD: from £15 to £20
Hours: breakfast 7am–10.30am, lunch 12noon–2pm, dinner 7pm–9.30pm, Sunday 6pm–10pm.
Cuisine: ENGLISH – à la carte menu: dishes include sauté of hare fillets, grilled duck breast with lime and gin sauce, pork fillet stuffed with York ham and blue Wensleydale cheese, beef steak and venison pie. Puddings include squidgy chocolate roll, banoffee pie, praline, coffee and Tia Maria pancakes. Yorkshire cheeses. Soup and sandwiches all day.
Cards: Visa, Access.
Other points: Sunday lunch, children welcome, pets allowed, garden, conferences.
Rooms: 3 single rooms, 7 double rooms, 5 twin rooms. All with TV, telephone, tea/coffee-making facilities.
Directions: 1 mile off A1, near Thirsk.
RAYMOND & EDWARD BOYNTON ☎ (01845) 567391 Fax (01845) 567212.

SHEPPARD'S HOTEL, RESTAURANT & BISTRO
Front Street, Sowerby, YO7 1JF

17th century brick buildings, ideally situated in Herriot Country. Sympathetically modernized, yet retaining a comfortable, country atmosphere, which is a joy to relax and unwind in. Excellent cuisine and service amid attractive surroundings.
DOUBLE ROOM: from £30 to £40
FOOD: from £15 to £20
Hours: breakfast 8.30am–9am, lunch 12noon–2pm, dinner 7pm–9.30pm, open all year.
Cuisine: ENGLISH / INTERNATIONAL – fresh local produce used. Restaurant and bistro.
Cards: Visa, Access.
Other points: licensed, Sunday lunch, children welcome.
Rooms: 7 double rooms, 1 triple room. All with TV, telephone, tea/coffee-making facilities.
Directions: off A19, into south-west corner of Thirsk, half a mile to Sowerby.
ROY SHEPPARD ☎ (01845) 523655
Fax (01845) 524720.

WHITBY • map 12C5

ANDERSONS
Silver Street, YO21 3AH

Centrally located, this bistro is popular for either a full meal or for a snack. Often gets very full in the evenings: booking recommended. Tables in the garden in summer.
FOOD: from £15 to £20 CLUB

Hours: lunch 11.30am–2.15pm, dinner 6.30pm–9.45pm, bar 10am–11pm.
Cuisine: MODERN ENGLISH – steaks with sauces, local fish dishes. Vegetarian menu available.
Cards: Visa, Access, Diners, AmEx.
Other points: open-air dining, Sunday lunch, children welcome, pets allowed.
Directions: Whitby is on A174 and A171; the bistro is located in the town centre.
DAVID WHISSON ☎ (01947) 605383.

THE MAGPIE CAFE
14 Pier Road, YO21 3PU
The McKenzie family have been serving superb fish in this historic building for nigh on 40 years. Window tables overlook the Abbey, 199 steps and picturesque harbour of Whitby. The restaurant is extremely popular with holiday-makers and locals alike. The food is always fresh and well cooked and the service friendly, quick and welcoming. Les Routiers Casserole Award 1991, 1992, 1993 and 1994.
FOOD: up to £15
Hours: meals all day 11.30am–6.30pm, closed end November until early March.
Cuisine: ENGLISH – fresh, local fish and shellfish straight off the quayside, up to 12 varieties each day including crab, lobster and salmon. Local ham, home-made steak pie and 30 home-made desserts.
Cards: Visa, Access.
Other points: Sunday lunch, children welcome.
Directions: Pier Road is main road from town centre to the beach and West Pier.
I. ROBSON, A. McKENZIE-ROBSON, S. & I. McKENZIE ☎ (01947) 602058.

SEACLIFFE HOTEL
North Promenade, West Cliff, YO21 3JX
A friendly, family-run hotel with a restaurant which is also open to non-residents. All food is of good quality and well presented at very reasonable prices. Tastefully decorated bedrooms, some with sea views and situated close to local attractions such as Whitby Abbey, the museum and the local golf course.
DOUBLE ROOM: from £20 to £30
FOOD: from £15 to £20 ★
Hours: breakfast 8am–9.30am, dinner 6pm–9pm, open all year.
Cuisine: ENGLISH – including fresh local seafood, steaks and vegetarian dishes.
Cards: Visa, Access, Diners, AmEx.
Other points: licensed, children welcome, pets allowed, open bank holidays, residents' lounge, residents' bar, vegetarian meals, parking.
Rooms: 1 single room, 15 double rooms, 3 twin rooms, 1 family room. All with en suite, TV, radio, telephone, tea/coffee-making facilities.
Directions: take A171 or A174 to Whitby. Follow signs to West Cliff.
J.A. PURCELL ☎ (01947) 603139 Fax (01947) 603139.

STAKESBY MANOR
Manor Close, High Stakesby, YO21 1HL
A lovely 17th century manor house, situated on the edge of Whitby, that has been owned and controlled by two generations of the Hodgson Family. Located in a quiet area approximately one mile from town centre, golf course and beach, Stakesby Manor offers well-cooked, tasty food, friendly, attentive service and comfortable accommodation in relaxed and attractive surroundings.
DOUBLE ROOM: from £20 to £30
SINGLE ROOM: from £35 to £45
FOOD: up to £15 CLUB
Hours: breakfast 8am–9am, dinner 7pm–9.30pm.
Cuisine: MODERN ENGLISH – three-course à la carte menu and table d'hôte, including salmon and lobster mousse, lobster cardinal, veal in leek and Stilton sauce.
Cards: Visa, Access, AmEx.
Other points: vegetarian meals, special diets, children welcome, garden, picnic lunches, functions, conferences, special breaks.
Rooms: 6 double rooms, 2 twin rooms. All with TV, radio, tea/coffee-making facilities.
Directions: off the A171.
MR & MRS HODGSON ☎ (01947) 602773.

TRENCHER'S RESTAURANT
New Quay Road, YO21 1DH
A family-run seafood restaurant in the historic fishing town of Whitby. Needless to say, fresh Whitby fish and seafoods are a speciality and are cooked to a high standard. Terry and his sisters Judy and Nicky have received thank-you letters from as far away as Europe and the USA.
FOOD: up to £15
Hours: meals all day 11am–12midnight, last orders 9pm, closed January and February.
Cuisine: SEAFOOD – fresh local fish, salad bar, freshly cut sandwiches, home-made desserts.
Other points: licensed, Sunday lunch, children welcome.
Directions: opposite the harbour offices and quayside car park, off main A174.
TERRY, JUDY & NICKY FOSTER ☎ (01947) 603212.

WHITE HOUSE HOTEL
Upgang Lane, YO21 3JJ
The hotel is situated adjacent to Whitby Golf Course, with panoramic views of Sandsend Bay. Whitby is a charming, picturesque fishing port with a history extending back 1,000 years. An ideal location for discovering an intriguing part of Yorkshire.
DOUBLE ROOM: from £20 to £30
FOOD: up to £15
Hours: breakfast 8.30am–10am, lunch 12noon–2pm, dinner 7pm–10pm.
Cuisine: ENGLISH – Yorkshire pudding with stew. 'Galley' five course dinner.
Cards: Visa, Access.
Other points: licensed, Sunday lunch, children welcome.
Directions: on the A174, beside Whitby Golf Course on the West Cliff.
THOMAS CAMPBELL ☎ (01947) 600469 Fax (01947) 821600.

WIGGLESWORTH • map 11E3

🍴 THE PLOUGH INN
Near Skipton, BD23 4RJ

This lovely country hotel is situated just two miles from the A65. Boasting early 18th century origins, the Plough Inn provides excellent food and service, comfortable furnishings and good service to meet all your needs. Good dining is offered in the bright conservatory restaurant.
DOUBLE ROOM: from £20 to £30
SINGLE ROOM: from £25 to £35
FOOD: up to £15
Hours: dinner 7pm–9.45pm, lunch 12noon–2pm.
Cuisine: ENGLISH – beef and cow-heel cobbler, seafood pancakes.
Cards: Visa, Access, Diners, AmEx.
Other points: licensed, Sunday lunch, children welcome.
Rooms: 7 double rooms, 3 twin rooms, 2 family rooms. All with TV, radio, telephone, tea/coffee-making facilities.
Directions: from the A65 at Long Preston, take the B6478 to Wigglesworth.
BRIAN GOODALL ☎ (01729) 840243.

YORK • map 12E5

🍴 ABBOTS MEWS HOTEL
6 Marygate Lane, Bootham, YO3 7DE

Situated in the centre of York, only minutes away from the city's historic attractions. The hotel was an original coachman's cottage with coach-house and stables, but was converted in 1976. The restaurant is renowned for its high standard of cuisine, and the service is very friendly and efficient.
DOUBLE ROOM: from £20 to £30
FOOD: up to £15 [CLUB]
Hours: breakfast 7.30am–9.30am, Sunday 8.30am–10am, lunch 12noon–2pm, dinner 7pm–9.30pm.
Cuisine: INTERNATIONAL – specialities include sautéed medallions of beef Hongroise, chicken Madras, stir-fried beef on oyster sauce. Bar lunches are also served weekdays.
Cards: Visa, Access, Diners, AmEx.
Other points: licensed, Sunday lunch, children welcome, garden, conferences.
Rooms: 20 double rooms, 19 twin rooms, 11 family rooms. All with TV, radio, tea/coffee-making facilities.
Directions: in centre of York. Close to Museum Gardens and Bootham Bar.
MR & MRS DEARNLEY ☎ (01904) 622395/ 634866.

🍺 THE ALICE HAWTHORN
Nun Monkton, YO5 8EW

An old cottage-style village pub, situated on the village green of the beautiful village of Nun Monkton, offering well-cooked food in restaurant and bar. The welcoming and friendly atmosphere of the main bar attracts both locals and visitors to the area.
FOOD: up to £15

Hours: lunch 12noon–2pm, dinner 7pm–9.30pm.
Cuisine: ENGLISH – home-cooked bar meals, using freshest produce available. Daily selection of vegetarian dishes.
Other points: licensed, open-air dining, Sunday lunch, no-smoking area, children welcome, garden, pets allowed.
Directions: off the main A59 at Skipbridge filling station.
MR S. WINSHIP ☎ (01423) 330303.

🏠 ASCOT HOUSE
80 East Parade, Heworth, YO3 7YH

An attractive Victorian guest house offering comfortable accommodation, a good home-cooked breakfast and a welcoming, homely atmosphere. Conveniently located for the historic town of York, York Minster, museums and the beautiful east coast.
DOUBLE ROOM: up to £20
Hours: breakfast 8.30am–9.30am (or on request).
Cards: Visa, Access.
Other points: parking, children welcome, no-smoking area, sauna, residents' lounge, vegetarian meals.
Rooms: 1 single room, 7 double rooms, 2 twin rooms, 5 family rooms. All with TV, tea/coffee-making facilities.
Directions: from outer ring road follow A1036 to city centre.
KEITH & JUNE WOOD ☎ (01904) 426826
[Fax] (01904) 413077.

🍴 THE BLACK BULL INN
Main Street, Escrick, YO4 6JP

This appealing cottage-style village inn close to York provides guests with comfortable accommodation in the recently refurbished bedrooms and fine food in the popular restaurant. Meals are also available in the bar, where the relaxed atmosphere provides a haven for many locals as well as passing travellers.
DOUBLE ROOM: from £20 to £30
FOOD: from £15 to £20
Hours: breakfast 7am–9am, lunch 12noon–2pm, dinner 6.30pm–10pm.
Cuisine: ENGLISH – traditional English cuisine, prepared and cooked to a high standard.
Cards: Visa, Access.
Other points: parking, children welcome, pets allowed, no-smoking area, vegetarian meals.
Rooms: 5 double rooms, 2 twin rooms, 1 family room. All with en suite, TV, radio, alarm, trouser-press, tea/coffee-making facilities.
Directions: 5 miles south of York on A19 towards Selby.
HUGH & ANNE BOWMAN ☎ (01904) 728745.

🏠 BYRON HOUSE HOTEL
7 Driffield Terrace, The Mount, YO2 2DD

Byron House provides a high standard of accommodation, a friendly atmosphere, and personal service in pleasant surroundings. Good food is served in the dining room, and guests can relax in the lounge with its licensed bar and selection of wines. Within walking distance of the hotel are many attractions, including the Minster.

DOUBLE ROOM: from £20 to £30
FOOD: from £15 to £20 ☆
Hours: breakfast 7.30am–9.30am, dinner 7pm, closed Christmas.
Cuisine: ENGLISH.
Cards: Visa, Access, Diners, AmEx.
Other points: children welcome, residents' lounge, vegetarian meals, baby-sitting, cots, left luggage, residents' bar, parking.
Rooms: 3 single rooms, 2 double rooms, 1 twin room, 4 family rooms. All with TV, radio, telephone, tea/coffee-making facilities.
Directions: A1036, signposted York west and Racecourse. Walking distance of centre.
DICK & JEAN TYSON ☎ (01904) 632525
Fax (01904) 639424.

■ CARLTON HOUSE HOTEL
134 The Mount, YO2 2AS
A cosy, family-run hotel, conveniently located close to the racecourse and all city-centre amenities. A popular choice for many visitors to York and the surrounding countryside.
DOUBLE ROOM: up to £20
SINGLE ROOM: up to £25
Hours: breakfast 7.45am–9.15am, closed Christmas.
Cuisine: BREAKFAST.
Other points: central heating, children welcome, residents' lounge.
Rooms: 1 single room, 4 double rooms, 5 twin rooms, 4 family rooms. All with TV, radio, tea/coffee-making facilities.
Directions: on the A1036 close to York station.
MALCOLM & LIZ GREAVES ☎ (01904) 622265.

■ DUKE OF CONNAUGHT HOTEL
Copmanthorpe Grange, YO2 3TN
The hotel is set in a fascinating location in York, encircled by 14th century walls, ancient streets and buildings and overlooked by the magnificent York Minster. With attractively 18th century-style furnishings and equipped with many modern facilities, guests are assured of a warm welcome and comfortable stay. There is a bright, airy lounge bar, and good access for disabled persons to all ground-floor rooms. An ideal base for touring the historic city of York.
DOUBLE ROOM: from £50
SINGLE ROOM: from £35 to £45
Hours: breakfast 8am–9.30am, dinner 7pm–10pm, closed Christmas.
Cuisine: ENGLISH.
Cards: Visa, Access, AmEx.
Other points: licensed, Sunday lunch, no-smoking area, disabled access, parking, vegetarian meals, afternoon tea, residents' lounge, garden, children welcome, cots.
Rooms: 5 double rooms, 5 family rooms. All with TV, telephone, tea/coffee-making facilities.
Directions: off A64 York–Leeds road; between Appleton Roebuck and Bishopthorpe, York.
JACK HUGHES ☎ (01904) 744318.

■ GRASMEAD HOUSE HOTEL
1 Scarcroft Hill, The Mount, YO2 1DF
A warm welcome and friendly service await guests at the Grasmead House, a small family-run hotel

situated just outside the city walls, within easy walking distance of the city centre attractions, the racecourse and the railway station. Restful nights are assured in the centrally-heated bedrooms, all with antique four-poster beds and en suite facilities, and some with direct views of the city walls and York Minster.
DOUBLE ROOM: from £20 to £30
SINGLE ROOM: from £55
Cards: Visa, Access, MasterCard, Switch.
Other points: licensed, parking, children welcome, no-smoking area, residents' lounge, vegetarian meals.
Rooms: 6 bedrooms. All with TV, radio, alarm, tea/coffee-making facilities.
Directions: Scarcroft Road is off the A1036, close to York Racecourse.
STANLEY & SUSAN LONG ☎ (01904) 629996
Fax (01904) 629996.

■ THE HAWNBY HOTEL
Hawnby, near Helmsley, YO6 5QS
Built in Yorkshire stone, the Hawnby Hotel was originally a drovers' inn in the 19th century. Decorated throughout to a high standard, this hotel enjoys the peace of the unspoilt surrounding countryside. A high degree of personal attention is afforded to all guests. Fishing is free for residents; tennis and pony-trekking can also be arranged locally.
DOUBLE ROOM: from £30 to £40
FOOD: up to £15
Hours: breakfast 8.30am–9.30am, lunch 12noon–2pm, dinner 7pm–8.30pm, closed February.
Cuisine: ENGLISH – traditional English cooking using home-grown produce when possible.
Cards: Visa, Access.
Other points: licensed, garden, special breaks.
Directions: off the B127, 8 miles from Helmsley.
LADY MEXBOROUGH ☎ (014396) 202
Fax (014396) 417.

■ HEDLEY HOUSE
3 Bootham Terrace, YO3 7DH
A Victorian residence within walking distance of the city of York. Family-run, the atmosphere is friendly and informal and complemented by good home-cooking.
DOUBLE ROOM: from £20 to £30
SINGLE ROOM: from £25 to £35
FOOD: up to £15
Hours: breakfast 8am–9am, dinner 6.30pm–7pm.
Cuisine: ENGLISH.
Cards: Visa, Access, AmEx.
Other points: children welcome, pets allowed, residents' lounge, vegetarian meals.
Rooms: 15 bedrooms.
Directions: off the A19, third turning on left away from Bootham Bar.
GRAHAM & SUSAN HARRAND ☎ (01904) 637404.

■ HUDSON'S HOTEL
60 Bootham, YO3 7BZ
A Victorian hotel in the city centre, only minutes from Bootham Bar, the Minster and the Roman Walls. The hotel was converted from two town

houses and now provides elegant accommodation and high-quality cuisine.
DOUBLE ROOM: from £30 to £40
FOOD: up to £15
Hours: breakfast 7.30am–9.30am, lunch by prior arrangement 12noon–2pm, dinner 6.30pm–9.30pm.
Cuisine: ENGLISH / CONTINENTAL – extensive à la carte menu served in the Below Stairs restaurant.
Cards: Visa, Access, Diners, AmEx.
Other points: Sunday lunch, children welcome.
Rooms: 1 single room, 15 double rooms, 10 twin rooms, 4 family rooms. All with satellite TV, telephone, tea/coffee-making facilities.
Directions: very close to Bootham Bar and York Minster.
C.R. HUDSON ☎ (01904) 621267
Fax (01904) 654719.

KITES RESTAURANT
13 Grape Lane, YO1 2HU
Tucked away in a small street very close to the Minster and Stonegate. Access to the restaurant is up a narrow staircase to the second floor. All herbs come from the proprietor's own herb garden. Local produce used where possible, including a good selection of unusual cheeses from the Dales. Well-chosen but affordable wine list.
FOOD: from £15 to £20 CLUB
Hours: lunch Saturday 12noon–1.45pm, dinner 6.30pm–10.30pm, closed Sunday.
Cuisine: INTERNATIONAL – innovative international menu: Thai stuffed crab, marinated duck breast with Chinese noodle and aubergine salad, wood pigeon and Cumberland sauce.
Cards: Visa, Access.
Other points: licensed, children welcome.
Directions: from Bootham Bar, follow Petergate to Low Petergate, then to Grape Lane.
MR C. WRIGHT ☎ (01904) 641750.

MOUNT ROYALE
The Mount, YO2 2DA
Gothic in appearance but mainly William IV in style, the Mount Royale has been tastefully decorated and furnished to retain its character. The atmosphere is further enhanced by the presence of the Old English garden, which can be seen from the restaurant. A very pleasant venue in which to enjoy good food and friendly, professional service.
DOUBLE ROOM: from £30 to £40
FOOD: from £20 to £25
Hours: breakfast 7.15am–9.30am, dinner 7pm–10.30pm.
Cuisine: INTERNATIONAL – including rack of lamb and duckling.
Cards: Visa, Access, Diners, AmEx.
Other points: licensed, children welcome, pets by prior arrangement, swimming pool, trimnasium, sauna, solarium.
Rooms: 13 double rooms, 10 twin rooms. All with TV, radio, telephone, tea/coffee-making facilities.
Directions: on A1036 past racecourse, up hill to traffic lights. On right side.
RICHARD & CHRISTINE OXTOBY ☎ (01904) 628856.

PLUNKETS RESTAURANT LTD
9 High Petergate, YO1 2EN
Plunkets is a cheerful restaurant set in a 17th century building near York Minster. It plays gentle jazz/disco music and is full of plants, prints and polished wooden tables.
FOOD: from £15 to £20
Hours: meals all day 11am–12noon, closed Christmas day and New Year's day.
Cuisine: INTERNATIONAL – dishes include fajitas, burritos, hamburgers, steaks, home-made pies, fresh salmon fishcakes, marinated chicken breasts, salads and various vegetarian dishes.
Other points: licensed, Sunday lunch, children welcome.
Directions: located on one of York's principal streets, near Bootham Bar.
TREVOR BARRINGTON WARD ☎ (01904) 637722.

RED LION MOTEL & COUNTRY INN
Upper Poppleton, YO2 6PR
A friendly, cheerful and welcoming country inn, offering fresh food amid pleasant surroundings. Ideally located for those who wish to tour the famous Yorkshire Dales, the Moors, or for visiting York itself and nearby Harrogate.
DOUBLE ROOM: from £20 to £30
FOOD: up to £15
Hours: breakfast 7.30am–9am, lunch 12noon–2pm, dinner 6.30pm–9.30pm, open all year.
Cuisine: ENGLISH – à la carte menu. offering a choice of good home-cooked dishes, including fresh Whitby fish. Vegetarian meals also available.
Cards: Visa, Access.
Other points: licensed, open-air dining, Sunday lunch, no-smoking area, children welcome, parking, garden, open bank holidays.
Rooms: 8 double rooms, 2 twin rooms, 8 family rooms. All with TV, telephone, tea/coffee-making facilities.
Directions: situated half a mile from the outskirts of York on the A59.
DOUGLAS MALTBY ☎ (01904) 781141
Fax (01904) 785143.

WHITE SWAN INN & RESTAURANT
Deighton, Escrick, YO2 6HA
A family-run country inn, with an intimate restaurant and comfortable bar area. Offers well-prepared and presented dishes at excellent value for money, in a very pleasant, friendly atmosphere.
FOOD: up to £15
Hours: Sunday lunch 12noon–2pm, bar meals 12noon–2pm, dinner 7pm–9.30pm, bar meals 7pm–9.30pm.
Cuisine: BRITISH – fillet of salmon in a piquant walnut sauce and half roast duckling available in restaurant. Steaks, salads, pies and special dishes of the day in the bar. Game available in season.
Cards: Visa, Access.
Other points: children welcome, open bank holidays, Sunday lunch.
Directions: on A19, 5 miles south of York.
MR & MRS WALKER ☎ (01904) 728287.

NORTHUMBERLAND

ALNMOUTH • map 12A4

FAMOUS SCHOONER HOTEL
Northumberland Street,
NE66 2RS

Listed Georgian coaching inn, situated only 100 yards from the beach, river and golf course. The Schooner is of ETB 4 Crown standard and is renowned for its superb food and extensive selection of real ales. Specializes in golf holidays.
DOUBLE ROOM: from £30 to £40
SINGLE ROOM: from £25 to £35
FOOD: up to £15 [CLUB] ☆
Hours: breakfast 7.30am–9.30am, lunch 12noon–3pm, dinner 7pm–11pm.
Cuisine: ENGLISH / FRENCH – superb English and French cuisine, also a 'Bistro' restaurant and conservatory.
Cards: Visa, Access, Diners, AmEx.
Other points: licensed, Sunday lunch, children welcome, garden, afternoon tea, pets allowed, squash, solarium, conservatory, conferences, free house.
Rooms: 23 bedrooms.
Directions: 100 yards from the 9-hole village golf course. 5 miles from A1, Alnwick exit.
MR ORDE ☎ (01665) 830216 [Fax] (01665) 830216.

ALNWICK • map 12A4

THE COTTAGE INN HOTEL
Dunstan Village, Craster,
NE66 3SZ

Recently modernized, The Cottage Inn is situated in the heart of the beautiful Northumbrian countryside, just a few minutes from the sea. Craster is the ideal base for touring the wealth of nearby historic buildings, which include Alnwick Castle and Wallington House. Hosts Lawrence and Shirley Jobling offer you good food, service and an olde-worlde atmosphere.
DOUBLE ROOM: from £20 to £30
FOOD: up to £15 ⊙
Hours: breakfast 8.30am–9.30am, Sunday lunch 12noon–2.30pm, bar meals 12noon–2.30pm, dinner 7pm–9.30pm, bar meals 6pm–9.30pm.
Cuisine: ENGLISH – a la carte, table d'hôte and extensive bar menu. Dishes may include pigeon, escalopes of venison, and monkfish in filo pastry. Vegetarian dishes.
Cards: Visa, Access.
Other points: licensed, open-air dining, Sunday lunch, no-smoking area, parking, children welcome, garden, open bank holidays, residents' bar, disabled access, listening device, cots.
Rooms: 2 double rooms, 8 twin rooms. All with TV, telephone, tea/coffee-making facilities.
Directions: 6 miles east of Alnwick and half a mile from Craster harbour.
LAWRENCE & SHIRLEY JOBLING ☎ (01665) 576658.

HOTSPUR HOTEL
Bondgate Without, NE66 1PR

A former coaching house converted into a comfortable, family-run hotel. There is a choice of dining in the restaurant or in the wine and food bar. Friendly and polite service.
DOUBLE ROOM: from £30 to £40
FOOD: from £15 to £20
Hours: lunch 12noon–2pm, dinner 7pm–9pm, closed Christmas day and New Year's day.
Cuisine: ENGLISH – steaks, wild salmon.
Cards: Visa, Access, Diners, AmEx.
Other points: licensed, Sunday lunch, children welcome, pets allowed, parking, vegetarian meals.
Directions: on B6346 just outside city wall approaching from A1.
MR D. COZENS ☎ (01665) 510101.

BELFORD • map 12A4

BLUE BELL
Market Square, NE70 7NE

A 17th century coaching inn set in the heart of a peaceful Northumbrian village. An ideal stopover for north/south travellers or those exploring Northumbria's wonderful beaches and historic castles.
DOUBLE ROOM: from £30 to £40
FOOD: from £15 to £20 [CLUB]
Hours: breakfast 8am–9.30am, lunch 12noon–2pm, dinner 7pm–9pm.
Cuisine: ENGLISH – fresh local produce; fish, lamb and game.
Cards: Visa, Access, AmEx.
Other points: open-air dining, Sunday lunch, children welcome, pets allowed, coaches by prior arrangement
Rooms: 1 single room, 8 double rooms, 8 twin rooms.
Directions: situated on the B6349 just off the A1.
MRS J. SHIRLEY ☎ (01668) 213543 [Fax] (01668) 213787.

BELLINGHAM • map 11B3

RIVERDALE HALL HOTEL
Bellingham, NE48 2JT

Undoubtedly one of Northumbria's most outstanding country house hotels, having been tastefully converted from a Victorian mansion. It stands in its own large grounds on the edge of the small town of Bellingham, close to the beautiful Northumberland National Park. The elegantly furnished restaurant provides a warm, relaxed setting in which to enjoy a high standard of cuisine, including regional specialities, complemented by well-chosen wines. It is a magnet for sports and leisure enthusiasts and an ideal base from which to tour the countryside and coastline and explore the many nearby attractions. Les Routiers Newcomer of the Year 1994.
DOUBLE ROOM: from £30 to £40

267

SINGLE ROOM: from £35 to £45
FOOD: from £15 to £20 [CLUB]
Hours: breakfast 7.45am–10am, lunch 12noon–2pm, dinner 6.45pm–9.30pm, bar snacks 6.45pm–9.30pm, open all year.
Cuisine: ENGLISH – with French influences: chicken au poivre, monkfish Thermidor, poached asparagus glazed with cheese.
Cards: Visa, Access, Diners, AmEx, Switch.
Other points: parking, children welcome, Sunday lunch, no-smoking area, afternoon tea, Sunday dinner, residents' lounge, residents' garden, vegetarian meals, open-air dining, pets allowed.
Rooms: 3 single rooms, 12 double rooms, 5 family rooms.
Directions: situated in Bellingham on the B6320, 17 miles north of Hexham, between Hadrian's Wall and Kielder Water and Forest.
MR J. COCKER ☎ (01434) 220254
[Fax] (01434) 220457.

BERWICK-UPON-TWEED
map 16E6

BLACK BULL INN
Main Street, Lowick, TD15 2UA

A 300-year-old Northumbrian pub with good local trade and excellent visitor trade in summer. Due to this pub's popularity, the proprietors, Anne and Tom Grundy, have expanded the food side of the business to offer larger dining room facilities, where real ales are also served. Booking is advised for evenings and weekends. A cottage attached to the pub, with independent access, provides accommodation for up to six people.
DOUBLE ROOM: from £20 to £30
SINGLE ROOM: from £25 to £35
FOOD: up to £15
Hours: lunch 12noon–2pm, dinner 6.30pm–9pm, closed Monday from October until Easter.
Cuisine: ENGLISH – well known for home-made pies and local fish. Children are welcome in the pub and dining room up till 8.30pm.
Cards: Visa, Access.
Other points: licensed, Sunday lunch, children catered for (please check for age limits), coaches by prior arrangement, limited disabled access.
Rooms: 2 double rooms, 1 twin room.
Directions: on B6353 between Coldstream and Holy Island.
ANNE & TOM GRUNDY ☎ (01289) 388228.

THE CAT INN
Cheswick, TD15 2RL

The Cat Inn is situated on the A1, four miles south of Berwick-on-Tweed, a Border town of great architectural diversity. Offering superb en suite accommodation and beautifully cooked meals, it is surrounded by open fields and is just 1½ miles from the sea. Close to excellent golfing and fishing facilities.
DOUBLE ROOM: up to £20
FOOD: up to £15
Hours: breakfast 9am–11am, closed Sunday afternoon 3pm–7pm, restaurant open all day.
Cuisine: ENGLISH.

Other points: licensed.
Directions: on the A1, 4 miles south of Berwick-upon-Tweed.
MR W.L. KEITH ☎ (01289) 387251
[Fax] (01289) 387251.

CORNHILL-ON-TWEED • map 16E6

TILLMOUTH PARK HOTEL
TD12 4UU

A country house hotel set in extensive grounds, with very comfortable surroundings, and food and accommodation of a high standard.
DOUBLE ROOM: from £40 to £50
FOOD: up to £15
Hours: breakfast 8am–9.45am, lunch 12.30am–2pm, dinner 7.30pm–9.30pm.
Cuisine: ENGLISH – Tweed salmon, local pheasant, Cheviot lamb.
Cards: Visa, Access, Diners, AmEx.
Other points: Sunday lunch, children welcome, pets allowed.
Rooms: 1 single room, 6 double rooms, 6 twin rooms, 1 family room. All with TV, radio, alarm, telephone, tea/coffee-making facilities.
Directions: on A698 Cornhill to Berwick-on-Tweed road. 3 miles from main A697.
R.M. DOLLERY ☎ (01890) 882255
[Fax] (01890) 882540.

WARK FARM HOUSE
Wark, TD12 4RE

This country house stands 200 yards from the pictuesque south bank of the River Tweed, set in two acres of garden, with views of the Cheviots to the south. You will be made to feel at home in spacious, comfortable accommodation, which is tastefully furnished and centrally heated. Conveniently located for Floors Castle, Paxton House, Chillingham Castle and many other places of interest.
DOUBLE ROOM: from £20 to £30
SINGLE ROOM: up to £25
Hours: breakfast 8am–9am.
Cuisine: ENGLISH – fresh local fare, imaginatively prepared and cooked. Evening meal up to £15.
Cards: Visa, Access, Diners, AmEx.
Other points: parking, children welcome, no-smoking, pets allowed, residents' lounge, garden, vegetarian meals, licensed.
Rooms: 2 single rooms, 2 twin rooms.
Directions: A697 to Cornhill-on-Tweed; B6350 is opposite Collingwood Arms and is signposted Wark and Carham. Wark Farm House is the first house on the right in Wark village.
DAVID & SHEILA HOGG ☎ (01890) 883570.

HADRIAN'S WALL • map 11B3

VALLUM LODGE
Military Road, Twice Brewed,
near Bardon Mill, NE47 7AN

Vallum Lodge Hotel is situated in peaceful countryside close to Hadrian's Wall on the edge of the Northumberland National Park. A warm welcome

always awaits from resident proprietors Jack and Christine Wright. There is a particular emphasis on cleanliness, comfort, relaxation and value for money, complemented by good, freshly-prepared food and appealing, newly decorated surroundings.
DOUBLE ROOM: from £20 to £30
SINGLE ROOM: up to £25
FOOD: up to £15
Hours: breakfast 8am–9am, dinner 7pm–8pm, closed December until January (inclusive).
Cuisine: ENGLISH – fresh home-cooking.
Other points: parking, no-smoking area, residents' lounge, garden, vegetarian meals.
Rooms: 7 bedrooms. All with radio, alarm, tea/coffee-making facilities.
Directions: 500 yards west of Once Brewed National Park Visitors' Centre on B6318.
MR & MRS WRIGHT ☎ (01434) 344248.

HEXHAM • map 11B3

BEAUMONT HOTEL
Beaumont Street, NE46 3LT
A busy, family-run hotel incorporating a wine bar and cocktail bar, the Park Restaurant and conference facilities. Close to the centre of this historic market town in the heart of Northumbria, the Beaumont is a popular hotel with tourists and businessmen.
DOUBLE ROOM: from £40 to £50
SINGLE ROOM: from £45 to £55
FOOD: from £15 to £20 [CLUB]
Hours: breakfast 7.30am–9.45am, lunch 12noon–2pm, bar meals 12noon–2pm, dinner 7pm–9.15pm, closed Christmas day and New Year's day.
Cuisine: FRENCH – steaks, pheasant, guinea fowl, lamb.
Cards: Visa, Access, Diners, AmEx.
Other points: licensed, Sunday lunch, children welcome, lift, baby-listening device, baby-sitting, cots, 24hr reception, parking, vegetarian meals, residents' bar, residents' lounge.
Rooms: 6 single rooms, 11 double rooms, 5 twin rooms, 1 family room. All with TV, radio, telephone, tea/coffee making facilities.
Directions: on the A69 overlooking the abbey and the park in the town centre.
MARTIN & LINDA OWEN ☎ (01434) 602331
[Fax] (01434) 602331.

COUNTY HOTEL
Priestpopple, NE46 1PS
A homely hotel, privately run by real Northumbrians who understand the meaning of real hospitality. Its old-fashioned atmosphere provides a warm, relaxing and comfortable retreat. Conveniently situated between train and bus stations.
DOUBLE ROOM: from £20 to £30
FOOD: up to £15
Hours: meals all day 7.30am–10pm, lunch 12.05pm–2.15pm, dinner 7pm–9.30pm.
Cuisine: ENGLISH – fresh, traditional British dishes.
Cards: Visa, Access, AmEx.
Other points: licensed, Sunday lunch, children welcome, coaches by prior arrangement, children welcome, baby-listening device, baby-sitting, cots, 24hr reception.

Rooms: 2 single rooms, 4 double rooms, 3 twin rooms. All TV, radio, telephone, tea/coffee-making facilities.
Directions: from A69, follow signs to Hexham. The hotel is on the main street.
MR KEN WATTS ☎ (01434) 602030.

LANGLEY CASTLE HOTEL
Langley on Tyne, NE47 5LU
Set in 10 acres of lush, mowed lawns surrounded by woodland, this fascinating 14th century castle combines contemporary conveniences with authentic reminiscences of yesteryear. The food is cooked to an extremely high standard and beautifully presented, with attention to detail. The spacious surroundings and sense of history make this a glorious setting for any visit.
DOUBLE ROOM: from £40 to £50
SINGLE ROOM: from £45 to £55
FOOD: from £15 to £20
Hours: breakfast 8am–9.30am, lunch 12noon–2pm dinner 7pm 9pm, bar meals 12noon 2pm.
Cuisine: FRENCH – imaginative menu, including daily specialities.
Cards: Visa, Access, Diners, AmEx.
Other points: licensed, Sunday lunch, afternoon tea, pets allowed, residents' lounge, children welcome, baby-listening device, cots.
Rooms: 6 double rooms, 2 twin rooms. All with TV, radio, alarm, telephone, tea/coffee-making facilities.
Directions: follow the A69 to Haydon Bridge, then A686 1½ miles to Langley.
ANTON PHILLIPS ☎ (01434) 688888
[Fax] (01434) 684019.

OTTERBURN • map 11A3

OTTERBURN TOWER HOTEL
Otterburn, NE19 1NP
An adapted, spacious, castellated country house in extensive grounds. Three-course menu and bar meals are offered in the traditionally furnished and wood-panelled dining room and lounges. Steeped in history – the hotel is reputedly haunted! Private fishing on 3½ miles of the River Rede.
DOUBLE ROOM: from £30 to £40
FOOD: up to £15 [CLUB]
Hours: open all day.
Cuisine: ENGLISH.
Cards: Visa, Access, Diners, AmEx.
Other points: Sunday lunch, children welcome, garden.
Directions: the entrance to the hotel is at the junction of the A696 and B6320.
PETER HARDING ☎ (01830) 20620.

ROTHBURY • map 12A4

COQUET VALE HOTEL
Station Road, NE65 7QW
A Victorian-type building constructed for the railways, it was previously called the Station Hotel. Situated on B6341, this hotel is very well placed for north/south travellers and for those wanting to

discover the delights of the area and the Borders.
DOUBLE ROOM: from £20 to £30
FOOD: from £15 to £20
Hours: breakfast 7.30am–9.30am, lunch 12noon–2pm, dinner 7pm–9pm.
Cuisine: ENGLISH / FRENCH – real Yorkshire pudding with onion gravy and baked halibut and salmon parcels. Pan-fried collops of venison.
Cards: Visa, Access.
Other points: open-air dining, Sunday lunch, children welcome, coaches by prior arrangement
Rooms: 4 double rooms, 14 twin rooms, 1 family room.
Directions: on the B6341.
JAMES M. CORRISH ☎ (01669) 20305
Fax (01669) 21500.

LES ROUTIERS ACCOMMODATION DIRECTORY

This handy directory is ideal for those looking for somewhere to stay at great value.
It lists a huge choice of *Les Routiers*-recommended places throughout the British Isles offering comfortable accommodation, good food and a warm welcome amid relaxed surroundings.

Available from selected
Les Routiers establishments
or direct from the publishers.

Price £2

SEAHOUSES • map 12A4

BEACH HOUSE HOTEL
Seafront, NE68 7SR

A small, friendly, family-run hotel, pleasantly situated overlooking the Farne Islands. The Beach House Hotel specializes in imaginative home-cooking and baking. Particularly suited to those looking for a quiet and comfortable holiday.
DOUBLE ROOM: from £30 to £40
SINGLE ROOM: from £35 to £45
FOOD: from £15 to £20
Hours: breakfast 8.30am–9.30am, dinner 7pm–8.30pm, closed November until March.
Cuisine: ENGLISH – local produce, e.g., game and fish including local kippers. Clootie dumpling.
Cards: Visa, Access.
Other points: licensed, no-smoking area, children welcome.
Directions: on the Seahouses to Bamburgh road.
MR & MRS F.R. CRAIGS ☎ (01665) 720337
Fax (01665) 720921.

THE LODGE
146 Main Street, NE68 7UA

The falcon sign of this small hotel makes it easy to spot. Styled along Scandinavian lines, with pine panelling and furniture throughout. Relaxing by the open fire in the convivial bar makes a perfect end to a day exploring this historic and beautiful area.

DOUBLE ROOM: from £20 to £30
SINGLE ROOM: from £25 to £35
FOOD: up to £15 CLUB
Hours: breakfast 8.30am–9.30am, lunch 12noon–2pm, dinner 6.30pm–9.30pm.
Cuisine: ENGLISH / SEAFOOD – local seafood.
Cards: Visa, Access, AmEx.
Other points: Sunday lunch, children catered for (please check for age limits), pets by prior arrangement, disabled access, vegetarian meals.
Rooms: 4 double rooms, 1 family room. All with TV, tea/coffee-making facilities.
Directions: on the main street in Seahouses (North Sunderland).
SELBY & JENIFER BROWN ☎ (01665) 720158.

ST AIDEN HOTEL & RESTAURANT
Seafront, Seahouses

Built of local sandstone, the St Aidan Hotel boasts an unrivalled position on the seafront of the spectacular Northumbrian coastline, just a short distance from the bustling fishing village of Seahouses. The well-appointed bedrooms have beautiful views, some towards the harbour, some towards the Farne Islands, Bamburgh Castle and Holy Island. A warm, welcoming atmosphere prevails.
DOUBLE ROOM: from £30 to £40
FOOD: up to £15
Hours: breakfast 8am–9.30am, dinner 6.30pm–8pm.
Cuisine: ENGLISH / INTERNATIONAL.
Cards: Visa, Access, Diners, AmEx.
Other points: children welcome, parking, limited disabled access, pets allowed, residents' lounge, garden, vegetarian meals.
Rooms: 9 bedrooms. All with en suite, TV, tea/coffee-making facilities.
Directions: 400 meters along seafront towards Bamburgh (next to filling station).
MR F. FORD-HUTCHINSON ☎ (01665) 720355 Fax (01665) 830333.

WARKWORTH • map 12A4

THE JACKDAW RESTAURANT
34 Castle Street, NE65 0UN

Attractive cottage-restaurant with a friendly atmosphere and home-cooking with locally purchased produce. The à la carte menu features a wide selection of traditional dishes, including mouthwatering sweets prepared daily. The menus change frequently. The fixed-price Sunday lunch is deservedly very popular.
FOOD: up to £15 CLUB
Hours: lunch 12.30am–2pm, dinner 7pm–9pm, closed Sunday evening, all day Monday, Thursday evening and January until mid-February.
Cuisine: ENGLISH – menu changes for lunch and dinner. All dishes are home-made.
Cards: Visa, Access, AmEx.
Other points: licensed, Sunday lunch, no-smoking area, children welcome, open bank holidays, morning coffee, afternoon tea.
Directions: 7 miles south of Alnwick on A1068 coast road.
RUPERT & GILLIAN BELL ☎ (01665) 711488.

SOUTH YORKSHIRE

DONCASTER • map 9A2

THE REGENT HOTEL, PARADE BAR & RESTAURANT
Regent Square, DN1 2DS
Established under the same family ownership for 60 years, this handsome town-centre Victorian building has the unique advantage of being situated in a small Regency park on the A638. Close to Doncaster racecourse and an ideal stopping place when travelling north or south.
DOUBLE ROOM: from £30 to £40
SINGLE ROOM: from £45 to £55
FOOD: from £15 to £20 [CLUB]
Hours: breakfast 7.30am–9am, lunch 12noon–2pm, dinner 6pm–10pm.
Cuisine: INTERNATIONAL – wide choice of menus and dishes includes table d'hôte, à la carte, steak house menu, Sunday lunch, Tapas and vegetarian dishes. Giant menu.
Cards: Visa, Access, Diners, AmEx.
Other points: licensed, Sunday lunch, children welcome, coaches by prior arrangement.
Directions: on the main A638 road through Doncaster.
MICHAEL LONGWORTH ☎ (01302) 364180.

ROTHERHAM • map 9A2

BRECON HOTEL
Moorgate Road, S60 2AY
A small, family-run hotel where you will find true Yorkshire hospitality. The restaurant enjoys a good reputation locally for its quality, generous portions and friendliness of service. With its good food, comfortable accommodation, welcoming service and value for money, Brecon Hotel is highly recommended.
DOUBLE ROOM: from £20 to £30
FOOD: up to £15 [CLUB]
Hours: breakfast 7.30am–9.30am, lunch 12noon–2pm, dinner 7pm–9.15pm.
Cuisine: ENGLISH – dishes may include beef stroganoff, roast chicken grand-mère, lamb cutlets with rosemary, salmon hollandaise. Bar meals. Traditional Sunday lunch.
Cards: Visa, Access, Diners, AmEx.
Other points: licensed, children welcome, pets allowed.
Rooms: 2 single rooms, 13 double rooms, 27 twin rooms.
Directions: off M1 junction 33. Half a mile past Rotherham General Hospital on A618.
DUNCAN CARR ☎ (01709) 828811
[Fax] (01709) 820213

THE ELTON HOTEL
Main Street, Bramley, S66 0SF
Situated only four miles from Rotherham, this is a popular spot for local business people at lunchtime and evening. The M18 is only half a mile away and the M1 and A1 are nearby, making this an ideal stopover for travellers. Catering also available for private functions, conferences and receptions. Winner of 'Rotherham in Bloom'.
DOUBLE ROOM: from £30 to £40
SINGLE ROOM: from £45 to £55
FOOD: from £15 to £20 [CLUB]
Hours: breakfast 7.15am–9am, lunch 12noon–2pm, Sunday 12noon–3.30pm, dinner 7pm–9.30pm.
Cuisine: ENGLISH / FRENCH.
Cards: Visa, Access, Diners, AmEx.
Other points: licensed, Sunday lunch, children welcome, baby-listening device, cots, 24hr reception, special weekend rates.
Rooms: 9 single rooms, 16 double rooms, 4 twin rooms. All with en suite, TV, radio, telephone, tea/coffee-making facilities.
Directions: M18 junction 1. From A631 in Bramley, take Ravenfield turn B6093, first left.
PETER & WYNA KEARY ☎ (01709) 545681
[Fax] (01709) 549100.

SHEFFIELD • map 9A2

HENRY'S CAFE BAR (SHEFFIELD)
Cambridge Street
A lively, popular café-bar serving an extensive range of international fast-food, American and non-alcoholic beers and speciality cocktails. The atmosphere is friendly and bustling.
FOOD: up to £15
Hours: meals all day 8am–7pm, closed Sunday.
Cuisine: INTERNATIONAL.
Cards: Visa, Access.
Other points: children welcome, open bank holidays, no-smoking area, afternoon teas, disabled access, vegetarian meals.
ALISTAIR AMIR ☎ (0114) 2752342.

THE OLD SIDINGS
91 Chesterfield Road, Dronfield, S18 6XE
An attractive Victorian pub with railway memorabilia throughout the Waiting Room lounge and Buffet Car dining room. Within the comfortable and welcoming surroundings there is a good choice of bar meals and snacks, lunchtime and evening, in both lounge and dining room, with the emphasis on traditional, country-style, home-made fare.
FOOD: up to £15
Hours: lunch 12noon–2.30pm, dinner 6pm–9.30pm.
Cuisine: ENGLISH – predominantly English. House speciality: Anne's home-made giant Yorkshire pudding. Large rump steaks. A large selection of vegetarian meals. Family budget menus and children's menu.
Cards: Visa, Access.
Other points: licensed, Sunday lunch, no-smoking area, children welcome, pets allowed, beer garden.
Directions: off main A61 on B6057. Next to only railway bridge in Dronfield.
WILLIAM & ANNE STANAWAY ☎ (01246) 410023.

NORTHERN ENGLAND • TYNE & WEAR

WESTBOURNE HOUSE HOTEL
25 Westbourne Road, S10 2QQ
A memorable, inexpensive country-house-style hotel offering a warm and friendly atmosphere, set in authentic period surroundings with beautiful gardens. The hotel is situated in a conservation area, close to the city centre and only a short walk from the universities, main hospitals and Botanical Gardens. Every room is furnished with antiques and decorated in Georgian, Victorian or Edwardian style.
DOUBLE ROOM: from £20 to £30
Hours: breakfast 7.30am–9am.
Cards: Visa, Access, AmEx.
Other points: parking, children welcome, pets allowed, residents' lounge, garden, vegetarian meals.
Rooms: 11 bedrooms. All with TV, radio, alarm, hair dryer, trouser-press, iron, tea/coffee-making facilities.
Directions: less than a mile south-west of the city centre, off A57 to Glossop.
MARY & MICHALL PRATT ☎ (0114) 2660109
[Fax] (0114) 2667778.

ZING VAA RESTAURANT
55 The Moor, S1 4PF
Genuine Cantonese dishes and atmosphere. Situated in the very heart of Sheffield's busy shopping area. Very popular with both locals, shoppers and business people. Parking is available at the rear of the restaurant.
FOOD: from £15 to £20
Hours: meals all day 12noon–11.45pm, closed Christmas day.
Cuisine: CANTONESE / PEKINESE – Cantonese and Peking cuisine, sliced fillet with king prawns marinated and cooked in a fruity sauce, duckling dishes.
Cards: Visa, Access, Diners, AmEx.
Other points: licensed, Sunday lunch, children welcome, parking.
Directions: situated in the heart of Sheffield shopping centre, opposite the bandstand.
ROGER CHEUNG ☎ (0114) 2722432
[Fax] (0114) 2729213.

TYNE & WEAR

GATESHEAD • map 12B4

BEAMISH PARK HOTEL
Beamish Burn Road, Marley Hill, NE16 5EG
Surrounded by some of the finest north-eastern heritage, the Beamish Park Hotel offers a perfect blend of food and accommodation in relaxing and comfortable surroundings. It is convenient for visiting the Beamish North of England Open Air Museum, the Metro Centre, Metroland, and Newcastle city centre. Perfect for an overnight stay or family break.
DOUBLE ROOM: up to £20
FOOD: up to £15
Hours: breakfast 7.30am–9.30am, lunch 12noon–2.30pm, dinner 7pm–10.15pm.
Cuisine: ENGLISH – à la carte and table d'hôte. Extensive choice of blackboard specials. Dishes include poached fillet of salmon, grilled duck breast, roast English lamb.
Cards: Visa, Access, Diners, AmEx.
Other points: licensed, Sunday lunch, children welcome, open bank holidays, parking, baby-sitting, cots, 24hr reception, foreign exchange.
Rooms: 9 single rooms, 24 double rooms, 4 twin rooms. All with TV, radio, telephone, tea/coffee-making facilities.

Directions: A1 to Chester-le-Street, then Stanley, taking A6076 to Gateshead.
WILLIAM WALKER ☎ (01207) 230666
[Fax] (01207) 281260.

NEWCASTLE-UPON-TYNE map 12B4

THE BLACK BULL
Matfen, NE20 0RP
Situated in the picturesque Northumbrian village of Matfen, deep in Hadrian's Wall country, this 200-year-old inn is a delight to visit, whatever the occasion. Sit outside and enjoy the scenery in summer, or experience the low beams and log fires in winter: whatever the season, you are guaranteed an intimate atmosphere and a warm welcome in this most traditional of country inns. Whether enjoying a quiet drink, staying for lunch or dinner in the à la carte restaurant or for a romantic weekend in one of the luxurious bedrooms, the Black Bull, with its view over the river and the village green, is a real find.
DOUBLE ROOM: from £20 to £30
SINGLE ROOM: from £25 to £35
FOOD: up to £15
Hours: breakfast 7.30am–9am (residents only), lunch 12noon–2pm, bar meals 12noon–2pm, dinner 7pm–9.30pm, bar meals 6.30pm–9pm.
Cuisine: ENGLISH – predominantly English, but with a wide variety of continental and vegetarian dishes and an excellent wine list.
Cards: Visa, Access, AmEx.
Other points: licensed, open-air dining, Sunday lunch, children welcome, disabled access, parking, garden, open bank holidays.

Rooms: 3 double rooms. All with TV, radio, tea/coffee-making facilities.
Directions: leave A69 at Corbridge to join B6318. 2 miles north of this road (follow signposts for Maften).
COLIN & MICHELE SCOTT ☎ (01661) 886330.

THE FERNCOURT HOTEL
34 Osborne Road, Jesmond, NE2 2AJ

An attractive, spacious hotel, with easy access to Hadrian's Wall and other local tourist attractions. Pleasant surroundings, comfortably furnished to appeal to business executives and holiday-makers alike. Well-prepared Tex-Mex food, attractively presented in a lively atmosphere. English Tourist Board 3 Crown Commended.
DOUBLE ROOM: from £20 to £30
FOOD: up to £15
Hours: breakfast 7am–9am, dinner (weekdays) 6.30pm–10.30pm, open all year.
Cuisine: TEX-MEX – large and varied menu, featuring authentic Texan and Mexican food; table d'hôte menu available weekdays.
Cards: Visa, Access, Diners, AmEx.
Other points: licensed, children welcome, vegetarian meals, pets allowed, parking.
Rooms: 1 single room, 3 double rooms, 10 twin rooms, 3 family rooms. All with TV, tea/coffee-making facilities.
Directions: off the A1058, left at roundabout onto Osborne Road.
MR CLARK ☎ (0191) 281 5418/281 5377 [Fax] (0191) 212 0783.

SACHINS
Forth Banks, NE1 3SG

An authentic Punjabi restaurant in a Grade II listed building situated at the head of the Forth Banks close to the River Tyne. The menu offers a range of speciality Punjabi dishes, flavoured with the freshest of produce with the delicate aromas of herbs and spices, prepared by one of the top Punjabi chefs in Britain. The atmosphere is relaxed and comfortable.
FOOD: from £15 to £20
Hours: lunch 12noon–2.15pm, dinner 6pm–11.15pm, closed Sunday.
Cuisine: PUNJABI – the fine menu offers a splendid array of the most exotic and enticing dishes.
Cards: Visa, Access, Diners, AmEx.
Other points: parking, children welcome, vegetarian meals, licensed.
Directions: easy to find behind the Central Station.
DINESH RAWLEY ☎ (0191) 261 9035/232 4660.

SURTEES HOTEL / WINGS RESTAURANT
12–16 Dean Street, NE1 1PG

A 100-year-old building which has been lovingly restored to its former glory, providing visitors to the city of Newcastle with a high degree of comfort, elegance and charm. Each one of the 27 beautifully decorated bedrooms has been individually and tastefully decorated to give a homely touch. Below the hotel is Wings Restaurant, which has been transformed into Newcastle's most interesting theme eatery, with an abundance of aeroplanes from ceiling to carpet. There are rooms which can be hired for meetings, full fax facilities and supervised car parking: everything you would expect from a first-class hotel.
DOUBLE ROOM: from £30 to £40
SINGLE ROOM: from £35 to £45
FOOD: up to £15
Hours: meals 5pm–11pm, meals all day (Saturday and Sunday) 8am–11pm.
Cuisine: INTERNATIONAL – Italian, French, American, Mexican, Oriental.
Cards: Visa, Access, Diners, AmEx, Switch.
Other points: licensed, Sunday lunch, children welcome, coaches by prior arrangement, functions.
Rooms: 12 single rooms, 9 double rooms, 6 twin rooms.
Directions: first exit off the Tyne Bridge, left and left again into Dean Street.
BRIAN MACKAY & JOHN MONK ☎ (0191) 261 7771 [Fax] (0191) 230 1322.

SOUTH SHIELDS • map 12B4

SEA HOTEL
Sea Road, NE33 2LD

This busy hotel is situated on the sea front in the heart of 'Catherine Cookson Country'. The hospitality, for which the region is renowned, is reflected in the friendly service.
DOUBLE ROOM: from £30 to £40
SINGLE ROOM: from £55
FOOD: up to £15
Hours: breakfast 7am–9.30am, lunch 12noon–2.30pm, dinner 7pm–9.30pm.
Cuisine: ENGLISH – traditional English menu using local produce and a French-based à la carte menu, both offering a wide choice of dishes.
Cards: Visa, Access, Diners, AmEx.
Other points: Sunday lunch, children welcome.
Rooms: 14 single rooms, 12 double rooms, 7 twin rooms.
Directions: on the seafront at A183 and A1018 junction.
MR JAMES, MR BASSETT & MR WATSON
☎ (0191) 427 0999 [Fax] (0191) 454 0500.

SUNDERLAND • map 12B4

MOWBRAY PARK HOTEL
Borough Road, SR1 1PR

A family-run private hotel located within five minutes' walk of the railway station, business and shopping areas and backing onto one of Sunderland's most impressive parks. The restaurant offers good food, well presented and at good value for money. Ideal for either a simple business lunch or for that special occasion.
DOUBLE ROOM: from £30 to £40

273

SINGLE ROOM: from £35 to £45
FOOD: from £15 to £20
Hours: breakfast 7am–10am, bar meals 12noon–2pm, dinner 7pm–10pm.
Cuisine: ENGLISH / CHINESE.
Cards: Visa, Access, Diners, AmEx.
Other points: licensed, Sunday lunch, children welcome, afternoon tea, pets allowed, residents' lounge, functions, conferences.
Rooms: 51 bedrooms.
Directions: centre of Sunderland, next to Mowbray Park, town museum and library.
EDWARD HUGHES ☎ (0191) 567 8221.

DISCOVER FRANCE FOR ONLY £9.99!

The *Les Routiers Guide to France* is the only official fully translated guide to the French *Routiers*, listing over 1,600 recommended restaurants, cafés and hotels throughout this alluring country.

Available from all good bookshops, or direct from the publishers, price £9.99.

THE PULLMAN LODGE HOTEL
Whitburn Road, Seaburn, SR6 8AA

A real dream for railway enthusiasts, this privately-owned and personally-run modern hotel is built in unique railway style, offering the visitor every modern convenience. It is situated on one of the north-east's most unspoilt beaches, close to some of Northumbria's finest heritage sites. Enjoy a drink in the Station Bar before retreating to the well-appointed Carriage Restaurant overlooking the rugged coastline, where you can choose from an à la carte menu using only the freshest produce and cooked to perfection. The Pullman also offers a complete wedding package, along with extensive conference and private function facilities.
DOUBLE ROOM: from £20 to £30
FOOD: up to £15 CLUB
Hours: breakfast 7am–10am, bar meals 12noon–3pm, dinner 7pm–10pm, bar meals 7pm–10pm.
Cuisine: ENGLISH – a range of choices on à la carte, table d'hôte menu and bar menu.
Cards: Visa, Access, Diners, AmEx.
Other points: parking, children welcome, Sunday lunch, open bank holidays, weekend breaks, disabled access, pets allowed, residents' lounge, vegetarian meals.
Rooms: 16 twin rooms, 8 family rooms with TV, radio, alarm, telephone, tea/coffee-making facilities.
DERRICK & PAULINE HARDY ☎ (0191) 529 2020 Fax (0191) 529 2077.

WHITLEY BAY • map 12B4

BRUNO'S RESTAURANTE ITALIANO
5 Victoria Crescent, Cullercoats, NE30 4PN

A lively Italian restaurant, popular with locals and holiday-makers because of the fine food and fun atmosphere. It is recommended you book for evening meals, as the restaurant does get very busy.
FOOD: from £20 to £25
Hours: dinner 6pm–11pm, closed Sunday.
Cuisine: ITALIAN – pizza, pasta, steaks and chicken dishes are among the house specialities.
Cards: Visa, Access.
Other points: children welcome, parking, disabled access, vegetarian meals.
Directions: on Cullercoats seafront overlooking Cullercoats Bay.
BRUNO & SUZY DIGENNARO ☎ (0191) 251 3065.

THE GRANGE RESTAURANT
East Holywell, NE27 0JJ

An 18th century farmhouse, which has been sympathetically extended to provide a relaxing, comfortable restaurant. Diners can choose from an extensive à la carte menu, created by one of the North's leading chefs, who uses only the freshest of local produce. Pre-dinner drinks can be enjoyed in the cocktail lounge. An excellent wine list is also available.
FOOD: from £20 to £25
Hours: lunch 11am–2pm, dinner 7pm–11pm, closed Sunday evening and Monday.
Cuisine: ENGLISH.
Cards: Visa, Access, Diners, AmEx.
Other points: parking, children welcome, disabled access, residents' lounge, vegetarian meals, Sunday lunch, open bank holidays.
Directions: near Earsdon village, Whitley Bay.
LYNN WAGNER ☎ (0191) 252 6980
Fax (0191) 252 0980.

YORK HOUSE HOTEL
30 Park Parade, NE26 1DX

A family-run hotel offering comfort, home-cooking and good service in a friendly atmosphere. A mid-terrace Victorian building in the town centre, the hotel is ideally situated for safe, sandy beaches, parks, indoor leisure pool and the shopping centre. Much thought has been given to the comfort of their guests, whether families on holiday or business people travelling in the area.
DOUBLE ROOM: up to £20
FOOD: up to £15
Hours: breakfast 7am–9.30am, dinner 6pm–7pm.
Cuisine: ENGLISH.
Cards: Visa, Access, AmEx.
Other points: 24hr reception, lounge, central heating, children welcome, baby-sitting, cots, disabled access.
Rooms: 1 single room, 3 double rooms, 2 twin rooms, 2 family rooms. All with TV, radio, alarm, telephone, tea/coffee-making facilities.
Directions: off A193 Park Avenue.
JUDY & MICHAEL RUDDY ☎ (0191) 252 8313 Fax (0191) 251 3953.

WEST YORKSHIRE

BINGLEY • map 12E4

OAKWOOD HALL HOTEL
Lady Lane, BD16 4AW
A family-run hotel set in a quiet woodland. The decor of the hotel is of a very high standard, with furnishings of great taste. A relaxed place to visit, serving superb food with unusual starters and sweets.
DOUBLE ROOM: from £30 to £40
SINGLE ROOM: from £35 to £45
FOOD: up to £15 [CLUB]
Hours: breakfast 7.30am–9.30am, lunch (except Sunday) 12noon–2pm, lunch Sunday 12.30am–2pm, dinner 7.30pm–9.30pm.
Cuisine: ENGLISH – à la carte menu, fixed three-course menu, bar meals and bar snacks.
Cards: Visa, Access, Diners, AmEx.
Other points: Sunday lunch, children welcome, garden, pets allowed, conferences, functions.
Rooms: 20 bedrooms.
Directions: off A650.
MRS K. BRASSINGTON ☎ (01274) 564123
[Fax] (01274) 561477.

ELLAND • map 9A1

BERTIES BISTRO
7–10 Town Hall, HX5 0EU
All menus and wine lists are on blackboards, which change every week. Fresh produce is always used, and the result is an excellent standard of well-cooked and presented food.
FOOD: up to £15
Hours: dinner 7pm–10.30pm, Saturday 6.30pm–11pm, Sunday 5pm–9pm, closed Monday.
Cuisine: ENGLISH / CONTINENTAL – salad of smoked turkey and quail eggs; tartlette of mushrooms, scallops and dill; griddled lamb steak with fresh basil and Berties bombe.
Other points: licensed, children welcome, parking.
Directions: Elland is 1 mile from exit 24 on the M62, next to the town hall.
MR G. BRETT WOODWARD ☎ (01422) 371724 [Fax] (01422) 372830.

HALIFAX • map 12E4

COLLYERS HOTEL
Burnley Road, Luddendenfoot, HX2 6AH
A former Victorian stone-built mill-owner's house, beautifully refurbished and overlooking the Calder Valley. Both accommodation and food are of a superb standard, the inspector remarking that it would be 'a pleasure to return'. Everything is beautifully clean, with pot pourri, plants and paintings adding to the charm of the furnishings. Friendly atmosphere.
DOUBLE ROOM: from £20 to £30
SINGLE ROOM: up to £25
FOOD: up to £15 [CLUB] ★
Hours: breakfast weekdays 7.30am–9am, weekends 8.30am–9.30am, morning coffee 10.30am–12noon, bar meals 12noon–2pm, lunch 12noon–2pm, afternoon tea 3.30pm–5pm, dinner 7pm–12midnight, last orders 9pm.
Cuisine: MODERN ENGLISH – à la carte menu includes dishes such as pork fillet in wine and coriander, scallops and scampi with basil and fillet steak Florentine. Vegetarian selection. Good wine list.
Cards: Visa, Access, Diners, AmEx.
Other points: Sunday lunch, children welcome, pets allowed, afternoon tea, baby-sitting, baby-listening device, cots, left luggage, residents' bar and lounge, parking, disabled access.
Rooms: 2 single rooms, 2 double rooms, 2 twin rooms. All with colour TV, radio, telephone, tea/coffee-making facilities, hair dryer. Most en suite.
Directions: leave M62 at exit 22 or 24, then to Sowerby Bridge, follow signs Burnley A646 to Luddendenfoot. Hotel on A646 in centre of village.
D.F. NORTHEY & N.A. SKELTON ☎ (01422) 882624 [Fax] (01422) 883897.

DUKE OF YORK INN
Brighouse & Denholmegate Road, Stone Chair, HX3 7LN
A former 17th century coaching inn, this establishment lavishly displays pots and pans from the ceiling. Tasty meals at value-for-money prices and a wide range of ales, spirits and malt whiskies are offered. Friendly, efficient staff help create the relaxed atmosphere, which is enjoyed by all ages.
DOUBLE ROOM: from £20 to £30
FOOD: up to £15
Hours: breakfast 7am–9am, lunch 12noon–2pm, dinner 5pm–9pm.
Cuisine: ENGLISH – home-cooked food, wide and varied menu. Daily specials.
Cards: Visa.
Other points: licensed, open-air dining, Sunday lunch, children welcome.
Rooms: 1 single room, 7 double rooms, 2 twin rooms, 2 family rooms. All with TV, tea/coffee making facilities, iron.
Directions: between Bradford and Halifax, 2 miles from M62 on main Howarth road.
STEPHEN WHITAKER ☎ (01422) 202056 [Fax] (01422) 206618.

IMPERIAL CROWN HOTEL
42–46 Horton Street, HX1 1BR
The hotel is under the personal supervision of the proprietors who, together with the local staff, take every care to look after their guests' comforts and needs. Within the atmosphere of informality and friendliness, the hotel provides an excellent standard of both food and accommodation. Well situated in the heart of historic Halifax. Extensive facilities for functions.
DOUBLE ROOM: from £30 to £40

SINGLE ROOM: from £45 to £55
FOOD: from £15 to £20
Hours: breakfast 7am–9am, bar snacks 5pm–10pm, dinner 7pm–10pm.
Cuisine: FRENCH – excellent French cuisine, à la carte and table d'hôte menus.
Cards: Visa, Access, Diners, AmEx.
Other points: licensed, Sunday lunch, children welcome, residents' lounge, functions, conferences.
Rooms: 26 single rooms, 4 double rooms, 6 twin rooms, 2 family rooms, 1 bridal suite, 2 executive suites.
Directions: M62 junction 24. Directly opposite main railway station in Halifax.
C. & C.H. TURCZAK ☎ (01422) 342342
Fax (01422) 349866.

ROCK INN HOTEL & CHURCHILL'S RESTAURANT
Holywell Green, HX4 9BS

A 17th century inn set in rural surroundings, recently refurbished to include large conservatory and patio areas. Open all day, every day. Close to Elland and Bradley Hall golf courses, with 'Last Of The Summer Wine' country just a few miles away. Ideal facilities for conferences and receptions, accommodating 160 people in comfort; choice of suites for smaller parties.
DOUBLE ROOM: from £30 to £40
FOOD: up to £15
Hours: breakfast 7am–9am, meals all day 12noon–10pm.
Cuisine: ENGLISH – steak à la Churchill's and traditional Sunday lunch.
Cards: Visa, Access, Diners, AmEx.
Other points: Sunday lunch, children welcome, pets allowed, vegetarian meals, residents' bar, residents' lounge, disabled access.
Rooms: 14 double rooms, 2 twin rooms, 1 triple room, 1 family room. All with satellite TV, radio, alarm, bar, telephone, tea/coffee-making facilities, hair dryer, trouser-press.
Directions: situated 1½ miles from junction 24 on the M62.
ROBERT VINSEN ☎ (01422) 379721
Fax (01422) 379110.

THE TREASURE HOUSE
Newlands Gate, Warley, HX2 7SU

Interestingly, the restaurant is four farmhouse cottages converted to become the attractive, spacious restaurant that it now is. The appealing interior provides diners with comfortable, relaxed surroundings to enjoy a fabulous meal and sample one of the many fine wines. The Treasure House is set in beautiful countryside, just 5 minutes from Halifax.
FOOD: from £15 to £20
Hours: lunch 12noon–2pm, dinner 7pm–10pm, check opening times in February and March.
Cuisine: ENGLISH / FRENCH – regularly changing menu. Good use of fresh local produce.
Cards: Visa, Access, AmEx, Switch, Delta.
Other points: parking, children welcome, vegetarian meals, traditional Sunday lunch.
Directions: take the Burnley road from Halifax and turn right into Windle Royd Lane, followed by Stocks Lane, into Warley Village.
GEOFFREY & SUSAN HODGSON ☎ (01422) 353278 Fax (01422) 353278.

HAWORTH • map 12E4

OLD WHITE LION HOTEL
West Lane, BD22 8DU

An old inn at the centre of this famous village, family-run for many years and featured in all major good-food guides. A convenient location for visitors to the Brontë Museum, parsonage and Worth Valley Steam Railway. Ideal centre for touring the Yorkshire Dales.
DOUBLE ROOM: from £20 to £30
SINGLE ROOM: from £35 to £45
FOOD: up to £15
Hours: breakfast 7am–9am, lunch 11.30am–2.30pm, dinner 6.30pm–9.30pm.
Cuisine: ENGLISH / INTERNATIONAL – Dover sole, fillet of Old England, seafood pie, and game in season.
Cards: Visa, Access, Diners, AmEx.
Other points: Sunday lunch, children welcome, coaches by prior arrangement.
Rooms: 15 bedrooms. All with en suite, TV, tea/coffee-making facilities, telephone and radio. Family rooms available.
Directions: off M62, take A629 through Halifax and turn off before Keighley.
MR KEITH BRADFORD ☎ (01535) 642313
Fax (01535) 646222.

HOLMFIRTH • map 9A1

LA GRENOUILLE
Stable Court, Huddersfield Road, HD7 1AZ

Formerly a coaching inn, this charming French restaurant is located in the heart of the 'Summer Wine Country'. Set in a comfortable, rustic and spacious setting, the restaurant has a lively and vibrant atmosphere. The cuisine is outstanding and is matched by pleasant service.
FOOD: from £15 to £20 CLUB
Hours: lunch 12noon–1.30pm, dinner 6.45pm–9.30pm, closed Sunday and Monday.
Cuisine: FRENCH – French country cooking, specializing in fresh fish and game. Vegetarian menu available. Table d'hôte menu Tuesday to Friday.
Other points: licensed, children welcome, air-conditioned, vegetarian meals.
Directions: off A6024. Just off main Hudds Road into Holmfirth. Near fire station.
CLIVE JONES ☎ (01484) 687955.

HUDDERSFIELD • map 9A1

ELM CREST GUEST HOTEL
2 Queens Road, HD2 2AG

A pleasant 1860s-built house with car park and attractive conservatory. The owners, Derek and

WEST YORKSHIRE • NORTHERN ENGLAND

Hilary Gee, prepare and cook all meals using only fresh local produce. Ideally located near town centre and other amenities.
DOUBLE ROOM: from £20 to £30
SINGLE ROOM: up to £25
FOOD: up to £15
Hours: breakfast 7.30am–8.30am, lunch 12noon–2pm, dinner 7pm–9.30pm.
Cuisine: ENGLISH – table d'hôte menu offering a good selection of interesting dishes. Fine selection of cheeses and wines.
Cards: Visa, Access, AmEx.
Other points: garden, afternoon tea, parking, left luggage.
Rooms: 3 single rooms, 2 double rooms, 3 twin rooms. All with TV, radio, telephone, tea/coffee-making facilities.
Directions: follow A629 ring road. Over traffic lights. Centre lane for right turn. Secure parking available.
DEREK & HILARY GEE ☎ (01484) 530990
[Fax] (01484) 516227.

HUDDERSFIELD HOTEL / ROSEMARY LANE BISTRO
HD1 1QT
The hotel is made up of a bistro, formal hotel, pub, wine bar, all-day brasserie and night club, all under the same roof. The Brasserie is air-conditioned and serves food from 10am, closing at 11pm, seven days a week.
DOUBLE ROOM: from £20 to £30
FOOD: up to £15
Hours: breakfast 7.30am–10am, brasserie 10am–11pm, lunch 12noon–2pm, dinner 7pm–11pm.
Cuisine: ENGLISH – grills, fish and British cooking.
Cards: Visa, Access, Diners, AmEx.
Other points: licensed, children welcome, coaches by prior arrangement.
Rooms: 16 single rooms, 20 double rooms, 17 twin rooms, 2 family rooms, 1 suite. All with TV, radio, alarm, telephone, tea/coffee-making facilities, heating, hair dryer, video, trouser-press.
Directions: off A62, on main ring road in town centre, opposite sports centre.
JOE MARSDEN ☎ (01484) 512111
[Fax] (01484) 435262.

THE LODGE HOTEL
48 Birkby Lodge Road, Birkby, HD2 2BG
A fine Victorian gentleman's residence, sympathetically restored as Huddersfield's first country house hotel and set in two acres of mature gardens. The 50-seater restaurant offers excellent and innovative cuisine using fresh seasonal foods, supplemented by an excellent wine list. An ideal venue for business luncheons, conferences, private functions and family Sunday lunch.
DOUBLE ROOM: from £20 to £30
SINGLE ROOM: from £45 to £55
FOOD: from £15 to £20
Hours: breakfast 7.30am–9.45am, lunch 12noon–2pm, dinner 7.30pm–9.45pm, closed 26th December until 28th December.
Cuisine: MODERN ENGLISH – fixed-price

speciality menus. Dishes to choose from include pan-fried venison, sautéed pork fillet, ballantine of duck. Vegetarian menu available.
Cards: Visa, Access, AmEx.
Other points: licensed, open-air dining, Sunday lunch, no-smoking area, afternoon tea, residents' lounge, garden, parking, children welcome, baby-listening device, cots, 24hr reception.
Rooms: 4 single rooms, 4 double rooms, 3 twin rooms. All with TV, radio, alarm, telephone, tea/coffee-making facilities.
Directions: 1 mile from Huddersfield town centre. 2 miles from M62 motorway.
GARRY & KEVIN BIRLEY ☎ (01484) 431001
[Fax] (01484) 421590.

THREE ACRES INN & RESTAURANT
Roydhouse, Shelley, HD8 8LR
Located in the picturesque rolling green countryside of the Pennine foothills, this recently extended 18th century coaching inn offers a comprehensive range of facilities and luxury accommodation. There are two restaurants, banqueting and conference facilities, and traditional bars, all offering a warm Yorkshire welcome.
DOUBLE ROOM: from £20 to £30
SINGLE ROOM: from £45 to £55
FOOD: from £15 to £20
Hours: breakfast 7am–9am, lunch 12noon–2pm, dinner 7pm–9.45pm.
Cuisine: ENGLISH / EUROPEAN.
Cards: Visa, Access, AmEx.
Other points: parking, children welcome, conference facilities, vegetarian meals, residents' garden.
Rooms: 20 bedrooms.
Directions: A635 or A642 off M1 or A642 from Huddersfield to Emley Moor Mast.
MR TRUELOVE & MR ORME ☎ (01484) 602606.

THE WHITE HOUSE
Slaithwaite, HD7 5TY
A 200-year-old pub situated on the Lancashire–Yorkshire packhorse route, with commanding views of the local countryside. The interior has been carefully restored with original flagstone floors, wooden beams and open fires.
DOUBLE ROOM: up to £20
FOOD: up to £15
Hours: breakfast 7.30am–9am, lunch 12noon–1.45pm, Sunday 12.15am–1.45pm, dinner 6pm–9.30pm.
Cuisine: ENGLISH – extensive menu served in the bar/restaurant with additional specialities and daily blackboard changes.
Cards: Visa, Access, Diners, AmEx.
Other points: Sunday lunch, children welcome, pets by prior arrangement.
Rooms: 1 single room, 6 double rooms, 1 twin room.
Directions: off B6107. Turn off A62 in Slaithwaite village.
MRS GILLIAN SWIFT ☎ (01484) 842245.

ILKLEY • map 12E4

COW & CALF HOTEL
Ilkley Moor, LS29 8BT
A country house on Ilkley Moor adjacent to the Cow and Calf Rocks, from which it takes its name. All bedrooms are fully en suite and offer a high standard of comfort, and well-cooked food is served lunchtime and evening. The restaurant has unrivalled views of Wharfedale, and the Moors, immortalized by the song On Ilkley Moor Baht 'at, are a mere 20 yards' walk away.
DOUBLE ROOM: from £30 to £40
FOOD: up to £15 CLUB
Hours: breakfast 7.30am–9.30am, lunch 12noon–2pm, dinner 7.15pm–9.30pm, closed Christmas day.
Cuisine: MODERN ENGLISH – à la carte menu in Panorama restaurant, e.g., Panorama pâté, chicken Panorama (chicken in chef's orange-and-tarragon sauce). Fish also available.
Cards: Visa, Access, Diners, AmEx.
Other points: Sunday lunch, children welcome, parking, residents' bar, residents' lounge.
Rooms: 17 twin rooms. All with TV, telephone, tea/coffee-making facilities.
Directions: located one mile off A65. Follow signs for Cow and Calf Rocks.
THE NORFOLK FAMILY ☎ (01943) 607335
Fax (01943) 816022.

LEEDS • map 12E4

AVALON GUEST HOUSE
132 Woodsley Road, LS2 9LZ
A Victorian family house situated close to the university. Comfortable and well maintained, the Avalon Guest House has a homely atmosphere. Popular with business travellers and visitors to the university.
DOUBLE ROOM: from £20 to £30
SINGLE ROOM: from £25 to £35
Hours: breakfast 7.30am–8.45am.
Cuisine: BREAKFAST.
Cards: Visa.
Other points: garden, pets allowed, cots, baby-sitting, disabled access, central heating.
Rooms: 4 single rooms, 1 double room, 3 twin rooms, 2 family rooms. All with TV, tea/coffee-making facilities.
Directions: one mile from the city centre in the university area.
ELIZABETH DEARDEN ☎ (0113) 2432848/2432545 Fax (0113) 2420649.

THE BUTLERS HOTEL
Cardigan Road, Headingley, LS6 3AG
Overlooking Headingley Cricket Gound and only two minutes from the city centre, this hotel offers excellent, luxurious accommodation and a friendly, welcoming atmosphere. The superbly-appointed licensed restaurant provides a wide choice of well-cooked dishes such as entrecôte au Paivie and chicken chasseur. An elegant, comfortable and welcoming place to stay.
DOUBLE ROOM: from £30 to £40
SINGLE ROOM: over £55
FOOD: up to £15
Hours: breakfast 7.30am–9am, lunch 12noon–2pm, dinner 7pm–9pm, bar meals 12noon–12midnight.
Cuisine: ENGLISH / FRENCH.
Cards: Visa, Access, Diners, AmEx.
Other points: children welcome, pets allowed, residents' lounge, afternoon tea, special breaks, vegetarian meals, baby-listening device, cots, 24hr reception, conferences, weekend breaks, parking.
Rooms: 3 single rooms, 2 double rooms, 2 twin rooms, 1 family room. All with en suite, TV, telephone.
Directions: link road between A65 Skipton and A660 Otley road. Next to Headingley Cicket Ground.
DAVID HARRY BUTLER ☎ (0113) 2744755
Fax (0113) 2744755.

THE NORDIC HOTEL
18 Kelso Road, LS2 9PR
A homely Victorian hotel, tastefully decorated throughout and offering comfortable accommodation and a warm welcome. Tetley Brewery Wharf is nearby for those interested in doing a brewery tour and pub trail; or for sports fanatics, Headlingley is also very close.
DOUBLE ROOM: up to £20
SINGLE ROOM: fro £25 to £35
FOOD: up to £15
Hours: breakfast 7.30am–8.30am, dinner 6pm–9pm, closed Christmas.
Cuisine: ENGLISH.
Cards: Visa, Access, AmEx.
Other points: parking, children welcome, residents' lounge, no-smoking area, afternoon teas, vegetarian meals.
Rooms: 6 single rooms, 3 double rooms, 3 twin rooms, 3 triple rooms, 1 family room. All with TV, tea/coffee-making facilities.
Directions: take the A660 from Leeds city centre. Turn left into Clarendon Road at the rear of Leeds University. Kelso Road is the third turning on the right.
ALLAN & NORAH SPENCE ☎ (0113) 2452357/2448261.

OLIVE TREE GREEK RESTAURANT
Oaklands, Rodley Lane, LS13 1NG
This is authentic food which encompasses many regional specialities, from the Greek mainland and the Greek islands to Cyprus. There are few Greek restaurants in the UK offering this fare, which is skilful and finely judged. The filo pastry parcels with chicken, feta cheese or prawn fillings are unrivalled. There are unusual dishes such as lamb stuffed with fruit, or spinach and feta, with true and balanced textures and flavours. The kitchen displays technical expertise, but the service is equally amiable, professional and friendly. The owners, George and his wife Vasoulla, have elevated the Greek cuisine to new heights; they have written newspaper articles and made numerous TV appearances, notably BBC's Food and Drink programme.

FOOD: from £15 to £20
Hours: lunch 12noon–2.30pm, dinner 6pm–11.30pm, closed Saturday lunch.
Cuisine: GREEK – choice of special meze including vegetarian and seafood, blackboard specials, home-made Greek pastries.
Cards: Visa, Access, AmEx.
Other points: licensed, Sunday lunch, children welcome.
Directions: by Rodley roundabout on the Leeds outer ring road.
GEORGE & VASOULLA PSARIAS ☎ (0113) 2569283.

PINEWOOD PRIVATE HOTEL
78 Potternewton Lane, L57 3LW
Set in a quiet residential area, the Pinewood offers a very good standard of cooking and accommodation. All food is cooked and prepared by the proprietors themselves, using fresh ingredients. Traditional standards of comfort and cleanliness are maintained at all times.
DOUBLE ROOM: from £20 to £30
SINGLE ROOM: from £25 to £35
FOOD: up to £15
Hours: breakfast weekdays 7.30am–8.30am, weekends 8.30am–9.30am, dinner 7.30pm.
Cuisine: MODERN ENGLISH – table d'hôte menu. Traditional home-cooking with a few surprises. Babotie, Jambalaya, chicken in lime with honey and almonds.
Cards: Visa, Access, AmEx.
Other points: licensed, weekend breaks, children welcome, residents' lounge, garden, vegetarian meals, street parking, cots, left luggage.
Rooms: 4 single rooms, 2 double rooms, 3 twin rooms, 1 family room. All with TV, radio, alarm, tea/coffee-making facilities.
Directions: leave Leeds on the A61 to Harrogate; approximately 2 miles from the centre on dual carriageway. Turn right at first roundabout, 600 yards on left.
CHARLES & WENDY STUBLEY ☎ (0113) 2622561. [Fax] (0113) 2622561.

SHIPLEY • map 12E4

THE CONNECTION
41 Westgate, BD18 3Q
A lively, family restaurant with eye-catching decor and a wide-ranging menu. Much frequented by locals and tourists alike.
FOOD: up to £15
Hours: dinner Monday–Friday 6pm–11pm, Saturday 5pm–11pm, Sunday 4pm–10pm.
Cuisine: INTERNATIONAL – hamburgers, pizzas, steaks, pancakes and chicken.
Cards: Visa.
Directions: on the corner of the A657 and Westgate.
S.R. JENNINGS ☎ (01274) 599461.

WAKEFIELD • map 9A2

THE CLOCK TOWER RESTAURANT
Town Hall, Wood Street, WF1 2HQ
The Town Hall was officially opened in 1880. The Clock Tower Restaurant was opened 108 years later and is located on the third floor of the Town Hall, directly under the clock tower itself. Formerly the members' dining room, the restaurant still retains the original oak panelling and carved plasterwork. The chefs pride themselves on producing and presenting interesting dishes from the regularly changing menu, using local suppliers and local produce.
FOOD: up to £15
Hours: lunch (Sunday–Friday) 12noon–2.30pm, dinner (Friday–Saturday) 7pm–11pm, closed 24th December until 31st December.
Cuisine: INTERNATIONAL – a wide selection of international meals, including traditional English, complemented by a comprehensive wine list.
Cards: Visa, Access.
Other points: children welcome, no-smoking area, vegetarian meals, traditional Sunday lunch, conference facilities.
Directions: in city centre.
WAKEFIELD M.D.C. ☎ (01924) 295130 [Fax] (01924) 295293.

WALES

Although part of Britain, Wales is as different from England as France is from Spain. It has its own language, history and heritage as well as its own culture and cuisine, and it is this difference, coupled with the traditional, warm Welsh welcome, that makes any visit here such a memorable and unique experience.

Award-winning Welsh cuisine is not hard to find, and uses only the very best of local produce. Here one can expect to find on the menu such dishes as honeyed Welsh lamb, Pembrokeshire turkey and Wye salmon, as well as a tremendous choice of cosmopolitan and continental dishes through to traditional roasts, quality home-made meals and light snacks.

We often wonder if the Welsh were thinking of *Les Routiers* when they composed *A Welcome in the Hillsides*, because there certainly is! Accommodation ranges from welcoming hill farms with spectacular views across sea and mountains to picturesque village inns in the heart of Snowdonia, from modern hotels with full facilities to first-class country and sporting hotels.

This area also has a wealth of interesting attractions and unusual places to visit, many of them unique, such as the Italianate village of Portmeirion, nestling on a secluded wooded hillside overlooking the Traeth Bach estuary, or the Centre for Alternative Technology, a 'green' village of the future in mid-Wales, where a host of environmentally friendly technologies are demonstrated.

The following counties are included in this chapter:

CLWYD	MID GLAMORGAN
DYFED	POWYS
GWENT	SOUTH GLAMORGAN
GWYNEDD	WEST GLAMORGAN

*C*LWYD

COLWYN BAY • map 7B3

CAFE NICOISE
124 Abergele Road, Colwyn Bay, LL29 7PS
Tastefully furnished restaurant, offering traditional and modern provincial cooking. Close to beach and other attractions, including Eirias Park, Conwy Castle, Great Orme and Llandudno.
FOOD: from £15 to £20
Hours: lunch 12noon–2pm, dinner 7pm–10pm, closed for lunch Sunday until Wednesday.
Cuisine: FRENCH – fillets of red mullet with roast peppers and basil, assiette du chef. A selection of 4 home-made desserts.
Cards: Visa, Access, Diners, AmEx.
Other points: licensed, children welcome, vegetarian meals, open bank holidays.
Directions: take the Old Colwyn exit from the A55. Situated on the main road through Colwyn Bay.
CARL SWIFT & LYNNE SWIFT ☎ (01492) 531555.

EDELWEISS HOTEL
Lawson Road, LL29 8HD
A 19th century country house set in its own wooded gardens and tucked away in central Colwyn Bay. Large car park, children's play area,

games room and solarium. Private pathway leading to the Promenade, Eirias Park, and the sports and leisure centre.
DOUBLE ROOM: up to £20
FOOD: up to £15
Hours: breakfast 7.45am–9.30am, lunch 12noon–2pm, dinner 6.30pm–9pm.
Cuisine: WELSH / ENGLISH – vegetarian meals, fresh vegetables, home-cut meats.
Cards: Visa, Access, Diners, AmEx.
Other points: pets allowed.
Directions: off the A55 and then the B5104.
IAN BURT ☎ (01492) 532314 Fax (01492) 534707.

NORTHWOOD HOTEL
47 Rhos Road, Rhos-on-Sea,
LL28 4RS
Centrally situated in the heart of attractive Rhos-on-Sea. Excellent tradition of fine cuisine with wide choice of menu. Special diets catered for. Ground-floor bedrooms. Special mini-break rates. Easter and Christmas house parties, golfing holidays arranged.
DOUBLE ROOM: up to £20
SINGLE ROOM: up to £25
FOOD: up to £15
Hours: breakfast 8.15am–9am, dinner 6.30pm–7pm.
Cuisine: BRITISH.
Cards: Visa, Access.
Other points: central heating, children welcome, pets allowed, residents' lounge, patio, residents' bar.
Rooms: 2 single rooms, 3 double rooms, 4 twin rooms, 3 family rooms. All with TV, clock/radio, tea/coffee-making facilities. Most rooms are en suite.
Directions: on Rhos Road, directly off the Promenade; turn opposite Rhos-on-Sea Tourist Information Centre.
GORDON & AGNES PALLISER ☎ (01492) 549931.

LLANGOLLEN • map 8B4

THE CHAIN BRIDGE HOTEL
Berwyn, LL20 8BS
The hotel nestles in one of the most picturesque localities in Wales, in a valley of serene and natural beauty shielded by the Berwyn and Eglwysig mountains. Situated on the banks of the River Dee, the hotel offers guests characteristic accommodation, a good restaurant with panoramic views, a cosy bar, and excellent facilities for weddings, functions and conferences.
DOUBLE ROOM: from £20 to £30
SINGLE ROOM: from £25 to £35
FOOD: up to £15
Hours: breakfast 7.30am–9.30am, lunch 12.30am–2pm, dinner 7.30pm–9pm.
Cuisine: ENGLISH / CONTINENTAL.
Cards: Visa, Access, Diners, AmEx, Switch.
Other points: parking, children welcome, pets allowed, no-smoking area, conference facilities,

residents' lounge, garden, vegetarian meals, traditional Sunday lunch, afternoon teas.
Rooms: 35 bedrooms. All with TV, telephone, radio, tea/coffee-making facilties.
Directions: 2 miles west of Llangollen, just off A5.
VICTOR BAKER ☎ (01978) 860215
Fax (01978) 861841.

GALES
18 Bridge Street, LL70 8PF
An 18th century establishment, opposite the River Dee, in the town famous for the International Eisteddfod. Over 250 wines, on- or off-sales. Limited-edition etchings and screen prints for sale. Overall winner of the Les Routiers / Mercier Wine List of the Year Award 1990.
DOUBLE ROOM: from £20 to £30
SINGLE ROOM: from £25 to £35
FOOD: up to £15
Hours: lunch 12noon–2pm, dinner 6pm–10pm, closed Sunday.
Cuisine: INTERNATIONAL – specializes in home-made soups and ice creams and offers a variety of dishes of the day.
Cards: Visa, Access.
Other points: open-air dining, children welcome, patio.
Rooms: 11 double rooms, 3 twin rooms. All en suite.
Directions: located in the town centre.
RICHARD & GILLIE GALE ☎ (01978) 860089
Fax (01978) 861313.

MOLD • map 8B4

CHEZ COLETTE
56 High Street, CH1 1BD
An attractive French family-run restaurant, offering fine traditional cuisine. The panelled decor is adorned with French paintings and complemented by soft background music, adding to the overall charm of this establishment, so popular with the locals. It is ideally situated for visits to the theatre and countryside walks, with the ancient parish church directly opposite.
FOOD: up to £15
Hours: lunch 11.30am–2pm, dinner 6pm–10pm, closed Sunday and Monday.
Cuisine: FRENCH – quality French provincial cuisine with table d'hôte and à la carte menus. Dishes may include mussels in garlic sauce, escargots, savoury pancake, navarin of lamb, poulet au Riesling, steak au poivre.
Cards: Visa, Access, AmEx.
Other points: licensed, children welcome.
Directions: A494, A541, top of Mold High Street, opposite the parish church.
JACQUES & COLETTE DUVAUCHELLE
☎ (01352) 759225.

THEATR CLWYD
Rakes Lane, CH7 1YA
Combine a meal with a visit to the theatre at the only theatre–restaurant recommended by Les Routiers. The meals are well-cooked and provide very fair value for money – reason enough for visiting

Theatr Clwyd at any time, for lunch or dinner, whether you wish to enjoy a play or just relax over a meal.
FOOD: up to £15
Hours: closed Sunday.
Cuisine: INTERNATIONAL – dishes may include tagliatelle carbonara, tarragon and lemon chicken, vegetarian chilli and trout Cleopatra. Menu changed monthly.
Cards: Visa, Access, Switch.
Other points: no-smoking area, children welcome, afternoon tea, conferences, functions.
Directions: situated on A494, half a mile outside Mold town. Signposted.
MR GORDON CARSON. LEISURE CATERING SERVICES LTD ☎ (01352) 759304 Fax (01352) 752302.

ST ASAPH • map 7B3

ORIEL HOUSE HOTEL
Upper Denbigh Road, LL17 0LW

Set in its own extensive grounds, this is a family-owned and run hotel. In these quiet, relaxed surroundings, you can enjoy well-prepared and presented meals. Comfortable accommodation and attractive decor. Good venue for wedding receptions and conferences.
DOUBLE ROOM: from £40 to £50
SINGLE ROOM: from £35 to £45
FOOD: up to £15 ☆
Hours: breakfast 7.15am–9.30am, lunch 11.30am–2pm, bar snacks 11am–2.30pm, dinner 7pm–9.30pm, bar snacks 6.15pm–10pm.
Cuisine: BRITISH – serving full à la carte menu, table d'hôte and bar snacks.
Cards: Visa, Access, Diners, AmEx.
Other points: licensed, Sunday lunch, children welcome, afternoon tea, pets allowed, garden, conferences, snooker room.
Rooms: 19 bedrooms. All with en suite, TV, radio, telephone, hair dryer, tea/coffee-making facilities.
Directions: A55 turn-off for Denbigh, left at cathedral, 1 mile on right.
MR & MRS WIGGIN & MR & MRS WOOD
☎ (01745) 582716 Fax (01745) 582716.

PLAS ELWY
The Roe, LL17 0LT

This is a small, friendly, family-run hotel, which provides modern facilities, yet retains the character and atmosphere of an establishment that dates back to 1850. The hotel offers a cosy bar, a delightful, intimate restaurant and 13 comfortable bedrooms.
DOUBLE ROOM: from £20 to £30
SINGLE ROOM: from £35 to £45
FOOD: from £15 to £20 CLUB ☆
Hours: breakfast 7.30am–9.15am, lunch 12noon–2.30pm, dinner 6.30pm–10pm.
Cuisine: BRITISH.
Cards: Visa, Access, Diners, AmEx, Eurocard.
Other points: parking, children welcome, vegetarian meals.
Rooms: 1 single room, 9 double rooms, 1 twin room, 1 triple room, 1 family room.
Directions: From the A55, take the A525 to St Asaph. Plas Elwy is the second building on the left-hand side.
MR & MRS P. WOOLLEY ☎ (01745) 582263/582089 Fax (01745) 583864.

TREFNANT • map 7B3

BRYN GLAS HOTEL
St Asaph Road, LL16 5UD

Set in the Vale of Clwyd, Bryn Glas is an ideal location as a base for touring the beautiful North Wales coast or just taking a relaxing break away. A home-cooked meal from the varied menu can be enjoyed in the dining room, then relax over a quiet drink in the lounge before retiring to one of the comfortable rooms for a restful night.
DOUBLE ROOM: from £20 to £30
SINGLE ROOM: from £25 to £35
FOOD: up to £15
Hours: breakfast 8am–9am, lunch 12noon–2pm, dinner 6pm–7.30pm.
Cuisine: BRITISH.
Other points: disabled access, children welcome, parking, pets allowed, residents' lounge, vegetarian meals, garden.
Directions: on A525, off A55 Expressway, 2½ miles from St Asaph and the same distance from Denbigh.
MS M. TIBBETTS ☎ (01745) 730868
Fax (01745) 730590.

WREXHAM • map 8B4

TREVOR ARMS HOTEL
Marford, near Wrexham, LL12 8TA

An old coaching inn, which maintains traditional pub hospitality together with a wide range of modern facilities and tempting menus at affordable prices. Excellent staff teamwork ensures a relaxed, no-fuss atmosphere in which to enjoy your meal. Comfortable accommodation, a safe children's play area and an outdoor barbecue. Very highly recommended by the Les Routiers inspector.
DOUBLE ROOM: up to £20
SINGLE ROOM: from £25 to £35
FOOD: up to £15
Hours: breakfast 7.30am–9am, lunch 12noon–2.30pm, dinner 6pm–10pm, Sunday 7pm–10pm.
Cuisine: BRITISH – extensive menu available in the restaurant and bar areas. Dishes may include king scampi, sirloin steak, salmon with lemon and tarragon. Daily specials.
Cards: Visa, Access.
Other points: licensed, open-air dining, Sunday lunch, no-smoking area, playland, afternoon tea.
Rooms: 2 single rooms, 12 double rooms, 3 twin rooms.
Directions: midway between Chester and Wrexham. A short distance off A483.
MARTIN & DENISE BENNETT ☎ (01244) 570436.

DYFED

ABERYSTWYTH • map 7D2

COURT ROYALE HOTEL
Eastgate, SY23 2AB
A hotel dating back to the early 19th century, tastefully restored and fitted with 20th century comforts. The restaurant, in mahogany finish, has its own character and offers an extensive à la carte selection. Close to the beach and town centre.
DOUBLE ROOM: from £20 to £30
FOOD: from £15 to £20
Hours: breakfast 8am–9.30am, lunch 12noon–2.30pm, bar meals 12noon–2.30pm, dinner 7pm–10pm, bar meals 7pm–10pm.
Cuisine: BRITISH – steaks.
Cards: Visa, Access, AmEx.
Other points: Sunday lunch, children welcome, pets allowed.
Directions: A44 or A487 to Aberystwyth; close to beach and town centre.
MR & MRS JENKINS ☎ (01970) 611722.

CARDIGAN • map 7E2

SKIPPERS
Tresaith Beach, SA43 2JL
Overlooking the unspoilt bay of Tresaith, this restaurant offers meals of 'outstanding quality' in a quiet, relaxed atmosphere. Efficient and friendly staff ensure an enjoyable meal. There is a definite nautical theme in the restaurant, which also has a log fire. Comfortable accommodation. Highly recommended.
DOUBLE ROOM: up to £20
FOOD: from £25 to £30
Hours: breakfast 7am–12noon, lunch 12noon–3pm, bar meals 12noon–3pm, dinner 6pm–11.30pm, last orders 9pm, closed January until Easter.
Cuisine: SEAFOOD / INTERNATIONAL – extensive home-made menu, which may feature oysters, fresh local crab and lobster, rack of lamb. Greek and Cypriot dishes a speciality.
Cards: Visa, Access.
Other points: licensed, open-air dining available, children welcome, afternoon tea, residents' lounge, residents' bar, vegetarian meals, pets allowed.
Rooms: 3 twin rooms. All with TV, radio, alarm, tea/coffee-making facilities.
Directions: B4333 to Aberporth, then unclassified road to Tresaith.
IAN & JANET DARROCH ☎ (01239) 810113
Fax (01239) 810176.

CARMARTHEN • map 3A3

THE COTHI BRIDGE HOTEL
Pontargothi, Nantgaredig, SA32 7NG
This family-run hotel is well located for travellers, offering good facilities and a pleasant family atmosphere. The dining room enjoys spectacular views over the river Cothi, while the bedrooms provide guests with comfortable accommodation. Many great attractions are located nearby.
DOUBLE ROOM: from £20 to £30
SINGLE ROOM: from £25 to £35
FOOD: up to £15 ☆
Hours: breakfast 7.30am–9am, lunch 12noon–2pm, dinner 7pm–9.30pm, bar snacks available throughout the day.
Cuisine: BRITISH – freshly prepared traditional meals. Grills a speciality.
Cards: Visa, Access, AmEx.
Other points: children welcome, pets allowed, parking, residents' lounge, garden, open-air dining, vegetarian meals.
Rooms: 2 single rooms, 6 double rooms, 2 twin rooms, 1 triple room, 1 family room. All with TV, tea-making facilities, telephone, room service.
Directions: situated on the A40, half-way between Carmarthen and Llandeilo.
MRS SANDY JONES ☎ (01267) 290251
Fax (01267) 290251.

THE FALCON
Lammas Street, SA31 3AP
An attractive hotel situated in the heart of the historic market town of Carmarthen. The hotel has been recently refurbished to a vey high standard throughout, offering excellent service by efficient staff in comfortable surroundings.
DOUBLE ROOM: from £20 to £30
SINGLE ROOM: from £35 to £45
FOOD: up to £15
Hours: breakfast 7.30am–10am, lunch 12noon–2.30pm, bar meals 12noon–2.30pm, dinner 6.30pm–9.30pm, closed Christmas day.
Cuisine: BRITISH / MODERN FRENCH.
Cards: Visa, Access, Diners, AmEx.
Other points: parking, residents' lounge, no-smoking area, traditional Sunday lunch, vegetarian meals.
Rooms: 4 single rooms, 3 double rooms, 7 twin rooms, 2 honeymoon suites. All with TV, telephone, radio, alarm, hair dryer, tea/coffee-making facilities.
Directions: take either the A40 or A48 into Carmarthen town centre. At the traffic lights, turn into Blue Street for Lammas Street.
MR & MRS EXTON ☎ (01267) 237152.

FISHGUARD • map 7E1

ABERGWAUN HOTEL
Market Square, SA65 9HA
This family-run hotel offers comfort throughout. Traditional home-cooked food, made from fresh local produce, is offered in the restaurant, and the 12 bedrooms are all well appointed, to provide a 'home away from home' aura. Situated in the heart of Fishguard, the hotel is a convenient stop for people on their way over to Ireland.

DOUBLE ROOM: from £20 to £30
SINGLE ROOM: up to £25
FOOD: up to £15
Hours: breakfast 7.30am 9.30am, lunch 12noon–2pm, dinner 7pm–9pm, bar snacks available throughout the day, closed Christmas day.
Cuisine: BRITISH – home-made food using fresh produce.
Cards: Visa, Access, Diners, AmEx.
Other points: children welcome, pets allowed, residents' lounge, vegetarian meals.
Rooms: 4 single rooms, 5 double rooms, 2 family rooms. All with TV, tea/coffee-making facilities.
Directions: located on the A40, in the main square of Fishguard.
MR R.L. COLLIER ☎ (01348) 872077.

THE HOPE & ANCHOR INN
Goodwick, SA64 0BP

This small, family-run inn overlooks the harbour and is conveniently placed for both the station and the Irish ferries. There are miles of beaches nearby, with a coastal path for walkers.
DOUBLE ROOM: up to £20
SINGLE ROOM: up to £25
FOOD: up to £15
Hours: lunch 12noon–2.30pm, dinner 7pm–10pm.
Cuisine: ENGLISH / WELSH.
Other points: open-air dining, Sunday lunch, children catered for (please check for age limits).
Rooms: 3 twin rooms. All with en suite, TV.
Directions: at end of A40.
MR T. McDONALD ☎ (01348) 872314.

HAVERFORDWEST • map 3A2

THE CASTLE HOTEL
Castle Square, SA62 2AA

The Castle Hotel, which has recently been refurbished, is ideally situated for touring the beautiful, rugged mountains and coastline of Pembrokeshire. Comfortably and attractively furnished.
DOUBLE ROOM: from £20 to £30
FOOD: up to £15
Hours: breakfast 7.30am–9.30am, lunch 12noon–2.45pm, dinner 7pm–10pm, bar meals 12noon–2.45pm, 7pm–9pm, open all year.
Cuisine: INTERNATIONAL – bistro-style menu. Dishes may include honey roasted chicken, pork and apricot stroganoff, nutty fettucini, rosemary lamb steak. Good selection of steaks. Vegetarian dishes.
Cards: Visa, Access.
Other points: licensed, Sunday lunch, children welcome, afternoon tea, vegetarian meals, weekend breaks.
Rooms: 2 single rooms, 3 double rooms, 2 twin rooms, 1 family room. All with TV, telephone.
Directions: turn off left at junction of A4076 and A40 over River Cleddau.
JULIET & PHILLIP LLEWELLYN ☎ (01437) 769322 Fax (01437) 769493.

ROCH GATE MOTEL
Roch, SA62 6AF

A modern motel, providing excellent personal service to both long- and short-term visitors. Tasty meals with an emphasis on healthy eating and comfortable accommodation. With an indoor swimming pool, family-sized Jacuzzi, solarium etc., there need never be a dull moment!
DOUBLE ROOM: from £30 to £40
FOOD: from £15 to £20 CLUB
Hours: breakfast 7.45am–9.30am, lunch 12noon–3pm, dinner 6pm–10pm.
Cuisine: CONTINENTAL – menu may feature tuna and prawn tagliatelle, cheese and walnut pasta bake, king prawns, and apple pie.
Cards: Visa, Access, AmEx.
Other points: licensed, Sunday lunch, children welcome, open bank holidays, pets allowed, sauna, gym facilities, Jacuzzi, solarium, swimming pool.
Directions: six miles out of Haverfordwest towards St David's.
JOHN SMITH ☎ (01437) 710435.

WOLFSCASTLE COUNTRY HOTEL
Wolf's Castle, SA62 5LZ

A country hotel where the traditional welcome of warmth, relaxation and friendliness has been maintained. Situated on a hillside amid beautiful countryside, this hotel offers a high standard of accommodation. The restaurant enjoys an enviable reputation locally for its excellent food, and imaginative bar meals are also available. A delightful hotel in which to stay or dine.
DOUBLE ROOM: from £30 to £40
FOOD: from £15 to £20
Hours: bar meals 12noon–2pm, 7pm–9pm, breakfast 7.30am–9.30am, dinner 7pm–9pm, lunch Sunday 12noon–2pm.
Cuisine: BRITISH – a blend of nouvelle cuisine and home-cooking. Predominantly fresh, local produce used. Traditional Sunday lunch. Good wine list.
Cards: Visa, Access, AmEx.
Other points: licensed, Sunday lunch, children welcome, residents' lounge, log fire, functions, patio, squash.
Rooms: 4 single rooms, 16 double rooms, 4 twin rooms.
Directions: A40. 6 miles north of Haverfordwest in village of Wolf's Castle.
ANDREW STIRLING ☎ (01437) 741225/741688 Fax (01437) 741383.

LAMPETER • map 7E2

PEPPERS RESTAURANT
14 High Street, SA48 7BG

Recently renovated and tastefully furnished, this bistro-style restaurant offers a cool, relaxed atmosphere in which to enjoy fine-quality food in spotlessly clean surroundings.
FOOD: up to £15
Hours: lunch 12noon–2.30pm, snacks all day 10am–9pm, closed Sunday, closed 23rd December until 3rd January.

DYFED • WALES

Cuisine: BRITISH / CONTINENTAL – daily changing menu, offering a good choice of typically bistro-style dishes, including vegetarian specialities and salads, all freshly prepared and cooked on the premises.
Other points: licensed, no-smoking area, children welcome, afternoon tea, morning tea.
Directions: follow A482 from Aberaeron or Lllanwrda, A485 from Carmarthen or Aberystwyth, or A475 from Newcastle Emlyn.
STEPHANIE WARNES ☎ (01570) 423796.

LITTLE HAVEN • map 3A2

THE NEST BISTRO
12 Grove Place, near Haverfordwest, SA62 3UG

A cosy bistro with a small cocktail bar, in an old rambling house in this unique seaside village. A wide choice of dishes such as Mexican turkey and breast of duck. Fresh local fish includes Dover sole, monkfish, stuffed fillets of lemon sole, and lobster. 100 yards from the beach and coastal path. Little Haven provides a picturesque base for touring or enjoying the many water sports.
DOUBLE ROOM: up to £20
FOOD: up to £15
Hours: lunch (high season only) 12noon–2.30pm, dinner (booking advisable) 6.30pm until late, last orders 10pm, closed Monday.
Cuisine: ENGLISH / CONTINENTAL – an imaginative menu with all dishes home-made, featuring fresh local fish, seafood and a selection of fine steaks. Extensive wine list. Welsh cheeseboard.
Cards: Visa, Access.
Other points: licensed, children welcome, parking.
Rooms: 2 double rooms, 2 twin rooms.
Directions: off the B4341 in Broad Haven.
PAUL & MARGARET MERRICK ☎ (01437) 781728.

LLANDOVERY • map 7E3

DROVERS RESTAURANT
9 Market Square, SA20 0AB

This attractive 18th century country-town pub has been tastefully modernized while retaining some of the more appealing of its original features. The comfortable bedrooms have all been lovingly decorated with period furniture. Excellent standards and cheerful, efficient service throughout make this a must when travelling in this most beautiful part of Wales.
DOUBLE ROOM: up to £20
FOOD: from £15 to £20
Hours: lunch 10.30am–2.30pm, dinner 6.30pm–9.30pm, restaurant closed Sunday evening and Monday.
Cuisine: WELSH – an excellent choice of high-quality dishes.
Cards: Visa, Access, Eurocard.
Other points: parking, children welcome, pets allowed, vegetarian meals, traditional Sunday lunch.

Rooms: 2 double rooms, 1 twin room. All with TV, tea/coffee-making facilities.
Directions: on A40, opposite the town hall in the centre of town.
MRS BLUD ☎ (01550) 21115.

THE ROYAL OAK INN
Rhandirmwyn, SA20 0NY

A 17th century village inn with restaurant, pool room and en suite accommodation. Near Brecon Beacons, RSPB Bird Reserve, Llyn Brianne dam and reservoir, fishing, riding and fabulous scenery. Just 40 minutes from the coast and 7 miles north of Llandovery.
DOUBLE ROOM: from £20 to £30
SINGLE ROOM: up to £25
FOOD: up to £15
Hours: breakfast 8am–9.30am, lunch 11.30am–3.30pm, dinner 6pm–10pm, bar meals 11.30am–3.30pm, 6pm–10.30pm.
Cuisine: ENGLISH – good-quality country food. Excellent value bar meals.
Cards: Visa, Access.
Other points: licensed, Sunday lunch, children catered for (please check for age limits), pets allowed, beer garden.
Rooms: 2 single rooms, 1 double room, 1 twin room, 1 family room. All with TV, tea/coffee-making facilities.
Directions: from Llandovery, follow signs to Llyn Brianne and Rhandirmwyn.
MR & MRS L.W. ALEXANDER ☎ (015506) 201 [Fax] (015506) 332.

LLANELLI • map 3A3

HENLLYS
Gorslas, SA14 7LH

Because of the excellent location of this restaurant, it is highly popular with travellers as well as the many locals, who come in droves to feast upon the many delights on offer. Although a Welsh restaurant, there is a distinct French provincial atmosphere, with excellent service to complement the fine food.
FOOD: from £20 to £25
Hours: Sunday lunch 12noon–4pm, dinner 6pm–11.30pm.
Cuisine: BRITISH – modern British cuisine with French influences. Fresh local seafood.
Other points: parking, children welcome, no-smoking area, vegetarian meals, traditional Sunday lunch.
Directions: M4 Cross Hands to Llandeilo road, drive for 1 mile, turn at Gorslas and then take second right.
RAYMOND WILLIAMS ☎ (01269) 844968.

MILFORD HAVEN • map 3A3

BELHAVEN HOUSE HOTEL & RESTAURANT
29 Hamilton Terrace, SA73 3JJ

A quiet hotel noted for its relaxed atmosphere. Six of the bedrooms overlook the attractive waterway. The restaurant offers a large selection of

scrumptious meals to cater for most tastes.
DOUBLE ROOM: from £20 to £30
FOOD: up to £15
Hours: breakfast 6am–10.30am, lunch 12noon–2pm, dinner 6.30pm–10pm.
Cuisine: BRITISH / CONTINENTAL – steaks, pavlovas, vegetarian dishes. Choice of over 40 main courses.
Cards: Visa.
Other points: licensed, Sunday lunch, children welcome, afternoon tea, coaches by prior arrangement
Rooms: 1 single room, 1 double room, 11 twin room, 4 family rooms.
Directions: on the front street, overlooking the haven, just past the monument.
MR & MRS HENRICKSEN ☎ (01646) 695983
[Fax] (01646) 690787.

NEW QUAY • map 7D2

BLACK LION HOTEL
Glanmor Terrace, SA45 9PT
Situated in the pretty resort of New Quay, with its sandy beach and fishing harbour, the Black Lion is a warm, friendly, family-run hotel. Most rooms are en suite, centrally heated, and have tea/coffee trays. The atmospheric old bar, dating back to 1680, has live music most weekends and bar snacks and meals available at lunchtime and evenings. Evening diners will enjoy 'Dylan's' restaurant, dedicated to the poet Dylan Thomas. During the summer months, meals are also served in the beer garden, which has panoramic views over Cardigan Bay. There is also a children's play area.
DOUBLE ROOM: from £20 to £30
SINGLE ROOM: from £25 to £35
FOOD: up to £15
Hours: breakfast 8.30am–10am, bar snacks 12noon–12.30am & 2.30pm–3pm, dinner 7pm–10pm, bar snacks 6pm–10pm.
Cuisine: BRITISH.
Other points: parking, children welcome, no-smoking area, pets allowed, residents' lounge, vegetarian meals, open-air dining.
Rooms: 10 double rooms, 1 twin room.
Directions: at centre of town on approach to harbour and beach.
THOMAS JAMES HUNTER ☎ (01545) 560209
[Fax] (01545) 560585.

TY HEN FARM HOTEL & LEISURE CENTRE
Llwyndafydd, near New Quay, SA44 6BZ
Situated in beautiful wooded countryside, near the spectacular Cardigan coast, this quiet stock-farm offers a choice of self-catering cottages or farm-hotel guest accommodation. Facilities in the area include riding, fishing and water sports. On-site leisure centre includes large indoor heated pool, fitness room, solarium, skittles, etc. Restaurant and bar. Smoking is restricted to cottages only. Private adult swimming lessons available.
DOUBLE ROOM: from £20 to £30
SINGLE ROOM: up to £25

FOOD: [CLUB] ☆
Hours: breakfast 8.30am–9.30am, dinner 6.30pm–8pm.
Cuisine: BRITISH.
Cards: Visa, Access.
Other points: central heating, children welcome, residents' lounge, garden, self-catering cottages, residents' bar, swimming pool, parking, disabled access.
Rooms: 5 bedrooms.
Directions: A487: follow signs to Llwyndafydd; with phone kiosk on left, go up hill approximately 1 mile, sharp right bend, then into 'No Through Road' on right. Entrance is 100 yards on right.
VERONICA KELLY ☎ (01545) 560346.

NEWCASTLE EMLYN • map 7E2

MAES-Y-DERW GUEST HOUSE & RESTAURANT
Cardigan Road, SA38 9RD
It is a well-known fact that if you want to find a good restaurant, dine where the locals dine – and with its excellent reputation, Maes-y-Derw is very popular with the locals. The imposing exterior of this Victorian country house and the impressive decor, furnishings and antiques inside will impress the most discerning tastes. Here you can be assured of tasteful, comfortable accommodation, superb food and charming hospitality.
DOUBLE ROOM: up to £20
SINGLE ROOM: up to £25
FOOD: from £15 to £20
Hours: breakfast 7.30am–9am, lunch 12noon–2.30pm, dinner 6.45pm–9.30pm.
Cuisine: FRENCH / INTERNATIONAL – very good local reputation for fresh, well-cooked food.
Other points: parking, children welcome, pets allowed, garden, vegetarian meals, traditional Sunday lunch, afternoon teas.
Rooms: 6 bedrooms. All with TV, tea/coffee-making facilities.
Directions: on A484 Carmarthen–Cardigan road. Between market town of Newcastle Emlyn and Cenarth Falls.
WYN & DIANE DAVIES ☎ (01239) 710860.

SAUNDERSFOOT • map 3A2

ST BRIDES HOTEL
St Brides Hill, SA69 9NH
Excellent location overlooking Carmarthen Bay. A very high standard is maintained in all aspects of the hotel, particularly with regard to the food and service.
DOUBLE ROOM: from £40 to £50
SINGLE ROOM: over £55
FOOD: from £15 to £20
Hours: breakfast 8am–10am, lunch 12noon–2pm, dinner 7pm–9.15pm, bar 12noon–11pm.
Cuisine: BRITISH / CONTINENTAL – specializing in locally caught fish, lobster and crab. Flambé dishes.
Cards: Visa, Access, Diners, AmEx.

Other points: licensed, Sunday lunch, children welcome, coaches by prior arrangement.
Rooms: 6 single rooms, 8 double rooms, 26 twin rooms, 5 executive suites. All with radio, bar, telephone, tea/coffee-making facilities, hair dryer, satellite TV.
Directions: from the A40, A477 or A476, follow signposts to Saundersfoot.
IAN BELL ☎ (01834) 812304 [Fax] (01834) 813303.

ST DAVID'S • map 7E1

HARBOUR HOUSE HOTEL & RESTAURANT
The Harbour, Solva, SA62 6UT
Nestled in the heart of the Pembrokeshire Coast National Park, yet standing at the head of a fiord. Decorated in soothing colours and comfortably furnished. Serving tastefully presented excellent meals in a quiet atmosphere.
DOUBLE ROOM: from £20 to £30
FOOD: from £15 to £20
Hours: breakfast 8.30am–10am, lunch 12noon–2.30pm, dinner 7pm–9pm.
Cuisine: BRITISH – dishes include trout pan-fried with capers, prawns and lemon, roast breast of duck with a blackberry and orange sauce.
Cards: Visa, Access.
Other points: licensed, Sunday lunch, children welcome, afternoon tea, pets allowed.
Directions: A487, 3 miles east of St David's.
PAUL HEMMING ☎ (01437) 721267.

RAMSEY HOUSE
Lower Moor, SA62 6RP
Ramsey House offers you a unique combination of professional hotel standards of accommodation and food service, coupled with the friendly, relaxing atmosphere of a pleasant country guest house. Situated just half a mile from St David's, with its 12th century cathedral, this guest house enjoys a quiet location on the road to Porthclais and is an ideal base for touring the area. Welsh Tourist Board 3 Crowns, 'highly commended'.
DOUBLE ROOM: from £20 to £30
FOOD: up to £15
Hours: breakfast 8am–8.30am, dinner 7pm.
Cuisine: WELSH – lamb steaks with laverbread and orange, 'Dragons Eggs', salmon with cucumber sauce.
Other points: garden, residents' lounge, pets allowed, parking, ground-floor rooms, vegetarian meals, picnic lunches.
Rooms: 5 double rooms, 2 twin rooms. All with tea/coffee-making facilities.
Directions: off A487, at centre of St David's Road from Cross Square, signposted Porthclais.
MAC & SANDRA THOMPSON ☎ (01437) 720321.

Y GLENNYDD GUEST HOUSE
51 Nun Street, SA62 6NU
A cosy guest house in the charming village city of St David's. Y Glennydd aims to make each guest's stay relaxed and comfortable. A full English breakfast, dinner, picnic baskets, etc. are available. Guests will also enjoy exploring this attractive area, famous for its cathedral, coastal path and offshore islands.
DOUBLE ROOM: up to £20
FOOD: up to £15
Hours: breakfast 8am–10am, dinner 7pm–8.30pm, closed January.
Cuisine: INTERNATIONAL – bistro licenced restaurant: à la carte and table d'hôte.
Cards: Visa, Access, Diners.
Other points: children welcome, residents' lounge, picnic lunches, street parking, public car park, residents' bar.
Rooms: 1 single room, 4 double rooms, 2 twin rooms, 3 family rooms. All with TV, tea/coffee-making facilities.
Directions: A487. Nun Street is part of the one-way system from Cross Square, next door to the fire station.
TIMOTHY & TRACEY FOSTER ☎ (01437) 720576 [Fax] (01437) 720104.

TENBY • map 3A2

ATLANTIC HOTEL
Esplanade, SA70 7DU
Fronted by magnificent gardens and with a spectacular view of the sea, this elegant Edwardian hotel fully deserves its loyal clientele. The rooms are richly furnished and fully fitted with an eye to comfort, the food is superbly prepared and presented with unobtrusive professionalism, and your every need is catered for.
DOUBLE ROOM: from £30 to £40
SINGLE ROOM: from £45 to £55
FOOD: from £15 to £20 [CLUB]
Hours: breakfast 8am–9.30am, bar meals 12noon–2pm, dinner 7pm–8.30pm, closed 20th December until 5th January.
Cuisine: WELSH / INTERNATIONAL – prepared using fresh local ingredients.
Cards: Visa, Access, AmEx.
Other points: licensed, Sunday lunch, children welcome, residents' lounge, garden.
Rooms: 4 single rooms, 22 double rooms, 5 twin rooms, 9 family rooms. All with TV, radio, telephone, tea/coffee-making facilities, baby-listening device, hair dryer, trouser-press.
Directions: follow A477 to Tenby, continue through town past 5 Arches.
DORIS & WILLIAM JAMES ☎ (01834) 842881/844176 [Fax] (01834) 842881 ext25.

FOURCROFT HOTEL
North Beach, SA70 8AP
Over 150 years old, the Fourcroft is situated in the most peaceful and select part of the town, with spectacular cliff-top gardens. A seafront hotel set above Tenby's Blue Flag North Beach, with magnificent views of Carmarthen Bay and Tenby Harbour.
DOUBLE ROOM: from £30 to £40
SINGLE ROOM: from £35 to £45
FOOD: up to £15 ☆
Hours: meals all day 8am–12midnight.

Cuisine: BRITISH – Pembrokeshire turkey, honeyed Welsh lamb, local salmon, trout and plaice, interesting bar lunches.
Cards: Visa, Access.
Other points: Sunday lunch, swimming pool, leisure centre, garden, parking.
Rooms: 6 single rooms, 16 double rooms, 16 twin rooms, 7 family rooms. All with TV, radio, telephone, tea/coffee-making facilities.
Directions: fork left after 'Welcome to Tenby' sign, double back along seafront, past information office.
THE OSBORNE FAMILY ☎ (01834) 842886 [Fax] (01834) 842888.

THE IMPERIAL HOTEL
The Paragon, SA70 7HR
Cliff-top location overlooking the South Beach towards St Catherine's and Caldy Islands. Private steps to the beach. The Imperial offers extensive menus and a good wine list, served by courteous staff in very pleasant surroundings. Three minutes' level walk to the town centre.
DOUBLE ROOM: from £20 to £30
SINGLE ROOM: from £25 to £35
FOOD: up to £15
Hours: breakfast 8am–9.30am, dinner 7pm–8.30pm, bar meals 11.30am–9pm.
Cuisine: ENGLISH – traditional English cuisine, with à la carte, table d'hôte and bar meals.
Cards: Visa, Access, Diners, AmEx, Switch.
Other points: licensed, Sunday lunch, children welcome, pets allowed, open bank holidays, functions, children welcome, baby-listening device, cots, 24hr reception, residents' lounge, residents' bar.
Rooms: 4 single rooms, 18 double rooms,

22 twin rooms. All with TV, radio, alarm, telephone, tea/coffee-making facilities. Executive rooms available.
Directions: M4, A40, A477 to Kilgetty, then A478.
JAN-ROELOF EGGENS ☎ (01834) 843737 [Fax] (01834) 844342.

WATERWYNCH HOUSE HOTEL
Waterwynch Bay, SA70 8TJ
Situated in the Pembrokshire Coast National Park, the hotel nestles in a secluded cove on the shore of Carmarthen Bay and is surrounded by its own 27 acres of woodland and private gardens. This attractive hotel offers a perfect base for walkers, bird-watchers, artists, fishing and golf.
DOUBLE ROOM: from £30 to £40
SINGLE ROOM: from £35 to £45
FOOD: up to £15
Hours: breakfast 8.30am–9.30am, dinner 6.30pm–8.30pm, closed November until March.
Cuisine: CONTINENTAL / BRITISH – attractively presented, freshly cooked dishes. Meals may be taken in the sun lounge.
Cards: Visa, Access.
Other points: children catered for (please check for age limits), parking, no-smoking area, residents' lounge, garden, vegetarian meals, traditional Sunday lunch.
Rooms: 17 bedrooms. All with TV, telephone, radio, alarm, hair dryer, tea/coffee-making facilities.
Directions: follow A478 from Kilgetty towards Tenby. Half a mile after leaving the New Hedges roundabout, take the signposted private-access road on the left to Waterwynch Bay.
GEOFF & BETTE HAMPTON ☎ (01834) 842464 [Fax] (01834) 845076.

GWENT

ABERGAVENNY • map 4A4

THE SWAN HOTEL
Cross Street, NP7 5ER
The hotel is situated adjacent to the bus station and within 10 minutes' walk from the railway station. It is centrally placed in the town, thus affording easy access to the M4. Very popular because of its excellent menu and reasonable prices.
DOUBLE ROOM: from £20 to £30
FOOD: up to £15
Hours: bar meals 12noon–2pm, dinner 7pm–9.30pm.
Cuisine: BRITISH – traditional home-cooking, e.g., Sunday lunch: roast beef with Yorkshire pud. Home-made pies, moussaka and fresh salads.
Cards: Visa, Access, AmEx.
Other points: Sunday lunch.
Rooms: 2 single rooms, 6 double rooms, 3 twin rooms. All with TV, radio, telephone, tea/coffee-making facilities.
Directions: next to bus station in Abergavenny.

IAN S. LITTLE ☎ (01873) 852829 [Fax] (01873) 852829.

CHEPSTOW • map 4A5

THE HUNTSMAN HOTEL
Chepstow, NP6 6B4
A small country hotel serving well-presented food in generous portions, with polite, unintrusive service. Three miles to Chepstow racecourse and golfing facilities.
DOUBLE ROOM: up to £20
FOOD: up to £15 ☆
Hours: breakfast 7.30am–10.30am, lunch 12noon–2pm, dinner 7pm–10pm.
Cuisine: BRITISH / CONTINENTAL – chicken in leek and Stilton sauce, in the restaurant. Breaded plaice, chicken chasseur and lasagne, in the bar.
Cards: Visa, Access, AmEx.
Other points: licensed, Sunday lunch, playland, pets allowed, functions.
Rooms: 3 single rooms, 3 double rooms, 2 twin

rooms, 2 family rooms. All with TV, radio, alarm, telephone, tea/coffee-making facilities.
Directions: approximately 4 miles out on the B4235 Chepstow to Usk road.
MR A.C. MOLES ☎ (01291) 641521.

CWMBRAN • map A4A

THE PARKWAY HOTEL & CONFERENCE CENTRE
Cwmbran Drive, NA44 3UW

Outstanding in all aspects, The Parkway is ideal for holiday-makers and business visitors alike. Designed on a Mediterranean theme, the hotel offers accommodation of a very high standard, first-class restaurant meals, a leisure complex, and excellent conference and banqueting facilities. Privately-owned and run, the service is excellent and a warm welcome is guaranteed. Highly recommended.
DOUBLE ROOM: from £30 to £40
SINGLE ROOM: from £55
FOOD: up to £15
Hours: breakfast 7am–9.30am, lunch 12noon–2.30pm, dinner 7pm–10pm.
Cuisine: BRITISH / MEDITERRANEAN – extensive choice such as River Wye salmon, lemon sole Walewska, grills, tournedos Rossini, Carvery. Open-air dining in the coffee shop at lunchtimes only.
Cards: Visa, Access, Diners, AmEx.
Other points: licensed, open-air dining, Sunday lunch, children catered for (please check for age limits), garden, residents' lounge, conferences, leisure centre, baby-listening device, cots, 24hr reception.
Rooms: 47 double rooms, 23 twin rooms. All with TV, radio, alarm, telephone, tea/coffee-making facilities, hair dryer, trouser-press.
Directions: off junction 26 of the M4, onto A4042. Left at roundabout onto A4051 (Cwmbran Drive). Third exit at next roundabout and first turning right.
JOHN WOODCOCK ☎ (01633) 871199
Fax (01633) 869160.

LLANTRISANT • map 4A5

THE GREYHOUND INN & HOTEL
Near Usk, NP5 1LE

The Greyhound was established as a country inn in 1845. Originally a 17th century farmhouse, with a stone stable block that has recently been converted into 10 bedrooms, all with en suite bathroom. Available in the dining room, or one of the two lounges, is a varied but inexpensive menu with an emphasis on home-cooking using traditional recipes. In the summer you can enjoy the beautiful surroundings in the beer garden, and in winter you can warm yourself by the real log fire. You can even shop for your country pine or antiques in the stone barn showroom.
DOUBLE ROOM: from £20 to £30
SINGLE ROOM: from £30 to £45
FOOD: up to £15
Hours: breakfast 7.15am–9.30am, lunch 12noon–2.15pm, dinner 6pm–10.30pm.

Cuisine: BRITISH – traditional home-cooking.
Cards: Visa, Access.
Other points: parking, children welcome, garden, open-air dining, vegetarian meals.
Rooms: 10 bedrooms. All with en suite, TV, telephone, radio, tea/coffee-making facilities.
Directions: take the A449 to Usk town centre. Enter the square and take the second on the left, following signs towards Llantrisant. The Greyhound may be found just over two miles down the road, on the right.
NICHOLAS DAVIES ☎ (01291) 672505/673447
Fax (01291) 673255.

THE ROYAL OAK
Near Usk, NP5 1LG

A 15th century residential inn situated on the A449, only 10 minutes' drive from junction 24 on the M4. An attractive, white-painted building standing in a well-kept cottage garden in the valley of the River Usk. In the summer the beer garden and the children's play area are in great demand.
DOUBLE ROOM: from £20 to £30
FOOD: from £15 to £20 CLUB
Hours: breakfast 7.30am–9.30am, bar meals 12noon–2pm, dinner 7.30pm–10pm, bar meals 7pm–10pm.
Cuisine: INTERNATIONAL – paella, beef Wellington.
Cards: Visa, Access, AmEx.
Other points: open-air dining, pets allowed, children welcome, coaches by prior arrangement.
Directions: near the A449.
MR GASCOINE ☎ (01291) 673317.

MONMOUTH • map 4A5

THE CROWN AT WHITEBROOK
Whitebrook, NP5 4TX

A small, intimate restaurant and hotel, remotely situated in beautiful scenery, five miles south of Monmouth and one mile from the River Wye. Sandra Bates specializes in creating original dishes from fresh local ingredients, and there is a good wine list. The cheerful hospitality of the proprietors and staff creates a relaxing, friendly atmosphere in which to dine or stay. Regional Newcomer of Year 1991.
DOUBLE ROOM: from £30 to £40
SINGLE ROOM: from £45 to £55
FOOD: from £20 to £25   CLUB ☆
Hours: breakfast 8am–9.30am, lunch 12noon–2pm, dinner 7pm–9pm, closed Christmas day and Boxing day.
Cuisine: FRENCH – specialities include quail boned and stuffed with a pork and sultana mousse. Local venison, salmon and Welsh lamb. All freshly cooked to order.
Cards: Visa, Access, Diners, AmEx.
Other points: licensed, Sunday lunch, children welcome, garden, pets allowed.
Rooms: 9 double rooms, 3 twin rooms.
Directions: off A466, 2 miles from Bigsweir Bridge. In the Whitebrook Valley.
ROGER & SANDRA BATES ☎ (01600) 860254
Fax (01600) 860607.

MONMOUTH PUNCH HOUSE
Agincourt Square, NP5 3BT

Situated in the centre of town and therefore enjoying both the local and the tourist trade. The restaurant overlooks Agincourt Square and its statues of Henry V and Charles Rolls. Throughout summer the building is festooned with hanging baskets.
FOOD: from £15 to £20
Hours: bar meals 11.30am–2.30pm, bar meals 6.30pm–9pm, lunch 11.30am–2pm.
Cuisine: BRITISH – traditional British dishes using finest, fresh local produce.
Cards: Visa, Access.
Other points: open-air dining, Sunday lunch, children welcome, coaches by prior arrangement.
Directions: situated on the A466, in the town centre.
MR W.J.L. WILLS ☎ (01600) 713855.

NEWPORT • map 4A5

VILLA DINO RESTAURANT
103 Chepstow Road, Maindee, NP9 8BY

This attractive Italian restaurant serves excellent food in a very relaxing and welcoming atmosphere. All dishes are freshly cooked to order and well presented. A small family business in a delightful Victorian setting. The service is outstanding – professional, efficient and very warm and courteous. Highly recommended: a winner of many awards.
FOOD: from £15 to £20
Hours: dinner 7pm–11pm, closed Sunday.
Cuisine: ITALIAN – a good choice of Italian dishes. Specialities include Chateaubriand bouquetière, filetto al Stilton. Fish, veal, beef, chicken, pasta and vegetarian. Something for everyone.
Cards: Visa, Access, Diners, AmEx.
Other points: licensed, disabled access, functions.
Directions: on the main road from Newport to Chepstow. Five minutes to rail station and motorway.
DINO GULOTTA ☎ (01633) 251267.

TINTERN • map 4A5

THE FOUNTAIN INN
Trellech Grange, NP6 6QW

A typical 17th century country inn where the food is prepared to order. The bar provides the focal point and, on a chilly day, a log fire provides a warm welcome. Real ales and whisky a speciality.
DOUBLE ROOM: up to £20
FOOD: up to £15 [CLUB]
Hours: lunch 12noon–3pm, Sunday 12noon–2pm, dinner 7pm–10.30pm, Sunday 7pm–9.30pm, closed Christmas evening only.
Cuisine: ENGLISH – dishes include jugged hare, Tudor roast, venison, rack of lamb.
Cards: Visa, Access.
Other points: licensed, Sunday lunch, children welcome, caravan facilities.
Rooms: 1 single room, 2 double rooms, 5 twin rooms, 2 family rooms.
Directions: off A466, 2 miles from Tintern Abbey. Turn by Royal George in Tintern and bear right around ponds.
CHRIS & JUDITH RABBITS ☎ (01291) 689303.

USK • map 4A5

See LLANTRISANT (Gwent), page 289.

GWYNEDD

ABERSOCH • map 7C2

TUDOR COURT HOTEL & RESTAURANT
Lôn Sarn Bach, LL53 7EB

Once the home of an old sea captain, but now extensively refurbished to provide a comfortable hotel with its own restaurant, offering fine cuisine using the best of local fresh produce. Sailing, golfing, fishing and many historical places of interest nearby. Open all Christmas and New Year. Mini-breaks and inclusive golf breaks arranged.
DOUBLE ROOM: from £20 to £30
SINGLE ROOM: from £25 to £35
FOOD: up to £15 [CLUB]
Hours: breakfast 8am–9am, lunch 12.30am–2pm, dinner 6.30pm–9.30pm.
Cuisine: FRENCH / ENGLISH – vegetarian meals also available.
Cards: Visa, Access, Diners.
Other points: parking, children welcome, afternoon teas, no-smoking area, disabled access, pets by prior arrangement, vegetarian meals.
Rooms: 1 single room, 4 double rooms, 2 twin rooms, 2 family rooms.
Directions: from Caernarfon or Porthmadog go to Pwllheli and drive along the coast to Abersoch. The hotel is on the right-hand side of the main road through the village.
MS J. JONES ☎ (01758) 713354 [Fax] (01758) 713354.

THE WHITE HOUSE HOTEL
Abersoch, LL53 7AG

Overlooking the picturesque harbour of Abersoch, Cardigan Bay and St Tudwal's Islands, this hotel is set back from the road in its own grounds. A warm welcome, comfortable accommodation and good food await you. The bedrooms have recently been modernized, and the elegant dining room is comfortable and spacious. A two-mile-long sandy beach is within easy walking distance.
DOUBLE ROOM: from £20 to £30
SINGLE ROOM: from £25 to £35
FOOD: from £15 to £20
Hours: bar meals 6.30pm–9.30pm, dinner 7pm–9pm.

Cuisine: BRITISH – bar menu and à la carte restaurant menu (evenings). Fresh local produce used wherever possible. Local lobsters and crabs, Welsh lamb and beef.
Cards: Visa, Access, Switch.
Other points: licensed, children welcome, garden, pets allowed, residents' lounge, baby-listening device, baby-sitting, cots available.
Rooms: 1 single room, 7 double rooms, 3 twin rooms, 1 family room. All with TV, radio, alarm, telephone, tea/coffee-making facilities.
Directions: A499, 7 miles from Pwllheli.
JAYNE & DAVID SMITH ☎ (01758) 713427
[Fax] (01758) 713512.

AMLWCH • map 7A2

LASTRA FARM HOTEL
Amlwch, LL68 9TF
Steeped in history, this delightful licensed country house hotel can accommodate any party, large or small. Situated in this most beautiful part of Wales, there is something for everyone, whether your interests lie with history or leisure activities. Lastra Farm Hotel is a great base for exploring Anglesey.
DOUBLE ROOM: from £20 to £30
SINGLE ROOM: from £25 to £35
FOOD: up to £15
Hours: breakfast 7.30am–9.30am, lunch 12noon–2pm, dinner 7pm–9.30pm.
Cuisine: BRITISH – freshly cooked British cuisine with a French influence. Game and lobster available in season.
Cards: Visa, Access, Switch.
Other points: parking, children welcome, pets allowed, residents' lounge, garden, vegetarian meals, traditional Sunday lunch.
Rooms: 1 single room, 5 double rooms, 1 twin room. All with TV, telephone, radio, tea/coffee-making facilities.
Directions: located near the sports centre in Amlwch, northern Anglesey.
MAURICE HUTCHINSON ☎ (01407) 830406
[Fax] (01407) 832552.

BALA • map 7C3

PLAS COCH HOTEL
High Street, LL23 7AB
This attractive stone building, dating back to 1780, sits in the centre of Bala near Bala Lake, surrounded by Snowdonia National Park. The restaurant lends itself to traditional Welsh cooking, with an emphasis on local produce and a choice of good wines.
DOUBLE ROOM: from £20 to £30
SINGLE ROOM: from £35 to £45
FOOD: up to £15 ☆
Hours: breakfast 8am–9am, lunch 12noon–2pm, dinner 7pm–8.30pm, closed Christmas day.
Cuisine: WELSH – à la carte menu, fixed three-course menu and bar menu.
Cards: Visa, Access, Diners, AmEx.
Other points: licensed, Sunday lunch, no-smoking area, children welcome, afternoon tea, baby-listening device, cots, left luggage, residents' bar, residents' lounge, vegetarian meals, parking.
Rooms: 1 single room, 4 double rooms, 1 twin room, 4 family rooms. All with TV, radio, alarm, telephone, tea/coffee-making facilities.
Directions: Bala is on the A494, 14 miles north of Dolgellau, 10 miles south of the A5.
MR & MRS EVANS ☎ (01678) 520309
[Fax] (01678) 521135.

BARMOUTH • map 7C3

LLWYNDU FARMHOUSE HOTEL
Llanaber, LL42 1RR
A delightful farmhouse dating from the early 17th century, with wonderful views of the sea and mountains of Cardigan Bay. You can savour the imaginative cuisine in an atmosphere of oak beams, inglenooks, candlelight and a little music. Licensed. Llwyndu was praised for its hospitality even in the 17th century, and a history of the house is available for guests. Occasional theme evenings for parties. All rooms have en suite bathrooms, TV, radio alarms, beverage facilities and great character. Four are in a converted barn next to the farmhouse.
DOUBLE ROOM: from £20 to £30
FOOD: up to £15
Hours: breakfast 8.30am–9.30am, dinner 6.30pm–9pm, open all year.
Cuisine: BRITISH – Taste of Wales (Blas ar Gymru) member. Local produce and seafood used in Welsh and international dishes: Welsh black beef and black olives with cardamom sauce, ham Llwyndu, old Welsh rarebit. Selection of Welsh cheeses. Good selection of vegetarian dishes also.
Cards: Visa.
Other points: licensed.
Rooms: 1 single room, 2 double rooms, 4 family rooms. All with TV, tea/coffee-making facilities, alarm.
Directions: 2 miles north of Barmouth on the A496.
PETER & PAULA THOMPSON ☎ (01341) 280144.

PANORAMA HOTEL
Panorama Road, LL42 1DG
A warm welcome awaits you at this friendly, family-run hotel, set in 2 acres of wooded grounds and overlooking the Mawddach estuary and Barmouth harbour. An excellent reputation for à la carte, table d'hôte and home-made bar meals, and a comprehensive wine list.
DOUBLE ROOM: from £20 to £30
SINGLE ROOM: from £25 to £35
FOOD: up to £15 [CLUB] ☆
Hours: breakfast 8.30am–9.30am, lunch 12noon–2pm, bar meals 12noon–2pm, dinner 7pm–9pm, bar meals 7pm–9pm.
Cuisine: BRITISH – home-made food.
Cards: Visa, Access.
Other points: open-air dining, Sunday lunch, pets allowed, children welcome, afternoon tea, vegetarian meals.
Rooms: 1 single room, 4 double rooms, 8 twin rooms, 4 family rooms.

WALES • GWYNEDD

Directions: Panorama Road is off the A496, half a mile east of Barmouth harbour.
MR & MRS FLAVELL & MR MORGAN
☎ (01341) 280550 Fax (01341) 280346.

BEDDGELERT • map 7B2

ROYAL GOAT HOTEL
Beddgelert, LL55 4YE

This Georgian building is situated in a charming little village in the heart of the Snowdonia National Park. The Royal Goat offers traditional Welsh hospitality in great comfort and style. The combination of excellent food, accommodation and service makes this hotel a pleasure to visit. Situated in town renowned for its 'Legend of Gelert', the faithful dog. Highly recommended.
DOUBLE ROOM: from £30 to £40
SINGLE ROOM: from £35 to £45
FOOD: up to £15
Hours: breakfast 7.45am–10am, lunch 12noon–2.30pm, dinner 7pm–10pm.
Cuisine: BRITISH – à la carte and fixed three-course menus. Serving fish, steak, duck and veal.
Cards: Visa, Access, Diners, AmEx.
Other points: licensed, Sunday lunch, no-smoking area, children welcome, garden, afternoon tea, pets allowed, car hire, pony-trekking, baby-listening device, baby-sitting, cots, 24hr reception, residents' lounge, residents' bar.
Rooms: 17 double rooms, 17 twin rooms. All with TV, radio, alarm, telephone, tea/coffee-making facilities.
Directions: located in the town centre.
IRENIE & EVAN ROBERTS ☎ (01766) 890224/890343 Fax (01766) 890422.

BETWS-Y-COED • map 7B3

ROYAL OAK HOTEL
Holyhead Road, LL24 OAY

Situated in a picturesque village in the heart of Snowdonia, the Royal Oak Hotel has been refurbished to provide excellent facilities and a high standard of comfort. All food is freshly made on the premises and can be enjoyed in the main dining room or in the more informal grill room. The newly opened Stables Bistro serves traditional bar food all day.
DOUBLE ROOM: from £30 to £40
FOOD: up to £15
Hours: breakfast 7.45am–9.30am, lunch 11.45am–2pm, dinner 5.30pm–9pm.
Cuisine: BRITISH – fresh fish, home-made soups, grilled steaks. Traditional bar food served in the new bar. Stables Bistro is open for meals all day 10.30am until 10.30pm.
Cards: Visa, Access, Diners, AmEx.
Other points: licensed, Sunday lunch, children welcome, coaches by prior arrangement, functions.
Rooms: 4 single rooms, 5 double rooms, 13 twin rooms, 5 family rooms. All with en suite, TV, telephone.
Directions: on the A5, in the centre of Betws-y-Coed.
☎ (01690) 710219 Fax (01690) 710603.

TY GWYN HOTEL
LL24 0SG

A delightful 16th century coaching inn, which has captured the charm and character of the period with low beams, antique furnishings and tasteful decor. An idyllic setting overlooking the River Conwy in this beautiful Welsh village. Excellent home-cooking ensures a strong local following. 1987 Routiers Newcomer of the Year winner.
DOUBLE ROOM: from £20 to £30
FOOD: up to £15
Hours: breakfast 8.15am–10am, lunch 12noon–2pm, bar meals 12noon–2pm, dinner 7pm–9.30pm, bar meals 7pm–9.30pm.
Cuisine: WELSH / CONTINENTAL – pheasant braised in a Beaujolais and wild mushroom sauce, fresh local wild salmon served with a basil and vermouth sauce, breast of chicken Rossini.
Cards: Visa, Access.
Other points: Sunday lunch, children welcome, pets allowed.
Rooms: 1 single room, 5 double rooms, 13 twin rooms.
Directions: on the A5 south of Betws-y-Coed.
JAMES & SHELAGH RATCLIFFE ☎ (01690) 710383/710787.

CAERNARFON • map 7B2

THE BLACK BOY INN
North-Gate Street, LL55 1RW

A 15th century inn situated within the walls of Caernarfon Castle. Good sea and game fishing. Ideal for yachting on inland tidal waters. Traditional home-cooking.
DOUBLE ROOM: up to £20
SINGLE ROOM: up to £25
FOOD: up to £15
Hours: lunch 12noon–2.30pm, dinner 6.30pm–9pm.
Cuisine: ENGLISH – traditional English cooking, e.g., roast beef, roast lamb and the trimmings. A la carte and table d'hôte menus.
Cards: Visa, Access, Diners.
Other points: Sunday lunch, children welcome.
Rooms: 2 single rooms, 4 double rooms, 4 twin rooms, 2 family room.
Directions: located in the town centre.
MR ROBERT WILLIAMS ☎ (01286) 673023.

VICTORIA HOUSE
13 Church Street, LL55 1SW

A Victorian terraced guest house offering comfortable accommodation in delightfully furnished surroundings. Snowdonia National Park and Caernarfon Castle are close by.
DOUBLE ROOM: up to £20
SINGLE ROOM: up to £25
Hours: breakfast 8am.
Cuisine: BREAKFAST.
Other points: children welcome, open bank holidays, pets (by arrangement), vegetarian meals.
Rooms: 2 single rooms, 4 double/twin rooms, 1 family room.
Directions: past castle entrance, turn right at end of street.
TERENCE & JANINE SMITH ☎ (01286) 673133.

CAPEL CURIG • map 7B3

COBDEN'S HOTEL & BRASSERIE
LL24 0EE

A 200-year-old country house hotel, set in the heart of Snowdonia. Comfortable, informal and fun; perfect for total rest and relaxation. Own 200-metre rock pool (clear running water) for swimming and fishing.
DOUBLE ROOM: from £20 to £30
SINGLE ROOM: from £25 to £35
FOOD: up to £15
Hours: lunch 12noon–2pm, dinner 6.30pm–9.30pm, Sunday 7pm–9pm.
Cuisine: earthy, international and healthy!
Cards: Visa, Access, AmEx.
Other points: licensed, Sunday lunch, children welcome, pets allowed, open bank holidays.
Rooms: 4 single rooms, 5 double rooms, 5 twin rooms, 2 family rooms. All with TV, tea/coffee-making facilities.
Directions: on A5, between Betws y Coed and Bangor.
THE GOODALL FAMILY ☎ (016904) 243/308
[Fax] (016904) 354.

CONWY • map 7B3

DEGANWY CASTLE HOTEL
Station Road, Deganwy, LL31 9DA

Originally a cottage and over 250 years old, the Deganwy Castle Hotel offers a magnificent view of Conwy estuary and castle. A main feature is the bar, which is built from beer barrels. Tourist packages are available. The many nearby places of interest include Conwy Castle, Bodnant Gardens and the beautiful Snowdonia National Park.
DOUBLE ROOM: from £20 to £30
FOOD: from £15 to £20 [CLUB]
Hours: breakfast 7am–9.30am, lunch 12noon–2.30pm, dinner 7pm–9.30pm.
Cuisine: BRITISH – à la carte and table d'hôte menus, offering an extensive choice of dishes. Vegetarian dishes also available.
Cards: Visa, Access, Diners, AmEx.
Other points: licensed, open-air dining, Sunday lunch, no-smoking area, children welcome, pets allowed, residents' lounge, garden, parking, afternoon tea.
Directions: proceed along A55 and take signposted turning to Deganwy.
DENNIS CHIN ☎ (01492) 583555 [Fax] (01492) 583555.

CRICCIETH • map 7C2

BRON EIFION COUNTRY HOUSE HOTEL
LL52 0SA

Built in the 1860s, Bron Eifion is set in the heart of the tranquil Welsh countryside. The hotel is surrounded by beautifully tended rose gardens and lawns with stonewalled terraces. The decor is of tasteful pine panelling, adding to the hotel's character. Meals are well prepared from fresh local produce.
DOUBLE ROOM: from £40 to £50
SINGLE ROOM: from £45 to £55
FOOD: from £20 to £25
Hours: breakfast 8am–9.30am, dinner 7pm–8.45pm (last orders), Sunday lunch 12noon–2pm.
Cuisine: BRITISH – à la carte menu, bar snacks, bar meals, fixed three-course menu and vegetarian meals.
Cards: Visa, Access, AmEx.
Other points: licensed, Sunday lunch, children welcome, garden, afternoon tea, conservatory, pets by arrangement, croquet, residents' lounge, residents' bar, vegetarian meals, disabled access.
Rooms: 9 double rooms, 6 twin rooms, 2 family rooms. All with en suite, TV, radio, telephone, tea/coffee-making facilities, trouser-press.
Directions: from the east on A497, through Criccieth. Hotel is ¼ mile on the right.
ALAN & CAROLE THOMPSON ☎ (01766) 522385 [Fax] (01766) 522003.

CAERWYLAN HOTEL
Beach Bank, LL52 0HW

Caerwylan is an imposing hotel and the only one in Criccieth situated on the promenade. The lounge and several of the bedroom windows look out across the sandy beaches to the sea, or to the castle. The food is traditional Welsh. The warm welcome offered by the Davies ensures many repeat bookings.
DOUBLE ROOM: up to £20
Hours: breakfast 8.45am–9.30am, dinner 6.45pm–7.30pm, closed mid-October until Easter.
Cuisine: WELSH.
Other points: pets allowed, children welcome, residents' lounge, TV lounge.
Rooms: 6 single rooms, 4 double rooms, 9 twin rooms, 7 family rooms. All with TV, radio, tea/coffee-making facilities.
Directions: off the A497 onto the B4411 to Criccieth. Hotel is on main promenade.
MR & MRS DAVIES ☎ (01766) 522547.

GLYN Y COED HOTEL
Porthmadog Road, LL52 0HL

A Victorian house overlooking the sea, mountains and castle. There is an attractive garden at the front with a small stream running through it. Family-run, a friendly, homely atmosphere prevails.
DOUBLE ROOM: from £20 to £30
SINGLE ROOM: up to £25
FOOD: up to £15
Hours: breakfast 8.30am–9am, lunch 12.30pm–1.30pm, dinner 6pm–6.30pm, closed Christmas day and New Year's eve.
Cuisine: BRITISH.
Other points: children welcome, pets allowed, residents' lounge, garden, baby-listening device, cots, 24hr reception.
Rooms: 2 single rooms, 3 double rooms, 2 twin room, 3 family rooms. All with en suite, TV, tea/coffee-making facilities.
Directions: Nearest hotel to Criccieth on A497 facing the sea.
MRS ANN REYNOLDS ☎ (01766) 522870 [Fax] (01766) 523341.

THE MOELWYN RESTAURANT WITH ROOMS
Mona Terrace, LL52 0HG

A Victorian, creeper-clad restaurant directly overlooking Cardigan Bay, with bar/lounge and well-appointed bedrooms. The restaurant serves English and French cuisine, including locally caught salmon. All food is carefully prepared and complemented by a comprehensive selection of wines. Public car park adjacent. Disabled access to restaurant only. Vegetarian menu.
DOUBLE ROOM: from £20 to £30
FOOD: up to £15
Hours: Sunday lunch 12.30am–2pm, dinner 7pm–9.30pm, closed January until March.
Cuisine: ENGLISH / FRENCH – seafood, salmon and lamb, interesting sauces and fresh vegetables. Home-made sweets. Lobster when available.
Cards: Visa, Access.
Other points: licensed, Sunday lunch, children welcome, pets by prior arrangement.
Directions: on the seafront.
MR & MRS PETER BOOTH ☎ (01766) 522500.

DOLGELLAU • map 7C3

CLIFTON HOUSE HOTEL
Smithfield Square, LL40 1ES

Dating from the 18th century when it was the County Gaol, the Clifton now offers a much warmer welcome as a hotel and restaurant. Mrs Dix, the chef, makes imaginative use of fresh local produce, and all the dishes are excellently cooked. The service is 'exemplary' and the warmth of the welcome is undoubtably genuine. Highly recommended for food and accommodation.
DOUBLE ROOM: from £20 to £30
SINGLE ROOM: from £25 to £35
FOOD: from £15 to £20
Hours: breakfast 8am–9.30am, dinner 7pm–9.30pm, closed January.
Cuisine: ENGLISH – interesting and varied menu featuring traditional and vegetarian dishes and using fresh, local produce.
Cards: Visa, Access.
Other points: licensed, garden, children welcome.
Rooms: 5 double rooms, 2 twin rooms.
Directions: A470. Centre of Dolgellau.
ROB & PAULINE DIX ☎ (01341) 422554.

HARLECH • map 7C2

CASTLE COTTAGE HOTEL & RESTAURANT
Pen Llech, LL46 2YL

An oak-beamed dining room and bar in one of the oldest houses in Harlech. Only 300 yards from the castle. International cuisine plus modestly priced wine list. Ideally situated for the Royal St David's Golf Course and surrounding area of natural beauty.
DOUBLE ROOM: from £20 to £30
SINGLE ROOM: up to £25
FOOD: from £15 to £20
Hours: Sunday lunch 12noon–2pm, dinner summer 7pm–9.30pm, winter 7pm–9pm.

Cuisine: INTERNATIONAL – dishes include local rack of lamb and honey and rosemary sauce. Brochette of scallops and smoked bacon, beurre blanc sauce.
Cards: Visa, Access, AmEx.
Other points: Sunday lunch, no-smoking area, children welcome.
Rooms: 2 single rooms, 2 double rooms, 2 twin rooms. All with en suite, radio, tea/coffee-making facilities.
Directions: on B4573 road to Porthmadog.
MR & MRS ROBERTS ☎ (01766) 780479.

THE CASTLE HOTEL
Castle Square, LL36 2YH

A family-run hotel open all year, offering a wide menu and warm, welcoming service. Local attractions include Harlech Castle, Cardigan Bay, a local golf club, Beddgelert copper mine and a dry ski slope. Nearby, Shell Island provides the opportunity for seal and bird spotting, and shell collecting.
DOUBLE ROOM: from £20 to £30
FOOD: from £15 to £20
Hours: meals all day in summer 12noon–11pm, lunch 12noon–3pm, dinner 7pm–11pm, last orders 10pm.
Cuisine: ENGLISH – pub menu, serving a range of dishes from Dover sole and steak tartare to cow pie, lasagne and the 'Kiddies Corner' selection.
Cards: Visa, Access.
Other points: licensed, Sunday lunch, no-smoking area, children welcome, pets allowed.
Rooms: 1 single room, 5 double rooms, 4 twin rooms. All with TV, telephone, tea/coffee-making facilities.
Directions: opposite the castle in the centre of Harlech, which is on the A496.
R.G. & T.M. SWINSCOE ☎ (01766) 780529.

HOLYHEAD • map 7B2

BULL HOTEL
London Road, Anglesey, LL65 3DP

A pleasant, cream-painted building on the main A5 road to Holyhead. There is a large, sheltered beer garden with children's play area outside, while inside, the main, informal eating area is separate from the bar. For those wishing to linger a while, the Bull offers comfortable accommodation.
DOUBLE ROOM: up to £20
SINGLE ROOM: from £25 to £35
FOOD: up to £15
Hours: breakfast 7.30am–9am, lunch 12noon–2pm, dinner 7pm–9.30pm, bar meals 12noon–9pm.
Cuisine: BRITISH – specials change daily.
Cards: Visa, Access.
Other points: open-air dining, Sunday lunch, pets allowed, children welcome, afternoon tea.
Rooms: 2 single rooms, 5 double rooms, 6 twin rooms, 2 family rooms.
Directions: situated 200 yards from Holyhead side traffic lights at A5025 junction.
DAVID HALL ☎ (01407) 740351.

VALLEY HOTEL
Station Road, Valley, LL65 3DU
This old coaching house has been newly decorated and refurbished to offer guests pleasurable surroundings while dining in the inviting restaurant or quenching a thirst in the cosy bar. Located in the beautiful Isle of Anglesey, there is always plenty to do, and the Valley Hotel is a good base for a relaxing weekend break or a family holiday.
DOUBLE ROOM: up to £20
SINGLE ROOM: from £25 to £35
FOOD: up to £15
Hours: breakfast 7am–9.30am, bar meals 12noon–2.30pm, dinner 7pm–9.30pm, bar meals 5.30pm–9pm.
Cuisine: BRITISH / FRENCH.
Cards: Visa, Access.
Other points: parking, children welcome, pets allowed, no-smoking area, conference facilities, garden, open-air dining, vegetarian meals, traditional Sunday lunch.
Rooms: 3 single rooms, 5 double rooms, 6 twin rooms, 2 triple rooms, 2 family rooms. All with en suite, TV, telephone, radio, alarm, tea/coffee-making facilities.
Directions: situated near the crossroads of the A5/A5025, five miles east of Holyhead.
DAVID HALL ☎ (01407) 740203 Fax (01407) 740686.

LLANBEDR • map 7C2

LLEW GLAS
LL45 2LD
Originally 'Yr Hen Feudy' (the old cowshed), today the Llew Glas brasserie is a popular, tastefully furnished brasserie with character beams and Trevor in full view cooking in the kitchen. All food is home-made and purchased locally and fresh. All lamb is Welsh, and baked goods are from their own bakery. Vegetarians and those with special diets are catered for. Many places of interest nearby.
FOOD: up to £15
Hours: dinner 6pm–10pm, open all year.
Cuisine: BRITISH – traditional home-cooked cuisine, using fresh local produce.
Cards: Visa.
Other points: licensed, open-air dining, no-smoking area, children welcome.
Directions: 3 miles south from Harlech. Turn left before bridge in centre of Llanbedr village on Cwm Bychan Road, which leads to the Roman Steps.
TREVOR & MARJ PHAROAH ☎ (01341) 23555.

LLANBEDROG • map 7C2

SHIP INN
Near Pwllheli, LL53 7PE
A public house serving very tasty food at good prices. It also has open views on three sides, with a protected area outside for diners. Celebrated for its flower displays, the gardens, which are attended by a professional gardener, give a particularly pleasant outlook.
FOOD: up to £15
Hours: lunch 12noon–3pm, dinner 6pm–9.45pm.
Cuisine: BRITISH – home-made pies, curries, local crab and lobster, salads, steaks.
Other points: parking, children welcome, no-smoking area, open-air dining, vegetarian meals.
Directions: approaching Llanbedrog from Pwllheli, take the sharp right towards Aberdaron.
BRIAN & PATRICIA WARD ☎ (01758) 740270.

LLANBERIS • map 7B2

LAKE VIEW HOTEL
Tan y Pant, LL55 4EL
The Lake View Hotel offers exceptional views of the surrounding terrain. Close to the narrow-gauge railways and Snowdonia National Park. A friendly hotel with a homely atmosphere.
DOUBLE ROOM: up to £20
FOOD: up to £15
Hours: breakfast 8.30am–9.30am, lunch 12noon–2pm, dinner 6.30pm–9pm, open all day.
Cuisine: ENGLISH – veal is a speciality, also fine steaks in home-made sauces. Local chef.
Cards: Visa, Access, Diners.
Other points: licensed, Sunday lunch, children welcome, coaches by prior arrangement
Rooms: 5 double rooms, 10 twin rooms, 4 family rooms.
Directions: on the A4086, on the Caernarfon side of Llanberis.
BRIAN TAYLOR & VAL TAYLOR ☎ (01286) 870422.

LLANDUDNO • map 7B3

AMBASSADOR HOTEL
Promenade, LL30 2NR
The Williams family have been in the hotel trade for 30 years and in that time have built up a regular return business. The two sun lounges are relaxing places to sit whatever the weather. Mini-breaks available throughout the year.
DOUBLE ROOM: from £20 to £30
SINGLE ROOM: up to £25
FOOD: up to £15
Hours: breakfast 8.30am–9.15am, bar meals 12noon–1.30pm, dinner 6.30pm–7.30pm, closed January.
Cuisine: BRITISH.
Other points: central heating, children welcome, residents' lounge, lift, bar, cots, disabled access, vegetarian meals, parking, residents' bar.
Rooms: 7 single rooms, 53 double/twin, 3 family rooms. All with TV, tea/coffee-making facilities.
Directions: leave A55; take A470 to Llandudno. Follow to Promenade, then turn left.
DAVID T. WILLIAMS ☎ (01492) 876886 Fax (01492) 876347.

CASANOVA RESTAURANT
18 Chapel Street, LL30 2SY
Situated in the heart of town. Gingham and red tablecloths, a cedar ceiling and lively music add to the bustling atmosphere. A very popular

restaurant: advance booking recommended.
FOOD: up to £15
Hours: dinner 6pm–10.30pm.
Cuisine: ITALIAN – e.g. calamari fritti, insalata Casanova, filetto al funghi.
Cards: Visa, Access.
Other points: licensed, children welcome, street parking.
Directions: off Gloddaeth Street opposite the English Presbyterian church.
MR K.R. BOONHAM ☎ (01492) 878426.

DUNOON HOTEL
Gloddaeth Street, LL30 2DW
Lavishly appointed with great attention to detail, the Dunoon exudes charm and comfort. It has been in the same family for over 40 years, which accounts for the care shown in the elegant accommodation and spacious restaurant. The Dunoon provides the ideal place to relax and enjoy good food, a civilized ambience and splendid facilities.
DOUBLE ROOM: from £30 to £40
FOOD: up to £15
Hours: breakfast 9am–10am, lunch 1pm–2pm, dinner 6.30pm–7.30pm.
Cuisine: BRITISH – table d'hôte, à la carte and bar meals. British cuisine specializing in fresh, local produce.
Cards: Visa, Access.
Other points: licensed, Sunday lunch, children welcome, garden, afternoon tea, pets allowed, solarium.
Rooms: 12 single rooms, 14 double rooms, 56 twin rooms, 12 family rooms.
Directions: off Mostyn Street, close to Promenade.
MR M.C. CHADDERTON ☎ (01492) 860787.

EMPIRE HOTEL
Church Walks, LL30 2HE
A family-run hotel located near the centre of this popular holiday resort. The Empire has developed a reputation for good food served in two separate restaurants, friendly service and leisure facilities. Luxury accommodation; all rooms have Jacuzzi baths.
DOUBLE ROOM: from £30 to £40
SINGLE ROOM: from £45 to £55
FOOD: up to £15
Hours: bar 11am–11pm.
Cuisine: BRITISH – Watkins & Co. serving traditional dishes; grill room/coffee shop, fish and roasts.
Cards: Visa, Access, Diners, AmEx.
Other points: licensed, Sunday lunch, no-smoking area, children welcome, roof patio garden, swimming pool, sauna.
Rooms: 58 bedrooms. All en suite.
Directions: Church Walks leads off the Promenade.
MR & MRS MADDOCKS ☎ (01492) 860555.

GLENORMES PRIVATE HOTEL
Central Promenade, LL30 1AR
This Grade II listed hotel is well positioned in the centre of the Promenade with easy access for shops, restaurants and theatres. You are assured of the best personal attention from the owners and the friendly staff, along with comfortable accommodation and good food.

DOUBLE ROOM: from £20 to £30
SINGLE ROOM: from £25 to £35
FOOD: up to £15
Hours: breakfst 8.30am–9am, dinner 6pm.
Cuisine: BRITISH – home-cooked table d'hôte menu.
Cards: Visa, Access.
Other points: parking, residents' lounge, no-smoking area, vegetarian meals, traditional Sunday lunch.
Rooms: 12 bedrooms. All with en suite, TV, tea/coffee-making facilities.
Directions: centre of Promenade, opposite beach.
TONY & JOANNE GIBSON ☎ (01492) 876643.

GRANBY GUEST HOUSE
Deganwy Avenue, LL30 2DD
Situated in a popular avenue just a short distance between both shores, shops, cinemas and entertainments. Family guest house with resident proprietors. Children welcome at reduced rates if sharing room with parents. Vegetarian, diabetic and coeliac diets catered for.
DOUBLE ROOM: up to £20
Hours: breakfast 9am–9.30am, dinner 6pm, last orders 4.30pm.
Cuisine: BREAKFAST.
Cards: Visa, Access.
Other points: children welcome, residents' lounge.
Directions: located in the centre of town, two blocks from Mostyn Street (main shops).
JUNE ROBERTS ☎ (01492) 76095.

HEADLANDS HOTEL
Hill Terrace, LL30 2LS
Situated above the town, but only a short walk to the beach and shops, Headlands Hotel offers superb views across the bay and Conwy estuary to the mountains of Snowdonia. Friendly service and home-cooked 5-course table d'hôte dinner make this a popular choice with tourists.
DOUBLE ROOM: from £20 to £30
SINGLE ROOM: from £25 to £35
FOOD: from £15 to £20
Hours: breakfast 8.30am–9.15am, bar meals 12noon–1.30pm, dinner 6.45pm–8pm, closed January and February.
Cuisine: BRITISH – a five-course table d'hôte menu is offered. Wide choice of dishes, using local produce, both traditional and classical. Vegetarian meals by arrangement.
Cards: Visa, Access, Diners, AmEx.
Other points: licensed, children welcome, pets by prior arrangement, bar, lounge, central heating.
Rooms: 4 single rooms, 8 double rooms, 3 twin rooms, 2 triple rooms. All with TV, radio, alarm, telephone, tea/coffee-making facilities.
Directions: at top of Hill Terrace, on the Great Orme in Llandudno.
MR & MRS WOODS ☎ (01492) 877485.

HEATH HOUSE HOTEL
Central Promenade, LL30 1AT
A restored, listed, family-run hotel on the seafront, part of the Victorian promenade of an unspoilt spa town. Ideal for a short stopover, a pleasant

mini-break or a traditional holiday, with the same friendly welcome all year round. Children most welcome.
DOUBLE ROOM: from £20 to £30
SINGLE ROOM: from £25 to £35
FOOD: up to £15
Hours: breakfast 8.30am–9.30am, dinner 6pm–7.30pm.
Cuisine: BRITISH – varied menus including traditional favourites. English breakfast. Comprehensive wine list. The dining room is air-conditioned and non-smoking.
Cards: Visa, Access, AmEx.
Other points: residents' lounge, baby-listening device, cots, high chairs, business facilities, entertainment, residents' bar, vegetarian meals.
Rooms: 2 single rooms, 3 double rooms, 3 twin rooms, 14 family rooms, 12 en suite. All with colour TV, radio, telephone, tea/coffee-making facilities, baby-listening device, central heating.
Directions: on the A546 (Promenade), 250 yards west of the conference centre
JOHN & MARY HODGES ☎ (01492) 876538 Fax (01492) 860307.

IMPERIAL HOTEL
The Promenade, LL30 1AP
A large hotel with many facilities including the Speakeasy Bar, based on 1920s American gangster style. Chantreys Restaurant plus Health & Fitness Centre.
DOUBLE ROOM: from £40 to £50
FOOD: from £15 to £20
Hours: lunch 12.30am–2pm, bar meals 12noon–2pm, dinner 6.30pm–9.30pm.
Cuisine: INTERNATIONAL – daily table d'hôte menu and monthly speciality menu.
Cards: Visa, Access, Diners, AmEx.
Other points: Sunday lunch, children welcome, coaches by prior arrangement
Rooms: 20 single rooms, 27 double rooms, 100 twin rooms, 4 family rooms.
Directions: on the Promenade.
MR GEOFFREY LOFTHOUSE ☎ (01492) 877466 Fax (01492) 878013.

RAVENHURST HOTEL
West Shore, LL30 2BB
The Ravenhurst is situated on the West Shore, which runs alongside the Conwy estuary. Wonderful views to Snowdonia and Anglesey. 50% of the bookings are from returning guests. No strangers – only friends you haven't met.
DOUBLE ROOM: from £20 to £30
FOOD: up to £15
Hours: breakfast 8.15am–10am, lunch 12.30am–2pm, bar meals 12noon–2pm, dinner 6.15pm–8pm, bar meals 5.45pm–11pm, closed from 30th November until 1st February.
Cuisine: BRITISH.
Cards: Visa, Access, Diners, AmEx.
Other points: central heating, children welcome, residents' lounge, garden, vegetarian meals, no-smoking area.
Rooms: 6 single rooms, 20 twin rooms, 3 family rooms. All with TV, tea/coffee-making facilities.
Directions: on the seafront. Llandudno West.

PETER, DAVID & KATHLEEN CARRINGTON
☎ (01492) 875525.

ROSE TOR HOTEL
124 Upper Mostyn Street, LL30 2SW
Family-run hotel with a very relaxed atmosphere. All the bedrooms have been individually styled and have colour TVs.
DOUBLE ROOM: up to £20
SINGLE ROOM: up to £25
FOOD: up to £15
Hours: breakfast 7.30am–9.15am, dinner 6pm–10.30pm.
Cuisine: BRITISH.
Cards: Visa, Access, Diners, AmEx.
Other points: central heating, residents' lounge, bar.
Rooms: 1 single room, 21 double rooms, 1 twin room, 3 family rooms. All with TV.
Directions: A546 or A470 to Llandudno.
MRS B. COTTON ☎ (01492) 870433.

SANDRINGHAM HOTEL
West Parade, West Shore, LL30 2BD
The bar has a definite naval flavour, with the cap bands of naval vessels and nautical seascapes on the walls. Situated in the centre of the West Shore, it is a real suntrap all day long and has unimpeded views of Anglesey and the Conwy estuary. Happy, family atmosphere.
DOUBLE ROOM: from £20 to £30
SINGLE ROOM: from £25 to £27
FOOD: up to £15
Hours: breakfast 8am–9.15am, lunch 12noon–2pm, dinner 6.30pm–8.30pm, open all year.
Cuisine: ENGLISH – concentration on fresh wholesome food such as home-made pies, lasagne, fish and roasts.
Cards: Visa, Access.
Other points: licensed, open-air dining, Sunday lunch, children welcome, residents' lounge, residents' bar.
Rooms: 3 single rooms, 7 double rooms, 5 twin rooms, 3 family rooms. All with telephone, tea/coffee-making facilities, heating, hair dryer, satellite TV.
Directions: on seafront of the quiet, sunny West Shore (not the main promenade).
MR & MRS D. KAVANAGH ☎ (01492) 876513/ 876447.

TYNEDALE PRIVATE HOTEL
Central Promenade, LL30 2XS
Situated in a premier position opposite The Bandstand with excellent views of Llandudno Bay, a warm welcome is assured for all guests. Food is very important here and every effort is made to select the best. Guests can relax and enjoy the magnificent views from a luxurious no-smoking lounge, or retire to the Sun Lounge for peace and quiet. There are two bars and two dance floors, both air-conditioned, and comfortable accommodation with many facilities.
DOUBLE ROOM: from £20 to £30
FOOD: up to £15
Hours: breakfast 8.15am–9.15am, bar snacks 12noon–2pm, dinner 6pm–7pm.

Cuisine: BRITISH.
Cards: Visa, Access.
Other points: parking, children welcome, no-smoking area, disabled access, residents' lounge, vegetarian meals.
Rooms: 56 bedrooms.
Directions: on Central Promenade opposite The Bandstand.
MR MICHAEL GOODEY ☎ (01492) 877426
[Fax] (01492) 871213.

🏨 WHITE COURT HOTEL
2 North Parade, LL30 2LP
An attractive hotel, well-situated adjacent to the pier, beach and shopping area. All bedrooms and the charming sitting room offer a very high standard of comfort, allowing guests to relax and enjoy the ambience of the hotel, which is completely non-smoking. The dining room is renowned for its good food and comprehensive wine list.
DOUBLE ROOM: from £20 to £30
FOOD: up to £15
Hours: breakfast 8am–9.30am, dinner 6.30pm–8.30pm, closed December and January.
Cuisine: BRITISH.
Cards: Visa, Access.
Other points: children welcome, residents' lounge.
Rooms: 9 double rooms, 3 twin rooms, 1 family room, 1 suite. All with TV, radio, alarm, telephone, tea/coffee-making facilities, toiletries.
Directions: near to cenotaph, adjacent to pier, beach and shopping area.
NATASHA & STEPHEN GARLINGE ☎ (01492) 876719 [Fax] (01492) 871583.

NEFYN • map 7C2

🏨 LION HOTEL
Tudweiliog, LL53 8ND
The hotel is situated in pleasant surroundings on the B4417, on the north coast of the Lleyn Peninsula. The staff are friendly and efficient and the food offers value for money.
DOUBLE ROOM: up to £20
SINGLE ROOM: up to £25
FOOD: up to £15
Hours: lunch 12noon–2pm, dinner 6pm–9.30pm, closed Sunday.
Cuisine: BRITISH – extensive three-course bar menu and home-made specials board.
Other points: open-air dining, no-smoking area, disabled access, children welcome, parking, playland, pets by prior arrangement, beer garden.
Rooms: 1 single room, 3 double room, 1 twin room.
Directions: on the B4417, 4 miles from Nefyn on the road to Aberdaron.
MRS LEE ☎ (01758) 770244.

PORTHMADOG • map 7C2

🍴 BLOSSOMS RESTAURANT
Borth-y-Gêst, LL49 9TP
Overlooking the bay at Borth-y-Gêst with Snowdonia in the distance, Blossoms Restaurant is part of the 'Heartbeat Wales' programme to promote healthy eating. Log fires and classical jazz or blues music set the atmosphere. It is a small restaurant, so booking is advisable.
FOOD: from £15 to £20
Hours: lunch (summer only) 12noon–2pm, dinner 7pm–10.30pm, closed Sunday.
Cuisine: MEDITERRANEAN – vegetarian dishes.
Cards: Visa, Access.
Other points: open-air dining, Sunday lunch, children welcome.
Directions: half a mile from A497 in the centre of Borth-y-Gêst.
PAUL DENHAM & MEG BROOK ☎ (01766) 513500.

🍴 Y LLONG – THE SHIP
Lombard Street, LL49 9AP
Built in 1824, this is the oldest public house in Porthmadog and is mentioned in many maritime books of the area. Having undergone extensive refurbishment, it still retains much of its original charm, with tiled floors, bench seats and a stone fireplace. Ideally situated for tourists and travellers. 'Heartbeat Wales Award', Vegetarian Good Food Guide, Good Beer Guide (CAMRA).
FOOD: up to £15
Hours: bar meals 12noon–2.15pm, 6.30pm–9.30pm, restaurant 5.30pm–11pm, closed Sunday.
Cuisine: CANTONESE / EUROPEAN – à la carte, plus extensive choice of Cantonese and Peking dishes. Daily changing specials, excellent vegetarian menu. Bar meals, snacks and traditional beers in both bars.
Cards: Visa, Access, Diners, AmEx.
Other points: licensed, no-smoking area, children catered for (restaurant only), parking, open bank holidays.
Directions: close to Porthmadog harbour.
ROBERT JONES & NIA JONES ☎ (01766) 512990/514415.

PWLLHELI • map 7C2

🍴 TWNTI SEAFOOD RESTAURANT
Rhydycladfy, LL53 7YH
Once the meeting place for the Monks Pilgrimage on their way to Bardsey Island, this family-run restaurant, tastefully converted from a barn, now offers real fires in winter and a warm and friendly atmosphere. It is ideally situated for visiting Caernarfon Castle, the Italianate village of Portmeirion, and the remote but beautiful wilderness of Snowdonia National Park.
FOOD: from £15 to £20
Hours: Sunday lunch 12noon–2pm, dinner 7pm until late, last orders 9pm, closed January and February.
Cuisine: BRITISH – à la carte menu, offering a wide choice of seafood dishes, all freshly prepared and cooked daily. Children's menu and vegetarian meals available if given 24 hours' notice.
Cards: Visa, Access.
Other points: licensed, Sunday lunch, children welcome, disabled access, open bank holidays.

Directions: from Pwllheli, left onto A497 for Nefyn. Turn left after rugby club.
KEITH JACKSON & STEPHEN WILLIAMS
☎ (01758) 740929.

TAL-Y-BONT • map 7B3

🛏 THE LODGE HOTEL
Near Conwy, LL32 8YX
An attractive and welcoming hotel and restaurant nestling in the Conwy Valley. The restaurant provides a relaxed and elegant setting in which to enjoy well-prepared traditional cuisine. Fresh local produce is used whenever possible, and most soft fruits and vegetables are grown in the hotel gardens.

DOUBLE ROOM: from £20 to £30
FOOD: up to £15
Hours: breakfast 8.15am–9.30am, lunch 12noon–2pm, dinner 7pm–9.30pm.
Cuisine: BRITISH – table d'hôte and à la carte menus. Local fish specialities. Vegetarian meals are also available.
Cards: Visa, Access.
Other points: licensed, open-air dining, Sunday lunch, children welcome, pets by prior arrangement, residents' bar, parking, vegetarian meals, disabled access.
Directions: follow A55 Expressway to Conwy. At castle, turn left for the B5106.
MR & MRS BALDON ☎ (01492) 660766
[Fax] (01492) 660534.

MID GLAMORGAN

BRIDGEND • map 4B4

🍽 ASHOKA TANDOORI
68 Nolton Street, CF31 3BP
Situated on the main road in Bridgend, the exterior suggests a Bengali connection. The interior is pleasantly decorated, with crisp, white tablecloths and unobtrusive background music. A popular restaurant.
FOOD: up to £15
Hours: lunch 12noon–2.30pm, dinner 5.30pm–12midnight.
Cuisine: INDIAN – rogon chicken special, meat masala, sag ghosht.
Cards: Visa, Access, Diners, AmEx.
Other points: open-air dining, children welcome.
Directions: situated on the main road in Bridgend.
MR MISPAK MIAH ☎ (01656) 650678.

LES ROUTIERS
Information & Bookings Line
☎ 0171 610 1856

PONTYPRIDD • map 4A4

🛏 MARKET TAVERN HOTEL
Market Street, CF37 2ST
A classic Victorian pub in the town centre, its upper half sympathetically converted into a hotel with an over 60-cover restaurant, offering traditional cuisine. Nearby attractions include Cardiff, with its museums and castle.
DOUBLE ROOM: up to £20
SINGLE ROOM: up to £25
FOOD: up to £15
Hours: breakfast 7.30am–9.30am; lunch 12noon–2.30pm; bar snacks 12noon–2.30pm, 7.30pm–11pm; dinner 7.30pm–9.30pm, Sunday 7pm–11pm; closed Christmas day.
Cuisine: BRITISH – traditional à la carte and table d'hôte menus.
Other points: children welcome, disabled access, residents' lounge, vegetarian meals, licensed.
Rooms: 2 single rooms, 3 double rooms, 6 twin rooms.
Directions: two minutes from Pontypridd intersection on A470.
PONTYPRIDD MARKET CO. ☎ (01443) 485331 [Fax] (01443) 402806.

POWYS

BRECON • map 7E3

🍽 LA BRASERIA & FORTUNA WINE BAR
22A High Street, LD3 7LA
An atmospheric wine bar and restaurant where the order of the day is char-grilled meals. Here you select the cut you wish to eat, and then it is cooked to your specifications before your very eyes. You only need to look at what is on offer here to see that only ingredients of the freshest

and finest quality are used. This is a real find!
FOOD: up to £15
Hours: dinner (Wednesday–Saturday) 6.30pm–10pm (last orders).
Cuisine: ENGLISH – charcoal grill.
Other points: children welcome, vegetarian meals.
Directions: on the High Street in the centre of town.
LYNTON & HEULWEN PHILLIPS ☎ (01874) 611313.

299

WALES • POWYS

🏨 PETERSTONE COURT
Llanhamlach Village, LD3 7YB

A listed Georgian manor house, which has been carefully restored to an outstanding country house hotel, nestling amid a breathtaking landscape in the Brecon Beacons National Park. Every effort has been made to ensure guests' comfort and relaxation, from the hotel's own high-standard leisure facilities to many thoughtfully provided extras. The surrounding countryside of mountains and waterfalls is highly regarded for country sports and outdoor pursuits. For business guests, there is a fully equipped boardroom for up to 16 persons.
DOUBLE ROOM: from £40 to £50
SINGLE ROOM: over £55
FOOD: up to £15
Hours: breakfast 7am, lunch 12noon–2.30pm, dinner 7pm–9.30pm, bar snacks 11am–10pm.
Cuisine: HAUTE CUISINE.
Cards: Visa, Access, Diners, AmEx.
Other points: licensed.
Rooms: 12 bedrooms. All luxury rooms with TV, radio, telephone, trouser-press, hair dryer.
Directions: 2 miles east of Brecon, towards Abergavenny.
MR M. TAYLOR ☎ (01874) 665387
[Fax] (01874) 665376.

LES ROUTIERS
Your assurance of Quality and Value

🏨 THE THREE COCKS HOTEL
Three Cocks, LD3 0SL

The Three Cocks stands in grounds of 1½ acres in the parish of Aberllynfi on the edge of the Brecon Beacons. The inn dates from the 15th century and has the unique distinction of being built around a tree, which can still be seen. It is complete with cobbled forecourt, mounting blocks, ivy-clad walls, great oak beams and log fires. Ideal location as a touring centre. Many clients come for the famous second-hand bookshops in Hay-on-Wye, and for other activities such as walking and pony-trekking. The superbly 'created' food comes highly recommended. The restaurant has a charming custom of serving second helpings of meat rather than overloading your plate at the start. The selection of fresh vegetables is served on a side plate.
DOUBLE ROOM: from £20 to £30
FOOD: from £20 to £25 ☆
Hours: breakfast 8am–9.30am, lunch 12noon–1.30pm, dinner 7pm–9pm.
Cuisine: CONTINENTAL – an accent on selected Belgian dishes, beautifully presented, using the finest fresh ingredients. The restaurant has been awarded 2 rosettes.
Cards: Visa, Access.
Other points: licensed, children welcome, residents' lounge, open bank holidays, afternoon tea, parking.
Rooms: 4 double rooms, 3 twin rooms.
Directions: between Hay-on-Wye and Brecon, on A438.
MR & MRS M. WINSTONE ☎ (01497) 847215.

LLANDRINDOD WELLS • map 7D3

🏨 SEVERN ARMS HOTEL
Penybont, LD1 5UA

A former coaching inn, ideally situated on a popular holiday route. The inn has an olde-worlde charm with a wealth of oak beams and a log fire which burns in the bar during winter. The Severn Arms is one of the best-known unaltered coaching houses in mid-Wales, but has been modernized inside to a high standard. Reduced rates on two golf courses. Six miles of fishing available.
DOUBLE ROOM: from £20 to £30
SINGLE ROOM: from £25 to £35
FOOD: up to £15
Hours: dinner 7pm–9.30pm, closed one week at Christmas.
Cuisine: ENGLISH – grills, roasts, home-made steak-and-kidney pie, cottage pie. Full à la carte menu and bar snacks are available seven days a week.
Cards: Visa, Access, Diners, AmEx.
Other points: licensed, Sunday lunch, children welcome, fishing, garden, caravan facilities.
Rooms: 3 double rooms, 1 twin room, 6 family rooms. All with en suite, TV, radio, telephone, tea/coffee-making facilities, hair dryer, trouser-press.
Directions: on A44, Rhayader to Leominster road.
GEOFF & TESSA LLOYD ☎ (01597) 851224/851344 [Fax] (01597) 851693.

LLANIDLOES • map 7D3

🏨 UNICORN HOTEL
Long Bridge Street, SY18 6EE

Set in an attractive terrace, this is an extremely popular and sociable hotel, both with tourists and local townsfolk. The service is efficient and helpful, complementing the welcoming atmosphere. This is an ideal base from which to tour the outstanding nearby countryside.
DOUBLE ROOM: up to £20
SINGLE ROOM: up to £25
FOOD: up to £15 [CLUB]
Hours: breakfast 7.30am–9am, bar meals 12noon–2pm, 7pm–9pm.
Cuisine: ENGLISH – table d'hôte menu offering traditional English fare. Vegetarian meals are also available.
Cards: Visa, Access, AmEx.
Other points: licensed, Sunday lunch, children welcome.
Rooms: 5 bedrooms.
Directions: situated in Llanidloes town centre.
CHRISTINE & DEREK HUMPHRIES ☎ (01686) 413167.

LLANWDDYN • map 8C4

🏨 LAKE VYRNWY HOTEL
Lake Vyrnwy, SY10 0LY

Lake Vyrnwy is everything you would expect from a unique first-class country house and sporting hotel, set in the heart of beautiful mid-Wales. The comfort of the hotel echoes the peace of the

surrounding countryside and its infinite views of outstanding natural beauty. A wide range of country pursuits is available on the estate's 24,000 acres. Own country pub in grounds.
DOUBLE ROOM: from £40 to £50
SINGLE ROOM: from £55
FOOD: from £20 to £25
Hours: breakfast 8.30am–9.30am, lunch 12.30am–2pm, dinner 7.30pm–9.30pm, bar meals 12.30am–2pm, 6.30pm–9pm, open all year.
Cuisine: BRITISH – award-winning traditional and innovative dishes. Hotel has daily changing menus, restaurant, and the estate's fish and game. Own market garden.
Cards: Visa, Access, Diners, AmEx.
Other points: licensed, Sunday lunch, no-smoking area, children welcome, pets allowed, afternoon tea, vegetarian meals, garden, residents' lounge, residents' bar.
Rooms: 2 single rooms, 21 double rooms, 14 twin rooms. All with TV, radio, telephone.
Directions: from Shrewsbury, A458 to Welshpool. Right onto B4393 to Lake Vyrnwy.
☎ (01691) 870692 Fax (01691) 870259.

MACHYNLLETH • map 7C3

LLUGWY HALL COUNTRY HOUSE HOTEL
Pennal, SY20 9JX

An exceptional hotel where the management and staff have created a unique experience. Here you will find that informality goes hand in hand with excellent cuisine, comfortable accommodation and impeccable standards of service. A superb hotel in this beautiful part of Wales, which comes highly recommended.
DOUBLE ROOM: from £30 to £40
SINGLE ROOM: from £45 to £55
FOOD: from £15 to £20
Hours: breakfast 8am–10am, lunch 12.30am–2pm, dinner 7pm–9pm.
Cuisine: FRENCH – predominantly French, with a few traditional Welsh dishes.
Cards: Visa, Access, Diners, AmEx.
Other points: parking, children welcome, pets allowed, conference facilities, residents' lounge, garden, open-air dining, vegetarian meals, traditional Sunday lunch, afternoon teas.
Rooms: 15 bedrooms. All with TV, telephone, radio, alarm, hair dryer, trouser-press, room service, baby-listening device, tea/coffee-making facilities.
Directions: take the main road, A493, from Machynlleth to Aberdovey, turn left before Pennal and the hotel is signed.
PAUL DAVIS ☎ (01654) 791228 Fax (01654) 791231.

THE WHITE LION COACHING INN
Heol Pentrerhedyn, SY20 8ND

The White Lion has been welcoming guests since the early 1000s. It was one of several coaching inns in town, and retains its original oak beams, inglenook fireplace and cobbled forecourt. Regular patrons appreciate the inn for its Dyffi salmon and traditional and innovative menus. Well worth a visit.
DOUBLE ROOM: from £20 to £30
SINGLE ROOM: from £25 to £35
FOOD: up to £15
Hours: lunch 12noon–2.30pm, dinner 6pm–9pm.
Cuisine: WELSH – traditional Welsh, including Sunday lunch. Bar meals.
Cards: Visa, Access.
Other points: licensed, Sunday lunch, children welcome, pets allowed, cots, disabled access, residents' bar, vegetarian meals.
Rooms: 9 bedrooms. All with TV, tea/coffee-making facilities. Some rooms are en suite.
Directions: hotel is on junction of A487 and A489 by the Victorian clock.
M.K. & J.F. QUICK ☎ (01654) 703455.

NEWTOWN • map 8D4

YESTERDAYS
Severn Square, SY16 2AG

A delightful restaurant and take-away situated in Severn Square, offering a wide range of traditional fare, including seafood, poultry, grills and light snacks. Easy access to historic Powis Castle, Elan Valley and the beautiful mid-Wales countryside.
FOOD: up to £15 CLUB
Hours: lunch 12noon–2.30pm, dinner 6.30pm–9.30pm.
Cuisine: ENGLISH.
Cards: Visa, Access, AmEx, Switch.
Other points: children welcome, Sunday lunch, open bank holidays, no-smoking area, disabled access, vegetarian meals.
Directions: from Barclays Bank along Severn Street, 80 yards to Severn Square.
JIM & MOYRA ASTON ☎ (01686) 622644.

TRECASTLE • map 7E3

CASTLE COACHING INN
Near Brecon, LD3 0UH

Nestling in the heart of the Brecon Beacons, this period hotel, once a coaching inn on the main West Wales to Ireland road, offers the perfect respite. There are bars and a lounge, offering glorious home-cooked meals, snacks and real ales in a warm, friendly setting. Awaiting a stone's throw away is the wild beauty of the Brecon Beacons National Park, where crystal waterfalls cascade over spectacular mountain scenery and streams babble through unspoilt villages. This is a must!
DOUBLE ROOM: from £20 to £30
FOOD: up to £15
Hours: breakfast 8am–10am, lunch 12noon–2pm, dinner 6.30pm–9.30pm.
Cuisine: BRITISH – fresh food cooked to order. Under-10s children's meals.
Cards: Visa, Access.
Other points: parking, children welcome, garden, open-air dining, vegetarian meals, traditional Sunday lunch.
Rooms: 7 double rooms, 2 twin rooms, 1 family

room. All with en suite, TV, telephone, radio, hair dryer, tea/coffee-making facilities.
Directions: on A40, 9 miles east of Llandovery, 12 miles west of Brecon.
DAVID & LORRAINE McKIE ☎ (01874) 636354
Fax (01874) 636457.

WELSHPOOL • map 8C4

THE LION HOTEL & RESTAURANT
Berriew, SY21 8PQ

Situated in a quiet village on the Welsh borders surrounded by beautiful countryside, the Lion Hotel is a delightful 17th century inn. The accommodation is of a high standard, and good food is served in both the bars and restaurant.
DOUBLE ROOM: from £40 to £50
SINGLE ROOM: from £45 to £55
FOOD: CLUB ☆
Hours: breakfast 8am–9.30am, lunch 12noon–2pm, dinner 7.30pm–9pm, bar meals 12noon–2pm, 7pm–9pm, open bank holidays.
Cuisine: BRITISH / CONTINENTAL – English, Welsh and continental cuisine. Dishes may include fillet of smoked trout with lemon and dill dressed salad, roast duck with vermouth and cranberry sauce, fillet of Welsh venison in a sauce of redberries, port, mushrooms and onions.
Cards: Visa, Access, Diners, AmEx.
Other points: licensed, Sunday lunch, children welcome.
Rooms: 5 double rooms, 1 twin room, 1 family room. All with TV, tea/coffee-making facilities.
Directions: in village centre.
MR & MRS THOMAS ☎ (01686) 640884
Fax (01686) 640604.

THE ROYAL OAK HOTEL
Welshpool, SY21 7DG

Situated in the heart of Welshpool, an historic Georgian Border town nestling in the rolling green countryside of the old county of Montgomeryshire, The Royal Oak Hotel and restaurant has been welcoming travellers for over 350 years. Once owned by the Earl of Powis, The Royal Oak has been in the same family for over 60 years and offers traditional cask ales, lunch/evening bar menus as well as table d'hôte, à la carte menus and over 100 wines in the Acorn Restaurant. The Powis Suite provides comfortable rooms for seminars, banquets and wedding receptions for up to 200 guests. Welshpool is home to Powis Castle, the famous Llanfair light railway and Powysland Canal Museum. Situated close to Offa's Dyke path, it makes an ideal centre for walking and exploring wildlife.
DOUBLE ROOM: from £30 to £40
FOOD: up to £15
Hours: breakfast 7.30am–9am, Sunday 8.30am–9.30am, lunch 12.30am–2.15pm, dinner 7pm–9pm, Saturday 7.30pm–9.15pm.
Cuisine: WELSH / ENGLISH – good, traditional local cooking, featuring lamb, roasts and grills, as well as modern English. Good-value popular bar menu.
Cards: Visa, Access, Diners, AmEx.
Other points: parking, children welcome, traditional Sunday lunch, open bank holidays, morning coffee, afternoon tea, disabled access, pets by arrangement, residents' lounge, residents' bar, vegetarian meals, conferences, functions.
Rooms: 8 single rooms, 7 double rooms, 7 twin rooms, 2 family rooms, 1 four-poster suite. All with en suite, TV, telephone, tea/coffee-making facilities.
Directions: junction of A483 and A458 in the very centre of Welshpool, at the only set of traffic lights.
MARGARET LANDGREBE ☎ (01938) 552217
Fax (01938) 552217.

SOUTH GLAMORGAN

CARDIFF • map 4B4

BENEDICTO'S
4 Windsor Place

Delightfully decorated throughout, this restaurant is highly regarded in the city by local businessmen and evening theatregoers. Both the à la carte and the table d'hôte menu offer a varied selection of well-prepared meals, complemented by a good wine list.
FOOD: from £15 to £20
Hours: lunch 12noon–2.30pm, dinner 6.30pm–11.30pm, closed Sunday evenings.
Cuisine: INTERNATIONAL – all dishes specially prepared to order using only the freshest produce.
Cards: Visa, Access, Diners, AmEx.
Other points: children welcome, vegetarian meals, traditional Sunday lunch.
Directions: Windsor Place is off Queen Street in Cardiff city centre, opposite the Capital Mall.
BEN LADO ☎ (01222) 371130.

CARDIFF WEST PAVILION LODGE AT CARDIFF WEST SERVICE AREA
Junction 33/A4232, M4 Motorway, near Pontyclun, CF7 8SA

The Lodge provides excellent accommodation at a competitive price and offers the facilities to make travelling a pleasure. Convenient for Cardiff Castle, Castell Coch, and Welsh Folk Museum at St Fagan's.
DOUBLE ROOM: from £20 to £30
FOOD: up to £15
Hours: open 24 hours.
Cuisine: BRITISH / INTERNATIONAL.
Other points: parking, children welcome, disabled access, vegetarian meals, forecourt shop.
Rooms: 50 bedrooms. All with en suite, satellite TV, telephone, radio, alarm, hair dryer, trouser-press, tea/coffee-making facilities.
Directions: at service area at junction 33 of the M4.
STEVEN NUNNEY ☎ (01222) 892255
Fax (01222) 892497.

WEST GLAMORGAN • WALES

HENRY'S CAFE BAR (CARDIFF)
Park Place
A trendy café-bar serving an extensive range of international food, American and non-alcoholic beers and speciality cocktails. Bustling, happy, friendly atmosphere.
FOOD: from £20 to £25
Hours: meals all day 9.30am–11pm, closed Sunday.
Cuisine: INTERNATIONAL.
Cards: Visa, Access.
Other points: children welcome, open bank holidays, no-smoking area, afternoon teas, disabled access, vegetarian meals.
Directions: adjacent to New Theatre.
☎ (01222) 224139.

WEST GLAMORGAN

ABERCRAF • map 3A3

MAES-Y-GWERNEN
School Road, Abercraf, Swansea Valley, SA9 1XD

LES ROUTIERS
GUEST HOUSE of the Year 1995

Maes-y-Gwernen is a well-appointed licensed guest house, situated in well-kept grounds in the upper Swansea Valley village of Abercraf. The Moore family offer good food and extremely comfortable, well-equipped accommodation to both tourists and business people, at rates that represent excellent value. (See special feature on page 12.)
DOUBLE ROOM: up to £20
SINGLE ROOM: up to £25
FOOD: up to £15
Hours: breakfast 7am–10am, lunch 12noon–2pm, dinner 6pm–8.30pm, open all year.
Cuisine: ENGLISH / FRENCH – meal times can be arranged to suit guests' requirements; everything is home-cooked on the premises, with special vegetarian menu available if required.
Cards: Visa, Access.
Other points: parking, children welcome, pets allowed, no-smoking area, conference facilities, residents' lounge, residents' bar, garden, vegetarian meals, traditional Sunday lunch.
Rooms: 5 double rooms, 2 twin rooms. All with TV, telephone, radio, alarm, hair dryer, trouser press, tea/coffee-making facilities.
Directions: 12 miles north of M4 junction 45, on A4067.
ELSIE MOORE ☎ (01639) 730218 Fax (01639) 730765.

GOWER • map 3A3

OXWICH BAY HOTEL
Oxwich Bay, near Swansea, SA3 1LS
The hotel is situated in its own grounds just ten yards from 2 glorious miles of safe, award-winning Oxwich Beach. Comfortable bedrooms, the majority of which have a sea view, provide an ideal base from which to explore the Gower peninsula.
DOUBLE ROOM: from £20 to £30
SINGLE ROOM: from £25 to £35
FOOD: up to £15
Hours: breakfast 8am–9.30am, bar meals 12noon–2.30pm, dinner 7pm–8.30pm, bar meals 6.30pm–9pm, bar meals all day weekends, July, August and any holiday period, closed Christmas day and Boxing day.
Cuisine: BRITISH – home-made sauces, e.g., steak chasseur, steak with pepper sauce.
Cards: Visa, Access.
Other points: licensed, open-air dining, Sunday lunch, children welcome, coach access.
Rooms: 13 bedrooms. All en suite.
Directions: from the A4118 take Oxwich turn, then left at Oxwich crossroads.
MR IAN WILLIAMS ☎ (01792) 390329
Fax (01792) 391254.

WORM'S HEAD HOTEL
Rhossili, SA3 1PP
Situated in a designated area of outstanding natural beauty at the westernmost tip of the Gower Peninsula, the hotel has a superb outlook over the majestic sweep of Rhossili Bay and the famous Worm's Head. The Worm's Head Hotel provides guests with well-appointed facilities in comfortable and tasteful surroundings and a very pleasant atmosphere.
DOUBLE ROOM: from £20 to £30
SINGLE ROOM: from £25 to £35
FOOD: up to £15
Hours: breakfast 8am–9.30am, lunch 12noon–2pm, bar meals 12noon–3pm, dinner 7pm–9pm, bar meals 7pm–9pm.
Cuisine: BRITISH – traditional home-style cooking.
Cards: Visa, Access, Switch.
Other points: parking, children welcome, pets allowed, disabled access, residents' lounge, garden, open-air dining, vegetarian meals, traditional Sunday lunch.
Rooms: 18 bedrooms. All with TV, tea/coffee-making facilities.
Directions: from Swansea, proceed along North Gower Road, past Swansea Airport, follow signs for Oxwich Bay; Rhossili is approximately 5 miles further on.
RHOSSILI HOTELS LTD ☎ (01792) 390512
Fax (01790) 391115.

SWANSEA • map 3A3

CEFN-BRYN
6 Uplands Crescent, Uplands, SA2 0PB
Built by a mariner a century ago, a calm, quiet atmosphere prevails throughout this vast, semi-

303

detached Victorian residence boasting some exceptional plasterwork. The rooms are clean, comfortable and spacious, with their own showers. Ideally situated for touring Mumbles and the Gower.
DOUBLE ROOM: from £20 to £30
SINGLE ROOM: up to £25
Hours: breakfast 7.30am–9am, closed Christmas and New Year.
Cuisine: BREAKFAST – full Welsh or continental breakfast.
Other points: children welcome, open bank holidays, no-smoking area, residents' lounge.
Rooms: 2 single rooms, 1 double room, 1 twin room, 2 family rooms.
Directions: on A4118, approximately 1 mile west of city centre.
ANN TELFER ☎ (01792) 466687.

THE SCHOONER
4 Prospect Place, SA1 1QP
Grade II listed building with wine bar, restaurant and function room. Situated in central Swansea on the fringe of the new Marina development and near the leisure centre.
FOOD: up to £15 [CLUB] ☆
Hours: lunch 12noon–2pm, bar meals 12noon–2pm, dinner 7pm–9.30pm, bar meals 7pm–7.30pm, closed Sunday evening.
Cuisine: INTERNATIONAL – fresh local produce, all home-cooked. Traditional Sunday lunches (booking advisable). Evening special menu changes monthly. Carvery meals most evenings.
Other points: Sunday lunch, no-smoking area, coaches by prior arrangement, vegetarian meals.
Directions: in the east of Swansea, close to Sainsbury's.
RAYMOND & CHRISTINE PARKMAN
☎ (01792) 649321.

SWANSEA PAVILION LODGE AT SWANSEA SERVICE AREA
Junction 47/A483, M4 Motorway, Penllergaer, SA4 1GT
The Lodge provides excellent accommodation at a competitive price and offers the facilities to make travelling a pleasure. Convenient for Swansea city centre and South Wales, or break your journey when using the ferries to Ireland.
DOUBLE ROOM: from £20 to £30
FOOD: up to £15
Hours: open 24 hours.
Cuisine: BRITISH / INTERNATIONAL.
Cards: Visa, Access, Diners, AmEx.
Other points: parking, children welcome, disabled access, forecourt shop.
Rooms: 50 bedrooms. All with en suite, satellite TV, telephone, radio, alarm, hair dryer, trouser-press, baby-listening device, tea/coffee-making facilities.
Directions: on the M4, at the service area of junction 47.
IAN STANTON ☎ (01792) 894894
[Fax] (01792) 898806.

SCOTLAND

Savour the wild beauty of the high, heather-covered mountains, sparkling blue lochs and rich green glens. Scotland is a land of legends and castles, perfected for the tourist, and *Les Routiers* has searched out many of the country's most excellent places to ensure that your visit leaves a lasting memory.

There are endless traditional Scottish specialities that will set the taste buds tingling, namely Tay salmon, Highland venison, prime Galloway beef, Solway duck, Aberdeen Angus steaks, Glenturret pâté, pheasant and grouse. Equally magnificent is the abundance of fresh fish and seafood: Arbroath smokies, lobster Thermidor, baked haddock, sea trout, Scotch cockles, and more.

Of course, no one could possibly visit Scotland without trying one of its famous whiskies, and there is a whisky trail that one can follow, sampling the products of Scotland's greatest distilleries. Or visit Campbeltown Loch, reputed in song to consist entirely of whisky.

Scotland's turbulent history has bequeathed a great legacy of famous monarchs and romantic palaces and castles. *Les Routiers* can't promise you will stay in a palace, but there are castles which carry our 'recommendation', and with it an outstanding choice of accommodation.

The following counties are included in this chapter:

BORDERS	LOTHIAN
CENTRAL	ORKNEY & SHETLAND
DUMFRIES & GALLOWAY	ISLANDS
FIFE	STRATHCLYDE
GRAMPIAN	TAYSIDE
HIGHLANDS	WESTERN ISLES

*B*ORDERS

BURNMOUTH • map 16E6

THE FLEMINGTON INN
TD14 5SL

An attractive, well-run pub directly on the A1 in the pretty fishing village of Burnmouth. This is the 'first and last' pub in Scotland. Presenting home-cooked meals made from fresh local produce at value-for-money prices, The Flemington Inn is very popular, especially with locals.
FOOD: up to £15
Hours: lunch 12noon–2.15pm, Sunday 12.30am–2.15pm, dinner 6.30pm–9pm.
Cuisine: SCOTTISH – traditional Scottish menu with good use of local seafood.

Other points: licensed, parking, children catered for (please check for age limits), vegetarian meals.
Directions: six miles north of Berwick-upon-Tweed on A1.
MR & MRS SMILLIE ☎ (018907) 81277.

GALASHIELS • map 16E5

ABBOTSFORD ARMS HOTEL
63 Stirling Street, TO1 1BY

A beautifully modernized family hotel 32 miles south of Edinburgh. Completely refurbished to a high standard.
DOUBLE ROOM: from £20 to £30

SINGLE ROOM: from £25 to £35
FOOD: up to £15 [CLUB]
Hours: breakfast 8am–10am, meals all day 12noon–9pm.
Cuisine: SCOTTISH – steak, chicken dishes.
Cards: Visa, Access.
Other points: licensed, Sunday lunch, children welcome, coaches by prior arrangement.
Rooms: 3 single rooms, 3 double rooms, 5 twin rooms, 3 family rooms. All with TV, tea/coffee-making facilities.
Directions: in Galashiels, opposite the bus station.
JAMES GORDON & CHRISTINA WILSON SCOTT ☎ (01896) 752517 [Fax] (01896) 750744.

HERGES
58 Island Street, TD1 1NY
Karen and Sandy Craig offer imaginative, good-value cuisine in a very friendly and relaxed atmosphere. A former yarn brokers' store, Herges has been expertly converted to form this attractive continental-style wine bar. The service is most courteous and efficient, and all dishes are freshly cooked to a high standard.
FOOD: up to £15 [CLUB]
Hours: lunch 12noon–2.30pm, dinner 6pm–12midnight, last orders 9.30pm, open from 5pm on Sunday, closed all day Monday.
Cuisine: CONTINENTAL – dishes may include baked rainbow trout, roast gigot of lamb, supreme of chicken Marengo. Also lighter snacks such as filled baked potatoes and croissants.
Cards: Visa, Access.
Other points: licensed, Sunday lunch, no-smoking area, children welcome.
Directions: A72 to Peebles, near the B&Q superstore.
KAREN & SANDY CRAIG ☎ (01896) 50400.

HAWICK • map 11A3

KIRKLANDS HOTEL
West Stewart Place, TD9 8BH
A charming, small hotel pleasantly situated in the beautiful Scottish borders. Ideal base for tourists and business people. Close to many attractions. Recommended by most leading hotel guides. Weekly terms and weekend breaks available. Colour brochure and tariff on request.
DOUBLE ROOM: from £30 to £40
SINGLE ROOM: from £45 to £55
FOOD: from £15 to £20 [CLUB]
Hours: lunch 12noon–2pm, dinner 7pm–9.30pm.
Cuisine: SCOTTISH / CONTINENTAL – excellent choice of Scottish and à la carte dishes. Table d'hôte and bar meals. Vegetarian dishes.
Cards: Visa, Access, Diners, AmEx.
Other points: open-air dining, no-smoking area, children welcome, garden, games room, library.
Rooms: 7 double rooms, 5 twin rooms.
Directions: 200 yards off the main A7, half a mile north of Hawick High Street.
MR B. NEWLAND ☎ (01450) 72263 [Fax] (01450) 370404.

MELROSE • map 16E5

BURTS HOTEL
Market Square, TD6 9PN
Built in 1722, Burts is a friendly, family-run hotel, renowned for its excellent cuisine, fine Scottish hospitality and everything you would expect of a first-class establishment. Situated in the heart of the Border country and convenient for visiting a wealth of stately homes, including Floors Castle. Nearby sporting activities include fishing, golfing, game-shooting and hill-walking. AA and RAC 3-star and Scottish Tourist Board 4 Crowns 'highly commended'.
DOUBLE ROOM: from £30 to £40
FOOD: from £15 to £20 [CLUB] ☆
Hours: breakfast 8am–9.30am, lunch 12.30am–2pm, bar meals 12noon–2pm, 6pm–9.30pm, dinner 7pm–9pm.
Cuisine: SCOTTISH – traditional Scottish fare. Dishes include filo parcels of Inverloch cheese with bacon and pears, plump west coast scallops wrapped in air-dried ham, trio of salmon (gravalax, poached and smoked salmon), roulade of Border lamb with celeriac and redcurrants, collage of Border game.
Cards: Visa, Access, Diners, AmEx.
Other points: licensed, open-air dining, Sunday lunch, parking, garden, residents' lounge, pets allowed, children welcome, baby-sitting, cots, left luggage.
Rooms: 8 single rooms, 4 double rooms, 8 twin rooms. All with TV, radio, telephone.
Directions: three miles from Galashiels, off A7. Two miles from A68, south of Earlston.
☎ (01896) 822285 [Fax] (01896) 822870.

PEEBLES • map 16E4

CRINGLETIE HOUSE HOTEL
EH45 8PL
Cringletie is a distinguished mansion house set well back in 28 acres of gardens and woodlands. The resident proprietors provide interesting and imaginative food, with fruit and vegetables in season from the hotel's extensive kitchen garden, which is featured in The Gourmet Garden by Geraldene Holt.
DOUBLE ROOM: from £40 to £50
SINGLE ROOM: from £45 to £55
FOOD: from £20 to £25
Hours: breakfast 8.15am–9.15am, lunch 1pm–1.45pm, dinner 7.30pm–8.30pm.
Cuisine: BRITISH – frequently-changing menu: all home-cooking. Afternoon tea including home-baking.
Cards: Visa, Access.
Other points: Sunday lunch, no-smoking area, children welcome.
Rooms: 1 single room, 4 double rooms, 8 twin rooms.
Directions: on the Edinburgh–Peebles road (A703), 2½ miles north of Peebles.
STANLEY & AILEEN MAGUIRE ☎ (01721) 730233 [Fax] (01721) 730244.

KINGSMUIR HOTEL
Springhill Road, EH45 9EP
A charming country house, built in the 1850s and set in leafy grounds in a quiet area, yet only 5 minutes' walk through parkland to the High Street. The resident proprietors take great pride in their 'Taste of Scotland' cuisine, to the delight of the many guests who have dined or stayed there. Winner of many local and regional awards.
DOUBLE ROOM: from £30 to £40
SINGLE ROOM: from £25 to £35
FOOD: up to £15
Hours: breakfast 8.30am–9.30am, lunch 12noon–2pm, bar meals 12noon–2pm, 7pm–9.30pm, dinner 7pm–9pm, closed Christmas day and New Year's day.
Cuisine: SCOTTISH – home-made soups, roasts, steak pie, sea and river fish, home-made desserts.
Cards: Visa, Access, AmEx.
Other points: licensed, Sunday lunch, pets allowed (dogs only), conferences, children welcome, baby listening device, baby-sitting, cots, foreign exchange, residents' lounge, residents' bar.
Rooms: 2 single rooms, 3 double rooms, 3 twin rooms, 1 triple room, 1 family room. All with en suite, TV, radio, alarm, telephone, tea/coffee-making facilities.
Directions: High Street, south over Tweed Bridge, Springhill Road and half a mile on the right.
ELIZABETH & NORMAN KERR ☎ (01721) 720151 [Fax] (01721) 721795.

PARK HOTEL
Innerleithen Road, EH45 8BA
A friendly hotel on the outskirts of Peebles, overlooking the River Tweed. Guests can enjoy attractive gardens, well-appointed bedrooms and the popular hotel restaurant. When available, guests can also benefit from the facilities at the Peebles Hydro Hotel (only 700 yards away): leisure centre with pool, saunas and Jacuzzi; squash courts; tennis courts and riding.
DOUBLE ROOM: from £30 to £40
SINGLE ROOM: from £45 to £55
FOOD: up to £15
Hours: breakfast 7.30am–10am, lunch 12noon–2pm, dinner 7pm–9pm, bar snacks 12noon–2pm, 6.30pm–9.30pm.
Cuisine: SCOTTISH – traditional cuisine featuring local produce such as smoked Scottish salmon and fresh local trout.
Cards: Visa, Access, Diners, AmEx.
Other points: licensed, Sunday lunch, pets allowed, garden, residents' lounge, leisure centre.
Rooms: 24 bedrooms. All en suite.
Directions: on the A72 south of Edinburgh.
LAWSON KEAY ☎ (01721) 720451 [Fax] (01721) 723510.

PEEBLES HOTEL HYDRO
Innerleithen Road, EH45 8LX
Few hotels offer facilities comparable to the Peebles Hydro, a resort hotel with a full range of indoor and outdoor recreation facilities. There is a superb range of top-value holiday packages all year round. Friendly staff and a warm welcome await you, and the quality of the food is excellent. Magnificent grounds of 30 acres. Sister to the Park Hotel, also in Peebles.
DOUBLE ROOM: from £40 to £50
FOOD: from £15 to £20
Hours: breakfast 8am–9.30am, lunch 12.45am–2pm, dinner 7.30pm–9pm, bar meals 12noon–3.30pm.
Cuisine: MODERN ENGLISH – table d'hôte dinner menu using local produce, e.g., roast leg of Border lamb with a coriander sauce. Separate vegetarian menu.
Cards: Visa, Access, Diners, AmEx.
Other points: licensed, Sunday lunch, no-smoking area, garden, leisure centre, residents' bar, residents' lounge, swimming pool, parking.
Rooms: 137 bedrooms. All with TV, telephone, tea/coffee-making facilities.
Directions: on the A72 Peebles to Galashiels road.
MR P.J. VAN DIJK ☎ (01721) 720602 [Fax] (01721) 722999.

VENLAW CASTLE HOTEL
Tweedale, EH45 8QG
Venlaw Castle, on the slopes of the Moorfoot Hills yet within five minutes from the centre of Peebles, is a family-owned hotel run in the country manner with the accent on personal attention. Reputed for their good-quality home-cooked dishes, using only the freshest produce, and for providing excellent accommodation, the Cumming family's hospitality is outstanding.
DOUBLE ROOM: from £20 to £30
SINGLE ROOM: from £25 to £35
FOOD: up to £15
Cuisine: ENGLISH – dishes include baked salmon served with hollandaise sauce, aubergine bake served with green salad. Trout, venison, fresh fish dishes, lemon sole bonne femme.
Cards: Visa, Access, Diners, AmEx.
Other points: children welcome, no-smoking area, garden, pets allowed, residents' bar, residents' lounge.
Rooms: 4 double rooms, 4 twin rooms, 4 family rooms.
Directions: A72, on the slopes of Moorfoot Hills, 5 minutes from town centre.
MR & MRS CUMMING ☎ (01721) 720384.

SELKIRK • map 16E5

PHILIPBURN HOUSE HOTEL & RESTAURANT
TD11 5LS
A charming 18th century house, carefully converted into a warm hostelry with very interesting gourmet cooking. Set in beautiful gardens amid superb historical buildings, abbeys and houses, this is the Borders' premier hotel for guided and unguided hill-walking.
DOUBLE ROOM: from £20 to £30
FOOD: up to £15   [CLUB]
Hours: breakfast 8am–9.30am, lunch 12.15am–2.15pm, bar meals 12.25am–2.15pm, dinner 7.30pm–9.30pm, bar meals 7pm–10pm.
Cuisine: SCOTTISH / FRENCH – innovative

Peebles
HOTEL HYDRO

WHETHER you're looking for a relaxing holiday or planning a business meeting or conference, the Peebles Hydro is the perfect choice.

Set in the heart of the beautiful Scottish Borders, the Hydro has every facility, both indoors and out, to help you relax and enjoy either a couple of days away from it all or a full week or two's holiday.

For business meetings and conferences the Hydro adds perhaps the most important feature of all - years of practical experience in providing organisers and delegates with precisely what they require.

And just 700 yards down the road our sister hotel, the Park, offers a haven of peace and quiet, yet with full use of all the facilities at the Hydro.

So for business or pleasure choose the Hydro or the Park - for comfort, service and a guarantee that we'll look after you.

For further details, please contact:

Peebles
HOTEL HYDRO

Pieter van Dijk
The Peebles Hotel Hydro,
Peebles EH45 8LX.
Tel: 0721 720602.

French and Scottish cooking, including local saddle of roe deer cassis and rosace of langoustines, Sachertorte. Unusual Scottish bar menu.
Cards: Visa, Access.
Other points: licensed, Sunday lunch, no-smoking area, children welcome, pets by prior arrangement, afternoon tea, open bank holidays, residents' lounge, garden.
Directions: near Selkirk rugby ground.
JIM HILL ☎ (01750) 720747 Fax (01750) 721690.

TWEEDSMUIR • map 11A2

THE CROOK INN
By Biggar, ML12 6QN
The Crook is Scotland's oldest licensed inn, which has been sympathetically updated over many years. This family-run establishment offers good food, comfortable accommodation and a very warm welcome. Ideally located for touring the beautiful Border country and a centre for country pursuits. Nearby Crafts Centre demonstrates a wide range of local crafts.
DOUBLE ROOM: from £20 to £30
FOOD: up to £15 CLUB
Hours: meals all day 8am–9.30pm.
Cuisine: BRITISH – dishes may include beef Stroganoff, roast duck, poached salmon steak. Bar meals include fish dishes and the very popular home-made steak pies.
Cards: Visa, Access, Diners, AmEx.
Other points: Sunday lunch, no-smoking area, children welcome, garden, afternoon tea, pets allowed, residents' lounge, residents' bar, parking.
Rooms: 8 twin rooms. All with tea/coffee-making facilities.
Directions: 17 miles north of Moffat on the A701, between Moffat and Edinburgh.
STUART & ANGELA REID ☎ (018997) 272 Fax (018997) 294.

CENTRAL

CRIANLARICH • map 15C3

THE ROD & REEL
Main Street, FK20 8QN
A family-run bar and restaurant, which offers a wide choice of good food at very reasonable prices. Personally run by Elspeth and Bill Paulin, you are assured a warm welcome and friendly service.
FOOD: up to £15
Hours: bar meals 12noon–9pm, dinner 6pm–9pm.
Cuisine: BRITISH – bar meals and à la carte menu. Menus based on the use of fresh fish and local game. Good incorporation of Scottish meat for roasts and steaks, and an extensive selection of vegetarian dishes.
Cards: Visa, Access.
Other points: licensed, children welcome.
Directions: in the centre of Crianlarich.
ELSPETH & BILL PAULIN ☎ (018383) 271 Fax (018383) 261.

DUNBLANE • map 15D3

STIRLING ARMS HOTEL
Stirling Road, FK15 9EP
Originally a 17th century coaching inn by the bridge over the Allan Water, this family-run hotel and restaurant has been extensively refurbished. The owners pride themselves on providing comfortable accommodation and excellent food in their Oak Room Restaurant. Good value for money. History records the inn's patronage by Robert Burns and the Duke of Argyle.
DOUBLE ROOM: from £20 to £30
FOOD: up to £15
Hours: breakfast 8am–9am, lunch 12noon–2.30pm, dinner 6pm–9pm.
Cuisine: SCOTTISH – modern Scottish/continental cuisine. Specialities include Gaelic steak. Bar meals.
Cards: Visa, Access, AmEx.
Other points: licensed, open-air dining, Sunday lunch, no-smoking area, children welcome, pets allowed, garden.
Directions: off B8033 Stirling–Perth road. Close to high street.
JANE & RICHARD CASTELOW ☎ (01786) 822156 Fax (01786) 825300.

KILLIN • map 15C3

CLACHAIG HOTEL
Gray Street, Falls of Dochart, FK21 8SL
A former 17th century coaching inn, overlooking the intimate Falls of Dochart. The intimate and characterful restaurant offers a wide choice of quality food. Trout and salmon fishing is available on the hotel's own private stretch of the River Dochart.
DOUBLE ROOM: up to £20
FOOD: up to £15 CLUB
Hours: breakfast 8.15am–9.15am, lunch 12noon–2.30pm, bar meals 12noon–3.30pm, dinner 6.30pm–9.30pm, bar meals 5.30pm–9.30pm.
Cuisine: SCOTTISH – trout, salmon, Highland beef steaks, venison.
Cards: Visa, Access.
Other points: open-air dining, Sunday lunch, no-smoking area, disabled access, children welcome, garden, afternoon tea, pets allowed.
Rooms: 1 single room, 4 double rooms, 9 twin rooms, 2 family rooms.
Directions: on A827 beside Falls of Dochart.
JOHN MALLINSON ☎ (01567) 820270.

LOCHEARNHEAD • map 15C3

LOCHEARNHEAD HOTEL
Lochside, FK19 8PT
This small country house beside Loch Earn forms part of a lochside water sports development, offering such sports as sailing, waterskiing and windsurfing. Coupled with the friendly atmosphere of the hotel and the superb home-cooking, this is a perfect place for water sports enthusiasts of all ages. Ideally central for golfers: access to 15 courses within the hour.
DOUBLE ROOM: from £20 to £30
FOOD: up to £15
Hours: breakfast 8.30am–9.30am, lunch 11am–2.30pm, dinner 7pm–9.30pm.
Cuisine: FRENCH – à la carte and three-course fixed menus. French.
Cards: Visa, Access, Diners, AmEx.
Other points: licensed, open-air dining, children welcome, afternoon tea, pets allowed, garden.
Rooms: 1 single room, 12 double rooms, 13 twin rooms. All with TV, tea/coffee-making facilities.
Directions: take the A84 from Oban; turn onto the A85 to Crieff.
ANGUS CAMERON ☎ (01567) 830229
Fax (01567) 830364.

STIRLING • map 15D3

STIRLING MANAGEMENT CENTRE
University of Stirling, FK9 4LA
Conveniently located in a splendid rural setting, Stirling Management Centre is an ideal venue for business conferences and training courses. Purpose-built meeting rooms, executive accommodation, sports and leisure facilities combined with the educational resources of a progressive, modern university ensure the success of your visit here.

DOUBLE ROOM: from £30 to £40
SINGLE ROOM: from £25 to £35
FOOD: from £15 to £20
Hours: breakfast 7.30am–9am, lunch 12.30am–2.30pm, dinner 6.30pm–8.30pm.
Cuisine: BRITISH.
Cards: Visa, Access.
Other points: parking, children welcome, no-smoking area, disabled access, vegetarian meals, garden.
Rooms: 75 bedrooms. All with en suite.
Directions: from the north, follow A9; from the south, follow A74, leading to the A80/M80.
MS G. McINTYRE ☎ (01786) 451666
Fax (01786) 450472.

TYNDRUM • map 15C2

CLIFTON COFFEE HOUSE
Tyndrum, FK20 8RY
Spacious self-service restaurant with adjoining shops, specializing in the best Scottish dishes, whisky and confectionery. Outstanding Scottish crafts. Extensive car park and filling station facilities.
FOOD: up to £15
Hours: meals all day 8.30am–5.30pm, closed January until end of March.
Cuisine: SCOTTISH – home-made soups, good country cooking including game pies, hot pots and casseroles, fresh and smoked salmon and extensive salad table.
Cards: Visa, Access, Diners, AmEx, Switch.
Other points: Sunday lunch, no-smoking area, children welcome.
Directions: Tyndrum is located on the A82. The Coffee House is in the middle of the village on the roadside.
I.L. WILKIE ☎ (01838) 400271 Fax (01838) 400330.

DUMFRIES & GALLOWAY

ANNAN • map 11B2

POWFOOT GOLF HOTEL
Links Avenue, Powfoot, DG12 5PN
Standing beside an 18-hole golf-course with fishing nearby on the River Annan, the Golf Hotel is a tempting prospect for sporting persons. With views over the unspoilt Powfoot Bay and with the countryside and history of south-west Scotland on the doorstep, it is an excellent centre for touring. Excellent wild-fowling from September to February.
DOUBLE ROOM: from £30 to £40
SINGLE ROOM: from £35 to £45
FOOD: up to £15 CLUB
Hours: breakfast 8am–9.30am, lunch 12noon–2pm, dinner 7pm–8.30pm, bar 11am–11pm, weekends 11am–12midnight.
Cuisine: SCOTTISH – traditional Scottish food, which is prepared where possible using local produce: for example, fresh Solway salmon, pheasant, venison, duck, prime Galloway beef.
Cards: Visa, Access, AmEx.
Other points: licensed, open-air dining, Sunday lunch, children welcome, beer garden, residents' lounge, residents' bar, foreign exchange.
Rooms: 1 single room, 3 double rooms, 14 twin rooms, 2 family rooms. All with TV, telephone, tea/coffee-making facilities.
Directions: on the B724 in Powfoot, next to the golf course.
ADAM T. GRIBBON ☎ (01461) 700254
Fax (01461) 700288.

DUMFRIES • map 11B2

HETLAND HALL HOTEL
Carrutherstown, DG1 4JX
Originally built as a manor house, then converted into a boarding school, Hetland Hall is now a

grand country house hotel and restaurant. Set in 45 acres of well-tended parklands with fine views over the Solway Firth. The restaurant serves an international menu in relaxed, informal surroundings. Chalet swimming pool, fitness suite and snooker are available.
DOUBLE ROOM: from £40 to £50
SINGLE ROOM: from £25 to £35
FOOD: from £15 to £20 ☆
Hours: breakfast 7.30am–9.30am, lunch 12noon–2pm, dinner 7pm–9.30pm, bar 12noon–11pm.
Cuisine: INTENATIONAL.
Cards: Visa, Access, Diners, AmEx.
Other points: open-air dining, Sunday lunch, no-smoking area, pets allowed, children welcome, afternoon tea, swimming pool, gym facilities, games room, residents' lounge, residents' bar, foreign exchange, disabled access, parking.
Rooms: 5 single rooms, 11 double rooms, 10 twin rooms. All with TV, radio, alarm, telephone, tea/coffee-making facilities, hair dryer.
Directions: hotel is located on the main A75, midway between Annan and Dumfries.
DAVID & MARY ALLEN ☎ (01387) 840201
Fax (01387) 840211.

GATEHOUSE OF FLEET
map 11B1

MURRAY ARMS HOTEL
High Street, DG7 2HY

A warm, welcoming inn where Robert Burns wrote Scots, Wha Hae. Gatehouse of Fleet is one of Scotland's scenic heritage areas, surrounded by unspoilt countryside. Residents enjoy free golf, tennis and fishing.
DOUBLE ROOM: from £30 to £40
SINGLE ROOM: from £35 to £45
FOOD: up to £15
Hours: meals all day 12noon–9.45pm.
Cuisine: SCOTTISH – Galloway beef, locally caught fish and smoked salmon, Scottish lamb, home-made soups and pâté. Vegetarian meals.
Cards: Visa, Access, Diners, AmEx.
Other points: Sunday lunch, no-smoking area, children catered for (please check for age limits), disabled access, residents' lounge, residents' bar.
Rooms: 1 single room, 6 double rooms, 5 twin rooms, 1 family room. All with TV, telephone, tea/coffee-making facilities.
Directions: off A75, 60 miles west of Carlisle between Dumfries and Stranraer.
MURRAY ARMS HOTEL LTD ☎ (01557) 814207 Fax (01557) 814370.

ISLE OF WHITHORN • map 11C1

STEAMPACKET HOTEL
Harbour Row, DG8 8LL

A small, family-run hotel with a distinct nautical atmosphere where all the bedrooms overlook the harbour. Good food served in friendly, comfortable surroundings.
DOUBLE ROOM: from £20 to £30
FOOD: up to £15
Hours: breakfast 8am–9.30am, lunch 12noon–2pm, dinner 7pm–9.30pm.
Cuisine: SCOTTISH – lobster a speciality.
Cards: Visa, Access.
Other points: licensed, Sunday lunch, pets allowed.
Rooms: 3 double rooms, 1 twin room, 1 family room. All with TV, telephone, tea/coffee-making facilities.
Directions: on quayside.
MR SCOULAR ☎ (01988) 500334.

KIRKCUDBRIGHT • map 11B1

SELKIRK ARMS HOTEL
Old High Street, DG6 4JG

Family-run hotel set in a picturesque town. Guests can enjoy friendly hospitality, with good food and comfortable accommodation. Free squash for residents. Short breaks also available at special rates. An ideal base to tour Galloway.
DOUBLE ROOM: from £30 to £40
FOOD: from £15 to £20
Hours: breakfast 7.30am–10am, lunch 12noon–2pm, dinner 7pm–9.30pm.
Cuisine: BRITISH – dishes include local seafood, scallops, turbot, brill. Beef and lamb dishes. A la carte and daily changing table d'hôte menus.
Cards: Visa, Access, Diners, AmEx.
Other points: Sunday lunch, children welcome.
Rooms: 5 single rooms, 5 double rooms, 15 twin rooms, 2 family rooms.
Directions: situated in the High Street.
MR E.J. MORRIS ☎ (01557) 330402
Fax (01557) 331639.

LOCKERBIE • map 11B2

LOCKERBIE MANOR COUNTRY HOTEL
Boreland Road, DG11 2RG

The Georgian mansion house retaining original Adam features, about half a mile north of Lockerbie, provides well-appointed bedrooms and comfortable public rooms. The cuisine is truly international: Eastern flavours and cooking styles blend easily with Western recipes to give a genuine East-meets-West experience that visitors will find truly unforgettable.
DOUBLE ROOM: from £40 to £50
FOOD: up to £15
Hours: breakfast 7.30am–9.30am, dinner 6.30pm–9.30pm.
Cuisine: INTERNATIONAL.
Cards: Visa, Access, AmEx.
Other points: licensed, open-air dining, traditional Sunday lunch, children welcome, pets allowed, afternoon tea, open bank holidays, residents' lounge, garden, parking, residents' bar, vegetarian meals.
Rooms: 28 twin rooms. All with telephone.
Directions: on the A74, 25 miles north of Carlisle. Follow B723 north, turn right.
JEFFREY YEH ☎ (01576) 202610 Fax (01576) 203046.

MOFFAT • map 11A2

BALMORAL HOTEL
High Street, DG10 9DL
Set in the picturesque Annan Valley, the Balmoral Hotel was once a coaching inn and frequented by Robert Burns. It is now a friendly, family-owned hotel offering comfortable accommodation, fine cuisine and welcoming, friendly service. The wide choice of dishes all offer very good value. Ideal place to relax in attractive surroundings and a warm, family atmosphere.
DOUBLE ROOM: from £20 to £30
FOOD: up to £15
Hours: breakfast 8am–9.30am, bar meals 12noon–2pm, dinner 6pm–9pm, bar meals 6pm–9pm.
Cuisine: BRITISH / FRENCH – traditional Scottish, English and French dishes. Specialities include venison, fresh salmon, fillet steak.
Cards: Visa, Access.
Other points: licensed, Sunday lunch, children welcome, pets allowed, residents' lounge.
Rooms: 3 single rooms, 5 double rooms, 7 twin rooms, 1 family room. All with tea/coffee-making facilities.
Directions: on the A701, on the main street in Moffat.
B. STOKES & FAMILY ☎ (01683) 20288
[Fax] (01683) 20451.

THE STAR HOTEL
44 High Street, DG10 9EF
Although this hotel is listed in the Guinness Book of Records as the narrowest detached hotel, the interior and welcome are heartwarming and wholesome. If you enjoy good food at great-value prices in splendidly comfortable surroundings, then this is the place for you.
DOUBLE ROOM: from £20 to £30
FOOD: up to £15
Hours: breakfast 8am–9.30am, lunch 12noon–2.30pm, dinner 5.30pm–9pm.
Cuisine: BRITISH / INTERNATIONAL – wide and varied menu, daily specials.
Cards: Visa, Access.
Other points: licensed, children welcome, afternoon tea, pets allowed, coaches by prior arrangement, functions, conferences.
Rooms: 4 double rooms, 2 twin rooms, 8 family rooms.
Directions: situated in the High Street.
MR HOUSE & MR LEIGHFIELD ☎ (01683) 20156.

NEW GALLOWAY • map 11B1

THE SMITHY
The High Street, DG7 3RN
As the name implies, this is a converted blacksmith's shop with a restaurant, craft shop and B&B accommodation in an attached cottage. In the summer, guests may dine outside beside the Mill Burn that flows through the property. This is the Official Tourist Information agency on behalf of the Dumfries & Galloway Tourist Board.

DOUBLE ROOM: up to £20
SINGLE ROOM: up to £25
FOOD: up to £15
Hours: 1st March until Easter 10am–6pm, Easter until 31st May 10am–8pm; meals 1st June until 30th September 10am–9pm, 1st October until 31st October 10am–7.30pm; closed 31st October until 1st March.
Cuisine: SCOTTISH – home-baking and cooking, trout in wine with almonds, home-made oatcakes and cheese, range of Scottish pâtés including wild garlic, smoked salmon, venison. Children and 'Grannie' portions available. A good range of Scottish wines.
Other points: parking, no-smoking area, children welcome, disabled access, vegetarian meals.
Rooms: 1 double room, 1 twin room.
Directions: on the A762 to Kirkcudbright.
MR & MRS McPHEE ☎ (016442) 269.

NEWTON STEWART • map 14C5

CROWN HOTEL
101 Queen Street, DG8 6JW
An attractive, cream, listed building carefully modernized in keeping with its character. The Crown Hotel has two private rods on the River Cree – a prime salmon river – and several salmon dishes on the menu as a result!
DOUBLE ROOM: from £20 to £30
FOOD: up to £15
Hours: breakfast 8am–9.30am, lunch 12noon–2.30pm, bar meals 12noon–2.30pm, dinner 6.30pm–8.30pm, bar meals 6pm–9pm.
Cuisine: INTERNATIONAL – a wide range of bar meals: chilli, curry, roast chicken, steaks.
Cards: Visa, Access.
Other points: licensed, Sunday lunch, no-smoking area, children welcome, baby-listening device, cots.
Rooms: 2 single, 6 double rooms, 2 twin rooms, 1 quad room. All with TV, telephone, tea/coffee-making facilities.
Directions: on the southern outskirts of town.
MR & MRS PRISE ☎ (01671) 2727.

INGLENOOK LICENSED RESTAURANT
43 Main Street, Glenluce, DG8 0PP
A small, intimate restaurant with a large inglenook fireplace. The menu offers an excellent choice of meals and snacks from 10am throughout the day until 9pm, all served within a friendly and relaxed atmosphere.
FOOD: up to £15 ★
Hours: meals all day 10am–9pm.
Cuisine: BRITISH – wide range of dishes with steak pie and Inglenook Mushrooms the house speciality. Full meals, snacks and drinks available.
Cards: Visa, Access.
Other points: Sunday lunch, children welcome, afternoon tea.
Directions: in Glenluce, 10 miles from Stranraer on the A75 to Dumfries.
ROY & DIANA FLETCHER ☎ (015813) 494.

THORNHILL • map 11A1

🏨 BUCCLEUGH & QUEENSBERRY HOTEL
112 Drumcanrigg Street, DG3 5LU

A family-run, comfortable hotel in the centre of Thornhill, surrounded by scenic Nithsdale. Built in 1855 by the Duke of Buccleuch, it provides a friendly, welcoming atmosphere and freshly prepared food in pleasant surroundings.
DOUBLE ROOM: up to £20
FOOD: up to £15
Hours: meals all day 10am–10.30pm.
Cuisine: ENGLISH / CONTINENTAL.
Cards: Visa, Access, Diners, AmEx.
Other points: parking, children welcome, afternoon teas, pets, residents' lounge, vegetarian meals.
Rooms: 12 twin rooms.
Directions: situated in the centre of Thornhill.
MR & MRS STACK ☎ (01848) 330215.

FIFE

AUCHTERMUCHTY • map 16C4

🏨 THE FOREST HILLS HOTEL
The Square, G11 6PT

A traditional 18th century inn situated in the town square of the former Royal Burgh of Auchtermuchty, once a busy weaving centre. There is a comfortable oak-beamed cocktail bar with copper-topped tables and ornate fireplace, which provides a cosy and intimate atmosphere. Nearby places of interest include Falkland, with its Royal Palace, and Freuchie. Function suite for up to 80 guests.
DOUBLE ROOM: from £20 to £30
SINGLE ROOM: from £35 to £45
FOOD: up to £15 [CLUB]
Hours: breakfast 8am–9am, Sunday 9am–10am, lunch 12.30am–2pm, bar snacks 12noon–2.15pm, dinner 7pm–9.15pm, bar snacks 6pm–10pm.
Cuisine: BRITISH / CONTINENTAL – table d'hôte and à la carte with some flambé dishes, complemented by an interesting wine list.
Cards: Visa, Access, Diners, AmEx.
Other points: parking, children welcome, Sunday lunch, open bank holidays, afternoon tea, pets allowed, residents' lounge, vegetarian meals, licensed, residents' bar.
Rooms: 2 single rooms, 3 double rooms, 3 twin rooms, 2 family rooms. All with TV, telephone, tea/coffee-making facilities, hair dryer, trouser-press.
Directions: 7 miles from Cupar and 6 miles from exit 8 of M90.
ERNST VAN BEUSEKOM ☎ (01337) 828318 [Fax] (01337) 828318.

BURNTISLAND • map 16D4

🏨 KINGSWOOD HOTEL
Kinghorn Road, KY3 9LL

Set in 2 acres of grounds with outstanding views across the River Forth towards Edinburgh. The hotel's ambience, tasteful furnishings and first-class cuisine all combine to make every visit an enjoyable experience.
DOUBLE ROOM: from £30 to £40
SINGLE ROOM: from £45 to £55
FOOD: from £15 to £20 [CLUB]
Hours: breakfast 7.30am–9am, lunch 12noon–3pm, dinner 7pm–9.30pm, bar meals 12noon–10pm.
Cuisine: SCOTTISH – full à la carte and table d'hôte menus available. Choices include cullen skink and fresh salmon.
Cards: Visa, Access.
Other points: licensed, open-air dining, Sunday lunch, no-smoking area, children welcome, pets by prior arrangement.
Rooms: 1 single room, 3 double rooms, 5 twin rooms, 1 family room.
Directions: on the A92 coast road, half-way between Kinghorn and Burntisland.
RANKIN & KATHRYN BELL ☎ (01592) 872329 [Fax] (01592) 873123.

CRAIL • map 16D5

🏨 MARINE HOTEL
54 Nethergate South, KY10 3TZ

Small family-run hotel, with eight en suite, well-appointed bedrooms, a residents' lounge and a restaurant serving à la carte and table d'hôte menus. Beautiful views of the Firth of Forth and the Isle of May can be enjoyed in the lounge bar, which has a patio leading into the garden.
DOUBLE ROOM: from £20 to £30
SINGLE ROOM: up to £25
FOOD: up to £15
Hours: breakfast 8.30am–9.30am, dinner 7pm–9pm, snacks all day.
Cuisine: SEAFOOD – local seafood (in season).
Cards: Visa, Access, Diners, AmEx.
Other points: licensed, Sunday lunch, pets allowed, afternoon tea.
Rooms: 3 double rooms, 4 twin rooms, 1 family room. All with en suite, TV, tea/coffee-making facilities.
Directions: on junction of B940 with A917, south-east of St Andrews. Follow signs for pottery.
IAIN & AILEEN GREENLEES ☎ (01333) 50207.

CUPAR • map 16C5

🏨 EDEN HOUSE HOTEL
2 Pitscottie Road, KY15 4HF

Built as a home for a Victorian merchant, this privately-owned hotel reflects the architectural grandeur of the period. Immaculately furnished throughout, it offers impeccable standards of

service and attention to detail for all its guests. A large conservatory restaurant is a new addition to this lovely place. Ideal for both the businessman and holiday-maker.
DOUBLE ROOM: from £20 to £30
SINGLE ROOM: from £35 to £45
FOOD: from £25 to £30
Hours: breakfast 7.30am–9.30am, bar snacks 12noon–2pm, dinner 6.30pm–9.30pm, bar snacks 6.30pm–9.30pm, closed Sunday lunch, closed Christmas.
Cuisine: BRITISH.
Cards: Visa, Access, AmEx.
Other points: children welcome, pets, disabled access, residents' lounge, garden, parking, vegetarian meals, open-air dining, residents' bar, cots, baby-listening device.
Rooms: 2 single rooms, 9 double rooms. All with TV, radio, alarm, telephone, tea/coffee-making facilities.
Directions: off A91 St Andrews road. East of Cupar, overlooking the park.
MR P.A. MEREDREW ☎ (01334) 652510.

DUNFERMLINE • map 16D4

HALFWAY HOUSE HOTEL
Kingseat, KY12 0TJ
Scotland is renowned for its long tradition of warm hospitality, and The Halfway House Hotel is no exception. Recently redecorated, the hotel is comfortable and welcoming, and the food in the bar and restaurant is well presented and served. Nearby Loch Fitty is famous for trout fishing, golf lovers can visit St Andrews and Gleneagles, and Edinburgh is only 30 minutes away. The hotel is 2 miles from the Scottish National Water Ski Centre and 4 miles from Knockhill Motor Racing Circuit.
DOUBLE ROOM: from £20 to £30
SINGLE ROOM: from £25 to £35
FOOD: up to £15
Hours: breakfast 7.30am–9.30am, lunch 12noon–3.30pm, bar meals 12noon–2pm, high tea Sunday 4pm–6pm, dinner 5.30pm–9.30pm, bar meals 5.30pm–9.30pm.
Cuisine: SCOTTISH – specialities include salmon gravadlax and a wide range of steaks.
Cards: Visa, Access.
Other points: licensed, Sunday lunch, children welcome, residents' lounge, golf nearby, residents' bar, parking, laundry, drying room.
Rooms: 3 double rooms, 9 twin rooms. All with TV, telephone, tea/coffee-making facilities.
Directions: take M90; exit 3 for Dunfermline. Travel 100 metres to next roundabout, turn right at sign for Retail Park; Kingseat is approximately one mile.
ANN WITHEYMAN & VIC PEGG ☎ (01383) 731661 [Fax] (01383) 621274.

FREUCHIE • map 16D4

THE LOMOND HILLS HOTEL
Parliament Square, KY7 7EY
Set in the quiet, picturesque village in the Howe of Fife, at the foot of the Lomond hills, this is a comfortable hotel dating back to 1753 and now upgraded to a high standard. Intimate candlelit restaurant, comfortable lounges, four-poster bedrooms and a leisure centre, which is free for guests' use.
DOUBLE ROOM: from £30 to £40
FOOD: up to £15 [CLUB]
Hours: breakfast 7.30am–9am, bar snacks 12noon–2.15pm, dinner 7pm–9.15pm, bar snacks 6pm–10pm.
Cuisine: BRITISH / CONTINENTAL – à la carte menu, with special menu of flamed dishes.
Other points: parking, children welcome, Sunday lunch, open bank holidays, disabled access, pets allowed, residents' lounge, vegetarian meals, garden, licensed, residents' bar, swimming pool.
Rooms: 2 single rooms, 8 double rooms, 10 twin rooms, 4 family rooms. All with TV, telephone, tea/coffee-making facilities.
Directions: in centre of Fife near Falkland, 14 miles from Kinross.
ERNST VAN BEUSEKOM ☎ (01337) 857329 [Fax] (01337) 857498.

GLENROTHES • map 16D4

TOWN HOUSE HOTEL
1 High Street, Markinch, KY7 6DQ
A family-run hotel bringing together traditional values and quality. Centrally situated in the Kingdom of Fife, ideal for sporting breaks and for family holidays. The Town House Hotel provides a warm welcome and good value for money.
DOUBLE ROOM: from £20 to £30
FOOD: up to £15
Hours: breakfast 7am–9am, lunch 12noon–2pm, dinner 6.15pm–8.30pm.
Cuisine: INTERNATIONAL – dishes may include chicken stir-fry, Tay salmon fillet, chicken tikka, Chinese sweet-and-sour pork, grilled steaks.
Cards: Visa, Access, Diners, AmEx.
Other points: licensed, Sunday lunch, no-smoking area, children welcome, pets allowed, special breaks, parking.
Rooms: 2 single rooms, 2 double rooms. All with TV, tea/coffee-making facilities.
Directions: B9130, opposite railway station in Markinch.
HARRY & LESLEY BAIN ☎ (01592) 758459.

LETHAM • map 16C4

FERNIE CASTLE HOTEL
Letham By Cupar, KY7 7RU
An ancient Scottish royal hunting lodge, dating from the mid-14th century, Fernie Castle retains many original features and an air of olde-worlde comfort. All restoration work is personally supervised by its current owner. Situated in the geographic centre of Fife, the surrounding area is equally attractive, and Falkland Palace, the Scottish Deer Centre and the Ladybank Golf Club are nearby.
DOUBLE ROOM: from £30 to £40
SINGLE ROOM: from £35 to £45

FOOD: up to £15 [CLUB]
Hours: breakfast 7.30am–10am, lunch, 12noon–2.30pm, dinner 6.30pm–9.30pm, bar meals and snacks 12noon–3pm, 6pm–10pm.
Cuisine: SCOTTISH – predominantly Scottish fare.
Cards: Visa, Access, AmEx.
Other points: licensed, open-air dining, Sunday lunch, residents' lounge, parking, open bank holidays, children welcome, baby-listening device, baby-sitting, cots.
Rooms: 4 single rooms, 6 double rooms, 5 twin rooms. All with TV, radio, alarm, telephone, tea/coffee-making facilities, hospitality tray, trouser-press.
Directions: half a mile north of Letham village on the A914.
NORMAN SMITH ☎ (01337) 810381
[Fax] (01337) 810422.

ROSYTH • map 16D4

GLADYER INN
Heath Road, Ridley Drive, KY11 2BT
A modern, purpose-built hotel with up-to-date facilities to match. The best of Scottish hospitality is extended to all guests whether staying overnight, dining or having a drink. Good value for money.
DOUBLE ROOM: from £20 to £30
FOOD: up to £15 [CLUB]
Hours: breakfast 7am–9.30am, lunch 12noon–2pm, dinner 7pm–9.30pm, bar meals 12noon–2pm, 7pm–9.30pm.
Cuisine: SCOTTISH – table d'hôte menu,
including traditional dishes.
Cards: Visa, Access, AmEx, Switch, Delta.
Other points: licensed, Sunday lunch, no-smoking area, children welcome, functions, pets allowed.
Rooms: 4 double rooms, 16 twin rooms, 1 family room. All with satellite TV, telephone, tea/coffee-making facilities.
Directions: from M90 junction 1 towards Kincardine Bridge, Ridley Drive on left.
JANET & JIM INNES ☎ (01383) 419977
[Fax] (01383) 411728.

ST ANDREWS • map 16C5

THE PANCAKE PLACE
177–9 South Street, KY16 9EE
A cheerful family restaurant serving satisfying meals at good value for money. Spacious surroundings and relaxed atmosphere. Famous golf-course, university and sea-life centre nearby. Also, beaches and cathedral ruins.
FOOD: up to £15
Hours: meals all day 9.30am–5.30pm, closed Christmas 25th December, 1st January.
Cuisine: SCOTTISH – pancakes in traditional Scottish style, savoury and sweet. Also baked potatoes, rice and monthly specials.
Other points: licensed, Sunday lunch, no-smoking area, children welcome.
Directions: towards the west port along South Street, near Madras College.
C.D. BURHOUSE ☎ (01334) 75671.

GRAMPIAN

ABERDEEN • map 16A6

BETTY BURKES
45 Langstane Place, AB1 2DJ
Betty Burkes is a stylish and interesting bar, which has been themed as a gentlemen's club, with old portrait paintings, wood panelling and leather seats. The massive carved eagle that dominates the entrance originated in America during the War Of Independence. There are display cabinets full of old bar and glass curios. Take in the bustling, local atmosphere.
FOOD: up to £15 [CLUB]
Hours: breakfast 10am–12noon, bar meals 12noon–9.30pm, Friday and Saturday 12noon–9pm.
Cuisine: ENGLISH / INTERNATIONAL – bar meals including deep-fried mushrooms, potato skins and home-made puddings.
Cards: Visa, Access, AmEx.
Other points: children welcome, open bank holidays.
Directions: in city centre, close to Union Street, Aberdeen's main street.
MIKE COOK ☎ (01224) 210359.

OLD MILL INN & RESTAURANT
South Deeside Road, Maryculter, AB1 0AX
An historic 200-year-old mill boasting original beams and timbers and set on the banks of the famous River Dee. It has been extensively refurbished to provide a high level of comfort and personal service in a friendly, welcoming atmosphere. There are many nearby places of interest to visit, including Royal Deeside and several whisky trails.
DOUBLE ROOM: from £20 to £30
SINGLE ROOM: from £25 to £35
FOOD: up to £15 ★
Hours: breakfast 7.30am–10am, dinner 5.30pm–10pm, lunch 12noon–2.30pm, open all day, 7.30am–11.30pm.
Cuisine: BRITISH / CONTINENTAL – titillate your taste-buds with the superb selection of traditional and innovative cuisine. Using only fresh, local produce, the house specialities are a must for the discerning diner. Menus change with the seasons.
Cards: Visa, Access, Diners, AmEx.
Other points: access to river fishing, golf, hill-walking, pony-trekking, parking, children welcome, Sunday lunch, open bank holidays, vegetarian meals.

Rooms: 1 single room, 3 double rooms, 2 twin rooms, 1 family room. All with TV, tea/coffee-making facilities.
Directions: from Aberdeen on south side of Dee Bridge, B9077 for 4 miles. The inn is 300 yards beyond Petercutler Bridge. Close to Story Book Glen.
VICTOR SANG ☎ (01224) 733212
Fax (01224) 732884.

ST MAGNUS COURT HOTEL
22 Guild Street, AB1 2NF
The St Magnus Court Hotel is a family-run hotel catering principally for the commercial sector. The accommodation is very comfortable, while the food is well cooked and prepared. Pleasant, relaxed atmosphere.
DOUBLE ROOM: from £20 to £30
SINGLE ROOM: from £35 to £45
FOOD: up to £15
Hours: breakfast 5.30am–9.30am, dinner 6pm–9pm, bar meals 12noon–10.30pm.
Cuisine: BRITISH – dishes include home-made soup of the day, rump steak garni, chicken fillet, omelettes, ice cream and fruit.
Cards: Visa, Access.
Other points: licensed, residents' bar, residents' lounge.
Rooms: 4 single rooms, 2 double rooms, 13 twin rooms, 1 family room. All with TV, telephone, tea/coffee-making facilities.
Directions: this commercial hotel is located in the centre of Aberdeen, directly opposite Aberdeen railway station.
BOB PAGE ☎ (01224) 589411 Fax (01224) 584352.

ALFORD • map 16A5

FORBES ARMS HOTEL
Brig of Alford, AB33 8QJ
Owned by the same family since 1894, the Forbes Arms Hotel lies on the banks of the River Don, just over the picturesque Brig of Alford, one mile from the town. It has a deserved reputation for its friendly service and has been completely refurbished with a splendid conservatory and spacious dining room, offering traditional Scottish cuisine and fine wines. An ideal base for touring north-east Scotland.
DOUBLE ROOM: from £20 to £30
FOOD: up to £15
Hours: breakfast 8.30am–9.30am, lunch 12noon–1.30pm, bar snacks 12noon–1.45pm, dinner 7pm–8.15pm, bar snacks 5pm–8.30pm.
Cuisine: SCOTTISH.
Cards: Visa, Access, Diners, AmEx.
Other points: children welcome, no-smoking area, pets disabled access, residents' lounge, garden, open-air dining, vegetarian meals, parking.
Directions: from Alford, take main A944 (signed Strathdon), and the hotel is located on the right after bridge over River Don.
CHARLES SPENCE ☎ (0197556) 2108
Fax (0197556) 3467.

BALLATER • map 16A5

ALEXANDRA HOTEL
12 Bridge Square, AB3 6QJ
An attractive, well-maintained exterior opens into a tastefully decorated hotel and restaurant. Table d'hôte and à la carte meals are offered with a touch of French cuisine. Close to Balmoral, Crathie church and distilleries. For anglers, there is fishing in the River Dee.
DOUBLE ROOM: from £20 to £30
FOOD: from £15 to £20
Hours: breakfast 8am–9.30am, lunch noon–2.15pm, dinner 6pm–9pm, bar 11am–midnight.
Cuisine: SCOTTISH / FRENCH – traditional Scottish and French: entrecôte au poivre, fillet steak Diane, trout with almonds, salmon, whole lemon sole, venison. Selection of cheese.
Cards: Visa, Access, Diners, AmEx.
Other points: licensed, central heating, children welcome, pets allowed, baby-listening device, cots, foreign exchange, left luggage, disabled access, vegetarian meals, parking.
Rooms: 7 bedrooms. All with en suite, TV, radio, telephone, tea/coffee-making facilities.
Directions: on the A93 Aberdeen to Braemar road, near the River Dee bridge.
ROBERT PATON ☎ (013397) 55376
Fax (013397) 55466.

AULD KIRK HOTEL
Braemar Road, AB35 5RQ
Converted from a church to a hotel in 1990, the original structure, including the front doors, bell tower and many of the windows, have been retained. The result is fascinating and well worth a visit. The resident proprietors provide a warm welcome, well-appointed accommodation, good food and good value.
DOUBLE ROOM: from £20 to £30
FOOD: from £15 to £20
Hours: breakfast 8.30am–9am, lunch 12noon–2pm, bar meals 11am–4pm, dinner 6.30pm–9pm, bar meals 4.30pm–9pm, open all year.
Cuisine: SCOTTISH – wide choice of meals from Royal Deeside salmon with hollandaise sauce to toasted sandwiches.
Cards: Visa, Access.
Other points: licensed, open-air dining, Sunday lunch, children welcome, afternoon tea, pets allowed, residents' lounge.
Directions: on main Braemar to Aberdeen road at northern end of Ballater. A93.
MONICE CHIVAS ☎ (013397) 55762.

BANCHORY • map 16A5

BANCHORY LODGE HOTEL
Banchory, AB31 3HS
At the confluence of the Feugh with the Dee, the Banchory Lodge is in a striking and historic setting, with the River Dee, a celebrated salmon river, running through the grounds. As well as salmon fishing, there is also ample opportunity for golfing, nearby forest walks and nature trails. An abundance of National Trust properties to visit nearby.

GRAMPIAN • SCOTLAND

DOUBLE ROOM: from £50
FOOD: from £25 to £30
Hours: bar 11am–2pm, bar 5pm–11pm, closed 12th December until 29th January.
Cuisine: SCOTTISH – prime Scottish beef, Dee salmon.
Cards: Visa, Access, AmEx.
Other points: children welcome, fishing, sauna.
Rooms: 8 double, 22 twin, 9 family rooms.
Directions: off the A93, 18 miles west of Aberdeen in Banchory, off Dee Street.
DUGALD JAFFRAY ☎ (0330) 822625/824777
[Fax] (0330) 825019.

BRAEMAR • map 16B4

CALLATER LODGE HOTEL
9 Glenshee Road, AB35 5YQ
A typical Victorian villa built from local granite and standing in one acre of mature grounds on the southern edge of Braemar. Peter and Mary Nelson have built up an enviable reputation for the warmth of their welcome and the excellence of their hospitality. There are two separate self-catering units also available, Callater Cottage and Callater Chalet. Ideal location for tourists, sportsmen and walkers.
DOUBLE ROOM: from £20 to £30
SINGLE ROOM: up to £25
FOOD: from £15 to £20
Hours: breakfast 8.30am, dinner 7.30pm.
Cuisine: BRITISH – fresh local produce is used extensively for the daily changing menu; 5 courses.
Cards: Visa, Eurocard, MasterCard.
Other points: parking, open bank holidays, no-smoking, pets allowed, residents' lounge, garden, licensed.
Rooms: 2 single, 3 double, 4 twin rooms.
Directions: on A93 (Perth to Aberdeen road), as it passes through Braemar.
PETER & MARY NELSON ☎ (013397) 41275
[Fax] (013397) 41275.

BUCKIE • map 18B5

MILL HOUSE HOTEL
Tynet, AB5 2HJ
A converted 18th-century water mill, offering all sporting and sightseeing activities. This hospitable, family-run establishment provides a relaxing atmosphere and is renowned for its excellent food and value. All 15 bedrooms are en suite with full modern facilities. Open all year.
DOUBLE ROOM: from £20 to £30
SINGLE ROOM: from £35 to £45
FOOD: up to £15 [CLUB]
Hours: breakfast 7.45am–9.30am, lunch 12noon–2pm, dinner 7pm–9pm.
Cuisine: SCOTTISH – à la carte: the speciality is Scottish cuisine from local produce.
Cards: Visa, Access, Diners, AmEx.
Other points: licensed, Sunday lunch, functions, special breaks, golf packages, vegetarian meals, residents' bar, residents' lounge, disabled access, children welcome.

Rooms: 7 single, 3 double, 1 family, 4 twin rooms. All with TV, radio, tea/coffee-making facilities.
Directions: on the A98, east of Elgin. Hotel located between Buckie and Fochabers.
GILL & PHIL SILVER ☎ (01542) 850233
[Fax] (01542) 850331.

CULLEN • map 18B5

BAYVIEW HOTEL
57 Seafield Street, AB5 2SU
A small, intimate hotel commanding spectacular views over the harbour, bay and Moray Firth, renowned for excellent food and personal service. The restaurant is open daily, and meals are also served in the bar at lunchtime and in the evening. The inspector declared the food 'excellently prepared and presented' and the rooms 'attractive and very comfortable'. Daily changing menu.
DOUBLE ROOM: from £20 to £30
FOOD: up to £15
Hours: breakfast 8am–9.30am, lunch 12noon–1.45pm, dinner 6.30pm–9pm.
Cuisine: SCOTTISH – restaurant part of 'Taste of Scotland' scheme, offering dishes such as fillet of salmon wrapped in pastry with lemon thyme. Good range of bar meals.
Cards: Visa, Access.
Other points: Sunday lunch.
Rooms: 1 single, 2 double, 1 family, 2 twin rooms. All with TV, telephone, tea/coffee-making facilities.
Directions: overlooking the harbour.
DAVID EVANS ☎ (01542) 041031.

GLENLIVET • map 16A4

MINMORE HOUSE
Glenlivet, AB37 9DB
Formerly the residence of George Smith, the founder of Glenlivet whisky, this is a family-run hotel with a relaxed atmosphere, log fires, fresh flowers and an abundance of peace and quiet. Surrounded by four acres of secluded walled gardens, the comfortable bedrooms are named after local Speyside malts. Hearty breakfasts begin the day, followed by sumptuous afternoon teas and a five-course dinner as the finale, from fresh salmon to fillet of venison. Glorious views over the glens.
DOUBLE ROOM: from £30 to £40
SINGLE ROOM: from £35 to £45
FOOD: from £15 to £20
Hours: breakfast 7.30am–10am, dinner, 8pm–8.30pm, closed November until April.
Cuisine: SCOTTISH – bookings are essential. Disabled access to restaurant only.
Cards: Visa, Access.
Other points: no-smoking area, parking, children welcome, limited disabled access, pets, residents' lounge, garden, vegetarian meals.
Rooms: 2 single, 5 double, 3 twin rooms.
Directions: A95 from Grantown, 15 miles and turn right onto B9008. Follow signs to the Glenlivet distillery, the hotel is adjacent.
BELINDA LUXMOORE ☎ (01807) 590378
[Fax] (01807) 590472.

317

INSCH • map 16A5

THE LODGE HOTEL
Old Rayne, AB5 6RY
Situated just off the main A96 Aberdeen–Inverness road, this family-run village hotel has superb views and offers a warm and friendly welcome. With a reputation for good food and generous portions, the hotel is frequented by locals, business people and holiday-makers. Being centrally situated, the hotel is an ideal base for touring the Grampian region and for visiting the numerous castles and distilleries in the area. It also provides a welcome opportunity for the weary traveller to enjoy some peace and tranquillity.
DOUBLE ROOM: from £20 to £30
SINGLE ROOM: from £25 to £35
FOOD: up to £15
Hours: breakfast 8am–9am, lunch 12noon–2.30pm, dinner weekdays 7pm–8pm, weekends 7pm–9pm.
Cuisine: ENGLISH / CONTINENTAL – daily changing menu with a selection of 46 different soups. Fresh local produce of beef, lamb, fish, salmon and seafood. Desserts are home-made, and the cheese platter is very good value. Special children's menu available.
Cards: Visa, Access, AmEx.
Other points: licensed, Sunday lunch, children welcome, pets allowed, vegetarian meals, residents' lounge, residents' bar.
Rooms: 1 single room, 1 double room, 4 twin rooms, 1 family room. All with en suite, TV, telephone, tea/coffee-making facilities, central heating, electric blankets, baby-listening facilities.
Directions: off the A96, 9 miles north of Inverurie, 12 miles south of Huntly.
MR & MRS NEIL ☎ (014645) 205/636.

PETERHEAD • map 18C6

BAYVIEW HOTEL
3 St Peter Street, AB4 6RR
Pleasant family-run hotel situated on the coastline of Scotland. Peterhead is the home of the largest fishing fleet in Europe, and during your visit you may have the opportunity to see the fish being landed. There is also a golf course nearby, and Aviemore and Inverness are just a short drive away.
DOUBLE ROOM: from £20 to £30
SINGLE ROOM: from 25 to £35
FOOD: up to £15
Hours: breakfast 7am–9.30am, lunch 12noon–2pm, dinner 5pm–8.30pm.
Cuisine: SCOTTISH – traditional Scottish cuisine: fresh fish and seafood, chicken, beef, pork and duck.
Cards: Visa, Access.
Other points: licensed, Sunday lunch, children welcome, pets allowed.
Rooms: 2 single, 11 double, 4 twin rooms.
Directions: off the A952 between Aberdeen and Fraserburgh.
MR JAMES ELDER ☎ (01779) 472523
[Fax] (01779) 479495.

STONEHAVEN • map 16B6

THE TOLBOOTH RESTAURANT
Kincardine, AB3 2JU
A building of historical interest, situated in the seaside holiday resort of Stonehaven, and offering good views across the working harbour. Excellent home-produced dishes using local produce, with the emphasis on local fish dishes. A major nearby tourist attraction is Dunotter Castle, setting for Franco Zefferelli's portrayal of Hamlet in 1990.
FOOD: from £15 to £20
Hours: lunch 12noon–2pm, dinner 7pm–9pm, closed Monday, closed January.
Cuisine: SEAFOOD – à la carte menu. Blue fin tuna steak, red snapper ravioli, monkfish casserole, loin of venison, all home-cooked using only fresh produce.
Cards: Visa.
Other points: licensed, Sunday lunch, children welcome, vegetarian meals.
Directions: 15 miles south of Aberdeen. In Stonehaven, follow harbour signs.
MOYA BOTHWELL ☎ (01569) 62287.

HIGHLANDS

ALTNAHARRA • map 17A3

ALTNAHARRA HOTEL
By Lairg, IV27 4UE
Privately owned and managed, Altnaharra offers a warm welcome and friendly atmosphere together with good food and comfortable accommodation. With its choice of refurbished bedrooms and two annex cottages, this hotel is ideal for families or a party of enthusiastic sports persons in the area to enjoy superb salmon and sea-trout fishing. Winter and spring breaks available.
DOUBLE ROOM: from £50
SINGLE ROOM: from £35 to £45
FOOD: from £15 to £20 ☆
Hours: breakfast 7.45am–9am, lunch 12noon–2pm, dinner 7.30pm–8.30pm, closed 17th October until 1st March.
Cuisine: SCOTTISH – prime Scottish beef and lamb, game, fresh local fish and seafood.
Cards: Visa, Access.
Other points: children welcome, garden, fishing, drying facilities, residents' lounge, residents' bar.
Rooms: 3 single rooms, 3 double rooms, 12 twin rooms. All with tea/coffee-making facilities.
Directions: off the A836 Lairg road; follow sign for Tongue.
ALTNAHARRA HOTEL LTD ☎ (0154981) 222
[Fax] (0154981) 222.

ARDEONAIG • map 18E4

🏨 ARDEONAIG HOTEL
South Loch Tayside, near Killin, FK21 8SU
This 17th century wayside inn is situated in Highland Perthshire on the southern shore of Loch Tay, midway betwen Killin and Kenmore, and enjoys impressive views of the Ben Lawers range. The hotel has it own salmon-fishing rights on Loch Tay, as well as fishing for trout and char. With a very high standard of accommodation and superb cuisine, this is a retreat not only for fishing enthusiasts, but for anyone wanting a break away.
DOUBLE ROOM: from £30 to £40
FOOD: from £20 to £25
Hours: breakfast 8am–10am, bar meals 12noon–2pm, dinner 7pm–9pm, bar meals 6pm–7pm.
Cuisine: SCOTTISH – superb award-winning cuisine.
Cards: Switch.
Other points: parking, pets allowed, conference facilities, residents' lounge, garden, vegetarian meals, afternoon teas.
Rooms: 16 bedrooms. All with tea/coffee-making facilities.
Directions: A84 north from Stirling, A9 north from Perth. The hotel is 7 miles from Killin and is well signposted. The road is unclassified, on south bank of Loch Tay.
ALAN & EILEEN MALONE ☎ (01567) 820400
Fax (01567) 820282.

AULTBEA • map 17B2

🏨 AULTBEA HOTEL
IV22 2HX
This 18th century family-run hotel is the perfect location from which to enjoy the wonders of the north-west Highlands. With exhilarating views, the hotel offers guests attractively furnished, well-appointed bedrooms, the intimate atmosphere and fine food in the Zetland Restaurant, a delightful patio and garden for dining in the warmer months, and friendly, attentive service. Opposite the hotel, the Waterside Bistro is open all day until 9pm and offers an attractive alternative to the restaurant.
DOUBLE ROOM: from £30 to £40
SINGLE ROOM: from £25 to £35
FOOD: from £15 to £20
Hours: breakfast 8am–11.30am, lunch 11am–3pm, bar meals 11am–3pm, dinner 7pm–9pm, bar meals 4.30pm–9pm.
Cuisine: SCOTTISH – a good selection: local seafood a speciality.
Cards: Visa, Access.
Other points: parking, children welcome, dogs allowed, residents' lounge, garden, open-air dining, vegetarian meals, traditional Sunday lunch, afternoon teas.
Rooms: 1 single room, 3 double rooms, 3 twin rooms, 1 family room. All with en suite, TV, telephone, radio, alarm, hair dryer, trouser-press, tea/coffee-making facilities.
Directions: A832, on the shore of Loch Ewe.
PETER & AVRIL NIETO ☎ (01445) 731201
Fax (01445) 731214.

HIGHLANDS • SCOTLAND

AVIEMORE • map 16A4

🏨 CAIRNGORM GUEST HOUSE
Grampian Road, PH22 1RP
A traditional stone mansion, the house has been skilfully extended to the rear to provide quality accommodation with full en suite facilities and central heating, to ensure you maximum privacy and comfort. This friendly, family-run guest house is an ideal place for a Highland break or holiday.
DOUBLE ROOM: up to £20
Hours: open all year.
Cards: Visa, Access.
Other points: parking, children welcome, no-smoking area, residents' lounge.
Rooms: 5 double rooms, 3 twin rooms, 1 family room. All with en suite, TV, tea/coffee-making facilities.
Directions: located in the main road of Aviemore, a short walk from the Aviemore Centre complex.
HARRY TANNOCK ☎ (01479) 010630
Fax (01479) 810630.

CAWDOR • map 18C4

🍽 CAWDOR TAVERN
The Lane, IV12 5XP
Situated near Cawdor Castle – made famous by Shakespeare's Macbeth – you'll find Cawdor Tavern. The focal point of this charming conservation village, only 15 minutes from Inverness, the Tavern is renowned for its traditional Scottish fare. The snug lounge bar, with a welcoming log fire and old oak panelling, has a vast selection of malt whiskies to tempt the connoisseur. There is also an interesting 40-bin wine list and a superb choice of beers, including real ales and a 'guest' beer. Open all year, there is a sunny patio for summer days, and children are always welcome. Run by Norman Sinclair, from the highly acclaimed Moorings Hotel in Fort William, you will see the same dedication for which The Moorings was voted 'AA Hotel of the Year for Scotland' 1994.
FOOD: from £15 to £20
Hours: lunch 12noon–2pm, dinner 6pm–9.30pm, open for morning coffee in summer.
Cuisine: SCOTTISH.
Cards: Visa, Access, MasterCard.
Other points: parking, children welcome, no-smoking area, open-air dining, vegetarian meals, traditional Sunday lunch.
Directions: half a mile from Cawdor Castle, on B9006, off A96 Inverness to Nairn road.
NORMAN SINCLAIR ☎ (01667) 404777
Fax (01667) 404777.

CONTIN • map 17C3

🏨 ACHILTY HOTEL
Contin By Strathpeffer, IV14 9EG
Family-run hotel, beautifully situated some 17 miles from Inverness, with spectacular views over the surrounding mountains. Private fishing rights

319

on River Blackwater, marvellous walks and scenery. Good comfortable accommodation. Popular restaurant and good bar meals featuring the best local produce and many French cordon bleu specialities. Warm welcome and good value.
DOUBLE ROOM: from £20 to £30
FOOD: up to £15 [CLUB]
Hours: breakfast 7.30am–9.30am, lunch 12noon–2.30pm, dinner 5.30pm–9.30pm, bar meals 12noon–2.30pm, 5.30pm–9.30pm, open all year.
Cuisine: BRITISH – à la carte and table d'hôte menus offering a good choice of traditional dishes. Vegetarians also catered for.
Cards: Visa, Access.
Other points: licensed, open-air dining, Sunday lunch, no-smoking area, children welcome, pets allowed, afternoon tea, residents' lounge, parking, disabled access, open bank holidays, cots, foreign exchange, fishing, vegetarian meals, residents' bar.
Rooms: 3 double rooms, 5 twin rooms, 3 triple rooms, 1 quad room. All with TV, tea/coffee-making facilities.
Directions: from Inverness, take A9, then A835 Ullapool road.
CLAUDE & HELENA PONTY ☎ (01997) 421355 [Fax] (01463) 792780.

CROMARTY • map 18B4

ROYAL HOTEL
Marine Terrace, IV11 8YN

A family-run hotel with attentive staff who guard their reputation for quality food and value for money with considerable pride – the best in Scottish hospitality. Cromarty is an unspoilt fishing village on the Black Isle, where relaxation and peace are guaranteed.
DOUBLE ROOM: from £20 to £30
SINGLE ROOM: from £25 to £35
FOOD: up to £15 🍽 [CLUB] ✭
Hours: breakfast 8am–9.30am, lunch 12noon–2pm, dinner 7pm–8.30pm, bar meals 12noon–2pm, 5.30pm–9.30pm.
Cuisine: SCOTTISH.
Cards: Visa, AmEx.
Other points: open-air dining, Sunday lunch, no-smoking area, children welcome, coaches by prior arrangement, residents' lounge, residents' bar.
Rooms: 3 single rooms, 5 double rooms, 2 twin rooms. All with en suite, TV, tea/coffee-making facilities, hair dryer.
Directions: off the A832 in Cromarty overlooking the beach and harbour.
YVONNE & STEWART MORRISON ☎ (01381) 600217.

DINGWALL • map 17C3

THE NATIONAL HOTEL
High Street, IV15 9HA

This Victorian hotel offers spacious accommodation, warmly decorated with wood panelling and comfortable furnishings, with convenient access to the spectacular Highland countryside. Traditional home-cooking is welcome after an invigorating day spent exploring the nearby sights.
DOUBLE ROOM: from £30 to £40
FOOD: up to £15
Hours: breakfast 7am–9.30am, lunch 12noon–2.30pm, dinner 7pm–9.30pm.
Cuisine: SCOTTISH – traditional home-cooking. Vegetarians catered for.
Cards: Visa, Access, Diners, AmEx.
Other points: licensed, Sunday lunch, children welcome, afternoon tea, residents' lounge.
Rooms: 51 bedrooms.
Directions: 12 miles north of Inverness.
BERNARD & ROSEMARIE JUSTICE ☎ (01349) 862166 [Fax] (01349) 865178.

DORNOCH • map 18B4

MALLIN HOUSE HOTEL
Church Street, IV25 3LP

A family-run hotel situated close to the famous golf course in Dornoch. Good food and a friendly atmosphere complement the high standard of accommodation. Choose from the à la carte, table d'hôte or bar meals menu. All dishes are freshly cooked to order and attractively presented. Good value for money. Especially popular with golfers and anglers.
DOUBLE ROOM: from £20 to £30
FOOD: from £15 to £20
Hours: breakfast 8.15am–10am, lunch 12noon–2.30pm, dinner 6.30pm–9pm.
Cuisine: ENGLISH – à la carte and table d'hôte menus. Dishes may include rack of spring lamb, lobster Thermidor. All dishes cooked to order. Good, imaginative bar meals.
Cards: Visa, Access, AmEx.
Other points: licensed, Sunday lunch, children welcome, pets allowed, garden.
Directions: in centre of Dornoch near to the famous golf course.
MALCOLM HOLDEN ☎ (01862) 810335.

DRUMNADROCHIT • map 17C3

LOCH NESS LODGE HOTEL
IV3 6TJ

A comfortable and friendly Highland lodge set in 8 acres of woodland near Loch Ness and Urquhart Castle. An ideal touring base for the Scottish Highlands. Regular Scottish entertainment. Loch Ness visitors' centre, giftshop, and Loch Ness cruises.
DOUBLE ROOM: from £30 to £40
FOOD: up to £15
Hours: breakfast 8am–10am, bar meals 11.30am–6pm, 6.30pm–9.30pm.
Cuisine: SCOTTISH – Aberdeen Angus steaks and fresh seafood. Carte du jour and full à la carte menus available. Bar snacks served in the bar/coffee shop. Children's menu. Home-baking.
Cards: Visa, Access, Diners, AmEx.
Other points: licensed, vegetarian meals, children welcome, pets allowed, afternoon tea, coaches by prior arrangement.

Telephone: (01952) 432274
Facsimile: (01952) 432308

THE VALLEY HOTEL

& "CHEZ MAW" RESTAURANT

A beautifully refurbished Georgian listed building set in its own secluded and spacious grounds.

Ironbridge, Near Telford, Shropshire, TF8 7DW

For full details see Shropshire, Telford

AVAILABLE NOW

LES ROUTIERS

PRICED AT £2.00

Accommodation Directory

THE HANDY DIRECTORY – ideal if you're looking for somewhere to stay at great value. It lists a huge choice of *Les Routiers*-recommended places throughout the British Isles offering comfortable accommodation and a warm welcome amid relaxed surroundings.

Available from selected Les Routiers establishments or direct from the publishers

Les Routiers

25 VANSTON PLACE LONDON SW6 1AZ TEL: 0171-385 6644 FAX: 0171-385 7136

LES ROUTIERS

For further information on

Les Routiers

or to book your accommodation...

telephone *(0171) 610 1856*

(Mondays to Fridays 9am-5pm)

(0171) 385 7136 *facsimile*

LES ROUTIERS   25 VANSTON PLACE   LONDON SW6 1AZ

APPLETON HALL
THE COUNTRY HOUSE HOTEL
APPLETON-LE-MOORS, NORTH YORKSHIRE, YO6 6TF
ELEGANCE • COMFORT • TRANQUILITY

Telephone: (01751) 417227 / 417452   Facsimile: (01751) 417540

For full details see North Yorkshire, Appleton-le-Moors

Rooms: 16 double rooms, 36 twin rooms, 2 triple rooms, 1 quad room. All with TV, telephone, tea/coffee-making facilities, hair dryer.
Directions: on the A831 Cannich to Inverness road.
D.W. SKINNER ☎ (01456) 450342
Fax (01456) 450429.

DUNBEATH • map 18A4

DUNBEATH HOTEL
KW6 6EB
Situated in a quiet Highland village with views to the sea, this old coaching inn, dating from around 1830, offers true character with modern comfort. An ideal opportunity for the visitor to sample the best of Highland produce, complemented by a fine wine list. Caithness itself has much to offer the visitor, with the Orkneys just off-shore and a wealth of sporting activities available. Scottish Tourist Board 3 Crowns 'commended'.
DOUBLE ROOM: from £30 to £40
SINGLE ROOM: from £35 to £45
FOOD: up to £15
Hours: breakfast 8am–9.30am, lunch 12noon–2.30pm, bar snacks 12noon–2.30pm, dinner 7pm–8pm, bar snacks 5pm–9pm, closed Christmas day and 1st January until 3rd January.
Cuisine: SCOTTISH – venison and salmon from local estates and seafood from northern harbours.
Cards: Visa, Access, Diners, AmEx.
Other points: licensed, Sunday lunch, no-smoking area, children welcome, afternoon tea, pets allowed, garden, parking, cots, 24hr reception, residents' lounge, residents' bar.
Rooms: 4 double rooms, 2 twin rooms. All with TV, radio, tea/coffee-making facilities.
Directions: north on A9 from Inverness; signs to Wick/Thurso; left at roadbridge over Dunbeath Water.
NEIL & PATRICIA BUCHANAN ☎ (01593) 731208 Fax (01593) 731242.

DURNESS • map 17A3

CAPE WRATH HOTEL
IV27 4SW
Originally built for the area tax official, this 200-year-old hotel is furnished in country house style, providing an ambience of comfort and relaxation. Popular with locals and tourists alike, It is an ideal location for visiting Balnakeil craft village and Smoo caves, and for exploring Cape Wrath.
DOUBLE ROOM: from £20 to £30
SINGLE ROOM: from £25 to £35
FOOD: up to £15
Hours: breakfast 8.30am, dinner 7.30pm, bar meals 12noon–2pm, closed November until Easter.
Cuisine: INTERNATIONAL – vegetarian meals by arrangement.
Cards: Visa, Access.
Other points: room service, vegetarian meals, residents' bar, residents' lounge.
Rooms: 11 bedrooms.

Directions: on A838, 2½ miles south of Durness.
MR J. WATSON ☎ (01971) 511212.

FORT AUGUSTUS • map 17C3

THE BRAE HOTEL
Fort Augustus, PH32 4DG
Originally a church manse, standing in its own landscaped grounds, this hotel offers a quiet, relaxing atmosphere with good food and drink. Some rooms offer a commanding view over the lochs nearby. The main nearby tourist attraction is Loch Ness, famous among monster-hunters.
DOUBLE ROOM: from £20 to £30
FOOD: from £15 to £20
Hours: breakfast 8.15am–9.15am, dinner 7pm–8.30pm.
Cuisine: BRITISH / INTERNATIONAL – table d'hôte menu, offering an imaginative selection of both national and international dishes of a very high standard, beautifully presented.
Cards: Visa, Access.
Other points: licensed, no-smoking area, vegetarian meals, special diets, children welcome, residents' lounge, pets allowed, parking.
Rooms: 3 single rooms, 2 double room, 3 twin rooms. All with en suite, TV, tea/coffee-making facilities.
Directions: on A82, 200 yards off main road, to the left of village.
ANDREW & MARI REIVE ☎ (01320) 366289 Fax (01320) 366702.

FORT WILLIAM • map 15B2

GUISACHAN HOUSE
Alma Road, PH35 6HA
Situated in a quiet location on the hillside above the town, affording panoramic views over Loch Linnhe and the Ardgow Hills. Tastefully decorated throughout, the guest house offers fresh, modern and comfortable accommodation, good food and friendly, homely service. An ideal base when touring the area.
DOUBLE ROOM: from £20 to £30
FOOD: up to £15
Hours: breakfast 7.45am–9am, dinner 6.30pm.
Cuisine: SCOTTISH – traditional home-cooking.
Cards: Visa, Access.
Other points: parking, children welcome, residents' lounge, vegetarian meals.
Rooms: 2 single rooms, 6 double rooms, 5 twin rooms, 4 family rooms. All with en suite, TV, tea/coffee-making facilities.
Directions: off Belford Road, near the swimming pool.
JOHN & ELIZABETH ROSIE ☎ (01397) 703797
Fax (01397) 703797.

ISLES OF GLENCOE HOTEL & LEISURE CENTRE
Ballachulish, PA39 4JY
The hotel nestles on the side of a peninsula reaching into Loch Leven, affording stunning views of sky, mountain and loch. It offers spacious,

well-appointed accommodation, good food and leisure facilities, including a heated swimming pool, sunbed and multi-gym. Water sports, walking and climbing can all be enjoyed, and there is an informal bistro bar in which to relax during the evenings.
DOUBLE ROOM: from £30 to £40
SINGLE ROOM: from £45 to £55
FOOD: from £15 to £20
Hours: breakfast 8am–10am, dinner 6pm–10pm, bar meals 11am–10pm.
Cuisine: SCOTTISH / CONTINENTAL – exciting and varied brasserie menu, also featuring traditional Scottish cuisine using fresh local produce, including venison. Restaurant and bistro bar.
Cards: Visa, Access, MasterCard.
Other points: licensed, open-air dining, no-smoking area, children welcome, afternoon tea, pets allowed, garden, leisure centre, swimming pool, residents' lounge, residents' bar, foreign exchange, disabled access, vegetarian meals, parking.
Rooms: 7 single rooms, 9 double room, 17 twin rooms, 6 family rooms. All with en suite, TV, telephone, tea/coffee-making facilities.
Directions: A82 Glasgow to Fort William road. On the loch side at Ballachulish.
GRAEME ROBERTSON ☎ (01855) 811602
Fax (01855) 811770.

THE MOORINGS HOTEL
Banavie, PH33 7LY

The Moorings Hotel lies alongside the Caledonian Canal at the famous Neptune's Staircase. With splendid panoramic views of Ben Nevis and Aonach Mor, The Moorings offers comfort and style, coupled with the convenience of a modern hotel. The bedrooms, lounge, bars and restaurant are all tastefully appointed. Here you will find elegant surroundings, courteous staff and a warm Highland atmosphere, suitably complemented by superb cuisine.
DOUBLE ROOM: from £30 to £40
SINGLE ROOM: from £45 to £55
FOOD: from £20 to £25
Hours: breakfast 7.30am–9.30am, lunch 12noon–2pm, dinner 7pm–9pm, closed Christmas day.
Cuisine: SCOTTISH – superb 'Taste of Scotland' dishes.
Cards: Visa, Access, Diners, AmEx.
Other points: parking, children welcome, conference facilities, residents' lounge, no-smoking area, garden, open-air dining, vegetarian meals, afternoon teas.
Rooms: 14 double rooms, 5 twin rooms, 1 triple room, 1 family room. All with en suite, TV, telephone, radio, alarm, baby-listening device, tea/coffee-making facilities.
Directions: leave A82 Fort William to Inverness road at A830 Mallaig road; turn left off A830 on to B8004. The hotel is on this road.
NORMAN SINCLAIR ☎ (01397) 772797
Fax (01397) 772441.

NEVISPORT RESTAURANT
High Street, PH33 6EJ

Situated in the Nevisport complex, which also includes a large mountaineering/sports shop and a craft and books department featuring many local crafts. Cafeteria-style system and Climbers Bar, the newest addition to the complex. Pull up a chair in front of the open fire and relax. The bar serves snacks, meals and real ales.
FOOD: up to £15
Hours: meals all day, summer from 9am–7.30pm, winter from 9am–5pm.
Cuisine: SCOTTISH – Scottish-influenced dishes, e.g., pan-fried Lochy trout.
Cards: Visa, Access, Diners, AmEx.
Other points: licensed, children welcome.
Directions: on the A82 within the Nevisport complex on the High Street.
IAIN SYKES & IAIN SUTHERLAND ☎ (01397) 704921.

TIGH-A-RIGH HOUSE
Onich, PH33 6SE

This small, family-run guest house, just beyond the village of Onich, is ideally suited for touring around the west coast of Scotland. The area is excellent for hill-walking and climbing, forest walks, fishing, yachting or canoeing, or just to admire the beautiful scenery. Tigh-a-Righ offers guests comfortable accommodation, good home-cooking, a well-stocked bar and Scottish hospitality at its best.
DOUBLE ROOM: from £20 to £30
FOOD: up to £15
Hours: breakfast 8.15am–9.15am, lunch 12.30am–2.30pm, dinner 7pm–8.45pm.
Cuisine: SCOTTISH – good-value, fresh, wholesome Scottish food.
Other points: parking, children welcome, pets allowed, residents' lounge, afternoon teas, vegetarian meals.
Rooms: 1 single room, 1 double room, 2 twin rooms, 2 family rooms. All with radio, hair dryer, tea/coffee-making facilities.
Directions: A82 Ballachyllish to Fort William road; on the north end of Onich village, 8 miles south of Fort William.
KATIE MacCALLUM ☎ (018553) 255.

GAIRLOCH • map 17B2

MILLCROFT HOTEL
Strath, IV21 2BZ

Small, family-run hotel in centre of village, with magnificent views of the mountains, islands and sea. Comfortable rooms and quality cooking, with an Italian head chef. Places of interest nearby include Inverewe Gardens, Gairloch Heritage Museum and Peinn Eighe National Nature Reserve.
DOUBLE ROOM: from £30 to £40
FOOD: from £15 to £20
Hours: breakfast 8am–9.30am, lunch 12noon–2pm, bar meals 12noon–10pm, dinner 6pm–9pm.
Cuisine: SCOTTISH – good choice using local produce, i.e., fresh local salmon, venison, home-baking and home-made jams when available.
Cards: Visa, Access.
Other points: licensed, Sunday lunch, children welcome, open bank holidays.
Directions: take B8021 off main road, signposted Melvaig. Hotel half a mile along.
BERNARDI HOWES ☎ (01445) 2376.

HIGHLANDS • SCOTLAND

STEADING RESTAURANT
Auchtercairn, IV21 2BZ
A coffee-house/restaurant in a delightful converted 19th century farm building, which retains much of its olde-worlde atmosphere. Adjoining the award-winning Gairloch Museum of West Highland Life, it offers good food, using local fresh produce such as seafood and venison. Self-service by day and waitress service in evenings.
FOOD: from £15 to £20
Hours: meals all day 9am–9pm, closed Sunday from October until March.
Cuisine: SCOTTISH – fresh local seafood and venison. Home-baked cakes and scones.
Other points: parking, children welcome, open bank holidays, afternoon tea, disabled access, vegetarian meals.
Directions: A832. From Inverness, 80 miles. At junction of A832 and B8031 in centre of Gairloch.
MR W.R. MURDOCH ☎ (01445) 2449.

WHINDLEY GUEST HOUSE
Auchtercairn, IV21 2BN
A comfortable, modern guest house, with glorious views over Gairloch Bay, which offers guests fresh, home-baked bread, warm, comfortable bedrooms and a relaxing atmosphere. Ideal holiday guest house, where you can relax with breakfast in bed before your day at the golf course or on the beach, both only a few minutes' drive away. Special winter breaks featuring spinning and weaving courses.
DOUBLE ROOM: from £20 to £30
Hours: breakfast 8.30am–9.15am, lunch 12.30am–2pm, dinner 7pm–8pm.
Cuisine: SCOTTISH.
Other points: children welcome, residents' lounge, vegetarian meals, special diets, picnic lunches, garden, patio.
Directions: uphill as you leave Gairloch on A832 towards Poolewe.
MICK & ELIZABETH PARK ☎ (01445) 2340.

GLENFINNAN • map 15B2

THE PRINCES HOUSE
Glenfinnan, PH37 4LT
Originally an old staging post on the road to the Isles, this stone-built building has enormous character with a good, homely atmosphere. The cuisine is mostly local, using the freshest of produce, complemented by a fine wine list. Ideal location for those seeking to get away from the pressures of modern-day life.
DOUBLE ROOM: from £30 to £40
SINGLE ROOM: from £35 to £45
FOOD: from £15 to £20
Hours: breakfast 8am–9am, dinner, 6.30pm–8.30pm, bar meals 12.30am–2.30pm, bar meals 5pm–9pm
Cuisine: SCOTTISH – blackboard and à la carte menus, offering salmon, venison, trout and fresh shellfish.
Cards: Visa, Access, AmEx, Switch.
Other points: licensed, no-smoking rooms, open bank holidays, pets allowed, residents' lounge, afternoon tea, children welcome, residents' bar, vegetarian meals, parking.

fishing, mountain bike hire.
Rooms: 6 double rooms, 3 twin rooms. All with TV, bar, telephone, tea/coffee-making facilities.
Directions: on the main Fort William to Mallaig road in the centre of Glenfinnan.
ROBERT & CAROLE HAWKES ☎ (01397) 722246 Fax (01397) 722307.

GLENMORISTON • map 15A2

CLUANIE INN
IV3 6YW
A converted coaching house, this inn offers good farmhouse cooking, comfortable accommodation and a warm welcome. With many beautiful walks through the mountains and glens, salmon and trout fishing, this is the ideal place to return to at the end of the day, with its cosy, relaxing atmosphere, fitness centre including sauna, and the very best in comfort. Highly recommended.
DOUBLE ROOM: from £30 to £40
SINGLE ROOM: from £25 to £35
FOOD: from £15 to £20
Hours: breakfast 8am–9.30am, lunch 12noon–2.30pm, dinner 6pm–9pm.
Cuisine: SCOTTISH – good farmhouse-style cooking.
Cards: Visa, Access.
Other points: licensed, Sunday lunch, children welcome, open bank holidays, pets allowed, garden, gym facilities, fishing.
Rooms: 13 bedrooms.
Directions: midway between Loch Ness and ferry terminal to Isle of Skye.
MR JOHN DOUGLAS CLINTON ☎ (01320) 340238.

GRANTOWN-ON-SPEY • map 18C4

THE BEN MHOR HOTEL
High Street, PH26 3EJ
Comfortable, family-run hotel in the heart of the Spey Valley. This is an ideal spot for the holiday-maker, with an 18-hole golf course, salmon fishing, bowling green and woods nearby. Offering good food and comfortable accommodation.
DOUBLE ROOM: from £20 to £30
FOOD: up to £15
Hours: breakfast 8am–9.30am, lunch 12.30am–2pm, dinner 7pm–9pm, bar meals 5.30pm–9pm,.
Cuisine: BRITISH / CONTINENTAL – meals made with an emphasis on local produce whenever possible. Dishes may include salmon en croute with dill sauce, Strathspey venison.
Cards: Visa, Access.
Other points: licensed, open-air dining, Sunday lunch, children welcome, open bank holidays, afternoon tea, pets allowed, residents' bar, residents' lounge, foreign exchange, disabled access, vegetarian meals.
Rooms: 3 single rooms, 3 double rooms, 16 twin rooms, 2 family rooms. All with TV, radio, tea/coffee-making facilities.
Directions: on the main street in the town centre.
CLIVE & FIONA WILLIAMSON ☎ (01479) 872056 Fax (01479) 873537.

323

CRAGGAN MILL RESTAURANT
PH26 3NT

An old watermill, Craggan Mill has a rustic feel, with candlelight, wooden tables and interesting relics from when the mill was still operating. All food is fresh and cooked to order by Mr Belleni, the owner. Well-cooked food at good-value prices, and the very best in friendly yet efficient service.
FOOD: from £15 to £20
Hours: dinner 6.30pm–10pm, closed 1st October until 14th October.
Cuisine: ITALIAN / BRITISH – house specialities include fillet of venison in a cream sauce.
Cards: Visa, Access.
Other points: licensed, children welcome.
Directions: on A95 Grantown to Aviemore road. One mile on south side of Grantown.
MR & MRS B. BELLENI ☎ (01479) 872288.

RAVENSCOURT HOUSE HOTEL
Seafield Avenue, PH26 3JG

Formerly a manse, this hotel is a delightful 19th century house, now tastefully restored and retaining most of its original features. The Orangery Restaurant is designed in period style and has a cosy, intimate atmosphere. The food is excellent, using local and regional fresh Scottish produce. Comfortable accommodation and good service; great value for money.
DOUBLE ROOM: from £30 to £40
FOOD: from £20 to £25
Hours: breakfast 8.30am–9am, lunch 12noon–2pm, dinner 7pm–9.30pm, closed January.
Cuisine: SCOTTISH – fine local produce with a French flair.
Cards: Visa, Access.
Other points: parking, children welcome, pets allowed, no-smoking area, residents' lounge, garden, open-air dining, vegetarian meals, afternoon teas.
Rooms: 1 single room, 2 double rooms, 2 twin rooms, 2 family rooms. All with TV, hair dryer, tea/coffee-making facilities.
Directions: just off the High Street, turn first left after Bank of Scotland.
CORINNE & DAVID WHALLEY ☎ (01479) 872286 [Fax] (01479) 873260.

HALKIRK • map 18A4

THE ULBSTER ARMS HOTEL
Bridge Street, KW12 6XY

Standing on the banks on the Thurso River at the centre of the village of Halkirk, this is a true sporting hotel. Both shooting and stalking can be arranged over a wide variety of moors, and also fly fishing on one of Scotland's finest 'fly only' salmon rivers. Other outdoor pursuits include bird-watching, photography, rambling, painting, geology, and much more.
DOUBLE ROOM: from £30 to £40
FOOD: from £15 to £20
Hours: breakfast 8am–9.30am, lunch 12.30am–1.45pm, dinner 7pm–8.45pm, open all year.
Cuisine: BRITISH – table d'hôte menu. Advance booking advisable for both lunch and dinner.

Cards: Visa, Access.
Other points: Sunday lunch, children welcome, pets allowed, afternoon tea, parking, open bank holidays.
Rooms: 9 single rooms, 3 double rooms, 13 twin rooms. All with TV, telephone, tea/coffee-making facilities.
Directions: from Inverness via A9 Perth to Latheronwheel. Turn left onto A895.
LOCHDHU HOTELS LTD ☎ (0184783) 206/641 [Fax] (0184783) 206/641.

HELMSDALE • map 18B4

BUNILLIDH RESTAURANT
2-4 Dunrobin Street, KW8 6JX

A pleasant, family-run restaurant offering good food and friendly service. Vakes, fresh lobster and crab from holding tanks complement the seafood specialities. There are spectacular views to be enjoyed all around.
FOOD: up to £15 [CLUB]
Hours: meals all day 9am–9pm.
Cuisine: SCOTTISH – good-value home-cooking. Langoustines (local prawn) cooked from live. Drinks licence and full wine list.
Cards: Visa.
Other points: parking, children welcome, open bank holidays, no-smoking area, afternoon tea, limited disabled access, vegetarian meals.
Directions: off A9, just past the visitors' centre, opposite Time Span.
EILEEN SHEWARD ☎ (014312) 457 [Fax] (014312) 205.

INVERGARRY • map 17D3

INVERGARRY HOTEL
PH35 4HG

A family-run Highland hotel offering comfortable accommodation, good food and friendly service. The interior decor is in keeping with the distinctive and attractive Victorian building and provides comfortable and relaxed surroundings. Well placed to enjoy the beauty of the Scottish Highlands, fishing, golf, skiing or visits to the distilleries.
DOUBLE ROOM: from £30 to £40
SINGLE ROOM: from £35 to £45
FOOD: up to £15 [CLUB]
Hours: breakfast 8.15am–9.30am, meals all day 9am–7pm, dinner 6.30pm–8.30pm, bar meals 12noon–2pm, 6pm–9pm.
Cuisine: SCOTTISH / INTERNATIONAL – bar meals, self-service restaurant meals, and dinner featuring Scottish and international dishes and using fresh, predominantly local produce.
Cards: Visa, Access, AmEx.
Other points: licensed, Sunday lunch, children welcome, afternoon tea, pets allowed, residents' lounge, garden, baby-listening device, cots, foreign exchange, residents' bar, vegetarian meals, real ale.
Rooms: 1 single room, 5 double rooms, 4 twin rooms. All with TV, telephone, tea/coffee-making facilities.

HIGHLANDS • SCOTLAND

Directions: from A82, take the A87 road for Kyle of Lochalsh. Hotel on the right.
MacCALLUM FAMILY ☎ (01809) 501206
[Fax] (01809) 501207.

INVERGORDON • map 18B4

KINCRAIG HOUSE HOTEL
IV19 0LF
Kincraig is a house of outstanding character, parts of which date back several centuries. Standing in its own grounds in an elevated position overlooking Cromarty Firth, it is ideal for both the business traveller and the holiday-maker. Spacious lounges, excellent food and friendly, personal service ensure any stay here is memorable.
FOOD: from £15 to £20
Hours: breakfast as required, bar snacks as required, lunch 12noon–2.30pm, dinner 6pm–10pm.
Cuisine: BRITISH.
Cards: Visa, Access, Diners, AmEx.
Other points: no-smoking area, children welcome, parking, pets, disabled access, vegetarian meals, open-air dining, residents' lounge, garden.
Rooms: 19 twin rooms.
Directions: travel north on the A9 beyond both signs for Invergordon and Alness, and you will find their sign on the left approximately 1 mile beyond the Alness bypass, on the A9.
MR H. DIXON ☎ (01349) 852587 [Fax] (01349) 852193.

INVERNESS • map 18C4

CULDUTHEL LODGE
14 Culduthel Road, IV2 4AG
A Georgian building set in its own grounds and enjoying views of the River Ness. The resident owners ensure that their guests enjoy a comfortable, relaxing stay. Tastefully decorated and furnished to a very high standard. Ideal touring base.
DOUBLE ROOM: from £30 to £40
SINGLE ROOM: from £35 to £45
FOOD: from £15 to £20
Hours: breakfast 8am–9am.
Cuisine: SCOTTISH – table d'hôte menu changes each day, offering delicious, freshly prepared food.
Cards: Visa, Access.
Other points: pets by prior arrangement, central heating, children welcome, cots, left luggage.
Rooms: 1 single room, 9 double rooms, 2 twin rooms. All with TV, telephone, hair dryer, radio, tea/coffee-making facilities, fresh fruit, flowers, sherry.
Directions: less than 1 mile from city centre. B861.
DAVID & MARION BONSOR ☎ (01463) 240089 [Fax] (01463) 240089.

HEATHMOUNT HOTEL
Kingsmill Road, IV2 3JU
A Victorian-style building featuring ornate ceilings and decorative panels. Extremely popular local hostelry, with busy restaurant and bars. The River Ness and Inverness Castle are within easy walking distance.

DOUBLE ROOM: from £20 to £30
FOOD: up to £15
Hours: breakfast 8am–10am, bar meals 12.15am–2.15pm, 5.45pm–9.15pm.
Cuisine: SCOTTISH / INTERNATIONAL – a good selection from the menu, including the Scottish speciality, haggis; also meals from the barbecue. Home-made pies, pasta and casseroles.
Cards: Visa, Access.
Other points: licensed.
Directions: follow sign for Hilton Culcabock, left after flyover, right at roundabout, straight through traffic lights, bearing left at mini-roundabout. At next set of lights, turn right into Kingsmill Road.
MR & MRS BUXTON ☎ (01463) 235877
[Fax] (01463) 715479.

LOCH NESS HOUSE HOTEL
Glen Urquhart Road, IV3 6JL
Overlooking the Caledonian Canal and the Torvean golf course, this family-owned and run hotel is ideal as a base for discovering the delights of Highland Scotland. A comfortable bar, dining room and residents' lounge await you after a day in the fresh air. Or join the locals in a ceilidh, held here most weekends. Loch Ness House is popular with locals and overseas visitors.
DOUBLE ROOM: from £30 to £40
FOOD: up to £15
Hours: breakfast 8am–9.30am, bar meals 12noon–2pm, dinner 7pm–9pm, bar meals 5.30pm–9pm, open all year.
Cuisine: SCOTTISH – à la carte and table d'hôte menus, offering traditional and new Scottish recipes, using only the freshest of local produce. Vegetarian dishes available.
Cards: Visa, Access, AmEx.
Other points: licensed, open-air dining, Sunday lunch, pets allowed, residents' lounge, garden, parking, disabled access, children welcome, baby-listening device, cots.
Rooms: 1 single room, 5 double rooms, 8 twin rooms, 7 triple rooms, 1 quad room. All with TV, radio, alarm, telephone, tea/coffee-making facilities.
Directions: 1½ miles west of Inverness city centre on A82.
ALLISTER MILROY ☎ (01463) 231248
[Fax] (01463) 239327.

ST ANN'S HOUSE
37 Harrowden Road, IV3 5QN
A small, friendly, family-run guest house set in a quiet residential area, 10 minutes' walk from the city centre. Here Betty and James offer their valued guests a warm, homely atmosphere, comfortable accommodation and good home-cooking. Popular attractions nearby include the Falls of Foyers and Loch Ness.
DOUBLE ROOM: up to £20
SINGLE ROOM: up to £25
FOOD: up to £15
Hours: breakfast 8am–9am, dinner 6pm–8pm.
Other points: parking, children welcome, pets allowed, no-smoking area, residents' lounge, garden, vegetarian meals.
Rooms: 1 single room, 1 double room, 2 twin

325

rooms, 2 family rooms. All with TV, hair dryer, tea/coffee-making facilities.
Directions: off Friars Bridge roundabout.
JAMES & BETTY GARDINER ☎ (01463) 236157.

ISLE OF SKYE • map 17C2

🍴 THE CASTLE MOIL RESTAURANT
Kyleakin, IV41 8PL
Comfortable restaurant serving reasonably priced snacks, lunches and evening meals. Just 300 yards from Skye ferry terminal, The Castle Moil is worthy of a visit to break your journey and to enjoy a good-value meal or snack.
FOOD: up to £15
Hours: breakfast all day, lunch 12noon–5pm, dinner 5pm–9.15pm, closed November to February, open bank holidays.
Cuisine: BRITISH / SEAFOOD – self-service during the day, table service in the evening. House speciality is seafood. Also salads, steaks, grills and all-day breakfast.
Cards: Visa, Access.
Other points: licensed, Sunday lunch, children welcome, meals all day, coaches by prior arrangement.
Directions: on the Skye side of the ferry.
ALEXANDER J.C. MacDIARMID ☎ (01599) 4164.

🛏 DUISDALE HOTEL
Isle Ornsay, Sleat, IV43 8QW
Built in a Scottish hunting lodge style, this family-run hotel is set in 25 acres, overlooking the Sound of Sleat. Offering good food and comfortable accommodation, Duisdale is ideal for fishing, walking or observing the wildlife. Frequented by mixed ages, the atmosphere is quiet and peaceful.
DOUBLE ROOM: from £30 to £40
FOOD: from £15 to £20 ☆
Hours: breakfast 8.30am–9.30am, lunch 12.30am–2pm, dinner 7.30pm–8.30pm.
Cuisine: SCOTTISH – dishes include platter of oak-smoked fish, casserole of venison and orange, Cloutie dumpling.
Cards: Visa, Access, AmEx.
Other points: licensed, bar lunches, children welcome, pets allowed, garden, morning coffee, afternoon tea, vegetarian meals, parking, residents' bar, residents' lounge.
Rooms: 3 single rooms, 4 double rooms, 8 twin rooms, 2 triple rooms, 2 family rooms. All with tea/coffee-making facilities, 14 rooms are en suite.
Directions: from Kyleakin ferry, take A850. At Skulamus, turn left onto A851.
MARGARET COLPUS ☎ (014713) 202 [Fax] (014713) 363.

🛏 DUNORIN HOUSE HOTEL
Herebost, Dunvegan, IV55 8GZ
A new hotel offering luxury accommodation to suit modern requirements. It is situated in the beautiful north-west corner of Skye, enjoying a magnificent panorama across Loch Roag to the Cuillin hills. The colour-coordinated ground-floor bedrooms and spacious corridors make it an ideal hotel for disabled persons. Already it has achieved a reputation for attention to traditional island recipes, all home-made and complemented by a select wine list. Joan and Alasdair look forward to providing you with a true taste of island culture and hospitality.
DOUBLE ROOM: from £30 to £40
SINGLE ROOM: from £35 to £45
FOOD: from £15 to £20
Hours: breakfast 8am–9am, dinner 6.45pm–9pm.
Cuisine: SCOTTISH.
Cards: Visa, Access, Eurocard, MasterCard.
Other points: parking, children welcome, open bank holidays, no-smoking area, disabled access, residents' lounge, vegetarian meals, garden.
Rooms: 2 single rooms, 6 double rooms, 2 family rooms. All with TV, tea/coffee-making facilities, heating.
Directions: from the ferry at Kyleakin, follow A850 to Sligachan, then A860 to Dunvegan. Turn left at Roag/Orbost junction. The hotel is 200 meters along on the right.
ALASDAIR & JOAN MacLEAN ☎ (0147022) 488.

🛏 FLODIGARRY COUNTRY HOUSE HOTEL
Staffin, IV51 9HZ
Magnificently situated with panoramic views across the sea to the Torridon mountains. Family-run, the hotel offers comfortable accommodation, Highland hospitality, and the best of traditional Scottish dishes and tempting specialities prepared from fresh local produce. The cottage next to the hotel was home to Flora MacDonald, who helped in the escape of Bonnie Prince Charlie.
DOUBLE ROOM: from £30 to £40
SINGLE ROOM: from £35 to £45
FOOD: from £15 to £20 ☜
Hours: breakfast 8.30am–10.30am, Sunday lunch, 12.30am–2.30pm, bar meals 11am–10.30pm, dinner 7pm–10pm.
Cuisine: SCOTTISH – local salmon, lobster, langoustines and other fine fresh seafood. Highland venison and game, along with the best of other fresh Scottish fare.
Cards: Visa, Access, Switch.
Other points: licensed, open-air dining, Sunday lunch, no-smoking area, children welcome, open bank holidays, afternoon tea, pets allowed, residents' lounge, residents' bar, disabled access, vegetarian meals, parking.
Rooms: 4 single rooms, 10 double rooms, 7 twin rooms, 2 family rooms. All with tea/coffee-making facilities.
Directions: take the A855 from Portree north for Staffin (20 miles). Signposted.
ANDREW & PAMELA BUTLER ☎ (01470) 552203 [Fax] (01470) 552301.

🛏 HOTEL EILEAN IARMAIN
Sleat, IV43 8QR
The hotel prides itself on continuing to provide a traditional welcome with blazing log fires, and expert cooking using fresh local produce. Friendly Gaelic-speaking management and staff. Each room has period furniture, offering special views of the

HIGHLANDS • SCOTLAND

sea and hills of Skye. All this in an idyllic and spectacular setting. Contact: Effie Kennedy (Manager).
DOUBLE ROOM: from £40 to £50
SINGLE ROOM: from £55
FOOD: from £20 to £25
Hours: breakfast 8.30am–9.30am, lunch 12.30am–2pm, bar meals 12noon–2.30pm, dinner 7.30pm–9pm, bar meals 6.30pm–9.30pm, open all year.
Cuisine: SCOTTISH – lobsters, scallops, mussels used on a regular basis. Own oyster beds. Best local game when in season. Exciting menus with fresh local produce. Extensive wine list.
Cards: Visa, Access, AmEx.
Other points: Sunday lunch, no-smoking area, children welcome, stalking, shooting, fishing, entertainment.
Rooms: 7 double rooms, 4 twin rooms, 1 family room. All with en suite, telephone. Non-smoking rooms available.
Directions: situated between Broadford and Armadale, with its ferry to Mallaig.
SIR IAIN NOBLE & LADY NOBLE ☎ (014713) 332 Fax (014713) 275.

KINLOCH LODGE
Sleat, IV43 8QY
Kinloch Lodge is the home of Lord and Lady MacDonald and family, who have turned their historic home into a small, comfortable hotel. The food is superb, and Lady MacDonald's cooking and attention to detail has earned great praise from some of the best-known gourmets and food writers. An ideal spot for a quiet, relaxing holiday and to enjoy the spectacular views.
DOUBLE ROOM: over £50
SINGLE ROOM: over £55
FOOD: from £25 to £30
Hours: breakfast 8.30am–9.30am, dinner 8pm, closed December until February.
Cuisine: MODERN ENGLISH – excellent table d'hôte menu. Main courses may include roast loin of pork with mushroom and vermouth sauce, smoked haddock roulade with scallops.
Cards: Visa, Access.
Other points: licensed, afternoon tea, pets by prior arrangement, residents' lounge, garden.
Rooms: 10 twin rooms.
Directions: 1 mile from A851. 6 miles south of Broadford and 8 miles north of Armadale.
LORD & LADY MacDONALD ☎ (014713) 214/333 Fax (014713) 277.

ROSEDALE HOTEL
Portree, IV51 9DB
A small hotel, created from a series of 19th century fishermen's dwellings, but with all modern comforts installed. An ideal base for exploring the surrounding area, with Dunvegan Castle and the Clan Donald centre close by.
DOUBLE ROOM: from £30 to £40
SINGLE ROOM: from £35 to £45
FOOD: from £15 to £20
Hours: breakfast 8am–9.30am, dinner 7pm–8.30pm, closed October until April.
Cuisine: SCOTTISH.

Cards: Visa, Access.
Other points: children welcome, pets allowed, residents' lounge, garden.
Rooms: 5 single rooms, 5 double rooms, 13 twin rooms. All with en suite, TV, radio, alarm, telephone, tea/coffee-making facilities.
Directions: centre of village. On harbour side, facing water.
H.M. ANDREW ☎ (01478) 613131 Fax (01478) 612531.

ROYAL HOTEL
Bank Street, Portree, IV51 9BU
From Portree's Royal Hotel, the whole of Skye is on the doorstep. With a coastline of more than 900 miles, the Isle of Skye enjoys a bountiful harvest from the sea: prawns, lobsters, oysters and salmon. From the hills, there is lamb or venison, and from the rich pastures, sizzling prime steaks. Most of the hotel's comfortably furnished bedrooms face the sea and have stunning views, making this a popular holiday retreat for families Leisure and fitness facilities available from January 1995.
DOUBLE ROOM: from £20 to £30
SINGLE ROOM: from £35 to £45
Hours: breakfast 7.30am–10am, lunch 12noon–2pm, bar snacks 12noon–2pm, dinner 7pm–9.30pm, bar snacks 5pm–7.30pm.
Cuisine: SCOTTISH.
Cards: Visa, Access.
Other points: parking, children welcome, no-smoking area, disabled access, pets, residents' lounge, vegetarian meals.
Rooms: 25 bedrooms.
Directions: off A850 to A855, ¼ mile on left-hand side, overlooking the harbour.
MacLEOD HOTELS LTD ☎ (01478) 612525 Fax (01478) 613198.

SKEABOST HOUSE HOTEL
Skeabost Bridge, IV51 9NP
A former Victorian shooting lodge set in 12 acres of secluded woodland and gardens. It is a comfortable and relaxing, family-run hotel with three lounges, cocktail bar and billiard room. The cuisine is excellent, using fresh, local produce. The hotel has a 9-hole golf-course and salmon and sea-trout fishing on River Snizort – all free to guests who stay three days or more.
DOUBLE ROOM: from £30 to £40
FOOD: from £15 to £20
Hours: breakfast 8.30am–9.30am, lunch 12noon–1.30pm, dinner 7pm–8.30pm, closed mid-October until April.
Cuisine: SCOTTISH – traditional Scottish cuisine using fresh, local ingredients.
Cards: Visa, Access.
Other points: licensed, open-air dining, Sunday lunch, no-smoking area, children welcome, pets allowed, afternoon tea, fishing.
Rooms: 7 single rooms, 8 double rooms, 26 twin rooms.
Directions: from Kyle of Lochalsh–Kyleakin ferry, 38 miles to Skeabost Bridge.
THE STUART & McNAB FAMILIES ☎ (0147032) 202 Fax (0147032) 454.

UIG HOTEL
Uig, Portree, IV51 9YE

An old coaching inn set on a hillside overlooking Loch Snizort. It is a family-run hotel offering excellent accommodation, good food and a warm welcome. The hotel has its own pony-trekking and self-catering apartments. Bargain breaks available.
DOUBLE ROOM: from £30 to £40
FOOD: from £15 to £20
Hours: breakfast 8am–9am, lunch 12.15am–1.45pm (buffet), dinner 7.15pm–8.15pm, closed mid-October until end of March.
Cuisine: BRITISH – traditional cuisine. House specialities are peat-smoked salmon, venison casserole, and bread-and-butter pudding.
Cards: Visa, Access, Diners, AmEx, Switch.
Other points: licensed, no-smoking area, children welcome, afternoon tea, pets by prior arrangement, garden.
Rooms: 5 single rooms, 3 double rooms, 9 twin rooms.
Directions: A856. On right-hand side of road approaching Uig from Portree.
GRACE GRAHAM & DAVID TAYLOR
☎ (01470) 542205 Fax (01470) 542308.

KINCRAIG • map 18C4

THE BOATHOUSE RESTAURANT
Loch Insh, PH21 1NU

Situated by Loch Insh, this restaurant is always a hub of activity because of the many sporting activities taking place, such as mountain biking, fishing, dry-slope skiing, sailing, skiing and canoeing. This restaurant offers a warm welcome, good, well-prepared food, and value for money.
DOUBLE ROOM: up to £20
FOOD: up to £15
Hours: meals all day 10am–10pm, last orders 9pm.
Cuisine: BRITISH – home-baking, fresh salads, fondues, bar meals served all day. A la carte evening menu. Barbeques every lunchtime (July–August). Children's menu.
Cards: Visa, Access.
Other points: licensed, open-air dining, Sunday lunch, no-smoking area, children welcome, dry ski slope, water sports, fishing.
Rooms: 18 twin rooms, 4 family rooms.
Directions: off A9 at Kingussie. Follow 'Loch Insh Watersports' sign at Kincraig.
MR & MRS C. FRESHWATER ☎ (01540) 651272 Fax (01540) 651208.

KINGUSSIE • map 18D4

THE ROYAL HOTEL
High Street, PH21 1HX

The Royal Hotel is in the centre of Kingussie in the beautiful Spey Valley. An ideal base for all types of outdoor activities, including skiing, and for touring the Highlands. The hotel is family-owned and run, offering good accommodation, good food and a warm welcome.
DOUBLE ROOM: from £20 to £30
FOOD: up to £15
Hours: breakfast 8am–9.30am, lunch 12noon–2pm, dinner 7pm–9.30pm.
Cuisine: SCOTTISH – three-course lunches, four-course table d'hôte dinner, à la carte. Traditional Scottish cuisine prepared from fresh local produce.
Cards: Visa, Access, Diners, AmEx.
Other points: licensed, Sunday lunch, no-smoking area, children welcome, garden, afternoon tea, pets allowed, foreign exchange, residents' lounge, residents' bar, vegetarian meals, parking, disabled access.
Rooms: 52 twin rooms. All with TV, bar, telephone, tea/coffee-making facilities.
Directions: Kingussie is just off the A9, 40 miles from Pitlochry and Inverness.
MRS JUSTICE ☎ (01540) 661898 Fax (01540) 661061.

KINLOCHLEVEN • map 17D3

MacDONALD HOTEL
Wades Road, PA40 4QL

This is a small, new, comfortable hotel, built in a traditional West Highland style, where the resident proprietors and staff pride themselves on a warm welcome and personal service. Good food and accommodation offer value for money.
DOUBLE ROOM: from £20 to £30
SINGLE ROOM: up to £25
FOOD: from £15 to £20
Hours: breakfast 8am–9am, bar meals 12noon–9pm, dinner 7pm–9pm, open bank holidays.
Cuisine: SCOTTISH – menu may feature rack of Scottish lamb glazed with honey and rosemary, medallions of local venison with a red wine sauce.
Cards: Visa, Access, Eurocard, MasterCard.
Other points: licensed, open-air dining, Sunday lunch, children welcome, waterside location, children welcome, cots, left luggage, fishing, foreign exchange, residents' bar, mountain bike hire.
Rooms: 4 double rooms, 5 twin rooms, 1 triple room. All with TV, tea/coffee-making facilities.
Directions: going north on A82, take turning at Glencoe village.
PETER & SUSAN MacDONALD ☎ (01855) 831539 Fax (01855) 831539.

KYLESKU • map 17A3

NEWTON LODGE
IV27 4HW

A large, comfortable guest house with all modern amenities, surrounded by an inspiring panorama of mountains and lochs. With a warm welcome, friendly service, good home-made food and outstanding accommodation, Newton Lodge is an ideal base for touring the beautiful Scottish countryside.
DOUBLE ROOM: from £20 to £30
SINGLE ROOM: from £25 to £35
FOOD: up to £15
Hours: breakfast 8.30am–9am, dinner 7pm–7.15pm, closed mid-October until March.

Cuisine: BRITISH – fresh fish caught on proprietor's own boat. Fresh seafood.
Cards: Visa, Access.
Other points: parking, pets allowed, residents' lounge, garden, no-smoking area.
Rooms: 2 single rooms, 4 double rooms, 2 twin rooms. All with TV, radio, alarm, hair dryer, tea/coffee-making facilities.
Directions: 1 mile south of Kylesku Bridge.
ANDREW & MYRA BRAUER ☎ (01971) 502070.

LOCHCARRON • map 17C2

ROCKVILLA HOTEL & RESTAURANT
Main Street, IV54 8YB

Situated in Lochcarron village centre, overlooking the mountains and loch beyond, this hotel provides an excellent centre from which to explore some of the most beautiful and romantic scenery in Scotland. It offers comfortable accommodation and friendly, personal service within a warm, homely atmosphere. Nearby scenic beauty spots abound, including superb views of Skye.
DOUBLE ROOM: from £20 to £30
FOOD: up to £15
Hours: breakfast 8am–9.15am, lunch 12noon–2pm, bar meals 12noon–2pm, dinner 6.30pm–9pm, bar meals 6pm–9pm.
Cuisine: SEAFOOD / ENGLISH – specializes in local freshly caught seafood, venison and the finest steaks. Daily changing à la carte menu, complemented by a comprehensive wine list.
Cards: Visa, Access.
Other points: licensed, Sunday lunch, no-smoking area, children welcome, parking.
Directions: located in the centre of the village of Lochcarron.
KENNETH & LORNA WHEELAN ☎ (015202) 379.

MALLAIG • map 17D2

MARINE HOTEL
Mallaig, PH41 4RG

The Marine Hotel is a comfortable, family-owned hotel. It overlooks Mallaig Harbour and is convenient for both rail and sea terminals. The West Highland line ends here, giving the train enthusiast an ideal opportunity to see steam trains at close quarters. All bedrooms have modern facilities, and the restaurant provides excellent bar meals and dinners, including fresh daily seafood and a good selection of malt whiskies. Arisaig and the beautiful Silver Sands of Morar, both ideal for bathing and picnics, are nearby.
DOUBLE ROOM: from £20 to £30
SINGLE ROOM: from £25 to £35
FOOD: from £15 to £20
Hours: breakfast 8am–9.30am, lunch on request, bar snacks 12noon–2pm, dinner 7pm–9pm, bar snacks 6pm–9.30pm.
Cuisine: SCOTTISH – simple fresh food of local origin, with an emphasis on fresh local seafood.
Cards: Visa, Access.

HIGHLANDS • SCOTLAND

Other points: parking, children catered for (please check for age limits), Sunday lunch, open bank holidays, no-smoking area, Sunday dinner, disabled access, residents' lounge, vegetarian meals.
Rooms: 21 bedrooms.
Directions: hotel is adjacent to rail station and first on right coming off main road.
MR E. & MRS D. IRONSIDE ☎ (01687) 462217 Fax (01687) 462821.

NAIRN • map 18C4

RAMLEH HOTEL & FINGAL'S RESTAURANT
Ramleh House, 2 Academy Street, IV12 4RJ

This is a family-run hotel and restaurant offering good food and comfortable accommodation. The restaurant features a new conservatory for that relaxed, friendly atmosphere. Close to the High Street, beach, two golf courses, harbour, and all amenities.
DOUBLE ROOM: from £20 to £30
SINGLE ROOM: up to £25
FOOD: from £15 to £20
Hours: breakfast 7.30am–9am, lunch 12noon–2.30pm, dinner 6.30pm–9.30pm.
Cuisine: BRITISH – a wide variety of dishes served, including fish and seafood, poultry and game, meat and also vegetarian meals. Desserts and a cheeseboard also on menu.
Cards: Visa, Access, AmEx.
Other points: licensed, children welcome, garden, residents' lounge, residents' bar.
Rooms: 3 single rooms, 2 double rooms, 4 twin rooms, 1 family room. All with TV, tea/coffee-making facilities, heating. Most rooms are en suite.
Directions: Nairn is on the A96 Aberdeen to Inverness road, 15 miles from Inverness.
GEORGE & CAROL WOODHOUSE ☎ (01667) 453551 Fax (01667) 456577.

NETHY BRIDGE • map 18C4

THE MOUNTVIEW HOTEL & HIGHLAND GAME RESTAURANT
Nethy Bridge, PH25 3EB

The hotel is situated in the beautiful Spey Valley, the centre for many attractions and central for touring the Highlands. Built in 1914 of granite and sandstone, the fully-licensed, small, family-run hotel is set in 2.5 acres of grounds on the edge of the Abernethy Forest, overlooking the Cairngorm Mountains. There is a wide selection of home-made dishes from the Highland Game and bar menus (including vegetarian and children's dishes), which can be enjoyed in front of a real log fire. Attractions nearby include golf, fishing, horse-riding, mountain biking, walking, climbing, skiing, summer and winter chair lifts to the top of the Cairngorms, the Osprey Hide at RSPB Reserve Loch Garten, Strathspey Steam Railway, and many more.
DOUBLE ROOM: up to £20
SINGLE ROOM: up to £25
FOOD: up to £15 CLUB

Hours: breakfast 8am–9am, lunch 12noon–2pm, dinner 6.30pm–9pm, weekends during season, or by arrangement.
Cuisine: BRITISH – à la carte menu in the restaurant and bar menu both include vegetarian and children's dishes.
Cards: Visa, Access.
Other points: licensed, open-air dining, children welcome, pets allowed.
Rooms: 7 bedrooms. All with en suite, TV, central heating. Tea/coffee-making facilities. All rooms have panoramic views.
Directions: take Aviemore Road off A9. Next village after Boat of Garten.
TRIXIE & STUART PARKINS ☎ (01479) 821248.

NEWTONMORE • map 18D4

BALAVIL SPORT HOTEL
Main Street, PH20 1DL
A family-run hotel situated in the centre of the village, offering a range of sporting amenities, including an indoor swimming pool. Recently renovated, the en suite bedrooms are spacious, airy and comfortable. Parties are welcomed. Good, fresh Scottish food served all day. Golf, bowling, tennis, fishing.
DOUBLE ROOM: from £20 to £30
SINGLE ROOM: from £35 to £45
FOOD: up to £15 ☆
Hours: breakfast 8am–9.30am, lunch 12noon–2.30pm, dinner 6.30pm–8.30pm, closed 1st January until 14th January.
Cuisine: SCOTTISH – home-style cooking using local Scottish produce. Includes Badenoch venison casserole, haggis, delicious pies, salmon and good home-baking.
Cards: Visa, Access.
Other points: licensed, Sunday lunch, no-smoking area, children welcome, pets allowed, parking, afternoon tea, residents' lounge, swimming pool, central heating, baby-listening device, cots, vegetarian meals, disabled access, residents' bar.
Rooms: 50 bedrooms. All with TV, telephone, tea/coffee-making facilities, alarm. Family rooms available, with children's discount.
Directions: A9, situated on the main road running through the village.
JIM & HELEN COYLE ☎ (01540) 673220
Fax (01540) 673773.

LODGE HOTEL
Laggan Road, PH20 1DG
The Lodge Hotel is an attractive former shooting lodge situated in two acres of open ground surrounded by pine trees. New bedrooms and a functions suite have been skilfully added to the original building. For guests' comfort, there are two tastefully decorated lounge bars. The hotel offers a wide selection of food, from sandwiches to an appetizing à la carte menu.
DOUBLE ROOM: from £20 to £30
FOOD: up to £15
Hours: breakfast 8.30am–9.30am, bar meals 12noon–3pm, dinner 6pm–9.30pm, bar meals 5pm–9.30pm.

Cuisine: BRITISH – specialities include venison and salmon steaks.
Cards: Visa, Access.
Other points: parking, children welcome, pets allowed, garden, open-air dining, vegetarian meals, traditional Sunday lunch, afternoon teas.
Rooms: 4 double rooms, 30 twin rooms, 1 family room. All with en suite, TV, tea/coffee-making facilities.
Directions: turn left into Laggan Road at south end of Newtonmore Main Street. The hotel is 100 yards along on the right.
EILEEN REID ☎ (01540) 673256 Fax (01540) 673898.

MAINS HOTEL
Main Street, PH20 1DF
A warm welcome awaits you at the Mains, a family-owned and run hotel, ideally situated in the attractive village of Newtonmore in the heart of the Spey Valley. This former coaching inn offers guests a pleasurable stay in the newly decorated bedrooms, good home-cooked food in the dining room, and polite, friendly service throughout.
DOUBLE ROOM: from £20 to £30
SINGLE ROOM: up to £25
FOOD: up to £15
Hours: breakfast 7.30am–9.30am, lunch 12noon–2pm, dinner 7pm–9.30pm, bar meals 12noon–9.30pm.
Cuisine: BRITISH – fresh home-cooked meals.
Cards: Visa, Access, Diners.
Other points: parking, children welcome, pets allowed, garden, residents' lounge, vegetarian meals.
Rooms: 2 single rooms, 12 double rooms, 15 twin rooms, 2 family rooms. All with en suite, TV, radio, tea/coffee-making facilities.
Directions: ¼ mile off A9, at the fork of Main Street and Laggan Road.
MR JUSTICE ☎ (01540) 673206.

POOLEWE • map 17B2

POOL HOUSE HOTEL
Near Gairloch, IV22 2LE
Situated in the heart of Wester Ross, at the head of Loch Ewe, Pool House Hotel offers an exciting alternative to those seeking a hotel base from which to explore the natural beauty of the Scottish Highlands. From the pleasant, candlelit restaurant, guests can watch otters, seals and cormorants feeding by day and night. The hotel has a unique, comfortable and friendly atmosphere in astonishingly beautiful surroundings. Renowned for its exceptional local fare.
DOUBLE ROOM: from £30 to £40
FOOD: up to £15
Hours: breakfast 7.45am–9.30am, bar snacks 12noon–9pm, dinner 7pm–9pm.
Cuisine: BRITISH.
Cards: Visa, Access.
Other points: licensed.
Directions: on main A832, on edge of River Ewe and Loch Ewe.
MR P.L. HARRISON ☎ (0144586) 272
Fax (0144586) 403.

HIGHLANDS • SCOTLAND

ROSEHALL • map 17B3

ACHNESS HOTEL
Sutherland, IV27 4BD
Formerly a turn-of-the-century farmhouse, the main building of the Achness Hotel is a highly successful conversion into a quadrangle, which allows parking outside the door of your room. Specially popular with holiday-makers and fishermen, the emphasis is on home-made meals, which no doubt is the reason for its popularity at lunchtimes.
DOUBLE ROOM: from £30 to £40
SINGLE ROOM: form £35 to £45
FOOD: from £20 to £25
Hours: breakfast 8.30am, bar meals 12.30am–2pm, dinner 8pm, bar meals 6pm–9pm.
Cuisine: ENGLISH – fixed-price menu, with an emphasis on home-made soups and sweets.
Cards: Visa, Access.
Other points: licensed, Sunday lunch, children welcome, pets allowed, afternoon tea, residents' lounge, parking, disabled access.
Rooms: 3 single rooms, 2 double rooms, 7 twin rooms. All with tea/coffee-making facilities.
Directions: situated off the A837 in Rosehall village. Well signposted.
NEIL GRAESSER & PARTNERS ☎ (01549) 441239 Fax (01549) 441324.

SCOURIE • map 17A3

EDDRACHILLES HOTEL
Badcall Bay, IV27 4TH
Eddrachilles Hotel stands in its own 320-acre estate in a magnificent situation at the head of the island-studded Badcall Bay. This is a family-run, comfortable hotel offering good food in friendly, relaxing surroundings. If you are looking for a peaceful, tranquil holiday, this hotel is well worth a visit.
DOUBLE ROOM: from £30 to £40
SINGLE ROOM: from £45 to £55
FOOD: up to £15
Hours: breakfast 8am–9am, dinner 6.30pm–8.30pm.
Cuisine: ENGLISH – dishes include salmon pâté, pepper steak, lemon sole meunière, and desserts such as blackberry and apple pie, rhum baba and pear Belle Hélène.
Cards: Visa, Access.
Other points: licensed.
Rooms: 11 bedrooms.
Directions: on A894, approximately 6 miles north of Kylesku Bridge.
MR & MRS A.C.M. WOOD ☎ (01971) 502080/502211 Fax (01971) 502477.

TAIN • map 18B4

MORANGIE HOUSE HOTEL
Morangie Road, IV19 1PY
A fine old Victorian mansion with luxurious rooms and stained-glass windows. Professionally managed yet friendly and welcoming, and offering an extensive range of menus to suit all tastes, with food of excellent quality. Reduced-price golf to residents. Tain Museum and 14th century church nearby.
DOUBLE ROOM: from £30 to £40
SINGLE ROOM: from £45 to £55
FOOD: up to £15 CLUB
Hours: breakfast 7am–10am, lunch 12noon–2.30pm, dinner 7pm–10pm, bar meals 12noon–2.30pm, bar meals 5pm–10pm.
Cuisine: SCOTTISH / CONTINENTAL – fresh seafood is the speciality. A la carte, table d'hôte and bar menus.
Cards: Visa, Access, Diners, AmEx.
Other points: licensed, Sunday lunch, children welcome.
Rooms: 4 single rooms, 7 double rooms, 2 twin rooms. All with TV, telephone, tea/coffee-making facilities, hair dryer, trouser-press.
Directions: north on A9, take last turn-off into Tain, on right-hand side.
AVRIL & JOHN WYNNE ☎ (01862) 892281 Fax (01862) 892872.

THURSO • map 18A4

THE CASTLE ARMS HOTEL
Mey, KW14 8XH
A former 19th century coaching inn, situated on the John o' Groats peninsula in the north coast village of Mey and only a short distance from the Queen Mother's Highland home, the Castle of Mey. In the evenings, relax in front of the Caithness flagstone fireplace and enjoy a wee dram from a choice of fine malt whiskies. A seal colony is just one of the main nearby attractions.
DOUBLE ROOM: from £20 to £30
FOOD: from £15 to £20
Hours: breakfast 8.30am–9.30am, lunch 12.30am–2pm, high tea 5.30pm–7.30pm, dinner 7pm–9pm, bar meals 5.30pm–9pm, open all year.
Cuisine: SCOTTISH – for dinner, a comprehensive table d'hôte menu is available, which includes locally caught fresh salmon, crab and succulent steaks. Extremely fine wine list.
Cards: Visa, Access.
Other points: open-air dining, Sunday lunch, children welcome, pets allowed, parking, afternoon tea, cots, left luggage, residents' lounge, residents' bar.
Rooms: 4 double rooms, 3 twin rooms, 1 triple room. All with TV, telephone, tea/coffee-making facilities.
Directions: 7 miles west of John o' Groats.
MRS MORRISON ☎ (0184785) 244 Fax (0184785) 244.

TONGUE • map 17A3

BEN LOYAL HOTEL
Main Street, IV27 4XE
Situated between Durness and Thurso, this small crofting village enjoys some of Scotland's most spectacular coastal and mountain scenery and wonderful, clean beaches. The warmth of

welcome and the genuine friendliness of the staff and proprietors add to its reputation as a mecca for fishermen and hill-walkers and a holiday/touring centre. A true sanctuary from the stresses of urban living.
DOUBLE ROOM: from £20 to £30
SINGLE ROOM: from £25 to £35
FOOD: from £15 to £20
Hours: breakfast 8am–9.15am, bar meals 12noon–2pm & 6pm–8.30pm, dinner 7pm–8pm.
Cuisine: SCOTTISH – traditional and modern Scottish cooking using fresh local produce.
Cards: Visa, Access.
Other points: licensed, no-smoking area, coaches by prior arrangement, vegetarian meals, cots.
Rooms: 3 single rooms, 4 double rooms, 5 twin rooms. All with TV, tea/coffee-making facilities.
Directions: at the junction of the A836 and A838 on the north Scottish coast.
MEL & PAULINE COOK ☎ (01847) 611216.

ULLAPOOL • map 17B3

BRAE GUEST HOUSE
Shore Street, IV26 2UJ
Situated on the seafront overlooking the harbour and Loch Broom, this a family-run guest house with all modern comforts to make your stay one of relaxed enjoyment. With a homely atmosphere and good, home-cooked meals, this is a good base or stopping-point for holiday-makers.
DOUBLE ROOM: up to £20
SINGLE ROOM: up to £25
FOOD: up to £15
Hours: closed October until May.
Other points: parking, residents' lounge.
Rooms: 9 double rooms. All with en suite, TV, tea/coffee-making facilities.
Directions: A835 from the south; the white-painted Brae is the first corner building as you approach the seafront area.
ROSANNE ROSS ☎ (01854) 612421.

CEILIDH PLACE
West Argyle Street, IV26 2TY
Originally two cottages, the buildings have been carefully renovated with quality fabrics and wood panelling to provide a relaxing, comfortable hotel with a friendly atmosphere. As the Gaelic name suggests, it is a 'place to meet, eat, talk or sing'.
There are regular concerts throughout the year: traditional music, with some folk, classical and jazz. Ullapool is a convenient centre from which to explore some of the finest mountain scenery in Scotland – but when you discover Ceilidh Place you will probably just want to stay and enjoy the fun and regular events! Special winter rates 27th October 1994 until 27th March 1995.
DOUBLE ROOM: from £40 to £50
FOOD: from £20 to £25
Hours: breakfast 8am–10am, bar snacks 10am–6pm, dinner 6.30pm–9.30pm, closed January.
Cuisine: SCOTTISH.
Cards: Visa, Access, Diners, AmEx.
Other points: parking, children welcome, no-smoking area, pets, residents' lounge, vegetarian meals.
Rooms: 2 single, 7 double, 4 twin rooms.
Directions: A835, first right after the pier.
JEAN & ROBERT URQUHART ☎ (01854) 612103 [Fax] (01854) 612886.

THE HARBOUR LIGHTS HOTEL
Garve Road, IV26 2SX
A family-run hotel and restaurant offering excellent food, a warm welcome and comfortable accommodation. The spacious lounge has a panoramic view of the harbour, Loch Broom and the surrounding hills, and the hotel is only a short walk from the centre of the old fishing port of Ullapool.
DOUBLE ROOM: from £20 to £30
SINGLE ROOM: from £35 to £45
FOOD: from £15 to £20
Hours: breakfast 8am–9am, bar meals 12noon–2pm, Sunday lunch 12.30am–2pm, dinner 7pm–9.30pm.
Cuisine: BRITISH – specialities include local salmon, seafood, Scotch beef and venison, turf and surf (fillet steak, with fresh scallops, prawn tails and shellfish sauce). Bar meals available from £2 to £10.
Cards: Visa, Access, AmEx.
Other points: licensed, Sunday lunch, children welcome, garden, afternoon tea, pets allowed, residents' lounge, residents' bar.
Rooms: 19 bedrooms. All with TV, tea/coffee-making facilities, telephone, hair dryer.
Directions: on the outskirts of Ullapool.
MARILYN & DANNY GORDON ☎ (01854) 612222.

*L*OTHIAN

DALKEITH • map 16E4

COUNTY HOTEL & RESTAURANT
152 High Street, EH22 1AY
Family-run for over 40 years, this hotel has a well-deserved reputation for friendly service, good food and value for money. Recently refurbished to provide additional bedrooms, a cocktail bar and bistro, two small meeting rooms and a well-designed function suite. Sporting and activity breaks such as golf, clay and game shooting, and much more, can be arranged. Ideal location for visiting Edinburgh and its many tourist attractions.
DOUBLE ROOM: from £20 to £30
FOOD: up to £15 [CLUB]
Hours: breakfast 7.30am–11.30am, meals all day 11.30am–10pm.

LOTHIAN • SCOTLAND

Cuisine: INTERNATIONAL – attractively presented fresh food.
Cards: Visa, Access.
Other points: children welcome, open bank holidays, no-smoking area, afternoon tea, disabled access, pets allowed, residents' lounge, vegetarian meals, functions, conferences.
Directions: 1 mile from Edinburgh city bypass, 7 miles south of Edinburgh on A68 or A7.
MR P. COPPOLA ☎ (0131) 663 3495
Fax (0131) 663 0208.

DUNBAR • map 16D5

REDHEUGH HOTEL
Bayswell Park, EH42 1AE
A warm, friendly welcome awaits you at the Redheugh Hotel, situated on the cliff top at Dunbar and with fine views over the Firth of Forth. Traditionally furnished, the hotel has a homely atmosphere and, with good food to match, you are sure of a relaxed stay. Golf and fishing packages can be arranged.
DOUBLE ROOM: from £20 to £30
SINGLE ROOM: from £25 to £35
FOOD: from £15 to £20
Hours: breakfast 7.30am–9am, dinner 7pm–8.30pm.
Cuisine: BRITISH – predominantly British cuisine. Menu changes daily. Specialities include local fish dishes, home-made casseroles and fresh fruit pies.
Cards: Visa, Access, Diners, AmEx.
Other points: licensed, pets allowed, golf, street parking, vegetarians meals.
Rooms: 2 single rooms, 3 double rooms, 3 twin rooms, 2 family rooms. All with TV, radio, bar, telephone, tea/coffee-making facilities.
Directions: on the cliff top at Dunbar.
MRS J. YOUNG ☎ (01368) 862793
Fax (01368) 862793.

EDINBURGH • map 16D4

AILSA CRAIG HOTEL
24 Royal Terrace, EH7 5AB
Originally built as family houses for affluent merchants from Leith, this Georgian house hotel retains many of its original features, while providing recently reburbished, modern accommodation in a centrally positioned, picturesque, tree-lined street. A warm, friendly atmosphere and comfortable rooms are ensured at the hotel.
DOUBLE ROOM: from £20 to £30
SINGLE ROOM: from £35 to £45
Hours: breakfast 7.45am–9am.
Cards: Visa, Access, Diners, AmEx.
Other points: children welcome, residents' lounge, garden
Rooms: 3 single rooms, 6 double rooms, 5 twin rooms, 4 family rooms. Rooms have all facilities.
Directions: turn left from Princes Street into Leith Street, go past the Playhouse Theatre and turn right. Waverley Station is 10 minutes' walk.
MRS CATHY HAMILTON ☎ (0131) 556 6055/556 1022 Fax (0131) 556 6055.

ALBANY HOTEL
39–43 Albany Street, EH1 3QY
A small, friendly hotel in a quiet area, yet only five minutes from Princes Street and the city centre. The fine Georgian exterior is matched by the elegantly refurbished interior. Under the personal supervision of the Swiss owner, all guests are assured a warm welcome. Comfortable bedrooms and excellent cuisine with a continental influence is served in the restaurant.
DOUBLE ROOM: from £40 to £50
FOOD: from £20 to £25
Hours: breakfast 7.30am–9.30am, lunch 12noon–2pm, dinner 6.30pm–9.30pm, bar meals 12noon–2pm, 6.30pm–9pm, closed Christmas day and New Year's day.
Cuisine: BRITISH – dishes may include noisettes of lamb, Scottish salmon steak, medallions of beef in a whisky sauce, garlic king prawns, Albany trio.
Cards: Visa, Access.
Other points: licensed, open-air dining, Sunday lunch, children welcome, conferences, pets allowed, residents' lounge.
Directions: city centre, behind bus station and St James Centre.
PAULINE MARIDOR ☎ (0131) 556 0397
Fax (0131) 557 6633.

BANGALORE TANDOORI
52 Home Street, EH3 9NA
Situated opposite the King's Theatre, the Bangalore restaurant is ideally placed for before- or after-theatre meals. The cuisine reflects a diverse range of tastes from the Indian peninsula, flavoured with an outstanding choice of herbs and spices using the finest fresh produce. Vegetarian dishes and special 3-course lunches are available.
FOOD: up to £15
Hours: lunch 12noon–2pm, dinner 5.30pm–12.30am, meals all day Friday and Saturday 12noon–1.30am.
Cuisine: INDIAN – all dishes are created from the finest fresh produce and freshly ground spices.
Cards: Visa, Access, AmEx.
Other points: children welcome, no-smoking area, vegetarian meals.
Directions: in Tollcross area, opposite King's Theatre.
MR M.R. KHAN ☎ (0131) 229 1348.

CELLAR No. 1
1a Chambers Street, EH1 1HR
A characteristic bistro-style wine bar with bare wooden floorboards and offering an interesting selection of dishes, including vegetarian, and an extensive choice of wines, spirits, liqueurs, beers and real ales.
FOOD: up to £15
Hours: lunch 12noon–2.30pm, bar meals 12noon–12midnight, dinner 6pm–10pm, snack meals available at all times, closed Sunday.
Cuisine: INTERNATIONAL – à la carte menu. Jambalaya, Persian-style lamb, baked salmon fillet, scampi Boscaiola. Vegetarian dishes. Extensive wine list. Booking advised.
Cards: Visa, Access, Switch.
Other points: licensed, vegetarian meals, open bank holidays, parking.

SCOTLAND • LOTHIAN

Directions: from east end of Princes Street, go south along North and South Bridge. Second on right.
MR F. MARTONI ☎ (0131) 220 4298.

■ GREENSIDE HOTEL
9 Royal Terrace, EH7 5AB
An attractive Georgian house hotel of a very high standard, decorated throughout in a tasteful classical style with spacious, comfortable accommodation. Delicious home-cooked evening meals are available to guests on request. Edinburgh Castle, Royal Mile, Carlton Hill and Princes Street are all within close proximity.
DOUBLE ROOM: from £20 to £30
SINGLE ROOM: from £25 to £35
Hours: breakfast 8am–9am.
Other points: children welcome, residents' lounge, garden.
Rooms: 3 single rooms, 3 double rooms, 4 twin rooms, 4 family rooms. All with en suite, TV, radio, alarm, hair dryer, tea/coffee-making facilities.
Directions: turn left from Princes Street into Leith Street, pass Playhouse Theatre and turn right.
JIM HOUSTON ☎ (0131) 557 0022/557 0121
[Fax] (0131) 557 0022.

■ HOWARD HOTEL
32–36 Great King Street, EH3 6QH
The Howard is situated in quiet seclusion among the city's elegant Georgian gardens and terraces. It was originally three private houses that were an integral part of Edinburgh's New Town. The classical facade gives no hint of the welcoming opulence within. Cross the threshold and it is clear that this hotel is quite unlike any other. A visit is highly recommended.
DOUBLE ROOM: over £50
SINGLE ROOM: over £50
FOOD: from £20 to £25
Hours: breakfast 7.30am–10am, dinner 7.30pm–9.30pm.
Cuisine: SCOTTISH / FRENCH.
Cards: Visa, Access, Diners, AmEx.
Other points: children welcome, parking, pets allowed, conference facilities, residents' lounge, no-smoking area, vegetarian meals.
Rooms: 16 bedrooms. All with TV, telephone, radio, alarm, hair dryer, trouser-press, room service.
Directions: proceed from Princes Street down Hanover/Dundas Street and take the fifth turn on the right.
MS G. THOMPSON ☎ (0131) 557 3500
[Fax] (0131) 557 6515.

■ LANCERS BRASSERIE
5 Hamilton Place, EH3 5BA
Lancers Brasserie has a good selection of French and Indian dishes at reasonable prices. Their warm welcome and helpful, efficient staff will make eating here a pleasurable experience.
FOOD: from £15 to £20
Hours: lunch 12noon–2.30pm, dinner 5.30pm–11.30pm.
Cuisine: INDIAN – Bengali and North Indian dishes, kurji lamb (48 hours' notice), vegetarian thali, Lancers assorted Tandoori, selection of French dishes.
Cards: Visa, Access, Diners, AmEx.
Other points: Sunday lunch, children catered for (please check for age limits).
Directions: in Stockbridge area of the city.
WALI UDDIN ☎ (0131) 332 3444/332 9559.

■ THE OLD BORDEAUX
47 Old Burdiehouse Road, EH17 8BJ
The principles of good food and friendly, efficient service in comfortable surroundings can be found at this pub on Edinburgh's southern boundary. Transformed from an original abode of exiled French silk weavers into today's warm, welcoming old-world inn, The Old Bordeaux is well worth a visit for its good food and service and very good value for money.
FOOD: up to £15 ✯
Hours: bar meals 10am–10pm, closed Christmas day and New Year's day.
Cuisine: BRITISH – an extensive choice of dishes such as fresh mussels, roast beef, steak pie. Daily specials include game, sea bass, salmon, salads and vegetarian meals.
Cards: Visa, Access, Diners, AmEx.
Other points: licensed, Sunday lunch, children welcome.
Directions: A701. Five miles south of city centre, adjacent to A720 city bypass.
LINDA & ALAN THOMSON & ADRIAN DEMPSEY ☎ (0131) 664 1734.

■ OSBOURNE HOTEL & SHELBOURNE LOUNGE
53–59 York Place, EH1 3JD
A city-centre hotel, ideally located near the main coach and rail stations and only a short walk from the castle, Palace, Royal Mile, Princes Street shops and gardens. The dining room offers meals to residents and groups. Visitors receive a warm welcome, and the service is polite and friendly.
DOUBLE ROOM: from £30 to £40
SINGLE ROOM: from £35 to £45
FOOD: up to £15
Hours: lunch 12noon–2pm, dinner 5.30pm–9pm.
Cuisine: CONTINENTAL – traditional pub meals.
Cards: Visa, Access, Diners, AmEx.
Other points: licensed, children welcome, pets by prior arrangement, residents' lounge, residents' bar.
Rooms: 13 single rooms, 12 double rooms, 12 twin rooms, 3 family rooms. All with en suite, TV, telephone, tea/coffee-making facilities.
Directions: in Edinburgh city centre. Follow Queen Street East onto York Place.
FEROZ WADIA ☎ (0131) 556 5577/556 2345
[Fax] (0131) 556 1012.

■ ROYAL CIRCUS HOTEL
19–21 Royal Circus, EH3 6TL
This traditionally furnished listed building close to the city centre in a select area offers many modern facilities. At the rear is a garden, which provides for alfresco dining and drinking. Other facilities include a bistro restaurant, comfortable lounge bar

and small function room. Within easy walking distance are the Castle, Royal Mile, Holyrood Palace and Botanical Gardens.
DOUBLE ROOM: from £20 to £30
SINGLE ROOM: from £25 to £35
FOOD: up to £15
Hours: breakfast 7.30am–9.30am, bar lunches 12noon–2pm, bar suppers 5.30pm–9pm, dinner 5.30pm–9pm.
Cuisine: CONTINENTAL.
Cards: Visa, Access, Diners, AmEx.
Other points: licensed.
Rooms: 29 bedrooms.
Directions: from Princes Street head down Fredrick Street and Howe Street to Royal Circus.
MR FEROZ WADIA ☎ (0131) 220 5000
Fax (0131) 220 2020.

SALISBURY VIEW HOTEL
64 Dalkeith Road, EH16 5AE
A spacious, family-run Georgian hotel situated approximately 5 minutes from the city centre, its fine shopping, the Princes Street gardens and Edinburgh Castle. The hotel overlooks Holyrood Park and the Royal Commonwealth Swimming Pool. There are eight well-appointed en suite bedrooms to ensure a comfortable stay and a large private car park with security night lights for peace of mind.
DOUBLE ROOM: from £20 to £30
SINGLE ROOM: from £25 to £35
FOOD: up to £15 ★
Hours: breakfast 8am–9.30am, dinner 6.30pm.
Cuisine: BRITISH – special diets can be catered for if notice is given.
Cards: Visa, Access, Diners.
Other points: parking, no-smoking area, residents' lounge, pets allowed, children welcome, vegetarian meals.
Rooms: 2 single rooms, 3 double rooms, 2 twin rooms, 1 family room. All with tea/coffee-making facilities, TV, telephone, radio.
Directions: located on the A7/A68, five minutes from the city centre.
KENNETH MEARCHENT ☎ (0131) 667 1133
Fax (0131) 667 1133.

THE TATTLER
23 Commercial Street, Leith, EH6 6JA
This 1992 winner of Les Routiers Pub of the Year is a traditional pub and restaurant, originally four derelict shops in the heart of the historic port of Leith. Tastefully decorated in Victorian/Edwardian style, The Tattler re-creates the glory of that era and offers a taste of Scotland to tourists, businessmen and locals alike.
FOOD: from £15 to £20 ★
Hours: meals all day Saturday and Sunday, lunch 12noon–2pm, dinner 6pm–10pm, bar meals 12noon–2pm, 6pm–10pm, closed Christmas day and New Year's day.
Cuisine: SCOTTISH – seafood, curries, casseroles and pies, vegetarian dishes. Border lamb, scampi, steaks, seafood, roast duckling.
Cards: Visa, Access, Diners, AmEx.
Other points: licensed, Sunday lunch, children welcome.

Directions: across from the Leith shore, opposite the historic Customs House.
LINDA & ALAN THOMSON & ADRIAN DEMPSEY ☎ (0131) 554 9999.

TERRACE HOTEL
37 Royal Terrace, EH7 5AH
This listed Georgian hotel is beautifully decorated in the style of the era. The bedrooms are large and gracious, with high ceilings and cornices. Fireplaces adorn both the bedrooms and dining room. As this hotel is centrally situated with easy access to most of Edinburgh's attractions, it is well worth a visit, with its panoramic views of the Firth of Forth.
DOUBLE ROOM: from £20 to £30
Hours: breakfast 8am–9am.
Cuisine: BREAKFAST – Scottish breakfast: choice of juices and cereals; eggs cooked to your specifications; oatcakes, toast, tea or coffee.
Cards: Visa, Access.
Other points: open bank holidays, residents' lounge, street parking, garden.
Rooms: 14 bedrooms. All with TV, tea/coffee-making facilities.
Directions: half a mile north-east of Princes Street. Near London Road.
ANNE & MICHAEL MANN ☎ (0131) 556 3423
Fax (0131) 556 2520.

TEX MEX
47 Hanover Street, EH2 2PJ
Authentic mix of 'Cross Border' Mexican and Texan dishes, all prepared on the premises using only fresh ingredients of the highest quality. The restaurant and bar are decorated with bright colours, and subtle lighting giving the feeling of being in sunnier climes. Situated just off Princes Street, there is a constant flow of people, and the restaurant tends to get very full in the evenings. Booking is essential on Friday and Saturday nights, and advisable on other evenings.
FOOD: up to £15 CLUB
Hours: meals all day 12noon–12midnight, closed Christmas and New Year's day.
Cuisine: MEXICAN / AMERICAN – e.g., nachos, flautas, carnitas, tortillas, burgers, home-made desserts and a wide selection of vegetarian meals. House speciality: flaming fajitas.
Cards: Visa, AmEx, MasterCard, Switch, Delta.
Other points: Sunday lunch, children welcome.
Directions: situated just off Princes Street, opposite The Mound.
DONALD & SARAH MAVOR ☎ (0131) 225 1796 Fax (0131) 557 5585.

THE TOWN HOUSE
65 Gilmore Place, EH3 9NU
A Victorian terraced town house on three floors. Built in 1876 as the manse for the church next door. Gilmore Place is situated opposite the King's Theatre and is within easy walking distance (15 minutes) of the city centre. It is also well placed on three city-centre bus routes.
DOUBLE ROOM: from £20 to £30
Hours: breakfast 8am–9am, open all year.
Cuisine: BREAKFAST.

SCOTLAND • LOTHIAN

Other points: central heating, no evening meal, children welcome, baby-sitting, left luggage.
Rooms: 1 single room, 1 double room, 1 twin room, 1 triple room. All with TV, tea/coffee-making facilities.
Directions: take A702 towards city centre, turn left at the King's Theatre.
MRS SUSAN VIRTUE ☎ (0131) 229 1985.

VERANDAH TANDOORI RESTAURANT
17 Dalry Road, EH11 2BQ
Winner of the Casserole Award in 1988, 1989, 1990, 1991, 1992, 1993 and 1994. The Verandah Restaurant is one of Edinburgh's most popular eating establishments, offering authentic Bangladeshi dishes. The light wicker chairs and the matching timber blinds further enhance the restaurant's already relaxed atmosphere.
FOOD: from £15 to £20
Hours: lunch 12noon–2.15pm, dinner 5pm–11.45pm.
Cuisine: INDIAN – lamb pasanda, chicken tikka massalla, Tandoori mixed.
Cards: Visa, Access, Diners.
Other points: Sunday lunch, children welcome.
Directions: close to Haymarket station in Edinburgh.
WALI TASAR UDDIN ☎ (0131) 337 5828
[Fax] (0131) 313 3853.

GULLANE • map 16D5

QUEENS HOTEL
Main Street, EH31 2AS
A family-run hotel situated in the picturesque village of Gullane. This is a welcoming and pleasant hotel with a good reputation, high standards, a relaxed atmosphere and friendly service. Golf and other packages are available.
DOUBLE ROOM: from £30 to £40
SINGLE ROOM: from £25 to £35
FOOD: up to £15 [CLUB]
Hours: breakfast 7am–9am, bar meals 12noon–10pm, dinner 7pm–10pm.
Cuisine: BRITISH – dinner menu may feature beef Wellington, baked halibut, steak caprice, chicken and mushroom crepe au gratin. Bar meals available all day.
Cards: Visa, Access, Diners, AmEx.
Other points: licensed, open-air dining, Sunday lunch, children welcome, afternoon tea, residents' lounge, garden.
Rooms: 35 bedrooms. All with TV, radio, alarm, telephone, tea/coffee-making facilities.
Directions: off A1. A6137 Haddington to Aberlady, A198 to Gullane.
ANN ROBERTSON ☎ (01620) 842275
[Fax] (01620) 842970.

LEADBURN • map 16E4

THE LEADBURN INN
West Linton, EH46 7BE
A country-style inn, the aptly named Carriage Restaurant is a luxurious converted railway carriage that re-creates the glory of the early trains. Only 25 minutes' drive from the centre of Edinburgh, the hotel is popular with business people, tourists and locals alike and was a winner of a Les Routiers Casserole Award in 1991.
DOUBLE ROOM: from £20 to £30
SINGLE ROOM: from £25 to £35
FOOD: up to £15 ☆
Hours: breakfast by arrangement, dinner 6pm–10pm, bar meals 12noon–10pm, closed Christmas day and New Year's day.
Cuisine: SCOTTISH – local game and seafood are the specialities. Good value for money; extensive menu.
Cards: Visa, Access, Diners, AmEx.
Other points: licensed, Sunday lunch, children welcome, pets by prior arrangement, residents' lounge, residents' bar, vegetarian meals, disabled access.
Rooms: 2 double rooms, 2 twin rooms, 2 family rooms.
Directions: from Edinburgh, take the A701 to Penicuik. Continue to Leadburn.
LINDA & ALAN THOMSON & ADRIAN DEMPSEY ☎ (01968) 672952.

LES ROUTIERS ACCOMMODATION DIRECTORY

This handy directory is ideal for those looking for somewhere to stay at great value.
It lists a huge choice of Les Routiers-recommended places throughout the British Isles offering comfortable accommodation, good food and a warm welcome amid relaxed surroundings.

Available from selected
Les Routiers establishments
or direct from the publishers.

Price £2

ROSLIN • map 16E4

OLD ORIGINAL ROSSLYN INN
EH25 9LE
This historic inn was first opened in 1827 and has remained open for business ever since. The village is in a rural area, and the inn's old-fashioned decor gives it a charming atmosphere.
DOUBLE ROOM: up to £20
FOOD: from £15 to £20 [CLUB]
Hours: breakfast 7.30am–9.30am, lunch 12noon–2pm, dinner 6pm–10pm, Saturday and Sunday 12noon–10pm.
Cuisine: BRITISH – grills, daily specials such as salmon vol au vents, grilled spring lamb, walnut sundae.
Cards: Visa, Access, Diners, AmEx.
Other points: open-air dining, Sunday lunch, children welcome, coaches by prior arrangement
Directions: just off A701, just outside Edinburgh.
MR G.A. HARRIS ☎ (0131) 440 2384.

ORKNEY & SHETLAND ISLANDS

KIRKWALL
Orkney • map 18B6

ALBERT HOTEL
Mounthoolie Lane, KW15 1JZ
A comfortable, family-run hotel in the centre of Kirkwall. Recently refurbished, the Albert Hotel is noted for its good food made from fresh local produce. An ideal place to stay when exploring these unique islands.
DOUBLE ROOM: from £30 to £40
FOOD: from £15 to £20 [CLUB]
Hours: breakfast 7.30am–9.30am, lunch 12noon–2pm, dinner 7pm–10pm, bar meals 12noon–2pm, 6pm–10pm, closed Christmas day and New Year's day.
Cuisine: ENGLISH / SEAFOOD – à la carte restaurant meals and bar meals made from fresh local produce. House speciality is the seafood platter and stables steak.
Cards: Visa, Access.
Other points: licensed, Sunday lunch, children welcome.
Rooms: 9 single, 5 double, 3 twin, 2 family rooms. All with TV, telephone, tea/coffee-making facilities.
Directions: in centre of Kirkwall, off Junction Road. Close to harbour.
ANJO CASEY ☎ (01856) 876000 [Fax] (01856) 875397.

KIRKWALL HOTEL
KW15 1LS
Orkney's largest hotel has, in its time, played host to a number of the crown heads of Europe. This fine historic hotel, overlooking the seafront and harbour, is justifiably popular with business and tourist clientele from around the world. The completely refurbished lounge and restaurant are ideal for relaxing or enjoying the exquisite Orkney cuisine. The Kirkwall Hotel is the perfect location for those who want to 'get away from it all', to discover the delights that Orkney has to offer.
DOUBLE ROOM: from £30 to £40
FOOD: from £15 to £20
Hours: breakfast 7am–9.30am, lunch 12noon–2pm, dinner 6.30pm–9pm.
Cuisine: BRITISH – Orkney cuisine including fresh local lobster, oysters, scallops and crab. Orkney steaks.
Other points: children welcome, pets allowed, vegetarian meals, satellite TV, residents' bar, residents' lounge.
Rooms: 44 bedrooms. All with TV, telephone, tea/coffee-making facilities.
Directions: situated on the main town harbour.
MR G. WILKINS ☎ (01856) 872232
[Fax] (01856) 872812.

STROMNESS
Orkney • map 18B6

STROMNESS HOTEL
Victoria Street, KW16 3AA
A comfortable hotel situated in the heart of the unique fishing port of Stromness, which is also the main ferry terminal between the mainland and Orkney. The hotel overlooks the harbour and Scapa Flow, which served as the British naval base for both World Wars. All bedrooms have modern facilities, and bar lunches are served daily in the lounge bar, which enjoys panoramic views.
DOUBLE ROOM: from £20 to £30
SINGLE ROOM: from £25 to £35
FOOD: from £15 to £20
Hours: bar snacks 12noon–2pm, 6.30pm–9.30pm, breakfast 7.15am–9.30am, dinner 7pm–9pm.
Cuisine: INTERNATIONAL.
Cards: Visa, Access.
Other points: parking, children welcome, open bank holidays, pets allowed, vegetarian meals, garden.
Rooms: 6 single rooms, 11 double rooms, 22 twin rooms.
Directions: the Stromness is situated at the main pier in Stromness, on the harbour.
☎ (01856) 850298 [Fax] (01856) 850610.

TANKERNESS
Orkney • map 18B6

QUOYBURRAY INN
Tankerness, KW17 2QU
Dating back 100 years, the Quoyburray was once a grain store and is now undergoing extensive renovations by the proprietor, whose aim is to build it up into a reputable out-of-town restaurant. Nearby places of interest include the Covenanters' Memorial.
FOOD: up to £15
Hours: bar snacks 12noon–2pm, dinner 6pm–9.30pm, closed Monday.
Cuisine: ENGLISH – traditional home-style cooking. Vegetarians catered for.
Cards: Visa, Access.
Other points: Sunday lunch, children welcome, open bank holidays, parking.
Directions: (A960) 5 miles east of Kirkwall.
JAMES & ISOBEL CURRIE ☎ (01856) 86255.

HILLSWICK
Shetland • map 18D6

ST MAGNUS BAY HOTEL
ZE2 9RW
A Norwegian mansion set amid the unspoiled coastal scenery of the Northmavine region of Shetland and overlooking St Magnus Bay. The accommodation is comfortable and the restaurant provides good meals, with particular emphasis on local seafood. An ideal hotel for families.
DOUBLE ROOM: from £30 to £40
FOOD: from £15 to £20
Hours: breakfast 6am–9am, bar meals 12.30am–2pm, 6.30pm–9pm.
Cuisine: SCOTTISH – traditional Scottish cuisine, with local seafood a speciality.

Cards: Visa, Access.
Other points: licensed, Sunday lunch, children welcome, afternoon tea, pets allowed, residents' lounge.
Directions: A970; end of road at Hillswick. 40 minutes' drive from Lerwick.
MR P. TITCOMB ☎ (0180623) 372
Fax (0180623) 373.

LERWICK
Shetland • map 18E6

SHETLAND HOTEL
Holmsgarth Road, Lerwick, ZE1 0PW
Warm hospitality is offered at this efficient, modern hotel overlooking Lerwick harbour, just three minutes from the ferry terminal. All rooms have the most up-to-date facilities for maximum comfort. Special package holidays are available, and conferences and private functions can be catered for.
DOUBLE ROOM: from £40 to £50
SINGLE ROOM: over £55
FOOD: from £15 to £20 CLUB
Cuisine: BRITISH.
Other points: children welcome, no-smoking area, disabled access, pets, vegetarian meals, parking, garden.
Rooms: 64 bedrooms.
Directions: situated at north end of Lerwick directly opposite ferry terminal.
LERWICK HARBOUR TRUST ☎ (01595) 695515 Fax (01595) 695828.

STRATHCLYDE

ARROCHAR • map 15D2

GREENBANK GUEST HOUSE & LICENSED RESTAURANT
G83 7AL
A small, family-run guest house and restaurant on the loch side. There is a good choice of meals available throughout the day, and the restaurant is licensed, with a selection of wines, beers and spirits. An excellent base for fishing, climbing, boating and touring. A friendly, relaxed atmosphere prevails, with fine food and accommodation at good value.
DOUBLE ROOM: up to £20
SINGLE ROOM: up to £25
FOOD: up to £15
Hours: meals all day 8am–9.30pm.
Cuisine: SCOTTISH – meals available all day. Dishes may include salmon steak, fresh-baked steak-and-kidney pie, fried Loch Fyne herring in oatmeal, curries, vegetarian dishes.
Other points: licensed, Sunday lunch, children welcome, pets allowed, garden, disabled access.
Rooms: 1 single room, 2 double rooms, 1 family room.
Directions: on the A83, opposite the famous Cobbler Mountain.
MR & MRS R. CLUER ☎ (01301) 702305.

AYR • map 14B5

FOUTERS BISTRO
2A Academy Street, KA7 1HS
Authentic cellar restaurant serving interesting French and British dishes using the best of local produce. Fouters Bistro is renowned for the high quality of its cuisine, steak and seafood specialities. Personally run by the proprietors. On-street parking opposite Town Hall.
FOOD: from £15 to £20 CLUB ☆
Hours: lunch 12noon–2pm, dinner 6.30pm–10.30pm, Sunday 7pm–10pm, closed 4 days over Christmas and 4 days over New Year.
Cuisine: SCOTTISH / FRENCH – fine Scottish produce cooked in the French style. Vegetarians welcomed and special diets catered for.
Cards: Visa, Access, Diners, AmEx.
Other points: children welcome.
Directions: opposite Town Hall, in a cobbled stone lane.
FRAN & LAURIE BLACK ☎ (01292) 261391.

THE KYLESTROME HOTEL
11 Miller Road, KA7 2AX
A large stone house in Ayr, which is in the heart of Burns Country. The seafront, railway station and town centre are a short walk away, and Prestwick Airport a few minutes' drive. The stylish restaurant provides a unique atmosphere in which to enjoy fine international cuisine.
DOUBLE ROOM: from £40 to £50
FOOD: from £15 to £20
Hours: breakfast 7.30am–9.30am, lunch 12noon–2pm, bar meals 12noon–2pm, high tea 5.30pm–7pm, dinner 7pm–10pm, bar meals 5.30pm–10pm.
Cuisine: SCOTTISH / SEAFOOD – fresh seafood, local produce. In the bar: lamb cutlets with minted pear. In the restaurant: steak, seafood (à la carte).
Cards: Visa, Access, Diners, AmEx.
Other points: licensed, Sunday lunch, no-smoking area, children welcome, conferences.
Rooms: 1 single room, 7 double rooms, 12 twin rooms.
Directions: on a main street in Ayr, near the railway station.
☎ (01292) 262474 Fax (01292) 260863.

OLD RACECOURSE HOTEL
2 Victoria Park, KA7 1HT
An attractive stone building in pleasant garden surroundings a mile from the town centre and minutes from the beach. The beautiful scenery of

Ayrshire is nearby, making this hotel a tempting base to return to. The hotel is justly proud of its fresh seafood and prime Scottish game.
DOUBLE ROOM: from £20 to £30
FOOD: from £15 to £20
Hours: breakfast 8am–9am, lunch 12noon–2pm, afternoon tea 3pm–5pm, high tea 5pm–7pm, dinner 7pm–9pm, bar meals 5pm–9pm.
Cuisine: SCOTTISH / SEAFOOD – specializing in fresh local seafood, game dishes and prime Scottish steaks.
Cards: Visa.
Other points: open-air dining, children welcome, pets allowed.
Rooms: 1 single room, 7 double rooms, 4 twin rooms. All with TV, tea/coffee-making facilities.
Directions: A70 or A719 to Ayr; 1 mile from town centre, close to beach.
JOHN & MARGARET NICOL ☎ (01292) 262873 [Fax] (01292) 267598.

TUDOR RESTAURANT
6–8 Beresford Terrace,
KA7 2EG

Now in its 27th year of operation, the reasonably-priced lunch, high tea menus and friendly staff make the Tudor a favourite with family parties. Children may choose from their own menus.
FOOD: up to £15
Hours: meals all day 9am–8pm, closed Sunday except July and August.
Cuisine: SCOTTISH – traditional Scottish high teas served with cakes and scones from own bakery.
Other points: no-smoking area, children welcome.
Directions: opposite Burn's Statue Square, off the A70 in the centre of Ayr.
KENNETH ANCELL ☎ (01292) 261404.

DALMALLY • map 15C2

GLENORCHY LODGE HOTEL
Near Oban, PA33 1AA

A small, family-run hotel in the village of Dalmally, offering warm, comfortable accommodation. Informal, lively bar and good bar meals served in generous portions. Ideal base for touring the area.
DOUBLE ROOM: from £20 to £30
FOOD: up to £15
Hours: breakfast 7am–9am, lunch 11am–2.30pm, dinner 5pm–9pm, closed Christmas day and New Year's day.
Cuisine: SCOTTISH – traditional cuisine using fresh Scottish produce such as Highland venison in a red wine sauce, local salmon, Awe trout, steaks.
Cards: Visa, Access, Diners, AmEx.
Other points: licensed, children welcome, afternoon tea, pets allowed, residents' lounge.
Rooms: 1 double room, 2 triple rooms, 2 family rooms. All with TV, radio, telephone, tea/coffee-making facilities.
Directions: A82 from Glasgow, A85 from Tyndrum. 16 miles Inverary, 25 miles Oban.
HECTOR & PATRICIA WHYTE ☎ (01838) 200312.

DUNOON • map 15D2

THE ARDTULLY HOTEL
297 Marine Parade, Hunter's Quay,
PA23 8HN

A family-run licensed hotel, set in its own grounds, in an elevated position affording outstanding views of the Clyde estuary and surrounding hills. The tastefully decorated rooms are well-appointed, and the high standard of friendly, polite service makes your stay unbeatable value for money.
DOUBLE ROOM: from £20 to £30
SINGLE ROOM: from £25 to £35
FOOD: up to £15
Hours: breakast 8am–9am, dinner 6pm–7pm.
Cuisine: BRITISH / INTERNATIONAL – the restaurant enjoys an excellent reputation and has been justifiably nominated for a 'Taste of Scotland' award.
Other points: children welcome, pets allowed, parking, no-smoking area, residents' lounge.
Rooms: 5 double rooms, 3 twin rooms, 2 family rooms. All with TV, tea/coffee-making facilities, room-service.
Directions: turn right after leaving the Western Ferries terminal. The Ardtully can be found 200 yards away on the Dunoon Seafront.
JAMES & JAN THOMAS ☎ (01369) 702478.

ARGYLL HOTEL
Argyll Street, PA23 7NE

A family-run hotel centrally situated overlooking Argyll Gardens and Dunoon Pier, also with splendid views over the Firth of Clyde. The hotel offers comfortable accommodation where you can relax in a warm and friendly atmosphere and enjoy traditional fare.
DOUBLE ROOM: from £20 to £30
SINGLE ROOM: from £25 to £35
FOOD: up to £15
Hours: meals all day (open to non-residents) 9.30am–9.30pm.
Cuisine: BRITISH.
Cards: Visa, Access.
Other points: children welcome, residents' lounge, vegetarian meals.
Rooms: 30 bedrooms. All with TV, radio, telephone, alarm, tea/coffee-making faiclities.
Directions: prominently situated in Dunoon town centre.
MR & MRS FLETCHER ☎ (01369) 2059.

ROYAL MARINE HOTEL
Marine Parade, Hunter's Quay, PA23 8HJ

A family-run country-style mansion with restaurant situated on the sea front, offering well-presented, good food, making special use of Scottish produce, especially local fresh seafood. Friendly, attentive service and comfortable accommodation. Easy access from Glasgow when using Western Ferries, as you will disembark immediately opposite the Royal Marine Hotel.
DOUBLE ROOM: from £20 to £30
SINGLE ROOM: from £25 to £35
FOOD: up to £15
Hours: breakfast 8am–9.30am, bar meals 12noon–8.30pm, dinner 7pm–8.30pm.

SCOTLAND • STRATHCLYDE

Cuisine: BRITISH / CONTINENTAL – roast haunch of venison, haddock auld reekie, venison in red wine sauce, fillet of plaice Valkyrie, baked salmon royale.
Cards: Visa, Access, Switch.
Other points: garden, residents' lounge, games room, afternoon tea, children welcome, baby-listening device, cots, foreign exchange, residents' bar, entertainment, dinner/dances.
Rooms: 9 single rooms, 13 double rooms, 11 twin rooms, 2 family rooms. All with en suite, TV, telephone, tea/coffee-making facilities, radio.
Directions: off A815 to Dunoon. On seafront, opposite Western Ferries terminal.
MR ARNOLD & MR GREIG ☎ (01369) 705810 Fax (01369) 702329.

LES ROUTIERS
Information & Bookings Line
☎ 0171 610 1856

EASDALE • map 15C1

THE HARBOUR RESTAURANT
By Oban, PA34 4RF

Situated in the picturesque village and harbour of Easdale, this stone-built cottage tearoom and restaurant offers home-baking, locally-caught seafood specialities and a warm, friendly atmosphere. Wander around the adjoining country shop and be delighted with locally-made clothes and crafts. Well worth a visit.
FOOD: up to £15
Hours: meals all day 10.30am–5pm, closed November until March (inclusive).
Cuisine: BRITISH – seafood, home-baking, soups.
Cards: Visa, Access, AmEx.
Other points: children welcome, pets allowed, no-smoking area, open-air dining, vegetarian meals, afternoon teas.
Directions: off the A816 south from Oban, then B844 to Seil Island and Easdale.
MICHAEL & CATHERINE SHAW ☎ (01852) 300349 Fax (01852) 300349.

INSHAIG PARK HOTEL (formerly Easdale)
By Oban, PA34 4RF

A fine Victorian house standing in its own grounds overlooking the sea and the islands, with truly wonderful views. This is a small, family-run, comfortable hotel in an idyllic location, with good food served by friendly, helpful staff.
DOUBLE ROOM: from £20 to £30
SINGLE ROOM: from £25 to £35
FOOD: up to £15
Hours: breakfast 8.30am–9.15am, dinner 7.30pm–8.30pm.
Cuisine: ENGLISH.
Other points: licensed, children welcome, garden, pets allowed.
Rooms: 3 double rooms, 3 twin rooms. All with TV, tea/coffee-making facilities.
Directions: 16 miles south of Oban on Seil Island.
B. & S. FLETCHER & G. & C. DALE ☎ (01852) 300256.

GLASGOW • map 15E3

EWINGTON HOTEL
132 Queen's Drive,
G42 8QW

Ideally situated overlooking Queen's Park in a Victorian crescent, this historic, listed terraced hotel offers accommodation of a high standard complemented by good food and an excellent wine list. For business people and tourists 'the Ewington' is a friendly hotel to stay in. Golfing parties catered for. Convenient for Burrell Gallery.
DOUBLE ROOM: from £30 to £40
SINGLE ROOM: from £55
FOOD: up to £15 CLUB
Hours: breakfast 7am–9.30am, lunch 12.30am, last orders 2pm, dinner from 6pm, last orders 9pm.
Cuisine: INTERNATIONAL / SCOTTISH – all prepared on premises from fresh produce daily, including vegetarian dishes. Excellent wine list.
Cards: Visa, Access, Diners, AmEx.
Other points: licensed, children welcome, pets allowed, afternoon tea, open all year, conferences, room service, baby-listening device, trouser press, hairdryers, residents' lounge, residents' bar, parking, vegetarian meals.
Rooms: 12 single rooms, 8 double rooms, 21 twin room, 1 triple room. All with TV, radio, alarm, telephone, tea/coffee-making facilities, hair dryer.
Directions: take junction 20 from M8 onto A77, through 4 sets of lights, then second left is Queen's Drive.
MARIE-CLARE WATSON (GENERAL MANAGER)
☎ (0141) 423 1152 Fax (0141) 422 2030.

LA FIORENTINA
2 Paisley Road West, G51 1LF

Situated in the West End of Glasgow, dining at La Riviera makes you feel you are in the Italian Riviera, surrounded by paintings and mirrors reflecting, from one to the other, seaside and villages. You are dining in a friendly atmosphere, decorated and maintained to a high-class standard. The specialities of the house include fish-veal pasta, seafood dishes and vegetarian, complemented by an extensive wine list.
FOOD: up to £15
Hours: lunch 12noon–2.15pm, dinner 5.30pm–11pm, closed Monday.
Cuisine: ITALIAN.
Cards: Visa, Access, Diners, AmEx.
Other points: parking, disabled access, vegetarian meals, children welcome.
MR PIEROTTI ☎ (0141) 420 1585 Fax (0141) 420 3090.

TURBAN TANDOORI RESTAURANT
2 Station Road, Giffnock, G46 8JD

One of Scotland's finest Tandoori restaurants, in a residential suburb of Glasgow.
FOOD: up to £15
Hours: dinner 5pm–12midnight, closed Christmas.
Cuisine: INDIAN – Tandoori dishes.
Cards: Visa, Access, AmEx.

Other points: Sunday lunch, children welcome, coaches by prior arrangement
Directions: close to the A726 and the A77.
KURBIR PUREWAL ☎ (0141) 638 0069.

THE WATERSIDE INN
Glasgow Road, By Barrhead, G53 7TH
Unusual for the area, this 19th century inn with lounge eating facilities, in a prime location on the Glasgow–Irvine road. Already famous for the quality of its international cuisine, which can be enjoyed in both the lounge and restaurant. Only the freshest produce is used and all food is prepared daily. A separate menu for the lounge, comprising the best that can be found in the area. Recently refurbished, it is worth a visit: you won't be disappointed.
FOOD: from £15 to £20
Hours: lunch 11.30am–2.30pm, dinner 6.30pm–10.30pm, bar meals 11.30am–9.30pm.
Cuisine: INTERNATIONAL – freshly-cooked meals.
Cards: Visa, Access, Diners, AmEx.
Other points: parking, children welcome, pets allowed, no-smoking area, vegetarian meals, traditional Sunday lunch.
Directions: 300 yards on A736 from The Hurlet.
LENNIE WILSON ☎ (01418) 812822.

ISLE OF ARRAN • map 14A4

CATACOL BAY HOTEL
Catacol, KA27 8HN
Small, comfortable, family-run hotel. Seafront location overlooking Kilbrannan Sound and Kintyre Peninsula. Ideally based for fishing, climbing, pony-trekking, walking, golfing, bird-watching. Island breaks available October to April.
DOUBLE ROOM: up to £20
SINGLE ROOM: up to £25
FOOD: up to £15
Hours: bar meals 12noon–10pm.
Cuisine: SCOTTISH / INTERNATIONAL – all home-cooking, using local produce; large portions.
Cards: Visa, Access, Diners, AmEx, Switch, Delta.
Other points: licensed, open all day, Sunday buffet, children welcome, pets allowed.
Rooms: 3 single rooms, 1 double room, 1 twin room, 2 family rooms.
Directions: on the A841, 1¼ miles south of Lochranza Pier.
DAVID C. ASHCROFT ☎ (01770) 830231
[Fax] (01770) 830350.

ISLE OF BUTE • map 14A5

CRAIGMORE HOTEL
48 Crichton Road, Rothesay, PA20 9JT
A private, family-run hotel and health club commanding spectacular views over the Firth of Clyde. The accent is on quality, service and value, and there is a professionally-designed restaurant and lounge bar providing an elegant and relaxing atmosphere. Bedrooms are traditionally furnished, notably the honeymoon suite with its four-poster. Guests may take full advantage of the health club facilities.

DOUBLE ROOM: from £20 to £30
SINGLE ROOM: from £25 to £35
FOOD: up to £15
Hours: breakfast 8.30am–9.30am, dinner 7pm–9pm.
Cuisine: SCOTTISH / ENGLISH.
Cards: Visa, Access.
Other points: parking, children welcome, pets allowed, gym facilities, sauna, Jacuzzi, sunbed, conference facilities, residents' lounge, vegetarian meals.
Rooms: 16 bedrooms. All with en suite, TV, hair dryer, iron, baby-listening device, tea/coffee-making facilities.
Directions: 1 mile south of ferry terminal, on an elevated position.
MR & MRS LLOYD ☎ (01700) 503533.

ISLE OF COLONSAY • map 15D1

ISLE OF COLONSAY HOTEL
PA61 7YP
There are few places in Britain that offer such a spectacular setting as Colonsay. A listed building, the hotel enjoys a fine reputation for its comfort and cuisine, which uses the best of local fresh produce. On Colonsay there is an abundance of wildlife, including golden eagles and a major Atlantic seal colony. Important pre-Christian remains and portions of the the ancient Caledonian forest still survive here. A magical place for all ages.
DOUBLE ROOM: from £40 to £50
SINGLE ROOM: from £45 to £55
FOOD: from £15 to £20 [CLUB]
Hours: breakfast 8.30am–9.30am, bar snacks 12.30am–1.30pm, 7pm–8.30pm, dinner 7.30pm, closed 5th November until 28th February.
Cuisine: SCOTTISH / INTERNATIONAL.
Cards: Visa, Access, Diners, AmEx.
Other points: parking, children welcome, open bank holidays, no-smoking area, afternoon tea, disabled access, pets allowed, residents' lounge, vegetarian meals, garden, residents' bar, foreign exchange.
Rooms: 3 single rooms, 2 double rooms, 4 twin rooms, 2 family rooms. All with TV, tea/coffee-making facilities. Most en suite.
Directions: ferry from Oban on Monday, Wednesday and Friday. Hotel is 400 yards west of the pier. A courtesy car meets all sailings.
KEVIN & CHRISTA BYRNE ☎ (01951) 200316
[Fax] (01951) 200353.

ISLE OF IONA • map 17E1

ARGYLL HOTEL
PA76 6SJ
A friendly hotel, right on the Iona seashore. Cars are not allowed on this tiny, unspoilt island and must be left at Fionnphort or Oban. Iona, with its brilliant waters, clear light and wealth of wildlife, has inspired poets and painters for centuries. When staying at the Argyll Hotel, guests are also sure to be inspired by the superb home-cooking and the comfort of the rooms.

SCOTLAND • STRATHCLYDE

DOUBLE ROOM: from £30 to £40
SINGLE ROOM: from £25 to £35
FOOD: from £15 to £20 [CLUB] ☆
Hours: breakfast 8.15am–9am, lunch 12.30am–1.30pm, dinner 7pm–7.30pm, closed 8th October until Easter.
Cuisine: SCOTTISH – Scottish fare, using fresh local produce, own vegetables in season and also offering vegetarian dishes made with wholefoods.
Cards: Visa, Access, Switch.
Other points: Sunday lunch, no-smoking area, children welcome, pets allowed, open bank holidays, residents' lounges, garden, sun lounge, open fires.
Rooms: 6 single rooms, 7 double/twin rooms, 2 family rooms. Most en suite with tea/coffee-making facilities.
Directions: ferry Oban–Craignure. Drive/bus to Fionnphort, then ferry to Iona.
MRS F. MENZIES ☎ (016817) 334
[Fax] (016817) 334.

ISLE OF MULL • map 15C1

GLENFORSA HOTEL
Salen, By Aros, PA72 6JW
Delightfully situated in six acres of secluded woodland, this timber chalet-style hotel offers tasty, well-presented meals in a warm atmosphere. Accommodation is to a high standard. An ideal base for touring, walking, climbing or fishing.
DOUBLE ROOM: from £30 to £40
SINGLE ROOM: from £35 to £45
FOOD: from £15 to £20 ☆
Hours: breakfast 8.30am–9.30am, bar meals 12noon–2pm, 6pm–8.30pm, dinner 7pm–8.30pm.
Cuisine: SCOTTISH/INTERNATIONAL – fixed-price four-course menu, bar snacks/meals and vegetarian meals.
Cards: Visa, Access, AmEx.
Other points: licensed, no-smoking area, children welcome, garden, pets allowed.
Rooms: 13 bedrooms.
Directions: off the ferry, turn right; 10 miles along the road.
JEAN & PAUL PRICE ☎ (01680) 300377
[Fax] (01680) 300535.

PENNYGHAEL HOTEL
Pennyghael, PA70 6HB
An original 17th century farm, this family-run hotel provides a warm, welcoming atmosphere with personal, friendly service in a setting of unparalleled beauty on the shores of Loch Scridain. The restaurant offers spectacular views over the loch. The Island of Mull is a beautiful wilderness of coastline, moorland and mountain, which also boasts two 9-hole golf courses.
DOUBLE ROOM: from £30 to £40
FOOD: from £15 to £20
Hours: breakfast 7.30am–9.30am, lunch 11.30am–6pm, dinner 6.30pm–8.30pm, closed winter.
Cuisine: BRITISH – dinner menu changes daily and offers the best of traditional cooking, including wild Carsaig salmon, prawns, scallops and venison. Vegetarian dishes also available by arrangement.

Cards: Visa, Access.
Other points: licensed, open-air dining, Sunday lunch, children welcome, pets allowed, parking, afternoon tea, pets allowed.
Rooms: 3 double rooms, 3 twin rooms. All with TV, telephone, tea/coffee-making facilities.
Directions: turn left off ferry from Oban.
JAMES BOWMAN ☎ (016814) 288.

THE WESTERN ISLES HOTEL
Tobermory, PA75 6PR
A magnificent Gothic-style building, personally run and commanding a spectacular position overlooking Tobermory Bay. The rooms also have marvellous views and are superbly furnished, offering a high standard of comfort. Excellent menu using fresh local produce, including lobster and venison. Perfect location for those wishing to 'get away from it all'.
DOUBLE ROOM: from £40 to £50
FOOD: from £20 to £25 🍲 [CLUB]
Hours: breakfast 8am–9.30am, bar snacks 12noon–1.45pm, dinner 7pm–8.30pm, closed 3rd January until 21st January.
Cuisine: BRITISH.
Other points: children welcome, residents' lounge, no-smoking area, pets, vegetarian meals, garden, parking.
Rooms: 24 twin rooms. All with TV, telephone, tea/coffee-making facilities.
Directions: above town of Tobermory.
SUE & MICHAEL FINK ☎ (01688) 302012
[Fax] (01688) 302297.

JOHNSTONE • map 15E3

LYNNHURST HOTEL
Park Road, PA5 8LS
An original old Scottish stone-built house, now considerably modernized. Off the A737, 10 minutes from Glasgow Airport. Golf courses nearby.
DOUBLE ROOM: from £30 to £40
SINGLE ROOM: from £35 to £45
FOOD: up to £15 [CLUB]
Hours: lunch 12noon–2pm, Sunday 12noon–3pm, dinner 6.30pm–9pm, Saturday 6.30pm–10pm.
Cuisine: BRITISH – table d'hôte menus, extensive à la carte, bar lunches/suppers.
Cards: Visa, Access.
Other points: licensed, Sunday lunch, children welcome.
Rooms: 11 single rooms, 8 double/twin rooms, 2 family rooms. All with en suite, TV, radio, telephone, tea/coffee-making facilities.
Directions: off the A737 in Park Road.
MR N. & MISS J. MacINTRYE ☎ (01505) 324331 [Fax] (01505) 324219.

KILMARNOCK • map 15E3

COFFEE CLUB
30 Bank Street, KA1 1AH
There is something for everyone here depending on your appetite, purse and time. There are three restaurants with separate menus, all housed under

one roof. Each has the same lively atmosphere and friendly staff. You may bring your own wine.
FOOD: up to £15
Hours: meals all day 9am–10pm, Sunday 12noon–5.30pm.
Cuisine: INTERNATIONAL – fast-food on ground floor, e.g., American-style hamburgers. Downstairs, full service for special coffees, grills, omelettes, fish, pasta and vegetarian dishes.
Cards: Visa, Access, AmEx.
Other points: street parking, children welcome, functions.
Directions: Bank Street is off John Finnie Street, close to BR and bus stations.
MR S. KAMMING & MR W. MacDONALD
☎ (01563) 22048.

KILWINNING • map 15E2

MONTGREENAN MANSION HOUSE HOTEL
Montgreenan Estate, near Ayr, KA13 7QZ
A magnificent 18th century mansion with original brass and marble fireplaces and decorative plasterwork; its character has been carefully retained. Set in 45 acres of unspoilt parkland, with tennis, croquet, golf and billiards available. Award-winning Scottish fare served in the restaurant. Scottish Tourist Board 4 Crowns 'highly commended'.
DOUBLE ROOM: from £40 to £50
SINGLE ROOM: from £55
FOOD: from £15 to £20
Hours: breakfast 7am–10.30am, lunch 12noon–2.30pm, dinner 7pm–9.30pm.
Cuisine: SCOTTISH – award-winning fresh Scottish fare.
Cards: Visa, Access, Diners, AmEx.
Other points: no-smoking area, children welcome.
Rooms: 2 single rooms, 8 double rooms, 21 twin room.
Directions: 4 miles north of Irvine on the A736.
THE DOBSON FAMILY ☎ (01294) 557733
Fax (01294) 850397.

LARGS • map 15E2

GLEN ELDON HOTEL
2 Barr Crescent, KA30 8PX
Largs is a popular family seaside resort, and the Glen Eldon Hotel caters for the needs of families on holiday. It is a family-run establishment at the north end of Largs, close to the sea front, swimming pool, sports centre and golf course and not far from the town centre.
DOUBLE ROOM: from £20 to £30
SINGLE ROOM: from £25 to £35
FOOD: up to £15
Hours: dinner – weekdays 7pm–7.45pm, Saturday 5pm–9pm, Sunday 5pm–7.45pm, closed mid-January until mid-March.
Cuisine: SCOTTISH – Scottish dishes including haggis, venison, salmon and daily specials.
Cards: Visa, Access, AmEx.

Other points: children welcome.
Rooms: 1 single room, 3 double rooms, 3 twin rooms, 2 family rooms. All with TV, telephone, tea/coffee-making facilities.
Directions: on A78, midway between Glasgow and Prestwick airports.
MARY PATON ☎ (01475) 673381/674094
Fax (010475) 673381.

THE MANOR PARK HOTEL
PA17 5HE
A well-kept, Grade B listed mansion house hotel with many architectural features, beautifully set in 15 acres of landscaped gardens on the coast overlooking the islands of the Firth of Clyde. Good food and accommodation make this an ideal base from which to tour, play golf or sail.
DOUBLE ROOM: from £40 to £50
FOOD: from £15 to £20 CLUB ☆
Hours: breakfast 7.30am–10am, lunch 12.30am–2.30pm, dinner 7pm–10.30pm.
Cuisine: SCOTTISH – all menus cooked to order using only fresh ingredients. Scottish dishes a speciality. Bar meals, table d'hôte plus extensive à la carte menu.
Cards: Visa, Access, Diners, AmEx.
Other points: licensed, open-air dining, Sunday lunch, children welcome, garden, afternoon tea.
Rooms: 2 single rooms, 7 double rooms, 22 twin rooms, 3 family rooms.
Directions: midway between Skelmorlie and Largs on the A78.
MR WILLIAMS (MANAGER) ☎ (01475) 520832
Fax (01475) 520832.

LOCHGILPHEAD • map 15D2

LOCHGAIR HOTEL
Lochgair, PA31 8SA
A family-run hotel offering a warm welcome to all discerning travellers who enjoy good food in friendly, comfortable surroundings. Situated in the village of Lochgair, only 200 yards from the loch, the hotel enjoys wonderful views. Ideal base for exploring the Western Highlands and Islands. Activities include trout fishing, sea angling, pony-trekking, golf and sailing.
DOUBLE ROOM: from £20 to £30
SINGLE ROOM: from £25 to £35
FOOD: up to £15
Hours: breakfast 8.30am–9.30am, bar meals 12.15am–2.15pm, dinner 6.30pm–9pm, bar meals 6.30pm–9pm.
Cuisine: INTERNATIONAL – local game dishes, spare ribs, home-made lasagne, chicken curry, beef stroganoff, haddock, trout, salmon and venison.
Cards: Visa, Access.
Other points: licensed, open-air dining, Sunday lunch, no-smoking area, yacht anchorage, children welcome, afternoon tea, residents' lounge.
Rooms: 2 single rooms, 6 double rooms, 5 twin rooms, 1 family room. Many rooms are en suite.
Directions: on A83 Glasgow to Campbeltown road. 7 miles north of Lochgilphead.
JOHN & ELSIE GALLOWAY ☎ (01546) 86333.

STAG HOTEL
Argyll Street, PA31 8NE

A family-run, modern hotel, ideally situated in scenic Argyll for a touring or residential holiday or a short break. Good food and comfortable accommodation in a relaxed, informal atmosphere. Free golf available on local course.
DOUBLE ROOM: from £20 to £30
FOOD: up to £15
Hours: breakfast 7.30am–9.30am, lunch 12noon–2.30pm, bar meals 12noon–2pm, dinner 7pm–9pm, bar meals 6pm–8.30pm.
Cuisine: SCOTTISH – traditional Scottish cuisine and bar meals.
Cards: Visa, Access.
Other points: licensed, Sunday lunch, residents' lounge, pets allowed, sauna, solarium, disabled access, baby-listening device, cots.
Rooms: 4 single rooms, 4 double rooms, 9 twin rooms. All with TV, radio, alarm, telephone, tea/coffee-making facilities.
Directions: take A83 from Inverary (23 miles) or A816 from Oban.
JOYCE & BILL ROSS, HEATHER & DREW McGLYN ☎ (01546) 602496 Fax (01546) 603549.

MOTHERWELL • map 15E3

THE MOORINGS HOUSE HOTEL
114 Hamilton Road, ML1 3DW

A family-run hotel dating from the 1880s, offering a warm, relaxed atmosphere. The restaurant is in keeping with the original house, and guests can choose from a wide selection of international dishes. All food is prepared under the supervision of the head chef, who uses fresh Scottish produce whenever possible. The meals offer good value for money, particularly at lunchtime.
DOUBLE ROOM: up to £20
FOOD: up to £15
Hours: breakfast 7am–9am, lunch 12noon–2pm, dinner 6.30pm–9pm.
Cuisine: FRENCH – table d'hôte and à la carte meals. Classic French cooking with an accent on the unusual.
Cards: Visa, Access, AmEx.
Other points: licensed, Sunday lunch, children welcome, afternoon tea, pets allowed, garden.
Rooms: 6 single rooms, 4 double rooms, 14 twin rooms.
Directions: Motherwell exit off M74. 500 yards past Strathclyde Country Park.
DAVID KERR ☎ (01698) 258131 Fax (01698) 254973.

OBAN • map 15C2

ARDS HOUSE
Connel, PA37 1PT

A family-owned guest house situated on the main Tyndrum to Oban road, with magnificent views over the Firth of Lorn and Morvern hills. An excellent touring base for the Highlands. All rooms are neatly furnished with most modern facilities, including central heating and colour television. There is an antique grand piano for more artistic guests.
DOUBLE ROOM: from £20 to £30
SINGLE ROOM: from £25 to £35
FOOD: up to £15
Hours: breakfast 8.15am–9am, dinner 7.15pm (later by arrangement).
Cuisine: BRITISH.
Cards: Visa, Access.
Other points: licensed, no-smoking.
Rooms: 6 bedrooms.
Directions: A85 Tyndrum to Oban road, 4 miles north of Oban on the main A85.
MR & MRS J. BOWMAN ☎ (01631 71) 255.

FALLS OF LORA HOTEL
Connel Ferry, PA37 1PB

An imposing Victorian building in its own grounds set back from the A85. 100 yards from Connel railway station, overlooking Loch Etive. The cocktail bar has a roaring log fire and over 100 whiskies to tempt you.
DOUBLE ROOM: from £30 to £40
SINGLE ROOM: from £35 to £45
FOOD: from £15 to £20 ☆
Hours: breakfast 8am–9.30am, lunch 12.30am–2pm, bistro meals 12.30am–2pm, 5pm–9.30pm, dinner 7pm–8pm, closed Christmas day, closed 1st January until 1st February.
Cuisine: SCOTTISH / CONTINENTAL – a seven-course Scottish dinner on most Thursdays.
Cards: Visa, Access, Diners, AmEx.
Other points: licensed, residents' lounge, no-smoking area, children welcome, baby-listening device, cots, residents' bar.
Rooms: 6 single rooms, 8 double rooms, 13 twin rooms, 3 quad rooms. All with TV, radio, alarm, telephone, tea/coffee-making facilities.
Directions: set back from A85, 5 miles before Oban, half a mile from Connel Bridge.
MRS C.M. WEBSTER ☎ (01631) 710483 Fax (01631) 710694.

FOXHOLES HOTEL
Cologin, Lerags, PA34 4SE

Foxholes is peacefully situated in its own grounds in a quiet Glen just three miles south of Oban, with magnificent views of the surrounding countryside. An ideal spot for those who want to 'escape from it all', it offers tastefully furnished accommodation, a six-course table d'hôte dinner menu and an à la carte menu using the finest of fresh local Scottish produce. A marvellous place for any family holiday or romantic weekend break.
DOUBLE ROOM: from £20 to £30
Hours: breakfast 8am–9am, dinner 7pm–8pm.
Cuisine: BRITISH – fresh local produce. Table d'hôte menu, à la carte menu available on request.
Other points: parking, residents' lounge, vegetarian meals, garden.
Rooms: 5 double rooms, 2 twin rooms.
Directions: south from Oban, take the A816 for approximately 2 miles, turn right to Lerags, follow the road for ¾ mile, then turn right and continue for ¼ mile.
MR G. & MRS J. WAUGH ☎ (01631) 64982.

STRATHCLYDE • SCOTLAND

LOCH ETIVE HOTEL
Connel Village, PA37 1PH

A stone cottage-style building, modernized to a high standard and set in its own gardens bordered by a small river. The hotel derives its name from the nearby Loch Etive, and several of the rooms have views over the loch. Traditional Scottish hospitality is found here.
DOUBLE ROOM: from £20 to £30
SINGLE ROOM: from £25 to £35
FOOD: up to £15 ☆
Hours: breakfast 8.15am–9am, dinner 7pm–7.30pm, dinner available May until August, closed November until April.
Cuisine: BREAKFAST – dinner available May to August.
Other points: central heating, children welcome, pets allowed, residents' lounge, parking.
Rooms: 6 twin rooms. All with TV, tea/coffee-making facilities.
Directions: 200 yards from the A85 in Connel village.
MISS FRANÇOISE WEBER ☎ (01631/71) 400
Fax (0163171) 680.

PAISLEY • map 15E3

BRABLOCH HOTEL
62 Renfrew Road, PA3 4RD

This pretty mansion house is set in 4 acres of land, conveniently situated within two miles of Glasgow Airport, on the outskirts of Paisley. The restaurant serves a good selection of French and English cuisine, accompanied by a wide selection of wines.
DOUBLE ROOM: from £40 to £50
FOOD: from £15 to £20
Hours: breakfast 7am–10am, lunch 12noon–2pm, dinner 7.30pm–10pm.
Cuisine: FRENCH / ENGLISH – à la carte, table d'hôte and bar menus. Duck à l'orange, scampi Provençal.
Cards: Visa, Access, AmEx.
Other points: licensed, Sunday lunch, no-smoking area, children welcome, garden, afternoon tea, foreign exchange, residents' bar, residents' lounge, disabled access, vegetarian meals.
Directions: on the A741. Less than a mile south of the M8, junction 27.
LEWIS GRANT ☎ (0141) 889 5577.

PRESTWICK • map 14B5

LE BISTRO
83 Main Street, KA9 1JS

A friendly, relaxed atmosphere prevails in this intimate restaurant, where you can enjoy a tasty meal from the select menu. Fresh local produce is always used where possible.
FOOD: up to £15 ☆
Hours: meals all day 8.30am–10.30pm (last orders).
Cuisine: BRITISH / FRENCH – theme nights monthly. A la carte available weekends. Special set menu only £11.95.
Cards: Visa, Access.
Other points: children welcome, no-smoking area, vegetarian meals.

Directions: Situated in Prestwick town centre on main Prestwick–Ayr Road.
MR F. SHEPHERD ☎ (01292) 671063.

STRACHUR • map 15D2

THE CREGGANS INN
PA27 8BX

Stupendous views over Loch Fyne. Genuine country lodge atmosphere of log fires, and own house malt whisky, 'McPhunns'. Private walks, deerstalking and fishing by arrangement. All the food is based on Lady MacLean's famous cookbook recipes. Only 1 hour from Glasgow. Also, via Gournock, ferry across Clyde and A815 to Strachur. 5 moorings are available on Loch Fyne in front of the inn. Special winter breaks are available from October to May.
DOUBLE ROOM: from £40 to £50
FOOD: from £15 to £20 CLUB
Hours: open all day 8am–12midnight.
Cuisine: SCOTTISH/FRENCH – home-made soups, rainbow trout, Aberdeen Angus steaks, poached salmon, local seafood table including oysters, smoked salmon and langoustines, wild game. Parties of up to 40 people can be catered for in the restaurant. High chair available.
Cards: Visa, Access, Diners, AmEx.
Other points: children welcome, residents' lounge, residents' bar.
Rooms: 17 twin/double rooms. All with en suite, TV, telephone, tea/coffee-making facilities.
Directions: from Arrochar, take A83, over the 'Rest and be Thankful', then the A815 to Strachur.
SIR FITZROY MacLEAN ☎ (0136986) 279
Fax (0136986) 637.

TAYNUILT • map 15C2

TAYCHREGGAN HOTEL
Kilchrenan, By Taynuilt, PA35 1HQ

LES ROUTIERS
NEWCOMER of the Year 1995

The Taychreggan Hotel is set in 25 acres of beautiful Scottish countryside on the shores of Loch Awe. A former drovers' inn has been sympathetically built around, so becoming the superb hotel it is today. The restaurant offers freshly prepared and well-presented cuisine, much of which is grown or caught locally. Experienced, friendly staff are always on hand to ensure your stay is as relaxing and memorable as possible. (See special feature on page 14.)
DOUBLE ROOM: from £30 to £40
SINGLE ROOM: from £35 to £45
FOOD: from £20 to £25 CLUB
Hours: breakfast 8.15am–9.30am, bar meals 12.30am–2pm, dinner 7.30pm–9pm.
Cuisine: EUROPEAN – the emphasis is on local produce. Vegetarian meals available by arrangement. Bar lunches can be taken in the courtyard.
Cards: Visa, Access, AmEx.
Other points: parking, dogs allowed, residents' lounge, vegetarian meals, open-air dining.
Rooms: 15 bedrooms.
Directions: located on the B845, about seven miles south of Taynuilt.
DR EUAN & MRS ANNIE PAUL ☎ (018663) 211/366 Fax (018663) 244.

345

TAYVALLICH • map 15D1

TAYVALLICH INN
By Lochgilphead, PA31 8PR
Tayvallich Inn is situated in one of the most beautiful and picturesque locations in Scotland. Mr Grafton and his staff offer a warm welcome and serve really good food. Steaks and locally caught mussels, prawns, scallops and lobsters are the house specialities.
FOOD: from £15 to £20
Hours: lunch 12noon–2pm, dinner 6pm–9pm, closed Monday from November until March.
Cuisine: BRITISH – traditional meals. House speciality is seafood.
Cards: Visa, Access.
Other points: licensed, open-air dining, Sunday lunch, children welcome, open bank holidays, pets allowed.
Directions: off the A816 Lochgilphead to Crinan road.
JOHN & PAT GRAFTON ☎ (015467) 282.

TAYSIDE

ABERFELDY • map 16C4

FORTINGALL HOTEL
Fortingall, PH15 2NQ
Fortingall, where the hotel is situated, has a yew tree reputed to be the oldest vegetation in Europe. The rooms have outstanding views of the hills, with the River Tay and Lyon in the foreground. Widely known for its cuisine, fully supported by an extensive wine list, this hotel provides a relaxing and enjoyable dinner.
DOUBLE ROOM: from £30 to £40
FOOD: from £20 to £25 [CLUB]
Hours: breakfast 7.30am–9.30am, lunch 12noon–2pm, dinner 7pm–9pm, closed November until February.
Cuisine: SCOTTISH / ITALIAN – home-cooking, using local produce, the specialities being seafood and some Italian dishes.
Cards: Visa, Access, AmEx.
Other points: licensed, central heating, children welcome, residents' lounge, garden.
Directions: off the A827 and B846, 8 miles from Aberfeldy.
MR ALAN SCHOFIELD ☎ (01887) 830367.

ARBROATH • map 16C5

HOTEL SEAFORTH
Dundee Road, DD11 1QF
A 19th century stone manor house with modern extension, offering a warm, family welcome. Hotel Seaforth is a convenient base for visiting the nearby glens and castles; or you could spend a few days relaxing in the hotel's leisure centre. Surrounded by fine golf courses. Sea and river angling.
DOUBLE ROOM: from £20 to £30
SINGLE ROOM: from £35 to £45
FOOD: up to £15
Hours: breakfast 7.30am–9.30am, lunch 12noon–2pm, dinner 7pm–10pm, meals all day Sunday 12.30am–8pm.
Cuisine: BRITISH – traditional menus, featuring many Scottish dishes and local seafood.
Cards: Visa, Access, Diners, AmEx.
Other points: licensed, Sunday lunch, children welcome, swimming pool, Jacuzzi, games room, ballroom, pets allowed, residents' bar.

Rooms: 3 single rooms, 6 double rooms, 8 twin rooms, 3 family rooms. All with TV, telephone, tea/coffee-making facilities.
Directions: on the promenade.
ROBERT & CHRISTINE TINDALL ☎ (01241) 872232 [Fax] (01241) 877437.

AUCHTERARDER • map 16C4

BLACKFORD HOTEL
Moray Street, Blackford, PH4 1QF
A small, comfortable, family-run hotel, situated in the village of Blackford in the heart of Tayside, known as Scotland's Golfing County. The building is a 19th century coaching inn, attractively and comfortably furnished. Only 2 miles from Gleneagles, Blackford Hotel provides good food, comfortable accommodation, welcoming service and a friendly atmosphere.
DOUBLE ROOM: from £20 to £30
FOOD: up to £15 [CLUB]
Hours: breakfast 8am–9am, lunch 12noon–2pm, dinner 6pm–9pm.
Cuisine: ENGLISH – two menus: one changes daily. Dishes may include chicken kiev, herring in oatmeal, gammon steak, T-bone steak, salads.
Cards: Visa, Access, Diners, AmEx.
Other points: licensed, Sunday lunch, children welcome, garden, afternoon tea, pets allowed, central heating.
Directions: just off the A9 in village of Blackford, 4 miles from Auchterarder.
MIKE & ROSEMARY TOMCZYNSKI ☎ (01764) 682497.

BLAIRGOWRIE • map 16C4

ANGUS HOTEL
46 Wellmeadow, PH10 6NQ
Situated in the centre of the country town of Blairgowrie, the hotel is well located for touring the surrounding countryside. With golf, skiing and fishing nearby and a heated indoor swimming pool, sauna and spa bath, the hotel has something to interest most visitors. Presenting tasty meals and offering accommodation of a high standard.
DOUBLE ROOM: from £20 to £30

FOOD: up to £15 [CLUB]
Hours: breakfast 8am–9.30am, dinner 7pm–8.30pm, bar meals 12noon–1.45pm, 7pm–8.30pm.
Cuisine: BRITISH – dishes may include smoked salmon with capers and lemon wedges. Pan-fried rainbow trout in almond butter. Filo tartlet with broccoli-and-mornay sauce.
Cards: Visa, Access, AmEx.
Other points: licensed, open-air dining, Sunday lunch, no-smoking area, children welcome, afternoon tea, pets allowed, conferences, swimming pool, sauna, spa bath.
Rooms: 16 single rooms, 21 double rooms, 40 twin rooms, 3 triple rooms, 4 family rooms. All with TV, telephone, tea/coffee-making facilities.
Directions: A93, Perth to Braemar road.
ARNOLD SCOTT ☎ (01250) 872455 [Fax] (01250) 875615.

THE GLENISLA HOTEL
Kirkton of Glenisla, PH11 8PH
Set in the centre of picturesque Glenisla, one of the famous Angus Glens, this 17th century coaching inn combines the best of the old with the new. Recently redecorated, the inn retains its old-world charm while offering guests modern en suite accommodation, a welcoming bar, and a gracious dining room with good, wholesome Scottish and English fare. Conveniently located to enjoy many nearby sporting activities and the spectacular sights of Perthshire, Angus and the Grampians.
DOUBLE ROOM: from £20 to £30
SINGLE ROOM: from £25 to £35
FOOD: up to £15
Hours: breakfast 8am–10am, bar meals 12.30am–2.30pm, dinner 6.30pm–8.30pm, bar meals 6.30pm–8.45pm (last orders).
Cuisine: BRISTISH – fresh local meats, seafood, game, freshwater fish. Menu changes daily.
Cards: Visa, Access, MasterCard.
Other points: parking, children welcome, pets allowed, residents' lounge, garden, open-air dining, vegetarian meals, traditional Sunday lunch, afternoon teas.
Rooms: 6 bedrooms. All with tea/coffee-making facilities.
Directions: 16 miles north of Blairgowrie, 12 miles north of Alyth on B951.
SIMON & LYNDY BLAKE ☎ (01575) 582223 [Fax] (01575) 582223.

ROSEMOUNT GOLF HOTEL
Golf Course Road, Rosemount, PH10 6LJ
Located in a quiet suburb on the south side of Blairgowrie, this small, family-run hotel stands well back from the road in its own gardens, secluded by mature trees and with ample parking to the rear. There is comfortable accommodation in the main house and the garden annex, as well as in two self-catering chalets. Good food is available in both the restaurant and the bar, where you can relax and enjoy the friendly atmosphere.
DOUBLE ROOM: from £20 to £30
FOOD: up to £15
Hours: breakfast 8am–9am, lunch 12noon–2.15pm, dinner 5pm–9.30pm.

Cuisine: BRITISH – well-cooked traditional meals.
Cards: Visa, Access, MasterCard.
Other points: parking, children welcome, no-smoking area, conference facilities, residents' lounge, vegetarian meals, traditional Sunday lunch.
Rooms: 2 double/family rooms, 10 twin rooms. All with en suite, TV, telephone, tea/coffee-making facilities.
Directions: from A93 approaching Blairgowrie from the south, turn right onto Golf Course Road. The hotel is on your left after half a mile.
KATHLEEN & EUAN WALKER ☎ (01250) 872604 [Fax] (01250) 874496.

CARNOUSTIE • map 16C5

STATION HOTEL
Carnoustie, DD7 6AR
Originally an old railway hotel, now extensively refurbished, providing comfortable accommodation and fine-quality food. Very popular with golfers. Nearby places of interest include Barry Mill and Broughty Ferry.
DOUBLE ROOM: from £20 to £30
SINGLE ROOM: from £25 to £35
Hours: breakfast 7.30am–9.30am, high tea 5pm–7pm, lunch 12noon–2pm, dinner 7.30pm–9pm.
Cuisine: ENGLISH – traditional cuisine. Separate high tea menu. Bar snacks. Children's menu. Vegetarian dishes.
Cards: Visa, Access, AmEx.
Other points: Sunday lunch, children welcome, pets allowed, afternoon tea, parking, open bank holidays.
Rooms: 9 bedrooms.
Directions: off the A92, near Carnoustie railway station.
ARTHUR CHRISTIESON & IVOR FARMER ☎ (01241) 852447.

CRIEFF • map 16C4

FOULFORD INN
PH7 3LN
Originally a drovers' meeting place and coaching inn, this family-run hotel has much to explain its continuing success: comfortable, affordable accommodation, good home-style cooking, a friendly and lively family atmosphere, and spectacular views of the southern Grampians. Good value for money.
DOUBLE ROOM: up to £20
FOOD: up to £15
Hours: breakfast 8am–9am, lunch 12.15am–2pm, dinner 5pm–9pm, bar meals 6.30pm–9pm, closed 1st February until 28th February, open bank holidays.
Cuisine: SCOTTISH – tasty, freshly prepared food, well-cooked to a high standard.
Cards: Visa, Access.
Other points: licensed, Sunday lunch, children welcome, afternoon tea, vegetarian meals, residents' lounge, garden, disabled access, pets allowed, own golf course.
Rooms: 2 single, 3 double, 4 twin rooms.

SCOTLAND • TAYSIDE

Directions: situated off A85, turn right at Gilmerton turn-off on A822.
MR BEAUMONT ☎ (01764) 652407.

🍴 SMUGGLERS RESTAURANT
The Hosh, PH7 4HA

Previously an old warehouse, the restaurant forms part of the visitors' Heritage Centre at the Glenturret distillery. The site incorporates an audiovisual theatre and a 3-D exhibition. Visitors can also take the opportunity to taste the whiskies. For groups of up to 60 persons, try the Pagoda Room.
FOOD: up to £15
Hours: lunch 12noon–3pm, meals all day 10am–4pm.
Cuisine: SCOTTISH – Glenturret pâté, Tay salmon, venison in whisky sauce, gaugers (gateaux flavoured with malt liqueur).
Cards: Visa, Access, AmEx.
Other points: licensed, open-air dining, no-smoking area, children welcome, coaches by prior arrangement
Directions: on the A85 in north-west Crieff, towards Comrie.
GLENTURRET DISTILLERY LTD ☎ (01764) 656565 [Fax] (01764) 654366.

DUNKELD • map 16C4

🏨 ATHOLL ARMS HOTEL
Bridgehead, PH8 0AQ

Built in 1790, the hotel stands at the head of the fine five-arched bridge built by Thomas Telford, which spans the River Tay. Once a coaching inn, it is now a privately-run hotel offering traditional Scottish hospitality. The comfortable lounge and public bar retain the character and atmosphere of gracious living, with open fires and friendly service. The hotel is an ideal base while touring this beautiful part of Scotland.
DOUBLE ROOM: from £20 to £30
SINGLE ROOM: up to £25
FOOD: up to £15
Hours: breakfast 8am–9am, lunch 12noon–2pm, dinner 6pm–8.45pm.
Cuisine: SCOTTISH – the chef/proprietor personally supervises the kitchen, which provides excellent, freshly prepared food.
Cards: Visa, Access, AmEx.
Other points: parking, children welcome, pets allowed, garden, vegetarian meals.
Rooms: 5 single rooms, 14 twin rooms, 1 family room. Tea/coffee-making facilities, hair dryer available. TV in some rooms.
Directions: on the A923 overlooking Dunkeld Bridge and the River Tay.
CALLUM & ANNIE DARBISHIRE ☎ (01350) 727219 [Fax] (01350) 727219.

EDZELL • map 16B5

🏨 PANMURE ARMS HOTEL
High Street, DDG 7TA

Behind its imposing facade, the Panmure Arms Hotel offers good food and warm hospitality. The accommodation is comfortable, and a lively atmosphere prevails.
DOUBLE ROOM: from £30 to £40
FOOD: up to £15 [CLUB]
Hours: bbreakfast 7.30am–9.30am, lunch 12noon–2pm, bar meals 12.30am–9.30pm, dinner 7pm–9pm, supper 6.30pm–9.30pm, Sunday roast 12.30am–7pm.
Cuisine: SCOTTISH – traditional Scottish cooking. Adventurous menu and large portions. Good value for money.
Cards: Visa, Access, Diners, AmEx.
Other points: licensed, Sunday lunch, children welcome, pets allowed, residents' lounge, open bank holidays.
Rooms: 2 single rooms, 15 double rooms, 24 twin rooms, 2 family rooms.
Directions: on main road through village.
MR CALE ☎ (01356) 648420 [Fax] (01356) 648588.

FORFAR • map 16C5

🏨 ROYAL HOTEL
Castle Street, DD8 3AE

Fine old coaching house in the centre of historic Forfar. All rooms are tastefully appointed with en suite facilities. The proprietors, both local, take special pride in making sure their guests enjoy excellent food in comfortable surroundings. The accommodation was extended and more rooms were added during 1994.
DOUBLE ROOM: from £30 to £40
FOOD: up to £15 [CLUB]
Hours: breakfast 7am–10am, lunch 12noon–2pm, dinner 7pm–9pm.
Cuisine: BRITISH – specialities include light fish mousse made from Arbroath smokies, prime Angus sirloin steak, venison and salmon from local rivers.
Cards: Visa, Access, Diners, AmEx.
Other points: licensed, Sunday lunch, children welcome, garden, gym facilities, Jacuzzi, swimming pool, functions, conferences.
Directions: off the A94, situated in the centre of Forfar.
ALISON & BRIAN BONNYMAN ☎ (01307) 462691 [Fax] (01307) 462691.

GLENSHEE • map 16B4

🏨 THE BLACKWATER INN
Glenshee By Blairgowrie, PH10 7LH

Nestling at the base of a steep hill in a landscaped heather and waterfall garden, this quaint old inn gives the impression that you have stepped back in time into Brigadoon! Situated on the main road to Balmoral, there is skiing, golf, fishing, stalking and hang-gliding available nearby.
DOUBLE ROOM: up to £20
FOOD: up to £15
Hours: breakfast (Sunday) 9am–10am, meals all day.
Cuisine: SCOTTISH / LOUISIANA – home-made pies, pastas, curries and Louisiana-style dishes. Daily specials.

Cards: Visa, Access.
Other points: children welcome, pets allowed, children welcome.
Directions: from south, take A93 Blairgowrie to Braemar road. 9 miles north of Blairgowrie on left-hand side of the road.
IVY BAILEY ☎ (01250) 882234.

KENMORE • map 15C3

CROFT-NA-CABER
Croft-na-Caber, PH15 2HW
A unique leisure village, set in the beautiful hills of Perthshire on the shores of Loch Tay. Comfortable accommodation in the hotel and in luxury log chalets, and good food, with the choice of good-value bar menus or dinner in the elegant Garden Restaurant. Relax and absorb the beauty and peace of Loch Tay, or enjoy the extensive choice of activities available on both land and loch.
DOUBLE ROOM: from £20 to £30
FOOD: up to £15
Hours: breakfast 8.30am–9.30am, light meals all day, lunch in restaurant 12.30am–2pm, dinner in restaurant 7pm–9pm.
Cuisine: SCOTTISH – first-class restaurant menu, with a selection of à la carte and table d'hôte available for lunch and dinner. Also a good selection of bar meals. 'Taste of Scotland'.
Cards: Visa, Access.
Other points: licensed, open-air dining, Sunday lunch, no-smoking area, children welcome, afternoon tea, pets allowed, water sports, special breaks, craft shop, coffee shop, parking, vegetarian meals, residents' bar, residents' lounge, disabled access.
Directions: A827 to Kenmore, then 500 yards along south side of Loch Tay.
CHARLES BARRATT ☎ (01887) 830236
[Fax] (01887) 830649.

KINROSS • map 16D4

BALGEDIE TOLL TAVERN
Wester Balgedie, KY13 7HE
An original toll house, with open fires, wooden beams and brasses giving a pleasant olde-worlde feel. The home-made food is excellent, and all guests are made to feel immediately welcome by the friendly and efficient staff. A very popular rendezvous, with many visitors travelling from far afield to enjoy the good food and convivial atmosphere.
FOOD: up to £15
Hours: lunch 12noon–2pm, dinner 5.30pm–9pm, bar 11am–3pm & 5pm–11pm.
Cuisine: BRITISH – comprehensive and imaginative menu with specials board; traditional dishes may include prime Scottish steaks with various garnishes, salmon and venison. Assorted home-made vegetarian dishes available.
Cards: Visa, Access.
Other points: licensed, open-air dining, parking, children welcome, beer garden, patio, real ales.
Directions: 1 mile south-east of junction 8 of the M90. North shore of Loch Leven in fork of A911 and B919.
ANDREW M. GLEBOCKI ☎ (01592) 840212.

KIRKLANDS HOTEL
High Street, KY13 7AN
This is an original coaching inn, fully refurbished to provide comfortable, modern accommodation and attractive surroundings in which to enjoy a home-cooked meal. There are many leisure activities nearby for the sports person, and for the holiday-maker, Lochleven Castle, the Scottish Falconry Centre and many other places of interest are within easy travelling distance.
DOUBLE ROOM: from £30 to £40
SINGLE ROOM: from £35 to £45
FOOD: up to £15
Hours: breakfast 7.30am–9am, bar meals 12noon–2pm, dinner 6pm–9pm.
Cuisine: SCOTTISH – fresh home-cooked meals.
Other points: parking, children welcome, no-smoking area, vegetarian meals.
Rooms: 3 double rooms, 5 twin rooms, 1 family room. All with en suite, TV, telephone, hair dryer, trouser-press, tea/coffee-making facilities.
Directions: M90 junction 6 to Kinross town centre, then turn left. The hotel is 50 yards along.
ROBERT & GAIL BOATH ☎ (01577) 863313
[Fax] (01577) 863313.

THE MUIRS INN KINROSS
49 Muirs, KY13 7AU
Situated on the 'Moorland of Kinross', this inn dates back to the 1800s, when it was originally a small farmhouse where the blacksmith lodged. The food is appetizing, well presented, generously portioned and of good quality, and the en suite accommodation is also of a very high standard. A unique feature is the vast array of real ales, beers, lagers, ciders, wines and spirits that this little inn stocks from all over the world, including its own-branded brewery-conditioned beers, and a connoisseurs' choice of around 130 malt whiskies. A truly fascinating place for business or pleasure. Loch Leven Castle, where Mary Queen of Scots was imprisoned, is nearby, as are 130 golf courses. All Scotland's major cities too are within driving distance.
DOUBLE ROOM: from £20 to £30
SINGLE ROOM: from £35 to £45
FOOD: up to £15 [CLUB] ☆
Hours: breakfast 7am–9am, Sunday 8am–10am, lunch 12noon–2pm, high tea 5pm–6pm, dinner 7pm–9pm, country supper 5pm–9pm, bar snacks 12noon–2pm, 7pm–10.30pm.
Cuisine: SCOTTISH – Scottish high teas also available.
Cards: Visa, Access, MasterCard.
Other points: parking, children welcome, high teas, disabled access, vegetarian meals, open-air dining.
Rooms: 3 double rooms, 2 twin rooms.
Directions: M90 exit junction 6, follow A922 (Milnathort) signs at T-junction; the inn is diagonally opposite on right.
THE INNKEEPER ☎ (01577) 862270
[Fax] (01577) 862270.

KIRKMICHAEL • map 16B4

THE LOG CABIN HOTEL
PH10 7NB

A large hotel built of whole Norwegian logs, set in the hills amid a majestic pine forest. Family-run, a definite après ski atmosphere prevails in winter. A superb four-course dinner can be enjoyed in the Edelweiss restaurant, while the Viking Bar serves a comprehensive selection of bar meals. A unique base from which to explore the Perthshire area.
DOUBLE ROOM: from £20 to £30
SINGLE ROOM: from £25 to £35
FOOD: up to £15
Hours: breakfast 8.45am–9.30am, lunch 12noon–1.45pm, dinner 7.30pm–8.45pm, open all year.
Cuisine: BRITISH – daily specials in the bar. Table d'hôte evening menu, using fresh local produce.
Cards: Visa, Access, Diners, AmEx.
Other points: licensed, open-air dining, Sunday lunch, children welcome, pets by prior arrangement, garden, disabled access.
Rooms: 5 double rooms, 4 twin rooms, 4 family rooms. All with radio, tea/coffee-making facilities.
Directions: off the A924. Equidistant from Pitlochry and Blairgowrie.
ALAN FINCH & DAPHNE KIRK ☎ (01250) 881288 Fax (01250) 881402.

MILNATHORT • map 16D4

THE THISTLE HOTEL
25-27 New Road, KY13 7XT

A small, residential country inn in a rural setting, only 1½ miles from Kinross and the M90 junction. Under the personal supervision of the managers, Mr and Mrs Quinn, The Thistle Hotel provides welcoming, friendly service and good food in the lounge bar and in the restaurant at weekends.
DOUBLE ROOM: up to £20
SINGLE ROOM: up to £25
FOOD: up to £15
Hours: breakfast 8am–9am, lunch 12noon–2pm, bar meals 12noon–2pm, 6pm–9pm, high tea weekends 5pm–7.30pm, dinner 6pm–9pm.
Cuisine: ENGLISH – specialities include steaks and home-made pâté. A la carte and bar meals. Home-made sweets, own sticky toffee pudding and apple toffee pecan pie.
Cards: Visa, Access.
Other points: licensed, Sunday lunch, children welcome, pets allowed.
Rooms: 1 single room, 1 double en suite, 2 twin rooms, 1 family room. All with TV, tea/coffee-making facilities.
Directions: M90 junction 6. A91 Perth to Stirling road in Milnathort.
MR J. HARLEY ☎ (01577) 863222.

MONTROSE • map 16B5

LINKS HOTEL
Mid Links, DD10 8RL

Recently refurbished to a high standard, the Links Hotel is located in a prime setting overlooking public gardens. The hotel is ideally suited for touring the east coast of Scotland and Grampians.
DOUBLE ROOM: from £30 to £40
SINGLE ROOM: from £35 to £45
FOOD: up to £15
Hours: breakfast 7.30am–9.30am, Sunday 8am–10am, dinner and bar suppers in the conservatory 12noon–2pm, 6.30pm–9.30pm, open all year, open bank holidays.
Cuisine: SCOTTISH – traditional cuisine. Traditional high tea every Sunday.
Cards: Visa, Access, Diners, AmEx.
Other points: licensed, Sunday lunch, children welcome, afternoon tea, residents' lounge, baby-listening device, baby-sitting, cots, 24hr reception, foreign exchange, left luggage.
Rooms: 3 single rooms, 7 double rooms, 10 twin rooms. All with TV, telephone, tea/coffee-making facilities, radio, alarm.
Directions: 2 minutes' walk from the town centre.
MR G.W. NINTEMAN ☎ (01674) 671000
Fax (01674) 672698.

PERTH • map 16C4

ALMONDBANK INN
Almondbank, PH1 3NH

Olde-worlde inn overlooking the River Almond in an attractive country village. Good food at very reasonable prices, friendly staff and a fun local atmosphere.
FOOD: up to £15
Hours: Lunch Monday–Saturday 12noon–2.15pm, Sunday 12.30am–9.15pm, bar tea Sunday–Thursday 5pm–10.30pm, Friday and Saturday 6.30pm–10pm.
Cuisine: ENGLISH – all fresh ingredients used: fresh melon, prawn and cheese salad, steaks, fresh salmon and prawn salad, plus a wide variety of special dishes.
Cards: Visa, Access.
Other points: licensed, Sunday lunch, children welcome, beer garden.
Directions: middle of main street of Almondbank village, about 3 miles from Perth.
MR & MRS C. LINDSAY ☎ (01738) 583242.

PITLOCHRY • map 16B4

ADDERLEY PRIVATE HOTEL
23 Tobergargan Road, PH16 5HG

Centrally situated, the Adderley Private Hotel and its sister hotel, Carra Beag Guest House, which is located 100 yards down the road, are both small, friendly hotels. They both have good accommodation and comfortable lounges in which to relax. A varied menu is on offer, vegetarian meals are available, and special diets can be catered for. This is a perfect base for touring, fishing, golfing, walking or simply relaxing.
DOUBLE ROOM: from £20 to £30
SINGLE ROOM: from £25 to £35
FOOD: up to £15
Hours: breakfast 8am–9am, dinner 6pm–6.30pm (residents only).

Other points: parking, children welcome, pets allowed, no-smoking area, residents' lounge.
Rooms: 1 single room, 2 double rooms, 1 twin room, 3 family rooms. All with en suite, satellite TV, tea/coffee-making facilities. Nine more rooms at the Carra Beag.
Directions: off A9 in Pitlochry, 200 metres from the town centre.
ARCHIE & MARY McGHIE ☎ (01769) 472433/ 472835.

🏨 CRAIGOWER HOTEL
134 Atholl Road, PH16 5AB
A delightful, family-run hotel occupying a prime position in the centre of Pitlochry, offering every comfort. Ideally situated within reach of all amenities, Pitlochry itself has much to offer, including golf, tennis, bowling, fishing, a cinema, and more. Nearby attractions include Blair Castle, the historic pass of Killiecrankie, and many breathtaking countryside walks.
DOUBLE ROOM: from £20 to £30
FOOD: up to £15
Hours: breakfast 8am–10am, morning coffee 10am–12noon, dinner 6.30pm–9.30pm, bar meals 9pm–11pm.
Cuisine: BRITISH – grilled rainbow trout, roast gigot of lamb, baked Madeira, choice of salads. Extensive wine list. Restaurant open all day for meals or snacks.
Cards: Visa, Access.
Other points: open-air dining, Sunday lunch, no-smoking area, pets allowed, afternoon tea, vegetarian meals, residents' lounge, garden, parking, children welcome, baby-listening device, cots, left luggage.
Rooms: 2 single rooms, 10 double rooms, 10 twin rooms, 4 triple rooms. All with TV, telephone, tea/coffee-making facilities.
Directions: Pitlochry, situated in the town centre.
ROBERT & JEAN WILSON ☎ (01796) 472590 [Fax] (01796) 472590.

🏨 GREEN PARK HOTEL
Clunie Bridge Road, PH16 5JY
This is a country house hotel situated on the banks of the lovely Loch Faskally, and although secluded, it is only five minutes' walk from the centre of the town. Popular with golfers because of the nearby golf course. Other facilities include fishing, sailing, golf and walking. Casserole Award winner 1990, 1991 and 1994.
DOUBLE ROOM: from £30 to £40
SINGLE ROOM: from £35 to £45
FOOD: from £15 to £20
Hours: dinner 6.30pm–8.30pm, bar meals 12noon–2.30pm, bar meals 6pm–8.30pm, closed November until mid-March.
Cuisine: SCOTTISH – Scottish cuisine, e.g., salmon, venison, Highland bonnets.
Cards: Visa, Access, Switch.
Other points: children welcome, no-smoking area, fishing.
Rooms: 2 single rooms, 12 double rooms, 23 twin rooms.
Directions: on the A924 in north-west Pitlochry, on the left as you leave town.
MR & MRS GRAHAM BROWN ☎ (01796) 473248 [Fax] (01796) 473520.

🏨 SCOTLAND'S HOTEL
Bonnethill Road, PH16 5BT
Centrally yet quietly located in picturesque Pitlochry, this friendly, family-owned and operated hotel enjoys a good reputation for comfortable bedrooms, fine food and attentive service. A new indoor leisure club features a 12-metre swimming pool, spa bath, solarium, sauna, mini-gym and beauty salon. Complimentary mini-bus to/from the Festival Theatre, railway station and golf course.
DOUBLE ROOM: from £30 to £40
FOOD: from £15 to £20
Hours: breakfast 7.30am–9.30am, lunch 12noon–2pm, dinner 6.30pm–8.30pm.
Cuisine: SCOTTISH – table d'hôte with ample choice. A la carte also available. Speciality: salmon.
Cards: Visa.
Other points: licensed, parking, children welcome, garden, children welcome, pets allowed, launderette, cots, bar.
Rooms: 13 single rooms, 1 double rooms, 23 twin rooms, 13 family rooms. All with TV, radio, telephone, tea/coffee-making facilities.
Directions: follow slip road from A9 or A924 into the centre of town. Turn off opposite Co-op, to find hotel on the right.
ERHARD J. PENKER & FAMILY ☎ (01796) 472292 [Fax] (01769) 473284.

WESTERN ISLES

ISLE OF BARRA • map 17D1

🏨 CASTLEBAY HOTEL
Castlebay, BA80 5XD
A small, family-run hotel in the main village overlooking the harbour and the Isle of Vatersay. Comfortable accommodation and good food. While visiting here you can enjoy walking, fishing or sailing. If you would rather relax, there are plenty of beautiful, secluded, sandy beaches to choose from.
DOUBLE ROOM: from £30 to £40
FOOD: from £15 to £20
Hours: breakfast 7.30am–9.30am, lunch 12.30am–2pm, bar meals 11am–9pm, dinner 6pm–9pm.
Cuisine: ENGLISH – traditional cuisine, with an emphasis on fresh fish. Dishes may include mussels in white wine sauce, lobster, chicken chasseur, strawberry gateau.
Cards: Visa, Access.
Other points: licensed, open-air dining, Sunday lunch, children welcome, afternoon tea, pets

SCOTLAND • WESTERN ISLES

allowed, special breaks, foreign exchange, residents' lounge, residents' bar, parking.
Rooms: 10 twin rooms. All with TV, telephone, tea/coffee-making facilities.
Directions: in the centre of Castlebay.
MR GEORGE MacLEOD ☎ (018714) 223.

ISLE OF BENBECULA • map 17C1

DARK ISLAND HOTEL
Liniclate, PA88 5PJ

Privately-owned hotel, offering comfortable, well-appointed accommodation, good food and service. Ideal holiday base, being well-situated for exploring adjacent islands: North Uist, Barra, Eriskay. Golf is available free of charge, and there is trout fishing on over 70 lochs. This is also the perfect place to stay if you are a keen archeologist or ornithologist.
DOUBLE ROOM: from £30 to £40
FOOD: from £15 to £20
Hours: bar meals 12noon, bar meals 6pm–10pm.
Cuisine: BRITISH – 'Taste of Scotland' cuisine, specialities seafood and shellfish. Also Laird's game casserole, Ben Mor mountain haggis and shepherd's grill.
Cards: Visa, Access.
Other points: children welcome, pets allowed, open bank holidays, residents' lounge.
Rooms: 8 single rooms, 22 double rooms, 13 twin rooms, 1 family room. All with TV, radio, alarm, tea/coffee-making facilities.
Directions: 4 miles from airport, 26 miles from ferry terminals (Loch Boisdale and Lochmaddy).
MR D.J. PETERANNA ☎ (01870) 603030
Fax (01870) 602347.

ISLE OF HARRIS • map 17B1

THE HARRIS HOTEL
Tarbert, Harris, PA85 3DL

An established family-run hotel. J.M. Barrie once stayed here and etched his initials in the dining-room window. The hotel is a perfect base for touring Harris and Lewis, and people return year after year to soak up the history, peace and unspoilt beauty of these dramatic islands.
DOUBLE ROOM: from £30 to £40
SINGLE ROOM: from £25 to £35
FOOD: CLUB
Hours: breakfast 8.30am–9.15am, lunch 12noon–2pm, dinner 7.30pm–9pm.
Cuisine: BRITISH.
Cards: Visa, Access.
Other points: central heating, children welcome, residents' lounge, garden.
Rooms: 1 single room, 6 double rooms, 15 twin rooms, 2 family rooms.
Directions: on the A859 central to village of Tarbert.
HELEN & JOHN MORRISON ☎ (01859) 2154/2425.

ISLE OF LEWIS • map 17A1

CORRAN VIEW GUEST HOUSE
22a Breasclete, Callanish, PA86 9EF

At Corran View you are assured of a friendly welcome. Christine and Alan's aim is to offer their guests comfort, good food and personal attention. Most rooms have a view over East Loch Roag and the surrounding Uig and Harris hills, where you can watch the sun go down. This location is ideal for touring, walking, sailing, fishing and sightseeing.
DOUBLE ROOM: from £20 to £30
FOOD: from £15 to £20
Hours: breakfast 8.30am, dinner 6.30pm, closed Christmas and New Year.
Cuisine: BRITISH – Hebridean seafood platter, local salmon, home-made soups and delicious sweets.
Cards: Visa, Access.
Other points: parking, children welcome, no-smoking area, residents' lounge, garden, vegetarian meals.
Rooms: 2 double rooms, 1 twin room. All with en suite, TV, radio, alarm, hair dryer, tea/coffee-making facilities.
Directions: off A858, approximately 2 miles north of Callanish Standing Stones. 18 miles from Stornoway, 40 miles from Tarbert ferry terminals.
CHRISTINE & ALAN HESLOP ☎ (01851) 621300.

NORTH UIST • map 17B1

LOCHMADDY HOTEL
Lochmaddy, PA82 5AA

Having undergone extensive restoration, this family-run sporting hotel offers good-quality food and comfortable accommodation in tastefully furnished surroundings. The Lochmaddy is ideally situated for access to nearby beaches, fishing lochs, bird reserves and archeological sites.
DOUBLE ROOM: from £30 to £40
SINGLE ROOM: from £35 to £45
FOOD: from £15 to £20
Hours: breakfast 8am–9.30am, bar meals 12noon–2pm, 5.30pm–9pm, dinner 6.30pm–9pm, open all year.
Cuisine: MODERN BRITISH – daily changing menus offering a wide selection of different dishes, including honey roast duck with apple and cranberry sauce, and salmon mornay.
Cards: Visa, Access, AmEx.
Other points: licensed, Sunday lunch, children welcome, pets allowed, afternoon tea, garden, residents' lounge, parking, baby-listening device, cots, residents' bar.
Rooms: 5 single rooms, 5 double rooms, 5 twin rooms. All with TV, radio, alarm, telephone, tea/coffee-making facilities.
Directions: 100 yards from Lochmaddy ferry terminal.
☎ (01876) 500331/500332 Fax (01876) 500210.

TELEPHONE

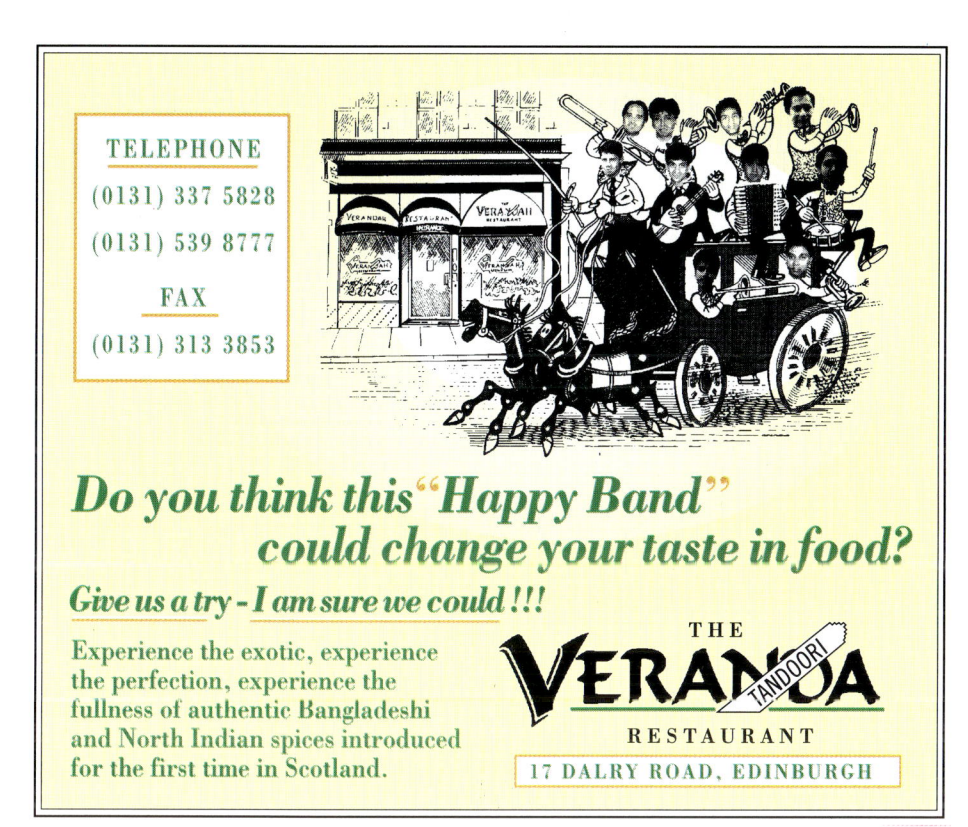

(0131) 337 5828

(0131) 539 8777

FAX

(0131) 313 3853

Do you think this "Happy Band" could change your taste in food?

Give us a try - I am sure we could !!!

Experience the exotic, experience the perfection, experience the fullness of authentic Bangladeshi and North Indian spices introduced for the first time in Scotland.

THE VERANDA TANDOORI RESTAURANT

17 DALRY ROAD, EDINBURGH

For full details see Lothian, Edinburgh

OUR FRENCH SELECTION

LES ROUTIERS 25 VANSTON PLACE LONDON SW6 1AZ

ROYAL MARINE HOTEL

And Garden Restaurant

Marine Parade, Hunter's Quay, Dunoon, Argyll PA23 8HJ

TEL: (01369) 705810 ◇ FAX: (01369) 702329

For full details see Strathclyde, Dunoon

The Falls of Lora Hotel

Connel Ferry, by Oban, Argyll PA37 1PB

Proprietor: Mrs C.M. Webster
Telephone: (01631) 710483 • Facsimile: (01631) 710694

For full details see Strathclyde, Oban

IRELAND

Ireland is excellent touring country – a world where time has stood still, a wild and enchanting landscape of emerald-green, windswept moors, remote lakes, ever-changing scenery and dramatic skies.

There are now 35 *Les Routiers* establishments throughout Ireland. Some have won major awards for their outstanding food and accommodation, but they all offer the same unmistakable warm, friendly welcome in the true Irish spirit. In recognition of their conscientious efforts to make every visitor feel welcome, and for providing excellent quality and value, *Les Routiers* has given its establishments in Ireland their very own award. (See page 15 for further details.)

The scenery in Ireland is as pleasing as the Irish hospitality itself. In the north, the famous Mountains of Mourne – idolized in song – with their twelve magnificent rounded summits are particularly worth seeing. The Sperrin Mountains are networked by tiny streams and roads where the walker and naturalist is often rewarded with sightings of golden plover and red grouse. The countryside is also scattered with many National Trust properties, such as Castle Coole, and Florence Court from which the yew tree originated.

Extraordinarily beautiful is the only way to describe southern Ireland. The breathtaking scenery varies immensely, from the lush inland pastures interspersed with tiny villages to the rugged coastal peninsulas and miles of golden, sandy beaches washed by the warm waters of the Gulf Stream. The warm coastal climate also provides some of Ireland's abundant seafood, such as mussels from West Cork and scallops from Kenmare Bay.

Baked Killyleagh trout, swordfish steaks, roast monkfish, guinea fowl, game terrine and lamb kebabs are just a few of the many exquisite dishes that the visitor can expect to find on the daily menu, alongside traditional British and adventurous continental choices.

Visitors seeking interesting places to visit and explore are spoilt for choice. Probably the most famous of all can be found in County Cork: Blarney Castle, with its Blarney Stone. Other regional attractions, to name but a few, include the Waterford Crystal Centre in County Waterford; Glendalough, a 6th century monastic settlement in the Wicklow Mountains; in County Cork, Fota House and Estate, Ireland's first wildlife park; the Irish Transport Museum at Killarney in County Kerry; and the Limerick City Gallery of Art.

Altogether, a charming land of equally charming people with a twinkle in their eye, who will welcome you as good friends – this is *Les Routiers* in Ireland.

Les Routiers establishments throughout Ireland listed in this chapter appear in the alphabetical order of their county:

CO. ANTRIM
CO. CLARE
CO. CORK
CO. DONEGAL
CO. DOWN
CO. DUBLIN
CO. FERMANAGH
CO. GALWAY
CO. KERRY
CO. KILKENNY
CO. LIMERICK
CO. LOUTH
CO. MAYO
CO. OFFALY
CO. SLIGO
CO. TYRONE
CO. WEXFORD

BELFAST
Co. Antrim • map 13D3

🍴 SAINTS & SCHOLARS LTD
3 University Street,
University & Malone, BT7 1FY

Highly popular and attractively furnished bistro-style restaurant on two floors, with a bar on each. The atmosphere is warm, welcoming and lively. Nearby places of interest include the Ulster Museum and Queens University.
FOOD: up to £15 [CLUB]
Hours: meals all day Monday to Saturday 12noon–11pm; Sunday lunch 12noon, dinner 5.30pm–9.30pm.
Cuisine: BRITISH – à la carte menu, combining traditional and modern dishes, complemented by a fine wine list. Vegetarian dishes available.
Cards: Visa, Access, Diners, AmEx.
Other points: licensed, Sunday lunch, children welcome, vegetarian meals, open bank holidays, parking.
Directions: situated on the left, off University Road, before Queens University.
DIRK LAKEMAN ☎ (01232) 325137
[Fax] (01232) 323240.

LES ROUTIERS
ACCOMMODATION DIRECTORY

This handy directory is ideal for those looking for somewhere to stay at great value.
It lists a huge choice of *Les Routiers*-recommended places throughout the British Isles offering comfortable accommodation, good food and a warm welcome amid relaxed surroundings.

Available from selected
Les Routiers establishments
or direct from the publishers.

Price £2

BUSHMILLS
Co. Antrim • map 13B3

🏨 HILLCREST COUNTRY HOUSE & RESTAURANT
306 Whitepark Road, BT57 8SN

An internationally renowned, award-winning guest house, offering comfortable and well-appointed accommodation in spacious en suite rooms, all with marvellous coastal or rural views. The restaurant offers traditional menus using the finest fresh ingredients, specializing in local seafood and game. Beautifully furnished throughout, and highly recommended. Les Routiers Restaurant of the Year: Ireland 1994.
DOUBLE ROOM: from £20 to £30
SINGLE ROOM: from £25 to £35
FOOD: from £15 to £20 🍷 🍴 [CLUB]
Hours: breakfast 8.30am–9.30am, lunch 12.30am–2.30pm, dinner 5pm–9pm, closed

Monday to Saturday 1st October until 31st April.
Cuisine: BRITISH – food and service of the highest standard.
Cards: Visa, Access.
Other points: parking, children catered for (please check for age limits), Sunday lunch, no-smoking area, disabled access, residents' lounge, vegetarian meals, garden.
Rooms: 1 double room, 3 twin rooms.
Directions: half a mile out of Bushmills village, on the main road to Giant's Causeway.
MR M. McKEEVER ☎ (012657) 31577
[Fax] (012657) 31577.

PORTRUSH
Co. Antrim • map 13B3

🏨 CAUSEWAY COAST HOTEL & CONFERENCE CENTRE
36 Ballyreagh Road, BT56 8LR

Overlooking the Atlantic Ocean and hills of Donegal, this is a new, well-furnished building. The atmosphere is busy and efficient, warm and friendly, with live music. Comfortable accommodation and conference facilities are provided.
DOUBLE ROOM: from £30 to £40
SINGLE ROOM: from £45 to £55
FOOD: up to £15 🍷
Hours: breakfast 7.30am–10am, bar snacks 12noon–2.30pm, dinner 7.30pm–9.30pm, bar snacks 5pm–9.30pm.
Cuisine: BRITISH.
Cards: Visa, Access, AmEx.
Other points: parking, children welcome, Sunday lunch, no-smoking area, afternoon teas, disabled access, residents' lounge, vegetarian meals.
Rooms: 21 bedrooms.
Directions: located on A2 coastal road between resorts of Portrush and Portstewart.
ALAN RICKETTS ☎ (01265) 822435
[Fax] (01265) 824495.

KILKEE
Co. Clare • map 19D1

🏨 HALPINS HOTEL
Erin Street

Overlooking old Victorian Kilkee, the tastefully refurbished Halpins Hotel offers quality, comfort and fine food. Close to Shannon Airport and Killimer car ferry, Kilkee is an excellent base when touring the West Coast. Facilities nearby include the Loop Drive, cliff walks, golf and angling. The owners offer the same quality service at Aberdeen Lodge in Dublin 4.
DOUBLE ROOM: from £20 to £30
FOOD: from £15 to £20
Hours: breakfast 8am–10am, dinner 7pm–9.30pm, closed January until 15th March.
Cuisine: CONTINENTAL – fresh seafood and meat dishes.
Cards: Visa, Access, Diners, AmEx.
Other points: parking, no-smoking area, conference facilities, residents' lounge, garden,

vegetarian meals, traditional Sunday lunch, afternoon teas.
Rooms: 2 single rooms, 3 double rooms, 3 twin rooms, 4 triple room. All with en suite, TV, telephone, radio, hair dryer, room service.
Directions: overlooking Kilkee Beach, 40 miles from Shannon Airport, 10 miles from Shann car ferry.
PAT HALPIN ☎ (065) 56032
Fax (065) 56317.

NEWMARKET-ON-FERGUS
Co. Clare • map 19D1

CARRYGERRY HOUSE HOTEL
Newmarket-on-Fergus

Carrygerry House is a 200-year-old manor house steeped in Irish history and tradition. The house was totally refurbished by Gerry and Ethnea Hughes, and they have added all the modern luxuries one associates with an international-standard hotel. Furnishings consist of valuable antiques and artworks collected over many years of travelling and visits to salesrooms. The restaurant offers fresh innovative cuisine, and the individually styled bedrooms offer comfort of the highest standard.
DOUBLE ROOM: from £30 to £40
FOOD: from £15 to £20
Hours: breakfast 7.30am–9.30am, bar meals 12noon–3pm, dinner 7.30pm–9.30pm.
Cuisine: CONTINENTAL.
Cards: Visa, Access, Diners, AmEx.
Other points: parking, children welcome, no-smoking area, residents' lounge, open-air dining, vegetarian meals.
Rooms: 2 single rooms, 6 double rooms, 4 twin rooms, 2 triple rooms. All with en suite, TV, telephone, room service.
Directions: off N18 to Shannon; at first traffic lights turn right to T-junction, take left and follow signposts.
GERRY HUGHES ☎ (061) 472339 Fax (061) 472123.

MALLOW
Co. Cork • map 19D2

SPRINGFORT HALL
Mallow

This elegant 18th century country manor house, surrounded by woodlands and landscaped gardens, makes an ideal venue for weddings, functions, conferences or just a break away from reality. Here you can relax in the spacious lounge with its open log fire, dine in the superb restaurant, or simply enjoy the comforts of the luxurious and spacious en suite bedrooms. This Grade A country house is owned and run by the Walsh family, who together with their professional and friendly staff ensure that your stay at Springfort Hall will be a memorable one.
DOUBLE ROOM: from £20 to £30
FOOD: from £15 to £20

Hours: breakfast 7.30am–10am, dinner 7pm–9.30pm.
Cuisine: BRITISH / CONTINENTAL.
Cards: Visa, Access, AmEx.
Other points: parking, children welcome, conference facilities, garden, vegetarian meals.
Rooms: 13 double rooms, 9 twin rooms, 2 family rooms. All with TV, telephone, radio, alarm, hair dryer, room service.
Directions: off the N20 main Cork–Limerick road.
MICHAEL & EILEEN WALSH ☎ (022) 21278
Fax (022) 21557.

BALLYBOFEY
Co. Donegal • map 13C1

JACKSON'S HOTEL
Ballybofey

Family-run since 1945, renowned for good food, welcoming hospitality and comfortable accommodation. The new leisure centre has a 22-metre swimming pool, hairdresser, creche, etc. The hotel is situated in its own gardens on the banks of the River Finn, opposite Drumboe Woods. Local amenities include trout, salmon and pike fishing, tennis, canoeing, hill-walking, golf and horse-riding. An ideal touring base.
DOUBLE ROOM: from £20 to £30
FOOD: up to £15
Cuisine: INTERNATIONAL.
Cards: Visa, Access, Diners, AmEx.
Other points: parking, children welcome, residents' lounge, vegetarian meals, gym facilities.
Rooms: 5 single rooms, 32 double rooms, 5 twin rooms, 30 family rooms. All with en suite, TV, telephone, hair dryer, trouser-press, room service.
Directions: 18 miles from Donegal town.
MARGARET & BARRY JACKSON ☎ (074) 31021 Fax (074) 31096.

LETTERKENNY
Co. Donegal • map 13C1

CASTLE GROVE COUNTRY HOUSE
Ramelton Road

Castle Grove is a 17th century mansion set in its own parkland overlooking Lough Swilly. It affords the discerning guest all the comforts of modern living while retaining the elegance of bygone days. It offers excellent cuisine to residents and non residents, using home-grown produce. You can golf, fish or shoot from Castle Grove. Shooting packages are available on request.
DOUBLE ROOM: from £40 to £50
FOOD: from £15 to £20
Hours: breakfast 8am–10.30am, dinner 6.30pm–9.30pm, closed 22nd December until 26th December and 9th January until 14th February.
Cuisine: FRENCH – classical cuisine.
Cards: Visa, Access, Diners, AmEx.
Other points: parking, no-smoking area, residents' lounge, garden, vegetarian meals, afternoon teas.
Rooms: 6 double rooms, 3 twin rooms. All with

en suite, telephone, room service.
Directions: 3 miles from Letterkenny–Ramelton road.
MS M. SWEENEY ☎ (074) 51118 Fax (074) 51384.

DUNDONALD
Co. Down • map 14D4

⇌ DUNDONALD OLD MILL
231 Belfast Road, near Belfast, BT16 0UE
This converted watermill is a very attractive and popular tourist spot, and is not only a restaurant but also a shop and garden centre. The restaurant offers olde-worlde charm, comfortable surroundings, delicious wholesome food and friendly hospitality. Well worth a visit.
FOOD: up to £15
Hours: lunch 11.30am–2.30pm, closed Christmas day, Boxing day, 12th July.
Cuisine: BRITISH – home-made traditional food.
Cards: Visa, Access.
Other points: parking, children welcome, no-smoking area, vegetarian meals, traditional Sunday lunch.
Directions: through Dundonald village on the way to Newtownards.
PETER SMYTH ☎ (01232) 480117 Fax (01232) 480217.

LES ROUTIERS
Information & Bookings Line
☎ 0171 610 1856

DUNDRUM
Co. Down • map 13E3

⇌ BUCK'S HEAD
77 Main Street, BT33 0LU
This is a country pub, dating back to the 18th century, which has been completely renovated, and a conservatory and beer garden have been added. The conservatory will seat private parties of 20 to 40 people. The dining room is panelled in beech and cherry wood, with an open fire and an atmosphere that is conducive to casual and intimate dining. The airy, bright conservatory looks out onto a patio and beer garden. Children are welcome until 7pm.
FOOD: from £15 to £20
Hours: lunch 12noon–2.30pm, bar meals 12noon–2.30pm, dinner 7pm–9.30pm, bar meals 5.30pm–7pm, closed Christmas day.
Cuisine: BRITISH – outstanding meals made from top-quality local ingredients and attractively presented.
Cards: Visa, Access, AmEx, MasterCard.
Other points: children welcome, open-air dining, vegetarian meals, traditional Sunday lunch.
Directions: Dundrum is located 3 miles from Newcastle on the main Belfast–Newcastle road.
MRS A.M. GRIFFITH ☎ (013967) 51868 Fax (013967) 51898.

HILLSBOROUGH
Co. Down • map 13D3

⇌ THE PLOUGH INN
The Square
A delightful olde-worlde restaurant, tastefully decorated, with many interesting nooks and recesses. The preparation and presentation of the food and the service of the staff are of the highest standard. A visit is highly recommended.

LES ROUTIERS
NEWCOMER of the Year IRELAND: 1995

FOOD: from £15 to £20
Hours: lunch 11.30am–11.30pm, dinner 6pm–11.30pm.
Cuisine: INTERNATIONAL – rustic home-cooking and international à la carte. Business lunches. Beer and herb garden. Wine bar.
Cards: Visa, Access, Diners, AmEx.
Other points: parking, conference facilities, no-smoking area, open-air dining, vegetarian meals.
Directions: follow signs to Hillsborough from the Sprucefield roundabout on the M1 Belfast to Dublin motorway.
MR D. PATTERSON ☎ (01846) 682985/682858.

KILKEEL
Co. Down • map 13E3

🏨 KILMOREY ARMS HOTEL
41–43 Greencastle Street, BT34 4BH
Situated in County Down exactly where 'the mountains of Mourne sweep down to the sea', this is the ideal location from which to experience an incredibly beautiful part of Ireland. This family-run hotel with many modern facilities offers an unobtrusive, relaxed and friendly atmosphere, with attention to detail at all times. Surrounded by breathtaking beauty, there are miles of pathways for walkers, sports, historic houses and nearby seaside resorts to visit.
DOUBLE ROOM: from £20 to £30
FOOD: up to £15
Hours: breakfast 7.30am–9.30am, lunch 12.30am–2.30pm, bar snacks 12noon–3pm, dinner 5.30pm–9pm, bar snacks 5pm–8pm.
Cuisine: INTERNATIONAL.
Cards: Visa, Access, Eurocard, MasterCard.
Other points: parking, children welcome, open bank holidays, no-smoking area, afternoon tea, disabled access, pets allowed, vegetarian meals, garden, adjoining bedrooms.
Rooms: 5 single rooms, 6 double rooms, 13 twin rooms, 3 family rooms.
Directions: on A2.
LINDSAY McMURRAY & HUGH & ROBERT GIFFEN ☎ (016937) 62220 Fax (016937) 65399.

KILLYLEAGH
Co. Down • map 14D4

🏨 DUFFERIN ARMS
35 High Street, BT30 9QF
The Dufferin Arms offers a warm welcome and a

friendly atmosphere for travellers and for businessmen. It is very popular and highly recommended. Ideal for visiting the many nearby attractions, including Killyleagh Castle, Strangford Lough and Delamont Country Park. Dufferin Arms also offers comfortable accommodation, self-catering apartments, and studios with a large lounge, country-style kitchen and access to barbeque and picnic table.
DOUBLE ROOM: up to £20
FOOD: from £15 to £20 [CLUB]
Hours: lunch 12.30am–2.30pm, Sunday brunch 12.30am–2.30pm, dinner and supper 7.30pm–9pm.
Cuisine: INTERNATIONAL – à la carte menu, offering baked Killyleagh trout, char-grilled steak and lamb kebabs, all with fresh seasonal vegetables. Excellent wine list.
Cards: Visa, Access.
Other points: licensed, music, children welcome, afternoon tea, open bank holidays, vegetarian meals, activities arranged.
Rooms: 7 bedrooms, 3 self-catering apartments.
Directions: located in front of Killyleagh Castle.
MORRIS CRAWFORD & KITTY STEWART
☎ (01396) 828229 [Fax] (01396) 828755.

LOUGHBRICKLAND
Co. Down • map 19B3

ROAD CHEF
179 Dublin Road, BT32
This old-world restaurant offers diners attractive surroundings in which to enjoy good food, excellent service and a relaxed, homely atmosphere. All dishes from the extensive menu, catering for all tastes, are made from the freshest local produce.
FOOD: up to £15
Hours: meals all day 8am–8pm, closed Christmas eve, Christmas day, Boxing day and New Year's day.
Cuisine: BRITISH – steaks, grills, snacks and light lunches. Good, wholesome food.
Other points: parking, children welcome, no-smoking area, vegetarian meals, afternoon teas, traditional Sunday lunch.
Directions: on main road between Belfast and Dublin, the T4 trunk road. Newry side of Loughbrickland.
FRANK DOWNEY ☎ (01762) 318366.

BALLSBRIDGE
Co. Dublin • map 19C3

ABERDEEN LODGE
53–55 Park Avenue, Aylesbury Road, Ballsbridge, Dublin 4
Sixteen tastefully furnished bedrooms await at this Edwardian hotel situated close to Dublin city centre. Run by the Halpin family, the house was designed with space and comfort in mind, together with old world charm and premier service.
DOUBLE ROOM: from £30 to £40
FOOD: from £15 to £20
Hours: breakfast 7am–10am, dinner 7pm–9.30pm.
Cuisine: CONTINENTAL – seafood, meat and vegetarian dishes.
Cards: Visa, Access, Diners, AmEx.
Other points: parking, children welcome, no-smoking area, gym facilities, conference facilities, residents' lounge, garden, vegetarian meals, afternoon teas.
Rooms: 4 double rooms, 8 twin rooms, 4 family rooms. All with en suite, TV, telephone, hair dryer, trouser-press.
Directions: Park Avenue, off Aylesbury Road, close to the Martello Tower.
PAT HALPIN ☎ (01) 2838155 [Fax] (01) 2837877.

MERRION HALL
54–56 Merrion Road, Ballsbridge, Dublin 4
An elegant Victorian red-brick house, situated in Ballsbridge, Dublin's most exclusive suburb, the centre of Dublin's embassy belt. Beautifully refurbished, the splendid dining room looks out onto landscaped gardens. Tastefully furnished TV and reading rooms are available. There is an enclosed car park within the grounds. Ideally situated 1½ miles from the city centre and adjacent to the Royal Dublin Society, Elm Park Golf Club, RTE Studios, St Vincent's Hospital and University College Dublin.
DOUBLE ROOM: from £30 to £40
Hours: closed 21st December until 3rd January.
Cards: Visa, Access.
Other points: parking, children welcome, residents' lounge, garden.
Rooms: 2 single rooms, 5 double rooms, 4 twin rooms, 4 family rooms. All with en suite, TV, telephone, hair dryer, tea/coffee-making facilities.
Directions: on route from Dublin Airport, via city centre and Merrion Road.
BETTY & PAUL SHEERAN ☎ (01) 6681426/ 6681825 [Fax] (01) 6684280.

HOWTH
Co. Dublin • map 19C3

HOWTH LODGE HOTEL
Howth
Overlooking Dublin Bay and the island of Ireland's Eye, Howth Lodge is owned and managed personally by the Hanratty family. Elegant restaurant with reputation for superb cuisine: fresh fish and charcoaled steaks a speciality. There are conference and banqueting facilities for up to 200 persons, with spectacular vistas of Claremont beach. Leisure club also available for guests' use (permission must be obtained for use of the gymnasium).
DOUBLE ROOM: from £40 to £50
FOOD: from £15 to £20
Hours: breakfast 7.30am–10am, bar meals 12.30am–2pm, dinner 7pm–9.30pm, bar meals 7pm–9.30pm, closed 24th December until 27th December (inclusive).
Cuisine: FRENCH – using fresh local produce.
Cards: Visa, Access, Diners, AmEx.

IRELAND • DUBLIN / FERMANAGH / GALWAY

Other points: parking, conference facilities, swimming pool, sauna, steam room, Jacuzzi, vegetarian meals, traditional Sunday lunch, afternoon teas.
Rooms: 35 double rooms, 5 twin rooms, 6 triple rooms. All with en suite, TV, telephone, radio, hair dryer, trouser-press, room service, tea/coffee-making facilities.
Directions: located on the main road from Dublin to Howth, only nine miles from Dublin city centre.
HANRATTY FAMILY ☎ (01) 8321010 [Fax] (01) 322268.

LUCAN
Co. Dublin • map 19C3

🏠 FINNSTOWN COUNTRY HOUSE HOTEL
Newcastle Road
Finnstown, a country house hotel set in 50 acres of woodland, with a nine-hole golf course, is one of the finest established manor houses in Co. Dublin. Enjoy the superb restaurant, drawing room and bar. The hotel's leisure facilities are available to residents and include a fully equipped gym, sauna, Turkish bath and swimming pool.
DOUBLE ROOM: over £50
FOOD: from £25 to £30
Hours: breakfast 7.30am–10am, lunch 12.30am–2.30pm, bar meals 12noon–2.30pm, dinner 7.30pm–9.45pm, bar meals 7.30pm–9.45pm.
Cuisine: INTERNATIONAL – superb classical cuisine.
Cards: Visa, Access, Diners, AmEx.
Other points: parking, children welcome, pets allowed, gym facilities, outdoor swimming pool, golf course, conference facilities, residents' lounge, garden, vegetarian meals, traditional Sunday lunch.
Rooms: 15 double rooms, 10 twin rooms. All with en suite, TV, telephone, hair dryer, trouser-press, room service, tea/coffee-making facilities.
Directions: 8 miles from Dublin city centre, just off the N4 or N7.
ELISABETH DUFFY ☎ (01) 6280644 [Fax] (01) 6281088.

ENNISKILLEN
Co. Fermanagh • map 13D1

🍴 FRANCOS
Queen Elizabeth Road, BT74 7DY
A popular restaurant with a distinctly warm and friendly continental atmosphere, where you can choose imaginative fresh food from an extensive menu. Ideal location for visiting and exploring the Lakeland Area.
FOOD: up to £15
Hours: meals all day 12noon–12midnight, open Sunday lunch, closed Christmas day.
Cuisine: COSMOPOLITAN – dishes may include roast monkfish, local wild salmon, guinea fowl, game terrine, duck breasts, swordfish steak. Fresh pizza and pastas.

Cards: Diners, AmEx.
Other points: licensed, no-smoking area, children welcome, pets allowed, vegetarian meals, disabled access.
Directions: on the A4 in the town centre, behind the town hall, on the river.
RUAIRI & FRANK SWEENEY & FAMILY
☎ (01365) 324424 [Fax] (01365) 323584.

🍴 OSCARS RESTAURANT
29 Belmore Street
A lovely little town-house restaurant situated in the centre of Enniskillen. Attractively decorated in pine, it has a friendly, fun atmosphere. Diners can choose from an extensive range of mouthwatering dishes. Nearby attractions include the Lakes of Fermanagh, Marble Arch Caves and Castle Coole.
FOOD: up to £15 [CLUB]
Hours: dinner 5pm–10.30pm, closed Christmas day.
Cuisine: INTERNATIONAL.
Cards: Visa, Access.
Other points: parking, children welcome, open bank holidays, disabled access, vegetarian meals.
Directions: Enniskillen town centre.
MR D. MAGEE ☎ (01365) 327037/326886.

CLIFDEN
Co. Galway • map 19C1

🏠 MALDUA GUEST HOUSE
Galway Road
A highly acclaimed family-run guest house in the heart of Connemara. A high standard of accommodation, with all bedrooms individually designed and well appointed. Local amenities include golf course, sea angling, fishing, horse-riding, cycling, walking and historical tours. A warm welcome awaits you at Maldua.
DOUBLE ROOM: from £20 to £30
Hours: breakfast 8am–9.30am, closed December.
Cards: Visa, Access, Eurocard, MasterCard.
Other points: parking, children welcome, no-smoking area, residents' lounge, garden.
Rooms: 1 single room, 4 double rooms, 2 twin rooms, 2 triple rooms. All with en suite, TV, telephone, radio, central heating, hair dryer, trouser-press, tea/coffee-making facilities.
Directions: N59 route from Galway city to Clifden.
IVOR & KATHLEEN DUANE ☎ (095) 21171 [Fax] (095) 21739.

OUGHTERARD
Co. Galway • map 19C1

🏠 ROSS LAKE HOUSE HOTEL
Rosscahill
Ross Lake House is a Georgian house situated at the end of a country road in a panoramic setiing. The hotel is owned by Henry and Elaine Reid, and the emphasis is on quality food served in a relaxed atmosphere. An ideal base for touring Connemara, fishing on Lough Corrib or golfing at Oughterard.

DOUBLE ROOM: from £30 to £40
FOOD: from £15 to £20
Hours: breakfast 8am–10am, dinner 7pm–9pm, closed 1st November until mid-March.
Cuisine: IRISH – quality ingredients used to produce quality dishes.
Cards: Visa, Access, Diners, AmEx.
Other points: parking, pets allowed, residents' lounge, garden, vegetarian meals.
Rooms: 1 single room, 12 double rooms. All with en suite, telephone, room service.
Directions: 14 miles from Galway city, 6 miles past Moycullen village.
HENRY & ELAINE REID ☎ (091) 80109
Fax (091) 80184.

CARAGH LAKE
Co. Kerry • map 19D1

CARAGH LODGE
Caragh Lake

Set in an award-winning garden one mile from the famous Ring of Kerry, you will find Caragh Lodge. This mid-Victorian house was originally built as a fishing lodge and is right on the shores of Caragh Lake, overlooking Macgillicuddy Reeks, home of Ireland's highest mountain. Mary Gaunt personally supervises the kitchen, and reservations for dinner are advisable because of the excellent reputation gained for providing superb cuisine. In keeping with its surroundings the lodge is furnished throughout with antiques, offering guests attractive, comfortable accommodation.
DOUBLE ROOM: from £40 to £50
FOOD: from £20 to £25
Hours: breakfast 8.30am–10.30am, dinner 7.30pm–8.30pm, closed mid-October until Easter.
Cuisine: IRISH – mouthwatering dishes prepared from fresh local produce.
Cards: Visa, Access.
Other points: parking, residents' lounge, garden, vegetarian meals, afternoon teas.
Rooms: 4 double rooms, 6 twin rooms. All with en suite, telephone, radio, alarm, hair dryer.
Directions: on the edge of Caragh Lake.
MARY GAUNT ☎ (066) 69115 Fax (066) 69316.

KENMARE
Co. Kerry • map 19E1

RIVERSDALE HOUSE HOTEL
Muxnaw

The hotel is ideally located right on the shores of Kenmare River, the only hotel in Kenmare with direct access to the sea. With its own carefully tended gardens of seven acres and just one kilometre from the town of Kenmare, the keynote is warmth, comfort and fine fare. The restaurant has an excellent reputation for seafood and shellfish specialities. All bedrooms are en suite, and the ground-floor rooms have direct access to the gardens. The hotel has its own tennis court. The best of Irish entertainment is provided in the

atmospheric bar, and admission is free to Cupids Nite Club for hotel guests.
DOUBLE ROOM: from £30 to £40
FOOD: from £15 to £20
Hours: breakfast 8am–10am, dinner 7pm–9.30pm, closed November until February.
Cuisine: BRITISH – a good selection of delicious, freshly cooked meals.
Cards: Visa, Access, Diners.
Other points: parking, children welcome, pets allowed, no-smoking area, conference facilities, residents' lounge, garden, open-air dining, vegetarian meals, traditional Sunday lunch, afternoon teas.
Rooms: 15 double rooms, 12 twin rooms, 3 triple rooms. All with en suite, TV, telephone, radio, hair dryer, trouser-press, room service, tea/coffee-making facilities.
Directions: at Kenmare ask or look for Glengarriff Road.
PEGGY O'SULLIVAN ☎ (064) 41299 Fax (064) 41075.

KILLARNEY
Co. Kerry • map 19D1

KATHLEEN'S COUNTRY HOUSE
Tralee Road, N22

Kathleen's is a delightful, family-run guest house where traditional hospitality and courteous, personal attention are a way of life. This house has been designed and built for comfort, and guests return again and again. Relaxation comes naturally here – the cares and pressures of modern living belong to another world. You are always assured of a warm welcome. Easy to get to, hard to leave!
DOUBLE ROOM: from £30 to £40
Hours: breakfast 7.45am–9.30am, closed 7th November until 17th March.
Cards: Visa, Access, AmEx.
Other points: parking, no-smoking area, residents' lounge, garden, lawn croquet, vegetarian meals.
Rooms: 6 double rooms, 7 twin rooms, 4 triple rooms. All with en suite, telephone, radio, hairdryer, trouser-press, tea/coffee-making facilities.
Directions: 3 kilometres north of Killarney on Killaney–Tralee road, N22.
KATHLEEN O'REGAN-SHEPPARD ☎ (064) 32810 Fax (064) 32340.

KILKENNY
Co. Kilkenny • map 19D2

BUTLER HOUSE
Patrick Street

Butler House is the dower house of Kilkenny Castle. Sweeping staircases, magnificent plastered ceilings, marble fireplaces and a walled garden are all features of this notable Georgian residence in the heart of medieval Kilkenny city. This is a room-and-breakfast experience the likes of which

you are unlikely to have experienced.
DOUBLE ROOM: from £30 to £40
Hours: breakfast 8am–10am.
Cards: Visa, Access, Diners, AmEx.
Other points: parking, children welcome, conference facilities, residents' lounge, garden.
Rooms: 1 single room, 4 double rooms, 8 twin rooms. All with en suite, TV, telephone, radio, hair dryer, trouser-press, tea/coffee-making facilities.
Directions: in the city centre, near Waterford Road.
☎ (056) 65707/22828 Fax (056) 65626.

ADARE
Co. Limerick • map 19D2

🛏 WOODLANDS HOUSE HOTEL
Knockanes, Adare

Set in its own private grounds, three kilometres from Adare, Woodlands House Hotel is owned and managed by Mary and Dick Fitzgerald. A comfortable 55-bedroom hotel, offering deluxe accommodation, executive suites and conference facilities. Its excellent cuisine, using the best of Golden Vale products, makes Woodlands Hotel a popular venue for weddings, functions, Sunday lunch and candlelit dinners. Convenient for many local sporting amenities. Special group rates available.
DOUBLE ROOM: from £20 to £30
FOOD: up to £15
Hours: breakfast 7.30am–10am, dinner 6.30pm–9.30pm, bar meals 12noon–10.30pm, closed 23rd December until 26th December.
Cuisine: IRISH – traditional dishes.
Cards: Visa, Access, Diners, AmEx.
Other points: parking, children welcome, conference facilities, garden, vegetarian meals, traditional Sunday lunch.
Rooms: 18 double rooms, 19 twin rooms, 2 family rooms, 4 suites. All with en suite, TV, telephone, radio, hair dryer, trouser-press, room service, baby-listening device, tea/coffee-making facilities.
Directions: off N21, 1½ miles north of Adare; look for signposts on the right.
DICK & MARY FITZGERALD ☎ (061) 396118/396553 Fax (061) 396073.

DROGHEDA
Co. Louth • map 19C3

🛏 BOYNE VALLEY HOTEL
Drogheda

A gracious country house on 16 acres of beautiful gardens and woodlands beside the historic town of Drogheda, 25 miles from Dublin and 20 miles from Dublin Airport. There is a new extension with deluxe rooms. The Cellar restaurant provides a wide selection of delicious meals, and they receive a daily supply of fresh fish. Nearby are the famous prehistoric sites of Newgrange, Dowth, Knowth and the medieval abbeys of Mellifont and Monasterboice. This family-run hotel offers a warm welcome and true Irish hospitality.
DOUBLE ROOM: from £30 to £40
FOOD: up to £15
Hours: breakfast 7am–11am, lunch 12.30am–2.30pm, bar meals 10am–5pm, dinner 6.30pm–10pm.
Cuisine: CONTINENTAL.
Cards: Visa, Access, Diners, AmEx, MasterCard.
Other points: parking, children welcome, pets allowed, no-smoking area, conference facilities, residents' lounge, garden, vegetarian meals, traditional Sunday lunch, afternoon teas.
Rooms: 7 single rooms, 18 double rooms, 9 twin rooms, 3 family rooms. All with en suite, TV, telephone, hairdryer, room service, tea/coffee-making facilities.
Directions: just south of Drogheda on the N1.
MICHAEL & ROSEMARY McNAMARA ☎ (041) 37737 Fax (041) 39188.

PONTOON
Co. Mayo • map 19B1

🛏 PONTOON BRIDGE HOTEL
Pontoon

Located on the sandy shores of Loughs Conn and Cullen, with panoramic surroundings. Excellent food and good-value wines in the Lakeside Restaurant. Nightly musical entertainment. This is Ireland's number-one angling centre for trout and salmon fishing, with guides, boats, rod hire, tackle, etc. Two- and four-day schools of fly-fishing, landscape-painting and cookery, all with professional tuition.
DOUBLE ROOM: from £20 to £30
FOOD: from £20 to £25
Hours: breakfast 8.30am–10am, Sunday lunch 1pm–3pm, dinner 7.30pm–9.30pm, bar meals all day.
Cuisine: INTERNATIONAL.
Cards: Visa, Access, Diners.
Other points: parking, children welcome, pets allowed, no-smoking area, conference facilities, residents' lounge, garden, open-air dining, vegetarian meals, traditional Sunday lunch, afternoon teas.
Rooms: 5 single rooms, 2 double rooms, 13 twin rooms, 15 family rooms. All with en suite, TV, telephone, radio, tea/coffee-making facilities.
Directions: from Dublin to Lonford N4, Lonford to Foxford N5, then to Pontoon.
BRENDAN & ANN GEARY ☎ (094) 56120/56688 Fax (094) 56120.

BIRR
Co. Offaly • map 19C2

🛏 COUNTY ARMS HOTEL
Railway Road

One of the finest examples of late Georgian architecture c.1810, its well-preserved interior features are outstanding. The atmosphere is warm, cosy and peaceful. The lavish hotel gardens and

glasshouses provide fresh herbs, fruit and vegetables for the various menus available at reasonable prices. Locally available, guests can enjoy golf, horse-riding, fishing, tennis and swimming in a heated indoor pool.
DOUBLE ROOM: from £30 to £40
FOOD: up to £15
Hours: closed 24th to 27th December (inclusive).
Cuisine: BRITISH – traditional home-cooking using fresh ingredients.
Cards: Visa, Access, Diners, AmEx.
Other points: parking, children welcome, pets allowed, conference facilities, squash courts, garden, open-air dining, vegetarian meals, traditional Sunday lunch, afternoon teas.
Rooms: 4 single rooms, 10 twin rooms, 4 family rooms. All with en suite, TV, telephone, room service, tea/coffee-making facilities.
Directions: in its own grounds in the town of Birr.
MR W LOUGHNANE ☎ (0509) 20791
Fax (0509) 21234.

COLLOONEY
Co. Sligo • map 19B2

MARKREE CASTLE
Collooney
Charles and Mary Cooper have restored Sligo's oldest inhabited house and made it a spectacular family hotel. Home of the Cooper family since 1640 and set in the middle of a large estate, Markree boasts spectacular plasterwork and a fine Irish oak staircase, yet has all the comforts of a three-star hotel. Good food, peace and quiet, lots of space and a warm family welcome await. Riding is also available on the estate.
DOUBLE ROOM: from £40 to £50
FOOD: from £20 to £25
Hours: breakfast 8.30am–10am, bar meals 1pm–2.30pm, dinner 7.30pm–9.30pm, closed February.
Cuisine: IRISH – country home-cooking.
Cards: Visa, Access, Diners, AmEx.
Other points: parking, children welcome, pets allowed, no-smoking area, conference facilities, residents' lounge, garden, vegetarian meals, traditional Sunday lunch, afternoon teas.
Rooms: 3 double rooms, 4 twin rooms, 7 family rooms. All with en suite, TV, telephone, hair dryer, room service, baby-listening device.
Directions: 1 mile east of N4, 7 miles south of Sligo town.
CHARLES & MARY COOPER ☎ (071) 67800
Fax (071) 67840.

COOKSTOWN
Co. Tyrone • map 13D2

GLENAVON HOUSE HOTEL
52 Drum Road, BT50 8JQ
An attractively furnished, modern, purpose-built hotel, where the emphasis is on healthy eating. The large hotel has managed to retain the intimate, friendly atmosphere that is only expected of much smaller hotels. The staff are also polite and efficient. An ideal location for a family holiday, with golf, fishing, riding and many historical places of interest nearby.
DOUBLE ROOM: from £20 to £30
SINGLE ROOM: from £35 to £45
FOOD: up to £15 CLUB
Hours: breakfast 7am–10am, lunch 12noon–5pm, dinner 5pm–10pm, bar snacks 10am–9.30pm.
Cuisine: BRITISH / CONTINENTAL.
Cards: Visa, Access, AmEx.
Other points: children welcome, parking, afternoon teas, disabled access, residents' lounge, vegetarian meals.
Rooms: 16 double rooms, 26 twin rooms, 11 family rooms.
Directions: on the A29, off the M1 or M2.
MR & MRS MORRIS ☎ (016487) 64949
Fax (016487) 64396.

DUNGANNON
Co. Tyrone • map 13D2

INN ON THE PARK
Moy Road, BT30 9QF
Set in 10 acres of mature, landscaped gardens, this was once the home of the Finneys, one of Ireland's dynastic linen families. Now extensively refurbished by the present owner, it prides itself on its standards of cuisine and service. A comprehensive wedding package is available, as well as attractively furnished function rooms catering for 6 to 250 persons. Own outdoor tennis court.
DOUBLE ROOM: from £30 to £40
FOOD: up to £15 CLUB
Hours: breakfast 7.30am–10.30am, lunch 12.30am–2.30pm, bar meals 12.30am–2.30pm, dinner 6pm–9.30pm, bar meals 2.30pm–10pm, closed Christmas.
Cuisine: IRISH – award-winning restaurant specializing in fresh local produce.
Cards: Visa, Access, Diners, AmEx.
Other points: licensed, Sunday lunch, no-smoking area, children welcome, pets allowed, parking, afternoon tea, special breaks.
Directions: junction 15 of M1 motorway; half a mile from Dungannon town.
ROBERT WATERSON ☎ (018687) 25151
Fax (018687) 24953.

OMAGH
Co. Tyrone • map 13D2

THE MELLON COUNTRY INN
134 Beltany Road, BT78 5RA
The extensive à la carte menu has been developed to suit both the cosmopolitan and regular clientele, offering dishes with recipes from all over Europe and complemented by more than 100 fine wines. One special feature of the dinner menu is a flambé dish. The restaurant also caters for 'late risers', offering traditional Ulster and continental breakfasts, coffee and scones from 10.30am, meals from 12noon, and early evening high-tea until 7.30pm. A special children's menu is also available.

361

IRELAND • WEXFORD

FOOD: from £15 to £20 ⇌ [CLUB]
Hours: à la carte 6.30pm–9.30pm, bar meals 12noon–5.30pm, breakfast 10.30am–12noon, dinner, 5.30pm–9.30pm, high tea and bistro 5.30pm–7.30pm, lunch 12noon–2.30pm.
Cuisine: BRITISH / CONTINENTAL – à la carte and table d'hôte menus. Dishes may include lobster and fillet steak with onions, lemon and garlic, fresh duckling in a puddle of peach sauce.
Cards: Visa, Access, Diners, AmEx.
Other points: licensed, open-air dining, Sunday lunch, no-smoking area, children welcome, pets allowed, vegetarian meals, garden, afternoon tea, parking.
Directions: half-way between Omagh and Newtonstewart. 1 mile from the Ulster American Folk Park.
KEN RUSSELL ☎ (016626) 61946
[Fax] (016626) 62245.

ROSSLARE HARBOUR
Co. Wexford • map 19D3

HOTEL ROSSLARE
Rosslare Harbour
Hotel Rosslare is the oldest hotel and catering establishment in the area and has been gracing the Rosslare Harbour skyline since 1907. It once traded under the quaint name of Pope's Tea and Boarding House. The open log fire in the lobby sets the tone of welcome you will receive from your hosts, Liam and Mary Griffin. The Portholes Bar offers a lively, friendly atmosphere, and the Captain's Table Restaurant, overlooking the harbour, offers a large range of excellent seafood and meat dishes. Squash court and sauna are available free to residents.
DOUBLE ROOM: from £30 to £40
FOOD: from £15 to £20
Hours: breakfast 7am–10am, lunch 12.30am–2.30pm, dinner 6pm–9pm.
Cuisine: BRITISH – seafood, grills.
Cards: Visa, Access, Diners, AmEx.
Other points: parking, children welcome, conference facilities, open-air dining, vegetarian meals, traditional Sunday lunch, afternoon teas.
Rooms: 11 double rooms, 5 twin rooms, 9 family rooms. All with TV, telephone, hair dryer, trouser-press, room service.
Directions: overlooking the harbour, third hotel on the left.
LIAM GRIFFIN ☎ (053) 33110 [Fax] (053) 33386.

ENTER THE
LES ROUTIERS
GRAND PRIZE DRAW...

AND WIN A FABULOUS STAY FOR TWO AT OUR HOTEL OF THE YEAR!

An exclusive opportunity
to participate in
our *Grand Prize Draw*.

Win two fabulous free nights for two
at the magnificent
Rangeworthy Court Hotel,
near Bristol.

Participation is simple – and fun too!

- ☐ Every time you visit a *Les Routiers* establishment offering a *Special Welcome Discount*, ask the manager or proprietor to tick off in your guidebook which discount you have taken advantage of – *either* 10% discount on food or accommodation, *or* a free bottle of house wine!

- ☐ KEEP YOUR RECEIPTS, as these will need to be attached to your *Grand Prize Draw Coupon* before returning it to us.

- ☐ There are over 140 *Les Routiers* establishments offering a *Special Welcome Discount*, which are listed overpage. There are no pre-set limits: you can visit any number that you choose, and collect as many ticks as you like.

Rules of the Grand Prize Draw:

The prizewinner will receive a stay of two consecutive nights' accommodation for two people at the Rangeworthy Court Hotel. Included is the cost of accommodation, bed and breakfast and evening meals only. Not included is the cost of travelling to and from the hotel, drinks or any additional expenses. The two-night stay must be taken between 2nd January 1996 and 31st May 1996. There will be no cash alternative.
The Draw is not open to *Les Routiers* employees or their families.
Your coupon must arrive at our offices **NO LATER THAN FRIDAY, 29 DECEMBER 1995**.

RANGEWORTHY COURT HOTEL

RANGEWORTHY COURT, first mentioned in 1167 as part of the manor of Thornbury, is set within its own grounds beside the church, amidst the rich farmlands and gently rolling countryside just south of the 'Edge' of the Cotswolds, offering some spectacular views across the Severn Estuary.

The hotel has an established tradition of high standards of hospitality and cleanliness, as well as the friendly, welcoming atmosphere of a fine old country house. On their arrival our winners will be warmly greeted by Mervyn and Lucia Gillett, the proprietors of Rangeworthy Court for the past 16 years, and can expect to be cosseted by the efficient, friendly staff throughout their stay.

An important feature of the hotel is its excellent cuisine, cooked mostly to traditional British recipes, including vegetarian and vegan dishes. The bedrooms are beautifully furnished and all are 'en suite', with a bath or shower and toilet, colour TV, in-house movies, and other comforts.

The Rangeworthy Court Hotel thrives on company. Here, all guests, particularly our winners, can be sure of a warm welcome and a truly memorable stay.

LES ROUTIERS GRAND PRIZE DRAW

Name: (Mr/Mrs/Miss/Ms):_____

Address:_____

_____ Daytime telephone number: _____

RETURN TO: *Les Routiers* GRAND PRIZE DRAW 25 Vanston Place, London SW6 1AZ

LES ROUTIERS ESTABLISHMENTS OFFERING SPECIAL WELCOME DISCOUNTS

Don't forget to take your guidebook with you and get your discounts ticked off by the proprietor or manager. KEEP YOUR RECEIPTS to attach to your Grand Prize Draw Coupon! All discounts are subject to individual establishments' regulations. Only one discount is permitted per person per visit.

	FOOD	ACCOM-MODATION	WINE

*L*ONDON

LONDON
BALZAC BISTRO Shepherds Bush W12	☐		
CAERNARVON HOTEL Ealing Common W5		☐	
HARROW HOTEL Harrow	☐	☐	
TRAPPERS RESTAURANT Putney SW15			☐
OLD CALCUTTA TANDOORI Oval SW9	☐		☐
RANI VEGETARIAN RESTAURANT Finchley N3	☐		
WINDMILL ON THE COMMON Clapham SW4		☐	

GREATER LONDON
FIDDLER'S RESTAURANT Harrow Weald			☐
ITALIAN PLACE BRASSERIE Teddington			☐
OAK LODGE HOTEL Enfield	☐		

*S*OUTH-EAST ENGLAND/EAST ANGLIA

BUCKINGHAMSHIRE
GEORGE INN Great Missenden	☐	☐	☐

HERTFORDSHIRE
BRITISH RAJ Royston			☐
REDCOATS FARMHOUSE HOTEL Hitchin		☐	

KENT
BOXLEY HOUSE HOTEL Maidstone	☐		
KINGSDOWN HOTEL Margate	☐	☐	
MOORINGS HOTEL Sevenoaks		☐	
THREE TUNS INN Staple, near Canterbury	☐	☐	☐

NORFOLK
GRANGE HOTEL Norwich	☐		☐

SUFFOLK
MARLBOROUGH HOTEL Felixstowe	☐		
OLD COUNTING HOUSE Haughley	☐		
SIX BELLS INN Bardwell	☐	☐	

	FOOD	ACCOM-MODATION	WINE
SURREY			
CRANLEIGH HOTEL Reigate	☐	☐	
MONGOLIAN RESTAURANT Godalming			☐
SUSSEX (EAST)			
HALLAND FORGE Halland	☐	☐	
MELFORD HALL HOTEL Brighton & Hove		☐	
POWDERMILLS HOTEL Battle			☐
SUSSEX (WEST)			
COUNTRYMAN INN Shipley			☐
INN THE PRIORY Haywards Heath	☐		
KINGSWAY HOTEL Worthing			☐

SOUTH-WEST ENGLAND

	FOOD	ACCOM-MODATION	WINE
AVON			
ARCHES HOTEL Bristol		☐	
RANGEWORTHY COURT HOTEL Rangeworthy	☐	☐	
SODBURY HOUSE HOTEL Old Sodbury		☐	
BERKSHIRE			
EDWARD COURT HOTEL Wokingham	☐	☐	☐
CORNWALL			
ALLHAYS COUNTRY HOUSE Looe		☐	
GROVE HOTEL Falmouth		☐	
MAER LODGE Bude	☐	☐	
NELSONS RESTAURANT Polperro			☐
PANDORA INN Mylor, Falmouth	☐		
PELYNT DAGGER RESTAURANT Looe	☐		
DEVON			
HEADLANDS HOTEL Ilfracombe			☐
ILFRACOMBE CARLTON HOTEL Ilfracombe			☐
LIVERMEAD CLIFF HOTEL Torquay	☐		
NEW COMMERCIAL INN Axminster	☐		
PRESTON HOUSE HOTEL Braunton		☐	
RIVERSFORD HOTEL Bideford	☐	☐	
ROSSLYN HOTEL Paignton		☐	
SHIP INN Axmouth	☐		
DORSET			
ANVIL Blandford	☐	☐	
BENNETT ARMS Shaftesbury		☐	
HENSLEIGH HOTEL Charmouth	☐		
HOTEL MON BIJOU Bournemouth	☐	☐	
KEERSBROOK HOTEL Lyme Regis	☐	☐	
MANOR HOTEL West Bexington, Dorchester		☐	
PEBBLES GUEST HOUSE Weymouth		☐	☐

	FOOD	ACCOM-MODATION	WINE

HAMPSHIRE
DEAN PARK HOTEL Bournemouth □
UPLANDS HOTEL Southsea □
WOODFALLS INN Woodfalls □ □ □
SOUTH GARDEN RESTAURANT Ramsey □

ISLE OF WIGHT
ST HELEN'S RESTAURANT St Helen's □

SOMERSET
LION AT PENNARD Glastonbury □
ROYAL OAK INN Winsford □ □
ROYAL OAK INN Withypool □

WILTSHIRE
ANTROBUS ARMS HOTEL Salisbury □
FINDERS KEEPERS Salisbury □
RIVERSIDE INN Bradford on Avon □
WOODBRIDGE INN North Newnton □

CENTRAL ENGLAND

CHESHIRE
LIBERTY CITY Adlington □

GLOUCESTERSHIRE
BELOW STAIRS Cheltenham □
GRAPEVINE HOTEL Stow-on-the-Wold □ □
WILD DUCK Ewen, Cirencester □

LINCOLNSHIRE
HILLCREST HOTEL Lincoln □
RED LION HOTEL Spalding □
WASHBOROUGH HALL HOTEL Washinborough, Lincoln □

NOTTINGHAMSHIRE
LION HOTEL Worksop □ □

OXFORDSHIRE
MOON AND SIXPENCE Hanwell, near Banbury □
SIX BELLS Warborough □

SHROPSHIRE
BOARS HEAD Bishops Castle □ □ □
DINHAM WEIR HOTEL Ludlow □ □
RAPHAELS RESTAURANT Shifnal □
SYDNEY HOUSE HOTEL Shrewsbury □

WARWICKSHIRE
EATON COURT HOTEL Leamington Spa □ □
ROSSINI RESTAURANT Alcester □

	FOOD	ACCOM-MODATION	WINE

WORCESTERSHIRE
CHEQUERS INN Pershore ☐
MOUNT PLEASANT HOTEL Great Malvern ☐ ☐ ☐

WEST MIDLANDS
SUTTON COURT HOTEL Sutton Coldfield, Birmingham ☐ ☐ ☐

NORTHERN ENGLAND

CLEVELAND
GOLDEN EAGLE HOTEL Thornaby ☐

COUNTY DURHAM
KENSINGTON HALL HOTEL Willington ☐

CUMBRIA
FINKLES RESTAURANT Kendal ☐
NEW INN Appleby-in-Westmoreland ☐
TEBAY MOUNTAIN LODGE HOTEL Penrith ☐
THORNBANK HOTEL Windermere ☐

DERBYSHIRE
KEGWORTH HOTEL Kegworth, Derby ☐

HUMBERSIDE
KINGSTOWN HOTEL Hull ☐

LANCASHIRE
SUNRAY Blackpool ☐ ☐

MERSEYSIDE
CRIMOND HOTEL Southport ☐
LEASOWE CASTLE Wirral ☐ ☐ ☐

NORTHUMBERLAND
FAMOUS SCHOONER Alnmouth ☐ ☐

YORKSHIRE (NORTH)
AMBASSADOR HOTEL Scarborough ☐
ANGEL INN Thirsk ☐
BUTLERS HOTEL Headingley, Leeds ☐ ☐ ☐
BYRON HOUSE HOTEL York ☐
KINGS HEAD HOTEL Malton ☐
MAYPOLE INN Skipton ☐
MILLERS RESTAURANT Stokesley ☐
SEAFIELD HOTEL Filey ☐
SEACLIFFE HOTEL Whitby ☐
WILLOW DENE HOTEL Scarborough ☐

YORKSHIRE (WEST)
COLLYERS HOTEL Halifax ☐

	FOOD	ACCOM-MODATION	WINE

WALES

CLWYD
ORIEL HOUSE HOTEL St Asaph   ☐   ☐
PLAS ELWY HOTEL & RESTAURANT St Asaph   ☐

DYFED
COTHI BRIDGE HOTEL Carmarthen   ☐
FOURCROFT HOTEL Tenby   ☐
SKIPPERS LEISURE LTD. Cardigan   ☐   ☐   ☐
TY HEN FARM New Quay   ☐

GWENT
CROWN AT WHITEBROOK Monmouth   ☐   ☐
HUNTSMAN HOTEL Chepstow   ☐   ☐

GWYNEDD
BULL HOTEL Holyhead   ☐
CLIFTON HOUSE HOTEL Dolgellau   ☐   ☐
PANORAMA HOTEL Barmouth   ☐
PLAS COCH HOTEL Bala   ☐

POWYS
LION HOTEL & RESTAURANT Berriew, near Welshpool   ☐
THREE COCKS HOTEL near Brecon   ☐

WEST GLAMORGAN
SCHOONER RESTAURANT Swansea   ☐   ☐

SCOTLAND

BORDERS
BURTS HOTEL Melrose   ☐
LEADBURN INN West Linton   ☐   ☐

DUMFRIES AND GALLOWAY
HETLAND HALL Carrutherstown   ☐   ☐
INGLENOOK RESTAURANT Newton Stewart   ☐
LOCKERBIE MANOR HOTEL Lockerbie   ☐   ☐   ☐

GRAMPIAN
AULD KIRK HOTEL Ballater   ☐
OLD MILL INN Maryculter, Aberdeen   ☐   ☐   ☐

HIGHLANDS
ALTNAHARA HOTEL Sutherland   ☐
DUISDALE HOTEL Sleat, Isle of Skye   ☐
ISLES OF GLENCOE HOTEL & LEISURE CENTRE Ballachulish ☐
PRINCE'S HOUSE Glenfinnan   ☐
RAMLEH HOTEL & FINGAL'S RESTAURANT Nairn   ☐

	FOOD	ACCOM-MODATION	WINE
HIGHLANDS (continued)			
ROYAL HOTEL Cromarty	☐	☐	
BALAVIL SPORT HOTEL Newtonmore, Inverness	☐		
LOTHIAN			
LEADBURN INN West Linton		☐	☐
OLD BORDEAUX Edinburgh			☐
SALISBURY VIEW HOTEL Edinburgh		☐	
TATTLER Edinburgh			☐
STRATHCLYDE			
ARGYLL HOTEL Isle of Iona			☐
CREGGANS INN Strachur		☐	
FALLS OF LORA Oban		☐	
FOUTERS Ayr	☐		
GLENFORSA HOTEL Salen by Aros, Isle of Mull		☐	
LE BISTRO Prestwick	☐		
LOCH ETIVE HOTEL near Oban	☐		
MANOR PARK HOTEL Skelmorlie, near Largs	☐		
TAYSIDE			
MUIRS INN Kinross		☐	

LES ROUTIERS

CLUB BON VIVEUR
The Ultimate Dining Scheme!

CLUB BON VIVEUR is an exciting nationwide scheme for diners, operated by *Les Routiers*, through which you are invited to rediscover the *Joie de Vivre* in hundreds of restaurants throughout the country, offering more than 23 types of international cuisine!

As a *Club Bon Viveur* cardholder, you are entitled to a range of substantial discounts and benefits, including reductions of up to 50% on food bills (subject to individual restaurants' restrictions), when dining with one or more guests. You can use your card as often as you wish, in any of the establishments listed in the *Joie de Vivre* Directory. The Directory will be sent to you with your Members' Pack, when you join.

Membership of *Club Bon Viveur* costs just £30 per annum, which can very quickly be recouped through discounts.

MEMBERSHIP BENEFITS INCLUDE:

- Discounted food prices when dining out
- The *Joie de Vivre* Directory for easy reference
- Discounts on purchases of *Les Routiers* guidebooks and publications
- Other promotional offers

To apply for your *Club Bon Viveur* membership, simply complete the application form (opposite) and return it with your payment of £30 to:

The Club Secretary
CLUB BON VIVEUR
25 Vanston Place
London SW6 1AZ

On page 381 near the back of this edition, you are invited to propose any restaurants you would like to recommend for the *Joie de Vivre* Directory, and also to record your comments and recommendations for this annual guide.

Your personal invitation . . .

To: Club Bon Viveur
25 Vanston Place, London SW6 1AZ
Telephone: 0171 385 6644 Fax: 0171 385 7136

Please enrol me in the Club Bon Viveur
National Dining Scheme, at an annual
subscription of £30.00 inc. VAT.
PLEASE COMPLETE IN BLOCK CAPITALS

Mr/Mrs/Ms/Miss

Forename

Surname

Address

Postcode

Telephone

Profession

THE ABOVE INFORMATION WILL BE KEPT IN THE STRICTEST
CONFIDENCE AND USED FOR INTERNAL PURPOSES ONLY.

I enclose my cheque for £30.00 inc. VAT, made payable to
Club Bon Viveur
Or
Charge my Access/Visa/Mastercard/Amex No.

IF YOU ARE INTRODUCING A NEW MEMBER,
PLEASE COMPLETE YOUR DETAILS BELOW

Expiry Date

Restaurant Name

Postcode

OR

Cardmember Name

Membership No.

Postcode

NOTES

NOTES

NOTES

NOTES

YOUR RECOMMENDATIONS

Do you have a favourite restaurant, inn, hotel or guest house that you would like to recommend to us – or possibly a restaurant that you have visited recently and would like to see included in the *Club Bon Viveur* dining scheme?

If so, please record your recommendations on the page below, so that we can arrange for one of our inspectors to call on them. Alternatively, if you have visited a *Les Routiers* establishment and are dissatisfied, we would still like to receive your comments. All correspondence is treated in the strictest confidence.

You may continue on a separate piece of paper, which should be attached to this page when returning it to us.

Establishment name: _____

Address: _____

_____

Establishment type (please circle):

| Restaurant | Public House | Hotel |
| Wine Bar/Bistro | B&B | Other |

Please circle: NOMINATION   COMPLAINT

Your comments: _____

_____

If recommending a restaurant for the *Joie de Vivre* Directory, please answer the following questions:

Type/s of cuisine: _____

Average price of a meal for two (excluding drinks): £ _____

Reason for your recommendation: _____

_____

Your name (Mr/Mrs/Ms/Miss): _____

Your address: _____

_____

CBV membership number (if applicable): _____

Signature: _____   Date: _____

Please return to: *LES ROUTIERS* 25 Vanston Place, London SW6 1AZ

INDEX OF *LES ROUTIERS* ESTABLISHMENTS

192 Restaurant see Notting Hill 40
51 Park Street see Bristol 102

A

A66 Motel 257
Abbey Bar & Courtyard Café 155
Abbey Bridge Inn 229
Abbots Mews Hotel 264
Abbotsford Arms Hotel 305
Abcone Hotel 38
Aberdeen Lodge 357
Abergwaun Hotel 283
Abingdon Arms 211
Academy Hotel 32
Achilty Hotel 319
Achness Hotel 331
Acorn Inn Hotel 143
Adderley Private Hotel 350
After Eight Restaurant 239
Agrah Indian Restaurant 240
Ailsa Craig Hotel 333
Albany Hotel 333
Albert Arms 91
Albert Hotel 337
Alessandria Hotel and Italian Restaurant 145
Alexandra Hotel 316
Alice Hawthorn 264
Allans Seafood Restaurant 145
Allhays Country House 111
Almondbank Inn 350
Altnaharra Hotel 318
Alverbank House Hotel 151
Alverton Manor 120
Ambassador Hotel see Llandudno 295
Ambassador Hotel see Scarborough 258
Ambassador Private Hotel 250
Anchor Inn see Cockwood 124
Anchor Inn see Sutton Gault 63
Anchor Inn Hotel 161
Ancient Shepherds 60
Andersons 262
Angel Inn see Longham 144
Angel Inn see Swalnes 32
Angel Inn see Thirsk 262
Angler's Rest 126
Anglesey Arms 93
Angus Hotel 346
Angus Hotel & Restaurant 230
Anne Port Bay Hotel 175

Anne-Marie at the 'Taste of the Taj' 34
Antonia's Bar Bistro 106
Antrobus Arms Hotel 170
Anvil Hotel and Restaurant 137
Appleton Hall Country House Hotel 252
Apsley House Hotel 98
Arches Hotel see Bristol 102
Arches Hotel see Ross-on-Wye 194
Arden House Hotel 254
Arden Tandoori Restaurant 217
Ardeonaig Hotel 319
Ards House 344
Ardtully Hotel 339
Argyll Hotel see Dunoon 339
Argyll Hotel see Isle of Iona 341
Arran House Hotel (Arran House) 45
Arties Mill 240
Arundel House Hotel 60
Ascot House 264
Ashburton Arms 129
Ashford Hotel & Restaurant 182
Ashley Hotel 41
Ashling Tara Hotel 52
Ashoka Tandoori 299
Asterisk Restaurant with Rooms 108
Atholl Arms Hotel 348
Atlantic Hotel 287
Atlas Hotel 38
Attenborough Hotel 258
Auld Kirk Hotel 316
Aultbea Hotel 319
Avalon Guest House 278
Avenue Hotel 154
Avoncroft Hotel 259

B

Babur Brasserie 36
Balavil Sport Hotel 330
Balcombe House Hotel 127
Balgedie Toll Tavern 349
Balmoral Hotel 312
Balzac Bistro 43
Banchory Lodge Hotel 316
Bangalore Tandoori 355
Barn Bistro 157
Bath Hotel 130
Bath Tasburgh Hotel 98
Battleborough Grange Country Hotel 160
Bay Horse 253
Bay Hotel 109

Bay Hotel & Restaurant 117
Bay View Court Hotel 137
Baycliffe Hotel 137
Bayley Arms 245
Bayview Hotel see Cullen 317
Bayview Hotel see Peterhead 318
Be My Guest 44
Beach Dunes Hotel 115
Beach House Hotel 270
Beaconwood Hotel 163
Beamish Park Hotel 272
Bear Hotel 168
Beauchamps Restaurant 40
Beaufort Hotel see Ormskirk 248
Beaufort Hotel see Portsmouth 153
Beaumont Hotel 269
Beaver Hotel 38
Beckmead House 235
Bedford Hotel 247
Beechcroft Hotel 147
Belfry Hotel 209
Belhaven House Hotel & Restaurant 285
Bell Bistro 216
Bell Cliff Restaurant 144
Bell Hotel & Restaurant 191
Bell Inn see Broadway 192
Bell Inn see Kersey 87
Bell Inn see Nottingham 205
Bell Inn see Rode 164
Bell Inn Hotel 63
Belle Plage Hotel 175
Belle Vue Hotel 151
Bellows Mill 56
Below Stairs Restaurant 186
Ben Loyal Hotel 331
Ben Mhor Hotel 323
Benedicto's 302
Benett Arms 146
Bensons Restaurant 144
Bent Arms 95
Bentley Brook Inn 182
Berkshire Hotel & Lillie Langtry Bar 175
Berties Bistro 275
Beswicks Restaurant 229
Betty Burkes 315
Bickenhall Hotel 45
Bickleigh Cottage Country Hotel 135
Billingham Arms Hotel 224
Bishops Bistro 225
Le Bistro see Prestwick 345
Le Bistro see Wirksworth 185
Black Boy Inn 292
Black Bull 272
Black Bull Inn see Berwick-upon-Tweed 268

383

Black Bull Inn see Brough Sowerby 229
Black Bull Inn see York 264
Black Horse 70
Black Lion Hotel 286
Blackford Hotel 346
Blacksmith's Arms Hotel 258
Blacksmiths Arms Inn 259
Blackwater Inn 348
Bleeding Heart Wine Bar 37
Blenheim Lodge 228
Blossoms Restaurant 298
Blue Ball Inn 134
Blue Bell 267
Blue Bell Restaurant 179
Blunsdon House Hotel 171
Bo-Peep Tea Rooms 186
Boars Head 212
Boathouse 181
Boathouse Restaurant 328
Bolholt 237
Bonnington in Bloomsbury 32
Boscean Country Hotel 119
Boskerris Hotel 118
Botany Bay Inne 149
La Bouffe 250
Bougie French Brasserie 132
Bowling Green Inn 184
Bowmans 212
Boxley House Hotel 77
Boyne Valley Hotel 360
Brabloch Hotel 345
Brackenborough Arms Hotel 200
Bradford Arms & Restaurant 212
Brae Guest House 332
Brae Hotel 321
Braemar Hotel 158
Bramcote Hall Hotel 138
La Braseria & Fortuna Wine Bar 299
La Brasserie 241
Brecon Hotel 271
Briarley Hotel 48
Bricks Restaurant 91
Bridge Guest House 135
Bridge Hotel see Buttermere 230
Bridge Hotel see Cambridge 60
Bridge Hotel see Greenford 49
Briggate Lodge Inn 241
Brighton Marina House Hotel 65
Britannia Lodge Hotel 254
British Raj Bangladeshi Restaurant 74
Brompton House 99
Bron Eifion Country House Hotel 293
Brook Lodge 218
Brook Meadow Hotel 180
Bruno's Restaurante Italiano 274
Brunswicks Restaurant 215
Bryn Glas Hotel 282
Bryn-y-Mor 175

Buccleugh & Queensberry Hotel 313
Buchan's 30
Buck's Head 356
Bull Hotel see Holyhead 294
Bull Hotel see Woodbridge 89
Bull Terrier 164
Bull's Head and Sussex Barn 93
Bulls Head 215
Bumbles Restaurant 47
Bunillidh Restaurant 324
Burley Court Hotel 138
Burlington Hotel 158
Burnt Wood House Hotel 64
Burton Cliff Hotel 141
Burts Hotel 306
Bushell's Arms 248
Busketts Lawn Hotel 152
Butler House 359
Butlers Hotel 278
Butt of Sherry 169
Byron House Hotel 264

C

La Cachette 55
Caerthillian 111
Caerwylan Hotel 293
Café De Bonheur 44
Le Café Des Amis Du Vin 34
Café in the Crypt 45
Café Niçoise 280
Café Rouge see Bayswater 31
Café Rouge see Chelsea 32
Café Rouge see Chiswick 33
Café Rouge see Ealing 35
Café Rouge see Fulham 36
Café Rouge see Hampstead 37
Café Rouge see Highgate 37
Café Rouge see Kensington 38
Café Rouge see Kew 39
Café Rouge see Knightsbridge 39
Café Rouge see London Bridge 40
Café Rouge see Maida Vale 40
Café Rouge see Notting Hill 40
Café Rouge see Putney 42
Café Rouge see Richmond 51
Café Rouge see Sheen 43
Café Rouge see Soho 43
Café Rouge see The City 44 and 44
Café Rouge see West End 45
Café Rouge see Wimbledon 47
Caffe Mamma 51
Cairngorm Guest House 319
Calcot Hotel 106
Caley Hall Motel & Restaurant 83
Calf's Head Hotel 245
Calico Café Bar Restaurant 44
Callater Lodge Hotel 317

Canary Café 99
Candlesticks Hotel & Restaurant 202
Cantley House Hotel / Maryline's Brasserie 107
Cape Wrath Hotel 321
Captain's Table 89
Caragh Lodge 359
Caravela Restaurant 249
Cardiff West Pavilion Lodge at Cardiff West Service Area 302
Carew Arms 164
Carlton House Hotel 265
Carnarvon Hotel 35
Carnson House Hotel 115
Carpenter's Arms 168
Carrington Hotel 105
Carrygerry House Hotel 355
Casa Tomas Ristorante 104
Casanova Restaurant 295
Castle Arms Hotel 331
Castle Coaching Inn 301
Castle Cottage Hotel & Restaurant 294
Castle Grove Country House 355
Castle Hotel see Harlech 294
Castle Hotel see Haverfordwest 284
Castle Inn see Edenbridge 76
Castle Inn see West Lulworth 147
Castle Inn Hotel 130
Castle Moil Restaurant 326
Castlebay Hotel 351
Cat Inn 268
Catacol Bay Hotel 341
Cathedral View Guest House 156
Causeway Coast Hotel & Conference Centre 354
Cawdor Tavern 319
Cefn-Bryn 303
Ceilidh Place 332
Cellar No. 1 333
Central Hotel 259
Chadwick Hotel & Leisure Complex 247
Chain Bridge Hotel 281
Charlotte Restaurant & Guest House 47
Charlotte's Place 35
Chase Lodge Hotel 50
Chaser Inn 80
Chatsworth 147
Chatsworth Hotel 67
Chauntry House Hotel 106
Chequers see Gedney Dyke 199
Chequers see Westoning 56
Chequers Inn 194
Le Chevalier 196
Cheyney Lodge Hotel 179
Chez Colette 281
Chez Ton Ton 61
Chine Hotel 138
Chinehurst Hotel 138
Chiswick Hotel 33
Christopher Hotel 107

384

Chy-an-Dour Hotel 118
Chy-an-Gwedhen 118
City Limits Restaurant & Wine Bar 32
Clachaig Hotel 309
Clare Hotel 86
Clarence Hotel 53
Clarendon Arms 217
Clarendon Hotel and Wight Mouse Inn 157
Cliff Hotel *see* Great Yarmouth 83
Cliff Hotel *see* Harwich 72
Cliffeside Hotel 139
Clifton Coffee House 310
Clifton House Hotel 294
Clock Tower Restaurant 279
Cluanie Inn 323
Coach House Hotel 203
Coasters Bar & Diner 243
Cobden's Hotel & Brasserie 293
Cobweb Tea Rooms 154
Cock & Bell Inn 87
Coffee Club 342
Colliers Arms 193
Collyers Hotel 275
Commodore Hotel 105
Compass Abbey Hotel 99
Compston House Hotel 227
Coniston Hotel 80
Coniston Lodge Hotel 230
Connection 279
Coombe Barton Inn 108
Coombe Farm 111
Copper Horse 259
Copper Kettle 232
Copper Skillet 142
Coquet Vale Hotel 269
Coriander Restaurant 139
Corisande Manor Hotel 113
Corkers Café Bar & Restaurant 145
Corner House *see* Lynmouth 130
Corner House *see* Taunton 164
Cornish Arms 117
Cornucopia 256
Corporation Arms 247
Corran View Guest House 352
Cosmopolitan Hotel 65
Cossington Mill 197
Cote Du Nord Hotel 175
Cothi Bridge Hotel 283
Cotswold Gateway 208
Cotswold Grange Hotel 187
Cottage Inn Hotel 267
Country Pie 211
Countryman at Trink 118
Countryman Inn 95
County Arms Hotel 360
County Hotel 269
County Hotel & Restaurant 332
Court Barn Country House Hotel 124
Court Hotel 99
Court House 96
Court Royale Hotel 283

Courtyard at the Blue Anchor 246
Cow & Calf Hotel 278
Cowick Barton Inn 126
Craggan Mill Restaurant 324
Craig Cleeve House 218
Craigmore Hotel 341
Craigower Hotel 351
Craigwell Hotel & Teddy's Restaurant 248
Cranbourne Hotel 133
Cranleigh Hotel 92
Crawford Hotel 201
Creggans Inn 345
Crescent Lodge Hotel 49
Crimond Hotel 250
Cringletie House Hotel 306
Croft-na-Caber 349
Crook Inn 309
Cross Keys Inn 100
Crossways Inn 165
Crown & Castle Hotel 88
Crown at Whitebrook 289
Crown Hotel *see* Bildeston 85
Crown Hotel *see* Chertsey 90
Crown Hotel *see* Downham Market 82
Crown Hotel *see* Faringdon 209
Crown Hotel *see* Newton Stewart 312
Crown Hotel *see* Skegness 201
Crown Hotel & Restaurant 85
Crown Inn *see* Chippenham 167
Crown Inn *see* Linton 62
Crown Inn *see* Old Dalby 198
Crown Inn Hotel 87
Crown of Crucis Hotel & Restaurant 187
La Cucina Restaurant 68
Culduthel Lodge 325
Culver Lodge Hotel 157
Cumberland Hotel *see* Bournemouth 139
Cumberland Hotel *see* Harrow 49

D

Dalesman Country Inn 234
Dalmacia House 36
Damson Dene Hotel 228
Dannah Farm Country Guest House 182
Dark Island Hotel 352
Dartmoor Halfway 122
Dean Park Hotel 139
Dedes Hotel and Wheel Inn, Pub and Restaurant 128
Deerstalker Restaurant 244
Deganwy Castle Hotel 293
Del Secolo 250
Dering Arms 78
Devonshire Hotel 136
Dino's (Mayfair) 40
Dixcart Hotel 174

Dog House Hotel 207
Dolphin Hotel 63
Don Pepe Restaurant 45
Donatello Restaurant 65
Donington Manor Hotel 196
Dorian House 100
Drake Court Hotel 57
Drovers Restaurant 285
Drusillas Park 64
Dufferin Arms 356
Duisdale Hotel 326
Duke of Connaught Hotel 265
Duke of Wellington Inn 256
Duke of York 70
Duke of York Inn 275
Duke William 77
Dunbeath Hotel 321
Dundonald Old Mill 356
Dunoon Hotel 296
Dunorin House Hotel 326
Durlston Court Hotel 139
Durrant House Hotel 122
Duxford Lodge Hotel 61

E

Eagle Lodge Hotel 202
Earl of March 94
Easington House & Farmhouse Restaurant 208
East Ayton Lodge Country Hotel & Restaurant 259
East Midlands Hotel 197
Eastern Promise Chinese Restaurant 110
Easton House 94
Eaton Court Hotel 217
Eddrachilles Hotel 331
Edelweiss Hotel 280
Eden House Hotel 313
Edgemoor Hotel 123
Edward Court Hotel 107
Edward Lear Hotel 45
Edward's Dining Room at Highfield House 171
Edwardian House Hotel 54
Edwards of Crick 203
Elizabethan Restaurant 184
Elm Crest Guest Hotel 276
Elm Grange Hotel 238
Elton Hotel 271
Embassy Hotel 140
Empire Hotel 296
English's Oyster Bar & Seafood Restaurant 65
Epchris Hotel 128
Epsom Downs Hotel 91
Euro and George Hotels 32
Ewington Hotel 340
Exmoor Sandpiper Inn 131
Exmoor White Horse Inn 161

F

Falcon 283
Falcon Hotel *see* Bude 108
Falcon Hotel *see* Uppingham 199

385

Falcon Inn 260
Falcon's Nest Hotel 242
Falls of Lora Hotel 344
Famous Schooner Hotel 267
Farmers Hotel 172
Ferncourt Hotel 273
Fernie Castle Hotel 314
Fernlea Hotel & Leisure Complex 247
Ferraris Restaurant 249
Feversham Arms Hotel 255
Fiddler's Restaurant 49
51 Park Street see Bristol 102
Finders Keepers 170
Finkles Restaurant 231
Finnstown Country House Hotel 358
La Fiorentina 340
Fisherman's Haunt Hotel 142
Fitzgeralds Restaurant 204
Flemings Hotel 222
Flemington Inn 305
Flintlock Inn 127
Flodigarry Country House Hotel 326
Food For Thought 34
Forbes Arms Hotel 316
Forest Hills Hotel 313
La Foret 153
Fortfield Hotel 134
Fortingall Hotel 346
Forton Pavilion Lodge at Forton Service Area 246
Foulford Inn 347
Fountain Court Hotel 220
Fountain Inn 290
Fountain Inn & Boxers Restaurant 165
Fourcroft Hotel 287
Fouters Bistro 338
Fox Inn 210
Fox Reformed 43
Foxholes Hotel 344
Francos 358
Francs Restaurant see Altrincham 236
Francs Restaurant see Chester 179
French Horn 56
Friends Restaurant 50
Fung-Shing 34

G

Gables Hotel 216
Gales 281
Galleon Restaurant 116
Gallon Pot 83
Game Larder Restaurant 155
Ganges 102
Ganges Restaurant 121
Garden Court Hotel 31
Gardens Hotel 238
Garlands 122
Garrick's at Maynard's 160
Garth Hotel 46
Gate Lodge Guest House 84
Gavin's Restaurant 42

George 57
George & Dragon see Kirkbymoorside 255
George & Dragon see Rowde 170
George & Dragon see West Wycombe 59
George and Dragon 170
George Hotel see Darlington 226
George Hotel see Frome 162
George Hotel see Leadenham 200
George Hotel see Loughborough 197
George Hotel & Restaurant 160
George Inn see Bridport 141
George Inn see Cambridge 186
Georges Hotel 100
Georgian House Hotel 236
Gilton Hotel 251
Giovanni's Restaurant 81
La Giralda 51
Gladyer Inn 315
Glaister's Garden Bistro 33
Glass Boat 102
Glen Eldon Hotel 343
Y Glennydd Guest House 287
Glenavon House Hotel 361
Glenforsa Hotel 342
Glenisla Hotel 347
Glenorchy Lodge Hotel 339
Glenormes Private Hotel 296
Glenthorne Hotel 176
Glyn y Coed Hotel 293
Goffs Park Hotel 94
Golden Eagle Hotel 225
Golden Grid Fish Restaurant 260
Gongoozler Restaurant 165
Gourmet Restaurant 48
Granby Guest House 296
Grand Hotel 225
La Grande Mare 174
Grange Hotel see Bournemouth 140
Grange Hotel see Bury St Edmunds 85
Grange Hotel see Newark-on-Trent 205
Grange Hotel see Norwich 84
Grange Restaurant 274
Grapevine Hotel 190
Grasmead House Hotel 265
Grasmere Court Hotel 103
Grassington House Hotel 253
Great Eastern Hotel 30
Great Northern Hotel 39
Great Western Hotel 113
Green Gables Guest House 235
Green Lawns Hotel 109
Green Man 76
Green Man Inn 192
Green Park Hotel 351
Greenbank Guest House & Licensed Restaurant 338

Greenside Hotel 334
Greenwood Lodge 176
La Grenouille 276
Gretna Hotel & Restaurant 227
Greyhound 69
Greyhound Hotel 155
Greyhound Inn see Burton on the Wolds 196
Greyhound Inn see Carlisle 230
Greyhound Inn & Hotel 289
Griffins Head 205
Grizedale Lodge Hotel & Restaurant 231
Grove Hotel 110
Grove House Hotel & Restaurant 251
Grundy's Restaurant 254
Guanock Hotel 84
Guisachan House 321
Gupshill Manor 192
Gyllyngvase House Hotel 110

H

Haddon House Hotel 142
Hagley Court Hotel 220
Halfway House Hotel 314
Halland Forge Hotel & Restaurant 69
Hallgarth Manor Hotel 226
Halpins Hotel 354
Hambledon Hotel 158
Hanover Square Wine Bar & Grill 47
Hansom Cabin 108
Harbour Bistro 242
Harbour House Hotel & Restaurant 287
Harbour Lights 112
Harbour Lights Hotel 332
Harbour Restaurant 340
Hare & Hounds see Cirencester 187
Hare & Hounds see Ledburn 57
Harestock Lodge Hotel & Restaurant 156
Harp 81
Harris Hotel 352
Harrow 107
Harrow Hotel 37
Harry Hare's Restaurant & Brasserie 188
Hartnoll Country House Hotel 135
Haven 206
Haven Hotel 145
Havenhurst Hotel 146
Hawnby Hotel 265
Hay-Way 183
Headland Hotel 113
Headlands Hotel see Ilfracombe 128
Headlands Hotel see Llandudno 296
Heath House Hotel 296
Heath Lodge Hotel 220

386

Heathfield 127
Heathmount Hotel 325
Hedley House 265
Hellenik Restaurant 33
Henllys 285
Henry Africa's Hothouse 103
Henry's Café Bar (Birmingham) 220
Henry's Café Bar (Bromley) 76
Henry's Café Bar (Cambridge) 60
Henry's Café Bar (Cardiff) 303
Henry's Café Bar (Covent Garden) 34
Henry's Café Bar (Manchester) 238
Henry's Café Bar (Piccadilly) 42
Henry's Café Bar (Richmond) 51
Henry's Café Bar (Sheffield) 271
Henry's Café Bar (Wapping) 44
Hensleigh Hotel 142
Herges 306
Hetland Hall Hotel 310
Hideaway Hotel 235
Highfield Hotel 232
Hill Foot Hotel 234
Hill's Tudor Rose Hotel 243
Hillcrest Country House & Restaurant 354
Hillcrest Hotel 200
Hilton Park Pavilion Lodge at Hilton Park Service Area 223
Hind's Head Hotel & Restaurant 249
Hobnails Inn 189
Hodgson's 38
Holbrook House Hotel 165
Holland Park Hotel 38
Hong Hong Restaurant 107
Hopcrofts Holt Hotel 210
Hope & Anchor Inn 284
Ye Horn's Inn 249
Horseshoe Inn see Burton upon Trent 215
Horseshoe Inn see Shipston on Stour 217
Hotel Eilean Iarmain 326
Hotel Gainsborough 149
Hotel Mon Bijou 140
Hotel Montville & Granny's Restaurant 194
Hotel Ristorante La Gondola 183
Hotel Rosslare 362
Hotel Rudyard 215
Hotel Seaforth 346
Hotspur Hotel 267
Housel Bay Hotel 120
Howard Arms 217
Howard Hotel 334
Howth Lodge Hotel 357
Huddersfield Hotel / Rosemary Lane Bistro 277
Hudson's Hotel 265

Hundred House Hotel, Restaurant & Inn 213
Hunters Arms Hotel 199
Hunters Restaurant 118
Huntsman Hotel 288
Hurdles Pub and Restaurant 150

I

Ilfracombe Carlton 128
Imperial Crown Hotel 275
Imperial Hotel see Great Yarmouth 83
Imperial Hotel see Llandudno 297
Imperial Hotel see Tenby 288
Imperial Hotel, Bars & Restaurant 174
Imperial Inn 129
Inchalla Hotel 173
Inglenook Licensed Restaurant 312
Inglewood Hotel 241
Ingoldsby Hotel 136
Inn at Freshford 104
Inn at Whitewell 245
Inn On the Green 132
Inn On the Moor 253
Inn On the Park 361
Inn The Priory 95
Inshaig Park Hotel 340
Invergarry Hotel 324
Isle of Colonsay Hotel 341
Isles of Glencoe Hotel & Leisure Centre 321
Italian Place Brasserie 53
Ivy House Hotel 232
Ivyside Hotel 78

J

Jack's Place 31
Jackdaw Restaurant 270
Jacklins Restaurant 71
Jackson's Hotel 355
Jallans 206
Jarvis Peacock Hotel 184
Jasper's Bun in the Oven 50
Jester Hotel 73
Jingle's Restaurant 136
Jingles 150
Joanna's 34
John H. Stracey 82
Johnscliffe Hotel & Restaurant 196
Jolly Huntsman 167
Jolly Sailors 82
Jubilee Inn 103
Judge Jeffreys Restaurant 142

K

Kathleen's Country House 359
Kea House Restaurant 120

Kegworth Hotel 184
Kempton House Hotel 65
Kendal Arms Hotel 232
Kensington Court Hotel 35
Kensington Hall Hotel 226
Kensington International Hotel 35
Kersbrook Hotel & Restaurant 144
Kilmorey Arms Hotel 356
Kimberley Hotel 65
Kincraig House Hotel 325
Kinfare Hotel & Restaurant 222
King William IV Freehouse & Restaurant 59
King's Arms Hotel & Clubroom Restaurant 252
Kings Arms Hotel see Hawkshead 231
Kings Arms Hotel see Reeth 257
Kings Arms Hotel see Salisbury 170
Kings Arms Hotel see Westerham 81
Kings Arms Inn 163
Kings Head 200
Kings Head Hotel see Cirencester 188
Kings Head Hotel see Malton 256
Kings Shade Coffee House 92
Kingsdown Hotel 78
Kingsmuir Hotel 307
Kingstons Black Horse Inn 240
Kingstown Hotel 240
Kingsway Hotel 96
Kingswood Hotel see Burntisland 313
Kingswood Hotel see Sidmouth 134
Kinloch Lodge 327
Kirklands Hotel see Hawick 306
Kirklands Hotel see Kinross 349
Kirkwall Hotel 337
Kitchen 116
Kitchins Bistro & Cellar Bar 232
Kites Restaurant 266
Knife & Cleaver 55
Knoll Hotel 229
Knotts Mill Country Lodge 233
Knutsford Pavilion Service Area 180
Krimo's 225
Kylestrome Hotel 338

L

Lady Godiva Hotel 221
Lairgate Hotel 239
Lake View Hotel 295
Lake Vyrnwy Hotel 300
Lamb Inn 189

387

Lamb Inn West Wittering 96
Lamb's 126
Lambsquay House Hotel 190
Lancers Brasserie 334
Landgate Bistro 68
Langham Hotel 254
Langley Castle Hotel 269
Langley's Bistro 155
Langstone Cliff Hotel 125
Lansdowne Hotel 136
Lansdowne Strand Hotel 166
Lastra Farm Hotel 291
Laws Hotel 55
Leadburn Inn 336
Leaside Hotel 56
Leasow House 192
Leasowe Castle 251
Leighton House 100
Lenchford Hotel 195
Liberty City 178
Lilmont Hotel 260
Limetree Restaurant and Hotel 77
Linden Hotel 103
Lindum Hotel 248
Links Hotel 350
Lion at Pennard 162
Lion Hotel see Dulverton 161
Lion Hotel see Nefyn 298
Lion Hotel see Worksop 207
Lion Hotel & Restaurant 302
Lions Court Restaurant & Hotel 150
Livermead Cliff Hotel 137
Llew Glas 295
Y Llong – The Ship 298
Llugwy Hall Country House Hotel 301
Llwyndu Farmhouse Hotel 291
Lobster Pot Hotel & Restaurant 176
Loch Etive Hotel 345
Loch Ness House Hotel 325
Loch Ness Lodge Hotel 320
Lochearnhead Hotel 310
Lochgair Hotel 343
Lochmaddy Hotel 352
Lockerbie Manor Country Hotel 311
Lodge 270
Lodge Hotel see Huddersfield 277
Lodge Hotel see Insch 318
Lodge Hotel see Newtonmore 330
Lodge Hotel see Tal-y-Bont 299
Log Cabin Hotel 350
Lomond Hills Hotel 314
London Continental Hotel 46
London Home To Home 35
London Hotel 191
Longland's Eating House 183
Longview Hotel & Restaurant 180
Loughpool Inn 194
Lundy House Hotel 131

Lyndhurst Hotel 220
Lynnhurst Hotel 342
Lynwood Guest House 115

M

MacDonald Hotel 328
Madeira Hall 159
La Madeleine 46
Mae-Mar Hotel 140
Maer Lodge Hotel 108
Maes-y-Derw Guest House & Restaurant 286
Maes-y-Gwernen 303
Magpie Café 263
Maid Marian Restaurant 204
Mains Hotel 330
Malbank Hotel 181
Maldua Guest House 358
Mallin House Hotel 320
Mamma Mia 179
Mandarin Restaurant 240
Mannings Hotel & Restaurant 81
Manor Arms 160
Manor Heath Hotel 260
Manor Hotel 143
Manor House 146
Manor House Hotel 125
Manor Park Hotel 343
Marche Restaurant – The Swiss Centre 46
Marcorrie 121
La Margherita Restaurant 155
Marine Hotel see Crail 313
Marine Hotel see Guernsey 174
Marine Hotel see Mallaig 329
Market Hotel 92
Market Tavern Hotel 299
Markington Hotel 48
Markree Castle 361
Marlborough Hotel 86
Marlowes Restaurant 218
Marshmallow 189
Martins Arms Inn 204
May House Restaurant 243
Mayflower Hotel 73
Mayflower Restaurant 250
Maypole Inn 256
Maytime Inn 207
Medway Pavilion Lodge at Medway Pavilion Service Area 77
Melford Hall Hotel 66
Mellon Country Inn 361
Merriemeade Hotel 136
Merrion Hall 357
Mews Wine Bar & Restaurant 195
Miami Hotel 70
Micawber's Restaurant 94
Midland Hotel 242
Milburn Arms Hotel 258
Miles House Restaurant 249
Mill at Oundle 204
Mill House Hotel 317
Mill House Hotel & Bishop's Cottage 144

Millbrook House 176
Millcroft Hotel 322
Miller of Mansfield Hotel 209
Miller's Arms 76
Millers Restaurant 261
Millers Wine Bar 201
Millslade Country House Hotel 131
Millstone Hotel 243
Ming 43
Minmore House 317
Mitre Hotel 49
Mitre House Hotel 42
Moat House Restaurant 216
Moelwyn Restaurant with Rooms 294
Moghul Palace 58
Molesworth Arms Hotel 121
Mongolian 92
Monmouth Punch House 290
Monroes 251
Mont Millais Hotel 177
Montgreenan Mansion House Hotel 343
Moon & Sixpence 208
Moonfleet Manor 148
Moonraker House 218
Moorings Hotel see Fort William 322
Moorings Hotel see Sevenoaks 79
Moorings House Hotel 344
Moorlands Hotel 253
Morangie House Hotel 331
Mornish Hotel 109
Morton's Fork 78
Motel Leeming 255
Mount Hotel 256
Mount Pleasant Hotel 192
Mount Royale 266
Mountview Hotel & Highland Game Restaurant 329
Mowbray Park Hotel 273
Mowlem Restaurant 147
Mr Bistro 112
Mr Chips Fish Restaurant 201
Muirs Inn Kinross 349
Murray Arms Hotel 311
Myra Restaurant 42
Mysore Indian Cuisine 58

N

Nag's Head 31
Nag's Head Hotel & Restaurant 262
Nanplough Farm 110
National Hotel 320
Natraj Tandoori (Nepalese & Indian Cuisine) 103
Le Nautique Restaurant 174
Navigation Inn see Milton Keynes 58
Navigation Inn see Wootton Wawen 219
Needhams Farm 237

Neeld Arms Inn 167
Nelson's Restaurant 116
Ness House Hotel 133
Nest Bistro 285
Netherwood Hotel 231
Neville's Cross Hotel 226
Nevisport Restaurant 322
New Commercial Inn 121
New Farm House 72
New Ferry Restaurant 205
New Inn see Appleby-in-Westmoreland 228
New Inn see Dorchester 143
New Inn Hotel 261
New Steine Hotel 66
Newington Manor Hotel & Restaurant 80
Newlands House 142
Newlyn Private Hotel 244
Newlyn Rex Hotel 244
Newton Lodge 328
Newtown House Hotel 151
No. 77 Wine Bar 47
Noel Arms Hotel 187
Nordic Hotel 278
Northern Hotel 64
Northgate House 84
Northwood Hotel 281

O

Oak Hall Hotel 140
Oak Lodge Hotel 48
Oaklands Hotel 157
Oakwood Hall Hotel 275
Office Wine Bar 81
Old Bell Hotel 172
Old Black Lion 193
Old Bordeaux 334
Old Calcutta 41
Old Chequers 88
Old Church House Inn 137
Old Cottage Restaurant 154
Old Counting House Restaurant 87
Old Court Hotel & Restaurant 194
Old Etonian Restaurant 50
Old Ferry Boat Inn 62
Old Forge Restaurant 69
Old Garden House 82
Old Green Man 50
Old Hall Hotel see Buxton 183
Old Hall Hotel see Frodsham 180
Old House at Home 167
Old Inn 163
Old Malt House Hotel 100
Old Manse Hotel 186
Old Mill Country House 115
Old Mill Guest House 151
Old Mill Hotel & Restaurant 238
Old Mill House 87
Old Mill Inn & Restaurant 315
Old New Inn 186
Old Original Rosslyn Inn 336

Old Park Hotel 159
Old Plough 69
Old Plough Inn 134
Old Queen's Head 71
Old Queens Head 58
Old Racecourse Hotel 338
Old Red Lion 62
Old Rose & Crown 57
Old School Hotel 117
Old Ship 206
Old Sidings 271
Old Stocks Hotel 191
Old Success Inn Hotel 111
Old Swan 58
Old Thatch Inn 126
Old Tollgate Restaurant & Hotel 95
Old Tudor Rectory 197
Old Vicarage Country House Hotel 236
Old Vine 69
Old White Hart Country Inn & Restaurant 198
Old White Lion Hotel 276
Ye Olde Salutation Inn 195
Ye Olde Toll House Restaurant 222
Oldfield House 235
Olive Tree Greek Restaurant 278
Oliver's Lodge Hotel & Restaurant 63
192 Restaurant see Notting Hill 40
Opposition Restaurant 218
Orepool Inn & Motel 189
Oriel House Hotel 282
Original Farmers Arms 246
Ormonde House 152
Osbourne Hotel & Shelbourne Lounge 334
Oscars 106
Oscars Restaurant 358
Ostrich Inn 82
Otterburn Tower Hotel 269
Oxwich Bay Hotel 303

P

Packe Arms 198
Packford's Hotel 53
Panborough Inn 163
Pancake Place 315
Pandora Inn 113
Panmure Arms Hotel 348
Panorama Hotel 291
Park Hall Hotel 185
Park Hotel 307
Park View Hotel 126
Parkend House Hotel 190
Parkgate Hotel 181
Parkway Hotel & Conference Centre 289
Parkwood Hotel 46
Peacock Hotel 86
Pearl De Mare Chinese Cuisine 105
Pearse House 74
Pearson Park Hotel 241
Peat Gate Head 257

Pebbles Guest House 148
Pedn-Olva Hotel & Restaurant 119
Peebles Hotel Hydro 307
Peelers Bistro 152
Pelynt Dagger Restaurant 112
Pembroke Arms Hotel 171
Pendower Beach House Hotel 120
Penkerris 117
Penny Farthing Hotel 153
Pennyghael Hotel 342
Penrhyn House Hotel 116
Pepper Mill Restaurant 243
Peppers Restaurant 284
Peterstone Court 300
Le Petit St Tropez 143
Pheasant 62
Pheasant Hotel 255
Pheasant Inn 228
Philipburn House Hotel & Restaurant 307
Piccadilly Restaurant 46
Pickwicks 210
Pinewood Private Hotel 279
Pinocchio 66
Pinocchio's Restaurant 220
Pissarro's Wine Bar 50
Plas Coch Hotel 291
Plas Elwy 282
Platters Restaurant 94
Plough Inn see Hathersage 184
Plough Inn see Hillsborough 356
Plough Inn see Wigglesworth 264
Plunkets Restaurant Ltd 266
Polash Restaurant 72
Pontoon Bridge Hotel 360
Pool House Hotel 330
Porky's 51
Port William 120
Porth Avallen Hotel 109
Il Portico 39
Portland Hotel 200
Portovino's Restaurant 79
La Poubelle 72
Powdermills Hotel 64
Powfoot Golf Hotel 310
Preston House Hotel 123
Princes House 323
Priory Hotel 101
Pullman Lodge Hotel 274
Punchbowl Inn 112

Q

Quayside Hotel 123
Queen's Hotel 141
Queens Hotel see Gullane 336
Queens Hotel see Keswick 232
Queensmead Hotel 158
Quiggins Restaurant 89
Quinn's Restaurant 229
Quoyburray Inn 337

389

R

Raddicombe Lodge 123
Ragged Cot Inn 191
Rainbow Café 104
Ramleh Hotel & Fingal's Restaurant 329
Ramsey House 287
Ramside Hall Hotel 226
Randell's Hotel & Leisure 261
Rangeworthy Court Hotel 105
Rani Vegetarian Restaurant 36
Raphaels Restaurant 214
Rascals Bistro 101
Rathlin House Hotel 135
Rattlebone Inn 171
Ravenhurst Hotel 297
Ravenscourt House Hotel 324
Red Lea Hotel 260
Red Lion *see* Didcot 209
Red Lion *see* Fernhurst 94
Red Lion *see* Worksop 207
Red Lion Hotel *see* Northampton 203
Red Lion Hotel *see* Spalding 202
Red Lion Inn *see* Banbury 208
Red Lion Inn *see* Rothley 198
Red Lion Inn / Le Baron Restaurant 202
Red Lion Motel & Country Inn 266
Redcliffe Hotel 132
Redcoats Farmhouse Hotel 74
Redheugh Hotel 333
Redland Hotel 179
Reedham Ferry & Inn 84
Regency Hotel 83
Regency Restaurant 66
Regent Hotel 60
Regent Hotel, Parade Bar & Restaurant 271
Renoirs 213
Rest & Be Thankful Inn 162
Restaurant Sebastian 213
Restaurant Twenty Seven 68
Retreat *see* Cheltenham 187
Retreat *see* Stourbridge 222
Rising Sun Hotel 130
River Terrace 51
Riverdale Country House Hotel 252
Riverdale Hall Hotel 267
Riversdale House Hotel 359
Riversford Hotel 122
Riverside Hotel 227
Riverside Inn Hotel & Restaurant 166
Rivington Pavilion Service Area 237
Road Chef 357
Robin Hood 71
Robin Hood Inn 248
Roch Gate Motel 284
Rock House Hotel 130
Rock Inn Hotel & Churchill's Restaurant 276
Rockvale Hotel 131
Rockvilla Hotel & Restaurant 329
Rod & Reel 309
Roebuck Inn 208
Rone House Hotel 124
Rookery 102
Rookery Hall Hotel 181
Rosco's Eating House 237
Rose & Crown *see* Alderney 173
Rose & Crown *see* Fletching 68
Rose & Crown *see* Ridgemont 56
Rose & Crown *see* Trent 147
Rose & Crown Freehouse 85
Rose & Crown Hotel 71
Rose & Crown Inn 190
Rose & Thistle 154
Rose Tor Hotel 297
Rosedale Hotel 327
Rosemount Golf Hotel 347
Roskarnon House Hotel 117
Roslin Hotel 73
Ross Lake House Hotel 358
Rossini Restaurant 216
Rosslyn Hotel 132
Rowton Hall Hotel 180
Royal Castle Hotel 125
Royal Circus Hotel 334
Royal Derwent Hotel 226
Royal Goat Hotel 292
Royal Hotel *see* Bognor Regis 93
Royal Hotel *see* Cromarty 320
Royal Hotel *see* Forfar 348
Royal Hotel *see* Isle of Skye 327
Royal Hotel *see* Kingussie 28
Royal Hotel *see* Winchester 156
Royal Lion Hotel 145
Royal Marine Hotel 339
Royal Oak *see* Carlisle 230
Royal Oak *see* Grantham 199
Royal Oak *see* Llantrisant 289
Royal Oak Hotel *see* Betws-y-Coed 292
Royal Oak Hotel *see* Welshpool 302
Royal Oak Inn *see* Exmoor 162
Royal Oak Inn *see* Llandovery 285
Royal Standard 75
Royal Standard of England 57
Rudloe Park Hotel & Restaurant 168
Rudstone Walk Farm 239
Ruislip Tandoori 52
Runshaw College School of Catering 247
Russ Hill Hotel 90
Russell Hotel 79
Rutland Arms 195

S

Sachins 273
Saffron Hotel 72
St Aiden Hotel & Restaurant 270
St Ann's House 325
St Brannocks House Hotel 128
St Brides Hotel 286
St Catherine's Lodge Hotel 66
St Giles Hotel 47
St Helen's Restaurant 159
St John's Lodge 235
St Magnus Bay Hotel 337
St Magnus Court Hotel 316
St Maur Hotel 159
St Peters Hotel 37
St Uny Hotel 119
Saints & Scholars Ltd 354
La Sala Romana 39
Saleem Bagh 215
Salisbury Arms Hotel 74
Salisbury View Hotel 335
Samratt Indian Cuisine 42
Sandbanks Hotel 145
Sandringham Hotel 297
Sandy Cove Hotel 124
Sawrey Hotel 231
La Scala Restaurant 91
Schooner 304
Scoffs Eating House 39
Scotch Corner Pavilion Lodge at Scotch Corner Service Area 257
Scotland's Hotel 351
Sea Cow Restaurant 148
Sea Hotel 273
Seacliffe Hotel 263
Seacourt Hotel 239
Seafarer Steak House & Fish Restaurant 153
Seafield Hotel 253
Seaview Hotel & Restaurant 157
Sefton Hotel 242
Selkirk Arms Hotel 311
Sentry Mead Hotel 159
Sequoia House Private Hotel 218
Seven Stars Inn 227
Sevenoaks Park Hotel 79
Sevens Wine Bar & Bistro 91
Severn Arms Hotel 300
Severn View Pavilion Lodge at Severn View Service Area 104
Shannon Court Hotel 254
Sharksfin Hotel & Restaurant 112
Shaven Crown Hotel 210
Shaw Hill Hotel, Golf & Country Club 244
Shelleys Cottage Hotel 131
Shelton Hall Hotel 213
Shepherd & Dog 71
Shepherds Inn 233
Sheppard's Hotel, Restaurant & Bistro 262
Shetland Hotel 338

390

Ship Inn see Axmouth 122
Ship Inn see Llanbedrog 295
Ship Inn see Rye 69
Ship Inn & Smugglers Restaurant 80
Ship Inn Restaurant 148
Shoulder of Mutton Inn see Middleton Tyas 256
Shoulder of Mutton Inn see Welford 204
Sidney House 193
Six Bells 211
Sixties Wine Bar 92
Skeabost House Hotel 327
Skidden House Hotel & Restaurant 119
Skippers 283
Sloop Inn 95
Sloping Deck Restaurant 125
Smeatons Tower Hotel 133
Smithy 312
Smoke House 88
Smoking Dog 169
Smugglers Cottage of Tolverne 116
Smugglers Restaurant see Birchington 75
Smugglers Restaurant see Crieff 348
Sodbury House Hotel 104
Sou'West Lodge Hotel 148
South Garden Cantonese & Pekinese Cuisine 154
South Lodge Hotel 70
South Sands Hotel 132
Southlands Hotel 260
Spinning Wheel Tavern 179
Sportsman's Inn 133
Sportsman's Restaurant & March Bank Hotel 233
Spotted Dog 78
Spread Eagle Hotel (Sawley) Ltd 245
Spread Eagle Restaurant 36
Springfield House Hotel & Restaurant 246
Springfort Hall 355
Springwells Hotel 96
Squirrel Inn 64
Stag Hotel 344
Stakesby Manor 263
Stanshope Hall 182
Stanton's Restaurant 110
Star 92
Star & Tipsy Toad Brewery 177
Star Hotel 312
Star Inn 203
Starlings Castle 213
Station Hotel 347
Staveley Arms (Spit Roast) 258
Steading Restaurant 323
Steampacket Hotel 311
Steels Corner House Restaurant 240
Stirling Arms Hotel 309

Stirling Management Centre 310
Stoke Lodge Hotel 125
Stone Manor Hotel 193
Strand Restaurant 201
Stromness Hotel 337
Studley Hotel 254
Stumbles Hotel & Restaurant 134
Stybeck Farm 234
Suffolk House 61
Sunningdale Hotel 148
Sunnybank Guest House 185
Sunray 244
Surfers Restaurant 252
Surtees Hotel / Wings Restaurant 273
Sutherland House Restaurant 89
Sutton Court Hotel 222
Sutton Hall 181
Sutton Staithe Hotel 85
Swan Hotel see Abergavenny 288
Swan Hotel see Arundel 93
Swan Hotel see Bampton 122
Swan Hotel see Bradford on Avon 166
Swan House Hotel 219
Swansea Pavilion Lodge at Swansea Service Area 304
Sydney House Hotel 214
Sysonby Knoll Hotel & Restaurant 198

T

Talbot Hotel 169
Tartar Frigate 75
Tatties 61
Tattler 335
Tavern at Tansley 185
Taychreggan Hotel 345
Tayvallich Inn 346
Tea Shoppe 161
Tebay Mountain Lodge Hotel 234
Terrace Hotel 335
Terrace Restaurant 221
La Terraza 36
Tex Mex 335
Thames Riviera Hotel 106
That Café 238
Thatched House Hotel 52
Theatr Clwyd 281
Thistle Hotel 350
Thornbank Hotel 235
Thornton Hall Hotel 251
Three Acres Inn & Restaurant 277
Three Cocks Hotel 300
Three Cranes 66
Three Crowns 167
Three Crowns Hotel 124
Three Hills 59
Three Horseshoes Inn & Restaurant 215
Three Tuns Inn see Canterbury 76

Three Tuns Inn see Osmotherley 257
Tigh-a-Righ House 322
Tillmouth Park Hotel 268
Le Toad and Stumps Bistro 150
Tolbooth Restaurant 318
Toll House Restaurant 204
Tophams Ebury Court 31
Torrs Hotel 128
Tower Hotel 72
Tower Hotel and Restaurant 73
Town House see Edinburgh 335
Town House see Nottingham 206
Town House Hotel 314
Trafalgar Hotel 129
Trappers 43
Trattoria Pescatore 133
Travellers Rest 61
Treasure House 276
Tregurrian Hotel 114
Trencher's Restaurant 263
Trevor Arms Hotel 282
Trewithen Restaurant 112
Trouville Hotel see Bournemouth 141
Trouville Hotel see Brighton & Hove 67
Tudor Court Hotel & Restaurant 290
Tudor Farmhouse Hotel 188
Tudor House Inn 219
Tudor Restaurant 339
Turban Tandoori Restaurant 340
Twnti Seafood Restaurant 298
Ty Gwyn Hotel 292
Ty Hen Farm Hotel & Leisure Centre 286
Tygwyn 114
Tynedale Private Hotel 297

U

Uig Hotel 328
Ulbster Arms Hotel 324
Unicorn Hotel 300
Union Hotel 115
Upland Park Hotel 153
Uplands 154
Upstairs Restaurant 129
Upton Lodge 74

V

Valentinos 221
Valley Hotel see Holyhead 295
Valley Hotel see Telford 214
Vallum Lodge 268
Venlaw Castle Hotel 307
Verandah Tandoori Restaurant 336
Victoria House 292

391

Victoria Inn 96
Villa Dino Restaurant 290
Village Pub 188
Village Tea Shop 76
Vine Inn 151
Vintner Café, Wine Bar 219

W

Wainstones Hotel 262
Walnut Tree Inn 160
Walton's Hotel 206
Warehouse Brasserie 71
Wark Farm House 268
Washingborough Hall Country House Hotel 200
Watergate Bay Hotel 114
Watergate Toll 237
Waters Edge Hotel 177
Waterside Inn 341
Watersplash Hotel 149
Waterwynch House Hotel 288
Waverley Hotel 86
Weary Friar Inn 116
Well Farm 135
Well House Restaurant & Hotel 211
Wellington Hotel 119
Wenlock Edge Inn 212
Wessex Royale Hotel 143
West Coombe Hotel 158
West Rocks Hotel 67
West Somerset Hotel 164
Westbourne House Hotel 272
Westbourne Lodge Hotel 221
Western Isles Hotel 342
Wheatsheaf Inn 168
Wherry Hotel 88
Whindley Guest House 323
Whipsiderry Hotel 114
White Court Hotel 298
White Hart 149
White Hart Hotel see Exeter 127
White Hart Hotel see Ford 168
White Hart Hotel see Lewes 68
White Hart Hotel see Stow-on-the-Wold 191
White Horse see Bury St Edmunds 86
White Horse see Stourpaine 146
White Horse Inn 208
White House 277
White House Hotel see Abersoch 290
White House Hotel see Kingsbridge 129
White House Hotel see Oxford 210
White House Hotel see Watford 75
White House Hotel see Whitby 263
White Lion see Market Drayton 212
White Lion see Tring 59
White Lion Coaching Inn 301
White Lodge Hotel 114
White Rose Hotel 152
White Swan Inn & Restaurant 266
White Tower Restaurant 244
Whitehall Hotel & Restaurant 245
Widbrook Grange 166
Wife of Bath Restaurant 102
Wild Duck Inn see Alton 214
Wild Duck Inn see Cirencester 188
William IV 90
Willow Dene 261
Willow Tree Inn 205
Windmill On the Common 33
Windsor House Hotel 97
Winston House Hotel 239
Winston Manor Hotel 67
Wish Tower Hotel 67
Withies 121
Wolfscastle Country Hotel 284
Wood Hall Hotel & Country Club 89
Woodbridge Inn 169
Woodfalls Inn 156
Woodland Park Hotel 236
Woodlands House Hotel 360
Woodlands Park Hotel 90
Woodside Farm Guest House 196
Woolverton House Hotel 165
Worm's Head Hotel 303
Wreay Farm Country Guest House 233
Wyndham Arms 189

Y

Yanwath Gate Inn 234
Yesterdays 301
Yew Tree Cottage Balti & Tandoori Restaurant 221
Yew Tree Country Restaurant 228
York House Hotel 274

Z

Zing Vaa Restaurant 272
La Zouch Restaurant 195

392

INDEX OF TOWN NAMES

A

Abercraf 303
Aberdeen 315
Aberfeldy 346
Abergavenny 288
Abersoch 290
Aberystwyth 283
Abingdon 207
Acle 81
Acton Trussell 216
Adare 360
Adlington 178
Alcester 216
Alderminster 216
Alderney 173
Aldgate 30
Aldham 71
Alford 316
Alfriston 64
Allensford 226
Almondbank 350
Alnmouth 267
Alnwick 267
Altnaharra 318
Alton 214
Altrincham 236
Alverstoke 151
Ambleside 227
Amesbury 170
Amlwch 291
Ampney Crucis 187
Andover 149
Annan 310
Appleby-in-Westmoreland 228
Appleton-le-Moors 252
Arbroath 346
Ardeonaig 319
Arreton 157
Arrochar 338
Arundel 93
Ashbourne 182
Ashby de la Zouch 195
Ashford 75
Ashford-in-the-Water 182
Askrigg 252
Asthall 207
Astwood 58
Auchterarder 346
Auchtercairn 323
Auchtermuchty 313
Aultbea 319
Aviemore 319
Axminster 121
Axmouth 122
Ayr 338

B

Badcall Bay 331
Bainbridge 252
Bakewell 182
Bala 291
Baldock 73
Ballachulish 321
Ballater 316
Ballsbridge 357
Ballybofey 355
Bampton 122
Banavie 322
Banbury 208
Banchory 316
Bardon Mill 268
Barmouth 291
Barnby-in-the-Willows 205
Barnsley 188
Barrhead 341
Bartlow 59
Barton-on-Sea 149
Bassenthwaite Lake 228
Bath 98
Battersea 30
Battle 64
Bayswater 31
Beaconsfield 57
Beaumont 175
Bedale 255
Beddgelert 292
Bedford 54
Beer 122
Belfast 354
Belford 267
Belgravia 31
Bellingham 267
Belper 182
Belton 197
Bere Ferrers 134
Berriew 302
Berrynarbor 124
Berwick-upon-Tweed 268
Berwyn 281
Bethersden 75
Betws-y-Coed 292
Beverley 239
Bexhill-on-Sea 64
Bickington 122
Bickleigh 135
Bideford 122
Biggleswade 55
Bildeston 85
Billericay 70
Billingham 224
Bingley 275
Birchington 75
Birmingham 220
Birr 360
Bishop Auckland 225
Bishop's Stortford 74
Bishops Castle 212
Bishopsgate 32
Blackburn 243
Blackford 346
Blackpool 243
Blackrod 236
Blackshaw Moor 215
Blairgowrie 346
Blandford Forum 137
Bletchingley 90
Blewbury 209
Bloomsbury 32
Bloxham 208
Blunsdon 171
Bodmin 108
Bognor Regis 93
Bolham 135
Bolton 236
Bolton-le-Sands 244
Bonchurch 159
Borrowdale 228
Borth-y-Gêst 298
Boscombe 138 140
Bothel 230
Bottesford 195
Bouley Bay 177
Bournemouth 137
Bourton-on-the-Water 186
Bovey Tracey 123
Bowness-on-Windermere 228
Boxley Village 77
Bracknell 106
Bradford on Avon 165
Braemar 317
Braithwaite 232
Bramber 95
Bramley 271
Brampton 228, 229
Brancaster Staithe 82
Braunton 123
Bray-on-Thames 106
Brecon 299
Brendon 131
Brent Knoll 160
Brentwood 70
Bressingham 82
Bridgend 299
Bridgwater 160
Bridlington 239
Bridport 141
Brig of Alford 316
Brigg 240
Brighton & Hove 65
Brinkworth 167
Bristol 102
Briston 82
Brixham 123
Broadstairs 75
Broadway 192
Brockenhurst 149
Bromley 76
Brough 239
Brough Sowerby 229
Broughton (Cheshire) 179
Broughton (Humberside) 241
Broughton-in-Furness 229
Brownhills 221
Buckie 317
Bude 108
Burford 208
Burnmouth 305
Burntisland 313
Burscough 248
Burton 167
Burton Bradstock 141

394

Burton on the Wolds 196
Burton upon Trent 215
Bury 237
Bury St Edmunds 85
Bushmills 354
Buttermere 230
Buxton 183

C

Cadnam 149
Caernarfon 292
Calcot 106
Callanish 352
Calne 166
Cambridge 60, 186
Cannock 215
Canterbury 76
Capel Curig 293
Caragh Lake 359
Carbis Bay 118, 119
Cardiff 302
Cardigan 283
Carlisle 230
Carlyon Bay 109
Carmarthen 283
Carnoustie 347
Carrutherstown 310
Carrville 226
Castel 174
Castle Acre 82
Castle Donington 196
Castlebay 351
Castlethorpe 240
Castleton 253
Catacol 341
Cawdor 319
Chagford 124
Chale 157
Charlwood 90
Charmouth 142
Chelmsford 70
Chelsea 32
Chelsworth 86
Cheltenham 186
Chepstow 288
Cherlton Bishop 126
Chertsey 90
Chesham 57
Chester 179
Cheswick 268
Chichester 93
Chiddingstone 76
Chideock 141
Chidham 94
Chilcompton 99
Childer Thornton 180
Chillington 129
Chippenham 167
Chipping Campden 187
Chiswick 33
Chittering 61
Chorley 244
Christchurch 142
Cirencester 187
The City 44
Clacton-on-Sea 71
Clapham (London) 33
Clapham (N. Yorks.) 261
Clare 86

Clawton 124
Clearwell 188
Cleethorpes 240
Clerkenwell 33
Clevedon 104
Clifden 358
Cliftonville 78
Clitheroe 245
Cloughton 259, 260
Clows Top 193
Cobham 90
Cockwood 124
Colchester 71
Coleford 189
Collooney 361
Cologin 344
Colston Bassett 204
Colwyn Bay 280
Combe Martin 124
Coniston 230
Connel 344, 345
Consett 226
Contin 319
Conwy 293
Conyer 80
Cookstown 361
Cordeaux Corner 200
Cornhill-on-Tweed 268
Corsham 168
Cossington 197
Cottingham 240
Countisbury 131
Covent Garden 34
Coventry 221
Coverack 109
Crail 313
Cranleigh 91
Craster 267
Crawley 94
Crewkerne 160
Crianlarich 309
Criccieth 293
Crick 203
Crieff 347
Cromarty 320
Crook 226
Croscombe 164
Crosthwaite 228
Crowborough 67
Crowcombe 164
Crowthorne 108
Croydon 48
Crystal Palace 34
Cullen 317
Cullercoats 274
Cullompton 125
Cupar 313
Cury 110
Cwmbran 289

D

Dalkeith 222
Dalmally 339
Darlington 226
Dartmouth 125
Darwen 245
Dawlish 125
Deganwy 293
Derby 183

Devizes 168
Didcot 209
Dingwall 320
Dolgellau 294
Doncaster 271
Dorchester 143
Dornoch 320
Douglas 241
Downham Market 82
Drayton 208
Drewsteignton 126
Drogheda 360
Dronfield 271
Droxford 150, 153
Drumnadrochit 320
Dublin 357
Dulverton 161
Dumfries 310
Dunbar 333
Dunbeath 321
Dunblane 309
Dundonald 356
Dundrum 356
Dunfermline 314
Dungannon 361
Dunkeld 348
Dunoon 339
Duns Tew 208
Dunstable 56
Dunster 161
Dunvegan 326
Durham 226
Durness 321
Dutton 249
Duxford 61

E

Ealing 34
Ealing Common 35
Earls Court 35
Earlsfield 44
Easdale 340
East Ayton 259
East Haddon 203
East Peckham 81
Eastbourne 67
Easton 145
Eaton Bray 56
Eccleston 246
Edenbridge 76
Edgbaston 220, 221
Edinburgh 333
Edwinstowe 204
Edzell 348
Elland 275
Ellerker 240
Ellesmere Port 180
Ely 61
Emsworth 150
Enfield 48
Enniskillen 358
Epsom 91
Erdington 220
Escrick 264, 266
Esher 91
Eton 107
Evershot 143
Eversley Cross 150
Ewen 188

Exebridge 161
Exeter 126
Exford 161
Exmoor 162
Exmoor National Park 162
Exmouth 127

F

Fairburn 253
Falls of Dochart 309
Falmouth 109
Far Sawrey 231
Faringdon 209
Farndon 205
Farnham 91
Felixstowe 86
Fenny Bentley 182
Fernhurst 94
Filey 253
Finchley 36
Fishbourne 93
Fishguard 283
Fladbury 194
Flax Bourton 103
Fletching 68
Ford 168
Fordingbridge 150
Forest Hill 36
Forfar 348
Fort Augustus 321
Fort William 321
Fortingall 346
Fowey 110
Fownhope 192
Framlingham 87
Freckleton 249
Freshford 104
Freuchie 314
Frilford Heath 207
Friston 88
Frodsham 180
Frome 162
Fulham 36

G

Gairloch 322
Galashiels 305
Gatehouse of Fleet 311
Gateshead 272
Geddington 203
Gedney Dyke 199
Gee Cross 237
Giddeahall 167
Giffnock 340
Gillingham 77
Glasgow 340
Glastonbury 162
Glenfield 197
Glenfinnan 323
Glenlivet 317
Glenluce 312
Glenmoriston 323
Glenrothes 314
Glenshee 348
Goathland 253
Godalming 92
Goodwick 284

Goosnargh 248, 249
Goring 209
Goring-by-Sea 96
Gorleston-on-Sea 83
Gorslas 285
Gosport 151
Gower 303
Grampound 110
Grange-over-Sands 231
Grantham 199
Grantown-on-Spey 323
Grassington 253
Great Broughton 262
Great Chishill 62
Great Eccleston 249
Great Malvern 192
Great Missenden 57
Great Rissington 189
Great Yarmouth 83
Greenford 49
Greenwich 36
Grittleton 167
Guernsey 174
Guildford 92
Gullane 336
Gunthorpe 204

H

Hadrian's Wall 268
Halifax 275
Halkirk 324
Halland 69
Halnaker 93
Hammersmith 36
Hampstead 37
Hampton Court 49
Hannington 151
Hanwell 208
Harborne 221
Harlech 294
Harome 255
Harrogate 254
Harrow 37, 49
Hartlepool 225
Hartoft End 258
Harwich 72
Hastings 68
Hathersage 183
Haughley 87
Havant 151
Haverfordwest 284
Hawick 306
Hawkshead 231
Hawnby 265
Haworth 276
Hay-on-Wye 193
Hayling Island 151
Haywards Heath 95
Headingley 278
Headington 210
Hedon 240
Helmsdale 324
Helmsley 255
Helston 110, 111
Henley-in-Arden 217
Hertford 74
Heworth 264
Hexham 269
High Wycombe 57

Highgate 37
Hillsborough 356
Hillswick 337
Hinckley 196
Hitchin 74
Holborn 37
Holbrook 165
Holland Park 38
Holmfirth 276
Holton 163
Holyhead 294
Holywell Green 276
Honiton 127
Horfield 102
Horseheath 62
Horsham 95
Horwich 237
Hoton 198
Houghton Conquest 55
Howth 357
Huddersfield 276
Hull 240
Hunstanton 83
Huntingdon 62
Hurst Green 245
Hyde (Glos.) 191
Hyde (Gtr. Manchester) 237

I

Ickham 77
Ilfracombe 128
Ilkley 278
Ilkley Moor 278
Ilmington 217
Insch 318
Invergarry 324
Invergordon 325
Inverness 325
Ipplepen 137
Ironbridge 214
Island of Sark 174
Isle of Arran 341
Isle of Barra 351
Isle of Benbecula 352
Isle of Bute 341
Isle of Colonsay 341
Isle of Harris 352
Isle of Iona 341
Isle of Lewis 352
Isle of Mull 342
Isle of Ornsay 326
Isle of Skye 326
Isle of Whithorn 311
Ivybridge 129, 133

J

Jersey 175
Jesmond 273
Johnstone 342

K

Kegworth 184
Kendal 231
Kenilworth 217
Kenmare 359

Kenmore 349
Kensington 38
Kersey 87
Keswick 232
Kettering 203
Kew 39 50
Keynsham 103
Kidderminster 193
Kilchrenan 345
Kilkee 354
Kilkeel 356
Kilkenny 359
Killarney 359
Killin 309
Killyleagh 356
Kilmarnock 342
Kilwinning 343
Kincardine 318
Kincraig 328
King's Cross 39
King's Lynn 84
Kingsbridge 129
Kingsclere 151
Kingseat 311
Kingston-upon-Thames 50
Kingswood 103
Kington St Michael 167
Kingussie 328
Kinlochleven 328
Kinross 349
Kinver 222
Kirkby Lonsdale 232
Kirkbymoorside 255
Kirkcudbright 311
Kirkmichael 350
Kirkton of Glenisla 347
Kirkwall 337
Knighton 212
Knightsbridge 39
Knutsford 180
Kyleakin 326
Kylesku 328

L

L'Etacq 176
Lacock 168
Lake Ullswater 233
Lake Vyrnwy 301
Lampeter 284
Lancaster 246
Land's End 111
Landford 170
Lanercost 229
Langham 71
Langley on Tyne 269
Lanreath 111
Largs 343
Leadburn 336
Leadenhall 40
Leadenham 200
Leatherhead 92
Ledburn 57
Lee on the Solent 151
Leeds 278
Leek 215
Leeming Bar 255
Leicester 196
Leith 335
Lerags 344

Lerwick 338
Letham 314
Letterkenny 355
Levenshulme 238
Lewes 68
Leyland 247
Lichfield 215
Lincoln 200
Lindfield 95
Liniclate 352
Linton 62
Little Haven 285
Little Petherick 115
Little Washbourne 189
Liverpool 250
Lizard 111
Llanaber 291
Llanbedr 295
Llanbedrog 295
Llanberis 295
Llandovery 285
Llandrindod Wells 300
Llandudno 295
Llanelli 205
Llangollen 281
Llanhamlach 300
Llanidloes 300
Llantrisant 289
Llanwddyn 300
Llanymynech 212
Llwyndafydd 286
Loch Insh 328
Lochcarron 329
Lochearnhead 310
Lochgair 343
Lochgilphead 343
Lochmaddy 352
Lockerbie 311
London Bridge 40
Long Melford 87
Long Preston 256
Longham 144
Longridge 247
Longtown 233
Looe 111
Lostwithiel 112
Loughborough 197
Loughbrickland 357
Louth 200
Low Row In Swaledale 257
Lowdham 206
Lower Green 217
Lowestoft 88
Lowick 268
Lucan 358
Luddendenfoot 275
Lulworth Cove 144
Luton 56
Lyddington 198
Lydford 130
Lyme Regis 144
Lymington 152
Lyndhurst 152
Lynmouth 130
Lynton 131
Lytham St-Annes 247

M

Macclesfield 181

Machynlleth 301
Maida Vale 40
Maidenhead 106
Maidstone 77
Maindee 290
Mallaig 329
Mallow 355
Malmesbury 169
Malton 256
Manchester 238
Mansfield 204
Marford 282
Margate 78
Market Drayton 212
Markinch 314
Marsh 127
Marston Green 220
Maryculter 315
Matfen 272
Matlock 184
Matlock Bath 185
Mawdesley 248
Mawgan Porth 114
Mayfair 40
Mellor 243
Melmerby 233
Melrose 306
Melton Mowbray 198
Mere 169
Mevagissey 112
Mey 331
Mid Lavant 94
Middleton Tyas 256
Mildenhall 88
Milford Haven 285
Milnathort 350
Milton Common 209
Milton Keynes 58
Minehead 163
Minster 78
Moffat 312
Mold 281
Monmouth 289
Montacute 163
Montrose 350
Moonfleet 148
Morecambe 248
Moreton 251
Moreton-in-Marsh 189
Mortehoe 131, 137
Motherwell 344
Much Wenlock 212
Muxnaw 359
Mylor Bridge 113

N

Nairn 329
Nantgaredig 283
Nantwich 181
Navenby 200
Nefyn 298
Nethy Bridge 329
Neville's Cross 226
New Galloway 312
New Quay 286
Newark-on-Trent 205
Newcastle Emlyn 286
Newcastle-under-Lyme 215
Newcastle-upon-Tyne 272

397

Newington 80
Newmarket-on-Fergus 355
Newport 157, 290
Newport Pagnell 58
Newquay 113
Newton Aycliffe 227
Newton Stewart 312
Newtonmore 330
Newtown (Powys) 301
Newtown (W. Midlands) 221
North Newnton 169
North Perrott 160
North Petherton 160
North Stainley 258
North Uist 352
North Wootton 165
Northallerton 256
Northam 122
Northampton 203
Norton (N. Yorks.) 256
Norton (Shropshire) 213
Norwich 84
Notting Hill 40
Nottingham 205
Nun Monkton 264
Nympsfield 190

O

Oban 344
Odiham 153
Old Bedhampton 151
Old Dalby 198
Old Rayne 318
Old Sodbury 104
Old Swinford 222
Olton 222
Omagh 361
Onich 322
Orford 88
Orkney 337
Ormskirk 248
Orton 234
Osmotherley 257
Oswestry 213
Otterburn 269
Oughterard 358
Oulton Broad 88
Oundle 204
Oval 41
Oxford 209
Oxwich Bay 303

P

Paddington 41
Padstow 115
Paignton 132
Paisley 345
Panborough 163
Parkend 190
Parkgate 181
Peebles 306
Pelynt 111
Pendoggett 117
Penn 58
Pennal 301
Pennyghael 342
Penrith 233

Penshurst 78
Penybont 300
Penzance 115
Perranporth 115
Pershore 194
Perth 350
Peterborough 63
Peterhead 318
Pewsey 169
Philleigh 116
Piccadilly 42
Pickhill 262
Piercebridge 226
Pillaton 116
Pilling 246
Pimperne 137
Pinner 50
Pitlochry 350
Pittington 226
Pluckley 78
Plymouth 132
Polperro 116
Pontoon 360
Pontypridd 299
Poole 145
Poolewe 330
Port Erin 242
Port Isaac 117
Porthmadog 298
Porthscatho 120
Portland 145
Portree 327, 328
Portrush 354
Portsmouth 153
Powfoot 310
Preston (Dorset) 148
Preston (Lancs.) 248
Prestwick 345
Princes Risborough 59
Putney 42
Pwllheli 298

R

Radstock 102
Rainham 51
Raithby-by-Spilsby 202
Ramsbottom 238
Ramsey 242
Ramsgate 78
Rangeworthy 105
Reading 106
Redditch 194
Reedham 84
Reeth 257
Reigate 92
Rhandirmwyn 285
Rhos-on-Sea 281
Rhossili 303
Rhydycladfy 298
Ribchester 249
Richmond (London) 51
Richmond (N. Yorks.) 256, 257
Ridgmont 56
Ringwood 154
Ripon 258
Risby 86
Roch 284
Rochdale 239

Roche 108
Rock 117
Rockbourne 154
Rode 164
Romsey 154
Rosedale Abbey 258
Rosehall 331
Rosemont 347
Roslin 336
Ross-on-Wye 194
Rosscahill 358
Rosslare Harbour 362
Rosyth 315
Rothbury 269
Rotherham 271
Rothesay 341
Rothley 198
Rowde 170
Rowsley 184
Royal Forest of Dean 190
Royal Leamington Spa 217
Royal Tunbridge Wells 79
Royston 74
Rudyard 215
Ruislip 52
Rye 68

S

Saffron Walden 72
Salen 342
Salisbury 170
Sampford Peverell 136
Sandown 157
Saundersfoot 286
Sawley 245
Saxmundham 88
Saxtead Green 87
Scarborough 258
Scotsby 230
Scotsdyke 233
Scourie 331
Scunthorpe 241
Seaburn 274
Seaford 69
Seahouses 270
Seamer 259
Seatoller 228
Seaton Carew 225
Seaview 157
Sedbergh 234
Selkirk 307
Sellack 194
Semington 171
Semley 146
Sennen Cove 111
Settle 261
Sevenoaks 79
Shaftesbury 146
Shaldon 133
Shanklin 158
Sheen 43
Sheffield 271
Shelley 277
Shelton 213
Shenstone 215
Shepherd's Bush 43
Sherborne 147
Sherston 171
Shetland 337-8

Shifnal 214
Shincliffe 227
Shipbourne 80
Shipley (W. Sussex) 95
Shipley (W. Yorks.) 279
Shipston on Stour 217
Shipton-under-Wychwood 210
Shoeburyness 72
Shottisham 89
Shottle 182
Shrawley 195
Shrewsbury 213
Sidford 134
Sidmouth 134
Sittingbourne 80
Skeabost 327
Skegness 201
Skipton 261
Slaithwaite 277
Sleaford 201
Sleat 326 327
Sling 189
Snettisham 85
Soho 43
Solihull 222
Solva 287
Souldern 210
South Hayling 151
South Molton 134
South Shields 273
Southampton 154
Southbourne 140
Southend-on-Sea 72
Southport 250
Southsea 153 154
Southwold 89
Sowerby 262
Spalding 202
Spilsby 202
Spinkhill 185
Springwood 238
St Agnes 117
St Andrews 315
St Anne's 173
St Asaph 282
St Clement 175
St David's 287
St Helen's 159
St Helier 175, 176, 177
St Ives (Cambs.) 62, 63
St Ives (Cornwall) 118
St Just 119
St Lawrence 159
St Martin 175
St Mawes 120
St Peter 177
St Peter Port 174
Staffin 326
Stafford 216
Staines 52
Stalham 85
Stamford 202
Stanshope 182
Staple 76
Stapleton 196
Steeple Aston 210
Steppingley 56
Steyning 95
Stirling 310
Stockbridge 155

Stoke Fleming 125
Stoke Newington 43
Stokesley 261
Stone 193
Stone Chair 275
Stonehaven 318
Stony Stratford 58
Stourbridge 222
Stourpaine 146
Stow-on-the-Wold 190
Strachur 345
Stratford-upon-Avon 218
Strath 322
Stromness 337
Stroud 191
Studland 146
Sulby 243
Sunderland 273
Sutton (Cambs.) 63
Sutton (Norfolk) 85
Sutton (Surrey) 52
Sutton Coldfield 222
Sutton Gault 63
Swanage 146
Swansea 303
Sway 152
Swayfield 199
Swindon 171
Sydenham 44
Symonds Yat 194

T

Tain 331
Tal-y-Bont 299
Tankerness 337
Tansley 185
Tarbert 352
Taunton 164
Tavistock 134
Taynuilt 345
Tayvallich 346
Teddington 53
Teignmouth 135
Telford 214
Tenby 287
Tewkesbury 192
Teynham 80
Thame 211
Thirlmere 234
Thirsk 262
Thornaby-on-Tees 225
Thornhill 313
Thornton Hough 251
Three Cocks 300
Throwleigh 135
Thurgarton 207
Thurso 331
Thurston 85
Timperley 236
Timsbury 100
Tintagel 120
Tintern 290
Tiverton 135
Tobermory 342
Tonbridge 80
Tongue 331
Topcliffe 262
Torquay 136
Torteval 174

Totland Bay 159
Totnes 137
Trecastle 301
Trefnant 282
Tregony 120
Trent 147
Tresaith 283
Tring 59
Trinity 175
Trowbridge 171
Truro 120
Tudweiliog 298
Turvey 55
Tweedsmuir 309
Twice Brewed 268
Twickenham 44
Tyndrum 310
Tynet 317

U

Uckfield 69
Uig 328
Ullapool 332
Ulverston 234
Upper Loughrigg 227
Upper Poppleton 266
Uppingham 199
Usk 289, 290

V

Valley 295
Ventnor 159

W

Wadebridge 121
Wadhurst 69
Wakefield 279
Wallasey 251
Walton-on-Thames 92
Wandsworth 44
Wapping 44
Warborough 211
Wark 268
Warkworth 270
Warley 276
Warminster 172
Warwick 219
Washingborough 200
Watchet 164
Waterbeach 60
Watermillock 233
Waterwynch Bay 288
Watford 74
Watlington 211
Welbury 256
Welford 204
Wells 164
Wells-next-the-Sea 85
Welshpool 302
Wenlock Edge 212
Weobley 195
West Bexington 143
West Charleton 129
West End 45
West Hampstead 47

West Ilsley 107
West Kirby 252
West Knighton 143
West Lavington 168
West Linton 336
West Lulworth 144, 147
West Marden 96
West Pennard 162
West Town 151
West Wittering 96
West Wycombe 59
Westcliff 72
Wester Balgedie 349
Westerham 81
Westgate-on-Sea 78
Westminster 47
Weston-super-Mare 105
Westoning 56
Weymouth 147
Whatton 205, 206
Wheddon Cross 162
Whitby 262
Whitebrook 289
Whitewell 245
Whitley Bay 274
Whitstable 81

Whittle-le-Woods 244
Wigglesworth 264
Willenhall 222
Willersey 192
Wilmcote 219
Wimbledon 47
Wincanton 165
Winchester 155
Windermere 235
Windsor 107
Winkton 142
Winsford 162
Winster 184
Winterborne Zelston 149
Wirksworth 185
Wirral 251
Witherslack 236
Withington 238
Withypool 162
Witney 211
Wix 72
Wokingham 107
Wolf's Castle 284
Wolverhampton 223

Woodbridge 89
Woodfalls 156
Woodford Green 53
Woodhall Spa 202
Woodlands 152
Woolacombe 131, 137
Woolverton 165
Wootton Wawen 219
Worcester 195
Worksop 207
Worleston 181
Worston 245
Worthing 96
Wrentham 89
Wrexham 282
Wrightington 249
Wymondham 199

Y

Yanwath 234
Yarbridge 157
Yardley 221
Yarmouth 160
York 264